INFORMATION RIGHTS

A PRACTITIONER'S GUIDE TO DATA PROTECTION, FREEDOM OF INFORMATION & OTHER INFORMATION RIGHTS

Fifth edition

VOLUME 2
MATERIALS

·HART·

OXFORD · LONDON · NEW YORK · NEW DELHI · SYDNEY

HART PUBLISHING

Bloomsbury Publishing Plc

Kemp House, Chawley Park, Cumnor Hill, Oxford, OX2 9PH, UK

1385 Broadway, New York, NY 10018, USA

HART PUBLISHING, the Hart/Stag logo, BLOOMSBURY and the Diana logo are
trademarks of Bloomsbury Publishing Plc

First published in Great Britain 2020
Reprinted 2020
Copyright © Philip Coppel, 2020

First published 2004
Second edition 2007
Third edition 2010
Fourth edition 2014

A catalogue record for this book is available from the British Library.

ISBN: HB: 978-1-50992-159-1 (Volume 1)
                978-1-50992-163-8 (Volume 2)
                978-1-50992-224-6 (2 Volume set)
       ePDF: 978-1-50992-248-2
       ePub: 978-1-50992-247-5

Typeset by Compuscript Ltd, Shannon
Printed and bound in Great Britain by CPI Group (UK) Ltd, Croydon CR0 4YY

To find out more about our authors and books visit www.hartpublishing.co.uk.
Here you will find extracts, author information, details of forthcoming events
and the option to sign up for our newsletters.

TABLE OF MATERIALS

Part I – Data Protection

Part II – Freedom of Information

Part III – Environmental Information

Part IV – Other Rights to Information

Part V – Data Protection (post-EU Exit Day)

Part VI – Data Protection (pre-25 May 2018)

Part VII – Procedural Material

Pt VIII – Procedural Material

Part I

Data Protection

Data Protection Act 2018

as amended to 1 February 2020

CONTENTS

PART 1
PRELIMINARY

PART 2
GENERAL PROCESSING

CHAPTER 1
SCOPE AND DEFINITIONS

CHAPTER 2
THE GDPR

Meaning of certain terms used in the GDPR

Lawfulness of processing

Special categories of personal data

Rights of the data subject

Restrictions on data subject's rights

Accreditation of certification providers

Transfers of personal data to third countries etc

PART 5
THE INFORMATION COMMISSIONER

PART 7
SUPPLEMENTARY AND FINAL PROVISION

SCHEDULES

Data Protection Act 2018

2018 CHAPTER 12

An Act to make provision for the regulation of the processing of information relating to individuals; to make provision in connection with the Information Commissioner's functions under certain regulations relating to information; to make provision for a direct marketing code of practice; and for connected purposes.

23rd May 2018

BE IT ENACTED by the Queen's most Excellent Majesty, by and with the advice and consent of the Lords Spiritual and Temporal, and Commons, in this present Parliament assembled, and by the authority of the same, as follows:—

PART 1
PRELIMINARY

Overview

1(1) This Act makes provision about the processing of personal data.

  (2) Most processing of personal data is subject to the GDPR.

  (3) Part 2 supplements the GDPR (see Chapter 2) and applies a broadly equivalent regime to certain types of processing to which the GDPR does not apply (see Chapter 3).

  (4) Part 3 makes provision about the processing of personal data by competent authorities for law enforcement purposes and implements the Law Enforcement Directive.

  (5) Part 4 makes provision about the processing of personal data by the intelligence services.

  (6) Part 5 makes provision about the Information Commissioner.

  (7) Part 6 makes provision about the enforcement of the data protection legislation.

  (8) Part 7 makes supplementary provision, including provision about the application of this Act to the Crown and to Parliament.

—— NOTES ——

Defined terms			
"the data protection legislation"	s 3(9)	"the Law Enforcement Directive"	s 3(12)
"the GDPR"	s 3(10)	"personal data"	s 3(2)
		"processing"	s 3(4)

Protection of personal data

2(1) The GDPR, the applied GDPR and this Act protect individuals with regard to the processing of personal data, in particular by—

  (a) requiring personal data to be processed lawfully and fairly, on the basis of the data subject's consent or another specified basis,

  (b) conferring rights on the data subject to obtain information about the processing of personal data and to require inaccurate personal data to be rectified, and

  (c) conferring functions on the Commissioner, giving the holder of that office responsibility for monitoring and enforcing their provisions.

(2) When carrying out functions under the GDPR, the applied GDPR and this Act, the Commissioner must have regard to the importance of securing an appropriate level of protection for personal data, taking account of the interests of data subjects, controllers and others and matters of general public interest.

—— NOTES ——

Defined terms		"the Law Enforcement Directive"	s 3(12)
"the applied GDPR"	s 3(11)	"personal data"	s 3(2)
"the GDPR"	s 3(10)	"processing"	s 3(4)

Terms relating to the processing of personal data

3(1) This section defines some terms used in this Act.

(2) "Personal data" means any information relating to an identified or identifiable living individual (subject to subsection (14)(c)).

(3) "Identifiable living individual" means a living individual who can be identified, directly or indirectly, in particular by reference to—

    (a) an identifier such as a name, an identification number, location data or an online identifier, or

    (b) one or more factors specific to the physical, physiological, genetic, mental, economic, cultural or social identity of the individual.

(4) "Processing", in relation to information, means an operation or set of operations which is performed on information, or on sets of information, such as—

    (a) collection, recording, organisation, structuring or storage,

    (b) adaptation or alteration,

    (c) retrieval, consultation or use,

    (d) disclosure by transmission, dissemination or otherwise making available,

    (e) alignment or combination, or

    (f) restriction, erasure or destruction,

(subject to subsection (14)(c) and sections 5(7), 29(2) and 82(3), which make provision about references to processing in the different Parts of this Act).

(5) "Data subject" means the identified or identifiable living individual to whom personal data relates.

(6) "Controller" and "processor", in relation to the processing of personal data to which Chapter 2 or 3 of Part 2, Part 3 or Part 4 applies, have the same meaning as in that Chapter or Part (see sections 5, 6, 32 and 83 and see also subsection (14)(d)).

(7) "Filing system" means any structured set of personal data which is accessible according to specific criteria, whether held by automated means or manually and whether centralised, decentralised or dispersed on a functional or geographical basis.

(8) "The Commissioner" means the Information Commissioner (see section 114).

(9) "The data protection legislation" means—

    (a) the GDPR,

    (b) the applied GDPR,

    (c) this Act,

    (d) regulations made under this Act, and

    (e) regulations made under section 2(2) of the European Communities Act 1972 which relate to the GDPR or the Law Enforcement Directive.

(10) "The GDPR" means Regulation (EU) 2016/679 of the European Parliament and of the Council of 27 April 2016 on the protection of natural persons with regard to the processing of personal data and on the free movement of such data (General Data Protection Regulation).

(11) "The applied GDPR" means the GDPR as applied by Chapter 3 of Part 2.

(12) "The Law Enforcement Directive" means Directive (EU) 2016/680 of the European Parliament and of the Council of 27 April 2016 on the protection of natural persons with regard to the processing of personal data by competent authorities for the purposes of the prevention, investigation, detection or prosecution of criminal offences or the execution of criminal penalties, and on the free movement of such data, and repealing Council Framework Decision 2008/977/JHA.

(13) "The Data Protection Convention" means the Convention for the Protection of Individuals with regard to Automatic Processing of Personal Data which was opened for signature on 28 January 1981, as amended up to the day on which this Act is passed.

(14) In Parts 5 to 7, except where otherwise provided—
    (a) references to the GDPR are to the GDPR read with Chapter 2 of Part 2 and include the applied GDPR read with Chapter 3 of Part 2 ;
    (b) references to Chapter 2 of Part 2, or to a provision of that Chapter, include that Chapter or that provision as applied by Chapter 3 of Part 2;
    (c) references to personal data, and the processing of personal data, are to personal data and processing to which Chapter 2 or 3 of Part 2, Part 3 or Part 4 applies;
    (d) references to a controller or processor are to a controller or processor in relation to the processing of personal data to which Chapter 2 or 3 of Part 2, Part 3 or Part 4 applies.

(15) There is an index of defined expressions in section 206.

PART 2
GENERAL PROCESSING

CHAPTER 1
SCOPE AND DEFINITIONS

Processing to which this Part applies

4(1) This Part is relevant to most processing of personal data.

(2) Chapter 2 of this Part—
    (a) applies to the types of processing of personal data to which the GDPR applies by virtue of Article 2 of the GDPR, and
    (b) supplements, and must be read with, the GDPR.

(3) Chapter 3 of this Part—
    (a) applies to certain types of processing of personal data to which the GDPR does not apply (see section 21), and
    (b) makes provision for a regime broadly equivalent to the GDPR to apply to such

processing.

——— NOTES ———

Defined terms		"personal data"	s 3(2)
"the GDPR"	s 3(10)	"processing"	s 3(4)

Definitions

5(1) Terms used in Chapter 2 of this Part and in the GDPR have the same meaning in Chapter 2 as they have in the GDPR.

(2) In subsection (1), the reference to a term's meaning in the GDPR is to its meaning in the GDPR read with any provision of Chapter 2 which modifies the term's meaning for the purposes of the GDPR.

(3) Subsection (1) is subject to any provision in Chapter 2 which provides expressly for the term to have a different meaning and to section 204.

(4) Terms used in Chapter 3 of this Part and in the applied GDPR have the same meaning in Chapter 3 as they have in the applied GDPR.

(5) In subsection (4), the reference to a term's meaning in the applied GDPR is to its meaning in the GDPR read with any provision of Chapter 2 (as applied by Chapter 3) or Chapter 3 which modifies the term's meaning for the purposes of the applied GDPR.

(6) Subsection (4) is subject to any provision in Chapter 2 (as applied by Chapter 3) or Chapter 3 which provides expressly for the term to have a different meaning.

(7) A reference in Chapter 2 or Chapter 3 of this Part to the processing of personal data is to processing to which the Chapter applies.

(8) Sections 3 and 205 include definitions of other expressions used in this Part.

——— NOTES ———

Defined terms		"personal data"	s 3(2)
"the applied GDPR"	s 3(11)	"processing"	s 3(4)
"the GDPR"	s 3(10)		

CHAPTER 2

THE GDPR

Meaning of certain terms used in the GDPR

Meaning of "controller"

6(1) The definition of "controller" in Article 4(7) of the GDPR has effect subject to—

    (a) subsection (2),

    (b) section 209, and

    (c) section 210.

(2) For the purposes of the GDPR, where personal data is processed only—

    (a) for purposes for which it is required by an enactment to be processed, and

    (b) by means by which it is required by an enactment to be processed,

the person on whom the obligation to process the data is imposed by the enactment (or, if different, one of the enactments) is the controller.

——— NOTES ———

Defined terms		"personal data"	s 3(2)
"enactment"	s 205(1)	"processing"	s 3(4)
"the GDPR"	s 3(10)	"processing of personal data"	s 5(7)

Meaning of "public authority" and "public body"

7(1) For the purposes of the GDPR, the following (and only the following) are "public authorities" and "public bodies" under the law of the United Kingdom—

    (a) a public authority as defined by the Freedom of Information Act 2000,

    (b) a Scottish public authority as defined by the Freedom of Information (Scotland) Act 2002 (asp 13), and

    (c) an authority or body specified or described by the Secretary of State in regulations,

subject to subsections (2), (3) and (4).

(2) An authority or body that falls within subsection (1) is only a "public authority" or "public body" for the purposes of the GDPR when performing a task carried out in the public interest or in the exercise of official authority vested in it.

(3) The references in subsection (1)(a) and (b) to public authorities and Scottish public authorities as defined by the Freedom of Information Act 2000 and the Freedom of Information (Scotland) Act 2002 (asp 13) do not include any of the following that fall within those definitions—

    (a) a parish council in England;

    (b) a community council in Wales;

    (c) a community council in Scotland;

    (d) a parish meeting constituted under section 13 of the Local Government Act 1972;

    (e) a community meeting constituted under section 27 of that Act;

    (f) charter trustees constituted—

        (i) under section 246 of that Act,

        (ii) under Part 1 of the Local Government and Public Involvement in Health Act 2007, or

        (iii) by the Charter Trustees Regulations 1996 (SI 1996/263).

(4) The Secretary of State may by regulations provide that a person specified or described in the regulations that is a public authority described in subsection (1)(a) or (b) is not a "public authority" or "public body" for the purposes of the GDPR.

(5) Regulations under this section are subject to the affirmative resolution procedure.

—— Notes ——

Defined terms	procedure"	s 182(7)
"the affirmative resolution	"the GDPR"	s 3(10)

Lawfulness of processing

Lawfulness of processing: public interest etc

8 In Article 6(1) of the GDPR (lawfulness of processing), the reference in point (e) to processing of personal data that is necessary for the performance of a task carried out in the public interest or in the exercise of the controller's official authority includes processing of personal data that is necessary for—

    (a) the administration of justice,

    (b) the exercise of a function of either House of Parliament,

    (c) the exercise of a function conferred on a person by an enactment or rule of law,

    (d) the exercise of a function of the Crown, a Minister of the Crown or a government department, or

    (e)   an activity that supports or promotes democratic engagement.

—— NOTES ——

Defined terms
"controller"   s 3(6)
"enactment"   s 205(1)
"the GDPR"   s 3(10)
"government department"   s 205(1)
"Minister of the Crown"   s 205(1)
"personal data"   s 3(2)
"processing"   s 3(4)
"processing of personal data"   s 5(7)

Child's consent in relation to information society services

9   In Article 8(1) of the GDPR (conditions applicable to child's consent in relation to information society services)—

    (a)   references to "16 years" are to be read as references to "13 years", and

    (b)   the reference to "information society services" does not include preventive or counselling services.

—— NOTES ——

Defined terms
"the GDPR"   s 3(10)

Special categories of personal data

Special categories of personal data and criminal convictions etc data

10(1) Subsections (2) and (3) make provision about the processing of personal data described in Article 9(1) of the GDPR (prohibition on processing of special categories of personal data) in reliance on an exception in one of the following points of Article 9(2)—

    (a)   point (b) (employment, social security and social protection);

    (b)   point (g) (substantial public interest);

    (c)   point (h) (health and social care);

    (d)   point (i) (public health);

    (e)   point (j) (archiving, research and statistics).

(2)   The processing meets the requirement in point (b), (h), (i) or (j) of Article 9(2) of the GDPR for authorisation by, or a basis in, the law of the United Kingdom or a part of the United Kingdom only if it meets a condition in Part 1 of Schedule 1.

(3)   The processing meets the requirement in point (g) of Article 9(2) of the GDPR for a basis in the law of the United Kingdom or a part of the United Kingdom only if it meets a condition in Part 2 of Schedule 1.

(4)   Subsection (5) makes provision about the processing of personal data relating to criminal convictions and offences or related security measures that is not carried out under the control of official authority.

(5)   The processing meets the requirement in Article 10 of the GDPR for authorisation by the law of the United Kingdom or a part of the United Kingdom only if it meets a condition in Part 1, 2 or 3 of Schedule 1.

(6)   The Secretary of State may by regulations—

    (a)   amend Schedule 1—

        (i)   by adding or varying conditions or safeguards, and

       (ii)   by omitting conditions or safeguards added by regulations under this section, and

    (b)   consequentially amend this section.

(7)   Regulations under this section are subject to the affirmative resolution procedure.

—— NOTES ——

Defined terms			
"the affirmative resolution		"personal data"	s 3(2)
procedure"	s 182(7)	"processing"	s 3(4)
"the GDPR"	s 3(10)	"processing of personal data"	s 5(7)

Special categories of personal data etc: supplementary

11(1)   For the purposes of Article 9(2)(h) of the GDPR (processing for health or social care purposes etc), the circumstances in which the processing of personal data is carried out subject to the conditions and safeguards referred to in Article 9(3) of the GDPR (obligation of secrecy) include circumstances in which it is carried out—

    (a)   by or under the responsibility of a health professional or a social work professional, or

    (b)   by another person who in the circumstances owes a duty of confidentiality under an enactment or rule of law.

(2)   In Article 10 of the GDPR and section 10, references to personal data relating to criminal convictions and offences or related security measures include personal data relating to—

    (a)   the alleged commission of offences by the data subject, or

    (b)   proceedings for an offence committed or alleged to have been committed by the data subject or the disposal of such proceedings, including sentencing.

—— NOTES ——

Defined terms			
"data subject"	s 3(5)	"personal data"	s 3(2)
"enactment"	s 205(1)	"processing"	s 3(4)
"the GDPR"	s 3(10)	"processing of personal data"	s 5(7)
"health professional"	s 204(1), (3), (4)	"social work professional"	s 204(2)

Rights of the data subject

Limits on fees that may be charged by controllers

12(1)   The Secretary of State may by regulations specify limits on the fees that a controller may charge in reliance on—

    (a)   Article 12(5) of the GDPR (reasonable fees when responding to manifestly unfounded or excessive requests), or

    (b)   Article 15(3) of the GDPR (reasonable fees for provision of further copies).

(2)   The Secretary of State may by regulations—

    (a)   require controllers of a description specified in the regulations to produce and publish guidance about the fees that they charge in reliance on those provisions, and

    (b)   specify what the guidance must include.

(3)   Regulations under this section are subject to the negative resolution procedure.

—— NOTES ——

Defined terms			
"controller"	s 3(6)	"the negative resolution procedure"	s 182(6)
"the GDPR"	s 3(10)	"publish"	s 205(1)

Obligations of credit reference agencies

13(1) This section applies where a controller is a credit reference agency (within the meaning of section 145(8) of the Consumer Credit Act 1974).

(2) The controller's obligations under Article 15(1) to (3) of the GDPR (confirmation of processing, access to data and safeguards for third country transfers) are taken to apply only to personal data relating to the data subject's financial standing, unless the data subject has indicated a contrary intention.

(3) Where the controller discloses personal data in pursuance of Article 15(1) to (3) of the GDPR, the disclosure must be accompanied by a statement informing the data subject of the data subject's rights under section 159 of the Consumer Credit Act 1974 (correction of wrong information).

—— NOTES ——

Defined terms		"the GDPR"	s 3(10)
"controller"	s 3(6)	"personal data"	s 3(2)
"data subject"	s 3(5)		

Automated decision-making authorised by law: safeguards

14(1) This section makes provision for the purposes of Article 22(2)(b) of the GDPR (exception from Article 22(1) of the GDPR for significant decisions based solely on automated processing that are authorised by law and subject to safeguards for the data subject's rights, freedoms and legitimate interests).

(2) A decision is a "significant decision" for the purposes of this section if, in relation to a data subject, it—
    (a) produces legal effects concerning the data subject, or
    (b) similarly significantly affects the data subject.

(3) A decision is a "qualifying significant decision" for the purposes of this section if—
    (a) it is a significant decision in relation to a data subject,
    (b) it is required or authorised by law, and
    (c) it does not fall within Article 22(2)(a) or (c) of the GDPR (decisions necessary to a contract or made with the data subject's consent).

(4) Where a controller takes a qualifying significant decision in relation to a data subject based solely on automated processing—
    (a) the controller must, as soon as reasonably practicable, notify the data subject in writing that a decision has been taken based solely on automated processing, and
    (b) the data subject may, before the end of the period of 1 month beginning with receipt of the notification, request the controller to—
        (i) reconsider the decision, or
        (ii) take a new decision that is not based solely on automated processing.

(5) If a request is made to a controller under subsection (4), the controller must, within the period described in Article 12(3) of the GDPR—
    (a) consider the request, including any information provided by the data subject that is relevant to it,
    (b) comply with the request, and
    (c) by notice in writing inform the data subject of—
        (i) the steps taken to comply with the request, and
        (ii) the outcome of complying with the request.

(6) In connection with this section, a controller has the powers and obligations under Article 12 of the GDPR (transparency, procedure for extending time for acting on request, fees, manifestly unfounded or excessive requests etc) that apply in connection with Article 22 of the GDPR.

(7) The Secretary of State may by regulations make such further provision as the Secretary of State considers appropriate to provide suitable measures to safeguard a data subject's rights, freedoms and legitimate interests in connection with the taking of qualifying significant decisions based solely on automated processing.

(8) Regulations under subsection (7)—
    (a) may amend this section, and
    (b) are subject to the affirmative resolution procedure.

—— NOTES ——

Defined terms		"data subject"	s 3(5)
"the affirmative resolution		"the GDPR"	s 3(10)
procedure"	s 182(7)	"processing"	s 3(4)
"controller"	s 3(6)		

Restrictions on data subject's rights

Exemptions etc

15(1) Schedules 2, 3 and 4 make provision for exemptions from, and restrictions and adaptations of the application of, rules of the GDPR.

(2) In Schedule 2—
    (a) Part 1 makes provision adapting or restricting the application of rules contained in Articles 13 to 21 and 34 of the GDPR in specified circumstances, as allowed for by Article 6(3) and Article 23(1) of the GDPR;
    (b) Part 2 makes provision restricting the application of rules contained in Articles 13 to 21 and 34 of the GDPR in specified circumstances, as allowed for by Article 23(1) of the GDPR;
    (c) Part 3 makes provision restricting the application of Article 15 of the GDPR where this is necessary to protect the rights of others, as allowed for by Article 23(1) of the GDPR;
    (d) Part 4 makes provision restricting the application of rules contained in Articles 13 to 15 of the GDPR in specified circumstances, as allowed for by Article 23(1) of the GDPR;
    (e) Part 5 makes provision containing exemptions or derogations from Chapters II, III, IV, V and VII of the GDPR for reasons relating to freedom of expression, as allowed for by Article 85(2) of the GDPR;
    (f) Part 6 makes provision containing derogations from rights contained in Articles 15, 16, 18, 19, 20 and 21 of the GDPR for scientific or historical research purposes, statistical purposes and archiving purposes, as allowed for by Article 89(2) and (3) of the GDPR.

(3) Schedule 3 makes provision restricting the application of rules contained in Articles 13 to 21 of the GDPR to health, social work, education and child abuse data, as allowed for by Article 23(1) of the GDPR.

(4) Schedule 4 makes provision restricting the application of rules contained in Articles 13

to 21 of the GDPR to information the disclosure of which is prohibited or restricted by an enactment, as allowed for by Article 23(1) of the GDPR.

(5) In connection with the safeguarding of national security and with defence, see Chapter 3 of this Part and the exemption in section 26.

—— NOTES ——

Defined terms
"the GDPR"   s 3(10)

Power to make further exemptions etc by regulations

16(1) The following powers to make provision altering the application of the GDPR may be exercised by way of regulations made by the Secretary of State under this section—

    (a) the power in Article 6(3) for Member State law to lay down a legal basis containing specific provisions to adapt the application of rules of the GDPR where processing is necessary for compliance with a legal obligation, for the performance of a task in the public interest or in the exercise of official authority;

    (b) the power in Article 23(1) to make a legislative measure restricting the scope of the obligations and rights mentioned in that Article where necessary and proportionate to safeguard certain objectives of general public interest;

    (c) the power in Article 85(2) to provide for exemptions or derogations from certain Chapters of the GDPR where necessary to reconcile the protection of personal data with the freedom of expression and information.

(2) Regulations under this section may—

    (a) amend Schedules 2 to 4—

      (i) by adding or varying provisions, and

      (ii) by omitting provisions added by regulations under this section, and

    (b) consequentially amend section 15.

(3) Regulations under this section are subject to the affirmative resolution procedure.

—— NOTES ——

Defined terms   "the GDPR"   s 3(10)
  "the affirmative resolution   "personal data"   s 3(2)
    procedure"   s 182(7)   "processing"   s 3(4)

Accreditation of certification providers

Accreditation of certification providers

17(1) Accreditation of a person as a certification provider is only valid when carried out by—

    (a) the Commissioner, or

    (b) the national accreditation body.

(2) The Commissioner may only accredit a person as a certification provider where the Commissioner—

    (a) has published a statement that the Commissioner will carry out such accreditation, and

    (b) has not published a notice withdrawing that statement.

(3) The national accreditation body may only accredit a person as a certification provider where the Commissioner—

    (a) has published a statement that the body may carry out such accreditation, and

    (b) has not published a notice withdrawing that statement.

(4) The publication of a notice under subsection (2)(b) or (3)(b) does not affect the validity of any accreditation carried out before its publication.

(5) Schedule 5 makes provision about reviews of, and appeals from, a decision relating to accreditation of a person as a certification provider.

(6) The national accreditation body may charge a reasonable fee in connection with, or incidental to, the carrying out of the body's functions under this section, Schedule 5 and Article 43 of the GDPR.

(7) The national accreditation body must provide the Secretary of State with such information relating to its functions under this section, Schedule 5 and Article 43 of the GDPR as the Secretary of State may reasonably require.

(8) In this section—

"certification provider" means a person who issues certification for the purposes of Article 42 of the GDPR;

"the national accreditation body" means the national accreditation body for the purposes of Article 4(1) of Regulation (EC) No 765/2008 of the European Parliament and of the Council of 9 July 2008 setting out the requirements for accreditation and market surveillance relating to the marketing of products and repealing Regulation (EEC) No 339/93.

─── NOTES ───

Defined terms		"the GDPR"	s 3(10)
"the Commissioner"	s 3(8)	"publish"	s 205(1)

Transfers of personal data to third countries etc

Transfers of personal data to third countries etc

18(1) The Secretary of State may by regulations specify, for the purposes of Article 49(1)(d) of the GDPR—

(a) circumstances in which a transfer of personal data to a third country or international organisation is to be taken to be necessary for important reasons of public interest, and

(b) circumstances in which a transfer of personal data to a third country or international organisation which is not required by an enactment is not to be taken to be necessary for important reasons of public interest.

(2) The Secretary of State may by regulations restrict the transfer of a category of personal data to a third country or international organisation where—

(a) the transfer is not authorised by an adequacy decision under Article 45(3) of the GDPR, and

(b) the Secretary of State considers the restriction to be necessary for important reasons of public interest.

(3) Regulations under this section—

(a) are subject to the made affirmative resolution procedure where the Secretary of State has made an urgency statement in respect of them;

(b) are otherwise subject to the affirmative resolution procedure.

(4) For the purposes of this section, an urgency statement is a reasoned statement that the Secretary of State considers it desirable for the regulations to come into force without

delay.

———— NOTES ————

Defined terms
"the affirmative resolution
  procedure"   s 182(7)
"enactment"   s 205(1)
"the GDPR"   s 3(10)

"international organisation" s 205(1)
"the made affirmative
  resolution procedure"   s 182(8)
"personal data"   s 3(2)

Specific processing situations

Processing for archiving, research and statistical purposes: safeguards

19(1)   This section makes provision about—

    (a)   processing of personal data that is necessary for archiving purposes in the public interest,

    (b)   processing of personal data that is necessary for scientific or historical research purposes, and

    (c)   processing of personal data that is necessary for statistical purposes.

(2)   Such processing does not satisfy the requirement in Article 89(1) of the GDPR for the processing to be subject to appropriate safeguards for the rights and freedoms of the data subject if it is likely to cause substantial damage or substantial distress to a data subject.

(3)   Such processing does not satisfy that requirement if the processing is carried out for the purposes of measures or decisions with respect to a particular data subject, unless the purposes for which the processing is necessary include the purposes of approved medical research.

(4)   In this section—

"approved medical research" means medical research carried out by a person who has approval to carry out that research from—

    (a)   a research ethics committee recognised or established by the Health Research Authority under Chapter 2 of Part 3 of the Care Act 2014, or

    (b)   a body appointed by any of the following for the purpose of assessing the ethics of research involving individuals—

        (i)   the Secretary of State, the Scottish Ministers, the Welsh Ministers, or a Northern Ireland department;

        (ii)   a relevant NHS body;

        (iii)   United Kingdom Research and Innovation or a body that is a Research Council for the purposes of the Science and Technology Act 1965;

        (iv)   an institution that is a research institution for the purposes of Chapter 4A of Part 7 of the Income Tax (Earnings and Pensions) Act 2003 (see section 457 of that Act);

"relevant NHS body" means—

    (a)   an NHS trust or NHS foundation trust in England,

    (b)   an NHS trust or Local Health Board in Wales,

    (c)   a Health Board or Special Health Board constituted under section 2 of the National Health Service (Scotland) Act 1978,

    (d)   the Common Services Agency for the Scottish Health Service, or

    (e)   any of the health and social care bodies in Northern Ireland falling within paragraphs (a) to (e) of section 1(5) of the Health and Social Care (Reform) Act (Northern Ireland) 2009 (c 1 (NI)).

(5) The Secretary of State may by regulations change the meaning of "approved medical research" for the purposes of this section, including by amending subsection (4).

(6) Regulations under subsection (5) are subject to the affirmative resolution procedure.

—— NOTES ——

Defined terms		"the GDPR"	s 3(10)
"the affirmative resolution		"personal data"	s 3(2)
procedure"	s 182(7)	"processing"	s 3(4)
"data subject"	s 3(5)	"processing of personal data"	s 5(7)

Minor definition

Meaning of "court"

20 Section 5(1) (terms used in this Chapter to have the same meaning as in the GDPR) does not apply to references in this Chapter to a court and, accordingly, such references do not include a tribunal.

—— NOTES ——

Defined terms	
"tribunal"	s 205(1)

CHAPTER 3
OTHER GENERAL PROCESSING

Scope

Processing to which this Chapter applies

21(1) This Chapter applies to the automated or structured processing of personal data in the course of—

   (a) an activity which is outside the scope of European Union law, or

   (b) an activity which falls within the scope of Article 2(2)(b) of the GDPR (common foreign and security policy activities),

provided that the processing is not processing by a competent authority for any of the law enforcement purposes (as defined in Part 3) or processing to which Part 4 (intelligence services processing) applies.

(2) This Chapter also applies to the manual unstructured processing of personal data held by an FOI public authority.

(3) This Chapter does not apply to the processing of personal data by an individual in the course of a purely personal or household activity.

(4) In this section—

   "the automated or structured processing of personal data" means—

      (a) the processing of personal data wholly or partly by automated means, and

      (b) the processing otherwise than by automated means of personal data which forms part of a filing system or is intended to form part of a filing system;

   "the manual unstructured processing of personal data" means the processing of personal data which is not the automated or structured processing of personal data.

(5) In this Chapter, "FOI public authority" means—

(a) a public authority as defined in the Freedom of Information Act 2000, or

(b) a Scottish public authority as defined in the Freedom of Information (Scotland) Act 2002 (asp 13).

(6) References in this Chapter to personal data "held" by an FOI public authority are to be interpreted—

(a) in relation to England and Wales and Northern Ireland, in accordance with section 3(2) of the Freedom of Information Act 2000, and

(b) in relation to Scotland, in accordance with section 3(2), (4) and (5) of the Freedom of Information (Scotland) Act 2002 (asp 13),

but such references do not include information held by an intelligence service (as defined in section 82) on behalf of an FOI public authority.

(7) But personal data is not to be treated as "held" by an FOI public authority for the purposes of this Chapter, where—

(a) section 7 of the Freedom of Information Act 2000 prevents Parts 1 to 5 of that Act from applying to the personal data, or

(b) section 7(1) of the Freedom of Information (Scotland) Act 2002 (asp 13) prevents that Act from applying to the personal data.

—— NOTES ——

Defined terms		"personal data"	s 3(2)
"filing system"	s 3(7)	"processing"	s 3(4)
"the GDPR"	s 3(10)	"processing of personal data"	s 5(7)

Application of the GDPR

Application of the GDPR to processing to which this Chapter applies

22(1) The GDPR applies to the processing of personal data to which this Chapter applies but as if its Articles were part of an Act extending to England and Wales, Scotland and Northern Ireland.

(2) Chapter 2 of this Part applies for the purposes of the applied GDPR as it applies for the purposes of the GDPR.

(3) In this Chapter, "the applied Chapter 2 " means Chapter 2 of this Part as applied by this Chapter.

(4) Schedule 6 contains provision modifying—

(a) the GDPR as it applies by virtue of subsection (1) (see Part 1);

(b) Chapter 2 of this Part as it applies by virtue of subsection (2) (see Part 2).

(5) A question as to the meaning or effect of a provision of the applied GDPR, or the applied Chapter 2 , is to be determined consistently with the interpretation of the equivalent provision of the GDPR, or Chapter 2 of this Part, as it applies otherwise than by virtue of this Chapter, except so far as Schedule 6 requires a different interpretation.

—— NOTES ——

Defined terms		"personal data"	s 3(2)
"the applied GDPR"	s 3(11)	"processing"	s 3(4)
"the GDPR"	s 3(10)	"processing of personal data"	s 5(7)

Power to make provision in consequence of regulations related to the GDPR

23(1) The Secretary of State may by regulations make provision in connection with the processing of personal data to which this Chapter applies which is equivalent to that made by GDPR regulations, subject to such modifications as the Secretary of State considers appropriate.

(2) In this section, "GDPR regulations" means regulations made under section 2(2) of the European Communities Act 1972 which make provision relating to the GDPR.

(3) Regulations under subsection (1) may apply a provision of GDPR regulations, with or without modification.

(4) Regulations under subsection (1) may amend or repeal a provision of—
    (a) the applied GDPR;
    (b) this Chapter;
    (c) Parts 5 to 7, in so far as they apply in relation to the applied GDPR.

(5) Regulations under this section are subject to the affirmative resolution procedure.

—— Notes ——

Defined terms		"personal data"	s 3(2)
"the affirmative resolution procedure"	182(7)	"processing"	s 3(4)
"the applied GDPR"	s 3(11)	"processing of personal data"	s 5(7)
"the GDPR"	s 3(10)		

Exemptions etc

Manual unstructured data held by FOI public authorities

24(1) The provisions of the applied GDPR and this Act listed in subsection (2) do not apply to personal data to which this Chapter applies by virtue of section 21(2) (manual unstructured personal data held by FOI public authorities).

(2) Those provisions are—
    (a) in Chapter II of the applied GDPR (principles)—
        (i) Article 5(1)(a) to (c), (e) and (f) (principles relating to processing, other than the accuracy principle),
        (ii) Article 6 (lawfulness),
        (iii) Article 7 (conditions for consent),
        (iv) Article 8(1) and (2) (child's consent),
        (v) Article 9 (processing of special categories of personal data),
        (vi) Article 10 (data relating to criminal convictions etc), and
        (vii) Article 11(2) (processing not requiring identification);
    (b) in Chapter III of the applied GDPR (rights of the data subject)—
        (i) Article 13(1) to (3) (personal data collected from data subject: information to be provided),
        (ii) Article 14(1) to (4) (personal data collected other than from data subject: information to be provided),
        (iii) Article 20 (right to data portability), and
        (iv) Article 21(1) (objections to processing);
    (c) in Chapter V of the applied GDPR, Articles 44 to 49 (transfers of personal data to third countries or international organisations);
    (d) sections 170 and 171 of this Act; (see also paragraph 1(2) of Schedule 18).

(3) In addition, the provisions of the applied GDPR listed in subsection (4) do not apply to personal data to which this Chapter applies by virtue of section 21(2) where the personal data relates to appointments, removals, pay, discipline, superannuation or other personnel

matters in relation to—

    (a) service in any of the armed forces of the Crown;

    (b) service in any office or employment under the Crown or under any public authority;

    (c) service in any office or employment, or under any contract for services, in respect of which power to take action, or to determine or approve the action taken, in such matters is vested in—

        (i) Her Majesty,

        (ii) a Minister of the Crown,

        (iii) the National Assembly for Wales,

        (iv) the Welsh Ministers,

        (v) a Northern Ireland Minister (within the meaning of the Freedom of Information Act 2000), or

        (vi) an FOI public authority.

(4) Those provisions are—

    (a) the remaining provisions of Chapters II and III (principles and rights of the data subject);

    (b) Chapter IV (controller and processor);

    (c) Chapter IX (specific processing situations).

(5) A controller is not obliged to comply with Article 15(1) to (3) of the applied GDPR (right of access by the data subject) in relation to personal data to which this Chapter applies by virtue of section 21(2) if—

    (a) the request under that Article does not contain a description of the personal data, or

    (b) the controller estimates that the cost of complying with the request so far as relating to the personal data would exceed the appropriate maximum.

(6) Subsection (5)(b) does not remove the controller's obligation to confirm whether or not personal data concerning the data subject is being processed unless the estimated cost of complying with that obligation alone in relation to the personal data would exceed the appropriate maximum.

(7) An estimate for the purposes of this section must be made in accordance with regulations under section 12(5) of the Freedom of Information Act 2000.

(8) In subsections (5) and (6), "the appropriate maximum" means the maximum amount specified by the Secretary of State by regulations.

(9) Regulations under subsection (8) are subject to the negative resolution procedure.

––––– NOTES –––––

Defined terms		"Minister of the Crown"	s 205(1)
"the applied GDPR"	s 3(11)	"the negative resolution procedure"	s 182(6)
"controller"	s 3(6)	"personal data"	s 3(2)
"data subject"	s 3(5)	"processing"	s 3(4)
"FOI public authority"	s 21(5)	"processing of personal data"	s 5(7)

Manual unstructured data used in longstanding historical research

25(1) The provisions of the applied GDPR listed in subsection (2) do not apply to personal data to which this Chapter applies by virtue of section 21(2) (manual unstructured personal data held by FOI public authorities) at any time when—

    (a) the personal data—

        (i) is subject to processing which was already underway immediately before 24 October 1998, and

       (ii) is processed only for the purposes of historical research, and

    (b) the processing is not carried out—

        (i) for the purposes of measures or decisions with respect to a particular data subject, or

       (ii) in a way that causes, or is likely to cause, substantial damage or substantial distress to a data subject.

(2) Those provisions are—

    (a) in Chapter II of the applied GDPR (principles), Article 5(1)(d) (the accuracy principle), and

    (b) in Chapter III of the applied GDPR (rights of the data subject)—

        (i) Article 16 (right to rectification), and

       (ii) Article 17(1) and (2) (right to erasure).

(3) The exemptions in this section apply in addition to the exemptions in section 24.

—— **NOTES** ——

Defined terms			
"the applied GDPR"	s 3(11)	"personal data"	s 3(2)
"data subject"	s 3(5)	"processing"	s 3(4)
		"processing of personal data"	s 5(7)

National security and defence exemption

26(1) A provision of the applied GDPR or this Act mentioned in subsection (2) does not apply to personal data to which this Chapter applies if exemption from the provision is required for—

    (a) the purpose of safeguarding national security, or

    (b) defence purposes.

(2) The provisions are—

    (a) Chapter II of the applied GDPR (principles) except for—

        (i) Article 5(1)(a) (lawful, fair and transparent processing), so far as it requires processing of personal data to be lawful;

       (ii) Article 6 (lawfulness of processing);

      (iii) Article 9 (processing of special categories of personal data);

    (b) Chapter III of the applied GDPR (rights of data subjects);

    (c) in Chapter IV of the applied GDPR—

        (i) Article 33 (notification of personal data breach to the Commissioner);

       (ii) Article 34 (communication of personal data breach to the data subject);

    (d) Chapter V of the applied GDPR (transfers of personal data to third countries or international organisations);

    (e) in Chapter VI of the applied GDPR—

        (i) Article 57(1)(a) and (h) (Commissioner's duties to monitor and enforce the applied GDPR and to conduct investigations);

       (ii) Article 58 (investigative, corrective, authorisation and advisory powers of Commissioner);

    (f) Chapter VIII of the applied GDPR (remedies, liabilities and penalties) except for—

        (i) Article 83 (general conditions for imposing administrative fines);

(ii) Article 84 (penalties);

    (g) in Part 5 of this Act—

        (i) in section 115 (general functions of the Commissioner), subsections (3)and (8);

        (ii) in section 115, subsection (9), so far as it relates to Article 58(2)(i) of the applied GDPR;

        (iii) section 119 (inspection in accordance with international obligations);

    (h) in Part 6 of this Act—

        (i) sections 142 to 154 and Schedule 15 (Commissioner's notices and powers of entry and inspection);

        (ii) sections 170 to 173 (offences relating to personal data);

    (i) in Part 7 of this Act, section 187 (representation of data subjects).

—— NOTES ——

Defined terms		"processing"	s 3(4)
"the applied GDPR"	s 3(11)	"processing of personal data"	s 5(7)
"personal data"	s 3(2)		

National security: certificate

27(1) Subject to subsection (3), a certificate signed by a Minister of the Crown certifying that exemption from all or any of the provisions listed in section 26(2) is, or at any time was, required in relation to any personal data for the purpose of safeguarding national security is conclusive evidence of that fact.

(2) A certificate under subsection (1)—

    (a) may identify the personal data to which it applies by means of a general description, and

    (b) may be expressed to have prospective effect.

(3) Any person directly affected by a certificate under subsection (1) may appeal to the Tribunal against the certificate.

(4) If, on an appeal under subsection (3), the Tribunal finds that, applying the principles applied by a court on an application for judicial review, the Minister did not have reasonable grounds for issuing a certificate, the Tribunal may—

    (a) allow the appeal, and

    (b) quash the certificate.

(5) Where, in any proceedings under or by virtue of the applied GDPR or this Act, it is claimed by a controller that a certificate under subsection (1) which identifies the personal data to which it applies by means of a general description applies to any personal data, another party to the proceedings may appeal to the Tribunal on the ground that the certificate does not apply to the personal data in question.

(6) But, subject to any determination under subsection (7), the certificate is to be conclusively presumed so to apply.

(7) On an appeal under subsection (5), the Tribunal may determine that the certificate does not so apply.

(8) A document purporting to be a certificate under subsection (1) is to be—

    (a) received in evidence, and

    (b) deemed to be such a certificate unless the contrary is proved.

(9) A document which purports to be certified by or on behalf of a Minister of the Crown as

a true copy of a certificate issued by that Minister under subsection (1) is—

    (a) in any legal proceedings, evidence of that certificate;

    (b) in any legal proceedings in Scotland, sufficient evidence of that certificate.

(10) The power conferred by subsection (1) on a Minister of the Crown is exercisable only by—

    (a) a Minister who is a member of the Cabinet, or

    (b) the Attorney General or the Advocate General for Scotland.

—— NOTES ——

Defined terms		"Minister of the Crown"	s 205(1)
"the applied GDPR"	s 3(11)	"personal data"	s 3(2)
"controller"	s 3(6)	"the Tribunal"	s 205(1)

National security and defence: modifications to Articles 9 and 32 of the applied GDPR

28(1) Article 9(1) of the applied GDPR (prohibition on processing of special categories of personal data) does not prohibit the processing of personal data to which this Chapter applies to the extent that the processing is carried out—

    (a) for the purpose of safeguarding national security or for defence purposes, and

    (b) with appropriate safeguards for the rights and freedoms of data subjects.

(2) Article 32 of the applied GDPR (security of processing) does not apply to a controller or processor to the extent that the controller or the processor (as the case may be) is processing personal data to which this Chapter applies for—

    (a) the purpose of safeguarding national security, or

    (b) defence purposes.

(3) Where Article 32 of the applied GDPR does not apply, the controller or the processor must implement security measures appropriate to the risks arising from the processing of the personal data.

(4) For the purposes of subsection (3), where the processing of personal data is carried out wholly or partly by automated means, the controller or the processor must, following an evaluation of the risks, implement measures designed to—

    (a) prevent unauthorised processing or unauthorised interference with the systems used in connection with the processing,

    (b) ensure that it is possible to establish the precise details of any processing that takes place,

    (c) ensure that any systems used in connection with the processing function properly and may, in the case of interruption, be restored, and

    (d) ensure that stored personal data cannot be corrupted if a system used in connection with the processing malfunctions.

—— NOTES ——

Defined terms		"personal data"	s 3(2)
"the applied GDPR"	s 3(11)	"processing"	s 3(4)
"controller"	s 3(6)	"processing of personal data"	s 5(7)
"data subject"	s 3(5)	"processor"	s 3(6)

PART 3
LAW ENFORCEMENT PROCESSING
CHAPTER 1
SCOPE AND DEFINITIONS

Scope

Processing to which this Part applies

29(1)   This Part applies to—

    (a)   the processing by a competent authority of personal data wholly or partly by automated means, and

    (b)   the processing by a competent authority otherwise than by automated means of personal data which forms part of a filing system or is intended to form part of a filing system.

  (2)   Any reference in this Part to the processing of personal data is to processing to which this Part applies.

  (3)   For the meaning of "competent authority", see section 30.

—— NOTES ——

Defined terms		"personal data"	s 3(2)
"filing system"	s 3(7)	"processing"	s 3(4)

Definitions

Meaning of "competent authority"

30(1)   In this Part, "competent authority" means—

    (a)   a person specified or described in Schedule 7, and

    (b)   any other person if and to the extent that the person has statutory functions for any of the law enforcement purposes.

  (2)   But an intelligence service is not a competent authority within the meaning of this Part.

  (3)   The Secretary of State may by regulations amend Schedule 7—

    (a)   so as to add or remove a person or description of person;

    (b)   so as to reflect any change in the name of a person specified in the Schedule.

  (4)   Regulations under subsection (3) which make provision of the kind described in subsection (3)(a) may also make consequential amendments of section 73(4)(b).

  (5)   Regulations under subsection (3) which make provision of the kind described in subsection (3)(a), or which make provision of that kind and of the kind described in subsection (3)(b), are subject to the affirmative resolution procedure.

  (6)   Regulations under subsection (3) which make provision only of the kind described in subsection (3)(b) are subject to the negative resolution procedure.

  (7)   In this section—

    "intelligence service" means—

      (a) the Security Service;

      (b) the Secret Intelligence Service;

      (c) the Government Communications Headquarters;

    "statutory function" means a function under or by virtue of an enactment.

—— NOTES ——

Defined terms		"enactment"	s 205(1)
"the affirmative resolution		"the law enforcement purposes"	s 31
procedure"	s 182(7)	"the negative resolution procedure"	s 182(6)

"The law enforcement purposes"

31   For the purposes of this Part, "the law enforcement purposes" are the purposes of the prevention, investigation, detection or prosecution of criminal offences or the execution of criminal penalties, including the safeguarding against and the prevention of threats to public security.

Meaning of "controller" and "processor"

32(1)   In this Part, "controller" means the competent authority which, alone or jointly with others—

(a)   determines the purposes and means of the processing of personal data, or

(b)   is the controller by virtue of subsection (2).

(2)   Where personal data is processed only—

(a)   for purposes for which it is required by an enactment to be processed, and

(b)   by means by which it is required by an enactment to be processed,

the competent authority on which the obligation to process the data is imposed by the enactment (or, if different, one of the enactments) is the controller.

(3)   In this Part, "processor" means any person who processes personal data on behalf of the controller (other than a person who is an employee of the controller).

—— NOTES ——

Defined terms		"personal data"	s 3(2)
"competent authority"	s 30	"processing"	s 3(4)
"employee"	s 33(1), (2)	"processing of personal data"	s 29(2)
"enactment"	s 205(1)		

Other definitions

33(1)   This section defines certain other expressions used in this Part.

(2)   "Employee", in relation to any person, includes an individual who holds a position (whether paid or unpaid) under the direction and control of that person.

(3)   "Personal data breach" means a breach of security leading to the accidental or unlawful destruction, loss, alteration, unauthorised disclosure of, or access to, personal data transmitted, stored or otherwise processed.

(4)   "Profiling" means any form of automated processing of personal data consisting of the use of personal data to evaluate certain personal aspects relating to an individual, in particular to analyse or predict aspects concerning that individual's performance at work, economic situation, health, personal preferences, interests, reliability, behaviour, location or movements.

(5)   "Recipient", in relation to any personal data, means any person to whom the data is disclosed, whether a third party or not, but it does not include a public authority to whom disclosure is or may be made in the framework of a particular inquiry in accordance with

the law.

(6) "Restriction of processing" means the marking of stored personal data with the aim of limiting its processing for the future.

(7) "Third country" means a country or territory other than a member State.

(8) Sections 3 and 205 include definitions of other expressions used in this Part.

—— NOTES ——

Defined terms		"processing"	s 3(4)
"personal data"	s 3(2)	"processing of personal data"	s 29(2)

CHAPTER 2
PRINCIPLES

Overview and general duty of controller

34(1) This Chapter sets out the six data protection principles as follows—

    (a) section 35(1) sets out the first data protection principle (requirement that processing be lawful and fair);

    (b) section 36(1) sets out the second data protection principle (requirement that purposes of processing be specified, explicit and legitimate);

    (c) section 37 sets out the third data protection principle (requirement that personal data be adequate, relevant and not excessive);

    (d) section 38(1) sets out the fourth data protection principle (requirement that personal data be accurate and kept up to date);

    (e) section 39(1) sets out the fifth data protection principle (requirement that personal data be kept for no longer than is necessary);

    (f) section 40 sets out the sixth data protection principle (requirement that personal data be processed in a secure manner).

(2) In addition—

    (a) each of sections 35, 36, 38 and 39 makes provision to supplement the principle to which it relates, and

    (b) sections 41 and 42 make provision about the safeguards that apply in relation to certain types of processing.

(3) The controller in relation to personal data is responsible for, and must be able to demonstrate, compliance with this Chapter.

—— NOTES ——

Defined terms		"personal data"	s 3(2)
"controller"	s 32(1), (2)	"processing"	s 3(4)

The first data protection principle

35(1) The first data protection principle is that the processing of personal data for any of the law enforcement purposes must be lawful and fair.

(2) The processing of personal data for any of the law enforcement purposes is lawful only if and to the extent that it is based on law and either—

    (a) the data subject has given consent to the processing for that purpose, or

    (b) the processing is necessary for the performance of a task carried out for that purpose by a competent authority.

(3)   In addition, where the processing for any of the law enforcement purposes is sensitive processing, the processing is permitted only in the two cases set out in subsections (4) and (5).

(4)   The first case is where—

    (a)   the data subject has given consent to the processing for the law enforcement purpose as mentioned in subsection (2)(a), and

    (b)   at the time when the processing is carried out, the controller has an appropriate policy document in place (see section 42).

(5)   The second case is where—

    (a)   the processing is strictly necessary for the law enforcement purpose,

    (b)   the processing meets at least one of the conditions in Schedule 8, and

    (c)   at the time when the processing is carried out, the controller has an appropriate policy document in place (see section 42).

(6)   The Secretary of State may by regulations amend Schedule 8—

    (a)   by adding conditions;

    (b)   by omitting conditions added by regulations under paragraph (a).

(7)   Regulations under subsection (6) are subject to the affirmative resolution procedure.

(8)   In this section, "sensitive processing" means—

    (a)   the processing of personal data revealing racial or ethnic origin, political opinions, religious or philosophical beliefs or trade union membership;

    (b)   the processing of genetic data, or of biometric data, for the purpose of uniquely identifying an individual;

    (c)   the processing of data concerning health;

    (d)   the processing of data concerning an individual's sex life or sexual orientation.

——— Notes ———

Defined terms		"data subject"	s 3(5)
"the affirmative resolution		"genetic data"	s 205(1)
procedure"	s 182(7)	"the law enforcement purposes"	s 31
"biometric data"	s 205(1)	"personal data"	s 3(2)
"competent authority"	s 30	"processing"	s 3(4)
"controller"	s 32(1), (2)	"processing of personal data"	s 29(2)
"data concerning health"	s 205(1)		

The second data protection principle

36(1) The second data protection principle is that—

    (a)   the law enforcement purpose for which personal data is collected on any occasion must be specified, explicit and legitimate, and

    (b)   personal data so collected must not be processed in a manner that is incompatible with the purpose for which it was collected.

(2)   Paragraph (b) of the second data protection principle is subject to subsections (3) and (4).

(3)   Personal data collected for a law enforcement purpose may be processed for any other law enforcement purpose (whether by the controller that collected the data or by another controller) provided that—

    (a)   the controller is authorised by law to process the data for the other purpose, and

(b) the processing is necessary and proportionate to that other purpose.

(4) Personal data collected for any of the law enforcement purposes may not be processed for a purpose that is not a law enforcement purpose unless the processing is authorised by law.

—— NOTES ——

Defined terms		"personal data"	s 3(2)
"controller"	s 32(1), (2)	"processing"	s 3(4)
"the law enforcement purposes"	s 31	"processing of personal data"	s 29(2)

The third data protection principle

37 The third data protection principle is that personal data processed for any of the law enforcement purposes must be adequate, relevant and not excessive in relation to the purpose for which it is processed.

—— NOTES ——

Defined terms		"processing"	s 3(4)
"the law enforcement purposes"	s 31	"processing of personal data"	s 29(2)
"personal data"	s 3(2)		

The fourth data protection principle

38(1) The fourth data protection principle is that—

(a) personal data processed for any of the law enforcement purposes must be accurate and, where necessary, kept up to date, and

(b) every reasonable step must be taken to ensure that personal data that is inaccurate, having regard to the law enforcement purpose for which it is processed, is erased or rectified without delay.

(2) In processing personal data for any of the law enforcement purposes, personal data based on facts must, so far as possible, be distinguished from personal data based on personal assessments.

(3) In processing personal data for any of the law enforcement purposes, a clear distinction must, where relevant and as far as possible, be made between personal data relating to different categories of data subject, such as—

(a) persons suspected of having committed or being about to commit a criminal offence;

(b) persons convicted of a criminal offence;

(c) persons who are or may be victims of a criminal offence;

(d) witnesses or other persons with information about offences.

(4) All reasonable steps must be taken to ensure that personal data which is inaccurate, incomplete or no longer up to date is not transmitted or made available for any of the law enforcement purposes.

(5) For that purpose—

(a) the quality of personal data must be verified before it is transmitted or made available,

(b) in all transmissions of personal data, the necessary information enabling the recipient to assess the degree of accuracy, completeness and reliability of the data and the extent to which it is up to date must be included, and

(c) if, after personal data has been transmitted, it emerges that the data was incorrect or that the transmission was unlawful, the recipient must be notified without delay.

—— NOTES ——

Defined terms		"personal data"	s 3(2)
"data subject"	s 3(5)	"processing"	s 3(4)
"inaccurate"	s 205(1)	"processing of personal data"	s 29(2)
"the law enforcement purposes"	s 31	"recipient"	s 33(1), (5)

The fifth data protection principle

39(1) The fifth data protection principle is that personal data processed for any of the law enforcement purposes must be kept for no longer than is necessary for the purpose for which it is processed.

(2) Appropriate time limits must be established for the periodic review of the need for the continued storage of personal data for any of the law enforcement purposes.

—— NOTES ——

Defined terms		"processing"	s 3(4)
"the law enforcement purposes"	s 31	"processing of personal data"	s 29(2)
"personal data"	s 3(2)		

The sixth data protection principle

40 The sixth data protection principle is that personal data processed for any of the law enforcement purposes must be so processed in a manner that ensures appropriate security of the personal data, using appropriate technical or organisational measures (and, in this principle, "appropriate security" includes protection against unauthorised or unlawful processing and against accidental loss, destruction or damage).

—— NOTES ——

Defined terms		"processing"	s 3(4)
"the law enforcement purposes"	s 31	"processing of personal data"	s 29(2)
"personal data"	s 3(2)		

Safeguards: archiving

41(1) This section applies in relation to the processing of personal data for a law enforcement purpose where the processing is necessary—
    (a) for archiving purposes in the public interest,
    (b) for scientific or historical research purposes, or
    (c) for statistical purposes.

(2) The processing is not permitted if—
    (a) it is carried out for the purposes of, or in connection with, measures or decisions with respect to a particular data subject, or
    (b) it is likely to cause substantial damage or substantial distress to a data subject.

—— NOTES ——

Defined terms		"personal data"	s 3(2)
"data subject"	s 3(5)	"processing"	s 3(4)
"the law enforcement purposes"	s 31	"processing of personal data"	s 29(2)

Safeguards: sensitive processing

42(1) This section applies for the purposes of section 35(4) and (5) (which require a controller to have an appropriate policy document in place when carrying out sensitive processing in reliance on the consent of the data subject or, as the case may be, in reliance on a condition specified in Schedule 8).

(2) The controller has an appropriate policy document in place in relation to the sensitive processing if the controller has produced a document which—

    (a) explains the controller's procedures for securing compliance with the data protection principles (see section 34(1)) in connection with sensitive processing in reliance on the consent of the data subject or (as the case may be) in reliance on the condition in question, and

    (b) explains the controller's policies as regards the retention and erasure of personal data processed in reliance on the consent of the data subject or (as the case may be) in reliance on the condition in question, giving an indication of how long such personal data is likely to be retained.

(3) Where personal data is processed on the basis that an appropriate policy document is in place, the controller must during the relevant period—

    (a) retain the appropriate policy document,

    (b) review and (if appropriate) update it from time to time, and

    (c) make it available to the Commissioner, on request, without charge.

(4) The record maintained by the controller under section 61(1) and, where the sensitive processing is carried out by a processor on behalf of the controller, the record maintained by the processor under section 61(3) must include the following information—

    (a) whether the sensitive processing is carried out in reliance on the consent of the data subject or, if not, which condition in Schedule 8 is relied on,

    (b) how the processing satisfies section 35 (lawfulness of processing), and

    (c) whether the personal data is retained and erased in accordance with the policies described in subsection (2)(b) and, if it is not, the reasons for not following those policies.

(5) In this section, "relevant period", in relation to sensitive processing in reliance on the consent of the data subject or in reliance on a condition specified in Schedule 8, means a period which—

    (a) begins when the controller starts to carry out the sensitive processing in reliance on the data subject's consent or (as the case may be) in reliance on that condition, and

    (b) ends at the end of the period of 6 months beginning when the controller ceases to carry out the processing.

—— NOTES ——

Defined terms		"processing"	s 3(4)
"the Commissioner"	s 3(8)	"processing of personal data"	s 29(2)
"controller"	s 32(1), (2)	"processor"	s 32(1), (3)
"data subject"	s 3(5)	"sensitive processing"	cf s 35(8)
"personal data"	s 3(2)		

CHAPTER 3
RIGHTS OF THE DATA SUBJECT

Overview and scope

Overview and scope

43(1) This Chapter—

(a) imposes general duties on the controller to make information available (see section 44);

(b) confers a right of access by the data subject (see section 45);

(c) confers rights on the data subject with respect to the rectification of personal data and the erasure of personal data or the restriction of its processing (see sections 46 to 48);

(d) regulates automated decision-making (see sections 49 and 50);

(e) makes supplementary provision (see sections 51 to 54).

(2) This Chapter applies only in relation to the processing of personal data for a law enforcement purpose.

(3) But sections 44 to 48 do not apply in relation to the processing of relevant personal data in the course of a criminal investigation or criminal proceedings, including proceedings for the purpose of executing a criminal penalty.

(4) In subsection (3), "relevant personal data" means personal data contained in a judicial decision or in other documents relating to the investigation or proceedings which are created by or on behalf of a court or other judicial authority.

(5) In this Chapter, "the controller", in relation to a data subject, means the controller in relation to personal data relating to the data subject.

—— NOTES ——

Defined terms		"personal data"	s 3(2)
controller"	s 32(1), (2)	"processing"	s 3(4)
"data subject"	s 3(5)	"processing of personal data"	s 29(2)
"the law enforcement purposes"	s 31	"restriction of processing"	s 33(1), (6)

Information: controller's general duties

Information: controller's general duties

44(1) The controller must make available to data subjects the following information (whether by making the information generally available to the public or in any other way)—

(a) the identity and the contact details of the controller;

(b) where applicable, the contact details of the data protection officer (see sections 69 to 71);

(c) the purposes for which the controller processes personal data;

(d) the existence of the rights of data subjects to request from the controller—

(i) access to personal data (see section 45),

(ii) rectification of personal data (see section 46), and

(iii) erasure of personal data or the restriction of its processing (see section 47);

(e) the existence of the right to lodge a complaint with the Commissioner and the contact details of the Commissioner.

(2) The controller must also, in specific cases for the purpose of enabling the exercise of a data subject's rights under this Part, give the data subject the following—

(a) information about the legal basis for the processing;

(b) information about the period for which the personal data will be stored or, where that is not possible, about the criteria used to determine that period;

(c) where applicable, information about the categories of recipients of the personal data (including recipients in third countries or international organisations);

(d) such further information as is necessary to enable the exercise of the data subject's rights under this Part.

(3) An example of where further information may be necessary as mentioned in subsection (2)(d) is where the personal data being processed was collected without the knowledge of the data subject.

(4) The controller may restrict, wholly or partly, the provision of information to the data subject under subsection (2) to the extent that and for so long as the restriction is, having regard to the fundamental rights and legitimate interests of the data subject, a necessary and proportionate measure to—

    (a) avoid obstructing an official or legal inquiry, investigation or procedure;

    (b) avoid prejudicing the prevention, detection, investigation or prosecution of criminal offences or the execution of criminal penalties;

    (c) protect public security;

    (d) protect national security;

    (e) protect the rights and freedoms of others.

(5) Where the provision of information to a data subject under subsection (2) is restricted, wholly or partly, the controller must inform the data subject in writing without undue delay—

    (a) that the provision of information has been restricted,

    (b) of the reasons for the restriction,

    (c) of the data subject's right to make a request to the Commissioner under section 51,

    (d) of the data subject's right to lodge a complaint with the Commissioner, and

    (e) of the data subject's right to apply to a court under section 167.

(6) Subsection (5)(a) and (b) do not apply to the extent that complying with them would undermine the purpose of the restriction.

(7) The controller must—

    (a) record the reasons for a decision to restrict (whether wholly or partly) the provision of information to a data subject under subsection (2), and

    (b) if requested to do so by the Commissioner, make the record available to the Commissioner.

—— NOTES ——

Defined terms		"personal data"	s 3(2)
"the Commissioner"	s 3(8)	"processing"	s 3(4)
"controller"	s 32(1), (2)	"processing of personal data"	s 29(2)
"the controller"	s 43(5)	"recipient"	s 33(1), (5)
"data subject"	s 3(5)	"restriction of processing"	s 33(1), (6)
"international organisation"	s 205(1)	"third country"	s 33(1), (7)

Data subject's right of access

Right of access by the data subject

45(1) A data subject is entitled to obtain from the controller—

    (a) confirmation as to whether or not personal data concerning him or her is being processed, and

    (b) where that is the case, access to the personal data and the information set out in subsection (2).

(2) That information is—

(a) the purposes of and legal basis for the processing;

(b) the categories of personal data concerned;

(c) the recipients or categories of recipients to whom the personal data has been disclosed (including recipients or categories of recipients in third countries or international organisations);

(d) the period for which it is envisaged that the personal data will be stored or, where that is not possible, the criteria used to determine that period;

(e) the existence of the data subject's rights to request from the controller—

   (i) rectification of personal data (see section 46), and

   (ii) erasure of personal data or the restriction of its processing (see section 47);

(f) the existence of the data subject's right to lodge a complaint with the Commissioner and the contact details of the Commissioner;

(g) communication of the personal data undergoing processing and of any available information as to its origin.

(3) Where a data subject makes a request under subsection (1), the information to which the data subject is entitled must be provided in writing —

   (a) without undue delay, and

   (b) in any event, before the end of the applicable time period (as to which see section 54).

(4) The controller may restrict, wholly or partly, the rights conferred by subsection (1) to the extent that and for so long as the restriction is, having regard to the fundamental rights and legitimate interests of the data subject, a necessary and proportionate measure to—

   (a) avoid obstructing an official or legal inquiry, investigation or procedure;

   (b) avoid prejudicing the prevention, detection, investigation or prosecution of criminal offences or the execution of criminal penalties;

   (c) protect public security;

   (d) protect national security;

   (e) protect the rights and freedoms of others.

(5) Where the rights of a data subject under subsection (1) are restricted, wholly or partly, the controller must inform the data subject in writing without undue delay—

   (a) that the rights of the data subject have been restricted,

   (b) of the reasons for the restriction,

   (c) of the data subject's right to make a request to the Commissioner under section 51,

   (d) of the data subject's right to lodge a complaint with the Commissioner, and

   (e) of the data subject's right to apply to a court under section 167.

(6) Subsection (5)(a) and (b) do not apply to the extent that the provision of the information would undermine the purpose of the restriction.

(7) The controller must—

   (a) record the reasons for a decision to restrict (whether wholly or partly) the rights of a data subject under subsection (1), and

   (b) if requested to do so by the Commissioner, make the record available to the Commissioner.

—— NOTES ——

Defined terms		"personal data"	s 3(2)
"the Commissioner"	s 3(8)	"processing"	s 3(4)
"controller"	s 32(1), (2)	"processing of personal data"	s 29(2)
"the controller"	s 43(5)	"recipient"	s 33(1), (5)
"data subject"	s 3(5)	"restriction of processing"	s 33(1), (6)
"international organisation"	s 205(1)	"third country"	s 33(1), (7)

Data subject's rights to rectification or erasure etc

Right to rectification

46(1)   The controller must, if so requested by a data subject, rectify without undue delay inaccurate personal data relating to the data subject.

(2)   Where personal data is inaccurate because it is incomplete, the controller must, if so requested by a data subject, complete it.

(3)   The duty under subsection (2) may, in appropriate cases, be fulfilled by the provision of a supplementary statement.

(4)   Where the controller would be required to rectify personal data under this section but the personal data must be maintained for the purposes of evidence, the controller must (instead of rectifying the personal data) restrict its processing.

—— NOTES ——

Defined terms		"personal data"	s 3(2)
"controller"	s 32(1), (2)	"processing"	s 3(4)
"the controller"	s 43(5)	"processing of personal data"	s 29(2)
"data subject"	s 3(5)	"restriction of processing"	s 33(1), (6)
"inaccurate"	s 205(1)		

Right to erasure or restriction of processing

47(1)   The controller must erase personal data without undue delay where—

    (a)   the processing of the personal data would infringe section 35, 36(1) to (3), 37, 38(1), 39(1), 40, 41 or 42, or

    (b)   the controller has a legal obligation to erase the data.

(2)   Where the controller would be required to erase personal data under subsection (1) but the personal data must be maintained for the purposes of evidence, the controller must (instead of erasing the personal data) restrict its processing.

(3)   Where a data subject contests the accuracy of personal data (whether in making a request under this section or section 46 or in any other way), but it is not possible to ascertain whether it is accurate or not, the controller must restrict its processing.

(4)   A data subject may request the controller to erase personal data or to restrict its processing (but the duties of the controller under this section apply whether or not such a request is made).

—— NOTES ——

Defined terms		"personal data"	s 3(2)
"controller"	s 32(1), (2)	"processing"	s 3(4)
"the controller"	s 43(5)	"processing of personal data"	s 29(2)
"data subject"	s 3(5)	"restriction of processing"	s 33(1), (6)

Rights under section 46 or 47: supplementary

48(1) Where a data subject requests the rectification or erasure of personal data or the restriction of its processing, the controller must inform the data subject in writing—

    (a) whether the request has been granted, and

    (b) if it has been refused—

        (i) of the reasons for the refusal,

        (ii) of the data subject's right to make a request to the Commissioner under section 51,

        (iii) of the data subject's right to lodge a complaint with the Commissioner, and

        (iv) of the data subject's right to apply to a court under section 167.

  (2) The controller must comply with the duty under subsection (1)—

    (a) without undue delay, and

    (b) in any event, before the end of the applicable time period (see section 54).

  (3) The controller may restrict, wholly or partly, the provision of information to the data subject under subsection (1)(b)(i) to the extent that and for so long as the restriction is, having regard to the fundamental rights and legitimate interests of the data subject, a necessary and proportionate measure to—

    (a) avoid obstructing an official or legal inquiry, investigation or procedure;

    (b) avoid prejudicing the prevention, detection, investigation or prosecution of criminal offences or the execution of criminal penalties;

    (c) protect public security;

    (d) protect national security;

    (e) protect the rights and freedoms of others.

  (4) Where the rights of a data subject under subsection (1) are restricted, wholly or partly, the controller must inform the data subject in writing without undue delay—

    (a) that the rights of the data subject have been restricted,

    (b) of the reasons for the restriction,

    (c) of the data subject's right to lodge a complaint with the Commissioner, and

    (d) of the data subject's right to apply to a court under section 167.

  (5) Subsection (4)(a) and (b) do not apply to the extent that the provision of the information would undermine the purpose of the restriction.

  (6) The controller must—

    (a) record the reasons for a decision to restrict (whether wholly or partly) the provision of information to a data subject under subsection (1)(b)(i), and

    (b) if requested to do so by the Commissioner, make the record available to the Commissioner.

  (7) Where the controller rectifies personal data, it must notify the competent authority (if any) from which the inaccurate personal data originated.

  (8) In subsection (7), the reference to a competent authority includes (in addition to a competent authority within the meaning of this Part) any person that is a competent authority for the purposes of the Law Enforcement Directive in a member State other than the United Kingdom.

  (9) Where the controller rectifies, erases or restricts the processing of personal data which has

PART I   *Data Protection Act 2018*
DATA PROTECTION MATERIAL   *Part 3 – Law Enforcement Processing*
                   Chapter 3 – Rights of the Data Subject

been disclosed by the controller—

 (a) the controller must notify the recipients, and

 (b) the recipients must similarly rectify, erase or restrict the processing of the personal data (so far as they retain responsibility for it).

(10) Where processing is restricted in accordance with section 47(3), the controller must inform the data subject before lifting the restriction.

—— NOTES ——

Defined terms		"the Law Enforcement Directive"	s 3(12)
"the Commissioner"	s 3(8)	"personal data"	s 3(2)
"competent authority"	s 30	"processing"	s 3(4)
(and note sub-s (8) of this section)		"processing of personal data"	s 29(2)
"controller"	ss 32(1), (2), 43(5)	"recipient"	s 33(1), (5)
"data subject"	s 3(5)	"restriction of processing"	s 33(1), (6)
"inaccurate"	s 205(1)		

Automated individual decision-making

Right not to be subject to automated decision-making

49(1) A controller may not take a significant decision based solely on automated processing unless that decision is required or authorised by law.

(2) A decision is a "significant decision" for the purpose of this section if, in relation to a data subject, it—

 (a) produces an adverse legal effect concerning the data subject, or

 (b) significantly affects the data subject.

—— NOTES ——

Defined terms		"data subject"	s 3(5)
"controller"	s 32(1), (2)		

Automated decision-making authorised by law: safeguards

50(1) A decision is a "qualifying significant decision" for the purposes of this section if—

 (a) it is a significant decision in relation to a data subject, and

 (b) it is required or authorised by law.

(2) Where a controller takes a qualifying significant decision in relation to a data subject based solely on automated processing—

 (a) the controller must, as soon as reasonably practicable, notify the data subject in writing that a decision has been taken based solely on automated processing, and

 (b) the data subject may, before the end of the period of 1 month beginning with receipt of the notification, request the controller to—

  (i) reconsider the decision, or

  (ii) take a new decision that is not based solely on automated processing.

(3) If a request is made to a controller under subsection (2), the controller must, before the end of the period of 1 month beginning with receipt of the request—

 (a) consider the request, including any information provided by the data subject that is relevant to it,

 (b) comply with the request, and

 (c) by notice in writing inform the data subject of—

  (i) the steps taken to comply with the request, and

(ii) the outcome of complying with the request.

(4) The Secretary of State may by regulations make such further provision as the Secretary of State considers appropriate to provide suitable measures to safeguard a data subject's rights, freedoms and legitimate interests in connection with the taking of qualifying significant decisions based solely on automated processing.

(5) Regulations under subsection (4)—

(a) may amend this section, and

(b) are subject to the affirmative resolution procedure.

(6) In this section "significant decision" has the meaning given by section 49(2).

—— NOTES ——

Defined terms		"the controller"	s 43(5)
"the affirmative resolution procedure"	s 182(7)	"data subject"	s 3(5)
"controller"	s 32(1), (2)	"processing"	s 3(4)

Supplementary

Exercise of rights through the Commissioner

51(1) This section applies where a controller—

(a) restricts under section 44(4) the information provided to the data subject under section 44(2) (duty of the controller to give the data subject additional information),

(b) restricts under section 45(4) the data subject's rights under section 45(1) (right of access), or

(c) refuses a request by the data subject for rectification under section 46 or for erasure or restriction of processing under section 47.

(2) The data subject may—

(a) where subsection (1)(a) or (b) applies, request the Commissioner to check that the restriction imposed by the controller was lawful;

(b) where subsection (1)(c) applies, request the Commissioner to check that the refusal of the data subject's request was lawful.

(3) The Commissioner must take such steps as appear to the Commissioner to be appropriate to respond to a request under subsection (2) (which may include the exercise of any of the powers conferred by sections 142 and 146).

(4) After taking those steps, the Commissioner must inform the data subject—

(a) where subsection (1)(a) or (b) applies, whether the Commissioner is satisfied that the restriction imposed by the controller was lawful;

(b) where subsection (1)(c) applies, whether the Commissioner is satisfied that the controller's refusal of the data subject's request was lawful.

(5) The Commissioner must also inform the data subject of the data subject's right to apply to a court under section 167.

(6) Where the Commissioner is not satisfied as mentioned in subsection (4)(a) or (b), the Commissioner may also inform the data subject of any further steps that the Commissioner is considering taking under Part 6 .

Form of provision of information etc

52(1)   The controller must take reasonable steps to ensure that any information that is required by this Chapter to be provided to the data subject is provided in a concise, intelligible and easily accessible form, using clear and plain language.

(2)   Subject to subsection (3), the information may be provided in any form, including electronic form.

(3)   Where information is provided in response to a request by the data subject under section 45, 46, 47 or 50, the controller must provide the information in the same form as the request where it is practicable to do so.

(4)   Where the controller has reasonable doubts about the identity of an individual making a request under section 45, 46 or 47, the controller may—

    (a)   request the provision of additional information to enable the controller to confirm the identity, and

    (b)   delay dealing with the request until the identity is confirmed.

(5)   Subject to section 53, any information that is required by this Chapter to be provided to the data subject must be provided free of charge.

(6)   The controller must facilitate the exercise of the rights of the data subject under sections 45 to 50.

Manifestly unfounded or excessive requests by the data subject

53(1)   Where a request from a data subject under section 45, 46, 47 or 50 is manifestly unfounded or excessive, the controller may—

    (a)   charge a reasonable fee for dealing with the request, or

    (b)   refuse to act on the request.

(2)   An example of a request that may be excessive is one that merely repeats the substance of previous requests.

(3)   In any proceedings where there is an issue as to whether a request under section 45, 46, 47 or 50 is manifestly unfounded or excessive, it is for the controller to show that it is.

(4)   The Secretary of State may by regulations specify limits on the fees that a controller may charge in accordance with subsection (1)(a).

(5)   Regulations under subsection (4) are subject to the negative resolution procedure.

Meaning of "applicable time period"

54(1) This section defines "the applicable time period" for the purposes of sections 45(3) (b) and 48(2)(b).

(2) "The applicable time period" means the period of 1 month, or such longer period as may be specified in regulations, beginning with the relevant time.

(3) "The relevant time" means the latest of the following—

　(a) when the controller receives the request in question;

　(b) when the controller receives the information (if any) requested in connection with a request under section 52(4);

　(c) when the fee (if any) charged in connection with the request under section 53 is paid.

(4) The power to make regulations under subsection (2) is exercisable by the Secretary of State.

(5) Regulations under subsection (2) may not specify a period which is longer than 3 months.

(6) Regulations under subsection (2) are subject to the negative resolution procedure.

—— NOTES ——

Defined terms		"the controller"	s 43(5)
"controller"	s 32(1), (2)	"the negative resolution procedure"	s 182(6)

CHAPTER 4
CONTROLLER AND PROCESSOR

Overview and scope

Overview and scope

55(1) This Chapter—

　(a) sets out the general obligations of controllers and processors (see sections 56 to 65);

　(b) sets out specific obligations of controllers and processors with respect to security (see section 66);

　(c) sets out specific obligations of controllers and processors with respect to personal data breaches (see sections 67 and 68);

　(d) makes provision for the designation, position and tasks of data protection officers (see sections 69 to 71).

(2) This Chapter applies only in relation to the processing of personal data for a law enforcement purpose.

(3) Where a controller is required by any provision of this Chapter to implement appropriate technical and organisational measures, the controller must (in deciding what measures are appropriate) take into account—

　(a) the latest developments in technology,

　(b) the cost of implementation,

　(c) the nature, scope, context and purposes of processing, and

　(d) the risks for the rights and freedoms of individuals arising from the processing.

Defined terms		"personal data breach"	s 33(1), (3)
"controller"	s 32(1), (2)	"processing"	s 3(4)
"the law enforcement purposes"	s 31	"processing of personal data"	s 29(2)
"personal data"	s 3(2)	"processor"	s 32(1), (3)

General obligations

General obligations of the controller

56(1)   Each controller must implement appropriate technical and organisational measures to ensure, and to be able to demonstrate, that the processing of personal data complies with the requirements of this Part.

(2)   Where proportionate in relation to the processing, the measures implemented to comply with the duty under subsection (1) must include appropriate data protection policies.

(3)   The technical and organisational measures implemented under subsection (1) must be reviewed and updated where necessary.

—— NOTES ——

Defined terms		"processing"	s 3(4)
"controller"	s 32(1), (2)	"processing of personal data"	s 29(2)
"personal data"	s 3(2)		

Data protection by design and default

57(1)   Each controller must implement appropriate technical and organisational measures which are designed—
    (a)   to implement the data protection principles in an effective manner, and
    (b)   to integrate into the processing itself the safeguards necessary for that purpose.

(2)   The duty under subsection (1) applies both at the time of the determination of the means of processing the data and at the time of the processing itself.

(3)   Each controller must implement appropriate technical and organisational measures for ensuring that, by default, only personal data which is necessary for each specific purpose of the processing is processed.

(4)   The duty under subsection (3) applies to—
    (a)   the amount of personal data collected,
    (b)   the extent of its processing,
    (c)   the period of its storage, and
    (d)   its accessibility.

(5)   In particular, the measures implemented to comply with the duty under subsection (3) must ensure that, by default, personal data is not made accessible to an indefinite number of people without an individual's intervention.

—— NOTES ——

Defined terms		"processing"	s 3(4)
"controller"	s 32(1), (2)	"processing of personal data"	s 29(2)
"personal data"	s 3(2)		

Joint controllers

58(1)   Where two or more competent authorities jointly determine the purposes and means of processing personal data, they are joint controllers for the purposes of this Part.

(2) Joint controllers must, in a transparent manner, determine their respective responsibilities for compliance with this Part by means of an arrangement between them, except to the extent that those responsibilities are determined under or by virtue of an enactment.

(3) The arrangement must designate the controller which is to be the contact point for data subjects.

—— NOTES ——

Defined terms			
"competent authority"	s 30	"enactment"	s 205(1)
"controller"	s 32(1), (2)	"personal data"	s 3(2)
"data subject"	s 3(5)	"processing"	s 3(4)
		"processing of personal data"	s 29(2)

Processors

59(1) This section applies to the use by a controller of a processor to carry out processing of personal data on behalf of the controller.

(2) The controller may use only a processor who provides guarantees to implement appropriate technical and organisational measures that are sufficient to secure that the processing will—

(a) meet the requirements of this Part, and

(b) ensure the protection of the rights of the data subject.

(3) The processor used by the controller may not engage another processor ("a sub-processor") without the prior written authorisation of the controller, which may be specific or general.

(4) Where the controller gives a general written authorisation to a processor, the processor must inform the controller if the processor proposes to add to the number of sub-processors engaged by it or to replace any of them (so that the controller has the opportunity to object to the proposal).

(5) The processing by the processor must be governed by a contract in writing between the controller and the processor setting out the following—

(a) the subject-matter and duration of the processing;

(b) the nature and purpose of the processing;

(c) the type of personal data and categories of data subjects involved;

(d) the obligations and rights of the controller and processor.

(6) The contract must, in particular, provide that the processor must—

(a) act only on instructions from the controller,

(b) ensure that the persons authorised to process personal data are subject to an appropriate duty of confidentiality,

(c) assist the controller by any appropriate means to ensure compliance with the rights of the data subject under this Part,

(d) at the end of the provision of services by the processor to the controller—

(i) either delete or return to the controller (at the choice of the controller) the personal data to which the services relate, and

(ii) delete copies of the personal data unless subject to a legal obligation to store the copies,

(e) make available to the controller all information necessary to demonstrate compliance with this section, and

    (f) comply with the requirements of this section for engaging sub-processors.

(7) The terms included in the contract in accordance with subsection (6)(a) must provide that the processor may transfer personal data to a third country or international organisation only if instructed by the controller to make the particular transfer.

(8) If a processor determines, in breach of this Part, the purposes and means of processing, the processor is to be treated for the purposes of this Part as a controller in respect of that processing.

—— NOTES ——

Defined terms		"processing"	s 3(4)
"controller"	s 32(1), (2)	"processing of personal data"	s 29(2)
"data subject"	s 3(5)	"processor"	s 32(3)
"international organisation"	s 205(1)	"third country"	s 33(1), (7)
"personal data"	s 3(2)		

Processing under the authority of the controller or processor

60 A processor, and any person acting under the authority of a controller or processor, who has access to personal data may not process the data except—

    (a) on instructions from the controller, or

    (b) to comply with a legal obligation.

—— NOTES ——

Defined terms		"processing"	s 3(4)
"controller"	s 32(1), (2)	"processing of personal data"	s 29(2)
"personal data"	s 3(2)	"processor"	s 32(3)

Records of processing activities

61(1) Each controller must maintain a record of all categories of processing activities for which the controller is responsible.

(2) The controller's record must contain the following information—

    (a) the name and contact details of the controller;

    (b) where applicable, the name and contact details of the joint controller;

    (c) where applicable, the name and contact details of the data protection officer;

    (d) the purposes of the processing;

    (e) the categories of recipients to whom personal data has been or will be disclosed (including recipients in third countries or international organisations);

    (f) a description of the categories of—

        (i) data subject, and

        (ii) personal data;

    (g) where applicable, details of the use of profiling;

    (h) where applicable, the categories of transfers of personal data to a third country or an international organisation;

    (i) an indication of the legal basis for the processing operations, including transfers, for which the personal data is intended;

    (j) where possible, the envisaged time limits for erasure of the different categories of personal data;

    (k) where possible, a general description of the technical and organisational security measures referred to in section 66.

(3) Each processor must maintain a record of all categories of processing activities carried out on behalf of a controller.

(4) The processor's record must contain the following information—

    (a) the name and contact details of the processor and of any other processors engaged by the processor in accordance with section 59(3);

    (b) the name and contact details of the controller on behalf of which the processor is acting;

    (c) where applicable, the name and contact details of the data protection officer;

    (d) the categories of processing carried out on behalf of the controller;

    (e) where applicable, details of transfers of personal data to a third country or an international organisation where explicitly instructed to do so by the controller, including the identification of that third country or international organisation;

    (f) where possible, a general description of the technical and organisational security measures referred to in section 66.

(5) The controller and the processor must make the records kept under this section available to the Commissioner on request.

———— NOTES ————

Defined terms

"the Commissioner"	s 3(8)	"processing"	s 3(4)
"controller"	s 32(1), (2)	"processing of personal data"	s 29(2)
"data subject"	s 3(5)	"processor"	s 32(3)
"international organisation"	s 205(1)	"profiling"	s 33(1), (4)
"personal data"	s 3(2)	"recipient"	s 33(1), (5)
		"third country"	s 33(1), (7)

Logging

62(1) A controller (or, where personal data is processed on behalf of the controller by a processor, the processor) must keep logs for at least the following processing operations in automated processing systems—

    (a) collection;

    (b) alteration;

    (c) consultation;

    (d) disclosure (including transfers);

    (e) combination;

    (f) erasure.

(2) The logs of consultation must make it possible to establish—

    (a) the justification for, and date and time of, the consultation, and

    (b) so far as possible, the identity of the person who consulted the data.

(3) The logs of disclosure must make it possible to establish—

    (a) the justification for, and date and time of, the disclosure, and

    (b) so far as possible—

        (i) the identity of the person who disclosed the data, and

        (ii) the identity of the recipients of the data.

(4) The logs kept under subsection (1) may be used only for one or more of the following purposes—

    (a) to verify the lawfulness of processing;

(b) to assist with self-monitoring by the controller or (as the case may be) the processor, including the conduct of internal disciplinary proceedings;

(c) to ensure the integrity and security of personal data;

(d) the purposes of criminal proceedings.

(5) The controller or (as the case may be) the processor must make the logs available to the Commissioner on request.

—— NOTES ——

Defined terms		"processing"	s 3(4)
"the Commissioner"	s 3(8)	"processing of personal data"	s 29(2)
"controller"	s 32(1), (2)	"processor"	s 32(3)
"personal data"	s 3(2)	"recipient"	s 33(1), (5)

Co-operation with the Commissioner

63 Each controller and each processor must co-operate, on request, with the Commissioner in the performance of the Commissioner's tasks.

—— NOTES ——

Defined terms		"controller"	s 32(1), (2)
"the Commissioner"	s 3(8)	"processor"	s 32(3)

Data protection impact assessment

64(1) Where a type of processing is likely to result in a high risk to the rights and freedoms of individuals, the controller must, prior to the processing, carry out a data protection impact assessment.

(2) A data protection impact assessment is an assessment of the impact of the envisaged processing operations on the protection of personal data.

(3) A data protection impact assessment must include the following—

(a) a general description of the envisaged processing operations;

(b) an assessment of the risks to the rights and freedoms of data subjects;

(c) the measures envisaged to address those risks;

(d) safeguards, security measures and mechanisms to ensure the protection of personal data and to demonstrate compliance with this Part, taking into account the rights and legitimate interests of the data subjects and other persons concerned.

(4) In deciding whether a type of processing is likely to result in a high risk to the rights and freedoms of individuals, the controller must take into account the nature, scope, context and purposes of the processing.

—— NOTES ——

Defined terms		"personal data"	s 3(2)
"controller"	s 32(1), (2)	"processing"	s 3(4)
"data subject"	s 3(5)	"processing of personal data"	s 29(2)

Prior consultation with the Commissioner

65(1) This section applies where a controller intends to create a filing system and process personal data forming part of it.

(2) The controller must consult the Commissioner prior to the processing if a data protection impact assessment prepared under section 64 indicates that the processing of the data would result in a high risk to the rights and freedoms of individuals (in the absence of measures to mitigate the risk).

(3) Where the controller is required to consult the Commissioner under subsection (2), the controller must give the Commissioner—

(a) the data protection impact assessment prepared under section 64, and

(b) any other information requested by the Commissioner to enable the Commissioner to make an assessment of the compliance of the processing with the requirements of this Part.

(4) Where the Commissioner is of the opinion that the intended processing referred to in subsection (1) would infringe any provision of this Part, the Commissioner must provide written advice to the controller and, where the controller is using a processor, to the processor.

(5) The written advice must be provided before the end of the period of 6 weeks beginning with receipt of the request for consultation by the controller or the processor.

(6) The Commissioner may extend the period of 6 weeks by a further period of 1 month, taking into account the complexity of the intended processing.

(7) If the Commissioner extends the period of 6 weeks, the Commissioner must—

(a) inform the controller and, where applicable, the processor of any such extension before the end of the period of 1 month beginning with receipt of the request for consultation, and

(b) provide reasons for the delay.

—— NOTES ——

Defined terms		"personal data"	s 3(2)
"the Commissioner"	s 3(8)	"processing"	s 3(4)
"controller"	s 32(1), (2)	"processing of personal data"	s 29(2)
"filing system"	s 3(7)	"processor"	s 32(3)

Obligations relating to security

Security of processing

66(1) Each controller and each processor must implement appropriate technical and organisational measures to ensure a level of security appropriate to the risks arising from the processing of personal data.

(2) In the case of automated processing, each controller and each processor must, following an evaluation of the risks, implement measures designed to—

(a) prevent unauthorised processing or unauthorised interference with the systems used in connection with it,

(b) ensure that it is possible to establish the precise details of any processing that takes place,

(c) ensure that any systems used in connection with the processing function properly and may, in the case of interruption, be restored, and

(d) ensure that stored personal data cannot be corrupted if a system used in connection with the processing malfunctions.

—— NOTES ——

Defined terms		"processing"	s 3(4)
"controller"	s 32(1), (2)	"processing of personal data"	s 29(2)
"personal data"	s 3(2)	"processor"	s 32(3)

Obligations relating to personal data breaches

Notification of a personal data breach to the Commissioner

67(1)   If a controller becomes aware of a personal data breach in relation to personal data for which the controller is responsible, the controller must notify the breach to the Commissioner—

(a)   without undue delay, and

(b)   where feasible, not later than 72 hours after becoming aware of it.

(2)   Subsection (1) does not apply if the personal data breach is unlikely to result in a risk to the rights and freedoms of individuals.

(3)   Where the notification to the Commissioner is not made within 72 hours, the notification must be accompanied by reasons for the delay.

(4)   Subject to subsection (5), the notification must include—

(a)   a description of the nature of the personal data breach including, where possible, the categories and approximate number of data subjects concerned and the categories and approximate number of personal data records concerned;

(b)   the name and contact details of the data protection officer or other contact point from whom more information can be obtained;

(c)   a description of the likely consequences of the personal data breach;

(d)   a description of the measures taken or proposed to be taken by the controller to address the personal data breach, including, where appropriate, measures to mitigate its possible adverse effects.

(5)   Where and to the extent that it is not possible to provide all the information mentioned in subsection (4) at the same time, the information may be provided in phases without undue further delay.

(6)   The controller must record the following information in relation to a personal data breach—

(a)   the facts relating to the breach,

(b)   its effects, and

(c)   the remedial action taken.

(7)   The information mentioned in subsection (6) must be recorded in such a way as to enable the Commissioner to verify compliance with this section.

(8)   Where a personal data breach involves personal data that has been transmitted by or to a person who is a controller under the law of another member State, the information mentioned in subsection (6) must be communicated to that person without undue delay.

(9)   If a processor becomes aware of a personal data breach (in relation to personal data processed by the processor), the processor must notify the controller without undue delay.

—— NOTES ——

Defined terms		"personal data breach"	s 33(1), (3)
"the Commissioner"		"processing"	s 3(4)
"controller"	s 32(1), (2)	"processing of personal data"	s 29(2)
"data subject"	s 3(5)	"processor"	s 32(3)
"personal data"	s 3(2)		

Communication of a personal data breach to the data subject

68(1)   Where a personal data breach is likely to result in a high risk to the rights and freedoms of individuals, the controller must inform the data subject of the breach without undue delay.

(2) The information given to the data subject must include the following—
   (a) a description of the nature of the breach;
   (b) the name and contact details of the data protection officer or other contact point from whom more information can be obtained;
   (c) a description of the likely consequences of the personal data breach;
   (d) a description of the measures taken or proposed to be taken by the controller to address the personal data breach, including, where appropriate, measures to mitigate its possible adverse effects.

(3) The duty under subsection (1) does not apply where—
   (a) the controller has implemented appropriate technological and organisational protection measures which were applied to the personal data affected by the breach,
   (b) the controller has taken subsequent measures which ensure that the high risk to the rights and freedoms of data subjects referred to in subsection (1) is no longer likely to materialise, or
   (c) it would involve a disproportionate effort.

(4) An example of a case which may fall within subsection (3)(a) is where measures that render personal data unintelligible to any person not authorised to access the data have been applied, such as encryption.

(5) In a case falling within subsection (3)(c) (but not within subsection (3)(a) or (b)), the information mentioned in subsection (2) must be made available to the data subject in another equally effective way, for example, by means of a public communication.

(6) Where the controller has not informed the data subject of the breach the Commissioner, on being notified under section 67 and after considering the likelihood of the breach resulting in a high risk, may—
   (a) require the controller to notify the data subject of the breach, or
   (b) decide that the controller is not required to do so because any of paragraphs (a) to (c) of subsection (3) applies.

(7) The controller may restrict, wholly or partly, the provision of information to the data subject under subsection (1) to the extent that and for so long as the restriction is, having regard to the fundamental rights and legitimate interests of the data subject, a necessary and proportionate measure to—
   (a) avoid obstructing an official or legal inquiry, investigation or procedure;
   (b) avoid prejudicing the prevention, detection, investigation or prosecution of criminal offences or the execution of criminal penalties;
   (c) protect public security;
   (d) protect national security;
   (e) protect the rights and freedoms of others.

(8) Subsection (6) does not apply where the controller's decision not to inform the data subject of the breach was made in reliance on subsection (7).

(9) The duties in section 52(1) and (2) apply in relation to information that the controller is required to provide to the data subject under this section as they apply in relation to

information that the controller is required to provide to the data subject under Chapter 3.

––––– NOTES –––––

Defined terms		"data subject"	s 3(5)
"the Commissioner"	s 3(8)	"personal data"	s 3(2)
"controller"	s 32(1), (2)	"personal data breach"	s 33(1), (3)

Data protection officers

Designation of a data protection officer

69(1) The controller must designate a data protection officer, unless the controller is a court, or other judicial authority, acting in its judicial capacity.

(2) When designating a data protection officer, the controller must have regard to the professional qualities of the proposed officer, in particular—
  (a) the proposed officer's expert knowledge of data protection law and practice, and
  (b) the ability of the proposed officer to perform the tasks mentioned in section 71.

(3) The same person may be designated as a data protection officer by several controllers, taking account of their organisational structure and size.

(4) The controller must publish the contact details of the data protection officer and communicate these to the Commissioner.

––––– NOTES –––––

| **Defined terms** | | "controller" | s 32(1), (2) |
| "the Commissioner" | s 3(8) | "publish" | s 205(1) |

Position of data protection officer

70(1) The controller must ensure that the data protection officer is involved, properly and in a timely manner, in all issues which relate to the protection of personal data.

(2) The controller must provide the data protection officer with the necessary resources and access to personal data and processing operations to enable the data protection officer to—
  (a) perform the tasks mentioned in section 71, and
  (b) maintain his or her expert knowledge of data protection law and practice.

(3) The controller—
  (a) must ensure that the data protection officer does not receive any instructions regarding the performance of the tasks mentioned in section 71;
  (b) must ensure that the data protection officer does not perform a task or fulfil a duty other than those mentioned in this Part where such task or duty would result in a conflict of interests;
  (c) must not dismiss or penalise the data protection officer for performing the tasks mentioned in section 71.

(4) A data subject may contact the data protection officer with regard to all issues relating to—
  (a) the processing of that data subject's personal data, or
  (b) the exercise of that data subject's rights under this Part.

(5) The data protection officer, in the performance of this role, must report to the highest management level of the controller.

—— NOTES ——

Defined terms		"personal data"	s 3(2)
"controller"	s 32(1), (2)	"processing"	s 3(4)
"data subject"	s 3(5)	"processing of personal data"	s 29(2)

Tasks of data protection officer

71(1) The controller must entrust the data protection officer with at least the following tasks—

(a) informing and advising the controller, any processor engaged by the controller, and any employee of the controller who carries out processing of personal data, of that person's obligations under this Part,

(b) providing advice on the carrying out of a data protection impact assessment under section 64 and monitoring compliance with that section,

(c) co-operating with the Commissioner,

(d) acting as the contact point for the Commissioner on issues relating to processing, including in relation to the consultation mentioned in section 65, and consulting with the Commissioner, where appropriate, in relation to any other matter,

(e) monitoring compliance with policies of the controller in relation to the protection of personal data, and

(f) monitoring compliance by the controller with this Part.

(2) In relation to the policies mentioned in subsection (1)(e), the data protection officer's tasks include—

(a) assigning responsibilities under those policies,

(b) raising awareness of those policies,

(c) training staff involved in processing operations, and

(d) conducting audits required under those policies.

(3) In performing the tasks set out in subsections (1) and (2), the data protection officer must have regard to the risks associated with processing operations, taking into account the nature, scope, context and purposes of processing.

—— NOTES ——

Defined terms		"personal data"	s 3(2)
"the Commissioner"	s 3(8)	"processing"	s 3(4)
"controller"	s 32(1), (2)	"processing of personal data"	s 29(2)
"employee"	s 33(1), (2)	"processor"	s 32(3)

CHAPTER 5
TRANSFERS OF PERSONAL DATA TO THIRD COUNTRIES ETC

Overview and interpretation

Overview and interpretation

72(1) This Chapter deals with the transfer of personal data to third countries or international organisations, as follows—

(a) sections 73 to 76 set out the general conditions that apply;

(b) section 77 sets out the special conditions that apply where the intended recipient of personal data is not a relevant authority in a third country or an international organisation;

(c) section 78 makes special provision about subsequent transfers of personal data.

(2) In this Chapter, "relevant authority", in relation to a third country, means any person

based in a third country that has (in that country) functions comparable to those of a competent authority.

────── NOTES ──────

Defined terms		"personal data"	s 3(2)
"competent authority"	s 30	"recipient"	s 33(1), (5)
"international organisation"	s 205(1)	"third country"	s 33(1), (7)

General principles for transfers

General principles for transfers of personal data

73(1) A controller may not transfer personal data to a third country or to an international organisation unless—

    (a) the three conditions set out in subsections (2) to (4) are met, and

    (b) in a case where the personal data was originally transmitted or otherwise made available to the controller or another competent authority by a member State other than the United Kingdom, that member State, or any person based in that member State which is a competent authority for the purposes of the Law Enforcement Directive, has authorised the transfer in accordance with the law of the member State.

(2) Condition 1 is that the transfer is necessary for any of the law enforcement purposes.

(3) Condition 2 is that the transfer—

    (a) is based on an adequacy decision (see section 74),

    (b) if not based on an adequacy decision, is based on there being appropriate safeguards (see section 75), or

    (c) if not based on an adequacy decision or on there being appropriate safeguards, is based on special circumstances (see section 76).

(4) Condition 3 is that—

    (a) the intended recipient is a relevant authority in a third country or an international organisation that is a relevant international organisation, or

    (b) in a case where the controller is a competent authority specified in any of paragraphs 5 to 17, 21, 24 to 28, 34 to 51, 54 and 56 of Schedule 7—

        (i) the intended recipient is a person in a third country other than a relevant authority, and

        (ii) the additional conditions in section 77 are met.

(5) Authorisation is not required as mentioned in subsection (1)(b) if—

    (a) the transfer is necessary for the prevention of an immediate and serious threat either to the public security of a member State or a third country or to the essential interests of a member State, and

    (b) the authorisation cannot be obtained in good time.

(6) Where a transfer is made without the authorisation mentioned in subsection (1)(b), the authority in the member State which would have been responsible for deciding whether to authorise the transfer must be informed without delay.

(7) In this section, "relevant international organisation" means an international organisation that carries out functions for any of the law enforcement purposes.

—— NOTES ——

Defined terms		"the law enforcement purposes"	s 31
"competent authority"	s 30	"personal data"	s 3(2)
"controller"	s 32(1), (2)	"recipient"	s 33(1), (5)
"international organisation"	s 205(1)	"relevant authority"	s 72(2)
"the Law Enforcement Directive"	s 3(12)	"third country"	s 33(1), (7)

Transfers on the basis of an adequacy decision

74 A transfer of personal data to a third country or an international organisation is based on an adequacy decision where—

   (a) the European Commission has decided, in accordance with Article 36 of the Law Enforcement Directive, that—

      (i) the third country or a territory or one or more specified sectors within that third country, or

      (ii) (as the case may be) the international organisation, ensures an adequate level of protection of personal data, and

   (b) that decision has not been repealed or suspended, or amended in a way that demonstrates that the Commission no longer considers there to be an adequate level of protection of personal data.

—— NOTES ——

Defined terms		"personal data"	s 3(2)
"international organisation"	s 205(1)	"third country"	s 33(1), (7)
"the Law Enforcement Directive"	s 3(12)		

Transfers on the basis of appropriate safeguards

75(1) A transfer of personal data to a third country or an international organisation is based on there being appropriate safeguards where—

   (a) a legal instrument containing appropriate safeguards for the protection of personal data binds the intended recipient of the data, or

   (b) the controller, having assessed all the circumstances surrounding transfers of that type of personal data to the third country or international organisation, concludes that appropriate safeguards exist to protect the data.

(2) The controller must inform the Commissioner about the categories of data transfers that take place in reliance on subsection (1)(b).

(3) Where a transfer of data takes place in reliance on subsection (1)—

   (a) the transfer must be documented,

   (b) the documentation must be provided to the Commissioner on request, and

   (c) the documentation must include, in particular—

      (i) the date and time of the transfer,

      (ii) the name of and any other pertinent information about the recipient,

      (iii) the justification for the transfer, and

      (iv) a description of the personal data transferred.

—— NOTES ——

Defined terms		"personal data"	s 3(2)
"the Commissioner"	s 3(8)	"recipient"	s 33(1), (5)
"controller"	s 32(1), (2)	"third country"	s 33(1), (7)
"international organisation"	s 205(1)		

Transfers on the basis of special circumstances

76(1) A transfer of personal data to a third country or international organisation is based on special circumstances where the transfer is necessary—

(a) to protect the vital interests of the data subject or another person,

(b) to safeguard the legitimate interests of the data subject,

(c) for the prevention of an immediate and serious threat to the public security of a member State or a third country,

(d) in individual cases for any of the law enforcement purposes, or

(e) in individual cases for a legal purpose.

(2) But subsection (1)(d) and (e) do not apply if the controller determines that fundamental rights and freedoms of the data subject override the public interest in the transfer.

(3) Where a transfer of data takes place in reliance on subsection (1)—

(a) the transfer must be documented,

(b) the documentation must be provided to the Commissioner on request, and

(c) the documentation must include, in particular—

(i) the date and time of the transfer,

(ii) the name of and any other pertinent information about the recipient,

(iii) the justification for the transfer, and

(iv) a description of the personal data transferred.

(4) For the purposes of this section, a transfer is necessary for a legal purpose if—

(a) it is necessary for the purpose of, or in connection with, any legal proceedings (including prospective legal proceedings) relating to any of the law enforcement purposes,

(b) it is necessary for the purpose of obtaining legal advice in relation to any of the law enforcement purposes, or

(c) it is otherwise necessary for the purposes of establishing, exercising or defending legal rights in relation to any of the law enforcement purposes.

—— NOTES ——

Defined terms		"the law enforcement purposes"	s 31
"the Commissioner"	s 3(8)	"personal data"	s 3(2)
"controller"	s 32(1), (2)	"recipient"	s 33(1), (5)
"data subject"	s 3(5)	"third country"	s 33(1), (7)
"international organisation"	s 205(1)		

Transfers to particular recipients

Transfers of personal data to persons other than relevant authorities

77(1) The additional conditions referred to in section 73(4)(b)(ii) are the following four conditions.

(2) Condition 1 is that the transfer is strictly necessary in a specific case for the performance of a task of the transferring controller as provided by law for any of the law enforcement purposes.

(3) Condition 2 is that the transferring controller has determined that there are no fundamental rights and freedoms of the data subject concerned that override the public interest necessitating the transfer.

(4) Condition 3 is that the transferring controller considers that the transfer of the personal

data to a relevant authority in the third country would be ineffective or inappropriate (for example, where the transfer could not be made in sufficient time to enable its purpose to be fulfilled).

(5) Condition 4 is that the transferring controller informs the intended recipient of the specific purpose or purposes for which the personal data may, so far as necessary, be processed.

(6) Where personal data is transferred to a person in a third country other than a relevant authority, the transferring controller must inform a relevant authority in that third country without undue delay of the transfer, unless this would be ineffective or inappropriate.

(7) The transferring controller must—
   (a) document any transfer to a recipient in a third country other than a relevant authority, and
   (b) inform the Commissioner about the transfer.

(8) This section does not affect the operation of any international agreement in force between member States and third countries in the field of judicial co-operation in criminal matters and police co-operation.

------ NOTES ------

Defined terms			
"the Commissioner"	s 3(8)	"processing"	s 3(4)
"controller"	s 32(1), (2)	"processing of personal data"	s 29(2)
"data subject"	s 3(5)	"recipient"	s 33(1), (5)
"the law enforcement purposes"	s 31	"relevant authority"	s 72(2)
"personal data"	s 3(2)	"third country"	s 33(1), (7)

Subsequent transfers

Subsequent transfers

78(1) Where personal data is transferred in accordance with section 73, the transferring controller must make it a condition of the transfer that the data is not to be further transferred to a third country or international organisation without the authorisation of the transferring controller or another competent authority.

(2) A competent authority may give an authorisation under subsection (1) only where the further transfer is necessary for a law enforcement purpose.

(3) In deciding whether to give the authorisation, the competent authority must take into account (among any other relevant factors)—
   (a) the seriousness of the circumstances leading to the request for authorisation,
   (b) the purpose for which the personal data was originally transferred, and
   (c) the standards for the protection of personal data that apply in the third country or international organisation to which the personal data would be transferred.

(4) In a case where the personal data was originally transmitted or otherwise made available to the transferring controller or another competent authority by a member State other than the United Kingdom, an authorisation may not be given under subsection (1) unless that member State, or any person based in that member State which is a competent authority for the purposes of the Law Enforcement Directive, has authorised the transfer in accordance with the law of the member State.

(5) Authorisation is not required as mentioned in subsection (4) if—

    (a) the transfer is necessary for the prevention of an immediate and serious threat either to the public security of a member State or a third country or to the essential interests of a member State, and

    (b) the authorisation cannot be obtained in good time.

(6) Where a transfer is made without the authorisation mentioned in subsection (4), the authority in the member State which would have been responsible for deciding whether to authorise the transfer must be informed without delay.

—— NOTES ——

Defined terms		"the Law Enforcement Directive"	s 3(12)
"competent authority"	s 30	"the law enforcement purposes"	s 31
"controller"	s 32(1), (2)	"personal data"	s 3(2)
"international organisation"	s 205(1)	"third country"	s 33(1), (7)

CHAPTER 6
SUPPLEMENTARY

National security: certificate

79(1) A Minister of the Crown may issue a certificate certifying, for the purposes of section 44(4), 45(4), 48(3) or 68(7), that a restriction is a necessary and proportionate measure to protect national security.

(2) The certificate may—

    (a) relate to a specific restriction (described in the certificate) which a controller has imposed or is proposing to impose under section 44(4), 45(4), 48(3) or 68(7), or

    (b) identify any restriction to which it relates by means of a general description.

(3) Subject to subsection (6), a certificate issued under subsection (1) is conclusive evidence that the specific restriction or (as the case may be) any restriction falling within the general description is, or at any time was, a necessary and proportionate measure to protect national security.

(4) A certificate issued under subsection (1) may be expressed to have prospective effect.

(5) Any person directly affected by the issuing of a certificate under subsection (1) may appeal to the Tribunal against the certificate.

(6) If, on an appeal under subsection (5), the Tribunal finds that, applying the principles applied by a court on an application for judicial review, the Minister did not have reasonable grounds for issuing the certificate, the Tribunal may —

    (a) allow the appeal, and

    (b) quash the certificate.

(7) Where in any proceedings under or by virtue of this Act, it is claimed by a controller that a restriction falls within a general description in a certificate issued under subsection (1), any other party to the proceedings may appeal to the Tribunal on the ground that the restriction does not fall within that description.

(8) But, subject to any determination under subsection (9), the restriction is to be conclusively presumed to fall within the general description.

(9) On an appeal under subsection (7), the Tribunal may determine that the certificate does

not so apply.

(10) A document purporting to be a certificate under subsection (1) is to be—
 (a) received in evidence, and
 (b) deemed to be such a certificate unless the contrary is proved.

(11) A document which purports to be certified by or on behalf of a Minister of the Crown as a true copy of a certificate issued by that Minister under subsection (1) is—
 (a) in any legal proceedings, evidence of that certificate, and
 (b) in any legal proceedings in Scotland, sufficient evidence of that certificate.

(12) The power conferred by subsection (1) on a Minister of the Crown is exercisable only by—
 (a) a Minister who is a member of the Cabinet, or
 (b) the Attorney General or the Advocate General for Scotland.

(13) No power conferred by any provision of Part 6 may be exercised in relation to the imposition of—
 (a) a specific restriction in a certificate under subsection (1), or
 (b) a restriction falling within a general description in such a certificate.

—— Notes ——

| Defined terms | | "Minister of the Crown" | s 205(1) |
| "controller" | s 32(1), (2) | "the Tribunal" | s 205(1) |

Special processing restrictions

80(1) Subsections (3) and (4) apply where, for a law enforcement purpose, a controller transmits or otherwise makes available personal data to an EU recipient or a non-EU recipient.

(2) In this section—
 "EU recipient" means—
  (a) a recipient in a member State other than the United Kingdom, or
  (b) an agency, office or body established pursuant to Chapters 4 and 5 of Title V of the Treaty on the Functioning of the European Union;
 "non-EU recipient" means—
  (a) a recipient in a third country, or
  (b) an international organisation.

(3) The controller must consider whether, if the personal data had instead been transmitted or otherwise made available within the United Kingdom to another competent authority, processing of the data by the other competent authority would have been subject to any restrictions by virtue of any enactment or rule of law.

(4) Where that would be the case, the controller must inform the EU recipient or non-EU recipient that the data is transmitted or otherwise made available subject to complianceby that person with the same restrictions (which must be set out in the information given to that person).

(5) Except as provided by subsection (4), the controller may not impose restrictions on the processing of personal data transmitted or otherwise made available by the controller to an EU recipient.

(6) Subsection (7) applies where—
 (a) a competent authority for the purposes of the Law Enforcement Directive in a

member State other than the United Kingdom transmits or otherwise makes available personal data to a controller for a law enforcement purpose, and

(b) the competent authority in the other member State informs the controller, in accordance with any law of that member State which implements Article 9(3) and (4) of the Law Enforcement Directive, that the data is transmitted or otherwise made available subject to compliance by the controller with restrictions set out by the competent authority.

(7) The controller must comply with the restrictions.

—— NOTES ——

Defined terms		"the law enforcement purposes"	s 31
"competent authority"	s 30	"personal data"	s 3(2)
"controller"	s 32(1), (2)	"processing"	s 3(4)
"enactment"	s 205(1)	"processing of personal data"	s 29(2)
"international organisation"	s 205(1)	"recipient"	s 33(1), (5)
"the Law Enforcement Directive"	s 3(12)	"third country"	s 33(1), (7)

Reporting of infringements

81(1) Each controller must implement effective mechanisms to encourage the reporting of an infringement of this Part.

(2) The mechanisms implemented under subsection (1) must provide that an infringement may be reported to any of the following persons—

(a) the controller;

(b) the Commissioner.

(3) The mechanisms implemented under subsection (1) must include—

(a) raising awareness of the protections provided by Part 4A of the Employment Rights Act 1996 and Part 5A of the Employment Rights (Northern Ireland) Order 1996 (SI 1996/1919 (NI 16)), and

(b) such other protections for a person who reports an infringement of this Part as the controller considers appropriate.

(4) A person who reports an infringement of this Part does not breach—

(a) an obligation of confidence owed by the person, or

(b) any other restriction on the disclosure of information (however imposed).

(5) Subsection (4) does not apply if or to the extent that the report includes a disclosure which is prohibited by any of Parts 1 to 7 or Chapter 1 of Part 9 of the Investigatory Powers Act 2016.

(6) Until the repeal of Part 1 of the Regulation of Investigatory Powers Act 2000 by paragraphs 45 and 54 of Schedule 10 to the Investigatory Powers Act 2016 is fully in force, subsection (5) has effect as if it included a reference to that Part.

—— NOTES ——

Defined terms		"controller"	s 32(1), (2)
"the Commissioner"	s 3(8)		

PART 4
INTELLIGENCE SERVICES PROCESSING

CHAPTER 1
SCOPE AND DEFINITIONS

Scope

Processing to which this Part applies

82(1) This Part applies to—

    (a) the processing by an intelligence service of personal data wholly or partly by automated means, and

    (b) the processing by an intelligence service otherwise than by automated means of personal data which forms part of a filing system or is intended to form part of a filing system.

  (2) In this Part, "intelligence service" means—

    (a) the Security Service;

    (b) the Secret Intelligence Service;

    (c) the Government Communications Headquarters.

  (3) A reference in this Part to the processing of personal data is to processing to which this Part applies.

—— NOTES ——

| **Defined terms** | | "personal data" | s 3(2) |
| "filing system" | s 3(7) | "processing" | s 3(4) |

Definitions

Meaning of "controller" and "processor"

83(1) In this Part, "controller" means the intelligence service which, alone or jointly with others—

    (a) determines the purposes and means of the processing of personal data, or

    (b) is the controller by virtue of subsection (2).

  (2) Where personal data is processed only—

    (a) for purposes for which it is required by an enactment to be processed, and

    (b) by means by which it is required by an enactment to be processed,

the intelligence service on which the obligation to process the data is imposed by the enactment (or, if different, one of the enactments) is the controller.

  (3) In this Part, "processor" means any person who processes personal data on behalf of the controller (other than a person who is an employee of the controller).

—— NOTES ——

Defined terms		"personal data"	s 3(2)
"employee"	s 84(1), (3)	"processing"	s 3(4)
"enactment"	s 205(1)	"processing of personal data"	s 82(3)
"intelligence service"	s 82(2)		

Other definitions

84(1) This section defines other expressions used in this Part.

  (2) "Consent", in relation to the processing of personal data relating to an individual, means

a freely given, specific, informed and unambiguous indication of the individual's wishes by which the individual, by a statement or by a clear affirmative action, signifies agreement to the processing of the personal data.

(3) "Employee", in relation to any person, includes an individual who holds a position (whether paid or unpaid) under the direction and control of that person.

(4) "Personal data breach" means a breach of security leading to the accidental or unlawful destruction, loss, alteration, unauthorised disclosure of, or access to, personal data transmitted, stored or otherwise processed.

(5) "Recipient", in relation to any personal data, means any person to whom the data is disclosed, whether a third party or not, but it does not include a person to whom disclosure is or may be made in the framework of a particular inquiry in accordance with the law.

(6) "Restriction of processing" means the marking of stored personal data with the aim of limiting its processing for the future.

(7) Sections 3 and 205 include definitions of other expressions used in this Part.

—— NOTES ——

Defined terms		"processing"	s 3(4)
"personal data"	s 3(2)	"processing of personal data"	s 82(3)

CHAPTER 2
PRINCIPLES

Overview

Overview

85(1) This Chapter sets out the six data protection principles as follows—
  (a) section 86 sets out the first data protection principle (requirement that processing be lawful, fair and transparent);
  (b) section 87 sets out the second data protection principle (requirement that the purposes of processing be specified, explicit and legitimate);
  (c) section 88 sets out the third data protection principle (requirement that personal data be adequate, relevant and not excessive);
  (d) section 89 sets out the fourth data protection principle (requirement that personal data be accurate and kept up to date);
  (e) section 90 sets out the fifth data protection principle (requirement that personal data be kept for no longer than is necessary);
  (f) section 91 sets out the sixth data protection principle (requirement that personal data be processed in a secure manner).

(2) Each of sections 86, 87 and 91 makes provision to supplement the principle to which it relates.

The data protection principles

The first data protection principle

86(1) The first data protection principle is that the processing of personal data must be—
  (a) lawful, and
  (b) fair and transparent.

(2) The processing of personal data is lawful only if and to the extent that—

(a) at least one of the conditions in Schedule 9 is met, and

(b) in the case of sensitive processing, at least one of the conditions in Schedule 10 is also met.

(3) The Secretary of State may by regulations amend Schedule 10—

    (a) by adding conditions;

    (b) by omitting conditions added by regulations under paragraph (a).

(4) Regulations under subsection (3) are subject to the affirmative resolution procedure.

(5) In determining whether the processing of personal data is fair and transparent, regard is to be had to the method by which it is obtained.

(6) For the purposes of subsection (5), data is to be treated as obtained fairly and transparently if it consists of information obtained from a person who—

    (a) is authorised by an enactment to supply it, or

    (b) is required to supply it by an enactment or by an international obligation of the United Kingdom.

(7) In this section, "sensitive processing" means—

    (a) the processing of personal data revealing racial or ethnic origin, political opinions, religious or philosophical beliefs or trade union membership;

    (b) the processing of genetic data for the purpose of uniquely identifying an individual;

    (c) the processing of biometric data for the purpose of uniquely identifying an individual;

    (d) the processing of data concerning health;

    (e) the processing of data concerning an individual's sex life or sexual orientation;

    (f) the processing of personal data as to—

        (i) the commission or alleged commission of an offence by an individual, or

        (ii) proceedings for an offence committed or alleged to have been committed by an individual, the disposal of such proceedings or the sentence of a court in such proceedings.

—— NOTES ——

Defined terms		"genetic data"	s 205(1)
"the affirmative resolution		"international obligation of the	
procedure"	s 182(7)	United Kingdom"	s 205(1)
"biometric data"	s 205(1)	"personal data"	s 3(2)
"data concerning health"	s 205(1)	"processing"	s 3(4)
"enactment"	s 205(1)	"processing of personal data"	s 82(3)

The second data protection principle

87(1) The second data protection principle is that—

    (a) the purpose for which personal data is collected on any occasion must be specified, explicit and legitimate, and

    (b) personal data so collected must not be processed in a manner that is incompatible with the purpose for which it is collected.

(2) Paragraph (b) of the second data protection principle is subject to subsections (3) and (4).

(3) Personal data collected by a controller for one purpose may be processed for any other purpose of the controller that collected the data or any purpose of another controller provided that—

(a) the controller is authorised by law to process the data for that purpose, and

(b) the processing is necessary and proportionate to that other purpose.

(4) Processing of personal data is to be regarded as compatible with the purpose for which it is collected if the processing—

    (a) consists of—

        (i) processing for archiving purposes in the public interest,

        (ii) processing for the purposes of scientific or historical research, or

        (iii) processing for statistical purposes, and

    (b) is subject to appropriate safeguards for the rights and freedoms of the data subject.

—— NOTES ——

Defined terms			
"controller"	s 83(1), (2)	"personal data"	s 3(2)
"data subject"	s 3(5)	"processing"	s 3(4)
		"processing of personal data"	s 82(3)

The third data protection principle

88 The third data protection principle is that personal data must be adequate, relevant and not excessive in relation to the purpose for which it is processed.

—— NOTES ——

Defined terms			
"personal data"	s 3(2)	"processing"	s 3(4)
		"processing of personal data"	s 82(3)

The fourth data protection principle

89 The fourth data protection principle is that personal data undergoing processing must be accurate and, where necessary, kept up to date.

—— NOTES ——

Defined terms			
"personal data"	s 3(2)	"processing"	s 3(4)
		"processing of personal data"	s 82(3)

The fifth data protection principle

90 The fifth data protection principle is that personal data must be kept for no longer than is necessary for the purpose for which it is processed.

—— NOTES ——

Defined terms			
"personal data"	s 3(2)	"processing"	s 3(4)
		"processing of personal data"	s 82(3)

The sixth data protection principle

91(1) The sixth data protection principle is that personal data must be processed in a manner that includes taking appropriate security measures as regards risks that arise from processing personal data.

(2) The risks referred to in subsection (1) include (but are not limited to) accidental or unauthorised access to, or destruction, loss, use, modification or disclosure of, personal data.

—— NOTES ——

Defined terms			
"personal data"	s 3(2)	"processing"	s 3(4)
		"processing of personal data"	s 82(3)

CHAPTER 3
RIGHTS OF THE DATA SUBJECT

Overview

Overview

92(1)   This Chapter sets out the rights of the data subject as follows—

(a)   section 93 deals with the information to be made available to the data subject;

(b)   sections 94 and 95 deal with the right of access by the data subject;

(c)   sections 96 and 97 deal with rights in relation to automated processing;

(d)   section 98 deals with the right to information about decision-making;

(e)   section 99 deals with the right to object to processing;

(f)   section 100 deals with rights to rectification and erasure of personal data.

(2)   In this Chapter, "the controller", in relation to a data subject, means the controller in relation to personal data relating to the data subject.

—— NOTES ——

Defined terms		"personal data"	s 3(2)
"controller"	s 83(1), (2)	"processing"	s 3(4)
"data subject"	s 3(5)		

Rights

Right to information

93(1)   The controller must give a data subject the following information—

(a)   the identity and the contact details of the controller;

(b)   the legal basis on which, and the purposes for which, the controller processes personal data;

(c)   the categories of personal data relating to the data subject that are being processed;

(d)   the recipients or the categories of recipients of the personal data (if applicable);

(e)   the right to lodge a complaint with the Commissioner and the contact details of the Commissioner;

(f)   how to exercise rights under this Chapter;

(g)   any other information needed to secure that the personal data is processed fairly and transparently.

(2)   The controller may comply with subsection (1) by making information generally available, where the controller considers it appropriate to do so.

(3)   The controller is not required under subsection (1) to give a data subject information that the data subject already has.

(4)   Where personal data relating to a data subject is collected by or on behalf of the controller from a person other than the data subject, the requirement in subsection (1) has effect, in relation to the personal data so collected, with the following exceptions—

(a)   the requirement does not apply in relation to processing that is authorised by an enactment;

(b)   the requirement does not apply in relation to the data subject if giving the information to the data subject would be impossible or involve disproportionate effort.

Defined terms		"enactment"	s 205(1)
"the Commissioner"	s 3(8)	"personal data"	s 3(2)
"controller"	s 83(1), (2)	"processing"	s 3(4)
"the controller"	s 92(2)	"processing of personal data"	s 82(3)
"data subject"	s 3(5)	"recipient"	s 84(1), (5)

Right of access

94(1) An individual is entitled to obtain from a controller—

    (a) confirmation as to whether or not personal data concerning the individual is being processed, and

    (b) where that is the case—

        (i) communication, in intelligible form, of the personal data of which that individual is the data subject, and

        (ii) the information set out in subsection (2).

(2) That information is—

    (a) the purposes of and legal basis for the processing;

    (b) the categories of personal data concerned;

    (c) the recipients or categories of recipients to whom the personal data has been disclosed;

    (d) the period for which the personal data is to be preserved;

    (e) the existence of a data subject's rights to rectification and erasure of personal data (see section 100);

    (f) the right to lodge a complaint with the Commissioner and the contact details of the Commissioner;

    (g) any information about the origin of the personal data concerned.

(3) A controller is not obliged to provide information under this section unless the controller has received such reasonable fee as the controller may require, subject to subsection (4).

(4) The Secretary of State may by regulations—

    (a) specify cases in which a controller may not charge a fee;

    (b) specify the maximum amount of a fee.

(5) Where a controller—

    (a) reasonably requires further information—

        (i) in order that the controller be satisfied as to the identity of the individual making a request under subsection (1), or

        (ii) to locate the information which that individual seeks, and

    (b) has informed that individual of that requirement,

the controller is not obliged to comply with the request unless the controller is supplied with that further information.

(6) Where a controller cannot comply with the request without disclosing information relating to another individual who can be identified from that information, the controller is not obliged to comply with the request unless—

    (a) the other individual has consented to the disclosure of the information to the individual making the request, or

    (b) it is reasonable in all the circumstances to comply with the request without the consent of the other individual.

(7) In subsection (6), the reference to information relating to another individual includes a reference to information identifying that individual as the source of the information sought by the request.

(8) Subsection (6) is not to be construed as excusing a controller from communicating so much of the information sought by the request as can be communicated without disclosing the identity of the other individual concerned, whether by the omission of names or other identifying particulars or otherwise.

(9) In determining for the purposes of subsection (6)(b) whether it is reasonable in all the circumstances to comply with the request without the consent of the other individual concerned, regard must be had, in particular, to—
    (a) any duty of confidentiality owed to the other individual,
    (b) any steps taken by the controller with a view to seeking the consent of the other individual,
    (c) whether the other individual is capable of giving consent, and
    (d) any express refusal of consent by the other individual.

(10) Subject to subsection (6), a controller must comply with a request under subsection (1)—
    (a) promptly, and
    (b) in any event before the end of the applicable time period.

(11) If a court is satisfied on the application of an individual who has made a request under subsection (1) that the controller in question has failed to comply with the request in contravention of this section, the court may order the controller to comply with the request.

(12) A court may make an order under subsection (11) in relation to a joint controller whose responsibilities are determined in an arrangement under section 104 only if the controller is responsible for compliance with the obligation to which the order relates.

(13) The jurisdiction conferred on a court by this section is exercisable by the High Court or, in Scotland, by the Court of Session.

(14) In this section—
    "the applicable time period" means—
        (a) the period of 1 month, or
        (b) such longer period, not exceeding 3 months, as may be specified in regulations made by the Secretary of State,
    beginning with the relevant time;
    "the relevant time", in relation to a request under subsection (1), means the latest of the following—
        (a) when the controller receives the request,
        (b) when the fee (if any) is paid, and
        (c) when the controller receives the information (if any) required under subsection (5) in connection with the request.

(15) Regulations under this section are subject to the negative resolution procedure.

Defined terms		"the negative resolution procedure"	s 182(6)
"the Commissioner"	s 3(8)	"personal data"	s 3(2)
"consent"	s 84(1), (2)	"processing"	s 3(4)
"controller"	s 83(1), (2)	"processing of personal data"	s 82(3)
"the controller"	s 92(2)	"recipient"	s 84(1), (5)
"data subject"	s 3(5)		

Right of access: supplementary

95(1) The controller must comply with the obligation imposed by section 94(1)(b)(i) by supplying the data subject with a copy of the information in writing unless—

    (a) the supply of such a copy is not possible or would involve disproportionate effort, or

    (b) the data subject agrees otherwise;

and where any of the information referred to in section 94(1)(b)(i) is expressed in terms which are not intelligible without explanation the copy must be accompanied by an explanation of those terms.

(2) Where a controller has previously complied with a request made under section 94 by an individual, the controller is not obliged to comply with a subsequent identical or similar request under that section by that individual unless a reasonable interval has elapsed between compliance with the previous request and the making of the current request.

(3) In determining for the purposes of subsection (2) whether requests under section 94 are made at reasonable intervals, regard must be had to—

    (a) the nature of the data,

    (b) the purpose for which the data is processed, and

    (c) the frequency with which the data is altered.

(4) The information to be supplied pursuant to a request under section 94 must be supplied by reference to the data in question at the time when the request is received, except that it may take account of any amendment or deletion made between that time and the time when the information is supplied, being an amendment or deletion that would have been made regardless of the receipt of the request.

(5) For the purposes of section 94(6) to (8), an individual can be identified from information to be disclosed to a data subject by a controller if the individual can be identified from—

    (a) that information, or

    (b) that and any other information that the controller reasonably believes the data subject making the request is likely to possess or obtain.

Defined terms		"data subject"	s 3(5)
"controller"	s 83(1), (2)	"processing"	s 3(4)
"the controller"	s 92(2)		

Right not to be subject to automated decision-making

96(1) The controller may not take a decision significantly affecting a data subject that is based solely on automated processing of personal data relating to the data subject.

(2) Subsection (1) does not prevent such a decision being made on that basis if—

    (a) the decision is required or authorised by law,

(b) the data subject has given consent to the decision being made on that basis, or

(c) the decision is a decision taken in the course of steps taken—

   (i) for the purpose of considering whether to enter into a contract with the data subject,

   (ii) with a view to entering into such a contract, or

   (iii) in the course of performing such a contract.

(3) For the purposes of this section, a decision that has legal effects as regards an individual is to be regarded as significantly affecting the individual.

—— NOTES ——

Defined terms		"data subject"	s 3(5)
"consent"	s 84(1), (2)	"personal data"	s 3(2)
"controller"	s 83(1), (2)	"processing"	s 3(4)
"the controller"	s 92(2)	"processing of personal data"	s 82(3)

Right to intervene in automated decision-making

97(1) This section applies where—

(a) the controller takes a decision significantly affecting a data subject that is based solely on automated processing of personal data relating to the data subject, and

(b) the decision is required or authorised by law.

(2) This section does not apply to such a decision if—

(a) the data subject has given consent to the decision being made on that basis, or

(b) the decision is a decision taken in the course of steps taken—

   (i) for the purpose of considering whether to enter into a contract with the data subject,

   (ii) with a view to entering into such a contract, or

   (iii) in the course of performing such a contract.

(3) The controller must as soon as reasonably practicable notify the data subject that such a decision has been made.

(4) The data subject may, before the end of the period of 1 month beginning with receipt of the notification, request the controller—

(a) to reconsider the decision, or

(b) to take a new decision that is not based solely on automated processing.

(5) If a request is made to the controller under subsection (4), the controller must, before the end of the period of 1 month beginning with receipt of the request—

(a) consider the request, including any information provided by the data subject that is relevant to it, and

(b) by notice in writing inform the data subject of the outcome of that consideration.

(6) For the purposes of this section, a decision that has legal effects as regards an individual is to be regarded as significantly affecting the individual.

—— NOTES ——

Defined terms		"data subject"	s 3(5)
"consent"	s 84(1), (2)	"personal data"	s 3(2)
"controller"	s 83(1), (2)	"processing"	s 3(4)
"the controller"	s 92(2)	"processing of personal data"	s 82(3)

Right to information about decision-making

98(1) Where—

    (a) the controller processes personal data relating to a data subject, and

    (b) results produced by the processing are applied to the data subject,

the data subject is entitled to obtain from the controller, on request, knowledge of the reasoning underlying the processing.

  (2) Where the data subject makes a request under subsection (1), the controller must comply with the request without undue delay.

—— NOTES ——

Defined terms		"personal data"	s 3(2)
"controller"	s 83(1), (2)	"processing"	s 3(4)
"the controller"	s 92(2)	"processing of personal data"	s 82(3)
"data subject"	s 3(5)		

Right to object to processing

99(1) A data subject is entitled at any time, by notice given to the controller, to require the controller—

    (a) not to process personal data relating to the data subject, or

    (b) not to process such data for a specified purpose or in a specified manner,

on the ground that, for specified reasons relating to the situation of the data subject, the processing in question is an unwarranted interference with the interests or rights of the data subject.

  (2) Where the controller—

    (a) reasonably requires further information—

       (i) in order that the controller be satisfied as to the identity of the individual giving notice under subsection (1), or

       (ii) to locate the data to which the notice relates, and

    (b) has informed that individual of that requirement,

the controller is not obliged to comply with the notice unless the controller is supplied with that further information.

  (3) The controller must, before the end of 21 days beginning with the relevant time, give a notice to the data subject—

    (a) stating that the controller has complied or intends to comply with the notice under subsection (1), or

    (b) stating the controller's reasons for not complying with the notice to any extent and the extent (if any) to which the controller has complied or intends to comply with the notice under subsection (1).

  (4) If the controller does not comply with a notice under subsection (1) to any extent, the data subject may apply to a court for an order that the controller take steps for complying with the notice.

  (5) If the court is satisfied that the controller should comply with the notice (or should comply to any extent), the court may order the controller to take such steps for complying with the notice (or for complying with it to that extent) as the court thinks fit.

  (6) A court may make an order under subsection (5) in relation to a joint controller whose responsibilities are determined in an arrangement under section 104 only if the controller

is responsible for compliance with the obligation to which the order relates.

(7) The jurisdiction conferred on a court by this section is exercisable by the High Court or, in Scotland, by the Court of Session.

(8) In this section, "the relevant time", in relation to a notice under subsection (1), means—

    (a) when the controller receives the notice, or

    (b) if later, when the controller receives the information (if any) required under subsection (2) in connection with the notice.

—— NOTES ——

Defined terms		"personal data"	s 3(2)
"controller"	s 83(1), (2)	"processing"	s 3(4)
"the controller"	s 92(2)	"processing of personal data"	s 82(3)
"data subject"	s 3(5)		

Rights to rectification and erasure

100(1) If a court is satisfied on the application of a data subject that personal data relating to the data subject is inaccurate, the court may order the controller to rectify that data without undue delay.

(2) If a court is satisfied on the application of a data subject that the processing of personal data relating to the data subject would infringe any of sections 86 to 91, the court may order the controller to erase that data without undue delay.

(3) If personal data relating to the data subject must be maintained for the purposes of evidence, the court may (instead of ordering the controller to rectify or erase the personal data) order the controller to restrict its processing without undue delay.

(4) If—

    (a) the data subject contests the accuracy of personal data, and

    (b) the court is satisfied that the controller is not able to ascertain whether the data is accurate or not,

the court may (instead of ordering the controller to rectify or erase the personal data) order the controller to restrict its processing without undue delay.

(5) A court may make an order under this section in relation to a joint controller whose responsibilities are determined in an arrangement under section 104 only if the controller is responsible for carrying out the rectification, erasure or restriction of processing that the court proposes to order.

(6) The jurisdiction conferred on a court by this section is exercisable by the High Court or, in Scotland, by the Court of Session.

—— NOTES ——

Defined terms		"personal data"	s 3(2)
"controller"	s 83(1), (2)	"processing"	s 3(4)
"the controller"	s 92(2)	"processing of personal data"	s 82(3)
"data subject"	s 3(5)	"restriction of processing"	s 84(1), (6)
"inaccurate"	s 205(1)		

CHAPTER 4
CONTROLLER AND PROCESSOR

Overview

Overview

101 This Chapter sets out—

    (a) the general obligations of controllers and processors (see sections 102 to 106);

    (b) specific obligations of controllers and processors with respect to security (see section 107);

    (c) specific obligations of controllers and processors with respect to personal data breaches (see section 108).

—— NOTES ——

Defined terms		"personal data breach"	s 84(1), (4)
"controller"	s 83(1), (2)	"processor"	s 83(3)

General obligations

General obligations of the controller

102 Each controller must implement appropriate measures—

    (a) to ensure, and

    (b) to be able to demonstrate, in particular to the Commissioner, that the processing of personal data complies with the requirements of this Part.

—— NOTES ——

Defined terms		"personal data"	s 3(2)
"the Commissioner"	s 3(8)	"processing"	s 3(4)
"controller"	s 83(1), (2)	"processing of personal data"	s 82(3)

Data protection by design

103(1) Where a controller proposes that a particular type of processing of personal data be carried out by or on behalf of the controller, the controller must, prior to the processing, consider the impact of the proposed processing on the rights and freedoms of data subjects.

  (2) A controller must implement appropriate technical and organisational measures which are designed to ensure that—

    (a) the data protection principles are implemented, and

    (b) risks to the rights and freedoms of data subjects are minimised.

—— NOTES ——

Defined terms		"personal data"	s 3(2)
"controller"	s 83(1), (2)	"processing"	s 3(4)
"data subject"	s 3(5)	"processing of personal data"	s 82(3)

Joint controllers

104(1) Where two or more intelligence services jointly determine the purposes and means of processing personal data, they are joint controllers for the purposes of this Part.

  (2) Joint controllers must, in a transparent manner, determine their respective responsibilities for compliance with this Part by means of an arrangement between them, except to the extent that those responsibilities are determined under or by virtue of an enactment.

  (3) The arrangement must designate the controller which is to be the contact point for data

subjects.

—— NOTES ——

Defined terms			
"controller"	s 83(1), (2)	"intelligence service"	s 82(2)
"data subject"	s 3(5)	"personal data"	s 3(2)
"enactment"	s 205(1)	"processing"	s 3(4)
		"processing of personal data"	s 82(3)

Processors

105(1) This section applies to the use by a controller of a processor to carry out processing of personal data on behalf of the controller.

(2) The controller may use only a processor who undertakes—

   (a) to implement appropriate measures that are sufficient to secure that the processing complies with this Part;

   (b) to provide to the controller such information as is necessary for demonstrating that the processing complies with this Part.

(3) If a processor determines, in breach of this Part, the purposes and means of processing, the processor is to be treated for the purposes of this Part as a controller in respect of that processing.

—— NOTES ——

Defined terms			
"controller"	s 83(1), (2)	"processing"	s 3(4)
"personal data"	s 3(2)	"processing of personal data"	s 82(3)
		"processor"	s 83(3)

Processing under the authority of the controller or processor

106 A processor, and any person acting under the authority of a controller or processor, who has access to personal data may not process the data except—

   (a) on instructions from the controller, or

   (b) to comply with a legal obligation.

—— NOTES ——

Defined terms			
"controller"	s 83(1), (2)	"processing"	s 3(4)
"personal data"	s 3(2)	"processing of personal data"	s 82(3)
		"processor"	s 83(3)

Obligations relating to security

Security of processing

107(1) Each controller and each processor must implement security measures appropriate to the risks arising from the processing of personal data.

(2) In the case of automated processing, each controller and each processor must, following an evaluation of the risks, implement measures designed to—

   (a) prevent unauthorised processing or unauthorised interference with the systems used in connection with it,

   (b) ensure that it is possible to establish the precise details of any processing that takes place,

   (c) ensure that any systems used in connection with the processing function properly and may, in the case of interruption, be restored, and

   (d) ensure that stored personal data cannot be corrupted if a system used in connection with the processing malfunctions.

Obligations relating to personal data breaches

Communication of a personal data breach

108(1) If a controller becomes aware of a serious personal data breach in relation to personal data for which the controller is responsible, the controller must notify the Commissioner of the breach without undue delay.

(2) Where the notification to the Commissioner is not made within 72 hours, the notification must be accompanied by reasons for the delay.

(3) Subject to subsection (4), the notification must include—
   (a) a description of the nature of the personal data breach including, where possible, the categories and approximate number of data subjects concerned and the categories and approximate number of personal data records concerned;
   (b) the name and contact details of the contact point from whom more information can be obtained;
   (c) a description of the likely consequences of the personal data breach;
   (d) a description of the measures taken or proposed to be taken by the controller to address the personal data breach, including, where appropriate, measures to mitigate its possible adverse effects.

(4) Where and to the extent that it is not possible to provide all the information mentioned in subsection (3) at the same time, the information may be provided in phases without undue further delay.

(5) If a processor becomes aware of a personal data breach (in relation to data processed by the processor), the processor must notify the controller without undue delay.

(6) Subsection (1) does not apply in relation to a personal data breach if the breach also constitutes a relevant error within the meaning given by section 231(9) of the Investigatory Powers Act 2016.

(7) For the purposes of this section, a personal data breach is serious if the breach seriously interferes with the rights and freedoms of a data subject.

CHAPTER 5
TRANSFERS OF PERSONAL DATA OUTSIDE THE UNITED KINGDOM

Transfers of personal data outside the United Kingdom

109(1) A controller may not transfer personal data to—
   (a) a country or territory outside the United Kingdom, or
   (b) an international organisation,

unless the transfer falls within subsection (2).

(2) A transfer of personal data falls within this subsection if the transfer is a necessary and proportionate measure carried out—

    (a) for the purposes of the controller's statutory functions, or

    (b) for other purposes provided for, in relation to the controller, in section 2(2)(a) of the Security Service Act 1989 or section 2(2)(a) or 4(2)(a) of the Intelligence Services Act 1994.

—— NOTES ——

Defined terms		"personal data"	s 3(2)
"controller"	s 83(1), (2)	"processing"	s 3(4)
"international organisation"	s 205(1)		

CHAPTER 6
EXEMPTIONS

National security

110(1) A provision mentioned in subsection (2) does not apply to personal data to which this Part applies if exemption from the provision is required for the purpose of safeguarding national security.

(2) The provisions are—

    (a) Chapter 2 (the data protection principles), except section 86(1)(a) and (2) and Schedules 9 and 10;

    (b) Chapter 3 (rights of data subjects);

    (c) in Chapter 4 , section 108 (communication of a personal data breach to the Commissioner);

    (d) in Part 5—

        (i) section 119 (inspection in accordance with international obligations);

        (ii) in Schedule 13 (other general functions of the Commissioner), paragraphs 1(a) and (g) and 2;

    (e) in Part 6—

        (i) sections 142 to 154 and Schedule 15 (Commissioner's notices and powers of entry and inspection);

        (ii) sections 170 to 173 (offences relating to personal data);

        (iii) sections 174 to 176 (provision relating to the special purposes).

—— NOTES ——

Defined terms	"personal data"	s 3(2)

National security: certificate

111(1) Subject to subsection (3), a certificate signed by a Minister of the Crown certifying that exemption from all or any of the provisions mentioned in section 110(2) is, or at any time was, required for the purpose of safeguarding national security in respect of any personal data is conclusive evidence of that fact.

(2) A certificate under subsection (1)—

    (a) may identify the personal data to which it applies by means of a general description, and

    (b) may be expressed to have prospective effect.

(3) Any person directly affected by the issuing of a certificate under subsection (1) may appeal to the Tribunal against the certificate.

(4) If on an appeal under subsection (3), the Tribunal finds that, applying the principles applied by a court on an application for judicial review, the Minister did not have reasonable grounds for issuing the certificate, the Tribunal may—

    (a) allow the appeal, and

    (b) quash the certificate.

(5) Where, in any proceedings under or by virtue of this Act, it is claimed by a controller that a certificate under subsection (1) which identifies the personal data to which it applies by means of a general description applies to any personal data, another party to the proceedings may appeal to the Tribunal on the ground that the certificate does not apply to the personal data in question.

(6) But, subject to any determination under subsection (7), the certificate is to be conclusively presumed so to apply.

(7) On an appeal under subsection (5), the Tribunal may determine that the certificate does not so apply.

(8) A document purporting to be a certificate under subsection (1) is to be—

    (a) received in evidence, and

    (b) deemed to be such a certificate unless the contrary is proved.

(9) A document which purports to be certified by or on behalf of a Minister of the Crown as a true copy of a certificate issued by that Minister under subsection (1) is—

    (a) in any legal proceedings, evidence of that certificate, and

    (b) in any legal proceedings in Scotland, sufficient evidence of that certificate.

(10) The power conferred by subsection (1) on a Minister of the Crown is exercisable only by—

    (a) a Minister who is a member of the Cabinet, or

    (b) the Attorney General or the Advocate General for Scotland.

—— NOTES ——

Defined terms		"personal data"	s 3(2)
"controller"	s 83(1), (2)	"the Tribunal"	s 205(1)
"Minister of the Crown"	s 205(1)		

Other exemptions

112 Schedule 11 provides for further exemptions.

Power to make further exemptions

113(1) The Secretary of State may by regulations amend Schedule 11—

    (a) by adding exemptions from any provision of this Part;

    (b) by omitting exemptions added by regulations under paragraph (a).

(2) Regulations under this section are subject to the affirmative resolution procedure.

—— NOTES ——

Defined terms	procedure"	s 182(7)
"the affirmative resolution		

PART 5
THE INFORMATION COMMISSIONER

The Commissioner

The Information Commissioner

114(1)   There is to continue to be an Information Commissioner.

(2)   Schedule 12 makes provision about the Commissioner.

General functions

General functions under the GDPR and safeguards

115(1)   The Commissioner is to be the supervisory authority in the United Kingdom for the purposes of Article 51 of the GDPR.

(2)   General functions are conferred on the Commissioner by—
    (a)   Article 57 of the GDPR (tasks), and
    (b)   Article 58 of the GDPR (powers),
(and see also the Commissioner's duty under section 2).

(3)   The Commissioner's functions in relation to the processing of personal data to which the GDPR applies include—
    (a) a duty to advise Parliament, the government and other institutions and bodies on legislative and administrative measures relating to the protection of individuals' rights and freedoms with regard to the processing of personal data, and
    (b) a power to issue, on the Commissioner's own initiative or on request, opinions to Parliament, the government or other institutions and bodies as well as to the public on any issue related to the protection of personal data.

(4)   The Commissioner's functions under Article 58 of the GDPR are subject to the safeguards in subsections (5) to (9).

(5)   The Commissioner's power under Article 58(1)(a) of the GDPR (power to require a controller or processor to provide information that the Commissioner requires for the performance of the Commissioner's tasks under the GDPR) is exercisable only by giving an information notice under section 142.

(6)   The Commissioner's power under Article 58(1)(b) of the GDPR (power to carry out data protection audits) is exercisable only in accordance with section 146.

(7)   The Commissioner's powers under Article 58(1)(e) and (f) of the GDPR (power to obtain information from controllers and processors and access to their premises) are exercisable only—
    (a)   in accordance with Schedule 15 (see section 154), or
    (b)   to the extent that they are exercised in conjunction with the power under Article 58(1)(b) of the GDPR, in accordance with section 146.

(8)   The following powers are exercisable only by giving an enforcement notice under section 149—
    (a)   the Commissioner's powers under Article 58(2)(c) to (g) and (j) of the GDPR (certain corrective powers);
    (b)   the Commissioner's powers under Article 58(2)(h) to order a certification body to withdraw, or not to issue, a certification under Articles 42 and 43 of the GDPR.

(9) The Commissioner's powers under Articles 58(2)(i) and 83 of the GDPR (administrative fines) are exercisable only by giving a penalty notice under section 155.

(10) This section is without prejudice to other functions conferred on the Commissioner, whether by the GDPR, this Act or otherwise.

—— NOTES ——

Defined terms		"personal data"	s 3(2), (14)(c)
"the Commissioner"	s 3(8)	"processing"	s 3(4), (14)(c)
"the GDPR"	s 3(10), (14)(a)		

Other general functions

116(1) The Commissioner—

    (a) is to be the supervisory authority in the United Kingdom for the purposes of Article 41 of the Law Enforcement Directive, and

    (b) is to continue to be the designated authority in the United Kingdom for the purposes of Article 13 of the Data Protection Convention.

(2) Schedule 13 confers general functions on the Commissioner in connection with processing to which the GDPR does not apply (and see also the Commissioner's duty under section 2).

(3) This section and Schedule 13 are without prejudice to other functions conferred on the Commissioner, whether by this Act or otherwise.

—— NOTES ——

Defined terms		"the GDPR"	s 3(10), (14)(a)
"the Commissioner"	s 3(8)	"the Law Enforcement Directive"	s 3(12)
"the Data Protection Convention"	s 3(13)	"processing"	s 3(4), (14)(c)

Competence in relation to courts etc

117 Nothing in this Act permits or requires the Commissioner to exercise functions in relation to the processing of personal data by—

    (a) an individual acting in a judicial capacity, or

    (b) a court or tribunal acting in its judicial capacity, (and see also Article 55(3) of the GDPR).

—— NOTES ——

Defined terms		"personal data"	s 3(2), (14)(c)
"the Commissioner"	s 3(8)	"processing"	s 3(4), (14)(c)
"the GDPR"	s 3(10), (14)(a)	"tribunal"	s 205(1)

International role

Co-operation and mutual assistance

118(1) Articles 60 to 62 of the GDPR confer functions on the Commissioner in relation to co-operation and mutual assistance between, and joint operations of, supervisory authorities under the GDPR.

(2) References to the GDPR in subsection (1) do not include the applied GDPR.

(3) Article 61 of the applied GDPR confers functions on the Commissioner in relation to co-operation with other supervisory authorities (as defined in Article 4(21) of the applied GDPR).

(4) Part 1 of Schedule 14 makes provision as to the functions to be carried out by the

Commissioner for the purposes of Article 50 of the Law Enforcement Directive (mutual assistance).

(5) Part 2 of Schedule 14 makes provision as to the functions to be carried out by the Commissioner for the purposes of Article 13 of the Data Protection Convention (co-operation between parties).

—— Notes ——

Defined terms		"the Data Protection Convention"	s 3(13)
"the applied GDPR"	s 3(11)	"the GDPR"	s 3(10), (14)(a)
"the Commissioner"	s 3(8)	"the Law Enforcement Directive"	s 3(12)

Inspection of personal data in accordance with international obligations

119(1) The Commissioner may inspect personal data where the inspection is necessary in order to discharge an international obligation of the United Kingdom, subject to the restriction in subsection (2).

(2) The power under subsection (1) is exercisable only if the personal data—
   (a) is processed wholly or partly by automated means, or
   (b) is processed otherwise than by automated means and forms part of a filing system or is intended to form part of a filing system.

(3) The power under subsection (1) includes power to inspect, operate and test equipment which is used for the processing of personal data.

(4) Before exercising the power under subsection (1), the Commissioner must by written notice inform the controller and any processor that the Commissioner intends to do so.

(5) Subsection (4) does not apply if the Commissioner considers that the case is urgent.

(6) It is an offence—
   (a) intentionally to obstruct a person exercising the power under subsection (1), or
   (b) to fail without reasonable excuse to give a person exercising that power any assistance the person may reasonably require.

(7) Paragraphs (c) and (d) of section 3(14) do not apply to references in this section to personal data, the processing of personal data, a controller or a processor.

—— Notes ——

Defined terms		"international obligation of the	
"the Commissioner"	s 3(8)	United Kingdom"	s 205(1)
"controller"	s 3(6)	"personal data"	s 3(2) (note sub-s 119(7))
(note sub-s 119(7) of this section)		"processing"	s 3(4) (note sub-s 119(7))
"filing system"	s 3(7)	"processor"	s 3(6) (note sub-s 119(7))

Further international role

120(1) The Commissioner must, in relation to third countries and international organisations, take appropriate steps to—
   (a) develop international co-operation mechanisms to facilitate the effective enforcement of legislation for the protection of personal data;
   (b) provide international mutual assistance in the enforcement of legislation for the protection of personal data, subject to appropriate safeguards for the protection of personal data and other fundamental rights and freedoms;
   (c) engage relevant stakeholders in discussion and activities aimed at furthering international co-operation in the enforcement of legislation for the protection of

personal data;

    (d) promote the exchange and documentation of legislation and practice for the protection of personal data, including legislation and practice relating to jurisdictional conflicts with third countries.

(2) Subsection (1) applies only in connection with the processing of personal data to which the GDPR does not apply; for the equivalent duty in connection with the processing of personal data to which the GDPR applies, see Article 50 of the GDPR (international co-operation for the protection of personal data).

(3) The Commissioner must carry out data protection functions which the Secretary of State directs the Commissioner to carry out for the purpose of enabling Her Majesty's Government in the United Kingdom to give effect to an international obligation of the United Kingdom.

(4) The Commissioner may provide an authority carrying out data protection functions under the law of a British overseas territory with assistance in carrying out those functions.

(5) The Secretary of State may direct that assistance under subsection (4) is to be provided on terms, including terms as to payment, specified or approved by the Secretary of State.

(6) In this section—

    "data protection functions" means functions relating to the protection of individuals with respect to the processing of personal data;

    "mutual assistance in the enforcement of legislation for the protection of personal data" includes assistance in the form of notification, complaint referral, investigative assistance and information exchange;

    "third country" means a country or territory that is not a member State.

(7) Section 3(14)(c) does not apply to references to personal data and the processing of personal data in this section.

────── NOTES ──────

Defined terms		the United Kingdom"	s 205(1)
"the Commissioner"	s 3(8)	"international organisation"	s 205(1)
"the GDPR"	s 3(10), (14)(a)	"personal data"	s 3(2) (note sub-s 120(7))
"international obligation of		"processing"	s 3(4) (note sub-s 120(7))

Codes of practice

Data-sharing code

121(1) The Commissioner must prepare a code of practice which contains—

    (a) practical guidance in relation to the sharing of personal data in accordance with the requirements of the data protection legislation, and

    (b) such other guidance as the Commissioner considers appropriate to promote good practice in the sharing of personal data.

(2) Where a code under this section is in force, the Commissioner may prepare amendments of the code or a replacement code.

(3) Before preparing a code or amendments under this section, the Commissioner must consult the Secretary of State and such of the following as the Commissioner considers appropriate—

    (a) trade associations;

(b) data subjects;

(c) persons who appear to the Commissioner to represent the interests of data subjects.

(4) A code under this section may include transitional provision or savings.

(5) In this section—

"good practice in the sharing of personal data" means such practice in the sharing of personal data as appears to the Commissioner to be desirable having regard to the interests of data subjects and others, including compliance with the requirements of the data protection legislation;

"the sharing of personal data" means the disclosure of personal data by transmission, dissemination or otherwise making it available;

"trade association" includes a body representing controllers or processors.

―――― NOTES ――――

Defined terms		"data subject"	s 3(5)
"the Commissioner"	s 3(8)	"personal data"	s 3(2), (14)(c)
"controller"	s 3(6), (14)(d)	"processor"	s 3(6), (14)(d)
"the data protection legislation"	s 3(9)		

Direct marketing code

122(1) The Commissioner must prepare a code of practice which contains—

(a) practical guidance in relation to the carrying out of direct marketing in accordance with the requirements of the data protection legislation and the Privacy and Electronic Communications (EC Directive) Regulations 2003 (SI 2003/2426), and

(b) such other guidance as the Commissioner considers appropriate to promote good practice in direct marketing.

(2) Where a code under this section is in force, the Commissioner may prepare amendments of the code or a replacement code.

(3) Before preparing a code or amendments under this section, the Commissioner must consult the Secretary of State and such of the following as the Commissioner considers appropriate—

(a) trade associations;

(b) data subjects;

(c) persons who appear to the Commissioner to represent the interests of data subjects.

(4) A code under this section may include transitional provision or savings.

(5) In this section—

"direct marketing" means the communication (by whatever means) of advertising or marketing material which is directed to particular individuals;

"good practice in direct marketing" means such practice in direct marketing as appears to the Commissioner to be desirable having regard to the interests of data subjects and others, including compliance with the requirements mentioned in subsection (1)(a);

"trade association" includes a body representing controllers or processors.

―――― NOTES ――――

Defined terms		"the data protection legislation"	s 3(9)
"the Commissioner"	s 3(8)	"data subject"	s 3(5)
"controller"	s 3(6), (14)(d)	"processor"	s 3(6), (14)(d)

Age-appropriate design code

123(1)   The Commissioner must prepare a code of practice which contains such guidance as the Commissioner considers appropriate on standards of age-appropriate design of relevant information society services which are likely to be accessed by children.

(2)   Where a code under this section is in force, the Commissioner may prepare amendments of the code or a replacement code.

(3)   Before preparing a code or amendments under this section, the Commissioner must consult the Secretary of State and such other persons as the Commissioner considers appropriate, including—

(a)   children,

(b)   parents,

(c)   persons who appear to the Commissioner to represent the interests of children,

(d)   child development experts, and

(e)   trade associations.

(4)   In preparing a code or amendments under this section, the Commissioner must have regard—

(a)   to the fact that children have different needs at different ages, and

(b)   to the United Kingdom's obligations under the United Nations Convention on the Rights of the Child.

(5)   A code under this section may include transitional provision or savings.

(6)   Any transitional provision included in the first code under this section must cease to have effect before the end of the period of 12 months beginning when the code comes into force.

(7)   In this section—

"age-appropriate design" means the design of services so that they are appropriate for use by, and meet the development needs of, children;

"information society services" has the same meaning as in the GDPR, but does not include preventive or counselling services;

"relevant information society services" means information society services which involve the processing of personal data to which the GDPR applies;

"standards of age-appropriate design of relevant information society services" means such standards of age-appropriate design of such services as appear to the Commissioner to be desirable having regard to the best interests of children;

"trade association" includes a body representing controllers or processors;

"the United Nations Convention on the Rights of the Child" means the Convention on the Rights of the Child adopted by the General Assembly of the United Nations on 20 November 1989 (including any Protocols to that Convention which are in force in relation to the United Kingdom), subject to any reservations, objections or interpretative declarations by the United Kingdom for the time being in force.

—— NOTES ——

Defined terms		"personal data"	s 3(2), (14)(c)
"the Commissioner"	s 3(8)	"processing"	s 3(4), (14)(c)
"controller"	s 3(6), (14)(d)	"processor"	s 3(6), (14)(d)
"the GDPR"	s 3(10), (14)(a)		

Data protection and journalism code

124(1)   The Commissioner must prepare a code of practice which contains—

   (a)   practical guidance in relation to the processing of personal data for the purposes of journalism in accordance with the requirements of the data protection legislation, and

   (b)   such other guidance as the Commissioner considers appropriate to promote good practice in the processing of personal data for the purposes of journalism.

   (2)   Where a code under this section is in force, the Commissioner may prepare amendments of the code or a replacement code.

   (3)   Before preparing a code or amendments under this section, the Commissioner must consult such of the following as the Commissioner considers appropriate—

   (a)   trade associations;

   (b)   data subjects;

   (c)   persons who appear to the Commissioner to represent the interests of data subjects.

   (4)   A code under this section may include transitional provision or savings.

   (5)   In this section—

   "good practice in the processing of personal data for the purposes of journalism" means such practice in the processing of personal data for those purposes as appears to the Commissioner to be desirable having regard to—

      (a)   the interests of data subjects and others, including compliance with the requirements of the data protection legislation, and

      (b)   the special importance of the public interest in the freedom of expression and information;

   "trade association" includes a body representing controllers or processors.

——— NOTES ———

Defined terms		"data subject"	s 3(5)
"the Commissioner"	s 3(8)	"personal data"	s 3(2), (14)(c)
"controller"	s 3(6), (14)(d)	"processing"	s 3(4), (14)(c)
"the data protection legislation"	s 3(9)	"processor"	s 3(6), (14)(d)

Approval of codes prepared under sections 121 to 124

125(1)   When a code is prepared under section 121, 122, 123 or 124—

   (a)   the Commissioner must submit the final version to the Secretary of State, and

   (b)   the Secretary of State must lay the code before Parliament.

   (2)   In relation to the first code under section 123—

   (a)   the Commissioner must prepare the code as soon as reasonably practicable and must submit it to the Secretary of State before the end of the period of 18 months beginning when this Act is passed, and

   (b)   the Secretary of State must lay it before Parliament as soon as reasonably practicable.

   (3)   If, within the 40-day period, either House of Parliament resolves not to approve a code prepared under section 121, 122, 123 or 124, the Commissioner must not issue the code.

   (4)   If no such resolution is made within that period—

   (a)   the Commissioner must issue the code, and

    (b) the code comes into force at the end of the period of 21 days beginning with the day on which it is issued.

(5) If, as a result of subsection (3), there is no code in force under section 121, 122, 123 or 124, the Commissioner must prepare another version of the code.

(6) Nothing in subsection (3) prevents another version of the code being laid before Parliament.

(7) In this section, "the 40-day period" means—
    (a) if the code is laid before both Houses of Parliament on the same day, the period of 40 days beginning with that day, or
    (b) if the code is laid before the Houses of Parliament on different days, the period of 40 days beginning with the later of those days.

(8) In calculating the 40-day period, no account is to be taken of any period during which Parliament is dissolved or prorogued or during which both Houses of Parliament are adjourned for more than 4 days.

(9) This section, other than subsections (2) and (5), applies in relation to amendments prepared under section 121, 122, 123 or 124 as it applies in relation to codes prepared under those sections.

—— NOTES ——

Defined terms   "the Commissioner"   s 3(8)

Publication and review of codes issued under section 125(4)

126(1) The Commissioner must publish a code issued under section 125(4).

(2) Where an amendment of a code is issued under section 125(4), the Commissioner must publish—
    (a) the amendment, or
    (b) the code as amended by it.

(3) The Commissioner must keep under review each code issued under section 125(4) for the time being in force.

(4) Where the Commissioner becomes aware that the terms of such a code could result in a breach of an international obligation of the United Kingdom, the Commissioner must exercise the power under section 121(2), 122(2), 123(2) or 124(2) with a view to remedying the situation.

—— NOTES ——

Defined terms		Kingdom"	s 205(1)
"the Commissioner"	s 3(8)	"publish"	s 205(1)
"international obligation of the United			

Effect of codes issued under section 125(4)

127(1) A failure by a person to act in accordance with a provision of a code issued under section 125(4) does not of itself make that person liable to legal proceedings in a court or tribunal.

(2) A code issued under section 125(4), including an amendment or replacement code, is admissible in evidence in legal proceedings.

(3) In any proceedings before a court or tribunal, the court or tribunal must take into account

a provision of a code issued under section 125(4) in determining a question arising in the proceedings if—

    (a) the question relates to a time when the provision was in force, and

    (b) the provision appears to the court or tribunal to be relevant to the question.

(4) Where the Commissioner is carrying out a function described in subsection (5), the Commissioner must take into account a provision of a code issued under section 125(4) in determining a question arising in connection with the carrying out of the function if—

    (a) the question relates to a time when the provision was in force, and

    (b) the provision appears to the Commissioner to be relevant to the question.

(5) Those functions are functions under—

    (a) the data protection legislation, or

    (b) the Privacy and Electronic Communications (EC Directive) Regulations 2003 (SI 2003/2426).

—— NOTES ——

Defined terms			
"the Commissioner"	s 3(8)	"the data protection legislation"	s 3(9)
		"tribunal"	s 205(1)

Other codes of practice

128(1) The Secretary of State may by regulations require the Commissioner—

    (a) to prepare appropriate codes of practice giving guidance as to good practice in the processing of personal data, and

    (b) to make them available to such persons as the Commissioner considers appropriate.

(2) Before preparing such codes, the Commissioner must consult such of the following as the Commissioner considers appropriate—

    (a) trade associations;

    (b) data subjects;

    (c) persons who appear to the Commissioner to represent the interests of data subjects.

(3) Regulations under this section—

    (a) must describe the personal data or processing to which the code of practice is to relate, and

    (b) may describe the persons or classes of person to whom it is to relate.

(4) Regulations under this section are subject to the negative resolution procedure.

(5) In this section—

    "good practice in the processing of personal data" means such practice in the processing of personal data as appears to the Commissioner to be desirable having regard to the interests of data subjects and others, including compliance with the requirements of the data protection legislation;

    "trade association" includes a body representing controllers or processors.

—— NOTES ——

Defined terms			
"the Commissioner"	s 3(8)	"the negative resolution procedure"	s 182(6)
"controller"	s 3(6), (14)(d)	"personal data"	s 3(2), (14)(c)
"the data protection legislation"	s 3(9)	"processing"	s 3(4), (14)(c)
"data subject"	s 3(5)	"processor"	s 3(6), (14)(d)

Consensual audits

Consensual audits

129(1) The Commissioner's functions under Article 58(1) of the GDPR and paragraph 1 of Schedule 13 include power, with the consent of a controller or processor, to carry out an assessment of whether the controller or processor is complying with good practice in the processing of personal data.

(2) The Commissioner must inform the controller or processor of the results of such an assessment.

(3) In this section, "good practice in the processing of personal data" has the same meaning as in section 128.

—— NOTES ——

Defined terms		"personal data"	s 3(2), (14)(c)
"the Commissioner"	s 3(8)	"processing"	s 3(4), (14)(c)
"controller"	s 3(6), (14)(d)	"processor"	s 3(6), (14)(d)
"the GDPR"	s 3(10), (14)(a)		

Records of national security certificates

Records of national security certificates

130(1) A Minister of the Crown who issues a certificate under section 27, 79 or 111 must send a copy of the certificate to the Commissioner.

(2) If the Commissioner receives a copy of a certificate under subsection (1), the Commissioner must publish a record of the certificate.

(3) The record must contain—
(a) the name of the Minister who issued the certificate,
(b) the date on which the certificate was issued, and
(c) subject to subsection (4), the text of the certificate.

(4) The Commissioner must not publish the text, or a part of the text, of the certificate if—
(a) the Minister determines that publishing the text or that part of the text—
(i) would be against the interests of national security,
(ii) would be contrary to the public interest, or
(iii) might jeopardise the safety of any person, and
(b) the Minister has notified the Commissioner of that determination.

(5) The Commissioner must keep the record of the certificate available to the public while the certificate is in force.

(6) If a Minister of the Crown revokes a certificate issued under section 27, 79 or 111, the Minister must notify the Commissioner.

—— NOTES ——

Defined terms		"Minister of the Crown"	s 205(1)
"the Commissioner"	s 3(8)	"publish"	s 205(1)

Information provided to the Commissioner

Disclosure of information to the Commissioner

131(1) No enactment or rule of law prohibiting or restricting the disclosure of information precludes a person from providing the Commissioner with information necessary for the discharge of the Commissioner's functions.

(2) But this section does not authorise the making of a disclosure which is prohibited by any of Parts 1 to 7 or Chapter 1 of Part 9 of the Investigatory Powers Act 2016.

(3) Until the repeal of Part 1 of the Regulation of Investigatory Powers Act 2000 by paragraphs 45 and 54 of Schedule 10 to the Investigatory Powers Act 2016 is fully in force, subsection (2) has effect as if it included a reference to that Part.

—— Notes ——

Defined terms		"enactment"	s 205(1)
"the Commissioner"	s 3(8)		

Confidentiality of information

132(1) A person who is or has been the Commissioner, or a member of the Commissioner's staff or an agent of the Commissioner, must not disclose information which—

   (a) has been obtained by, or provided to, the Commissioner in the course of, or for the purposes of, the discharging of the Commissioner's functions,

   (b) relates to an identified or identifiable individual or business, and

   (c) is not available to the public from other sources at the time of the disclosure and has not previously been available to the public from other sources,

unless the disclosure is made with lawful authority.

(2) For the purposes of subsection (1), a disclosure is made with lawful authority only if and to the extent that—

   (a) the disclosure was made with the consent of the individual or of the person for the time being carrying on the business,

   (b) the information was obtained or provided as described in subsection (1)(a) for the purpose of its being made available to the public (in whatever manner),

   (c) the disclosure was made for the purposes of, and is necessary for, the discharge of one or more of the Commissioner's functions,

   (d) the disclosure was made for the purposes of, and is necessary for, the discharge of an EU obligation,

   (e) the disclosure was made for the purposes of criminal or civil proceedings, however arising, or

   (f) having regard to the rights, freedoms and legitimate interests of any person, the disclosure was necessary in the public interest.

(3) It is an offence for a person knowingly or recklessly to disclose information in contravention of subsection (1).

—— Notes ——

Defined terms	"the Commissioner"	s 3(8)

Guidance about privileged communications

133(1) The Commissioner must produce and publish guidance about—

   (a) how the Commissioner proposes to secure that privileged communications which the Commissioner obtains or has access to in the course of carrying out the Commissioner's functions are used or disclosed only so far as necessary for carrying out those functions, and

   (b) how the Commissioner proposes to comply with restrictions and prohibitions on obtaining or having access to privileged communications which are imposed by an enactment.

(2) The Commissioner—

    (a) may alter or replace the guidance, and

    (b) must publish any altered or replacement guidance.

(3) The Commissioner must consult the Secretary of State before publishing guidance under this section (including altered or replacement guidance).

(4) The Commissioner must arrange for guidance under this section (including altered or replacement guidance) to be laid before Parliament.

(5) In this section, "privileged communications" means—

    (a) communications made—

        (i) between a professional legal adviser and the adviser's client, and

        (ii) in connection with the giving of legal advice to the client with respect to legal obligations, liabilities or rights, and

    (b) communications made—

        (i) between a professional legal adviser and the adviser's client or between such an adviser or client and another person,

        (ii) in connection with or in contemplation of legal proceedings, and

        (iii) for the purposes of such proceedings.

(6) In subsection (5)—

    (a) references to the client of a professional legal adviser include references to a person acting on behalf of the client, and

    (b) references to a communication include—

        (i) a copy or other record of the communication, and

        (ii) anything enclosed with or referred to in the communication if made as described in subsection (5)(a)(ii) or in subsection (5)(b)(ii) and (iii).

—— NOTES ——

Defined terms		"enactment"	s 205(1)
"the Commissioner"	s 3(8)	"publish"	s 205(1)

Fees

Fees for services

134 The Commissioner may require a person other than a data subject or a data protection officer to pay a reasonable fee for a service provided to the person, or at the person's request, which the Commissioner is required or authorised to provide under the data protection legislation.

—— NOTES ——

Defined terms		"the data protection legislation"	s 3(9)
"the Commissioner"	s 3(8)	"data subject"	s 3(5)

Manifestly unfounded or excessive requests by data subjects etc

135(1) Where a request to the Commissioner from a data subject or a data protection officer is manifestly unfounded or excessive, the Commissioner may—

    (a) charge a reasonable fee for dealing with the request, or

    (b) refuse to act on the request.

(2) An example of a request that may be excessive is one that merely repeats the substance of previous requests.

(3) In any proceedings where there is an issue as to whether a request described in subsection

(1) is manifestly unfounded or excessive, it is for the Commissioner to show that it is.

(4) Subsections (1) and (3) apply only in cases in which the Commissioner does not already have such powers and obligations under Article 57(4) of the GDPR.

—— NOTES ——

| **Defined terms** | | "data subject" | s 3(5) |
| "the Commissioner" | s 3(8) | "the GDPR" | s 3(10), (14)(a) |

Guidance about fees

136(1) The Commissioner must produce and publish guidance about the fees the Commissioner proposes to charge in accordance with—

(a) section 134 or 135, or

(b) Article 57(4) of the GDPR.

(2) Before publishing the guidance, the Commissioner must consult the Secretary of State.

—— NOTES ——

| **Defined terms** | | "the GDPR" | s 3(10), (14)(a) |
| "the Commissioner" | s 3(8) | "publish" | s 205(1) |

Charges

Charges payable to the Commissioner by controllers

137(1) The Secretary of State may by regulations require controllers to pay charges of an amount specified in the regulations to the Commissioner.

(2) Regulations under subsection (1) may require a controller to pay a charge regardless of whether the Commissioner has provided, or proposes to provide, a service to the controller.

(3) Regulations under subsection (1) may—

(a) make provision about the time or times at which, or period or periods within which, a charge must be paid;

(b) make provision for cases in which a discounted charge is payable;

(c) make provision for cases in which no charge is payable;

(d) make provision for cases in which a charge which has been paid is to be refunded.

(4) In making regulations under subsection (1), the Secretary of State must have regard to the desirability of securing that the charges payable to the Commissioner under such regulations are sufficient to offset—

(a) expenses incurred by the Commissioner in discharging the Commissioner's functions—

(i) under the data protection legislation,

(ii) under the Data Protection Act 1998,

(iii) under or by virtue of sections 108 and 109 of the Digital Economy Act 2017, and

(iv) under or by virtue of the Privacy and Electronic Communications (EC Directive) Regulations 2003 (SI 2003/2426),

(b) any expenses of the Secretary of State in respect of the Commissioner so far as attributable to those functions,

(c) to the extent that the Secretary of State considers appropriate, any deficit previously incurred (whether before or after the passing of this Act) in respect of the expenses mentioned in paragraph (a), and

(d) to the extent that the Secretary of State considers appropriate, expenses incurred by the Secretary of State in respect of the inclusion of any officers or staff of the Commissioner in any scheme under section 1 of the Superannuation Act 1972 or section 1 of the Public Service Pensions Act 2013.

(5) The Secretary of State may from time to time require the Commissioner to provide information about the expenses referred to in subsection (4)(a).

(6) The Secretary of State may by regulations make provision—
    (a) requiring a controller to provide information to the Commissioner, or
    (b) enabling the Commissioner to require a controller to provide information to the Commissioner,
for either or both of the purposes mentioned in subsection (7).

(7) Those purposes are—
    (a) determining whether a charge is payable by the controller under regulations under subsection (1);
    (b) determining the amount of a charge payable by the controller.

(8) The provision that may be made under subsection (6)(a) includes provision requiring a controller to notify the Commissioner of a change in the controller's circumstances of a kind specified in the regulations.

––––– NOTES –––––

| **Defined terms** | | "controller" | s 3(6), (14)(d) |
| "the Commissioner" | s 3(8) | "the data protection legislation" | s 3(9) |

Regulations under section 137: supplementary

138(1) Before making regulations under section 137(1) or (6), the Secretary of State must consult such representatives of persons likely to be affected by the regulations as the Secretary of State thinks appropriate (and see also section 182).

(2) The Commissioner—
    (a) must keep under review the working of regulations under section 137(1) or (6), and
    (b) may from time to time submit proposals to the Secretary of State for amendments to be made to the regulations.

(3) The Secretary of State must review the working of regulations under section 137(1) or (6)—
    (a) at the end of the period of 5 years beginning with the making of the first set of regulations under section 108 of the Digital Economy Act 2017, and
    (b) at the end of each subsequent 5 year period.

(4) Regulations under section 137(1) are subject to the negative resolution procedure if—
    (a) they only make provision increasing a charge for which provision is made by previous regulations under section 137(1) or section 108(1) of the Digital Economy Act 2017, and
    (b) they do so to take account of an increase in the retail prices index since the previous regulations were made.

(5) Subject to subsection (4), regulations under section 137(1) or (6) are subject to the affirmative resolution procedure.

(6) In subsection (4), "the retail prices index" means—
    (a) the general index of retail prices (for all items) published by the Statistics Board, or

(b) where that index is not published for a month, any substitute index or figures published by the Board.

(7) Regulations under section 137(1) or (6) may not apply to—

(a) Her Majesty in her private capacity,

(b) Her Majesty in right of the Duchy of Lancaster, or

(c) the Duke of Cornwall.

—— NOTES ——

Defined terms		"the Commissioner"	s 3(8)
"the affirmative resolution		"the negative resolution procedure"	s 182(6)
procedure"	s 182(7)		

Reports etc

Reporting to Parliament

139(1) The Commissioner must—

(a) produce a general report on the carrying out of the Commissioner's functions annually,

(b) arrange for it to be laid before Parliament, and

(c) publish it.

(2) The report must include the annual report required under Article 59 of the GDPR.

(3) The Commissioner may produce other reports relating to the carrying out of the Commissioner's functions and arrange for them to be laid before Parliament.

—— NOTES ——

| **Defined terms** | | "the GDPR" | s 3(10), (14)(a) |
| "the Commissioner" | s 3(8) | "publish" | s 205(1) |

Publication by the Commissioner

140 A duty under this Act for the Commissioner to publish a document is a duty for the Commissioner to publish it, or to arrange for it to be published, in such form and manner as the Commissioner considers appropriate.

—— NOTES ——

| **Defined terms** | | "publish" | s 205(1) |
| "the Commissioner" | s 3(8) | | |

Notices from the Commissioner

141(1) This section applies in relation to a notice authorised or required by this Act to be given to a person by the Commissioner.

(2) The notice may be given to an individual—

(a) by delivering it to the individual,

(b) by sending it to the individual by post addressed to the individual at his or her usual or last-known place of residence or business, or

(c) by leaving it for the individual at that place.

(3) The notice may be given to a body corporate or unincorporate—

(a) by sending it by post to the proper officer of the body at its principal office, or

(b) by addressing it to the proper officer of the body and leaving it at that office.

(4) The notice may be given to a partnership in Scotland—

(a) by sending it by post to the principal office of the partnership, or

(b) by addressing it to that partnership and leaving it at that office.

(5) The notice may be given to the person by other means, including by electronic means, with the person's consent.

(6) In this section—

"principal office", in relation to a registered company, means its registered office;

"proper officer", in relation to any body, means the secretary or other executive officer charged with the conduct of its general affairs;

"registered company" means a company registered under the enactments relating to companies for the time being in force in the United Kingdom.

(7) This section is without prejudice to any other lawful method of giving a notice.

—— NOTES ——

Defined terms "enactment" s 205(1)
"the Commissioner" s 3(8)

PART 6
ENFORCEMENT

Information notices

Information notices

142(1) The Commissioner may, by written notice (an "information notice")—

(a) require a controller or processor to provide the Commissioner with information that the Commissioner reasonably requires for the purposes of carrying out the Commissioner's functions under the data protection legislation, or

(b) require any person to provide the Commissioner with information that the Commissioner reasonably requires for the purposes of—

(i) investigating a suspected failure of a type described in section 149(2) or a suspected offence under this Act, or

(ii) determining whether the processing of personal data is carried out by an individual in the course of a purely personal or household activity.

(2) An information notice must state—

(a) whether it is given under subsection (1)(a), (b)(i) or (b)(ii), and

(b) why the Commissioner requires the information.

(3) An information notice—

(a) may specify or describe particular information or a category of information;

(b) may specify the form in which the information must be provided;

(c) may specify the time at which, or the period within which, the information must be provided;

(d) may specify the place where the information must be provided; (but see the restrictions in subsections (5) to (7)).

(4) An information notice must provide information about—

(a) the consequences of failure to comply with it, and

(b) the rights under sections 162 and 164 (appeals etc).

(5) An information notice may not require a person to provide information before the end of the period within which an appeal can be brought against the notice.

(6) If an appeal is brought against an information notice, the information need not be provided pending the determination or withdrawal of the appeal.

(7) If an information notice—

    (a) states that, in the Commissioner's opinion, the information is required urgently, and

    (b) gives the Commissioner's reasons for reaching that opinion,

subsections (5) and (6) do not apply but the notice must not require the information to be provided before the end of the period of 24 hours beginning when the notice is given.

(8) The Commissioner may cancel an information notice by written notice to the person to whom it was given.

(9) In subsection (1), in relation to a person who is a controller or processor for the purposes of the GDPR, the reference to a controller or processor includes a representative of a controller or processor designated under Article 27 of the GDPR (representatives of controllers or processors not established in the European Union).

(10) Section 3(14)(c) does not apply to the reference to the processing of personal data in subsection (1)(b).

—— NOTES ——

Defined terms

"the Commissioner"	s 3(8)
"controller" s 3(6), (14)(d) (note sub-s 142(9))	
"the data protection legislation"	s 3(9)
"the GDPR"	s 3(10), (14)(a)
"personal data"	s 3(2) (note sub-s 142(10))
"processing"	s 3(4) (note sub-s 142(10))
"processor" s 3(6), (14)(d) (note sub-s 142(9))	
"representative"	s 181

Information notices: restrictions

143(1) The Commissioner may not give an information notice with respect to the processing of personal data for the special purposes unless—

    (a) a determination under section 174 with respect to the data or the processing has taken effect, or

    (b) the Commissioner—

        (i) has reasonable grounds for suspecting that such a determination could be made, and

        (ii) the information is required for the purposes of making such a determination.

(2) An information notice does not require a person to give the Commissioner information to the extent that requiring the person to do so would involve an infringement of the privileges of either House of Parliament.

(3) An information notice does not require a person to give the Commissioner information in respect of a communication which is made—

    (a) between a professional legal adviser and the adviser's client, and

    (b) in connection with the giving of legal advice to the client with respect to obligations, liabilities or rights under the data protection legislation.

(4) An information notice does not require a person to give the Commissioner information in respect of a communication which is made—

    (a) between a professional legal adviser and the adviser's client or between such an adviser or client and another person,

    (b) in connection with or in contemplation of proceedings under or arising out of the data protection legislation, and

    (c) for the purposes of such proceedings.

(5) In subsections (3) and (4), references to the client of a professional legal adviser include references to a person acting on behalf of the client.

(6) An information notice does not require a person to provide the Commissioner with information if doing so would, by revealing evidence of the commission of an offence expose the person to proceedings for that offence.

(7) The reference to an offence in subsection (6) does not include an offence under—

    (a) this Act;

    (b) section 5 of the Perjury Act 1911 (false statements made otherwise than on oath);

    (c) section 44(2) of the Criminal Law (Consolidation) (Scotland) Act 1995 (false statements made otherwise than on oath);

    (d) Article 10 of the Perjury (Northern Ireland) Order 1979 (SI 1979/1714 (NI 19)) (false statutory declarations and other false unsworn statements).

(8) An oral or written statement provided by a person in response to an information notice may not be used in evidence against that person on a prosecution for an offence under this Act (other than an offence under section 144) unless in the proceedings—

    (a) in giving evidence the person provides information inconsistent with the statement, and

    (b) evidence relating to the statement is adduced, or a question relating to it is asked, by that person or on that person's behalf.

(9) In subsection (6), in relation to an information notice given to a representative of a controller or processor designated under Article 27 of the GDPR, the reference to the person providing the information being exposed to proceedings for an offence includes a reference to the controller or processor being exposed to such proceedings.

——— NOTES ———

Defined terms		"personal data"	s 3(2) (note also s 142(10))
"the Commissioner"	s 3(8)	"processing"	s 3(4) (note also s 142(10))
"controller"	s 3(6), (14)(d)	"processor"	s 3(6), (14)(d)
"the data protection legislation"	s 3(9)	"representative"	s 181
"the GDPR"	s 3(10), (14)(a)	"the special purposes"	s 174(1)
"information notice"	ss 142(1), 181		

False statements made in response to information notices

144 It is an offence for a person, in response to an information notice—

    (a) to make a statement which the person knows to be false in a material respect, or

    (b) recklessly to make a statement which is false in a material respect.

——— NOTES ———

Defined terms		"information notice"	ss 142(1), 181

Information orders

145(1) This section applies if, on an application by the Commissioner, a court is satisfied that a person has failed to comply with a requirement of an information notice.

(2) The court may make an order requiring the person to provide to the Commissioner some

or all of the following—

    (a) information referred to in the information notice;

    (b) other information which the court is satisfied the Commissioner requires, having regard to the statement included in the notice in accordance with section 142(2)(b).

(3) The order—

    (a) may specify the form in which the information must be provided,

    (b) must specify the time at which, or the period within which, the information must be provided, and

    (c) may specify the place where the information must be provided.

—— NOTES ——

Assessment notices

Assessment notices

146(1) The Commissioner may by written notice (an "assessment notice") require a controller or processor to permit the Commissioner to carry out an assessment of whether the controller or processor has complied or is complying with the data protection legislation.

(2) An assessment notice may require the controller or processor to do any of the following—

    (a) permit the Commissioner to enter specified premises;

    (b) direct the Commissioner to documents on the premises that are of a specified description;

    (c) assist the Commissioner to view information of a specified description that is capable of being viewed using equipment on the premises;

    (d) comply with a request from the Commissioner for a copy (in such form as may be requested) of—

        (i) the documents to which the Commissioner is directed;

        (ii) the information which the Commissioner is assisted to view;

    (e) direct the Commissioner to equipment or other material on the premises which is of a specified description;

    (f) permit the Commissioner to inspect or examine the documents, information, equipment or material to which the Commissioner is directed or which the Commissioner is assisted to view;

    (g) provide the Commissioner with an explanation of such documents, information, equipment or material;

    (h) permit the Commissioner to observe the processing of personal data that takes place on the premises;

    (i) make available for interview by the Commissioner a specified number of people of a specified description who process personal data on behalf of the controller, not exceeding the number who are willing to be interviewed.

(3) In subsection (2), references to the Commissioner include references to the Commissioner's officers and staff.

(4) An assessment notice must, in relation to each requirement imposed by the notice, specify the time or times at which, or period or periods within which, the requirement must be complied with (but see the restrictions in subsections (6) to (9)).

(5) An assessment notice must provide information about—

    (a) the consequences of failure to comply with it, and

    (b) the rights under sections 162 and 164 (appeals etc).

(6) An assessment notice may not require a person to do anything before the end of the period within which an appeal can be brought against the notice.

(7) If an appeal is brought against an assessment notice, the controller or processor need not comply with a requirement in the notice pending the determination or withdrawal of the appeal.

(8) If an assessment notice—

    (a) states that, in the Commissioner's opinion, it is necessary for the controller or processor to comply with a requirement in the notice urgently,

    (b) gives the Commissioner's reasons for reaching that opinion, and

    (c) does not meet the conditions in subsection (9)(a) to (d),

subsections (6) and (7) do not apply but the notice must not require the controller or processor to comply with the requirement before the end of the period of 7 days beginning when the notice is given.

(9) If an assessment notice—

    (a) states that, in the Commissioner's opinion, there are reasonable grounds for suspecting that a controller or processor has failed or is failing as described in section 149(2) or that an offence under this Act has been or is being committed,

    (b) indicates the nature of the suspected failure or offence,

    (c) does not specify domestic premises,

    (d) states that, in the Commissioner's opinion, it is necessary for the controller or processor to comply with a requirement in the notice in less than 7 days, and

    (e) gives the Commissioner's reasons for reaching that opinion, subsections (6) and (7) do not apply.

(10) The Commissioner may cancel an assessment notice by written notice to the controller or processor to whom it was given.

(11) Where the Commissioner gives an assessment notice to a processor, the Commissioner must, so far as reasonably practicable, give a copy of the notice to each controller for whom the processor processes personal data.

(12) In this section—

    "domestic premises" means premises, or a part of premises, used as a dwelling;

    "specified" means specified in an assessment notice.

—— NOTES ——

Defined terms		"personal data"	s 3(2), (14)(c)
"the Commissioner" s 3(8) (note sub-s 146(3))		"processing"	s 3(4), (14)(c)
"controller"	s 3(6), (14)(d)	"processor"	s 3(6), (14)(d)
"the data protection legislation"	s 3(9)		

Assessment notices: restrictions

147(1) An assessment notice does not require a person to do something to the extent that requiring the person to do it would involve an infringement of the privileges of either House of Parliament.

(2) An assessment notice does not have effect so far as compliance would result in the disclosure of a communication which is made—

    (a) between a professional legal adviser and the adviser's client, and

(b) in connection with the giving of legal advice to the client with respect to obligations, liabilities or rights under the data protection legislation.

(3) An assessment notice does not have effect so far as compliance would result in the disclosure of a communication which is made—

(a) between a professional legal adviser and the adviser's client or between such an adviser or client and another person,

(b) in connection with or in contemplation of proceedings under or arising out of the data protection legislation, and

(c) for the purposes of such proceedings.

(4) In subsections (2) and (3)—

(a) references to the client of a professional legal adviser include references to a person acting on behalf of such a client, and

(b) references to a communication include—

(i) a copy or other record of the communication, and

(ii) anything enclosed with or referred to in the communication if made as described in subsection (2)(b) or in subsection (3)(b) and (c).

(5) The Commissioner may not give a controller or processor an assessment notice with respect to the processing of personal data for the special purposes.

(6) The Commissioner may not give an assessment notice to—

(a) a body specified in section 23(3) of the Freedom of Information Act 2000 (bodies dealing with security matters), or

(b) the Office for Standards in Education, Children's Services and Skills in so far as it is a controller or processor in respect of information processed for the purposes of functions exercisable by Her Majesty's Chief Inspector of Education, Children's Services and Skills by virtue of section 5(1)(a) of the Care Standards Act 2000.

—— NOTES ——

Defined terms		"personal data"	s 3(2), (14)(c)
"assessment notice"	ss 146(1), 181	"processing"	s 3(4), (14)(c)
"the Commissioner"	s 3(8)	"processor"	s 3(6), (14)(d)
"controller"	s 3(6), (14)(d)	"the special purposes"	s 174(1)
"the data protection legislation"	s 3(9)		

Information notices and assessment notices: destruction of documents etc
Destroying or falsifying information and documents etc

148(1) This section applies where a person—

(a) has been given an information notice requiring the person to provide the Commissioner with information, or

(b) has been given an assessment notice requiring the person to direct the Commissioner to a document, equipment or other material or to assist the Commissioner to view information.

(2) It is an offence for the person—

(a) to destroy or otherwise dispose of, conceal, block or (where relevant) falsify all or part of the information, document, equipment or material, or

(b) to cause or permit the destruction, disposal, concealment, blocking or (where relevant) falsification of all or part of the information, document, equipment or material,

with the intention of preventing the Commissioner from viewing, or being provided with or directed to, all or part of the information, document, equipment or material.

(3) It is a defence for a person charged with an offence under subsection (2) to prove that the destruction, disposal, concealment, blocking or falsification would have occurred in the absence of the person being given the notice.

—— NOTES ——

Enforcement notices

Enforcement notices

149(1) Where the Commissioner is satisfied that a person has failed, or is failing, as described in subsection (2), (3), (4) or (5), the Commissioner may give the person a written notice (an "enforcement notice") which requires the person—

(a) to take steps specified in the notice, or

(b) to refrain from taking steps specified in the notice, or both (and see also sections 150 and 151).

(2) The first type of failure is where a controller or processor has failed, or is failing, to comply with any of the following—

(a) a provision of Chapter II of the GDPR or Chapter 2 of Part 3 or Chapter 2 of Part 4 of this Act (principles of processing);

(b) a provision of Articles 12 to 22 of the GDPR or Part 3 or 4 of this Act conferring rights on a data subject;

(c) a provision of Articles 25 to 39 of the GDPR or section 64 or 65 of this Act (obligations of controllers and processors);

(d) a requirement to communicate a personal data breach to the Commissioner or a data subject under section 67, 68 or 108 of this Act;

(e) the principles for transfers of personal data to third countries, non-Convention countries and international organisations in Articles 44 to 49 of the GDPR or in sections 73 to 78 or 109 of this Act.

(3) The second type of failure is where a monitoring body has failed, or is failing, to comply with an obligation under Article 41 of the GDPR (monitoring of approved codes of conduct).

(4) The third type of failure is where a person who is a certification provider—

(a) does not meet the requirements for accreditation,

(b) has failed, or is failing, to comply with an obligation under Article 42 or 43 of the GDPR (certification of controllers and processors), or

(c) has failed, or is failing, to comply with any other provision of the GDPR (whether in the person's capacity as a certification provider or otherwise).

(5) The fourth type of failure is where a controller has failed, or is failing, to comply with regulations under section 137.

(6) An enforcement notice given in reliance on subsection (2), (3) or (5) may only impose requirements which the Commissioner considers appropriate for the purpose of remedying the failure.

(7) An enforcement notice given in reliance on subsection (4) may only impose requirements which the Commissioner considers appropriate having regard to the failure (whether or not for the purpose of remedying the failure).

(8) The Secretary of State may by regulations confer power on the Commissioner to give an enforcement notice in respect of other failures to comply with the data protection legislation.

(9) Regulations under this section—

    (a) may make provision about the giving of an enforcement notice in respect of the failure, including by amending this section and sections 150 to 152,

    (b) may make provision about the giving of an information notice, an assessment notice or a penalty notice, or about powers of entry and inspection, in connection with the failure, including by amending sections 142, 143, 146, 147 and 155 to 157 and Schedules 15 and 16, and

    (c) are subject to the affirmative resolution procedure.

——— NOTES ———

Defined terms			
"the affirmative resolution		"data subject"	s 3(5)
procedure"	s 182(7)	"the GDPR"	s 3(10), (14)(a)
"the Commissioner"	s 3(8)	"international organisation"	s 205(1)
"controller"	s 3(6), (14)(d)	"personal data"	s 3(2), (14)(c)
"the data protection legislation"	s 3(9)	"processor"	s 3(6), (14)(d)

Enforcement notices: supplementary

150(1) An enforcement notice must—

    (a) state what the person has failed or is failing to do, and

    (b) give the Commissioner's reasons for reaching that opinion.

(2) In deciding whether to give an enforcement notice in reliance on section 149(2), the Commissioner must consider whether the failure has caused or is likely to cause any person damage or distress.

(3) In relation to an enforcement notice given in reliance on section 149(2), the Commissioner's power under section 149(1)(b) to require a person to refrain from taking specified steps includes power—

    (a) to impose a ban relating to all processing of personal data, or

    (b) to impose a ban relating only to a specified description of processing of personal data, including by specifying one or more of the following—

        (i) a description of personal data;

        (ii) the purpose or manner of the processing;

        (iii) the time when the processing takes place.

(4) An enforcement notice may specify the time or times at which, or period or periods within which, a requirement imposed by the notice must be complied with (but see the restrictions in subsections (6) to (8)).

(5) An enforcement notice must provide information about—

    (a) the consequences of failure to comply with it, and

    (b) the rights under sections 162 and 164 (appeals etc).

(6) An enforcement notice must not specify a time for compliance with a requirement in the notice which falls before the end of the period within which an appeal can be brought against the notice.

(7) If an appeal is brought against an enforcement notice, a requirement in the notice need

not be complied with pending the determination or withdrawal of the appeal.

(8) If an enforcement notice—

    (a) states that, in the Commissioner's opinion, it is necessary for a requirement to be complied with urgently, and

    (b) gives the Commissioner's reasons for reaching that opinion,

subsections (6) and (7) do not apply but the notice must not require the requirement to be complied with before the end of the period of 24 hours beginning when the notice is given.

(9) In this section, "specified" means specified in an enforcement notice.

—— NOTES ——

Defined terms		"personal data"	s 3(2), (14)(c)
"the Commissioner"	s 3(8)	"processing"	s 3(4), (14)(c)
"enforcement notice"	ss 149(1), 181		

Enforcement notices: rectification and erasure of personal data etc

151(1) Subsections (2) and (3) apply where an enforcement notice is given in respect of a failure by a controller or processor—

    (a) to comply with a data protection principle relating to accuracy, or

    (b) to comply with a data subject's request to exercise rights under Article 16, 17 or 18 of the GDPR (right to rectification, erasure or restriction on processing) or section 46, 47 or 100 of this Act.

(2) If the enforcement notice requires the controller or processor to rectify or erase inaccurate personal data, it may also require the controller or processor to rectify or erase any other data which—

    (a) is held by the controller or processor, and

    (b) contains an expression of opinion which appears to the Commissioner to be based on the inaccurate personal data.

(3) Where a controller or processor has accurately recorded personal data provided by the data subject or a third party but the data is inaccurate, the enforcement notice may require the controller or processor—

    (a) to take steps specified in the notice to ensure the accuracy of the data,

    (b) if relevant, to secure that the data indicates the data subject's view that the data is inaccurate, and

    (c) to supplement the data with a statement of the true facts relating to the matters dealt with by the data that is approved by the Commissioner,

(as well as imposing requirements under subsection (2)).

(4) When deciding what steps it is reasonable to specify under subsection (3)(a), the Commissioner must have regard to the purpose for which the data was obtained and further processed.

(5) Subsections (6) and (7) apply where—

    (a) an enforcement notice requires a controller or processor to rectify or erase personal data, or

    (b) the Commissioner is satisfied that the processing of personal data which has been rectified or erased by the controller or processor involved a failure described in subsection (1).

(6) An enforcement notice may, if reasonably practicable, require the controller or processor

to notify third parties to whom the data has been disclosed of the rectification or erasure.

(7) In determining whether it is reasonably practicable to require such notification, the Commissioner must have regard, in particular, to the number of people who would have to be notified.

(8) In this section, "data protection principle relating to accuracy" means the principle in—

(a) Article 5(1)(d) of the GDPR,

(b) section 38(1) of this Act, or

(c) section 89 of this Act.

—— Notes ——

Defined terms		"the GDPR"	s 3(10), (14)(a)
"the Commissioner"	s 3(8)	"inaccurate"	s 205(1)
"controller"	s 3(6), (14)(d)	"personal data"	s 3(2), (14)(c)
"data subject"	s 3(5)	"processing"	s 3(4), (14)(c)
"enforcement notice"	ss 149(1), 181	"processor"	s 3(6), (14)(d)

Enforcement notices: restrictions

152(1) The Commissioner may not give a controller or processor an enforcement notice in reliance on section 149(2) with respect to the processing of personal data for the special purposes unless—

(a) a determination under section 174 with respect to the data or the processing has taken effect, and

(b) a court has granted leave for the notice to be given.

(2) A court must not grant leave for the purposes of subsection (1)(b) unless it is satisfied that—

(a) the Commissioner has reason to suspect a failure described in section 149(2) which is of substantial public importance, and

(b) the controller or processor has been given notice of the application for leave in accordance with rules of court or the case is urgent.

(3) An enforcement notice does not require a person to do something to the extent that requiring the person to do it would involve an infringement of the privileges of either House of Parliament.

(4) In the case of a joint controller in respect of the processing of personal data to which Part 3 or 4 applies whose responsibilities for compliance with that Part are determined in an arrangement under section 58 or 104, the Commissioner may only give the controller an enforcement notice in reliance on section 149(2) if the controller is responsible for compliance with the provision, requirement or principle in question.

—— Notes ——

Defined terms		"personal data"	s 3(2), (14)(c)
"the Commissioner"	s 3(8)	"processing"	s 3(4), (14)(c)
"controller"	s 3(6), (14)(d)	"processor"	s 3(6), (14)(d)
"enforcement notice"	ss 149(1), 181	"the special purposes"	s 174(1)

Enforcement notices: cancellation and variation

153(1) The Commissioner may cancel or vary an enforcement notice by giving written notice to the person to whom it was given.

(2) A person to whom an enforcement notice is given may apply in writing to the

Commissioner for the cancellation or variation of the notice.

(3) An application under subsection (2) may be made only—

(a) after the end of the period within which an appeal can be brought against the notice, and

(b) on the ground that, by reason of a change of circumstances, one or more of the provisions of that notice need not be complied with in order to remedy the failure identified in the notice.

—— NOTES ——

Defined terms		"enforcement notice"	ss 149(1), 181
"the Commissioner"	s 3(8)		

Powers of entry and inspection

Powers of entry and inspection

154 Schedule 15 makes provision about powers of entry and inspection.

Penalties

Penalty notices

155(1) If the Commissioner is satisfied that a person—

(a) has failed or is failing as described in section 149(2), (3), (4) or (5), or

(b) has failed to comply with an information notice, an assessment notice or an enforcement notice,

the Commissioner may, by written notice (a "penalty notice"), require the person to pay to the Commissioner an amount in sterling specified in the notice.

(2) Subject to subsection (4), when deciding whether to give a penalty notice to a person and determining the amount of the penalty, the Commissioner must have regard to the following, so far as relevant—

(a) to the extent that the notice concerns a matter to which the GDPR applies, the matters listed in Article 83(1) and (2) of the GDPR;

(b) to the extent that the notice concerns another matter, the matters listed in subsection (3).

(3) Those matters are—

(a) the nature, gravity and duration of the failure;

(b) the intentional or negligent character of the failure;

(c) any action taken by the controller or processor to mitigate the damage or distress suffered by data subjects;

(d) the degree of responsibility of the controller or processor, taking into account technical and organisational measures implemented by the controller or processor in accordance with section 57, 66, 103 or 107;

(e) any relevant previous failures by the controller or processor;

(f) the degree of co-operation with the Commissioner, in order to remedy the failure and mitigate the possible adverse effects of the failure;

(g) the categories of personal data affected by the failure;

(h) the manner in which the infringement became known to the Commissioner, including whether, and if so to what extent, the controller or processor notified the Commissioner of the failure;

(i) the extent to which the controller or processor has complied with previous enforcement notices or penalty notices;

(j) adherence to approved codes of conduct or certification mechanisms;

(k) any other aggravating or mitigating factor applicable to the case, including financial benefits gained, or losses avoided, as a result of the failure (whether directly or indirectly);

(l) whether the penalty would be effective, proportionate and dissuasive.

(4) Subsections (2) and (3) do not apply in the case of a decision or determination relating to a failure described in section 149(5).

(5) Schedule 16 makes further provision about penalty notices, including provision requiring the Commissioner to give a notice of intent to impose a penalty and provision about payment, variation, cancellation and enforcement.

(6) The Secretary of State may by regulations—

(a) confer power on the Commissioner to give a penalty notice in respect of other failures to comply with the data protection legislation, and

(b) provide for the maximum penalty that may be imposed in relation to such failures to be either the standard maximum amount or the higher maximum amount.

(7) Regulations under this section—

(a) may make provision about the giving of penalty notices in respect of the failure,

(b) may amend this section and sections 156 to 158, and

(c) are subject to the affirmative resolution procedure.

(8) In this section, "higher maximum amount" and "standard maximum amount" have the same meaning as in section 157.

—— NOTES ——

Defined terms				
"the affirmative resolution procedure"	s 182(7)	"data subject"	s 3(5)	
"assessment notice"	ss 146(1), 181	"enforcement notice"	ss 149(1), 181	
"the Commissioner"	s 3(8)	"the GDPR"	s 3(10), (14)(a)	
"controller"	s 3(6), (14)(d)	"information notice"	ss 142(1), 181	
"the data protection legislation"	s 3(9)	"personal data"	s 3(2), (14)(c)	
		"processor"	s 3(6), (14)(d)	

Penalty notices: restrictions

156(1) The Commissioner may not give a controller or processor a penalty notice in reliance on section 149(2) with respect to the processing of personal data for the special purposes unless—

(a) a determination under section 174 with respect to the data or the processing has taken effect, and

(b) a court has granted leave for the notice to be given.

(2) A court must not grant leave for the purposes of subsection (1)(b) unless it is satisfied that—

(a) the Commissioner has reason to suspect a failure described in section 149(2) which is of substantial public importance, and

(b) the controller or processor has been given notice of the application for leave in accordance with rules of court or the case is urgent.

(3) The Commissioner may not give a controller or processor a penalty notice with respect to the processing of personal data where the purposes and manner of the processing are determined by or on behalf of either House of Parliament.

(4) The Commissioner may not give a penalty notice to—

    (a) the Crown Estate Commissioners, or

    (b) a person who is a controller by virtue of section 209(4) (controller for the Royal Household etc).

(5) In the case of a joint controller in respect of the processing of personal data to which Part 3 or 4 applies whose responsibilities for compliance with that Part are determined in an arrangement under section 58 or 104, the Commissioner may only give the controller a penalty notice in reliance on section 149(2) if the controller is responsible for compliance with the provision, requirement or principle in question.

—— NOTES ——

Defined terms		"personal data"	s 3(2), (14)(c)
"the Commissioner"	s 3(8)	"processing"	s 3(4), (14)(c)
"controller"	s 3(6), (14)(d)	"processor"	s 3(6), (14)(d)
"penalty notice"	ss 155(1), 181	"the special purposes"	s 174(1)

Maximum amount of penalty

157(1) In relation to an infringement of a provision of the GDPR, the maximum amount of the penalty that may be imposed by a penalty notice is—

    (a) the amount specified in Article 83 of the GDPR, or

    (b) if an amount is not specified there, the standard maximum amount.

(2) In relation to an infringement of a provision of Part 3 of this Act, the maximum amount of the penalty that may be imposed by a penalty notice is—

    (a) in relation to a failure to comply with section 35, 36, 37, 38(1), 39(1), 40, 44, 45, 46, 47, 48, 49, 52, 53, 73, 74, 75, 76, 77 or 78, the higher maximum amount, and

    (b) otherwise, the standard maximum amount.

(3) In relation to an infringement of a provision of Part 4 of this Act, the maximum amount of the penalty that may be imposed by a penalty notice is—

    (a) in relation to a failure to comply with section 86, 87, 88, 89, 90, 91, 93, 94, 100 or 109, the higher maximum amount, and

    (b) otherwise, the standard maximum amount.

(4) In relation to a failure to comply with an information notice, an assessment notice or an enforcement notice, the maximum amount of the penalty that may be imposed by a penalty notice is the higher maximum amount.

(5) The "higher maximum amount" is—

    (a) in the case of an undertaking, 20 million Euros or 4% of the undertaking's total annual worldwide turnover in the preceding financial year, whichever is higher, or

    (b) in any other case, 20 million Euros.

(6) The "standard maximum amount" is—

    (a) in the case of an undertaking, 10 million Euros or 2% of the undertaking's total annual worldwide turnover in the preceding financial year, whichever is higher, or

    (b) in any other case, 10 million Euros.

(7) The maximum amount of a penalty in sterling must be determined by applying the spot rate of exchange set by the Bank of England on the day on which the penalty notice is

given.

Defined terms		"the GDPR"	s 3(10), (14)(a)
"assessment notice"	ss 146(1), 181	"information notice"	ss 142(1), 181
"enforcement notice"	ss 149(1), 181	"penalty notice"	ss 155(1), 181

Fixed penalties for non-compliance with charges regulations

158(1) The Commissioner must produce and publish a document specifying the amount of the penalty for a failure to comply with regulations made under section 137.

(2) The Commissioner may specify different amounts for different types of failure.

(3) The maximum amount that may be specified is 150% of the highest charge payable by a controller in respect of a financial year in accordance with the regulations, disregarding any discount available under the regulations.

(4) The Commissioner—

    (a) may alter or replace the document, and

    (b) must publish any altered or replacement document.

(5) Before publishing a document under this section (including any altered or replacement document), the Commissioner must consult—

    (a) the Secretary of State, and

    (b) such other persons as the Commissioner considers appropriate.

(6) The Commissioner must arrange for a document published under this section (including any altered or replacement document) to be laid before Parliament.

Defined terms		"controller"	s 3(6), (14)(d)
"the Commissioner"	s 3(8)	"publish"	s 205(1)

Amount of penalties: supplementary

159(1) For the purposes of Article 83 of the GDPR and section 157, the Secretary of State may by regulations—

    (a) provide that a person of a description specified in the regulations is or is not an undertaking, and

    (b) make provision about how an undertaking's turnover is to be determined.

(2) For the purposes of Article 83 of the GDPR, section 157 and section 158, the Secretary of State may by regulations provide that a period is or is not a financial year.

(3) Regulations under this section are subject to the affirmative resolution procedure.

Defined terms	"the GDPR"	s 3(10), (14)(a)
the affirmative resolution procedure" s 182(7)		

Guidance

Guidance about regulatory action

160(1) The Commissioner must produce and publish guidance about how the Commissioner proposes to exercise the Commissioner's functions in connection with—

    (a) information notices,

    (b) assessment notices,

    (c) enforcement notices, and

(d) penalty notices.

(2) The Commissioner may produce and publish guidance about how the Commissioner proposes to exercise the Commissioner's other functions under this Part.

(3) In relation to information notices, the guidance must include—

(a) provision specifying factors to be considered in determining the time at which, or the period within which, information is to be required to be provided;

(b) provision about the circumstances in which the Commissioner would consider it appropriate to give an information notice to a person in reliance on section 142(7) (urgent cases);

(c) provision about how the Commissioner will determine how to proceed if a person does not comply with an information notice.

(4) In relation to assessment notices, the guidance must include—

(a) provision specifying factors to be considered in determining whether to give an assessment notice to a person;

(b) provision about the circumstances in which the Commissioner would consider it appropriate to give an assessment notice in reliance on section 146(8) or (9) (urgent cases);

(c) provision specifying descriptions of documents or information that—

(i) are not to be examined or inspected in accordance with an assessment notice, or

(ii) are to be so examined or inspected only by a person of a description specified in the guidance;

(d) provision about the nature of inspections and examinations carried out in accordance with an assessment notice;

(e) provision about the nature of interviews carried out in accordance with an assessment notice;

(f) provision about the preparation, issuing and publication by the Commissioner of assessment reports in respect of controllers and processors that have been given assessment notices;

(g) provision about how the Commissioner will determine how to proceed if a person does not comply with an assessment notice.

(5) The guidance produced in accordance with subsection (4)(c) must include provisions that relate to—

(a) documents and information concerning an individual's physical or mental health;

(b) documents and information concerning the provision of social care for an individual.

(6) In relation to enforcement notices, the guidance must include—

(a) provision specifying factors to be considered in determining whether to give an enforcement notice to a person;

(b) provision about the circumstances in which the Commissioner would consider it appropriate to give an enforcement notice to a person in reliance on section 150(8) (urgent cases);

(c) provision about how the Commissioner will determine how to proceed if a person does not comply with an enforcement notice.

(7) In relation to penalty notices, the guidance must include—

(a) provision about the circumstances in which the Commissioner would consider it appropriate to issue a penalty notice;

   (b) provision about the circumstances in which the Commissioner would consider it appropriate to allow a person to make oral representations about the Commissioner's intention to give the person a penalty notice;

   (c) provision explaining how the Commissioner will determine the amount of penalties;

   (d) provision about how the Commissioner will determine how to proceed if a person does not comply with a penalty notice.

(8)   The Commissioner—

   (a) may alter or replace guidance produced under this section, and

   (b) must publish any altered or replacement guidance.

(9)   Before producing guidance under this section (including any altered or replacement guidance), the Commissioner must consult—

   (a) the Secretary of State, and

   (b) such other persons as the Commissioner considers appropriate.

(10) Section 161 applies in relation to the first guidance under subsection (1).

(11) The Commissioner must arrange for other guidance under this section (including any altered or replacement guidance) to be laid before Parliament.

(12) In this section, "social care" has the same meaning as in Part 1 of the Health and Social Care Act 2008 (see section 9(3) of that Act).

—— NOTES ——

Defined terms		"information notice"	ss 142(1), 181
"assessment notice"	ss 146(1), 181	"penalty notice"	ss 155(1), 181
"the Commissioner"	s 3(8)	"processor"	s 3(6), (14)(d)
"controller"	s 3(6), (14)(d)	"publish"	s 205(1)
"enforcement notice"	ss 149(1), 181		

Approval of first guidance about regulatory action

161(1) When the first guidance is produced under section 160(1)—

   (a) the Commissioner must submit the final version to the Secretary of State, and

   (b) the Secretary of State must lay the guidance before Parliament.

(2)   If, within the 40-day period, either House of Parliament resolves not to approve the guidance—

   (a) the Commissioner must not issue the guidance, and

   (b) the Commissioner must produce another version of the guidance (and this section applies to that version).

(3)   If, within the 40-day period, no such resolution is made—

   (a) the Commissioner must issue the guidance, and

   (b) the guidance comes into force at the end of the period of 21 days beginning with the day on which it is issued.

(4)   Nothing in subsection (2)(a) prevents another version of the guidance being laid before Parliament.

(5)   In this section, "the 40-day period" means—

   (a) if the guidance is laid before both Houses of Parliament on the same day, the period of 40 days beginning with that day, or

(b) if the guidance is laid before the Houses of Parliament on different days, the period of 40 days beginning with the later of those days.

(6) In calculating the 40-day period, no account is to be taken of any period during which Parliament is dissolved or prorogued or during which both Houses of Parliament are adjourned for more than 4 days.

—— NOTES ——

Defined terms   "the Commissioner"   s 3(8)

Appeals etc

Rights of appeal

162(1) A person who is given any of the following notices may appeal to the Tribunal—
    (a) an information notice;
    (b) an assessment notice;
    (c) an enforcement notice;
    (d) a penalty notice;
    (e) a penalty variation notice.

(2) A person who is given an enforcement notice may appeal to the Tribunal against the refusal of an application under section 153 for the cancellation or variation of the notice.

(3) A person who is given a penalty notice or a penalty variation notice may appeal to the Tribunal against the amount of the penalty specified in the notice, whether or not the person appeals against the notice.

(4) Where a determination is made under section 174 in respect of the processing of personal data, the controller or processor may appeal to the Tribunal against the determination.

—— NOTES ——

Defined terms			
"assessment notice"	ss 146(1), 181	"penalty variation notice"	s 181, Sch 16, para 7(1)
"controller"	s 3(6), (14)(d)	"personal data"	s 3(2), (14)(c)
"enforcement notice"	ss 149(1), 181	"processing"	s 3(4), (14)(c)
"information notice"	ss 142(1), 181	"processor"	s 3(6), (14)(d)
"penalty notice"	ss 155(1), 181	"the Tribunal"	s 205(1)

Determination of appeals

163(1) Subsections (2) to (4) apply where a person appeals to the Tribunal under section 162(1) or (3).

(2) The Tribunal may review any determination of fact on which the notice or decision against which the appeal is brought was based.

(3) If the Tribunal considers—
    (a) that the notice or decision against which the appeal is brought is not in accordance with the law, or
    (b) to the extent that the notice or decision involved an exercise of discretion by the Commissioner, that the Commissioner ought to have exercised the discretion differently,
the Tribunal must allow the appeal or substitute another notice or decision which the Commissioner could have given or made.

(4) Otherwise, the Tribunal must dismiss the appeal.

(5)   On an appeal under section 162(2), if the Tribunal considers that the enforcement notice ought to be cancelled or varied by reason of a change in circumstances, the Tribunal must cancel or vary the notice.

(6)   On an appeal under section 162(4), the Tribunal may cancel the Commissioner's determination.

—— Notes ——

| Defined terms | | "enforcement notice" | ss 149(1), 181 |
| "the Commissioner" | s 3(8) | "the Tribunal" | s 205(1) |

Applications in respect of urgent notices

164(1)   This section applies where an information notice, an assessment notice or an enforcement notice given to a person contains an urgency statement.

(2)   The person may apply to the court for either or both of the following—
   (a)   the disapplication of the urgency statement in relation to some or all of the requirements of the notice;
   (b)   a change to the time at which, or the period within which, a requirement of the notice must be complied with.

(3)   On an application under subsection (2), the court may do any of the following—
   (a)   direct that the notice is to have effect as if it did not contain the urgency statement;
   (b)   direct that the inclusion of the urgency statement is not to have effect in relation to a requirement of the notice;
   (c)   vary the notice by changing the time at which, or the period within which, a requirement of the notice must be complied with;
   (d)   vary the notice by making other changes required to give effect to a direction under paragraph (a) or (b) or in consequence of a variation under paragraph (c).

(4)   The decision of the court on an application under this section is final.

(5)   In this section, "urgency statement" means—
   (a)   in relation to an information notice, a statement under section 142(7)(a),
   (b)   in relation to an assessment notice, a statement under section 146(8)(a) or (9) (d), and
   (c)   in relation to an enforcement notice, a statement under section 150(8)(a).

—— Notes ——

| Defined terms | | "enforcement notice" | ss 149(1), 181 |
| "assessment notice" | ss 146(1), 181 | "information notice" | ss 142(1), 181 |

Complaints

Complaints by data subjects

165(1)   Articles 57(1)(f) and (2) and 77 of the GDPR (data subject's right to lodge a complaint) confer rights on data subjects to complain to the Commissioner if the data subject considers that, in connection with personal data relating to him or her, there is an infringement of the GDPR.

(2)   A data subject may make a complaint to the Commissioner if the data subject considers that, in connection with personal data relating to him or her, there is an infringement of Part 3 or 4 of this Act.

(3)   The Commissioner must facilitate the making of complaints under subsection (2) by

taking steps such as providing a complaint form which can be completed electronically and by other means.

(4) If the Commissioner receives a complaint under subsection (2), the Commissioner must—

    (a) take appropriate steps to respond to the complaint,

    (b) inform the complainant of the outcome of the complaint,

    (c) inform the complainant of the rights under section 166, and

    (d) if asked to do so by the complainant, provide the complainant with further information about how to pursue the complaint.

(5) The reference in subsection (4)(a) to taking appropriate steps in response to a complaint includes—

    (a) investigating the subject matter of the complaint, to the extent appropriate, and

    (b) informing the complainant about progress on the complaint, including about whether further investigation or co-ordination with another supervisory authority or foreign designated authority is necessary.

(6) If the Commissioner receives a complaint relating to the infringement of a data subject's rights under provisions adopted by a member State other than the United Kingdom pursuant to the Law Enforcement Directive, the Commissioner must—

    (a) send the complaint to the relevant supervisory authority for the purposes of that Directive,

    (b) inform the complainant that the Commissioner has done so, and

    (c) if asked to do so by the complainant, provide the complainant with further information about how to pursue the complaint.

(7) In this section—

    "foreign designated authority" means an authority designated for the purposes of Article 13 of the Data Protection Convention by a party, other than the United Kingdom, which is bound by that Convention;

    "supervisory authority" means a supervisory authority for the purposes of Article 51 of the GDPR or Article 41 of the Law Enforcement Directive in a member State other than the United Kingdom.

—— NOTES ——

Defined terms		"the GDPR"	s 3(10), (14)(a)
"the Commissioner"	s 3(8)	"the Law Enforcement Directive"	s 3(12)
"the Data Protection Convention"	s 3(13)	"personal data"	s 3(2), (14)(c)
"data subject"	s 3(5)		

Orders to progress complaints

166(1) This section applies where, after a data subject makes a complaint under section 165 or Article 77 of the GDPR, the Commissioner—

    (a) fails to take appropriate steps to respond to the complaint,

    (b) fails to provide the complainant with information about progress on the complaint, or of the outcome of the complaint, before the end of the period of 3 months beginning when the Commissioner received the complaint, or

    (c) if the Commissioner's consideration of the complaint is not concluded during that period, fails to provide the complainant with such information during a subsequent period of 3 months.

(2) The Tribunal may, on an application by the data subject, make an order requiring the Commissioner—

(a) to take appropriate steps to respond to the complaint, or

(b) to inform the complainant of progress on the complaint, or of the outcome of the complaint, within a period specified in the order.

(3) An order under subsection (2)(a) may require the Commissioner—

    (a) to take steps specified in the order;

    (b) to conclude an investigation, or take a specified step, within a period specified in the order.

(4) Section 165(5) applies for the purposes of subsections (1)(a) and (2)(a) as it applies for the purposes of section 165(4)(a).

—— Notes ——

Defined terms		"the GDPR"	s 3(10), (14)(a)
"the Commissioner"	s 3(8)	"the Tribunal"	s 205(1)
"data subject"	s 3(5)		

Remedies in the court

Compliance orders

167(1) This section applies if, on an application by a data subject, a court is satisfied that there has been an infringement of the data subject's rights under the data protection legislation in contravention of that legislation.

(2) A court may make an order for the purposes of securing compliance with the data protection legislation which requires the controller in respect of the processing, or a processor acting on behalf of that controller—

    (a) to take steps specified in the order, or

    (b) to refrain from taking steps specified in the order.

(3) The order may, in relation to each step, specify the time at which, or the period within which, it must be taken.

(4) In subsection (1)—

    (a) the reference to an application by a data subject includes an application made in exercise of the right under Article 79(1) of the GDPR (right to an effective remedy against a controller or processor);

    (b) the reference to the data protection legislation does not include Part 4 of this Act or regulations made under that Part.

(5) In relation to a joint controller in respect of the processing of personal data to which Part 3 applies whose responsibilities are determined in an arrangement under section 58, a court may only make an order under this section if the controller is responsible for compliance with the provision of the data protection legislation that is contravened.

—— Notes ——

Defined terms		"the GDPR"	s 3(10), (14)(a)
"controller"	s 3(6), (14)(d)	"personal data"	s 3(2), (14)(c)
"the data protection legislation"		"processing"	s 3(4), (14)(c)
	s 3(9) (note sub-s 167(4)(b))	"processor"	s 3(6), (14)(d)
"data subject"	s 3(5)		

Compensation for contravention of the GDPR

168(1) In Article 82 of the GDPR (right to compensation for material or non-material damage), "non-material damage" includes distress.

(2) Subsection (3) applies where—

    (a) in accordance with rules of court, proceedings under Article 82 of the GDPR are brought by a representative body on behalf of a person, and

    (b) a court orders the payment of compensation.

(3) The court may make an order providing for the compensation to be paid on behalf of the person to—

    (a) the representative body, or

    (b) such other person as the court thinks fit.

—— NOTES ——

Defined terms		"representative body"	s 187(5)
"the GDPR"	s 3(10), (14)(a)		

Compensation for contravention of other data protection legislation

169(1) A person who suffers damage by reason of a contravention of a requirement of the data protection legislation, other than the GDPR, is entitled to compensation for that damage from the controller or the processor, subject to subsections (2) and (3).

(2) Under subsection (1)—

    (a) a controller involved in processing of personal data is liable for any damage caused by the processing, and

    (b) a processor involved in processing of personal data is liable for damage caused by the processing only if the processor—

        (i) has not complied with an obligation under the data protection legislation specifically directed at processors, or

        (ii) has acted outside, or contrary to, the controller's lawful instructions.

(3) A controller or processor is not liable as described in subsection (2) if the controller or processor proves that the controller or processor is not in any way responsible for the event giving rise to the damage.

(4) A joint controller in respect of the processing of personal data to which Part 3 or 4 applies whose responsibilities are determined in an arrangement under section 58 or 104 is only liable as described in subsection (2) if the controller is responsible for compliance with the provision of the data protection legislation that is contravened.

(5) In this section, "damage" includes financial loss and damage not involving financial loss, such as distress.

—— NOTES ——

Defined terms		"personal data"	s 3(2), (14)(c)
"controller"	s 3(6), (14)(d)	"processing"	s 3(4), (14)(c)
"the data protection legislation"	s 3(9)	"processor"	s 3(6), (14)(d)
"the GDPR"	s 3(10), (14)(a)		

Offences relating to personal data

Unlawful obtaining etc of personal data

170(1) It is an offence for a person knowingly or recklessly—

    (a) to obtain or disclose personal data without the consent of the controller,

    (b) to procure the disclosure of personal data to another person without the consent of the controller, or

    (c) after obtaining personal data, to retain it without the consent of the person who was the controller in relation to the personal data when it was obtained.

(2) It is a defence for a person charged with an offence under subsection (1) to prove that the obtaining, disclosing, procuring or retaining—

    (a) was necessary for the purposes of preventing or detecting crime,

    (b) was required or authorised by an enactment, by a rule of law or by the order of a court or tribunal, or

    (c) in the particular circumstances, was justified as being in the public interest.

(3) It is also a defence for a person charged with an offence under subsection (1) to prove that—

    (a) the person acted in the reasonable belief that the person had a legal right to do the obtaining, disclosing, procuring or retaining,

    (b) the person acted in the reasonable belief that the person would have had the consent of the controller if the controller had known about the obtaining, disclosing, procuring or retaining and the circumstances of it, or

    (c) the person acted—

        (i) for the special purposes,

        (ii) with a view to the publication by a person of any journalistic, academic, artistic or literary material, and

        (iii) in the reasonable belief that in the particular circumstances the obtaining, disclosing, procuring or retaining was justified as being in the public interest.

(4) It is an offence for a person to sell personal data if the person obtained the data in circumstances in which an offence under subsection (1) was committed.

(5) It is an offence for a person to offer to sell personal data if the person—

    (a) has obtained the data in circumstances in which an offence under subsection (1) was committed, or

    (b) subsequently obtains the data in such circumstances.

(6) For the purposes of subsection (5), an advertisement indicating that personal data is or may be for sale is an offer to sell the data.

(7) In this section—

    (a) references to the consent of a controller do not include the consent of a person who is a controller by virtue of Article 28(10) of the GDPR or section 59(8) or 105(3) of this Act (processor to be treated as controller in certain circumstances);

    (b) where there is more than one controller, such references are references to the consent of one or more of them.

—— NOTES ——

Defined terms		"personal data"	s 3(2), (14)(c)
"controller"	s 3(6), (14)(d)	"publish"	s 205(1)
"enactment"	s 205(1)	"the special purposes"	s 174(1)
"the GDPR"	s 3(10), (14)(a)	"tribunal"	s 205(1)

Re-identification of de-identified personal data

171(1) It is an offence for a person knowingly or recklessly to re-identify information that is de-identified personal data without the consent of the controller responsible for de-identifying the personal data.

(2) For the purposes of this section and section 172—

    (a) personal data is "de-identified" if it has been processed in such a manner that it can no longer be attributed, without more, to a specific data subject;

    (b) a person "re-identifies" information if the person takes steps which result in the information no longer being de-identified within the meaning of paragraph (a).

(3) It is a defence for a person charged with an offence under subsection (1) to prove that the re-identification—

    (a) was necessary for the purposes of preventing or detecting crime,

    (b) was required or authorised by an enactment, by a rule of law or by the order of a court or tribunal, or

    (c) in the particular circumstances, was justified as being in the public interest.

(4) It is also a defence for a person charged with an offence under subsection (1) to prove that—

    (a) the person acted in the reasonable belief that the person—

        (i) is the data subject to whom the information relates,

        (ii) had the consent of that data subject, or

        (iii) would have had such consent if the data subject had known about the re-identification and the circumstances of it,

    (b) the person acted in the reasonable belief that the person—

        (i) is the controller responsible for de-identifying the personal data,

        (ii) had the consent of that controller, or

        (iii) would have had such consent if that controller had known about the re-identification and the circumstances of it,

    (c) the person acted—

        (i) for the special purposes,

        (ii) with a view to the publication by a person of any journalistic, academic, artistic or literary material, and

        (iii) in the reasonable belief that in the particular circumstances the re-identification was justified as being in the public interest, or

    (d) the effectiveness testing conditions were met (see section 172).

(5) It is an offence for a person knowingly or recklessly to process personal data that is information that has been re-identified where the person does so—

    (a) without the consent of the controller responsible for de-identifying the personal data, and

    (b) in circumstances in which the re-identification was an offence under subsection (1).

(6) It is a defence for a person charged with an offence under subsection (5) to prove that the processing—

    (a) was necessary for the purposes of preventing or detecting crime,

    (b) was required or authorised by an enactment, by a rule of law or by the order of a court or tribunal, or

    (c) in the particular circumstances, was justified as being in the public interest.

(7) It is also a defence for a person charged with an offence under subsection (5) to prove that—

    (a) the person acted in the reasonable belief that the processing was lawful,

    (b) the person acted in the reasonable belief that the person—

        (i) had the consent of the controller responsible for de-identifying the personal data, or

        (ii) would have had such consent if that controller had known about the processing and the circumstances of it, or

(c) the person acted—

  (i) for the special purposes,

  (ii) with a view to the publication by a person of any journalistic, academic, artistic or literary material, and

  (iii) in the reasonable belief that in the particular circumstances the processing was justified as being in the public interest.

(8) In this section—

  (a) references to the consent of a controller do not include the consent of a person who is a controller by virtue of Article 28(10) of the GDPR or section 59(8) or 105(3) of this Act (processor to be treated as controller in certain circumstances);

  (b) where there is more than one controller, such references are references to the consent of one or more of them.

—— NOTES ——

Defined terms		"personal data"	s 3(2), (14)(c)
"controller"	s 3(6), (14)(d)	"processing"	s 3(4), (14)(c)
"data subject"	s 3(5)	"publish"	s 205(1)
"enactment"	s 205(1)	"the special purposes"	s 174(1)
"the GDPR"	s 3(10), (14)(a)	"tribunal"	s 205(1)

Re-identification: effectiveness testing conditions

172(1) For the purposes of section 171, in relation to a person who re-identifies information that is de-identified personal data, "the effectiveness testing conditions" means the conditions in subsections (2) and (3).

(2) The first condition is that the person acted—

  (a) with a view to testing the effectiveness of the de-identification of personal data,

  (b) without intending to cause, or threaten to cause, damage or distress to a person, and

  (c) in the reasonable belief that, in the particular circumstances, re-identifying the information was justified as being in the public interest.

(3) The second condition is that the person notified the Commissioner or the controller responsible for de-identifying the personal data about the re-identification—

  (a) without undue delay, and

  (b) where feasible, not later than 72 hours after becoming aware of it.

(4) Where there is more than one controller responsible for de-identifying personal data, the requirement in subsection (3) is satisfied if one or more of them is notified.

—— NOTES ——

Defined terms		"de-identified"	s 171(2)(a)
"the Commissioner"	s 3(8)	"personal data"	s 3(2), (14)(c)
"controller"	s 3(6), (14)(d)	"re-identifies"	s 171(2)(b)

Alteration etc of personal data to prevent disclosure to data subject

173(1) Subsection (3) applies where—

  (a) a request has been made in exercise of a data subject access right, and

  (b) the person making the request would have been entitled to receive information in response to that request.

(2) In this section, "data subject access right" means a right under—

(a) Article 15 of the GDPR (right of access by the data subject);

(b) Article 20 of the GDPR (right to data portability);

(c) section 45 of this Act (law enforcement processing: right of access by the data subject);

(d) section 94 of this Act (intelligence services processing: right of access by the data subject).

(3) It is an offence for a person listed in subsection (4) to alter, deface, block, erase, destroy or conceal information with the intention of preventing disclosure of all or part of the information that the person making the request would have been entitled to receive.

(4) Those persons are—

(a) the controller, and

(b) a person who is employed by the controller, an officer of the controller or subject to the direction of the controller.

(5) It is a defence for a person charged with an offence under subsection (3) to prove that—

(a) the alteration, defacing, blocking, erasure, destruction or concealment of the information would have occurred in the absence of a request made in exercise of a data subject access right, or

(b) the person acted in the reasonable belief that the person making the request was not entitled to receive the information in response to the request.

——— Notes ———

Defined terms		"data subject"	s 3(5)
"controller"	s 3(6), (14)(d)	"the GDPR"	s 3(10), (14)(a)

The special purposes

The special purposes

174(1) In this Part, "the special purposes" means one or more of the following—

(a) the purposes of journalism;

(b) academic purposes;

(c) artistic purposes;

(d) literary purposes.

(2) In this Part, "special purposes proceedings" means legal proceedings against a controller or processor which relate, wholly or partly, to personal data processed for the special purposes and which are—

(a) proceedings under section 167 (including proceedings on an application under Article 79 of the GDPR), or

(b) proceedings under Article 82 of the GDPR or section 169.

(3) The Commissioner may make a written determination, in relation to the processing of personal data, that—

(a) the personal data is not being processed only for the special purposes;

(b) the personal data is not being processed with a view to the publication by a person of journalistic, academic, artistic or literary material which has not previously been published by the controller.

(4) The Commissioner must give written notice of the determination to the controller and the processor.

(5) The notice must provide information about the rights of appeal under section 162.

(6) The determination does not take effect until one of the following conditions is satisfied—

    (a) the period for the controller or the processor to appeal against the determination has ended without an appeal having been brought, or

    (b) an appeal has been brought against the determination and—

        (i) the appeal and any further appeal in relation to the determination has been decided or has otherwise ended, and

        (ii) the time for appealing against the result of the appeal or further appeal has ended without another appeal having been brought.

—— NOTES ——

Defined terms		"personal data"	s 3(2), (14)(c)
"the Commissioner"	s 3(8)	"processing"	s 3(4), (14)(c)
"controller"	s 3(6), (14)(d)	"processor"	s 3(6), (14)(d)
"the GDPR"	s 3(10), (14)(a)	"publish"	s 205(1)

Provision of assistance in special purposes proceedings

175(1) An individual who is a party, or prospective party, to special purposes proceedings may apply to the Commissioner for assistance in those proceedings.

(2) As soon as reasonably practicable after receiving an application under subsection (1), the Commissioner must decide whether, and to what extent, to grant it.

(3) The Commissioner must not grant the application unless, in the Commissioner's opinion, the case involves a matter of substantial public importance.

(4) If the Commissioner decides not to provide assistance, the Commissioner must, as soon as reasonably practicable, notify the applicant of the decision, giving reasons for the decision.

(5) If the Commissioner decides to provide assistance, the Commissioner must—

    (a) as soon as reasonably practicable, notify the applicant of the decision, stating the extent of the assistance to be provided, and

    (b) secure that the person against whom the proceedings are, or are to be, brought is informed that the Commissioner is providing assistance.

(6) The assistance that may be provided by the Commissioner includes—

    (a) paying costs in connection with the proceedings, and

    (b) indemnifying the applicant in respect of liability to pay costs, expenses or damages in connection with the proceedings.

(7) In England and Wales or Northern Ireland, the recovery of expenses incurred by the Commissioner in providing an applicant with assistance under this section (as taxed or assessed in accordance with rules of court) is to constitute a first charge for the benefit of the Commissioner—

    (a) on any costs which, by virtue of any judgment or order of the court, are payable to the applicant by any other person in respect of the matter in connection with which the assistance is provided, and

    (b) on any sum payable to the applicant under a compromise or settlement arrived at in connection with that matter to avoid, or bring to an end, any proceedings.

(8) In Scotland, the recovery of such expenses (as taxed or assessed in accordance with rules of court) is to be paid to the Commissioner, in priority to other debts—

    (a) out of any expenses which, by virtue of any judgment or order of the court, are payable to the applicant by any other person in respect of the matter in connection with which the assistance is provided, and

(b) out of any sum payable to the applicant under a compromise or settlement arrived at in connection with that matter to avoid, or bring to an end, any proceedings.

––––– NOTES –––––

Defined terms		"special purposes proceedings"	s 174(2)
"the Commissioner"	s 3(8)		

Staying special purposes proceedings

176(1) In any special purposes proceedings before a court, if the controller or processor claims, or it appears to the court, that any personal data to which the proceedings relate—

(a) is being processed only for the special purposes,

(b) is being processed with a view to the publication by any person of journalistic, academic, artistic or literary material, and

(c) has not previously been published by the controller, the court must stay or, in Scotland, sist the proceedings.

(2) In considering, for the purposes of subsection (1)(c), whether material has previously been published, publication in the immediately preceding 24 hours is to be ignored.

(3) Under subsection (1), the court must stay or sist the proceedings until either of the following conditions is met—

(a) a determination of the Commissioner under section 174 with respect to the personal data or the processing takes effect;

(b) where the proceedings were stayed or sisted on the making of a claim, the claim is withdrawn.

––––– NOTES –––––

Defined terms		"processor"	s 3(6), (14)(d)
"the Commissioner"	s 3(8)	"publish"	s 205(1)
"controller"	s 3(6), (14)(d)	"the special purposes"	s 174(1)
"personal data"	s 3(2), (14)(c)	"special purposes proceedings"	s 174(2)
"processing"	s 3(4), (14)(c)		

Guidance about how to seek redress against media organisations

177(1) The Commissioner must produce and publish guidance about the steps that may be taken where an individual considers that a media organisation is failing or has failed to comply with the data protection legislation.

(2) In this section, "media organisation" means a body or other organisation whose activities consist of or include journalism.

(3) The guidance must include provision about relevant complaints procedures, including—

(a) who runs them,

(b) what can be complained about, and

(c) how to make a complaint.

(4) For the purposes of subsection (3), relevant complaints procedures include procedures for making complaints to the Commissioner, the Office of Communications, the British Broadcasting Corporation and other persons who produce or enforce codes of practice for media organisations.

(5) The guidance must also include provision about—

    (a) the powers available to the Commissioner in relation to a failure to comply with the data protection legislation,

    (b) when a claim in respect of such a failure may be made before a court and how to make such a claim,

    (c) alternative dispute resolution procedures,

    (d) the rights of bodies and other organisations to make complaints and claims on behalf of data subjects, and

    (e) the Commissioner's power to provide assistance in special purpose proceedings.

(6) The Commissioner—

    (a) may alter or replace the guidance, and

    (b) must publish any altered or replacement guidance.

(7) The Commissioner must produce and publish the first guidance under this section before the end of the period of 1 year beginning when this Act is passed.

—— Notes ——

Defined terms			
"the Commissioner"	s 3(8)	"data subject"	s 3(5)
"the data protection legislation"	s 3(9)	"publish"	s 205(1)
		"special purposes proceedings"	s 174(2)

Review of processing of personal data for the purposes of journalism

178(1) The Commissioner must—

    (a) review the extent to which, during each review period, the processing of personal data for the purposes of journalism complied with—

        (i) the data protection legislation, and

        (ii) good practice in the processing of personal data for the purposes of journalism,

    (b) prepare a report of the review, and

    (c) submit the report to the Secretary of State.

(2) In this section—

    "good practice in the processing of personal data for the purposes of journalism" has the same meaning as in section 124;

    "review period" means—

    (a) the period of 4 years beginning with the day on which Chapter 2 of Part 2 of this Act comes into force, and

    (b) each subsequent period of 5 years beginning with the day after the day on which the previous review period ended.

(3) The Commissioner must start a review under this section, in respect of a review period, within the period of 6 months beginning when the review period ends.

(4) The Commissioner must submit the report of a review under this section to the Secretary of State—

    (a) in the case of the first review, before the end of the period of 18 months beginning when the Commissioner started the review, and

    (b) in the case of each subsequent review, before the end of the period of 12 months beginning when the Commissioner started the review.

(5) The report must include consideration of the extent of compliance (as described in subsection (1)(a)) in each part of the United Kingdom.

(6) The Secretary of State must—
    (a) lay the report before Parliament, and
    (b) send a copy of the report to—
        (i) the Scottish Ministers,
        (ii) the Welsh Ministers, and
        (iii) the Executive Office in Northern Ireland.

(7) Schedule 17 makes further provision for the purposes of a review under this section.

—— NOTES ——

Defined terms		"the data protection legislation"	s 3(9)
"Chapter 2 of Part 2"	s 3(14)(b)	"personal data"	s 3(2), (14)(c)
"the Commissioner"	s 3(8)	"processing"	s 3(4), (14)(c)

Effectiveness of the media's dispute resolution procedures

179(1) The Secretary of State must, before the end of each review period, lay before Parliament a report produced by the Secretary of State or an appropriate person on—
    (a) the use of relevant alternative dispute resolution procedures, during that period, in cases involving a failure, or alleged failure, by a relevant media organisation to comply with the data protection legislation, and
    (b) the effectiveness of those procedures in such cases.

(2) In this section—
    "appropriate person" means a person who the Secretary of State considers has appropriate experience and skills to produce a report described in subsection (1);
    "relevant alternative dispute resolution procedures" means alternative dispute resolution procedures provided by persons who produce or enforce codes of practice for relevant media organisations;
    "relevant media organisation" means a body or other organisation whose activities consist of or include journalism, other than a broadcaster;
    "review period" means—
        (a) the period of 3 years beginning when this Act is passed, and
        (b) each subsequent period of 3 years.

(3) The Secretary of State must send a copy of the report to—
    (a) the Scottish Ministers,
    (b) the Welsh Ministers, and
    (c) the Executive Office in Northern Ireland.

—— NOTES ——

Defined terms	"the data protection legislation"	s 3(9)

Jurisdiction of courts

Jurisdiction

180(1) The jurisdiction conferred on a court by the provisions listed in subsection (2) is exercisable—
    (a) in England and Wales, by the High Court or the county court,
    (b) in Northern Ireland, by the High Court or a county court, and
    (c) in Scotland, by the Court of Session or the sheriff, subject to subsections (3) and (4).

(2) Those provisions are—

   (a)   section 145 (information orders);

   (b)   section 152 (enforcement notices and processing for the special purposes);

   (c)   section 156 (penalty notices and processing for the special purposes);

   (d)   section 167 and Article 79 of the GDPR (compliance orders);

   (e)   sections 168 and 169 and Article 82 of the GDPR (compensation).

(3) In relation to the processing of personal data to which Part 4 applies, the jurisdiction conferred by the provisions listed in subsection (2) is exercisable only by the High Court or, in Scotland, the Court of Session.

(4) In relation to an information notice which contains a statement under section 142(7), the jurisdiction conferred on a court by section 145 is exercisable only by the High Court or, in Scotland, the Court of Session.

(5) The jurisdiction conferred on a court by section 164 (applications in respect of urgent notices) is exercisable only by the High Court or, in Scotland, the Court of Session.

—— NOTES ——

Defined terms		"information notice"	ss 142(1), 181
"the GDPR"	s 3(10), (14)(a)	"personal data"	s 3(2)

Definitions

Interpretation of Part 6

181 In this Part—

"assessment notice" has the meaning given in section 146;

"certification provider" has the meaning given in section 17;

"enforcement notice" has the meaning given in section 149;

"information notice" has the meaning given in section 142;

"penalty notice" has the meaning given in section 155;

"penalty variation notice" has the meaning given in Schedule 16;

"representative", in relation to a controller or processor, means a person designated by the controller or processor under Article 27 of the GDPR to represent the controller or processor with regard to the controller's or processor's obligations under the GDPR.

—— NOTES ——

Defined terms		"the GDPR"	s 3(10), (14)(a)
"controller"	s 3(6), (14)(d)	"processor"	s 3(6), (14)(d)

PART 7
SUPPLEMENTARY AND FINAL PROVISION

Regulations under this Act

Regulations and consultation

182(1) Regulations under this Act are to be made by statutory instrument.

(2) Before making regulations under this Act, the Secretary of State must consult—

   (a)   the Commissioner, and

   (b)   such other persons as the Secretary of State considers appropriate.

(3) Subsection (2) does not apply to regulations made under—

   (a)   section 23;

   (b)   section 30;

(c) section 211;

(d) section 212;

(e) section 213;

(f) paragraph 15 of Schedule 2.

(4) Subsection (2) does not apply to regulations made under section 18 where the Secretary of State has made an urgency statement in respect of them.

(5) Regulations under this Act may—

(a) make different provision for different purposes;

(b) include consequential, supplementary, incidental, transitional, transitory or saving provision.

(6) Where regulations under this Act are subject to "the negative resolution procedure" the statutory instrument containing the regulations is subject to annulment in pursuance of a resolution of either House of Parliament.

(7) Where regulations under this Act are subject to "the affirmative resolution procedure" the regulations may not be made unless a draft of the statutory instrument containing them has been laid before Parliament and approved by a resolution of each House of Parliament.

(8) Where regulations under this Act are subject to "the made affirmative resolution procedure"—

(a) the statutory instrument containing the regulations must be laid before Parliament after being made, together with the urgency statement in respect of them, and

(b) the regulations cease to have effect at the end of the period of 120 days beginning with the day on which the instrument is made, unless within that period the instrument is approved by a resolution of each House of Parliament.

(9) In calculating the period of 120 days, no account is to be taken of any time during which—

(a) Parliament is dissolved or prorogued, or

(b) both Houses of Parliament are adjourned for more than 4 days.

(10) Where regulations cease to have effect as a result of subsection (8), that does not—

(a) affect anything previously done under the regulations, or

(b) prevent the making of new regulations.

(11) Any provision that may be included in regulations under this Act subject to the negative resolution procedure may be made by regulations subject to the affirmative resolution procedure or the made affirmative resolution procedure.

(12) If a draft of a statutory instrument containing regulations under section 7 would, apart from this subsection, be treated for the purposes of the standing orders of either House of Parliament as a hybrid instrument, it is to proceed in that House as if it were not such an instrument.

(13) A requirement under a provision of this Act to consult may be satisfied by consultation before, as well as by consultation after, the provision comes into force.

(14) In this section, "urgency statement" has the meaning given in section 18(4).

—— NOTES ——

Defined terms   "the Commissioner"   s 3(8)

Changes to the Data Protection Convention

Power to reflect changes to the Data Protection Convention

183(1)   The Secretary of State may by regulations make such provision as the Secretary of State considers necessary or appropriate in connection with an amendment of, or an instrument replacing, the Data Protection Convention which has effect, or is expected to have effect, in the United Kingdom.

(2)   The power under subsection (1) includes power—

(a)   to amend or replace the definition of "the Data Protection Convention" in section 3;

(b)   to amend Chapter 3 of Part 2 of this Act;

(c)   to amend Part 4 of this Act;

(d)   to make provision about the functions of the Commissioner, courts or tribunals in connection with processing of personal data to which Chapter 3 of Part 2 or Part 4 of this Act applies, including provision amending Parts 5 to 7 of this Act;

(e)   to make provision about the functions of the Commissioner in connection with the Data Protection Convention or an instrument replacing that Convention, including provision amending Parts 5 to 7 of this Act;

(f)   to consequentially amend this Act.

(3)   Regulations under this section are subject to the affirmative resolution procedure.

(4)   Regulations under this section may not be made after the end of the period of 3 years beginning with the day on which this Act is passed.

—— NOTES ——

Defined terms			
"the affirmative resolution procedure"s	182(7)	"personal data"	s 3(2), (14)(c)
"the Commissioner"	s 3(8)	"processing"	s 3(4), (14)(c)
"the Data Protection Convention"	s 3(13)	"tribunal"	s 205(1)

Rights of the data subject

Prohibition of requirement to produce relevant records

184(1)   It is an offence for a person ("P1") to require another person to provide P1 with, or give P1 access to, a relevant record in connection with—

(a)   the recruitment of an employee by P1,

(b)   the continued employment of a person by P1, or

(c)   a contract for the provision of services to P1.

(2)   It is an offence for a person ("P2") to require another person to provide P2 with, or give P2 access to, a relevant record if—

(a)   P2 is involved in the provision of goods, facilities or services to the public or a section of the public, and

(b)   the requirement is a condition of providing or offering to provide goods, facilities or services to the other person or to a third party.

(3)   It is a defence for a person charged with an offence under subsection (1) or (2) to prove that imposing the requirement—

(a)   was required or authorised by an enactment, by a rule of law or by the order of a court or tribunal, or

(b)   in the particular circumstances, was justified as being in the public interest.

(4) The imposition of the requirement referred to in subsection (1) or (2) is not to be regarded as justified as being in the public interest on the ground that it would assist in the prevention or detection of crime, given Part 5 of the Police Act 1997 (certificates of criminal records etc).

(5) In subsections (1) and (2), the references to a person who requires another person to provide or give access to a relevant record include a person who asks another person to do so—

    (a) knowing that, in the circumstances, it would be reasonable for the other person to feel obliged to comply with the request, or

    (b) being reckless as to whether, in the circumstances, it would be reasonable for the other person to feel obliged to comply with the request,

and the references to a "requirement" in subsections (3) and (4) are to be interpreted accordingly.

(6) In this section—

"employment" means any employment, including—

    (a) work under a contract for services or as an office-holder,

    (b) work under an apprenticeship,

    (c) work experience as part of a training course or in the course of training for employment, and

    (d) voluntary work,

and "employee" is to be interpreted accordingly;

"relevant record" has the meaning given in Schedule 18 and references to a relevant record include—

    (a) a part of such a record, and

    (b) a copy of, or of part of, such a record.

—— NOTES ——

Defined terms   "tribunal"   s 205(1)
   "enactment"   s 205(1)

Avoidance of certain contractual terms relating to health records

185(1) A term or condition of a contract is void in so far as it purports to require an individual to supply another person with a record which—

    (a) consists of the information contained in a health record, and

    (b) has been or is to be obtained by a data subject in the exercise of a data subject access right.

(2) A term or condition of a contract is also void in so far as it purports to require an individual to produce such a record to another person.

(3) The references in subsections (1) and (2) to a record include a part of a record and a copy of all or part of a record.

(4) In this section, "data subject access right" means a right under—

    (a) Article 15 of the GDPR (right of access by the data subject);

    (b) Article 20 of the GDPR (right to data portability);

    (c) section 45 of this Act (law enforcement processing: right of access by the data subject);

    (d) section 94 of this Act (intelligence services processing: right of access by the data subject).

——— Notes ———

| Defined terms | | "the GDPR" | s 3(10), (14)(a) |
| "data subject" | s 3(5) | "health record" | s 205(1) |

Data subject's rights and other prohibitions and restrictions

186(1) An enactment or rule of law prohibiting or restricting the disclosure of information, or authorising the withholding of information, does not remove or restrict the obligations and rights provided for in the provisions listed in subsection (2), except as provided by or under the provisions listed in subsection (3).

(2) The provisions providing obligations and rights are—

    (a) Chapter III of the GDPR (rights of the data subject),

    (b) Chapter 3 of Part 3 of this Act (law enforcement processing: rights of the data subject), and

    (c) Chapter 3 of Part 4 of this Act (intelligence services processing: rights of the data subject).

(3) The provisions providing exceptions are—

    (a) in Chapter 2 of Part 2 of this Act, sections 15 and 16 and Schedules 2, 3 and 4,

    (b) in Chapter 3 of Part 2 of this Act, sections 23, 24, 25 and 26,

    (c) in Part 3 of this Act, sections 44(4), 45(4) and 48(3), and

    (d) in Part 4 of this Act, Chapter 6.

——— Notes ———

| Defined terms | | "the GDPR" | s 3(10), (14)(a) |
| "enactment" | s 205(1) | | |

Representation of data subjects

Representation of data subjects with their authority

187(1) In relation to the processing of personal data to which the GDPR applies—

    (a) Article 80(1) of the GDPR (representation of data subjects) enables a data subject to authorise a body or other organisation which meets the conditions set out in that Article to exercise the data subject's rights under Articles 77, 78 and 79 of the GDPR (rights to lodge complaints and to an effective judicial remedy) on the data subject's behalf, and

    (b) a data subject may also authorise such a body or organisation to exercise the data subject's rights under Article 82 of the GDPR (right to compensation).

(2) In relation to the processing of personal data to which the GDPR does not apply, a body or other organisation which meets the conditions in subsections (3) and (4), if authorised to do so by a data subject, may exercise some or all of the following rights of a data subject on the data subject's behalf—

    (a) rights under section 165(2), (4)(d) and (6)(c) (complaints to the Commissioner);

    (b) rights under section 166(2) (orders for the Commissioner to progress complaints);

    (c) rights under section 167(1) (compliance orders);

    (d) the right to bring judicial review proceedings against the Commissioner.

(3) The first condition is that the body or organisation, by virtue of its constitution or an enactment—

    (a) is required (after payment of outgoings) to apply the whole of its income and any capital it expends for charitable or public purposes,

(b) is prohibited from directly or indirectly distributing amongst its members any part of its assets (otherwise than for charitable or public purposes), and

(c) has objectives which are in the public interest.

(4) The second condition is that the body or organisation is active in the field of protection of data subjects' rights and freedoms with regard to the protection of their personal data.

(5) In this Act, references to a "representative body", in relation to a right of a data subject, are to a body or other organisation authorised to exercise the right on the data subject's behalf under Article 80 of the GDPR or this section.

—— NOTES ——

Defined terms		"the GDPR"	s 3(10), (14)(a)
"the Commissioner"	s 3(8)	"personal data"	s 3(2), (14)(c)
"data subject"	s 3(5)	"processing"	s 3(4), (14)(c)
"enactment"	s 205(1)		

Representation of data subjects with their authority: collective proceedings

188(1) The Secretary of State may by regulations make provision for representative bodies to bring proceedings before a court or tribunal in England and Wales or Northern Ireland combining two or more relevant claims.

(2) In this section, "relevant claim", in relation to a representative body, means a claim in respect of a right of a data subject which the representative body is authorised to exercise on the data subject's behalf under Article 80(1) of the GDPR or section 187.

(3) The power under subsection (1) includes power—

(a) to make provision about the proceedings;

(b) to confer functions on a person, including functions involving the exercise of a discretion;

(c) to make different provision in relation to England and Wales and in relation to Northern Ireland.

(4) The provision mentioned in subsection (3)(a) includes provision about—

(a) the effect of judgments and orders;

(b) agreements to settle claims;

(c) the assessment of the amount of compensation;

(d) the persons to whom compensation may or must be paid, including compensation not claimed by the data subject;

(e) costs.

(5) Regulations under this section are subject to the negative resolution procedure.

—— NOTES ——

Defined terms		"the negative resolution procedure"	s 182(6)
"data subject"	s 3(5)	"representative body"	s 187(5)
"the GDPR"	s 3(10), (14)(a)	"tribunal"	s 205(1)

Duty to review provision for representation of data subjects

189(1) Before the end of the review period, the Secretary of State must—

(a) review the matters listed in subsection (2) in relation to England and Wales and Northern Ireland,

(b) prepare a report of the review, and

(c) lay a copy of the report before Parliament.

(2) Those matters are—

(a) the operation of Article 80(1) of the GDPR,

(b) the operation of section 187,

(c) the merits of exercising the power under Article 80(2) of the GDPR (power to enable a body or other organisation which meets the conditions in Article 80(1) of the GDPR to exercise some or all of a data subject's rights under Articles 77, 78 and 79 of the GDPR without being authorised to do so by the data subject),

(d) the merits of making equivalent provision in relation to data subjects' rights under Article 82 of the GDPR (right to compensation), and

(e) the merits of making provision for a children's rights organisation to exercise some or all of a data subject's rights under Articles 77, 78, 79 and 82 of the GDPR on behalf of a data subject who is a child, with or without being authorised to do so by the data subject.

(3) "The review period" is the period of 30 months beginning when section 187 comes into force.

(4) In carrying out the review, the Secretary of State must—

(a) consider the particular needs of children separately from the needs of adults,

(b) have regard to the fact that children have different needs at different stages of development,

(c) carry out an analysis of the particular challenges that children face in authorising, and deciding whether to authorise, other persons to act on their behalf under Article 80(1) of the GDPR or section 187,

(d) consider the support and advice available to children in connection with the exercise of their rights under Articles 77, 78, 79 and 82 of the GDPR by another person on their behalf and the merits of making available other support or advice, and

(e) have regard to the United Kingdom's obligations under the United Nations Convention on the Rights of the Child.

(5) Before preparing the report under subsection (1), the Secretary of State must consult the Commissioner and such other persons as the Secretary of State considers appropriate, including—

(a) persons active in the field of protection of data subjects' rights and freedoms with regard to the protection of their personal data,

(b) children and parents,

(c) children's rights organisations and other persons who appear to the Secretary of State to represent the interests of children,

(d) child development experts, and

(e) trade associations.

(6) In this section—

"children's rights organisation" means a body or other organisation which—

(a) is active in representing the interests of children, and

(b) has objectives which are in the public interest;

"trade association" includes a body representing controllers or processors;

"the United Nations Convention on the Rights of the Child" means the Convention on the Rights of the Child adopted by the General Assembly of the United Nations on 20 November 1989 (including any Protocols to that Convention which are in force in relation to the United Kingdom), subject to any reservations, objections or interpretative declarations by the United Kingdom for the time being in force.

—— Notes ——

Defined terms		"the GDPR"	s 3(10), (14)(a)
"the Commissioner"	s 3(8)	"personal data"	s 3(2), (14)(c)
"controller"	s 3(6), (14)(d)	"processor"	s 3(6), (14)(d)
"data subject"	s 3(5)		

Post-review powers to make provision about representation of data subjects

190(1) After the report under section 189(1) is laid before Parliament, the Secretary of State may by regulations—

(a) exercise the powers under Article 80(2) of the GDPR in relation to England and Wales and Northern Ireland,

(b) make provision enabling a body or other organisation which meets the conditions in Article 80(1) of the GDPR to exercise a data subject's rights under Article 82 of the GDPR in England and Wales and Northern Ireland without being authorised to do so by the data subject, and

(c) make provision described in section 189(2)(e) in relation to the exercise in England and Wales and Northern Ireland of the rights of a data subject who is a child.

(2) The powers under subsection (1) include power—

(a) to make provision enabling a data subject to prevent a body or other organisation from exercising, or continuing to exercise, the data subject's rights;

(b) to make provision about proceedings before a court or tribunal where a body or organisation exercises a data subject's rights;

(c) to make provision for bodies or other organisations to bring proceedings before a court or tribunal combining two or more claims in respect of a right of a data subject;

(d) to confer functions on a person, including functions involving the exercise of a discretion;

(e) to amend sections 166 to 168, 180, 187, 203, 205 and 206;

(f) to insert new sections and Schedules into Part 6 or 7 ;

(g) to make different provision in relation to England and Wales and in relation to Northern Ireland.

(3) The powers under subsection (1)(a) and (b) include power to make provision in relation to data subjects who are children or data subjects who are not children or both.

(4) The provision mentioned in subsection (2)(b) and (c) includes provision about—

(a) the effect of judgments and orders;

(b) agreements to settle claims;

(c) the assessment of the amount of compensation;

(d) the persons to whom compensation may or must be paid, including compensation not claimed by the data subject;

(e) costs.

(5) Regulations under this section are subject to the affirmative resolution procedure.

—— Notes ——

Defined terms		"data subject"	s 3(5)
"the affirmative resolution		"the GDPR"	s 3(10), (14)(a)
procedure"	s 182(7)	"tribunal"	s 205(1)

Framework for Data Processing by Government

Framework for Data Processing by Government

191(1) The Secretary of State may prepare a document, called the Framework for Data Processing by Government, which contains guidance about the processing of personal data in connection with the exercise of functions of—

(a) the Crown, a Minister of the Crown or a United Kingdom government department, and

(b) a person with functions of a public nature who is specified or described in regulations made by the Secretary of State.

(2) The document may make provision relating to all of those functions or only to particular functions or persons.

(3) The document may not make provision relating to, or to the functions of, a part of the Scottish Administration, the Welsh Government, a Northern Ireland Minister or a Northern Ireland department.

(4) The Secretary of State may from time to time prepare amendments of the document or a replacement document.

(5) Before preparing a document or amendments under this section, the Secretary of State must consult—

(a) the Commissioner, and

(b) any other person the Secretary of State considers it appropriate to consult.

(6) Regulations under subsection (1)(b) are subject to the negative resolution procedure.

(7) In this section, "Northern Ireland Minister" includes the First Minister and deputy First Minister in Northern Ireland.

——— NOTES ———

Defined terms		"the negative resolution procedure" s 182(6)
"the Commissioner"	s 3(8)	"personal data" s 3(2), (14)(c)
"Minister of the Crown"	s 205(1)	"processing" s 3(4), (14)(c)

Approval of the Framework

192(1) Before issuing a document prepared under section 191, the Secretary of State must lay it before Parliament.

(2) If, within the 40-day period, either House of Parliament resolves not to approve the document, the Secretary of State must not issue it.

(3) If no such resolution is made within that period—

(a) the Secretary of State must issue the document, and

(b) the document comes into force at the end of the period of 21 days beginning with the day on which it is issued.

(4) Nothing in subsection (2) prevents another version of the document being laid before Parliament.

(5) In this section, "the 40-day period" means—

(a) if the document is laid before both Houses of Parliament on the same day, the period of 40 days beginning with that day, or

(b) if the document is laid before the Houses of Parliament on different days, the period of 40 days beginning with the later of those days.

(6) In calculating the 40-day period, no account is to be taken of any period during which Parliament is dissolved or prorogued or during which both Houses of Parliament are adjourned for more than 4 days.

(7) This section applies in relation to amendments prepared under section 191 as it applies in relation to a document prepared under that section.

Publication and review of the Framework

193(1) The Secretary of State must publish a document issued under section 192(3).

(2) Where an amendment of a document is issued under section 192(3), the Secretary of State must publish—
   (a) the amendment, or
   (b) the document as amended by it.

(3) The Secretary of State must keep under review the document issued under section 192(3) for the time being in force.

(4) Where the Secretary of State becomes aware that the terms of such a document could result in a breach of an international obligation of the United Kingdom, the Secretary of State must exercise the power under section 191(4) with a view to remedying the situation.

—— NOTES ——

Defined terms			
"international obligation of		the United Kingdom"	s 205(1)
		"publish"	s 205(1)

Effect of the Framework

194(1) When carrying out processing of personal data which is the subject of a document issued under section 192(3) which is for the time being in force, a person must have regard to the document.

(2) A failure to act in accordance with a provision of such a document does not of itself make a person liable to legal proceedings in a court or tribunal.

(3) A document issued under section 192(3), including an amendment or replacement document, is admissible in evidence in legal proceedings.

(4) In any legal proceedings before a court or tribunal, the court or tribunal must take into account a provision of any document issued under section 192(3) in determining a question arising in the proceedings if—
   (a) the question relates to a time when the provision was in force, and
   (b) the provision appears to the court or tribunal to be relevant to the question.

(5) In determining a question arising in connection with the carrying out of any of the Commissioner's functions, the Commissioner must take into account a provision of a document issued under section 192(3) if—
   (a) the question relates to a time when the provision was in force, and
   (b) the provision appears to the Commissioner to be relevant to the question.

—— NOTES ——

Defined terms			
"the Commissioner"	s 3(8)	"processing"	s 3(4), (14)(c)
"personal data"	s 3(2), (14)(c)	"tribunal"	s 205(1)

Data-sharing: HMRC and reserve forces

Reserve forces: data-sharing by HMRC

195(1)   The Reserve Forces Act 1996 is amended as follows.

(2)   After section 125 insert—

"125A Supply of contact details by HMRC

(1)   This subsection applies to contact details for—

(a)   a member of an ex-regular reserve force, or

(b)   a person to whom section 66 (officers and former servicemen liable to recall) applies,

which are held by HMRC in connection with a function of HMRC.

(2)   HMRC may supply contact details to which subsection (1) applies to the Secretary of State for the purpose of enabling the Secretary of State—

(a)   to contact a member of an ex-regular reserve force in connection with the person's liability, or potential liability, to be called out for service under Part 6;

(b)   to contact a person to whom section 66 applies in connection with the person's liability, or potential liability, to be recalled for service under Part 7.

(3)   Where a person's contact details are supplied under subsection (2) for a purpose described in that subsection, they may also be used for defence purposes connected with the person's service (whether past, present or future) in the reserve forces or regular services.

(4)   In this section, "HMRC" means Her Majesty's Revenue and Customs.

125B   Prohibition on disclosure of contact details supplied under section 125A

(1)   A person who receives information supplied under section 125A may not disclose it except with the consent of the Commissioners for Her Majesty's Revenue and Customs (which may be general or specific).

(2)   A person who contravenes subsection (1) is guilty of an offence.

(3)   It is a defence for a person charged with an offence under this section to prove that the person reasonably believed—

(a)   that the disclosure was lawful, or

(b)   that the information had already lawfully been made available to the public.

(4)   Subsections (4) to (7) of section 19 of the Commissioners for Revenue and Customs Act 2005 apply to an offence under this section as they apply to an offence under that section.

(5)   Nothing in section 107 or 108 (institution of proceedings and evidence) applies in relation to an offence under this section.

125C   Data protection

(1)   Nothing in section 125A or 125B authorises the making of a disclosure which contravenes the data protection legislation.

(2)   In this section, "the data protection legislation" has the same meaning as in the Data Protection Act 2018 (see section 3 of that Act)."

Offences

Penalties for offences

196(1)   A person who commits an offence under section 119 or 173 or paragraph 15 of Schedule 15 is liable—

    (a) on summary conviction in England and Wales, to a fine;

    (b) on summary conviction in Scotland or Northern Ireland, to a fine not exceeding level 5 on the standard scale.

(2) A person who commits an offence under section 132, 144, 148, 170, 171 or 184 is liable—

    (a) on summary conviction in England and Wales, to a fine;

    (b) on summary conviction in Scotland or Northern Ireland, to a fine not exceeding the statutory maximum;

    (c) on conviction on indictment, to a fine.

(3) Subsections (4) and (5) apply where a person is convicted of an offence under section 170 or 184.

(4) The court by or before which the person is convicted may order a document or other material to be forfeited, destroyed or erased if—

    (a) it has been used in connection with the processing of personal data, and

    (b) it appears to the court to be connected with the commission of the offence, subject to subsection (5).

(5) If a person, other than the offender, who claims to be the owner of the material, or to be otherwise interested in the material, applies to be heard by the court, the court must not make an order under subsection (4) without giving the person an opportunity to show why the order should not be made.

—— NOTES ——

Defined terms
    "personal data"   s 3(2), (14)(c)

"processing"   s 3(4), (14)(c)

Prosecution

197(1) In England and Wales, proceedings for an offence under this Act may be instituted only—

    (a) by the Commissioner, or

    (b) by or with the consent of the Director of Public Prosecutions.

(2) In Northern Ireland, proceedings for an offence under this Act may be instituted only—

    (a) by the Commissioner, or

    (b) by or with the consent of the Director of Public Prosecutions for Northern Ireland.

(3) Subject to subsection (4), summary proceedings for an offence under section 173 (alteration etc of personal data to prevent disclosure) may be brought within the period of 6 months beginning with the day on which the prosecutor first knew of evidence that, in the prosecutor's opinion, was sufficient to bring the proceedings.

(4) Such proceedings may not be brought after the end of the period of 3 years beginning with the day on which the offence was committed.

(5) A certificate signed by or on behalf of the prosecutor and stating the day on which the 6 month period described in subsection (3) began is conclusive evidence of that fact.

(6) A certificate purporting to be signed as described in subsection (5) is to be treated as so signed unless the contrary is proved.

(7) In relation to proceedings in Scotland, section 136(3) of the Criminal Procedure (Scotland) Act 1995 (deemed date of commencement of proceedings) applies for the purposes of this section as it applies for the purposes of that section.

Liability of directors etc

198(1) Subsection (2) applies where—

    (a) an offence under this Act has been committed by a body corporate, and

    (b) it is proved to have been committed with the consent or connivance of or to be attributable to neglect on the part of—

        (i) a director, manager, secretary or similar officer of the body corporate, or

        (ii) a person who was purporting to act in such a capacity.

  (2) The director, manager, secretary, officer or person, as well as the body corporate, is guilty of the offence and liable to be proceeded against and punished accordingly.

  (3) Where the affairs of a body corporate are managed by its members, subsections (1) and (2) apply in relation to the acts and omissions of a member in connection with the member's management functions in relation to the body as if the member were a director of the body corporate.

  (4) Subsection (5) applies where—

    (a) an offence under this Act has been committed by a Scottish partnership, and

    (b) the contravention in question is proved to have occurred with the consent or connivance of, or to be attributable to any neglect on the part of, a partner.

  (5) The partner, as well as the partnership, is guilty of the offence and liable to be proceeded against and punished accordingly.

Recordable offences

199(1) The National Police Records (Recordable Offences) Regulations 2000 (SI 2000/1139) have effect as if the offences under the following provisions were listed in the Schedule to the Regulations—

    (a) section 119;

    (b) section 132;

    (c) section 144;

    (d) section 148;

    (e) section 170;

    (f) section 171;

    (g) section 173;

    (h) section 184;

    (i) paragraph 15 of Schedule 15.

  (2) Regulations under section 27(4) of the Police and Criminal Evidence Act 1984 (recordable offences) may repeal subsection (1).

Guidance about PACE codes of practice

200(1) The Commissioner must produce and publish guidance about how the Commissioner proposes to perform the duty under section 67(9) of the Police and Criminal Evidence Act 1984 (duty to have regard to codes of practice under that Act when investigating offences and charging offenders) in connection with offences under this Act.

  (2) The Commissioner—

(a) may alter or replace the guidance, and

(b) must publish any altered or replacement guidance.

(3) The Commissioner must consult the Secretary of State before publishing guidance under this section (including any altered or replacement guidance).

(4) The Commissioner must arrange for guidance under this section (including any altered or replacement guidance) to be laid before Parliament.

—— NOTES ——

Defined terms		"publish"	s 205(1)
"the Commissioner"	s 3(8)		

The Tribunal

Disclosure of information to the Tribunal

201(1) No enactment or rule of law prohibiting or restricting the disclosure of information precludes a person from providing the First-tier Tribunal or the Upper Tribunal with information necessary for the discharge of—

(a) its functions under the data protection legislation, or

(b) its other functions relating to the Commissioner's acts and omissions.

(2) But this section does not authorise the making of a disclosure which is prohibited by any of Parts 1 to 7 or Chapter 1 of Part 9 of the Investigatory Powers Act 2016.

(3) Until the repeal of Part 1 of the Regulation of Investigatory Powers Act 2000 by paragraphs 45 and 54 of Schedule 10 to the Investigatory Powers Act 2016 is fully in force, subsection (2) has effect as if it included a reference to that Part.

—— NOTES ——

Defined terms		"the data protection legislation"	s 3(9)
"the Commissioner"	s 3(8)	"enactment"	s 205(1)

Proceedings in the First-tier Tribunal: contempt

202(1) This section applies where—

(a) a person does something, or fails to do something, in relation to proceedings before the First-tier Tribunal—

    (i) on an appeal under section 27, 79, 111 or 162, or

    (ii) for an order under section 166, and

(b) if those proceedings were proceedings before a court having power to commit for contempt, the act or omission would constitute contempt of court.

(2) The First-tier Tribunal may certify the offence to the Upper Tribunal.

(3) Where an offence is certified under subsection (2), the Upper Tribunal may—

(a) inquire into the matter, and

(b) deal with the person charged with the offence in any manner in which it could deal with the person if the offence had been committed in relation to the Upper Tribunal.

(4) Before exercising the power under subsection (3)(b), the Upper Tribunal must—

(a) hear any witness who may be produced against or on behalf of the person charged with the offence, and

(b) hear any statement that may be offered in defence.

Tribunal Procedure Rules

203(1)   Tribunal Procedure Rules may make provision for regulating—

  (a)   the exercise of the rights of appeal conferred by section 27, 79, 111 or 162, and

  (b)   the exercise of the rights of data subjects under section 166, including their exercise by a representative body.

  (2)   In relation to proceedings involving the exercise of those rights, Tribunal Procedure Rules may make provision about—

  (a)   securing the production of material used for the processing of personal data, and

  (b)   the inspection, examination, operation and testing of equipment or material used in connection with the processing of personal data.

—— NOTES ——

Defined terms		"processing"	s 3(4), (14)(c)
"data subject"	s 3(5)	"representative body"	s 187(5)
"personal data"	s 3(2), (14)(c)		

Interpretation

Meaning of "health professional" and "social work professional"

204(1)   In this Act, "health professional" means any of the following—

  (a)   a registered medical practitioner;

  (b)   a registered nurse or midwife;

  (c)   a registered dentist within the meaning of the Dentists Act 1984 (see section 53 of that Act);

  (d)   a registered dispensing optician or a registered optometrist within the meaning of the Opticians Act 1989 (see section 36 of that Act);

  (e)   a registered osteopath with the meaning of the Osteopaths Act 1993 (see section 41 of that Act);

  (f)   a registered chiropractor within the meaning of the Chiropractors Act 1994 (see section 43 of that Act);

  (g)   a person registered as a member of a profession to which the Health Professions Order 2001 (SI 2002/254) for the time being extends;

  (h)   a registered pharmacist or a registered pharmacy technician within the meaning of the Pharmacy Order 2010 (SI 2010/231) (see article 3 of that Order);

  (i)   a registered person within the meaning of the Pharmacy (Northern Ireland) Order 1976 (SI 1976/1213 (NI 22)) (see Article 2 of that Order);

  (j)   a child psychotherapist;

  (k)   a scientist employed by a health service body as head of a department.

  (2)   In this Act, "social work professional" means any of the following—

  (a)   a person registered as a social worker in the register maintained by Social Work England under section 39(1) of the Children and Social Work Act 2017;]

  (b)   a person registered as a social worker in the register maintained by Social Care Wales under section 80 of the Regulation and Inspection of Social Care (Wales) Act 2016 (anaw 2);

  (c)   a person registered as a social worker in the register maintained by the Scottish Social Services Council under section 44 of the Regulation of Care (Scotland) Act 2001 (asp 8);

  (d)   a person registered as a social worker in the register maintained by the Northern Ireland Social Care Council under section 3 of the Health and Personal Social Services Act Northern Ireland) 2001 (c. 3 (NI)).

(3) In subsection (1)(a) "registered medical practitioner" includes a person who is provisionally registered under section 15 or 21 of the Medical Act 1983 and is engaged in such employment as is mentioned in subsection (3) of that section.

(4) In subsection (1)(k) "health service body" means any of the following—

(a) the Secretary of State in relation to the exercise of functions under section 2A or 2B of, or paragraph 7C, 8 or 12 of Schedule 1 to, the National Health Service Act 2006;

(b) a local authority in relation to the exercise of functions under section 2B or 111 of, or any of paragraphs 1 to 7B or 13 of Schedule 1 to, the National Health Service Act 2006;

(c) a National Health Service trust first established under section 25 of the National Health Service Act 2006;

(d) a Special Health Authority established under section 28 of the National Health Service Act 2006;

(e) an NHS foundation trust;

(f) the National Institute for Health and Care Excellence;

(g) the Health and Social Care Information Centre;

(h) a National Health Service trust first established under section 5 of the National Health Service and Community Care Act 1990;

(i) a Local Health Board established under section 11 of the National Health Service (Wales) Act 2006;

(j) a National Health Service trust first established under section 18 of the National Health Service (Wales) Act 2006;

(k) a Special Health Authority established under section 22 of the National Health Service (Wales) Act 2006;

(l) a Health Board within the meaning of the National Health Service (Scotland) Act 1978;

(m) a Special Health Board within the meaning of the National Health Service (Scotland) Act 1978;

(n) a National Health Service trust first established under section 12A of the National Health Service (Scotland) Act 1978;

(o) the managers of a State Hospital provided under section 102 of the National Health Service (Scotland) Act 1978;

(p) the Regional Health and Social Care Board established under section 7 of the Health and Social Care (Reform) Act (Northern Ireland) 2009 (c. 1 (N.I));

(q) a special health and social care agency established under the Health and Personal Social Services (Special Agencies) (Northern Ireland) Order 1990 (SI 1990/247 (NI 3));

(r) a Health and Social Care trust established under Article 10 of the Health and Personal Social Services (Northern Ireland) Order 1991 (SI 1991/194 (NI 1)).

General interpretation

205(1) In this Act—

"biometric data" means personal data resulting from specific technical processing relating to the physical, physiological or behavioural characteristics of an individual, which allows or confirms the unique identification of that individual, such as facial images or dactyloscopic data;

"data concerning health" means personal data relating to the physical or mental health of an individual, including the provision of health care services, which reveals information about his or her health status;

"enactment" includes—

    (a) an enactment passed or made after this Act,

    (b) an enactment comprised in subordinate legislation,

    (c) an enactment comprised in, or in an instrument made under, a Measure or Act of the National Assembly for Wales,

    (d) an enactment comprised in, or in an instrument made under, an Act of the Scottish Parliament, and

    (e) an enactment comprised in, or in an instrument made under, Northern Ireland legislation;

"genetic data" means personal data relating to the inherited or acquired genetic characteristics of an individual which gives unique information about the physiology or the health of that individual and which results, in particular, from an analysis of a biological sample from the individual in question;

"government department" includes the following (except in the expression "United Kingdom government department")—

    (a) a part of the Scottish Administration;

    (b) a Northern Ireland department;

    (c) the Welsh Government;

    (d) a body or authority exercising statutory functions on behalf of the Crown;

"health record" means a record which—

    (a) consists of data concerning health, and

    (b) has been made by or on behalf of a health professional in connection with the diagnosis, care or treatment of the individual to whom the data relates;

"inaccurate", in relation to personal data, means incorrect or misleading as to any matter of fact;

"international obligation of the United Kingdom" includes—

    (a) an EU obligation, and

    (b) an obligation that arises under an international agreement or arrangement to which the United Kingdom is a party;

"international organisation" means an organisation and its subordinate bodies governed by international law, or any other body which is set up by, or on the basis of, an agreement between two or more countries;

"Minister of the Crown" has the same meaning as in the Ministers of the Crown Act 1975;

"publish" means make available to the public or a section of the public (and related expressions are to be read accordingly);

"subordinate legislation" has the meaning given in the Interpretation Act 1978;

"tribunal" means any tribunal in which legal proceedings may be brought; "the Tribunal", in relation to an application or appeal under this Act, means—

    (a) the Upper Tribunal, in any case where it is determined by or under Tribunal Procedure Rules that the Upper Tribunal is to hear the application or appeal, or

    (b) the First-tier Tribunal, in any other case.

(2) References in this Act to a period expressed in hours, days, weeks, months or years are to be interpreted in accordance with Article 3 of Regulation (EEC, Euratom) No 1182/71 of the Council of 3 June 1971 determining the rules applicable to periods, dates and time limits, except in—

(a) section 125(4), (7) and (8);

(b) section 161(3), (5) and (6);

(c) section 176(2);

(d) section 178(2);

(e) section 182(8) and (9);

(f) section 183(4);

(g) section 192(3), (5) and (6);

(h) section 197(3) and (4);

(i) paragraph 23(4) and (5) of Schedule 1;

(j) paragraphs 5(4) and 6(4) of Schedule 3;

(k) Schedule 5;

(l) paragraph 11(5) of Schedule 12;

(m) Schedule 15;

(and the references in section 5 to terms used in Chapter 2 or 3 of Part 2 do not include references to a period expressed in hours, days, weeks, months or years).

(3) Section 3(14)(b) (interpretation of references to Chapter 2 of Part 2 in Parts 5 to 7) and the amendments in Schedule 19 which make equivalent provision are not to be treated as implying a contrary intention for the purposes of section 20(2) of the Interpretation Act 1978, or any similar provision in another enactment, as it applies to other references to, or to a provision of, Chapter 2 of Part 2 of this Act.

———— NOTES ————

Defined terms		"personal data"	s 3(2), (14)(c)
"health professional"	s 204(1), (3), (4)	"processing"	s 3(4), (14)(c)

Index of defined expressions

206 The Table below lists provisions which define or otherwise explain terms defined for this Act, for a Part of this Act or for Chapter 2 or 3 of Part 2 of this Act.

the affirmative resolution procedure	section 182
the applied Chapter 2 (in Chapter 3 of Part 2)	section 22
the applied GDPR	section 3
assessment notice (in Part 6)	section 181
biometric data	section 205
certification provider (in Part 6)	section 181
the Commissioner	section 3
competent authority (in Part 3)	section 30
consent (in Part 4)	section 84
controller	section 3
data concerning health	section 205
the Data Protection Convention	section 3
the data protection legislation	section 3
data subject	section 3
employee (in Parts 3 and 4)	sections 33 and 84
enactment	section 205

filing system	section 3
FOI public authority (in Chapter 3 of Part 2)	section 21
the GDPR	section 2
genetic data	section 205
government department	section 205
health professional	section 204
health record	section 205
identifiable living individual	section 3
inaccurate	section 205
information notice (in Part 6)	section 181
intelligence service (in Part 4)	section 82
international obligation of the United Kingdom	section 205
the Law Enforcement Directive	section 3
the law enforcement purposes (in Part 3)	section 31
the made affirmative resolution procedure	section 182
Minister of the Crown	section 205
the negative resolution procedure	section 182
penalty notice (in Part 6)	section 181
penalty variation notice (in Part 6)	section 181
personal data	section 3
personal data breach (in Parts 3 and 4)	sections 33 and 84
processing	section 3
processor	section 3
profiling (in Part 3)	section 33
public authority (in the GDPR and Part 2)	section 7
public body (in the GDPR and Part 2)	section 7
publish	section 205
recipient (in Parts 3 and 4)	sections 33 and 84
representative (in Part 60	section 181
representative body (in relation to a right of a data subject)	section 187
restriction of processing (in Parts 3 and 4)	sections 33 and 84
social work professional	section 204
the special purposes (in Part 6)	section 174

subordinate legislation	section 205
third country (in Part 3)	section 33
tribunal	section 205
the Tribunal	section 205

—— NOTES ——

Defined terms   "Chapter 2 of Part 2"   s 3(14)(b)

Territorial application

Territorial application of this Act

207(1) This Act applies only to processing of personal data described in subsections (2) and (3).

(2) It applies to the processing of personal data in the context of the activities of an establishment of a controller or processor in the United Kingdom, whether or not the processing takes place in the United Kingdom.

(3) It also applies to the processing of personal data to which Chapter 2 of Part 2 (the GDPR) applies where—

    (a) the processing is carried out in the context of the activities of an establishment of a controller or processor in a country or territory that is not a member State, whether or not the processing takes place in such a country or territory,

    (b) the personal data relates to a data subject who is in the United Kingdom when the processing takes place, and

    (c) the processing activities are related to—

        (i) the offering of goods or services to data subjects in the United Kingdom, whether or not for payment, or

        (ii) the monitoring of data subjects' behaviour in the United Kingdom.

(4) Subsections (1) to (3) have effect subject to any provision in or made under section 120 providing for the Commissioner to carry out functions in relation to other processing of personal data.

(5) Section 3(14)(c) does not apply to the reference to the processing of personal data in subsection (2).

(6) The reference in subsection (3) to Chapter 2 of Part 2 (the GDPR) does not include that Chapter as applied by Chapter 3 of Part 2 (the applied GDPR).

(7) In this section, references to a person who has an establishment in the United Kingdom include the following—

    (a) an individual who is ordinarily resident in the United Kingdom,

    (b) a body incorporated under the law of the United Kingdom or a part of the United Kingdom,

    (c) a partnership or other unincorporated association formed under the law of the United Kingdom or a part of the United Kingdom, and

    (d) a person not within paragraph (a), (b) or (c) who maintains, and carries on activities through, an office, branch or agency or other stable arrangements in the United Kingdom,

and references to a person who has an establishment in another country or territory have a corresponding meaning.

—— Notes ——

Defined terms
 "the Commissioner"   s 3(8)
 "controller"   s 3(6), (14)(d)
 "data subject"   s 3(5)

"personal data"   s 3(2), (14)(c)
"processing"   s 3(4), (14)(c) (note sub-s 207(5))
"processor"   s 3(6), (14)(d)

General

Children in Scotland

208(1) Subsections (2) and (3) apply where a question falls to be determined in Scotland as to the legal capacity of a person aged under 16 to—

 (a) exercise a right conferred by the data protection legislation, or

 (b) give consent for the purposes of the data protection legislation.

(2) The person is to be taken to have that capacity where the person has a general understanding of what it means to exercise the right or give such consent.

(3) A person aged 12 or over is to be presumed to be of sufficient age and maturity to have such understanding, unless the contrary is shown.

—— Notes ——

Defined terms   "the data protection legislation"   s 3(9)

Application to the Crown

209(1) This Act binds the Crown.

(2) For the purposes of the GDPR and this Act, each government department is to be treated as a person separate from the other government departments (to the extent that is not already the case).

(3) Where government departments are not able to enter into contracts with each other, a provision of the GDPR or this Act that would require relations between them to be governed by a contract (or other binding legal act) in writing is to be treated as satisfied if the relations are the subject of a memorandum of understanding between them.

(4) Where the purposes for which and the manner in which personal data is, or is to be, processed are determined by a person acting on behalf of the Royal Household, the Duchy of Lancaster or the Duchy of Cornwall, the controller in respect of that data for the purposes of the GDPR and this Act is—

 (a) in relation to the Royal Household, the Keeper of the Privy Purse,

 (b) in relation to the Duchy of Lancaster, such person as the Chancellor of the Duchy appoints, and

 (c) in relation to the Duchy of Cornwall, such person as the Duke of Cornwall, or the possessor for the time being of the Duchy of Cornwall, appoints.

(5) Different persons may be appointed under subsection (4)(b) or (c) for different purposes.

(6) As regards criminal liability—

 (a) a government department is not liable to prosecution under this Act;

 (b) nothing in subsection (4) makes a person who is a controller by virtue of that subsection liable to prosecution under this Act;

 (c) a person in the service of the Crown is liable to prosecution under the provisions of this Act listed in subsection (7).

(7) Those provisions are—
  (a) section 119;
  (b) section 170;
  (c) section 171;
  (d) section 173;
  (e) paragraph 15 of Schedule 15.

—— NOTES ——

Defined terms		"personal data"	s 3(2), (14)(c)
"controller"	s 3(6), (14)(d)	"processing"	s 3(4), (14)(c)
"the GDPR"	s 3(10), (14)(a)	"processor"	s 3(6), (14)(d)
"government department"	s 205(1)		

Application to Parliament

210(1) Parts 1, 2 and 5 to 7 of this Act apply to the processing of personal data by or on behalf of either House of Parliament.

(2) Where the purposes for which and the manner in which personal data is, or is to be, processed are determined by or on behalf of the House of Commons, the controller in respect of that data for the purposes of the GDPR and this Act is the Corporate Officer of that House.

(3) Where the purposes for which and the manner in which personal data is, or is to be, processed are determined by or on behalf of the House of Lords, the controller in respect of that data for the purposes of the GDPR and this Act is the Corporate Officer of that House.

(4) Subsections (2) and (3) do not apply where the purposes for which and the manner in which the personal data is, or is to be, processed are determined by or on behalf of the Intelligence and Security Committee of Parliament.

(5) As regards criminal liability—
  (a) nothing in subsection (2) or (3) makes the Corporate Officer of the House of Commons or the Corporate Officer of the House of Lords liable to prosecution under this Act;
  (b) a person acting on behalf of either House of Parliament is liable to prosecution under the provisions of this Act listed in subsection (6).

(6) Those provisions are—
  (a) section 170;
  (b) section 171;
  (c) section 173;
  (d) paragraph 15 of Schedule 15.

—— NOTES ——

Defined terms		"personal data"	s 3(2), (14)(c)
"controller"	s 3(6), (14)(d)	"processing"	s 3(4), (14)(c)
"the GDPR"	s 3(10), (14)(a)		

Minor and consequential provision

211(1) In Schedule 19—
  (a) Part 1 contains minor and consequential amendments of primary legislation;
  (b) Part 2 contains minor and consequential amendments of other legislation;

    (c)   Part 3 contains consequential modifications of legislation;

    (d)   Part 4 contains supplementary provision.

(2)   The Secretary of State may by regulations make provision that is consequential on any provision made by this Act.

(3)   Regulations under subsection (2)—

    (a)   may include transitional, transitory or saving provision;

    (b)   may amend, repeal or revoke an enactment.

(4)   The reference to an enactment in subsection (3)(b) does not include an enactment passed or made after the end of the Session in which this Act is passed.

(5)   Regulations under this section that amend, repeal or revoke primary legislation are subject to the affirmative resolution procedure.

(6)   Any other regulations under this section are subject to the negative resolution procedure.

(7)   In this section, "primary legislation" means—

    (a)   an Act;

    (b)   an Act of the Scottish Parliament;

    (c)   a Measure or Act of the National Assembly for Wales;

    (d)   Northern Ireland legislation.

—— NOTES ——

Defined terms
"the affirmative resolution procedure"   s 182(7)

"enactment"   s 205(1) (note sub-s 211(4))
"the negative resolution procedure"   s 182(6)

Final

Commencement

212(1)   Except as provided by subsections (2) and (3), this Act comes into force on such day as the Secretary of State may by regulations appoint.

(2)   This section and the following provisions come into force on the day on which this Act is passed—

    (a)   sections 1 and 3;

    (b)   section 182;

    (c)   sections 204, 205 and 206;

    (d)   sections 209 and 210;

    (e)   sections 213(2), 214 and 215;

    (f)   any other provision of this Act so far as it confers power to make regulations or Tribunal Procedure Rules or is otherwise necessary for enabling the exercise of such a power on or after the day on which this Act is passed.

(3)   The following provisions come into force at the end of the period of 2 months beginning when this Act is passed—

    (a)   section 124;

    (b)   sections 125, 126 and 127, so far as they relate to a code prepared under section 124;

    (c)   section 177;

    (d)   section 178 and Schedule 17;

    (e)   section 179.

(4)   Regulations under this section may make different provision for different areas.

Transitional provision

213(1) Schedule 20 contains transitional, transitory and saving provision.

(2) The Secretary of State may by regulations make transitional, transitory or saving provision in connection with the coming into force of any provision of this Act or with the GDPR beginning to apply, including provision amending or repealing a provision of Schedule 20.

(3) Regulations under this section that amend or repeal a provision of Schedule 20 are subject to the negative resolution procedure.

—— NOTES ——

Defined terms		"the negative resolution procedure" s 182(6)
"the GDPR"	s 3(10), (14)(a)	

Extent

214(1) This Act extends to England and Wales, Scotland and Northern Ireland, subject to—
    (a) subsections (2) to (5), and
    (b) paragraph 12 of Schedule 12.

(2) Section 199 extends to England and Wales only.

(3) Sections 188, 189 and 190 extend to England and Wales and Northern Ireland only.

(4) An amendment, repeal or revocation made by this Act has the same extent in the United Kingdom as the enactment amended, repealed or revoked.

(5) This subsection and the following provisions also extend to the Isle of Man—
    (a) paragraphs 332 and 434 of Schedule 19;
    (b) sections 211(1), 212(1) and 213(2), so far as relating to those paragraphs.

(6) Where there is a power to extend a part of an Act by Order in Council to any of the Channel Islands, the Isle of Man or any of the British overseas territories, the power may be exercised in relation to an amendment or repeal of that part which is made by or under this Act.

Short title

215 This Act may be cited as the Data Protection Act 2018.

———————————

Data Protection Act 2018
Schedule 1 – Special Categories of Personal Data & Criminal Conviction etc Data
Conditions Relating to Employment, Health and Research

SCHEDULES

SCHEDULE 1   Section 10
SPECIAL CATEGORIES OF PERSONAL DATA AND CRIMINAL CONVICTIONS ETC DATA

PART 1
CONDITIONS RELATING TO EMPLOYMENT, HEALTH AND RESEARCH ETC

Employment, social security and social protection

1(1)   This condition is met if—

    (a)   the processing is necessary for the purposes of performing or exercising obligations or rights which are imposed or conferred by law on the controller or the data subject in connection with employment, social security or social protection, and

    (b)   when the processing is carried out, the controller has an appropriate policy document in place (see paragraph 39 in Part 4 of this Schedule).

  (2)   See also the additional safeguards in Part 4 of this Schedule.

  (3)   In this paragraph—

"social security" includes any of the branches of social security listed in Article 3(1) of Regulation (EC) No 883/2004 of the European Parliament and of the Council on the co-ordination of social security systems (as amended from time to time);

"social protection" includes an intervention described in Article 2(b) of Regulation (EC) 458/2007 of the European Parliament and of the Council of 25 April 2007 on the European system of integrated social protection statistics (ESSPROS) (as amended from time to time).

Health or social care purposes

2(1)   This condition is met if the processing is necessary for health or social care purposes.

  (2)   In this paragraph "health or social care purposes" means the purposes of—

    (a)   preventive or occupational medicine,

    (b)   the assessment of the working capacity of an employee,

    (c)   medical diagnosis,

    (d)   the provision of health care or treatment,

    (e)   the provision of social care, or

    (f)   the management of health care systems or services or social care systems or services.

  (3)   See also the conditions and safeguards in Article 9(3) of the GDPR (obligations of secrecy) and section 11(1).

Public health

3   This condition is met if the processing—

    (a)   is necessary for reasons of public interest in the area of public health, and

    (b)   is carried out—

      (i)   by or under the responsibility of a health professional, or

      (ii)   by another person who in the circumstances owes a duty of confidentiality under an enactment or rule of law.

Research etc

4   This condition is met if the processing—

    (a) is necessary for archiving purposes, scientific or historical research purposes or statistical purposes,

    (b) is carried out in accordance with Article 89(1) of the GDPR (as supplemented by section 19), and

    (c) is in the public interest.

——— **NOTES** ———

Defined terms		"the GDPR"	s 3(10)
"controller"	s 3(6)	"health professional"	s 204(1), (3), (4)
"data subject"	s 3(5)	"processing"	s 3(4)
"enactment"	s 205(1)		

PART 2
SUBSTANTIAL PUBLIC INTEREST CONDITIONS

Requirement for an appropriate policy document when relying on conditions in this Part

5(1)   Except as otherwise provided, a condition in this Part of this Schedule is met only if, when the processing is carried out, the controller has an appropriate policy document in place (see paragraph 39 in Part 4 of this Schedule).

(2)   See also the additional safeguards in Part 4 of this Schedule.

Statutory etc and government purposes

6(1)   This condition is met if the processing—

    (a) is necessary for a purpose listed in sub-paragraph (2), and

    (b) is necessary for reasons of substantial public interest.

(2)   Those purposes are—

    (a) the exercise of a function conferred on a person by an enactment or rule of law;

    (b) the exercise of a function of the Crown, a Minister of the Crown or a government department.

Administration of justice and parliamentary purposes

7   This condition is met if the processing is necessary—

    (a) for the administration of justice, or

    (b) for the exercise of a function of either House of Parliament.

Equality of opportunity or treatment

8(1)   This condition is met if the processing—

    (a) is of a specified category of personal data, and

    (b) is necessary for the purposes of identifying or keeping under review the existence or absence of equality of opportunity or treatment between groups of people specified in relation to that category with a view to enabling such equality to be promoted or maintained, subject to the exceptions in sub-paragraphs (3) to (5).

(2)   In sub-paragraph (1), "specified" means specified in the following table—

Category of personal data	Groups of people (in relation to a category of personal data)
Personal data revealing racial or ethnic origin	People of different racial or ethnic origins
Personal data revealing religious or philosophical beliefs	People holding different religious or philosophical beliefs
Data concerning health	People with different states of physical or mental health
Personal data concerning an individual's sexual orientation	People of different sexual orientation

(3) Processing does not meet the condition in sub-paragraph (1) if it is carried out for the purposes of measures or decisions with respect to a particular data subject.

(4) Processing does not meet the condition in sub-paragraph (1) if it is likely to cause substantial damage or substantial distress to an individual.

(5) Processing does not meet the condition in sub-paragraph (1) if—
    (a) an individual who is the data subject (or one of the data subjects) has given notice in writing to the controller requiring the controller not to process personal data in respect of which the individual is the data subject (and has not given notice in writing withdrawing that requirement),
    (b) the notice gave the controller a reasonable period in which to stop processing such data, and
    (c) that period has ended.

Racial and ethnic diversity at senior levels of organisations
9(1) This condition is met if the processing—
    (a) is of personal data revealing racial or ethnic origin,
    (b) is carried out as part of a process of identifying suitable individuals to hold senior positions in a particular organisation, a type of organisation or organisations generally,
    (c) is necessary for the purposes of promoting or maintaining diversity in the racial and ethnic origins of individuals who hold senior positions in the organisation or organisations, and
    (d) can reasonably be carried out without the consent of the data subject, subject to the exception in sub-paragraph (3).

(2) For the purposes of sub-paragraph (1)(d), processing can reasonably be carried out without the consent of the data subject only where—
    (a) the controller cannot reasonably be expected to obtain the consent of the data subject, and
    (b) the controller is not aware of the data subject withholding consent.

(3) Processing does not meet the condition in sub-paragraph (1) if it is likely to cause substantial damage or substantial distress to an individual.

(4) For the purposes of this paragraph, an individual holds a senior position in an organisation if the individual—

      (a) holds a position listed in sub-paragraph (5), or

      (b) does not hold such a position but is a senior manager of the organisation.

(5) Those positions are—

      (a) a director, secretary or other similar officer of a body corporate;

      (b) a member of a limited liability partnership;

      (c) a partner in a partnership within the Partnership Act 1890, a limited partnership registered under the Limited Partnerships Act 1907 or an entity of a similar character formed under the law of a country or territory outside the United Kingdom.

(6) In this paragraph, "senior manager", in relation to an organisation, means a person who plays a significant role in—

      (a) the making of decisions about how the whole or a substantial part of the organisation's activities are to be managed or organised, or

      (b) the actual managing or organising of the whole or a substantial part of those activities.

(7) The reference in sub-paragraph (2)(b) to a data subject withholding consent does not include a data subject merely failing to respond to a request for consent.

Preventing or detecting unlawful acts

10(1) This condition is met if the processing—

      (a) is necessary for the purposes of the prevention or detection of an unlawful act,

      (b) must be carried out without the consent of the data subject so as not to prejudice those purposes, and

      (c) is necessary for reasons of substantial public interest.

(2) If the processing consists of the disclosure of personal data to a competent authority, or is carried out in preparation for such disclosure, the condition in sub-paragraph (1) is met even if, when the processing is carried out, the controller does not have an appropriate policy document in place (see paragraph 5 of this Schedule).

(3) In this paragraph—

      "act" includes a failure to act;

      "competent authority" has the same meaning as in Part 3 of this Act (see section 30).

Protecting the public against dishonesty etc

11(1) This condition is met if the processing—

      (a) is necessary for the exercise of a protective function,

      (b) must be carried out without the consent of the data subject so as not to prejudice the exercise of that function, and

      (c) is necessary for reasons of substantial public interest.

(2) In this paragraph, "protective function" means a function which is intended to protect members of the public against—

      (a) dishonesty, malpractice or other seriously improper conduct,

      (b) unfitness or incompetence,

      (c) mismanagement in the administration of a body or association, or

      (d) failures in services provided by a body or association.

Regulatory requirements relating to unlawful acts and dishonesty etc

12(1)   This condition is met if—

    (a)   the processing is necessary for the purposes of complying with, or assisting other persons to comply with, a regulatory requirement which involves a person taking steps to establish whether another person has—

        (i)   committed an unlawful act, or

        (ii)   been involved in dishonesty, malpractice or other seriously improper conduct,

    (b)   in the circumstances, the controller cannot reasonably be expected to obtain the consent of the data subject to the processing, and

    (c)   the processing is necessary for reasons of substantial public interest.

  (2)   In this paragraph—

    "act" includes a failure to act; "regulatory requirement" means—

      (a) a requirement imposed by legislation or by a person in exercise of a function conferred by legislation, or

      (b) a requirement forming part of generally accepted principles of good practice relating to a type of body or an activity.

Journalism etc in connection with unlawful acts and dishonesty etc

13(1)   This condition is met if—

    (a)   the processing consists of the disclosure of personal data for the special purposes,

    (b)   it is carried out in connection with a matter described in sub-paragraph (2),

    (c)   it is necessary for reasons of substantial public interest,

    (d)   it is carried out with a view to the publication of the personal data by any person, and

    (e)   the controller reasonably believes that publication of the personal data would be in the public interest.

  (2)   The matters mentioned in sub-paragraph (1)(b) are any of the following (whether alleged or established)—

    (a)   the commission of an unlawful act by a person;

    (b)   dishonesty, malpractice or other seriously improper conduct of a person;

    (c)   unfitness or incompetence of a person;

    (d)   mismanagement in the administration of a body or association;

    (e)   a failure in services provided by a body or association.

  (3)   The condition in sub-paragraph (1) is met even if, when the processing is carried out, the controller does not have an appropriate policy document in place (see paragraph 5 of this Schedule).

  (4)   In this paragraph—

    "act" includes a failure to act;

    "the special purposes" means—

      (a) the purposes of journalism;

      (b) academic purposes;

      (c) artistic purposes;

      (d) literary purposes.

Preventing fraud

14(1)   This condition is met if the processing—

(a) is necessary for the purposes of preventing fraud or a particular kind of fraud, and

(b) consists of—

    (i) the disclosure of personal data by a person as a member of an anti- fraud organisation,

    (ii) the disclosure of personal data in accordance with arrangements made by an anti-fraud organisation, or

    (iii) the processing of personal data disclosed as described in sub- paragraph (i) or (ii).

(2) In this paragraph, "anti-fraud organisation" has the same meaning as in section 68 of the Serious Crime Act 2007.

Suspicion of terrorist financing or money laundering

15 This condition is met if the processing is necessary for the purposes of making a disclosure in good faith under either of the following—

(a) section 21CA of the Terrorism Act 2000 (disclosures between certain entities within regulated sector in relation to suspicion of commission of terrorist financing offence or for purposes of identifying terrorist property);

(b) section 339ZB of the Proceeds of Crime Act 2002 (disclosures within regulated sector in relation to suspicion of money laundering).

Support for individuals with a particular disability or medical condition

16(1) This condition is met if the processing—

(a) is carried out by a not-for-profit body which provides support to individuals with a particular disability or medical condition,

(b) is of a type of personal data falling within sub-paragraph (2) which relates to an individual falling within sub-paragraph (3),

(c) is necessary for the purposes of—

    (i) raising awareness of the disability or medical condition, or

    (ii) providing support to individuals falling within sub-paragraph (3) or enabling such individuals to provide support to each other,

(d) can reasonably be carried out without the consent of the data subject, and

(e) is necessary for reasons of substantial public interest.

(2) The following types of personal data fall within this sub-paragraph—

(a) personal data revealing racial or ethnic origin;

(b) genetic data or biometric data;

(c) data concerning health;

(d) personal data concerning an individual's sex life or sexual orientation.

(3) An individual falls within this sub-paragraph if the individual is or has been a member of the body mentioned in sub-paragraph (1)(a) and—

(a) has the disability or condition mentioned there, has had that disability or condition or has a significant risk of developing that disability or condition, or

(b) is a relative or carer of an individual who satisfies paragraph (a) of this sub-paragraph.

(4) For the purposes of sub-paragraph (1)(d), processing can reasonably be carried out without the consent of the data subject only where—

(a) the controller cannot reasonably be expected to obtain the consent of the data subject, and

    (b) the controller is not aware of the data subject withholding consent.

(5) In this paragraph—

    "carer" means an individual who provides or intends to provide care for another individual other than—

        (a)   under or by virtue of a contract, or

        (b)   as voluntary work;

    "disability" has the same meaning as in the Equality Act 2010 (see section 6 of, and Schedule 1 to, that Act).

(6) The reference in sub-paragraph (4)(b) to a data subject withholding consent does not include a data subject merely failing to respond to a request for consent.

Counselling etc

17(1) This condition is met if the processing—

    (a) is necessary for the provision of confidential counselling, advice or support or of another similar service provided confidentially,

    (b) is carried out without the consent of the data subject for one of the reasons listed in sub-paragraph (2), and

    (c) is necessary for reasons of substantial public interest.

(2) The reasons mentioned in sub-paragraph (1)(b) are—

    (a) in the circumstances, consent to the processing cannot be given by the data subject;

    (b) in the circumstances, the controller cannot reasonably be expected to obtain the consent of the data subject to the processing;

    (c) the processing must be carried out without the consent of the data subject because obtaining the consent of the data subject would prejudice the provision of the service mentioned in sub-paragraph (1)(a).

Safeguarding of children and of individuals at risk

18(1) This condition is met if—

    (a) the processing is necessary for the purposes of—

        (i) protecting an individual from neglect or physical, mental or emotional harm, or

        (ii) protecting the physical, mental or emotional well-being of an individual,

    (b) the individual is—

        (i) aged under 18, or

        (ii) aged 18 or over and at risk,

    (c) the processing is carried out without the consent of the data subject for one of the reasons listed in sub-paragraph (2), and

    (d) the processing is necessary for reasons of substantial public interest.

(2) The reasons mentioned in sub-paragraph (1)(c) are—

    (a) in the circumstances, consent to the processing cannot be given by the data subject;

    (b) in the circumstances, the controller cannot reasonably be expected to obtain the consent of the data subject to the processing;

    (c) the processing must be carried out without the consent of the data subject because obtaining the consent of the data subject would prejudice the provision of the protection mentioned in sub-paragraph (1)(a).

(3) For the purposes of this paragraph, an individual aged 18 or over is "at risk" if the controller has reasonable cause to suspect that the individual—

    (a) has needs for care and support,

    (b) is experiencing, or at risk of, neglect or physical, mental or emotional harm, and

    (c) as a result of those needs is unable to protect himself or herself against the neglect or harm or the risk of it.

(4) In sub-paragraph (1)(a), the reference to the protection of an individual or of the well-being of an individual includes both protection relating to a particular individual and protection relating to a type of individual.

Safeguarding of economic well-being of certain individuals

19(1) This condition is met if the processing—

    (a) is necessary for the purposes of protecting the economic well-being of an individual at economic risk who is aged 18 or over,

    (b) is of data concerning health,

    (c) is carried out without the consent of the data subject for one of the reasons listed in sub-paragraph (2), and

    (d) is necessary for reasons of substantial public interest.

(2) The reasons mentioned in sub-paragraph (1)(c) are—

    (a) in the circumstances, consent to the processing cannot be given by the data subject;

    (b) in the circumstances, the controller cannot reasonably be expected to obtain the consent of the data subject to the processing;

    (c) the processing must be carried out without the consent of the data subject because obtaining the consent of the data subject would prejudice the provision of the protection mentioned in sub-paragraph (1)(a).

(3) In this paragraph, "individual at economic risk" means an individual who is less able to protect his or her economic well-being by reason of physical or mental injury, illness or disability.

Insurance

20(1) This condition is met if the processing—

    (a) is necessary for an insurance purpose,

    (b) is of personal data revealing racial or ethnic origin, religious or philosophical beliefs or trade union membership, genetic data or data concerning health, and

    (c) is necessary for reasons of substantial public interest, subject to sub-paragraphs (2) and (3).

(2) Sub-paragraph (3) applies where—

    (a) the processing is not carried out for the purposes of measures or decisions with respect to the data subject, and

    (b) the data subject does not have and is not expected to acquire—

        (i) rights against, or obligations in relation to, a person who is an insured person under an insurance contract to which the insurance purpose mentioned in sub-paragraph (1)(a) relates, or

        (ii) other rights or obligations in connection with such a contract.

(3) Where this sub-paragraph applies, the processing does not meet the condition in sub-paragraph (1) unless, in addition to meeting the requirements in that sub-paragraph, it can reasonably be carried out without the consent of the data subject.

(4) For the purposes of sub-paragraph (3), processing can reasonably be carried out without the consent of the data subject only where—

   (a) the controller cannot reasonably be expected to obtain the consent of the data subject, and

   (b) the controller is not aware of the data subject withholding consent.

(5) In this paragraph—

   "insurance contract" means a contract of general insurance or long-term insurance;

   "insurance purpose" means—

     (a) advising on, arranging, underwriting or administering an insurance contract,

     (b) administering a claim under an insurance contract, or

     (c) exercising a right, or complying with an obligation, arising in connection with an insurance contract, including a right or obligation arising under an enactment or rule of law.

(6) The reference in sub-paragraph (4)(b) to a data subject withholding consent does not include a data subject merely failing to respond to a request for consent.

(7) Terms used in the definition of "insurance contract" in sub-paragraph (5) and also in an order made under section 22 of the Financial Services and Markets Act 2000 (regulated activities) have the same meaning in that definition as they have in that order.

Occupational pensions

21(1) This condition is met if the processing—

   (a) is necessary for the purpose of making a determination in connection with eligibility for, or benefits payable under, an occupational pension scheme,

   (b) is of data concerning health which relates to a data subject who is the parent, grandparent, great-grandparent or sibling of a member of the scheme,

   (c) is not carried out for the purposes of measures or decisions with respect to the data subject, and

   (d) can reasonably be carried out without the consent of the data subject.

(2) For the purposes of sub-paragraph (1)(d), processing can reasonably be carried out without the consent of the data subject only where—

   (a) the controller cannot reasonably be expected to obtain the consent of the data subject, and

   (b) the controller is not aware of the data subject withholding consent.

(3) In this paragraph—

   "occupational pension scheme" has the meaning given in section 1 of the Pension Schemes Act 1993;

   "member", in relation to a scheme, includes an individual who is seeking to become a member of the scheme.

(4) The reference in sub-paragraph (2)(b) to a data subject withholding consent does not include a data subject merely failing to respond to a request for consent.

Political parties

22(1)   This condition is met if the processing—

    (a)   is of personal data revealing political opinions,

    (b)   is carried out by a person or organisation included in the register maintained under section 23 of the Political Parties, Elections and Referendums Act 2000, and

    (c)   is necessary for the purposes of the person's or organisation's political activities, subject to the exceptions in sub-paragraphs (2) and (3).

  (2)   Processing does not meet the condition in sub-paragraph (1) if it is likely to cause substantial damage or substantial distress to a person.

  (3)   Processing does not meet the condition in sub-paragraph (1) if—

    (a)   an individual who is the data subject (or one of the data subjects) has given notice in writing to the controller requiring the controller not to process personal data in respect of which the individual is the data subject (and has not given notice in writing withdrawing that requirement),

    (b)   the notice gave the controller a reasonable period in which to stop processing such data, and

    (c)   that period has ended.

  (4)   In this paragraph, "political activities" include campaigning, fund-raising, political surveys and case-work.

Elected representatives responding to requests

23(1)   This condition is met if—

    (a)   the processing is carried out—

      (i)   by an elected representative or a person acting with the authority of such a representative,

      (ii)   in connection with the discharge of the elected representative's functions, and

      (iii)   in response to a request by an individual that the elected representative take action on behalf of the individual, and

    (b)   the processing is necessary for the purposes of, or in connection with, the action reasonably taken by the elected representative in response to that request, subject to sub-paragraph (2).

  (2)   Where the request is made by an individual other than the data subject, the condition in sub-paragraph (1) is met only if the processing must be carried out without the consent of the data subject for one of the following reasons—

    (a)   in the circumstances, consent to the processing cannot be given by the data subject;

    (b)   in the circumstances, the elected representative cannot reasonably be expected to obtain the consent of the data subject to the processing;

    (c)   obtaining the consent of the data subject would prejudice the action taken by the elected representative;

    (d)   the processing is necessary in the interests of another individual and the data subject has withheld consent unreasonably.

  (3)   In this paragraph, "elected representative" means—

    (a)   a member of the House of Commons;

    (b)   a member of the National Assembly for Wales;

    (c)   a member of the Scottish Parliament;

    (d)   a member of the Northern Ireland Assembly;

    (e)   a member of the European Parliament elected in the United Kingdom;

    (f)   an elected member of a local authority within the meaning of section 270(1) of the Local Government Act 1972, namely—

        (i)   in England, a county council, a district council, a London borough council or a parish council;

        (ii) in Wales, a county council, a county borough council or a community council;

    (g) an elected mayor of a local authority within the meaning of Part 1A or 2 of the Local Government Act 2000;

    (h) a mayor for the area of a combined authority established under section 103 of the Local Democracy, Economic Development and Construction Act 2009;

    (i)   the Mayor of London or an elected member of the London Assembly;

    (j)   an elected member of—

        (i)   the Common Council of the City of London, or

        (ii) the Council of the Isles of Scilly;

    (k) an elected member of a council constituted under section 2 of the Local Government etc (Scotland) Act 1994;

    (l)   an elected member of a district council within the meaning of the Local Government Act (Northern Ireland) 1972 (c. 9 (NI));

    (m) a police and crime commissioner.

(4)   For the purposes of sub-paragraph (3), a person who is—

    (a) a member of the House of Commons immediately before Parliament is dissolved,

    (b) a member of the National Assembly for Wales immediately before that Assembly is dissolved,

    (c) a member of the Scottish Parliament immediately before that Parliament is dissolved, or

    (d) a member of the Northern Ireland Assembly immediately before that Assembly is dissolved,

is to be treated as if the person were such a member until the end of the fourth day after the day on which the subsequent general election in relation to that Parliament or Assembly is held.

(5)   For the purposes of sub-paragraph (3), a person who is an elected member of the Common Council of the City of London and whose term of office comes to an end at the end of the day preceding the annual Wardmotes is to be treated as if he or she were such a member until the end of the fourth day after the day on which those Wardmotes are held.

Disclosure to elected representatives

24(1) This condition is met if—

    (a) the processing consists of the disclosure of personal data—

        (i)   to an elected representative or a person acting with the authority of such a representative, and

        (ii) in response to a communication to the controller from that representative or person which was made in response to a request from an individual,

    (b) the personal data is relevant to the subject matter of that communication, and

    (c) the disclosure is necessary for the purpose of responding to that communication, subject to sub-paragraph (2).

(2)   Where the request to the elected representative came from an individual other than the data subject, the condition in sub-paragraph (1) is met only if the disclosure must be made without the consent of the data subject for one of the following reasons—

    (a)   in the circumstances, consent to the processing cannot be given by the data subject;

    (b)   in the circumstances, the elected representative cannot reasonably be expected to obtain the consent of the data subject to the processing;

    (c)   obtaining the consent of the data subject would prejudice the action taken by the elected representative;

    (d)   the processing is necessary in the interests of another individual and the data subject has withheld consent unreasonably.

(3)   In this paragraph, "elected representative" has the same meaning as in paragraph 23.

Informing elected representatives about prisoners

25(1)   This condition is met if—

    (a)   the processing consists of the processing of personal data about a prisoner for the purpose of informing a member of the House of Commons, a member of the National Assembly for Wales or a member of the Scottish Parliament about the prisoner, and

    (b)   the member is under an obligation not to further disclose the personal data.

(2)   The references in sub-paragraph (1) to personal data about, and to informing someone about, a prisoner include personal data about, and informing someone about, arrangements for the prisoner's release.

(3)   In this paragraph—

    "prison" includes a young offender institution, a remand centre, a secure training centre or a secure college;

    "prisoner" means a person detained in a prison.

Publication of legal judgments

26   This condition is met if the processing—

    (a)   consists of the publication of a judgment or other decision of a court or tribunal, or

    (b)   is necessary for the purposes of publishing such a judgment or decision.

Anti-doping in sport

27(1)   This condition is met if the processing is necessary—

    (a)   for the purposes of measures designed to eliminate doping which are undertaken by or under the responsibility of a body or association that is responsible for eliminating doping in a sport, at a sporting event or in sport generally, or

    (b)   for the purposes of providing information about doping, or suspected doping, to such a body or association.

(2)   The reference in sub-paragraph (1)(a) to measures designed to eliminate doping includes measures designed to identify or prevent doping.

(3)   If the processing consists of the disclosure of personal data to a body or association described in sub-paragraph (1)(a), or is carried out in preparation for such disclosure, the

Data Protection Act 2018
Schedule 1 – Special Categories of Personal Data & Criminal Conviction etc Data
Part 3 – Additional Conditions relating to Criminal Convictions etc

condition in sub-paragraph (1) is met even if, when the processing is carried out, the controller does not have an appropriate policy document in place (see paragraph 5 of this Schedule).

Standards of behaviour in sport

28(1) This condition is met if the processing—

    (a) is necessary for the purposes of measures designed to protect the integrity of a sport or a sporting event,

    (b) must be carried out without the consent of the data subject so as not to prejudice those purposes, and

    (c) is necessary for reasons of substantial public interest.

  (2) In sub-paragraph (1)(a), the reference to measures designed to protect the integrity of a sport or a sporting event is a reference to measures designed to protect a sport or a sporting event against—

    (a) dishonesty, malpractice or other seriously improper conduct, or

    (b) failure by a person participating in the sport or event in any capacity to comply with standards of behaviour set by a body or association with responsibility for the sport or event.

—— NOTES ——

Defined terms

"biometric data"	s 205(1)	"government department"	s 205(1)
"controller"	s 3(6)	"Minister of the Crown"	s 205(1)
"court"	s 20	"personal data"	s 3(2)
"data concerning health"	s 205(1)	"processing"	s 3(4)
"data subject"	s 3(5)	"processing of personal data"	s 5(7)
"enactment"	s 205(1)	"publish"	s 205(1)
"genetic data"	s 205(1)	"tribunal"	s 205(1)

PART 3
ADDITIONAL CONDITIONS RELATING TO CRIMINAL CONVICTIONS ETC

Consent

29 This condition is met if the data subject has given consent to the processing.

Protecting individual's vital interests

30 This condition is met if—

    (a) the processing is necessary to protect the vital interests of an individual, and

    (b) the data subject is physically or legally incapable of giving consent.

Processing by not-for-profit bodies

31 This condition is met if the processing is carried out—

    (a) in the course of its legitimate activities with appropriate safeguards by a foundation, association or other not-for-profit body with a political, philosophical, religious or trade union aim, and

    (b) on condition that—

      (i) the processing relates solely to the members or to former members of the body or to persons who have regular contact with it in connection with its purposes, and

      (ii) the personal data is not disclosed outside that body without the consent of the data subjects.

Personal data in the public domain

32 This condition is met if the processing relates to personal data which is manifestly made public by the data subject.

Legal claims

33 This condition is met if the processing—

(a) is necessary for the purpose of, or in connection with, any legal proceedings (including prospective legal proceedings),

(b) is necessary for the purpose of obtaining legal advice, or

(c) is otherwise necessary for the purposes of establishing, exercising or defending legal rights.

Judicial acts

34 This condition is met if the processing is necessary when a court or tribunal is acting in its judicial capacity.

Administration of accounts used in commission of indecency offences involving children

35(1) This condition is met if—

(a) the processing is of personal data about a conviction or caution for an offence listed in sub-paragraph (2),

(b) the processing is necessary for the purpose of administering an account relating to the payment card used in the commission of the offence or cancelling that payment card, and

(c) when the processing is carried out, the controller has an appropriate policy document in place (see paragraph 39 in Part 4 of this Schedule).

(2) Those offences are an offence under—

(a) section 1 of the Protection of Children Act 1978 (indecent photographs of children),

(b) Article 3 of the Protection of Children (Northern Ireland) Order 1978 (SI 1978/1047 (NI 17)) (indecent photographs of children),

(c) section 52 of the Civic Government (Scotland) Act 1982 (indecent photographs etc of children),

(d) section 160 of the Criminal Justice Act 1988 (possession of indecent photograph of child),

(e) Article 15 of the Criminal Justice (Evidence etc) (Northern Ireland) Order 1988 (SI 1988/1847 (NI 17)) (possession of indecent photograph of child), or

(f) section 62 of the Coroners and Justice Act 2009 (possession of prohibited images of children),

or incitement to commit an offence under any of those provisions.

(3) See also the additional safeguards in Part 4 of this Schedule.

(4) In this paragraph—

"caution" means a caution given to a person in England and Wales or Northern Ireland in respect of an offence which, at the time when the caution is given, is admitted;

"conviction" has the same meaning as in the Rehabilitation of Offenders Act 1974 or the Rehabilitation of Offenders (Northern Ireland) Order 1978 (SI 1978/1908 (NI

27));

"payment card" includes a credit card, a charge card and a debit card.

Extension of conditions in Part 2 of this Schedule referring to substantial public interest

36 This condition is met if the processing would meet a condition in Part 2 of this Schedule but for an express requirement for the processing to be necessary for reasons of substantial public interest.

Extension of insurance conditions

37 This condition is met if the processing—

 (a) would meet the condition in paragraph 20 in Part 2 of this Schedule (the "insurance condition"), or

 (b) would meet the condition in paragraph 36 by virtue of the insurance condition,

but for the requirement for the processing to be processing of a category of personal data specified in paragraph 20(1)(b).

—— NOTES ——

Defined terms		"personal data"	s 3(2)
"controller"	s 3(6)	"processing"	s 3(4)
"court"	s 20	"processing of personal data"	s 5(7)
"data subject"	s 3(5)	"tribunal"	s 205(1)

PART 4
APPROPRIATE POLICY DOCUMENT AND ADDITIONAL SAFEGUARDS

Application of this Part of this Schedule

38 This Part of this Schedule makes provision about the processing of personal data carried out in reliance on a condition in Part 1, 2 or 3 of this Schedule which requires the controller to have an appropriate policy document in place when the processing is carried out.

Requirement to have an appropriate policy document in place

39 The controller has an appropriate policy document in place in relation to the processing of personal data in reliance on a condition described in paragraph 38 if the controller has produced a document which—

 (a) explains the controller's procedures for securing compliance with the principles in Article 5 of the GDPR (principles relating to processing of personal data) in connection with the processing of personal data in reliance on the condition in question, and

 (b) explains the controller's policies as regards the retention and erasure of personal data processed in reliance on the condition, giving an indication of how long such personal data is likely to be retained.

Additional safeguard: retention of appropriate policy document

40(1) Where personal data is processed in reliance on a condition described in paragraph 38, the controller must during the relevant period—

 (a) retain the appropriate policy document,

 (b) review and (if appropriate) update it from time to time, and

 (c) make it available to the Commissioner, on request, without charge.

(2) "Relevant period", in relation to the processing of personal data in reliance on a condition described in paragraph 38, means a period which—

    (a) begins when the controller starts to carry out processing of personal data in reliance on that condition, and

    (b) ends at the end of the period of 6 months beginning when the controller ceases to carry out such processing.

Additional safeguard: record of processing

41   A record maintained by the controller, or the controller's representative, under Article 30 of the GDPR in respect of the processing of personal data in reliance on a condition described in paragraph 38 must include the following information—

    (a) which condition is relied on,

    (b) how the processing satisfies Article 6 of the GDPR (lawfulness of processing), and

    (c) whether the personal data is retained and erased in accordance with the policies described in paragraph 39(b) and, if it is not, the reasons for not following those policies.

—— NOTES ——

Defined terms			
"the Commissioner"	s 3(8)	"personal data"	s 3(2)
"controller"	s 3(6)	"processing"	s 3(4)
"the GDPR"	s 3(10)	"processing of personal data"	s 5(7)

SCHEDULE 2
Section 15

EXEMPTIONS ETC FROM THE GDPR

PART 1
ADAPTATIONS AND RESTRICTIONS BASED ON ARTICLES 6(3) AND 23(1)

GDPR provisions to be adapted or restricted: "the listed GDPR provisions"

1   In this Part of this Schedule, "the listed GDPR provisions" means—

    (a) the following provisions of the GDPR (the rights and obligations in which may be restricted by virtue of Article 23(1) of the GDPR)—

       (i) Article 13(1) to (3) (personal data collected from data subject: information to be provided);

      (ii) Article 14(1) to (4) (personal data collected other than from data subject: information to be provided);

     (iii) Article 15(1) to (3) (confirmation of processing, access to data and safeguards for third country transfers);

     (iv) Article 16 (right to rectification);

      (v) Article 17(1) and (2) (right to erasure);

     (vi) Article 18(1) (restriction of processing);

    (vii) Article 19 (notification obligation regarding rectification or erasure of personal data or restriction of processing);

   (viii) Article 20(1) and (2) (right to data portability);

     (ix) Article 21(1) (objections to processing);

      (x) Article 5 (general principles) so far as its provisions correspond to the rights and obligations provided for in the provisions mentioned in sub-paragraphs

Data Protection Act 2018
Schedule 2 – Exemptions etc from the GDPR
Part 1 – Adaptations & Restrictions based on Articles 6(2) and 21

         (i) to (ix); and

    (b) the following provisions of the GDPR (the application of which may be adapted by virtue of Article 6(3) of the GDPR)—

        (i) Article 5(1)(a) (lawful, fair and transparent processing), other than the lawfulness requirements set out in Article 6;

        (ii) Article 5(1)(b) (purpose limitation).

Crime and taxation: general

2(1) The listed GDPR provisions and Article 34(1) and (4) of the GDPR (communication of personal data breach to the data subject) do not apply to personal data processed for any of the following purposes—

    (a) the prevention or detection of crime,

    (b) the apprehension or prosecution of offenders, or

    (c) the assessment or collection of a tax or duty or an imposition of a similar nature,

to the extent that the application of those provisions would be likely to prejudice any of the matters mentioned in paragraphs (a) to (c).

(2) Sub-paragraph (3) applies where—

    (a) personal data is processed by a person ("Controller 1") for any of the purposes mentioned in sub-paragraph (1)(a) to (c), and

    (b) another person ("Controller 2") obtains the data from Controller 1 for the purpose of discharging statutory functions and processes it for the purpose of discharging statutory functions.

(3) Controller 2 is exempt from the obligations in the following provisions of the GDPR—

    (a) Article 13(1) to (3) (personal data collected from data subject: information to be provided),

    (b) Article 14(1) to (4) (personal data collected other than from data subject: information to be provided),

    (c) Article 15(1) to (3) (confirmation of processing, access to data and safeguards for third country transfers), and

    (d) Article 5 (general principles) so far as its provisions correspond to the rights and obligations provided for in the provisions mentioned in paragraphs (a) to (c),

to the same extent that Controller 1 is exempt from those obligations by virtue of sub-paragraph (1).

Crime and taxation: risk assessment systems

3(1) The GDPR provisions listed in sub-paragraph (3) do not apply to personal data which consists of a classification applied to the data subject as part of a risk assessment system falling within sub-paragraph (2) to the extent that the application of those provisions would prevent the system from operating effectively.

(2) A risk assessment system falls within this sub-paragraph if—

    (a) it is operated by a government department, a local authority or another authority administering housing benefit, and

    (b) it is operated for the purposes of—

        (i) the assessment or collection of a tax or duty or an imposition of a similar nature, or

        (ii) the prevention or detection of crime or apprehension or prosecution of offenders, where the offence concerned involves the unlawful use of public money or an unlawful claim for payment out of public money.

(3) The GDPR provisions referred to in sub-paragraph (1) are the following provisions of the GDPR (the rights and obligations in which may be restricted by virtue of Article 23(1) of the GDPR)—

(a) Article 13(1) to (3) (personal data collected from data subject: information to be provided);

(b) Article 14(1) to (4) (personal data collected other than from data subject: information to be provided);

(c) Article 15(1) to (3) (confirmation of processing, access to data and safeguards for third country transfers);

(d) Article 5 (general principles) so far as its provisions correspond to the rights and obligations provided for in the provisions mentioned in paragraphs (a) to (c).

Immigration

4(1) The GDPR provisions listed in sub-paragraph (2) do not apply to personal data processed for any of the following purposes—

(a) the maintenance of effective immigration control, or

(b) the investigation or detection of activities that would undermine the maintenance of effective immigration control,

to the extent that the application of those provisions would be likely to prejudice any of the matters mentioned in paragraphs (a) and (b).

(2) The GDPR provisions referred to in sub-paragraph (1) are the following provisions of the GDPR (the rights and obligations in which may be restricted by virtue of Article 23(1) of the GDPR)—

(a) Article 13(1) to (3) (personal data collected from data subject: information to be provided);

(b) Article 14(1) to (4) (personal data collected other than from data subject: information to be provided);

(c) Article 15(1) to (3) (confirmation of processing, access to data and safeguards for third country transfers);

(d) Article 17(1) and (2) (right to erasure);

(e) Article 18(1) (restriction of processing);

(f) Article 21(1) (objections to processing);

(g) Article 5 (general principles) so far as its provisions correspond to the rights and obligations provided for in the provisions mentioned in sub-paragraphs (a) to (f).

(That is, the listed GDPR provisions other than Article 16 (right to rectification), Article 19 (notification obligation regarding rectification or erasure of personal data or restriction of processing) and Article 20(1) and (2) (right to data portability) and, subject to sub-paragraph (2)(g) of this paragraph, the provisions of Article 5 listed in paragraph 1(b).)

(3) Sub-paragraph (4) applies where—

(a) personal data is processed by a person ("Controller 1"), and

(b) another person ("Controller 2") obtains the data from Controller 1 for any of the purposes mentioned in sub-paragraph (1)(a) and (b) and processes it for any of those purposes.

(4) Controller 1 is exempt from the obligations in the following provisions of the GDPR—

(a) Article 13(1) to (3) (personal data collected from data subject: information to be

Data Protection Act 2018
Schedule 2 – Exemptions etc from the GDPR
Part 2 – Restrictions based on Article23(1): restriction of rules in Articles 13-21 and 34

provided),

(b) Article 14(1) to (4) (personal data collected other than from data subject: information to be provided),

(c) Article 15(1) to (3) (confirmation of processing, access to data and safeguards for third country transfers), and

(d) Article 5 (general principles) so far as its provisions correspond to the rights and obligations provided for in the provisions mentioned in paragraphs (a) to (c),

to the same extent that Controller 2 is exempt from those obligations by virtue of sub-paragraph (1).

Information required to be disclosed by law etc or in connection with legal proceedings

5(1) The listed GDPR provisions do not apply to personal data consisting of information that the controller is obliged by an enactment to make available to the public, to the extent that the application of those provisions would prevent the controller from complying with that obligation.

(2) The listed GDPR provisions do not apply to personal data where disclosure of the data is required by an enactment, a rule of law or an order of a court or tribunal, to the extent that the application of those provisions would prevent the controller from making the disclosure.

(3) The listed GDPR provisions do not apply to personal data where disclosure of the data—

(a) is necessary for the purpose of, or in connection with, legal proceedings (including prospective legal proceedings),

(b) is necessary for the purpose of obtaining legal advice, or

(c) is otherwise necessary for the purposes of establishing, exercising or defending legal rights,

to the extent that the application of those provisions would prevent the controller from making the disclosure.

—— NOTES ——

Defined terms		"government department"	s 205(1)
"controller"	s 3(6)	"personal data"	s 3(2)
"court"	s 20	"processing"	s 3(4)
"data subject"	s 3(5)	"processing of personal data"	s 5(7)
"enactment"	s 205(1)	"tribunal"	s 205(1)
"the GDPR"	s 3(10)		

PART 2
RESTRICTIONS BASED ON ARTICLE 23(1):
RESTRICTIONS OF RULES IN ARTICLES 13 TO 21 AND 34

GDPR provisions to be restricted: "the listed GDPR provisions"

6 In this Part of this Schedule, "the listed GDPR provisions" means the following provisions of the GDPR (the rights and obligations in which may be restricted by virtue of Article 23(1) of the GDPR)—

(a) Article 13(1) to (3) (personal data collected from data subject: information to be provided);

(b) Article 14(1) to (4) (personal data collected other than from data subject: information to be provided);

    (c) Article 15(1) to (3) (confirmation of processing, access to data and safeguards for third country transfers);

    (d) Article 16 (right to rectification);

    (e) Article 17(1) and (2) (right to erasure);

    (f) Article 18(1) (restriction of processing);

    (g) Article 19 (notification obligation regarding rectification or erasure of personal data or restriction of processing);

    (h) Article 20(1) and (2) (right to data portability);

    (i) Article 21(1) (objections to processing);

    (j) Article 5 (general principles) so far as its provisions correspond to the rights and obligations provided for in the provisions mentioned in sub-paragraphs (a) to (i).

Functions designed to protect the public etc

7   The listed GDPR provisions do not apply to personal data processed for the purposes of discharging a function that—

    (a) is designed as described in column 1 of the Table, and

    (b) meets the condition relating to the function specified in column 2 of the Table,

to the extent that the application of those provisions would be likely to prejudice the proper discharge of the function.

TABLE

Description of function design	Condition
1. The function is designed to protect members of the public against— (a) financial loss due to dishonesty, malpractice or other seriously improper conduct by, or the unfitness or incompetence of, persons concerned in the provision of banking, insurance, investment or other financial services or in the management of bodies corporate, or (b) financial loss due to the conduct of discharged or undischarged bankrupts.	The function is— (a) conferred on a person by an enactment, (b) a function of the Crown, a Minister of the Crown or a government department, or (c) of a public nature, and is exercised in the public interest.
2. The function is designed to protect members of the public against— (a) dishonesty, malpractice or other seriously improper conduct, or (b) unfitness or incompetence.	The function is— (a) conferred on a person by an enactment, (b) a function of the Crown, a Minister of the Crown or a government department, or (c) of a public nature, and is exercised in the public interest.
3. The function is designed— (a) to protect charities or community interest companies against misconduct or mismanagement	The function is— (a) conferred on a person by an enactment, (b) a function of the Crown, a

Data Protection Act 2018
Schedule 2 – Exemptions etc from the GDPR
Part 2 – Restrictions based on Article23(1): restriction of rules in Articles 13-21 and 34

(whether by trustees, directors or other persons) in their administration, (b) to protect the property of charities or community interest companies from loss or misapplication, or (c) to recover the property of charities or community interest companies.	Minister of the Crown or a government department, or (c) of a public nature, and is exercised in the public interest.
4. The function is designed— (a) to secure the health, safety and welfare of persons at work, or (b) to protect persons other than those at work against risk to health or safety arising out of or in connection with the action of persons at work.	The function is— (a) conferred on a person by an enactment, (b) a function of the Crown, a Minister of the Crown or a government department, or (c) of a public nature, and is exercised in the public interest.
5. The function is designed to protect members of the public against— (a) maladministration by public bodies, (b) failures in services provided by public bodies, or (c) a failure of a public body to provide a service which it is a function of the body to provide.	The function is conferred by any enactment on— (a) the Parliamentary Commissioner for Administration, (b) the Commissioner for Local Administration in England, (c) the Health Service Commissioner for England, (d) the Public Services Ombudsman for Wales, (e) the Northern Ireland Public Services Ombudsman, (f) the Prison Ombudsman for Northern Ireland, or (g) the Scottish Public Services Ombudsman.
6. The function is designed— (a) to protect members of the public against conduct which may adversely affect their interests by persons carrying on a business, (b) to regulate agreements or conduct which have as their object or effect the prevention, restriction or distortion of competition in	The function is conferred on the Competition and Markets Authority by an enactment.

connection with any commercial
activity, or

(c) to regulate conduct on the part of
one or more undertakings which
amounts to the abuse of a dominant
position in a market.

Audit functions

8(1) The listed GDPR provisions do not apply to personal data processed for the purposes of
discharging a function listed in sub-paragraph (2) to the extent that the application of
those provisions would be likely to prejudice the proper discharge of the function.

(2) The functions are any function that is conferred by an enactment on—

(a) the Comptroller and Auditor General;

(b) the Auditor General for Scotland;

(c) the Auditor General for Wales;

(d) the Comptroller and Auditor General for Northern Ireland.

Functions of the Bank of England

9(1) The listed GDPR provisions do not apply to personal data processed for the purposes of
discharging a relevant function of the Bank of England to the extent that the application
of those provisions would be likely to prejudice the proper discharge of the function.

(2) "Relevant function of the Bank of England" means—

(a) a function discharged by the Bank acting in its capacity as a monetary authority
(as defined in section 244(2)(c) and (2A) of the Banking Act 2009);

(b) a public function of the Bank within the meaning of section 349 of the Financial
Services and Markets Act 2000;

(c) a function conferred on the Prudential Regulation Authority by or under the
Financial Services and Markets Act 2000 or by another enactment.

Regulatory functions relating to legal services, the health service and children's services

10(1) The listed GDPR provisions do not apply to personal data processed for the purposes of
discharging a function listed in sub-paragraph (2) to the extent that the application of
those provisions would be likely to prejudice the proper discharge of the function.

(2) The functions are—

(a) a function of the Legal Services Board;

(b) the function of considering a complaint under the scheme established under Part
6 of the Legal Services Act 2007 (legal complaints);

(c) the function of considering a complaint under—

(i) section 14 of the NHS Redress Act 2006,

(ii) section 113(1) or (2) or section 114(1) or (3) of the Health and Social Care
(Community Health and Standards) Act 2003,

(iii) section 24D or 26 of the Children Act 1989, or

(iv) Part 2A of the Public Services Ombudsman (Wales) Act 2005 [F4or Part 5 of
the Public Services Ombudsman (Wales) Act 2019];

(d) the function of considering a complaint or representations under Chapter 1 of Part

Data Protection Act 2018
Schedule 2 – Exemptions etc from the GDPR
Part 2 – Restrictions based on Article23(1): restriction of rules in Articles 13-21 and 34

10 of the Social Services and Well-being (Wales) Act 2014 (anaw 4).

Regulatory functions of certain other persons

11   The listed GDPR provisions do not apply to personal data processed for the purposes of discharging a function that—

(a)   is a function of a person described in column 1 of the Table, and

(b)   is conferred on that person as described in column 2 of the Table,

to the extent that the application of those provisions would be likely to prejudice the proper discharge of the function.

TABLE

Person on whom function is conferred	*How function is conferred*
1. The Commissioner	By or under— (a) the data protection legislation; (b) the Freedom of Information Act 2000; (c) section 244 of the Investigatory Powers Act 2016; (d) the Privacy and Electronic Communications (EC Directive) Regulations 2003 (SI 2003/2426); (e) the Environmental Information Regulations 2004 (SI 2004/3391); (f) the INSPIRE Regulations 2009 (SI 2009/3157); (g) Regulation (EU) No 910/2014 of the European Parliament and of the Council of 23 July 2014 on electronic identification and trust services for electronic transactions in the internal market and repealing Directive 1999/93/EC; (h) the Re-use of Public Sector Information Regulations 2015 (S I 2015/1415); (i) the Electronic Identification and Trust Services for Electronic Transactions Regulations 2016 (S I 2016/696).
2. The Scottish Information Commissioner	By or under— (a) the Freedom of Information (Scotland) Act 2002 (asp 13); (b) the Environmental Information (Scotland) Regulations 2004 (SSI 2004/520); (c) the INSPIRE (Scotland) Regulations 2009 (SSI 2009/440).

3. The Pension Ombudsman	By or under Part 10 of the Pension Schemes Act 1993 or any corresponding legislation having equivalent effect in Northern Ireland.
4. The Board of the Pension Protection Fund	By or under sections 206 to 208 of the Pensions Act 2004 or any corresponding legislation having equivalent effect in Northern Ireland.
5. The Ombudsman for the Board of the Pension Protection Fund	By or under any of sections 209 to 218 or 286(1) of the Pensions Act 2004 or any corresponding legislation having equivalent effect in Northern Ireland.
6. The Pensions Regulator	By an enactment.
7. The Financial Conduct Authority	By or under the Financial Services and Markets Act 2000 or by another enactment.
8. The Financial Ombudsman	By or under Part 16 of the Financial Services and Markets Act 2000.
9. The investigator of complaints against the financial regulators	By or under Part 6 of the Financial Services Act 2012.
10. A consumer protection enforcer, other than the Competition and Markets Authority	By or under the CPC Regulation.
11. The monitoring officer of a relevant authority	By or under the Local Government and Housing Act 1989.
12. The monitoring officer of a relevant Welsh authority	By or under the Local Government Act 2000.
13. The Public Services Ombudsman for Wales	By or under the Local Government Act 2000.
14. The Charity Commission	By or under— (a) the Charities Act 1992; (b) the Charities Act 2006; (c) the Charities Act 2011.

12 In the Table in paragraph 11—
     "consumer protection enforcer" has the same meaning as "CPC enforcer" in section

Data Protection Act 2018
Schedule 2 – Exemptions etc from the GDPR
Part 2 – Restrictions based on Article23(1): restriction of rules in Articles 13-21 and 34

213(5A) of the Enterprise Act 2002;

the "CPC Regulation" has the meaning given in section 235A of the Enterprise Act 2002;

the "Financial Ombudsman" means the scheme operator within the meaning of Part 16 of the Financial Services and Markets Act 2000 (see section 225 of that Act);

the "investigator of complaints against the financial regulators" means the person appointed under section 84(1)(b) of the Financial Services Act 2012; "relevant authority" has the same meaning as in section 5 of the Local Government and Housing Act 1989, and "monitoring officer", in relation to such an authority, means a person designated as such under that section;

"relevant Welsh authority" has the same meaning as "relevant authority" in section 49(6) of the Local Government Act 2000, and "monitoring officer", in relation to such an authority, has the same meaning as in Part 3 of that Act.

Parliamentary privilege

13   The listed GDPR provisions and Article 34(1) and (4) of the GDPR (communication of personal data breach to the data subject) do not apply to personal data where this is required for the purpose of avoiding an infringement of the privileges of either House of Parliament.

Judicial appointments, judicial independence and judicial proceedings

14(1)   The listed GDPR provisions do not apply to personal data processed for the purposes of assessing a person's suitability for judicial office or the office of Queen's Counsel.

(2)   The listed GDPR provisions do not apply to personal data processed by—

    (a)   an individual acting in a judicial capacity, or

    (b)   a court or tribunal acting in its judicial capacity.

(3)   As regards personal data not falling within sub-paragraph (1) or (2), the listed GDPR provisions do not apply to the extent that the application of those provisions would be likely to prejudice judicial independence or judicial proceedings.

Crown honours, dignities and appointments

15(1)   The listed GDPR provisions do not apply to personal data processed for the purposes of the conferring by the Crown of any honour or dignity.

(2)   The listed GDPR provisions do not apply to personal data processed for the purposes of assessing a person's suitability for any of the following offices—

    (a)   archbishops and diocesan and suffragan bishops in the Church of England;

    (b)   deans of cathedrals of the Church of England;

    (c)   deans and canons of the two Royal Peculiars;

    (d)   the First and Second Church Estates Commissioners;

    (e)   lord-lieutenants;

    (f)   Masters of Trinity College and Churchill College, Cambridge;

    (g)   the Provost of Eton;

    (h)   the Poet Laureate;

    (i)   the Astronomer Royal.

(3)   The Secretary of State may by regulations amend the list in sub-paragraph (2) to—

    (a) remove an office, or

    (b) add an office to which appointments are made by Her Majesty.

(4) Regulations under sub-paragraph (3) are subject to the affirmative resolution procedure.

--- NOTES ---

Defined terms		"government department"	s 205(1)
"the affirmative resolution procedure"	182(7)	"Minister of the Crown"	s 205(1)
"the Commissioner"	s 3(8)	"personal data"	s 3(2)
"court"	s 20	"processing"	s 3(4)
"the data protection legislation"	s 3(9)	"processing of personal data"	s 5(7)
"enactment"	s 205(1)	"tribunal"	s 205(1)
"the GDPR"	s 3(10)		

PART 3
RESTRICTION BASED ON ARTICLE 23(1): PROTECTION OF RIGHTS OF OTHERS

Protection of the rights of others: general

16(1) Article 15(1) to (3) of the GDPR (confirmation of processing, access to data and safeguards for third country transfers), and Article 5 of the GDPR so far as its provisions correspond to the rights and obligations provided for in Article 15(1) to (3), do not oblige a controller to disclose information to the data subject to the extent that doing so would involve disclosing information relating to another individual who can be identified from the information.

(2) Sub-paragraph (1) does not remove the controller's obligation where—

    (a) the other individual has consented to the disclosure of the information to the data subject, or

    (b) it is reasonable to disclose the information to the data subject without the consent of the other individual.

(3) In determining whether it is reasonable to disclose the information without consent, the controller must have regard to all the relevant circumstances, including—

    (a) the type of information that would be disclosed,

    (b) any duty of confidentiality owed to the other individual,

    (c) any steps taken by the controller with a view to seeking the consent of the other individual,

    (d) whether the other individual is capable of giving consent, and

    (e) any express refusal of consent by the other individual.

(4) For the purposes of this paragraph—

    (a) "information relating to another individual" includes information identifying the other individual as the source of information;

    (b) an individual can be identified from information to be provided to a data subject by a controller if the individual can be identified from—

        (i) that information, or

        (ii) that information and any other information that the controller reasonably believes the data subject is likely to possess or obtain.

Assumption of reasonableness for health workers, social workers and education workers

17(1) For the purposes of paragraph 16(2)(b), it is to be considered reasonable for a controller

Data Protection Act 2018
Schedule 2 – Exemptions etc from the GDPR
Part 3 – Restriction based on Article 23(1): Protection of rights of others

to disclose information to a data subject without the consent of the other individual where—

    (a) the health data test is met,

    (b) the social work data test is met, or

    (c) the education data test is met.

(2) The health data test is met if—

    (a) the information in question is contained in a health record, and

    (b) the other individual is a health professional who has compiled or contributed to the health record or who, in his or her capacity as a health professional, has been involved in the diagnosis, care or treatment of the data subject.

(3) The social work data test is met if—

    (a) the other individual is—

        (i) a children's court officer,

       (ii) a person who is or has been employed by a person or body referred to in paragraph 8 of Schedule 3 in connection with functions exercised in relation to the information, or

      (iii) a person who has provided for reward a service that is similar to a service provided in the exercise of any relevant social services functions, and

    (b) the information relates to the other individual in an official capacity or the other individual supplied the information—

        (i) in an official capacity, or

       (ii) in a case within paragraph (a)(iii), in connection with providing the service mentioned in paragraph (a)(iii).

(4) The education data test is met if—

    (a) the other individual is an education-related worker, or

    (b) the other individual is employed by an education authority (within the meaning of the Education (Scotland) Act 1980) in pursuance of its functions relating to education and—

        (i) the information relates to the other individual in his or her capacity as such an employee, or

       (ii) the other individual supplied the information in his or her capacity as such an employee.

(5) In this paragraph—

    "children's court officer" means a person referred to in paragraph 8(1)(q), (r), (s), (t) or (u) of Schedule 3;

    "education-related worker" means a person referred to in paragraph 14(4)(a) or (b) or 16(4)(a), (b) or (c) of Schedule 3 (educational records);

    "relevant social services functions" means functions specified in paragraph 8(1)(a), (b), (c) or (d) of Schedule 3.

────── NOTES ──────

Defined terms		"the GDPR"	s 3(10)
"controller"	s 3(6)	"health professional"	s 204(1), (3), (4)
"data subject"	s 3(5)	"health record"	s 205(1)

PART 4

RESTRICTIONS BASED ON ARTICLE 23(1):
RESTRICTIONS OF RULES IN ARTICLES 13 TO 15

GDPR provisions to be restricted: "the listed GDPR provisions"

18   In this Part of this Schedule, "the listed GDPR provisions" means the following provisions of the GDPR (the rights and obligations in which may be restricted by virtue of Article 23(1) of the GDPR)—

    (a)   Article 13(1) to (3) (personal data collected from data subject: information to be provided);

    (b)   Article 14(1) to (4) (personal data collected other than from data subject: information to be provided);

    (c)   Article 15(1) to (3) (confirmation of processing, access to data and safeguards for third country transfers);

    (d)   Article 5 (general principles) so far as its provisions correspond to the rights and obligations provided for in the provisions mentioned in sub-paragraphs (a) to (c).

Legal professional privilege

19   The listed GDPR provisions do not apply to personal data that consists of—

    (a)   information in respect of which a claim to legal professional privilege or, in Scotland, confidentiality of communications, could be maintained in legal proceedings, or

    (b)   information in respect of which a duty of confidentiality is owed by a professional legal adviser to a client of the adviser.

Self incrimination

20(1)   A person need not comply with the listed GDPR provisions to the extent that compliance would, by revealing evidence of the commission of an offence, expose the person to proceedings for that offence.

    (2)   The reference to an offence in sub-paragraph (1) does not include an offence under—

        (a)   this Act,

        (b)   section 5 of the Perjury Act 1911 (false statements made otherwise than on oath),

        (c)   section 44(2) of the Criminal Law (Consolidation) (Scotland) Act 1995 (false statements made otherwise than on oath), or

        (d)   Article 10 of the Perjury (Northern Ireland) Order 1979 (SI 1979/1714 (NI 19)) (false statutory declarations and other false unsworn statements).

    (3)   Information disclosed by any person in compliance with Article 15 of the GDPR is not admissible against the person in proceedings for an offence under this Act.

Corporate finance

21(1)   The listed GDPR provisions do not apply to personal data processed for the purposes of or in connection with a corporate finance service provided by a relevant person to the extent that either Condition A or Condition B is met.

    (2)   Condition A is that the application of the listed GDPR provisions would be likely to affect the price of an instrument.

    (3)   Condition B is that—

        (a)   the relevant person reasonably believes that the application of the listed GDPR

Data Protection Act 2018
Schedule 2 – Exemptions etc from the GDPR
Part 4 – Restrictions based on Article 23(1): Restrictions on rules in Articles 13-15

provisions to the personal data in question could affect a decision of a person—

    (i) whether to deal in, subscribe for or issue an instrument, or

    (ii) whether to act in a way likely to have an effect on a business activity (such as an effect on the industrial strategy of a person, the capital structure of an undertaking or the legal or beneficial ownership of a business or asset), and

  (b) the application of the listed GDPR provisions to that personal data would have a prejudicial effect on the orderly functioning of financial markets or the efficient allocation of capital within the economy.

(4) In this paragraph—

    "corporate finance service" means a service consisting in—

      (a) underwriting in respect of issues of, or the placing of issues of, any instrument,

      (b) services relating to such underwriting, or

      (c) advice to undertakings on capital structure, industrial strategy and related matters and advice and service relating to mergers and the purchase of undertakings;

    "instrument" means an instrument listed in section C of Annex 1 to Directive 2004/39/EC of the European Parliament and of the Council of 21 April 2004 on markets in financial instruments, and references to an instrument include an instrument not yet in existence but which is to be or may be created;

    "price" includes value;

    "relevant person" means—

      (a) a person who, by reason of a permission under Part 4A of the Financial Services and Markets Act 2000, is able to carry on a corporate finance service without contravening the general prohibition;

      (b) an EEA firm of the kind mentioned in paragraph 5(a) or (b) of Schedule 3 to that Act which has qualified for authorisation under paragraph 12 of that Schedule, and may lawfully carry on a corporate finance service;

      (c) a person who is exempt from the general prohibition in respect of any corporate finance service—

        (i) as a result of an exemption order made under section 38(1) of that Act, or

        (ii) by reason of section 39(1) of that Act (appointed representatives);

      (d) a person, not falling within paragraph (a), (b) or (c), who may lawfully carry on a corporate finance service without contravening the general prohibition;

      (e) a person who, in the course of employment, provides to their employer a service falling within paragraph (b) or (c) of the definition of "corporate finance service";

      (f) a partner who provides to other partners in the partnership a service falling within either of those paragraphs.

(5) In the definition of "relevant person" in sub-paragraph (4), references to "the general prohibition" are to the general prohibition within the meaning of section 19 of the Financial Services and Markets Act 2000.

Management forecasts

22 The listed GDPR provisions do not apply to personal data processed for the purposes of management forecasting or management planning in relation to a business or other

activity to the extent that the application of those provisions would be likely to prejudice the conduct of the business or activity concerned.

Negotiations

23   The listed GDPR provisions do not apply to personal data that consists of records of the intentions of the controller in relation to any negotiations with the data subject to the extent that the application of those provisions would be likely to prejudice those negotiations.

Confidential references

24   The listed GDPR provisions do not apply to personal data consisting of a reference given (or to be given) in confidence for the purposes of—
     (a)   the education, training or employment (or prospective education, training or employment) of the data subject,
     (b)   the placement (or prospective placement) of the data subject as a volunteer,
     (c)   the appointment (or prospective appointment) of the data subject to any office, or
     (d)   the provision (or prospective provision) by the data subject of any service.

Exam scripts and exam marks

25(1)   The listed GDPR provisions do not apply to personal data consisting of information recorded by candidates during an exam.

(2)   Where personal data consists of marks or other information processed by a controller—
      (a)   for the purposes of determining the results of an exam, or
      (b)   in consequence of the determination of the results of an exam,
      the duty in Article 12(3) or (4) of the GDPR for the controller to provide information requested by the data subject within a certain time period, as it applies to Article 15 of the GDPR (confirmation of processing, access to data and safeguards for third country transfers), is modified as set out in sub-paragraph (3).

(3)   Where a question arises as to whether the controller is obliged by Article 15 of the GDPR to disclose personal data, and the question arises before the day on which the exam results are announced, the controller must provide the information mentioned in Article 12(3) or (4)—
      (a)   before the end of the period of 5 months beginning when the question arises, or
      (b)   if earlier, before the end of the period of 40 days beginning with the announcement of the results.

(4)   In this paragraph, "exam" means an academic, professional or other examination used for determining the knowledge, intelligence, skill or ability of a candidate and may include an exam consisting of an assessment of the candidate's performance while undertaking work or any other activity.

(5)   For the purposes of this paragraph, the results of an exam are treated as announced when they are first published or, if not published, first communicated to the candidate.

—— NOTES ——

Defined terms			
"controller"	s 3(6)	"personal data"	s 3(2)
"data subject"	s 3(5)	"processing"	s 3(4)
"the GDPR"	s 3(10)	"processing of personal data"	s 5(7)
		"publish"	s 205(1)

Data Protection Act 2018
Schedule 2 – Exemptions etc from the GDPR
Part 5 – Exemptions etc based on Article 85(2) for reasons of freedom of expression

PART 5

EXEMPTIONS ETC BASED ON ARTICLE 85(2) FOR REASONS OF
FREEDOM OF EXPRESSION AND INFORMATION

Journalistic, academic, artistic and literary purposes

26(1)   In this paragraph, "the special purposes" means one or more of the following—

    (a)   the purposes of journalism;

    (b)   academic purposes;

    (c)   artistic purposes;

    (d)   literary purposes.

(2)   Sub-paragraph (3) applies to the processing of personal data carried out for the special purposes if—

    (a)   the processing is being carried out with a view to the publication by a person of journalistic, academic, artistic or literary material, and

    (b)   the controller reasonably believes that the publication of the material would be in the public interest.

(3)   The listed GDPR provisions do not apply to the extent that the controller reasonably believes that the application of those provisions would be incompatible with the special purposes.

(4)   In determining whether publication would be in the public interest the controller must take into account the special importance of the public interest in the freedom of expression and information.

(5)   In determining whether it is reasonable to believe that publication would be in the public interest, the controller must have regard to any of the codes of practice or guidelines listed in sub-paragraph (6) that is relevant to the publication in question.

(6)   The codes of practice and guidelines are—

    (a)   BBC Editorial Guidelines;

    (b)   Ofcom Broadcasting Code;

    (c)   Editors' Code of Practice.

(7)   The Secretary of State may by regulations amend the list in sub-paragraph (6).

(8)   Regulations under sub-paragraph (7) are subject to the affirmative resolution procedure.

(9)   For the purposes of this paragraph, the listed GDPR provisions are the following provisions of the GDPR (which may be exempted or derogated from by virtue of Article 85(2) of the GDPR)—

    (a)   in Chapter II of the GDPR (principles)—

        (i)   Article 5(1)(a) to (e) (principles relating to processing);

       (ii)   Article 6 (lawfulness);

      (iii)   Article 7 (conditions for consent);

      (iv)   Article 8(1) and (2) (child's consent);

       (v)   Article 9 (processing of special categories of data);

      (vi)   Article 10 (data relating to criminal convictions etc);

     (vii)   Article 11(2) (processing not requiring identification);

    (b)   in Chapter III of the GDPR (rights of the data subject)—

        (i)   Article 13(1) to (3) (personal data collected from data subject: information to be provided);

    (ii) Article 14(1) to (4) (personal data collected other than from data subject: information to be provided);

   (iii) Article 15(1) to (3) (confirmation of processing, access to data and safeguards for third country transfers);

   (iv) Article 16 (right to rectification);

    (v) Article 17(1) and (2) (right to erasure);

   (vi) Article 18(1)(a), (b) and (d) (restriction of processing);

  (vii) Article 19 (notification obligation regarding rectification or erasure of personal data or restriction of processing);

  (viii) Article 20(1) and (2) (right to data portability);

   (ix) Article 21(1) (objections to processing);

  (c) in Chapter IV of the GDPR (controller and processor)—

    (i) Article 34(1) and (4) (communication of personal data breach to the data subject);

   (ii) Article 36 (requirement for controller to consult Commissioner prior to high risk processing);

  (d) in Chapter V of the GDPR (transfers of data to third countries etc), Article 44 (general principles for transfers);

  (e) in Chapter VII of the GDPR (co-operation and consistency)—

    (i) Articles 60 to 62 (co-operation);

   (ii) Articles 63 to 67 (consistency).

—— **NOTES** ——

Defined terms			
"the affirmative resolution procedure"	s 182(7)	"personal data"	s 3(2)
"controller"	s 3(6)	"processing"	s 3(4)
"the GDPR"	s 3(10)	"processing of personal data"	s 5(7)
		"publish"	s 205(1)

PART 6
DEROGATIONS ETC BASED ON ARTICLE 89 FOR RESEARCH, STATISTICS AND ARCHIVING

Research and statistics

27(1) The listed GDPR provisions do not apply to personal data processed for—

  (a) scientific or historical research purposes, or

  (b) statistical purposes,

to the extent that the application of those provisions would prevent or seriously impair the achievement of the purposes in question.

This is subject to sub-paragraph (3).

  (2) For the purposes of this paragraph, the listed GDPR provisions are the following provisions of the GDPR (the rights in which may be derogated from by virtue of Article 89(2) of the GDPR)—

  (a) Article 15(1) to (3) (confirmation of processing, access to data and safeguards for third country transfers);

  (b) Article 16 (right to rectification);

  (c) Article 18(1) (restriction of processing);

  (d) Article 21(1) (objections to processing).

  (3) The exemption in sub-paragraph (1) is available only where—

(a) the personal data is processed in accordance with Article 89(1) of the GDPR (as supplemented by section 19), and

(b) as regards the disapplication of Article 15(1) to (3), the results of the research or any resulting statistics are not made available in a form which identifies a data subject.

Archiving in the public interest

28(1) The listed GDPR provisions do not apply to personal data processed for archiving purposes in the public interest to the extent that the application of those provisions would prevent or seriously impair the achievement of those purposes.
This is subject to sub-paragraph (3).

(2) For the purposes of this paragraph, the listed GDPR provisions are the following provisions of the GDPR (the rights in which may be derogated from by virtue of Article 89(3) of the GDPR)—

(a) Article 15(1) to (3) (confirmation of processing, access to data and safeguards for third country transfers);

(b) Article 16 (right to rectification);

(c) Article 18(1) (restriction of processing);

(d) Article 19 (notification obligation regarding rectification or erasure of personal data or restriction of processing);

(e) Article 20(1) (right to data portability);

(f) Article 21(1) (objections to processing).

(3) The exemption in sub-paragraph (1) is available only where the personal data is processed in accordance with Article 89(1) of the GDPR (as supplemented by section 19).

------ NOTES ------

Defined terms		"personal data"	s 3(2)
"data subject"	s 3(5)	"processing"	s 3(4)
"the GDPR"	s 3(10)	"processing of personal data"	s 5(7)

SCHEDULE 3   Section 15

EXEMPTIONS ETC FROM THE GDPR: HEALTH, SOCIAL WORK, EDUCATION AND CHILD ABUSE DATA

PART 1
GDPR PROVISIONS TO BE RESTRICTED

1 In this Schedule "the listed GDPR provisions" means the following provisions of the GDPR (the rights and obligations in which may be restricted by virtue of Article 23(1) of the GDPR)—

(a) Article 13(1) to (3) (personal data collected from data subject: information to be provided);

(b) Article 14(1) to (4) (personal data collected other than from data subject: information to be provided);

(c) Article 15(1) to (3) (confirmation of processing, access to data and safeguards for third country transfers);

(d) Article 16 (right to rectification);

(e) Article 17(1) and (2) (right to erasure);

(f) Article 18(1) (restriction of processing);

(g) Article 20(1) and (2) (right to data portability);

(h) Article 21(1) (objections to processing);

(i) Article 5 (general principles) so far as its provisions correspond to the rights and obligations provided for in the provisions mentioned in sub-paragraphs (a) to (h).

—— Notes ——

Defined terms   "the GDPR"   s 3(10)

PART 2
HEALTH DATA

Definitions

2(1) In this Part of this Schedule—

"the appropriate health professional", in relation to a question as to whether the serious harm test is met with respect to data concerning health, means—

(a) the health professional who is currently or was most recently responsible for the diagnosis, care or treatment of the data subject in connection with the matters to which the data relates,

(b) where there is more than one such health professional, the health professional who is the most suitable to provide an opinion on the question, or

(c) a health professional who has the necessary experience and qualifications to provide an opinion on the question, where—

(i) there is no health professional available falling within paragraph (a) or (b), or

(ii) the controller is the Secretary of State and data is processed in connection with the exercise of the functions conferred on the Secretary of State by or under the Child Support Act 1991 and the Child Support Act 1995, or the Secretary of State's functions in relation to social security or war pensions, or

(iii) the controller is the Department for Communities in Northern Ireland and data is processed in connection with the exercise of the functions conferred on the Department by or under the Child Support (Northern Ireland) Order 1991 (SI 1991/2628 (NI 23)) and the Child Support (Northern Ireland) Order 1995 (SI 1995/2702 (NI 13));

"war pension" has the same meaning as in section 25 of the Social Security Act 1989 (establishment and functions of war pensions committees).

(2) For the purposes of this Part of this Schedule, the "serious harm test" is met with respect to data concerning health if the application of Article 15 of the GDPR to the data would be likely to cause serious harm to the physical or mental health of the data subject or another individual.

Exemption from the listed GDPR provisions: data processed by a court

3(1) The listed GDPR provisions do not apply to data concerning health if—

(a) it is processed by a court,

(b) it consists of information supplied in a report or other evidence given to the court in the course of proceedings to which rules listed in subparagraph (2) apply, and

(c) in accordance with those rules, the data may be withheld by the court in whole or in part from the data subject.

(2) Those rules are—

    (a) the Magistrates' Courts (Children and Young Persons) Rules (Northern Ireland) 1969 (SR (NI) 1969 No 221);

    (b) the Magistrates' Courts (Children and Young Persons) Rules 1992 (SI 1992/2071 (L 17));

    (c) the Family Proceedings Rules (Northern Ireland) 1996 (SR (NI) 1996 No 322);

    (d) the Magistrates' Courts (Children (Northern Ireland) Order 1995) Rules (Northern Ireland) 1996 (SR (NI) 1996 No 323);

    (e) the Act of Sederunt (Child Care and Maintenance Rules) 1997 (SI 1997/291 (S 19));

    (f) the Sheriff Court Adoption Rules 2009;

    (g) the Family Procedure Rules 2010 (SI 2010/2955 (L 17));

    (h) the Children's Hearings (Scotland) Act 2011 (Rules of Procedure in Children's Hearings) Rules 2013 (SSI 2013/194).

Exemption from the listed GDPR provisions: data subject's expectations and wishes

4(1) This paragraph applies where a request for data concerning health is made in exercise of a power conferred by an enactment or rule of law and—

    (a) in relation to England and Wales or Northern Ireland, the data subject is an individual aged under 18 and the person making the request has parental responsibility for the data subject,

    (b) in relation to Scotland, the data subject is an individual aged under 16 and the person making the request has parental responsibilities for the data subject, or

    (c) the data subject is incapable of managing his or her own affairs and the person making the request has been appointed by a court to manage those affairs.

(2) The listed GDPR provisions do not apply to data concerning health to the extent that complying with the request would disclose information—

    (a) which was provided by the data subject in the expectation that it would not be disclosed to the person making the request,

    (b) which was obtained as a result of any examination or investigation to which the data subject consented in the expectation that the information would not be so disclosed, or

    (c) which the data subject has expressly indicated should not be so disclosed.

(3) The exemptions under sub-paragraph (2)(a) and (b) do not apply if the data subject has expressly indicated that he or she no longer has the expectation mentioned there.

Exemption from Article 15 of the GDPR: serious harm

5(1) Article 15(1) to (3) of the GDPR (confirmation of processing, access to data and safeguards for third country transfers) do not apply to data concerning health to the extent that the serious harm test is met with respect to the data.

(2) A controller who is not a health professional may not rely on sub-paragraph (1) to withhold data concerning health unless the controller has obtained an opinion from the person who appears to the controller to be the appropriate health professional to the effect that the serious harm test is met with respect to the data.

(3) An opinion does not count for the purposes of sub-paragraph (2) if—

    (a) it was obtained before the beginning of the relevant period, or

    (b) it was obtained during that period but it is reasonable in all the circumstances to re-consult the appropriate health professional.

(4) In this paragraph, "the relevant period" means the period of 6 months ending with the day on which the opinion would be relied on.

Restriction of Article 15 of the GDPR: prior opinion of appropriate health professional

6(1) Article 15(1) to (3) of the GDPR (confirmation of processing, access to data and safeguards for third country transfers) do not permit the disclosure of data concerning health by a controller who is not a health professional unless the controller has obtained an opinion from the person who appears to the controller to be the appropriate health professional to the effect that the serious harm test is not met with respect to the data.

(2) Sub-paragraph (1) does not apply to the extent that the controller is satisfied that the data concerning health has already been seen by, or is within the knowledge of, the data subject.

(3) An opinion does not count for the purposes of sub-paragraph (1) if—

    (a) it was obtained before the beginning of the relevant period, or

    (b) it was obtained during that period but it is reasonable in all the circumstances to re-consult the appropriate health professional.

(4) In this paragraph, "the relevant period" means the period of 6 months ending with the day on which the opinion would be relied on.

—— Notes ——

Defined terms		"the GDPR"	s 3(10)
"controller"	s 3(6)	"health professional"	s 204(1), (3), (4)
"court"	s 20	"the listed GDPR	
"data concerning health"	s 205(1)	provisions"	Sch 3, Pt 1, para 1
"data subject"	s 3(5)	"processing"	s 3(4)
"enactment"	s 205(1)		

PART 3
SOCIAL WORK DATA

Definitions

7(1) In this Part of this Schedule—

    "education data" has the meaning given by paragraph 17 of this Schedule; "Health and Social Care trust" means a Health and Social Care trust established under the Health and Personal Social Services (Northern Ireland) Order 1991 (SI 1991/194 (NI 1));

    "Principal Reporter" means the Principal Reporter appointed under the Children's Hearings (Scotland) Act 2011 (asp 1), or an officer of the Scottish Children's Reporter Administration to whom there is delegated under paragraph 10(1) of Schedule 3 to that Act any function of the Principal Reporter;

    "social work data" means personal data which—

      (a) is data to which paragraph 8 applies, but

      (b) is not education data or data concerning health.

(2) For the purposes of this Part of this Schedule, the "serious harm test" is met with respect to social work data if the application of Article 15 of the GDPR to the data would be

Data Protection Act 2018
Schedule 3 – Exemptions etc from the GDPR: health, social work, education & child abuse data
Part 3 – Social work data

likely to prejudice carrying out social work, because it would be likely to cause serious harm to the physical or mental health of the data subject or another individual.

(3) In sub-paragraph (2), "carrying out social work" is to be taken to include doing any of the following—

   (a) the exercise of any functions mentioned in paragraph 8(1)(a), (d), (f) to (j), (m), (p), (s), (t), (u), (v) or (w);

   (b) the provision of any service mentioned in paragraph 8(1)(b), (c) or (k);

   (c) the exercise of the functions of a body mentioned in paragraph 8(1)(e) or a person mentioned in paragraph 8(1)(q) or (r).

(4) In this Part of this Schedule, a reference to a local authority, in relation to data processed or formerly processed by it, includes a reference to the Council of the Isles of Scilly, in relation to data processed or formerly processed by the Council in connection with any functions mentioned in paragraph 8(1)(a)(ii) which are or have been conferred on the Council by an enactment.

8(1) This paragraph applies to personal data falling within any of the following descriptions—

   (a) data processed by a local authority—

      (i) in connection with its social services functions (within the meaning of the Local Authority Social Services Act 1970 or the Social Services and Well-being (Wales) Act 2014 (anaw 4)) or any functions exercised by local authorities under the Social Work (Scotland) Act 1968 or referred to in section 5(1B) of that Act, or

      (ii) in the exercise of other functions but obtained or consisting of information obtained in connection with any of the functions mentioned in sub-paragraph (i);

   (b) data processed by the Regional Health and Social Care Board—

      (i) in connection with the provision of social care within the meaning of section 2(5) of the Health and Social Care (Reform) Act (Northern Ireland) 2009 (c. 1 (NI)), or

      (ii) in the exercise of other functions but obtained or consisting of information obtained in connection with the provision of that care;

   (c) data processed by a Health and Social Care trust—

      (i) in connection with the provision of social care within the meaning of section 2(5) of the Health and Social Care (Reform) Act (Northern Ireland) 2009 (c. 1 (NI)) on behalf of the Regional Health and Social Care Board by virtue of an authorisation made under Article 3(1) of the Health and Personal Social Services (Northern Ireland) Order 1994 (SI 1994/429 (NI 2)), or

      (ii) in the exercise of other functions but obtained or consisting of information obtained in connection with the provision of that care;

   (d) data processed by a council in the exercise of its functions under Part 2 of Schedule 9 to the Health and Social Services and Social Security Adjudications Act 1983;

   (e) data processed by—

      (i) a probation trust established under section 5 of the Offender Management Act 2007, or

      (ii) the Probation Board for Northern Ireland established by the Probation Board

(Northern Ireland) Order 1982 (SI 1982/713 (NI 10));

(f) data processed by a local authority in the exercise of its functions under section 36 of the Children Act 1989 or Chapter 2 of Part 6 of the Education Act 1996, so far as those functions relate to ensuring that children of compulsory school age (within the meaning of section 8 of the Education Act 1996) receive suitable education whether by attendance at school or otherwise;

(g) data processed by the Education Authority in the exercise of its functions under Article 55 of the Children (Northern Ireland) Order 1995 (SI 1995/755 (NI 2)) or Article 45 of, and Schedule 13 to, the Education and Libraries (Northern Ireland) Order 1986 (SI 1986/594 (NI 3)), so far as those functions relate to ensuring that children of compulsory school age (within the meaning of Article 46 of the Education and Libraries (Northern Ireland) Order 1986) receive efficient full-time education suitable to their age, ability and aptitude and to any special educational needs they may have, either by regular attendance at school or otherwise;

(h) data processed by an education authority in the exercise of its functions under sections 35 to 42 of the Education (Scotland) Act 1980 so far as those functions relate to ensuring that children of school age (within the meaning of section 31 of the Education (Scotland) Act 1980) receive efficient education suitable to their age, ability and aptitude, whether by attendance at school or otherwise;

(i) data relating to persons detained in a hospital at which high security psychiatric services are provided under section 4 of the National Health Service Act 2006 and processed by a Special Health Authority established under section 28 of that Act in the exercise of any functions similar to any social services functions of a local authority;

(j) data relating to persons detained in special accommodation provided under Article 110 of the Mental Health (Northern Ireland) Order 1986 (SI 1986/595 (NI 4)) and processed by a Health and Social Care trust in the exercise of any functions similar to any social services functions of a local authority;

(k) data which—

    (i) is processed by the National Society for the Prevention of Cruelty to Children, or by any other voluntary organisation or other body designated under this paragraph by the Secretary of State or the Department of Health in Northern Ireland, and

    (ii) appears to the Secretary of State or the Department, as the case may be, to be processed for the purposes of the provision of any service similar to a service provided in the exercise of any functions specified in paragraph (a), (b), (c) or (d);

(l) data processed by a body mentioned in sub-paragraph (2)—

    (i) which was obtained, or consists of information which was obtained, from an authority or body mentioned in any of paragraphs (a) to (k) or from a government department, and

    (ii) in the case of data obtained, or consisting of information obtained, from an authority or body mentioned in any of paragraphs (a) to (k), fell within any of those paragraphs while processed by the authority or body;

(m) data processed by a National Health Service trust first established under section 25 of the National Health Service Act 2006, section 18 of the National Health Service (Wales) Act 2006 or section 5 of the National Health Service and Community Care Act 1990 in the exercise of any functions similar to any social services functions of a local authority;

Data Protection Act 2018
Schedule 3 – Exemptions etc from the GDPR: health, social work, education & child abuse data
Part 3 – Social work data

(n) data processed by an NHS foundation trust in the exercise of any functions similar to any social services functions of a local authority;

(o) data processed by a government department—
    (i) which was obtained, or consists of information which was obtained, from an authority or body mentioned in any of paragraphs (a) to (n), and
    (ii) which fell within any of those paragraphs while processed by that authority or body;

(p) data processed for the purposes of the functions of the Secretary of State pursuant to section 82(5) of the Children Act 1989;

(q) data processed by—
    (i) a children's guardian appointed under Part 16 of the Family Procedure Rules 2010 (SI 2010/2955 (L 17)),
    (ii) a guardian ad litem appointed under Article 60 of the Children (Northern Ireland) Order 1995 (SI 1995/755 (NI 2)) or Article 66 of the Adoption (Northern Ireland) Order 1987 (SI 1987/2203 (NI 22)), or
    (iii) a safeguarder appointed under section 30(2) or 31(3) of the Children's Hearings (Scotland) Act 2011 (asp 1);

(r) data processed by the Principal Reporter;

(s) data processed by an officer of the Children and Family Court Advisory and Support Service for the purpose of the officer's functions under section 7 of the Children Act 1989 or Part 16 of the Family Procedure Rules 2010 (SI 2010/2955 (L. 17));

(t) data processed by the Welsh family proceedings officer for the purposes of the functions under section 7 of the Children Act 1989 or Part 16 of the Family Procedure Rules 2010;

(u) data processed by an officer of the service appointed as guardian ad litem under Part 16 of the Family Procedure Rules 2010;

(v) data processed by the Children and Family Court Advisory and Support Service for the purpose of its functions under section 12(1) and (2) and section 13(1), (2) and (4) of the Criminal Justice and Court Services Act 2000;

(w) data processed by the Welsh Ministers for the purposes of their functions under section 35(1) and (2) and section 36(1), (2), (4), (5) and (6) of the Children Act 2004;

(x) data processed for the purposes of the functions of the appropriate Minister pursuant to section 12 of the Adoption and Children Act 2002 (independent review of determinations).

(2) The bodies referred to in sub-paragraph (1)(l) are—

(a) a National Health Service trust first established under section 25 of the National Health Service Act 2006 or section 18 of the National Health Service (Wales) Act 2006;

(b) a National Health Service trust first established under section 5 of the National Health Service and Community Care Act 1990;

(c) an NHS foundation trust;

(d) a clinical commissioning group established under section 14D of the National Health Service Act 2006;

(e) the National Health Service Commissioning Board;

(f) a Local Health Board established under section 11 of the National Health Service (Wales) Act 2006;

(g) a Health Board established under section 2 of the National Health Service

(Scotland) Act 1978.

Exemption from the listed GDPR provisions: data processed by a court

9(1)   The listed GDPR provisions do not apply to data that is not education data or data concerning health if—

    (a)   it is processed by a court,

    (b)   it consists of information supplied in a report or other evidence given to the court in the course of proceedings to which rules listed in subparagraph (2) apply, and

    (c)   in accordance with any of those rules, the data may be withheld by the court in whole or in part from the data subject.

  (2)   Those rules are—

    (a)   the Magistrates' Courts (Children and Young Persons) Rules (Northern Ireland) 1969 (SR (NI) 1969 No 221);

    (b)   the Magistrates' Courts (Children and Young Persons) Rules 1992 (SI 1992/2071 (L 17));

    (c)   the Family Proceedings Rules (Northern Ireland) 1996 (SR (NI) 1996 No 322);

    (d)   the Magistrates' Courts (Children (Northern Ireland) Order 1995) Rules (Northern Ireland) 1996 (SR (NI) 1996 No 323);

    (e)   the Act of Sederunt (Child Care and Maintenance Rules) 1997 (SI 1997/291 (S 19));

    (f)   the Sheriff Court Adoption Rules 2009;

    (g)   the Family Procedure Rules 2010 (SI 2010/2955 (L 17));

    (h)   the Children's Hearings (Scotland) Act 2011 (Rules of Procedure in Children's Hearings) Rules 2013 (SSI 2013/194).

Exemption from the listed GDPR provisions: data subject's expectations and wishes

10(1)   This paragraph applies where a request for social work data is made in exercise of a power conferred by an enactment or rule of law and—

    (a)   in relation to England and Wales or Northern Ireland, the data subject is an individual aged under 18 and the person making the request has parental responsibility for the data subject,

    (b)   in relation to Scotland, the data subject is an individual aged under 16 and the person making the request has parental responsibilities for the data subject, or

    (c)   the data subject is incapable of managing his or her own affairs and the person making the request has been appointed by a court to manage those affairs.

  (2)   The listed GDPR provisions do not apply to social work data to the extent that complying with the request would disclose information—

    (a)   which was provided by the data subject in the expectation that it would not be disclosed to the person making the request,

    (b)   which was obtained as a result of any examination or investigation to which the data subject consented in the expectation that the information would not be so disclosed, or

    (c)   which the data subject has expressly indicated should not be so disclosed.

  (3)   The exemptions under sub-paragraph (2)(a) and (b) do not apply if the data subject has expressly indicated that he or she no longer has the expectation mentioned there.

Exemption from Article 15 of the GDPR: serious harm

11   Article 15(1) to (3) of the GDPR (confirmation of processing, access to data and safeguards

for third country transfers) do not apply to social work data to the extent that the serious harm test is met with respect to the data.

Restriction of Article 15 of the GDPR: prior opinion of Principal Reporter

12(1) This paragraph applies where—

  (a) a question arises as to whether a controller who is a social work authority is obliged by Article 15(1) to (3) of the GDPR (confirmation of processing, access to data and safeguards for third country transfers) to disclose social work data, and

  (b) the data—

    (i) originated from or was supplied by the Principal Reporter acting in pursuance of the Principal Reporter's statutory duties, and

    (ii) is not data which the data subject is entitled to receive from the Principal Reporter.

(2) The controller must inform the Principal Reporter of the fact that the question has arisen before the end of the period of 14 days beginning when the question arises.

(3) Article 15(1) to (3) of the GDPR (confirmation of processing, access to data and safeguards for third country transfers) do not permit the controller to disclose the data to the data subject unless the Principal Reporter has informed the controller that, in the opinion of the Principal Reporter, the serious harm test is not met with respect to the data.

(4) In this paragraph "social work authority" means a local authority for the purposes of the Social Work (Scotland) Act 1968.

―――― NOTES ――――

Defined terms		"government department"	s 205(1)
"controller"	s 3(6)	"the listed GDPR provisions"	
"court"	s 20		Sch 3, Pt 1, para 1
"data concerning health"	s 205(1)	"personal data"	s 3(2)
"data subject"	s 3(5)	"processing"	s 3(4)
"enactment"	s 205(1)	"processing of personal data"	s 5(7)
"the GDPR"	s 3(10)		

PART 4
EDUCATION DATA

Educational records

13 In this Part of this Schedule "educational record" means a record to which paragraph 14, 15 or 16 applies.

14(1) This paragraph applies to a record of information which—

  (a) is processed by or on behalf of the proprietor of, or a teacher at, a school in England and Wales specified in sub-paragraph (3),

  (b) relates to an individual who is or has been a pupil at the school, and

  (c) originated from, or was supplied by or on behalf of, any of the persons specified in sub-paragraph (4).

(2) But this paragraph does not apply to information which is processed by a teacher solely for the teacher's own use.

(3) The schools referred to in sub-paragraph (1)(a) are—

  (a) a school maintained by a local authority;

(b) an Academy school;

(c) an alternative provision Academy;

(d) an independent school that is not an Academy school or an alternative provision Academy;

(e) a non-maintained special school.

(4) The persons referred to in sub-paragraph (1)(c) are—

    (a) an employee of the local authority which maintains the school;

    (b) in the case of—

        (i) a voluntary aided, foundation or foundation special school (within the meaning of the School Standards and Framework Act 1998),

        (ii) an Academy school,

        (iii) an alternative provision Academy,

        (iv) an independent school that is not an Academy school or an alternative provision Academy, or

        (v) a non-maintained special school,

a teacher or other employee at the school (including an educational psychologist engaged by the proprietor under a contract for services);

    (c) the pupil to whom the record relates;

    (d) a parent, as defined by section 576(1) of the Education Act 1996, of that pupil.

(5) In this paragraph—

"independent school" has the meaning given by section 463 of the Education Act 1996;

"local authority" has the same meaning as in that Act (see sections 579(1) and 581 of that Act);

"non-maintained special school" has the meaning given by section 337A of that Act;

"proprietor" has the meaning given by section 579(1) of that Act.

15(1) This paragraph applies to a record of information which is processed—

    (a) by an education authority in Scotland, and

    (b) for the purpose of the relevant function of the authority.

(2) But this paragraph does not apply to information which is processed by a teacher solely for the teacher's own use.

(3) For the purposes of this paragraph, information processed by an education authority is processed for the purpose of the relevant function of the authority if the processing relates to the discharge of that function in respect of a person—

    (a) who is or has been a pupil in a school provided by the authority, or

    (b) who receives, or has received, further education provided by the authority.

(4) In this paragraph "the relevant function" means, in relation to each education authority, its function under section 1 of the Education (Scotland) Act 1980 and section 7(1) of the Self-Governing Schools etc. (Scotland) Act 1989.

16(1) This paragraph applies to a record of information which—

    (a) is processed by or on behalf of the Board of Governors, proprietor or trustees of, or a teacher at, a school in Northern Ireland specified in sub-paragraph (3),

    (b) relates to an individual who is or has been a pupil at the school, and

    (c) originated from, or was supplied by or on behalf of, any of the persons specified in sub-paragraph (4).

(2) But this paragraph does not apply to information which is processed by a teacher solely for the teacher's own use.

(3) The schools referred to in sub-paragraph (1)(a) are—
    (a) a grant-aided school;
    (b) an independent school.

(4) The persons referred to in sub-paragraph (1)(c) are—
    (a) a teacher at the school;
    (b) an employee of the Education Authority, other than a teacher at the school;
    (c) an employee of the Council for Catholic Maintained Schools, other than a teacher at the school;
    (d) the pupil to whom the record relates;
    (e) a parent, as defined by Article 2(2) of the Education and Libraries (Northern Ireland) Order 1986 (SI 1986/594 (NI 3)).

(5) In this paragraph, "grant-aided school", "independent school", "proprietor" and "trustees" have the same meaning as in the Education and Libraries (Northern Ireland) Order 1986 (SI 1986/594 (NI 3)).

Other definitions

17(1) In this Part of this Schedule—
    "education authority" and "further education" have the same meaning as in the Education (Scotland) Act 1980;
    "education data" means personal data consisting of information which—
        (a) constitutes an educational record, but
        (b) is not data concerning health;
    "Principal Reporter" means the Principal Reporter appointed under the Children's Hearings (Scotland) Act 2011 (asp 1), or an officer of the Scottish Children's Reporter Administration to whom there is delegated under paragraph 10(1) of Schedule 3 to that Act any function of the Principal Reporter;
    "pupil" means—
        (a) in relation to a school in England and Wales, a registered pupil within the meaning of the Education Act 1996,
        (b) in relation to a school in Scotland, a pupil within the meaning of the Education (Scotland) Act 1980, and
        (c) in relation to a school in Northern Ireland, a registered pupil within the meaning of the Education and Libraries (Northern Ireland) Order 1986 (SI 1986/594 (NI 3));
    "school"—
        (a) in relation to England and Wales, has the same meaning as in the Education Act 1996,
        (b) in relation to Scotland, has the same meaning as in the Education (Scotland) Act 1980, and
        (c) in relation to Northern Ireland, has the same meaning as in the Education and Libraries (Northern Ireland) Order 1986;
    "teacher" includes—
        (a) in Great Britain, head teacher, and

(b) in Northern Ireland, the principal of a school.

(2) For the purposes of this Part of this Schedule, the "serious harm test" is met with respect to education data if the application of Article 15 of the GDPR to the data would be likely to cause serious harm to the physical or mental health of the data subject or another individual.

Exemption from the listed GDPR provisions: data processed by a court

18(1) The listed GDPR provisions do not apply to education data if—

(a) it is processed by a court,

(b) it consists of information supplied in a report or other evidence given to the court in the course of proceedings to which rules listed in subparagraph (2) apply, and

(c) in accordance with those rules, the data may be withheld by the court in whole or in part from the data subject.

(2) Those rules are—

(a) the Magistrates' Courts (Children and Young Persons) Rules (Northern Ireland) 1969 (SR (NI) 1969 No 221);

(b) the Magistrates' Courts (Children and Young Persons) Rules 1992 (SI 1992/2071 (L 17));

(c) the Family Proceedings Rules (Northern Ireland) 1996 (SR (NI) 1996 No 322);

(d) the Magistrates' Courts (Children (Northern Ireland) Order 1995) Rules (Northern Ireland) 1996 (SR (NI) 1996 No 323);

(e) the Act of Sederunt (Child Care and Maintenance Rules) 1997 (SI 1997/291 (S 19));

(f) the Sheriff Court Adoption Rules 2009;

(g) the Family Procedure Rules 2010 (SI 2010/2955 (L 17));

(h) the Children's Hearings (Scotland) Act 2011 (Rules of Procedure in Children's Hearings) Rules 2013 (SSI 2013/194).

Exemption from Article 15 of the GDPR: serious harm

19 Article 15(1) to (3) of the GDPR (confirmation of processing, access to data and safeguards for third country transfers) do not apply to education data to the extent that the serious harm test is met with respect to the data.

Restriction of Article 15 of the GDPR: prior opinion of Principal Reporter

20(1) This paragraph applies where—

(a) a question arises as to whether a controller who is an education authority is obliged by Article 15(1) to (3) of the GDPR (confirmation of processing, access to data and safeguards for third country transfers) to disclose education data, and

(b) the controller believes that the data—

(i) originated from or was supplied by or on behalf of the Principal Reporter acting in pursuance of the Principal Reporter's statutory duties, and

(ii) is not data which the data subject is entitled to receive from the Principal Reporter.

(2) The controller must inform the Principal Reporter of the fact that the question has arisen before the end of the period of 14 days beginning when the question arises.

(3) Article 15(1) to (3) of the GDPR (confirmation of processing, access to data and safeguards for third country transfers) do not permit the controller to disclose the data to the data

Data Protection Act 2018
Schedule 3 – Exemptions etc from the GDPR: health, social work, education & child abuse data
Part 5 – Child abuse data

subject unless the Principal Reporter has informed the controller that, in the opinion of the Principal Reporter, the serious harm test is not met with respect to the data.

—— NOTES ——

Defined terms		"the listed GDPR provisions"	
"controller"	s 3(6)		Sch 3, Pt 1, para 1
"court"	s 20	"personal data"	s 3(2)
"data concerning health"	s 205(1)	"processing"	s 3(4)
"data subject"	s 3(5)	"processing of personal data"	s 5(7)
"the GDPR"	s 3(10)		

PART 5
CHILD ABUSE DATA

Exemption from Article 15 of the GDPR: child abuse data

21(1)   This paragraph applies where a request for child abuse data is made in exercise of a power conferred by an enactment or rule of law and—

    (a)   the data subject is an individual aged under 18 and the person making the request has parental responsibility for the data subject, or

    (b)   the data subject is incapable of managing his or her own affairs and the person making the request has been appointed by a court to manage those affairs.

(2)   Article 15(1) to (3) of the GDPR (confirmation of processing, access to data and safeguards for third country transfers) do not apply to child abuse data to the extent that the application of that provision would not be in the best interests of the data subject.

(3)   "Child abuse data" is personal data consisting of information as to whether the data subject is or has been the subject of, or may be at risk of, child abuse.

(4)   For this purpose, "child abuse" includes physical injury (other than accidental injury) to, and physical and emotional neglect, ill-treatment and sexual abuse of, an individual aged under 18.

(5)   This paragraph does not apply in relation to Scotland.

—— NOTES ——

Defined terms		"enactment"	s 205(1)
"court"	s 20	"the GDPR"	s 3(10)
"data subject"	s 3(5)	"personal data"	s 3(2)

SCHEDULE 4   Section 15
EXEMPTIONS ETC FROM THE GDPR: DISCLOSURE PROHIBITED
OR RESTRICTED BY AN ENACTMENT

GDPR provisions to be restricted: "the listed GDPR provisions"

1   In this Schedule "the listed GDPR provisions" means the following provisions of the GDPR (the rights and obligations in which may be restricted by virtue of Article 23(1) of the GDPR)—

    (a)   Article 15(1) to (3) (confirmation of processing, access to data and safeguards for third country transfers);

    (b)   Article 5 (general principles) so far as its provisions correspond to the rights and obligations provided for in Article 15(1) to (3).

Human fertilisation and embryology information

2   The listed GDPR provisions do not apply to personal data consisting of information the disclosure of which is prohibited or restricted by any of sections 31, 31ZA to 31ZE and 33A to 33D of the Human Fertilisation and Embryology Act 1990.

Adoption records and reports

3(1)   The listed GDPR provisions do not apply to personal data consisting of information the disclosure of which is prohibited or restricted by an enactment listed in sub- paragraph (2), (3) or (4).

(2)   The enactments extending to England and Wales are—

    (a)   regulation 14 of the Adoption Agencies Regulations 1983 (SI 1983/1964);

    (b)   regulation 41 of the Adoption Agencies Regulations 2005 (SI 2005/389);

    (c)   regulation 42 of the Adoption Agencies (Wales) Regulations 2005 (SI 2005/1313 (W 95));

    (d)   rules 5, 6, 9, 17, 18, 21, 22 and 53 of the Adoption Rules 1984 (SI 1984/265);

    (e)   rules 24, 29, 30, 65, 72, 73, 77, 78 and 83 of the Family Procedure (Adoption) Rules 2005 (SI 2005/2795 (L 22));

    (f)   in the Family Procedure Rules 2010 (SI 2010/2955 (L 17)), rules 14.6, 14.11, 14.12, 14.13, 14.14, 14.24, 16.20 (so far as it applies to a children's guardian appointed in proceedings to which Part 14 of those Rules applies), 16.32 and 16.33 (so far as it applies to a children and family reporter in proceedings to which Part 14 of those Rules applies).

(3)   The enactments extending to Scotland are—

    (a)   regulation 23 of the Adoption Agencies (Scotland) Regulations 1996 (SI 1996/3266 (S 254));

    (b)   rule 67.3 of the Act of Sederunt (Rules of the Court of Session 1994) 1994 (SI 1994/1443 (S 69));

    (c)   rules 10.3, 17.2, 21, 25, 39, 43.3, 46.2 and 47 of the Act of Sederunt (Sheriff Court Rules Amendment) (Adoption and Children (Scotland) Act 2007) 2009 (SSI 2009/284);

    (d)   sections 53 and 55 of the Adoption and Children (Scotland) Act 2007 (asp 4);

    (e)   regulation 28 of the Adoption Agencies (Scotland) Regulations 2009 (SSI 2009/154);

    (f)   regulation 3 of the Adoption (Disclosure of Information and Medical Information about Natural Parents) (Scotland) Regulations 2009 (SSI 2009/268).

(4)   The enactments extending to Northern Ireland are—

    (a)   Articles 50 and 54 of the Adoption (Northern Ireland) Order 1987 (SI 1987/2203 (NI 22));

    (b)   rule 53 of Order 84 of the Rules of the Court of Judicature (Northern Ireland) 1980 (SR. (NI) 1980 No 346);

    (c)   rules 4A.4(5), 4A.5(1), 4A.6(6), 4A.22(5) and 4C.7 of Part IVA of the Family Proceedings Rules (Northern Ireland) 1996 (SR (NI) 1996 No 322).

Statements of special educational needs

4(1)   The listed GDPR provisions do not apply to personal data consisting of information the disclosure of which is prohibited or restricted by an enactment listed in sub- paragraph

(2).

(2) The enactments are—

    (a) regulation 17 of the Special Educational Needs and Disability Regulations 2014 (SI 2014/1530);

    (b) regulation 10 of the Additional Support for Learning (Co-ordinated Support Plan) (Scotland) Amendment Regulations 2005 (SSI 2005/518);

    (c) regulation 22 of the Education (Special Educational Needs) Regulations (Northern Ireland) 2005 (SR (NI) 2005 No 384).

Parental order records and reports

5(1) The listed GDPR provisions do not apply to personal data consisting of information the disclosure of which is prohibited or restricted by an enactment listed in sub- paragraph (2), (3) or (4).

(2) The enactments extending to England and Wales are—

    (a) sections 60, 77, 78 and 79 of the Adoption and Children Act 2002, as applied with modifications by regulation 2 of and Schedule 1 to the Human Fertilisation and Embryology (Parental Orders) Regulations 2010 (SI 2010/985) in relation to parental orders made under—

        (i) section 30 of the Human Fertilisation and Embryology Act 1990, or

        (ii) section 54 of the Human Fertilisation and Embryology Act 2008;

    (b) rules made under section 144 of the Magistrates' Courts Act 1980 by virtue of section 141(1) of the Adoption and Children Act 2002, as applied with modifications by regulation 2 of and Schedule 1 to the Human Fertilisation and Embryology (Parental Orders) Regulations 2010, so far as the rules relate to—

        (i) the appointment and duties of the parental order reporter, and

        (ii) the keeping of registers and the custody, inspection and disclosure of documents and information relating to parental order proceedings or related proceedings;

    (c) rules made under section 75 of the Courts Act 2003 by virtue of section 141(1) of the Adoption and Children Act 2002, as applied with modifications by regulation 2 of Schedule 1 to the Human Fertilisation and Embryology (Parental Orders) Regulations 2010 (SI 2010/985), so far as the rules relate to—

        (i) the appointment and duties of the parental order reporter, and

        (ii) the keeping of registers and the custody, inspection and disclosure of documents and information relating to parental order proceedings or related proceedings.

(3) The enactments extending to Scotland are—

    (a) sections 53 and 55 of the Adoption and Children (Scotland) Act 2007 (asp 4), as applied with modifications by regulation 4 of and Schedule 3 to the Human Fertilisation and Embryology (Parental Orders) Regulations 2010 2010/985) in relation to parental orders made under—

        (i) section 30 of the Human Fertilisation and Embryology Act 1990, or

        (ii) section 54 of the Human Fertilisation and Embryology Act 2008;

    (b) rules 2.47 and 2.59 of the Act of Sederunt (Child Care and Maintenance Rules) 1997 (SI 1997/291 (S 19));

    (c) rules 21 and 25 of the Sheriff Court Adoption Rules 2009.

(4) The enactments extending to Northern Ireland are—

(a) Articles 50 and 54 of the Adoption (Northern Ireland) Order 1987 (SI 1987/2203 (NI 22)), as applied with modifications by regulation 3 of and Schedule 2 to the Human Fertilisation and Embryology (Parental Orders) Regulations 2010 in respect of parental orders made under—

    (i) section 30 of the Human Fertilisation and Embryology Act 1990, or

    (ii) section 54 of the Human Fertilisation and Embryology Act 2008;

(b) rules 4, 5 and 16 of Order 84A of the Rules of the Court of Judicature (Northern Ireland) 1980 (SR (NI) 1980 No 346);

(c) rules 3, 4 and 15 of Order 50A of the County Court Rules (Northern Ireland) 1981 (SR (NI) 1981 No 225).

Information provided by Principal Reporter for children's hearing

6   The listed GDPR provisions do not apply to personal data consisting of information the disclosure of which is prohibited or restricted by any of the following enactments—

(a) section 178 of the Children's Hearings (Scotland) Act 2011 (asp 1);

(b) the Children's Hearings (Scotland) Act 2011 (Rules of Procedure in Children's Hearings) Rules 2013 (SSI 2013/194).

———— NOTES ————

Defined terms	"personal data"	s 3(2)
"the GDPR" s 3(10)		

SCHEDULE 5
Section 17

ACCREDITATION OF CERTIFICATION PROVIDERS: REVIEWS AND APPEALS

Introduction

1(1)   This Schedule applies where—

(a) a person ("the applicant") applies to an accreditation authority for accreditation as a certification provider, and

(b) is dissatisfied with the decision on that application.

(2)   In this Schedule—

"accreditation authority" means—

    (a) the Commissioner, or

    (b) the national accreditation body;

"certification provider" and "national accreditation body" have the same meaning as in section 17.

Review

2(1)   The applicant may ask the accreditation authority to review the decision.

(2)   The request must be made in writing before the end of the period of 28 days beginning with the day on which the person receives written notice of the accreditation authority's decision.

(3)   The request must specify—

(a) the decision to be reviewed, and

(b) the reasons for asking for the review.

(4)   The request may be accompanied by additional documents which the applicant wants the accreditation authority to take into account for the purposes of the review.

(5) If the applicant makes a request in accordance with sub-paragraphs (1) to (4), the accreditation authority must—

    (a) review the decision, and

    (b) inform the applicant of the outcome of the review in writing before the end of the period of 28 days beginning with the day on which the request for a review is received.

Right to appeal

3(1) If the applicant is dissatisfied with the decision on the review under paragraph 2, the applicant may ask the accreditation authority to refer the decision to an appeal panel constituted in accordance with paragraph 4.

(2) The request must be made in writing before the end of the period of 3 months beginning with the day on which the person receives written notice of the decision on the review.

(3) A request must specify—

    (a) the decision to be referred to the appeal panel, and

    (b) the reasons for asking for it to be referred.

(4) The request may be accompanied by additional documents which the applicant wants the appeal panel to take into account.

(5) The applicant may discontinue an appeal at any time by giving notice in writing to the accreditation authority.

Appeal panel

4(1) If the applicant makes a request in accordance with paragraph 3, an appeal panel must be established in accordance with this paragraph.

(2) An appeal panel must consist of a chair and at least two other members.

(3) Where the request relates to a decision of the Commissioner—

    (a) the Secretary of State may appoint one person to be a member of the appeal panel other than the chair, and

    (b) subject to paragraph (a), the Commissioner must appoint the members of the appeal panel.

(4) Where the request relates to a decision of the national accreditation body—

    (a) the Secretary of State—

        (i) may appoint one person to be a member of the appeal panel other than the chair, or

        (ii) may direct the Commissioner to appoint one person to be a member of the appeal panel other than the chair, and

    (b) subject to paragraph (a), the chair of the national accreditation body must appoint the members of the appeal panel.

(5) A person may not be a member of an appeal panel if the person—

    (a) has a commercial interest in the decision referred to the panel,

    (b) has had any prior involvement in any matters relating to the decision, or

    (c) is an employee or officer of the accreditation authority.

(6) The Commissioner may not be a member of an appeal panel to which a decision of the Commissioner is referred.

(7) The applicant may object to all or any of the members of the appeal panel appointed under sub-paragraph (3) or (4).

(8) If the applicant objects to a member of the appeal panel under sub-paragraph (7), the person who appointed that member must appoint a replacement.

(9) The applicant may not object to a member of the appeal panel appointed under sub-paragraph (8).

Hearing

5(1) If the appeal panel considers it necessary, a hearing must be held at which both the applicant and the accreditation authority may be represented.

(2) Any additional documents which the applicant or the accreditation authority want the appeal panel to take into account must be submitted to the chair of the appeal panel at least 5 working days before the hearing.

(3) The appeal panel may allow experts and witnesses to give evidence at a hearing.

Decision following referral to appeal panel

6(1) The appeal panel must, before the end of the period of 28 days beginning with the day on which the appeal panel is established in accordance with paragraph 4—
    (a) make a reasoned recommendation in writing to the accreditation authority, and
    (b) give a copy of the recommendation to the applicant.

(2) For the purposes of sub-paragraph (1), where there is an objection under paragraph 4(7), an appeal panel is not to be taken to be established in accordance with paragraph 4 until the replacement member is appointed (or, if there is more than one objection, until the last replacement member is appointed).

(3) The accreditation authority must, before the end of the period of 3 working days beginning with the day on which the authority receives the recommendation—
    (a) make a reasoned final decision in writing, and
    (b) give a copy of the decision to the applicant.

(4) Where the accreditation authority is the national accreditation body, the recommendation must be given to, and the final decision must be made by, the chief executive of that body.

Meaning of "working day"

7 In this Schedule, "working day" means any day other than—
    (a) Saturday or Sunday,
    (b) Christmas Day or Good Friday, or
    (c) a day which is a bank holiday under the Banking and Financial Dealings Act 1971 in any part of the United Kingdom.

—— NOTES ——

Defined terms   "the Commissioner"   s 3(8)

Data Protection Act 2018
Schedule 6 – The applied GDPR and the applied Chapter 2
Part 1: modifications to the GDPR

SCHEDULE 6   Section 22
THE APPLIED GDPR AND THE APPLIED CHAPTER 2

PART 1
MODIFICATIONS TO THE GDPR

Introductory

1   In its application by virtue of section 22(1), the GDPR has effect as if it were modified as
     follows.

References to the GDPR and its provisions

2(1)   References to "this Regulation" and to provisions of the GDPR have effect as references
        to the applied GDPR and to the provisions of the applied GDPR.

 (2)   But sub-paragraph (1) does not have effect—
        (a) in the case of the references which are modified or inserted by paragraphs 9(f)(ii),
             15(b), 16(a)(ii), 35, 36(a) and (e)(ii) and 38(a)(i);
        (b) in relation to the references in points (a) and (b) of paragraph 2 of Article 61, as
             inserted by paragraph 49.

References to Union law and Member State law

3(1)   References to "Union law", "Member State law", "the law of a Member State" and
        "Union or Member State law" have effect as references to domestic law.

 (2)   Sub-paragraph (1) is subject to the specific modifications made in this Part of this
        Schedule.

 (3)   In this paragraph, "domestic law" means the law of the United Kingdom, or of a part of
        the United Kingdom, and includes law in the form of an enactment, an instrument made
        under Her Majesty's prerogative or a rule of law.

References to the Union and to Member States

4(1)   References to "the Union", "a Member State" and "Member States" have effect as
        references to the United Kingdom.

 (2)   Sub-paragraph (1) is subject to the specific modifications made in this Part of this
        Schedule (including paragraph 3(1)).

References to supervisory authorities

5(1)   References to a "supervisory authority", a "competent supervisory authority" or
        "supervisory authorities", however expressed, have effect as references to the
        Commissioner.

 (2)   Sub-paragraph (1) does not apply to the references in—
        (a) Article 4(21) as modified by paragraph 9(f);
        (b) Article 57(1)(h);
        (c) Article 61(1) inserted by paragraph 49.

 (3)   Sub-paragraph (1) is also subject to the specific modifications made in this Part of this
        Schedule.

References to the national parliament

6   References to "the national parliament" have effect as references to both Houses of Parliament.

Chapter I of the GDPR (general provisions)

7   For Article 2 (material scope) substitute—

"2   This Regulation applies to the processing of personal data to which Chapter 3 of Part 2 of the 2018 Act applies (see section 21 of that Act)."

8   For Article 3 substitute—

"Article 3

Territorial application

Subsections (1), (2) and (7) of section 207 of the 2018 Act have effect for the purposes of this Regulation as they have effect for the purposes of that Act but as if the following were omitted—

(a) in subsection (1), the reference to subsection (3), and

(b) in subsection (7), the words following paragraph (d)."

9   In Article 4 (definitions)—

(a)   in paragraph (7) (meaning of "controller"), for "; where the purposes and means of such processing are determined by Union or Member State law, the controller or the specific criteria for its nomination may be provided for by Union or Member State law" substitute " , subject to section 6 of the 2018 Act (meaning of "controller")";

(b)   after paragraph (7) insert—

"(7A) "the 2018 Act" means the Data Protection Act 2018 as applied by section 22 of that Act and further modified by section 3 of that Act.";

(c)   omit paragraph (16) (meaning of "main establishment");

(d)   omit paragraph (17) (meaning of "representative");

(e)   in paragraph (20) (meaning of "binding corporate rules"), for "on the territory of a Member State" substitute " in the United Kingdom";

(f)   in paragraph (21) (meaning of "supervisory authority")—

(i)   after "a Member State" insert " (other than the United Kingdom)";

(ii)   for "Article 51" substitute " Article 51 of the GDPR";

(g)   after paragraph (21) insert—

"(21A) "the Commissioner" means the Information Commissioner (see section 114 of the 2018 Act);";

(h)   omit paragraph (22) (meaning of "supervisory authority concerned");

(i)   omit paragraph (23) (meaning of "cross-border processing");

(j)   omit paragraph (24) (meaning of "relevant and reasoned objection");

(k)   after paragraph (26) insert—

"(27) "the GDPR" has the meaning given in section 3(10) of the 2018 Act.

(28) "domestic law" has the meaning given in paragraph 3(3) of Schedule 6 to the 2018 Act."

Chapter II of the GDPR (principles)

10   In Article 6 (lawfulness of processing)—

(a)   omit paragraph 2;

(b)   in paragraph 3, for the first subparagraph substitute—

Data Protection Act 2018
Schedule 6 – The applied GDPR and the applied Chapter 2
Part 1: modifications to the GDPR

"In addition to the provision made in section 15 of and Part 1 of Schedule 2 to the 2018 Act, a legal basis for the processing referred to in point (c) and (e) of paragraph 1 may be laid down by the Secretary of State in regulations (see section 16 of the 2018 Act).";

    (c) in paragraph 3, in the second subparagraph, for "The Union or the Member State law shall" substitute " The regulations must".

11 In Article 8 (conditions applicable to child's consent in relation to information society services)—

    (a) in paragraph 1, for the second subparagraph substitute—

        "This paragraph is subject to section 9 of the 2018 Act.";

    (b) in paragraph 3, for "the general contract law of Member States" substitute " the general law of contract as it operates in domestic law".

12 In Article 9 (processing of special categories of personal data)—

    (a) in paragraph 2(a), omit ", except where Union or Member State law provide that the prohibition referred to in paragraph 1 may not be lifted by the data subject";

    (b) in paragraph 2(b), for "Union or Member State law" substitute " domestic law (see section 10 of the 2018 Act)";

    (c) in paragraph 2, for point (g) substitute—

        "(g) processing is necessary for reasons of substantial public interest and is authorised by domestic law (see section 10 of the 2018 Act);";

    (d) in paragraph 2(h), for "Union or Member State law" substitute " domestic law (see section 10 of the 2018 Act)";

    (e) in paragraph 2(i), for "Union or Member State law" insert " domestic law (see section 10 of the 2018 Act);";

    (f) in paragraph 2, for point (j) substitute—

        "(j) processing is necessary for archiving purposes in the public interest, scientific or historical research purposes or statistical purposes in accordance with Article 89(1) (as supplemented by section 19 of the 2018 Act) and is authorised by domestic law (see section 10 of that Act).";

    (g) in paragraph 3, for "national competent bodies", in both places, substitute " a national competent body of the United Kingdom";

    (h) omit paragraph 4.

13 In Article 10 (processing of personal data relating to criminal convictions and offences), in the first sentence, for "Union or Member State law providing for appropriate safeguards for the rights and freedoms of data subjects" substitute " domestic law (see section 10 of the 2018 Act)".

Section 1 of Chapter III of the GDPR (rights of the data subject: transparency and modalities)

14 In Article 12 (transparent information etc for the exercise of the rights of the data subject), omit paragraph 8.

Section 2 of Chapter III of the GDPR (rights of the data subject: information and access to personal data)

15 In Article 13 (personal data collected from data subject: information to be provided), in paragraph 1—

    (a) in point (a), omit "and, where applicable, of the controller's representative";

   (b) in point (f), after "the Commission" insert " pursuant to Article 45(3) of the GDPR".

16 In Article 14 (personal data collected other than from data subject: information to be provided)—

   (a) in paragraph 1—
       (i)   in point (a), omit "and, where applicable, of the controller's representative";
       (ii) in point (f), after "the Commission" insert " pursuant to Article 45(3) of the GDPR";
   (b) in paragraph 5(c), for "Union or Member State law to which the controller is subject" substitute " a rule of domestic law".

Section 3 of Chapter III of the GDPR (rights of the data subject: rectification and erasure)

17 In Article 17 (right to erasure ('right to be forgotten'))—

   (a) in paragraph 1(e), for "in Union or Member State law to which the controller is subject" substitute " under domestic law";
   (b) in paragraph 3(b), for "by Union or Member State law to which the controller is subject" substitute " under domestic law".

18 In Article 18 (right to restriction of processing), in paragraph 2, for "of the Union or of a Member State" substitute " of the United Kingdom".

Section 4 of Chapter III of the GDPR (rights of the data subject: right to object and automated individual decision-making)

19 In Article 21 (right to object), in paragraph 5, omit ", and notwithstanding Directive 2002/58/EC,".

20 In Article 22 (automated individual decision-making, including profiling), for paragraph 2(b) substitute—

   "(b) is a qualifying significant decision for the purposes of section 14 of the 2018 Act; or".

Section 5 of Chapter III of the GDPR (rights of the data subject: restrictions)

21 In Article 23 (restrictions), in paragraph 1—

   (a) for "Union or Member State law to which the data controller or processor is subject" substitute " In addition to the provision made by section 15 of and Schedules 2, 3 and 4 to the 2018 Act, the Secretary of State";
   (b) in point (e), for "of the Union or of a Member State", in both places, substitute " of the United Kingdom";
   (c) after point (j) insert—
        "See section 16 of the 2018 Act."

Section 1 of Chapter IV of the GDPR (controller and processor: general obligations)

22 In Article 26 (joint controllers), in paragraph 1, for "Union or Member State law to which the controllers are subject" substitute " domestic law".

23 Omit Article 27 (representatives of controllers or processors not established in the Union).

Data Protection Act 2018
Schedule 6 – The applied GDPR and the applied Chapter 2
Part 1: modifications to the GDPR

24 In Article 28 (processor)—

    (a) in paragraph 3, in point (a), for "Union or Member State law to which the processor is subject" substitute " domestic law";

    (b) in paragraph 3, in the second subparagraph, for "other Union or Member State data protection provisions" substitute " any other rule of domestic law relating to data protection";

    (c) in paragraph 6, for "paragraphs 7 and 8" substitute " paragraph 8";

    (d) omit paragraph 7;

    (e) in paragraph 8, omit "and in accordance with the consistency mechanism referred to in Article 63".

25 In Article 30 (records of processing activities)—

    (a) in paragraph 1, in the first sentence, omit "and, where applicable, the controller's representative,";

    (b) in paragraph 1, in point (a), omit ", the controller's representative";

    (c) in paragraph 1, in point (g), after "32(1)" insert " or section 28(3) of the 2018 Act";

    (d) in paragraph 2, in the first sentence, omit "and, where applicable, the processor's representative";

    (e) in paragraph 2, in point (a), omit "the controller's or the processor's representative, and";

    (f) in paragraph 2, in point (d), after "32(1)" insert " or section 28(3) of the 2018 Act";

    (g) in paragraph 4, omit "and, where applicable, the controller's or the processor's representative,".

26 In Article 31 (co-operation with the supervisory authority), omit "and, where applicable, their representatives,".

Section 3 of Chapter IV of the GDPR (controller and processor: data protection impact assessment and prior consultation)

27 In Article 35 (data protection impact assessment), omit paragraphs 4, 5, 6 and 10.

28 In Article 36 (prior consultation)—

    (a) for paragraph 4 substitute—

        "4 The Secretary of State must consult the Commissioner during the preparation of any proposal for a legislative measure which relates to processing.";

    (b) omit paragraph 5.

Section 4 of Chapter IV of the GDPR (controller and processor: data protection officer)

29 In Article 37 (designation of data protection officers), omit paragraph 4.

30 In Article 39 (tasks of the data protection officer), in paragraph 1(a) and (b), for "other Union or Member State data protection provisions" substitute " other rules of domestic law relating to data protection".

Section 5 of Chapter IV of the GDPR (controller and processor: codes of conduct and certification)

31 In Article 40 (codes of conduct)—

    (a) in paragraph 1, for "The Member States, the supervisory authorities, the Board

and the Commission shall" substitute " The Commissioner must";
   (b) omit paragraph 3;
   (c) in paragraph 6, omit ", and where the code of conduct concerned does not relate to processing activities in several Member States";
   (d) omit paragraphs 7 to 11.

32   In Article 41 (monitoring of approved codes of conduct), omit paragraph 3.

33   In Article 42 (certification)—
   (a) in paragraph 1—
      (i) for "The Member States, the supervisory authorities, the Board and the Commission" substitute " The Commissioner";
      (ii) omit ", in particular at Union level,";
   (b) omit paragraph 2;
   (c) in paragraph 5, omit "or by the Board pursuant to Article 63. Where the criteria are approved by the Board, this may result in a common certification, the European Data Protection Seal";
   (d) omit paragraph 8.

34   In Article 43 (certification bodies)—
   (a) in paragraph 1, in the second sentence, for "Member States shall ensure that those certification bodies are" substitute " Those certification bodies must be";
   (b) in paragraph 2, in point (b), omit "or by the Board pursuant to Article 63";
   (c) in paragraph 3, omit "or by the Board pursuant to Article 63";
   (d) in paragraph 6, omit the second and third sentences;
   (e) omit paragraphs 8 and 9.

Chapter V of the GDPR (transfers of data to third countries or international organisations)
35   In Article 45 (transfers on the basis of an adequacy decision)—
   (a) in paragraph 1, after "decided" insert " in accordance with Article 45 of the GDPR";
   (b) after paragraph 1 insert—
   "1A But a transfer of personal data to a third country or international organisation must not take place under paragraph 1, if the Commission's decision in relation to the third country (including a territory or sector within it) or the international organisation—
      (a)   is suspended,
      (b)   has been amended, or
      (c)   has been repealed,
   by the Commission under Article 45(5) of the GDPR.";
   (c) omit paragraphs 2 to 8;
   (d) in paragraph 9, for "of this Article" substitute " of Article 45 of the GDPR".

36   In Article 46 (transfers subject to appropriate safeguards)—
   (a) in paragraph 1, for "Article 45(3)" substitute " Article 45(3) of the GDPR";
   (b) in paragraph 2, omit point (c);
   (c) in paragraph 2, in point (d), omit "and approved by the Commission pursuant to the examination procedure referred to in Article 93(2)";
   (d) omit paragraph 4;

Data Protection Act 2018
Schedule 6 – The applied GDPR and the applied Chapter 2
Part 1: modifications to the GDPR

    (e) in paragraph 5—

        (i) in the first sentence, for "a Member State or supervisory authority" substitute " the Commissioner";

        (ii) in the second sentence, for "this Article" substitute " Article 46 of the GDPR".

37   In Article 47 (binding corporate rules)—

    (a) in paragraph 1, in the first sentence, omit "in accordance with the consistency mechanism set out in Article 63";

    (b) in paragraph 2, in point (e), for "the competent courts of the Member States" substitute " a court";

    (c) in paragraph 2, in point (f), for "on the territory of a Member State" substitute " in the United Kingdom";

    (d) omit paragraph 3.

38   In Article 49 (derogations for specific situations)—

    (a) in paragraph 1, in the first sentence—

        (i) for "Article 45(3)" substitute " Article 45(3) of the GDPR";

        (ii) for "Article 46" substitute " Article 46 of this Regulation";

    (b) in paragraph 4, for "Union law or in the law of the Member State to which the controller is subject" substitute " domestic law (see section 18 of the 2018 Act which makes certain provision about the public interest)";

    (c) for paragraph 5 substitute—

on 18(2) of the 2018 Act."

39   In Article 50 (international co-operation for the protection of personal data), omit "the Commission and".

Section 1 of Chapter VI of the GDPR (independent supervisory authorities: independent status)

40   In Article 51 (supervisory authority)—

    (a) in paragraph 1—

        (i) for "Each Member State shall provide for one or more independent public authorities to be" substitute " The Commissioner is";

        (ii) omit "and to facilitate the free flow of personal data within the Union ('supervisory authority')";

    (b) omit paragraphs 2 to 4.

41   In Article 52 (independence)—

    (a) in paragraph 2—

        (i) for "The member or members of each supervisory authority" substitute " The Commissioner";

        (ii) for "their", in both places, substitute "the Commissioner's";

    (b) in paragraph 3—

        (i) for "Member or members of each supervisory authority" substitute " The Commissioner";

        (ii) for "their", in both places, substitute "the Commissioner's";

    (c) omit paragraphs 4 to 6.

42   Omit Article 53 (general conditions for the members of the supervisory authority).

43 Omit Article 54 (rules on the establishment of the supervisory authority).

Section 2 of Chapter VI of the GDPR (independent supervisory authorities: competence, tasks and powers)

44 In Article 55 (competence)—
   (a) in paragraph 1, omit "on the territory of its own Member State";
   (b) omit paragraph 2.

45 Omit Article 56 (competence of the lead supervisory authority).

46 In Article 57 (tasks)—
   (a) in paragraph 1, in the first sentence, for "each supervisory authority shall on its territory" substitute " the Commissioner is to";
   (b) in paragraph 1, in point (e), omit "and, if appropriate, cooperate with the supervisory authorities in other Member States to that end";
   (c) in paragraph 1, in point (f), omit "or coordination with another supervisory authority";
   (d) in paragraph 1, omit points (g), (k) and (t);
   (e) after paragraph 1 insert—
      "1A In this Article and Article 58, references to "this Regulation" have effect as references to this Regulation and section 28(3) of the 2018 Act."

47 In Article 58 (powers)—
   (a) in paragraph 1, in point (a), omit ", and, where applicable, the controller's or the processor's representative";
   (b) in paragraph 1, in point (f), for "Union or Member State procedural law" substitute " domestic law";
   (c) in paragraph 3, in point (b), for "the Member State government" substitute " the Secretary of State";
   (d) in paragraph 3, omit point (c);
   (e) omit paragraphs 4 to 6.

48 In Article 59 (activity reports)—
   (a) for ", the government and other authorities as designated by Member State law" substitute " and the Secretary of State";
   (b) omit ", to the Commission and to the Board".

Chapter VII of the GDPR (co-operation and consistency)

49 For Articles 60 to 76 substitute—
   "Article 61
   Co-operation with other supervisory authorities etc
   1 The Commissioner may, in connection with carrying out the Commissioner's functions under this Regulation—
      (a) co-operate with, provide assistance to and seek assistance from other supervisory authorities;
      (b) conduct joint operations with other supervisory authorities, including joint investigations and joint enforcement measures.
   2 The Commissioner must, in carrying out the Commissioner's functions under this Regulation, have regard to—

Data Protection Act 2018
Schedule 6 – The applied GDPR and the applied Chapter 2
Part 1: modifications to the GDPR

(a) decisions, advice, guidelines, recommendations and best practices issued by the European Data Protection Board established under Article 68 of the GDPR;

(b) any implementing acts adopted by the Commission under Article 67 of the GDPR (exchange of information)."

Chapter VIII of the GDPR (remedies, liability and penalties)

50   In Article 77 (right to lodge a complaint with a supervisory authority)—

    (a) in paragraph 1, omit "in particular in the Member State of his or her habitual residence, place of work or place of the alleged infringement";

    (b) in paragraph 2, for "The supervisory authority with which the complaint has been lodged" substitute " The Commissioner".

51   In Article 78 (right to an effective judicial remedy against a supervisory authority)—

    (a) omit paragraph 2;

    (b) for paragraph 3 substitute—

        "3 Proceedings against the Commissioner are to be brought before a court in the United Kingdom.";

    (c) omit paragraph 4.

52   In Article 79 (right to an effective judicial remedy against a controller or processor), for paragraph 2 substitute—

    "2 Proceedings against a controller or a processor are to be brought before a court (see section 180 of the 2018 Act)."

53   In Article 80 (representation of data subjects)—

    (a) in paragraph 1, omit "where provided for by Member State law";

    (b) in paragraph 2, for "Member States" substitute " The Secretary of State";

    (c) after that paragraph insert—

        "3 The power under paragraph 2 may only be exercised by making regulations under section 190 of the 2018 Act."

54   Omit Article 81 (suspension of proceedings).

55   In Article 82 (right to compensation and liability), for paragraph 6 substitute—

    "6 Proceedings for exercising the right to receive compensation are to be brought before a court (see section 180 of the 2018 Act)."

56   In Article 83 (general conditions for imposing administrative fines)—

    (a) in paragraph 5, in point (d), for "pursuant to Member State law adopted under Chapter IX" substitute " under Part 5 or 6 of Schedule 2 to the 2018 Act or under regulations made under section 16 of that Act";

    (b) in paragraph 7—

        (i) for "each Member State" substitute " the Secretary of State";

        (ii) for "that Member State" substitute " the United Kingdom";

    (c) for paragraph 8 substitute—

        "8   Section 115(9) of the 2018 Act makes provision about the exercise of the Commissioner's powers under this Article.";

(d) omit paragraph 9.

57 In Article 84 (penalties)—
    (a) for paragraph 1 substitute—
        "1 The rules on other penalties applicable to infringements of this Regulation are set out in the 2018 Act (see in particular Part 6 (enforcement)).";
    (b) omit paragraph 2.

Chapter IX of the GDPR (provisions relating to specific processing situations)
58 In Article 85 (processing and freedom of expression and information)—
    (a) omit paragraph 1;
    (b) in paragraph 2, for "Member States shall" substitute " the Secretary of State, in addition to the relevant provisions, may by way of regulations (see section 16 of the 2018 Act),";
    (c) in paragraph 2, at the end insert—
        "In this paragraph, "the relevant provisions" means section 15 of and Part 5 of Schedule 2 to the 2018 Act.";
    (d) omit paragraph 3.

59 In Article 86 (processing and public access to official documents), for "Union or Member State law to which the public authority or body is subject" substitute " domestic law".

60 Omit Article 87 (processing of national identification number).

61 Omit Article 88 (processing in the context of employment).

62 In Article 89 (safeguards and derogations relating to processing for archiving purposes etc)—
    (a) in paragraph 2, for "Union or Member State law may" substitute " the Secretary of State, in addition to the relevant provisions, may in regulations (see section 16 of the 2018 Act)";
    (b) in paragraph 3, for "Union or Member State law may" substitute " the Secretary of State, in addition to the relevant provisions, may in regulations (see section 16 of the 2018 Act)";
    (c) after paragraph 3 insert—
        "3A In this Article "the relevant provisions" means section 15 of and Part 6 of Schedule 2 to the 2018 Act."

63 Omit Article 90 (obligations of secrecy).

64 Omit Article 91 (existing data protection rules of churches and religious associations).

Chapter X of the GDPR (delegated acts and implementing acts)
65 Omit Article 92 (exercise of the delegation).

66 Omit Article 93 (committee procedure).

Chapter XI of the GDPR (final provisions)

Data Protection Act 2018
Schedule 6 – The applied GDPR and the applied Chapter 2
Part 2: modifications to Chapter 2 of Part 2

67   Omit Article 94 (repeal of Directive 95/46/EC).

68   Omit Article 95 (relationship with Directive 2002/58/EC).

69   In Article 96 (relationship with previously concluded Agreements), for "by Member States" substitute " by the United Kingdom or the Commissioner".

70   Omit Article 97 (Commission reports).

71   Omit Article 98 (Commission reviews).

72   Omit Article 99 (entry into force and application).

—— Notes ——

Defined terms		"enactment"	s 205(1)
"the applied GDPR"	s 3(11)	"the GDPR"	s 3(10)
"the Commissioner"	s 3(8)		

PART 2
Modifications to Chapter 2 of Part 2

Introductory

73   In its application by virtue of section 22(2), Chapter 2 of Part 2 has effect as if it were modified as follows.

General modifications

74(1)   References to Chapter 2 of Part 2 and the provisions of that Chapter have effect as references to the applied Chapter 2 and the provisions of the applied Chapter 2 .

(2)   References to the GDPR and to the provisions of the GDPR have effect as references to the applied GDPR and to the provisions of the applied GDPR, except in section 18(2)(a).

(3)   References to the processing of personal data to which Chapter 2 applies have effect as references to the processing of personal data to which Chapter 3 applies.

Exemptions

75   In section 16 (power to make further exemptions etc by regulations), in subsection (1)(a), for "Member State law" substitute " the Secretary of State".

—— Notes ——

Defined terms		"personal data"	s 3(2)
"the applied Chapter 2"	s 22(3)	"processing"	s 3(4)
"the applied GDPR"	s 3(11)		

SCHEDULE 7
Competent Authorities

Section 30

1   Any United Kingdom government department other than a non-ministerial government department.

2 The Scottish Ministers.

3 Any Northern Ireland department.

4 The Welsh Ministers.

Chief officers of police and other policing bodies

5 The chief constable of a police force maintained under section 2 of the Police Act 1996.

6 The Commissioner of Police of the Metropolis.

7 The Commissioner of Police for the City of London.

8 The Chief Constable of the Police Service of Northern Ireland.

9 The chief constable of the Police Service of Scotland.

10 The chief constable of the British Transport Police.

11 The chief constable of the Civil Nuclear Constabulary.

12 The chief constable of the Ministry of Defence Police.

13 The Provost Marshal of the Royal Navy Police.

14 The Provost Marshal of the Royal Military Police.

15 The Provost Marshal of the Royal Air Force Police.

16 The chief officer of—

    (a) a body of constables appointed under provision incorporating section 79 of the Harbours, Docks, and Piers Clauses Act 1847;

    (b) a body of constables appointed under an order made under section 14 of the Harbours Act 1964;

    (c) the body of constables appointed under section 154 of the Port of London Act 1968 (c.xxxii).

17 A body established in accordance with a collaboration agreement under section 22A of the Police Act 1996.

18 The Director General of the Independent Office for Police Conduct.

19 The Police Investigations and Review Commissioner.

20 The Police Ombudsman for Northern Ireland.

Other authorities with investigatory functions

21 The Commissioners for Her Majesty's Revenue and Customs.

22 The Welsh Revenue Authority.

23 Revenue Scotland.

24 The Director General of the National Crime Agency.

25 The Director of the Serious Fraud Office.

26 The Director of Border Revenue.

27 The Financial Conduct Authority.

28 The Health and Safety Executive.

29 The Competition and Markets Authority.

30 The Gas and Electricity Markets Authority.

31 The Food Standards Agency.

32 Food Standards Scotland.

33 Her Majesty's Land Registry.

34 The Criminal Cases Review Commission.

35 The Scottish Criminal Cases Review Commission.

Authorities with functions relating to offender management

36 A provider of probation services (other than the Secretary of State), acting in pursuance of arrangements made under section 3(2) of the Offender Management Act 2007.

37 The Youth Justice Board for England and Wales.

38 The Parole Board for England and Wales.

39 The Parole Board for Scotland.

40 The Parole Commissioners for Northern Ireland.

41 The Probation Board for Northern Ireland.

42 The Prisoner Ombudsman for Northern Ireland.

43 A person who has entered into a contract for the running of, or part of—

    (a) a prison or young offender institution under section 84 of the Criminal Justice Act 1991, or

    (b) a secure training centre under section 7 of the Criminal Justice and Public Order Act 1994.

44 A person who has entered into a contract with the Secretary of State—

    (a) under section 80 of the Criminal Justice Act 1991 for the purposes of prisoner escort arrangements, or

    (b) under paragraph 1 of Schedule 1 to the Criminal Justice and Public Order Act 1994 for the purposes of escort arrangements.

45 A person who is, under or by virtue of any enactment, responsible for securing the electronic monitoring of an individual.

46 A youth offending team established under section 39 of the Crime and Disorder Act 1998.

The Director of Public Prosecutions.

The Director of Public Prosecutions for Northern Ireland.

The Lord Advocate.

A procurator Fiscal.

The Director of Service Prosecutions.

The Information Commissioner.

The Scottish Information Commissioner.

The Scottish Courts and Tribunal Service.

The Crown agent.

56 A court or tribunal.

―――― NOTES ――――

Defined terms			
"enactment"	s 205(1)	"government department"	s 205(1)
		"tribunal"	s 205(1)

SCHEDULE 8
CONDITIONS FOR SENSITIVE PROCESSING UNDER PART 3

Section 35(5)

Statutory etc purposes

1 This condition is met if the processing—

    (a) is necessary for the exercise of a function conferred on a person by an enactment or rule of law, and

    (b) is necessary for reasons of substantial public interest.

Administration of justice

2 This condition is met if the processing is necessary for the administration of justice.

Protecting individual's vital interests

3   This condition is met if the processing is necesary to protect the vital interests of the data subject or of another individual.

Safeguarding of children and of individuals at risk

4(1)   This condition is met if—

    (a)   the processing is necessary for the purpose of—

        (i)   protecting an individual from neglect or physic mental or emotional harm, or

        (ii)   protecting the physical, mental or emotional well-l of an individual,

    (b)   the individual is—

        (i)   aged under 18, or

        (ii)   aged 18 or over and at risk,

    (c)   the processing is carried out without the consent of the data sub, ne of the reasons listed in sub-paragraph (2), and

    (d)   the processing is necessary for reasons of substantial public interes

(2)   The reasons mentioned in sub-paragraph (1)(c) are—

    (a)   in the circumstances, consent to the processing cannot be given b subject;

    (b)   in the circumstances, the controller cannot reasonably be expected to ot consent of the data subject to the processing;

    (c)   the processing must be carried out without the consent of the data subject be obtaining the consent of the data subject would prejudice the provision of protection mentioned in sub-paragraph (1)(a).

(3)   For the purposes of this paragraph, an individual aged 18 or over is "at risk" if the controller has reasonable cause to suspect that the individual—

    (a)   has needs for care and support,

    (b)   is experiencing, or at risk of, neglect or physical, mental or emotional harm, and

    (c)   as a result of those needs is unable to protect himself or herself against the neglect or harm or the risk of it.

(4)   In sub-paragraph (1)(a), the reference to the protection of an individual or of the well-being of an individual includes both protection relating to a particular individual and protection relating to a type of individual.

Personal data already in the public domain

5   This condition is met if the processing relates to personal data which is manifestly made public by the data subject.

Legal claims

6   This condition is met if the processing—

    (a)   is necessary for the purpose of, or in connection with, any legal proceedings (including prospective legal proceedings),

    (b)   is necessary for the purpose of obtaining legal advice, or

    (c)   is otherwise necessary for the purposes of establishing, exercising or defending legal rights.

Judicial acts

7   This condition is met if the processing is necessary when a court or other judicial

Protecting individual's vital interests

3 This condition is met if the processing is necessary to protect the vital interests of the data subject or of another individual.

Safeguarding of children and of individuals at risk

4(1) This condition is met if—

   (a) the processing is necessary for the purposes of—

      (i) protecting an individual from neglect or physical, mental or emotional harm, or

      (ii) protecting the physical, mental or emotional well-being of an individual,

   (b) the individual is—

      (i) aged under 18, or

      (ii) aged 18 or over and at risk,

   (c) the processing is carried out without the consent of the data subject for one of the reasons listed in sub-paragraph (2), and

   (d) the processing is necessary for reasons of substantial public interest.

(2) The reasons mentioned in sub-paragraph (1)(c) are—

   (a) in the circumstances, consent to the processing cannot be given by the data subject;

   (b) in the circumstances, the controller cannot reasonably be expected to obtain the consent of the data subject to the processing;

   (c) the processing must be carried out without the consent of the data subject because obtaining the consent of the data subject would prejudice the provision of the protection mentioned in sub-paragraph (1)(a).

(3) For the purposes of this paragraph, an individual aged 18 or over is "at risk" if the controller has reasonable cause to suspect that the individual—

   (a) has needs for care and support,

   (b) is experiencing, or at risk of, neglect or physical, mental or emotional harm, and

   (c) as a result of those needs is unable to protect himself or herself against the neglect or harm or the risk of it.

(4) In sub-paragraph (1)(a), the reference to the protection of an individual or of the well-being of an individual includes both protection relating to a particular individual and protection relating to a type of individual.

Personal data already in the public domain

5 This condition is met if the processing relates to personal data which is manifestly made public by the data subject.

Legal claims

6 This condition is met if the processing—

   (a) is necessary for the purpose of, or in connection with, any legal proceedings (including prospective legal proceedings),

   (b) is necessary for the purpose of obtaining legal advice, or

   (c) is otherwise necessary for the purposes of establishing, exercising or defending legal rights.

Judicial acts

7 This condition is met if the processing is necessary when a court or other judicial

government department, or

    (e) for the exercise of any other functions of a public nature exercised in the public interest by a person.

6(1) The processing is necessary for the purposes of legitimate interests pursued by—

    (a) the controller, or

    (b) the third party or parties to whom the data is disclosed.

  (2) Sub-paragraph (1) does not apply where the processing is unwarranted in any particular case because of prejudice to the rights and freedoms or legitimate interests of the data subject.

  (3) In this paragraph, "third party", in relation to personal data, means a person other than the data subject, the controller or a processor or other person authorised to process personal data for the controller or processor.

—— NOTES ——

Defined terms		"Minister of the Crown"	s 205(1)
"consent"	s 84(1), (2)	"personal data"	s 3(2)
"controller"	s 83(1), (2)	"processing"	s 3(4)
"data subject"	s 3(5)	"processing of personal data"	s 82(3)
"enactment"	s 205(1)	"processor"	s 83(3)
"government department"	s 205(1)		

SCHEDULE 10

Section 86

CONDITIONS FOR SENSITIVE PROCESSING UNDER PART 4

Consent to particular processing

1 The data subject has given consent to the processing,

Right or obligation relating to employment

2 The processing is necessary for the purposes of exercising or performing any right or obligation which is conferred or imposed by an enactment or rule of law on the controller in connection with employment.

Vital interests of a person

3 The processing is necessary—

    (a) in order to protect the vital interests of the data subject or of another person, in a case where—

        (i) consent cannot be given by or on behalf of the data subject, or

        (ii) the controller cannot reasonably be expected to obtain the consent of the data subject, or

    (b) in order to protect the vital interests of another person, in a case where consent by or on behalf of the data subject has been unreasonably withheld.

Safeguarding of children and of individuals at risk

4(1) This condition is met if—

    (a) the processing is necessary for the purposes of—

        (i) protecting an individual from neglect or physical, mental or emotional harm, or

> > (ii) protecting the physical, mental or emotional well-being of an individual,
>
> (b) the individual is—
>
> > (i) aged under 18, or
> >
> > (ii) aged 18 or over and at risk,
>
> (c) the processing is carried out without the consent of the data subject for one of the reasons listed in sub-paragraph (2), and
>
> (d) the processing is necessary for reasons of substantial public interest.

(2) The reasons mentioned in sub-paragraph (1)(c) are—

> (a) in the circumstances, consent to the processing cannot be given by the data subject;
>
> (b) in the circumstances, the controller cannot reasonably be expected to obtain the consent of the data subject to the processing;
>
> (c) the processing must be carried out without the consent of the data subject because obtaining the consent of the data subject would prejudice the provision of the protection mentioned in sub-paragraph (1)(a).

(3) For the purposes of this paragraph, an individual aged 18 or over is "at risk" if the controller has reasonable cause to suspect that the individual—

> (a) has needs for care and support,
>
> (b) is experiencing, or at risk of, neglect or physical, mental or emotional harm, and
>
> (c) as a result of those needs is unable to protect himself or herself against the neglect or harm or the risk of it.

(4) In sub-paragraph (1)(a), the reference to the protection of an individual or of the well-being of an individual includes both protection relating to a particular individual and protection relating to a type of individual.

Data already published by data subject

5 The information contained in the personal data has been made public as a result of steps deliberately taken by the data subject.

Legal proceedings etc

6 The processing—

> (a) is necessary for the purpose of, or in connection with, any legal proceedings (including prospective legal proceedings),
>
> (b) is necessary for the purpose of obtaining legal advice, or
>
> (c) is otherwise necessary for the purposes of establishing, exercising or defending legal rights.

Administration of justice, parliamentary, statutory etc and government purposes

7 The processing is necessary—

> (a) for the administration of justice,
>
> (b) for the exercise of any functions of either House of Parliament,
>
> (c) for the exercise of any functions conferred on any person by an enactment or rule of law, or
>
> (d) for the exercise of any functions of the Crown, a Minister of the Crown or a government department.

Medical purposes

8(1) The processing is necessary for medical purposes and is undertaken by—

    (a) a health professional, or

    (b) a person who in the circumstances owes a duty of confidentiality which is equivalent to that which would arise if that person were a health professional.

(2) In this paragraph, "medical purposes" includes the purposes of preventative medicine, medical diagnosis, medical research, the provision of care and treatment and the management of healthcare services.

Equality

9(1) The processing—

    (a) is of sensitive personal data consisting of information as to racial or ethnic origin,

    (b) is necessary for the purpose of identifying or keeping under review the existence or absence of equality of opportunity or treatment between persons of different racial or ethnic origins, with a view to enabling such equality to be promoted or maintained, and

    (c) is carried out with appropriate safeguards for the rights and freedoms of data subjects.

(2) In this paragraph, "sensitive personal data" means personal data the processing of which constitutes sensitive processing (see section 86(7)).

—— NOTES ——

Defined terms		"health professional"	s 204(1), (3), (4)
"consent"	s 84(1), (2)	"Minister of the Crown"	s 205(1)
"controller"	s 83(1), (2)	"personal data"	s 3(2)
"data subject"	s 3(5)	"processing"	s 3(4)
"enactment"	s 205(1)	"processing of personal data"	s 82(3)
"government department"	s 205(1)		

SCHEDULE 11   Section 112
OTHER EXEMPTIONS UNDER PART 4

Preliminary

1 In this Schedule, "the listed provisions" means—

    (a) Chapter 2 of Part 4 (the data protection principles), except section 86(1)(a) and (2) and Schedules 9 and 10;

    (b) Chapter 3 of Part 4 (rights of data subjects);

    (c) in Chapter 4 of Part 4 , section 108 (communication of personal data breach to the Commissioner).

Crime

2 The listed provisions do not apply to personal data processed for any of the following purposes—

    (a) the prevention and detection of crime, or

    (b) the apprehension and prosecution of offenders,

to the extent that the application of the listed provisions would be likely to prejudice any of the matters mentioned in paragraph (a) or (b).

Information required to be disclosed by law etc or in connection with legal proceedings

3(1) The listed provisions do not apply to personal data consisting of information that the controller is obliged by an enactment to make available to the public, to the extent that the application of the listed provisions would prevent the controller from complying with that obligation.

(2) The listed provisions do not apply to personal data where disclosure of the data is required by an enactment, a rule of law or the order of a court, to the extent that the application of the listed provisions would prevent the controller from making the disclosure.

(3) The listed provisions do not apply to personal data where disclosure of the data—
    (a) is necessary for the purpose of, or in connection with, legal proceedings (including prospective legal proceedings),
    (b) is necessary for the purpose of obtaining legal advice, or
    (c) is otherwise necessary for the purposes of establishing, exercising or defending legal rights,
to the extent that the application of the listed provisions would prevent the controller from making the disclosure.

Parliamentary privilege

4 The listed provisions do not apply to personal data where this is required for the purpose of avoiding an infringement of the privileges of either House of Parliament.

Judicial proceedings

5 The listed provisions do not apply to personal data to the extent that the application of the listed provisions would be likely to prejudice judicial proceedings.

Crown honours and dignities

6 The listed provisions do not apply to personal data processed for the purposes of the conferring by the Crown of any honour or dignity.

Armed forces

7 The listed provisions do not apply to personal data to the extent that the application of the listed provisions would be likely to prejudice the combat effectiveness of any of the armed forces of the Crown.

Economic well-being

8 The listed provisions do not apply to personal data to the extent that the application of the listed provisions would be likely to prejudice the economic well-being of the United Kingdom.

Legal professional privilege

9 The listed provisions do not apply to personal data that consists of—
    (a) information in respect of which a claim to legal professional privilege or, in Scotland, confidentiality of communications, could be maintained in legal proceedings, or
    (b) information in respect of which a duty of confidentiality is owed by a professional legal adviser to a client of the adviser.

Negotiations

10 The listed provisions do not apply to personal data that consists of records of the

intentions of the controller in relation to any negotiations with the data subject to the extent that the application of the listed provisions would be likely to prejudice the negotiations.

Confidential references given by the controller

11   The listed provisions do not apply to personal data consisting of a reference given (or to be given) in confidence by the controller for the purposes of—

    (a)   the education, training or employment (or prospective education, training or employment) of the data subject,

    (b)   the appointment (or prospective appointment) of the data subject to any office, or

    (c)   the provision (or prospective provision) by the data subject of any service.

Exam scripts and marks

12(1)   The listed provisions do not apply to personal data consisting of information recorded by candidates during an exam.

    (2)   Where personal data consists of marks or other information processed by a controller—

        (a)   for the purposes of determining the results of an exam, or

        (b)   in consequence of the determination of the results of an exam, section 94 has effect subject to sub-paragraph (3).

    (3)   Where the relevant time falls before the results of the exam are announced, the period mentioned in section 94(10)(b) is extended until the earlier of—

        (a)   the end of the period of 5 months beginning with the relevant time, and

        (b)   the end of the period of 40 days beginning with the announcement of the results.

    (4)   In this paragraph—

        "exam" means an academic, professional or other examination used for determining the knowledge, intelligence, skill or ability of a candidate and may include an exam consisting of an assessment of the candidate's performance while undertaking work or any other activity;

        "the relevant time" has the same meaning as in section 94.

    (5)   For the purposes of this paragraph, the results of an exam are treated as announced when they are first published or, if not published, first communicated to the candidate.

Research and statistics

13(1)   The listed provisions do not apply to personal data processed for—

        (a)   scientific or historical research purposes, or

        (b)   statistical purposes,

    to the extent that the application of those provisions would prevent or seriously impair the achievement of the purposes in question.

    (2)   The exemption in sub-paragraph (1) is available only where—

        (a)   the personal data is processed subject to appropriate safeguards for the rights and freedoms of data subjects, and

        (b)   the results of the research or any resulting statistics are not made available in a form which identifies a data subject.

Archiving in the public interest

14(1)   The listed provisions do not apply to personal data processed for archiving purposes in the public interest to the extent that the application of those provisions would prevent or seriously impair the achievement of those purposes.

(2) The exemption in sub-paragraph (1) is available only where the personal data is processed subject to appropriate safeguards for the rights and freedoms of data subjects.

—— NOTES ——

Defined terms		"personal data"	s 3(2)
"controller"	s 83(1), (2)	"processing"	s 3(4)
"data subject"	s 3(5)	"processing of personal data"	s 82(3)
"enactment"	s 205(1)	"publish"	s 205(1)

SCHEDULE 12   Section 114
THE INFORMATION COMMISSIONER

Status and capacity

1(1) The Commissioner is to continue to be a corporation sole.

(2) The Commissioner and the Commissioner's officers and staff are not to be regarded as servants or agents of the Crown.

Appointment

2(1) The Commissioner is to be appointed by Her Majesty by Letters Patent.

(2) No recommendation may be made to Her Majesty for the appointment of a person as the Commissioner unless the person concerned has been selected on merit on the basis of fair and open competition.

(3) The Commissioner is to hold office for such term not exceeding 7 years as may be determined at the time of the Commissioner's appointment, subject to paragraph 3.

(4) A person cannot be appointed as the Commissioner more than once.

Resignation and removal

3(1) The Commissioner may be relieved of office by Her Majesty at the Commissioner's own request.

(2) The Commissioner may be removed from office by Her Majesty on an Address from both Houses of Parliament.

(3) No motion is to be made in either House of Parliament for such an Address unless a Minister of the Crown has presented a report to that House stating that the Minister is satisfied that one or both of the following grounds is made out—
  (a) the Commissioner is guilty of serious misconduct;
  (b) the Commissioner no longer fulfils the conditions required for the performance of the Commissioner's functions.

Salary etc

4(1) The Commissioner is to be paid such salary as may be specified by a resolution of the House of Commons.

(2) There is to be paid in respect of the Commissioner such pension as may be specified by a resolution of the House of Commons.

(3) A resolution for the purposes of this paragraph may—

(a) specify the salary or pension,

(b) specify the salary or pension and provide for it to be increased by reference to such variables as may be specified in the resolution, or

(c) provide that the salary or pension is to be the same as, or calculated on the same basis as, that payable to, or in respect of, a person employed in a specified office under, or in a specified capacity in the service of, the Crown.

(4) A resolution for the purposes of this paragraph may take effect from—

    (a) the date on which it is passed, or

    (b) from an earlier date or later date specified in the resolution.

(5) A resolution for the purposes of this paragraph may make different provision in relation to the pension payable to, or in respect of, different holders of the office of Commissioner.

(6) A salary or pension payable under this paragraph is to be charged on and issued out of the Consolidated Fund.

(7) In this paragraph, "pension" includes an allowance or gratuity and a reference to the payment of a pension includes a reference to the making of payments towards the provision of a pension.

Officers and staff

5(1) The Commissioner—

    (a) must appoint one or more deputy commissioners, and

    (b) may appoint other officers and staff.

(2) The Commissioner is to determine the remuneration and other conditions of service of people appointed under this paragraph.

(3) The Commissioner may pay pensions, allowances or gratuities to, or in respect of, people appointed under this paragraph, including pensions, allowances or gratuities paid by way of compensation in respect of loss of office or employment.

(4) The references in sub-paragraph (3) to paying pensions, allowances or gratuities includes making payments towards the provision of pensions, allowances or gratuities.

(5) In making appointments under this paragraph, the Commissioner must have regard to the principle of selection on merit on the basis of fair and open competition.

(6) The Employers' Liability (Compulsory Insurance) Act 1969 does not require insurance to be effected by the Commissioner.

Carrying out of the Commissioner's functions by officers and staff

6(1) The functions of the Commissioner are to be carried out by the deputy commissioner or deputy commissioners if—

    (a) there is a vacancy in the office of the Commissioner, or

    (b) the Commissioner is for any reason unable to act.

(2) When the Commissioner appoints a second or subsequent deputy commissioner, the Commissioner must specify which deputy commissioner is to carry out which of the Commissioner's functions in the circumstances referred to in sub-paragraph (1).

(3) A function of the Commissioner may, to the extent authorised by the Commissioner, be carried out by any of the Commissioner's officers or staff.

Authentication of the seal of the Commissioner

7   The application of the seal of the Commissioner is to be authenticated by—

    (a)   the Commissioner's signature, or

    (b)   the signature of another person authorised for the purpose.

Presumption of authenticity of documents issued by the Commissioner

8   A document purporting to be an instrument issued by the Commissioner and to be—

    (a)   duly executed under the Commissioner's seal, or

    (b)   signed by or on behalf of the Commissioner,

is to be received in evidence and is to be deemed to be such an instrument unless the contrary is shown.

Money

9   The Secretary of State may make payments to the Commissioner out of money provided by Parliament.

Fees etc and other sums

10(1)   All fees, charges, penalties and other sums received by the Commissioner in carrying out the Commissioner's functions are to be paid by the Commissioner to the Secretary of State.

(2)   Sub-paragraph (1) does not apply where the Secretary of State, with the consent of the Treasury, otherwise directs.

(3)   Any sums received by the Secretary of State under sub-paragraph (1) are to be paid into the Consolidated Fund.

Accounts

11(1)   The Commissioner must—

    (a)   keep proper accounts and other records in relation to the accounts, and

    (b)   prepare in respect of each financial year a statement of account in such form as the Secretary of State may direct.

(2)   The Commissioner must send a copy of the statement to the Comptroller and Auditor General—

    (a)   on or before 31 August next following the end of the year to which the statement relates, or

    (b)   on or before such earlier date after the end of that year as the Treasury may direct.

(3)   The Comptroller and Auditor General must examine, certify and report on the statement.

(4)   The Commissioner must arrange for copies of the statement and the Comptroller and Auditor General's report to be laid before Parliament.

(5)   In this paragraph, "financial year" means a period of 12 months beginning with 1 April.

Scotland

12   Paragraphs 1(1), 7 and 8 do not extend to Scotland.

—— Notes ——

Defined terms		"Minister of the Crown"	s 205(1)
"the Commissioner"	s 3(8)		

SCHEDULE 13   Section 116
OTHER GENERAL FUNCTIONS OF THE COMMISSIONER

General tasks

1(1) The Commissioner must—

(a) monitor and enforce Parts 3 and 4 of this Act;

(b) promote public awareness and understanding of the risks, rules, safeguards and rights in relation to processing of personal data to which those Parts apply;

(c) advise Parliament, the government and other institutions and bodies on legislative and administrative measures relating to the protection of individuals' rights and freedoms with regard to processing of personal data to which those Parts apply;

(d) promote the awareness of controllers and processors of their obligations under Parts 3 and 4 of this Act;

(e) on request, provide information to a data subject concerning the exercise of the data subject's rights under Parts 3 and 4 of this Act and, if appropriate, co-operate with LED supervisory authorities and foreign designated authorities to provide such information;

(f) co-operate with LED supervisory authorities and foreign designated authorities with a view to ensuring the consistency of application and enforcement of the Law Enforcement Directive and the Data Protection Convention, including by sharing information and providing mutual assistance;

(g) conduct investigations on the application of Parts 3 and 4 of this Act, including on the basis of information received from an LED supervisory authority, a foreign designated authority or another public authority;

(h) monitor relevant developments to the extent that they have an impact on the protection of personal data, including the development of information and communication technologies;

(i) contribute to the activities of the European Data Protection Board established by the GDPR in connection with the processing of personal data to which the Law Enforcement Directive applies.

(2) Section 3(14)(c) does not apply to the reference to personal data in sub-paragraph (1) (h).

General powers

2 The Commissioner has the following investigative, corrective, authorisation and advisory powers in relation to processing of personal data to which Part 3 or 4 of this Act applies—

(a) to notify the controller or the processor of an alleged infringement of Part 3 or 4 of this Act;

(b) to issue warnings to a controller or processor that intended processing operations are likely to infringe provisions of Part 3 or 4 of this Act;

(c) to issue reprimands to a controller or processor where processing operations have infringed provisions of Part 3 or 4 of this Act;

(d) to issue, on the Commissioner's own initiative or on request, opinions to Parliament, the government or other institutions and bodies as well as to the public on any issue related to the protection of personal data.

Definitions

3   In this Schedule—

"foreign designated authority" means an authority designated for the purposes of Article 13 of the Data Protection Convention by a party, other than the United Kingdom, which is bound by that Convention;

"LED supervisory authority" means a supervisory authority for the purposes of Article 41 of the Law Enforcement Directive in a member State other than the United Kingdom.

—— Notes ——

Defined terms			
"the Commissioner"	s 3(8)	"the Law Enforcement Directive"	s 3(12)
"controller"	s 3(6), (14)(d)	"personal data"	
"the Data Protection Convention"	s 3(13)		s 3(2), (14)(c) (and note para 1(2))
"data subject"	s 3(5)	"processing"	s 3(4), (14)(c)
"the GDPR"	s 3(10), (14)(a)	"processor"	s 3(6), (14)(d)

SCHEDULE 14

Section 118

CO-OPERATION AND MUTUAL ASSISTANCE

PART 1

LAW ENFORCEMENT DIRECTIVE

Co-operation

1(1)   The Commissioner may provide information or assistance to an LED supervisory authority to the extent that, in the opinion of the Commissioner, providing that information or assistance is necessary for the performance of the recipient's data protection functions.

(2)   The Commissioner may ask an LED supervisory authority to provide information or assistance which the Commissioner requires for the performance of the Commissioner's data protection functions.

(3)   In this paragraph, "data protection functions" means functions relating to the protection of individuals with respect to the processing of personal data.

Requests for information and assistance from LED supervisory authorities

2(1)   This paragraph applies where the Commissioner receives a request from an LED supervisory authority for information or assistance referred to in Article 41 of the Law Enforcement Directive and the request—

(a)   explains the purpose of and reasons for the request, and

(b)   contains all other information necessary to enable the Commissioner to respond.

(2)   The Commissioner must—

(a)   take all appropriate measures required to reply to the request without undue delay and, in any event, before the end of the period of 1 month beginning with receipt of the request, and

(b)   inform the LED supervisory authority of the results or, as the case may be, of the progress of the measures taken in order to respond to the request.

(3) The Commissioner must not refuse to comply with the request unless—

   (a) the Commissioner does not have power to do what is requested, or

   (b) complying with the request would infringe the Law Enforcement Directive, EU legislation or the law of the United Kingdom or a part of the United Kingdom.

(4) If the Commissioner refuses to comply with a request from an LED supervisory authority, the Commissioner must inform the authority of the reasons for the refusal.

(5) As a general rule, the Commissioner must provide information requested by LED supervisory authorities by electronic means using a standardised format.

Fees

3(1) Subject to sub-paragraph (2), any information or assistance that is required to be provided by this Part of this Schedule must be provided free of charge.

(2) The Commissioner may enter into agreements with other LED supervisory authorities for the Commissioner and other authorities to indemnify each other for expenditure arising from the provision of assistance in exceptional circumstances.

Restrictions on use of information

4 Where the Commissioner receives information from an LED supervisory authority as a result of a request under paragraph 1(2), the Commissioner may use the information only for the purposes specified in the request.

LED supervisory authority

5 In this Part of this Schedule, "LED supervisory authority" means a supervisory authority for the purposes of Article 41 of the Law Enforcement Directive in a member State other than the United Kingdom.

––––– NOTES –––––

Defined terms		"personal data"	s 3(2), (14)(c)
"the Commissioner"	s 3(8)	"processing"	s 3(4), (14)(c)
"the Law Enforcement Directive"	s 3(12)		

PART 2
DATA PROTECTION CONVENTION

Co-operation between the Commissioner and foreign designated authorities

6(1) The Commissioner must, at the request of a foreign designated authority—

   (a) provide that authority with such information referred to in Article 13(3)(a) of the Data Protection Convention (information on law and administrative practice in the field of data protection) as is the subject of the request, and

   (b) take appropriate measures in accordance with Article 13(3)(b) of the Data Protection Convention for providing that authority with information relating to the processing of personal data in the United Kingdom.

(2) The Commissioner may ask a foreign designated authority—

   (a) to provide the Commissioner with information referred to in Article 13(3) of the Data Protection Convention, or

   (b) to take appropriate measures to provide such information.

Assisting persons resident outside the UK with requests under Article 14 of the Convention

7(1) This paragraph applies where a request for assistance in exercising any of the rights referred to in Article 8 of the Data Protection Convention in the United Kingdom is made by a person resident outside the United Kingdom, including where the request is forwarded to the Commissioner through the Secretary of State or a foreign designated authority.

(2) The Commissioner must take appropriate measures to assist the person to exercise those rights.

Assisting UK residents with requests under Article 8 of the Convention

8(1) This paragraph applies where a request for assistance in exercising any of the rights referred to in Article 8 of the Data Protection Convention in a country or territory (other than the United Kingdom) specified in the request is—

    (a) made by a person resident in the United Kingdom, and

    (b) submitted through the Commissioner under Article 14(2) of the Convention.

(2) If the Commissioner is satisfied that the request contains all necessary particulars referred to in Article 14(3) of the Data Protection Convention, the Commissioner must send the request to the foreign designated authority in the specified country or territory.

(3) Otherwise, the Commissioner must, where practicable, notify the person making the request of the reasons why the Commissioner is not required to assist.

Restrictions on use of information

9 Where the Commissioner receives information from a foreign designated authority as a result of—

    (a) a request made by the Commissioner under paragraph 6(2), or

    (b) a request received by the Commissioner under paragraph 6(1) or 7,

the Commissioner may use the information only for the purposes specified in the request.

Foreign designated authority

10 In this Part of this Schedule, "foreign designated authority" means an authority designated for the purposes of Article 13 of the Data Protection Convention by a party, other than the United Kingdom, which is bound by that Data Protection Convention.

—— NOTES ——

Defined terms		"personal data"	s 3(2), (14)(c)
"the Commissioner"	s 3(8)	"processing"	s 3(4), (14)(c)
"the Data Protection Convention"	s 3(13)		

SCHEDULE 15   Section 154
POWERS OF ENTRY AND INSPECTION

Issue of warrants in connection with non-compliance and offences

1(1) This paragraph applies if a judge of the High Court, a circuit judge or a District Judge (Magistrates' Courts) is satisfied by information on oath supplied by the Commissioner that—

    (a) there are reasonable grounds for suspecting that—

        (i) a controller or processor has failed or is failing as described in section 149(2), or

        (ii) an offence under this Act has been or is being committed, and

    (b) there are reasonable grounds for suspecting that evidence of the failure or of the commission of the offence is to be found on premises specified in the information or is capable of being viewed using equipment on such premises.

(2) The judge may grant a warrant to the Commissioner.

Issue of warrants in connection with assessment notices

2(1) This paragraph applies if a judge of the High Court, a circuit judge or a District Judge (Magistrates' Courts) is satisfied by information on oath supplied by the Commissioner that a controller or processor has failed to comply with a requirement imposed by an assessment notice.

(2) The judge may, for the purpose of enabling the Commissioner to determine whether the controller or processor has complied or is complying with the data protection legislation, grant a warrant to the Commissioner in relation to premises that were specified in the assessment notice.

Restrictions on issuing warrants: processing for the special purposes

3 A judge must not issue a warrant under this Schedule in respect of personal data processed for the special purposes unless a determination under section 174 with respect to the data or the processing has taken effect.

Restrictions on issuing warrants: procedural requirements

4(1) A judge must not issue a warrant under this Schedule unless satisfied that—

    (a) the conditions in sub-paragraphs (2) to (4) are met,

    (b) compliance with those conditions would defeat the object of entry to the premises in question, or

    (c) the Commissioner requires access to the premises in question urgently.

(2) The first condition is that the Commissioner has given 7 days' notice in writing to the occupier of the premises in question demanding access to the premises.

(3) The second condition is that—

    (a) access to the premises was demanded at a reasonable hour and was unreasonably refused, or

    (b) entry to the premises was granted but the occupier unreasonably refused to comply with a request by the Commissioner or the Commissioner's officers or staff to be allowed to do any of the things referred to in paragraph 5.

(4) The third condition is that, since the refusal, the occupier of the premises—

    (a) has been notified by the Commissioner of the application for the warrant, and

    (b) has had an opportunity to be heard by the judge on the question of whether or not the warrant should be issued.

(5) In determining whether the first condition is met, an assessment notice given to the occupier is to be disregarded.

Content of warrants

5(1) A warrant issued under this Schedule must authorise the Commissioner or any of the Commissioner's officers or staff—

    (a) to enter the premises,

   (b) to search the premises, and

   (c) to inspect, examine, operate and test any equipment found on the premises which is used or intended to be used for the processing of personal data.

(2) A warrant issued under paragraph 1 must authorise the Commissioner or any of the Commissioner's officers or staff—

   (a) to inspect and seize any documents or other material found on the premises which may be evidence of the failure or offence mentioned in that paragraph,

   (b) to require any person on the premises to provide, in an appropriate form, a copy of information capable of being viewed using equipment on the premises which may be evidence of that failure or offence,

   (c) to require any person on the premises to provide an explanation of any document or other material found on the premises and of any information capable of being viewed using equipment on the premises, and

   (d) to require any person on the premises to provide such other information as may reasonably be required for the purpose of determining whether the controller or processor has failed or is failing as described in section 149(2).

(3) A warrant issued under paragraph 2 must authorise the Commissioner or any of the Commissioner's officers or staff—

   (a) to inspect and seize any documents or other material found on the premises which may enable the Commissioner to determine whether the controller or processor has complied or is complying with the data protection legislation,

   (b) to require any person on the premises to provide, in an appropriate form, a copy of information capable of being viewed using equipment on the premises which may enable the Commissioner to make such a determination,

   (c) to require any person on the premises to provide an explanation of any document or other material found on the premises and of any information capable of being viewed using equipment on the premises, and

   (d) to require any person on the premises to provide such other information as may reasonably be required for the purpose of determining whether the controller or processor has complied or is complying with the data protection legislation.

(4) A warrant issued under this Schedule must authorise the Commissioner or any of the Commissioner's officers or staff to do the things described in sub-paragraphs (1) to (3) at any time in the period of 7 days beginning with the day on which the warrant is issued.

(5) For the purposes of this paragraph, a copy of information is in an "appropriate form" if—

   (a) it can be taken away, and

   (b) it is visible and legible or it can readily be made visible and legible.

Copies of warrants

6 A judge who issues a warrant under this Schedule must—

   (a) issue two copies of it, and

   (b) certify them clearly as copies.

Execution of warrants: reasonable force

7 A person executing a warrant issued under this Schedule may use such reasonable force as may be necessary.

Execution of warrants: time when executed

8   A warrant issued under this Schedule may be executed only at a reasonable hour, unless it appears to the person executing it that there are grounds for suspecting that exercising it at a reasonable hour would defeat the object of the warrant.

Execution of warrants: occupier of premises

9(1) If an occupier of the premises in respect of which a warrant is issued under this Schedule is present when the warrant is executed, the person executing the warrant must—

   (a) show the occupier the warrant, and

   (b) give the occupier a copy of it.

 (2) Otherwise, a copy of the warrant must be left in a prominent place on the premises.

Execution of warrants: seizure of documents etc

10(1) This paragraph applies where a person executing a warrant under this Schedule seizes something.

 (2) The person must, on request—

   (a) give a receipt for it, and

   (b) give an occupier of the premises a copy of it.

 (3) Sub-paragraph (2)(b) does not apply if the person executing the warrant considers that providing a copy would result in undue delay.

 (4) Anything seized may be retained for so long as is necessary in all the circumstances.

Matters exempt from inspection and seizure: privileged communications

11(1) The powers of inspection and seizure conferred by a warrant issued under this Schedule are not exercisable in respect of a communication which is made—

   (a) between a professional legal adviser and the adviser's client, and

   (b) in connection with the giving of legal advice to the client with respect to obligations, liabilities or rights under the data protection legislation.

 (2) The powers of inspection and seizure conferred by a warrant issued under this Schedule are not exercisable in respect of a communication which is made—

   (a) between a professional legal adviser and the adviser's client or between such an adviser or client and another person,

   (b) in connection with or in contemplation of proceedings under or arising out of the data protection legislation, and

   (c) for the purposes of such proceedings.

 (3) Sub-paragraphs (1) and (2) do not prevent the exercise of powers conferred by a warrant issued under this Schedule in respect of—

   (a) anything in the possession of a person other than the professional legal adviser or the adviser's client, or

   (b) anything held with the intention of furthering a criminal purpose.

 (4) The references to a communication in sub-paragraphs (1) and (2) include—

   (a) a copy or other record of the communication, and

   (b) anything enclosed with or referred to in the communication if made as described in sub-paragraph (1)(b) or in sub-paragraph (2)(b) and (c).

 (5) In sub-paragraphs (1) to (3), the references to the client of a professional legal adviser

include a person acting on behalf of such a client.

Matters exempt from inspection and seizure: Parliamentary privilege

12   The powers of inspection and seizure conferred by a warrant issued under this Schedule are not exercisable where their exercise would involve an infringement of the privileges of either House of Parliament.

Partially exempt material

13(1)   This paragraph applies if a person in occupation of premises in respect of which a warrant is issued under this Schedule objects to the inspection or seizure of any material under the warrant on the grounds that it consists partly of matters in respect of which those powers are not exercisable.

(2)   The person must, if the person executing the warrant so requests, provide that person with a copy of so much of the material as is not exempt from those powers.

Return of warrants

14(1)   Where a warrant issued under this Schedule is executed—

(a)   it must be returned to the court from which it was issued after being executed, and

(b)   the person by whom it is executed must write on the warrant a statement of the powers that have been exercised under the warrant.

(2)   Where a warrant issued under this Schedule is not executed, it must be returned to the court from which it was issued within the time authorised for its execution.

Offences

15(1)   It is an offence for a person—

(a)   intentionally to obstruct a person in the execution of a warrant issued under this Schedule, or

(b)   to fail without reasonable excuse to give a person executing such a warrant such assistance as the person may reasonably require for the execution of the warrant.

(2)   It is an offence for a person—

(a)   to make a statement in response to a requirement under paragraph 5(2)(c) or (d) or (3)(c) or (d) which the person knows to be false in a material respect, or

(b)   recklessly to make a statement in response to such a requirement which is false in a material respect.

Self-incrimination

16(1)   An explanation given, or information provided, by a person in response to a requirement under paragraph 5(2)(c) or (d) or (3)(c) or (d) may only be used in evidence against that person—

(a)   on a prosecution for an offence under a provision listed in sub-paragraph (2), or

(b)   on a prosecution for any other offence where—

(i)   in giving evidence that person makes a statement inconsistent with that explanation or information, and

(ii)   evidence relating to that explanation or information is adduced, or a question relating to it is asked, by that person or on that person's behalf.

(2)   Those provisions are —

(a)   paragraph 15,

   (b) section 5 of the Perjury Act 1911 (false statements made otherwise than on oath),

   (c) section 44(2) of the Criminal Law (Consolidation) (Scotland) Act 1995 (false statements made otherwise than on oath), or

   (d) Article 10 of the Perjury (Northern Ireland) Order 1979 (SI 1979/1714 (NI19)) (false statutory declarations and other false unsworn statements).

Vessels, vehicles etc

17 In this Schedule—

   (a) "premises" includes a vehicle, vessel or other means of transport, and

   (b) references to the occupier of premises include the person in charge of a vehicle, vessel or other means of transport.

Scotland

18 In the application of this Schedule to Scotland—

   (a) references to a judge of the High Court have effect as if they were references to a judge of the Court of Session,

   (b) references to a circuit judge have effect as if they were references to the sheriff or the summary sheriff,

   (c) references to information on oath have effect as if they were references to evidence on oath, and

   (d) references to the court from which the warrant was issued have effect as if they were references to the sheriff clerk.

Northern Ireland

19 In the application of this Schedule to Northern Ireland—

   (a) references to a circuit judge have effect as if they were references to a county court judge, and

   (b) references to information on oath have effect as if they were references to a complaint on oath.

—— NOTES ——

Defined terms		"personal data"	s 3(2), (14)(c)
"assessment notice"	ss 146(1), 181	"processing"	s 3(4), (14)(c)
"the Commissioner"	s 3(8)	"processor"	s 3(6), (14)(d)
"controller"	s 3(6), (14)(d)	"the special purposes"	s 174(1)
"the data protection legislation"	s 3(9)		

SCHEDULE 16   Section 155
PENALTIES

Meaning of "penalty"

1 In this Schedule, "penalty" means a penalty imposed by a penalty notice.

Notice of intent to impose penalty

2(1) Before giving a person a penalty notice, the Commissioner must, by written notice (a "notice of intent") inform the person that the Commissioner intends to give a penalty notice.

  (2) The Commissioner may not give a penalty notice to a person in reliance on a notice of intent after the end of the period of 6 months beginning when the notice of intent is given,

subject to sub-paragraph (3).

(3) The period for giving a penalty notice to a person may be extended by agreement between the Commissioner and the person.

Contents of notice of intent

3(1) A notice of intent must contain the following information—

    (a) the name and address of the person to whom the Commissioner proposes to give a penalty notice;

    (b) the reasons why the Commissioner proposes to give a penalty notice (see sub-paragraph (2));

    (c) an indication of the amount of the penalty the Commissioner proposes to impose, including any aggravating or mitigating factors that the Commissioner proposes to take into account.

(2) The information required under sub-paragraph (1)(b) includes—

    (a) a description of the circumstances of the failure, and

    (b) where the notice is given in respect of a failure described in section 149(2), the nature of the personal data involved in the failure.

(3) A notice of intent must also—

    (a) state that the person may make written representations about the Commissioner's intention to give a penalty notice, and

    (b) specify the period within which such representations may be made.

(4) The period specified for making written representations must be a period of not less than 21 days beginning when the notice of intent is given.

(5) If the Commissioner considers that it is appropriate for the person to have an opportunity to make oral representations about the Commissioner's intention to give a penalty notice, the notice of intent must also—

    (a) state that the person may make such representations, and

    (b) specify the arrangements for making such representations and the time at which, or the period within which, they may be made.

Giving a penalty notice

4(1) The Commissioner may not give a penalty notice before a time, or before the end of a period, specified in the notice of intent for making oral or written representations.

(2) When deciding whether to give a penalty notice to a person and determining the amount of the penalty, the Commissioner must consider any oral or written representations made by the person in accordance with the notice of intent.

Contents of penalty notice

5(1) A penalty notice must contain the following information—

    (a) the name and address of the person to whom it is addressed;

    (b) details of the notice of intent given to the person;

    (c) whether the Commissioner received oral or written representations in accordance with the notice of intent;

    (d) the reasons why the Commissioner proposes to impose the penalty (see sub-paragraph (2));

    (e) the reasons for the amount of the penalty, including any aggravating or mitigating factors that the Commissioner has taken into account;

    (f)   details of how the penalty is to be paid;

    (g)   details of the rights of appeal under section 162;

    (h)   details of the Commissioner's enforcement powers under this Schedule.

(2)   The information required under sub-paragraph (1)(d) includes—

    (a)   a description of the circumstances of the failure, and

    (b)   where the notice is given in respect of a failure described in section 149(2), the nature of the personal data involved in the failure.

Period for payment of penalty

6(1)   A penalty must be paid to the Commissioner within the period specified in the penalty notice.

(2)   The period specified must be a period of not less than 28 days beginning when the penalty notice is given.

Variation of penalty

7(1)   The Commissioner may vary a penalty notice by giving written notice (a "penalty variation notice") to the person to whom it was given.

(2)   A penalty variation notice must specify—

    (a)   the penalty notice concerned, and

    (b)   how it is varied.

(3)   A penalty variation notice may not—

    (a)   reduce the period for payment of the penalty;

    (b)   increase the amount of the penalty;

    (c)   otherwise vary the penalty notice to the detriment of the person to whom it was given.

(4)   If—

    (a)   a penalty variation notice reduces the amount of the penalty, and

    (b)   when that notice is given, an amount has already been paid that exceeds the amount of the reduced penalty,

the Commissioner must repay the excess.

Cancellation of penalty

8(1)   The Commissioner may cancel a penalty notice by giving written notice to the person to whom it was given.

(2)   If a penalty notice is cancelled, the Commissioner—

    (a)   may not take any further action under section 155 or this Schedule in relation to the failure to which that notice relates, and

    (b)   must repay any amount that has been paid in accordance with that notice.

Enforcement of payment

9(1)   The Commissioner must not take action to recover a penalty unless—

    (a)   the period specified in accordance with paragraph 6 has ended,

    (b)   any appeals against the penalty notice have been decided or otherwise ended,

    (c)   if the penalty notice has been varied, any appeals against the penalty variation notice have been decided or otherwise ended, and

(d)   the period for the person to whom the penalty notice was given to appeal against the penalty, and any variation of it, has ended.

(2)   In England and Wales, a penalty is recoverable—
   (a)   if the county court so orders, as if it were payable under an order of that court;
   (b)   if the High Court so orders, as if it were payable under an order of that court.

(3)   In Scotland, a penalty may be enforced in the same manner as an extract registered decree arbitral bearing a warrant for execution issued by the sheriff court of any sheriffdom in Scotland.

(4)   In Northern Ireland, a penalty is recoverable—
   (a)   if a county court so orders, as if it were payable under an order of that court;
   (b)   if the High Court so orders, as if it were payable under an order of that court.

—— Notes ——

Defined terms		"penalty notice"	ss 155(1), 181
"the Commissioner"	s 3(8)	"personal data"	s 3(2), (14)(c)

SCHEDULE 17
Section 178

Review of Processing of Personal Data for the Purposes of Journalism

Interpretation

1   In this Schedule—
   "relevant period" means—
   (a)   the period of 18 months beginning when the Commissioner starts the first review under section 178, and
   (b)   the period of 12 months beginning when the Commissioner starts a subsequent review under that section;
   "the relevant review", in relation to a relevant period, means the review under section 178 which the Commissioner must produce a report about by the end of that period.

Information notices

2(1)   This paragraph applies where the Commissioner gives an information notice during a relevant period.

(2)   If the information notice—
   (a)   states that, in the Commissioner's opinion, the information is required for the purposes of the relevant review, and
   (b)   gives the Commissioner's reasons for reaching that opinion,
   subsections (5) and (6) of section 142 do not apply but the notice must not require the information to be provided before the end of the period of 24 hours beginning when the notice is given.

Assessment notices

3(1)   Sub-paragraph (2) applies where the Commissioner gives an assessment notice to a person during a relevant period.

(2)   If the assessment notice—
   (a)   states that, in the Commissioner's opinion, it is necessary for the controller or processor to comply with a requirement in the notice for the purposes of the

relevant review, and

(b) gives the Commissioner's reasons for reaching that opinion,

subsections (6) and (7) of section 146 do not apply but the notice must not require the controller or processor to comply with the requirement before the end of the period of 7 days beginning when the notice is given.

(3) During a relevant period, section 147 has effect as if for subsection (5) there were substituted—

"(5) The Commissioner may not give a controller or processor an assessment notice with respect to the processing of personal data for the special purposes unless a determination under section 174 with respect to the data or the processing has taken effect."

Applications in respect of urgent notices

4 Section 164 applies where an information notice or assessment notice contains a statement under paragraph 2(2)(a) or 3(2)(a) as it applies where such a notice contains a statement under section 142(7)(a) or 146(8)(a).

—— NOTES ——

Defined terms		"personal data"	s 3(2), (14)(c)
"assessment notice"	ss 146(1), 181	"processing"	s 3(4), (14)(c)
"the Commissioner"	s 3(8)	"processor"	s 3(6), (14)(d)
"controller"	s 3(6), (14)(d)	"the special purposes"	s 174(1)
"information notice"	ss 142(1), 181		

SCHEDULE 18   Section 184
RELEVANT RECORDS

Relevant records

1(1) In section 184, "relevant record" means—

(a) a relevant health record (see paragraph 2),

(b) a relevant record relating to a conviction or caution (see paragraph 3), or

(c) a relevant record relating to statutory functions (see paragraph 4).

(2) A record is not a "relevant record" to the extent that it relates, or is to relate, only to personal data which falls within section 21(2) (manual unstructured personal data held by FOI public authorities).

Relevant health records

2 "Relevant health record" means a health record which has been or is to be obtained by a data subject in the exercise of a data subject access right.

Relevant records relating to a conviction or caution

3(1) "Relevant record relating to a conviction or caution" means a record which—

(a) has been or is to be obtained by a data subject in the exercise of a data subject access right from a person listed in sub-paragraph (2), and

(b) contains information relating to a conviction or caution.

(2) Those persons are—

(a) the chief constable of a police force maintained under section 2 of the Police Act 1996;

(b) the Commissioner of Police of the Metropolis;

(c)   the Commissioner of Police for the City of London;

(d)   the Chief Constable of the Police Service of Northern Ireland;

(e)   the chief constable of the Police Service of Scotland;

(f)   the Director General of the National Crime Agency;

(g)   the Secretary of State.

(3)   In this paragraph—

"caution" means a caution given to a person in England and Wales or Northern Ireland in respect of an offence which, at the time when the caution is given, is admitted;

"conviction" has the same meaning as in the Rehabilitation of Offenders Act 1974 or the Rehabilitation of Offenders (Northern Ireland) Order 1978 (SI 1978/1908 (NI 27)).

Relevant records relating to statutory functions

4(1)   "Relevant record relating to statutory functions" means a record which—

(a)   has been or is to be obtained by a data subject in the exercise of a data subject access right from a person listed in sub-paragraph (2), and

(b)   contains information relating to a relevant function in relation to that person.

(2)   Those persons are—

(a)   the Secretary of State;

(b)   the Department for Communities in Northern Ireland;

(c)   the Department of Justice in Northern Ireland;

(d)   the Scottish Ministers;

(e)   the Disclosure and Barring Service.

(3)   In relation to the Secretary of State, the "relevant functions" are—

(a)   the Secretary of State's functions in relation to a person sentenced to detention under—

(i)   section 92 of the Powers of Criminal Courts (Sentencing) Act 2000,

(ii)   section 205(2) or 208 of the Criminal Procedure (Scotland) Act 1995, or

(iii)   Article 45 of the Criminal Justice (Children) (Northern Ireland) Order 1998 (SI 1998/1504 (NI 9));

(b)   the Secretary of State's functions in relation to a person imprisoned or detained under—

(i)   the Prison Act 1952,

(ii)   the Prisons (Scotland) Act 1989, or

(iii)   the Prison Act (Northern Ireland) 1953 (c. 18 (NI));

(c)   the Secretary of State's functions under—

(i)   the Social Security Contributions and Benefits Act 1992,

(ii)   the Social Security Administration Act 1992,

(iii)   the Jobseekers Act 1995,

(iv)   Part 5 of the Police Act 1997,

(v)   Part 1 of the Welfare Reform Act 2007, or

(vi)   Part 1 of the Welfare Reform Act 2012.

(4)   In relation to the Department for Communities in Northern Ireland, the "relevant functions" are its functions under—

(a)   the Social Security Contributions and Benefits (Northern Ireland) Act 1992,

(b)   the Social Security Administration (Northern Ireland) Act 1992,

     (c) the Jobseekers (Northern Ireland) Order 1995 (SI 1995/2705 (NI 15)), or

     (d) Part 1 of the Welfare Reform Act (Northern Ireland) 2007 (c. 2 (NI)).

(5) In relation to the Department of Justice in Northern Ireland, the "relevant functions" are its functions under Part 5 of the Police Act 1997.

(6) In relation to the Scottish Ministers, the "relevant functions" are their functions under

     (a) Part 5 of the Police Act 1997, or

     (b) Parts 1 and 2 of the Protection of Vulnerable Groups (Scotland) Act 2007 (asp 14).

(7) In relation to the Disclosure and Barring Service, the "relevant functions" are its functions under—

     (a) Part 5 of the Police Act 1997,

     (b) the Safeguarding Vulnerable Groups Act 2006, or

     (c) the Safeguarding Vulnerable Groups (Northern Ireland) Order 2007 (SI 2007/1351 (NI 11)).

Data subject access right

5 In this Schedule, "data subject access right" means a right under—

     (a) Article 15 of the GDPR (right of access by the data subject);

     (b) Article 20 of the GDPR (right to data portability);

     (c) section 45 of this Act (law enforcement processing: right of access by the data subject);

     (d) section 94 of this Act (intelligence services processing: right of access by the data subject).

Records stating that personal data is not processed

6 For the purposes of this Schedule, a record which states that a controller is not processing personal data relating to a particular matter is to be taken to be a record containing information relating to that matter.

Power to amend

7(1) The Secretary of State may by regulations amend this Schedule.

(2) Regulations under this paragraph are subject to the affirmative resolution procedure.

—— NOTES ——

Defined terms		"the GDPR"	s 3(10), (14)(a)
"the affirmative resolution		"health record"	s 205(1)
procedure"	s 182(7)	"personal data"	s 3(2), (14)(c)
"controller"	s 3(6), (14)(d)	"processing"	s 3(4), (14)(c)
"data subject"	s 3(5)		

SCHEDULE 19   Section 211

MINOR AND CONSEQUENTIAL AMENDMENTS

Not reproduced

SCHEDULE 20   Section 213
TRANSITIONAL PROVISION ETC

PART 1
GENERAL

Interpretation

1(1) In this Schedule—

"the 1984 Act" means the Data Protection Act 1984;

"the 1998 Act" means the Data Protection Act 1998;

"the 2014 Regulations" means the Criminal Justice and Data Protection (Protocol No 36) Regulations 2014 (SI 2014/3141);

"data controller" has the same meaning as in the 1998 Act (see section 1 of that Act);

"the old data protection principles" means the principles set out in—

(a) Part 1 of Schedule 1 to the 1998 Act, and

(b) regulation 30 of the 2014 Regulations.

(2) A provision of the 1998 Act that has effect by virtue of this Schedule is not, by virtue of that, part of the data protection legislation (as defined in section 3).

—— NOTES ——

Defined terms   s 3(9) (and note para 1(2))
"the data protection legislation"

PART 2
RIGHTS OF DATA SUBJECTS

Right of access to personal data under the 1998 Act

2(1) The repeal of sections 7 to 9A of the 1998 Act (right of access to personal data) does not affect the application of those sections after the relevant time in a case in which a data controller received a request under section 7 of that Act (right of access to personal data) before the relevant time.

(2) The repeal of sections 7 and 8 of the 1998 Act and the revocation of regulation 44 of the 2014 Regulations (which applies those sections with modifications) do not affect the application of those sections and that regulation after the relevant time in a case in which a UK competent authority received a request under section 7 of the 1998 Act (as applied by that regulation) before the relevant time.

(3) The revocation of the relevant regulations, or their amendment by Schedule 19 to this Act, and the repeals and revocation mentioned in sub-paragraphs (1) and (2), do not affect the application of the relevant regulations after the relevant time in a case described in those sub-paragraphs.

(4) In this paragraph—

"the relevant regulations" means—

(a) the Data Protection (Subject Access) (Fees and Miscellaneous Provisions) Regulations 2000 (SI 2000/191);

(b) regulation 4 of, and Schedule 1 to, the Consumer Credit (Credit Reference Agency) Regulations 2000 (SI 2000/290);

(c) regulation 3 of the Freedom of Information and Data Protection (Appropriate Limit and Fees) Regulations 2004 (SI 2004/3244);

"the relevant time" means the time when the repeal of section 7 of the 1998 Act comes into force;

"UK competent authority" has the same meaning as in Part 4 of the 2014 Regulations (see regulation 27 of those Regulations).

Right to prevent processing likely to cause damage or distress under the 1998 Act

3(1) The repeal of section 10 of the 1998 Act (right to prevent processing likely to cause damage or distress) does not affect the application of that section after the relevant time in a case in which an individual gave notice in writing to a data controller under that section before the relevant time.

(2) In this paragraph, "the relevant time" means the time when the repeal of section 10 of the 1998 Act comes into force.

Right to prevent processing for purposes of direct marketing under the 1998 Act

4(1) The repeal of section 11 of the 1998 Act (right to prevent processing for purposes of direct marketing) does not affect the application of that section after the relevant time in a case in which an individual gave notice in writing to a data controller under that section before the relevant time.

(2) In this paragraph, "the relevant time" means the time when the repeal of section 11 of the 1998 Act comes into force.

Automated processing under the 1998 Act

5(1) The repeal of section 12 of the 1998 Act (rights in relation to automated decision-taking) does not affect the application of that section after the relevant time in relation to a decision taken by a person before that time if—

(a) in taking the decision the person failed to comply with section 12(1) of the 1998 Act, or

(b) at the relevant time—

(i) the person had not taken all of the steps required under section 12(2) or (3) of the 1998 Act, or

(ii) the period specified in section 12(2)(b) of the 1998 Act (for an individual to require a person to reconsider a decision) had not expired.

(2) In this paragraph, "the relevant time" means the time when the repeal of section 12 of the 1998 Act comes into force.

Compensation for contravention of the 1998 Act or Part 4 of the 2014 Regulations

6(1) The repeal of section 13 of the 1998 Act (compensation for failure to comply with certain requirements) does not affect the application of that section after the relevant time in relation to damage or distress suffered at any time by reason of an act or omission before the relevant time.

(2) The revocation of regulation 45 of the 2014 Regulations (right to compensation) does not affect the application of that regulation after the relevant time in relation to damage or distress suffered at any time by reason of an act or omission before the relevant time.

(3) "The relevant time" means—

(a) in sub-paragraph (1), the time when the repeal of section 13 of the 1998 Act comes into force;

(b) in sub-paragraph (2), the time when the revocation of regulation 45 of the 2014 Regulation comes into force.

Rectification, blocking, erasure and destruction under the 1998 Act

7(1) The repeal of section 14(1) to (3) and (6) of the 1998 Act (rectification, blocking, erasure and destruction of inaccurate personal data) does not affect the application of those provisions after the relevant time in a case in which an application was made under subsection (1) of that section before the relevant time.

(2) The repeal of section 14(4) to (6) of the 1998 Act (rectification, blocking, erasure and destruction: risk of further contravention in circumstances entitling data subject to compensation under section 13 of the 1998 Act) does not affect the application of those provisions after the relevant time in a case in which an application was made under subsection (4) of that section before the relevant time.

(3) In this paragraph, "the relevant time" means the time when the repeal of section 14 of the 1998 Act comes into force.

Jurisdiction and procedure under the 1998 Act

8 The repeal of section 15 of the 1998 Act (jurisdiction and procedure) does not affect the application of that section in connection with sections 7 to 14 of the 1998 Act as they have effect by virtue of this Schedule.

Exemptions under the 1998 Act

9(1) The repeal of Part 4 of the 1998 Act (exemptions) does not affect the application of that Part after the relevant time in connection with a provision of Part 2 of the 1998 Act as it has effect after that time by virtue of paragraphs 2 to 7 of this Schedule.

(2) The revocation of the relevant Orders, and the repeal mentioned in subparagraph (1), do not affect the application of the relevant Orders after the relevant time in connection with a provision of Part 2 of the 1998 Act as it has effect as described in sub-paragraph (1).

(3) In this paragraph—
　　"the relevant Orders" means—
　　　　(a) the Data Protection (Corporate Finance Exemption) Order 2000 (SI 2000/184);
　　　　(b) the Data Protection (Subject Access Modification) (Health) Order 2000 (SI 2000/413);
　　　　(c) the Data Protection (Subject Access Modification) (Education) Order 2000 (SI 2000/414);
　　　　(d) the Data Protection (Subject Access Modification) (Social Work) Order 2000 (SI 2000/415);
　　　　(e) the Data Protection (Crown Appointments) Order 2000 (SI 2000/416);
　　　　(f) Data Protection (Miscellaneous Subject Access Exemptions) Order 2000 (SI 2000/419);
　　　　(g) Data Protection (Designated Codes of Practice) (No 2) Order 2000 (SI 2000/1864);
　　"the relevant time" means the time when the repeal of the provision of Part 2 of the 1998 Act in question comes into force.

(4) As regards certificates issued under section 28(2) of the 1998 Act, see Part 5 of this Schedule.

Prohibition by this Act of requirement to produce relevant records

10(1) In Schedule 18 to this Act, references to a record obtained in the exercise of a data subject access right include a record obtained at any time in the exercise of a right under section 7 of the 1998 Act.

(2) In section 184 of this Act, references to a "relevant record" include a record which does not fall within the definition in Schedule 18 to this Act (read with sub-paragraph (1)) but which, immediately before the relevant time, was a "relevant record" for the purposes of section 56 of the 1998 Act.

(3) In this paragraph, "the relevant time" means the time when the repeal of section 56 of the 1998 Act comes into force.

Avoidance under this Act of certain contractual terms relating to health records

11 In section 185 of this Act, references to a record obtained in the exercise of a data subject access right include a record obtained at any time in the exercise of a right under section 7 of the 1998 Act.

—— NOTES ——

Defined terms		"the 2014 Regulations"	Sch 20, Pt 1, para 1(1)
"data controller"	Sch 20, Pt 1, para 1(1)		
"the 1998 Act"	Sch 20, Pt 1, para 1(1)		

PART 3
THE GDPR AND PART 2 OF THIS ACT

Exemptions from the GDPR: restrictions of rules in Articles 13 to 15 of the GDPR

12 In paragraph 20(2) of Schedule 2 to this Act (self-incrimination), the reference to an offence under this Act includes an offence under the 1998 Act or the 1984 Act.

Manual unstructured data held by FOI public authorities

13 Until the first regulations under section 24(8) of this Act come into force, "the appropriate maximum" for the purposes of that section is—

(a) where the controller is a public authority listed in Part 1 of Schedule 1 to the Freedom of Information Act 2000, £600, and

(b) otherwise, £450.

—— NOTES ——

Defined terms		"the 1998 Act"	Sch 20, Pt 1, para 1(1)
"the 1984 Act"	Sch 20, Pt 1, para 1(1)		

PART 4
LAW ENFORCEMENT AND INTELLIGENCE SERVICES PROCESSING

Logging

14(1) In relation to an automated processing system set up before 6 May 2016, subsections (1) to (3) of section 62 of this Act do not apply if and to the extent that compliance with them would involve disproportionate effort.

(2) Sub-paragraph (1) ceases to have effect at the beginning of 6 May 2023.

Regulation 50 of the 2014 Regulations (disapplication of the 1998 Act)

15 Nothing in this Schedule, read with the revocation of regulation 50 of the 2014

Regulations, has the effect of applying a provision of the 1998 Act to the processing of personal data to which Part 4 of the 2014 Regulations applies in a case in which that provision did not apply before the revocation of that regulation.

Maximum fee for data subject access requests to intelligence services

16   Until the first regulations under section 94(4)(b) of this Act come into force, the maximum amount of a fee that may be required by a controller under that section is £10.

——— NOTES ———

Defined terms				Sch 20, Pt 1, para 1(1)
"the 1998 Act"	Sch 20, Pt 1, para 1(1)	"personal data"		s 3(2), (14)(c)
"the 2014 Regulations"		"processing"		s 3(4), (14)(c)

PART 5
NATIONAL SECURITY CERTIFICATES

National security certificates: processing of personal data under the 1998 Act

17(1)   The repeal of section 28(2) to (12) of the 1998 Act does not affect the application of those provisions after the relevant time with respect to the processing of personal data to which the 1998 Act (including as it has effect by virtue of this Schedule) applies.

(2)   A certificate issued under section 28(2) of the 1998 Act continues to have effect after the relevant time with respect to the processing of personal data to which the 1998 Act (including as it has effect by virtue of this Schedule) applies.

(3)   Where a certificate continues to have effect under sub-paragraph (2) after the relevant time, it may be revoked or quashed in accordance with section 28 of the 1998 Act after the relevant time.

(4)   In this paragraph, "the relevant time" means the time when the repeal of section 28 of the 1998 Act comes into force.

National security certificates: processing of personal data under the 2018 Act

18(1)   This paragraph applies to a certificate issued under section 28(2) of the 1998 Act (an "old certificate") which has effect immediately before the relevant time.

(2)   If and to the extent that the old certificate provides protection with respect to personal data which corresponds to protection that could be provided by a certificate issued under section 27, 79 or 111 of this Act, the old certificate also has effect to that extent after the relevant time as if—

(a)   it were a certificate issued under one or more of sections 27, 79 and 111 (as the case may be),

(b)   it provided protection in respect of that personal data in relation to the corresponding provisions of this Act or the applied GDPR, and

(c)   where it has effect as a certificate issued under section 79, it certified that each restriction in question is a necessary and proportionate measure to protect national security.

(3)   Where an old certificate also has effect as if it were a certificate issued under one or more of sections 27, 79 and 111, that section has, or those sections have, effect accordingly in relation to the certificate.

(4)   Where an old certificate has an extended effect because of sub-paragraph (2), section 130

of this Act does not apply in relation to it.

(5) An old certificate that has an extended effect because of sub-paragraph (2) provides protection only with respect to the processing of personal data that occurs during the period of 1 year beginning with the relevant time (and a Minister of the Crown may curtail that protection by wholly or partly revoking the old certificate).

(6) For the purposes of this paragraph—

    (a) a reference to the protection provided by a certificate issued under—

        (i) section 28(2) of the 1998 Act, or

        (ii) section 27, 79 or 111 of this Act,

    is a reference to the effect of the evidence that is provided by the certificate;

    (b) protection provided by a certificate under section 28(2) of the 1998 Act is to be regarded as corresponding to protection that could be provided by a certificate under section 27, 79 or 111 of this Act where, in respect of provision in the 1998 Act to which the certificate under section 28(2) relates, there is corresponding provision in this Act or the applied GDPR to which a certificate under section 27, 79 or 111 could relate.

(7) In this paragraph, "the relevant time" means the time when the repeal of section 28 of the 1998 Act comes into force.

——— Notes ———

Defined terms		"Minister of the Crown"	s 205(1)
"the 1998 Act"	Sch 20, Pt 1, para 1(1)	"personal data"	s 3(2), (14)(c)
"the applied GDPR"	s 3(11)	"processing"	s 3(4), (14)(c)

PART 6
The Information Commissioner

Appointment etc

19(1) On and after the relevant day, the individual who was the Commissioner immediately before that day—

    (a) continues to be the Commissioner,

    (b) is to be treated as having been appointed under Schedule 12 to this Act, and

    (c) holds office for the period—

        (i) beginning with the relevant day, and

        (ii) lasting for 7 years less a period equal to the individual's precommencement term.

(2) On and after the relevant day, a resolution passed by the House of Commons for the purposes of paragraph 3 of Schedule 5 to the 1998 Act (salary and pension of Commissioner), and not superseded before that day, is to be treated as having been passed for the purposes of paragraph 4 of Schedule 12 to this Act.

(3) In this paragraph—

    "pre-commencement term", in relation to an individual, means the period during which the individual was the Commissioner before the relevant day;

    "the relevant day" means the day on which Schedule 12 to this Act comes into force.

Accounts

20(1) The repeal of paragraph 10 of Schedule 5 to the 1998 Act does not affect the duties of the Commissioner and the Comptroller and Auditor General under that paragraph in respect of the Commissioner's statement of account for the financial year beginning with 1 April 2017.

(2) The Commissioner's duty under paragraph 11 of Schedule 12 to this Act to prepare a statement of account for each financial year includes a duty to do so for the financial year beginning with 1 April 2018.

Annual report

21(1) The repeal of section 52(1) of the 1998 Act (annual report) does not affect the Commissioner's duty under that subsection to produce a general report on the exercise of the Commissioner's functions under the 1998 Act during the period of 1 year beginning with 1 April 2017 and to lay it before Parliament.

(2) The repeal of section 49 of the Freedom of Information Act 2000 (annual report) does not affect the Commissioner's duty under that section to produce a general report on the exercise of the Commissioner's functions under that Act during the period of 1 year beginning with 1 April 2017 and to lay it before Parliament.

(3) The first report produced by the Commissioner under section 139 of this Act must relate to the period of 1 year beginning with 1 April 2018.

Fees etc received by the Commissioner

22(1) The repeal of Schedule 5 to the 1998 Act (Information Commissioner) does not affect the application of paragraph 9 of that Schedule after the relevant time to amounts received by the Commissioner before the relevant time.

(2) In this paragraph, "the relevant time" means the time when the repeal of Schedule 5 to the 1998 Act comes into force.

23 Paragraph 10 of Schedule 12 to this Act applies only to amounts received by the Commissioner after the time when that Schedule comes into force.

Functions in connection with the Data Protection Convention

24(1) The repeal of section 54(2) of the 1998 Act (functions to be discharged by the Commissioner for the purposes of Article 13 of the Data Protection Convention), and the revocation of the Data Protection (Functions of Designated Authority) Order 2000 (SI 2000/186), do not affect the application of articles 1 to 5 of that Order after the relevant time in relation to a request described in those articles which was made before that time.

(2) The references in paragraph 9 of Schedule 14 to this Act (Data Protection Convention: restrictions on use of information) to requests made or received by the Commissioner under paragraph 6 or 7 of that Schedule include a request made or received by the Commissioner under article 3 or 4 of the Data Protection (Functions of Designated Authority) Order 2000 (SI 2000/ 186).

(3) The repeal of section 54(7) of the 1998 Act (duty to notify the European Commission of certain approvals and authorisations) does not affect the application of that provision after the relevant time in relation to an approval or authorisation granted before the relevant time.

(4) In this paragraph, "the relevant time" means the time when the repeal of section 54 of the 1998 Act comes into force.

Co-operation with the European Commission: transfers of personal data outside the EEA

25(1) The repeal of section 54(3) of the 1998 Act (co-operation by the Commissioner with the European Commission etc), and the revocation of the Data Protection (International Co-operation) Order 2000 (SI 2000/190), do not affect the application of articles 1 to 4 of that Order after the relevant time in relation to transfers that took place before the relevant time.

(2) In this paragraph—

"the relevant time" means the time when the repeal of section 54 of the 1998 Act comes into force;

"transfer" has the meaning given in article 2 of the Data Protection (International Co-operation) Order 2000 (SI 2000/190).

Charges payable to the Commissioner by controllers

26(1) The Data Protection (Charges and Information) Regulations 2018 (SI 2018/ 480) have effect after the relevant time (until revoked) as if they were made under section 137 of this Act.

(2) In this paragraph, "the relevant time" means the time when section 137 of this Act comes into force.

Requests for assessment

27(1) The repeal of section 42 of the 1998 Act (requests for assessment) does not affect the application of that section after the relevant time in a case in which the Commissioner received a request under that section before the relevant time, subject to sub-paragraph (2).

(2) The Commissioner is only required to make an assessment of acts and omissions that took place before the relevant time.

(3) In this paragraph, "the relevant time" means the time when the repeal of section 42 of the 1998 Act comes into force.

Codes of practice

28(1) The repeal of section 52E of the 1998 Act (effect of codes of practice) does not affect the application of that section after the relevant time in relation to legal proceedings or to the exercise of the Commissioner's functions under the 1998 Act as it has effect by virtue of this Schedule.

(2) In section 52E of the 1998 Act, as it has effect by virtue of this paragraph, the references to the 1998 Act include that Act as it has effect by virtue of this Schedule.

(3) For the purposes of subsection (3) of that section, as it has effect by virtue of this paragraph, the data-sharing code and direct marketing code in force immediately before the relevant time are to be treated as having continued in force after that time.

(4) In this paragraph—

"the data-sharing code" and "the direct marketing code" mean the codes respectively prepared under sections 52A and 52AA of the 1998 Act and issued under section 52B(5) of that Act;

"the relevant time" means the time when the repeal of section 52E of the 1998 Act comes into force.

—— NOTES ——

Defined terms   "the Commissioner"   s 3(8)
   "the 1998 Act"   Sch 20, Pt 1, para 1(1)

PART 7
ENFORCEMENT ETC UNDER THE 1998 ACT

Interpretation of this Part

29(1) In this Part of this Schedule, references to contravention of the sixth data protection principle sections are to relevant contravention of any of sections 7, 10, 11 or 12 of the 1998 Act, as they continue to have effect by virtue of this Schedule after their repeal (and references to compliance with the sixth data protection principle sections are to be read accordingly).

(2) In sub-paragraph (1), "relevant contravention" means contravention in a manner described in paragraph 8 of Part 2 of Schedule 1 to the 1998 Act (sixth data protection principle).

Information notices

30(1) The repeal of section 43 of the 1998 Act (information notices) does not affect the application of that section after the relevant time in a case in which—

   (a) the Commissioner served a notice under that section before the relevant time (and did not cancel it before that time), or

   (b) the Commissioner requires information after the relevant time for the purposes of—

      (i) responding to a request made under section 42 of the 1998 Act before that time,

      (ii) determining whether a data controller complied with the old data protection principles before that time, or

      (iii) determining whether a data controller complied with the sixth data protection principle sections after that time.

(2) In section 43 of the 1998 Act, as it has effect by virtue of this paragraph—

   (a) the reference to an offence under section 47 of the 1998 Act includes an offence under section 144 of this Act, and

   (b) the references to an offence under the 1998 Act include an offence under this Act.

(3) In this paragraph, "the relevant time" means the time when the repeal of section 43 of the 1998 Act comes into force.

Special information notices

31(1) The repeal of section 44 of the 1998 Act (special information notices) does not affect the application of that section after the relevant time in a case in which—

   (a) the Commissioner served a notice under that section before the relevant time (and did not cancel it before that time), or

   (b) the Commissioner requires information after the relevant time for the purposes of—

      (i) responding to a request made under section 42 of the 1998 Act before that time, or

      (ii) ascertaining whether section 44(2)(a) or (b) of the 1998 Act was satisfied before that time.

(2) In section 44 of the 1998 Act, as it has effect by virtue of this paragraph—

  (a) the reference to an offence under section 47 of the 1998 Act includes an offence under section 144 of this Act, and

  (b) the references to an offence under the 1998 Act include an offence under this Act.

(3) In this paragraph, "the relevant time" means the time when the repeal of section 44 of the 1998 Act comes into force.

Assessment notices

32(1) The repeal of sections 41A and 41B of the 1998 Act (assessment notices) does not affect the application of those sections after the relevant time in a case in which—

  (a) the Commissioner served a notice under section 41A of the 1998 Act before the relevant time (and did not cancel it before that time), or

  (b) the Commissioner considers it appropriate, after the relevant time, to investigate—

    (i) whether a data controller complied with the old data protection principles before that time, or

    (ii) whether a data controller complied with the sixth data protection principle sections after that time.

(2) The revocation of the Data Protection (Assessment Notices) (Designation of National Health Service Bodies) Order 2014 (SI 2014/3282), and the repeals mentioned in sub-paragraph (1), do not affect the application of that Order in a case described in sub-paragraph (1).

(3) Sub-paragraph (1) does not enable the Secretary of State, after the relevant time, to make an order under section 41A(2)(b) or (c) of the 1998 Act (data controllers on whom an assessment notice may be served) designating a public authority or person for the purposes of that section.

(4) Section 41A of the 1998 Act, as it has effect by virtue of sub-paragraph (1), has effect as if subsections (8) and (11) (duty to review designation orders) were omitted.

(5) The repeal of section 41C of the 1998 Act (code of practice about assessment notice) does not affect the application, after the relevant time, of the code issued under that section and in force immediately before the relevant time in relation to the exercise of the Commissioner's functions under and in connection with section 41A of the 1998 Act, as it has effect by virtue of subparagraph (1).

(6) In this paragraph, "the relevant time" means the time when the repeal of section 41A of the 1998 Act comes into force.

Enforcement notices

33(1) The repeal of sections 40 and 41 of the 1998 Act (enforcement notices) does not affect the application of those sections after the relevant time in a case in which—

  (a) the Commissioner served a notice under section 40 of the 1998 Act before the relevant time (and did not cancel it before that time), or

  (b) the Commissioner is satisfied, after that time, that a data controller —

    (i) contravened the old data protection principles before that time, or

    (ii) contravened the sixth data protection principle sections after that time.

(2) In this paragraph, "the relevant time" means the time when the repeal of section 40 of

the 1998 Act comes into force.

Determination by Commissioner as to the special purposes

34(1) The repeal of section 45 of the 1998 Act (determination by Commissioner as to the special purposes) does not affect the application of that section after the relevant time in a case in which—

    (a) the Commissioner made a determination under that section before the relevant time, or

    (b) the Commissioner considers it appropriate, after the relevant time, to make a determination under that section.

  (2) In this paragraph, "the relevant time" means the time when the repeal of section 45 of the 1998 Act comes into force.

Restriction on enforcement in case of processing for the special purposes

35(1) The repeal of section 46 of the 1998 Act (restriction on enforcement in case of processing for the special purposes) does not affect the application of that section after the relevant time in relation to an enforcement notice or information notice served under the 1998 Act—

    (a) before the relevant time, or

    (b) after the relevant time in reliance on this Schedule.

  (2) In this paragraph, "the relevant time" means the time when the repeal of section 46 of the 1998 Act comes into force.

Offences

36(1) The repeal of sections 47, 60 and 61 of the 1998 Act (offences of failing to comply with certain notices and of providing false information etc in response to a notice) does not affect the application of those sections after the relevant time in connection with an information notice, special information notice or enforcement notice served under Part 5 of the 1998 Act—

    (a) before the relevant time, or

    (b) after that time in reliance on this Schedule.

  (2) In this paragraph, "the relevant time" means the time when the repeal of section 47 of the 1998 Act comes into force.

Powers of entry

37(1) The repeal of sections 50, 60 and 61 of, and Schedule 9 to, the 1998 Act (powers of entry) does not affect the application of those provisions after the relevant time in a case in which—

    (a) a warrant issued under that Schedule was in force immediately before the relevant time,

    (b) before the relevant time, the Commissioner supplied information on oath for the purposes of obtaining a warrant under that Schedule but that had not been considered by a circuit judge or a District Judge (Magistrates' Courts), or

    (c) after the relevant time, the Commissioner supplies information on oath to a circuit judge or a District Judge (Magistrates' Courts) in respect of—

        (i) a contravention of the old data protection principles before the relevant time;

        (ii) a contravention of the sixth data protection principle sections after the relevant time;

(iii) the commission of an offence under a provision of the 1998 Act (including as the provision has effect by virtue of this Schedule);

(iv) a failure to comply with a requirement imposed by an assessment notice issued under section 41A the 1998 Act (including as it has effect by virtue of this Schedule).

(2) In paragraph 16 of Schedule 9 to the 1998 Act, as it has effect by virtue of this paragraph, the reference to an offence under paragraph 12 of that Schedule includes an offence under paragraph 15 of Schedule 15 to this Act.

(3) In this paragraph, "the relevant time" means the time when the repeal of Schedule 9 to the 1998 Act comes into force.

(4) Paragraphs 14 and 15 of Schedule 9 to the 1998 Act (application of that Schedule to Scotland and Northern Ireland) apply for the purposes of this paragraph as they apply for the purposes of that Schedule.

Monetary penalties

38(1) The repeal of sections 55A, 55B, 55D and 55E of the 1998 Act (monetary penalties) does not affect the application of those provisions after the relevant time in a case in which—

(a) the Commissioner served a monetary penalty notice under section 55A of the 1998 Act before the relevant time,

(b) the Commissioner served a notice of intent under section 55B of the 1998 Act before the relevant time, or

(c) the Commissioner considers it appropriate, after the relevant time, to serve a notice mentioned in paragraph (a) or (b) in respect of—

(i) a contravention of section 4(4) of the 1998 Act before the relevant time, or

(ii) a contravention of the sixth data protection principle sections after the relevant time.

(2) The revocation of the relevant subordinate legislation, and the repeals mentioned in sub-paragraph (1), do not affect the application of the relevant subordinate legislation (or of provisions of the 1998 Act applied by them) after the relevant time in a case described in sub-paragraph (1).

(3) Guidance issued under section 55C of the 1998 Act (guidance about monetary penalty notices) which is in force immediately before the relevant time continues in force after that time for the purposes of the Commissioner's exercise of functions under sections 55A and 55B of the 1998 Act as they have effect by virtue of this paragraph.

(4) In this paragraph—
"the relevant subordinate legislation" means—

(a) the Data Protection (Monetary Penalties) (Maximum Penalty and Notices) Regulations 2010 (SI 2010/31);

(b) the Data Protection (Monetary Penalties) Order 2010 (SI 2010/910);
"the relevant time" means the time when the repeal of section 55A of the 1998 Act comes into force.

Appeals

39(1) The repeal of sections 48 and 49 of the 1998 Act (appeals) does not affect the application of those sections after the relevant time in relation to a notice served under the 1998 Act or a determination made under section 45 of that Act—

   (a) before the relevant time, or

   (b) after that time in reliance on this Schedule.

(2) In this paragraph, "the relevant time" means the time when the repeal of section 48 of the 1998 Act comes into force.

Exemptions

40(1) The repeal of section 28 of the 1998 Act (national security) does not affect the application of that section after the relevant time for the purposes of a provision of Part 5 of the 1998 Act as it has effect after that time by virtue of the preceding paragraphs of this Part of this Schedule.

(2) In this paragraph, "the relevant time" means the time when the repeal of the provision of Part 5 of the 1998 Act in question comes into force.

(3) As regards certificates issued under section 28(2) of the 1998 Act, see Part 5 of this Schedule.

Tribunal Procedure Rules

41(1) The repeal of paragraph 7 of Schedule 6 to the 1998 Act (Tribunal Procedure Rules) does not affect the application of that paragraph, or of rules made under that paragraph, after the relevant time in relation to the exercise of rights of appeal conferred by section 28 or 48 of the 1998 Act, as they have effect by virtue of this Schedule.

(2) Part 3 of Schedule 19 to this Act does not apply for the purposes of Tribunal Procedure Rules made under paragraph 7(1)(a) of Schedule 6 to the 1998 Act as they apply, after the relevant time, in relation to the exercise of rights of appeal described in sub-paragraph (1).

(3) In this paragraph, "the relevant time" means the time when the repeal of paragraph 7 of Schedule 6 to the 1998 Act comes into force.

Obstruction etc

42(1) The repeal of paragraph 8 of Schedule 6 to the 1998 Act (obstruction etc in proceedings before the Tribunal) does not affect the application of that paragraph after the relevant time in relation to an act or omission in relation to proceedings under the 1998 Act (including as it has effect by virtue of this Schedule).

(2) In this paragraph, "the relevant time" means the time when the repeal of paragraph 8 of Schedule 6 to the 1998 Act comes into force.

Enforcement etc under the 2014 Regulations

43(1) The references in the preceding paragraphs of this Part of this Schedule to provisions of the 1998 Act include those provisions as applied, with modifications, by regulation 51 of the 2014 Regulations (other functions of the Commissioner).

(2) The revocation of regulation 51 of the 2014 Regulations does not affect the application of those provisions of the 1998 Act (as so applied) as described in those paragraphs.

—— Notes ——

Defined terms		"the Commissioner"	s 3(8)
"the 1998 Act"	Sch 20, Pt 1, para 1(1)	"data controller"	Sch 20, Pt 1, para 1(1)
"the 2014 Regulations"		"the old data protection principles"	
	Sch 20, Pt 1, para 1(1)		Sch 20, Pt 1, para 1(1)

PART 8
ENFORCEMENT ETC UNDER THIS ACT

Information notices

44 In section 143 of this Act—

    (a) the reference to an offence under section 144 of this Act includes an offence under section 47 of the 1998 Act (including as it has effect by virtue of this Schedule), and

    (b) the references to an offence under this Act include an offence under the 1998 Act (including as it has effect by virtue of this Schedule) or the 1984 Act.

Powers of entry

45 In paragraph 16 of Schedule 15 to this Act (powers of entry: self-incrimination), the reference to an offence under paragraph 15 of that Schedule includes an offence under paragraph 12 of Schedule 9 to the 1998 Act (including as it has effect by virtue of this Schedule).

Tribunal Procedure Rules

46(1) Tribunal Procedure Rules made under paragraph 7(1)(a) of Schedule 6 to the 1998 Act (appeal rights under the 1998 Act) and in force immediately before the relevant time have effect after that time as if they were also made under section 203 of this Act.

  (2) In this paragraph, "the relevant time" means the time when the repeal of paragraph 7(1)(a) of Schedule 6 to the 1998 Act comes into force.

—— NOTES ——

Defined terms   "the 1998 Act"   Sch 20, Pt 1, para 1(1)
    "the 1984 Act"   Sch 20, Pt 1, para 1(1)

PART 9
OTHER ENACTMENTS

Powers to disclose information to the Commissioner

47(1) The following provisions (as amended by Schedule 19 to this Act) have effect after the relevant time as if the matters they refer to included a matter in respect of which the Commissioner could exercise a power conferred by a provision of Part 5 of the 1998 Act, as it has effect by virtue of this Schedule—

    (a) section 11AA(1)(a) of the Parliamentary Commissioner Act 1967 (disclosure of information by Parliamentary Commissioner);

    (b) sections 33A(1)(a) and 34O(1)(a) of the Local Government Act 1974 (disclosure of information by Local Commissioner);

    (c) section 18A(1)(a) of the Health Service Commissioners Act 1993 (disclosure of information by Health Service Commissioner);

    (d) paragraph 1 of the entry for the Information Commissioner in Schedule 5 to the Scottish Public Services Ombudsman Act 2002 (asp11) (disclosure of information by the Ombudsman);

    (e) section 34X(3)(a) of the Public Services Ombudsman (Wales) Act 2005 (disclosure of information by the Ombudsman);

    (f) section 18(6)(a) of the Commissioner for Older People (Wales) Act 2006 (disclosure of information by the Commissioner);

    (g) section 22(3)(a) of the Welsh Language (Wales) Measure 2011 (nawm 1) (disclosure of information by the Welsh Language Commissioner);

    (h) section 49(3)(a) of the Public Services Ombudsman Act (Northern Ireland) 2016

(c. 4 (NI)) (disclosure of information by the Ombudsman);

   (i)   section 44(3)(a) of the Justice Act (Northern Ireland) 2016 (c. 21 (NI)) (disclosure of information by the Prison Ombudsman for Northern Ireland).

(2)   The following provisions (as amended by Schedule 19 to this Act) have effect after the relevant time as if the offences they refer to included an offence under any provision of the 1998 Act other than paragraph 12 of Schedule 9 to that Act (obstruction of execution of warrant)—

   (a)   section 11AA(1)(b) of the Parliamentary Commissioner Act 1967;

   (b)   sections 33A(1)(b) and 34O(1)(b) of the Local Government Act 1974;

   (c)   section 18A(1)(b) of the Health Service Commissioners Act 1993;

   (d)   paragraph 2 of the entry for the Information Commissioner in Schedule 5 to the Scottish Public Services Ombudsman Act 2002 (asp 11);

   (e)   section 34X(5) of the Public Services Ombudsman (Wales) Act 2005 (disclosure of information by the Ombudsman);

   (f)   section 18(8) of the Commissioner for Older People (Wales) Act 2006;

   (g)   section 22(5) of the Welsh Language (Wales) Measure 2011 (nawm 1);

   (h)   section 49(5) of the Public Services Ombudsman Act (Northern Ireland) 2016 (c. 4 (NI));

   (i)   section 44(3)(b) of the Justice Act (Northern Ireland) 2016 (c. 21 (NI)).

(3)   In this paragraph, "the relevant time", in relation to a provision of a section or Schedule listed in sub-paragraph (1) or (2), means the time when the amendment of the section or Schedule by Schedule 19 to this Act comes into force.

Codes etc required to be consistent with the Commissioner's data-sharing code

48(1)   This paragraph applies in relation to the code of practice issued under each of the following provisions—

   (a)   section 19AC of the Registration Service Act 1953 (code of practice about disclosure of information by civil registration officials);

   (b)   section 43 of the Digital Economy Act 2017 (code of practice about disclosure of information to improve public service delivery);

   (c)   section 52 of that Act (code of practice about disclosure of information to reduce debt owed to the public sector);

   (d)   section 60 of that Act (code of practice about disclosure of information to combat fraud against the public sector);

   (e)   section 70 of that Act (code of practice about disclosure of information for research purposes).

(2)   During the relevant period, the code of practice does not have effect to the extent that it is inconsistent with the code of practice prepared under section 121 of this Act (data-sharing code) and issued under section 125(4) of this Act (as altered or replaced from time to time).

(3)   In this paragraph, "the relevant period", in relation to a code issued under a section mentioned in sub-paragraph (1), means the period—

   (a)   beginning when the amendments of that section in Schedule 19 to this Act come into force, and

   (b)   ending when the code is first reissued under that section.

49(1)   This paragraph applies in relation to the original statement published under section 45E of the Statistics and Registration Service Act 2007 (statement of principles and procedures in connection with access to information by the Statistics Board).

(2) During the relevant period, the statement does not have effect to the extent that it is inconsistent with the code of practice prepared under section 121 of this Act (data-sharing code) and issued under section 125(4) of this Act (as altered or replaced from time to time).

(3) In this paragraph, "the relevant period" means the period—

    (a) beginning when the amendments of section 45E of the Statistics and Registration Service Act 2007 in Schedule 19 to this Act come into force, and

    (b) ending when the first revised statement is published under that section.

Consumer Credit Act 1974

50 In section 159(1)(a) of the Consumer Credit Act 1974 (correction of wrong information) (as amended by Schedule 19 to this Act), the reference to information given under Article 15(1) to (3) of the GDPR includes information given at any time under section 7 of the 1998 Act.

Freedom of Information Act 2000

51 Paragraphs 52 to 55 make provision about the Freedom of Information Act 2000 ("the 2000 Act").

52(1) This paragraph applies where a request for information was made to a public authority under the 2000 Act before the relevant time.

(2) To the extent that the request is dealt with after the relevant time, the amendments of sections 2 and 40 of the 2000 Act in Schedule 19 to this Act have effect for the purposes of determining whether the authority deals with the request in accordance with Part 1 of the 2000 Act.

(3) To the extent that the request was dealt with before the relevant time—

    (a) the amendments of sections 2 and 40 of the 2000 Act in Schedule 19 to this Act do not have effect for the purposes of determining whether the authority dealt with the request in accordance with Part 1 of the 2000 Act, but

    (b) the powers of the Commissioner and the Tribunal, on an application or appeal under the 2000 Act, do not include power to require the authority to take steps which it would not be required to take in order to comply with Part 1 of the 2000 Act as amended by Schedule 19 to this Act.

(4) In this paragraph—

    "public authority" has the same meaning as in the 2000 Act;

    "the relevant time" means the time when the amendments of sections 2 and 40 of the 2000 Act in Schedule 19 to this Act come into force.

53(1) Tribunal Procedure Rules made under paragraph 7(1)(b) of Schedule 6 to the 1998 Act (appeal rights under the 2000 Act) and in force immediately before the relevant time have effect after that time as if they were also made under section 61 of the 2000 Act (as inserted by Schedule 19 to this Act).

(2) In this paragraph, "the relevant time" means the time when the repeal of paragraph 7(1)(b) of Schedule 6 to the 1998 Act comes into force.

54(1) The repeal of paragraph 8 of Schedule 6 to the 1998 Act (obstruction etc in proceedings before the Tribunal) does not affect the application of that paragraph after the relevant time in relation to an act or omission before that time in relation to an appeal under the 2000 Act.

(2) In this paragraph, "the relevant time" means the time when the repeal of paragraph 8 of Schedule 6 to the 1998 Act comes into force.

55(1) The amendment of section 77 of the 2000 Act in Schedule 19 to this Act (offence of altering etc record with intent to prevent disclosure: omission of reference to section 7 of the 1998 Act) does not affect the application of that section after the relevant time in relation to a case in which—

(a) the request for information mentioned in section 77(1) of the 2000 Act was made before the relevant time, and

(b) when the request was made, section 77(1)(b) of the 2000 Act was satisfied by virtue of section 7 of the 1998 Act.

(2) In this paragraph, "the relevant time" means the time when the repeal of section 7 of the 1998 Act comes into force.

Freedom of Information (Scotland) Act 2002

56(1) This paragraph applies where a request for information was made to a Scottish public authority under the Freedom of Information (Scotland) Act 2002 ("the 2002 Act") before the relevant time.

(2) To the extent that the request is dealt with after the relevant time, the amendments of the 2002 Act in Schedule 19 to this Act have effect for the purposes of determining whether the authority deals with the request in accordance with Part 1 of the 2002 Act.

(3) To the extent that the request was dealt with before the relevant time—

(a) the amendments of the 2002 Act in Schedule 19 to this Act do not have effect for the purposes of determining whether the authority dealt with the request in accordance with Part 1 of the 2002 Act, but

(b) the powers of the Scottish Information Commissioner and the Court of Session, on an application or appeal under the 2002 Act, do not include power to require the authority to take steps which it would not be required to take in order to comply with Part 1 of the 2002 Act as amended by Schedule 19 to this Act.

(4) In this paragraph—
"Scottish public authority" has the same meaning as in the 2002 Act; "the relevant time" means the time when the amendments of the 2002 Act in Schedule 19 to this Act come into force.

Access to Health Records (Northern Ireland) Order 1993 (SI 1993/1250 (NI 4))

57 Until the first regulations under Article 5(4)(a) of the Access to Health Records (Northern Ireland) Order 1993 (as amended by Schedule 19 to this Act) come into force, the maximum amount of a fee that may be required for giving access under that Article is £10.

Privacy and Electronic Communications (EC Directive) Regulations 2003 (SI 2003/2450)

58(1) The repeal of a provision of the 1998 Act does not affect its operation for the purposes of the Privacy and Electronic Communications (EC Directive) Regulations 2003 ("the PECR 2003") (see regulations 2, 31 and 31B of, and Schedule 1 to, those Regulations).

(2) Where subordinate legislation made under a provision of the 1998 Act is in force immediately before the repeal of that provision, neither the revocation of the subordinate legislation nor the repeal of the provision of the 1998 Act affect the application of the subordinate legislation for the purposes of the PECR 2003 after that time.

(3) Part 3 of Schedule 19 to this Act (modifications) does not have effect in relation to the PECR 2003.

(4) Part 7 of this Schedule does not have effect in relation to the provisions of the 1998 Act as applied by the PECR 2003.

Health and Personal Social Services (Quality, Improvement and Regulation) (Northern Ireland) Order 2003 (SI 2003/431 (NI 9))

59 Part 3 of Schedule 19 to this Act (modifications) does not have effect in relation to the reference to an accessible record within the meaning of section 68 of the 1998 Act in Article 43 of the Health and Personal Social Services (Quality, Improvement and Regulation) (Northern Ireland) Order 2003.

Environmental Information Regulations 2004 (SI 2004/3391)

60(1) This paragraph applies where a request for information was made to a public authority under the Environmental Information Regulations 2004 ("the 2004 Regulations") before the relevant time.

(2) To the extent that the request is dealt with after the relevant time, the amendments of the 2004 Regulations in Schedule 19 to this Act have effect for the purposes of determining whether the authority deals with the request in accordance with Parts 2 and 3 of those Regulations.

(3) To the extent that the request was dealt with before the relevant time—

(a) the amendments of the 2004 Regulations in Schedule 19 to this Act do not have effect for the purposes of determining whether the authority dealt with the request in accordance with Parts 2 and 3 of those Regulations, but

(b) the powers of the Commissioner and the Tribunal, on an application or appeal under the 2000 Act (as applied by the 2004 Regulations), do not include power to require the authority to take steps which it would not be required to take in order to comply with Parts 2 and 3 of those Regulations as amended by Schedule 19 to this Act.

(4) In this paragraph—

"public authority" has the same meaning as in the 2004 Regulations; "the relevant time" means the time when the amendments of the 2004 Regulations in Schedule 19 to this Act come into force.

Environmental Information (Scotland) Regulations 2004 (SSI 2004/520)

61(1) This paragraph applies where a request for information was made to a Scottish public authority under the Environmental Information (Scotland) Regulations 2004 ("the 2004 Regulations") before the relevant time.

(2) To the extent that the request is dealt with after the relevant time, the amendments of the 2004 Regulations in Schedule 19 to this Act have effect for the purposes of determining

whether the authority deals with the request in accordance with those Regulations.

(3) To the extent that the request was dealt with before the relevant time—

    (a) the amendments of the 2004 Regulations in Schedule 19 to this Act do not have effect for the purposes of determining whether the authority dealt with the request in accordance with those Regulations, but

    (b) the powers of the Scottish Information Commissioner and the Court of Session, on an application or appeal under the 2002 Act (as applied by the 2004 Regulations), do not include power to require the authority to take steps which it would not be required to take in order to comply with those Regulations as amended by Schedule 19 to this Act.

(4) In this paragraph—

    "Scottish public authority" has the same meaning as in the 2004 Regulations;

    "the relevant time" means the time when the amendments of the 2004 Regulations in Schedule 19 to this Act come into force.

—— Notes ——

Defined terms				
"the 1998 Act"	Sch 20, Pt 1, para 1(1)	"the Commissioner"		s 3(8)
		"the Tribunal"		s 205(1)

General Data Protection Regulation

This table of contents is not part of the official text

CONTENTS

RECITALS

CHAPTER I – GENERAL PROVISIONS

CHAPTER II – PRINCIPLES

CHAPTER III – RIGHTS OF THE DATA SUBJECT

Section 1 – Transparency & Modalities

Section 2 – Information & Access to Personal Data

Section 3 – Rectification & Erasure

Section 4 – Right to Object and Automated Individual Decision-Making

Chapter IV – Controller and Processor

Chapter V – Transfers of Personal data to Third Countries or International Organisations

Chapter VI – Independent Supervisory Authorities

**REGULATION (EU) 2016/679 OF THE EUROPEAN
PARLIAMENT AND OF THE COUNCIL
of 27 April 2016
on the protection of natural persons with regard to the processing
of personal data and on the free movement of such data,
and repealing Directive 95/46/EC (General Data Protection Regulation)**

THE EUROPEAN PARLIAMENT AND THE COUNCIL OF THE EUROPEAN UNION,

Having regard to the Treaty on the Functioning of the European Union, and in particular Article 16 thereof,

Having regard to the proposal from the European Commission,

After transmission of the draft legislative act to the national parliaments,

Having regard to the opinion of the European Economic and Social Committee,

Having regard to the opinion of the Committee of the Regions,

Acting in accordance with the ordinary legislative procedure,

Whereas:

(1)   The protection of natural persons in relation to the processing of personal data is a fundamental right. Article 8(1) of the Charter of Fundamental Rights of the European Union (the 'Charter') and Article 16(1) of the Treaty on the Functioning of the European Union (TFEU) provide that everyone has the right to the protection of personal data concerning him or her.

(2)   The principles of, and rules on the protection of natural persons with regard to the processing of their personal data should, whatever their nationality or residence, respect their fundamental rights and freedoms, in particular their right to the protection of personal data. This Regulation is intended to contribute to the accomplishment of an area of freedom, security and justice and of an economic union, to economic and social progress, to the strengthening and the convergence of the economies within the internal market, and to the well-being of natural persons.

(3)   Directive 95/46/EC of the European Parliament and of the Council seeks to harmonise the protection of fundamental rights and freedoms of natural persons in respect of processing activities and to ensure the free flow of personal data between Member States.

(4)   The processing of personal data should be designed to serve mankind. The right to the protection of personal data is not an absolute right; it must be considered in relation to its function in society and be balanced against other fundamental rights, in accordance with the principle of proportionality. This Regulation respects all fundamental rights and observes the freedoms and principles recognised in the Charter as enshrined in the Treaties, in particular the respect for private and family life, home and communications, the protection of personal data, freedom of thought, conscience and religion, freedom of

expression and information, freedom to conduct a business, the right to an effective remedy and to a fair trial, and cultural, religious and linguistic diversity.

(5) The economic and social integration resulting from the functioning of the internal market has led to a substantial increase in cross-border flows of personal data. The exchange of personal data between public and private actors, including natural persons, associations and undertakings across the Union has increased. National authorities in the Member States are being called upon by Union law to cooperate and exchange personal data so as to be able to perform their duties or carry out tasks on behalf of an authority in another Member State.

(6) Rapid technological developments and globalisation have brought new challenges for the protection of personal data. The scale of the collection and sharing of personal data has increased significantly. Technology allows both private companies and public authorities to make use of personal data on an unprecedented scale in order to pursue their activities. Natural persons increasingly make personal information available publicly and globally. Technology has transformed both the economy and social life, and should further facilitate the free flow of personal data within the Union and the transfer to third countries and international organisations, while ensuring a high level of the protection of personal data.

(7) Those developments require a strong and more coherent data protection framework in the Union, backed by strong enforcement, given the importance of creating the trust that will allow the digital economy to develop across the internal market. Natural persons should have control of their own personal data. Legal and practical certainty for natural persons, economic operators and public authorities should be enhanced.

(8) Where this Regulation provides for specifications or restrictions of its rules by Member State law, Member States may, as far as necessary for coherence and for making the national provisions comprehensible to the persons to whom they apply, incorporate elements of this Regulation into their national law.

(9) The objectives and principles of Directive 95/46/EC remain sound, but it has not prevented fragmentation in the implementation of data protection across the Union, legal uncertainty or a widespread public perception that there are significant risks to the protection of natural persons, in particular with regard to online activity. Differences in the level of protection of the rights and freedoms of natural persons, in particular the right to the protection of personal data, with regard to the processing of personal data in the Member States may prevent the free flow of personal data throughout the Union. Those differences may therefore constitute an obstacle to the pursuit of economic activities at the level of the Union, distort competition and impede authorities in the discharge of their responsibilities under Union law. Such a difference in levels of protection is due to the existence of differences in the implementation and application of Directive 95/46/EC.

(10) In order to ensure a consistent and high level of protection of natural persons and to remove the obstacles to flows of personal data within the Union, the level of protection of the rights and freedoms of natural persons with regard to the processing of such data should be equivalent in all Member States. Consistent and homogenous application of the rules for the protection of the fundamental rights and freedoms of natural persons

with regard to the processing of personal data should be ensured throughout the Union. Regarding the processing of personal data for compliance with a legal obligation, for the performance of a task carried out in the public interest or in the exercise of official authority vested in the controller, Member States should be allowed to maintain or introduce national provisions to further specify the application of the rules of this Regulation. In conjunction with the general and horizontal law on data protection implementing Directive 95/46/EC, Member States have several sector-specific laws in areas that need more specific provisions. This Regulation also provides a margin of manoeuvre for Member States to specify its rules, including for the processing of special categories of personal data ('sensitive data'). To that extent, this Regulation does not exclude Member State law that sets out the circumstances for specific processing situations, including determining more precisely the conditions under which the processing of personal data is lawful.

(11) Effective protection of personal data throughout the Union requires the strengthening and setting out in detail of the rights of data subjects and the obligations of those who process and determine the processing of personal data, as well as equivalent powers for monitoring and ensuring compliance with the rules for the protection of personal data and equivalent sanctions for infringements in the Member States.

(12) Article 16(2) TFEU mandates the European Parliament and the Council to lay down the rules relating to the protection of natural persons with regard to the processing of personal data and the rules relating to the free movement of personal data.

(13) In order to ensure a consistent level of protection for natural persons throughout the Union and to prevent divergences hampering the free movement of personal data within the internal market, a Regulation is necessary to provide legal certainty and transparency for economic operators, including micro, small and medium-sized enterprises, and to provide natural persons in all Member States with the same level of legally enforceable rights and obligations and responsibilities for controllers and processors, to ensure consistent monitoring of the processing of personal data, and equivalent sanctions in all Member States as well as effective cooperation between the supervisory authorities of different Member States. The proper functioning of the internal market requires that the free movement of personal data within the Union is not restricted or prohibited for reasons connected with the protection of natural persons with regard to the processing of personal data. To take account of the specific situation of micro, small and medium-sized enterprises, this Regulation includes a derogation for organisations with fewer than 250 employees with regard to record-keeping. In addition, the Union institutions and bodies, and Member States and their supervisory authorities, are encouraged to take account of the specific needs of micro, small and medium-sized enterprises in the application of this Regulation. The notion of micro, small and medium-sized enterprises should draw from Article 2 of the Annex to Commission Recommendation 2003/361/EC.

(14) The protection afforded by this Regulation should apply to natural persons, whatever their nationality or place of residence, in relation to the processing of their personal data. This Regulation does not cover the processing of personal data which concerns legal persons and in particular undertakings established as legal persons, including the name and the form of the legal person and the contact details of the legal person.

(15) In order to prevent creating a serious risk of circumvention, the protection of natural persons should be technologically neutral and should not depend on the techniques used. The protection of natural persons should apply to the processing of personal data by automated means, as well as to manual processing, if the personal data are contained or are intended to be contained in a filing system. Files or sets of files, as well as their cover pages, which are not structured according to specific criteria should not fall within the scope of this Regulation.

(16) This Regulation does not apply to issues of protection of fundamental rights and freedoms or the free flow of personal data related to activities which fall outside the scope of Union law, such as activities concerning national security. This Regulation does not apply to the processing of personal data by the Member States when carrying out activities in relation to the common foreign and security policy of the Union.

(17) Regulation (EC) No 45/2001 of the European Parliament and of the Council applies to the processing of personal data by the Union institutions, bodies, offices and agencies. Regulation (EC) No 45/2001 and other Union legal acts applicable to such processing of personal data should be adapted to the principles and rules established in this Regulation and applied in the light of this Regulation. In order to provide a strong and coherent data protection framework in the Union, the necessary adaptations of Regulation (EC) No 45/2001 should follow after the adoption of this Regulation, in order to allow application at the same time as this Regulation.

(18) This Regulation does not apply to the processing of personal data by a natural person in the course of a purely personal or household activity and thus with no connection to a professional or commercial activity. Personal or household activities could include correspondence and the holding of addresses, or social networking and online activity undertaken within the context of such activities. However, this Regulation applies to controllers or processors which provide the means for processing personal data for such personal or household activities.

(19) The protection of natural persons with regard to the processing of personal data by competent authorities for the purposes of the prevention, investigation, detection or prosecution of criminal offences or the execution of criminal penalties, including the safeguarding against and the prevention of threats to public security and the free movement of such data, is the subject of a specific Union legal act. This Regulation should not, therefore, apply to processing activities for those purposes. However, personal data processed by public authorities under this Regulation should, when used for those purposes, be governed by a more specific Union legal act, namely Directive (EU) 2016/680 of the European Parliament and of the Council. Member States may entrust competent authorities within the meaning of Directive (EU) 2016/680 with tasks which are not necessarily carried out for the purposes of the prevention, investigation, detection or prosecution of criminal offences or the execution of criminal penalties, including the safeguarding against and prevention of threats to public security, so that the processing of personal data for those other purposes, in so far as it is within the scope of Union law, falls within the scope of this Regulation. With regard to the processing of personal data by those competent authorities for purposes falling within scope of this Regulation, Member States should be able to maintain or introduce more specific provisions to adapt the application of the rules of this Regulation. Such provisions may determine more

precisely specific requirements for the processing of personal data by those competent authorities for those other purposes, taking into account the constitutional, organisational and administrative structure of the respective Member State. When the processing of personal data by private bodies falls within the scope of this Regulation, this Regulation should provide for the possibility for Member States under specific conditions to restrict by law certain obligations and rights when such a restriction constitutes a necessary and proportionate measure in a democratic society to safeguard specific important interests including public security and the prevention, investigation, detection or prosecution of criminal offences or the execution of criminal penalties, including the safeguarding against and the prevention of threats to public security. This is relevant for instance in the framework of anti-money laundering or the activities of forensic laboratories.

(20) While this Regulation applies, inter alia, to the activities of courts and other judicial authorities, Union or Member State law could specify the processing operations and processing procedures in relation to the processing of personal data by courts and other judicial authorities. The competence of the supervisory authorities should not cover the processing of personal data when courts are acting in their judicial capacity, in order to safeguard the independence of the judiciary in the performance of its judicial tasks, including decision-making. It should be possible to entrust supervision of such data processing operations to specific bodies within the judicial system of the Member State, which should, in particular ensure compliance with the rules of this Regulation, enhance awareness among members of the judiciary of their obligations under this Regulation and handle complaints in relation to such data processing operations.

(21) This Regulation is without prejudice to the application of Directive 2000/31/EC of the European Parliament and of the Council, in particular of the liability rules of intermediary service providers in Articles 12 to 15 of that Directive. That Directive seeks to contribute to the proper functioning of the internal market by ensuring the free movement of information society services between Member States.

(22) Any processing of personal data in the context of the activities of an establishment of a controller or a processor in the Union should be carried out in accordance with this Regulation, regardless of whether the processing itself takes place within the Union. Establishment implies the effective and real exercise of activity through stable arrangements. The legal form of such arrangements, whether through a branch or a subsidiary with a legal personality, is not the determining factor in that respect.

(23) In order to ensure that natural persons are not deprived of the protection to which they are entitled under this Regulation, the processing of personal data of data subjects who are in the Union by a controller or a processor not established in the Union should be subject to this Regulation where the processing activities are related to offering goods or services to such data subjects irrespective of whether connected to a payment. In order to determine whether such a controller or processor is offering goods or services to data subjects who are in the Union, it should be ascertained whether it is apparent that the controller or processor envisages offering services to data subjects in one or more Member States in the Union. Whereas the mere accessibility of the controller's, processor's or an intermediary's website in the Union, of an email address or of other contact details, or the use of a language generally used in the third country where the controller is established, is insufficient to ascertain such intention, factors such as the use of a language or a

currency generally used in one or more Member States with the possibility of ordering goods and services in that other language, or the mentioning of customers or users who are in the Union, may make it apparent that the controller envisages offering goods or services to data subjects in the Union.

(24) The processing of personal data of data subjects who are in the Union by a controller or processor not established in the Union should also be subject to this Regulation when it is related to the monitoring of the behaviour of such data subjects in so far as their behaviour takes place within the Union. In order to determine whether a processing activity can be considered to monitor the behaviour of data subjects, it should be ascertained whether natural persons are tracked on the internet including potential subsequent use of personal data processing techniques which consist of profiling a natural person, particularly in order to take decisions concerning her or him or for analysing or predicting her or his personal preferences, behaviours and attitudes.

(25) Where Member State law applies by virtue of public international law, this Regulation should also apply to a controller not established in the Union, such as in a Member State's diplomatic mission or consular post.

(26) The principles of data protection should apply to any information concerning an identified or identifiable natural person. Personal data which have undergone pseudonymisation, which could be attributed to a natural person by the use of additional information should be considered to be information on an identifiable natural person. To determine whether a natural person is identifiable, account should be taken of all the means reasonably likely to be used, such as singling out, either by the controller or by another person to identify the natural person directly or indirectly. To ascertain whether means are reasonably likely to be used to identify the natural person, account should be taken of all objective factors, such as the costs of and the amount of time required for identification, taking into consideration the available technology at the time of the processing and technological developments. The principles of data protection should therefore not apply to anonymous information, namely information which does not relate to an identified or identifiable natural person or to personal data rendered anonymous in such a manner that the data subject is not or no longer identifiable. This Regulation does not therefore concern the processing of such anonymous information, including for statistical or research purposes.

(27) This Regulation does not apply to the personal data of deceased persons. Member States may provide for rules regarding the processing of personal data of deceased persons.

(28) The application of pseudonymisation to personal data can reduce the risks to the data subjects concerned and help controllers and processors to meet their data-protection obligations. The explicit introduction of 'pseudonymisation' in this Regulation is not intended to preclude any other measures of data protection.

(29) In order to create incentives to apply pseudonymisation when processing personal data, measures of pseudonymisation should, whilst allowing general analysis, be possible within the same controller when that controller has taken technical and organisational measures necessary to ensure, for the processing concerned, that this Regulation is implemented, and that additional information for attributing the personal data to a specific data subject

is kept separately. The controller processing the personal data should indicate the authorised persons within the same controller.

(30) Natural persons may be associated with online identifiers provided by their devices, applications, tools and protocols, such as internet protocol addresses, cookie identifiers or other identifiers such as radio frequency identification tags. This may leave traces which, in particular when combined with unique identifiers and other information received by the servers, may be used to create profiles of the natural persons and identify them.

(31) Public authorities to which personal data are disclosed in accordance with a legal obligation for the exercise of their official mission, such as tax and customs authorities, financial investigation units, independent administrative authorities, or financial market authorities responsible for the regulation and supervision of securities markets should not be regarded as recipients if they receive personal data which are necessary to carry out a particular inquiry in the general interest, in accordance with Union or Member State law. The requests for disclosure sent by the public authorities should always be in writing, reasoned and occasional and should not concern the entirety of a filing system or lead to the interconnection of filing systems. The processing of personal data by those public authorities should comply with the applicable data-protection rules according to the purposes of the processing.

(32) Consent should be given by a clear affirmative act establishing a freely given, specific, informed and unambiguous indication of the data subject's agreement to the processing of personal data relating to him or her, such as by a written statement, including by electronic means, or an oral statement. This could include ticking a box when visiting an internet website, choosing technical settings for information society services or another statement or conduct which clearly indicates in this context the data subject's acceptance of the proposed processing of his or her personal data. Silence, pre-ticked boxes or inactivity should not therefore constitute consent. Consent should cover all processing activities carried out for the same purpose or purposes. When the processing has multiple purposes, consent should be given for all of them. If the data subject's consent is to be given following a request by electronic means, the request must be clear, concise and not unnecessarily disruptive to the use of the service for which it is provided.

(33) It is often not possible to fully identify the purpose of personal data processing for scientific research purposes at the time of data collection. Therefore, data subjects should be allowed to give their consent to certain areas of scientific research when in keeping with recognised ethical standards for scientific research. Data subjects should have the opportunity to give their consent only to certain areas of research or parts of research projects to the extent allowed by the intended purpose.

(34) Genetic data should be defined as personal data relating to the inherited or acquired genetic characteristics of a natural person which result from the analysis of a biological sample from the natural person in question, in particular chromosomal, deoxyribonucleic acid (DNA) or ribonucleic acid (RNA) analysis, or from the analysis of another element enabling equivalent information to be obtained.

(35) Personal data concerning health should include all data pertaining to the health status of

a data subject which reveal information relating to the past, current or future physical or mental health status of the data subject. This includes information about the natural person collected in the course of the registration for, or the provision of, health care services as referred to in Directive 2011/24/EU of the European Parliament and of the Council to that natural person; a number, symbol or particular assigned to a natural person to uniquely identify the natural person for health purposes; information derived from the testing or examination of a body part or bodily substance, including from genetic data and biological samples; and any information on, for example, a disease, disability, disease risk, medical history, clinical treatment or the physiological or biomedical state of the data subject independent of its source, for example from a physician or other health professional, a hospital, a medical device or an in vitro diagnostic test.

(36) The main establishment of a controller in the Union should be the place of its central administration in the Union, unless the decisions on the purposes and means of the processing of personal data are taken in another establishment of the controller in the Union, in which case that other establishment should be considered to be the main establishment. The main establishment of a controller in the Union should be determined according to objective criteria and should imply the effective and real exercise of management activities determining the main decisions as to the purposes and means of processing through stable arrangements. That criterion should not depend on whether the processing of personal data is carried out at that location. The presence and use of technical means and technologies for processing personal data or processing activities do not, in themselves, constitute a main establishment and are therefore not determining criteria for a main establishment. The main establishment of the processor should be the place of its central administration in the Union or, if it has no central administration in the Union, the place where the main processing activities take place in the Union. In cases involving both the controller and the processor, the competent lead supervisory authority should remain the supervisory authority of the Member State where the controller has its main establishment, but the supervisory authority of the processor should be considered to be a supervisory authority concerned and that supervisory authority should participate in the cooperation procedure provided for by this Regulation. In any case, the supervisory authorities of the Member State or Member States where the processor has one or more establishments should not be considered to be supervisory authorities concerned where the draft decision concerns only the controller. Where the processing is carried out by a group of undertakings, the main establishment of the controlling undertaking should be considered to be the main establishment of the group of undertakings, except where the purposes and means of processing are determined by another undertaking.

(37) A group of undertakings should cover a controlling undertaking and its controlled undertakings, whereby the controlling undertaking should be the undertaking which can exert a dominant influence over the other undertakings by virtue, for example, of ownership, financial participation or the rules which govern it or the power to have personal data protection rules implemented. An undertaking which controls the processing of personal data in undertakings affiliated to it should be regarded, together with those undertakings, as a group of undertakings.

(38) Children merit specific protection with regard to their personal data, as they may be less aware of the risks, consequences and safeguards concerned and their rights in relation to

the processing of personal data. Such specific protection should, in particular, apply to the use of personal data of children for the purposes of marketing or creating personality or user profiles and the collection of personal data with regard to children when using services offered directly to a child. The consent of the holder of parental responsibility should not be necessary in the context of preventive or counselling services offered directly to a child.

(39) Any processing of personal data should be lawful and fair. It should be transparent to natural persons that personal data concerning them are collected, used, consulted or otherwise processed and to what extent the personal data are or will be processed. The principle of transparency requires that any information and communication relating to the processing of those personal data be easily accessible and easy to understand, and that clear and plain language be used. That principle concerns, in particular, information to the data subjects on the identity of the controller and the purposes of the processing and further information to ensure fair and transparent processing in respect of the natural persons concerned and their right to obtain confirmation and communication of personal data concerning them which are being processed. Natural persons should be made aware of risks, rules, safeguards and rights in relation to the processing of personal data and how to exercise their rights in relation to such processing. In particular, the specific purposes for which personal data are processed should be explicit and legitimate and determined at the time of the collection of the personal data. The personal data should be adequate, relevant and limited to what is necessary for the purposes for which they are processed. This requires, in particular, ensuring that the period for which the personal data are stored is limited to a strict minimum. Personal data should be processed only if the purpose of the processing could not reasonably be fulfilled by other means. In order to ensure that the personal data are not kept longer than necessary, time limits should be established by the controller for erasure or for a periodic review. Every reasonable step should be taken to ensure that personal data which are inaccurate are rectified or deleted. Personal data should be processed in a manner that ensures appropriate security and confidentiality of the personal data, including for preventing unauthorised access to or use of personal data and the equipment used for the processing.

(40) In order for processing to be lawful, personal data should be processed on the basis of the consent of the data subject concerned or some other legitimate basis, laid down by law, either in this Regulation or in other Union or Member State law as referred to in this Regulation, including the necessity for compliance with the legal obligation to which the controller is subject or the necessity for the performance of a contract to which the data subject is party or in order to take steps at the request of the data subject prior to entering into a contract.

(41) Where this Regulation refers to a legal basis or a legislative measure, this does not necessarily require a legislative act adopted by a parliament, without prejudice to requirements pursuant to the constitutional order of the Member State concerned. However, such a legal basis or legislative measure should be clear and precise and its application should be foreseeable to persons subject to it, in accordance with the case-law of the Court of Justice of the European Union (the 'Court of Justice') and the European Court of Human Rights.

(42) Where processing is based on the data subject's consent, the controller should be able to

demonstrate that the data subject has given consent to the processing operation. In particular in the context of a written declaration on another matter, safeguards should ensure that the data subject is aware of the fact that and the extent to which consent is given. In accordance with Council Directive 93/13/EEC a declaration of consent pre-formulated by the controller should be provided in an intelligible and easily accessible form, using clear and plain language and it should not contain unfair terms. For consent to be informed, the data subject should be aware at least of the identity of the controller and the purposes of the processing for which the personal data are intended. Consent should not be regarded as freely given if the data subject has no genuine or free choice or is unable to refuse or withdraw consent without detriment.

(43) In order to ensure that consent is freely given, consent should not provide a valid legal ground for the processing of personal data in a specific case where there is a clear imbalance between the data subject and the controller, in particular where the controller is a public authority and it is therefore unlikely that consent was freely given in all the circumstances of that specific situation. Consent is presumed not to be freely given if it does not allow separate consent to be given to different personal data processing operations despite it being appropriate in the individual case, or if the performance of a contract, including the provision of a service, is dependent on the consent despite such consent not being necessary for such performance.

(44) Processing should be lawful where it is necessary in the context of a contract or the intention to enter into a contract.

(45) Where processing is carried out in accordance with a legal obligation to which the controller is subject or where processing is necessary for the performance of a task carried out in the public interest or in the exercise of official authority, the processing should have a basis in Union or Member State law. This Regulation does not require a specific law for each individual processing. A law as a basis for several processing operations based on a legal obligation to which the controller is subject or where processing is necessary for the performance of a task carried out in the public interest or in the exercise of an official authority may be sufficient. It should also be for Union or Member State law to determine the purpose of processing. Furthermore, that law could specify the general conditions of this Regulation governing the lawfulness of personal data processing, establish specifications for determining the controller, the type of personal data which are subject to the processing, the data subjects concerned, the entities to which the personal data may be disclosed, the purpose limitations, the storage period and other measures to ensure lawful and fair processing. It should also be for Union or Member State law to determine whether the controller performing a task carried out in the public interest or in the exercise of official authority should be a public authority or another natural or legal person governed by public law, or, where it is in the public interest to do so, including for health purposes such as public health and social protection and the management of health care services, by private law, such as a professional association.

(46) The processing of personal data should also be regarded to be lawful where it is necessary to protect an interest which is essential for the life of the data subject or that of another natural person. Processing of personal data based on the vital interest of another natural person should in principle take place only where the processing cannot be manifestly based on another legal basis. Some types of processing may serve both important grounds

of public interest and the vital interests of the data subject as for instance when processing is necessary for humanitarian purposes, including for monitoring epidemics and their spread or in situations of humanitarian emergencies, in particular in situations of natural and man-made disasters.

(47) The legitimate interests of a controller, including those of a controller to which the personal data may be disclosed, or of a third party, may provide a legal basis for processing, provided that the interests or the fundamental rights and freedoms of the data subject are not overriding, taking into consideration the reasonable expectations of data subjects based on their relationship with the controller. Such legitimate interest could exist for example where there is a relevant and appropriate relationship between the data subject and the controller in situations such as where the data subject is a client or in the service of the controller. At any rate the existence of a legitimate interest would need careful assessment including whether a data subject can reasonably expect at the time and in the context of the collection of the personal data that processing for that purpose may take place. The interests and fundamental rights of the data subject could in particular override the interest of the data controller where personal data are processed in circumstances where data subjects do not reasonably expect further processing. Given that it is for the legislator to provide by law for the legal basis for public authorities to process personal data, that legal basis should not apply to the processing by public authorities in the performance of their tasks. The processing of personal data strictly necessary for the purposes of preventing fraud also constitutes a legitimate interest of the data controller concerned. The processing of personal data for direct marketing purposes may be regarded as carried out for a legitimate interest.

(48) Controllers that are part of a group of undertakings or institutions affiliated to a central body may have a legitimate interest in transmitting personal data within the group of undertakings for internal administrative purposes, including the processing of clients' or employees' personal data. The general principles for the transfer of personal data, within a group of undertakings, to an undertaking located in a third country remain unaffected.

(49) The processing of personal data to the extent strictly necessary and proportionate for the purposes of ensuring network and information security, i.e. the ability of a network or an information system to resist, at a given level of confidence, accidental events or unlawful or malicious actions that compromise the availability, authenticity, integrity and confidentiality of stored or transmitted personal data, and the security of the related services offered by, or accessible via, those networks and systems, by public authorities, by computer emergency response teams (CERTs), computer security incident response teams (CSIRTs), by providers of electronic communications networks and services and by providers of security technologies and services, constitutes a legitimate interest of the data controller concerned. This could, for example, include preventing unauthorised access to electronic communications networks and malicious code distribution and stopping 'denial of service' attacks and damage to computer and electronic communication systems.

(50) The processing of personal data for purposes other than those for which the personal data were initially collected should be allowed only where the processing is compatible with the purposes for which the personal data were initially collected. In such a case, no legal basis separate from that which allowed the collection of the personal data is required. If

the processing is necessary for the performance of a task carried out in the public interest or in the exercise of official authority vested in the controller, Union or Member State law may determine and specify the tasks and purposes for which the further processing should be regarded as compatible and lawful. Further processing for archiving purposes in the public interest, scientific or historical research purposes or statistical purposes should be considered to be compatible lawful processing operations. The legal basis provided by Union or Member State law for the processing of personal data may also provide a legal basis for further processing. In order to ascertain whether a purpose of further processing is compatible with the purpose for which the personal data are initially collected, the controller, after having met all the requirements for the lawfulness of the original processing, should take into account, inter alia: any link between those purposes and the purposes of the intended further processing; the context in which the personal data have been collected, in particular the reasonable expectations of data subjects based on their relationship with the controller as to their further use; the nature of the personal data; the consequences of the intended further processing for data subjects; and the existence of appropriate safeguards in both the original and intended further processing operations. Where the data subject has given consent or the processing is based on Union or Member State law which constitutes a necessary and proportionate measure in a democratic society to safeguard, in particular, important objectives of general public interest, the controller should be allowed to further process the personal data irrespective of the compatibility of the purposes. In any case, the application of the principles set out in this Regulation and in particular the information of the data subject on those other purposes and on his or her rights including the right to object, should be ensured. Indicating possible criminal acts or threats to public security by the controller and transmitting the relevant personal data in individual cases or in several cases relating to the same criminal act or threats to public security to a competent authority should be regarded as being in the legitimate interest pursued by the controller. However, such transmission in the legitimate interest of the controller or further processing of personal data should be prohibited if the processing is not compatible with a legal, professional or other binding obligation of secrecy.

(51) Personal data which are, by their nature, particularly sensitive in relation to fundamental rights and freedoms merit specific protection as the context of their processing could create significant risks to the fundamental rights and freedoms. Those personal data should include personal data revealing racial or ethnic origin, whereby the use of the term 'racial origin' in this Regulation does not imply an acceptance by the Union of theories which attempt to determine the existence of separate human races. The processing of photographs should not systematically be considered to be processing of special categories of personal data as they are covered by the definition of biometric data only when processed through a specific technical means allowing the unique identification or authentication of a natural person. Such personal data should not be processed, unless processing is allowed in specific cases set out in this Regulation, taking into account that Member States law may lay down specific provisions on data protection in order to adapt the application of the rules of this Regulation for compliance with a legal obligation or for the performance of a task carried out in the public interest or in the exercise of official authority vested in the controller. In addition to the specific requirements for such processing, the general principles and other rules of this Regulation should apply, in particular as regards the conditions for lawful processing. Derogations from the general prohibition for processing such special categories of personal data should be explicitly

provided, inter alia, where the data subject gives his or her explicit consent or in respect of specific needs in particular where the processing is carried out in the course of legitimate activities by certain associations or foundations the purpose of which is to permit the exercise of fundamental freedoms.

(52) Derogating from the prohibition on processing special categories of personal data should also be allowed when provided for in Union or Member State law and subject to suitable safeguards, so as to protect personal data and other fundamental rights, where it is in the public interest to do so, in particular processing personal data in the field of employment law, social protection law including pensions and for health security, monitoring and alert purposes, the prevention or control of communicable diseases and other serious threats to health. Such a derogation may be made for health purposes, including public health and the management of health-care services, especially in order to ensure the quality and cost-effectiveness of the procedures used for settling claims for benefits and services in the health insurance system, or for archiving purposes in the public interest, scientific or historical research purposes or statistical purposes. A derogation should also allow the processing of such personal data where necessary for the establishment, exercise or defence of legal claims, whether in court proceedings or in an administrative or out-of-court procedure.

(53) Special categories of personal data which merit higher protection should be processed for health-related purposes only where necessary to achieve those purposes for the benefit of natural persons and society as a whole, in particular in the context of the management of health or social care services and systems, including processing by the management and central national health authorities of such data for the purpose of quality control, management information and the general national and local supervision of the health or social care system, and ensuring continuity of health or social care and cross-border healthcare or health security, monitoring and alert purposes, or for archiving purposes in the public interest, scientific or historical research purposes or statistical purposes, based on Union or Member State law which has to meet an objective of public interest, as well as for studies conducted in the public interest in the area of public health. Therefore, this Regulation should provide for harmonised conditions for the processing of special categories of personal data concerning health, in respect of specific needs, in particular where the processing of such data is carried out for certain health-related purposes by persons subject to a legal obligation of professional secrecy. Union or Member State law should provide for specific and suitable measures so as to protect the fundamental rights and the personal data of natural persons. Member States should be allowed to maintain or introduce further conditions, including limitations, with regard to the processing of genetic data, biometric data or data concerning health. However, this should not hamper the free flow of personal data within the Union when those conditions apply to cross-border processing of such data.

(54) The processing of special categories of personal data may be necessary for reasons of public interest in the areas of public health without consent of the data subject. Such processing should be subject to suitable and specific measures so as to protect the rights and freedoms of natural persons. In that context, 'public health' should be interpreted as defined in Regulation (EC) No 1338/2008 of the European Parliament and of the Council, namely all elements related to health, namely health status, including morbidity and disability, the determinants having an effect on that health status, health care needs,

resources allocated to health care, the provision of, and universal access to, health care as well as health care expenditure and financing, and the causes of mortality. Such processing of data concerning health for reasons of public interest should not result in personal data being processed for other purposes by third parties such as employers or insurance and banking companies.

(55) Moreover, the processing of personal data by official authorities for the purpose of achieving the aims, laid down by constitutional law or by international public law, of officially recognised religious associations, is carried out on grounds of public interest.

(56) Where in the course of electoral activities, the operation of the democratic system in a Member State requires that political parties compile personal data on people's political opinions, the processing of such data may be permitted for reasons of public interest, provided that appropriate safeguards are established.

(57) If the personal data processed by a controller do not permit the controller to identify a natural person, the data controller should not be obliged to acquire additional information in order to identify the data subject for the sole purpose of complying with any provision of this Regulation. However, the controller should not refuse to take additional information provided by the data subject in order to support the exercise of his or her rights. Identification should include the digital identification of a data subject, for example through authentication mechanism such as the same credentials, used by the data subject to log-in to the on-line service offered by the data controller.

(58) The principle of transparency requires that any information addressed to the public or to the data subject be concise, easily accessible and easy to understand, and that clear and plain language and, additionally, where appropriate, visualisation be used. Such information could be provided in electronic form, for example, when addressed to the public, through a website. This is of particular relevance in situations where the proliferation of actors and the technological complexity of practice make it difficult for the data subject to know and understand whether, by whom and for what purpose personal data relating to him or her are being collected, such as in the case of online advertising. Given that children merit specific protection, any information and communication, where processing is addressed to a child, should be in such a clear and plain language that the child can easily understand.

(59) Modalities should be provided for facilitating the exercise of the data subject's rights under this Regulation, including mechanisms to request and, if applicable, obtain, free of charge, in particular, access to and rectification or erasure of personal data and the exercise of the right to object. The controller should also provide means for requests to be made electronically, especially where personal data are processed by electronic means. The controller should be obliged to respond to requests from the data subject without undue delay and at the latest within one month and to give reasons where the controller does not intend to comply with any such requests.

(60) The principles of fair and transparent processing require that the data subject be informed of the existence of the processing operation and its purposes. The controller should provide the data subject with any further information necessary to ensure fair and transparent processing taking into account the specific circumstances and context in

which the personal data are processed. Furthermore, the data subject should be informed of the existence of profiling and the consequences of such profiling. Where the personal data are collected from the data subject, the data subject should also be informed whether he or she is obliged to provide the personal data and of the consequences, where he or she does not provide such data. That information may be provided in combination with standardised icons in order to give in an easily visible, intelligible and clearly legible manner, a meaningful overview of the intended processing. Where the icons are presented electronically, they should be machine-readable.

(61) The information in relation to the processing of personal data relating to the data subject should be given to him or her at the time of collection from the data subject, or, where the personal data are obtained from another source, within a reasonable period, depending on the circumstances of the case. Where personal data can be legitimately disclosed to another recipient, the data subject should be informed when the personal data are first disclosed to the recipient. Where the controller intends to process the personal data for a purpose other than that for which they were collected, the controller should provide the data subject prior to that further processing with information on that other purpose and other necessary information. Where the origin of the personal data cannot be provided to the data subject because various sources have been used, general information should be provided.

(62) However, it is not necessary to impose the obligation to provide information where the data subject already possesses the information, where the recording or disclosure of the personal data is expressly laid down by law or where the provision of information to the data subject proves to be impossible or would involve a disproportionate effort. The latter could in particular be the case where processing is carried out for archiving purposes in the public interest, scientific or historical research purposes or statistical purposes. In that regard, the number of data subjects, the age of the data and any appropriate safeguards adopted should be taken into consideration.

(63) A data subject should have the right of access to personal data which have been collected concerning him or her, and to exercise that right easily and at reasonable intervals, in order to be aware of, and verify, the lawfulness of the processing. This includes the right for data subjects to have access to data concerning their health, for example the data in their medical records containing information such as diagnoses, examination results, assessments by treating physicians and any treatment or interventions provided. Every data subject should therefore have the right to know and obtain communication in particular with regard to the purposes for which the personal data are processed, where possible the period for which the personal data are processed, the recipients of the personal data, the logic involved in any automatic personal data processing and, at least when based on profiling, the consequences of such processing. Where possible, the controller should be able to provide remote access to a secure system which would provide the data subject with direct access to his or her personal data. That right should not adversely affect the rights or freedoms of others, including trade secrets or intellectual property and in particular the copyright protecting the software. However, the result of those considerations should not be a refusal to provide all information to the data subject. Where the controller processes a large quantity of information concerning the data subject, the controller should be able to request that, before the information is delivered, the data subject specify the information or processing activities to which the request

relates.

(64) The controller should use all reasonable measures to verify the identity of a data subject who requests access, in particular in the context of online services and online identifiers. A controller should not retain personal data for the sole purpose of being able to react to potential requests.

(65) A data subject should have the right to have personal data concerning him or her rectified and a 'right to be forgotten' where the retention of such data infringes this Regulation or Union or Member State law to which the controller is subject. In particular, a data subject should have the right to have his or her personal data erased and no longer processed where the personal data are no longer necessary in relation to the purposes for which they are collected or otherwise processed, where a data subject has withdrawn his or her consent or objects to the processing of personal data concerning him or her, or where the processing of his or her personal data does not otherwise comply with this Regulation. That right is relevant in particular where the data subject has given his or her consent as a child and is not fully aware of the risks involved by the processing, and later wants to remove such personal data, especially on the internet. The data subject should be able to exercise that right notwithstanding the fact that he or she is no longer a child. However, the further retention of the personal data should be lawful where it is necessary, for exercising the right of freedom of expression and information, for compliance with a legal obligation, for the performance of a task carried out in the public interest or in the exercise of official authority vested in the controller, on the grounds of public interest in the area of public health, for archiving purposes in the public interest, scientific or historical research purposes or statistical purposes, or for the establishment, exercise or defence of legal claims.

(66) To strengthen the right to be forgotten in the online environment, the right to erasure should also be extended in such a way that a controller who has made the personal data public should be obliged to inform the controllers which are processing such personal data to erase any links to, or copies or replications of those personal data. In doing so, that controller should take reasonable steps, taking into account available technology and the means available to the controller, including technical measures, to inform the controllers which are processing the personal data of the data subject's request.

(67) Methods by which to restrict the processing of personal data could include, inter alia, temporarily moving the selected data to another processing system, making the selected personal data unavailable to users, or temporarily removing published data from a website. In automated filing systems, the restriction of processing should in principle be ensured by technical means in such a manner that the personal data are not subject to further processing operations and cannot be changed. The fact that the processing of personal data is restricted should be clearly indicated in the system.

(68) To further strengthen the control over his or her own data, where the processing of personal data is carried out by automated means, the data subject should also be allowed to receive personal data concerning him or her which he or she has provided to a controller in a structured, commonly used, machine-readable and interoperable format, and to transmit it to another controller. Data controllers should be encouraged to develop interoperable formats that enable data portability. That right should apply where

the data subject provided the personal data on the basis of his or her consent or the processing is necessary for the performance of a contract. It should not apply where processing is based on a legal ground other than consent or contract. By its very nature, that right should not be exercised against controllers processing personal data in the exercise of their public duties. It should therefore not apply where the processing of the personal data is necessary for compliance with a legal obligation to which the controller is subject or for the performance of a task carried out in the public interest or in the exercise of an official authority vested in the controller. The data subject's right to transmit or receive personal data concerning him or her should not create an obligation for the controllers to adopt or maintain processing systems which are technically compatible. Where, in a certain set of personal data, more than one data subject is concerned, the right to receive the personal data should be without prejudice to the rights and freedoms of other data subjects in accordance with this Regulation. Furthermore, that right should not prejudice the right of the data subject to obtain the erasure of personal data and the limitations of that right as set out in this Regulation and should, in particular, not imply the erasure of personal data concerning the data subject which have been provided by him or her for the performance of a contract to the extent that and for as long as the personal data are necessary for the performance of that contract. Where technically feasible, the data subject should have the right to have the personal data transmitted directly from one controller to another.

(69) Where personal data might lawfully be processed because processing is necessary for the performance of a task carried out in the public interest or in the exercise of official authority vested in the controller, or on grounds of the legitimate interests of a controller or a third party, a data subject should, nevertheless, be entitled to object to the processing of any personal data relating to his or her particular situation. It should be for the controller to demonstrate that its compelling legitimate interest overrides the interests or the fundamental rights and freedoms of the data subject.

(70) Where personal data are processed for the purposes of direct marketing, the data subject should have the right to object to such processing, including profiling to the extent that it is related to such direct marketing, whether with regard to initial or further processing, at any time and free of charge. That right should be explicitly brought to the attention of the data subject and presented clearly and separately from any other information.

(71) The data subject should have the right not to be subject to a decision, which may include a measure, evaluating personal aspects relating to him or her which is based solely on automated processing and which produces legal effects concerning him or her or similarly significantly affects him or her, such as automatic refusal of an online credit application or e-recruiting practices without any human intervention. Such processing includes 'profiling' that consists of any form of automated processing of personal data evaluating the personal aspects relating to a natural person, in particular to analyse or predict aspects concerning the data subject's performance at work, economic situation, health, personal preferences or interests, reliability or behaviour, location or movements, where it produces legal effects concerning him or her or similarly significantly affects him or her. However, decision-making based on such processing, including profiling, should be allowed where expressly authorised by Union or Member State law to which the controller is subject, including for fraud and tax-evasion monitoring and prevention purposes conducted in accordance with the regulations, standards and recommendations

of Union institutions or national oversight bodies and to ensure the security and reliability of a service provided by the controller, or necessary for the entering or performance of a contract between the data subject and a controller, or when the data subject has given his or her explicit consent. In any case, such processing should be subject to suitable safeguards, which should include specific information to the data subject and the right to obtain human intervention, to express his or her point of view, to obtain an explanation of the decision reached after such assessment and to challenge the decision. Such measure should not concern a child. In order to ensure fair and transparent processing in respect of the data subject, taking into account the specific circumstances and context in which the personal data are processed, the controller should use appropriate mathematical or statistical procedures for the profiling, implement technical and organisational measures appropriate to ensure, in particular, that factors which result in inaccuracies in personal data are corrected and the risk of errors is minimised, secure personal data in a manner that takes account of the potential risks involved for the interests and rights of the data subject and that prevents, inter alia, discriminatory effects on natural persons on the basis of racial or ethnic origin, political opinion, religion or beliefs, trade union membership, genetic or health status or sexual orientation, or that result in measures having such an effect. Automated decision-making and profiling based on special categories of personal data should be allowed only under specific conditions.

(72) Profiling is subject to the rules of this Regulation governing the processing of personal data, such as the legal grounds for processing or data protection principles. The European Data Protection Board established by this Regulation (the 'Board') should be able to issue guidance in that context.

(73) Restrictions concerning specific principles and the rights of information, access to and rectification or erasure of personal data, the right to data portability, the right to object, decisions based on profiling, as well as the communication of a personal data breach to a data subject and certain related obligations of the controllers may be imposed by Union or Member State law, as far as necessary and proportionate in a democratic society to safeguard public security, including the protection of human life especially in response to natural or manmade disasters, the prevention, investigation and prosecution of criminal offences or the execution of criminal penalties, including the safeguarding against and the prevention of threats to public security, or of breaches of ethics for regulated professions, other important objectives of general public interest of the Union or of a Member State, in particular an important economic or financial interest of the Union or of a Member State, the keeping of public registers kept for reasons of general public interest, further processing of archived personal data to provide specific information related to the political behaviour under former totalitarian state regimes or the protection of the data subject or the rights and freedoms of others, including social protection, public health and humanitarian purposes. Those restrictions should be in accordance with the requirements set out in the Charter and in the European Convention for the Protection of Human Rights and Fundamental Freedoms.

(74) The responsibility and liability of the controller for any processing of personal data carried out by the controller or on the controller's behalf should be established. In particular, the controller should be obliged to implement appropriate and effective measures and be able to demonstrate the compliance of processing activities with this Regulation, including the effectiveness of the measures. Those measures should take into

account the nature, scope, context and purposes of the processing and the risk to the rights and freedoms of natural persons.

(75) The risk to the rights and freedoms of natural persons, of varying likelihood and severity, may result from personal data processing which could lead to physical, material or non-material damage, in particular: where the processing may give rise to discrimination, identity theft or fraud, financial loss, damage to the reputation, loss of confidentiality of personal data protected by professional secrecy, unauthorised reversal of pseudonymisation, or any other significant economic or social disadvantage; where data subjects might be deprived of their rights and freedoms or prevented from exercising control over their personal data; where personal data are processed which reveal racial or ethnic origin, political opinions, religion or philosophical beliefs, trade union membership, and the processing of genetic data, data concerning health or data concerning sex life or criminal convictions and offences or related security measures; where personal aspects are evaluated, in particular analysing or predicting aspects concerning performance at work, economic situation, health, personal preferences or interests, reliability or behaviour, location or movements, in order to create or use personal profiles; where personal data of vulnerable natural persons, in particular of children, are processed; or where processing involves a large amount of personal data and affects a large number of data subjects.

(76) The likelihood and severity of the risk to the rights and freedoms of the data subject should be determined by reference to the nature, scope, context and purposes of the processing. Risk should be evaluated on the basis of an objective assessment, by which it is established whether data processing operations involve a risk or a high risk.

(77) Guidance on the implementation of appropriate measures and on the demonstration of compliance by the controller or the processor, especially as regards the identification of the risk related to the processing, their assessment in terms of origin, nature, likelihood and severity, and the identification of best practices to mitigate the risk, could be provided in particular by means of approved codes of conduct, approved certifications, guidelines provided by the Board or indications provided by a data protection officer. The Board may also issue guidelines on processing operations that are considered to be unlikely to result in a high risk to the rights and freedoms of natural persons and indicate what measures may be sufficient in such cases to address such risk.

(78) The protection of the rights and freedoms of natural persons with regard to the processing of personal data require that appropriate technical and organisational measures be taken to ensure that the requirements of this Regulation are met. In order to be able to demonstrate compliance with this Regulation, the controller should adopt internal policies and implement measures which meet in particular the principles of data protection by design and data protection by default. Such measures could consist, inter alia, of minimising the processing of personal data, pseudonymising personal data as soon as possible, transparency with regard to the functions and processing of personal data, enabling the data subject to monitor the data processing, enabling the controller to create and improve security features. When developing, designing, selecting and using applications, services and products that are based on the processing of personal data or process personal data to fulfil their task, producers of the products, services and applications should be encouraged to take into account the right to data protection when

developing and designing such products, services and applications and, with due regard to the state of the art, to make sure that controllers and processors are able to fulfil their data protection obligations. The principles of data protection by design and by default should also be taken into consideration in the context of public tenders.

(79) The protection of the rights and freedoms of data subjects as well as the responsibility and liability of controllers and processors, also in relation to the monitoring by and measures of supervisory authorities, requires a clear allocation of the responsibilities under this Regulation, including where a controller determines the purposes and means of the processing jointly with other controllers or where a processing operation is carried out on behalf of a controller.

(80) Where a controller or a processor not established in the Union is processing personal data of data subjects who are in the Union whose processing activities are related to the offering of goods or services, irrespective of whether a payment of the data subject is required, to such data subjects in the Union, or to the monitoring of their behaviour as far as their behaviour takes place within the Union, the controller or the processor should designate a representative, unless the processing is occasional, does not include processing, on a large scale, of special categories of personal data or the processing of personal data relating to criminal convictions and offences, and is unlikely to result in a risk to the rights and freedoms of natural persons, taking into account the nature, context, scope and purposes of the processing or if the controller is a public authority or body. The representative should act on behalf of the controller or the processor and may be addressed by any supervisory authority. The representative should be explicitly designated by a written mandate of the controller or of the processor to act on its behalf with regard to its obligations under this Regulation. The designation of such a representative does not affect the responsibility or liability of the controller or of the processor under this Regulation. Such a representative should perform its tasks according to the mandate received from the controller or processor, including cooperating with the competent supervisory authorities with regard to any action taken to ensure compliance with this Regulation. The designated representative should be subject to enforcement proceedings in the event of non-compliance by the controller or processor.

(81) To ensure compliance with the requirements of this Regulation in respect of the processing to be carried out by the processor on behalf of the controller, when entrusting a processor with processing activities, the controller should use only processors providing sufficient guarantees, in particular in terms of expert knowledge, reliability and resources, to implement technical and organisational measures which will meet the requirements of this Regulation, including for the security of processing. The adherence of the processor to an approved code of conduct or an approved certification mechanism may be used as an element to demonstrate compliance with the obligations of the controller. The carrying-out of processing by a processor should be governed by a contract or other legal act under Union or Member State law, binding the processor to the controller, setting out the subject-matter and duration of the processing, the nature and purposes of the processing, the type of personal data and categories of data subjects, taking into account the specific tasks and responsibilities of the processor in the context of the processing to be carried out and the risk to the rights and freedoms of the data subject. The controller and processor may choose to use an individual contract or standard contractual clauses which are adopted either directly by the Commission or by a supervisory authority in

accordance with the consistency mechanism and then adopted by the Commission. After the completion of the processing on behalf of the controller, the processor should, at the choice of the controller, return or delete the personal data, unless there is a requirement to store the personal data under Union or Member State law to which the processor is subject.

(82) In order to demonstrate compliance with this Regulation, the controller or processor should maintain records of processing activities under its responsibility. Each controller and processor should be obliged to cooperate with the supervisory authority and make those records, on request, available to it, so that it might serve for monitoring those processing operations.

(83) In order to maintain security and to prevent processing in infringement of this Regulation, the controller or processor should evaluate the risks inherent in the processing and implement measures to mitigate those risks, such as encryption. Those measures should ensure an appropriate level of security, including confidentiality, taking into account the state of the art and the costs of implementation in relation to the risks and the nature of the personal data to be protected. In assessing data security risk, consideration should be given to the risks that are presented by personal data processing, such as accidental or unlawful destruction, loss, alteration, unauthorised disclosure of, or access to, personal data transmitted, stored or otherwise processed which may in particular lead to physical, material or non-material damage.

(84) In order to enhance compliance with this Regulation where processing operations are likely to result in a high risk to the rights and freedoms of natural persons, the controller should be responsible for the carrying-out of a data protection impact assessment to evaluate, in particular, the origin, nature, particularity and severity of that risk. The outcome of the assessment should be taken into account when determining the appropriate measures to be taken in order to demonstrate that the processing of personal data complies with this Regulation. Where a data-protection impact assessment indicates that processing operations involve a high risk which the controller cannot mitigate by appropriate measures in terms of available technology and costs of implementation, a consultation of the supervisory authority should take place prior to the processing.

(85) A personal data breach may, if not addressed in an appropriate and timely manner, result in physical, material or non-material damage to natural persons such as loss of control over their personal data or limitation of their rights, discrimination, identity theft or fraud, financial loss, unauthorised reversal of pseudonymisation, damage to reputation, loss of confidentiality of personal data protected by professional secrecy or any other significant economic or social disadvantage to the natural person concerned. Therefore, as soon as the controller becomes aware that a personal data breach has occurred, the controller should notify the personal data breach to the supervisory authority without undue delay and, where feasible, not later than 72 hours after having become aware of it, unless the controller is able to demonstrate, in accordance with the accountability principle, that the personal data breach is unlikely to result in a risk to the rights and freedoms of natural persons. Where such notification cannot be achieved within 72 hours, the reasons for the delay should accompany the notification and information may be provided in phases without undue further delay.

(86) The controller should communicate to the data subject a personal data breach, without undue delay, where that personal data breach is likely to result in a high risk to the rights and freedoms of the natural person in order to allow him or her to take the necessary precautions. The communication should describe the nature of the personal data breach as well as recommendations for the natural person concerned to mitigate potential adverse effects. Such communications to data subjects should be made as soon as reasonably feasible and in close cooperation with the supervisory authority, respecting guidance provided by it or by other relevant authorities such as law-enforcement authorities. For example, the need to mitigate an immediate risk of damage would call for prompt communication with data subjects whereas the need to implement appropriate measures against continuing or similar personal data breaches may justify more time for communication.

(87) It should be ascertained whether all appropriate technological protection and organisational measures have been implemented to establish immediately whether a personal data breach has taken place and to inform promptly the supervisory authority and the data subject. The fact that the notification was made without undue delay should be established taking into account in particular the nature and gravity of the personal data breach and its consequences and adverse effects for the data subject. Such notification may result in an intervention of the supervisory authority in accordance with its tasks and powers laid down in this Regulation.

(88) In setting detailed rules concerning the format and procedures applicable to the notification of personal data breaches, due consideration should be given to the circumstances of that breach, including whether or not personal data had been protected by appropriate technical protection measures, effectively limiting the likelihood of identity fraud or other forms of misuse. Moreover, such rules and procedures should take into account the legitimate interests of law-enforcement authorities where early disclosure could unnecessarily hamper the investigation of the circumstances of a personal data breach.

(89) Directive 95/46/EC provided for a general obligation to notify the processing of personal data to the supervisory authorities. While that obligation produces administrative and financial burdens, it did not in all cases contribute to improving the protection of personal data. Such indiscriminate general notification obligations should therefore be abolished, and replaced by effective procedures and mechanisms which focus instead on those types of processing operations which are likely to result in a high risk to the rights and freedoms of natural persons by virtue of their nature, scope, context and purposes. Such types of processing operations may be those which in, particular, involve using new technologies, or are of a new kind and where no data protection impact assessment has been carried out before by the controller, or where they become necessary in the light of the time that has elapsed since the initial processing.

(90) In such cases, a data protection impact assessment should be carried out by the controller prior to the processing in order to assess the particular likelihood and severity of the high risk, taking into account the nature, scope, context and purposes of the processing and the sources of the risk. That impact assessment should include, in particular, the measures, safeguards and mechanisms envisaged for mitigating that risk, ensuring the protection of personal data and demonstrating compliance with this Regulation.

(91)   This should in particular apply to large-scale processing operations which aim to process a considerable amount of personal data at regional, national or supranational level and which could affect a large number of data subjects and which are likely to result in a high risk, for example, on account of their sensitivity, where in accordance with the achieved state of technological knowledge a new technology is used on a large scale as well as to other processing operations which result in a high risk to the rights and freedoms of data subjects, in particular where those operations render it more difficult for data subjects to exercise their rights. A data protection impact assessment should also be made where personal data are processed for taking decisions regarding specific natural persons following any systematic and extensive evaluation of personal aspects relating to natural persons based on profiling those data or following the processing of special categories of personal data, biometric data, or data on criminal convictions and offences or related security measures. A data protection impact assessment is equally required for monitoring publicly accessible areas on a large scale, especially when using optic-electronic devices or for any other operations where the competent supervisory authority considers that the processing is likely to result in a high risk to the rights and freedoms of data subjects, in particular because they prevent data subjects from exercising a right or using a service or a contract, or because they are carried out systematically on a large scale. The processing of personal data should not be considered to be on a large scale if the processing concerns personal data from patients or clients by an individual physician, other health care professional or lawyer. In such cases, a data protection impact assessment should not be mandatory.

(92)   There are circumstances under which it may be reasonable and economical for the subject of a data protection impact assessment to be broader than a single project, for example where public authorities or bodies intend to establish a common application or processing platform or where several controllers plan to introduce a common application or processing environment across an industry sector or segment or for a widely used horizontal activity.

(93)   In the context of the adoption of the Member State law on which the performance of the tasks of the public authority or public body is based and which regulates the specific processing operation or set of operations in question, Member States may deem it necessary to carry out such assessment prior to the processing activities.

(94)   Where a data protection impact assessment indicates that the processing would, in the absence of safeguards, security measures and mechanisms to mitigate the risk, result in a high risk to the rights and freedoms of natural persons and the controller is of the opinion that the risk cannot be mitigated by reasonable means in terms of available technologies and costs of implementation, the supervisory authority should be consulted prior to the start of processing activities. Such high risk is likely to result from certain types of processing and the extent and frequency of processing, which may result also in a realisation of damage or interference with the rights and freedoms of the natural person. The supervisory authority should respond to the request for consultation within a specified period. However, the absence of a reaction of the supervisory authority within that period should be without prejudice to any intervention of the supervisory authority in accordance with its tasks and powers laid down in this Regulation, including the power to prohibit processing operations. As part of that consultation process, the outcome of a

data protection impact assessment carried out with regard to the processing at issue may be submitted to the supervisory authority, in particular the measures envisaged to mitigate the risk to the rights and freedoms of natural persons.

(95) The processor should assist the controller, where necessary and upon request, in ensuring compliance with the obligations deriving from the carrying out of data protection impact assessments and from prior consultation of the supervisory authority.

(96) A consultation of the supervisory authority should also take place in the course of the preparation of a legislative or regulatory measure which provides for the processing of personal data, in order to ensure compliance of the intended processing with this Regulation and in particular to mitigate the risk involved for the data subject.

(97) Where the processing is carried out by a public authority, except for courts or independent judicial authorities when acting in their judicial capacity, where, in the private sector, processing is carried out by a controller whose core activities consist of processing operations that require regular and systematic monitoring of the data subjects on a large scale, or where the core activities of the controller or the processor consist of processing on a large scale of special categories of personal data and data relating to criminal convictions and offences, a person with expert knowledge of data protection law and practices should assist the controller or processor to monitor internal compliance with this Regulation. In the private sector, the core activities of a controller relate to its primary activities and do not relate to the processing of personal data as ancillary activities. The necessary level of expert knowledge should be determined in particular according to the data processing operations carried out and the protection required for the personal data processed by the controller or the processor. Such data protection officers, whether or not they are an employee of the controller, should be in a position to perform their duties and tasks in an independent manner.

(98) Associations or other bodies representing categories of controllers or processors should be encouraged to draw up codes of conduct, within the limits of this Regulation, so as to facilitate the effective application of this Regulation, taking account of the specific characteristics of the processing carried out in certain sectors and the specific needs of micro, small and medium enterprises. In particular, such codes of conduct could calibrate the obligations of controllers and processors, taking into account the risk likely to result from the processing for the rights and freedoms of natural persons.

(99) When drawing up a code of conduct, or when amending or extending such a code, associations and other bodies representing categories of controllers or processors should consult relevant stakeholders, including data subjects where feasible, and have regard to submissions received and views expressed in response to such consultations.

(100) In order to enhance transparency and compliance with this Regulation, the establishment of certification mechanisms and data protection seals and marks should be encouraged, allowing data subjects to quickly assess the level of data protection of relevant products and services.

(101) Flows of personal data to and from countries outside the Union and international organisations are necessary for the expansion of international trade and international

cooperation. The increase in such flows has raised new challenges and concerns with regard to the protection of personal data. However, when personal data are transferred from the Union to controllers, processors or other recipients in third countries or to international organisations, the level of protection of natural persons ensured in the Union by this Regulation should not be undermined, including in cases of onward transfers of personal data from the third country or international organisation to controllers, processors in the same or another third country or international organisation. In any event, transfers to third countries and international organisations may only be carried out in full compliance with this Regulation. A transfer could take place only if, subject to the other provisions of this Regulation, the conditions laid down in the provisions of this Regulation relating to the transfer of personal data to third countries or international organisations are complied with by the controller or processor.

(102) This Regulation is without prejudice to international agreements concluded between the Union and third countries regulating the transfer of personal data including appropriate safeguards for the data subjects. Member States may conclude international agreements which involve the transfer of personal data to third countries or international organisations, as far as such agreements do not affect this Regulation or any other provisions of Union law and include an appropriate level of protection for the fundamental rights of the data subjects.

(103) The Commission may decide with effect for the entire Union that a third country, a territory or specified sector within a third country, or an international organisation, offers an adequate level of data protection, thus providing legal certainty and uniformity throughout the Union as regards the third country or international organisation which is considered to provide such level of protection. In such cases, transfers of personal data to that third country or international organisation may take place without the need to obtain any further authorisation. The Commission may also decide, having given notice and a full statement setting out the reasons to the third country or international organisation, to revoke such a decision.

(104) In line with the fundamental values on which the Union is founded, in particular the protection of human rights, the Commission should, in its assessment of the third country, or of a territory or specified sector within a third country, take into account how a particular third country respects the rule of law, access to justice as well as international human rights norms and standards and its general and sectoral law, including legislation concerning public security, defence and national security as well as public order and criminal law. The adoption of an adequacy decision with regard to a territory or a specified sector in a third country should take into account clear and objective criteria, such as specific processing activities and the scope of applicable legal standards and legislation in force in the third country. The third country should offer guarantees ensuring an adequate level of protection essentially equivalent to that ensured within the Union, in particular where personal data are processed in one or several specific sectors. In particular, the third country should ensure effective independent data protection supervision and should provide for cooperation mechanisms with the Member States' data protection authorities, and the data subjects should be provided with effective and enforceable rights and effective administrative and judicial redress.

(105) Apart from the international commitments the third country or international organisation

has entered into, the Commission should take account of obligations arising from the third country's or international organisation's participation in multilateral or regional systems in particular in relation to the protection of personal data, as well as the implementation of such obligations. In particular, the third country's accession to the Council of Europe Convention of 28 January 1981 for the Protection of Individuals with regard to the Automatic Processing of Personal Data and its Additional Protocol should be taken into account. The Commission should consult the Board when assessing the level of protection in third countries or international organisations.

(106) The Commission should monitor the functioning of decisions on the level of protection in a third country, a territory or specified sector within a third country, or an international organisation, and monitor the functioning of decisions adopted on the basis of Article 25(6) or Article 26(4) of Directive 95/46/EC. In its adequacy decisions, the Commission should provide for a periodic review mechanism of their functioning. That periodic review should be conducted in consultation with the third country or international organisation in question and take into account all relevant developments in the third country or international organisation. For the purposes of monitoring and of carrying out the periodic reviews, the Commission should take into consideration the views and findings of the European Parliament and of the Council as well as of other relevant bodies and sources. The Commission should evaluate, within a reasonable time, the functioning of the latter decisions and report any relevant findings to the Committee within the meaning of Regulation (EU) No 182/2011 of the European Parliament and of the Council as established under this Regulation, to the European Parliament and to the Council.

(107) The Commission may recognise that a third country, a territory or a specified sector within a third country, or an international organisation no longer ensures an adequate level of data protection. Consequently the transfer of personal data to that third country or international organisation should be prohibited, unless the requirements in this Regulation relating to transfers subject to appropriate safeguards, including binding corporate rules, and derogations for specific situations are fulfilled. In that case, provision should be made for consultations between the Commission and such third countries or international organisations. The Commission should, in a timely manner, inform the third country or international organisation of the reasons and enter into consultations with it in order to remedy the situation.

(108) In the absence of an adequacy decision, the controller or processor should take measures to compensate for the lack of data protection in a third country by way of appropriate safeguards for the data subject. Such appropriate safeguards may consist of making use of binding corporate rules, standard data protection clauses adopted by the Commission, standard data protection clauses adopted by a supervisory authority or contractual clauses authorised by a supervisory authority. Those safeguards should ensure compliance with data protection requirements and the rights of the data subjects appropriate to processing within the Union, including the availability of enforceable data subject rights and of effective legal remedies, including to obtain effective administrative or judicial redress and to claim compensation, in the Union or in a third country. They should relate in particular to compliance with the general principles relating to personal data processing, the principles of data protection by design and by default. Transfers may also be carried out by public authorities or bodies with public authorities or bodies in third countries or

with international organisations with corresponding duties or functions, including on the basis of provisions to be inserted into administrative arrangements, such as a memorandum of understanding, providing for enforceable and effective rights for data subjects. Authorisation by the competent supervisory authority should be obtained when the safeguards are provided for in administrative arrangements that are not legally binding.

(109) The possibility for the controller or processor to use standard data-protection clauses adopted by the Commission or by a supervisory authority should prevent controllers or processors neither from including the standard data-protection clauses in a wider contract, such as a contract between the processor and another processor, nor from adding other clauses or additional safeguards provided that they do not contradict, directly or indirectly, the standard contractual clauses adopted by the Commission or by a supervisory authority or prejudice the fundamental rights or freedoms of the data subjects. Controllers and processors should be encouraged to provide additional safeguards via contractual commitments that supplement standard protection clauses.

(110) A group of undertakings, or a group of enterprises engaged in a joint economic activity, should be able to make use of approved binding corporate rules for its international transfers from the Union to organisations within the same group of undertakings, or group of enterprises engaged in a joint economic activity, provided that such corporate rules include all essential principles and enforceable rights to ensure appropriate safeguards for transfers or categories of transfers of personal data.

(111) Provisions should be made for the possibility for transfers in certain circumstances where the data subject has given his or her explicit consent, where the transfer is occasional and necessary in relation to a contract or a legal claim, regardless of whether in a judicial procedure or whether in an administrative or any out-of-court procedure, including procedures before regulatory bodies. Provision should also be made for the possibility for transfers where important grounds of public interest laid down by Union or Member State law so require or where the transfer is made from a register established by law and intended for consultation by the public or persons having a legitimate interest. In the latter case, such a transfer should not involve the entirety of the personal data or entire categories of the data contained in the register and, when the register is intended for consultation by persons having a legitimate interest, the transfer should be made only at the request of those persons or, if they are to be the recipients, taking into full account the interests and fundamental rights of the data subject.

(112) Those derogations should in particular apply to data transfers required and necessary for important reasons of public interest, for example in cases of international data exchange between competition authorities, tax or customs administrations, between financial supervisory authorities, between services competent for social security matters, or for public health, for example in the case of contact tracing for contagious diseases or in order to reduce and/or eliminate doping in sport. A transfer of personal data should also be regarded as lawful where it is necessary to protect an interest which is essential for the data subject's or another person's vital interests, including physical integrity or life, if the data subject is incapable of giving consent. In the absence of an adequacy decision, Union or Member State law may, for important reasons of public interest, expressly set limits to the transfer of specific categories of data to a third country or an international

organisation. Member States should notify such provisions to the Commission. Any transfer to an international humanitarian organisation of personal data of a data subject who is physically or legally incapable of giving consent, with a view to accomplishing a task incumbent under the Geneva Conventions or to complying with international humanitarian law applicable in armed conflicts, could be considered to be necessary for an important reason of public interest or because it is in the vital interest of the data subject.

(113) Transfers which can be qualified as not repetitive and that only concern a limited number of data subjects, could also be possible for the purposes of the compelling legitimate interests pursued by the controller, when those interests are not overridden by the interests or rights and freedoms of the data subject and when the controller has assessed all the circumstances surrounding the data transfer. The controller should give particular consideration to the nature of the personal data, the purpose and duration of the proposed processing operation or operations, as well as the situation in the country of origin, the third country and the country of final destination, and should provide suitable safeguards to protect fundamental rights and freedoms of natural persons with regard to the processing of their personal data. Such transfers should be possible only in residual cases where none of the other grounds for transfer are applicable. For scientific or historical research purposes or statistical purposes, the legitimate expectations of society for an increase of knowledge should be taken into consideration. The controller should inform the supervisory authority and the data subject about the transfer.

(114) In any case, where the Commission has taken no decision on the adequate level of data protection in a third country, the controller or processor should make use of solutions that provide data subjects with enforceable and effective rights as regards the processing of their data in the Union once those data have been transferred so that that they will continue to benefit from fundamental rights and safeguards.

(115) Some third countries adopt laws, regulations and other legal acts which purport to directly regulate the processing activities of natural and legal persons under the jurisdiction of the Member States. This may include judgments of courts or tribunals or decisions of administrative authorities in third countries requiring a controller or processor to transfer or disclose personal data, and which are not based on an international agreement, such as a mutual legal assistance treaty, in force between the requesting third country and the Union or a Member State. The extraterritorial application of those laws, regulations and other legal acts may be in breach of international law and may impede the attainment of the protection of natural persons ensured in the Union by this Regulation. Transfers should only be allowed where the conditions of this Regulation for a transfer to third countries are met. This may be the case, inter alia, where disclosure is necessary for an important ground of public interest recognised in Union or Member State law to which the controller is subject.

(116) When personal data moves across borders outside the Union it may put at increased risk the ability of natural persons to exercise data protection rights in particular to protect themselves from the unlawful use or disclosure of that information. At the same time, supervisory authorities may find that they are unable to pursue complaints or conduct investigations relating to the activities outside their borders. Their efforts to work together in the cross-border context may also be hampered by insufficient preventative

or remedial powers, inconsistent legal regimes, and practical obstacles like resource constraints. Therefore, there is a need to promote closer cooperation among data protection supervisory authorities to help them exchange information and carry out investigations with their international counterparts. For the purposes of developing international cooperation mechanisms to facilitate and provide international mutual assistance for the enforcement of legislation for the protection of personal data, the Commission and the supervisory authorities should exchange information and cooperate in activities related to the exercise of their powers with competent authorities in third countries, based on reciprocity and in accordance with this Regulation.

(117) The establishment of supervisory authorities in Member States, empowered to perform their tasks and exercise their powers with complete independence, is an essential component of the protection of natural persons with regard to the processing of their personal data. Member States should be able to establish more than one supervisory authority, to reflect their constitutional, organisational and administrative structure.

(118) The independence of supervisory authorities should not mean that the supervisory authorities cannot be subject to control or monitoring mechanisms regarding their financial expenditure or to judicial review.

(119) Where a Member State establishes several supervisory authorities, it should establish by law mechanisms for ensuring the effective participation of those supervisory authorities in the consistency mechanism. That Member State should in particular designate the supervisory authority which functions as a single contact point for the effective participation of those authorities in the mechanism, to ensure swift and smooth cooperation with other supervisory authorities, the Board and the Commission.

(120) Each supervisory authority should be provided with the financial and human resources, premises and infrastructure necessary for the effective performance of their tasks, including those related to mutual assistance and cooperation with other supervisory authorities throughout the Union. Each supervisory authority should have a separate, public annual budget, which may be part of the overall state or national budget.

(121) The general conditions for the member or members of the supervisory authority should be laid down by law in each Member State and should in particular provide that those members are to be appointed, by means of a transparent procedure, either by the parliament, government or the head of State of the Member State on the basis of a proposal from the government, a member of the government, the parliament or a chamber of the parliament, or by an independent body entrusted under Member State law. In order to ensure the independence of the supervisory authority, the member or members should act with integrity, refrain from any action that is incompatible with their duties and should not, during their term of office, engage in any incompatible occupation, whether gainful or not. The supervisory authority should have its own staff, chosen by the supervisory authority or an independent body established by Member State law, which should be subject to the exclusive direction of the member or members of the supervisory authority.

(122) Each supervisory authority should be competent on the territory of its own Member State to exercise the powers and to perform the tasks conferred on it in accordance with this

Regulation. This should cover in particular the processing in the context of the activities of an establishment of the controller or processor on the territory of its own Member State, the processing of personal data carried out by public authorities or private bodies acting in the public interest, processing affecting data subjects on its territory or processing carried out by a controller or processor not established in the Union when targeting data subjects residing on its territory. This should include handling complaints lodged by a data subject, conducting investigations on the application of this Regulation and promoting public awareness of the risks, rules, safeguards and rights in relation to the processing of personal data.

(123) The supervisory authorities should monitor the application of the provisions pursuant to this Regulation and contribute to its consistent application throughout the Union, in order to protect natural persons in relation to the processing of their personal data and to facilitate the free flow of personal data within the internal market. For that purpose, the supervisory authorities should cooperate with each other and with the Commission, without the need for any agreement between Member States on the provision of mutual assistance or on such cooperation.

(124) Where the processing of personal data takes place in the context of the activities of an establishment of a controller or a processor in the Union and the controller or processor is established in more than one Member State, or where processing taking place in the context of the activities of a single establishment of a controller or processor in the Union substantially affects or is likely to substantially affect data subjects in more than one Member State, the supervisory authority for the main establishment of the controller or processor or for the single establishment of the controller or processor should act as lead authority. It should cooperate with the other authorities concerned, because the controller or processor has an establishment on the territory of their Member State, because data subjects residing on their territory are substantially affected, or because a complaint has been lodged with them. Also where a data subject not residing in that Member State has lodged a complaint, the supervisory authority with which such complaint has been lodged should also be a supervisory authority concerned. Within its tasks to issue guidelines on any question covering the application of this Regulation, the Board should be able to issue guidelines in particular on the criteria to be taken into account in order to ascertain whether the processing in question substantially affects data subjects in more than one Member State and on what constitutes a relevant and reasoned objection.

(125) The lead authority should be competent to adopt binding decisions regarding measures applying the powers conferred on it in accordance with this Regulation. In its capacity as lead authority, the supervisory authority should closely involve and coordinate the supervisory authorities concerned in the decision-making process. Where the decision is to reject the complaint by the data subject in whole or in part, that decision should be adopted by the supervisory authority with which the complaint has been lodged.

(126) The decision should be agreed jointly by the lead supervisory authority and the supervisory authorities concerned and should be directed towards the main or single establishment of the controller or processor and be binding on the controller and processor. The controller or processor should take the necessary measures to ensure compliance with this Regulation and the implementation of the decision notified by the

lead supervisory authority to the main establishment of the controller or processor as regards the processing activities in the Union.

(127) Each supervisory authority not acting as the lead supervisory authority should be competent to handle local cases where the controller or processor is established in more than one Member State, but the subject matter of the specific processing concerns only processing carried out in a single Member State and involves only data subjects in that single Member State, for example, where the subject matter concerns the processing of employees' personal data in the specific employment context of a Member State. In such cases, the supervisory authority should inform the lead supervisory authority without delay about the matter. After being informed, the lead supervisory authority should decide, whether it will handle the case pursuant to the provision on cooperation between the lead supervisory authority and other supervisory authorities concerned ('one-stop-shop mechanism'), or whether the supervisory authority which informed it should handle the case at local level. When deciding whether it will handle the case, the lead supervisory authority should take into account whether there is an establishment of the controller or processor in the Member State of the supervisory authority which informed it in order to ensure effective enforcement of a decision vis-à-vis the controller or processor. Where the lead supervisory authority decides to handle the case, the supervisory authority which informed it should have the possibility to submit a draft for a decision, of which the lead supervisory authority should take utmost account when preparing its draft decision in that one-stop-shop mechanism.

(128) The rules on the lead supervisory authority and the one-stop-shop mechanism should not apply where the processing is carried out by public authorities or private bodies in the public interest. In such cases the only supervisory authority competent to exercise the powers conferred to it in accordance with this Regulation should be the supervisory authority of the Member State where the public authority or private body is established.

(129) In order to ensure consistent monitoring and enforcement of this Regulation throughout the Union, the supervisory authorities should have in each Member State the same tasks and effective powers, including powers of investigation, corrective powers and sanctions, and authorisation and advisory powers, in particular in cases of complaints from natural persons, and without prejudice to the powers of prosecutorial authorities under Member State law, to bring infringements of this Regulation to the attention of the judicial authorities and engage in legal proceedings. Such powers should also include the power to impose a temporary or definitive limitation, including a ban, on processing. Member States may specify other tasks related to the protection of personal data under this Regulation. The powers of supervisory authorities should be exercised in accordance with appropriate procedural safeguards set out in Union and Member State law, impartially, fairly and within a reasonable time. In particular each measure should be appropriate, necessary and proportionate in view of ensuring compliance with this Regulation, taking into account the circumstances of each individual case, respect the right of every person to be heard before any individual measure which would affect him or her adversely is taken and avoid superfluous costs and excessive inconveniences for the persons concerned. Investigatory powers as regards access to premises should be exercised in accordance with specific requirements in Member State procedural law, such as the requirement to obtain a prior judicial authorisation. Each legally binding measure of the supervisory authority should be in writing, be clear and unambiguous, indicate the

supervisory authority which has issued the measure, the date of issue of the measure, bear the signature of the head, or a member of the supervisory authority authorised by him or her, give the reasons for the measure, and refer to the right of an effective remedy. This should not preclude additional requirements pursuant to Member State procedural law. The adoption of a legally binding decision implies that it may give rise to judicial review in the Member State of the supervisory authority that adopted the decision.

(130) Where the supervisory authority with which the complaint has been lodged is not the lead supervisory authority, the lead supervisory authority should closely cooperate with the supervisory authority with which the complaint has been lodged in accordance with the provisions on cooperation and consistency laid down in this Regulation. In such cases, the lead supervisory authority should, when taking measures intended to produce legal effects, including the imposition of administrative fines, take utmost account of the view of the supervisory authority with which the complaint has been lodged and which should remain competent to carry out any investigation on the territory of its own Member State in liaison with the competent supervisory authority.

(131) Where another supervisory authority should act as a lead supervisory authority for the processing activities of the controller or processor but the concrete subject matter of a complaint or the possible infringement concerns only processing activities of the controller or processor in the Member State where the complaint has been lodged or the possible infringement detected and the matter does not substantially affect or is not likely to substantially affect data subjects in other Member States, the supervisory authority receiving a complaint or detecting or being informed otherwise of situations that entail possible infringements of this Regulation should seek an amicable settlement with the controller and, if this proves unsuccessful, exercise its full range of powers. This should include: specific processing carried out in the territory of the Member State of the supervisory authority or with regard to data subjects on the territory of that Member State; processing that is carried out in the context of an offer of goods or services specifically aimed at data subjects in the territory of the Member State of the supervisory authority; or processing that has to be assessed taking into account relevant legal obligations under Member State law.

(132) Awareness-raising activities by supervisory authorities addressed to the public should include specific measures directed at controllers and processors, including micro, small and medium-sized enterprises, as well as natural persons in particular in the educational context.

(133) The supervisory authorities should assist each other in performing their tasks and provide mutual assistance, so as to ensure the consistent application and enforcement of this Regulation in the internal market. A supervisory authority requesting mutual assistance may adopt a provisional measure if it receives no response to a request for mutual assistance within one month of the receipt of that request by the other supervisory authority.

(134) Each supervisory authority should, where appropriate, participate in joint operations with other supervisory authorities. The requested supervisory authority should be obliged to respond to the request within a specified time period.

(135) In order to ensure the consistent application of this Regulation throughout the Union, a consistency mechanism for cooperation between the supervisory authorities should be established. That mechanism should in particular apply where a supervisory authority intends to adopt a measure intended to produce legal effects as regards processing operations which substantially affect a significant number of data subjects in several Member States. It should also apply where any supervisory authority concerned or the Commission requests that such matter should be handled in the consistency mechanism. That mechanism should be without prejudice to any measures that the Commission may take in the exercise of its powers under the Treaties.

(136) In applying the consistency mechanism, the Board should, within a determined period of time, issue an opinion, if a majority of its members so decides or if so requested by any supervisory authority concerned or the Commission. The Board should also be empowered to adopt legally binding decisions where there are disputes between supervisory authorities. For that purpose, it should issue, in principle by a two-thirds majority of its members, legally binding decisions in clearly specified cases where there are conflicting views among supervisory authorities, in particular in the cooperation mechanism between the lead supervisory authority and supervisory authorities concerned on the merits of the case, in particular whether there is an infringement of this Regulation.

(137) There may be an urgent need to act in order to protect the rights and freedoms of data subjects, in particular when the danger exists that the enforcement of a right of a data subject could be considerably impeded. A supervisory authority should therefore be able to adopt duly justified provisional measures on its territory with a specified period of validity which should not exceed three months.

(138) The application of such mechanism should be a condition for the lawfulness of a measure intended to produce legal effects by a supervisory authority in those cases where its application is mandatory. In other cases of cross-border relevance, the cooperation mechanism between the lead supervisory authority and supervisory authorities concerned should be applied and mutual assistance and joint operations might be carried out between the supervisory authorities concerned on a bilateral or multilateral basis without triggering the consistency mechanism.

(139) In order to promote the consistent application of this Regulation, the Board should be set up as an independent body of the Union. To fulfil its objectives, the Board should have legal personality. The Board should be represented by its Chair. It should replace the Working Party on the Protection of Individuals with Regard to the Processing of Personal Data established by Directive 95/46/EC. It should consist of the head of a supervisory authority of each Member State and the European Data Protection Supervisor or their respective representatives. The Commission should participate in the Board's activities without voting rights and the European Data Protection Supervisor should have specific voting rights. The Board should contribute to the consistent application of this Regulation throughout the Union, including by advising the Commission, in particular on the level of protection in third countries or international organisations, and promoting cooperation of the supervisory authorities throughout the Union. The Board should act independently when performing its tasks.

(140) The Board should be assisted by a secretariat provided by the European Data Protection Supervisor. The staff of the European Data Protection Supervisor involved in carrying out the tasks conferred on the Board by this Regulation should perform its tasks exclusively under the instructions of, and report to, the Chair of the Board.

(141) Every data subject should have the right to lodge a complaint with a single supervisory authority, in particular in the Member State of his or her habitual residence, and the right to an effective judicial remedy in accordance with Article 47 of the Charter if the data subject considers that his or her rights under this Regulation are infringed or where the supervisory authority does not act on a complaint, partially or wholly rejects or dismisses a complaint or does not act where such action is necessary to protect the rights of the data subject. The investigation following a complaint should be carried out, subject to judicial review, to the extent that is appropriate in the specific case. The supervisory authority should inform the data subject of the progress and the outcome of the complaint within a reasonable period. If the case requires further investigation or coordination with another supervisory authority, intermediate information should be given to the data subject. In order to facilitate the submission of complaints, each supervisory authority should take measures such as providing a complaint submission form which can also be completed electronically, without excluding other means of communication.

(142) Where a data subject considers that his or her rights under this Regulation are infringed, he or she should have the right to mandate a not-for-profit body, organisation or association which is constituted in accordance with the law of a Member State, has statutory objectives which are in the public interest and is active in the field of the protection of personal data to lodge a complaint on his or her behalf with a supervisory authority, exercise the right to a judicial remedy on behalf of data subjects or, if provided for in Member State law, exercise the right to receive compensation on behalf of data subjects. A Member State may provide for such a body, organisation or association to have the right to lodge a complaint in that Member State, independently of a data subject's mandate, and the right to an effective judicial remedy where it has reasons to consider that the rights of a data subject have been infringed as a result of the processing of personal data which infringes this Regulation. That body, organisation or association may not be allowed to claim compensation on a data subject's behalf independently of the data subject's mandate.

(143) Any natural or legal person has the right to bring an action for annulment of decisions of the Board before the Court of Justice under the conditions provided for in Article 263 TFEU. As addressees of such decisions, the supervisory authorities concerned which wish to challenge them have to bring action within two months of being notified of them, in accordance with Article 263 TFEU. Where decisions of the Board are of direct and individual concern to a controller, processor or complainant, the latter may bring an action for annulment against those decisions within two months of their publication on the website of the Board, in accordance with Article 263 TFEU. Without prejudice to this right under Article 263 TFEU, each natural or legal person should have an effective judicial remedy before the competent national court against a decision of a supervisory authority which produces legal effects concerning that person. Such a decision concerns in particular the exercise of investigative, corrective and authorisation powers by the supervisory authority or the dismissal or rejection of complaints. However, the right to an effective judicial remedy does not encompass measures taken by supervisory

authorities which are not legally binding, such as opinions issued by or advice provided by the supervisory authority. Proceedings against a supervisory authority should be brought before the courts of the Member State where the supervisory authority is established and should be conducted in accordance with that Member State's procedural law. Those courts should exercise full jurisdiction, which should include jurisdiction to examine all questions of fact and law relevant to the dispute before them. Where a complaint has been rejected or dismissed by a supervisory authority, the complainant may bring proceedings before the courts in the same Member State. In the context of judicial remedies relating to the application of this Regulation, national courts which consider a decision on the question necessary to enable them to give judgment, may, or in the case provided for in Article 267 TFEU, must, request the Court of Justice to give a preliminary ruling on the interpretation of Union law, including this Regulation. Furthermore, where a decision of a supervisory authority implementing a decision of the Board is challenged before a national court and the validity of the decision of the Board is at issue, that national court does not have the power to declare the Board's decision invalid but must refer the question of validity to the Court of Justice in accordance with Article 267 TFEU as interpreted by the Court of Justice, where it considers the decision invalid. However, a national court may not refer a question on the validity of the decision of the Board at the request of a natural or legal person which had the opportunity to bring an action for annulment of that decision, in particular if it was directly and individually concerned by that decision, but had not done so within the period laid down in Article 263 TFEU.

(144) Where a court seized of proceedings against a decision by a supervisory authority has reason to believe that proceedings concerning the same processing, such as the same subject matter as regards processing by the same controller or processor, or the same cause of action, are brought before a competent court in another Member State, it should contact that court in order to confirm the existence of such related proceedings. If related proceedings are pending before a court in another Member State, any court other than the court first seized may stay its proceedings or may, on request of one of the parties, decline jurisdiction in favour of the court first seized if that court has jurisdiction over the proceedings in question and its law permits the consolidation of such related proceedings. Proceedings are deemed to be related where they are so closely connected that it is expedient to hear and determine them together in order to avoid the risk of irreconcilable judgments resulting from separate proceedings.

(145) For proceedings against a controller or processor, the plaintiff should have the choice to bring the action before the courts of the Member States where the controller or processor has an establishment or where the data subject resides, unless the controller is a public authority of a Member State acting in the exercise of its public powers.

(146) The controller or processor should compensate any damage which a person may suffer as a result of processing that infringes this Regulation. The controller or processor should be exempt from liability if it proves that it is not in any way responsible for the damage. The concept of damage should be broadly interpreted in the light of the case-law of the Court of Justice in a manner which fully reflects the objectives of this Regulation. This is without prejudice to any claims for damage deriving from the violation of other rules in Union or Member State law. Processing that infringes this Regulation also includes processing that infringes delegated and implementing acts adopted in accordance with this Regulation and Member State law specifying rules of this Regulation. Data subjects

should receive full and effective compensation for the damage they have suffered. Where controllers or processors are involved in the same processing, each controller or processor should be held liable for the entire damage. However, where they are joined to the same judicial proceedings, in accordance with Member State law, compensation may be apportioned according to the responsibility of each controller or processor for the damage caused by the processing, provided that full and effective compensation of the data subject who suffered the damage is ensured. Any controller or processor which has paid full compensation may subsequently institute recourse proceedings against other controllers or processors involved in the same processing.

(147) Where specific rules on jurisdiction are contained in this Regulation, in particular as regards proceedings seeking a judicial remedy including compensation, against a controller or processor, general jurisdiction rules such as those of Regulation (EU) No 1215/2012 of the European Parliament and of the Council should not prejudice the application of such specific rules.

(148) In order to strengthen the enforcement of the rules of this Regulation, penalties including administrative fines should be imposed for any infringement of this Regulation, in addition to, or instead of appropriate measures imposed by the supervisory authority pursuant to this Regulation. In a case of a minor infringement or if the fine likely to be imposed would constitute a disproportionate burden to a natural person, a reprimand may be issued instead of a fine. Due regard should however be given to the nature, gravity and duration of the infringement, the intentional character of the infringement, actions taken to mitigate the damage suffered, degree of responsibility or any relevant previous infringements, the manner in which the infringement became known to the supervisory authority, compliance with measures ordered against the controller or processor, adherence to a code of conduct and any other aggravating or mitigating factor. The imposition of penalties including administrative fines should be subject to appropriate procedural safeguards in accordance with the general principles of Union law and the Charter, including effective judicial protection and due process.

(149) Member States should be able to lay down the rules on criminal penalties for infringements of this Regulation, including for infringements of national rules adopted pursuant to and within the limits of this Regulation. Those criminal penalties may also allow for the deprivation of the profits obtained through infringements of this Regulation. However, the imposition of criminal penalties for infringements of such national rules and of administrative penalties should not lead to a breach of the principle of ne bis in idem, as interpreted by the Court of Justice.

(150) In order to strengthen and harmonise administrative penalties for infringements of this Regulation, each supervisory authority should have the power to impose administrative fines. This Regulation should indicate infringements and the upper limit and criteria for setting the related administrative fines, which should be determined by the competent supervisory authority in each individual case, taking into account all relevant circumstances of the specific situation, with due regard in particular to the nature, gravity and duration of the infringement and of its consequences and the measures taken to ensure compliance with the obligations under this Regulation and to prevent or mitigate the consequences of the infringement. Where administrative fines are imposed on an undertaking, an undertaking should be understood to be an undertaking in accordance

with Articles 101 and 102 TFEU for those purposes. Where administrative fines are imposed on persons that are not an undertaking, the supervisory authority should take account of the general level of income in the Member State as well as the economic situation of the person in considering the appropriate amount of the fine. The consistency mechanism may also be used to promote a consistent application of administrative fines. It should be for the Member States to determine whether and to which extent public authorities should be subject to administrative fines. Imposing an administrative fine or giving a warning does not affect the application of other powers of the supervisory authorities or of other penalties under this Regulation.

(151) The legal systems of Denmark and Estonia do not allow for administrative fines as set out in this Regulation. The rules on administrative fines may be applied in such a manner that in Denmark the fine is imposed by competent national courts as a criminal penalty and in Estonia the fine is imposed by the supervisory authority in the framework of a misdemeanour procedure, provided that such an application of the rules in those Member States has an equivalent effect to administrative fines imposed by supervisory authorities. Therefore the competent national courts should take into account the recommendation by the supervisory authority initiating the fine. In any event, the fines imposed should be effective, proportionate and dissuasive.

(152) Where this Regulation does not harmonise administrative penalties or where necessary in other cases, for example in cases of serious infringements of this Regulation, Member States should implement a system which provides for effective, proportionate and dissuasive penalties. The nature of such penalties, criminal or administrative, should be determined by Member State law.

(153) Member States law should reconcile the rules governing freedom of expression and information, including journalistic, academic, artistic and or literary expression with the right to the protection of personal data pursuant to this Regulation. The processing of personal data solely for journalistic purposes, or for the purposes of academic, artistic or literary expression should be subject to derogations or exemptions from certain provisions of this Regulation if necessary to reconcile the right to the protection of personal data with the right to freedom of expression and information, as enshrined in Article 11 of the Charter. This should apply in particular to the processing of personal data in the audiovisual field and in news archives and press libraries. Therefore, Member States should adopt legislative measures which lay down the exemptions and derogations necessary for the purpose of balancing those fundamental rights. Member States should adopt such exemptions and derogations on general principles, the rights of the data subject, the controller and the processor, the transfer of personal data to third countries or international organisations, the independent supervisory authorities, cooperation and consistency, and specific data-processing situations. Where such exemptions or derogations differ from one Member State to another, the law of the Member State to which the controller is subject should apply. In order to take account of the importance of the right to freedom of expression in every democratic society, it is necessary to interpret notions relating to that freedom, such as journalism, broadly.

(154) This Regulation allows the principle of public access to official documents to be taken into account when applying this Regulation. Public access to official documents may be considered to be in the public interest. Personal data in documents held by a public

authority or a public body should be able to be publicly disclosed by that authority or body if the disclosure is provided for by Union or Member State law to which the public authority or public body is subject. Such laws should reconcile public access to official documents and the reuse of public sector information with the right to the protection of personal data and may therefore provide for the necessary reconciliation with the right to the protection of personal data pursuant to this Regulation. The reference to public authorities and bodies should in that context include all authorities or other bodies covered by Member State law on public access to documents. Directive 2003/98/EC of the European Parliament and of the Council leaves intact and in no way affects the level of protection of natural persons with regard to the processing of personal data under the provisions of Union and Member State law, and in particular does not alter the obligations and rights set out in this Regulation. In particular, that Directive should not apply to documents to which access is excluded or restricted by virtue of the access regimes on the grounds of protection of personal data, and parts of documents accessible by virtue of those regimes which contain personal data the re-use of which has been provided for by law as being incompatible with the law concerning the protection of natural persons with regard to the processing of personal data.

(155) Member State law or collective agreements, including 'works agreements', may provide for specific rules on the processing of employees' personal data in the employment context, in particular for the conditions under which personal data in the employment context may be processed on the basis of the consent of the employee, the purposes of the recruitment, the performance of the contract of employment, including discharge of obligations laid down by law or by collective agreements, management, planning and organisation of work, equality and diversity in the workplace, health and safety at work, and for the purposes of the exercise and enjoyment, on an individual or collective basis, of rights and benefits related to employment, and for the purpose of the termination of the employment relationship.

(156) The processing of personal data for archiving purposes in the public interest, scientific or historical research purposes or statistical purposes should be subject to appropriate safeguards for the rights and freedoms of the data subject pursuant to this Regulation. Those safeguards should ensure that technical and organisational measures are in place in order to ensure, in particular, the principle of data minimisation. The further processing of personal data for archiving purposes in the public interest, scientific or historical research purposes or statistical purposes is to be carried out when the controller has assessed the feasibility to fulfil those purposes by processing data which do not permit or no longer permit the identification of data subjects, provided that appropriate safeguards exist (such as, for instance, pseudonymisation of the data). Member States should provide for appropriate safeguards for the processing of personal data for archiving purposes in the public interest, scientific or historical research purposes or statistical purposes. Member States should be authorised to provide, under specific conditions and subject to appropriate safeguards for data subjects, specifications and derogations with regard to the information requirements and rights to rectification, to erasure, to be forgotten, to restriction of processing, to data portability, and to object when processing personal data for archiving purposes in the public interest, scientific or historical research purposes or statistical purposes. The conditions and safeguards in question may entail specific procedures for data subjects to exercise those rights if this is appropriate in the light of the purposes sought by the specific processing along with technical and

organisational measures aimed at minimising the processing of personal data in pursuance of the proportionality and necessity principles. The processing of personal data for scientific purposes should also comply with other relevant legislation such as on clinical trials.

(157) By coupling information from registries, researchers can obtain new knowledge of great value with regard to widespread medical conditions such as cardiovascular disease, cancer and depression. On the basis of registries, research results can be enhanced, as they draw on a larger population. Within social science, research on the basis of registries enables researchers to obtain essential knowledge about the long-term correlation of a number of social conditions such as unemployment and education with other life conditions. Research results obtained through registries provide solid, high-quality knowledge which can provide the basis for the formulation and implementation of knowledge-based policy, improve the quality of life for a number of people and improve the efficiency of social services. In order to facilitate scientific research, personal data can be processed for scientific research purposes, subject to appropriate conditions and safeguards set out in Union or Member State law.

(158) Where personal data are processed for archiving purposes, this Regulation should also apply to that processing, bearing in mind that this Regulation should not apply to deceased persons. Public authorities or public or private bodies that hold records of public interest should be services which, pursuant to Union or Member State law, have a legal obligation to acquire, preserve, appraise, arrange, describe, communicate, promote, disseminate and provide access to records of enduring value for general public interest. Member States should also be authorised to provide for the further processing of personal data for archiving purposes, for example with a view to providing specific information related to the political behaviour under former totalitarian state regimes, genocide, crimes against humanity, in particular the Holocaust, or war crimes.

(159) Where personal data are processed for scientific research purposes, this Regulation should also apply to that processing. For the purposes of this Regulation, the processing of personal data for scientific research purposes should be interpreted in a broad manner including for example technological development and demonstration, fundamental research, applied research and privately funded research. In addition, it should take into account the Union's objective under Article 179(1) TFEU of achieving a European Research Area. Scientific research purposes should also include studies conducted in the public interest in the area of public health. To meet the specificities of processing personal data for scientific research purposes, specific conditions should apply in particular as regards the publication or otherwise disclosure of personal data in the context of scientific research purposes. If the result of scientific research in particular in the health context gives reason for further measures in the interest of the data subject, the general rules of this Regulation should apply in view of those measures.

(160) Where personal data are processed for historical research purposes, this Regulation should also apply to that processing. This should also include historical research and research for genealogical purposes, bearing in mind that this Regulation should not apply to deceased persons.

(161) For the purpose of consenting to the participation in scientific research activities in clinical

trials, the relevant provisions of Regulation (EU) No 536/2014 of the European Parliament and of the Council should apply.

(162) Where personal data are processed for statistical purposes, this Regulation should apply to that processing. Union or Member State law should, within the limits of this Regulation, determine statistical content, control of access, specifications for the processing of personal data for statistical purposes and appropriate measures to safeguard the rights and freedoms of the data subject and for ensuring statistical confidentiality. Statistical purposes mean any operation of collection and the processing of personal data necessary for statistical surveys or for the production of statistical results. Those statistical results may further be used for different purposes, including a scientific research purpose. The statistical purpose implies that the result of processing for statistical purposes is not personal data, but aggregate data, and that this result or the personal data are not used in support of measures or decisions regarding any particular natural person.

(163) The confidential information which the Union and national statistical authorities collect for the production of official European and official national statistics should be protected. European statistics should be developed, produced and disseminated in accordance with the statistical principles as set out in Article 338(2) TFEU, while national statistics should also comply with Member State law. Regulation (EC) No 223/2009 of the European Parliament and of the Council provides further specifications on statistical confidentiality for European statistics.

(164) As regards the powers of the supervisory authorities to obtain from the controller or processor access to personal data and access to their premises, Member States may adopt by law, within the limits of this Regulation, specific rules in order to safeguard the professional or other equivalent secrecy obligations, in so far as necessary to reconcile the right to the protection of personal data with an obligation of professional secrecy. This is without prejudice to existing Member State obligations to adopt rules on professional secrecy where required by Union law.

(165) This Regulation respects and does not prejudice the status under existing constitutional law of churches and religious associations or communities in the Member States, as recognised in Article 17 TFEU.

(166) In order to fulfil the objectives of this Regulation, namely to protect the fundamental rights and freedoms of natural persons and in particular their right to the protection of personal data and to ensure the free movement of personal data within the Union, the power to adopt acts in accordance with Article 290 TFEU should be delegated to the Commission. In particular, delegated acts should be adopted in respect of criteria and requirements for certification mechanisms, information to be presented by standardised icons and procedures for providing such icons. It is of particular importance that the Commission carry out appropriate consultations during its preparatory work, including at expert level. The Commission, when preparing and drawing-up delegated acts, should ensure a simultaneous, timely and appropriate transmission of relevant documents to the European Parliament and to the Council.

(167) In order to ensure uniform conditions for the implementation of this Regulation, implementing powers should be conferred on the Commission when provided for by this

Regulation. Those powers should be exercised in accordance with Regulation (EU) No 182/2011. In that context, the Commission should consider specific measures for micro, small and medium-sized enterprises.

(168) The examination procedure should be used for the adoption of implementing acts on standard contractual clauses between controllers and processors and between processors; codes of conduct; technical standards and mechanisms for certification; the adequate level of protection afforded by a third country, a territory or a specified sector within that third country, or an international organisation; standard protection clauses; formats and procedures for the exchange of information by electronic means between controllers, processors and supervisory authorities for binding corporate rules; mutual assistance; and arrangements for the exchange of information by electronic means between supervisory authorities, and between supervisory authorities and the Board.

(169) The Commission should adopt immediately applicable implementing acts where available evidence reveals that a third country, a territory or a specified sector within that third country, or an international organisation does not ensure an adequate level of protection, and imperative grounds of urgency so require.

(170) Since the objective of this Regulation, namely to ensure an equivalent level of protection of natural persons and the free flow of personal data throughout the Union, cannot be sufficiently achieved by the Member States and can rather, by reason of the scale or effects of the action, be better achieved at Union level, the Union may adopt measures, in accordance with the principle of subsidiarity as set out in Article 5 of the Treaty on European Union (TEU). In accordance with the principle of proportionality as set out in that Article, this Regulation does not go beyond what is necessary in order to achieve that objective.

(171) Directive 95/46/EC should be repealed by this Regulation. Processing already under way on the date of application of this Regulation should be brought into conformity with this Regulation within the period of two years after which this Regulation enters into force. Where processing is based on consent pursuant to Directive 95/46/EC, it is not necessary for the data subject to give his or her consent again if the manner in which the consent has been given is in line with the conditions of this Regulation, so as to allow the controller to continue such processing after the date of application of this Regulation. Commission decisions adopted and authorisations by supervisory authorities based on Directive 95/46/EC remain in force until amended, replaced or repealed.

(172) The European Data Protection Supervisor was consulted in accordance with Article 28(2) of Regulation (EC) No 45/2001 and delivered an opinion on 7 March 2012.

(173) This Regulation should apply to all matters concerning the protection of fundamental rights and freedoms vis-à-vis the processing of personal data which are not subject to specific obligations with the same objective set out in Directive 2002/58/EC of the European Parliament and of the Council, including the obligations on the controller and the rights of natural persons. In order to clarify the relationship between this Regulation and Directive 2002/58/EC, that Directive should be amended accordingly. Once this Regulation is adopted, Directive 2002/58/EC should be reviewed in particular in order to ensure consistency with this Regulation,

HAVE ADOPTED THIS REGULATION:

CHAPTER I – GENERAL PROVISIONS

Article 1   Subject-matter and objectives

1. This Regulation lays down rules relating to the protection of natural persons with regard to the processing of personal data and rules relating to the free movement of personal data.

2. This Regulation protects fundamental rights and freedoms of natural persons and in particular their right to the protection of personal data.

3. The free movement of personal data within the Union shall be neither restricted nor prohibited for reasons connected with the protection of natural persons with regard to the processing of personal data.

—— NOTES ——

Defined terms		Relevant recitals
personal data	Art 4(1)	(1), (2), (3), (4), (5), (6), (7), (8), (9), (12), (170)
processing	Art 4(2)	

LED equivalent
Arts 1, 2

Article 2   Material scope

1. This Regulation applies to the processing of personal data wholly or partly by automated means and to the processing other than by automated means of personal data which form part of a filing system or are intended to form part of a filing system.

2. This Regulation does not apply to the processing of personal data:
    (a) in the course of an activity which falls outside the scope of Union law;
    (b) by the Member States when carrying out activities which fall within the scope of Chapter 2 of Title V of the TEU;
    (c) by a natural person in the course of a purely personal or household activity;
    (d) by competent authorities for the purposes of the prevention, investigation, detection or prosecution of criminal offences or the execution of criminal penalties, including the safeguarding against and the prevention of threats to public security.

3. For the processing of personal data by the Union institutions, bodies, offices and agencies, Regulation (EC) No 45/2001 applies. Regulation (EC) No 45/2001 and other Union legal acts applicable to such processing of personal data shall be adapted to the principles and rules of this Regulation in accordance with Article 98.

4. This Regulation shall be without prejudice to the application of Directive 2000/31/EC, in particular of the liability rules of intermediary service providers in Articles 12 to 15 of that Directive.

—— NOTES ——

Defined terms		Relevant recitals
filing system	Art 4(6)	(14), (15), (16), (17), (18), (19), (20), (21)
personal data	Art 4(1)	
supervisory authority	Art 4(22)	**LED equivalent**
		Arts 1, 2, 3

Article 3   Territorial scope

1. This Regulation applies to the processing of personal data in the context of the activities of an establishment of a controller or a processor in the Union, regardless of whether the

processing takes place in the Union or not.

2. This Regulation applies to the processing of personal data of data subjects who are in the Union by a controller or processor not established in the Union, where the processing activities are related to:

    (a) the offering of goods or services, irrespective of whether a payment of the data subject is required, to such data subjects in the Union; or

    (b) the monitoring of their behaviour as far as their behaviour takes place within the Union.

3. This Regulation applies to the processing of personal data by a controller not established in the Union, but in a place where Member State law applies by virtue of public international law.

—— NOTES ——

Defined terms		Relevant recitals
controller	Art 4(7)	(22), (23), (24), (25)
personal data	Art 4(1)	
processing	Art 4(2)	**LED equivalent**
processor	Art 4(8)	n/a

Article 4   Definitions

For the purposes of this Regulation:

(1) 'personal data' means any information relating to an identified or identifiable natural person ('data subject'); an identifiable natural person is one who can be identified, directly or indirectly, in particular by reference to an identifier such as a name, an identification number, location data, an online identifier or to one or more factors specific to the physical, physiological, genetic, mental, economic, cultural or social identity of that natural person;

(2) 'processing' means any operation or set of operations which is performed on personal data or on sets of personal data, whether or not by automated means, such as collection, recording, organisation, structuring, storage, adaptation or alteration, retrieval, consultation, use, disclosure by transmission, dissemination or otherwise making available, alignment or combination, restriction, erasure or destruction;

(3) 'restriction of processing' means the marking of stored personal data with the aim of limiting their processing in the future;

(4) 'profiling' means any form of automated processing of personal data consisting of the use of personal data to evaluate certain personal aspects relating to a natural person, in particular to analyse or predict aspects concerning that natural person's performance at work, economic situation, health, personal preferences, interests, reliability, behaviour, location or movements;

(5) 'pseudonymisation' means the processing of personal data in such a manner that the personal data can no longer be attributed to a specific data subject without the use of additional information, provided that such additional information is kept separately and is subject to technical and organisational measures to ensure that the personal data are not attributed to an identified or identifiable natural person;

(6) 'filing system' means any structured set of personal data which are accessible according to specific criteria, whether centralised, decentralised or dispersed on a functional or geographical basis;

(7) 'controller' means the natural or legal person, public authority, agency or other body which, alone or jointly with others, determines the purposes and means of the processing of personal data; where the purposes and means of such processing are determined by Union or Member State law, the controller or the specific criteria for its nomination may be provided for by Union or Member State law;

(8) 'processor' means a natural or legal person, public authority, agency or other body which processes personal data on behalf of the controller;

(9) 'recipient' means a natural or legal person, public authority, agency or another body, to which the personal data are disclosed, whether a third party or not. However, public authorities which may receive personal data in the framework of a particular inquiry in accordance with Union or Member State law shall not be regarded as recipients; the processing of those data by those public authorities shall be in compliance with the applicable data protection rules according to the purposes of the processing;

(10) 'third party' means a natural or legal person, public authority, agency or body other than the data subject, controller, processor and persons who, under the direct authority of the controller or processor, are authorised to process personal data;

(11) 'consent' of the data subject means any freely given, specific, informed and unambiguous indication of the data subject's wishes by which he or she, by a statement or by a clear affirmative action, signifies agreement to the processing of personal data relating to him or her;

(12) 'personal data breach' means a breach of security leading to the accidental or unlawful destruction, loss, alteration, unauthorised disclosure of, or access to, personal data transmitted, stored or otherwise processed;

(13) 'genetic data' means personal data relating to the inherited or acquired genetic characteristics of a natural person which give unique information about the physiology or the health of that natural person and which result, in particular, from an analysis of a biological sample from the natural person in question;

(14) 'biometric data' means personal data resulting from specific technical processing relating to the physical, physiological or behavioural characteristics of a natural person, which allow or confirm the unique identification of that natural person, such as facial images or dactyloscopic data;

(15) 'data concerning health' means personal data related to the physical or mental health of a natural person, including the provision of health care services, which reveal information about his or her health status;

(16) 'main establishment' means:
    (a) as regards a controller with establishments in more than one Member State, the place of its central administration in the Union, unless the decisions on the purposes and means of the processing of personal data are taken in another establishment of the controller in the Union and the latter establishment has the power to have such decisions implemented, in which case the establishment having taken such decisions is to be considered to be the main establishment;
    (b) as regards a processor with establishments in more than one Member State, the place of its central administration in the Union, or, if the processor has no central administration in the Union, the establishment of the processor in the Union where the main processing activities in the context of the activities of an establishment of

the processor take place to the extent that the processor is subject to specific obligations under this Regulation;

(17) 'representative' means a natural or legal person established in the Union who, designated by the controller or processor in writing pursuant to Article 27, represents the controller or processor with regard to their respective obligations under this Regulation;

(18) 'enterprise' means a natural or legal person engaged in an economic activity, irrespective of its legal form, including partnerships or associations regularly engaged in an economic activity;

(19) 'group of undertakings' means a controlling undertaking and its controlled undertakings;

(20) 'binding corporate rules' means personal data protection policies which are adhered to by a controller or processor established on the territory of a Member State for transfers or a set of transfers of personal data to a controller or processor in one or more third countries within a group of undertakings, or group of enterprises engaged in a joint economic activity;

(21) 'supervisory authority' means an independent public authority which is established by a Member State pursuant to Article 51;

(22) 'supervisory authority concerned' means a supervisory authority which is concerned by the processing of personal data because:
    (a) the controller or processor is established on the territory of the Member State of that supervisory authority;
    (b) data subjects residing in the Member State of that supervisory authority are substantially affected or likely to be substantially affected by the processing; or
    (c) a complaint has been lodged with that supervisory authority;

(23) 'cross-border processing' means either:
    (a) processing of personal data which takes place in the context of the activities of establishments in more than one Member State of a controller or processor in the Union where the controller or processor is established in more than one Member State; or
    (b) processing of personal data which takes place in the context of the activities of a single establishment of a controller or processor in the Union but which substantially affects or is likely to substantially affect data subjects in more than one Member State.

(24) 'relevant and reasoned objection' means an objection to a draft decision as to whether there is an infringement of this Regulation, or whether envisaged action in relation to the controller or processor complies with this Regulation, which clearly demonstrates the significance of the risks posed by the draft decision as regards the fundamental rights and freedoms of data subjects and, where applicable, the free flow of personal data within the Union;

(25) 'information society service' means a service as defined in point (b) of Article 1(1) of Directive (EU) 2015/1535 of the European Parliament and of the Council;

(26) 'international organisation' means an organisation and its subordinate bodies governed by public international law, or any other body which is set up by, or on the basis of, an agreement between two or more countries.

—— NOTES ——

Relevant recitals
(26), (27), (30), (34), (35)

LED equivalent
Art 3(1), (5), (12), (13), (14)

CHAPTER II – PRINCIPLES

Article 5   Principles relating to processing of personal data

1.   Personal data shall be:

(a)   processed lawfully, fairly and in a transparent manner in relation to the data subject ('lawfulness, fairness and transparency');

(b)   collected for specified, explicit and legitimate purposes and not further processed in a manner that is incompatible with those purposes; further processing for archiving purposes in the public interest, scientific or historical research purposes or statistical purposes shall, in accordance with Article 89(1), not be considered to be incompatible with the initial purposes ('purpose limitation');

(c)   adequate, relevant and limited to what is necessary in relation to the purposes for which they are processed ('data minimisation');

(d)   accurate and, where necessary, kept up to date; every reasonable step must be taken to ensure that personal data that are inaccurate, having regard to the purposes for which they are processed, are erased or rectified without delay ('accuracy');

(e)   kept in a form which permits identification of data subjects for no longer than is necessary for the purposes for which the personal data are processed; personal data may be stored for longer periods insofar as the personal data will be processed solely for archiving purposes in the public interest, scientific or historical research purposes or statistical purposes in accordance with Article 89(1) subject to implementation of the appropriate technical and organisational measures required by this Regulation in order to safeguard the rights and freedoms of the data subject ('storage limitation');

(f)   processed in a manner that ensures appropriate security of the personal data, including protection against unauthorised or unlawful processing and against accidental loss, destruction or damage, using appropriate technical or organisational measures ('integrity and confidentiality').

2.   The controller shall be responsible for, and be able to demonstrate compliance with, paragraph 1 ('accountability').

—— NOTES ——

Defined terms
controller   Art 4(7)
personal data   Art 4(1)
processing   Art 4(2)

Relevant recitals
(39)

LED equivalent
Arts 4, 9(1), (2), 13, 19, 29

Article 6   Lawfulness of processing

1.   Processing shall be lawful only if and to the extent that at least one of the following applies:

(a)   the data subject has given consent to the processing of his or her personal data for one or more specific purposes;

(b)   processing is necessary for the performance of a contract to which the data subject is party or in order to take steps at the request of the data subject prior to entering into a contract;

(c) processing is necessary for compliance with a legal obligation to which the controller is subject;

(d) processing is necessary in order to protect the vital interests of the data subject or of another natural person;

(e) processing is necessary for the performance of a task carried out in the public interest or in the exercise of official authority vested in the controller;

(f) processing is necessary for the purposes of the legitimate interests pursued by the controller or by a third party, except where such interests are overridden by the interests or fundamental rights and freedoms of the data subject which require protection of personal data, in particular where the data subject is a child.

Point (f) of the first subparagraph shall not apply to processing carried out by public authorities in the performance of their tasks.

2. Member States may maintain or introduce more specific provisions to adapt the application of the rules of this Regulation with regard to processing for compliance with points (c) and (e) of paragraph 1 by determining more precisely specific requirements for the processing and other measures to ensure lawful and fair processing including for other specific processing situations as provided for in Chapter IX.

3. The basis for the processing referred to in point (c) and (e) of paragraph 1 shall be laid down by:

(a) Union law; or

(b) Member State law to which the controller is subject.

The purpose of the processing shall be determined in that legal basis or, as regards the processing referred to in point (e) of paragraph 1, shall be necessary for the performance of a task carried out in the public interest or in the exercise of official authority vested in the controller. That legal basis may contain specific provisions to adapt the application of rules of this Regulation, inter alia: the general conditions governing the lawfulness of processing by the controller; the types of data which are subject to the processing; the data subjects concerned; the entities to, and the purposes for which, the personal data may be disclosed; the purpose limitation; storage periods; and processing operations and processing procedures, including measures to ensure lawful and fair processing such as those for other specific processing situations as provided for in Chapter IX. The Union or the Member State law shall meet an objective of public interest and be proportionate to the legitimate aim pursued.

4. Where the processing for a purpose other than that for which the personal data have been collected is not based on the data subject's consent or on a Union or Member State law which constitutes a necessary and proportionate measure in a democratic society to safeguard the objectives referred to in Article 23(1), the controller shall, in order to ascertain whether processing for another purpose is compatible with the purpose for which the personal data are initially collected, take into account, inter alia:

(a) any link between the purposes for which the personal data have been collected and the purposes of the intended further processing;

(b) the context in which the personal data have been collected, in particular regarding the relationship between data subjects and the controller;

(c) the nature of the personal data, in particular whether special categories of personal data are processed, pursuant to Article 9, or whether personal data related to criminal convictions and offences are processed, pursuant to Article 10;

(d) the possible consequences of the intended further processing for data subjects;

(e) the existence of appropriate safeguards, which may include encryption or pseudonymisation.

—— NOTES ——

Defined terms		Relevant recitals
consent	Art 4(11)	(40), (41), (43), (44), (45), (46), (47), (48), (49),
controller	Art 4(7)	(50)
personal data	Art 4(1)	
processing	Art 4(2)	**LED equivalent**
pseudonymisation	Art 4(5)	Arts 4, 5, 8, 9
third party	Art 4(10)	

Article 7 Conditions for consent

1. Where processing is based on consent, the controller shall be able to demonstrate that the data subject has consented to processing of his or her personal data.

2. If the data subject's consent is given in the context of a written declaration which also concerns other matters, the request for consent shall be presented in a manner which is clearly distinguishable from the other matters, in an intelligible and easily accessible form, using clear and plain language. Any part of such a declaration which constitutes an infringement of this Regulation shall not be binding.

3. The data subject shall have the right to withdraw his or her consent at any time. The withdrawal of consent shall not affect the lawfulness of processing based on consent before its withdrawal. Prior to giving consent, the data subject shall be informed thereof. It shall be as easy to withdraw as to give consent.

4. When assessing whether consent is freely given, utmost account shall be taken of whether, inter alia, the performance of a contract, including the provision of a service, is conditional on consent to the processing of personal data that is not necessary for the performance of that contract.

—— NOTES ——

Defined terms		Relevant recitals
consent	Art 4(11)	(42), (43)
controller	Art 4(7)	
personal data	Art 4(1)	**LED equivalent**
processing	Art 4(2)	Recitals (35), (37)

Article 8 Conditions applicable to child's consent in relation to information society services

1. Where point (a) of Article 6(1) applies, in relation to the offer of information society services directly to a child, the processing of the personal data of a child shall be lawful where the child is at least 16 years old. Where the child is below the age of 16 years, such processing shall be lawful only if and to the extent that consent is given or authorised by the holder of parental responsibility over the child.
   Member States may provide by law for a lower age for those purposes provided that such lower age is not below 13 years.

2. The controller shall make reasonable efforts to verify in such cases that consent is given or authorised by the holder of parental responsibility over the child, taking into consideration available technology.

3. Paragraph 1 shall not affect the general contract law of Member States such as the rules on the validity, formation or effect of a contract in relation to a child.

Defined terms		Relevant recitals
consent	Art 4(11)	(38)
controller	Art 4(7)	
information society services	Art 4(25)	**LED equivalent**
personal data	Art 4(1)	Arts 13, 20
processing	Art 4(2)	

Article 9   Processing of special categories of personal data

1. Processing of personal data revealing racial or ethnic origin, political opinions, religious or philosophical beliefs, or trade union membership, and the processing of genetic data, biometric data for the purpose of uniquely identifying a natural person, data concerning health or data concerning a natural person's sex life or sexual orientation shall be prohibited.

2. Paragraph 1 shall not apply if one of the following applies:

    (a) the data subject has given explicit consent to the processing of those personal data for one or more specified purposes, except where Union or Member State law provide that the prohibition referred to in paragraph 1 may not be lifted by the data subject;

    (b) processing is necessary for the purposes of carrying out the obligations and exercising specific rights of the controller or of the data subject in the field of employment and social security and social protection law in so far as it is authorised by Union or Member State law or a collective agreement pursuant to Member State law providing for appropriate safeguards for the fundamental rights and the interests of the data subject;

    (c) processing is necessary to protect the vital interests of the data subject or of another natural person where the data subject is physically or legally incapable of giving consent;

    (d) processing is carried out in the course of its legitimate activities with appropriate safeguards by a foundation, association or any other not-for-profit body with a political, philosophical, religious or trade union aim and on condition that the processing relates solely to the members or to former members of the body or to persons who have regular contact with it in connection with its purposes and that the personal data are not disclosed outside that body without the consent of the data subjects;

    (e) processing relates to personal data which are manifestly made public by the data subject;

    (f) processing is necessary for the establishment, exercise or defence of legal claims or whenever courts are acting in their judicial capacity;

    (g) processing is necessary for reasons of substantial public interest, on the basis of Union or Member State law which shall be proportionate to the aim pursued, respect the essence of the right to data protection and provide for suitable and specific measures to safeguard the fundamental rights and the interests of the data subject;

    (h) processing is necessary for the purposes of preventive or occupational medicine, for the assessment of the working capacity of the employee, medical diagnosis, the provision of health or social care or treatment or the management of health or social care systems and services on the basis of Union or Member State law or pursuant to contract with a health professional and subject to the conditions and safeguards referred to in paragraph 3;

(i) processing is necessary for reasons of public interest in the area of public health, such as protecting against serious cross-border threats to health or ensuring high standards of quality and safety of health care and of medicinal products or medical devices, on the basis of Union or Member State law which provides for suitable and specific measures to safeguard the rights and freedoms of the data subject, in particular professional secrecy;

(j) processing is necessary for archiving purposes in the public interest, scientific or historical research purposes or statistical purposes in accordance with Article 89(1) based on Union or Member State law which shall be proportionate to the aim pursued, respect the essence of the right to data protection and provide for suitable and specific measures to safeguard the fundamental rights and the interests of the data subject.

3. Personal data referred to in paragraph 1 may be processed for the purposes referred to in point (h) of paragraph 2 when those data are processed by or under the responsibility of a professional subject to the obligation of professional secrecy under Union or Member State law or rules established by national competent bodies or by another person also subject to an obligation of secrecy under Union or Member State law or rules established by national competent bodies.

4. Member States may maintain or introduce further conditions, including limitations, with regard to the processing of genetic data, biometric data or data concerning health.

—— NOTES ——

Defined terms		Relevant recitals
biometric data	Art 4(14)	(10), (51), (52), (53), (54), (55), (56)
consent	Art 4(11)	
controller	Art 4(7)	**LED equivalent**
data concerning health	Art 4(15)	Arts 10, 11, 19, 24, 27, 29
genetic data	Art 4(13)	
personal data	Art 4(1)	
processing	Art 4(2)	

Article 10   Processing of personal data relating to criminal convictions and offences

Processing of personal data relating to criminal convictions and offences or related security measures based on Article 6(1) shall be carried out only under the control of official authority or when the processing is authorised by Union or Member State law providing for appropriate safeguards for the rights and freedoms of data subjects. Any comprehensive register of criminal convictions shall be kept only under the control of official authority.

—— NOTES ——

Defined terms		Relevant recitals
personal data	Art 4(1)	(19)
processing	Art 4(2)	
		LED equivalent
		Arts 1, 2, 3

Article 11   Processing which does not require identification

1. If the purposes for which a controller processes personal data do not or do no longer require the identification of a data subject by the controller, the controller shall not be

obliged to maintain, acquire or process additional information in order to identify the data subject for the sole purpose of complying with this Regulation.

2. Where, in cases referred to in paragraph 1 of this Article, the controller is able to demonstrate that it is not in a position to identify the data subject, the controller shall inform the data subject accordingly, if possible. In such cases, Articles 15 to 20 shall not apply except where the data subject, for the purpose of exercising his or her rights under those articles, provides additional information enabling his or her identification.

—— NOTES ——

Defined terms		Relevant recitals
controller	Art 4(7)	(26), (57)
personal data	Art 4(1)	
processing	Art 4(2)	**LED equivalent**
		n/a

CHAPTER III – RIGHTS OF THE DATA SUBJECT

Section 1 – Transparency and modalities

Article 12   Transparent information, communication and modalities for the exercise of the rights of the data subject

1. The controller shall take appropriate measures to provide any information referred to in Articles 13 and 14 and any communication under Articles 15 to 22 and 34 relating to processing to the data subject in a concise, transparent, intelligible and easily accessible form, using clear and plain language, in particular for any information addressed specifically to a child. The information shall be provided in writing, or by other means, including, where appropriate, by electronic means. When requested by the data subject, the information may be provided orally, provided that the identity of the data subject is proven by other means.

2. The controller shall facilitate the exercise of data subject rights under Articles 15 to 22. In the cases referred to in Article 11(2), the controller shall not refuse to act on the request of the data subject for exercising his or her rights under Articles 15 to 22, unless the controller demonstrates that it is not in a position to identify the data subject.

3. The controller shall provide information on action taken on a request under Articles 15 to 22 to the data subject without undue delay and in any event within one month of receipt of the request. That period may be extended by two further months where necessary, taking into account the complexity and number of the requests. The controller shall inform the data subject of any such extension within one month of receipt of the request, together with the reasons for the delay. Where the data subject makes the request by electronic form means, the information shall be provided by electronic means where possible, unless otherwise requested by the data subject.

4. If the controller does not take action on the request of the data subject, the controller shall inform the data subject without delay and at the latest within one month of receipt of the request of the reasons for not taking action and on the possibility of lodging a complaint with a supervisory authority and seeking a judicial remedy.

5. Information provided under Articles 13 and 14 and any communication and any actions taken under Articles 15 to 22 and 34 shall be provided free of charge. Where requests

General Data Protection Regulation
Chapter III – Rights of the Data Subject
Section 2 – Information & access to personal data

from a data subject are manifestly unfounded or excessive, in particular because of their repetitive character, the controller may either:

    (a) charge a reasonable fee taking into account the administrative costs of providing the information or communication or taking the action requested; or

    (b) refuse to act on the request.

The controller shall bear the burden of demonstrating the manifestly unfounded or excessive character of the request.

6. Without prejudice to Article 11, where the controller has reasonable doubts concerning the identity of the natural person making the request referred to in Articles 15 to 21, the controller may request the provision of additional information necessary to confirm the identity of the data subject.

7. The information to be provided to data subjects pursuant to Articles 13 and 14 may be provided in combination with standardised icons in order to give in an easily visible, intelligible and clearly legible manner a meaningful overview of the intended processing. Where the icons are presented electronically they shall be machine-readable.

8. The Commission shall be empowered to adopt delegated acts in accordance with Article 92 for the purpose of determining the information to be presented by the icons and the procedures for providing standardised icons.

—— Notes ——

Defined terms		Relevant recitals
controller	Art 4(7)	(11), (58), (59), (60), (63), (166)
personal data	Art 4(1)	
processing	Art 4(2)	**LED equivalent**
		Arts 11, 12, 13, 14, 15, 16, 17, 18, 31

Section 2 – Information and access to personal data

Article 13   **Information to be provided where personal data are collected from the data subject**

1. Where personal data relating to a data subject are collected from the data subject, the controller shall, at the time when personal data are obtained, provide the data subject with all of the following information:

    (a) the identity and the contact details of the controller and, where applicable, of the controller's representative;

    (b) the contact details of the data protection officer, where applicable;

    (c) the purposes of the processing for which the personal data are intended as well as the legal basis for the processing;

    (d) where the processing is based on point (f) of Article 6(1), the legitimate interests pursued by the controller or by a third party;

    (e) the recipients or categories of recipients of the personal data, if any;

    (f) where applicable, the fact that the controller intends to transfer personal data to a third country or international organisation and the existence or absence of an adequacy decision by the Commission, or in the case of transfers referred to in Article 46 or 47, or the second subparagraph of Article 49(1), reference to the appropriate or suitable safeguards and the means by which to obtain a copy of them or where they have been made available.

2. In addition to the information referred to in paragraph 1, the controller shall, at the time

when personal data are obtained, provide the data subject with the following further information necessary to ensure fair and transparent processing:

    (a) the period for which the personal data will be stored, or if that is not possible, the criteria used to determine that period;

    (b) the existence of the right to request from the controller access to and rectification or erasure of personal data or restriction of processing concerning the data subject or to object to processing as well as the right to data portability;

    (c) where the processing is based on point (a) of Article 6(1) or point (a) of Article 9(2), the existence of the right to withdraw consent at any time, without affecting the lawfulness of processing based on consent before its withdrawal;

    (d) the right to lodge a complaint with a supervisory authority;

    (e) whether the provision of personal data is a statutory or contractual requirement, or a requirement necessary to enter into a contract, as well as whether the data subject is obliged to provide the personal data and of the possible consequences of failure to provide such data;

    (f) the existence of automated decision-making, including profiling, referred to in Article 22(1) and (4) and, at least in those cases, meaningful information about the logic involved, as well as the significance and the envisaged consequences of such processing for the data subject.

3.   Where the controller intends to further process the personal data for a purpose other than that for which the personal data were collected, the controller shall provide the data subject prior to that further processing with information on that other purpose and with any relevant further information as referred to in paragraph 2.

4.   Paragraphs 1, 2 and 3 shall not apply where and insofar as the data subject already has the information.

—— NOTES ——

Defined terms		supervisory authority	Art 4(22)
consent	Art 4(11)	third party	Art 4(10)
controller	Art 4(7)		
international organisation	Art 4(26)	**Relevant recitals**	
personal data	Art 4(1)	(60), (61), (62)	
processing	Art 4(2)		
profiling	Art 4(4)	**LED equivalent**	
recipient	Art 4(9)	Arts 13	
representative	Art 4(17)		
restriction of processing	Art 4(3)		

Article 14   Information to be provided where personal data have not been obtained from the data subject

1.   Where personal data have not been obtained from the data subject, the controller shall provide the data subject with the following information:

    (a) the identity and the contact details of the controller and, where applicable, of the controller's representative;

    (b) the contact details of the data protection officer, where applicable;

    (c) the purposes of the processing for which the personal data are intended as well as the legal basis for the processing;

    (d) the categories of personal data concerned;

    (e) the recipients or categories of recipients of the personal data, if any;

    (f) where applicable, that the controller intends to transfer personal data to a recipient in a third country or international organisation and the existence or absence of an

General Data Protection Regulation
Chapter III – Rights of the Data Subject
Section 2 – Information & access to personal data

adequacy decision by the Commission, or in the case of transfers referred to in Article 46 or 47, or the second subparagraph of Article 49(1), reference to the appropriate or suitable safeguards and the means to obtain a copy of them or where they have been made available.

2. In addition to the information referred to in paragraph 1, the controller shall provide the data subject with the following information necessary to ensure fair and transparent processing in respect of the data subject:

   (a) the period for which the personal data will be stored, or if that is not possible, the criteria used to determine that period;

   (b) where the processing is based on point (f) of Article 6(1), the legitimate interests pursued by the controller or by a third party;

   (c) the existence of the right to request from the controller access to and rectification or erasure of personal data or restriction of processing concerning the data subject and to object to processing as well as the right to data portability;

   (d) where processing is based on point (a) of Article 6(1) or point (a) of Article 9(2), the existence of the right to withdraw consent at any time, without affecting the lawfulness of processing based on consent before its withdrawal;

   (e) the right to lodge a complaint with a supervisory authority;

   (f) from which source the personal data originate, and if applicable, whether it came from publicly accessible sources;

   (g) the existence of automated decision–making, including profiling, referred to in Article 22(1) and (4) and, at least in those cases, meaningful information about the logic involved, as well as the significance and the envisaged consequences of such processing for the data subject.

3. The controller shall provide the information referred to in paragraphs 1 and 2:

   (a) within a reasonable period after obtaining the personal data, but at the latest within one month, having regard to the specific circumstances in which the personal data are processed;

   (b) if the personal data are to be used for communication with the data subject, at the latest at the time of the first communication to that data subject; or

   (c) if a disclosure to another recipient is envisaged, at the latest when the personal data are first disclosed.

4. Where the controller intends to further process the personal data for a purpose other than that for which the personal data were obtained, the controller shall provide the data subject prior to that further processing with information on that other purpose and with any relevant further information as referred to in paragraph 2.

5. Paragraphs 1 to 4 shall not apply where and insofar as:

   (a) the data subject already has the information;

   (b) the provision of such information proves impossible or would involve a disproportionate effort, in particular for processing for archiving purposes in the public interest, scientific or historical research purposes or statistical purposes, subject to the conditions and safeguards referred to in Article 89(1) or in so far as the obligation referred to in paragraph 1 of this Article is likely to render impossible or seriously impair the achievement of the objectives of that processing. In such cases the controller shall take appropriate measures to protect the data subject's rights and freedoms and legitimate interests, including making the information publicly available;

(c) obtaining or disclosure is expressly laid down by Union or Member State law to which the controller is subject and which provides appropriate measures to protect the data subject's legitimate interests; or

(d) where the personal data must remain confidential subject to an obligation of professional secrecy regulated by Union or Member State law, including a statutory obligation of secrecy.

—— NOTES ——

Defined terms		supervisory authority	Art 4(22)
consent	Art 4(11)	third party	Art 4(10)
controller	Art 4(7)		
international organisation	Art 4(26)	**Relevant recitals**	
personal data	Art 4(1)	(60), (61), (62)	
processing	Art 4(2)		
profiling	Art 4(4)	**LED equivalent**	
recipient	Art 4(9)	Art 13	
representative	Art 4(17)		
restriction of processing	Art 4(3)		

Article 15   Right of access by the data subject

1. The data subject shall have the right to obtain from the controller confirmation as to whether or not personal data concerning him or her are being processed, and, where that is the case, access to the personal data and the following information:

   (a) the purposes of the processing;

   (b) the categories of personal data concerned;

   (c) the recipients or categories of recipient to whom the personal data have been or will be disclosed, in particular recipients in third countries or international organisations;

   (d) where possible, the envisaged period for which the personal data will be stored, or, if not possible, the criteria used to determine that period;

   (e) the existence of the right to request from the controller rectification or erasure of personal data or restriction of processing of personal data concerning the data subject or to object to such processing;

   (f) the right to lodge a complaint with a supervisory authority;

   (g) where the personal data are not collected from the data subject, any available information as to their source;

   (h) the existence of automated decision-making, including profiling, referred to in Article 22(1) and (4) and, at least in those cases, meaningful information about the logic involved, as well as the significance and the envisaged consequences of such processing for the data subject.

2. Where personal data are transferred to a third country or to an international organisation, the data subject shall have the right to be informed of the appropriate safeguards pursuant to Article 46 relating to the transfer.

3. The controller shall provide a copy of the personal data undergoing processing. For any further copies requested by the data subject, the controller may charge a reasonable fee based on administrative costs. Where the data subject makes the request by electronic means, and unless otherwise requested by the data subject, the information shall be provided in a commonly used electronic form.

4. The right to obtain a copy referred to in paragraph 3 shall not adversely affect the rights and freedoms of others.

—— NOTES ——

Defined terms		supervisory authority	Art 4(22)
controller	Art 4(7)		
international organisation	Art 4(26)	**Relevant recitals**	
personal data	Art 4(1)	(58), (59), (63), (64)	
processing	Art 4(2)		
profiling	Art 4(4)	**LED equivalent**	
recipient	Art 4(9)	Arts 12, 14, 15	
restriction of processing	Art 4(3)		

Section 3 – Rectification and erasure

Article 16 Right to rectification

The data subject shall have the right to obtain from the controller without undue delay the rectification of inaccurate personal data concerning him or her. Taking into account the purposes of the processing, the data subject shall have the right to have incomplete personal data completed, including by means of providing a supplementary statement.

—— NOTES ——

Defined terms		**Relevant recitals**	
controller	Art 4(7)	(39), (65)	
personal data	Art 4(1)		
processing	Art 4(2)	**LED equivalent**	
		Arts 4(1)(d), 13(1)(e), 16, 17	

Article 17 Right to erasure ('right to be forgotten')

1. The data subject shall have the right to obtain from the controller the erasure of personal data concerning him or her without undue delay and the controller shall have the obligation to erase personal data without undue delay where one of the following grounds applies:

    (a) the personal data are no longer necessary in relation to the purposes for which they were collected or otherwise processed;

    (b) the data subject withdraws consent on which the processing is based according to point (a) of Article 6(1), or point (a) of Article 9(2), and where there is no other legal ground for the processing;

    (c) the data subject objects to the processing pursuant to Article 21(1) and there are no overriding legitimate grounds for the processing, or the data subject objects to the processing pursuant to Article 21(2);

    (d) the personal data have been unlawfully processed;

    (e) the personal data have to be erased for compliance with a legal obligation in Union or Member State law to which the controller is subject;

    (f) the personal data have been collected in relation to the offer of information society services referred to in Article 8(1).

2. Where the controller has made the personal data public and is obliged pursuant to paragraph 1 to erase the personal data, the controller, taking account of available technology and the cost of implementation, shall take reasonable steps, including technical measures, to inform controllers which are processing the personal data that the data subject has requested the erasure by such controllers of any links to, or copy or replication of, those personal data.

3. Paragraphs 1 and 2 shall not apply to the extent that processing is necessary:

(a) for exercising the right of freedom of expression and information;

(b) for compliance with a legal obligation which requires processing by Union or Member State law to which the controller is subject or for the performance of a task carried out in the public interest or in the exercise of official authority vested in the controller;

(c) for reasons of public interest in the area of public health in accordance with points (h) and (i) of Article 9(2) as well as Article 9(3);

(d) for archiving purposes in the public interest, scientific or historical research purposes or statistical purposes in accordance with Article 89(1) in so far as the right referred to in paragraph 1 is likely to render impossible or seriously impair the achievement of the objectives of that processing; or

(e) for the establishment, exercise or defence of legal claims.

——— NOTES ———

Defined terms		Relevant recitals
consent	Art 4(11)	(65), (66)
controller	Art 4(7)	
information society services	Art 4(25)	**LED equivalent**
personal data	Art 4(1)	Art 16
processing	Art 4(2)	

Article 18   Right to restriction of processing

1. The data subject shall have the right to obtain from the controller restriction of processing where one of the following applies:

    (a) the accuracy of the personal data is contested by the data subject, for a period enabling the controller to verify the accuracy of the personal data;

    (b) the processing is unlawful and the data subject opposes the erasure of the personal data and requests the restriction of their use instead;

    (c) the controller no longer needs the personal data for the purposes of the processing, but they are required by the data subject for the establishment, exercise or defence of legal claims;

    (d) the data subject has objected to processing pursuant to Article 21(1) pending the verification whether the legitimate grounds of the controller override those of the data subject.

2. Where processing has been restricted under paragraph 1, such personal data shall, with the exception of storage, only be processed with the data subject's consent or for the establishment, exercise or defence of legal claims or for the protection of the rights of another natural or legal person or for reasons of important public interest of the Union or of a Member State.

3. A data subject who has obtained restriction of processing pursuant to paragraph 1 shall be informed by the controller before the restriction of processing is lifted.

——— NOTES ———

Defined terms		Relevant recitals
consent	Art 4(11)	(67), (156)
controller	Art 4(7)	
personal data	Art 4(1)	
processing	Art 4(2)	**LED equivalent**
restriction of processing	Art 4(3)	Arts 3(3), 16

General Data Protection Regulation
Chapter III – Rights of the Data Subject
Section 4 – Right to object & automated decision-making

Article 19   Notification obligation regarding rectification or erasure of personal data or restriction of processing

The controller shall communicate any rectification or erasure of personal data or restriction of processing carried out in accordance with Article 16, Article 17(1) and Article 18 to each recipient to whom the personal data have been disclosed, unless this proves impossible or involves disproportionate effort. The controller shall inform the data subject about those recipients if the data subject requests it.

—— Notes ——

Defined terms		Relevant recitals
controller	Art 4(7)	n/a
personal data	Art 4(1)	
processing	Art 4(2)	**LED equivalent**
recipient	Art 4(9)	Arts 16(6)
restriction of processing	Art 4(3)	

Article 20   Right to data portability

1. The data subject shall have the right to receive the personal data concerning him or her, which he or she has provided to a controller, in a structured, commonly used and machine-readable format and have the right to transmit those data to another controller without hindrance from the controller to which the personal data have been provided, where:

    (a) the processing is based on consent pursuant to point (a) of Article 6(1) or point (a) of Article 9(2) or on a contract pursuant to point (b) of Article 6(1); and

    (b) the processing is carried out by automated means.

2. In exercising his or her right to data portability pursuant to paragraph 1, the data subject shall have the right to have the personal data transmitted directly from one controller to another, where technically feasible.

3. The exercise of the right referred to in paragraph 1 of this Article shall be without prejudice to Article 17. That right shall not apply to processing necessary for the performance of a task carried out in the public interest or in the exercise of official authority vested in the controller.

4. The right referred to in paragraph 1 shall not adversely affect the rights and freedoms of others.

—— Notes ——

Defined terms		Relevant recitals
consent	Art 4(11)	(68), (73), (156)
personal data	Art 4(1)	
processing	Art 4(2)	**LED equivalent**
		Arts 12, 13, 14, 15, 16, 17, 18

Section 4 – Right to object and automated individual decision-making

Article 21   Right to object

1. The data subject shall have the right to object, on grounds relating to his or her particular situation, at any time to processing of personal data concerning him or her which is based on point (e) or (f) of Article 6(1), including profiling based on those provisions. The controller shall no longer process the personal data unless the controller demonstrates compelling legitimate grounds for the processing which override the interests, rights and

freedoms of the data subject or for the establishment, exercise or defence of legal claims.

2.   Where personal data are processed for direct marketing purposes, the data subject shall have the right to object at any time to processing of personal data concerning him or her for such marketing, which includes profiling to the extent that it is related to such direct marketing.

3.   Where the data subject objects to processing for direct marketing purposes, the personal data shall no longer be processed for such purposes.

4.   At the latest at the time of the first communication with the data subject, the right referred to in paragraphs 1 and 2 shall be explicitly brought to the attention of the data subject and shall be presented clearly and separately from any other information.

5.   In the context of the use of information society services, and notwithstanding Directive 2002/58/EC, the data subject may exercise his or her right to object by automated means using technical specifications.

6.   Where personal data are processed for scientific or historical research purposes or statistical purposes pursuant to Article 89(1), the data subject, on grounds relating to his or her particular situation, shall have the right to object to processing of personal data concerning him or her, unless the processing is necessary for the performance of a task carried out for reasons of public interest.

——— NOTES ———

Defined terms		Relevant recitals
controller	Art 4(7)	(69), (70)
information society services	Art 4(25)	
personal data	Art 4(1)	**LED equivalent**
processing	Art 4(2)	Art 16
profiling	Art 4(4)	

Article 22   Automated individual decision-making, including profiling

1.   The data subject shall have the right not to be subject to a decision based solely on automated processing, including profiling, which produces legal effects concerning him or her or similarly significantly affects him or her.

2.   Paragraph 1 shall not apply if the decision:
     (a) is necessary for entering into, or performance of, a contract between the data subject and a data controller;
     (b) is authorised by Union or Member State law to which the controller is subject and which also lays down suitable measures to safeguard the data subject's rights and freedoms and legitimate interests; or
     (c) is based on the data subject's explicit consent.

3.   In the cases referred to in points (a) and (c) of paragraph 2, the data controller shall implement suitable measures to safeguard the data subject's rights and freedoms and legitimate interests, at least the right to obtain human intervention on the part of the controller, to express his or her point of view and to contest the decision.

4.   Decisions referred to in paragraph 2 shall not be based on special categories of personal data referred to in Article 9(1), unless point (a) or (g) of Article 9(2) applies and suitable measures to safeguard the data subject's rights and freedoms and legitimate interests are in place.

——— NOTES ———

Defined terms

consent	Art 4(11)
controller	Art 4(7)
personal data	Art 4(1)
processing	Art 4(2)
profiling	Art 4(4)

Relevant recitals
(4), (24), (38), (60), (63), (71), (72), (73), (91)

LED equivalent
Arts 3(4), 4(1)(a), 11, 12, 24, 27

Section 5 – Restrictions

Article 23   Restrictions

1. Union or Member State law to which the data controller or processor is subject may restrict by way of a legislative measure the scope of the obligations and rights provided for in Articles 12 to 22 and Article 34, as well as Article 5 in so far as its provisions correspond to the rights and obligations provided for in Articles 12 to 22, when such a restriction respects the essence of the fundamental rights and freedoms and is a necessary and proportionate measure in a democratic society to safeguard:

    (a) national security;

    (b) defence;

    (c) public security;

    (d) the prevention, investigation, detection or prosecution of criminal offences or the execution of criminal penalties, including the safeguarding against and the prevention of threats to public security;

    (e) other important objectives of general public interest of the Union or of a Member State, in particular an important economic or financial interest of the Union or of a Member State, including monetary, budgetary and taxation a matters, public health and social security;

    (f) the protection of judicial independence and judicial proceedings;

    (g) the prevention, investigation, detection and prosecution of breaches of ethics for regulated professions;

    (h) a monitoring, inspection or regulatory function connected, even occasionally, to the exercise of official authority in the cases referred to in points (a) to (e) and (g);

    (i) the protection of the data subject or the rights and freedoms of others;

    (j) the enforcement of civil law claims.

2. In particular, any legislative measure referred to in paragraph 1 shall contain specific provisions at least, where relevant, as to:

    (a) the purposes of the processing or categories of processing;

    (b) the categories of personal data;

    (c) the scope of the restrictions introduced;

    (d) the safeguards to prevent abuse or unlawful access or transfer;

    (e) the specification of the controller or categories of controllers;

    (f) the storage periods and the applicable safeguards taking into account the nature, scope and purposes of the processing or categories of processing;

    (g) the risks to the rights and freedoms of data subjects; and

    (h) the right of data subjects to be informed about the restriction, unless that may be prejudicial to the purpose of the restriction.

—— NOTES ——

Defined terms		**Relevant recitals**
consent	Art 4(11)	(73)
personal data	Art 4(1)	
processing	Art 4(2)	**LED equivalent**
processor	Art 4(8)	Arts 13(3), 15, 16(4)

CHAPTER IV – CONTROLLER AND PROCESSOR

Section 1 – General obligations

Article 24   Responsibility of the controller

1. Taking into account the nature, scope, context and purposes of processing as well as the risks of varying likelihood and severity for the rights and freedoms of natural persons, the controller shall implement appropriate technical and organisational measures to ensure and to be able to demonstrate that processing is performed in accordance with this Regulation. Those measures shall be reviewed and updated where necessary.

2. Where proportionate in relation to processing activities, the measures referred to in paragraph 1 shall include the implementation of appropriate data protection policies by the controller.

3. Adherence to approved codes of conduct as referred to in Article 40 or approved certification mechanisms as referred to in Article 42 may be used as an element by which to demonstrate compliance with the obligations of the controller.

—— NOTES ——

Defined terms		**Relevant recitals**
controller	Art 4(7)	(74), (75), (76), (77)
processing	Art 4(2)	
		LED equivalent
		Arts 19, 20, 24, 25, 27, 29, 32, 33, 34

Article 25   Data protection by design and by default

1. Taking into account the state of the art, the cost of implementation and the nature, scope, context and purposes of processing as well as the risks of varying likelihood and severity for rights and freedoms of natural persons posed by the processing, the controller shall, both at the time of the determination of the means for processing and at the time of the processing itself, implement appropriate technical and organisational measures, such as pseudonymisation, which are designed to implement data-protection principles, such as data minimisation, in an effective manner and to integrate the necessary safeguards into the processing in order to meet the requirements of this Regulation and protect the rights of data subjects.

2. The controller shall implement appropriate technical and organisational measures for ensuring that, by default, only personal data which are necessary for each specific purpose of the processing are processed. That obligation applies to the amount of personal data collected, the extent of their processing, the period of their storage and their accessibility. In particular, such measures shall ensure that by default personal data are not made accessible without the individual's intervention to an indefinite number of natural persons.

3. An approved certification mechanism pursuant to Article 42 may be used as an element

to demonstrate compliance with the requirements set out in paragraphs 1 and 2 of this Article.

—— NOTES ——

Defined terms		Relevant recitals
controller	Art 4(7)	(78)
personal data	Art 4(1)	
processing	Art 4(2)	**LED equivalent**
pseudonymisation	Art 4(5)	Arts 4(4), 19, 20, 22, 24(1)(i), 25, 27, 29, 31(3)(a)

Article 26   Joint controllers

1. Where two or more controllers jointly determine the purposes and means of processing, they shall be joint controllers. They shall in a transparent manner determine their respective responsibilities for compliance with the obligations under this Regulation, in particular as regards the exercising of the rights of the data subject and their respective duties to provide the information referred to in Articles 13 and 14, by means of an arrangement between them unless, and in so far as, the respective responsibilities of the controllers are determined by Union or Member State law to which the controllers are subject. The arrangement may designate a contact point for data subjects.

2. The arrangement referred to in paragraph 1 shall duly reflect the respective roles and relationships of the joint controllers vis-à-vis the data subjects. The essence of the arrangement shall be made available to the data subject.

3. Irrespective of the terms of the arrangement referred to in paragraph 1, the data subject may exercise his or her rights under this Regulation in respect of and against each of the controllers.

—— NOTES ——

Defined terms		Relevant recitals
processing	Art 4(2)	(79)
		LED equivalent
		Arts 3, 19, 21

Article 27   Representatives of controllers or processors not established in the Union

1. Where Article 3(2) applies, the controller or the processor shall designate in writing a representative in the Union.

2. The obligation laid down in paragraph 1 of this Article shall not apply to:
    (a) processing which is occasional, does not include, on a large scale, processing of special categories of data as referred to in Article 9(1) or processing of personal data relating to criminal convictions and offences referred to in Article 10, and is unlikely to result in a risk to the rights and freedoms of natural persons, taking into account the nature, context, scope and purposes of the processing; or
    (b) a public authority or body.

3. The representative shall be established in one of the Member States where the data subjects, whose personal data are processed in relation to the offering of goods or services to them, or whose behaviour is monitored, are.

4. The representative shall be mandated by the controller or processor to be addressed in

addition to or instead of the controller or the processor by, in particular, supervisory authorities and data subjects, on all issues related to processing, for the purposes of ensuring compliance with this Regulation.

5.   The designation of a representative by the controller or processor shall be without prejudice to legal actions which could be initiated against the controller or the processor themselves.

——— NOTES ———

Defined terms		Relevant recitals
controller	Art 4(7)	(80)
personal data	Art 4(1)	
processing	Art 4(2)	**LED equivalent**
processor	Art 4(8)	n/a
representative	Art 4(17)	

Article 28   Processor

1.   Where processing is to be carried out on behalf of a controller, the controller shall use only processors providing sufficient guarantees to implement appropriate technical and organisational measures in such a manner that processing will meet the requirements of this Regulation and ensure the protection of the rights of the data subject.

2.   The processor shall not engage another processor without prior specific or general written authorisation of the controller. In the case of general written authorisation, the processor shall inform the controller of any intended changes concerning the addition or replacement of other processors, thereby giving the controller the opportunity to object to such changes.

3.   Processing by a processor shall be governed by a contract or other legal act under Union or Member State law, that is binding on the processor with regard to the controller and that sets out the subject-matter and duration of the processing, the nature and purpose of the processing, the type of personal data and categories of data subjects and the obligations and rights of the controller. That contract or other legal act shall stipulate, in particular, that the processor:

   (a) processes the personal data only on documented instructions from the controller, including with regard to transfers of personal data to a third country or an international organisation, unless required to do so by Union or Member State law to which the processor is subject; in such a case, the processor shall inform the controller of that legal requirement before processing, unless that law prohibits such information on important grounds of public interest;

   (b) ensures that persons authorised to process the personal data have committed themselves to confidentiality or are under an appropriate statutory obligation of confidentiality;

   (c) takes all measures required pursuant to Article 32;

   (d) respects the conditions referred to in paragraphs 2 and 4 for engaging another processor;

   (e) taking into account the nature of the processing, assists the controller by appropriate technical and organisational measures, insofar as this is possible, for the fulfilment of the controller's obligation to respond to requests for exercising the data subject's rights laid down in Chapter III;

   (f) assists the controller in ensuring compliance with the obligations pursuant to Articles 32 to 36 taking into account the nature of processing and the information available to the processor;

(g) at the choice of the controller, deletes or returns all the personal data to the controller after the end of the provision of services relating to processing, and deletes existing copies unless Union or Member State law requires storage of the personal data;

(h) makes available to the controller all information necessary to demonstrate compliance with the obligations laid down in this Article and allow for and contribute to audits, including inspections, conducted by the controller or another auditor mandated by the controller.

With regard to point (h) of the first subparagraph, the processor shall immediately inform the controller if, in its opinion, an instruction infringes this Regulation or other Union or Member State data protection provisions.

4. Where a processor engages another processor for carrying out specific processing activities on behalf of the controller, the same data protection obligations as set out in the contract or other legal act between the controller and the processor as referred to in paragraph 3 shall be imposed on that other processor by way of a contract or other legal act under Union or Member State law, in particular providing sufficient guarantees to implement appropriate technical and organisational measures in such a manner that the processing will meet the requirements of this Regulation. Where that other processor fails to fulfil its data protection obligations, the initial processor shall remain fully liable to the controller for the performance of that other processor's obligations.

5. Adherence of a processor to an approved code of conduct as referred to in Article 40 or an approved certification mechanism as referred to in Article 42 may be used as an element by which to demonstrate sufficient guarantees as referred to in paragraphs 1 and 4 of this Article.

6. Without prejudice to an individual contract between the controller and the processor, the contract or the other legal act referred to in paragraphs 3 and 4 of this Article may be based, in whole or in part, on standard contractual clauses referred to in paragraphs 7 and 8 of this Article, including when they are part of a certification granted to the controller or processor pursuant to Articles 42 and 43.

7. The Commission may lay down standard contractual clauses for the matters referred to in paragraph 3 and 4 of this Article and in accordance with the examination procedure referred to in Article 93(2).

8. A supervisory authority may adopt standard contractual clauses for the matters referred to in paragraph 3 and 4 of this Article and in accordance with the consistency mechanism referred to in Article 63.

9. The contract or the other legal act referred to in paragraphs 3 and 4 shall be in writing, including in electronic form.

10. Without prejudice to Articles 82, 83 and 84, if a processor infringes this Regulation by determining the purposes and means of processing, the processor shall be considered to be a controller in respect of that processing.

Defined terms		Relevant recitals
controller	Art 4(7)	(81)
international organisation	Art 4(26)	
personal data	Art 4(1)	**LED equivalent**
processing	Art 4(2)	Arts 3, 22, 24, 26, 28, 29, 30, 54
processor	Art 4(8)	
supervisory authority	Art 4(22)	

Article 29   Processing under the authority of the controller or processor

The processor and any person acting under the authority of the controller or of the processor, who has access to personal data, shall not process those data except on instructions from the controller, unless required to do so by Union or Member State law.

Defined terms		Relevant recitals
controller	Art 4(7)	(81)
personal data	Art 4(1)	
processing	Art 4(2)	**LED equivalent**
processor	Art 4(8)	Arts 23

Article 30   Records of processing activities

1. Each controller and, where applicable, the controller's representative, shall maintain a record of processing activities under its responsibility. That record shall contain all of the following information:

    (a) the name and contact details of the controller and, where applicable, the joint controller, the controller's representative and the data protection officer;

    (b) the purposes of the processing;

    (c) a description of the categories of data subjects and of the categories of personal data;

    (d) the categories of recipients to whom the personal data have been or will be disclosed including recipients in third countries or international organisations;

    (e) where applicable, transfers of personal data to a third country or an international organisation, including the identification of that third country or international organisation and, in the case of transfers referred to in the second subparagraph of Article 49(1), the documentation of suitable safeguards;

    (f) where possible, the envisaged time limits for erasure of the different categories of data;

    (g) where possible, a general description of the technical and organisational security measures referred to in Article 32(1).

2. Each processor and, where applicable, the processor's representative shall maintain a record of all categories of processing activities carried out on behalf of a controller, containing:

    (a) the name and contact details of the processor or processors and of each controller on behalf of which the processor is acting, and, where applicable, of the controller's or the processor's representative, and the data protection officer;

    (b) the categories of processing carried out on behalf of each controller;

    (c) where applicable, transfers of personal data to a third country or an international organisation, including the identification of that third country or international organisation and, in the case of transfers referred to in the second subparagraph of Article 49(1), the documentation of suitable safeguards;

(d) where possible, a general description of the technical and organisational security measures referred to in Article 32(1).

3. The records referred to in paragraphs 1 and 2 shall be in writing, including in electronic form.

4. The controller or the processor and, where applicable, the controller's or the processor's representative, shall make the record available to the supervisory authority on request.

5. The obligations referred to in paragraphs 1 and 2 shall not apply to an enterprise or an organisation employing fewer than 250 persons unless the processing it carries out is likely to result in a risk to the rights and freedoms of data subjects, the processing is not occasional, or the processing includes special categories of data as referred to in Article 9(1) or personal data relating to criminal convictions and offences referred to in Article 10.

———— NOTES ————

Defined terms		supervisory authority	Art 4(22)
controller	Art 4(7)		
enterprise	Art 4(18)	**Relevant recitals**	
international organisation	Art 4(26)	(82)	
personal data	Art 4(1)		
processing	Art 4(2)	**LED equivalent**	
processor	Art 4(8)	Arts 19, 24, 25, 29, 32	
recipient	Art 4(9)		
representative	Art 4(17)		

Article 31   Cooperation with the supervisory authority

The controller and the processor and, where applicable, their representatives, shall cooperate, on request, with the supervisory authority in the performance of its tasks.

———— NOTES ————

Defined terms		**Relevant recitals**
controller	Art 4(7)	(82)
personal data	Art 4(1)	
processor	Art 4(8)	**LED equivalent**
representative	Art 4(17)	Arts 26, 46, 47
supervisory authority	Art 4(22)	

Section 2 – Security of personal data

Article 32   Security of processing

1. Taking into account the state of the art, the costs of implementation and the nature, scope, context and purposes of processing as well as the risk of varying likelihood and severity for the rights and freedoms of natural persons, the controller and the processor shall implement appropriate technical and organisational measures to ensure a level of security appropriate to the risk, including inter alia as appropriate:

    (a) the pseudonymisation and encryption of personal data;

    (b) the ability to ensure the ongoing confidentiality, integrity, availability and resilience of processing systems and services;

    (c) the ability to restore the availability and access to personal data in a timely manner in the event of a physical or technical incident;

    (d) a process for regularly testing, assessing and evaluating the effectiveness of technical and organisational measures for ensuring the security of the processing.

2.   In assessing the appropriate level of security account shall be taken in particular of the risks that are presented by processing, in particular from accidental or unlawful destruction, loss, alteration, unauthorised disclosure of, or access to personal data transmitted, stored or otherwise processed.

3.   Adherence to an approved code of conduct as referred to in Article 40 or an approved certification mechanism as referred to in Article 42 may be used as an element by which to demonstrate compliance with the requirements set out in paragraph 1 of this Article.

4.   The controller and processor shall take steps to ensure that any natural person acting under the authority of the controller or the processor who has access to personal data does not process them except on instructions from the controller, unless he or she is required to do so by Union or Member State law.

—— NOTES ——

Defined terms		Relevant recitals
controller	Art 4(7)	(83)
personal data	Art 4(1)	
processing	Art 4(2)	**LED equivalent**
processor	Art 4(8)	Arts 3(11), 4(1)(f), 24(1)(i), 29, 30, 31
pseudonymisation	Art 4(5)	

Article 33   Notification of a personal data breach to the supervisory authority

1.   In the case of a personal data breach, the controller shall without undue delay and, where feasible, not later than 72 hours after having become aware of it, notify the personal data breach to the supervisory authority competent in accordance with Article 55, unless the personal data breach is unlikely to result in a risk to the rights and freedoms of natural persons. Where the notification to the supervisory authority is not made within 72 hours, it shall be accompanied by reasons for the delay.

2.   The processor shall notify the controller without undue delay after becoming aware of a personal data breach.

3.   The notification referred to in paragraph 1 shall at least:
     (a) describe the nature of the personal data breach including where possible, the categories and approximate number of data subjects concerned and the categories and approximate number of personal data records concerned;
     (b) communicate the name and contact details of the data protection officer or other contact point where more information can be obtained;
     (c) describe the likely consequences of the personal data breach;
     (d) describe the measures taken or proposed to be taken by the controller to address the personal data breach, including, where appropriate, measures to mitigate its possible adverse effects.

4.   Where, and in so far as, it is not possible to provide the information at the same time, the information may be provided in phases without undue further delay.

5.   The controller shall document any personal data breaches, comprising the facts relating to the personal data breach, its effects and the remedial action taken. That documentation shall enable the supervisory authority to verify compliance with this Article.

—— Notes ——

Defined terms		Relevant recitals
controller	Art 4(7)	(85), (87)
personal data	Art 4(1)	
personal data breach	Art 4(12)	**LED equivalent**
processor	Art 4(8)	Arts 30, 31, 51(1)
supervisory authority	Art 4(22)	

Article 34   Communication of a personal data breach to the data subject

1. When the personal data breach is likely to result in a high risk to the rights and freedoms of natural persons, the controller shall communicate the personal data breach to the data subject without undue delay.

2. The communication to the data subject referred to in paragraph 1 of this Article shall describe in clear and plain language the nature of the personal data breach and contain at least the information and measures referred to in points (b), (c) and (d) of Article 33(3).

3. The communication to the data subject referred to in paragraph 1 shall not be required if any of the following conditions are met:
    (a) the controller has implemented appropriate technical and organisational protection measures, and those measures were applied to the personal data affected by the personal data breach, in particular those that render the personal data unintelligible to any person who is not authorised to access it, such as encryption;
    (b) the controller has taken subsequent measures which ensure that the high risk to the rights and freedoms of data subjects referred to in paragraph 1 is no longer likely to materialise;
    (c) it would involve disproportionate effort. In such a case, there shall instead be a public communication or similar measure whereby the data subjects are informed in an equally effective manner.

4. If the controller has not already communicated the personal data breach to the data subject, the supervisory authority, having considered the likelihood of the personal data breach resulting in a high risk, may require it to do so or may decide that any of the conditions referred to in paragraph 3 are met.

—— Notes ——

Defined terms		Relevant recitals
controller	Art 4(7)	(86), (87), (88)
personal data	Art 4(1)	
personal data breach	Art 4(12)	**LED equivalent**
supervisory authority	Art 4(22)	Arts 13(3), 30, 31, 51(1)

Section 3 – Data protection impact assessment and prior consultation

Article 35   Data protection impact assessment

1. Where a type of processing in particular using new technologies, and taking into account the nature, scope, context and purposes of the processing, is likely to result in a high risk to the rights and freedoms of natural persons, the controller shall, prior to the processing, carry out an assessment of the impact of the envisaged processing operations on the protection of personal data. A single assessment may address a set of similar processing operations that present similar high risks.

2. The controller shall seek the advice of the data protection officer, where designated, when

carrying out a data protection impact assessment.

3. A data protection impact assessment referred to in paragraph 1 shall in particular be required in the case of:

    (a) a systematic and extensive evaluation of personal aspects relating to natural persons which is based on automated processing, including profiling, and on which decisions are based that produce legal effects concerning the natural person or similarly significantly affect the natural person;

    (b) processing on a large scale of special categories of data referred to in Article 9(1), or of personal data relating to criminal convictions and offences referred to in Article 10; or

    (c) a systematic monitoring of a publicly accessible area on a large scale.

4. The supervisory authority shall establish and make public a list of the kind of processing operations which are subject to the requirement for a data protection impact assessment pursuant to paragraph 1. The supervisory authority shall communicate those lists to the Board referred to in Article 68.

5. The supervisory authority may also establish and make public a list of the kind of processing operations for which no data protection impact assessment is required. The supervisory authority shall communicate those lists to the Board.

6. Prior to the adoption of the lists referred to in paragraphs 4 and 5, the competent supervisory authority shall apply the consistency mechanism referred to in Article 63 where such lists involve processing activities which are related to the offering of goods or services to data subjects or to the monitoring of their behaviour in several Member States, or may substantially affect the free movement of personal data within the Union.

7. The assessment shall contain at least:

    (a) a systematic description of the envisaged processing operations and the purposes of the processing, including, where applicable, the legitimate interest pursued by the controller;

    (b) an assessment of the necessity and proportionality of the processing operations in relation to the purposes;

    (c) an assessment of the risks to the rights and freedoms of data subjects referred to in paragraph 1; and

    (d) the measures envisaged to address the risks, including safeguards, security measures and mechanisms to ensure the protection of personal data and to demonstrate compliance with this Regulation taking into account the rights and legitimate interests of data subjects and other persons concerned.

8. Compliance with approved codes of conduct referred to in Article 40 by the relevant controllers or processors shall be taken into due account in assessing the impact of the processing operations performed by such controllers or processors, in particular for the purposes of a data protection impact assessment.

9. Where appropriate, the controller shall seek the views of data subjects or their representatives on the intended processing, without prejudice to the protection of commercial or public interests or the security of processing operations.

10. Where processing pursuant to point (c) or (e) of Article 6(1) has a legal basis in Union law or in the law of the Member State to which the controller is subject, that law regulates the specific processing operation or set of operations in question, and a data protection impact

assessment has already been carried out as part of a general impact assessment in the context of the adoption of that legal basis, paragraphs 1 to 7 shall not apply unless Member States deem it to be necessary to carry out such an assessment prior to processing activities.

11. Where necessary, the controller shall carry out a review to assess if processing is performed in accordance with the data protection impact assessment at least when there is a change of the risk represented by processing operations.

—— NOTES ——

Defined terms		supervisory authority	Art 4(22)
controller	Art 4(7)		
personal data	Art 4(1)	**Relevant recitals**	
processing	Art 4(2)	(75), (84), (89), (90), (91), (92), (93)	
processor	Art 4(8)		
profiling	Art 4(4)	**LED equivalent**	
representative	Art 4(17)	Arts 19, 20, 27, 28	

Article 36   Prior consultation

1. The controller shall consult the supervisory authority prior to processing where a data protection impact assessment under Article 35 indicates that the processing would result in a high risk in the absence of measures taken by the controller to mitigate the risk.

2. Where the supervisory authority is of the opinion that the intended processing referred to in paragraph 1 would infringe this Regulation, in particular where the controller has insufficiently identified or mitigated the risk, the supervisory authority shall, within period of up to eight weeks of receipt of the request for consultation, provide written advice to the controller and, where applicable to the processor, and may use any of its powers referred to in Article 58. That period may be extended by six weeks, taking into account the complexity of the intended processing. The supervisory authority shall inform the controller and, where applicable, the processor, of any such extension within one month of receipt of the request for consultation together with the reasons for the delay. Those periods may be suspended until the supervisory authority has obtained information it has requested for the purposes of the consultation.

3. When consulting the supervisory authority pursuant to paragraph 1, the controller shall provide the supervisory authority with:
   (a) where applicable, the respective responsibilities of the controller, joint controllers and processors involved in the processing, in particular for processing within a group of undertakings;
   (b) the purposes and means of the intended processing;
   (c) the measures and safeguards provided to protect the rights and freedoms of data subjects pursuant to this Regulation;
   (d) where applicable, the contact details of the data protection officer;
   (e) the data protection impact assessment provided for in Article 35; and
   (f) any other information requested by the supervisory authority.

4. Member States shall consult the supervisory authority during the preparation of a proposal for a legislative measure to be adopted by a national parliament, or of a regulatory measure based on such a legislative measure, which relates to processing.

5. Notwithstanding paragraph 1, Member State law may require controllers to consult with, and obtain prior authorisation from, the supervisory authority in relation to processing by

a controller for the performance of a task carried out by the controller in the public interest, including processing in relation to social protection and public health.

—— NOTES ——

Defined terms		**Relevant recitals**
controller	Art 4(7)	(84), (89), (94), (95), (96)
group of undertakings	Art 4(19)	
processing	Art 4(2)	**LED equivalent**
processor	Art 4(8)	Arts 19, 27, 28
supervisory authority	Art 4(22)	

Section 4 – Data protection officer

Article 37   Designation of the data protection officer

1. The controller and the processor shall designate a data protection officer in any case where:

    (a) the processing is carried out by a public authority or body, except for courts acting in their judicial capacity;

    (b) the core activities of the controller or the processor consist of processing operations which, by virtue of their nature, their scope and/or their purposes, require regular and systematic monitoring of data subjects on a large scale; or

    (c) the core activities of the controller or the processor consist of processing on a large scale of special categories of data pursuant to Article 9 and personal data relating to criminal convictions and offences referred to in Article 10.

2. A group of undertakings may appoint a single data protection officer provided that a data protection officer is easily accessible from each establishment.

3. Where the controller or the processor is a public authority or body, a single data protection officer may be designated for several such authorities or bodies, taking account of their organisational structure and size.

4. In cases other than those referred to in paragraph 1, the controller or processor or associations and other bodies representing categories of controllers or processors may or, where required by Union or Member State law shall, designate a data protection officer. The data protection officer may act for such associations and other bodies representing controllers or processors.

5. The data protection officer shall be designated on the basis of professional qualities and, in particular, expert knowledge of data protection law and practices and the ability to fulfil the tasks referred to in Article 39.

6. The data protection officer may be a staff member of the controller or processor, or fulfil the tasks on the basis of a service contract.

7. The controller or the processor shall publish the contact details of the data protection officer and communicate them to the supervisory authority.

—— NOTES ——

Defined terms		**Relevant recitals**
controller	Art 4(7)	(97)
group of undertakings	Art 4(19)	
personal data	Art 4(1)	**LED equivalent**
processing	Art 4(2)	Art 32
processor	Art 4(8)	
supervisory authority	Art 4(22)	

Article 38   Position of the data protection officer

1. The controller and the processor shall ensure that the data protection officer is involved, properly and in a timely manner, in all issues which relate to the protection of personal data.

2. The controller and processor shall support the data protection officer in performing the tasks referred to in Article 39 by providing resources necessary to carry out those tasks and access to personal data and processing operations, and to maintain his or her expert knowledge.

3. The controller and processor shall ensure that the data protection officer does not receive any instructions regarding the exercise of those tasks. He or she shall not be dismissed or penalised by the controller or the processor for performing his tasks. The data protection officer shall directly report to the highest management level of the controller or the processor.

4. Data subjects may contact the data protection officer with regard to all issues related to processing of their personal data and to the exercise of their rights under this Regulation.

5. The data protection officer shall be bound by secrecy or confidentiality concerning the performance of his or her tasks, in accordance with Union or Member State law.

6. The data protection officer may fulfil other tasks and duties. The controller or processor shall ensure that any such tasks and duties do not result in a conflict of interests.

–––––– NOTES ––––––

Defined terms		Relevant recitals
controller	Art 4(7)	(97)
personal data	Art 4(1)	
processing	Art 4(2)	**LED equivalent**
processor	Art 4(8)	Arts 33

Article 39   Tasks of the data protection officer

1. The data protection officer shall have at least the following tasks:

    (a) to inform and advise the controller or the processor and the employees who carry out processing of their obligations pursuant to this Regulation and to other Union or Member State data protection provisions;

    (b) to monitor compliance with this Regulation, with other Union or Member State data protection provisions and with the policies of the controller or processor in relation to the protection of personal data, including the assignment of responsibilities, awareness-raising and training of staff involved in processing operations, and the related audits;

    (c) to provide advice where requested as regards the data protection impact assessment and monitor its performance pursuant to Article 35;

    (d) to cooperate with the supervisory authority;

    (e) to act as the contact point for the supervisory authority on issues relating to processing, including the prior consultation referred to in Article 36, and to consult, where appropriate, with regard to any other matter.

2. The data protection officer shall in the performance of his or her tasks have due regard to the risk associated with processing operations, taking into account the nature, scope, context and purposes of processing.

Defined terms		Relevant recitals
controller	Art 4(7)	(77), (97)
personal data	Art 4(1)	
processing	Art 4(2)	**LED equivalent**
processor	Art 4(8)	Arts 34
supervisory authority	Art 4(22)	

Section 5 – Codes of conduct and certification

Article 40   Codes of conduct

1. The Member States, the supervisory authorities, the Board and the Commission shall encourage the drawing up of codes of conduct intended to contribute to the proper application of this Regulation, taking account of the specific features of the various processing sectors and the specific needs of micro, small and medium-sized enterprises.

2. Associations and other bodies representing categories of controllers or processors may prepare codes of conduct, or amend or extend such codes, for the purpose of specifying the application of this Regulation, such as with regard to:
   (a) fair and transparent processing;
   (b) the legitimate interests pursued by controllers in specific contexts;
   (c) the collection of personal data;
   (d) the pseudonymisation of personal data;
   (e) the information provided to the public and to data subjects;
   (f) the exercise of the rights of data subjects;
   (g) the information provided to, and the protection of, children, and the manner in which the consent of the holders of parental responsibility over children is to be obtained;
   (h) the measures and procedures referred to in Articles 24 and 25 and the measures to ensure security of processing referred to in Article 32;
   (i) the notification of personal data breaches to supervisory authorities and the communication of such personal data breaches to data subjects;
   (j) the transfer of personal data to third countries or international organisations; or
   (k) out-of-court proceedings and other dispute resolution procedures for resolving disputes between controllers and data subjects with regard to processing, without prejudice to the rights of data subjects pursuant to Articles 77 and 79.

3. In addition to adherence by controllers or processors subject to this Regulation, codes of conduct approved pursuant to paragraph 5 of this Article and having general validity pursuant to paragraph 9 of this Article may also be adhered to by controllers or processors that are not subject to this Regulation pursuant to Article 3 in order to provide appropriate safeguards within the framework of personal data transfers to third countries or international organisations under the terms referred to in point (e) of Article 46(2). Such controllers or processors shall make binding and enforceable commitments, via contractual or other legally binding instruments, to apply those appropriate safeguards including with regard to the rights of data subjects.

4. A code of conduct referred to in paragraph 2 of this Article shall contain mechanisms which enable the body referred to in Article 41(1) to carry out the mandatory monitoring of compliance with its provisions by the controllers or processors which undertake to apply it, without prejudice to the tasks and powers of supervisory authorities competent pursuant to Article 55 or 56.

5. Associations and other bodies referred to in paragraph 2 of this Article which intend to prepare a code of conduct or to amend or extend an existing code shall submit the draft code, amendment or extension to the supervisory authority which is competent pursuant to Article 55. The supervisory authority shall provide an opinion on whether the draft code, amendment or extension complies with this Regulation and shall approve that draft code, amendment or extension if it finds that it provides sufficient appropriate safeguards.

6. Where the draft code, or amendment or extension is approved in accordance with paragraph 5, and where the code of conduct concerned does not relate to processing activities in several Member States, the supervisory authority shall register and publish the code.

7. Where a draft code of conduct relates to processing activities in several Member States, the supervisory authority which is competent pursuant to Article 55 shall, before approving the draft code, amendment or extension, submit it in the procedure referred to in Article 63 to the Board which shall provide an opinion on whether the draft code, amendment or extension complies with this Regulation or, in the situation referred to in paragraph 3 of this Article, provides appropriate safeguards.

8. Where the opinion referred to in paragraph 7 confirms that the draft code, amendment or extension complies with this Regulation, or, in the situation referred to in paragraph 3, provides appropriate safeguards, the Board shall submit its opinion to the Commission.

9. The Commission may, by way of implementing acts, decide that the approved code of conduct, amendment or extension submitted to it pursuant to paragraph 8 of this Article have general validity within the Union. Those implementing acts shall be adopted in accordance with the examination procedure set out in Article 93(2).

10. The Commission shall ensure appropriate publicity for the approved codes which have been decided as having general validity in accordance with paragraph 9.

11. The Board shall collate all approved codes of conduct, amendments and extensions in a register and shall make them publicly available by way of appropriate means.

–––––– NOTES ––––––

Defined terms
consent	Art 4(11)	
controller	Art 4(7)	
enterprise	Art 4(18)	
international organisation	Art 4(26)	
personal data	Art 4(1)	
personal data breach	Art 4(12)	
processing	Art 4(2)	
processor	Art 4(8)	

pseudonymisation   Art 4(5)
supervisory authority   Art 4(22)

Relevant recitals
(77), (81), (98), (99), (168)

LED equivalent
n/a

Article 41   Monitoring of approved codes of conduct

1. Without prejudice to the tasks and powers of the competent supervisory authority under Articles 57 and 58, the monitoring of compliance with a code of conduct pursuant to Article 40 may be carried out by a body which has an appropriate level of expertise in relation to the subject-matter of the code and is accredited for that purpose by the competent supervisory authority.

2. A body as referred to in paragraph 1 may be accredited to monitor compliance with a code of conduct where that body has:

    (a) demonstrated its independence and expertise in relation to the subject-matter of the code to the satisfaction of the competent supervisory authority;

    (b) established procedures which allow it to assess the eligibility of controllers and processors concerned to apply the code, to monitor their compliance with its provisions and to periodically review its operation;

    (c) established procedures and structures to handle complaints about infringements of the code or the manner in which the code has been, or is being, implemented by a controller or processor, and to make those procedures and structures transparent to data subjects and the public; and

    (d) demonstrated to the satisfaction of the competent supervisory authority that its tasks and duties do not result in a conflict of interests.

3. The competent supervisory authority shall submit the draft criteria for accreditation of a body as referred to in paragraph 1 of this Article to the Board pursuant to the consistency mechanism referred to in Article 63.

4. Without prejudice to the tasks and powers of the competent supervisory authority and the provisions of Chapter VIII, a body as referred to in paragraph 1 of this Article shall, subject to appropriate safeguards, take appropriate action in cases of infringement of the code by a controller or processor, including suspension or exclusion of the controller or processor concerned from the code. It shall inform the competent supervisory authority of such actions and the reasons for taking them.

5. The competent supervisory authority shall revoke the accreditation of a body as referred to in paragraph 1 if the conditions for accreditation are not, or are no longer, met or where actions taken by the body infringe this Regulation.

6. This Article shall not apply to processing carried out by public authorities and bodies.

—— NOTES ——

Defined terms		Relevant recitals	
controller	Art 4(7)	(77), (81), (98), (168)	
processing	Art 4(2)		
processor	Art 4(8)	**LED equivalent**	
supervisory authority	Art 4(22)	Arts 13, 20	

Article 42   Certification

1. The Member States, the supervisory authorities, the Board and the Commission shall encourage, in particular at Union level, the establishment of data protection certification mechanisms and of data protection seals and marks, for the purpose of demonstrating compliance with this Regulation of processing operations by controllers and processors. The specific needs of micro, small and medium-sized enterprises shall be taken into account.

2. In addition to adherence by controllers or processors subject to this Regulation, data protection certification mechanisms, seals or marks approved pursuant to paragraph 5 of this Article may be established for the purpose of demonstrating the existence of appropriate safeguards provided by controllers or processors that are not subject to this Regulation pursuant to Article 3 within the framework of personal data transfers to third countries or international organisations under the terms referred to in point (f) of Article 46(2). Such controllers or processors shall make binding and enforceable commitments, via contractual or other legally binding instruments, to apply those appropriate safeguards, including with regard to the rights of data subjects.

3. The certification shall be voluntary and available via a process that is transparent.

4. A certification pursuant to this Article does not reduce the responsibility of the controller or the processor for compliance with this Regulation and is without prejudice to the tasks and powers of the supervisory authorities which are competent pursuant to Article 55 or 56.

5. A certification pursuant to this Article shall be issued by the certification bodies referred to in Article 43 or by the competent supervisory authority, on the basis of criteria approved by that competent supervisory authority pursuant to Article 58(3) or by the Board pursuant to Article 63. Where the criteria are approved by the Board, this may result in a common certification, the European Data Protection Seal.

6. The controller or processor which submits its processing to the certification mechanism shall provide the certification body referred to in Article 43, or where applicable, the competent supervisory authority, with all information and access to its processing activities which are necessary to conduct the certification procedure.

7. Certification shall be issued to a controller or processor for a maximum period of three years and may be renewed, under the same conditions, provided that the relevant requirements continue to be met. Certification shall be withdrawn, as applicable, by the certification bodies referred to in Article 43 or by the competent supervisory authority where the requirements for the certification are not or are no longer met.

8. The Board shall collate all certification mechanisms and data protection seals and marks in a register and shall make them publicly available by any appropriate means.

─── NOTES ───

Defined terms		Relevant recitals
controller	Art 4(7)	(100)
enterprise	Art 4(18)	
personal data	Art 4(1)	**LED equivalent**
processing	Art 4(2)	n/a
processor	Art 4(8)	
supervisory authority	Art 4(22)	

Article 43   Certification bodies

1. Without prejudice to the tasks and powers of the competent supervisory authority under Articles 57 and 58, certification bodies which have an appropriate level of expertise in relation to data protection shall, after informing the supervisory authority in order to allow it to exercise its powers pursuant to point (h) of Article 58(2) where necessary, issue and renew certification. Member States shall ensure that those certification bodies are accredited by one or both of the following:

    (a) the supervisory authority which is competent pursuant to Article 55 or 56;

    (b) the national accreditation body named in accordance with Regulation (EC) No 765/2008 of the European Parliament and of the Council in accordance with EN-ISO/IEC 17065/2012 and with the additional requirements established by the supervisory authority which is competent pursuant to Article 55 or 56.

2. Certification bodies referred to in paragraph 1 shall be accredited in accordance with that paragraph only where they have:

    (a) demonstrated their independence and expertise in relation to the subject-matter of the certification to the satisfaction of the competent supervisory authority;

(b) undertaken to respect the criteria referred to in Article 42(5) and approved by the supervisory authority which is competent pursuant to Article 55 or 56 or by the Board pursuant to Article 63;

(c) established procedures for the issuing, periodic review and withdrawal of data protection certification, seals and marks;

(d) established procedures and structures to handle complaints about infringements of the certification or the manner in which the certification has been, or is being, implemented by the controller or processor, and to make those procedures and structures transparent to data subjects and the public; and

(e) demonstrated, to the satisfaction of the competent supervisory authority, that their tasks and duties do not result in a conflict of interests.

3. The accreditation of certification bodies as referred to in paragraphs 1 and 2 of this Article shall take place on the basis of criteria approved by the supervisory authority which is competent pursuant to Article 55 or 56 or by the Board pursuant to Article 63. In the case of accreditation pursuant to point (b) of paragraph 1 of this Article, those requirements shall complement those envisaged in Regulation (EC) No 765/2008 and the technical rules that describe the methods and procedures of the certification bodies.

4. The certification bodies referred to in paragraph 1 shall be responsible for the proper assessment leading to the certification or the withdrawal of such certification without prejudice to the responsibility of the controller or processor for compliance with this Regulation. The accreditation shall be issued for a maximum period of five years and may be renewed on the same conditions provided that the certification body meets the requirements set out in this Article.

5. The certification bodies referred to in paragraph 1 shall provide the competent supervisory authorities with the reasons for granting or withdrawing the requested certification.

6. The requirements referred to in paragraph 3 of this Article and the criteria referred to in Article 42(5) shall be made public by the supervisory authority in an easily accessible form. The supervisory authorities shall also transmit those requirements and criteria to the Board. The Board shall collate all certification mechanisms and data protection seals in a register and shall make them publicly available by any appropriate means.

7. Without prejudice to Chapter VIII, the competent supervisory authority or the national accreditation body shall revoke an accreditation of a certification body pursuant to paragraph 1 of this Article where the conditions for the accreditation are not, or are no longer, met or where actions taken by a certification body infringe this Regulation.

8. The Commission shall be empowered to adopt delegated acts in accordance with Article 92 for the purpose of specifying the requirements to be taken into account for the data protection certification mechanisms referred to in Article 42(1).

9. The Commission may adopt implementing acts laying down technical standards for certification mechanisms and data protection seals and marks, and mechanisms to promote and recognise those certification mechanisms, seals and marks. Those implementing acts shall be adopted in accordance with the examination procedure referred to in Article 93(2).

—— NOTES ——

Defined terms		supervisory authority	Art 4(22)
controller	Art 4(7)		
personal data	Art 4(1)	**Relevant recitals**	
processor	Art 4(8)	(100)	

CHAPTER V – TRANSFERS OF PERSONAL DATA TO THIRD COUNTRIES OR INTERNATIONAL ORGANISATIONS

Article 44   General principle for transfers

Any transfer of personal data which are undergoing processing or are intended for processing after transfer to a third country or to an international organisation shall take place only if, subject to the other provisions of this Regulation, the conditions laid down in this Chapter are complied with by the controller and processor, including for onward transfers of personal data from the third country or an international organisation to another third country or to another international organisation. All provisions in this Chapter shall be applied in order to ensure that the level of protection of natural persons guaranteed by this Regulation is not undermined.

—— NOTES ——

Defined terms		Relevant recitals	
controller	Art 4(7)	(6), (101), (102)	
international organisation	Art 4(26)		
personal data	Art 4(1)	**LED equivalent**	
processing	Art 4(2)	Art 35	
processor	Art 4(8)		

Article 45   Transfers on the basis of an adequacy decision

1. A transfer of personal data to a third country or an international organisation may take place where the Commission has decided that the third country, a territory or one or more specified sectors within that third country, or the international organisation in question ensures an adequate level of protection. Such a transfer shall not require any specific authorisation.

2. When assessing the adequacy of the level of protection, the Commission shall, in particular, take account of the following elements:

    (a) the rule of law, respect for human rights and fundamental freedoms, relevant legislation, both general and sectoral, including concerning public security, defence, national security and criminal law and the access of public authorities to personal data, as well as the implementation of such legislation, data protection rules, professional rules and security measures, including rules for the onward transfer of personal data to another third country or international organisation which are complied with in that country or international organisation, case-law, as well as effective and enforceable data subject rights and effective administrative and judicial redress for the data subjects whose personal data are being transferred;

    (b) the existence and effective functioning of one or more independent supervisory authorities in the third country or to which an international organisation is subject, with responsibility for ensuring and enforcing compliance with the data protection rules, including adequate enforcement powers, for assisting and advising the data subjects in exercising their rights and for cooperation with the supervisory authorities of the Member States; and

(c) the international commitments the third country or international organisation concerned has entered into, or other obligations arising from legally binding conventions or instruments as well as from its participation in multilateral or regional systems, in particular in relation to the protection of personal data.

3. The Commission, after assessing the adequacy of the level of protection, may decide, by means of implementing act, that a third country, a territory or one or more specified sectors within a third country, or an international organisation ensures an adequate level of protection within the meaning of paragraph 2 of this Article. The implementing act shall provide for a mechanism for a periodic review, at least every four years, which shall take into account all relevant developments in the third country or international organisation. The implementing act shall specify its territorial and sectoral application and, where applicable, identify the supervisory authority or authorities referred to in point (b) of paragraph 2 of this Article. The implementing act shall be adopted in accordance with the examination procedure referred to in Article 93(2).

4. The Commission shall, on an ongoing basis, monitor developments in third countries and international organisations that could affect the functioning of decisions adopted pursuant to paragraph 3 of this Article and decisions adopted on the basis of Article 25(6) of Directive 95/46/EC.

5. The Commission shall, where available information reveals, in particular following the review referred to in paragraph 3 of this Article, that a third country, a territory or one or more specified sectors within a third country, or an international organisation no longer ensures an adequate level of protection within the meaning of paragraph 2 of this Article, to the extent necessary, repeal, amend or suspend the decision referred to in paragraph 3 of this Article by means of implementing acts without retro-active effect. Those implementing acts shall be adopted in accordance with the examination procedure referred to in Article 93(2).
On duly justified imperative grounds of urgency, the Commission shall adopt immediately applicable implementing acts in accordance with the procedure referred to in Article 93(3).

6. The Commission shall enter into consultations with the third country or international organisation with a view to remedying the situation giving rise to the decision made pursuant to paragraph 5.

7. A decision pursuant to paragraph 5 of this Article is without prejudice to transfers of personal data to the third country, a territory or one or more specified sectors within that third country, or the international organisation in question pursuant to Articles 46 to 49.

8. The Commission shall publish in the Official Journal of the European Union and on its website a list of the third countries, territories and specified sectors within a third country and international organisations for which it has decided that an adequate level of protection is or is no longer ensured.

9. Decisions adopted by the Commission on the basis of Article 25(6) of Directive 95/46/EC shall remain in force until amended, replaced or repealed by a Commission Decision adopted in accordance with paragraph 3 or 5 of this Article.

——— Notes ———

Defined terms		Relevant recitals
international organisation	Art 4(26)	(102), (103), (104), (105), (106), (107)
supervisory authority	Art 4(22)	

LED equivalent
Arts 35, 36, 51(1)(g)

Article 46   Transfers subject to appropriate safeguards

1. In the absence of a decision pursuant to Article 45(3), a controller or processor may transfer personal data to a third country or an international organisation only if the controller or processor has provided appropriate safeguards, and on condition that enforceable data subject rights and effective legal remedies for data subjects are available.

2. The appropriate safeguards referred to in paragraph 1 may be provided for, without requiring any specific authorisation from a supervisory authority, by:
    (a) a legally binding and enforceable instrument between public authorities or bodies;
    (b) binding corporate rules in accordance with Article 47;
    (c) standard data protection clauses adopted by the Commission in accordance with the examination procedure referred to in Article 93(2);
    (d) standard data protection clauses adopted by a supervisory authority and approved by the Commission pursuant to the examination procedure referred to in Article 93(2);
    (e) an approved code of conduct pursuant to Article 40 together with binding and enforceable commitments of the controller or processor in the third country to apply the appropriate safeguards, including as regards data subjects' rights; or
    (f) an approved certification mechanism pursuant to Article 42 together with binding and enforceable commitments of the controller or processor in the third country to apply the appropriate safeguards, including as regards data subjects' rights.

3. Subject to the authorisation from the competent supervisory authority, the appropriate safeguards referred to in paragraph 1 may also be provided for, in particular, by:
    (a) contractual clauses between the controller or processor and the controller, processor or the recipient of the personal data in the third country or international organisation; or
    (b) provisions to be inserted into administrative arrangements between public authorities or bodies which include enforceable and effective data subject rights.

4. The supervisory authority shall apply the consistency mechanism referred to in Article 63 in the cases referred to in paragraph 3 of this Article.

5. Authorisations by a Member State or supervisory authority on the basis of Article 26(2) of Directive 95/46/EC shall remain valid until amended, replaced or repealed, if necessary, by that supervisory authority. Decisions adopted by the Commission on the basis of Article 26(4) of Directive 95/46/EC shall remain in force until amended, replaced or repealed, if necessary, by a Commission Decision adopted in accordance with paragraph 2 of this Article.

——— NOTES ———

Defined terms		Relevant recitals
binding corporate rules	Art 4(20)	(108), (109), (114)
controller	Art 4(7)	
international organisation	Art 4(26)	**LED equivalent**
personal data	Art 4(1)	Art 37
processor	Art 4(8)	
recipient	Art 4(9)	
supervisory authority	Art 4(22)	

Article 47   Binding corporate rules

1. The competent supervisory authority shall approve binding corporate rules in accordance with the consistency mechanism set out in Article 63, provided that they:

   (a) are legally binding and apply to and are enforced by every member concerned of the group of undertakings, or group of enterprises engaged in a joint economic activity, including their employees;

   (b) expressly confer enforceable rights on data subjects with regard to the processing of their personal data; and

   (c) fulfil the requirements laid down in paragraph 2.

2. The binding corporate rules referred to in paragraph 1 shall specify at least:

   (a) the structure and contact details of the group of undertakings, or group of enterprises engaged in a joint economic activity and of each of its members;

   (b) the data transfers or set of transfers, including the categories of personal data, the type of processing and its purposes, the type of data subjects affected and the identification of the third country or countries in question;

   (c) their legally binding nature, both internally and externally;

   (d) the application of the general data protection principles, in particular purpose limitation, data minimisation, limited storage periods, data quality, data protection by design and by default, legal basis for processing, processing of special categories of personal data, measures to ensure data security, and the requirements in respect of onward transfers to bodies not bound by the binding corporate rules;

   (e) the rights of data subjects in regard to processing and the means to exercise those rights, including the right not to be subject to decisions based solely on automated processing, including profiling in accordance with Article 22, the right to lodge a complaint with the competent supervisory authority and before the competent courts of the Member States in accordance with Article 79, and to obtain redress and, where appropriate, compensation for a breach of the binding corporate rules;

   (f) the acceptance by the controller or processor established on the territory of a Member State of liability for any breaches of the binding corporate rules by any member concerned not established in the Union; the controller or the processor shall be exempt from that liability, in whole or in part, only if it proves that that member is not responsible for the event giving rise to the damage;

   (g) how the information on the binding corporate rules, in particular on the provisions referred to in points (d), (e) and (f) of this paragraph is provided to the data subjects in addition to Articles 13 and 14;

   (h) the tasks of any data protection officer designated in accordance with Article 37 or any other person or entity in charge of the monitoring compliance with the binding corporate rules within the group of undertakings, or group of enterprises engaged in a joint economic activity, as well as monitoring training and complaint-handling;

(i) the complaint procedures;

(j) the mechanisms within the group of undertakings, or group of enterprises engaged in a joint economic activity for ensuring the verification of compliance with the binding corporate rules. Such mechanisms shall include data protection audits and methods for ensuring corrective actions to protect the rights of the data subject. Results of such verification should be communicated to the person or entity referred to in point (h) and to the board of the controlling undertaking of a group of undertakings, or of the group of enterprises engaged in a joint economic activity, and should be available upon request to the competent supervisory authority;

(k) the mechanisms for reporting and recording changes to the rules and reporting those changes to the supervisory authority;

(l) the cooperation mechanism with the supervisory authority to ensure compliance by any member of the group of undertakings, or group of enterprises engaged in a joint economic activity, in particular by making available to the supervisory authority the results of verifications of the measures referred to in point (j);

(m) the mechanisms for reporting to the competent supervisory authority any legal requirements to which a member of the group of undertakings, or group of enterprises engaged in a joint economic activity is subject in a third country which are likely to have a substantial adverse effect on the guarantees provided by the binding corporate rules; and

(n) the appropriate data protection training to personnel having permanent or regular access to personal data.

3.   The Commission may specify the format and procedures for the exchange of information between controllers, processors and supervisory authorities for binding corporate rules within the meaning of this Article. Those implementing acts shall be adopted in accordance with the examination procedure set out in Article 93(2).

——— NOTES ———

Defined terms		supervisory authority	Art 4(22)
binding corporate rules	Art 4(20)		
controller	Art 4(7)	**Relevant recitals**	
enterprise	Art 4(18)	(110)	
group of undertakings	Art 4(19)		
personal data	Art 4(1)	**LED equivalent**	
processing	Art 4(2)	n/a	
processor	Art 4(8)		
profiling	Art 4(4)		

Article 48   Transfers or disclosures not authorised by Union law

Any judgment of a court or tribunal and any decision of an administrative authority of a third country requiring a controller or processor to transfer or disclose personal data may only be recognised or enforceable in any manner if based on an international agreement, such as a mutual legal assistance treaty, in force between the requesting third country and the Union or a Member State, without prejudice to other grounds for transfer pursuant to this Chapter.

——— NOTES ———

Defined terms		**Relevant recitals**
controller	Art 4(7)	(102), (115)
personal data	Art 4(1)	
processor	Art 4(8)	

Article 49   Derogations for specific situations

1. In the absence of an adequacy decision pursuant to Article 45(3), or of appropriate safeguards pursuant to Article 46, including binding corporate rules, a transfer or a set of transfers of personal data to a third country or an international organisation shall take place only on one of the following conditions:

    (a) the data subject has explicitly consented to the proposed transfer, after having been informed of the possible risks of such transfers for the data subject due to the absence of an adequacy decision and appropriate safeguards;

    (b) the transfer is necessary for the performance of a contract between the data subject and the controller or the implementation of pre-contractual measures taken at the data subject's request;

    (c) the transfer is necessary for the conclusion or performance of a contract concluded in the interest of the data subject between the controller and another natural or legal person;

    (d) the transfer is necessary for important reasons of public interest;

    (e) the transfer is necessary for the establishment, exercise or defence of legal claims;

    (f) the transfer is necessary in order to protect the vital interests of the data subject or of other persons, where the data subject is physically or legally incapable of giving consent;

    (g) the transfer is made from a register which according to Union or Member State law is intended to provide information to the public and which is open to consultation either by the public in general or by any person who can demonstrate a legitimate interest, but only to the extent that the conditions laid down by Union or Member State law for consultation are fulfilled in the particular case.

    Where a transfer could not be based on a provision in Article 45 or 46, including the provisions on binding corporate rules, and none of the derogations for a specific situation referred to in the first subparagraph of this paragraph is applicable, a transfer to a third country or an international organisation may take place only if the transfer is not repetitive, concerns only a limited number of data subjects, is necessary for the purposes of compelling legitimate interests pursued by the controller which are not overridden by the interests or rights and freedoms of the data subject, and the controller has assessed all the circumstances surrounding the data transfer and has on the basis of that assessment provided suitable safeguards with regard to the protection of personal data. The controller shall inform the supervisory authority of the transfer. The controller shall, in addition to providing the information referred to in Articles 13 and 14, inform the data subject of the transfer and on the compelling legitimate interests pursued.

2. A transfer pursuant to point (g) of the first subparagraph of paragraph 1 shall not involve the entirety of the personal data or entire categories of the personal data contained in the register. Where the register is intended for consultation by persons having a legitimate interest, the transfer shall be made only at the request of those persons or if they are to be the recipients.

3. Points (a), (b) and (c) of the first subparagraph of paragraph 1 and the second subparagraph thereof shall not apply to activities carried out by public authorities in the exercise of their public powers.

4. The public interest referred to in point (d) of the first subparagraph of paragraph 1 shall be recognised in Union law or in the law of the Member State to which the controller is subject.

5.   In the absence of an adequacy decision, Union or Member State law may, for important reasons of public interest, expressly set limits to the transfer of specific categories of personal data to a third country or an international organisation. Member States shall notify such provisions to the Commission.

6.   The controller or processor shall document the assessment as well as the suitable safeguards referred to in the second subparagraph of paragraph 1 of this Article in the records referred to in Article 30.

—— NOTES ——

Defined terms

binding corporate rules	Art 4(20)	
consent	Art 4(11)	
controller	Art 4(7)	
international organisation	Art 4(26)	
personal data	Art 4(1)	
processor	Art 4(8)	
recipient	Art 4(9)	

supervisory authority   Art 4(22)

Relevant recitals
(111), (112), (113), (114)

LED equivalent
Arts 38, 39

Article 50   International cooperation for the protection of personal data

In relation to third countries and international organisations, the Commission and supervisory authorities shall take appropriate steps to:

(a)   develop international cooperation mechanisms to facilitate the effective enforcement of legislation for the protection of personal data;

(b)   provide international mutual assistance in the enforcement of legislation for the protection of personal data, including through notification, complaint referral, investigative assistance and information exchange, subject to appropriate safeguards for the protection of personal data and other fundamental rights and freedoms;

(c)   engage relevant stakeholders in discussion and activities aimed at furthering international cooperation in the enforcement of legislation for the protection of personal data;

(d)   promote the exchange and documentation of personal data protection legislation and practice, including on jurisdictional conflicts with third countries.

—— NOTES ——

Defined terms
international organisation   Art 4(26)
personal data   Art 4(1)

Relevant recitals
(102), (116)

LED equivalent
Arts 40, 51(1)

CHAPTER VI – INDEPENDENT SUPERVISORY AUTHORITIES

Section 1 – Independent status

Article 51   Supervisory authority

1.   Each Member State shall provide for one or more independent public authorities to be responsible for monitoring the application of this Regulation, in order to protect the fundamental rights and freedoms of natural persons in relation to processing and to facilitate the free flow of personal data within the Union ('supervisory authority').

2. Each supervisory authority shall contribute to the consistent application of this Regulation throughout the Union. For that purpose, the supervisory authorities shall cooperate with each other and the Commission in accordance with Chapter VII.

3. Where more than one supervisory authority is established in a Member State, that Member State shall designate the supervisory authority which is to represent those authorities in the Board and shall set out the mechanism to ensure compliance by the other authorities with the rules relating to the consistency mechanism referred to in Article 63.

4. Each Member State shall notify to the Commission the provisions of its law which it adopts pursuant to this Chapter, by 25 May 2018 and, without delay, any subsequent amendment affecting them.

—— NOTES ——

Defined terms		Relevant recitals
personal data	Art 4(1)	(117), (119), (122), (123)
processing	Art 4(2)	
supervisory authority	Art 4(22)	**LED equivalent**
		Art 41

Article 52   Independence

1. Each supervisory authority shall act with complete independence in performing its tasks and exercising its powers in accordance with this Regulation.

2. The member or members of each supervisory authority shall, in the performance of their tasks and exercise of their powers in accordance with this Regulation, remain free from external influence, whether direct or indirect, and shall neither seek nor take instructions from anybody.

3. Member or members of each supervisory authority shall refrain from any action incompatible with their duties and shall not, during their term of office, engage in any incompatible occupation, whether gainful or not.

4. Each Member State shall ensure that each supervisory authority is provided with the human, technical and financial resources, premises and infrastructure necessary for the effective performance of its tasks and exercise of its powers, including those to be carried out in the context of mutual assistance, cooperation and participation in the Board.

5. Each Member State shall ensure that each supervisory authority chooses and has its own staff which shall be subject to the exclusive direction of the member or members of the supervisory authority concerned.

6. Each Member State shall ensure that each supervisory authority is subject to financial control which does not affect its independence and that it has separate, public annual budgets, which may be part of the overall state or national budget.

—— NOTES ——

Defined terms		Relevant recitals
supervisory authority concerned	Art 4(21)	(117), (118), (120), (121)
supervisory authority	Art 4(22)	
		LED equivalent
		Art 42

Article 53   General conditions for the members of the supervisory authority

1. Member States shall provide for each member of their supervisory authorities to be appointed by means of a transparent procedure by:
    — their parliament;
    — their government;
    — their head of State; or
    — an independent body entrusted with the appointment under Member State law.

2. Each member shall have the qualifications, experience and skills, in particular in the area of the protection of personal data, required to perform its duties and exercise its powers.

3. The duties of a member shall end in the event of the expiry of the term of office, resignation or compulsory retirement, in accordance with the law of the Member State concerned.

4. A member shall be dismissed only in cases of serious misconduct or if the member no longer fulfils the conditions required for the performance of the duties.

------ NOTES ------

Defined terms		**Relevant recitals**
personal data	Art 4(1)	(121)
supervisory authority	Art 4(22)	

LED equivalent
Arts 3(15), 41, 42, 43, 44

Article 54   Rules on the establishment of the supervisory authority

1. Each Member State shall provide by law for all of the following:
    (a) the establishment of each supervisory authority;
    (b) the qualifications and eligibility conditions required to be appointed as member of each supervisory authority;
    (c) the rules and procedures for the appointment of the member or members of each supervisory authority;
    (d) the duration of the term of the member or members of each supervisory authority of no less than four years, except for the first appointment after 24 May 2016, part of which may take place for a shorter period where that is necessary to protect the independence of the supervisory authority by means of a staggered appointment procedure;
    (e) whether and, if so, for how many terms the member or members of each supervisory authority is eligible for reappointment;
    (f) the conditions governing the obligations of the member or members and staff of each supervisory authority, prohibitions on actions, occupations and benefits incompatible therewith during and after the term of office and rules governing the cessation of employment.

2. The member or members and the staff of each supervisory authority shall, in accordance with Union or Member State law, be subject to a duty of professional secrecy both during and after their term of office, with regard to any confidential information which has come to their knowledge in the course of the performance of their tasks or exercise of their powers. During their term of office, that duty of professional secrecy shall in particular apply to reporting by natural persons of infringements of this Regulation.

——— NOTES ———

Defined terms
supervisory authority   Art 4(22)

Relevant recitals
(117), (121)

LED equivalent
Arts 3(15), 41, 42, 43, 44

Section 2 – Competence, tasks and powers

Article 55   Competence

1. Each supervisory authority shall be competent for the performance of the tasks assigned to and the exercise of the powers conferred on it in accordance with this Regulation on the territory of its own Member State.

2. Where processing is carried out by public authorities or private bodies acting on the basis of point (c) or (e) of Article 6(1), the supervisory authority of the Member State concerned shall be competent. In such cases Article 56 does not apply.

3. Supervisory authorities shall not be competent to supervise processing operations of courts acting in their judicial capacity.

——— NOTES ———

Defined terms
processing   Art 4(2)
supervisory authority   Art 4(22)

Relevant recitals
(20), (122), (128)

LED equivalent
Art 45

Article 56   Competence of the lead supervisory authority

1. Without prejudice to Article 55, the supervisory authority of the main establishment or of the single establishment of the controller or processor shall be competent to act as lead supervisory authority for the cross-border processing carried out by that controller or processor in accordance with the procedure provided in Article 60.

2. By derogation from paragraph 1, each supervisory authority shall be competent to handle a complaint lodged with it or a possible infringement of this Regulation, if the subject matter relates only to an establishment in its Member State or substantially affects data subjects only in its Member State.

3. In the cases referred to in paragraph 2 of this Article, the supervisory authority shall inform the lead supervisory authority without delay on that matter. Within a period of three weeks after being informed the lead supervisory authority shall decide whether or not it will handle the case in accordance with the procedure provided in Article 60, taking into account whether or not there is an establishment of the controller or processor in the Member State of which the supervisory authority informed it.

4. Where the lead supervisory authority decides to handle the case, the procedure provided in Article 60 shall apply. The supervisory authority which informed the lead supervisory authority may submit to the lead supervisory authority a draft for a decision. The lead supervisory authority shall take utmost account of that draft when preparing the draft decision referred to in Article 60(3).

5. Where the lead supervisory authority decides not to handle the case, the supervisory authority which informed the lead supervisory authority shall handle it according to

Articles 61 and 62.

6.   The lead supervisory authority shall be the sole interlocutor of the controller or processor for the cross-border processing carried out by that controller or processor.

—— Notes ——

Defined terms		**Relevant recitals**
controller	Art 4(7)	(124), (125), (126), (127), (128)
cross-border processing	Art 4(23)	
main establishment	Art 4(16)	**LED equivalent**
processing	Art 4(2)	n/a
processor	Art 4(8)	
profiling	Art 4(4)	
supervisory authority	Art 4(22)	

Article 57   Tasks

1.   Without prejudice to other tasks set out under this Regulation, each supervisory authority shall on its territory:

(a) monitor and enforce the application of this Regulation;

(b) promote public awareness and understanding of the risks, rules, safeguards and rights in relation to processing. Activities addressed specifically to children shall receive specific attention;

(c) advise, in accordance with Member State law, the national parliament, the government, and other institutions and bodies on legislative and administrative measures relating to the protection of natural persons' rights and freedoms with regard to processing;

(d) promote the awareness of controllers and processors of their obligations under this Regulation;

(e) upon request, provide information to any data subject concerning the exercise of their rights under this Regulation and, if appropriate, cooperate with the supervisory authorities in other Member States to that end;

(f) handle complaints lodged by a data subject, or by a body, organisation or association in accordance with Article 80, and investigate, to the extent appropriate, the subject matter of the complaint and inform the complainant of the progress and the outcome of the investigation within a reasonable period, in particular if further investigation or coordination with another supervisory authority is necessary;

(g) cooperate with, including sharing information and provide mutual assistance to, other supervisory authorities with a view to ensuring the consistency of application and enforcement of this Regulation;

(h) conduct investigations on the application of this Regulation, including on the basis of information received from another supervisory authority or other public authority;

(i) monitor relevant developments, insofar as they have an impact on the protection of personal data, in particular the development of information and communication technologies and commercial practices;

(j) adopt standard contractual clauses referred to in Article 28(8) and in point (d) of Article 46(2);

(k) establish and maintain a list in relation to the requirement for data protection impact assessment pursuant to Article 35(4);

    (l) give advice on the processing operations referred to in Article 36(2);

    (m) encourage the drawing up of codes of conduct pursuant to Article 40(1) and provide an opinion and approve such codes of conduct which provide sufficient safeguards, pursuant to Article 40(5);

    (n) encourage the establishment of data protection certification mechanisms and of data protection seals and marks pursuant to Article 42(1), and approve the criteria of certification pursuant to Article 42(5);

    (o) where applicable, carry out a periodic review of certifications issued in accordance with Article 42(7);

    (p) draft and publish the criteria for accreditation of a body for monitoring codes of conduct pursuant to Article 41 and of a certification body pursuant to Article 43;

    (q) conduct the accreditation of a body for monitoring codes of conduct pursuant to Article 41 and of a certification body pursuant to Article 43;

    (r) authorise contractual clauses and provisions referred to in Article 46(3);

    (s) approve binding corporate rules pursuant to Article 47;

    (t) contribute to the activities of the Board;

    (u) keep internal records of infringements of this Regulation and of measures taken in accordance with Article 58(2); and

    (v) fulfil any other tasks related to the protection of personal data.

2.   Each supervisory authority shall facilitate the submission of complaints referred to in point (f) of paragraph 1 by measures such as a complaint submission form which can also be completed electronically, without excluding other means of communication.

3.   The performance of the tasks of each supervisory authority shall be free of charge for the data subject and, where applicable, for the data protection officer.

4.   Where requests are manifestly unfounded or excessive, in particular because of their repetitive character, the supervisory authority may charge a reasonable fee based on administrative costs, or refuse to act on the request. The supervisory authority shall bear the burden of demonstrating the manifestly unfounded or excessive character of the request.

—— NOTES ——

Defined terms		**Relevant recitals**
binding corporate rules	Art 4(20)	(122), (123), (129)
controller	Art 4(7)	
personal data	Art 4(1)	**LED equivalent**
processing	Art 4(2)	Arts 3(15), 17, 28, 40, 41, 42(1), 45, 46, 47, 50,
processor	Art 4(8)	51, 52

Article 58   Powers

1.   Each supervisory authority shall have all of the following investigative powers:

    (a) to order the controller and the processor, and, where applicable, the controller's or the processor's representative to provide any information it requires for the performance of its tasks;

    (b) to carry out investigations in the form of data protection audits;

    (c) to carry out a review on certifications issued pursuant to Article 42(7);

    (d) to notify the controller or the processor of an alleged infringement of this Regulation;

    (e) to obtain, from the controller and the processor, access to all personal data and to all information necessary for the performance of its tasks;

(f) to obtain access to any premises of the controller and the processor, including to any data processing equipment and means, in accordance with Union or Member State procedural law.

2. Each supervisory authority shall have all of the following corrective powers:

   (a) to issue warnings to a controller or processor that intended processing operations are likely to infringe provisions of this Regulation;

   (b) to issue reprimands to a controller or a processor where processing operations have infringed provisions of this Regulation;

   (c) to order the controller or the processor to comply with the data subject's requests to exercise his or her rights pursuant to this Regulation;

   (d) to order the controller or processor to bring processing operations into compliance with the provisions of this Regulation, where appropriate, in a specified manner and within a specified period;

   (e) to order the controller to communicate a personal data breach to the data subject;

   (f) to impose a temporary or definitive limitation including a ban on processing;

   (g) to order the rectification or erasure of personal data or restriction of processing pursuant to Articles 16, 17 and 18 and the notification of such actions to recipients to whom the personal data have been disclosed pursuant to Article 17(2) and Article 19;

   (h) to withdraw a certification or to order the certification body to withdraw a certification issued pursuant to Articles 42 and 43, or to order the certification body not to issue certification if the requirements for the certification are not or are no longer met;

   (i) to impose an administrative fine pursuant to Article 83, in addition to, or instead of measures referred to in this paragraph, depending on the circumstances of each individual case;

   (j) to order the suspension of data flows to a recipient in a third country or to an international organisation.

3. Each supervisory authority shall have all of the following authorisation and advisory powers:

   (a) to advise the controller in accordance with the prior consultation procedure referred to in Article 36;

   (b) to issue, on its own initiative or on request, opinions to the national parliament, the Member State government or, in accordance with Member State law, to other institutions and bodies as well as to the public on any issue related to the protection of personal data;

   (c) to authorise processing referred to in Article 36(5), if the law of the Member State requires such prior authorisation;

   (d) to issue an opinion and approve draft codes of conduct pursuant to Article 40(5);

   (e) to accredit certification bodies pursuant to Article 43;

   (f) to issue certifications and approve criteria of certification in accordance with Article 42(5);

   (g) to adopt standard data protection clauses referred to in Article 28(8) and in point (d) of Article 46(2);

   (h) to authorise contractual clauses referred to in point (a) of Article 46(3);

   (i) to authorise administrative arrangements referred to in point (b) of Article 46(3);

   (j) to approve binding corporate rules pursuant to Article 47.

4.   The exercise of the powers conferred on the supervisory authority pursuant to this Article shall be subject to appropriate safeguards, including effective judicial remedy and due process, set out in Union and Member State law in accordance with the Charter.

5.   Each Member State shall provide by law that its supervisory authority shall have the power to bring infringements of this Regulation to the attention of the judicial authorities and where appropriate, to commence or engage otherwise in legal proceedings, in order to enforce the provisions of this Regulation.

6.   Each Member State may provide by law that its supervisory authority shall have additional powers to those referred to in paragraphs 1, 2 and 3. The exercise of those powers shall not impair the effective operation of Chapter VII.

—— NOTES ——

Defined terms			
binding corporate rules	Art 4(20)	restriction of processing	Art 4(3)
controller	Art 4(7)	supervisory authority	Art 4(22)
international organisation	Art 4(26)	**Relevant recitals**	
personal data	Art 4(1)	(129), (148), (150)	
personal data breach	Art 4(12)		
processing	Art 4(2)	**LED equivalent**	
processor	Art 4(8)	Arts 3(15), 28, 41, 43, 45, 46, 51, 53	
recipient	Art 4(9)		

Article 59   Activity reports

Each supervisory authority shall draw up an annual report on its activities, which may include a list of types of infringement notified and types of measures taken in accordance with Article 58(2). Those reports shall be transmitted to the national parliament, the government and other authorities as designated by Member State law. They shall be made available to the public, to the Commission and to the Board.

—— NOTES ——

Defined terms		**Relevant recitals**
supervisory authority	Art 4(22)	n/a

LED equivalent
Art 49

CHAPTER VII – COOPERATION AND CONSISTENCY

Section 1 – Cooperation

Article 60   Cooperation between the lead supervisory authority and the other supervisory authorities concerned

1.   The lead supervisory authority shall cooperate with the other supervisory authorities concerned in accordance with this Article in an endeavour to reach consensus. The lead supervisory authority and the supervisory authorities concerned shall exchange all relevant information with each other.

2.   The lead supervisory authority may request at any time other supervisory authorities concerned to provide mutual assistance pursuant to Article 61 and may conduct joint operations pursuant to Article 62, in particular for carrying out investigations or for monitoring the implementation of a measure concerning a controller or processor established in another Member State.

3. The lead supervisory authority shall, without delay, communicate the relevant information on the matter to the other supervisory authorities concerned. It shall without delay submit a draft decision to the other supervisory authorities concerned for their opinion and take due account of their views.

4. Where any of the other supervisory authorities concerned within a period of four weeks after having been consulted in accordance with paragraph 3 of this Article, expresses a relevant and reasoned objection to the draft decision, the lead supervisory authority shall, if it does not follow the relevant and reasoned objection or is of the opinion that the objection is not relevant or reasoned, submit the matter to the consistency mechanism referred to in Article 63.

5. Where the lead supervisory authority intends to follow the relevant and reasoned objection made, it shall submit to the other supervisory authorities concerned a revised draft decision for their opinion. That revised draft decision shall be subject to the procedure referred to in paragraph 4 within a period of two weeks.

6. Where none of the other supervisory authorities concerned has objected to the draft decision submitted by the lead supervisory authority within the period referred to in paragraphs 4 and 5, the lead supervisory authority and the supervisory authorities concerned shall be deemed to be in agreement with that draft decision and shall be bound by it.

7. The lead supervisory authority shall adopt and notify the decision to the main establishment or single establishment of the controller or processor, as the case may be and inform the other supervisory authorities concerned and the Board of the decision in question, including a summary of the relevant facts and grounds. The supervisory authority with which a complaint has been lodged shall inform the complainant on the decision.

8. By derogation from paragraph 7, where a complaint is dismissed or rejected, the supervisory authority with which the complaint was lodged shall adopt the decision and notify it to the complainant and shall inform the controller thereof.

9. Where the lead supervisory authority and the supervisory authorities concerned agree to dismiss or reject parts of a complaint and to act on other parts of that complaint, a separate decision shall be adopted for each of those parts of the matter. The lead supervisory authority shall adopt the decision for the part concerning actions in relation to the controller, shall notify it to the main establishment or single establishment of the controller or processor on the territory of its Member State and shall inform the complainant thereof, while the supervisory authority of the complainant shall adopt the decision for the part concerning dismissal or rejection of that complaint, and shall notify it to that complainant and shall inform the controller or processor thereof.

10. After being notified of the decision of the lead supervisory authority pursuant to paragraphs 7 and 9, the controller or processor shall take the necessary measures to ensure compliance with the decision as regards processing activities in the context of all its establishments in the Union. The controller or processor shall notify the measures taken for complying with the decision to the lead supervisory authority, which shall inform the other supervisory authorities concerned.

11. Where, in exceptional circumstances, a supervisory authority concerned has reasons to

consider that there is an urgent need to act in order to protect the interests of data subjects, the urgency procedure referred to in Article 66 shall apply.

12. The lead supervisory authority and the other supervisory authorities concerned shall supply the information required under this Article to each other by electronic means, using a standardised format.

—— NOTES ——

Defined terms		supervisory authority	Art 4(22)
controller	Art 4(7)		
main establishment	Art 4(16)	**Relevant recitals**	
processing	Art 4(2)	(130), (131)	
processor	Art 4(8)		
relevant and reasoned objection	Art 4(24)	**LED equivalent**	
supervisory authority concerned	Art 4(21)	Arts 40, 46(1), 50	

Article 61   Mutual assistance

1. Supervisory authorities shall provide each other with relevant information and mutual assistance in order to implement and apply this Regulation in a consistent manner, and shall put in place measures for effective cooperation with one another. Mutual assistance shall cover, in particular, information requests and supervisory measures, such as requests to carry out prior authorisations and consultations, inspections and investigations.

2. Each supervisory authority shall take all appropriate measures required to reply to a request of another supervisory authority without undue delay and no later than one month after receiving the request. Such measures may include, in particular, the transmission of relevant information on the conduct of an investigation.

3. Requests for assistance shall contain all the necessary information, including the purpose of and reasons for the request. Information exchanged shall be used only for the purpose for which it was requested.

4. The requested supervisory authority shall not refuse to comply with the request unless:
   (a) it is not competent for the subject-matter of the request or for the measures it is requested to execute; or
   (b) compliance with the request would infringe this Regulation or Union or Member State law to which the supervisory authority receiving the request is subject.

5. The requested supervisory authority shall inform the requesting supervisory authority of the results or, as the case may be, of the progress of the measures taken in order to respond to the request. The requested supervisory authority shall provide reasons for any refusal to comply with a request pursuant to paragraph 4.

6. Requested supervisory authorities shall, as a rule, supply the information requested by other supervisory authorities by electronic means, using a standardised format.

7. Requested supervisory authorities shall not charge a fee for any action taken by them pursuant to a request for mutual assistance. Supervisory authorities may agree on rules to indemnify each other for specific expenditure arising from the provision of mutual assistance in exceptional circumstances.

8. Where a supervisory authority does not provide the information referred to in paragraph 5 of this Article within one month of receiving the request of another supervisory authority, the requesting supervisory authority may adopt a provisional measure on the territory of its Member State in accordance with Article 55(1). In that case, the urgent

need to act under Article 66(1) shall be presumed to be met and require an urgent binding decision from the Board pursuant to Article 66(2).

9. The Commission may, by means of implementing acts, specify the format and procedures for mutual assistance referred to in this Article and the arrangements for the exchange of information by electronic means between supervisory authorities, and between supervisory authorities and the Board, in particular the standardised format referred to in paragraph 6 of this Article. Those implementing acts shall be adopted in accordance with the examination procedure referred to in Article 93(2).

––––– Notes –––––

Defined terms		Relevant recitals
supervisory authority	Art 4(22)	(123), (133), (138)

LED equivalent
Arts 40, 46(1), 47(1), 50

Article 62   Joint operations of supervisory authorities

1. The supervisory authorities shall, where appropriate, conduct joint operations including joint investigations and joint enforcement measures in which members or staff of the supervisory authorities of other Member States are involved.

2. Where the controller or processor has establishments in several Member States or where a significant number of data subjects in more than one Member State are likely to be substantially affected by processing operations, a supervisory authority of each of those Member States shall have the right to participate in joint operations. The supervisory authority which is competent pursuant to Article 56(1) or (4) shall invite the supervisory authority of each of those Member States to take part in the joint operations and shall respond without delay to the request of a supervisory authority to participate.

3. A supervisory authority may, in accordance with Member State law, and with the seconding supervisory authority's authorisation, confer powers, including investigative powers on the seconding supervisory authority's members or staff involved in joint operations or, in so far as the law of the Member State of the host supervisory authority permits, allow the seconding supervisory authority's members or staff to exercise their investigative powers in accordance with the law of the Member State of the seconding supervisory authority. Such investigative powers may be exercised only under the guidance and in the presence of members or staff of the host supervisory authority. The seconding supervisory authority's members or staff shall be subject to the Member State law of the host supervisory authority.

4. Where, in accordance with paragraph 1, staff of a seconding supervisory authority operate in another Member State, the Member State of the host supervisory authority shall assume responsibility for their actions, including liability, for any damage caused by them during their operations, in accordance with the law of the Member State in whose territory they are operating.

5. The Member State in whose territory the damage was caused shall make good such damage under the conditions applicable to damage caused by its own staff. The Member State of the seconding supervisory authority whose staff has caused damage to any person in the territory of another Member State shall reimburse that other Member State in full any sums it has paid to the persons entitled on their behalf.

6. Without prejudice to the exercise of its rights vis-à-vis third parties and with the exception of paragraph 5, each Member State shall refrain, in the case provided for in paragraph 1, from requesting reimbursement from another Member State in relation to damage referred to in paragraph 4.

7. Where a joint operation is intended and a supervisory authority does not, within one month, comply with the obligation laid down in the second sentence of paragraph 2 of this Article, the other supervisory authorities may adopt a provisional measure on the territory of its Member State in accordance with Article 55. In that case, the urgent need to act under Article 66(1) shall be presumed to be met and require an opinion or an urgent binding decision from the Board pursuant to Article 66(2).

—— NOTES ——

Defined terms		Relevant recitals
controller	Art 4(7)	(116), (134), (138)
processing	Art 4(2)	
processor	Art 4(8)	**LED equivalent**
supervisory authority	Art 4(22)	Arts 40, 46, 47, 50
third party	Art 4(10)	

Section 2 – Consistency

Article 63   Consistency mechanism

In order to contribute to the consistent application of this Regulation throughout the Union, the supervisory authorities shall cooperate with each other and, where relevant, with the Commission, through the consistency mechanism as set out in this Section.

—— NOTES ——

Defined terms		Relevant recitals
supervisory authority	Art 4(22)	(135), (138)

LED equivalent
Arts 41(2), 51

Article 64   Opinion of the Board

1. The Board shall issue an opinion where a competent supervisory authority intends to adopt any of the measures below. To that end, the competent supervisory authority shall communicate the draft decision to the Board, when it:

   (a) aims to adopt a list of the processing operations subject to the requirement for a data protection impact assessment pursuant to Article 35(4);

   (b) concerns a matter pursuant to Article 40(7) whether a draft code of conduct or an amendment or extension to a code of conduct complies with this Regulation;

   (c) aims to approve the criteria for accreditation of a body pursuant to Article 41(3) or a certification body pursuant to Article 43(3);

   (d) aims to determine standard data protection clauses referred to in point (d) of Article 46(2) and in Article 28(8);

   (e) aims to authorise contractual clauses referred to in point (a) of Article 46(3); or

   (f) aims to approve binding corporate rules within the meaning of Article 47.

2. Any supervisory authority, the Chair of the Board or the Commission may request that any matter of general application or producing effects in more than one Member State be examined by the Board with a view to obtaining an opinion, in particular where a competent supervisory authority does not comply with the obligations for mutual

assistance in accordance with Article 61 or for joint operations in accordance with Article 62.

3. In the cases referred to in paragraphs 1 and 2, the Board shall issue an opinion on the matter submitted to it provided that it has not already issued an opinion on the same matter. That opinion shall be adopted within eight weeks by simple majority of the members of the Board. That period may be extended by a further six weeks, taking into account the complexity of the subject matter. Regarding the draft decision referred to in paragraph 1 circulated to the members of the Board in accordance with paragraph 5, a member which has not objected within a reasonable period indicated by the Chair, shall be deemed to be in agreement with the draft decision.

4. Supervisory authorities and the Commission shall, without undue delay, communicate by electronic means to the Board, using a standardised format any relevant information, including as the case may be a summary of the facts, the draft decision, the grounds which make the enactment of such measure necessary, and the views of other supervisory authorities concerned.

5. The Chair of the Board shall, without undue, delay inform by electronic means:
   (a) the members of the Board and the Commission of any relevant information which has been communicated to it using a standardised format. The secretariat of the Board shall, where necessary, provide translations of relevant information; and
   (b) the supervisory authority referred to, as the case may be, in paragraphs 1 and 2, and the Commission of the opinion and make it public.

6. The competent supervisory authority shall not adopt its draft decision referred to in paragraph 1 within the period referred to in paragraph 3.

7. The supervisory authority referred to in paragraph 1 shall take utmost account of the opinion of the Board and shall, within two weeks after receiving the opinion, communicate to the Chair of the Board by electronic means whether it will maintain or amend its draft decision and, if any, the amended draft decision, using a standardised format.

8. Where the supervisory authority concerned informs the Chair of the Board within the period referred to in paragraph 7 of this Article that it does not intend to follow the opinion of the Board, in whole or in part, providing the relevant grounds, Article 65(1) shall apply.

—— Notes ——

Defined terms		Relevant recitals	
binding corporate rules	Art 4(20)	(135), (136), (138)	
processing	Art 4(2)		
supervisory authority concerned	Art 4(21)	**LED equivalent**	
supervisory authority	Art 4(22)	n/a	

Article 65 Dispute resolution by the Board

1. In order to ensure the correct and consistent application of this Regulation in individual cases, the Board shall adopt a binding decision in the following cases:
   (a) where, in a case referred to in Article 60(4), a supervisory authority concerned has raised a relevant and reasoned objection to a draft decision of the lead authority or the lead authority has rejected such an objection as being not relevant or reasoned. The binding decision shall concern all the matters which are the subject

of the relevant and reasoned objection, in particular whether there is an infringement of this Regulation;

(b) where there are conflicting views on which of the supervisory authorities concerned is competent for the main establishment;

(c) where a competent supervisory authority does not request the opinion of the Board in the cases referred to in Article 64(1), or does not follow the opinion of the Board issued under Article 64. In that case, any supervisory authority concerned or the Commission may communicate the matter to the Board.

2. The decision referred to in paragraph 1 shall be adopted within one month from the referral of the subject-matter by a two-thirds majority of the members of the Board. That period may be extended by a further month on account of the complexity of the subject-matter. The decision referred to in paragraph 1 shall be reasoned and addressed to the lead supervisory authority and all the supervisory authorities concerned and binding on them.

3. Where the Board has been unable to adopt a decision within the periods referred to in paragraph 2, it shall adopt its decision within two weeks following the expiration of the second month referred to in paragraph 2 by a simple majority of the members of the Board. Where the members of the Board are split, the decision shall by adopted by the vote of its Chair.

4. The supervisory authorities concerned shall not adopt a decision on the subject matter submitted to the Board under paragraph 1 during the periods referred to in paragraphs 2 and 3.

5. The Chair of the Board shall notify, without undue delay, the decision referred to in paragraph 1 to the supervisory authorities concerned. It shall inform the Commission thereof. The decision shall be published on the website of the Board without delay after the supervisory authority has notified the final decision referred to in paragraph 6.

6. The lead supervisory authority or, as the case may be, the supervisory authority with which the complaint has been lodged shall adopt its final decision on the basis of the decision referred to in paragraph 1 of this Article, without undue delay and at the latest by one month after the Board has notified its decision. The lead supervisory authority or, as the case may be, the supervisory authority with which the complaint has been lodged, shall inform the Board of the date when its final decision is notified respectively to the controller or the processor and to the data subject. The final decision of the supervisory authorities concerned shall be adopted under the terms of Article 60(7), (8) and (9). The final decision shall refer to the decision referred to in paragraph 1 of this Article and shall specify that the decision referred to in that paragraph will be published on the website of the Board in accordance with paragraph 5 of this Article. The final decision shall attach the decision referred to in paragraph 1 of this Article.

—— NOTES ——

Defined terms		supervisory authority	Art 4(22)
controller	Art 4(7)		
main establishment	Art 4(16)	**Relevant recitals**	
processor	Art 4(8)	(136), (143)	
relevant and reasoned objection	Art 4(24)		
supervisory authority concerned	Art 4(21)	**LED equivalent**	
		n/a	

Article 66   Urgency procedure

1. In exceptional circumstances, where a supervisory authority concerned considers that there is an urgent need to act in order to protect the rights and freedoms of data subjects, it may, by way of derogation from the consistency mechanism referred to in Articles 63, 64 and 65 or the procedure referred to in Article 60, immediately adopt provisional measures intended to produce legal effects on its own territory with a specified period of validity which shall not exceed three months. The supervisory authority shall, without delay, communicate those measures and the reasons for adopting them to the other supervisory authorities concerned, to the Board and to the Commission.

2. Where a supervisory authority has taken a measure pursuant to paragraph 1 and considers that final measures need urgently be adopted, it may request an urgent opinion or an urgent binding decision from the Board, giving reasons for requesting such opinion or decision.

3. Any supervisory authority may request an urgent opinion or an urgent binding decision, as the case may be, from the Board where a competent supervisory authority has not taken an appropriate measure in a situation where there is an urgent need to act, in order to protect the rights and freedoms of data subjects, giving reasons for requesting such opinion or decision, including for the urgent need to act.

4. By derogation from Article 64(3) and Article 65(2), an urgent opinion or an urgent binding decision referred to in paragraphs 2 and 3 of this Article shall be adopted within two weeks by simple majority of the members of the Board.

------ NOTES ------

Defined terms		**Relevant recitals**
supervisory authority concerned	Art 4(21)	(137), (138)
supervisory authority	Art 4(22)	

Article 67   Exchange of information

The Commission may adopt implementing acts of general scope in order to specify the arrangements for the exchange of information by electronic means between supervisory authorities, and between supervisory authorities and the Board, in particular the standardised format referred to in Article 64.

Those implementing acts shall be adopted in accordance with the examination procedure referred to in Article 93(2).

------ NOTES ------

Defined terms		**Relevant recitals**
representative	Art 4(17)	(168)
restriction of processing	Art 4(3)	
supervisory authority	Art 4(22)	**LED equivalent**
		Art 50(8)

Section 3 – European data protection board

Article 68   European Data Protection Board

1. The European Data Protection Board (the 'Board') is hereby established as a body of the Union and shall have legal personality.

2. The Board shall be represented by its Chair.

3. The Board shall be composed of the head of one supervisory authority of each Member

State and of the European Data Protection Supervisor, or their respective representatives.

4.   Where in a Member State more than one supervisory authority is responsible for monitoring the application of the provisions pursuant to this Regulation, a joint representative shall be appointed in accordance with that Member State's law.

5.   The Commission shall have the right to participate in the activities and meetings of the Board without voting right. The Commission shall designate a representative. The Chair of the Board shall communicate to the Commission the activities of the Board.

6.   In the cases referred to in Article 65, the European Data Protection Supervisor shall have voting rights only on decisions which concern principles and rules applicable to the Union institutions, bodies, offices and agencies which correspond in substance to those of this Regulation.

—— NOTES ——

Defined terms		**LED equivalent**
supervisory authority	Art 4(22)	Art 51

Relevant recitals
(139)

Article 69   Independence

1.   The Board shall act independently when performing its tasks or exercising its powers pursuant to Articles 70 and 71.

2.   Without prejudice to requests by the Commission referred to in point (b) of Article 70(1) and in Article 70(2), the Board shall, in the performance of its tasks or the exercise of its powers, neither seek nor take instructions from anybody.

—— NOTES ——

Defined terms	**Relevant recitals**
n/a	(139)

LED equivalent
n/a

Article 70   Tasks of the Board

1.   The Board shall ensure the consistent application of this Regulation. To that end, the Board shall, on its own initiative or, where relevant, at the request of the Commission, in particular:

(a) monitor and ensure the correct application of this Regulation in the cases provided for in Articles 64 and 65 without prejudice to the tasks of national supervisory authorities;

(b) advise the Commission on any issue related to the protection of personal data in the Union, including on any proposed amendment of this Regulation;

(c) advise the Commission on the format and procedures for the exchange of information between controllers, processors and supervisory authorities for binding corporate rules;

(d) issue guidelines, recommendations, and best practices on procedures for erasing links, copies or replications of personal data from publicly available communication services as referred to in Article 17(2);

(e) examine, on its own initiative, on request of one of its members or on request of the Commission, any question covering the application of this Regulation and issue guidelines, recommendations and best practices in order to encourage consistent application of this Regulation;

(f) issue guidelines, recommendations and best practices in accordance with point (e) of this paragraph for further specifying the criteria and conditions for decisions based on profiling pursuant to Article 22(2);

(g) issue guidelines, recommendations and best practices in accordance with point (e) of this paragraph for establishing the personal data breaches and determining the undue delay referred to in Article 33(1) and (2) and for the particular circumstances in which a controller or a processor is required to notify the personal data breach;

(h) issue guidelines, recommendations and best practices in accordance with point (e) of this paragraph as to the circumstances in which a personal data breach is likely to result in a high risk to the rights and freedoms of the natural persons referred to in Article 34(1).

(i) issue guidelines, recommendations and best practices in accordance with point (e) of this paragraph for the purpose of further specifying the criteria and requirements for personal data transfers based on binding corporate rules adhered to by controllers and binding corporate rules adhered to by processors and on further necessary requirements to ensure the protection of personal data of the data subjects concerned referred to in Article 47;

(j) issue guidelines, recommendations and best practices in accordance with point (e) of this paragraph for the purpose of further specifying the criteria and requirements for the personal data transfers on the basis of Article 49(1);

(k) draw up guidelines for supervisory authorities concerning the application of measures referred to in Article 58(1), (2) and (3) and the setting of administrative fines pursuant to Article 83;

(l) review the practical application of the guidelines, recommendations and best practices referred to in points (e) and (f);

(m) issue guidelines, recommendations and best practices in accordance with point (e) of this paragraph for establishing common procedures for reporting by natural persons of infringements of this Regulation pursuant to Article 54(2);

(n) encourage the drawing-up of codes of conduct and the establishment of data protection certification mechanisms and data protection seals and marks pursuant to Articles 40 and 42;

(o) carry out the accreditation of certification bodies and its periodic review pursuant to Article 43 and maintain a public register of accredited bodies pursuant to Article 43(6) and of the accredited controllers or processors established in third countries pursuant to Article 42(7);

(p) specify the requirements referred to in Article 43(3) with a view to the accreditation of certification bodies under Article 42;

(q) provide the Commission with an opinion on the certification requirements referred to in Article 43(8);

(r) provide the Commission with an opinion on the icons referred to in Article 12(7);

(s) provide the Commission with an opinion for the assessment of the adequacy of the level of protection in a third country or international organisation, including for the assessment whether a third country, a territory or one or more specified sectors within that third country, or an international organisation no longer ensures an adequate level of protection. To that end, the Commission shall provide the Board with all necessary documentation, including correspondence with the government of the third country, with regard to that third country, territory or specified sector, or with the international organisation.

(t) issue opinions on draft decisions of supervisory authorities pursuant to the consistency mechanism referred to in Article 64(1), on matters submitted pursuant to Article 64(2) and to issue binding decisions pursuant to Article 65, including in cases referred to in Article 66;

(u) promote the cooperation and the effective bilateral and multilateral exchange of information and best practices between the supervisory authorities;

(v) promote common training programmes and facilitate personnel exchanges between the supervisory authorities and, where appropriate, with the supervisory authorities of third countries or with international organisations;

(w) promote the exchange of knowledge and documentation on data protection legislation and practice with data protection supervisory authorities worldwide.

(x) issue opinions on codes of conduct drawn up at Union level pursuant to Article 40(9); and

(y) maintain a publicly accessible electronic register of decisions taken by supervisory authorities and courts on issues handled in the consistency mechanism.

2. Where the Commission requests advice from the Board, it may indicate a time limit, taking into account the urgency of the matter.

3. The Board shall forward its opinions, guidelines, recommendations, and best practices to the Commission and to the committee referred to in Article 93 and make them public.

4. The Board shall, where appropriate, consult interested parties and give them the opportunity to comment within a reasonable period. The Board shall, without prejudice to Article 76, make the results of the consultation procedure publicly available.

—— NOTES ——

Defined terms		Relevant recitals
binding corporate rules	Art 4(20)	(124), (136), (139), (172)
controller	Art 4(7)	
international organisation	Art 4(26)	**LED equivalent**
personal data	Art 4(1)	Arts 46, 47, 51
personal data breach	Art 4(12)	
processor	Art 4(8)	
profiling	Art 4(4)	

Article 71   Reports

1. The Board shall draw up an annual report regarding the protection of natural persons with regard to processing in the Union and, where relevant, in third countries and international organisations. The report shall be made public and be transmitted to the European Parliament, to the Council and to the Commission.

2. The annual report shall include a review of the practical application of the guidelines, recommendations and best practices referred to in point (l) of Article 70(1) as well as of the binding decisions referred to in Article 65.

—— NOTES ——

Defined terms		Relevant recitals
international organisation	Art 4(26)	(100), (139)
processing	Art 4(2)	
		LED equivalent
		Arts 49, 62

Article 72   Procedure

1. The Board shall take decisions by a simple majority of its members, unless otherwise provided for in this Regulation.

2. The Board shall adopt its own rules of procedure by a two–thirds majority of its members and organise its own operational arrangements.

—— NOTES ——

Defined terms	Relevant recitals
n/a	n/a

Article 73   Chair

1. The Board shall elect a chair and two deputy chairs from amongst its members by simple majority.

2. The term of office of the Chair and of the deputy chairs shall be five years and be renewable once.

—— NOTES ——

Defined terms	Relevant recitals
n/a	n/a

Article 74   Tasks of the Chair

1. The Chair shall have the following tasks:
    (a) to convene the meetings of the Board and prepare its agenda;
    (b) to notify decisions adopted by the Board pursuant to Article 65 to the lead supervisory authority and the supervisory authorities concerned;
    (c) to ensure the timely performance of the tasks of the Board, in particular in relation to the consistency mechanism referred to in Article 63.

2. The Board shall lay down the allocation of tasks between the Chair and the deputy chairs in its rules of procedure.

—— NOTES ——

Defined terms		Relevant recitals
supervisory authority concerned	Art 4(21)	n/a
supervisory authority	Art 4(22)	

Article 75   Secretariat

1. The Board shall have a secretariat, which shall be provided by the European Data Protection Supervisor.

2. The secretariat shall perform its tasks exclusively under the instructions of the Chair of the Board.

3. The staff of the European Data Protection Supervisor involved in carrying out the tasks conferred on the Board by this Regulation shall be subject to separate reporting lines from the staff involved in carrying out tasks conferred on the European Data Protection Supervisor.

4. Where appropriate, the Board and the European Data Protection Supervisor shall establish and publish a Memorandum of Understanding implementing this Article, determining the terms of their cooperation, and applicable to the staff of the European

Data Protection Supervisor involved in carrying out the tasks conferred on the Board by this Regulation.

5. The secretariat shall provide analytical, administrative and logistical support to the Board.

6. The secretariat shall be responsible in particular for:
    (a) the day-to-day business of the Board;
    (b) communication between the members of the Board, its Chair and the Commission;
    (c) communication with other institutions and the public;
    (d) the use of electronic means for the internal and external communication;
    (e) the translation of relevant information;
    (f) the preparation and follow-up of the meetings of the Board;
    (g) the preparation, drafting and publication of opinions, decisions on the settlement of disputes between supervisory authorities and other texts adopted by the Board.

—— NOTES ——

Defined terms	Relevant recitals
n/a	(118), (140)

Article 76   Confidentiality

1. The discussions of the Board shall be confidential where the Board deems it necessary, as provided for in its rules of procedure.

2. Access to documents submitted to members of the Board, experts and representatives of third parties shall be governed by Regulation (EC) No 1049/2001 of the European Parliament and of the Council.

—— NOTES ——

Defined terms		Relevant recitals
representative	Art 4(17)	n/a
third party	Art 4(10)	

CHAPTER VIII – REMEDIES, LIABILITY AND PENALTIES

Article 77   Right to lodge a complaint with a supervisory authority

1. Without prejudice to any other administrative or judicial remedy, every data subject shall have the right to lodge a complaint with a supervisory authority, in particular in the Member State of his or her habitual residence, place of work or place of the alleged infringement if the data subject considers that the processing of personal data relating to him or her infringes this Regulation.

2. The supervisory authority with which the complaint has been lodged shall inform the complainant on the progress and the outcome of the complaint including the possibility of a judicial remedy pursuant to Article 78.

—— NOTES ——

Defined terms		Relevant recitals
personal data	Art 4(1)	(141), (146)
processing	Art 4(2)	
supervisory authority	Art 4(22)	**LED equivalent**
		Arts 52

Article 78 Right to an effective judicial remedy against a supervisory authority

1. Without prejudice to any other administrative or non-judicial remedy, each natural or legal person shall have the right to an effective judicial remedy against a legally binding decision of a supervisory authority concerning them.

2. Without prejudice to any other administrative or non-judicial remedy, each data subject shall have the right to a an effective judicial remedy where the supervisory authority which is competent pursuant to Articles 55 and 56 does not handle a complaint or does not inform the data subject within three months on the progress or outcome of the complaint lodged pursuant to Article 77.

3. Proceedings against a supervisory authority shall be brought before the courts of the Member State where the supervisory authority is established.

4. Where proceedings are brought against a decision of a supervisory authority which was preceded by an opinion or a decision of the Board in the consistency mechanism, the supervisory authority shall forward that opinion or decision to the court.

—— Notes ——

Defined terms		Relevant recitals
supervisory authority	Art 4(22)	(141), (143), (147)

LED equivalent
Art 53

Article 79 Right to an effective judicial remedy against a controller or processor

1. Without prejudice to any available administrative or non-judicial remedy, including the right to lodge a complaint with a supervisory authority pursuant to Article 77, each data subject shall have the right to an effective judicial remedy where he or she considers that his or her rights under this Regulation have been infringed as a result of the processing of his or her personal data in non-compliance with this Regulation.

2. Proceedings against a controller or a processor shall be brought before the courts of the Member State where the controller or processor has an establishment. Alternatively, such proceedings may be brought before the courts of the Member State where the data subject has his or her habitual residence, unless the controller or processor is a public authority of a Member State acting in the exercise of its public powers.

—— Notes ——

Defined terms		Relevant recitals
controller	Art 4(7)	(145), (147)
personal data	Art 4(1)	
processing	Art 4(2)	**LED equivalent**
processor	Art 4(8)	Arts 54
supervisory authority	Art 4(22)	

Article 80 Representation of data subjects

1. The data subject shall have the right to mandate a not-for-profit body, organisation or association which has been properly constituted in accordance with the law of a Member State, has statutory objectives which are in the public interest, and is active in the field of the protection of data subjects' rights and freedoms with regard to the protection of their personal data to lodge the complaint on his or her behalf, to exercise the rights referred

to in Articles 77, 78 and 79 on his or her behalf, and to exercise the right to receive compensation referred to in Article 82 on his or her behalf where provided for by Member State law.

2. Member States may provide that any body, organisation or association referred to in paragraph 1 of this Article, independently of a data subject's mandate, has the right to lodge, in that Member State, a complaint with the supervisory authority which is competent pursuant to Article 77 and to exercise the rights referred to in Articles 78 and 79 if it considers that the rights of a data subject under this Regulation have been infringed as a result of the processing.

—— NOTES ——

Defined terms		Relevant recitals
personal data	Art 4(1)	(142)
processing	Art 4(2)	
supervisory authority	Art 4(22)	**LED equivalent**
		Arts 55

Article 81   Suspension of proceedings

1. Where a competent court of a Member State has information on proceedings, concerning the same subject matter as regards processing by the same controller or processor, that are pending in a court in another Member State, it shall contact that court in the other Member State to confirm the existence of such proceedings.

2. Where proceedings concerning the same subject matter as regards processing of the same controller or processor are pending in a court in another Member State, any competent court other than the court first seized may suspend its proceedings.

3. Where those proceedings are pending at first instance, any court other than the court first seized may also, on the application of one of the parties, decline jurisdiction if the court first seized has jurisdiction over the actions in question and its law permits the consolidation thereof.

—— NOTES ——

Defined terms		Relevant recitals
controller	Art 4(7)	(144)
processing	Art 4(2)	
processor	Art 4(8)	

Article 82   Right to compensation and liability

1. Any person who has suffered material or non-material damage as a result of an infringement of this Regulation shall have the right to receive compensation from the controller or processor for the damage suffered.

2. Any controller involved in processing shall be liable for the damage caused by processing which infringes this Regulation. A processor shall be liable for the damage caused by processing only where it has not complied with obligations of this Regulation specifically directed to processors or where it has acted outside or contrary to lawful instructions of the controller.

3. A controller or processor shall be exempt from liability under paragraph 2 if it proves that it is not in any way responsible for the event giving rise to the damage.

4. Where more than one controller or processor, or both a controller and a processor, are

involved in the same processing and where they are, under paragraphs 2 and 3, responsible for any damage caused by processing, each controller or processor shall be held liable for the entire damage in order to ensure effective compensation of the data subject.

5.   Where a controller or processor has, in accordance with paragraph 4, paid full compensation for the damage suffered, that controller or processor shall be entitled to claim back from the other controllers or processors involved in the same processing that part of the compensation corresponding to their part of responsibility for the damage, in accordance with the conditions set out in paragraph 2.

6.   Court proceedings for exercising the right to receive compensation shall be brought before the courts competent under the law of the Member State referred to in Article 79(2).

—— Notes ——

Defined terms		Relevant recitals
controller	Art 4(7)	(145), (146), (147)
processing	Art 4(2)	
processor	Art 4(8)	**LED equivalent**
		Arts 52, 53, 54, 56

Article 83   General conditions for imposing administrative fines

1.   Each supervisory authority shall ensure that the imposition of administrative fines pursuant to this Article in respect of infringements of this Regulation referred to in paragraphs 4, 5 and 6 shall in each individual case be effective, proportionate and dissuasive.

2.   Administrative fines shall, depending on the circumstances of each individual case, be imposed in addition to, or instead of, measures referred to in points (a) to (h) and (j) of Article 58(2). When deciding whether to impose an administrative fine and deciding on the amount of the administrative fine in each individual case due regard shall be given to the following:

   (a) the nature, gravity and duration of the infringement taking into account the nature scope or purpose of the processing concerned as well as the number of data subjects affected and the level of damage suffered by them;

   (b) the intentional or negligent character of the infringement;

   (c) any action taken by the controller or processor to mitigate the damage suffered by data subjects;

   (d) the degree of responsibility of the controller or processor taking into account technical and organisational measures implemented by them pursuant to Articles 25 and 32;

   (e) any relevant previous infringements by the controller or processor;

   (f) the degree of cooperation with the supervisory authority, in order to remedy the infringement and mitigate the possible adverse effects of the infringement;

   (g) the categories of personal data affected by the infringement;

   (h) the manner in which the infringement became known to the supervisory authority, in particular whether, and if so to what extent, the controller or processor notified the infringement;

   (i) where measures referred to in Article 58(2) have previously been ordered against the controller or processor concerned with regard to the same subject-matter, compliance with those measures;

   (j) adherence to approved codes of conduct pursuant to Article 40 or approved certification mechanisms pursuant to Article 42; and

(k) any other aggravating or mitigating factor applicable to the circumstances of the case, such as financial benefits gained, or losses avoided, directly or indirectly, from the infringement.

3. If a controller or processor intentionally or negligently, for the same or linked processing operations, infringes several provisions of this Regulation, the total amount of the administrative fine shall not exceed the amount specified for the gravest infringement.

4. Infringements of the following provisions shall, in accordance with paragraph 2, be subject to administrative fines up to 10,000,000 EUR, or in the case of an undertaking, up to 2 % of the total worldwide annual turnover of the preceding financial year, whichever is higher:

(a) the obligations of the controller and the processor pursuant to Articles 8, 11, 25 to 39 and 42 and 43;

(b) the obligations of the certification body pursuant to Articles 42 and 43;

(c) the obligations of the monitoring body pursuant to Article 41(4).

5. Infringements of the following provisions shall, in accordance with paragraph 2, be subject to administrative fines up to 20 000 000 EUR, or in the case of an undertaking, up to 4 % of the total worldwide annual turnover of the preceding financial year, whichever is higher:

(a) the basic principles for processing, including conditions for consent, pursuant to Articles 5, 6, 7 and 9;

(b) the data subjects' rights pursuant to Articles 12 to 22;

(c) the transfers of personal data to a recipient in a third country or an international organisation pursuant to Articles 44 to 49;

(d) any obligations pursuant to Member State law adopted under Chapter IX;

(e) non-compliance with an order or a temporary or definitive limitation on processing or the suspension of data flows by the supervisory authority pursuant to Article 58(2) or failure to provide access in violation of Article 58(1).

6. Non-compliance with an order by the supervisory authority as referred to in Article 58(2) shall, in accordance with paragraph 2 of this Article, be subject to administrative fines up to 20 000 000 EUR, or in the case of an undertaking, up to 4 % of the total worldwide annual turnover of the preceding financial year, whichever is higher.

7. Without prejudice to the corrective powers of supervisory authorities pursuant to Article 58(2), each Member State may lay down the rules on whether and to what extent administrative fines may be imposed on public authorities and bodies established in that Member State.

8. The exercise by the supervisory authority of its powers under this Article shall be subject to appropriate procedural safeguards in accordance with Union and Member State law, including effective judicial remedy and due process.

9. Where the legal system of the Member State does not provide for administrative fines, this Article may be applied in such a manner that the fine is initiated by the competent supervisory authority and imposed by competent national courts, while ensuring that those legal remedies are effective and have an equivalent effect to the administrative fines imposed by supervisory authorities. In any event, the fines imposed shall be effective, proportionate and dissuasive. Those Member States shall notify to the Commission the provisions of their laws which they adopt pursuant to this paragraph by 25 May 2018 and,

without delay, any subsequent amendment law or amendment affecting them.

—— NOTES ——

Defined terms		supervisory authority	Art 4(22)
consent	Art 4(11)		
controller	Art 4(7)	**Relevant recitals**	
international organisation	Art 4(26)	(13), (148), (149), (150), (151), 152	
personal data	Art 4(1)		
processing	Art 4(2)	**LED equivalent**	
processor	Art 4(8)	Arts 53, 57	
recipient	Art 4(9)		

Article 84   Penalties

1. Member States shall lay down the rules on other penalties applicable to infringements of this Regulation in particular for infringements which are not subject to administrative fines pursuant to Article 83, and shall take all measures necessary to ensure that they are implemented. Such penalties shall be effective, proportionate and dissuasive.

2. Each Member State shall notify to the Commission the provisions of its law which it adopts pursuant to paragraph 1, by 25 May 2018 and, without delay, any subsequent amendment affecting them.

—— NOTES ——

Defined terms		**Relevant recitals**
processing	Art 4(2)	(149), (150), (151), (152)

LED equivalent
Art 57

CHAPTER IX – PROVISIONS RELATING TO SPECIFIC PROCESSING SITUATIONS

Article 85   Processing and freedom of expression and information

1. Member States shall by law reconcile the right to the protection of personal data pursuant to this Regulation with the right to freedom of expression and information, including processing for journalistic purposes and the purposes of academic, artistic or literary expression.

2. For processing carried out for journalistic purposes or the purpose of academic artistic or literary expression, Member States shall provide for exemptions or derogations from Chapter II (principles), Chapter III (rights of the data subject), Chapter IV (controller and processor), Chapter V (transfer of personal data to third countries or international organisations), Chapter VI (independent supervisory authorities), Chapter VII (cooperation and consistency) and Chapter IX (specific data processing situations) if they are necessary to reconcile the right to the protection of personal data with the freedom of expression and information.

3. Each Member State shall notify to the Commission the provisions of its law which it has adopted pursuant to paragraph 2 and, without delay, any subsequent amendment law or amendment affecting them.

Defined terms		processor	Art 4(8)
controller	Art 4(7)		
international organisation	Art 4(26)	**Relevant recitals**	
personal data	Art 4(1)	(4), (153)	
processing	Art 4(2)		

Article 86 Processing and public access to official documents

Personal data in official documents held by a public authority or a public body or a private body for the performance of a task carried out in the public interest may be disclosed by the authority or body in accordance with Union or Member State law to which the public authority or body is subject in order to reconcile public access to official documents with the right to the protection of personal data pursuant to this Regulation.

Defined terms		**Relevant recitals**
personal data	Art 4(1)	(154)
processing	Art 4(2)	

Article 87 Processing of the national identification number

Member States may further determine the specific conditions for the processing of a national identification number or any other identifier of general application. In that case the national identification number or any other identifier of general application shall be used only under appropriate safeguards for the rights and freedoms of the data subject pursuant to this Regulation.

Defined terms		**Relevant recitals**
processing	Art 4(2)	n/a

Article 88 Processing in the context of employment

1. Member States may, by law or by collective agreements, provide for more specific rules to ensure the protection of the rights and freedoms in respect of the processing of employees' personal data in the employment context, in particular for the purposes of the recruitment, the performance of the contract of employment, including discharge of obligations laid down by law or by collective agreements, management, planning and organisation of work, equality and diversity in the workplace, health and safety at work, protection of employer's or customer's property and for the purposes of the exercise and enjoyment, on an individual or collective basis, of rights and benefits related to employment, and for the purpose of the termination of the employment relationship.

2. Those rules shall include suitable and specific measures to safeguard the data subject's human dignity, legitimate interests and fundamental rights, with particular regard to the transparency of processing, the transfer of personal data within a group of undertakings, or a group of enterprises engaged in a joint economic activity and monitoring systems at the work place.

3. Each Member State shall notify to the Commission those provisions of its law which it adopts pursuant to paragraph 1, by 25 May 2018 and, without delay, any subsequent amendment affecting them.

—— Notes ——

Defined terms		processing	Art 4(2)
enterprise	Art 4(18)		
group of undertakings	Art 4(19)	**Relevant recitals**	
personal data	Art 4(1)	(155)	

Article 89 Safeguards and derogations relating to processing for archiving purposes in the public interest, scientific or historical research purposes or statistical purposes

1.   Processing for archiving purposes in the public interest, scientific or historical research purposes or statistical purposes, shall be subject to appropriate safeguards, in accordance with this Regulation, for the rights and freedoms of the data subject. Those safeguards shall ensure that technical and organisational measures are in place in particular in order to ensure respect for the principle of data minimisation. Those measures may include pseudonymisation provided that those purposes can be fulfilled in that manner. Where those purposes can be fulfilled by further processing which does not permit or no longer permits the identification of data subjects, those purposes shall be fulfilled in that manner.

2.   Where personal data are processed for scientific or historical research purposes or statistical purposes, Union or Member State law may provide for derogations from the rights referred to in Articles 15, 16, 18 and 21 subject to the conditions and safeguards referred to in paragraph 1 of this Article in so far as such rights are likely to render impossible or seriously impair the achievement of the specific purposes, and such derogations are necessary for the fulfilment of those purposes.

3.   Where personal data are processed for archiving purposes in the public interest, Union or Member State law may provide for derogations from the rights referred to in Articles 15, 16, 18, 19, 20 and 21 subject to the conditions and safeguards referred to in paragraph 1 of this Article in so far as such rights are likely to render impossible or seriously impair the achievement of the specific purposes, and such derogations are necessary for the fulfilment of those purposes.

4.   Where processing referred to in paragraphs 2 and 3 serves at the same time another purpose, the derogations shall apply only to processing for the purposes referred to in those paragraphs.

—— Notes ——

Defined terms		**Relevant recitals**
personal data	Art 4(1)	(156), (157), (158), (159), (160), (161), (162),
processing	Art 4(2)	(163)
processor	Art 4(8)	
pseudonymisation	Art 4(5)	**LED equivalent**
		Arts 4, 9

Article 90 Obligations of secrecy

1.   Member States may adopt specific rules to set out the powers of the supervisory authorities laid down in points (e) and (f) of Article 58(1) in relation to controllers or processors that are subject, under Union or Member State law or rules established by national competent bodies, to an obligation of professional secrecy or other equivalent obligations of secrecy where this is necessary and proportionate to reconcile the right of the protection of personal data with the obligation of secrecy. Those rules shall apply only with regard to personal data which the controller or processor has received as a result of or has obtained

in an activity covered by that obligation of secrecy.

2.   Each Member State shall notify to the Commission the rules adopted pursuant to paragraph 1, by 25 May 2018 and, without delay, any subsequent amendment affecting them.

—— NOTES ——

Defined terms		Relevant recitals
controller	Art 4(7)	(164)
personal data	Art 4(1)	
processor	Art 4(8)	

Article 91   Existing data protection rules of churches and religious associations

1.   Where in a Member State, churches and religious associations or communities apply, at the time of entry into force of this Regulation, comprehensive rules relating to the protection of natural persons with regard to processing, such rules may continue to apply, provided that they are brought into line with this Regulation.

2.   Churches and religious associations which apply comprehensive rules in accordance with paragraph 1 of this Article shall be subject to the supervision of an independent supervisory authority, which may be specific, provided that it fulfils the conditions laid down in Chapter VI of this Regulation.

—— NOTES ——

Defined terms		Relevant recitals
processing	Art 4(2)	(4)
supervisory authority	Art 4(22)	

CHAPTER X – DELEGATED ACTS AND IMPLEMENTING ACTS

Article 92   Exercise of the delegation

1.   The power to adopt delegated acts is conferred on the Commission subject to the conditions laid down in this Article.

2.   The delegation of power referred to in Article 12(8) and Article 43(8) shall be conferred on the Commission for an indeterminate period of time from 24 May 2016.

3.   The delegation of power referred to in Article 12(8) and Article 43(8) may be revoked at any time by the European Parliament or by the Council. A decision of revocation shall put an end to the delegation of power specified in that decision. It shall take effect the day following that of its publication in the Official Journal of the European Union or at a later date specified therein. It shall not affect the validity of any delegated acts already in force.

4.   As soon as it adopts a delegated act, the Commission shall notify it simultaneously to the European Parliament and to the Council.

5.   A delegated act adopted pursuant to Article 12(8) and Article 43(8) shall enter into force only if no objection has been expressed by either the European Parliament or the Council within a period of three months of notification of that act to the European Parliament and the Council or if, before the expiry of that period, the European Parliament and the Council have both informed the Commission that they will not object. That period shall be extended by three months at the initiative of the European Parliament or of the

Council.

—— NOTES ——

Defined terms	Relevant recitals
n/a	(166)

Article 93   Committee procedure

1. The Commission shall be assisted by a committee. That committee shall be a committee within the meaning of Regulation (EU) No 182/2011.

2. Where reference is made to this paragraph, Article 5 of Regulation (EU) No 182/2011 shall apply.

3. Where reference is made to this paragraph, Article 8 of Regulation (EU) No 182/2011, in conjunction with Article 5 thereof, shall apply.

—— NOTES ——

Defined terms	Relevant recitals
n/a	(167), (168), (169)

CHAPTER XI – FINAL PROVISIONS

Article 94   Repeal of Directive 95/46/EC

1. Directive 95/46/EC is repealed with effect from 25 May 2018.

2. References to the repealed Directive shall be construed as references to this Regulation. References to the Working Party on the Protection of Individuals with regard to the Processing of Personal Data established by Article 29 of Directive 95/46/EC shall be construed as references to the European Data Protection Board established by this Regulation.

—— NOTES ——

Defined terms		Relevant recitals
personal data	Art 4(1)	(171)
processing	Art 4(2)	

Article 95   Relationship with Directive 2002/58/EC

This Regulation shall not impose additional obligations on natural or legal persons in relation to processing in connection with the provision of publicly available electronic communications services in public communication networks in the Union in relation to matters for which they are subject to specific obligations with the same objective set out in Directive 2002/58/EC.

—— NOTES ——

Defined terms		Relevant recitals
processing	Art 4(2)	(173)

Article 96   Relationship with previously concluded Agreements

International agreements involving the transfer of personal data to third countries or international organisations which were concluded by Member States prior to 24 May 2016, and which comply with Union law as applicable prior to that date, shall remain in force until amended, replaced or revoked.

—— NOTES ——

Defined terms		Relevant recitals
international organisation	Art 4(26)	n/a
personal data	Art 4(1)	
		LED equivalent
		Art 61

Article 97   Commission reports

1. By 25 May 2020 and every four years thereafter, the Commission shall submit a report on the evaluation and review of this Regulation to the European Parliament and to the Council. The reports shall be made public.

2. In the context of the evaluations and reviews referred to in paragraph 1, the Commission shall examine, in particular, the application and functioning of:

    (a) Chapter V on the transfer of personal data to third countries or international organisations with particular regard to decisions adopted pursuant to Article 45(3) of this Regulation and decisions adopted on the basis of Article 25(6) of Directive 95/46/EC;

    (b) Chapter VII on cooperation and consistency.

3. For the purpose of paragraph 1, the Commission may request information from Member States and supervisory authorities.

4. In carrying out the evaluations and reviews referred to in paragraphs 1 and 2, the Commission shall take into account the positions and findings of the European Parliament, of the Council, and of other relevant bodies or sources.

5. The Commission shall, if necessary, submit appropriate proposals to amend this Regulation, in particular taking into account of developments in information technology and in the light of the state of progress in the information society.

—— NOTES ——

Defined terms		Relevant recitals
international organisation	Art 4(26)	n/a
personal data	Art 4(1)	

Article 98   Review of other Union legal acts on data protection

The Commission shall, if appropriate, submit legislative proposals with a view to amending other Union legal acts on the protection of personal data, in order to ensure uniform and consistent protection of natural persons with regard to processing. This shall in particular concern the rules relating to the protection of natural persons with regard to processing by Union institutions, bodies, offices and agencies and on the free movement of such data.

—— NOTES ——

Defined terms		Relevant recitals
personal data	Art 4(1)	(17), (173)
processing	Art 4(2)	

Article 99   Entry into force and application

1. This Regulation shall enter into force on the twentieth day following that of its publication in the Official Journal of the European Union.

2. It shall apply from 25 May 2018.

This Regulation shall be binding in its entirety and directly applicable in all Member States.

Done at Brussels, 27 April 2016.

For the European Parliament
The President
M SCHULZ

For the Council
The President
J A HENNIS-PLASSCHAERT

Law Enforcement Directive

This table of contents is not part of the official text

Contents

Recitals

Chapter I – General Provisions

Chapter II – Principles

Chapter III – Rights of the Data Subject

Chapter IV – Controller and Processor

Section 1 – General obligations

CHAPTER IX – IMPLEMENTING ACTS

58   Committee procedure

CHAPTER X – FINAL PROVISIONS

59   Repeal of Framework Decision 2008/977/JHA
60   Union legal acts already in force
61   judicial cooperation in criminal matters and police cooperation
62   Commission reports
63   Transposition
64   Entry into force
65   Addressees

THE EUROPEAN PARLIAMENT AND THE COUNCIL OF THE EUROPEAN UNION,

Having regard to the Treaty on the Functioning of the European Union, and in particular Article 16(2) thereof,

Having regard to the proposal from the European Commission,

After transmission of the draft legislative act to the national parliaments,

Having regard to the opinion of the Committee of the Regions,

Acting in accordance with the ordinary legislative procedure,

Whereas:

(1)   The protection of natural persons in relation to the processing of personal data is a fundamental right. Article 8(1) of the Charter of Fundamental Rights of the European Union ('the Charter') and Article 16(1) of the Treaty on the Functioning of the European Union (TFEU) provide that everyone has the right to the protection of personal data concerning him or her.

(2)   The principles of, and rules on the protection of natural persons with regard to the processing of their personal data should, whatever their nationality or residence, respect their fundamental rights and freedoms, in particular their right to the protection of personal data. This Directive is intended to contribute to the accomplishment of an area of freedom, security and justice.

(3)   Rapid technological developments and globalisation have brought new challenges for the protection of personal data. The scale of the collection and sharing of personal data has increased significantly. Technology allows personal data to be processed on an unprecedented scale in order to pursue activities such as the prevention, investigation, detection or prosecution of criminal offences or the execution of criminal penalties.

(4)   The free flow of personal data between competent authorities for the purposes of the prevention, investigation, detection or prosecution of criminal offences or the execution

376

of criminal penalties, including the safeguarding against and the prevention of threats to public security within the Union and the transfer of such personal data to third countries and international organisations, should be facilitated while ensuring a high level of protection of personal data. Those developments require the building of a strong and more coherent framework for the protection of personal data in the Union, backed by strong enforcement.

(5) Directive 95/46/EC of the European Parliament and of the Council applies to all processing of personal data in Member States in both the public and the private sectors. However, it does not apply to the processing of personal data in the course of an activity which falls outside the scope of Community law, such as activities in the areas of judicial cooperation in criminal matters and police cooperation.

(6) Council Framework Decision 2008/977/JHA applies in the areas of judicial cooperation in criminal matters and police cooperation. The scope of application of that Framework Decision is limited to the processing of personal data transmitted or made available between Member States.

(7) Ensuring a consistent and high level of protection of the personal data of natural persons and facilitating the exchange of personal data between competent authorities of Members States is crucial in order to ensure effective judicial cooperation in criminal matters and police cooperation. To that end, the level of protection of the rights and freedoms of natural persons with regard to the processing of personal data by competent authorities for the purposes of the prevention, investigation, detection or prosecution of criminal offences or the execution of criminal penalties, including the safeguarding against and the prevention of threats to public security, should be equivalent in all Member States. Effective protection of personal data throughout the Union requires the strengthening of the rights of data subjects and of the obligations of those who process personal data, as well as equivalent powers for monitoring and ensuring compliance with the rules for the protection of personal data in the Member States.

(8) Article 16(2) TFEU mandates the European Parliament and the Council to lay down the rules relating to the protection of natural person s with regard to the processing of personal data and the rules relating to the free movement of personal data.

(9) On that basis, Regulation (EU) 2016/679 of the European Parliament and of the Council lays down general rules to protect natural persons in relation to the processing of personal data and to ensure the free movement of personal data within the Union.

(10) In Declaration No 21 on the protection of personal data in the fields of judicial cooperation in criminal matters and police cooperation, annexed to the final act of the intergovernmental conference which adopted the Treaty of Lisbon, the conference acknowledged that specific rules on the protection of personal data and the free movement of personal data in the fields of judicial cooperation in criminal matters and police cooperation based on Article 16 TFEU may prove necessary because of the specific nature of those fields.

(11) It is therefore appropriate for those fields to be addressed by a directive that lays down the specific rules relating to the protection of natural persons with regard to the processing

of personal data by competent authorities for the purposes of the prevention, investigation, detection or prosecution of criminal offences or the execution of criminal penalties, including the safeguarding against and the prevention of threats to public security, respecting the specific nature of those activities. Such competent authorities may include not only public authorities such as the judicial authorities, the police or other law-enforcement authorities but also any other body or entity entrusted by Member State law to exercise public authority and public powers for the purposes of this Directive. Where such a body or entity processes personal data for purposes other than for the purposes of this Directive, Regulation (EU) 2016/679 applies. Regulation (EU) 2016/679 therefore applies in cases where a body or entity collects personal data for other purposes and further processes those personal data in order to comply with a legal obligation to which it is subject. For example, for the purposes of investigation detection or prosecution of criminal offences financial institutions retain certain personal data which are processed by them, and provide those personal data only to the competent national authorities in specific cases and in accordance with Member State law. A body or entity which processes personal data on behalf of such authorities within the scope of this Directive should be bound by a contract or other legal act and by the provisions applicable to processors pursuant to this Directive, while the application of Regulation (EU) 2016/679 remains unaffected for the processing of personal data by the processor outside the scope of this Directive.

(12) The activities carried out by the police or other law-enforcement authorities are focused mainly on the prevention, investigation, detection or prosecution of criminal offences, including police activities without prior knowledge if an incident is a criminal offence or not. Such activities can also include the exercise of authority by taking coercive measures such as police activities at demonstrations, major sporting events and riots. They also include maintaining law and order as a task conferred on the police or other law-enforcement authorities where necessary to safeguard against and prevent threats to public security and to fundamental interests of the society protected by law which may lead to a criminal offence. Member States may entrust competent authorities with other tasks which are not necessarily carried out for the purposes of the prevention, investigation, detection or prosecution of criminal offences, including the safeguarding against and the prevention of threats to public security, so that the processing of personal data for those other purposes, in so far as it is within the scope of Union law, falls within the scope of Regulation (EU) 2016/679.

(13) A criminal offence within the meaning of this Directive should be an autonomous concept of Union law as interpreted by the Court of Justice of the European Union (the 'Court of Justice').

(14) Since this Directive should not apply to the processing of personal data in the course of an activity which falls outside the scope of Union law, activities concerning national security, activities of agencies or units dealing with national security issues and the processing of personal data by the Member States when carrying out activities which fall within the scope of Chapter 2 of Title V of the Treaty on European Union (TEU) should not be considered to be activities falling within the scope of this Directive.

(15) In order to ensure the same level of protection for natural persons through legally enforceable rights throughout the Union and to prevent divergences hampering the

exchange of personal data between competent authorities, this Directive should provide for harmonised rules for the protection and the free movement of personal data processed for the purposes of the prevention, investigation, detection or prosecution of criminal offences or the execution of criminal penalties, including the safeguarding against and the prevention of threats to public security. The approximation of Member States' laws should not result in any lessening of the personal data protection they afford but should, on the contrary, seek to ensure a high level of protection within the Union. Member States should not be precluded from providing higher safeguards than those established in this Directive for the protection of the rights and freedoms of the data subject with regard to the processing of personal data by competent authorities.

(16) This Directive is without prejudice to the principle of public access to official documents. Under Regulation (EU) 2016/679 personal data in official documents held by a public authority or a public or private body for the performance of a task carried out in the public interest may be disclosed by that authority or body in accordance with Union or Member State law to which the public authority or body is subject in order to reconcile public access to official documents with the right to the protection of personal data.

(17) The protection afforded by this Directive should apply to natural persons, whatever their nationality or place of residence, in relation to the processing of their personal data.

(18) In order to prevent creating a serious risk of circumvention, the protection of natural persons should be technologically neutral and should not depend on the techniques used. The protection of natural persons should apply to the processing of personal data by automated means, as well as to manual processing, if the personal data are contained or are intended to be contained in a filing system. Files or sets of files, as well as their cover pages, which are not structured according to specific criteria should not fall within the scope of this Directive.

(19) Regulation (EC) No 45/2001 of the European Parliament and of the Council applies to the processing of personal data by the Union institutions, bodies, offices and agencies. Regulation (EC) No 45/2001 and other Union legal acts applicable to such processing of personal data should be adapted to the principles and rules established in Regulation (EU) 2016/679.

(20) This Directive does not preclude Member States from specifying processing operations and processing procedures in national rules on criminal procedures in relation to the processing of personal data by courts and other judicial authorities, in particular as regards personal data contained in a judicial decision or in records in relation to criminal proceedings.

(21) The principles of data protection should apply to any information concerning an identified or identifiable natural person. To determine whether a natural person is identifiable, account should be taken of all the means reasonably likely to be used, such as singling out, either by the controller or by another person to identify the natural person directly or indirectly. To ascertain whether means are reasonably likely to be used to identify the natural person, account should be taken of all objective factors, such as the costs of and the amount of time required for identification, taking into consideration the available technology at the time of the processing and technological developments. The

principles of data protection should therefore not apply to anonymous information, namely information which does not relate to an identified or identifiable natural person or to personal data rendered anonymous in such a manner that the data subject is no longer identifiable.

(22) Public authorities to which personal data are disclosed in accordance with a legal obligation for the exercise of their official mission, such as tax and customs authorities, financial investigation units, independent administrative authorities, or financial market authorities responsible for the regulation and supervision of securities markets should not be regarded as recipients if they receive personal data which are necessary to carry out a particular inquiry in the general interest, in accordance with Union or Member State law. The requests for disclosure sent by the public authorities should always be in writing, reasoned and occasional and should not concern the entirety of a filing system or lead to the interconnection of filing systems. The processing of personal data by those public authorities should comply with the applicable data protection rules according to the purposes of the processing.

(23) Genetic data should be defined as personal data relating to the inherited or acquired genetic characteristics of a natural person which give unique information about the physiology or health of that natural person and which result from the analysis of a biological sample from the natural person in question, in particular chromosomal, deoxyribonucleic acid (DNA) or ribonucleic acid (RNA) analysis, or from the analysis of another element enabling equivalent information to be obtained. Considering the complexity and sensitivity of genetic information, there is a great risk of misuse and re-use for various purposes by the controller. Any discrimination based on genetic features should in principle be prohibited.

(24) Personal data concerning health should include all data pertaining to the health status of a data subject which reveal information relating to the past, current or future physical or mental health status of the data subject. This includes information about the natural person collected in the course of the registration for, or the provision of, health care services as referred to in Directive 2011/24/EU of the European Parliament and of the Council to that natural person; a number, symbol or particular assigned to a natural person to uniquely identify the natural person for health purposes; information derived from the testing or examination of a body part or bodily substance, including from genetic data and biological samples; and any information on, for example, a disease, disability, disease risk, medical history, clinical treatment or the physiological or biomedical state of the data subject independent of its source, for example from a physician or other health professional, a hospital, a medical device or an in vitro diagnostic test.

(25) All Member States are affiliated to the International Criminal Police Organisation (Interpol). To fulfil its mission, Interpol receives, stores and circulates personal data to assist competent authorities in preventing and combating international crime. It is therefore appropriate to strengthen cooperation between the Union and Interpol by promoting an efficient exchange of personal data whilst ensuring respect for fundamental rights and freedoms regarding the automatic processing of personal data. Where personal data are transferred from the Union to Interpol, and to countries which have delegated members to Interpol, this Directive, in particular the provisions on international transfers, should apply. This Directive should be without prejudice to the specific rules laid down

in Council Common Position 2005/69/JHA and Council Decision 2007/533/JHA.

(26) Any processing of personal data must be lawful, fair and transparent in relation to the natural persons concerned, and only processed for specific purposes laid down by law. This does not in itself prevent the law-enforcement authorities from carrying out activities such as covert investigations or video surveillance. Such activities can be done for the purposes of the prevention, investigation, detection or prosecution of criminal offences or the execution of criminal penalties, including the safeguarding against and the prevention of threats to public security, as long as they are laid down by law and constitute a necessary and proportionate measure in a democratic society with due regard for the legitimate interests of the natural person concerned. The data protection principle of fair processing is a distinct notion from the right to a fair trial as defined in Article 47 of the Charter and in Article 6 of the European Convention for the Protection of Human Rights and Fundamental Freedoms (ECHR). Natural persons should be made aware of risks, rules, safeguards and rights in relation to the processing of their personal data and how to exercise their rights in relation to the processing. In particular, the specific purposes for which the personal data are processed should be explicit and legitimate and determined at the time of the collection of the personal data. The personal data should be adequate and relevant for the purposes for which they are processed. It should, in particular, be ensured that the personal data collected are not excessive and not kept longer than is necessary for the purpose for which they are processed. Personal data should be processed only if the purpose of the processing could not reasonably be fulfilled by other means. In order to ensure that the data are not kept longer than necessary, time limits should be established by the controller for erasure or for a periodic review. Member States should lay down appropriate safeguards for personal data stored for longer periods for archiving in the public interest, scientific, statistical or historical use.

(27) For the prevention, investigation and prosecution of criminal offences, it is necessary for competent authorities to process personal data collected in the context of the prevention, investigation, detection or prosecution of specific criminal offences beyond that context in order to develop an understanding of criminal activities and to make links between different criminal offences detected.

(28) In order to maintain security in relation to processing and to prevent processing in infringement of this Directive, personal data should be processed in a manner that ensures an appropriate level of security and confidentiality, including by preventing unauthorised access to or use of personal data and the equipment used for the processing, and that takes into account available state of the art and technology, the costs of implementation in relation to the risks and the nature of the personal data to be protected.

(29) Personal data should be collected for specified, explicit and legitimate purposes within the scope of this Directive and should not be processed for purposes incompatible with the purposes of the prevention, investigation, detection or prosecution of criminal offences or the execution of criminal penalties, including the safeguarding against and the prevention of threats to public security. If personal data are processed by the same or another controller for a purpose within the scope of this Directive other than that for which it has been collected, such processing should be permitted under the condition that such processing is authorised in accordance with applicable legal provisions and is necessary for and proportionate to that other purpose.

(30) The principle of accuracy of data should be applied while taking account of the nature and purpose of the processing concerned. In particular in judicial proceedings, statements containing personal data are based on the subjective perception of natural persons and are not always verifiable. Consequently, the requirement of accuracy should not appertain to the accuracy of a statement but merely to the fact that a specific statement has been made.

(31) It is inherent to the processing of personal data in the areas of judicial cooperation in criminal matters and police cooperation that personal data relating to different categories of data subjects are processed. Therefore, a clear distinction should, where applicable and as far as possible, be made between personal data of different categories of data subjects such as: suspects; persons convicted of a criminal offence; victims and other parties, such as witnesses; persons possessing relevant information or contacts; and associates of suspects and convicted criminals. This should not prevent the application of the right of presumption of innocence as guaranteed by the Charter and by the ECHR, as interpreted in the case-law of the Court of Justice and by the European Court of Human Rights respectively.

(32) The competent authorities should ensure that personal data which are inaccurate, incomplete or no longer up to date are not transmitted or made available. In order to ensure the protection of natural persons, the accuracy, completeness or the extent to which the personal data are up to date and the reliability of the personal data transmitted or made available, the competent authorities should, as far as possible, add necessary information in all transmissions of personal data.

(33) Where this Directive refers to Member State law, a legal basis or a legislative measure, this does not necessarily require a legislative act adopted by a parliament, without prejudice to requirements pursuant to the constitutional order of the Member State concerned. However, such a Member State law, legal basis or legislative measure should be clear and precise and its application foreseeable for those subject to it, as required by the case-law of the Court of Justice and the European Court of Human Rights. Member State law regulating the processing of personal data within the scope of this Directive should specify at least the objectives, the personal data to be processed, the purposes of the processing and procedures for preserving the integrity and confidentiality of personal data and procedures for its destruction, thus providing sufficient guarantees against the risk of abuse and arbitrariness.

(34) The processing of personal data by competent authorities for the purposes of the prevention, investigation, detection or prosecution of criminal offences or the execution of criminal penalties, including the safeguarding against and the prevention of threats to public security, should cover any operation or set of operations which are performed upon personal data or sets of personal data for those purposes, whether by automated means or otherwise, such as collection, recording, organisation, structuring, storage, adaptation or alteration, retrieval, consultation, use, alignment or combination, restriction of processing, erasure or destruction. In particular, the rules of this Directive should apply to the transmission of personal data for the purposes of this Directive to a recipient not subject to this Directive. Such a recipient should encompass a natural or legal person, public authority, agency or any other body to which personal data are lawfully disclosed

by the competent authority. Where personal data were initially collected by a competent authority for one of the purposes of this Directive, Regulation (EU) 2016/679 should apply to the processing of those data for purposes other than the purposes of this Directive where such processing is authorised by Union or Member State law. In particular, the rules of Regulation (EU) 2016/679 should apply to the transmission of personal data for purposes outside the scope of this Directive. For the processing of personal data by a recipient that is not a competent authority or that is not acting as such within the meaning of this Directive and to which personal data are lawfully disclosed by a competent authority, Regulation (EU) 2016/679 should apply. While implementing this Directive, Member States should also be able to further specify the application of the rules of Regulation (EU) 2016/679, subject to the conditions set out therein.

(35) In order to be lawful, the processing of personal data under this Directive should be necessary for the performance of a task carried out in the public interest by a competent authority based on Union or Member State law for the purposes of the prevention, investigation, detection or prosecution of criminal offences or the execution of criminal penalties, including the safeguarding against and the prevention of threats to public security. Those activities should cover the protection of vital interests of the data subject. The performance of the tasks of preventing, investigating, detecting or prosecuting criminal offences institutionally conferred by law to the competent authorities allows them to require or order natural persons to comply with requests made. In such a case, the consent of the data subject, as defined in Regulation (EU) 2016/679, should not provide a legal ground for processing personal data by competent authorities. Where the data subject is required to comply with a legal obligation, the data subject has no genuine and free choice, so that the reaction of the data subject could not be considered to be a freely given indication of his or her wishes. This should not preclude Member States from providing, by law, that the data subject may agree to the processing of his or her personal data for the purposes of this Directive, such as DNA tests in criminal investigations or the monitoring of his or her location with electronic tags for the execution of criminal penalties.

(36) Member States should provide that where Union or Member State law applicable to the transmitting competent authority provides for specific conditions applicable in specific circumstances to the processing of personal data, such as the use of handling codes, the transmitting competent authority should inform the recipient of such personal data of those conditions and the requirement to respect them. Such conditions could, for example, include a prohibition against transmitting the personal data further to others, or using them for purposes other than those for which they were transmitted to the recipient, or informing the data subject in the case of a limitation of the right of information without the prior approval of the transmitting competent authority. Those obligations should also apply to transfers by the transmitting competent authority to recipients in third countries or international organisations. Member States should ensure that the transmitting competent authority does not apply such conditions to recipients in other Member States or to agencies, offices and bodies established pursuant to Chapters 4 and 5 of Title V of the TFEU other than those applicable to similar data transmissions within the Member State of that competent authority.

(37) Personal data which are, by their nature, particularly sensitive in relation to fundamental rights and freedoms merit specific protection as the context of their processing could

create significant risks to the fundamental rights and freedoms. Those personal data should include personal data revealing racial or ethnic origin, whereby the use of the term 'racial origin' in this Directive does not imply an acceptance by the Union of theories which attempt to determine the existence of separate human races. Such personal data should not be processed, unless processing is subject to appropriate safeguards for the rights and freedoms of the data subject laid down by law and is allowed in cases authorised by law; where not already authorised by such a law, the processing is necessary to protect the vital interests of the data subject or of another person; or the processing relates to data which are manifestly made public by the data subject. Appropriate safeguards for the rights and freedoms of the data subject could include the possibility to collect those data only in connection with other data on the natural person concerned, the possibility to secure the data collected adequately, stricter rules on the access of staff of the competent authority to the data and the prohibition of transmission of those data. The processing of such data should also be allowed by law where the data subject has explicitly agreed to the processing that is particularly intrusive to him or her. However, the consent of the data subject should not provide in itself a legal ground for processing such sensitive personal data by competent authorities.

(38) The data subject should have the right not to be subject to a decision evaluating personal aspects relating to him or her which is based solely on automated processing and which produces adverse legal effects concerning, or significantly affects, him or her. In any case, such processing should be subject to suitable safeguards, including the provision of specific information to the data subject and the right to obtain human intervention, in particular to express his or her point of view, to obtain an explanation of the decision reached after such assessment or to challenge the decision. Profiling that results in discrimination against natural persons on the basis of personal data which are by their nature particularly sensitive in relation to fundamental rights and freedoms should be prohibited under the conditions laid down in Articles 21 and 52 of the Charter.

(39) In order to enable him or her to exercise his or her rights, any information to the data subject should be easily accessible, including on the website of the controller, and easy to understand, using clear and plain language. Such information should be adapted to the needs of vulnerable persons such as children.

(40) Modalities should be provided for facilitating the exercise of the data subject's rights under the provisions adopted pursuant to this Directive, including mechanisms to request and, if applicable, obtain, free of charge, in particular, access to and rectification or erasure of personal data and restriction of processing. The controller should be obliged to respond to requests of the data subject without undue delay, unless the controller applies limitations to data subject rights in accordance with this Directive. Moreover, if requests are manifestly unfounded or excessive, such as where the data subject unreasonably and repetitiously requests information or where the data subject abuses his or her right to receive information, for example, by providing false or misleading information when making the request, the controller should be able to charge a reasonable fee or refuse to act on the request.

(41) Where the controller requests the provision of additional information necessary to confirm the identity of the data subject, that information should be processed only for that specific purpose and should not be stored for longer than needed for that purpose.

(42) At least the following information should be made available to the data subject: the identity of the controller, the existence of the processing operation, the purposes of the processing, the right to lodge a complaint and the existence of the right to request from the controller access to and rectification or erasure of personal data or restriction of processing. This could take place on the website of the competent authority. In addition, in specific cases and in order to enable the exercise of his or her rights, the data subject should be informed of the legal basis for the processing and of how long the data will be stored, in so far as such further information is necessary, taking into account the specific circumstances in which the data are processed, to guarantee fair processing in respect of the data subject.

(43) A natural person should have the right of access to data which has been collected concerning him or her, and to exercise this right easily and at reasonable intervals, in order to be aware of and verify the lawfulness of the processing. Every data subject should therefore have the right to know, and obtain communications about, the purposes for which the data are processed, the period during which the data are processed and the recipients of the data, including those in third countries. Where such communications include information as to the origin of the personal data, the information should not reveal the identity of natural persons, in particular confidential sources. For that right to be complied with, it is sufficient that the data subject be in possession of a full summary of those data in an intelligible form, that is to say a form which allows that data subject to become aware of those data and to verify that they are accurate and processed in accordance with this Directive, so that it is possible for him or her to exercise the rights conferred on him or her by this Directive. Such a summary could be provided in the form of a copy of the personal data undergoing processing.

(44) Member States should be able to adopt legislative measures delaying, restricting or omitting the information to data subjects or restricting, wholly or partly, the access to their personal data to the extent that and as long as such a measure constitutes a necessary and proportionate measure in a democratic society with due regard for the fundamental rights and the legitimate interests of the natural person concerned, to avoid obstructing official or legal inquiries, investigations or procedures, to avoid prejudicing the prevention, investigation, detection or prosecution of criminal offences or the execution of criminal penalties, to protect public security or national security, or to protect the rights and freedoms of others. The controller should assess, by way of a concrete and individual examination of each case, whether the right of access should be partially or completely restricted.

(45) Any refusal or restriction of access should in principle be set out in writing to the data subject and include the factual or legal reasons on which the decision is based.

(46) Any restriction of the rights of the data subject must comply with the Charter and with the ECHR, as interpreted in the case-law of the Court of Justice and by the European Court of Human Rights respectively, and in particular respect the essence of those rights and freedoms.

(47) A natural person should have the right to have inaccurate personal data concerning him or her rectified, in particular where it relates to facts, and the right to erasure where the

processing of such data infringes this Directive. However, the right to rectification should not affect, for example, the content of a witness testimony. A natural person should also have the right to restriction of processing where he or she contests the accuracy of personal data and its accuracy or inaccuracy cannot be ascertained or where the personal data have to be maintained for purpose of evidence. In particular, instead of erasing personal data, processing should be restricted if in a specific case there are reasonable grounds to believe that erasure could affect the legitimate interests of the data subject. In such a case, restricted data should be processed only for the purpose which prevented their erasure. Methods to restrict the processing of personal data could include, inter alia, moving the selected data to another processing system, for example for archiving purposes, or making the selected data unavailable. In automated filing systems the restriction of processing should in principle be ensured by technical means. The fact that the processing of personal data is restricted should be indicated in the system in such a manner that it is clear that the processing of the personal data is restricted. Such rectification or erasure of personal data or restriction of processing should be communicated to recipients to whom the data have been disclosed and to the competent authorities from which the inaccurate data originated. The controllers should also abstain from further dissemination of such data.

(48) Where the controller denies a data subject his or her right to information, access to or rectification or erasure of personal data or restriction of processing, the data subject should have the right to request that the national supervisory authority verify the lawfulness of the processing. The data subject should be informed of that right. Where the supervisory authority acts on behalf of the data subject, the data subject should be informed by the supervisory authority at least that all necessary verifications or reviews by the supervisory authority have taken place. The supervisory authority should also inform the data subject of the right to seek a judicial remedy.

(49) Where the personal data are processed in the course of a criminal investigation and court proceedings in criminal matters, Member States should be able to provide that the exercise the right to information, access to and rectification or erasure of personal data and restriction of processing is carried out in accordance with national rules on judicial proceedings.

(50) The responsibility and liability of the controller for any processing of personal data carried out by the controller or on the controller's behalf should be established. In particular, the controller should be obliged to implement appropriate and effective measures and should be able to demonstrate that processing activities are in compliance with this Directive. Such measures should take into account the nature, scope, context and purposes of the processing and the risk to the rights and freedoms of natural persons. The measures taken by the controller should include drawing up and implementing specific safeguards in respect of the treatment of personal data of vulnerable natural persons, such as children.

(51) The risk to the rights and freedoms of natural persons, of varying likelihood and severity, may result from data processing which could lead to physical, material or non-material damage, in particular: where the processing may give rise to discrimination, identity theft or fraud, financial loss, damage to the reputation, loss of confidentiality of data protected by professional secrecy, unauthorised reversal of pseudonymisation or any other

significant economic or social disadvantage; where data subjects might be deprived of their rights and freedoms or from exercising control over their personal data; where personal data are processed which reveal racial or ethnic origin, political opinions, religion or philosophical beliefs or trade union membership; where genetic data or biometric data are processed in order to uniquely identify a person or where data concerning health or data concerning sex life and sexual orientation or criminal convictions and offences or related security measures are processed; where personal aspects are evaluated, in particular analysing and predicting aspects concerning performance at work, economic situation, health, personal preferences or interests, reliability or behaviour, location or movements, in order to create or use personal profiles; where personal data of vulnerable natural persons, in particular children, are processed; or where processing involves a large amount of personal data and affects a large number of data subjects.

(52) The likelihood and severity of the risk should be determined by reference to the nature, scope, context and purposes of the processing. Risk should be evaluated on the basis of an objective assessment, through which it is established whether data-processing operations involve a high risk. A high risk is a particular risk of prejudice to the rights and freedoms of data subjects.

(53) The protection of the rights and freedoms of natural persons with regard to the processing of personal data requires that appropriate technical and organisational measures are taken, to ensure that the requirements of this Directive are met. The implementation of such measures should not depend solely on economic considerations. In order to be able to demonstrate compliance with this Directive, the controller should adopt internal policies and implement measures which adhere in particular to the principles of data protection by design and data protection by default. Where the controller has carried out a data protection impact assessment pursuant to this Directive, the results should be taken into account when developing those measures and procedures. The measures could consist, inter alia, of the use of pseudonymisation, as early as possible. The use of pseudonymisation for the purposes of this Directive can serve as a tool that could facilitate, in particular, the free flow of personal data within the area of freedom, security and justice.

(54) The protection of the rights and freedoms of data subjects as well as the responsibility and liability of controllers and processors, also in relation to the monitoring by and measures of supervisory authorities, requires a clear attribution of the responsibilities set out in this Directive, including where a controller determines the purposes and means of the processing jointly with other controllers or where a processing operation is carried out on behalf of a controller.

(55) The carrying-out of processing by a processor should be governed by a legal act including a contract binding the processor to the controller and stipulating, in particular, that the processor should act only on instructions from the controller. The processor should take into account the principle of data protection by design and by default.

(56) In order to demonstrate compliance with this Directive, the controller or processor should maintain records regarding all categories of processing activities under its responsibility. Each controller and processor should be obliged to cooperate with the supervisory

authority and make those records available to it on request, so that they might serve for monitoring those processing operations. The controller or the processor processing personal data in non-automated processing systems should have in place effective methods of demonstrating the lawfulness of the processing, of enabling self-monitoring and of ensuring data integrity and data security, such as logs or other forms of records.

(57) Logs should be kept at least for operations in automated processing systems such as collection, alteration, consultation, disclosure including transfers, combination or erasure. The identification of the person who consulted or disclosed personal data should be logged and from that identification it should be possible to establish the justification for the processing operations. The logs should solely be used for the verification of the lawfulness of the processing, self-monitoring, for ensuring data integrity and data security and criminal proceedings. Self-monitoring also includes internal disciplinary proceedings of competent authorities.

(58) A data protection impact assessment should be carried out by the controller where the processing operations are likely to result in a high risk to the rights and freedoms of data subjects by virtue of their nature, scope or purposes, which should include, in particular, the measures, safeguards and mechanisms envisaged to ensure the protection of personal data and to demonstrate compliance with this Directive. Impact assessments should cover relevant systems and processes of processing operations, but not individual cases.

(59) In order to ensure effective protection of the rights and freedoms of data subjects, the controller or processor should consult the supervisory authority, in certain cases, prior to the processing.

(60) In order to maintain security and to prevent processing that infringes this Directive, the controller or processor should evaluate the risks inherent in the processing and should implement measures to mitigate those risks, such as encryption. Such measures should ensure an appropriate level of security, including confidentiality and take into account the state of the art, the costs of implementation in relation to the risk and the nature of the personal data to be protected. In assessing data security risks, consideration should be given to the risks that are presented by data processing, such as the accidental or unlawful destruction, loss, alteration or unauthorised disclosure of or access to personal data transmitted, stored or otherwise processed, which may, in particular, lead to physical, material or non-material damage. The controller and processor should ensure that the processing of personal data is not carried out by unauthorised persons.

(61) A personal data breach may, if not addressed in an appropriate and timely manner, result in physical, material or non-material damage to natural persons such as loss of control over their personal data or limitation of their rights, discrimination, identity theft or fraud, financial loss, unauthorised reversal of pseudonymisation, damage to reputation, loss of confidentiality of personal data protected by professional secrecy or any other significant economic or social disadvantage to the natural person concerned. Therefore, as soon as the controller becomes aware that a personal data breach has occurred, the controller should notify the personal data breach to the supervisory authority without undue delay and, where feasible, not later than 72 hours after having become aware of it, unless the controller is able to demonstrate, in accordance with the accountability principle, that the personal data breach is unlikely to result in a risk to the rights and freedoms of natural

persons. Where such notification cannot be achieved within 72 hours, the reasons for the delay should accompany the notification and information may be provided in phases without undue further delay.

(62) Natural persons should be informed without undue delay where the personal data breach is likely to result in a high risk to the rights and freedoms of natural persons, in order to allow them to take the necessary precautions. The communication should describe the nature of the personal data breach and include recommendations for the natural person concerned to mitigate potential adverse effects. Communication to data subjects should be made as soon as reasonably feasible, in close cooperation with the supervisory authority, and respecting guidance provided by it or other relevant authorities. For example, the need to mitigate an immediate risk of damage would call for a prompt communication to data subjects, whereas the need to implement appropriate measures against continuing or similar data breaches may justify more time for the communication. Where avoiding obstruction of official or legal inquiries, investigations or procedures, avoiding prejudice to the prevention, detection, investigation or prosecution of criminal offences or the execution of criminal penalties, protecting public security, protecting national security or protecting the rights and freedoms of others cannot be achieved by delaying or restricting the communication of a personal data breach to the natural person concerned, such communication could, in exceptional circumstances, be omitted.

(63) The controller should designate a person who would assist it in monitoring internal compliance with the provisions adopted pursuant to this Directive, except where a Member State decides to exempt courts and other independent judicial authorities when acting in their judicial capacity. That person could be a member of the existing staff of the controller who received special training in data protection law and practice in order to acquire expert knowledge in that field. The necessary level of expert knowledge should be determined, in particular, according to the data processing carried out and the protection required for the personal data processed by the controller. His or her task could be carried out on a part-time or full-time basis. A data protection officer may be appointed jointly by several controllers, taking into account their organisational structure and size, for example in the case of shared resources in central units. That person can also be appointed to different positions within the structure of the relevant controllers. That person should help the controller and the employees processing personal data by informing and advising them on compliance with their relevant data protection obligations. Such data protection officers should be in a position to perform their duties and tasks in an independent manner in accordance with Member State law.

(64) Member States should ensure that a transfer to a third country or to an international organisation takes place only if necessary for the prevention, investigation, detection or prosecution of criminal offences or the execution of criminal penalties, including the safeguarding against and the prevention of threats to public security, and that the controller in the third country or international organisation is an authority competent within the meaning of this Directive. A transfer should be carried out only by competent authorities acting as controllers, except where processors are explicitly instructed to transfer on behalf of controllers. Such a transfer may take place in cases where the Commission has decided that the third country or international organisation in question ensures an adequate level of protection, where appropriate safeguards have been provided, or where derogations for specific situations apply. Where personal data are

transferred from the Union to controllers, to processors or to other recipients in third countries or international organisations, the level of protection of natural persons provided for in the Union by this Directive should not be undermined, including in cases of onward transfers of personal data from the third country or international organisation to controllers or processors in the same or in another third country or international organisation.

(65) Where personal data are transferred from a Member State to third countries or international organisations, such a transfer should, in principle, take place only after the Member State from which the data were obtained has given its authorisation to the transfer. The interests of efficient law-enforcement cooperation require that where the nature of a threat to the public security of a Member State or a third country or to the essential interests of a Member State is so immediate as to render it impossible to obtain prior authorisation in good time, the competent authority should be able to transfer the relevant personal data to the third country or international organisation concerned without such a prior authorisation. Member States should provide that any specific conditions concerning the transfer should be communicated to third countries or international organisations. Onward transfers of personal data should be subject to prior authorisation by the competent authority that carried out the original transfer. When deciding on a request for the authorisation of an onward transfer, the competent authority that carried out the original transfer should take due account of all relevant factors, including the seriousness of the criminal offence, the specific conditions subject to which, and the purpose for which, the data was originally transferred, the nature and conditions of the execution of the criminal penalty, and the level of personal data protection in the third country or an international organisation to which personal data are onward transferred. The competent authority that carried out the original transfer should also be able to subject the onward transfer to specific conditions. Such specific conditions can be described, for example, in handling codes.

(66) The Commission should be able to decide with effect for the entire Union that certain third countries, a territory or one or more specified sectors within a third country, or an international organisation, offer an adequate level of data protection, thus providing legal certainty and uniformity throughout the Union as regards the third countries or international organisations which are considered to provide such a level of protection. In such cases, transfers of personal data to those countries should be able to take place without the need to obtain any specific authorisation, except where another Member State from which the data were obtained has to give its authorisation to the transfer.

(67) In line with the fundamental values on which the Union is founded, in particular the protection of human rights, the Commission should, in its assessment of the third country, or of a territory or specified sector within a third country, take into account how a particular third country respects the rule of law, access to justice as well as international human rights norms and standards and its general and sectoral law, including legislation concerning public security, defence and national security, as well as public order and criminal law. The adoption of an adequacy decision with regard to a territory or a specified sector in a third country should take into account clear and objective criteria, such as specific processing activities and the scope of applicable legal standards and legislation in force in the third country. The third country should offer guarantees ensuring an adequate level of protection essentially equivalent to that ensured within the

Union, in particular where data are processed in one or several specific sectors. In particular, the third country should ensure effective independent data protection supervision and provide for cooperation mechanisms with the Member States' data protection authorities, and the data subjects should be provided with effective and enforceable rights and effective administrative and judicial redress.

(68) Apart from the international commitments the third country or international organisation has entered into, the Commission should also take account of obligations arising from the third country's or international organisation's participation in multilateral or regional systems, in particular in relation to the protection of personal data, as well as the implementation of such obligations. In particular the third country's accession to the Council of Europe Convention of 28 January 1981 for the Protection of Individuals with regard to the Automatic Processing of Personal Data and its Additional Protocol should be taken into account. The Commission should consult with the European Data Protection Board established by Regulation (EU) 2016/679 (the 'Board') when assessing the level of protection in third countries or international organisations. The Commission should also take into account any relevant Commission adequacy decision adopted in accordance with Article 45 of Regulation (EU) 2016/679.

(69) The Commission should monitor the functioning of decisions on the level of protection in a third country, a territory or a specified sector within a third country, or an international organisation. In its adequacy decisions, the Commission should provide for a periodic review mechanism of their functioning. That periodic review should be undertaken in consultation with the third country or international organisation in question and should take into account all relevant developments in the third country or international organisation.

(70) The Commission should also be able to recognise that a third country, a territory or a specified sector within a third country, or an international organisation, no longer ensures an adequate level of data protection. Consequently, the transfer of personal data to that third country or international organisation should be prohibited unless the requirements in this Directive relating to transfers subject to appropriate safeguards and derogations for specific situations are fulfilled. Provision should be made for procedures for consultations between the Commission and such third countries or international organisations. The Commission should, in a timely manner, inform the third country or international organisation of the reasons and enter into consultations with it in order to remedy the situation.

(71) Transfers not based on such an adequacy decision should be allowed only where appropriate safeguards have been provided in a legally binding instrument which ensures the protection of personal data or where the controller has assessed all the circumstances surrounding the data transfer and, on the basis of that assessment, considers that appropriate safeguards with regard to the protection of personal data exist. Such legally binding instruments could, for example, be legally binding bilateral agreements which have been concluded by the Member States and implemented in their legal order and which could be enforced by their data subjects, ensuring compliance with data protection requirements and the rights of the data subjects, including the right to obtain effective administrative or judicial redress. The controller should be able to take into account cooperation agreements concluded between Europol or Eurojust and third countries

which allow for the exchange of personal data when carrying out the assessment of all the circumstances surrounding the data transfer. The controller should be able to also take into account the fact that the transfer of personal data will be subject to confidentiality obligations and the principle of specificity, ensuring that the data will not be processed for other purposes than for the purposes of the transfer. In addition, the controller should take into account that the personal data will not be used to request, hand down or execute a death penalty or any form of cruel and inhuman treatment. While those conditions could be considered to be appropriate safeguards allowing the transfer of data, the controller should be able to require additional safeguards.

(72) Where no adequacy decision or appropriate safeguards exist, a transfer or a category of transfers could take place only in specific situations, if necessary to protect the vital interests of the data subject or another person, or to safeguard legitimate interests of the data subject where the law of the Member State transferring the personal data so provides; for the prevention of an immediate and serious threat to the public security of a Member State or a third country; in an individual case for the purposes of the prevention, investigation, detection or prosecution of criminal offences or the execution of criminal penalties, including the safeguarding against and the prevention of threats to public security; or in an individual case for the establishment, exercise or defence of legal claims. Those derogations should be interpreted restrictively and should not allow frequent, massive and structural transfers of personal data, or large-scale transfers of data, but should be limited to data strictly necessary. Such transfers should be documented and should be made available to the supervisory authority on request in order to monitor the lawfulness of the transfer.

(73) Competent authorities of Member States apply bilateral or multilateral international agreements in force, concluded with third countries in the field of judicial cooperation in criminal matters and police cooperation, for the exchange of relevant information to allow them to perform their legally assigned tasks. In principle, this takes place through, or at least with, the cooperation of the authorities competent in the third countries concerned for the purposes of this Directive, sometimes even in the absence of a bilateral or multilateral international agreement. However, in specific individual cases, the regular procedures requiring contacting such an authority in the third country may be ineffective or inappropriate, in particular because the transfer could not be carried out in a timely manner, or because that authority in the third country does not respect the rule of law or international human rights norms and standards, so that competent authorities of Member States could decide to transfer personal data directly to recipients established in those third countries. This may be the case where there is an urgent need to transfer personal data to save the life of a person who is in danger of becoming a victim of a criminal offence or in the interest of preventing an imminent perpetration of a crime, including terrorism. Even if such a transfer between competent authorities and recipients established in third countries should take place only in specific individual cases, this Directive should provide for conditions to regulate such cases. Those provisions should not be considered to be derogations from any existing bilateral or multilateral international agreements in the field of judicial cooperation in criminal matters and police cooperation. Those rules should apply in addition to the other rules of this Directive, in particular those on the lawfulness of processing and Chapter V.

(74) Where personal data move across borders it may put at increased risk the ability of

natural persons to exercise data protection rights to protect themselves from the unlawful use or disclosure of those data. At the same time, supervisory authorities may find that they are unable to pursue complaints or conduct investigations relating to the activities outside their borders. Their efforts to work together in the cross-border context may also be hampered by insufficient preventative or remedial powers and inconsistent legal regimes. Therefore, there is a need to promote closer cooperation among data protection supervisory authorities to help them exchange information with their foreign counterparts.

(75) The establishment in Member States of supervisory authorities that are able to exercise their functions with complete independence is an essential component of the protection of natural persons with regard to the processing of their personal data. The supervisory authorities should monitor the application of the provisions adopted pursuant to this Directive and should contribute to their consistent application throughout the Union in order to protect natural persons with regard to the processing of their personal data. To that end, the supervisory authorities should cooperate with each other and with the Commission.

(76) Member States may entrust a supervisory authority already established under Regulation (EU) 2016/679 with the responsibility for the tasks to be performed by the national supervisory authorities to be established under this Directive.

(77) Member States should be allowed to establish more than one supervisory authority to reflect their constitutional, organisational and administrative structure. Each supervisory authority should be provided with the financial and human resources, premises and infrastructure, which are necessary for the effective performance of their tasks, including for the tasks related to mutual assistance and cooperation with other supervisory authorities throughout the Union. Each supervisory authority should have a separate, public annual budget, which may be part of the overall state or national budget.

(78) Supervisory authorities should be subject to independent control or monitoring mechanisms regarding their financial expenditure, provided that such financial control does not affect their independence.

(79) The general conditions for the member or members of the supervisory authority should be laid down by Member State law and should in particular provide that those members should be either appointed by the parliament or the government or the head of State of the Member State based on a proposal from the government or a member of the government, or the parliament or its chamber, or by an independent body entrusted by Member State law with the appointment by means of a transparent procedure. In order to ensure the independence of the supervisory authority, the member or members should act with integrity, should refrain from any action incompatible with their duties and should not, during their term of office, engage in any incompatible occupation, whether gainful or not. In order to ensure the independence of the supervisory authority, the staff should be chosen by the supervisory authority which may include an intervention by an independent body entrusted by Member State law.

(80) While this Directive applies also to the activities of national courts and other judicial authorities, the competence of the supervisory authorities should not cover the processing

of personal data where courts are acting in their judicial capacity, in order to safeguard the independence of judges in the performance of their judicial tasks. That exemption should be limited to judicial activities in court cases and not apply to other activities where judges might be involved in accordance with Member State law. Member States should also be able to provide that the competence of the supervisory authority does not cover the processing of personal data of other independent judicial authorities when acting in their judicial capacity, for example public prosecutor's office. In any event, the compliance with the rules of this Directive by the courts and other independent judicial authorities is always subject to independent supervision in accordance with Article 8(3) of the Charter.

(81) Each supervisory authority should handle complaints lodged by any data subject and should investigate the matter or transmit it to the competent supervisory authority. The investigation following a complaint should be carried out, subject to judicial review, to the extent that is appropriate in the specific case. The supervisory authority should inform the data subject of the progress and the outcome of the complaint within a reasonable period. If the case requires further investigation or coordination with another supervisory authority, intermediate information should be provided to the data subject.

(82) In order to ensure effective, reliable and consistent monitoring of compliance with and enforcement of this Directive throughout the Union pursuant to the TFEU as interpreted by the Court of Justice, the supervisory authorities should have in each Member State the same tasks and effective powers, including investigative, corrective, and advisory powers which constitute necessary means to perform their tasks. However, their powers should not interfere with specific rules for criminal proceedings, including investigation and prosecution of criminal offences, or the independence of the judiciary. Without prejudice to the powers of prosecutorial authorities under Member State law, supervisory authorities should also have the power to bring infringements of this Directive to the attention of the judicial authorities or to engage in legal proceedings. The powers of supervisory authorities should be exercised in accordance with appropriate procedural safeguards laid down by Union and Member State law, impartially, fairly and within a reasonable time. In particular each measure should be appropriate, necessary and proportionate in view of ensuring compliance with this Directive, taking into account the circumstances of each individual case, respect the right of every person to be heard before any individual measure that would adversely affect the person concerned is taken, and avoiding superfluous costs and excessive inconvenience to the person concerned. Investigative powers as regards access to premises should be exercised in accordance with specific requirements in Member State law, such as the requirement to obtain a prior judicial authorisation. The adoption of a legally binding decision should be subject to judicial review in the Member State of the supervisory authority that adopted the decision.

(83) The supervisory authorities should assist one another in performing their tasks and provide mutual assistance, so as to ensure the consistent application and enforcement of the provisions adopted pursuant to this Directive.

(84) The Board should contribute to the consistent application of this Directive throughout the Union, including advising the Commission and promoting the cooperation of the supervisory authorities throughout the Union.

(85) Every data subject should have the right to lodge a complaint with a single supervisory authority and to an effective judicial remedy in accordance with Article 47 of the Charter where the data subject considers that his or her rights under provisions adopted pursuant to this Directive are infringed or where the supervisory authority does not act on a complaint, partially or wholly rejects or dismisses a complaint or does not act where such action is necessary to protect the rights of the data subject. The investigation following a complaint should be carried out, subject to judicial review, to the extent that is appropriate in the specific case. The competent supervisory authority should inform the data subject of the progress and the outcome of the complaint within a reasonable period. If the case requires further investigation or coordination with another supervisory authority, intermediate information should be provided to the data subject. In order to facilitate the submission of complaints, each supervisory authority should take measures such as providing a complaint submission form which can also be completed electronically, without excluding other means of communication.

(86) Each natural or legal person should have the right to an effective judicial remedy before the competent national court against a decision of a supervisory authority which produces legal effects concerning that person. Such a decision concerns in particular the exercise of investigative, corrective and authorisation powers by the supervisory authority or the dismissal or rejection of complaints. However, that right does not encompass other measures of supervisory authorities which are not legally binding, such as opinions issued by or advice provided by the supervisory authority. Proceedings against a supervisory authority should be brought before the courts of the Member State where the supervisory authority is established and should be conducted in accordance with Member State law. Those courts should exercise full jurisdiction which should include jurisdiction to examine all questions of fact and law relevant to the dispute before it.

(87) Where a data subject considers that his or her rights under this Directive are infringed, he or she should have the right to mandate a body which aims to protect the rights and interests of data subjects in relation to the protection of their personal data and is constituted according to Member State law to lodge a complaint on his or her behalf with a supervisory authority and to exercise the right to a judicial remedy. The right of representation of data subjects should be without prejudice to Member State procedural law which may require mandatory representation of data subjects by a lawyer, as defined in Council Directive 77/249/EEC, before national courts.

(88) Any damage which a person may suffer as a result of processing that infringes the provisions adopted pursuant to this Directive should be compensated by the controller or any other authority competent under Member State law. The concept of damage should be broadly interpreted in the light of the case-law of the Court of Justice in a manner which fully reflects the objectives of this Directive. This is without prejudice to any claims for damage deriving from the violation of other rules in Union or Member State law. When reference is made to processing that is unlawful or that infringes the provisions adopted pursuant to this Directive it also covers processing that infringes implementing acts adopted pursuant to this Directive. Data subjects should receive full and effective compensation for the damage that they have suffered.

(89) Penalties should be imposed on any natural or legal person, whether governed by private

or public law, who infringes this Directive. Member States should ensure that the penalties are effective, proportionate and dissuasive and should take all measures to implement the penalties.

(90) In order to ensure uniform conditions for the implementation of this Directive, implementing powers should be conferred on the Commission with regard to the adequate level of protection afforded by a third country, a territory or a specified sector within a third country, or an international organisation and the format and procedures for mutual assistance and the arrangements for the exchange of information by electronic means between supervisory authorities, and between supervisory authorities and the Board. Those powers should be exercised in accordance with Regulation (EU) No 182/2011 of the European Parliament and of the Council.

(91) The examination procedure should be used for the adoption of implementing acts on the adequate level of protection afforded by a third country, a territory or a specified sector within a third country, or an international organisation and on the format and procedures for mutual assistance and the arrangements for the exchange of information by electronic means between supervisory authorities, and between supervisory authorities and the Board, given that those acts are of a general scope.

(92) The Commission should adopt immediately applicable implementing acts where, in duly justified cases relating to a third country, a territory or a specified sector within a third country, or an international organisation which no longer ensure an adequate level of protection, imperative grounds of urgency so require.

(93) Since the objectives of this Directive, namely to protect the fundamental rights and freedoms of natural persons and in particular their right to the protection of personal data and to ensure the free exchange of personal data by competent authorities within the Union, cannot be sufficiently achieved by the Member States and can rather, by reason of the scale or effects of the action, be better achieved at Union level, the Union may adopt measures, in accordance with the principle of subsidiarity as set out in Article 5 of the TEU. In accordance with the principle of proportionality as set out in that Article, this Directive does not go beyond what is necessary in order to achieve those objectives

(94) Specific provisions of acts of the Union adopted in the field of judicial cooperation in criminal matters and police cooperation which were adopted prior to the date of the adoption of this Directive, regulating the processing of personal data between Member States or the access of designated authorities of Member States to information systems established pursuant to the Treaties, should remain unaffected, such as, for example, the specific provisions concerning the protection of personal data applied pursuant to Council Decision 2008/615/JHA, or Article 23 of the Convention on Mutual Assistance in Criminal Matters between the Member States of the European Union. Since Article 8 of the Charter and Article 16 TFEU require that the fundamental right to the protection of personal data be ensured in a consistent manner throughout the Union, the Commission should evaluate the situation with regard to the relationship between this Directive and the acts adopted prior to the date of adoption of this Directive regulating the processing of personal data between Member States or the access of designated authorities of Member States to information systems established pursuant to the Treaties, in order to assess the need for alignment of those specific provisions with this Directive.

Where appropriate, the Commission should make proposals with a view to ensuring consistent legal rules relating to the processing of personal data.

(95) In order to ensure a comprehensive and consistent protection of personal data in the Union, international agreements which were concluded by Member States prior to the date of entry into force of this Directive and which comply with the relevant Union law applicable prior to that date should remain in force until amended, replaced or revoked.

(96) Member States should be allowed a period of not more than two years from the date of entry into force of this Directive to transpose it. Processing already under way on that date should be brought into conformity with this Directive within the period of two years after which this Directive enters into force. However, where such processing complies with the Union law applicable prior to the date of entry into force of this Directive, the requirements of this Directive concerning the prior consultation of the supervisory authority should not apply to the processing operations already under way on that date given that those requirements, by their very nature, are to be met prior to the processing. Where Member States use the longer implementation period expiring seven years after the date of entry into force of this Directive for meeting the logging obligations for automated processing systems set up prior to that date, the controller or the processor should have in place effective methods for demonstrating the lawfulness of the data processing, for enabling self-monitoring and for ensuring data integrity and data security, such as logs or other forms of records.

(97) This Directive is without prejudice to the rules on combating the sexual abuse and sexual exploitation of children and child pornography as laid down in Directive 2011/93/EU of the European Parliament and of the Council.

(98) Framework Decision 2008/977/JHA should therefore be repealed.

(99) In accordance with Article 6a of Protocol No 21 on the position of the United Kingdom and Ireland in respect of the area of freedom, security and justice, as annexed to the TEU and to the TFEU, the United Kingdom and Ireland are not bound by the rules laid down in this Directive which relate to the processing of personal data by the Member States when carrying out activities which fall within the scope of Chapter 4 or Chapter 5 of Title V of Part Three of the TFEU where the United Kingdom and Ireland are not bound by the rules governing the forms of judicial cooperation in criminal matters or police cooperation which require compliance with the provisions laid down on the basis of Article 16 TFEU.

(100) In accordance with Articles 2 and 2a of Protocol No 22 on the position of Denmark, as annexed to the TEU and to the TFEU, Denmark is not bound by the rules laid down in this Directive or subject to their application which relate to the processing of personal data by the Member States when carrying out activities which fall within the scope of Chapter 4 or Chapter 5 of Title V of Part Three of the TFEU. Given that this Directive builds upon the Schengen acquis, under Title V of Part Three of the TFEU, Denmark, in accordance with Article 4 of that Protocol, is to decide within six months after adoption of this Directive whether it will implement it in its national law.

(101) As regards Iceland and Norway, this Directive constitutes a development of provisions of

the Schengen acquis, as provided for by the Agreement concluded by the Council of the European Union and the Republic of Iceland and the Kingdom of Norway concerning the association of those two States with the implementation, application and development of the Schengen acquis.

(102) As regards Switzerland, this Directive constitutes a development of provisions of the Schengen acquis, as provided for by the Agreement between the European Union, the European Community and the Swiss Confederation concerning the association of the Swiss Confederation with the implementation, application and development of the Schengen acquis.

(103) As regards Liechtenstein, this Directive constitutes a development of provisions of the Schengen acquis, as provided for by the Protocol between the European Union, the European Community, the Swiss Confederation and the Principality of Liechtenstein on the accession of the Principality of Liechtenstein to the Agreement between the European Union, the European Community and the Swiss Confederation on the Swiss Confederation's association with the implementation, application and development of the Schengen acquis.

(104) This Directive respects the fundamental rights and observes the principles recognised in the Charter as enshrined in the TFEU, in particular the right to respect for private and family life, the right to the protection of personal data, the right to an effective remedy and to a fair trial. Limitations placed on those rights are in accordance with Article 52(1) of the Charter as they are necessary to meet objectives of general interest recognised by the Union or the need to protect the rights and freedoms of others.

(105) In accordance with the Joint Political Declaration of 28 September 2011 of Member States and the Commission on explanatory documents, Member States have undertaken to accompany, in justified cases, the notification of their transposition measures with one or more documents explaining the relationship between the components of a directive and the corresponding parts of national transposition measures. With regard to this Directive, the legislator considers the transmission of such documents to be justified.

(106) The European Data Protection Supervisor was consulted in accordance with Article 28(2) of Regulation (EC) No 45/2001 and delivered an opinion on 7 March 2012.

(107) This Directive should not preclude Member States from implementing the exercise of the rights of data subjects on information, access to and rectification or erasure of personal data and restriction of processing in the course of criminal proceedings, and their possible restrictions thereto, in national rules on criminal procedure,

HAVE ADOPTED THIS DIRECTIVE:

CHAPTER I – GENERAL PROVISIONS

Article 1 Subject-matter and objectives

1. This Directive lays down the rules relating to the protection of natural persons with regard to the processing of personal data by competent authorities for the purposes of the prevention, investigation, detection or prosecution of criminal offences or the execution

of criminal penalties, including the safeguarding against and the prevention of threats to public security.

2. In accordance with this Directive, Member States shall:
   (a) protect the fundamental rights and freedoms of natural persons and in particular their right to the protection of personal data; and
   (b) ensure that the exchange of personal data by competent authorities within the Union, where such exchange is required by Union or Member State law, is neither restricted nor prohibited for reasons connected with the protection of natural persons with regard to the processing of personal data.

3. This Directive shall not preclude Member States from providing higher safeguards than those established in this Directive for the protection of the rights and freedoms of the data subject with regard to the processing of personal data by competent authorities.

Article 2 Scope

1. This Directive applies to the processing of personal data by competent authorities for the purposes set out in Article 1(1).

2. This Directive applies to the processing of personal data wholly or partly by automated means, and to the processing other than by automated means of personal data which form part of a filing system or are intended to form part of a filing system.

3. This Directive does not apply to the processing of personal data:
   (a) in the course of an activity which falls outside the scope of Union law;
   (b) by the Union institutions, bodies, offices and agencies.

Article 3 Definitions

For the purposes of this Directive:

(1) 'personal data' means any information relating to an identified or identifiable natural person ('data subject'); an identifiable natural person is one who can be identified, directly or indirectly, in particular by reference to an identifier such as a name, an identification number, location data, an online identifier or to one or more factors specific to the physical, physiological, genetic, mental, economic, cultural or social identity of that natural person;

(2) 'processing' means any operation or set of operations which is performed on personal data or on sets of personal data, whether or not by automated means, such as collection, recording, organisation, structuring, storage, adaptation or alteration, retrieval, consultation, use, disclosure by transmission, dissemination or otherwise making available, alignment or combination, restriction, erasure or destruction;

(3) 'restriction of processing' means the marking of stored personal data with the aim of limiting their processing in the future;

(4) 'profiling' means any form of automated processing of personal data consisting of the use of personal data to evaluate certain personal aspects relating to a natural person, in particular to analyse or predict aspects concerning that natural person's performance at work, economic situation, health, personal preferences, interests, reliability, behaviour, location or movements;

(5) 'pseudonymisation' means the processing of personal data in such a manner that the personal data can no longer be attributed to a specific data subject without the use of

additional information, provided that such additional information is kept separately and is subject to technical and organisational measures to ensure that the personal data are not attributed to an identified or identifiable natural person;

(6) 'filing system' means any structured set of personal data which are accessible according to specific criteria, whether centralised, decentralised or dispersed on a functional or geographical basis;

(7) 'competent authority' means:
    (a) any public authority competent for the prevention, investigation, detection or prosecution of criminal offences or the execution of criminal penalties, including the safeguarding against and the prevention of threats to public security; or
    (b) any other body or entity entrusted by Member State law to exercise public authority and public powers for the purposes of the prevention, investigation, detection or prosecution of criminal offences or the execution of criminal penalties, including the safeguarding against and the prevention of threats to public security;

(8) 'controller' means the competent authority which, alone or jointly with others, determines the purposes and means of the processing of personal data; where the purposes and means of such processing are determined by Union or Member State law, the controller or the specific criteria for its nomination may be provided for by Union or Member State law;

(9) 'processor' means a natural or legal person, public authority, agency or other body which processes personal data on behalf of the controller;

(10) 'recipient' means a natural or legal person, public authority, agency or another body, to which the personal data are disclosed, whether a third party or not. However, public authorities which may receive personal data in the framework of a particular inquiry in accordance with Member State law shall not be regarded as recipients; the processing of those data by those public authorities shall be in compliance with the applicable data protection rules according to the purposes of the processing;

(11) 'personal data breach' means a breach of security leading to the accidental or unlawful destruction, loss, alteration, unauthorised disclosure of, or access to, personal data transmitted, stored or otherwise processed;

(12) 'genetic data' means personal data, relating to the inherited or acquired genetic characteristics of a natural person which give unique information about the physiology or the health of that natural person and which result, in particular, from an analysis of a biological sample from the natural person in question;

(13) 'biometric data' means personal data resulting from specific technical processing relating to the physical, physiological or behavioural characteristics of a natural person, which allow or confirm the unique identification of that natural person, such as facial images or dactyloscopic data;

(14) 'data concerning health' means personal data related to the physical or mental health of a natural person, including the provision of health care services, which reveal information about his or her health status;

(15) 'supervisory authority' means an independent public authority which is established by a Member State pursuant to Article 41;

(16) 'international organisation' means an organisation and its subordinate bodies governed by public international law, or any other body which is set up by, or on the basis of, an

agreement between two or more countries.

CHAPTER II – PRINCIPLES

Article 4 Principles relating to processing of personal data

1. Member States shall provide for personal data to be:
   (a) processed lawfully and fairly;
   (b) collected for specified, explicit and legitimate purposes and not processed in a manner that is incompatible with those purposes;
   (c) adequate, relevant and not excessive in relation to the purposes for which they are processed;
   (d) accurate and, where necessary, kept up to date; every reasonable step must be taken to ensure that personal data that are inaccurate, having regard to the purposes for which they are processed, are erased or rectified without delay;
   (e) kept in a form which permits identification of data subjects for no longer than is necessary for the purposes for which they are processed;
   (f) processed in a manner that ensures appropriate security of the personal data, including protection against unauthorised or unlawful processing and against accidental loss, destruction or damage, using appropriate technical or organisational measures.

2. Processing by the same or another controller for any of the purposes set out in Article 1(1) other than that for which the personal data are collected shall be permitted in so far as:
   (a) the controller is authorised to process such personal data for such a purpose in accordance with Union or Member State law; and
   (b) processing is necessary and proportionate to that other purpose in accordance with Union or Member State law.

3. Processing by the same or another controller may include archiving in the public interest, scientific, statistical or historical use, for the purposes set out in Article 1(1), subject to appropriate safeguards for the rights and freedoms of data subjects.

4. The controller shall be responsible for, and be able to demonstrate compliance with, paragraphs 1, 2 and 3.

Article 5 Time-limits for storage and review

Member States shall provide for appropriate time limits to be established for the erasure of personal data or for a periodic review of the need for the storage of personal data. Procedural measures shall ensure that those time limits are observed.

Article 6 Distinction between different categories of data subject

Member States shall provide for the controller, where applicable and as far as possible, to make a clear distinction between personal data of different categories of data subjects, such as:
   (a) persons with regard to whom there are serious grounds for believing that they have committed or are about to commit a criminal offence;
   (b) persons convicted of a criminal offence;
   (c) victims of a criminal offence or persons with regard to whom certain facts give rise to reasons for believing that he or she could be the victim of a criminal offence; and
   (d) other parties to a criminal offence, such as persons who might be called on to testify in investigations in connection with criminal offences or subsequent criminal

proceedings, persons who can provide information on criminal offences, or contacts or associates of one of the persons referred to in points (a) and (b).

Article 7   Distinction between personal data and verification of quality of personal data

1. Member States shall provide for personal data based on facts to be distinguished, as far as possible, from personal data based on personal assessments.

2. Member States shall provide for the competent authorities to take all reasonable steps to ensure that personal data which are inaccurate, incomplete or no longer up to date are not transmitted or made available. To that end, each competent authority shall, as far as practicable, verify the quality of personal data before they are transmitted or made available. As far as possible, in all transmissions of personal data, necessary information enabling the receiving competent authority to assess the degree of accuracy, completeness and reliability of personal data, and the extent to which they are up to date shall be added.

3. If it emerges that incorrect personal data have been transmitted or personal data have been unlawfully transmitted, the recipient shall be notified without delay. In such a case, the personal data shall be rectified or erased or processing shall be restricted in accordance with Article 16.

Article 8   Lawfulness of processing

1. Member States shall provide for processing to be lawful only if and to the extent that processing is necessary for the performance of a task carried out by a competent authority for the purposes set out in Article 1(1) and that it is based on Union or Member State law.

2. Member State law regulating processing within the scope of this Directive shall specify at least the objectives of processing, the personal data to be processed and the purposes of the processing.

Article 9   Specific processing conditions

1. Personal data collected by competent authorities for the purposes set out in Article 1(1) shall not be processed for purposes other than those set out in Article 1(1) unless such processing is authorised by Union or Member State law. Where personal data are processed for such other purposes, Regulation (EU) 2016/679 shall apply unless the processing is carried out in an activity which falls outside the scope of Union law.

2. Where competent authorities are entrusted by Member State law with the performance of tasks other than those performed for the purposes set out in Article 1(1), Regulation (EU) 2016/679 shall apply to processing for such purposes, including for archiving purposes in the public interest, scientific or historical research purposes or statistical purposes, unless the processing is carried out in an activity which falls outside the scope of Union law.

3. Member States shall, where Union or Member State law applicable to the transmitting competent authority provides specific conditions for processing, provide for the transmitting competent authority to inform the recipient of such personal data of those conditions and the requirement to comply with them.

4. Member States shall provide for the transmitting competent authority not to apply conditions pursuant to paragraph 3 to recipients in other Member States or to agencies, offices and bodies established pursuant to Chapters 4 and 5 of Title V of the TFEU other

than those applicable to similar transmissions of data within the Member State of the transmitting competent authority.

Article 10   Processing of special categories of personal data

Processing of personal data revealing racial or ethnic origin, political opinions, religious or philosophical beliefs, or trade union membership, and the processing of genetic data, biometric data for the purpose of uniquely identifying a natural person, data concerning health or data concerning a natural person's sex life or sexual orientation shall be allowed only where strictly necessary, subject to appropriate safeguards for the rights and freedoms of the data subject, and only:

    (a) where authorised by Union or Member State law;

    (b) to protect the vital interests of the data subject or of another natural person; or

    (c) where such processing relates to data which are manifestly made public by the data subject.

Article 11   Automated individual decision-making

1.   Member States shall provide for a decision based solely on automated processing, including profiling, which produces an adverse legal effect concerning the data subject or significantly affects him or her, to be prohibited unless authorised by Union or Member State law to which the controller is subject and which provides appropriate safeguards for the rights and freedoms of the data subject, at least the right to obtain human intervention on the part of the controller.

2.   Decisions referred to in paragraph 1 of this Article shall not be based on special categories of personal data referred to in Article 10, unless suitable measures to safeguard the data subject's rights and freedoms and legitimate interests are in place.

3.   Profiling that results in discrimination against natural persons on the basis of special categories of personal data referred to in Article 10 shall be prohibited, in accordance with Union law.

CHAPTER III – RIGHTS OF THE DATA SUBJECT

Article 12   Communication and modalities for exercising the rights of the data subject

1.   Member States shall provide for the controller to take reasonable steps to provide any information referred to in Article 13 and make any communication with regard to Articles 11, 14 to 18 and 31 relating to processing to the data subject in a concise, intelligible and easily accessible form, using clear and plain language. The information shall be provided by any appropriate means, including by electronic means. As a general rule, the controller shall provide the information in the same form as the request.

2.   Member States shall provide for the controller to facilitate the exercise of the rights of the data subject under Articles 11 and 14 to 18.

3.   Member States shall provide for the controller to inform the data subject in writing about the follow up to his or her request without undue delay.

4.   Member States shall provide for the information provided under Article 13 and any communication made or action taken pursuant to Articles 11, 14 to 18 and 31 to be provided free of charge. Where requests from a data subject are manifestly unfounded or excessive, in particular because of their repetitive character, the controller may either:

(a) charge a reasonable fee, taking into account the administrative costs of providing the information or communication or taking the action requested; or

(b) refuse to act on the request.

The controller shall bear the burden of demonstrating the manifestly unfounded or excessive character of the request.

5. Where the controller has reasonable doubts concerning the identity of the natural person making a request referred to in Article 14 or 16, the controller may request the provision of additional information necessary to confirm the identity of the data subject.

Article 13   Information to be made available or given to the data subject

1. Member States shall provide for the controller to make available to the data subject at least the following information:

(a) the identity and the contact details of the controller;

(b) the contact details of the data protection officer, where applicable;

(c) the purposes of the processing for which the personal data are intended;

(d) the right to lodge a complaint with a supervisory authority and the contact details of the supervisory authority;

(e) the existence of the right to request from the controller access to and rectification or erasure of personal data and restriction of processing of the personal data concerning the data subject.

2. In addition to the information referred to in paragraph 1, Member States shall provide by law for the controller to give to the data subject, in specific cases, the following further information to enable the exercise of his or her rights:

(a) the legal basis for the processing;

(b) the period for which the personal data will be stored, or, where that is not possible, the criteria used to determine that period;

(c) where applicable, the categories of recipients of the personal data, including in third countries or international organisations;

(d) where necessary, further information, in particular where the personal data are collected without the knowledge of the data subject.

3. Member States may adopt legislative measures delaying, restricting or omitting the provision of the information to the data subject pursuant to paragraph 2 to the extent that, and for as long as, such a measure constitutes a necessary and proportionate measure in a democratic society with due regard for the fundamental rights and the legitimate interests of the natural person concerned, in order to:

(a) avoid obstructing official or legal inquiries, investigations or procedures;

(b) avoid prejudicing the prevention, detection, investigation or prosecution of criminal offences or the execution of criminal penalties;

(c) protect public security;

(d) protect national security;

(e) protect the rights and freedoms of others.

4. Member States may adopt legislative measures in order to determine categories of processing which may wholly or partly fall under any of the points listed in paragraph 3.

Article 14   Right of access by the data subject

Subject to Article 15, Member States shall provide for the right of the data subject to obtain from the controller confirmation as to whether or not personal data concerning him or her are being processed, and, where that is the case, access to the personal data and the following information:

(a) the purposes of and legal basis for the processing;

(b) the categories of personal data concerned;

(c) the recipients or categories of recipients to whom the personal data have been disclosed, in particular recipients in third countries or international organisations;

(d) where possible, the envisaged period for which the personal data will be stored, or, if not possible, the criteria used to determine that period;

(e) the existence of the right to request from the controller rectification or erasure of personal data or restriction of processing of personal data concerning the data subject;

(f) the right to lodge a complaint with the supervisory authority and the contact details of the supervisory authority;

(g) communication of the personal data undergoing processing and of any available information as to their origin.

Article 15   Limitations to the right of access

1. Member States may adopt legislative measures restricting, wholly or partly, the data subject's right of access to the extent that, and for as long as such a partial or complete restriction constitutes a necessary and proportionate measure in a democratic society with due regard for the fundamental rights and legitimate interests of the natural person concerned, in order to:

(a) avoid obstructing official or legal inquiries, investigations or procedures;

(b) avoid prejudicing the prevention, detection, investigation or prosecution of criminal offences or the execution of criminal penalties;

(c) protect public security;

(d) protect national security;

(e) protect the rights and freedoms of others.

2. Member States may adopt legislative measures in order to determine categories of processing which may wholly or partly fall under points (a) to (e) of paragraph 1.

3. In the cases referred to in paragraphs 1 and 2, Member States shall provide for the controller to inform the data subject, without undue delay, in writing of any refusal or restriction of access and of the reasons for the refusal or the restriction. Such information may be omitted where the provision thereof would undermine a purpose under paragraph 1. Member States shall provide for the controller to inform the data subject of the possibility of lodging a complaint with a supervisory authority or seeking a judicial remedy.

4. Member States shall provide for the controller to document the factual or legal reasons on which the decision is based. That information shall be made available to the supervisory authorities.

Article 16   Right to rectification or erasure of personal data and restriction of processing

1. Member States shall provide for the right of the data subject to obtain from the controller without undue delay the rectification of inaccurate personal data relating to him or her. Taking into account the purposes of the processing, Member States shall provide for the data subject to have the right to have incomplete personal data completed, including by means of providing a supplementary statement.

2. Member States shall require the controller to erase personal data without undue delay and provide for the right of the data subject to obtain from the controller the erasure of personal data concerning him or her without undue delay where processing infringes the provisions adopted pursuant to Article 4, 8 or 10, or where personal data must be erased in order to comply with a legal obligation to which the controller is subject.

3. Instead of erasure, the controller shall restrict processing where:
   (a) the accuracy of the personal data is contested by the data subject and their accuracy or inaccuracy cannot be ascertained; or
   (b) the personal data must be maintained for the purposes of evidence.
   Where processing is restricted pursuant to point (a) of the first subparagraph, the controller shall inform the data subject before lifting the restriction of processing.

4. Member States shall provide for the controller to inform the data subject in writing of any refusal of rectification or erasure of personal data or restriction of processing and of the reasons for the refusal. Member States may adopt legislative measures restricting, wholly or partly, the obligation to provide such information to the extent that such a restriction constitutes a necessary and proportionate measure in a democratic society with due regard for the fundamental rights and legitimate interests of the natural person concerned in order to:
   (a) avoid obstructing official or legal inquiries, investigations or procedures;
   (b) avoid prejudicing the prevention, detection, investigation or prosecution of criminal offences or the execution of criminal penalties;
   (c) protect public security;
   (d) protect national security;
   (e) protect the rights and freedoms of others.
   Member States shall provide for the controller to inform the data subject of the possibility of lodging a complaint with a supervisory authority or seeking a judicial remedy.

5. Member States shall provide for the controller to communicate the rectification of inaccurate personal data to the competent authority from which the inaccurate personal data originate.

6. Member States shall, where personal data has been rectified or erased or processing has been restricted pursuant to paragraphs 1, 2 and 3, provide for the controller to notify the recipients and that the recipients shall rectify or erase the personal data or restrict processing of the personal data under their responsibility.

Article 17   Exercise of rights by the data subject and verification by the supervisory authority

1. In the cases referred to in Article 13(3), Article 15(3) and Article 16(4) Member States shall adopt measures providing that the rights of the data subject may also be exercised through the competent supervisory authority.

2. Member States shall provide for the controller to inform the data subject of the possibility of exercising his or her rights through the supervisory authority pursuant to paragraph 1.

3. Where the right referred to in paragraph 1 is exercised, the supervisory authority shall inform the data subject at least that all necessary verifications or a review by the supervisory authority have taken place. The supervisory authority shall also inform the data subject of his or her right to seek a judicial remedy.

Article 18   Rights of the data subject in criminal investigations and proceedings

Member States may provide for the exercise of the rights referred to in Articles 13, 14 and 16 to be carried out in accordance with Member State law where the personal data are contained in a judicial decision or record or case file processed in the course of criminal investigations and proceedings.

CHAPTER IV – CONTROLLER AND PROCESSOR

Section 1   General obligations

Article 19   Obligations of the controller

1. Member States shall provide for the controller, taking into account the nature, scope, context and purposes of processing as well as the risks of varying likelihood and severity for the rights and freedoms of natural persons, to implement appropriate technical and organisational measures to ensure and to be able to demonstrate that processing is performed in accordance with this Directive. Those measures shall be reviewed and updated where necessary.

2. Where proportionate in relation to the processing activities, the measures referred to in paragraph 1 shall include the implementation of appropriate data protection policies by the controller.

Article 20   Data protection by design and by default

1. Member States shall provide for the controller, taking into account the state of the art, the cost of implementation and the nature, scope, context and purposes of processing, as well as the risks of varying likelihood and severity for rights and freedoms of natural persons posed by the processing, both at the time of the determination of the means for processing and at the time of the processing itself, to implement appropriate technical and organisational measures, such as pseudonymisation, which are designed to implement data protection principles, such as data minimisation, in an effective manner and to integrate the necessary safeguards into the processing, in order to meet the requirements of this Directive and protect the rights of data subjects.

2. Member States shall provide for the controller to implement appropriate technical and organisational measures ensuring that, by default, only personal data which are necessary for each specific purpose of the processing are processed. That obligation applies to the amount of personal data collected, the extent of their processing, the period of their storage and their accessibility. In particular, such measures shall ensure that by default personal data are not made accessible without the individual's intervention to an indefinite number of natural persons.

Article 21   Joint controllers

1. Member States shall, where two or more controllers jointly determine the purposes and means of processing, provide for them to be joint controllers. They shall, in a transparent manner, determine their respective responsibilities for compliance with this Directive, in particular as regards the exercise of the rights of the data subject and their respective duties to provide the information referred to in Article 13, by means of an arrangement between them unless, and in so far as, the respective responsibilities of the controllers are determined by Union or Member State law to which the controllers are subject. The

arrangement shall designate the contact point for data subjects. Member States may designate which of the joint controllers can act as a single contact point for data subjects to exercise their rights.

2. Irrespective of the terms of the arrangement referred to in paragraph 1, Member States may provide for the data subject to exercise his or her rights under the provisions adopted pursuant to this Directive in respect of and against each of the controllers.

Article 22   Processor

1. Member States shall, where processing is to be carried out on behalf of a controller, provide for the controller to use only processors providing sufficient guarantees to implement appropriate technical and organisational measures in such a manner that the processing will meet the requirements of this Directive and ensure the protection of the rights of the data subject.

2. Member States shall provide for the processor not to engage another processor without prior specific or general written authorisation by the controller. In the case of general written authorisation, the processor shall inform the controller of any intended changes concerning the addition or replacement of other processors, thereby giving the controller the opportunity to object to such changes.

3. Member States shall provide for the processing by a processor to be governed by a contract or other legal act under Union or Member State law, that is binding on the processor with regard to the controller and that sets out the subject-matter and duration of the processing, the nature and purpose of the processing, the type of personal data and categories of data subjects and the obligations and rights of the controller. That contract or other legal act shall stipulate, in particular, that the processor:
   (a) acts only on instructions from the controller;
   (b) ensures that persons authorised to process the personal data have committed themselves to confidentiality or are under an appropriate statutory obligation of confidentiality;
   (c) assists the controller by any appropriate means to ensure compliance with the provisions on the data subject's rights;
   (d) at the choice of the controller, deletes or returns all the personal data to the controller after the end of the provision of data processing services, and deletes existing copies unless Union or Member State law requires storage of the personal data;
   (e) makes available to the controller all information necessary to demonstrate compliance with this Article;
   (f) complies with the conditions referred to in paragraphs 2 and 3 for engaging another processor.

4. The contract or the other legal act referred to in paragraph 3 shall be in writing, including in an electronic form.

5. If a processor determines, in infringement of this Directive, the purposes and means of processing, that processor shall be considered to be a controller in respect of that processing.

Article 23   Processing under the authority of the controller or processor

Member States shall provide for the processor and any person acting under the authority of the controller or of the processor, who has access to personal data, not to process those data except on instructions from the controller, unless required to do so by Union or Member State law.

Article 24   Records of processing activities

1. Member States shall provide for controllers to maintain a record of all categories of processing activities under their responsibility. That record shall contain all of the following information:

    (a) the name and contact details of the controller and, where applicable, the joint controller and the data protection officer;

    (b) the purposes of the processing;

    (c) the categories of recipients to whom the personal data have been or will be disclosed including recipients in third countries or international organisations;

    (d) a description of the categories of data subject and of the categories of personal data;

    (e) where applicable, the use of profiling;

    (f) where applicable, the categories of transfers of personal data to a third country or an international organisation;

    (g) an indication of the legal basis for the processing operation, including transfers, for which the personal data are intended;

    (h) where possible, the envisaged time limits for erasure of the different categories of personal data;

    (i) where possible, a general description of the technical and organisational security measures referred to in Article 29(1).

2. Member States shall provide for each processor to maintain a record of all categories of processing activities carried out on behalf of a controller, containing:

    (a) the name and contact details of the processor or processors, of each controller on behalf of which the processor is acting and, where applicable, the data protection officer;

    (b) the categories of processing carried out on behalf of each controller;

    (c) where applicable, transfers of personal data to a third country or an international organisation where explicitly instructed to do so by the controller, including the identification of that third country or international organisation;

    (d) where possible, a general description of the technical and organisational security measures referred to in Article 29(1).

3. The records referred to in paragraphs 1 and 2 shall be in writing, including in electronic form.

    The controller and the processor shall make those records available to the supervisory authority on request.

Article 25   Logging

1. Member States shall provide for logs to be kept for at least the following processing operations in automated processing systems: collection, alteration, consultation, disclosure including transfers, combination and erasure. The logs of consultation and disclosure shall make it possible to establish the justification, date and time of such operations and, as far as possible, the identification of the person who consulted or disclosed personal data, and the identity of the recipients of such personal data.

2. The logs shall be used solely for verification of the lawfulness of processing, self-

monitoring, ensuring the integrity and security of the personal data, and for criminal proceedings.

3.   The controller and the processor shall make the logs available to the supervisory authority on request.

Article 26   Cooperation with the supervisory authority

Member States shall provide for the controller and the processor to cooperate, on request, with the supervisory authority in the performance of its tasks on request.

Article 27   Data protection impact assessment

1.   Where a type of processing, in particular, using new technologies, and taking into account the nature, scope, context and purposes of the processing is likely to result in a high risk to the rights and freedoms of natural persons, Member States shall provide for the controller to carry out, prior to the processing, an assessment of the impact of the envisaged processing operations on the protection of personal data.

2.   The assessment referred to in paragraph 1 shall contain at least a general description of the envisaged processing operations, an assessment of the risks to the rights and freedoms of data subjects, the measures envisaged to address those risks, safeguards, security measures and mechanisms to ensure the protection of personal data and to demonstrate compliance with this Directive, taking into account the rights and legitimate interests of the data subjects and other persons concerned.

Article 28   Prior consultation of the supervisory authority

1.   Member States shall provide for the controller or processor to consult the supervisory authority prior to processing which will form part of a new filing system to be created, where:

    (a) a data protection impact assessment as provided for in Article 27 indicates that the processing would result in a high risk in the absence of measures taken by the controller to mitigate the risk; or

    (b) the type of processing, in particular, where using new technologies, mechanisms or procedures, involves a high risk to the rights and freedoms of data subjects.

2.   Member States shall provide for the supervisory authority to be consulted during the preparation of a proposal for a legislative measure to be adopted by a national parliament or of a regulatory measure based on such a legislative measure, which relates to processing.

3.   Member States shall provide that the supervisory authority may establish a list of the processing operations which are subject to prior consultation pursuant to paragraph 1.

4.   Member States shall provide for the controller to provide the supervisory authority with the data protection impact assessment pursuant to Article 27 and, on request, with any other information to allow the supervisory authority to make an assessment of the compliance of the processing and in particular of the risks for the protection of personal data of the data subject and of the related safeguards.

5.   Member States shall, where the supervisory authority is of the opinion that the intended processing referred to in paragraph 1 of this Article would infringe the provisions adopted pursuant to this Directive, in particular where the controller has insufficiently identified or mitigated the risk, provide for the supervisory authority to provide, within a period of up to six weeks of receipt of the request for consultation, written advice to the controller

and, where applicable, to the processor, and may use any of its powers referred to in Article 47. That period may be extended by a month, taking into account the complexity of the intended processing. The supervisory authority shall inform the controller and, where applicable, the processor of any such extension within one month of receipt of the request for consultation, together with the reasons for the delay.

Section 2   Security of personal data

Article 29   Security of processing

1.   Member States shall provide for the controller and the processor, taking into account the state of the art, the costs of implementation and the nature, scope, context and purposes of the processing as well as the risk of varying likelihood and severity for the rights and freedoms of natural persons, to implement appropriate technical and organisational measures to ensure a level of security appropriate to the risk, in particular as regards the processing of special categories of personal data referred to in Article 10.

2.   In respect of automated processing, each Member State shall provide for the controller or processor, following an evaluation of the risks, to implement measures designed to:

   (a) deny unauthorised persons access to processing equipment used for processing ('equipment access control');

   (b) prevent the unauthorised reading, copying, modification or removal of data media ('data media control');

   (c) prevent the unauthorised input of personal data and the unauthorised inspection, modification or deletion of stored personal data ('storage control');

   (d) prevent the use of automated processing systems by unauthorised persons using data communication equipment ('user control');

   (e) ensure that persons authorised to use an automated processing system have access only to the personal data covered by their access authorisation ('data access control');

   (f) ensure that it is possible to verify and establish the bodies to which personal data have been or may be transmitted or made available using data communication equipment ('communication control');

   (g) ensure that it is subsequently possible to verify and establish which personal data have been input into automated processing systems and when and by whom the personal data were input ('input control');

   (h) prevent the unauthorised reading, copying, modification or deletion of personal data during transfers of personal data or during transportation of data media ('transport control');

   (i) ensure that installed systems may, in the case of interruption, be restored ('recovery');

   (j) ensure that the functions of the system perform, that the appearance of faults in the functions is reported ('reliability') and that stored personal data cannot be corrupted by means of a malfunctioning of the system ('integrity').

Article 30   Notification of a personal data breach to the supervisory authority

1.   Member States shall, in the case of a personal data breach, provide for the controller to notify without undue delay and, where feasible, not later than 72 hours after having become aware of it, the personal data breach to the supervisory authority, unless the personal data breach is unlikely to result in a risk to the rights and freedoms of natural

persons. Where the notification to the supervisory authority is not made within 72 hours, it shall be accompanied by reasons for the delay.

2. The processor shall notify the controller without undue delay after becoming aware of a personal data breach.

3. The notification referred to in paragraph 1 shall at least:
    (a) describe the nature of the personal data breach including, where possible, the categories and approximate number of data subjects concerned and the categories and approximate number of personal data records concerned;
    (b) communicate the name and contact details of the data protection officer or other contact point where more information can be obtained;
    (c) describe the likely consequences of the personal data breach;
    (d) describe the measures taken or proposed to be taken by the controller to address the personal data breach, including, where appropriate, measures to mitigate its possible adverse effects.

4. Where, and in so far as, it is not possible to provide the information at the same time, the information may be provided in phases without undue further delay.

5. Member States shall provide for the controller to document any personal data breaches referred to in paragraph 1, comprising the facts relating to the personal data breach, its effects and the remedial action taken. That documentation shall enable the supervisory authority to verify compliance with this Article.

6. Member States shall, where the personal data breach involves personal data that have been transmitted by or to the controller of another Member State, provide for the information referred to in paragraph 3 to be communicated to the controller of that Member State without undue delay.

Article 31 Communication of a personal data breach to the data subject

1. Member States shall, where the personal data breach is likely to result in a high risk to the rights and freedoms of natural persons, provide for the controller to communicate the personal data breach to the data subject without undue delay.

2. The communication to the data subject referred to in paragraph 1 of this Article shall describe in clear and plain language the nature of the personal data breach and shall contain at least the information and measures referred to in points (b), (c) and (d) of Article 30(3).

3. The communication to the data subject referred to in paragraph 1 shall not be required if any of the following conditions are met:
    (a) the controller has implemented appropriate technological and organisational protection measures, and those measures were applied to the personal data affected by the personal data breach, in particular those that render the personal data unintelligible to any person who is not authorised to access it, such as encryption;
    (b) the controller has taken subsequent measures which ensure that the high risk to the rights and freedoms of data subjects referred to in paragraph 1 is no longer likely to materialise;
    (c) it would involve a disproportionate effort. In such a case, there shall instead be a public communication or a similar measure whereby the data subjects are informed in an equally effective manner.

4. If the controller has not already communicated the personal data breach to the data subject, the supervisory authority, having considered the likelihood of the personal data breach resulting in a high risk, may require it to do so, or may decide that any of the conditions referred to in paragraph 3 are met.

5. The communication to the data subject referred to in paragraph 1 of this Article may be delayed, restricted or omitted subject to the conditions and on the grounds referred to in Article 13(3).

Section 3   Data protection officer
Article 32   Designation of the data protection officer

1. Member States shall provide for the controller to designate a data protection officer. Member States may exempt courts and other independent judicial authorities when acting in their judicial capacity from that obligation.

2. The data protection officer shall be designated on the basis of his or her professional qualities and, in particular, his or her expert knowledge of data protection law and practice and ability to fulfil the tasks referred to in Article 34.

3. A single data protection officer may be designated for several competent authorities, taking account of their organisational structure and size.

4. Member States shall provide for the controller to publish the contact details of the data protection officer and communicate them to the supervisory authority.

Article 33   Position of the data protection officer

1. Member States shall provide for the controller to ensure that the data protection officer is involved, properly and in a timely manner, in all issues which relate to the protection of personal data.

2. The controller shall support the data protection officer in performing the tasks referred to in Article 34 by providing resources necessary to carry out those tasks and access to personal data and processing operations, and to maintain his or her expert knowledge.

Article 34   Tasks of the data protection officer

Member States shall provide for the controller to entrust the data protection officer at least with the following tasks:

(a) to inform and advise the controller and the employees who carry out processing of their obligations pursuant to this Directive and to other Union or Member State data protection provisions;

(b) to monitor compliance with this Directive, with other Union or Member State data protection provisions and with the policies of the controller in relation to the protection of personal data, including the assignment of responsibilities, awareness-raising and training of staff involved in processing operations, and the related audits;

(c) to provide advice where requested as regards the data protection impact assessment and monitor its performance pursuant to Article 27;

(d) to cooperate with the supervisory authority;

(e) to act as the contact point for the supervisory authority on issues relating to processing, including the prior consultation referred to in Article 28, and to consult, where appropriate, with regard to any other matter.

CHAPTER V – TRANSFERS OF PERSONAL DATA TO
THIRD COUNTRIES OR INTERNATIONAL ORGANISATIONS

Article 35   General principles for transfers of personal data

1.   Member States shall provide for any transfer by competent authorities of personal data which are undergoing processing or are intended for processing after transfer to a third country or to an international organisation including for onward transfers to another third country or international organisation to take place, subject to compliance with the national provisions adopted pursuant to other provisions of this Directive, only where the conditions laid down in this Chapter are met, namely:

(a) the transfer is necessary for the purposes set out in Article 1(1);

(b) the personal data are transferred to a controller in a third country or international organisation that is an authority competent for the purposes referred to in Article 1(1);

(c) where personal data are transmitted or made available from another Member State, that Member State has given its prior authorisation to the transfer in accordance with its national law;

(d) the Commission has adopted an adequacy decision pursuant to Article 36, or, in the absence of such a decision, appropriate safeguards have been provided or exist pursuant to Article 37, or, in the absence of an adequacy decision pursuant to Article 36 and of appropriate safeguards in accordance with Article 37, derogations for specific situations apply pursuant to Article 38; and

(e) in the case of an onward transfer to another third country or international organisation, the competent authority that carried out the original transfer or another competent authority of the same Member State authorises the onward transfer, after taking into due account all relevant factors, including the seriousness of the criminal offence, the purpose for which the personal data was originally transferred and the level of personal data protection in the third country or an international organisation to which personal data are onward transferred.

2.   Member States shall provide for transfers without the prior authorisation by another Member State in accordance with point (c) of paragraph 1 to be permitted only if the transfer of the personal data is necessary for the prevention of an immediate and serious threat to public security of a Member State or a third country or to essential interests of a Member State and the prior authorisation cannot be obtained in good time. The authority responsible for giving prior authorisation shall be informed without delay.

3.   All provisions in this Chapter shall be applied in order to ensure that the level of protection of natural persons ensured by this Directive is not undermined.

Article 36   Transfers on the basis of an adequacy decision

1.   Member States shall provide that a transfer of personal data to a third country or an international organisation may take place where the Commission has decided that the third country, a territory or one or more specified sectors within that third country, or the international organisation in question ensures an adequate level of protection. Such a transfer shall not require any specific authorisation.

2.   When assessing the adequacy of the level of protection, the Commission shall, in particular, take account of the following elements:

(a) the rule of law, respect for human rights and fundamental freedoms, relevant legislation, both general and sectoral, including concerning public security, defence, national security and criminal law and the access of public authorities to personal data, as well as the implementation of such legislation, data protection rules, professional rules and security measures, including rules for the onward transfer of personal data to another third country or international organisation, which are complied with in that country or international organisation, case-law, as well as effective and enforceable data subject rights and effective administrative and judicial redress for the data subjects whose personal data are transferred;

(b) the existence and effective functioning of one or more independent supervisory authorities in the third country or to which an international organisation is subject, with responsibility for ensuring and enforcing compliance with data protection rules, including adequate enforcement powers, for assisting and advising data subjects in exercising their rights and for cooperation with the supervisory authorities of the Member States; and

(c) the international commitments the third country or international organisation concerned has entered into, or other obligations arising from legally binding conventions or instruments as well as from its participation in multilateral or regional systems, in particular in relation to the protection of personal data.

3. The Commission, after assessing the adequacy of the level of protection, may decide, by means of implementing act, that a third country, a territory or one or more specified sectors within a third country, or an international organisation ensures an adequate level of protection within the meaning of paragraph 2 of this Article. The implementing act shall provide a mechanism for periodic review, at least every four years, which shall take into account all relevant developments in the third country or international organisation. The implementing act shall specify its territorial and sectoral application and, where applicable, identify the supervisory authority or authorities referred to in point (b) of paragraph 2 of this Article. The implementing act shall be adopted in accordance with the examination procedure referred to in Article 58(2).

4. The Commission shall, on an ongoing basis, monitor developments in third countries and international organisations that could affect the functioning of decisions adopted pursuant to paragraph 3.

5. The Commission shall, where available information reveals, in particular following the review referred to in paragraph 3 of this Article, that a third country, a territory or one or more specified sectors within a third country, or an international organisation no longer ensures an adequate level of protection within the meaning of paragraph 2 of this Article, to the extent necessary, repeal, amend or suspend the decision referred to in paragraph 3 of this Article by means of implementing acts without retro-active effect. Those implementing acts shall be adopted in accordance with the examination procedure referred to in Article 58(2).
On duly justified imperative grounds of urgency, the Commission shall adopt immediately applicable implementing acts in accordance with the procedure referred to in Article 58(3).

6. The Commission shall enter into consultations with the third country or international organisation with a view to remedying the situation giving rise to the decision made pursuant to paragraph 5.

7. Member States shall provide for a decision pursuant to paragraph 5 to be without prejudice to transfers of personal data to the third country, the territory or one or more specified sectors within that third country, or the international organisation in question

pursuant to Articles 37 and 38.

8.   The Commission shall publish in the Official Journal of the European Union and on its website a list of the third countries, territories and specified sectors within a third country and international organisations for which it has decided that an adequate level of protection is or is no longer ensured.

Article 37   Transfers subject to appropriate safeguards

1.   In the absence of a decision pursuant to Article 36(3), Member States shall provide that a transfer of personal data to a third country or an international organisation may take place where:

> (a) appropriate safeguards with regard to the protection of personal data are provided for in a legally binding instrument; or
>
> (b) the controller has assessed all the circumstances surrounding the transfer of personal data and concludes that appropriate safeguards exist with regard to the protection of personal data.

2.   The controller shall inform the supervisory authority about categories of transfers under point (b) of paragraph 1.

3.   When a transfer is based on point (b) of paragraph 1, such a transfer shall be documented and the documentation shall be made available to the supervisory authority on request, including the date and time of the transfer, information about the receiving competent authority, the justification for the transfer and the personal data transferred.

Article 38   Derogations for specific situations

1.   In the absence of an adequacy decision pursuant to Article 36, or of appropriate safeguards pursuant to Article 37, Member States shall provide that a transfer or a category of transfers of personal data to a third country or an international organisation may take place only on the condition that the transfer is necessary:

> (a) in order to protect the vital interests of the data subject or another person;
>
> (b) to safeguard legitimate interests of the data subject, where the law of the Member State transferring the personal data so provides;
>
> (c) for the prevention of an immediate and serious threat to public security of a Member State or a third country;
>
> (d) in individual cases for the purposes set out in Article 1(1); or
>
> (e) in an individual case for the establishment, exercise or defence of legal claims relating to the purposes set out in Article 1(1).

2.   Personal data shall not be transferred if the transferring competent authority determines that fundamental rights and freedoms of the data subject concerned override the public interest in the transfer set out in points (d) and (e) of paragraph 1.

3.   Where a transfer is based on paragraph 1, such a transfer shall be documented and the documentation shall be made available to the supervisory authority on request, including the date and time of the transfer, information about the receiving competent authority, the justification for the transfer and the personal data transferred.

Article 39   Transfers of personal data to recipients established in third countries

1.   By way of derogation from point (b) of Article 35(1) and without prejudice to any international agreement referred to in paragraph 2 of this Article, Union or Member State

law may provide for the competent authorities referred to in point (7)(a) of Article 3, in individual and specific cases, to transfer personal data directly to recipients established in third countries only if the other provisions of this Directive are complied with and all of the following conditions are fulfilled:

(a) the transfer is strictly necessary for the performance of a task of the transferring competent authority as provided for by Union or Member State law for the purposes set out in Article 1(1);

(b) the transferring competent authority determines that no fundamental rights and freedoms of the data subject concerned override the public interest necessitating the transfer in the case at hand;

(c) the transferring competent authority considers that the transfer to an authority that is competent for the purposes referred to in Article 1(1) in the third country is ineffective or inappropriate, in particular because the transfer cannot be achieved in good time;

(d) the authority that is competent for the purposes referred to in Article 1(1) in the third country is informed without undue delay, unless this is ineffective or inappropriate;

(e) the transferring competent authority informs the recipient of the specified purpose or purposes for which the personal data are only to be processed by the latter provided that such processing is necessary.

2. An international agreement referred to in paragraph 1 shall be any bilateral or multilateral international agreement in force between Member States and third countries in the field of judicial cooperation in criminal matters and police cooperation.

3. The transferring competent authority shall inform the supervisory authority about transfers under this Article.

4. Where a transfer is based on paragraph 1, such a transfer shall be documented.

Article 40   International cooperation for the protection of personal data

In relation to third countries and international organisations, the Commission and Member States shall take appropriate steps to:

(a) develop international cooperation mechanisms to facilitate the effective enforcement of legislation for the protection of personal data;

(b) provide international mutual assistance in the enforcement of legislation for the protection of personal data, including through notification, complaint referral, investigative assistance and information exchange, subject to appropriate safeguards for the protection of personal data and other fundamental rights and freedoms;

(c) engage relevant stakeholders in discussion and activities aimed at furthering international cooperation in the enforcement of legislation for the protection of personal data;

(d) promote the exchange and documentation of personal data protection legislation and practice, including on jurisdictional conflicts with third countries.

CHAPTER VI – INDEPENDENT SUPERVISORY AUTHORITIES

Section 1   Independent status
Article 41   Supervisory authority

1. Each Member State shall provide for one or more independent public authorities to be responsible for monitoring the application of this Directive, in order to protect the fundamental rights and freedoms of natural persons in relation to processing and to facilitate the free flow of personal data within the Union ('supervisory authority').

2. Each supervisory authority shall contribute to the consistent application of this Directive throughout the Union. For that purpose, the supervisory authorities shall cooperate with each other and with the Commission in accordance with Chapter VII.

3. Member States may provide for a supervisory authority established under Regulation (EU) 2016/679 to be the supervisory authority referred to in this Directive and to assume responsibility for the tasks of the supervisory authority to be established under paragraph 1 of this Article.

4. Where more than one supervisory authority is established in a Member State, that Member State shall designate the supervisory authority which are to represent those authorities in the Board referred to in Article 51.

Article 42   Independence

1. Each Member State shall provide for each supervisory authority to act with complete independence in performing its tasks and exercising its powers in accordance with this Directive.

2. Member States shall provide for the member or members of their supervisory authorities in the performance of their tasks and exercise of their powers in accordance with this Directive, to remain free from external influence, whether direct or indirect, and that they shall neither seek nor take instructions from anybody.

3. Members of Member States' supervisory authorities shall refrain from any action incompatible with their duties and shall not, during their term of office, engage in any incompatible occupation, whether gainful or not.

4. Each Member State shall ensure that each supervisory authority is provided with the human, technical and financial resources, premises and infrastructure necessary for the effective performance of its tasks and exercise of its powers, including those to be carried out in the context of mutual assistance, cooperation and participation in the Board.

5. Each Member State shall ensure that each supervisory authority chooses and has its own staff which shall be subject to the exclusive direction of the member or members of the supervisory authority concerned.

6. Each Member State shall ensure that each supervisory authority is subject to financial control which does not affect its independence and that it has separate, public annual budgets, which may be part of the overall state or national budget.

Article 43   General conditions for the members of the supervisory authority

1. Member States shall provide for each member of their supervisory authorities to be appointed by means of a transparent procedure by:
    — their parliament;
    — their government;
    — their head of State; or
    — an independent body entrusted with the appointment under Member State law.

2. Each member shall have the qualifications, experience and skills, in particular in the area

of the protection of personal data, required to perform their duties and exercise their powers.

3. The duties of a member shall end in the event of the expiry of the term of office, resignation or compulsory retirement, in accordance with the law of the Member State concerned.

4. A member shall be dismissed only in cases of serious misconduct or if the member no longer fulfils the conditions required for the performance of the duties.

Article 44   Rules on the establishment of the supervisory authority

1. Each Member State shall provide by law for all of the following:
   (a) the establishment of each supervisory authority;
   (b) the qualifications and eligibility conditions required to be appointed as a member of each supervisory authority;
   (c) the rules and procedures for the appointment of the member or members of each supervisory authority;
   (d) the duration of the term of the member or members of each supervisory authority of not less than four years, except for the first appointment after 6 May 2016, part of which may take place for a shorter period where that is necessary to protect the independence of the supervisory authority by means of a staggered appointment procedure;
   (e) whether and, if so, for how many terms the member or members of each supervisory authority is eligible for reappointment;
   (f) the conditions governing the obligations of the member or members and staff of each supervisory authority, prohibitions on actions, occupations and benefits incompatible therewith during and after the term of office and rules governing the cessation of employment.

2. The member or members and the staff of each supervisory authority shall, in accordance with Union or Member State law, be subject to a duty of professional secrecy both during and after their term of office, with regard to any confidential information which has come to their knowledge in the course of the performance of their tasks or the exercise of their powers. During their term of office, that duty of professional secrecy shall in particular apply to reporting by natural persons of infringements of this Directive.

Section 2   Competence, tasks and powers
Article 45   Competence

1. Each Member State shall provide for each supervisory authority to be competent for the performance of the tasks assigned to, and for the exercise of the powers conferred on, it in accordance with this Directive on the territory of its own Member State.

2. Each Member State shall provide for each supervisory authority not to be competent for the supervision of processing operations of courts when acting in their judicial capacity. Member States may provide for their supervisory authority not to be competent to supervise processing operations of other independent judicial authorities when acting in their judicial capacity.

Article 46   Tasks

1. Each Member State shall provide, on its territory, for each supervisory authority to:

(a) monitor and enforce the application of the provisions adopted pursuant to this Directive and its implementing measures;

(b) promote public awareness and understanding of the risks, rules, safeguards and rights in relation to processing;

(c) advise, in accordance with Member State law, the national parliament, the government and other institutions and bodies on legislative and administrative measures relating to the protection of natural persons' rights and freedoms with regard to processing;

(d) promote the awareness of controllers and processors of their obligations under this Directive;

(e) upon request, provide information to any data subject concerning the exercise of their rights under this Directive and, if appropriate, cooperate with the supervisory authorities in other Member States to that end;

(f) deal with complaints lodged by a data subject, or by a body, organisation or association in accordance with Article 55, and investigate, to the extent appropriate, the subject-matter of the complaint and inform the complainant of the progress and the outcome of the investigation within a reasonable period, in particular if further investigation or coordination with another supervisory authority is necessary;

(g) check the lawfulness of processing pursuant to Article 17, and inform the data subject within a reasonable period of the outcome of the check pursuant to paragraph 3 of that Article or of the reasons why the check has not been carried out;

(h) cooperate with, including by sharing information, and provide mutual assistance to other supervisory authorities, with a view to ensuring the consistency of application and enforcement of this Directive;

(i) conduct investigations on the application of this Directive, including on the basis of information received from another supervisory authority or other public authority;

(j) monitor relevant developments insofar as they have an impact on the protection of personal data, in particular the development of information and communication technologies;

(k) provide advice on the processing operations referred to in Article 28; and

(l) contribute to the activities of the Board.

2.   Each supervisory authority shall facilitate the submission of complaints referred to in point (f) of paragraph 1 by measures such as providing a complaint submission form which can also be completed electronically, without excluding other means of communication.

3.   The performance of the tasks of each supervisory authority shall be free of charge for the data subject and for the data protection officer.

4.   Where a request is manifestly unfounded or excessive, in particular because it is repetitive, the supervisory authority may charge a reasonable fee based on its administrative costs, or may refuse to act on the request. The supervisory authority shall bear the burden of demonstrating that the request is manifestly unfounded or excessive.

Article 47   Powers

1.   Each Member State shall provide by law for each supervisory authority to have effective investigative powers. Those powers shall include at least the power to obtain from the controller and the processor access to all personal data that are being processed and to all

information necessary for the performance of its tasks.

2. Each Member State shall provide by law for each supervisory authority to have effective corrective powers such as, for example:

    (a) to issue warnings to a controller or processor that intended processing operations are likely to infringe the provisions adopted pursuant to this Directive;

    (b) to order the controller or processor to bring processing operations into compliance with the provisions adopted pursuant to this Directive, where appropriate, in a specified manner and within a specified period, in particular by ordering the rectification or erasure of personal data or restriction of processing pursuant to Article 16;

    (c) to impose a temporary or definitive limitation, including a ban, on processing.

3. Each Member State shall provide by law for each supervisory authority to have effective advisory powers to advise the controller in accordance with the prior consultation procedure referred to in Article 28 and to issue, on its own initiative or on request, opinions to its national parliament and its government or, in accordance with its national law, to other institutions and bodies as well as to the public on any issue related to the protection of personal data.

4. The exercise of the powers conferred on the supervisory authority pursuant to this Article shall be subject to appropriate safeguards, including effective judicial remedy and due process, as set out in Union and Member State law in accordance with the Charter.

5. Each Member State shall provide by law for each supervisory authority to have the power to bring infringements of provisions adopted pursuant to this Directive to the attention of judicial authorities and, where appropriate, to commence or otherwise engage in legal proceedings, in order to enforce the provisions adopted pursuant to this Directive.

Article 48   Reporting of infringements

Member States shall provide for competent authorities to put in place effective mechanisms to encourage confidential reporting of infringements of this Directive.

Article 49   Activity reports

Each supervisory authority shall draw up an annual report on its activities, which may include a list of types of infringement notified and types of penalties imposed. Those reports shall be transmitted to the national parliament, the government and other authorities as designated by Member State law. They shall be made available to the public, the Commission and the Board.

CHAPTER VII – COOPERATION

Article 50   Mutual assistance

1. Each Member State shall provide for their supervisory authorities to provide each other with relevant information and mutual assistance in order to implement and apply this Directive in a consistent manner, and to put in place measures for effective cooperation with one another. Mutual assistance shall cover, in particular, information requests and supervisory measures, such as requests to carry out consultations, inspections and investigations.

2. Each Member States shall provide for each supervisory authority to take all appropriate measures required to reply to a request of another supervisory authority without undue

delay and no later than one month after receiving the request. Such measures may include, in particular, the transmission of relevant information on the conduct of an investigation.

3. Requests for assistance shall contain all the necessary information, including the purpose of and reasons for the request. Information exchanged shall be used only for the purpose for which it was requested.

4. The requested supervisory authority shall not refuse to comply with the request unless:
   (a) it is not competent for the subject-matter of the request or for the measures it is requested to execute; or
   (b) compliance with the request would infringe this Directive or Union or Member State law to which the supervisory authority receiving the request is subject.

5. The requested supervisory authority shall inform the requesting supervisory authority of the results or, as the case may be, of the progress of the measures taken in order to respond to the request. The requested supervisory authority shall provide reasons for any refusal to comply with a request pursuant to paragraph 4.

6. Requested supervisory authorities shall, as a rule, supply the information requested by other supervisory authorities by electronic means, using a standardised format.

7. Requested supervisory authorities shall not charge a fee for any action taken by them pursuant to a request for mutual assistance. Supervisory authorities may agree on rules to indemnify each other for specific expenditure arising from the provision of mutual assistance in exceptional circumstances.

8. The Commission may, by means of implementing acts, specify the format and procedures for mutual assistance referred to in this Article and the arrangements for the exchange of information by electronic means between supervisory authorities, and between supervisory authorities and the Board. Those implementing acts shall be adopted in accordance with the examination procedure referred to in Article 58(2).

Article 51   Tasks of the Board

1. The Board established by Regulation (EU) 2016/679 shall perform all of the following tasks in relation to processing within the scope of this Directive:
   (a) advise the Commission on any issue related to the protection of personal data in the Union, including on any proposed amendment of this Directive;
   (b) examine, on its own initiative, on request of one of its members or on request of the Commission, any question covering the application of this Directive and issue guidelines, recommendations and best practices in order to encourage consistent application of this Directive;
   (c) draw up guidelines for supervisory authorities concerning the application of measures referred to in Article 47(1) and (3);
   (d) issue guidelines, recommendations and best practices in accordance with point (b) of this subparagraph for establishing personal data breaches and determining the undue delay referred to in Article 30(1) and (2) and for the particular circumstances in which a controller or a processor is required to notify the personal data breach;
   (e) issue guidelines, recommendations and best practices in accordance with point (b) of this subparagraph as to the circumstances in which a personal data breach is likely to result in a high risk to the rights and freedoms of natural persons as

referred to in Article 31(1);

(f) review the practical application of the guidelines, recommendations and best practices referred to in points (b) and (c);

(g) provide the Commission with an opinion for the assessment of the adequacy of the level of protection in a third country, a territory or one or more specified sectors within a third country, or an international organisation, including for the assessment whether such a third country, territory, specified sector, or international organisation no longer ensures an adequate level of protection;

(h) promote the cooperation and the effective bilateral and multilateral exchange of information and best practices between the supervisory authorities;

(i) promote common training programmes and facilitate personnel exchanges between the supervisory authorities and, where appropriate, with the supervisory authorities of third countries or with international organisations;

(j) promote the exchange of knowledge and documentation on data protection law and practice with data protection supervisory authorities worldwide.

With regard to point (g) of the first subparagraph, the Commission shall provide the Board with all necessary documentation, including correspondence with the government of the third country, with the territory or specified sector within that third country, or with the international organisation.

2. Where the Commission requests advice from the Board, it may indicate a time limit, taking into account the urgency of the matter.

3. The Board shall forward its opinions, guidelines, recommendations and best practices to the Commission and to the committee referred to in Article 58(1) and make them public.

4. The Commission shall inform the Board of the action it has taken following opinions, guidelines, recommendations and best practices issued by the Board.

CHAPTER VIII – REMEDIES, LIABILITY AND PENALTIES

Article 52   Right to lodge a complaint with a supervisory authority

1. Without prejudice to any other administrative or judicial remedy, Member States shall provide for every data subject to have the right to lodge a complaint with a single supervisory authority, if the data subject considers that the processing of personal data relating to him or her infringes provisions adopted pursuant to this Directive.

2. Member States shall provide for the supervisory authority with which the complaint has been lodged to transmit it to the competent supervisory authority, without undue delay if the complaint is not lodged with the supervisory authority that is competent pursuant to Article 45(1). The data subject shall be informed about the transmission.

3. Member States shall provide for the supervisory authority with which the complaint has been lodged to provide further assistance on request of the data subject.

4. The data subject shall be informed by the competent supervisory authority of the progress and the outcome of the complaint, including of the possibility of a judicial remedy pursuant to Article 53.

Article 53   Right to an effective judicial remedy against a supervisory authority

1. Without prejudice to any other administrative or non-judicial remedy, Member States

shall provide for the right of a natural or legal person to an effective judicial remedy against a legally binding decision of a supervisory authority concerning them.

2. Without prejudice to any other administrative or non-judicial remedy, each data subject shall have the right to an effective judicial remedy where the supervisory authority which is competent pursuant to Article 45(1) does not handle a complaint or does not inform the data subject within three months of the progress or outcome of the complaint lodged pursuant to Article 52.

3. Member States shall provide for proceedings against a supervisory authority to be brought before the courts of the Member State where the supervisory authority is established.

Article 54 Right to an effective judicial remedy against a controller or processor

Without prejudice to any available administrative or non-judicial remedy, including the right to lodge a complaint with a supervisory authority pursuant to Article 52, Member States shall provide for the right of a data subject to an effective judicial remedy where he or she considers that his or her rights laid down in provisions adopted pursuant to this Directive have been infringed as a result of the processing of his or her personal data in non-compliance with those provisions.

Article 55 Representation of data subjects

Member States shall, in accordance with Member State procedural law, provide for the data subject to have the right to mandate a not-for-profit body, organisation or association which has been properly constituted in accordance with Member State law, has statutory objectives which are in the public interest and is active in the field of protection of data subject's rights and freedoms with regard to the protection of their personal data to lodge the complaint on his or her behalf and to exercise the rights referred to in Articles 52, 53 and 54 on his or her behalf.

Article 56 Right to compensation

Member States shall provide for any person who has suffered material or non-material damage as a result of an unlawful processing operation or of any act infringing national provisions adopted pursuant to this Directive to have the right to receive compensation for the damage suffered from the controller or any other authority competent under Member State law.

Article 57 Penalties

Member States shall lay down the rules on penalties applicable to infringements of the provisions adopted pursuant to this Directive and shall take all measures necessary to ensure that they are implemented. The penalties provided for shall be effective, proportionate and dissuasive.

CHAPTER IX – IMPLEMENTING ACTS

Article 58 Committee procedure

1. The Commission shall be assisted by the committee established by Article 93 of Regulation (EU) 2016/679. That committee shall be a committee within the meaning of Regulation (EU) No 182/2011.

2. Where reference is made to this paragraph, Article 5 of Regulation (EU) No 182/2011 shall apply.

3. Where reference is made to this paragraph, Article 8 of Regulation (EU) No 182/2011, in conjunction with Article 5 thereof, shall apply.

CHAPTER X – FINAL PROVISIONS

Article 59   Repeal of Framework Decision 2008/977/JHA

1. Framework Decision 2008/977/JHA is repealed with effect from 6 May 2018.

2. References to the repealed Decision referred to in paragraph 1 shall be construed as references to this Directive.

Article 60   Union legal acts already in force

The specific provisions for the protection of personal data in Union legal acts that entered into force on or before 6 May 2016 in the field of judicial cooperation in criminal matters and police cooperation, which regulate processing between Member States and the access of designated authorities of Member States to information systems established pursuant to the Treaties within the scope of this Directive, shall remain unaffected.

Article 61   Relationship with previously concluded international agreements in the field of judicial cooperation in criminal matters and police cooperation

International agreements involving the transfer of personal data to third countries or international organisations which were concluded by Member States prior to 6 May 2016 and which comply with Union law as applicable prior to that date shall remain in force until amended, replaced or revoked.

Article 62   Commission reports

1. By 6 May 2022, and every four years thereafter, the Commission shall submit a report on the evaluation and review of this Directive to the European Parliament and to the Council. The reports shall be made public.

2. In the context of the evaluations and reviews referred to in paragraph 1, the Commission shall examine, in particular, the application and functioning of Chapter V on the transfer of personal data to third countries or international organisations with particular regard to decisions adopted pursuant to Article 36(3) and Article 39.

3. For the purposes of paragraphs 1 and 2, the Commission may request information from Member States and supervisory authorities.

4. In carrying out the evaluations and reviews referred to in paragraphs 1 and 2, the Commission shall take into account the positions and findings of the European Parliament, of the Council and of other relevant bodies or sources.

5. The Commission shall, if necessary, submit appropriate proposals with a view to amending this Directive, in particular taking account of developments in information technology and in the light of the state of progress in the information society.

6. By 6 May 2019, the Commission shall review other legal acts adopted by the Union which regulate processing by the competent authorities for the purposes set out in Article 1(1) including those referred to in Article 60, in order to assess the need to align them with this

Directive and to make, where appropriate, the necessary proposals to amend those acts to ensure a consistent approach to the protection of personal data within the scope of this Directive.

Article 63   Transposition

1.   Member States shall adopt and publish, by 6 May 2018, the laws, regulations and administrative provisions necessary to comply with this Directive. They shall forthwith notify to the Commission the text of those provisions. They shall apply those provisions from 6 May 2018.

When Member States adopt those provisions, they shall contain a reference to this Directive or shall be accompanied by such a reference on the occasion of their official publication. Member States shall determine how such reference is to be made.

2.   By way of derogation from paragraph 1, a Member State may provide, exceptionally, where it involves disproportionate effort, for automated processing systems set up before 6 May 2016 to be brought into conformity with Article 25(1) by 6 May 2023.

3.   By way of derogation from paragraphs 1 and 2 of this Article, a Member State may, in exceptional circumstances, bring an automated processing system as referred to in paragraph 2 of this Article into conformity with Article 25(1) within a specified period after the period referred to in paragraph 2 of this Article, if it would otherwise cause serious difficulties for the operation of that particular automated processing system. The Member State concerned shall notify the Commission of the grounds for those serious difficulties and the grounds for the specified period within which it shall bring that particular automated processing system into conformity with Article 25(1). The specified period shall in any event not be later than 6 May 2026.

4.   Member States shall communicate to the Commission the text of the main provisions of national law which they adopt in the field covered by this Directive.

Article 64   Entry into force

This Directive shall enter into force on the day following that of its publication in the Official Journal of the European Union.

Article 65   Addressees

This Directive is addressed to the Member States.

Done at Brussels, 27 April 2016.

For the European Parliament
The President
M SCHULZ

For the Council
The President
J A HENNIS-PLASSCHAERT

Convention for the Protection of Individuals with regard to Automatic Processing of Personal Data

Strasbourg, 28.I.1981

Preamble

The member States of the Council of Europe, signatory hereto,

Considering that the aim of the Council of Europe is to achieve greater unity between its members, based in particular on respect for the rule of law, as well as human rights and fundamental freedoms;

Considering that it is desirable to extend the safeguards for everyone's rights and fundamental freedoms, and in particular the right to the respect for privacy, taking account of the increasing flow across frontiers of personal data undergoing automatic processing;

Reaffirming at the same time their commitment to freedom of information regardless of frontiers;

Recognising that it is necessary to reconcile the fundamental values of the respect for privacy and the free flow of information between peoples,

Have agreed as follows:

Chapter I – General provisions

Article 1 – Object and purpose

The purpose of this Convention is to secure in the territory of each Party for every individual, whatever his nationality or residence, respect for his rights and fundamental freedoms, and in particular his right to privacy, with regard to automatic processing of personal data relating to him ("data protection").

Article 2 – Definitions

For the purposes of this Convention:

    a   "personal data" means any information relating to an identified or identifiable individual ("data subject");

    b   "automated data file" means any set of data undergoing automatic processing;

    c   "automatic processing" includes the following operations if carried out in whole or in part by automated means: storage of data, carrying out of logical and/or arithmetical operations on those data, their alteration, erasure, retrieval or dissemination;

    d   "controller of the file" means the natural or legal person, public authority, agency or any other body who is competent according to the national law to decide what should be the purpose of the automated data file, which categories of personal data should be stored and which operations should be applied to them.

Article 3 – Scope

1   The Parties undertake to apply this Convention to automated personal data files and automatic processing of personal data in the public and private sectors.

2   Any State may, at the time of signature or when depositing its instrument of ratification, acceptance, approval or accession, or at any later time, give notice by a declaration

addressed to the Secretary General of the Council of Europe:

    a   that it will not apply this Convention to certain categories of automated personal data files, a list of which will be deposited. In this list it shall not include, however, categories of automated data files subject under its domestic law to data protection provisions. Consequently, it shall amend this list by a new declaration whenever additional categories of automated personal data files are subjected to data protection provisions under its domestic law;

    b   that it will also apply this Convention to information relating to groups of persons, associations, foundations, companies, corporations and any other bodies consisting directly or indirectly of individuals, whether or not such bodies possess legal personality;

    c   hat it will also apply this Convention to personal data files which are not processed automatically.

3   Any State which has extended the scope of this Convention by any of the declarations provided for in sub-paragraph 2.b or c above may give notice in the said declaration that such extensions shall apply only to certain categories of personal data files, a list of which will be deposited.

4   Any Party which has excluded certain categories of automated personal data files by a declaration provided for in sub-paragraph 2.a above may not claim the application of this Convention to such categories by a Party which has not excluded them.

5   Likewise, a Party which has not made one or other of the extensions provided for in subparagraphs 2.b and c above may not claim the application of this Convention on these points with respect to a Party which has made such extensions.

6   The declarations provided for in paragraph 2 above shall take effect from the moment of the entry into force of the Convention with regard to the State which has made them if they have been made at the time of signature or deposit of its instrument of ratification, acceptance, approval or accession, or three months after their receipt by the Secretary General of the Council of Europe if they have been made at any later time. These declarations may be withdrawn, in whole or in part, by a notification addressed to the Secretary General of the Council of Europe. Such withdrawals shall take effect three months after the date of receipt of such notification.

Chapter II – Basic principles for data protection

Article 4 – Duties of the Parties

1   Each Party shall take the necessary measures in its domestic law to give effect to the basic principles for data protection set out in this chapter.

2   These measures shall be taken at the latest at the time of entry into force of this Convention in respect of that Party.

Article 5 – Quality of data

Personal data undergoing automatic processing shall be:

    a   obtained and processed fairly and lawfully;

    b   stored for specified and legitimate purposes and not used in a way incompatible with those purposes;

c   adequate, relevant and not excessive in relation to the purposes for which they are stored;

d   accurate and, where necessary, kept up to date;

e   preserved in a form which permits identification of the data subjects for no longer than is required for the purpose for which those data are stored.

Article 6 – Special categories of data

Personal data revealing racial origin, political opinions or religious or other beliefs, as well as personal data concerning health or sexual life, may not be processed automatically unless domestic law provides appropriate safeguards. The same shall apply to personal data relating to criminal convictions.

Article 7 – Data security

Appropriate security measures shall be taken for the protection of personal data stored in automated data files against accidental or unauthorised destruction or accidental loss as well as against unauthorised access, alteration or dissemination.

Article 8 – Additional safeguards for the data subject

Any person shall be enabled:

a   to establish the existence of an automated personal data file, its main purposes, as well as the identity and habitual residence or principal place of business of the controller of the file;

b   to obtain at reasonable intervals and without excessive delay or expense confirmation of whether personal data relating to him are stored in the automated data file as well as communication to him of such data in an intelligible form;

c   to obtain, as the case may be, rectification or erasure of such data if these have been processed contrary to the provisions of domestic law giving effect to the basic principles set out in Articles 5 and 6 of this Convention;

d   to have a remedy if a request for confirmation or, as the case may be, communication, rectification or erasure as referred to in paragraphs b and c of this article is not complied with.

Article 9 – Exceptions and restrictions

1   No exception to the provisions of Articles 5, 6 and 8 of this Convention shall be allowed except within the limits defined in this article.

2   Derogation from the provisions of Articles 5, 6 and 8 of this Convention shall be allowed when such derogation is provided for by the law of the Party and constitutes a necessary measure in a democratic society in the interests of:

a   protecting State security, public safety, the monetary interests of the State or the suppression of criminal offences;

b   protecting the data subject or the rights and freedoms of others.

3   Restrictions on the exercise of the rights specified in Article 8, paragraphs b, c and d, may be provided by law with respect to automated personal data files used for statistics or for scientific research purposes when there is obviously no risk of an infringement of the privacy of the data subjects.

Article 10 – Sanctions and remedies

Each Party undertakes to establish appropriate sanctions and remedies for violations of provisions of domestic law giving effect to the basic principles for data protection set out in this chapter.

Article 11 – Extended protection

None of the provisions of this chapter shall be interpreted as limiting or otherwise affecting the possibility for a Party to grant data subjects a wider measure of protection than that stipulated in this Convention.

Chapter III – Transborder data flows

Article 12 – Transborder flows of personal data and domestic law

1   The following provisions shall apply to the transfer across national borders, by whatever medium, of personal data undergoing automatic processing or collected with a view to their being automatically processed.

2   A Party shall not, for the sole purpose of the protection of privacy, prohibit or subject to special authorisation transborder flows of personal data going to the territory of another Party. 3 Nevertheless, each Party shall be entitled to derogate from the provisions of paragraph 2:
     a   insofar as its legislation includes specific regulations for certain categories of personal data or of automated personal data files, because of the nature of those data or those files, except where the regulations of the other Party provide an equivalent protection;
     b   when the transfer is made from its territory to the territory of a non-Contracting State through the intermediary of the territory of another Party, in order to avoid such transfers resulting in circumvention of the legislation of the Party referred to at the beginning of this paragraph.

Chapter IV – Mutual assistance

Article 13 – Co-operation between Parties

1   The Parties agree to render each other mutual assistance in order to implement this Convention.

2   For that purpose:
     a   each Party shall designate one or more authorities, the name and address of each of which it shall communicate to the Secretary General of the Council of Europe;
     b   each Party which has designated more than one authority shall specify in its communication referred to in the previous sub-paragraph the competence of each authority.

3   An authority designated by a Party shall at the request of an authority designated by another Party:
     a   furnish information on its law and administrative practice in the field of data protection;
     b   take, in conformity with its domestic law and for the sole purpose of protection of privacy, all appropriate measures for furnishing factual information relating to specific automatic processing carried out in its territory, with the exception

however of the personal data being processed.

Article 14 – Assistance to data subjects resident abroad

1 Each Party shall assist any person resident abroad to exercise the rights conferred by its domestic law giving effect to the principles set out in Article 8 of this Convention.

2 When such a person resides in the territory of another Party he shall be given the option of submitting his request through the intermediary of the authority designated by that Party.

3 The request for assistance shall contain all the necessary particulars, relating inter alia to:
   a   the name, address and any other relevant particulars identifying the person making the request;
   b   the automated personal data file to which the request pertains, or its controller;
   c   the purpose of the request.

Article 15 – Safeguards concerning assistance rendered by designated authorities

1 An authority designated by a Party which has received information from an authority designated by another Party either accompanying a request for assistance or in reply to its own request for assistance shall not use that information for purposes other than those specified in the request for assistance.

2 Each Party shall see to it that the persons belonging to or acting on behalf of the designated authority shall be bound by appropriate obligations of secrecy or confidentiality with regard to that information.

3 In no case may a designated authority be allowed to make under Article 14, paragraph 2, a request for assistance on behalf of a data subject resident abroad, of its own accord and without the express consent of the person concerned.

Article 16 – Refusal of requests for assistance

A designated authority to which a request for assistance is addressed under Articles 13 or 14 of this Convention may not refuse to comply with it unless:
   a   the request is not compatible with the powers in the field of data protection of the authorities responsible for replying;
   b   the request does not comply with the provisions of this Convention;
   c   compliance with the request would be incompatible with the sovereignty, security or public policy (ordre public) of the Party by which it was designated, or with the rights and fundamental freedoms of persons under the jurisdiction of that Party.

Article 17 – Costs and procedures of assistance

1 Mutual assistance which the Parties render each other under Article 13 and assistance they render to data subjects abroad under Article 14 shall not give rise to the payment of any costs or fees other than those incurred for experts and interpreters. The latter costs or fees shall be borne by the Party which has designated the authority making the request for assistance.

2 The data subject may not be charged costs or fees in connection with the steps taken on his behalf in the territory of another Party other than those lawfully payable by residents of that Party.

3   Other details concerning the assistance relating in particular to the forms and procedures and the languages to be used, shall be established directly between the Parties concerned.

Chapter V – Consultative Committee

Article 18 – Composition of the committee

1   A Consultative Committee shall be set up after the entry into force of this Convention.

2   Each Party shall appoint a representative to the committee and a deputy representative. Any member State of the Council of Europe which is not a Party to the Convention shall have the right to be represented on the committee by an observer.

3   The Consultative Committee may, by unanimous decision, invite any non-member State of the Council of Europe which is not a Party to the Convention to be represented by an observer at a given meeting.

Article 19 – Functions of the committee

The Consultative Committee:

    a   may make proposals with a view to facilitating or improving the application of the Convention;

    b   may make proposals for amendment of this Convention in accordance with Article 21;

    c   shall formulate its opinion on any proposal for amendment of this Convention which is referred to it in accordance with Article 21, paragraph 3;

    d   may, at the request of a Party, express an opinion on any question concerning the application of this Convention.

Article 20 – Procedure

1   The Consultative Committee shall be convened by the Secretary General of the Council of Europe. Its first meeting shall be held within twelve months of the entry into force of this Convention. It shall subsequently meet at least once every two years and in any case when one-third of the representatives of the Parties request its convocation.

2   A majority of representatives of the Parties shall constitute a quorum for a meeting of the Consultative Committee.

3   After each of its meetings, the Consultative Committee shall submit to the Committee of Ministers of the Council of Europe a report on its work and on the functioning of the Convention.

4   Subject to the provisions of this convention, the Consultative Committee shall draw up its own Rules of Procedure.

Chapter VI – Amendments

Article 21 – Amendments

1   Amendments to this Convention may be proposed by a Party, the Committee of Ministers of the Council of Europe or the Consultative Committee.

2   Any proposal for amendment shall be communicated by the Secretary General of the Council of Europe to the member States of the Council of Europe and to every non-member State which has acceded to or has been invited to accede to this Convention in accordance with the provisions of Article 23.

3   Moreover, any amendment proposed by a Party or the Committee of Ministers shall be communicated to the Consultative Committee, which shall submit to the Committee of Ministers its opinion on that proposed amendment.

4   The Committee of Ministers shall consider the proposed amendment and any opinion submitted by the Consultative Committee and may approve the amendment.

5   The text of any amendment approved by the Committee of Ministers in accordance with paragraph 4 of this article shall be forwarded to the Parties for acceptance.

6   Any amendment approved in accordance with paragraph 4 of this article shall come into force on the thirtieth day after all Parties have informed the Secretary General of their acceptance thereof.

Chapter VII – Final clauses

Article 22 – Entry into force

1   This Convention shall be open for signature by the member States of the Council of Europe. It is subject to ratification, acceptance or approval. Instruments of ratification, acceptance or approval shall be deposited with the Secretary General of the Council of Europe.

2   This Convention shall enter into force on the first day of the month following the expiration of a period of three months after the date on which five member States of the Council of Europe have expressed their consent to be bound by the Convention in accordance with the provisions of the preceding paragraph.

3   In respect of any member State which subsequently expresses its consent to be bound by it, the Convention shall enter into force on the first day of the month following the expiration of a period of three months after the date of deposit of the instrument of ratification, acceptance or approval.

Article 23 – Accession by non-member States

1   After the entry into force of this Convention, the Committee of Ministers of the Council of Europe may invite any State not a member of the Council of Europe to accede to this Convention by a decision taken by the majority provided for in Article 20.d of the Statute of the Council of Europe and by the unanimous vote of the representatives of the Contracting States entitled to sit on the committee.

2   In respect of any acceding State, the Convention shall enter into force on the first day of the month following the expiration of a period of three months after the date of deposit of the instrument of accession with the Secretary General of the Council of Europe.

Article 24 – Territorial clause

1   Any State may at the time of signature or when depositing its instrument of ratification,

acceptance, approval or accession, specify the territory or territories to which this Convention shall apply.

2   Any State may at any later date, by a declaration addressed to the Secretary General of the Council of Europe, extend the application of this Convention to any other territory specified in the declaration. In respect of such territory the Convention shall enter into force on the first day of the month following the expiration of a period of three months after the date of receipt of such declaration by the Secretary General.

3   Any declaration made under the two preceding paragraphs may, in respect of any territory specified in such declaration, be withdrawn by a notification addressed to the Secretary General. The withdrawal shall become effective on the first day of the month following the expiration of a period of six months after the date of receipt of such notification by the Secretary General.

Article 25 – Reservations

No reservation may be made in respect of the provisions of this Convention.

Article 26 – Denunciation

1   Any Party may at any time denounce this Convention by means of a notification addressed to the Secretary General of the Council of Europe.

2   Such denunciation shall become effective on the first day of the month following the expiration of a period of six months after the date of receipt of the notification by the Secretary General.

Article 27 – Notifications

The Secretary General of the Council of Europe shall notify the member States of the Council and any State which has acceded to this Convention of

a   any signature;

b   the deposit of any instrument of ratification, acceptance, approval or accession;

c   any date of entry into force of this Convention in accordance with Articles 22, 23 and 24;

d   any other act, notification or communication relating to this Convention.

In witness whereof the undersigned, being duly authorised thereto, have signed this Convention.

Done at Strasbourg, the 28th day of January 1981, in English and in French, both texts being equally authoritative, in a single copy which shall remain deposited in the archives of the Council of Europe. The Secretary General of the Council of Europe shall transmit certified copies to each member State of the Council of Europe and to any State invited to accede to this Convention.

Modernised Convention regarding Automatic Processing of Personal Data (2018)

*being the Convention regarding Automatic Processing of Personal Data (1981)
as amended by Protocol adopted by Committee of Ministers on 18 May 2018
and opened for signature on 10 October 2018*[1]

Preamble

The member States of the Council of Europe, and the other signatories hereto,

Considering that the aim of the Council of Europe is to achieve greater unity between its members, based in particular on respect for the rule of law, as well as human rights and fundamental freedoms;

Considering that it is necessary to secure the human dignity and protection of the human rights and fundamental freedoms of every individual and, given the diversification, intensification and globalisation of data processing and personal data flows, personal autonomy based on a person's right to control of his or her personal data and the processing of such data;

Recalling that the right to protection of personal data is to be considered in respect of its role in society and that it has to be reconciled with other human rights and fundamental freedoms, including freedom of expression;

Considering that this Convention permits account to be taken, in the implementation of the rules laid down therein, of the principle of the right of access to official documents;

Recognising that it is necessary to promote at the global level the fundamental values of respect for privacy and protection of personal data, thereby contributing to the free flow of information between people;

Recognising the interest of a reinforcement of international co-operation between the Parties to the Convention,

Have agreed as follows:

CHAPTER I – GENERAL PROVISIONS

Article 1 – Object and purpose
The purpose of this Convention is to protect every individual, whatever his or her nationality or residence, with regard to the processing of their personal data, thereby contributing to respect for his or her human rights and fundamental freedoms, and in particular the right to privacy.

---

[1] As at 1 February 2020, the Modernised Convention is not in force. It will come into force on ratification by all Parties to Convention 108, or on 11 October 2023 if there are 38 Parties to the Protocol at this date.

Article 2 – Definitions

For the purposes of this Convention:

    a. "personal data" means any information relating to an identified or identifiable individual ("data subject");

    b. "data processing" means any operation or set of operations performed on personal data, such as the collection, storage, preservation, alteration, retrieval, disclosure, making available, erasure, or destruction of, or the carrying out of logical and/or arithmetical operations on such data;

    c. Where automated processing is not used, "data processing" means an operation or set of operations performed upon personal data within a structured set of such data which are accessible or retrievable according to specific criteria;

    d. "controller" means the natural or legal person, public authority, service, agency or any other body which, alone or jointly with others, has decision-making power with respect to data processing;

    e. "recipient" means a natural or legal person, public authority, service, agency or any other body to whom data are disclosed or made available;

    f. "processor" means a natural or legal person, public authority, service, agency or any other body which processes personal data on behalf of the controller.

Article 3 – Scope

1.   Each Party undertakes to apply this Convention to data processing subject to its jurisdiction in the public and private sectors, thereby securing every individual's right to protection of his or her personal data.

2.   This Convention shall not apply to data processing carried out by an individual in the course of purely personal or household activities.

CHAPTER II – BASIC PRINCIPLES FOR THE PROTECTION OF PERSONAL DATA

Article 4 – Duties of the Parties

1.   Each Party shall take the necessary measures in its law to give effect to the provisions of this Convention and secure their effective application.

2.   These measures shall be taken by each Party and shall have come into force by the time of ratification or of accession to this Convention.

3.   Each Party undertakes:

    a. to allow the Convention Committee provided for in Chapter VI to evaluate the effectiveness of the measures it has taken in its law to give effect to the provisions of this Convention; and

    b. to contribute actively to this evaluation process.

Article 5 – Legitimacy of data processing and quality of data

1.   Data processing shall be proportionate in relation to the legitimate purpose pursued and reflect at all stages of the processing a fair balance between all interests concerned, whether public or private, and the rights and freedoms at stake.

2.   Each Party shall provide that data processing can be carried out on the basis of the free, specific, informed and unambiguous consent of the data subject or of some other

legitimate basis laid down by law.

3. Personal data undergoing processing shall be processed lawfully.

4. Personal data undergoing processing shall be:
   a. processed fairly and in a transparent manner;
   b. collected for explicit, specified and legitimate purposes and not processed in a way incompatible with those purposes; further processing for archiving purposes in the public interest, scientific or historical research purposes or statistical purposes is, subject to appropriate safeguards, compatible with those purposes;
   c. adequate, relevant and not excessive in relation to the purposes for which they are processed;
   d. accurate and, where necessary, kept up to date;
   e. preserved in a form which permits identification of data subjects for no longer than is necessary for the purposes for which those data are processed.

Article 6 – Special categories of data

1. The processing of:
   - genetic data;
   - personal data relating to offences, criminal proceedings and convictions, and related security measures;
   - biometric data uniquely identifying a person;
   - personal data for the information they reveal relating to racial or ethnic origin, political opinions, trade-union membership, religious or other beliefs, health or sexual life,

   shall only be allowed where appropriate safeguards are enshrined in law, complementing those of this Convention.

2. Such safeguards shall guard against the risks that the processing of sensitive data may present for the interests, rights and fundamental freedoms of the data subject, notably a risk of discrimination.

Article 7 – Data security

1. Each Party shall provide that the controller, and, where applicable the processor, takes appropriate security measures against risks such as accidental or unauthorised access to, destruction, loss, use, modification or disclosure of personal data.

2. Each Party shall provide that the controller notifies, without delay, at least the competent supervisory authority within the meaning of Article 15 of this Convention, of those data breaches which may seriously interfere with the rights and fundamental freedoms of data subjects.

Article 8 – Transparency of processing

1. Each Party shall provide that the controller informs the data subjects of:
   a. his or her identity and habitual residence or establishment;
   b. the legal basis and the purposes of the intended processing;
   c. the categories of personal data processed;
   d. the recipients or categories of recipients of the personal data, if any; and
   e. the means of exercising the rights set out in Article 9,

   as well as any necessary additional information in order to ensure fair and transparent processing of the personal data.

2.   Paragraph 1 shall not apply where the data subject already has the relevant information.

3.   Where the personal data are not collected from the data subjects, the controller shall not be required to provide such information where the processing is expressly prescribed by law or this proves to be impossible or involves disproportionate efforts.

Article 9 – Rights of the data subject

1.   Every individual shall have a right:
      a. not to be subject to a decision significantly affecting him or her based solely on an automated processing of data without having his or her views taken into consideration;
      b. to obtain, on request, at reasonable intervals and without excessive delay or expense, confirmation of the processing of personal data relating to him or her, the communication in an intelligible form of the data processed, all available information on their origin, on the preservation period as well as any other information that the controller is required to provide in order to ensure the transparency of processing in accordance with Article 8, paragraph 1;
      c. to obtain, on request, knowledge of the reasoning underlying data processing where the results of such processing are applied to him or her;
      d. to object at any time, on grounds relating to his or her situation, to the processing of personal data concerning him or her unless the controller demonstrates legitimate grounds for the processing which override his or her interests or rights and fundamental freedoms;
      e. to obtain, on request, free of charge and without excessive delay, rectification or erasure, as the case may be, of such data if these are being, or have been, processed contrary to the provisions of this Convention;
      f. to have a remedy under Article 12 where his or her rights under this Convention have been violated;
      g. to benefit, whatever his or her nationality or residence, from the assistance of a supervisory authority within the meaning of Article 15, in exercising his or her rights under this Convention.

2.   Paragraph 1.a shall not apply if the decision is authorised by a law to which the controller is subject and which also lays down suitable measures to safeguard the data subject's rights, freedoms and legitimate interests.

Article 10 – Additional obligations

1.   Each Party shall provide that controllers and, where applicable, processors, take all appropriate measures to comply with the obligations of this Convention and be able to demonstrate, subject to the domestic legislation adopted in accordance with Article 11, paragraph 3, in particular to the competent supervisory authority provided for in Article 15, that the data processing under their control is in compliance with the provisions of this Convention.

2.   Each Party shall provide that controllers and, where applicable, processors, examine the likely impact of intended data processing on the rights and fundamental freedoms of data subjects prior to the commencement of such processing, and shall design the data processing in such a manner as to prevent or minimise the risk of interference with those

rights and fundamental freedoms.

3. Each Party shall provide that controllers, and, where applicable, processors, implement technical and organisational measures which take into account the implications of the right to the protection of personal data at all stages of the data processing.

4. Each Party may, having regard to the risks arising for the interests, rights and fundamental freedoms of the data subjects, adapt the application of the provisions of paragraphs 1, 2 and 3 in the law giving effect to the provisions of this Convention, according to the nature and volume of the data, the nature, scope and purpose of the processing and, where appropriate, the size of the controller or processor.

Article 11 – Exceptions and restrictions

1. No exception to the provisions set out in this Chapter shall be allowed except to the provisions of Article 5 paragraph 4, Article 7 paragraph 2, Article 8 paragraph 1 and Article 9, when such an exception is provided for by law, respects the essence of the fundamental rights and freedoms and constitutes a necessary and proportionate measure in a democratic society for:
   a. the protection of national security, defense, public safety, important economic and financial interests of the State, the impartiality and independence of the judiciary or the prevention, investigation and prosecution of criminal offences and the execution of criminal penalties, and other essential objectives of general public interest;
   b. the protection of the data subject or the rights and fundamental freedoms of others, notably freedom of expression.

2. Restrictions on the exercise of the provisions specified in Articles 8 and 9 may be provided for by law with respect to data processing for archiving purposes in the public interest, scientific or historical research purposes or statistical purposes when there is no recognisable risk of infringement of the rights and fundamental freedoms of data subjects.

3. In addition to the exceptions allowed for in paragraph 1 of this article, with reference to processing activities for national security and defense purposes, each Party may provide, by law and only to the extent that it constitutes a necessary and proportionate measure in a democratic society to fulfill such aim, exceptions to Article 4 paragraph 3, Article 14 paragraphs 5 and 6 and Article 15, paragraph 2, litterae a, b, c and d.
   This is without prejudice to the requirement that processing activities for national security and defense purposes are subject to independent and effective review and supervision under the domestic legislation of the respective Party.

Article 12 – Sanctions and remedies

Each Party undertakes to establish appropriate judicial and non-judicial sanctions and remedies for violations of the provisions of this Convention.

Article 13 – Extended protection

None of the provisions of this chapter shall be interpreted as limiting or otherwise affecting the possibility for a Party to grant data subjects a wider measure of protection than that stipulated in this Convention.

CHAPTER III – TRANSBORDER FLOWS OF PERSONAL DATA

Article 14 – Transborder flows of personal data

1. A Party shall not, for the sole purpose of the protection of personal data, prohibit or subject to special authorisation the transfer of such data to a recipient who is subject to the jurisdiction of another Party to the Convention. Such a Party may, however, do so if there is a real and serious risk that the transfer to another Party, or from that other Party to a non-Party, would lead to circumventing the provisions of the Convention. A Party may also do so, if bound by harmonised rules of protection shared by States belonging to a regional international organisation.

2. When the recipient is subject to the jurisdiction of a State or international organisation which is not Party to this Convention, the transfer of personal data may only take place where an appropriate level of protection based on the provisions of this Convention is secured.

3. An appropriate level of protection can be secured by:
    a. the law of that State or international organisation, including the applicable international treaties or agreements; or
    b. ad hoc or approved standardised safeguards provided by legally-binding and enforceable instruments adopted and implemented by the persons involved in the transfer and further processing.

4. Notwithstanding the provisions of the previous paragraphs, each Party may provide that the transfer of personal data may take place if:
    a. the data subject has given explicit, specific and free consent, after being informed of risks arising in the absence of appropriate safeguards; or
    b. the specific interests of the data subject require it in the particular case; or
    c. prevailing legitimate interests, in particular important public interests, are provided for by law and such transfer constitutes a necessary and proportionate measure in a democratic society; or
    d. it constitutes a necessary and proportionate measure in a democratic society for freedom of expression.
    5. Each Party shall provide that the competent supervisory authority within the meaning of Article 15 of this Convention is provided with all relevant information concerning the transfers of data referred to in paragraph 3.b and, upon request, paragraphs 4.b and 4.c.

6. Each Party shall also provide that the supervisory authority is entitled to request that the person who transfers data demonstrates the effectiveness of the safeguards or the existence of prevailing legitimate interests and that the supervisory authority may, in order to protect the rights and fundamental freedoms of data subjects, prohibit such transfers, suspend them or subject them to condition.

CHAPTER IV – SUPERVISORY AUTHORITIES

Article 15 – Supervisory authorities

1   Each Party shall provide for one or more authorities to be responsible for ensuring compliance with the provisions of this Convention.

2   To this end, such authorities:
   a. shall have powers of investigation and intervention;
   b. shall perform the functions relating to transfers of data provided for under Article 14, notably the approval of standardised safeguards;
   c. shall have powers to issue decisions with respect to violations of the provisions of this Convention and may, in particular, impose administrative sanctions;
   d. shall have the power to engage in legal proceedings or to bring to the attention of the competent judicial authorities violations of the provisions of this Convention;
   e. shall promote:
      i.   public awareness of their functions and powers as well as their activities;
      ii.   public awareness of the rights of data subjects and the exercise of such rights;
      iii. awareness of controllers and processors of their responsibilities under this Convention;
         specific attention shall be given to the data protection rights of children and other vulnerable individuals.

3.   The competent supervisory authorities shall be consulted on proposals for any legislative or administrative measures which provide for the processing of personal data.

4.   Each competent supervisory authority shall deal with requests and complaints lodged by data subjects concerning their data protection rights and shall keep data subjects informed of progress.

5.   The supervisory authorities shall act with complete independence and impartiality in performing their duties and exercising their powers and in doing so shall neither seek nor accept instructions.

6.   Each Party shall ensure that the supervisory authorities are provided with the resources necessary for the effective performance of their functions and exercise of their powers.

7.   Each supervisory authority shall prepare and publish a periodical report outlining its activities.

8.   Members and staff of the supervisory authorities shall be bound by obligations of confidentiality with regard to confidential information to which they have access, or have had access to, in the performance of their duties and exercise of their powers.

9.   Decisions of the supervisory authorities may be subject to appeal through the courts.

10.   The supervisory authorities shall not be competent with respect to processing carried out by bodies when acting in their judicial capacity.

CHAPTER V – CO-OPERATION AND MUTUAL ASSISTANCE

Article 16 – Designation of supervisory authorities

1.   The Parties agree to co-operate and render each other mutual assistance in order to implement this Convention.

2.   For that purpose:
   a. each Party shall designate one or more supervisory authorities within the meaning of Article 15 of this Convention, the name and address of each of which it shall

communicate to the Secretary General of the Council of Europe;

b. each Party which has designated more than one supervisory authority shall specify the competence of each authority in its communication referred to in the previous littera.

Article 17 – Forms of co-operation

1. The supervisory authorities shall co-operate with one another to the extent necessary for the performance of their duties and exercise of their powers, in particular by:

   a. providing mutual assistance by exchanging relevant and useful information and co-operating with each other under the condition that, as regards the protection of personal data, all the rules and safeguards of this Convention are complied with;

   b. co-ordinating their investigations or interventions, or conducting joint actions;

   c. providing information and documentation on their law and administrative practice relating to data protection.

2. The information referred to in paragraph 1 shall not include personal data undergoing processing unless such data are essential for co-operation, or where the data subject concerned has given explicit, specific, free and informed consent to its provision.

3. In order to organise their co-operation and to perform the duties set out in the preceding paragraphs, the supervisory authorities of the Parties shall form a network.

Article 18 – Assistance to data subjects

1. Each Party shall assist any data subject, whatever his or her nationality or residence, to exercise his or her rights under Article 9 of this Convention.

2. Where a data subject resides on the territory of another Party, he or she shall be given the option of submitting the request through the intermediary of the supervisory authority designated by that Party.

3. The request for assistance shall contain all the necessary particulars, relating inter alia to:

   a. the name, address and any other relevant particulars identifying the data subject making the request;

   b. the processing to which the request pertains, or its controller;

   c. the purpose of the request.

Article 19 – Safeguards

1. A supervisory authority which has received information from another supervisory authority, either accompanying a request or in reply to its own request, shall not use that information for purposes other than those specified in the request.

2. In no case may a supervisory authority be allowed to make a request on behalf of a data subject of its own accord and without the express approval of the data subject concerned.

Article 20 – Refusal of requests

A supervisory authority to which a request is addressed under Article 17 of this Convention may not refuse to comply with it unless:

   a. the request is not compatible with its powers;

   b. the request does not comply with the provisions of this Convention;

   c. compliance with the request would be incompatible with the sovereignty, national security or public order of the Party by which it was designated, or with the rights and fundamental freedoms of individuals under the jurisdiction of that Party.

Article 21 – Costs and procedures

1. Co-operation and mutual assistance which the Parties render each other under Article 17 and assistance they render to data subjects under Articles 9 and 18 shall not give rise to the payment of any costs or fees other than those incurred for experts and interpreters. The latter costs or fees shall be borne by the Party making the request.

2. The data subject may not be charged costs or fees in connection with the steps taken on his or her behalf in the territory of another Party other than those lawfully payable by residents of that Party.

3. Other details concerning the co-operation and assistance, relating in particular to the forms and procedures and the languages to be used, shall be established directly between the Parties concerned.

CHAPTER VI – CONVENTION COMMITTEE

Article 22 – Composition of the committee

1. A Convention Committee shall be set up after the entry into force of this Convention.

2. Each Party shall appoint a representative to the committee and a deputy representative. Any member State of the Council of Europe which is not a Party to the Convention shall have the right to be represented on the committee by an observer.

3. The Convention Committee may, by a decision taken by a majority of two-thirds of the representatives of the Parties, invite an observer to be represented at its meetings.

4. Any Party which is not a member of the Council of Europe shall contribute to the funding of the activities of the Convention Committee according to the modalities established by the Committee of Ministers in agreement with that Party.

Article 23 – Functions of the committee

The Convention Committee:
   a. may make recommendations with a view to facilitating or improving the application of the Convention;
   b. may make proposals for amendment of this Convention in accordance with Article 25;
   c. shall formulate its opinion on any proposal for amendment of this Convention which is referred to it in accordance with Article 25, paragraph 3;
   d. may express an opinion on any question concerning the interpretation or application of this Convention;
   e. shall prepare, before any new accession to the Convention, an opinion for the Committee of Ministers relating to the level of personal data protection of the candidate for accession and, where necessary, recommend measures to take to reach compliance with the provisions of this Convention;
   f. may, at the request of a State or an international organisation, evaluate whether the level of personal data protection the former provides is in compliance with the provisions of this Convention and, where necessary, recommend measures to be

taken to reach such compliance;

g. may develop or approve models of standardised safeguards referred to in Article 14;

h. shall review the implementation of this Convention by the Parties and recommend measures to be taken in the case where a Party is not in compliance with this Convention;

i. shall facilitate, where necessary, the friendly settlement of all difficulties related to the application of this Convention.

Article 24 – Procedure

1. The Convention Committee shall be convened by the Secretary General of the Council of Europe. Its first meeting shall be held within twelve months of the entry into force of this Convention. It shall subsequently meet at least once a year, and in any case when one-third of the representatives of the Parties request its convocation.

2. After each of its meetings, the Convention Committee shall submit to the Committee of Ministers of the Council of Europe a report on its work and on the functioning of this Convention.

3. The voting arrangements in the Convention Committee are laid down in the elements for the Rules of Procedure appended to Protocol CETS No. [223].

4. The Convention Committee shall draw up the other elements of its Rules of Procedure and establish, in particular, the procedures for evaluation and review referred to in Article 4, paragraph 3, and Article 23, litterae e, f and h on the basis of objective criteria.

CHAPTER VII – AMENDMENTS

Article 25 – Amendments

1. Amendments to this Convention may be proposed by a Party, the Committee of Ministers of the Council of Europe or the Convention Committee.

2. Any proposal for amendment shall be communicated by the Secretary General of the Council of Europe to the Parties to this Convention, to the other member States of the Council of Europe, to the European Union and to every non-member State or international organisation which has been invited to accede to this Convention in accordance with the provisions of Article 27.

3. Moreover, any amendment proposed by a Party or the Committee of Ministers shall be communicated to the Convention Committee, which shall submit to the Committee of Ministers its opinion on that proposed amendment.

4. The Committee of Ministers shall consider the proposed amendment and any opinion submitted by the Convention Committee and may approve the amendment.

5. The text of any amendment approved by the Committee of Ministers in accordance with paragraph 4 of this article shall be forwarded to the Parties for acceptance.

6. Any amendment approved in accordance with paragraph 4 of this article shall come into force on the thirtieth day after all Parties have informed the Secretary General of their acceptance thereof.

7.   Moreover, the Committee of Ministers may, after consulting the Convention Committee, decide unanimously that a particular amendment shall enter into force at the expiration of a period of three years from the date on which it has been opened to acceptance, unless a Party notifies the Secretary General of the Council of Europe of an objection to its entry into force. If such an objection is notified, the amendment shall enter into force on the first day of the month following the date on which the Party to this Convention which has notified the objection has deposited its instrument of acceptance with the Secretary General of the Council of Europe.

CHAPTER VIII – FINAL CLAUSES

Article 26 – Entry into force

1.   This Convention shall be open for signature by the member States of the Council of Europe and by the European Union. It is subject to ratification, acceptance or approval. Instruments of ratification, acceptance or approval shall be deposited with the Secretary General of the Council of Europe.

2.   This Convention shall enter into force on the first day of the month following the expiration of a period of three months after the date on which five member States of the Council of Europe have expressed their consent to be bound by the Convention in accordance with the provisions of the preceding paragraph.

3.   In respect of any Party which subsequently expresses its consent to be bound by it, the Convention shall enter into force on the first day of the month following the expiration of a period of three months after the date of deposit of the instrument of ratification, acceptance or approval.

Article 27 – Accession by non-member States or international organisations

1.   After the entry into force of this Convention, the Committee of Ministers of the Council of Europe may, after consulting the Parties to this Convention and obtaining their unanimous agreement, and in light of the opinion prepared by the Convention Committee in accordance with Article 23.e, invite any State not a member of the Council of Europe or an international organisation to accede to this Convention by a decision taken by the majority provided for in Article 20.d of the Statute of the Council of Europe and by the unanimous vote of the representatives of the Contracting States entitled to sit on the Committee of Ministers.

2.   In respect of any State or international organisation acceding to this Convention according to paragraph 1 above, the Convention shall enter into force on the first day of the month following the expiration of a period of three months after the date of deposit of the instrument of accession with the Secretary General of the Council of Europe.

Article 28 – Territorial clause

1.   Any State, the European Union or other international organisation may, at the time of signature or when depositing its instrument of ratification, acceptance, approval or accession, specify the territory or territories to which this Convention shall apply.

2.   Any State, the European Union or other international organisation may, at any later date, by a declaration addressed to the Secretary General of the Council of Europe, extend the

application of this Convention to any other territory specified in the declaration. In respect of such territory the Convention shall enter into force on the first day of the month following the expiration of a period of three months after the date of receipt of such declaration by the Secretary General.

3. Any declaration made under the two preceding paragraphs may, in respect of any territory specified in such declaration, be withdrawn by a notification addressed to the Secretary General. The withdrawal shall become effective on the first day of the month following the expiration of a period of six months after the date of receipt of such notification by the Secretary General.

Article 29 – Reservations

No reservation may be made in respect of the provisions of this Convention.

Article 30 – Denunciation

1. Any Party may at any time denounce this Convention by means of a notification addressed to the Secretary General of the Council of Europe.

2. Such denunciation shall become effective on the first day of the month following the expiration of a period of six months after the date of receipt of the notification by the Secretary General.

Article 31 – Notifications

The Secretary General of the Council of Europe shall notify the member States of the Council and any Party to this Convention of:
   a. any signature;
   b. the deposit of any instrument of ratification, acceptance, approval or accession;
   c. any date of entry into force of this Convention in accordance with Articles 26, 27 and 28;
   d. any other act, notification or communication relating to this Convention.

Appendix to the Protocol: Elements for the Rules of Procedure of the Convention Committee

1. Each Party has a right to vote and shall have one vote.

2. A two-thirds majority of representatives of the Parties shall constitute a quorum for the meetings of the Convention Committee. In case the amending Protocol to the Convention enters into force in accordance with its Article 37 (2) before its entry into force in respect of all Contracting States to the Convention, the quorum for the meetings of the Convention Committee shall be no less than 34 Parties to the Protocol.

3. The decisions under Article 23 shall be taken by a four-fifths majority. The decisions pursuant to Article 23 littera h shall be taken by a four-fifths majority, including a majority of the votes of States Parties not members of a regional integration organisation that is a Party to the Convention.

4. Where the Convention Committee takes decisions pursuant to Article 23 littera h, the Party concerned by the review shall not vote. Whenever such a decision concerns a matter falling within the competence of a regional integration organisation, neither the organisation nor its member States shall vote.

5. Decisions concerning procedural issues shall be taken by a simple majority.

6. Regional integration organisations, in matters within their competence, may exercise their right to vote in the Convention Committee, with a number of votes equal to the number of their member States that are Parties to the Convention. Such an organisation shall not exercise its right to vote if any of its member States exercises its right.

7. In case of vote, all Parties must be informed of the subject and time for the vote, as well as whether the vote will be exercised by the Parties individually or by a regional integration organisation on behalf of its member States.

8. The Convention Committee may further amend its rules of procedure by a two-thirds majority, except for the voting arrangements which may only be amended by unanimous vote of the Parties and to which Article 25 of the Convention applies.

OECD

Revised Guidelines Governing the Protection of Privacy and Transborder Flows of Personal Data (2013)

PART ONE – GENERAL

Definitions

1. For the purposes of these Guidelines:
    a) "Data controller" means a party who, according to national law, is competent to decide about the contents and use of personal data regardless of whether or not such data are collected, stored, processed or disseminated by that party or by an agent on its behalf.
    b) "Personal data" means any information relating to an identified or identifiable individual (data subject).
    c) "Laws protecting privacy" means national laws or regulations, the enforcement of which has the effect of protecting personal data consistent with these Guidelines.
    d) "Privacy enforcement authority" means any public body, as determined by each Member country, that is responsible for enforcing laws protecting privacy, and that has powers to conduct investigations or pursue enforcement proceedings.
    e) "Transborder flows of personal data" means movements of personal data across national borders.

Scope of Guidelines

2. These Guidelines apply to personal data, whether in the public or private sectors, which, because of the manner in which they are processed, or because of their nature or the context in which they are used, pose a risk to privacy and individual liberties.

3. The principles in these Guidelines are complementary and should be read as a whole. They should not be interpreted:
    a) as preventing the application of different protective measures to different categories of personal data, depending upon their nature and the context in which they are collected, stored, processed or disseminated; or
    b) in a manner which unduly limits the freedom of expression.

4. Exceptions to these Guidelines, including those relating to national sovereignty, national security and public policy ("ordre public"), should be:
    a) as few as possible, and
    b) made known to the public.

5. In the particular case of federal countries the observance of these Guidelines may be affected by the division of powers in the federation.

6. These Guidelines should be regarded as minimum standards which can be supplemented by additional measures for the protection of privacy and individual liberties, which may impact transborder flows of personal data.

Part Two – Basic Principles of National Application

Collection Limitation Principle

7. There should be limits to the collection of personal data and any such data should be obtained by lawful and fair means and, where appropriate, with the knowledge or consent of the data subject.

Data Quality Principle

8. Personal data should be relevant to the purposes for which they are to be used, and, to the extent necessary for those purposes, should be accurate, complete and kept up-to-date.

Purpose Specification Principle

9. The purposes for which personal data are collected should be specified not later than at the time of data collection and the subsequent use limited to the fulfilment of those purposes or such others as are not incompatible with those purposes and as are specified on each occasion of change of purpose.

Use Limitation Principle

10. Personal data should not be disclosed, made available or otherwise used for purposes other than those specified in accordance with Paragraph 9 except:
    a) with the consent of the data subject; or
    b) by the authority of law.

Security Safeguards Principle

11. Personal data should be protected by reasonable security safeguards against such risks as loss or unauthorised access, destruction, use, modification or disclosure of data.

Openness Principle

12. There should be a general policy of openness about developments, practices and policies with respect to personal data. Means should be readily available of establishing the existence and nature of personal data, and the main purposes of their use, as well as the identity and usual residence of the data controller.

Individual Participation Principle

13. Individuals should have the right:
    a) to obtain from a data controller, or otherwise, confirmation of whether or not the data controller has data relating to them;
    b) to have communicated to them, data relating to them
        i. within a reasonable time;
        ii. at a charge, if any, that is not excessive;
        iii. in a reasonable manner; and
        iv. in a form that is readily intelligible to them;
    c) to be given reasons if a request made under subparagraphs (a) and (b) is denied, and to be able to challenge such denial; and
    d) to challenge data relating to them and, if the challenge is successful to have the data erased, rectified, completed or amended.

Accountability Principle

14. A data controller should be accountable for complying with measures which give effect to

the principles stated above.

PART THREE – IMPLEMENTING ACCOUNTABILITY

15. A data controller should:
    a) Have in place a privacy management programme that:
       i. gives effect to these Guidelines for all personal data under its control;
       ii. is tailored to the structure, scale, volume and sensitivity of its operations;
       iii. provides for appropriate safeguards based on privacy risk assessment;
       iv. is integrated into its governance structure and establishes internal oversight mechanisms;
       v. includes plans for responding to inquiries and incidents;
       vi. is updated in light of ongoing monitoring and periodic assessment;
    b) Be prepared to demonstrate its privacy management programme as appropriate, in particular at the request of a competent privacy enforcement authority or another entity responsible for promoting adherence to a code of conduct or similar arrangement giving binding effect to these Guidelines; and
    c) Provide notice, as appropriate, to privacy enforcement authorities or other relevant authorities where there has been a significant security breach affecting personal data. Where the breach is likely to adversely affect data subjects, a data controller should notify affected data subjects.

PART FOUR – BASIC PRINCIPLES OF INTERNATIONAL APPLICATION: FREE FLOW AND LEGITIMATE RESTRICTIONS

16. A data controller remains accountable for personal data under its control without regard to the location of the data.

17. A Member country should refrain from restricting transborder flows of personal data between itself and another country where (a) the other country substantially observes these Guidelines or (b) sufficient safeguards exist, including effective enforcement mechanisms and appropriate measures put in place by the data controller, to ensure a continuing level of protection consistent with these Guidelines.

18. Any restrictions to transborder flows of personal data should be proportionate to the risks presented, taking into account the sensitivity of the data, and the purpose and context of the processing.

PART FIVE – NATIONAL IMPLEMENTATION

19. In implementing these Guidelines, Member countries should:
    a) develop national privacy strategies that reflect a co-ordinated approach across governmental bodies;
    b) adopt laws protecting privacy;
    c) establish and maintain privacy enforcement authorities with the governance, resources and technical expertise necessary to exercise their powers effectively and to make decisions on an objective, impartial and consistent basis;
    d) encourage and support self-regulation, whether in the form of codes of conduct or otherwise;
    e) provide for reasonable means for individuals to exercise their rights;

f) provide for adequate sanctions and remedies in case of failures to comply with laws protecting privacy;

g) consider the adoption of complementary measures, including education and awareness raising, skills development, and the promotion of technical measures which help to protect privacy;

h) consider the role of actors other than data controllers, in a manner appropriate to their individual role; and

i) ensure that there is no unfair discrimination against data subjects.

PART SIX – INTERNATIONAL CO-OPERATION AND INTEROPERABILITY

20. Member countries should take appropriate measures to facilitate crossborder privacy law enforcement co-operation, in particular by enhancing information sharing among privacy enforcement authorities.

21. Member countries should encourage and support the development of international arrangements that promote interoperability among privacy frameworks that give practical effect to these Guidelines.

22. Member countries should encourage the development of internationally comparable metrics to inform the policy making process related to privacy and transborder flows of personal data.

23. Member countries should make public the details of their observance of these Guidelines.

Data Protection (Charges and Information) Regulations 2018
(SI 2018/480)

Made: 11th April 2018

The Secretary of State makes the following Regulations in exercise of the powers conferred by sections 108(1) and (5) and 110(6) of the Digital Economy Act 2017

The Secretary of State makes these Regulations—
(a) after consultation in accordance with section 109(1) of that Act; and
(b) having regard to the matters specified in section 109(2) of that Act.

In accordance with section 110(2) of that Act, a draft of this instrument was laid before Parliament and approved by a resolution of each House of Parliament.

Citation, commencement and interpretation

1(1)   These Regulations may be cited as the Data Protection (Charges and Information) Regulations 2018 and come into force on 25th May 2018.

(2)   In these Regulations—

"business" includes any trade or profession;

"charge period" has the meaning given in regulation 2(6);

"data controller" means a person who is a controller for the purposes of Parts 5 to 7 of the Data Protection Act 2018 (see section 3(6) and (14) of that Act);

"data controller's financial year" means—
(a)   if the data controller has been in existence for less than 12 months, the period of its existence, or
(b)   in any other case, the most recent financial year of the data controller that ended prior to the first day of the charge period in respect of which information is being provided, or a charge is being paid, pursuant to regulation 2;

"exempt processing" has the meaning given in the Schedule;

"financial year", in paragraph (b) of the definition of "data controller's financial year"—
(a)   in relation to a company, is determined in accordance with section 390 of the Companies Act 2006,
(b)   in relation to a limited liability partnership, is determined in accordance with section 390 of the Companies Act 2006 as applied by regulation 7 of the Limited Liability Partnerships (Accounts and Audit) (Application of Companies Act 2006) Regulations 2008, and
(c)   in relation to any other case, means the period, covering 12 consecutive months, over which a data controller determines income and expenditure;

"member of staff" means any—
(a)   employee,
(b)   worker within the meaning given in section 296 of the Trade Union and Labour Relations (Consolidation) Act 1992,
(c)   office holder, or
(d)   partner;

"number of members of staff" means the number calculated by—

> (a) ascertaining for each completed month of the data controller's financial year the total number of persons who have been members of staff of the data controller in that month,
>
> (b) adding together the monthly totals, and
>
> (c) dividing by the number of months in the data controller's financial year;

"personal data" has the same meaning as in Parts 5 to 7 of the Data Protection Act 2018 (see section 3(2) and (14) of that Act);

"processing", in relation to personal data, means an operation or set of operations which is performed on personal data;

"public authority" means a public authority as defined by the Freedom of Information Act 2000 or a Scottish public authority as defined by the Freedom of Information (Scotland) Act 2002;

"turnover"—

> (a) in relation to a company, has the meaning given in section 474 of the Companies Act 2006,
>
> (b) in relation to a limited liability partnership, has the meaning given in section 474 of the Companies Act 2006 as applied by regulation 32 of the Limited Liability Partnerships (Accounts and Audit) (Application of Companies Act 2006) Regulations 2008, and
>
> (c) in relation to any other case, means the amounts derived by the data controller from the provision of goods and services falling within the data controller's ordinary activities, after deduction of—
>
> > (i) trade discounts,
> >
> > (ii) value added tax, and
> >
> > (iii) any other taxes based on the amounts so derived.

"Data controller" for the purposes of these Regulations is defined by s.108(8) of the Digital Economy Act 2017.

Requirements on data controllers

2(1) A data controller must comply with the requirements of this regulation unless all of the processing of personal data they undertake is exempt processing.

(2) Within the first 21 days of each charge period a data controller must pay a charge to the Information Commissioner, determined in accordance with regulation 3.

(3) Within the first 21 days of each charge period a data controller must provide to the Information Commissioner the following information, as of the first day of each charge period—

(a) the name and address of the data controller;

(b) whether the number of members of staff of the data controller is—
> (i) less than or equal to 10,
> (ii) greater than 10 but less than or equal to 250, or
> (iii) greater than 250;

(c) whether the turnover for the data controller's financial year is—
> (i) less than or equal to £632,000,
> (ii) greater than £632,000 but less than or equal to £36 million, or
> (iii) greater than £36 million; and

(d) whether the data controller is a public authority.

(4) Paragraph (3)(c) does not apply to a data controller that is a public authority.

(5)   For the purposes of paragraph (3)(a)—
    (a) the address of a registered company is that of its registered office, and
    (b) the address of a person (other than a registered company) carrying on a business
       is that of the person's principal place of business in the UK.

(6)   In this regulation—
    "charge period" means—
       (a) for a person who is a data controller immediately before 25th May 2018
          and has paid a fee pursuant to section 18(5) or 19(4) of the Data Protection
          Act 1998—
            (i) the period of 12 months beginning on the date which is 12
               months after the date on which that fee was most recently
               received by the Information Commissioner, and
            (ii) each subsequent period of 12 months;
       (b) for a person who is a data controller immediately before 25th May 2018 but
          has not paid a fee pursuant to section 18(5) or 19(4) of the Data Protection
          Act 1998—
            (i) the period of 12 months beginning on 25th May 2018, and
            (ii) each subsequent period of 12 months; or
       (c) for a person who becomes a data controller on or after 25th May 2018—
            (i) the period of 12 months beginning on the date on which the
               person becomes a data controller, and
            (ii) each subsequent period of 12 months;
    "registered company" means a company registered under the Companies Acts as
    defined by section 2(1) of the Companies Act 2006.

Amount of charge payable under regulation 2

3(1)   For the purposes of regulation 2(2), the charge payable by a data controller in—
    (a) tier 1 (micro organisations), is £40;
    (b) tier 2 (small and medium organisations), is £60;
    (c) tier 3 (large organisations), is £2,900.

(2)   For the purposes of this regulation, a data controller is, subject to paragraph (3)—
    (a) in tier 1 if—
       (i) it has a turnover of less than or equal to £632,000 for the data controller's
         financial year,
       (ii) the number of members of staff of the data controller is less than or equal
         to 10,
       (iii) it is a charity, or
       (iv) it is a small occupational pension scheme;
    (b) in tier 2 if it is not in tier 1 and—
       (i) it has a turnover of less than or equal to £36 million for the data controller's
         financial year, or
       (ii) the number of members of staff of the data controller is less than or equal
         to 250;
    (c) in tier 3 if it is not in tier 1 or tier 2.

(3)   Paragraphs (2)(a)(i) and (2)(b)(i) are to be disregarded in relation to a public authority.

(4)   For the purposes of regulation 3(2), the turnover and number of members of staff is
determined on the first day of the charge period to which the charge relates.

(5)   The applicable charge in paragraph (1) is reduced by £5.00 for a data controller that makes payment of the charge by direct debit.

(6)   In this regulation—

"charity"—

    (i)   in relation to England and Wales, has the meaning given in section 1 of the Charities Act 2011,

    (ii)   in relation to Scotland, means a body entered in the Scottish Charity Register maintained under section 3 of the Charity and Trustee Investment (Scotland) Act 2005 , and

    (iii)   in relation to Northern Ireland, has the meaning given in section 1 of the Charities Act (Northern Ireland) 2008 ;

"small occupational pension scheme" has the meaning given in regulation 4 of the Occupational and Personal Pension Schemes (Consultation by Employers and Miscellaneous Amendment) Regulations 2006.

Requirements in respect of partnerships

4(1)   In any case in which two or more persons carrying on a business in partnership are the data controllers in respect of personal data for the purposes of that business, the requirements of regulation 2 may be satisfied in respect of those persons in the name of the firm.

(2)   Where the requirements of regulation 2 are satisfied in the name of a firm under paragraph (1) above—

    (a) the name to be specified for the purposes of regulation 2(3)(a) is the name of that firm, and

    (b) the address to be specified for the purposes of regulation 2(3)(a) is the address of that firm's principal place of business.

(3)   For the purposes of regulations 2 and 3, references to the turnover and number of members of staff of a data controller which is a partnership are references to the turnover and number of members of staff of the firm as a whole.

Requirements in respect of the governing body of, and head teacher at, any school

5(1)   In any case in which a governing body of a school and a head teacher at a school are both data controllers for the purposes of that school, the requirements of regulation 2 may be satisfied in respect of that governing body and head teacher in the name of the school.

(2)   Where the requirements of regulation 2 are satisfied in the name of a school under paragraph (1) above, the name and address to be specified for the purposes of regulation 2(3)(a) are those of the school.

(3)   For the purposes of this regulation, in the definition of "number of members of staff" in regulation 1(2) any reference to a data controller is to be treated as a reference to the school.

(4)   In this regulation—

"head teacher" includes, in Northern Ireland, the principal of a school;

"school"—

    (a) in relation to England and Wales, has the same meaning as in the Education Act 1996,

(b) in relation to Scotland, has the same meaning as in the Education (Scotland) Act 1980, and

(c) in relation to Northern Ireland, has the same meaning as in the Education and Libraries (Northern Ireland) Order 1986.

Crown application

6 These Regulations bind the Crown but do not apply to—

(a) Her Majesty in Her private capacity,

(b) Her Majesty in right of the Duchy of Lancaster, or

(c) the Duke of Cornwall.

Margot James
Minister of State
Department for Digital, Culture, Media and Sport

SCHEDULE
EXEMPT PROCESSING

Regulation 2(1)

Interpretation

1 In this Schedule—

"elected representative" has the meaning given in paragraph 23(3)(a) to (d) and (f) to (m) of Schedule 1 to the Data Protection Act 2018;

"judge" includes—

(a) a justice of the peace (or, in Northern Ireland, a lay magistrate),

(b) a member of a tribunal, and

(c) a clerk or other officer entitled to exercise the jurisdiction of a court or tribunal;

"public register" means any register which, pursuant to a requirement imposed—

(a) by or under any enactment, or

(b) in pursuance of any international agreement,

is open to public inspection or open to any inspection by any person having a legitimate interest.

Exempt processing

2(1) For the purposes of regulation 2(1), processing of personal data is exempt processing if it—

(a) falls within one or more of the descriptions of processing set out in sub-paragraph (2), or

(b) does not fall within one or more of those descriptions solely by virtue of the fact that disclosure of the personal data is made for one of the reasons set out in sub-paragraph (3).

(2) The processing is—

(a) of personal data which is not being processed wholly or partly by automated means or recorded with the intention that it should be processed wholly or partly by automated means;

(b) undertaken by a data controller for the purposes of their personal, family or household affairs, including—

    (i)   the processing of personal data for recreational purposes, and

    (ii)   the capturing of images, in a public space, containing personal data;

(c) for the purpose of the maintenance of a public register;

(d) for the purposes of matters of administration in relation to the members of staff and volunteers of, or persons working under any contract for services provided to, the data controller;

(e) for the purposes of advertising, marketing and public relations in respect of the data controller's business, activity, goods or services;

(f) subject to sub-paragraph (4), for the purposes of—

    (i)   keeping accounts, or records of purchases, sales or other transactions,

    (ii)   deciding whether to accept any person as a customer or supplier, or

    (iii)   making financial or financial management forecasts,

in relation to any activity carried on by the data controller;

(g) carried out by a body or association which is not established or conducted for profit and which carries out the processing for the purposes of establishing or maintaining membership or support for the body or association, or providing or administering activities for individuals who are either a member of the body or association or who have regular contact with it;

(h) carried out by—

    (i)   a judge, or

    (ii)   a person acting on the instructions, or on behalf, of a judge,

for the purposes of exercising judicial functions including the functions of appointment, discipline, administration or leadership of judges; or

(i) carried out by—

    (i)   a member of the House of Lords who is entitled to receive writs of summons to attend that House, or

    (ii)   a person acting on the instructions, or on behalf, of such a member,

for the purposes of exercising the member's functions as such;

(j) carried out by—

    (i)   an elected representative, or

    (ii)   a person acting on the instructions, or on behalf, of such a representative,

for the purposes of exercising the elected representative's functions as such;

(k) carried out by—

    (i)   a person seeking to become (or remain) an elected representative (a "prospective representative"), or

    (ii)   a person acting on the instructions, or on behalf, of a prospective representative,

in connection with any activity which can be reasonably regarded as intended to promote or procure the election (or re-election) of the prospective representative.

(3)   The disclosure is—

(a) required by or under any enactment, by any rule of law or by the order of a court;

(b) made for the purposes of—

    (i)   the prevention or detection of crime,

    (ii)   the apprehension or prosecution of offenders, or

    (iii)   the assessment or collection of any tax or duty or of any imposition of a similar nature,

and not otherwise being able to make the disclosure would be likely to prejudice any of the matters in (i) to (iii) above;

(c) necessary—

(i)   for the purpose of, or in connection with, any legal proceedings (including prospective legal proceedings), or

(ii)   for the purposes of obtaining legal advice,

or is otherwise necessary for the purposes of establishing, exercising or defending legal rights; or

(d) required for the purpose of avoiding an infringement of the privileges of either House of Parliament.

(4)   The processing of personal data by or obtained from a credit reference agency (within the meaning of section 145(8) of the Consumer Credit Act 1974) does not fall within the description of processing set out in sub-paragraph (2)(f).

Table of statutory codes and statutory guidance required to be produced by the Information Commissioner under DPA 2018

DPA 2018	Title	Status as at 1 February 2020	
s 121(1)	Data-sharing code	15/7/19 Draft for consultation issued.	
s 122(1)	Direct marketing code	8/1/20 Draft for consultation issued.	
s 123(1)	Age-appropriate design code	21/1/20 Submitted to government under s 125(1)(a). Yet to be laid before Parliament.	
s 124(1)	Data protection and journalism code	Nil prepared.	
s 128(1)	Other statutorily required codes	n/a	
s 133(1)	Guidance about privileged communications	July 2018: laid before Parliament under s 133(4). See: HL Paper 185.	In force.
s 136(1)	Guidance about fees	Nil prepared. A pre-DPA 2018 version of 21/2/18 stated an intention to update it prior to 25/5/18, but has yet to materialise.	
s 158	Penalties for non-payment of fees	July 2018: laid before Parliament under s 158(6). See: HL Paper 185.	In force.
s 160	Guidance about regulatory action	July 2018: first guidance laid before Parliament under ss 160(11), 161(1)(b). See: HL Paper 185.	"Approved" November 2018. Date issued by Information Commissioner under s 161(3)(a): unclear. Date coming into force under s 161(3)(b): unclear.
s 177	Guidance about redress against media organisation	Nil prepared.	
s 200	Guidance about PACE Code	Nil prepared.	

Regulatory Action Policy

Information Commissioner's Office

Contents

2

Commissioner's foreword

As Information Commissioner, I'm responsible for regulating a wide range of legislation in the UK.

I'm both an educator and an ombudsman, and in most situations this is enough. But sometimes the carrot of education goes unheeded and regulators must use their stick – so I also have the ability to take enforcement action and apply sanctions when warranted.

My office has a range of enforcement and sanctioning powers, from light to severe – from letters warning against intended processing of data to monetary penalties of up to 4% of global turnover for the most serious and harmful contraventions.

These are significant powers, and we must use them predictably, consistently and judiciously. As Information Commissioner, I always try to select the most suitable regulatory tool by assessing the nature and seriousness of a failure, the sensitivity of the subject matter, whether and how individuals have been affected, the novelty and duration of the concerns, the public interest, and whether other regulatory authorities are already taking action on the matter. This all links back to my Information Rights Strategic Plan - my office's five-year programme of key regulatory priorities

Organisations should be able to predict how my office will carry out its regulatory activity, which is why we have developed this Regulatory Action Policy. We have drafted it with due regard to concerns raised during our public consultation in spring 2018. We'll continue to review the policy's effectiveness, and adjust it as needed. We'll also produce more communications for specific sectors to help them understand how the ICO will seek to regulate them.

I believe this regulatory action policy shows how the ICO acts both as a strong defender of individuals' information rights and as an enabler of organisations seeking to use data responsibly and safely. Those who are subject to ICO regulatory action should be in no doubt that we will pursue failures under the law in a way that is transparent, consistent and proportionate.

Ultimately my office exists to uphold individuals' information rights in the digital age. Our refreshed Regulatory Action Policy sets out how I will do this.

Elizabeth Denham
Information Commissioner

3

Overview

Our Regulatory Action Policy sits under the umbrella of our Information Rights Strategic Plan for 2017-2021[1] which sets out the Information Commissioner's mission to increase the trust the public has in government, public bodies and the private sector: trust in transparency, in the digital economy and in digital public service delivery.

The purpose of this Policy is to provide direction and focus for those we regulate, the public and our staff about our chosen approach to regulatory action. This will help ICO achieve the goals we set out in our Strategic Plan, and complements our International Strategy 2017-2021.

This Policy sets out a risk-based approach to taking regulatory action against organisations and individuals that have breached the provisions of the data protection, freedom of information and other legislation, set out in our Aims below. As with earlier versions of the policy it focusses on areas of highest risk and most harm and the principles we apply in exercising our powers.

The ICO's approach is designed to help create an environment within which, on the one hand, data subjects are protected, while ensuring that, on the other hand, business is able to operate and innovate efficiently in the digital age. We will be as robust as we need to be in upholding the law, whilst ensuring that commercial enterprise is not constrained by red tape, or concern that sanctions will be used disproportionately. We will work with others where it makes sense to do so, and where joint application of activity can achieve the best result and protection.

---

[1] https://ico.org.uk/media/about-the-ico/documents/2014134/20170413icoinformationrightsstrategicplan2017to2021v10.pdf

4

Aims

This Policy seeks to:

- set out the nature of the ICO's various powers in one place and to be clear and consistent about when and how we use them[2];

- ensure that we take fair, proportionate and timely regulatory action with a view to guaranteeing that individuals' information rights are properly protected;

- guide the ICO and our staff in ensuring that any regulatory action is targeted, proportionate and effective; and

- assist delivery of the six goals of the Information Rights Strategic Plan and uphold information rights effectively for individuals in the digital age.

In addition, by issuing this Policy we are:

- fulfilling our statutory obligation to provide guidance as to how we propose to exercise our functions in connection with information notices, assessment notices, enforcement notices, and penalty notices.[3]

- providing additional statutory guidance about how we propose to exercise our other enforcement functions.[4]

- fulfilling our statutory obligation[5] to provide guidance as to how we propose to:

    (a) secure that privileged communications which we obtain or have access to in the course of carrying out our functions are used or disclosed only so far as necessary for carrying out those functions, and

    (b) comply with restrictions and prohibitions on obtaining or having access to privileged communications which are imposed by an enactment.

---

[2] Although see also the ICO Prosecution Policy Statement in relation to the prosecution of offences primarily under the Data Protection Act 1998, Data Protection Act 2018 and Freedom of Information Act 2000. Last published in May 2018.

[3] See S160(1) Data Protection Act 2018
[4] See S160(2) Data Protection Act 2018
[5] See S133 Data Protection Act 2018

5

- fulfilling our statutory obligation to produce and publish a document specifying the amount of the penalty for a failure to pay the data protection fees required under the Data Protection (Charges and Information) Regulations 2018.[6]

Objectives of regulatory action

When considering whether to take action, and in carrying it out, we will seek to meet the following five objectives:

Objective 1

To respond swiftly and effectively to breaches of legislation which fall within the ICO's remit, focussing on (i) those involving highly sensitive information, (ii) those adversely affecting large groups of individuals, and/or (iii) those impacting vulnerable individuals.

Objective 2

To be effective, proportionate, dissuasive and consistent in our application of sanctions, targeting our most significant powers (i) for organisations and individuals suspected of repeated or wilful misconduct or serious failures to take proper steps to protect personal data, and (ii) where formal regulatory action serves as an important deterrent to those who risk non-compliance with the law.

Objective 3

In line with legislative provisions, promote compliance with the law through the promotion of good practice and provision of targeted advice on how to comply with all aspects of the legislation.

Objective 4

To be proactive in identifying and mitigating new or emerging risks arising from technological and societal change.

Objective 5

To work with other regulators and interested parties constructively, at home and abroad, recognising the interconnected nature of the technological landscape in which we operate and the nature of data flows in the expanding digital economy. Our aim is to establish effective networks with other regulators to cut down on regulatory burden and red tape.

We will implement these objectives by exercising our statutory powers in the following ways:

---

[6] See S158 Data Protection Act 2018

6

- we will take action proportionately, we will exercise discretion as to when, in what manner, and to what extent enforcement is required;

- we will be selective when exercising this discretion, looking at the features and context of each case, as well as applying our resources more broadly to the areas of greatest risk and potential or actual harm to the community;

- we will apply our fining and other enforcement powers where they are effective, proportionate and dissuasive (to both the individual or organisation receiving the fine and more generally to those processing personal data;

- we will effectively deploy our intelligence products and technology to allow us to recognise and promptly tackle emerging threats; and

- we will seek to manage risks by sharing information effectively.

Where we are invoking our criminal prosecution powers we will do so by reference to the ICO Prosecution Policy Statement.

In applying the regulatory principles we will ensure that we always seek to meet our obligations under the Regulators' Code[7], the Victims' Code[8] and the Children Act 2004. We will also take account of the GDPR's requirements for greater consistency across Europe when determining the appropriate type and level of regulatory response in our data protection remit.

Legislative basis underpinning the ICO's regulatory activity

We are empowered to take various regulatory actions for breaches of the following legislation:

- Data Protection Act 2018 (DPA);

- General Data Protection Regulation[9] (GDPR);

- Privacy and Electronic Communications (EC Directive) Regulations 2003[10] (PECR);

- Freedom of Information Act 2000 (FOIA);

---

[7] Published in April 2014 and laid before Parliament in accordance with section 23 of the Legislative and Regulatory Reform Act 2006.
[8] The Code of Practice for Victims of Crime, also known as the Victims' Code, was established by the Domestic Violence, Crime and Victims Act 2004 and came into effect in 2006. It was revised in 2013 to reflect the commitments in the EU Victims' Directive 2012/29/EU, and updated again in 2015. The Victims' Code also reflects parts of the Human Trafficking and Child Sexual Exploitation EU Directives.
[9] Regulation (EU)2016/679
[10] S.I. 2003/2426

7

- Environmental Information Regulations 2004 (EIR)[11];

- Environmental Protection Public Sector Information Regulations 2009;[12]

- Investigatory Powers Act 2016;

- Re-use of Public Sector Information Regulations 2015[13];

- Enterprise Act 2002;

- The Network and Information Systems Regulations 2018 (NIS)[14]; and

- Electronic Identification, Authentication and Trust Services Regulation (e-IDAS)[15] [16].

Our regulatory activity

Our regulatory activity (and activity in support of regulatory activity) includes:

- conducting assessments of compliance with the DPA and GDPR (which we refer to in this Policy as the 'data protection legislation'), PECR, e-IDAS, NIS, FOIA and EIR;

- issuing information notices;

- issuing 'urgent' information notices under the DPA, requiring individuals, controllers or processors to provide information on not less than 24 hours' notice;

- applying for a court order requiring compliance with the information notice issued under the DPA, if the recipient does not provide a full and timely response;

- issuing assessment notices under DPA;

- issuing 'urgent' assessment notices under the DPA, requiring controllers or processors to allow us to undertake an assessment of whether they are compliant with the data protection legislation, on not less than 7 days notice;

- issuing no-notice (or short notice) assessment notices under the DPA where we have reasonable grounds to suspect that the controller or processor has failed or is failing to comply with certain provisions of the

---

[11] S.I. 2004/3391
[12] S.I. 2009/3157. Also known as the INSPIRE Regulations 2009.
[13] S.I. 2015/1415
[14] S.I. 2018/506, implementing Directive (EU) 2016/1148
[15] Regulation (EU) 910/2014
[16] Readers should bear in mind that this list may be extended as new legislation is introduced following the publication of this Policy.

8

data protection legislation[17] or has committed or is committing an offence under the DPA, allowing us to undertake an assessment on less than 7 days notice;

- producing codes of practice about data sharing and direct marketing, and any other codes of practice that we are required to produce under the legislation we cover;
- conducting assessments of cross-border data transfers and corporate groups' binding corporate rules;
- overseeing data protection impact assessments;
- conducting audits and assessments under IPA and other information rights legislation;
- overseeing the establishment of data protection certification mechanisms;
- encouraging the development of codes of conduct, and accrediting bodies to monitor compliance with codes of conduct;
- requiring a controller or digital service provider to inform an individual of a personal data breach;
- issuing a warning where proposed action threatens non-compliance with data protection legislation;
- issuing a reprimand for infringements of relevant data protection legislation;
- issuing practice recommendations under FOIA and EIR and decision notices detailing the outcome of an ICO investigation into an individual's case under FOIA or EIR;
- issuing enforcement notices orders requiring specific actions by an individual or organisation to resolve breaches (including potential breaches) of applicable information rights obligations. An 'urgent' enforcement notice under the DPA may be used to require action to resolve breaches or potential breaches of the data protection legislation, on not less than 24 hours' notice;
- certifying contempt of court should an authority fail to comply with an information notice, decision notice or enforcement notice under FOIA and EIR;
- administering fines by way of penalty notices in the circumstances set out in section 155 of the DPA;

---

[17] Set out in S149(2) of the Data Protection Act 2018

9

- administering fixed penalties for failing to meet specific obligations (e.g. a failure to pay the relevant fee to the ICO); and

- prosecuting criminal offences before the courts.

We will provide a suite of guidance to organisations and individuals about how to comply with the law and support this with advice. This can take the form of letters of advice, compliance meetings, presentations, conferences and advice sessions, in addition to advice provided via our telephone contact centre, web chat and on our website.

The full range of our enforcement powers, together with the regulatory actions associated with those powers, and the legislation we regulate, is set out on our website.

Selecting the appropriate regulatory activity for breaches of information rights

We will adopt a selective approach to the action we take. When deciding whether and how to respond to breaches of information rights obligations, we will consider criteria including[18]:

- the nature and seriousness of the breach or potential breach (including, for example, whether any critical national infrastructure or service is involved);

- where relevant, the categories of personal data affected (including whether any special categories of personal data are involved) and the level of any privacy intrusion;

- the number of individuals affected, the extent of any exposure to physical, financial or psychological harm, and, where it is an issue, the degree of intrusion into their privacy;

- whether the issue raises new or repeated issues, or concerns that technological security measures are not protecting the personal data;

- the gravity and duration of a breach or potential breach;

- whether the organisation or individual involved is representative of a sector or group, raising the possibility of similar issues arising again across that group or sector if not addressed;

- the cost of measures to mitigate any risk, issue or harm;

---

[18] Note that this set of criteria is not intended to be exhaustive.

10

- the public interest in regulatory action being taken (for example, to provide an effective deterrent against future breaches or clarify or test an issue in dispute);

- whether another regulator, law enforcement bodies or competent authority is already taking (or has already taken) action in respect of the same matter; and

- in relevant cases, the expressed opinions of the European Data Protection Board.

We also reserve the right to take into account any aggravating or mitigating factors where relevant, for example[19]:

Aggravating Factors

- whether the attitude and conduct of the individual or organisation concerned suggests an intentional, wilful or negligent approach to compliance or unlawful business or operating model;

- whether relevant advice, warnings, consultation feedback, conditions or guidance from the ICO and/or the Data Protection Officer (for data protection cases) has not been followed;

- in data protection cases, whether the relevant individual or organisation is certified by a body that has been accredited under Article 43 of the GDPR or has failed to follow an approved or statutory code of conduct;

- the relevant individual or organisation's prior regulatory history, including pattern, number and type of complaints about the issue;

- the vulnerability, if any, of the individuals affected, in particular by virtue of their age or other protected characteristic under the Equality Act 2010;

- the state and nature of any protective or preventative measures and technology available, including by design;

- the manner in which the breach or issue became known to the ICO and, if relevant, failure or delay by the relevant individual or organisation to notify the ICO of the breach or issue; and

- any financial (including budgetary) benefits gained or financial losses avoided by the relevant individual or organisation, directly or indirectly.

Mitigating factors

- any action taken by a relevant individual or organisation to mitigate or minimise any damage (including delay) suffered by individuals;

---

[19] As above, it should be noted that this list of factors is not intended to be exhaustive.

11

- in data protection cases, whether the relevant individual or organisation has followed an approved or statutory code of conduct

- the state and nature of any protective or preventative measures and technology available; and

- early notification by the relevant individual or organisation to the ICO of the breach or issue.

As a matter of course, we will typically invite comments from those we regulate[20] about the application of regulatory action where are taking action at the upper end of the scale, save where it is inappropriate to do so (for example, where a matter is particularly urgent or there is a need for wider protection of others from harm).

In line with our commitment to transparency and accountability, we will be as open as possible about our regulatory, and, where relevant, enforcement work. We will normally publish details about the volume and types of cases we pursue and the outcomes we achieve. In particular, we will report on those relating to corrective measures, sanctions, fines or civil monetary penalties, enforcement notices or orders, fixed penalty notices and prosecutions. We may also publish case study examples to illustrate good practice or learning.

We will be particularly careful to ensure that redaction of confidential, personally sensitive or commercially sensitive information is properly considered when publishing details of specific cases. We will also set our internal service performance measures to focus on impacts and outcomes rather than any prescribed sanction or regulatory activity levels.

A hierarchy of regulatory action

We will consider each case on its merits and within the context of any compliance breach (or risk of such breach). However, as a general principle, the more serious, high-impact, intentional, wilful, neglectful or repeated breaches can expect stronger regulatory action. Breaches involving novel or invasive technology, or a high degree of intrusion into the privacy of individuals, without having done a full Data Protection Impact Assessment and taken appropriate mitigating action and/or which should have been reported to the ICO[21] but was not, can also expect to attract regulatory attention at the upper end of the scale.

---

[20] Such representations are invited from individuals and organisations against whom the ICO is considering taking enforcement action, rather than from complainants.
[21] See Art 36 GDPR

12

Our regulatory approach generally represents a range of measures. This spans observation, intelligence gathering and monitoring through to individual case and appeal considerations, as well as application of audit/assessment or inspection powers to better understand an issue, and, then, finally investigation and sanction where we need to look at and address the detail of an incident.

In this way, as issues or patterns of issues escalate in frequency or severity then we will use more significant powers in response. This does not mean however that we cannot use our most significant powers immediately in serious or high-risk cases where there is a direct need to protect the public from harm.

Our approach will also encourage and reward compliance. Those who self-report, who engage with us to resolve issues and who can demonstrate strong information rights accountability arrangements, can expect us to take these into account when deciding how to respond.

We will also provide opportunities for innovative products, services or concepts to be tested with appropriate regulatory oversight and safeguards, so that innovation and development is not over-burdened.

International regulatory action

Given the extent of international data flows and their importance to the economy[22], as well as the extra-territorial nature of the GDPR, we will take action in support of our International Strategy and in line with our cooperation and consistency mechanism obligations under the GDPR.

This approach means that in cases involving cross-border information flows we will liaise internationally with other supervisory authorities. We will do so to identify the most appropriate regulatory response, including identifying any lead authority or other concerned supervisory authorities under the GDPR (usually where the controller's 'main establishment' is based), as well as to share information to assist investigations, provide mutual aid and secure appropriate regulatory outcomes.

We already have a significant international standing, being an active participant in the:

- European Data Protection Board;
- British Islands and Irish Data Protection Authorities network;
- Common Thread Network;

---

[22] *The exchange and protection of personal data, A future partnership paper*, HMSO 2017

13

- Global Privacy Enforcement Network;
- International Conference of Data Protection and Privacy Commissioners;
- International Conference of Information Commissioners;
- Organisation for Economic Co-operation and Development;
- Unsolicited Communications Enforcement Network (formerly known as the London Action Plan); and
- Council of Europe Convention 108 signatories.

More details about these groups and their role is on our website.

In addition, we have direct contact with a range of data protection authorities on individual cases and systemic issues (such as the privacy issues arising from app development or connected toys). We share intelligence, information, threat analyses, tactics, guidance and learning with these groups. Where appropriate we coordinate our investigative and evidence gathering activity with these partners; this may be either jointly or individually depending on the circumstances of the case.

We also have operational protocols and memoranda of understanding with our international partners in support of this policy, and we will continue to keep these updated. We publish more information about them on our website [link].

Working with others to take effective action

In addition to our international work we often work with a range of other regulators and agencies to deliver our remit. This includes:

- National Cyber Security Centre, in our role as a NIS competent authority, and in the immediate response phase to cyber-attacks which lead to breaches of personal data;
- other NIS competent authorities, such as the Drinking Water Authority, Office of Communications, and Civil Aviation Authority;
- law enforcement, including the National Crime Agency, in cases involving the theft or criminal misuse of personal data; and
- sector and consumer regulators, including, the Financial Conduct Authority and the Competition and Markets Authority Competitions and Marketing;

As with our international work we share intelligence, threat analyses, insight, and tactics with these groups, and we refer relevant cases where they fall within their jurisdiction as well as our own. Where we undertake joint regulatory

14

or investigative work we coordinate our activity to ensure a proportionate burden on those being regulated (e.g. minimising duplication of evidence gathering/information requests). These arrangements are set out in protocols and memoranda of understanding published on our website.

We also do additional work in support of our regulatory action where it is necessary to give effect to that action. For example, where a company seeks to avoid a financial penalty through complex liability structures or by dissolution, we will pursue matters via winding-up orders or by referral to the Insolvency Service. We have achieved success in obtaining disqualification of directors and winding-up orders to disrupt those who repeatedly break the rules, and we will expand our work in this area.

Statutory Guidance:

This section applies in addition to the general guidance and policies set out in this document as to our approach to regulatory action.

When we will issue Information Notices

An information notice is a formal request for a controller, processor or individual to provide us with information, within a specified time frame, to assist us with our investigations. In some circumstances it may be a criminal offence to provide a response which is false in any material respect.

We may serve an information notice at our discretion in any investigation. We will have regard to what action is appropriate and proportionate, and criteria including:

- the risk of harm to individuals or the level of intrusion into their privacy potentially posed by the events or data processing under investigation;
- the utility of requiring a formal response within a defined time period;
- the utility of testing responses, by the fact that it is an offence to deliberately or recklessly make a false statement in a material respect in response; and
- the public interest in the response.

When deciding the period for compliance with information notices, in particular whether or not to issue an 'urgent' information notice, we will have regard to what action is appropriate and proportionate and criteria including:

- the extent to which urgent investigation may prevent or limit the risk of serious harm to individuals or serious intrusion into their privacy. For example requesting an early report on a serious data security breach in

15

order for the ICO to advise the controller on and validate appropriate notification to data subjects and appropriate mitigation of the breach.
- the extent to which urgent investigation may prevent the sanitisation, alteration, destruction, concealment, blocking, falsifying, or removal of relevant evidence of data processing;
- the scope of the notice, that is the scope of questions or requests in an information notice;
- the additional burden on the recipient in having to comply with a notice urgently;
- the impact on the rights of the recipient, should the ICO obtain information under an urgent information notice (which may be by court order), prior to an appeal being heard by the Information Tribunal;
- the length of time of the investigation. For example, it may be appropriate and proportionate to issue an urgent information notice during a long running investigation where the questions are limited and the response may bring the investigation closer to completion; and
- the comparative effectiveness of other investigatory powers of the ICO.

If a recipient of an information notice does not fully respond within the applicable time period, whether urgent or not, the Commissioner will promptly apply for a court order requiring a response. The Commissioner may decide not to make such application, having regard to criteria including:

- the reasons for non-compliance with the information notice;
- any commitments given by the recipient to responding to the information notice;
- whether the information has been or is likely to be obtained from another source;
- the comparative effectiveness of other investigatory and enforcement powers of the ICO. For example, the ICO may decide it has sufficient evidence to move to an enforcement action in any event; and
- the public interest.

The Commissioner will also consider whether or not to issue a Penalty Notice (see below).

When we will issue Assessment Notices

The DPA contains a provision for the ICO to issue an 'assessment notice'[23]. This is, essentially, a notice which is issued by the ICO to a controller or processor to allow us to investigate whether the controller or processor is compliant with data protection legislation. The notice may, for example, require the controller

---

[23] Section 146 of the DPA

or processor to give us access to premises and specified documentation and equipment.

We may serve an assessment notice at our discretion in any investigation into compliance with the data protection legislation. We will have regard to what action is appropriate and proportionate, and criteria including:

- where we have conducted a risk assessment or other regulatory action, there is a probability that personal data is not being processed in compliance with the data protection legislation, together with a likelihood of damage or distress to individuals;

- it is necessary to verify compliance with an enforcement notice;

- communications with or information (e.g. news reports, statutory reporting or publications) about the controller or processor suggest that they are not processing personal data in compliance with the data protection legislation; and

- the controller or processor has failed to respond to an information notice within an appropriate time.

When determining the risks of non-compliance we will consider one or more of the factors for regulatory action. We will also consider other relevant information, such as reports by whistle-blowers, and any data privacy impact assessments that may have been carried out.

When deciding the period for compliance with assessment notices, in particular whether or not to issue an 'urgent', 'no-notice' or 'short-notice' assessment notice, we will have regard to what action is appropriate and proportionate, and criteria including:

- the extent to which urgent investigation may prevent or limit the risk of serious harm to individuals or serious intrusion into their privacy;
- the extent to which urgent investigation may prevent the sanitisation, alteration, destruction, concealment, blocking, falsifying, or removal of relevant evidence of data processing;
- the scope of the notice, that is the scope of our requests in an assessment notice;
- the additional burden on the recipient in having to comply with a notice urgently, on no-notice or on short-notice;
- the impact on the rights of the recipient should the ICO gain access to its premises and data processing activities urgently, without notice or on short notice, and without the opportunity to appeal and/or for an appeal to be heard by the Information Tribunal;

17

- the length of time of the investigation. For example, it may be appropriate and proportionate to issue an urgent assessment notice during a long running investigation where the requests are limited and the response may bring the investigation closer to completion; and
- the comparative effectiveness of other investigatory powers of the ICO.

Assessments of documents, including handling of health and social care records

We may require access to the specified documents and information, or classes of documents and information, which define and explain how obligations have been met under the legislation, and the governance controls in place to measure compliance.

Although not an exhaustive list this could include, for example:

- Strategies
- Policies
- Procedures
- Guidance
- Codes of practice
- Training material
- Protocols
- Frameworks
- Memoranda of understanding
- Contracts
- Privacy statements
- Privacy impact assessments
- Control data
- Job descriptions

We may also need access to specified personal data or classes of personal data, and to evidence that it is being handled in compliance with the policies and procedures which ensure compliance with the legislation. The level of access will only be enough to assess compliance.

We do require access to information which:

- is subject to legal professional privilege (see below);

- has a high level of commercial sensitivity;

- is exempt information as defined by section 23 FOIA (information supplied by, or relating to bodies dealing with security matters); or

18

- is exempt from the DPA, by virtue of a national security certificate[24].

We recognise that there might also be legitimate concerns about other information which relates to issues of national security, international relations or sensitive activities. In these cases it will generally be possible to audit data protection compliance without access to such information. Where it is necessary and appropriate, we will ensure that properly vetted members of staff inspect such information. We have memoranda of understanding with relevant agencies to provide access and understanding of this type of material.

Individuals can contact us to request that, if an assessment notice requires access to such information, this access be limited to the minimum required to adequately assess their compliance with the legislation. They may also request other access conditions. Such requests must be made within 28 days of the notice, unless the assessment is to be conducted on shorter notice, in which case, as soon as reasonably possible.

We may need to view health and social care records. If we do, we will respect the confidentiality of this data, and will limit access to the minimum required to adequately assess compliance. We will not take the content of these off-site, neither will we copy or transcribe them into working notes, and we will not include them in any reporting of the assessment.

Inspection and examinations during assessments

Inspections and examinations are key review elements of the assessment. They help us to identify objective evidence of compliance, and how policies and procedures have been implemented.

These reviews of personal data, and associated logs and audit trails, may consider both manually and electronically stored data, including data stored centrally, locally and on mobile devices and media.

We use these reviews to evaluate how an organisation:

- obtains, stores, organises, adapts or alters information (eg policies and procedures) or personal data;
- ensures the confidentiality, integrity and availability of the data or service it provides;
- retrieves, consults, or uses the information or personal data;
- discloses personal data by transmitting or disseminating or otherwise making the data available; and

---

[24] Section 27 of the DPA

19

- weeds and destroys personal data.

The review may also cover management/control information, to monitor and record how personal data is being processed, and to measure how a controller meets their wider obligations under the legislation.

The review may evaluate physical and IT-related security measures, including how personal data is stored and disposed of.

The review and evaluation process may take place on site as part of a discussion with staff to demonstrate 'practice', or independently by way of sampling by auditors. If information is held electronically we may require the controller to provide manual copies or facilitate direct access.

Any direct access would be limited to the identified records, would only be done locally and would be for a limited and agreed time.

Data reviewed as part of the review and evaluation process, but not specifically identified in the assessment notice, may only be taken off the controller's site with the controller's permission.

Interviews carried out during assessments

Interviews will consist of discussions with:

- staff and contractors;
- any processor's staff; and
- staff of relevant service providers as specified in the assessment notice.

We conduct interviews to develop further understanding of working practices and/or awareness of regulatory obligations. Departmental managers, operational staff, support staff (e.g. IT staff, security staff) as well as staff involved with information and information governance may be interviewed.

Where possible we will schedule and agree interviews with the controller or processor before the on-site audit. We will give a schedule of areas to be covered before the audit, and will discuss and agree the level and grade of staff to be interviewed (e.g. managers, operational staff etc.). Individuals should be advised by the target organisation in advance of their required participation.

We will use questions to understand individual roles and processes followed or managed, specifically referring to the handling of personal data and its security. Some questions may cover training and awareness, but they will not be framed as a test, nor are they intended to catch people out.

20

Interviews may be conducted at an individual's desk or in a separate room dependent upon circumstances, and whether there is a need to observe the working environment or examine information and records. Interviews will normally be 'one-to-one', but sometimes it may be appropriate to include a number of staff in an interview – where, for example, there are shared responsibilities. Auditors will take notes during the interviews.

Given the nature of interviews we do not consider it necessary for interviewees to be accompanied by third parties, but we will not object where it is reasonably recommended.

We will make every effort to restrict interviews to staff identified within the agreed schedule. But when it becomes clear during an audit that access to additional staff may be necessary, we will arrange this with the consent of the controller. Similarly, the schedule will not prevent us having confirmatory conversations with a consenting third party, for example where the third party is close to a desk-side discussion.

Interviews are to help in assessing compliance. They do not form part of, or provide information for, any individual disciplinary or criminal investigation. Should evidence of criminal activity by an individual emerge during an interview, the interview will be halted.

Individuals' names may be used in distribution lists and the acknowledgements sections of reports, but they will not be referenced in the body of any report. Job titles may be used where appropriate.

Publication of assessment reports

We will follow the procedure set out in our Communicating our Regulatory and Enforcement Activity Policy when publishing assessment reports.

If a recipient of an information notice does not fully respond within the applicable time period, whether urgent or not, the Commissioner will promptly apply for a court order requiring a response. The Commissioner may decide not to make such application, having regard to criteria including:

- the reasons for non-compliance with the information notice;
- any commitments given by the recipient to responding to the information notice;
- whether the information has been or is likely to be obtained from another source;

21

- the comparative effectiveness of other investigatory and enforcement powers of the ICO. For example, the ICO may decide it has sufficient evidence to move to an enforcement action in any event; and
- the public interest.

If a controller or processor fails to comply with an Assessment Notice, the Commissioner will consider whether or not to issue a Penalty Notice (see below).

Privileged communications

We do not require access to information which is subject to legal professional privilege. Where we receive such privileged information we will respect the confidentiality of this information and any particular sensitivities. We will handle all such privileged communications in accordance with the Attorney Generals Guidelines.

When we will issue Enforcement Notices

Enforcement notices may be issued in the circumstances set out in section 149 of the DPA or Regulation 17 of the NIS Regulations. For example, where a controller or processor has breached one of the data protection principles, where a certification provider or monitoring body for a code of conduct is failing to meet their obligations, or where a relevant digital service provider has suffered a failing as set out in Regulation 17 of the NIS Regulations.

The purpose of an enforcement notice is to mandate action (or halt action, such as processing or transfer) to bring about compliance with information rights and/or remedy a breach. Failure to comply with an enforcement notice invites further action, including the possibility of the ICO issuing a civil monetary penalty.

Enforcement notices will usually be appropriate where specific correcting action (or its prevention) may be required. Although this is not an exhaustive list, an enforcement notice may be required in such circumstances as:

- repeated failure to meet information rights obligations or timescales for them (e.g. repeatedly delayed subject access requests);
- where processing or transfer of information to a third country fails (or risks failing) to meet the requirements of the data protection legislation;
- where there is an ongoing NIS incident requiring action by a digital service provider;

22

- there is a need for the ICO to require communication of a data security breach to those who have been affected by it; or

- there is a need for correcting action by a certification body or monitoring body to ensure that they meet their obligations.

The notice will set out:

- who is required to take the action and why;
- the specifics of the action to be taken;
- how to report that the action has been taken;
- the timescales that apply for that action; and,
- any appeal / challenge process that applies.

When deciding whether to issue an enforcement notice, we will have regard to the factors set out above, including the presence of any mitigating or aggravating factors.

Timescales set out in an enforcement notice will usually reflect the imminence of proposed action that could lead to a breach of obligations, the severity and scale of any breach/failings, and the feasibility (including lead times) of any correcting measures or technology.

In addition, when deciding whether or not to issue an 'urgent' enforcement notice, and in deciding the period for compliance with such notice, we will consider whether urgent action by the recipient (to take specific steps or to stop specific processing of personal data) is appropriate and proportionate having regard to criteria including:

- the extent to which such urgent action may prevent or limit the risk of serious harm to individuals or serious intrusion into their privacy. For example requesting a controller stops using personal data for a specific purpose or takes action to protect personal data from security breaches;
- the scope of the enforcement notice;
- the additional burden or impact on the recipient in having to comply with an urgent enforcement notice within the period specified; and
- the comparative effectiveness of other enforcement powers of the ICO.

If a controller or processor fails to comply with an enforcement notice, the Commissioner will also consider whether or not to issue a Penalty Notice (see below).

Penalty Notices

The ICO's aim in applying penalty notices is to ensure compliance with legislation and information rights obligations. To do this, penalties must provide

23

an appropriate sanction for any breach of information rights or legislation, as well as act as an effective deterrent.

Our decision whether to impose a penalty at all; **and** the decision as to the amount of the penalty in a case will involve consideration of the following factors:

- the nature, gravity and duration of the failure;
- The intentional character of the failure or the extent of negligence involved;
- any action taken by the controller or processor to mitigate the damage or distress suffered by the data subjects;
- the degree of responsibility of the controller or processor, taking into account technical and organisational measures implemented by the controller or processor in accordance with the GDPR and sections 57, 66, 103 and 107 of the DPA;
- any relevant previous failures by the controller or processor;
- the degree of co-operation with the Commissioner, in order to remedy the failure and mitigate the possible adverse risks of the failure;
- the categories of personal data affected by the failure;
- the manner in which the infringement became known to the Commissioner, including whether, and if so to what extent, the controller or processor notified the Commissioner of the failure;
- the extent to which the controller or processor has complied with previous enforcement notices or penalty notices;
- adherence to approved codes of conduct or certification mechanisms;
- any other aggravating or mitigating factor applicable to the case, including financial benefits gained, or losses avoided, as a result of the failure (whether directly or indirectly);
- whether the penalty would be effective, proportionate and dissuasive.

When a Penalty Notice will be appropriate

In the majority of cases we will reserve our powers for the most serious cases, representing the most severe breaches of information rights obligations. These will typically involve wilful, deliberate or negligent acts, or repeated breaches of information rights obligations, causing harm or damage to individuals. In considering the degree of harm or damage we may consider that, where there

24

is a lower level of impact across a large number of individuals, the totality of that damage or harm may be substantial, and may require a sanction.

This means that each case will be assessed objectively on its own merits. But our hierarchy and risk-based approach mean that it is more likely that a penalty will be imposed where, for example:

- a number of individuals have been affected;
- there has been a degree of damage or harm (which may include distress and/or embarrassment);
- sensitive personal data has been involved;
- there has been a failure to comply with an information notice, an assessment notice or an enforcement notice
- there has been a repeated breach of obligations or a failure to rectify a previously identified problem or follow previous recommendations.;
- wilful action (including inaction) is a feature of the case;
- there has been a failure to apply reasonable measures (including relating to privacy by design) to mitigate any breach (or the possibility of it); and
- there has been a failure to implement the accountability provisions of the GDPR.

When oral representations will be appropriate

Before issuing a penalty we will advise the target that we intend to levy a penalty by issuing a notice of intent (NOI). The NOI will set out the circumstances of any breach, our investigation findings and the proposed level of penalty, along with a rationale for the penalty and any proposed enforcement notice requirements.

Representations will be taken from the proposed target about the imposition of the penalty and its level. The target will be allowed at least 21 calendar days to make these representations.

In addition, we may allow an organisation or individual subject to an NOI to submit representations orally during a face-face meeting at our office. However, this is discretionary and only relevant in cases that are considered by us to be exceptional. It is likely that these could be appropriate in circumstances where:

- the central facts of any breach or failing are in dispute;
- the integrity of any technical witness evidence is in dispute;

25

- there is a requirement to make reasonable adjustments under the Equality Act 2010; or

- the consideration of 'harm' elements of a case would benefit from evidence from those affected.

During these meetings, representatives of the target of the NOI are able to explain in person how the privacy concerns and breaches occurred, submit mitigating factors, what they have (or plan to do) to achieve compliance and the reasons why they believe that the ICO should not take the intended regulatory action. A request for a reduction in the size of the penalty may also be submitted during the oral representations.

If an organisation or individual thinks that their circumstances warrant oral representations of this nature, they can explain why they think this extra step is justified in their written representations. In particular, the ICO will need to understand what oral representations will add to the regulatory process. We will then decide whether or not to invite the target to a face-face meeting.

However, it is unlikely that we will agree to take oral representations in a case that is principally technical in nature. In such cases, it is normally more appropriate to consider complex technical representations in writing.

Where appropriate, we will also have regard to representations (including from any Concerned Supervisory Authorities elsewhere in the EU where the ICO is the lead Supervisory Authority or the Data Protection Board itself) under the cooperation and consistency mechanisms of the GDPR in setting the final amount of any penalty. These representations will be taken after the consideration of representations of the target of the penalty but before the final setting of any penalty level and following the procedures set out in relevant Data Protection Board rules of procedure.

For very significant penalties (expected to be those over the threshold of £1M) a panel comprising non-executive advisors to the Commissioner's Office may be convened by the Commissioner to consider the investigation findings and any representations made, before making a recommendation to the Commissioner as to any penalty level to be applied. It will be the Commissioner's final decision as to the level of penalty applied. The panel may comprise technical experts in areas relevant to the case under consideration.

Once all representations have been fully considered we will confirm any penalty notice in writing. We will also advise those subject to penalties of any relevant rights of appeal that apply to their case.

26

What will be the amount of any penalty

Where we have discretion to set the amount of any penalty in the context of our regulatory work, we will approach setting any penalty level, within the legislative bands, on the basis of the following mechanism:

Step 1. An 'initial element' removing any financial gain from the breach.

Step 2. Adding in an element to censure the breach based on its scale and severity, taking into account the considerations identified at section 155(2)-(4) of the DPA.

Step 3. Adding in an element to reflect any aggravating factors.

Step 4. Adding in an amount for deterrent effect to others.

Step 5. Reducing the amount (save that in the initial element) to reflect any mitigating factors, including ability to pay (financial hardship).

In data protection cases (including NIS cases) involving failures to meet data security obligations we will consider the breach separately from the failure to report. In all other cases we will adopt a 'whole case' approach when setting the penalty level.

Generally, the amount will be higher where:

- vulnerable individuals or critical national infrastructure are affected;
- there has been deliberate action for financial or personal gain;
- advice, guidance, recommendations or warnings (including those from a data protection officer or the ICO) have been ignored or not acted upon;
- there has been a high degree of intrusion into the privacy of a data subject;
- there has been a failure to cooperate with an ICO investigation or enforcement notice; and
- there is a pattern of poor regulatory history by the target of the investigation.

Fixed penalties

27

Certain legislation provides for set penalties to be applied for failing to meet specific obligations (for example, a failure to pay the relevant fee to the ICO). Where those provisions apply, we will levy those penalties in accordance with the law.

For the purposes of section 155 of the DPA, the fixed penalty payable by a controller for any type of failure to pay a data protection fee in accordance with the Data Protection (Charges and Information) Regulations 2018, are [25]:

(a) tier 1 (micro organisations), is £400;

(b) tier 2 (small and medium organisations), is £600;

(c) tier 3 (large organisations), is £4,000.

We reserve the right to increase this amount up to a statutory maximum of £4,350[26] for data controllers in respect of a failure to provide the ICO with sufficient information to determine the appropriate fee/exemption, depending on aggravating factors (for example, a failure to engage or co-operate with the ICO).

Cost recovery

We will not consider our own investigative or regulatory costs in the application of a penalty calculation. All monetary penalties will be payable for the benefit of HM Treasury and the Consolidated Fund.

NIS provides that the ICO should develop, by 2020, a mechanism to recover its costs in regulating Digital Service Providers (DSPs). The ICO will produce separate guidance on how it proposes to do this, in consultation with relevant DSPs.

Effectiveness of regulatory action

Our Information Rights Strategy sets out the measures we apply to the effectiveness of our work.

We will report annually to Parliament about our work, including our regulatory activity and, where needed, our formal enforcement actions. This may also include reporting on specific issues identified with individual organisations,

---

[25] The tiers are as defined in the Data Protection (Charges and Information) Regulations 2018

28

sectors or public authorities where systemic information rights problems have
been identified and addressed.

Evaluation and next steps

We will keep this Policy under review and evaluate it regularly and at least at
the end of the Information Rights Strategic Plan timeline. We will update it to
reflect any amendments to legislation, including any implementation of an
updated e-Privacy Regulation, and once the final settlement between the EU
and the UK post-Brexit is confirmed.

29

Part II

Freedom of Information

Freedom of Information Act 2000

(as amended to 1 February 2020)

CHAPTER 36

An Act to make provision for the disclosure of information held by public authorities or by persons providing services for them and to amend the Data Protection Act 1998 and the Public Records Act 1958; and for connected purposes.

30 November 2000

BE IT ENACTED by the Queen's most Excellent Majesty, by and with the advice and consent of the Lords Spiritual and Temporal, and Commons, in this present Parliament assembled, and by the authority of the same, as follows:—

PART I
ACCESS TO INFORMATION HELD BY PUBLIC AUTHORITIES

PART II
EXEMPT INFORMATION

PART III
GENERAL FUNCTIONS OF MINISTER FOR THE CABINET OFFICE, SECRETARY OF STATE AND INFORMATION COMMISSIONER

PART IV
ENFORCEMENT

PART V
APPEALS

SCHEDULE 1
Public Authorities

SCHEDULE 2
The Commissioner and the Tribunal

SCHEDULE 3
Powers of Entry and Inspection

SCHEDULE 4
.....

SCHEDULE 5
Amendments of Public Records Legislation

SCHEDULE 6
Further Amendments of Data Protection Act 1998

SCHEDULE 7
Disclosure of Information by Ombudsmen

SCHEDULE 8
Repeals

PART I
ACCESS TO INFORMATION HELD BY PUBLIC AUTHORITIES

Right to information

General right of access to information held by public authorities

1(1) Any person making a request for information to a public authority is entitled—

    (a)   to be informed in writing by the public authority whether it holds information of the description specified in the request, and

    (b)   if that is the case, to have that information communicated to him.

(2) Subsection (1) has effect subject to the following provisions of this section and to the provisions of sections 2, 9, 12 and 14.

(3) Where a public authority—

    (a)   reasonably requires further information in order to identify and locate the information requested, and

    (b)   has informed the applicant of that requirement,

the authority is not obliged to comply with subsection (1) unless it is supplied with that further information.

(4) The information—

    (a)   in respect of which the applicant is to be informed under subsection (1)(a), or

    (b)   which is to be communicated under subsection (1)(b),

is the information in question held at the time when the request is received, except that account may be taken of any amendment or deletion made between that time and the time when the information is to be communicated under subsection (1)(b), being an amendment or deletion that would have been made regardless of the receipt of the request.

(5) A public authority is to be taken to have complied with subsection (1)(a) in relation to any information if it has communicated the information to the applicant in accordance with subsection (1)(b).

(6) In this Act, the duty of a public authority to comply with subsection (1)(a) is referred to as "the duty to confirm or deny".

NOTES

Scottish public authority equivalent
  FOI(S)A s 1

Defined terms
  "applicant": s 84

"duty to confirm or deny": subs (6)
"information": s 84
"public authority": s 3(1)
"request for information": s 8

Effect of the exemptions in Part II

2(1) Where any provision of Part II states that the duty to confirm or deny does not arise in relation to any information, the effect of the provision is that where either—

    (a)   the provision confers absolute exemption, or

    (b)   in all the circumstances of the case, the public interest in maintaining the exclusion of the duty to confirm or deny outweighs the public interest in disclosing whether the public authority holds the information,

section 1(1)(a) does not apply.

(2) In respect of any information which is exempt information by virtue of any provision of Part II, section 1(1)(b) does not apply if or to the extent that—

    (a)   the information is exempt information by virtue of a provision conferring absolute exemption, or

    (b)   in all the circumstances of the case, the public interest in maintaining the exemption outweighs the public interest in disclosing the information.

(3)   For the purposes of this section, the following provisions of Part II (and no others) are to be regarded as conferring absolute exemption—

    (a)   section 21,

    (b)   section 23,

    (c)   section 32,

    (d)   section 34,

    (e)   section 36 so far as relating to information held by the House of Commons or the House of Lords,

    (ea)   in section 37, paragraphs (a) to (ab) of subsection (1), and subsection (2) so far as relating to those paragraphs,

    (f)   section 40(1)

    (fa)   section 40 (2) so far as relating to cases where the first condition referred to in that subsection is satisfied,

    (g)   section 41, and

    (h)   section 44.

NOTES

Scottish public authority equivalent
FOI(S)A s 2

Defined terms
"duty to confirm or deny": s 1(6)
"exempt information": s 84 and Pt II

Public authorities

3(1)   In this Act "public authority" means—

    (a)   subject to section 4(4), any body which, any other person who, or the holder of any office which—

        (i)   is listed in Schedule 1, or

        (ii)   is designated by order under section 5, or

    (b)   a publicly-owned company as defined by section 6.

(2)   For the purposes of this Act, information is held by a public authority if—

    (a)   it is held by the authority, otherwise than on behalf of another person, or

    (b)   it is held by another person on behalf of the authority.

NOTES

Scottish public authority equivalent
FOI(S)A s 2

Defined terms
"information": s 84
"public authority": subs (1)

Amendment of Schedule 1

4(1)   The Secretary of State or the Minister for the Cabinet Office may by order amend Schedule 1 by adding to that Schedule a reference to any body or the holder of any office which (in either case) is not for the time being listed in that Schedule but as respects which both the first and the second conditions below are satisfied.

(2)   The first condition is that the body or office—

    (a)   is established by virtue of Her Majesty's prerogative or by an enactment or by subordinate legislation, or

    (b)   is established in any other way by a Minister of the Crown in his capacity as

Minister, by a government department or by the Welsh Ministers, the First Minister for Wales or the Counsel General to the Welsh Assembly Government.

(3) The second condition is—

    (a) in the case of a body, that the body is wholly or partly constituted by appointment made by the Crown, by a Minister of the Crown, by a government department or by the Welsh Ministers, the First Minister for Wales or the Counsel General to the Welsh Assembly Government, or

    (b) in the case of an office, that appointments to the office are made by the Crown, by a Minister of the Crown, by a government department or by the Welsh Ministers, the First Minister for Wales or the Counsel General to the Welsh Assembly Government.

(4) If either the first or the second condition above ceases to be satisfied as respects any body or office which is listed in Part VI or VII of Schedule 1, that body or the holder of that office shall cease to be a public authority by virtue of the entry in question.

(5) The Secretary of State or the Minister for the Cabinet Office may by order amend Schedule 1 by removing from Part VI or VII of that Schedule an entry relating to any body or office—

    (a) which has ceased to exist, or

    (b) as respects which either the first or the second condition above has ceased to be satisfied.

(6) An order under subsection (1) may relate to a specified person or office or to persons or offices falling within a specified description.

(7) Before making an order under subsection (1), the Secretary of State or the Minister for the Cabinet Office shall—

    (a) if the order adds to Part II, III, IV or VI of Schedule 1 a reference to—

        (i) a body whose functions are exercisable only or mainly in or as regards Wales, or

        (ii) the holder of an office whose functions are exercisable only or mainly in or as regards Wales, consult the Welsh Ministers, and

    (b) if the order relates to a body which, or the holder of any office who, if the order were made, would be a Northern Ireland public authority, consult the First Minister and deputy First Minister in Northern Ireland.

(8) This section has effect subject to section 80.

(9) In this section "Minister of the Crown" includes a Northern Ireland Minister.

NOTES

Scottish public authority equivalent
  FOI(S)A s 4

Defined terms
  "public authority": s 3(1)

Subordinate legislation
  Numerous regulations have been made adding and removing public authorities from the first schedule

Further power to designate public authorities

5(1) The Secretary of State or the Minister for the Cabinet Office may by order designate as a public authority for the purposes of this Act any person who is neither listed in Schedule 1 nor capable of being added to that Schedule by an order under section 4(1), but who—

(a) appears to the Secretary of State or the Minister for the Cabinet Office to exercise functions of a public nature, or

(b) is providing under a contract made with a public authority any service whose provision is a function of that authority.

(2) An order under this section may designate a specified person or office or persons or offices falling within a specified description.

(3) Before making an order under this section, the Secretary of State or the Minister for the Cabinet Office shall consult every person to whom the order relates, or persons appearing to him to represent such persons.

(4) This section has effect subject to section 80.

NOTES

Scottish public authority equivalent
  FOI(S)A s 5

Defined terms
  "public authority": s 3(1)

Subordinate legislation
  Freedom of Information (Designation as Public Authorities) Order 2011, SI 2011/2598
  Freedom of Information (Designation as Public Authorities) Order 2015, SI 2015/851

Publicly-owned companies

6(1) A company is a "publicly-owned company" for the purposes of section 3(1)(b) if—

  (a) it is wholly owned by the Crown, or

  (b) it is wholly owned by the wider public sector, or

  (c) it is wholly owned by the Crown and the wider public sector.

(2) For the purposes of this section—

  (a) a company is wholly owned by the Crown if, and only if, every member is a person falling within sub-paragraph (i) or (ii)—

    (i) a Minister of the Crown, government department or company wholly owned by the Crown, or

    (ii) a person acting on behalf of a Minister of the Crown, government department or company wholly owned by the Crown,

  (b) a company is wholly owned by the wider public sector if, and only if, every member is a person falling within sub-paragraph (i) or (ii)-

    (i) a relevant public authority or a company wholly owned by the wider public sector, or

    (ii) a person acting on behalf of a relevant public authority or of a company wholly owned by the wider public sector, and

  (c) a company is wholly owned by the Crown and the wider public sector if, and only if, condition A, B or C is met.

(2A) In subsection (2)(c)

  (a) condition A is met if—

    (i) at least one member is a person falling within subsection (2)(a)(i) or (ii),

    (ii) at least one member is a person falling within subsection (2)(b)(i) or (ii), and

    (iii) every member is a person falling within subsection (2)(a)(i) or (ii) or (b)(i) or (ii),

  (b) condition B is met if-

    (i) at least one member is a person falling within subsection (2)(a)(i) or (ii) or (b)(i) or (ii),

(ii) at least one member is a company wholly owned by the Crown and the wider public sector, and

(iii) every member is a person falling within subsection (2)(a)(i) or (ii) or (b)(i) or (ii) or a company wholly owned by the Crown and the wider public sector, and

(c) condition C is met if every member is a company wholly owned by the Crown and the wider public sector.

(3) In this section—

"company" includes any body corporate;

"Minister of the Crown" includes a Northern Ireland Minister;

"relevant public authority" means any public authority listed in Schedule 1 other than—

(a) a government department, or

(b) any authority which is listed only in relation to particular information.

NOTES

Scottish public authority equivalent
    FOI(S)A s 6

Defined terms
    "company": subs (3)

"government department": s 84
"Minister of the Crown": subs.(3), s 84 of the Ministers of the Crown Act 1975 (c.26)
"Northern Ireland Minister": s 84
"public authority": s 3(1)

Public authorities to which Act has limited application

7(1) Where a public authority is listed in Schedule 1 only in relation to information of a specified description, nothing in Parts I to V of this Act applies to any other information held by the authority.

(2) An order under section 4(1) may, in adding an entry to Schedule 1, list the public authority only in relation to information of a specified description.

(3) The Secretary of State or the Minister for the Cabinet Office may by order amend Schedule 1—

(a) by limiting to information of a specified description the entry relating to any public authority, or

(b) by removing or amending any limitation to information of a specified description which is for the time being contained in any entry.

(4) Before making an order under subsection (3), the Secretary of State or the Minister for the Cabinet Office shall—

(a) if the order relates to the National Assembly for Wales or a Welsh public authority referred to in section 83(1)(b)(ii) (subsidiary of the Assembly Commission), consult the Presiding Officer of the National Assembly for Wales,

(aa) if the order relates to the Welsh Assembly Government or a Welsh public authority other than one referred to in section 83(1)(b)(ii), consult the First Minister for Wales,

(b) if the order relates to the Northern Ireland Assembly, consult the Presiding Officer of that Assembly, and

(c) if the order relates to a Northern Ireland department or a Northern Ireland public authority, consult the First Minister and deputy First Minister in Northern Ireland.

(5) An order under section 5(1)(a) must specify the functions of the public authority designated

by the order with respect to which the designation is to have effect; and nothing in Parts I to V of this Act applies to information which is held by the authority but does not relate to the exercise of those functions.

(6) An order under section 5(1)(b) must specify the services provided under contract with respect to which the designation is to have effect; and nothing in Parts I to V of this Act applies to information which is held by the public authority designated by the order but does not relate to the provision of those services.

(7) Nothing in Parts I to V of this Act applies in relation to any information held by a publicly-owned company which is excluded information in relation to that company.

(8) In subsection (7) "excluded information", in relation to a publicly-owned company, means information which is of a description specified in relation to that company in an order made by the Secretary of State or the Minister for the Cabinet Office for the purposes of this subsection.

(9) In this section "publicly-owned company" has the meaning given by section 6.

NOTES

Scottish public authority equivalent
  FOI(S)A s 7

Defined terms
  "excluded information": subs (8)
  "information": s 84
  "publicly owned company": subs (9), s 6

"public authority": s 3(1)

Subordinate legislation
  Freedom of Information (Additional Public Authorities) Order 2002, SI 2002/2623
  Freedom of Information (Additional Public Authorities) Order 2003, SI 2003/1882

Request for information

8(1) In this Act any reference to a "request for information" is a reference to such a request which—

    (a)   is in writing,

    (b)   states the name of the applicant and an address for correspondence, and

    (c)   describes the information requested.

(2) For the purposes of subsection (1)(a), a request is to be treated as made in writing where the text of the request—

    (a)   is transmitted by electronic means,

    (b)   is received in legible form, and

    (c)   is capable of being used for subsequent reference.

NOTES

Scottish public authority equivalent
  FOI(S)A s 8

Defined terms
  "applicant": s 84
  "information": s 84

Fees

9(1) A public authority to whom a request for information is made may, within the period for complying with section 1(1), give the applicant a notice in writing (in this Act referred to as a "fees notice") stating that a fee of an amount specified in the notice is to be charged by the authority for complying with section 1(1).

(2) Where a fees notice has been given to the applicant, the public authority is not obliged to comply with section 1(1) unless the fee is paid within the period of three months beginning with the day on which the fees notice is given to the applicant.

(3) Subject to subsection (5), any fee under this section must be determined by the public authority in accordance with regulations made by the Minister for the Cabinet Office.

(4) Regulations under subsection (3) may, in particular, provide—

    (a)   that no fee is to be payable in prescribed cases,

    (b)   that any fee is not to exceed such maximum as may be specified in, or determined in accordance with, the regulations, and

    (c)   that any fee is to be calculated in such manner as may be prescribed by the regulations.

(5) Subsection (3) does not apply where provision is made by or under any enactment as to the fee that may be charged by the public authority for the disclosure of the information.

NOTES

Scottish public authority equivalent
  FOI(S)A s 9

Defined terms
  "applicant": s 84
  "fees notice": subs (1)
  "public authority": s 3(1)

"request for information": s 8

Subordinate legislation
Freedom of Information and Data Protection (Appropriate Limit and Fees) Regulations 2004, SI 2004/3244

Time for compliance with request

10(1) Subject to subsections (2) and (3), a public authority must comply with section 1(1) promptly and in any event not later than the twentieth working day following the date of receipt.

(2) Where the authority has given a fees notice to the applicant and the fee is paid in accordance with section 9(2), the working days in the period beginning with the day on which the fees notice is given to the applicant and ending with the day on which the fee is received by the authority are to be disregarded in calculating for the purposes of subsection (1) the twentieth working day following the date of receipt.

(3) If, and to the extent that—

    (a)   section 1(1)(a) would not apply if the condition in section 2(1)(b) were satisfied, or

    (b)   section 1(1)(b) would not apply if the condition in section 2(2)(b) were satisfied,

the public authority need not comply with section 1(1)(a) or (b) until such time as is reasonable in the circumstances; but this subsection does not affect the time by which any notice under section 17(1) must be given.

(4) The Minister for the Cabinet Office may by regulations provide that subsections (1) and (2) are to have effect as if any reference to the twentieth working day following the date of receipt were a reference to such other day, not later than the sixtieth working day following the date of receipt, as may be specified in, or determined in accordance with, the regulations.

(5) Regulations under subsection (4) may—

    (a)   prescribe different days in relation to different cases, and

    (b)   confer a discretion on the Commissioner.

(6) In this section—

  "the date of receipt" means—

    (a)   the day on which the public authority receives the request for information, or

(b)   if later, the day on which it receives the information referred to in section 1(3);
"working day" means any day other than a Saturday, a Sunday, Christmas Day, Good
Friday or a day which is a bank holiday under the Banking and Financial Dealings Act
1971 in any part of the United Kingdom.

NOTES

Scottish public authority equivalent
  FOI(S)A s 10

Defined terms
  "applicant": s 84
  "date of receipt": subs (6)
  "fees notice": s 9(1)
  "information": s 84
  "public authority": s 3(1)
  "request for information": s 8
  "working day": subs (6)

Subordinate legislation
  Freedom of Information (Time for Compliance
  with Request) Regulations 2004, SI 2004/3364.
  The Freedom of Information (Time for
  Compliance with Request) Regulations 2009,
  which apply to a request for information that is
  received by the managers of a controlled school,
  voluntary school, grant-maintained integrated
  school or pupil referral unit
  The Freedom of Information (Time for
  Compliance with Request) Regulations 2010,
  which apply to a request for information that is
  received by the proprietor of an Academy

Means by which communication to be made

11(1)   Where, on making his request for information, the applicant expresses a preference for
communication by any one or more of the following means, namely—

    (a)   the provision to the applicant of a copy of the information in permanent form
or in another form acceptable to the applicant,

    (b)   the provision to the applicant of a reasonable opportunity to inspect a record
containing the information, and

    (c)   the provision to the applicant of a digest or summary of the information in
permanent form or in another form acceptable to the applicant,

the public authority shall so far as reasonably practicable give effect to that preference.

(1A)   Where-

    (a)   an applicant makes a request for information to a public authority in respect of
information that is, or forms part of, a dataset held by the public authority, and

    (b)   on making the request for information, the applicant expresses a preference for
communication by means of the provision to the applicant of a copy of the
information in electronic form,

the public authority must, so far as reasonably practicable, provide the information to the
applicant in an electronic form which is capable of re-use.

(2)   In determining for the purposes of this section whether it is reasonably practicable to
communicate information by particular means, the public authority may have regard to
all the circumstances, including the cost of doing so.

(3)   Where the public authority determines that it is not reasonably practicable to comply with
any preference expressed by the applicant in making his request, the authority shall notify
the applicant of the reasons for its determination.

(4)   Subject to subsection (1) or (1A), a public authority may comply with a request by
communicating information by any means which are reasonable in the circumstances.

(5)   In this Act 'dataset' means information comprising a collection of information held in
electronic form where all or most of the information in the collection—

    (a)   has been obtained or recorded for the purpose of providing a public authority
with information in connection with the provision of a service by the authority

or the carrying out of any other function of the authority,

    (b)   is factual information which—

        (i)   is not the product of analysis or interpretation other than calculation, and

        (ii) is not an official statistic (within the meaning given by section 6(1) of the Statistics and Registration Service Act 2007), and

    (c)   remains presented in a way that (except for the purpose of forming part of the collection) has not been organised, adapted or otherwise materially altered since it was obtained or recorded.

NOTES

Scottish public authority equivalent
  FOI(S)A s 11
Defined terms
  "applicant": s 84

"information": s 84
"public authority": s 3(1)
"request for information": s 8

Release of datasets for re-use

11A(1) This section applies where—

    (a)   a person makes a request for information to a public authority in respect of information that is, or forms part of, a dataset held by the authority,

    (b)   any of the dataset or part of a dataset so requested is a relevant copyright work,

    (c)   the public authority is the only owner of the relevant copyright work, and

    (d)   the public authority is communicating the relevant copyright work to the applicant in accordance with this Act.

(1A) But if the whole of the relevant copyright work is a document to which the Re-use of Public Sector Information Regulations 2015 apply, this section does not apply to the relevant copyright work.

(1B) If part of the relevant copyright work is a document to which those Regulations apply--

    (a)   this section does not apply to that part, but

    (b)   this section does apply to the part to which the Regulations do not apply (and references in the following provisions of this section to the relevant copyright work are to be read as references to that part).

(2) When communicating the relevant copyright work to the applicant, the public authority must make the relevant copyright work available for re-use by the applicant in accordance with the terms of the specified licence.

(3) The public authority may exercise any power that it has by virtue of regulations under section 11B to charge a fee in connection with making the relevant copyright work available for re-use in accordance with subsection (2).

(4) Nothing in this section or section 11B prevents a public authority which is subject to a duty under subsection (2) from exercising any power that it has by or under an enactment other than this Act to charge a fee in connection with making the relevant copyright work available for re-use.

(5) Where a public authority intends to charge a fee (whether in accordance with regulations under section 11B or as mentioned in subsection (4)) in connection with making a relevant copyright work available for re-use by an applicant, the authority must give the applicant a notice in writing (in this section referred to as a "re-use fee notice") stating that a fee of an amount specified in, or determined in accordance with, the notice is to be charged by

the authority in connection with complying with subsection (2).

(6) Where a re-use fee notice has been given to the applicant, the public authority is not obliged to comply with subsection (2) while any part of the fee which is required to be paid is unpaid.

(7) Where a public authority intends to charge a fee as mentioned in subsection (4), the re-use fee notice may be combined with any other notice which is to be given under the power which enables the fee to be charged.

(8) In this section—

"copyright owner" has the meaning given by Part 1 of the Copyright, Designs and Patents Act 1988 (see section 173 of that Act);

"copyright work" has the meaning given by Part 1 of the Act of 1988 (see section 1(2) of that Act);

"database" has the meaning given by section 3A of the Act of 1988;

"database right" has the same meaning as in Part 3 of the Copyright and Rights in Databases Regulations 1997 (S.I. 1997/3032);

"owner", in relation to a relevant copyright work, means—

(a) the copyright owner, or

(b) the owner of the database right in the database;

"relevant copyright work" means

(a) a copyright work, or

(b) a database subject to a database right,

but excludes a relevant Crown work or a relevant Parliamentary work;

"relevant Crown work" means—

(a) a copyright work in relation to which the Crown is the copyright owner, or

(b) a database in relation to which the Crown is the owner of the database right;

"relevant Parliamentary work" means—

(a) a copyright work in relation to which the House of Commons or the House of Lords is the copyright owner, or

(b) a database in relation to which the House of Commons or the House of Lords is the owner of the database right;

"the specified licence" is the licence specified by the Minister of the Cabinet Office in a code of practice issued under section 45, and the Minister of the Cabinet Office may specify different licences for different purposes.

NOTES

Defined terms
"applicant": s 84
"information": s 84

"public authority": s 3(1)
"request for information": s 8

Power to charge fees in relation to release of datasets for re-use

11B(1) The Minister for the Cabinet Office may, with the consent of the Treasury, make provision by regulations about the charging of fees by public authorities in connection with making relevant copyright works available for re-use under section 11A(2) or by virtue of section 19(2A)(c).

(2) Regulations under this section may, in particular—

(a) prescribe cases in which fees may, or may not, be charged,

(b) prescribe the amount of any fee payable or provide for any such amount to be determined in such manner as may be prescribed,

(c) prescribe, or otherwise provide for, times at which fees, or parts of fees, are payable,

(d) require the provision of information about the manner in which amounts of fees are determined,

(e) make different provision for different purposes.

(3) Regulations under this section may, in prescribing the amount of any fee payable or providing for any such amount to be determined in such manner as may be prescribed, provide for a reasonable return on investment.

(4) In this section "relevant copyright work" has the meaning given by section 11A(8).

NOTES

Defined terms
"applicant": s 84
"information": s 84
"public authority": s 3(1)
"request for information": s 8

Subordinate legislation
Freedom of Information (Release of Datasets for Re-use) (Fees) Regulations 2013, SI 2013/1977

Exemption where cost of compliance exceeds appropriate limit

12(1) Section 1(1) does not oblige a public authority to comply with a request for information if the authority estimates that the cost of complying with the request would exceed the appropriate limit.

(2) Subsection (1) does not exempt the public authority from its obligation to comply with paragraph (a) of section 1(1) unless the estimated cost of complying with that paragraph alone would exceed the appropriate limit.

(3) In subsections (1) and (2) "the appropriate limit" means such amount as may be prescribed, and different amounts may be prescribed in relation to different cases.

(4) The Minister for the Cabinet Office may by regulations provide that, in such circumstances as may be prescribed, where two or more requests for information are made to a public authority—

(a) by one person, or

(b) by different persons who appear to the public authority to be acting in concert or in pursuance of a campaign,

the estimated cost of complying with any of the requests is to be taken to be the estimated total cost of complying with all of them.

(5) The Minister for the Cabinet Office may by regulations make provision for the purposes of this section as to the costs to be estimated and as to the manner in which they are to be estimated.

NOTES

Scottish public authority equivalent
FOI(S)A s 12

Defined terms
"appropriate limit": subs (3)
"public authority": s 3(1)

"request for information": s 8

Subordinate legislation
Freedom of Information and Data Protection (Appropriate Limit and Fees) Regulations 2004, SI 2004/3244.

Fees for disclosure where cost of compliance exceeds appropriate limit

13(1) A public authority may charge for the communication of any information whose communication—

    (a)   is not required by section 1(1) because the cost of complying with the request for information exceeds the amount which is the appropriate limit for the purposes of section 12(1) and (2), and

    (b)   is not otherwise required by law,

such fee as may be determined by the public authority in accordance with regulations made by the Minister for the Cabinet Office.

(2)   Regulations under this section may, in particular, provide—

    (a)   that any fee is not to exceed such maximum as may be specified in, or determined in accordance with, the regulations, and

    (b)   that any fee is to be calculated in such manner as may be prescribed by the regulations.

(3)   Subsection (1) does not apply where provision is made by or under any enactment as to the fee that may be charged by the public authority for the disclosure of the information.

NOTES

Scottish public authority equivalent
    FOI(S)A s 13

Defined terms
    "appropriate limit": s 12(3)
    "information": s 84

"public authority": s 3(1)

Subordinate legislation
Freedom of Information and Data Protection (Appropriate Limit and Fees) Regulations 2004, SI 2004/3244.

Vexatious or repeated requests

14(1)   Section 1(1) does not oblige a public authority to comply with a request for information if the request is vexatious.

(2)   Where a public authority has previously complied with a request for information which was made by any person, it is not obliged to comply with a subsequent identical or substantially similar request from that person unless a reasonable interval has elapsed between compliance with the previous request and the making of the current request.

NOTES

Scottish public authority equivalent
    FOI(S)A s 14

Defined terms
    "public authority": s 3(1)
    "request for information": s 8

Special provisions relating to public records transferred to Public Record Office, etc

15(1)   Where—

    (a)   the appropriate records authority receives a request for information which relates to information which is, or if it existed would be, contained in a transferred public record, and

    (b)   either of the conditions in subsection (2) is satisfied in relation to any of that information,

that authority shall, within the period for complying with section 1(1), send a copy of the request to the responsible authority.

(2)   The conditions referred to in subsection (1)(b) are—

    (a)   that the duty to confirm or deny is expressed to be excluded only by a provision of Part II not specified in subsection (3) of section 2, and

    (b)   that the information is exempt information only by virtue of a provision of Part

II not specified in that subsection.

(3) On receiving the copy, the responsible authority shall, within such time as is reasonable in all the circumstances, inform the appropriate records authority of the determination required by virtue of subsection (3) or (4) of section 66.

(4) In this Act "transferred public record" means a public record which has been transferred—

(a) to the Public Record Office,

(b) to another place of deposit appointed by the Secretary of State under the Public Records Act 1958, or

(c) to the Public Record Office of Northern Ireland.

(5) In this Act—

"appropriate records authority", in relation to a transferred public record, means—

(a) in a case falling within subsection (4)(a), the Public Record Office,

(b) in a case falling within subsection (4)(b), the Secretary of State, and

(c) in a case falling within subsection (4)(c), the Public Record Office of Northern Ireland;

"responsible authority", in relation to a transferred public record, means—

(a) in the case of a record transferred as mentioned in subsection (4)(a) or (b) from a government department in the charge of a Minister of the Crown, the Minister of the Crown who appears to the Secretary of State to be primarily concerned,

(b) in the case of a record transferred as mentioned in subsection (4)(a) or (b) from any other person, the person who appears to the Secretary of State to be primarily concerned,

(c) in the case of a record transferred to the Public Record Office of Northern Ireland from a government department in the charge of a Minister of the Crown, the Minister of the Crown who appears to the appropriate Northern Ireland Minister to be primarily concerned,

(d) in the case of a record transferred to the Public Record Office of Northern Ireland from a Northern Ireland department, the Northern Ireland Minister who appears to the appropriate Northern Ireland Minister to be primarily concerned, or

(e) in the case of a record transferred to the Public Record Office of Northern Ireland from any other person, the person who appears to the appropriate Northern Ireland Minister to be primarily concerned.

NOTES

Scottish public authority equivalent
FOI(S)A s 22

Defined terms
"appropriate records authority": subs (5)
"public record": s 84 of the Public Records Act 1958 (c 51), Public Records Act (Northern Ireland) 1923

"responsible authority": subs (5)
"request for information": s 8
"transferred public record": subs (5)

Duty to provide advice and assistance

16(1) It shall be the duty of a public authority to provide advice and assistance, so far as it would be reasonable to expect the authority to do so, to persons who propose to make, or have made, requests for information to it.

(2) Any public authority which, in relation to the provision of advice or assistance in any case, conforms with the code of practice under section 45 is to be taken to comply with the duty imposed by subsection (1) in relation to that case.

NOTES

Scottish public authority equivalent
  FOI(S)A s 15

Defined terms
  "public authority": s 3(1)
  "request for information": s 8

Refusal of request

17(1) A public authority which, in relation to any request for information, is to any extent relying on a claim that any provision of Part II relating to the duty to confirm or deny is relevant to the request or on a claim that information is exempt information must, within the time for complying with section 1(1), give the applicant a notice which—

    (a) states that fact,

    (b) specifies the exemption in question, and

    (c) states (if that would not otherwise be apparent) why the exemption applies.

(2) Where—

    (a) in relation to any request for information, a public authority is, as respects any information, relying on a claim—

        (i) that any provision of Part II which relates to the duty to confirm or deny and is not specified in section 2(3) is relevant to the request, or

        (ii) that the information is exempt information only by virtue of a provision not specified in section 2(3), and

    (b) at the time when the notice under subsection (1) is given to the applicant, the public authority (or, in a case falling within section 66(3) or (4), the responsible authority) has not yet reached a decision as to the application of subsection (1)(b) or (2)(b) of section 2,

the notice under subsection (1) must indicate that no decision as to the application of that provision has yet been reached and must contain an estimate of the date by which the authority expects that such a decision will have been reached.

(3) A public authority which, in relation to any request for information, is to any extent relying on a claim that subsection (1)(b) or (2)(b) of section 2 applies must, either in the notice under subsection (1) or in a separate notice given within such time as is reasonable in the circumstances, state the reasons for claiming—

    (a) that, in all the circumstances of the case, the public interest in maintaining the exclusion of the duty to confirm or deny outweighs the public interest in disclosing whether the authority holds the information, or

    (b) that, in all the circumstances of the case, the public interest in maintaining the exemption outweighs the public interest in disclosing the information.

(4) A public authority is not obliged to make a statement under subsection (1)(c) or (3) if, or to the extent that, the statement would involve the disclosure of information which would itself be exempt information.

(5) A public authority which, in relation to any request for information, is relying on a claim that section 12 or 14 applies must, within the time for complying with section 1(1), give the applicant a notice stating that fact.

(6) Subsection (5) does not apply where—

    (a)   the public authority is relying on a claim that section 14 applies,

    (b)   the authority has given the applicant a notice, in relation to a previous request for information, stating that it is relying on such a claim, and

    (c)   it would in all the circumstances be unreasonable to expect the authority to serve a further notice under subsection (5) in relation to the current request.

(7) A notice under subsection (1), (3) or (5) must—

    (a)   contain particulars of any procedure provided by the public authority for dealing with complaints about the handling of requests for information or state that the authority does not provide such a procedure, and

    (b)   contain particulars of the right conferred by section 50.

NOTES

Scottish public authority equivalent
  FOI(S)A s 16

Defined terms
  "duty to confirm or deny": s 1(6)

"exempt information": s 84 and Part II
"public authority": s 3(1)
"request for information": s 8
"responsible authority": s 15(5)

The Information Commissioner

18(1) ....

(3) In this Act—

    (a)   the Information Commissioner is referred to as "the Commissioner"

(4) Schedule 2 (which makes provision consequential on subsections (1) and (2) and amendments of the Data Protection Act 1998 relating to the extension by this Act of the functions of the Commissioner and the Tribunal) has effect.

NOTES

Scottish public authority equivalent
  None

Defined terms
  "Commissioner": subs (3)
  "Information Commissioner": subs (1)

Publication schemes

19(1) It shall be the duty of every public authority—

    (a)   to adopt and maintain a scheme which relates to the publication of information by the authority and is approved by the Commissioner (in this Act referred to as a "publication scheme"),

    (b)   to publish information in accordance with its publication scheme, and

    (c)   from time to time to review its publication scheme.

(2) A publication scheme must—

    (a)   specify classes of information which the public authority publishes or intends to publish,

    (b)   specify the manner in which information of each class is, or is intended to be, published, and

    (c)   specify whether the material is, or is intended to be, available to the public free of charge or on payment.

(2A) A publication scheme must, in particular, include a requirement for the public authority concerned-

    (a)   to publish—

    (i)   any dataset held by the authority in relation to which a person makes a request for information to the authority, and

    (ii)   any up-dated version held by the authority of such a dataset,

unless the authority is satisfied that it is not appropriate for the dataset to be published,

    (b)   where reasonably practicable, to publish any dataset the authority publishes by virtue of paragraph (a) in an electronic form which is capable of re-use,

    (c)   subject to subsections (2AA) and 2(AB) where any information in a dataset published by virtue of paragraph (a) is a relevant copyright work in relation to which the authority is the only owner, to make the information available for re-use in accordance with the terms of the specified licence.

(2AA)   If the whole of the relevant copyright work is a document to which the Re-use of Public Sector Information Regulations 2015 apply, subsections (2A(c) and (2B) to (2F) do not apply to the relevant copyright work.

(2AB)   If part of the relevant copyright work is a document to which those Regulations apply–

    (a)   subsections (2A)(c) and (2B) to (2F) do not apply to that part, but

    (b)   those provisions do apply to the part to which Regulations do not apply (and references in the following provisions of this section to the relevant copyright work are to be read as references to that part).

(2B)   The public authority may exercise any power that it has by virtue of regulations under section 11B to charge a fee in connection with making the relevant copyright work available for re-use in accordance with a requirement imposed by virtue of subsection (2A)(c).

(2C)   Nothing in this section or section 11B prevents a public authority which is subject to such a requirement from exercising any power that it has by or under an enactment other than this Act to charge a fee in connection with making the relevant copyright work available for re-use.

(2D)   Where a public authority intends to charge a fee (whether in accordance with regulations under section 11B or as mentioned in subsection (2C)) in connection with making a relevant copyright work available for re-use by an applicant, the authority must give the applicant a notice in writing (in this section referred to as a "re-use fee notice") stating that a fee of an amount specified in, or determined in accordance with, the notice is to be charged by the authority in connection with complying with the requirement imposed by virtue of subsection (2A)(c).

(2E)   Where a re-use fee notice has been given to the applicant, the public authority is not obliged to comply with the requirement imposed by virtue of subsection (2A)(c) while any part of the fee which is required to be paid is unpaid.

(2F)   Where a public authority intends to charge a fee as mentioned in subsection (2C), the re-use fee notice may be combined with any other notice which is to be given under the power which enables the fee to be charged.

(3)   In adopting or reviewing a publication scheme, a public authority shall have regard to the public interest—

    (a)   in allowing public access to information held by the authority, and

    (b)   in the publication of reasons for decisions made by the authority.

(4)   A public authority shall publish its publication scheme in such manner as it thinks fit.

(5)   The Commissioner may, when approving a scheme, provide that his approval is to expire at the end of a specified period.

(6)   Where the Commissioner has approved the publication scheme of any public authority, he may at any time give notice to the public authority revoking his approval of the scheme as from the end of the period of six months beginning with the day on which the notice is given.

(7)   Where the Commissioner—
    (a)   refuses to approve a proposed publication scheme, or
    (b)   revokes his approval of a publication scheme,
he must give the public authority a statement of his reasons for doing so.

(8)   In this section—
    "copyright owner" has the meaning given by Part 1 of the Copyright, Designs and Patents Act 1988 (see section 173 of that Act);
    "copyright work" has the meaning given by Part 1 of the Act of 1988 (see section 1(2) of that Act);
    "database" has the meaning given by section 3A of the Act of 1988;
    "database right" has the same meaning as in Part 3 of the Copyright and Rights in Databases Regulations 1997 (SI 1997/3032);
    "owner", in relation to a relevant copyright work, means—
      (a)   the copyright owner, or
      (b)   the owner of the database right in the database;
    "relevant copyright work" means—
      (a)   a copyright work, or
      (b)   a database subject to a database right,
    but excludes a relevant Crown work or a relevant Parliamentary work;
    "relevant Crown work" means—
      (a)   a copyright work in relation to which the Crown is the copyright owner, or
      (b)   a database in relation to which the Crown is the owner of the database right;
    "relevant Parliamentary work" means—
      (a)   a copyright work in relation to which the House of Commons or the House of Lords is the copyright owner, or
      (b)   a database in relation to which the House of Commons or the House of Lords is the owner of the database right;
    "the specified licence" has the meaning given by section 11A(8).

NOTES

Scottish public authority equivalent
FOI(S)A s 23

Defined terms
"Commissioner": s 18(3)
"information": s 84
"public authority": s 3(1)
"publication scheme": subs (1)

Model publication schemes

20(1)   The Commissioner may from time to time approve, in relation to public authorities falling within particular classes, model publication schemes prepared by him or by other persons.

(2)   Where a public authority falling within the class to which an approved model scheme relates adopts such a scheme without modification, no further approval of the

Commissioner is required so long as the model scheme remains approved; and where such an authority adopts such a scheme with modifications, the approval of the Commissioner is required only in relation to the modifications.

(3) The Commissioner may, when approving a model publication scheme, provide that his approval is to expire at the end of a specified period.

(4) Where the Commissioner has approved a model publication scheme, he may at any time publish, in such manner as he thinks fit, a notice revoking his approval of the scheme as from the end of the period of six months beginning with the day on which the notice is published.

(5) Where the Commissioner refuses to approve a proposed model publication scheme on the application of any person, he must give the person who applied for approval of the scheme a statement of the reasons for his refusal.

(6) Where the Commissioner refuses to approve any modifications under subsection (2), he must give the public authority a statement of the reasons for his refusal.

(7) Where the Commissioner revokes his approval of a model publication scheme, he must include in the notice under subsection (4) a statement of his reasons for doing so.

NOTES

Scottish public authority equivalent
FOI(S)A s 24

Defined terms
"Commissioner": s 18(3)
"public authority": s 3(1)
"publication scheme": s 19(1)

PART II
EXEMPT INFORMATION

Information accessible to applicant by other means

21(1) Information which is reasonably accessible to the applicant otherwise than under section 1 is exempt information.

(2) For the purposes of subsection (1)—
 (a) information may be reasonably accessible to the applicant even though it is accessible only on payment, and
 (b) information is to be taken to be reasonably accessible to the applicant if it is information which the public authority or any other person is obliged by or under any enactment to communicate (otherwise than by making the information available for inspection) to members of the public on request, whether free of charge or on payment.

(3) For the purposes of subsection (1), information which is held by a public authority and does not fall within subsection (2)(b) is not to be regarded as reasonably accessible to the applicant merely because the information is available from the public authority itself on request, unless the information is made available in accordance with the authority's publication scheme and any payment required is specified in, or determined in accordance with, the scheme.

NOTES

Scottish public authority equivalent
FOI(S)A s 25

Exemption type
Absolute: s 2(3)(a)

Defined terms
  "applicant": s 84
  "exempt information": s 84
  "information": s 84
  "publication scheme": s 19(1)
  "public authority": s 3(1)

Information intended for future publication

22(1) Information is exempt information if—

   (a) the information is held by the public authority with a view to its publication, by the authority or any other person, at some future date (whether determined or not),

   (b) the information was already held with a view to such publication at the time when the request for information was made, and

   (c) it is reasonable in all the circumstances that the information should be withheld from disclosure until the date referred to in paragraph (a).

(2) The duty to confirm or deny does not arise if, or to the extent that, compliance with section 1(1)(a) would involve the disclosure of any information (whether or not already recorded) which falls within subsection (1).

NOTES

Scottish public authority equivalent
  FOI(S)A s 27

Exemption type
  Not absolute: s 2(3)

Defined terms
  "duty to confirm or deny": s 16
  "exempt information": s 84
  "information": s 84
  "public authority": s 3(1)

Research

22A(1) Information obtained in the course of, or derived from, a programme of research, is exempt information if—

   (a) the programme is continuing with a view to the publication, by a public authority or any other person, of a report of the research (whether or not including a statement of that information), and,

   (b) disclosure of the information under this Act before the date of publication would, or would be likely to, prejudice–

      (i) the programme,

      (ii) the interests of any individual participating in the programme,

      (iii) the interests of the authority which holds the information, or.

      (iv) the interests of the authority mentioned in paragraph (a) (if it is a different authority from that which holds the information).

(2) The duty to confirm or deny does not arise in relation to information which is (or if it were held by the public authority would be) exempt information by virtue of subsection (1) if, or the extent that, compliance with subsection 1(1)(a) would, or would be likely to, prejudice any of the matters mentioned in subsection (1)(b).

NOTES

Scottish public authority equivalent
  Nil

Exemption type
  Not absolute: s 2(3)

Defined terms
  "duty to confirm or deny": s 16
  "exempt information": s 84
  "held": s 3(2)
  "information": s 84
  "public authority": s 3(1)

Information supplied by, or relating to, bodies dealing with security matters

23(1) Information held by a public authority is exempt information if it was directly or indirectly supplied to the public authority by, or relates to, any of the bodies specified in subsection (3).

(2) A certificate signed by a Minister of the Crown certifying that the information to which it applies was directly or indirectly supplied by, or relates to, any of the bodies specified in subsection (3) shall, subject to section 60, be conclusive evidence of that fact.

(3) The bodies referred to in subsections (1) and (2) are—

    (a)   the Security Service,

    (b)   the Secret Intelligence Service,

    (c)   the Government Communications Headquarters,

    (d)   the special forces,

    (e)   the Tribunal established under section 65 of the Regulation of Investigatory Powers Act 2000,

    (f)   the Tribunal established under section 7 of the Interception of Communications Act 1985,

    (g)   the Tribunal established under section 5 of the Security Service Act 1989,

    (h)   the Tribunal established under section 9 of the Intelligence Services Act 1994,

    (i)   the Security Vetting Appeals Panel,

    (j)   the Security Commission,

    (k)   the National Criminal Intelligence Service,

    (l)   the Service Authority for the National Criminal Intelligence Service,

    (m)   the Serious Organised Crime Agency,

    (n)   the National Crime Agency, and

    (o)   the Intelligence and Security Committee of Parliament.

(4) In subsection (3)(c) "the Government Communications Headquarters" includes any unit or part of a unit of the armed forces of the Crown which is for the time being required by the Secretary of State to assist the Government Communications Headquarters in carrying out its functions.

(5) The duty to confirm or deny does not arise if, or to the extent that, compliance with section 1(1)(a) would involve the disclosure of any information (whether or not already recorded) which was directly or indirectly supplied to the public authority by, or relates to, any of the bodies specified in subsection (3).

NOTES

Scottish public authority equivalent
  None

Exemption type
  Absolute: s 2(3)(b)

Defined terms
  "duty to confirm or deny": s 1(6)
  "exempt information": s 84
  "information": s 84
  "Minister of the Crown": s 84 of the Ministers of the Crown Act 1975
  "public authority": s 3(1)

National security

24(1) Information which does not fall within section 23(1) is exempt information if exemption from section 1(1)(b) is required for the purpose of safeguarding national security.

(2) The duty to confirm or deny does not arise if, or to the extent that, exemption from section 1(1)(a) is required for the purpose of safeguarding national security.

(3) A certificate signed by a Minister of the Crown certifying that exemption from section 1(1)(b), or from section 1(1)(a) and (b), is, or at any time was, required for the purpose of safeguarding national security shall, subject to section 60, be conclusive evidence of that fact.

(4) A certificate under subsection (3) may identify the information to which it applies by means of a general description and may be expressed to have prospective effect.

NOTES

Scottish public authority equivalent
FOI(S)A s 31

Exemption type
Not absolute: s 2(3)

Defined terms
"duty to confirm or deny": s 1(6)
"exempt information": s 84
"information": s 84
"Minister of the Crown": s 84, Ministers of the Crown Act 1975
"special forces": s 84

Certificates under ss 23 and 24: supplementary provisions

25(1) A document purporting to be a certificate under section 23(2) or 24(3) shall be received in evidence and deemed to be such a certificate unless the contrary is proved.

(2) A document which purports to be certified by or on behalf of a Minister of the Crown as a true copy of a certificate issued by that Minister under section 23(2) or 24(3) shall in any legal proceedings be evidence (or, in Scotland, sufficient evidence) of that certificate.

(3) The power conferred by section 23(2) or 24(3) on a Minister of the Crown shall not be exercisable except by a Minister who is a member of the Cabinet or by the Attorney General, the Advocate General for Scotland or the Attorney General for Northern Ireland.

NOTES

Scottish public authority equivalent
None

Defined terms
"Minister of the Crown": s.84, Ministers of the Crown Act 1975

Defence

26(1) Information is exempt information if its disclosure under this Act would, or would be likely to, prejudice—
　　(a)　the defence of the British Islands or of any colony, or
　　(b)　the capability, effectiveness or security of any relevant forces.

(2) In subsection (1)(b) "relevant forces" means—
　　(a)　the armed forces of the Crown, and
　　(b)　any forces co-operating with those forces,
or any part of any of those forces.

(3) The duty to confirm or deny does not arise if, or to the extent that, compliance with section 1(1)(a) would, or would be likely to, prejudice any of the matters mentioned in subsection (1).

NOTES

Scottish public authority equivalent
FOI(S)A s 31

Exemption type
Not absolute: s 2(3)

Defined terms
"duty to confirm or deny": s 1(6)
"exempt information": s 84
"information": s 84
"relevant forces": subs.(2)

International relations

27(1) Information is exempt information if its disclosure under this Act would, or would be likely to, prejudice—

(a) relations between the United Kingdom and any other State,

(b) relations between the United Kingdom and any international organisation or international court,

(c) the interests of the United Kingdom abroad, or

(d) the promotion or protection by the United Kingdom of its interests abroad.

(2) Information is also exempt information if it is confidential information obtained from a State other than the United Kingdom or from an international organisation or international court.

(3) For the purposes of this section, any information obtained from a State, organisation or court is confidential at any time while the terms on which it was obtained require it to be held in confidence or while the circumstances in which it was obtained make it reasonable for the State, organisation or court to expect that it will be so held.

(4) The duty to confirm or deny does not arise if, or to the extent that, compliance with section 1(1)(a)—

(a) would, or would be likely to, prejudice any of the matters mentioned in subsection (1), or

(b) would involve the disclosure of any information (whether or not already recorded) which is confidential information obtained from a State other than the United Kingdom or from an international organisation or international court.

(5) In this section—

"international court" means any international court which is not an international organisation and which is established—

(a) by a resolution of an international organisation of which the United Kingdom is a member, or

(b) by an international agreement to which the United Kingdom is a party;

"international organisation" means any international organisation whose members include any two or more States, or any organ of such an organisation;

"State" includes the government of any State and any organ of its government, and references to a State other than the United Kingdom include references to any territory outside the United Kingdom.

NOTES

Scottish public authority equivalent FOI(S)A s 32	**Defined terms** "duty to confirm or deny": s 1(6) "exempt information": s 84
	"information": s 84
Exemption type Not absolute: s 2(3)	"international court": subs (5) "international organisation": subs (5) "State": subs 5

Relations within the United Kingdom

28(1) Information is exempt information if its disclosure under this Act would, or would be likely to, prejudice relations between any administration in the United Kingdom and any other such administration.

(2) In subsection (1) "administration in the United Kingdom" means—

(a)   the government of the United Kingdom,

(b)   the Scottish Administration,

(c)   the Executive Committee of the Northern Ireland Assembly, or

(d)   the Welsh Assembly Government.

(3)   The duty to confirm or deny does not arise if, or to the extent that, compliance with section 1(1)(a) would, or would be likely to, prejudice any of the matters mentioned in subsection (1).

NOTES

Scottish public authority equivalent
   FOI(S)A s 28

Exemption type
   Not absolute: s 2(3)

Defined terms
   "administration in the United Kingdom": subs (2)
   "duty to confirm or deny": s 1(6)
   "exempt information": s 84
   "information": s 84

The economy

29(1)   Information is exempt information if its disclosure under this Act would, or would be likely to, prejudice—

(a)   the economic interests of the United Kingdom or of any part of the United Kingdom, or

(b)   the financial interests of any administration in the United Kingdom, as defined by section 28(2).

(2)   The duty to confirm or deny does not arise if, or to the extent that, compliance with section 1(1)(a) would, or would be likely to, prejudice any of the matters mentioned in subsection (1).

NOTES

Scottish public authority equivalent
   FOI(S)A s 33

Exemption type
   Not absolute: s 2(3)

Defined terms
   "duty to confirm or deny": s 1(6)
   "exempt information": s 84
   "information": s 84

Investigations and proceedings conducted by public authorities

30(1)   Information held by a public authority is exempt information if it has at any time been held by the authority for the purposes of—

(a)   any investigation which the public authority has a duty to conduct with a view to it being ascertained—

(i)   whether a person should be charged with an offence, or

(ii)   whether a person charged with offence is guilty of it,

(b)   any investigation which is conducted by the authority and in the circumstances may lead to a decision by the authority to institute criminal proceedings which the authority has power to conduct, or

(c)   any criminal proceedings which the authority has power to conduct.

(2)   Information held by a public authority is exempt information if—

(a)   it was obtained or recorded by the authority for the purposes of its functions relating to—

(i)   investigations falling within subsection (1)(a) or (b),

(ii)   criminal proceedings which the authority has power to conduct,

(iii)   investigations (other than investigations falling within subsection (1)(a) or (b)) which are conducted by the authority for any of the purposes specified in section 31(2) and either by virtue of Her Majesty's prerogative or by virtue of powers conferred by or under any enactment, or

(iv) civil proceedings which are brought by or on behalf of the authority and arise out of such investigations, and

(b) it relates to the obtaining of information from confidential sources.

(3) The duty to confirm or deny does not arise in relation to information which is (or if it were held by the public authority would be) exempt information by virtue of subsection (1) or (2).

(4) In relation to the institution or conduct of criminal proceedings or the power to conduct them, references in subsection (1)(b) or (c) and subsection (2)(a) to the public authority include references—

(a) to any officer of the authority,

(b) in the case of a government department other than a Northern Ireland department, to the Minister of the Crown in charge of the department, and

(c) in the case of a Northern Ireland department, to the Northern Ireland Minister in charge of the department.

(5) In this section—

"criminal proceedings" includes service law proceedings (as defined by section 324(5) of the Armed Forces Act 2006);

"offence" includes a service offence (as defined by section 50 of that Act).

(6) In the application of this section to Scotland—

(a) in subsection (1)(b), for the words from "a decision" to the end there is substituted "a decision by the authority to make a report to the procurator fiscal for the purpose of enabling him to determine whether criminal proceedings should be instituted",

(b) in subsections (1)(c) and (2)(a)(ii) for "which the authority has power to conduct" there is substituted "which have been instituted in consequence of a report made by the authority to the procurator fiscal", and

(c) for any reference to a person being charged with an offence there is substituted a reference to the person being prosecuted for the offence.

NOTES

Scottish public authority equivalent
FOI(S)A s 34

Exemption type
Not absolute: s 2(3)

Defined terms
"criminal proceedings": subs (5)

"duty to confirm or deny": s 1(6)
"enactment": s 84
"exempt information": s 84
"held": s 3(2)
"information": s 84
"Northern Ireland Minister": s 84
"public authority": s 3(1)

Law enforcement

31(1) Information which is not exempt information by virtue of section 30 is exempt information if its disclosure under this Act would, or would be likely to, prejudice—

(a) the prevention or detection of crime,

(b) the apprehension or prosecution of offenders,

(c) the administration of justice,

(d) the assessment or collection of any tax or duty or of any imposition of a similar nature,

(e) the operation of the immigration controls,

(f) the maintenance of security and good order in prisons or in other institutions where persons are lawfully detained,

(g) the exercise by any public authority of its functions for any of the purposes specified in subsection (2),

(h) any civil proceedings which are brought by or on behalf of a public authority and arise out of an investigation conducted, for any of the purposes specified in subsection (2), by or on behalf of the authority by virtue of Her Majesty's prerogative or by virtue of powers conferred by or under an enactment, or

(i) any inquiry held under the Inquiries into Fatal Accidents and Sudden Deaths etc (Scotland) Act 2016 to the extent that the inquiry arises out of an investigation conducted, for any of the purposes specified in subsection (2), by or on behalf of the authority by virtue of Her Majesty's prerogative or by virtue of powers conferred by or under an enactment.

(2) The purposes referred to in subsection (1)(g) to (i) are—

(a) the purpose of ascertaining whether any person has failed to comply with the law,

(b) the purpose of ascertaining whether any person is responsible for any conduct which is improper,

(c) the purpose of ascertaining whether circumstances which would justify regulatory action in pursuance of any enactment exist or may arise,

(d) the purpose of ascertaining a person's fitness or competence in relation to the management of bodies corporate or in relation to any profession or other activity which he is, or seeks to become, authorised to carry on,

(e) the purpose of ascertaining the cause of an accident,

(f) the purpose of protecting charities against misconduct or mismanagement (whether by trustees or other persons) in their administration,

(g) the purpose of protecting the property of charities from loss or misapplication,

(h) the purpose of recovering the property of charities,

(i) the purpose of securing the health, safety and welfare of persons at work, and

(j) the purpose of protecting persons other than persons at work against risk to health or safety arising out of or in connection with the actions of persons at work.

(3) The duty to confirm or deny does not arise if, or to the extent that, compliance with section 1(1)(a) would, or would be likely to, prejudice any of the matters mentioned in subsection (1).

NOTES

Scottish public authority equivalent
FOI(S)A s 35

Exemption type
Not absolute: s 2(3)

Defined terms
"duty to confirm or deny": s 1(6)
"enactment": s 84
"exempt information": s 84
"information": s 84
"public authority": s 3(1)

Court records, etc

32(1) Information held by a public authority is exempt information if it is held only by virtue of being contained in—

(a) any document filed with, or otherwise placed in the custody of, a court for the purposes of proceedings in a particular cause or matter,

   (b)   any document served upon, or by, a public authority for the purposes of proceedings in a particular cause or matter, or

   (c)   any document created by—

        (i)   a court, or

        (ii)   a member of the administrative staff of a court,

for the purposes of proceedings in a particular cause or matter.

(2)   Information held by a public authority is exempt information if it is held only by virtue of being contained in—

   (a)   any document placed in the custody of a person conducting an inquiry or arbitration, for the purposes of the inquiry or arbitration, or

   (b)   any document created by a person conducting an inquiry or arbitration, for the purposes of the inquiry or arbitration.

(3)   The duty to confirm or deny does not arise in relation to information which is (or if it were held by the public authority would be) exempt information by virtue of this section.

(4)   In this section—

   (a)   "court" includes any tribunal or body exercising the judicial power of the State,

   (b)   "proceedings in a particular cause or matter" includes any inquest or any investigation under Part 1 of the Coroners and Justice Act 2009, any inquest under the Coroners Act (Northern Ireland) 1959 and any post-mortem examination,

   (c)   "inquiry" means any inquiry or hearing held under any provision contained in, or made under, an enactment, and

   (d)   except in relation to Scotland, "arbitration" means any arbitration to which Part I of the Arbitration Act 1996 applies.

NOTES

Scottish public authority equivalent
  FOI(S)A s 37

Exemption type
  Absolute: s 2(3)(c)

Defined terms
  "arbitration": subs.(4), Arbitration Act 1996
  "court": subs.(4)

"duty to confirm or deny": s 1(6)
"exempt information": s 84
"held": s 3(2)
"information": s 84
"inquiry": subs.(4)
"proceedings in any cause or matter": subs.(4)
"public authority": s 84

Audit functions

33(1)   This section applies to any public authority which has functions in relation to—

   (a)   the audit of the accounts of other public authorities, or

   (b)   the examination of the economy, efficiency and effectiveness with which other public authorities use their resources in discharging their functions.

(2)   Information held by a public authority to which this section applies is exempt information if its disclosure would, or would be likely to, prejudice the exercise of any of the authority's functions in relation to any of the matters referred to in subsection (1).

(3)   The duty to confirm or deny does not arise in relation to a public authority to which this section applies if, or to the extent that, compliance with section 1(1)(a) would, or would be likely to, prejudice the exercise of any of the authority's functions in relation to any of the matters referred to in subsection (1).

NOTES

Scottish public authority equivalent
   FOI(S)A s 40

Exemption type
   Not absolute: s 2(3)

Defined terms
   "duty to confirm or deny": s 1(6)
   "exempt information": s 84
   "held": s 3(2)
   "information": s 84
   "public authority": s 84

Parliamentary privilege

34(1) Information is exempt information if exemption from section 1(1)(b) is required for the purpose of avoiding an infringement of the privileges of either House of Parliament.

(2) The duty to confirm or deny does not apply if, or to the extent that, exemption from section 1(1)(a) is required for the purpose of avoiding an infringement of the privileges of either House of Parliament.

(3) A certificate signed by the appropriate authority certifying that exemption from section 1(1)(b), or from section 1(1)(a) and (b), is, or at any time was, required for the purpose of avoiding an infringement of the privileges of either House of Parliament shall be conclusive evidence of that fact.

(4) In subsection (3) "the appropriate authority" means—
    (a) in relation to the House of Commons, the Speaker of that House, and
    (b) in relation to the House of Lords, the Clerk of the Parliaments.

NOTES

Scottish public authority equivalent
   None

Exemption type
   Absolute: s 2(3)(d)

Defined terms
   "duty to confirm or deny": s 1(3)
   "exempt information": s 84
   "information": s 84

Formulation of government policy, etc

35(1) Information held by a government department or by the Welsh Assembly Government is exempt information if it relates to—
    (a) the formulation or development of government policy,
    (b) Ministerial communications,
    (c) the provision of advice by any of the Law Officers or any request for the provision of such advice, or
    (d) the operation of any Ministerial private office.

(2) Once a decision as to government policy has been taken, any statistical information used to provide an informed background to the taking of the decision is not to be regarded—
    (a) for the purposes of subsection (1)(a), as relating to the formulation or development of government policy, or
    (b) for the purposes of subsection (1)(b), as relating to Ministerial communications.

(3) The duty to confirm or deny does not arise in relation to information which is (or if it were held by the public authority would be) exempt information by virtue of subsection (1).

(4) In making any determination required by section 2(1)(b) or (2)(b) in relation to information which is exempt information by virtue of subsection (1)(a), regard shall be had to the particular public interest in the disclosure of factual information which has been used, or is intended to be used, to provide an informed background to decision-taking.

(5)   In this section—

"government policy" includes the policy of the Executive Committee of the Northern Ireland Assembly and the policy of the Welsh Assembly Government;

"the Law Officers" means the Attorney General, the Solicitor General, the Advocate General for Scotland, the Lord Advocate, the Solicitor General for Scotland, the Counsel General to the Welsh Assembly Government and the Attorney General for Northern Ireland;

"Ministerial communications" means any communications—

(a)   between Ministers of the Crown,

(b)   between Northern Ireland Ministers, including Northern Ireland junior Ministers, or

(c)   between members of the Welsh Assembly Government,

and includes, in particular, proceedings of the Cabinet or of any committee of the Cabinet, proceedings of the Executive Committee of the Northern Ireland Assembly, and proceedings of the Cabinet or any committee of the Cabinet of the Welsh Assembly Government;

"Ministerial private office" means any part of a government department which provides personal administrative support to a Minister of the Crown, to a Northern Ireland Minister or a Northern Ireland junior Minister or any part of the administration of the Welsh Assembly Government providing personal administrative support to the members of the Welsh Assembly Government;

"Northern Ireland junior Minister" means a member of the Northern Ireland Assembly appointed as a junior Minister under section 19 of the Northern Ireland Act 1998.

Scottish public authority equivalent
FOI(S)A s 29

Exemption type
Not absolute: s 2(3)

Defined terms
"duty to confirm or deny": s 1(6)
"exempt information": s 84
"government department": s 84

"government policy": subs (6)
"held": s 3(2)
"information": s 84
"Law Officer": subs (6)
"Minister of the Crown": s 84, Ministers of the Crown Act 1975
"Ministerial communication": subs (6)
"Ministerial private office": subs (6)
"Northern Ireland junior Minister": subs (6)
"Northern Ireland Minister": s 84

Prejudice to effective conduct of public affairs

36(1)   This section applies to—

(a)   information which is held by a government department or by the Welsh Assembly Government and is not exempt information by virtue of section 35, and

(b)   information which is held by any other public authority.

(2)   Information to which this section applies is exempt information if, in the reasonable opinion of a qualified person, disclosure of the information under this Act—

(a)   would, or would be likely to, prejudice—

(i)   the maintenance of the convention of the collective responsibility of Ministers of the Crown, or

(ii)   the work of the Executive Committee of the Northern Ireland Assembly, or

(iii)   the work of the Cabinet of the Welsh Assembly Government,

    (b)   would, or would be likely to, inhibit—

        (i)   the free and frank provision of advice, or

        (ii)   the free and frank exchange of views for the purposes of deliberation, or

    (c)   would otherwise prejudice, or would be likely otherwise to prejudice, the effective conduct of public affairs.

(3)   The duty to confirm or deny does not arise in relation to information to which this section applies (or would apply if held by the public authority) if, or to the extent that, in the reasonable opinion of a qualified person, compliance with section 1(1)(a) would, or would be likely to, have any of the effects mentioned in subsection (2).

(4)   In relation to statistical information, subsections (2) and (3) shall have effect with the omission of the words "in the reasonable opinion of a qualified person".

(5)   In subsections (2) and (3) "qualified person"—

    (a)   in relation to information held by a government department in the charge of a Minister of the Crown, means any Minister of the Crown,

    (b)   in relation to information held by a Northern Ireland department, means the Northern Ireland Minister in charge of the department,

    (c)   in relation to information held by any other government department, means the commissioners or other person in charge of that department,

    (d)   in relation to information held by the House of Commons, means the Speaker of that House,

    (e)   in relation to information held by the House of Lords, means the Clerk of the Parliaments,

    (f)   in relation to information held by the Northern Ireland Assembly, means the Presiding Officer,

    (g)   in relation to information held by the Welsh Assembly Government, means the Welsh Ministers or the Counsel General to the Welsh Assembly Government,

    (ga)   in relation to information held by the National Assembly for Wales, means the Presiding Officer of the National Assembly for Wales,

    (gb)   in relation to information held by any Welsh public authority (other than one referred to in section 83(1)(b)(ii) (subsidiary of the Assembly Commission), the Auditor General for Wales, the Wales Audit Office or the Public Services Ombudsman for Wales), means—

        (i)   the public authority, or

        (ii)   any officer or employee of the authority authorised by the Welsh Ministers or the Counsel General to the Welsh Assembly Government",

    (gc)   in relation to information held by a Welsh public authority referred to in section 83(1)(b)(ii), means—

        (i)   the public authority, or

        (ii)   any officer or employee of the authority authorised by the Presiding Officer of the National Assembly for Wales,

    (i)   in relation to information held by the National Audit Office or the Comptroller and Auditor General, means the Comptroller and Auditor General,

    (j)   in relation to information held by the Northern Ireland Audit Office, means the Comptroller and Auditor General for Northern Ireland,

    (k)   in relation to information held by the Auditor General for Wales or the Wales Audit Office, means the Auditor General for Wales,

    (ka)   in relation to information held by the Public Services Ombudsman for Wales, means the Public Services Ombudsman for Wales,

(l)   in relation to information held by any Northern Ireland public authority other than the Northern Ireland Audit Office, means—

    (i)   the public authority, or

    (ii)   any officer or employee of the authority authorised by the First Minister and deputy First Minister in Northern Ireland acting jointly,

(m)   in relation to information held by the Greater London Authority, means the Mayor of London,

(n)   in relation to information held by a functional body within the meaning of the Greater London Authority Act 1999, means the chairman of that functional body, and

(o)   in relation to information held by any public authority not falling within any of paragraphs (a) to (n), means—

    (i)   a Minister of the Crown,

    (ii)   the public authority, if authorised for the purposes of this section by a Minister of the Crown, or

    (iii)   any officer or employee of the public authority who is authorised for the purposes of this section by a Minister of the Crown.

(6)   Any authorisation for the purposes of this section—

    (a)   may relate to a specified person or to persons falling within a specified class,

    (b)   may be general or limited to particular classes of case, and

    (c)   may be granted subject to conditions.

(7)   A certificate signed by the qualified person referred to in subsection (5)(d) or (e) above certifying that in his reasonable opinion—

    (a)   disclosure of information held by either House of Parliament, or

    (b)   compliance with section 1(1)(a) by either House,

would, or would be likely to, have any of the effects mentioned in subsection (2) shall be conclusive evidence of that fact.

NOTES

Scottish public authority equivalent
  FOI(S)A s 30

Exemption type
  Absolute, so far as relates to information held by the House of Commons or House of Lords, not absolute otherwise: s 2(3)(e)

Defined terms
  "duty to confirm or deny": s 1(6)

"exempt information": s 84
"government department": s 84
"held": s 3(2)
"information": s 84
"Minister of the Crown": s 84, Ministers of the Crown Act 1975
"Northern Ireland Minister": s 84
"public authority": s 3(1)
"qualified person": subs (5)

Communications with Her Majesty, etc and honours

37(1)   Information is exempt information if it relates to—

    (a)   communications with the Sovereign,

    (aa)   communications with the heir to, or the person who is for the time being second in line of succession to, the Throne,

    (ab)   communications with a person who has subsequently acceded to the Throne or become heir to, or second in line to, the Throne,

    (ac)   communications with other members of the Royal Family (other than communications which fall within any of paragraphs (a) to (ab) because they are made or received on behalf of a person falling within any of those paragraphs), and

> (ad)　communications with the Royal Household (other than communications which fall within any of paragraphs (a) to (ac) because they are made or received on behalf of a person falling within any of those paragraphs), or
>
> (b)　the conferring by the Crown of any honour or dignity.

(2)　The duty to confirm or deny does not arise in relation to information which is (or if it were held by the public authority would be) exempt information by virtue of subsection (1).

NOTES

Scottish public authority equivalent
　FOI(S)A s 41

52(2), Sch 7 para 2; SI 2011/46, art.3(b)(i) (with art 4)

Exemption type
　Originally not absolute: s 2(3)
　Paras 1(a)-(ab) and (2) now absolute: s 2(3)(ea) inserted 19 January 2011 by Constitutional Reform and Governance Act 2010 ss 46(1),

Defined terms
　"duty to confirm or deny": s 1(6)
　"exempt information": s 84
　"information": s 84

Health and safety

38(1)　Information is exempt information if its disclosure under this Act would, or would be likely to—

> (a)　endanger the physical or mental health of any individual, or
>
> (b)　endanger the safety of any individual.

(2)　The duty to confirm or deny does not arise if, or to the extent that, compliance with section 1(1)(a) would, or would be likely to, have either of the effects mentioned in subsection (1).

NOTES

Scottish public authority equivalent
　FOI(S)A s 39

Defined terms
　"duty to confirm or deny": s 1(6)
　"exempt information": s 84
　"information": s 84

Exemption type
　Not absolute: s 2(3)

Environmental information

39(1)　Information is exempt information if the public authority holding it—

> (a)　is obliged by environmental information regulations to make the information available to the public in accordance with the regulations, or
>
> (b)　would be so obliged but for any exemption contained in the regulations.

(1A)　In subsection (1) "environmental information regulations" means—

> (a)　regulations made under section 74, or
>
> (b)　regulations made under section 2(2) of the European Communities Act 1972 for the purpose of implementing any EU obligation relating to public access to, and the dissemination of, information on the environment.

(2)　The duty to confirm or deny does not arise in relation to information which is (or if it were held by the public authority would be) exempt information by virtue of subsection (1).

(3)　Subsection (1)(a) does not limit the generality of section 21(1).

NOTES

Scottish public authority equivalent
　FOI(S)A s s 39

Exemption type
　Not absolute: s 2(3)

Defined terms
"duty to confirm or deny": s 1(6)
"exempt information": s 84
"held": s 3(2)
"information": s 84
"public authority": s 3(1)

Personal information

40(1)   Any information to which a request for information relates is exempt information if it constitutes personal data of which the applicant is the data subject.

(2)   Any information to which a request for information relates is also exempt information if—

(a)   it constitutes personal data which does not fall within subsection (1), and

(b)   either the first, second or third condition below is satisfied.

(3A)   The first condition is that the disclosure of the information to a member of the public otherwise than under this Act—

(a)   would contravene any of the data protection principles, or

(b)   would do so if the exemptions in section 24(1) of the Data Protection Act 2018 (manual unstructured data held by public authorities) were disregarded.

(3B)   The second condition is that the disclosure of the information to a member of the public otherwise than under this Act would contravene Article 21 of the GDPR (general processing: right to object to processing).

(4A)   The third condition is that--

(a)   on a request under Article 15(1) of the GDPR (general processing: right of access by the data subject) for access to personal data, the information would be withheld in reliance on provision made by or under section 15, 16 or 26 of, or Schedule 2, 3 or 4 to, the Data Protection Act 2018, or

(b)   on a request under section 45(1)(b) of that Act (law enforcement processing: right of access by the data subject), the information would be withheld in reliance on subsection (4) of that section.

(5A)   The duty to confirm or deny does not arise in relation to information which is (or if it were held by the public authority would be) exempt information by virtue of subsection (1).

(5B)   The duty to confirm or deny does not arise in relation to other information if or to the extent that any of the following applies--

(a)   giving a member of the public the confirmation or denial that would have to be given to comply with section 1(1)(a)--

(i)   would (apart from this Act) contravene any of the data protection principles, or

(ii)   would do so if the exemptions in section 24(1) of the Data Protection Act 2018 (manual unstructured data held by public authorities) were disregarded;

(b)   giving a member of the public the confirmation or denial that would have to be given to comply with section 1(1)(a) would (apart from this Act) contravene Article 21 of the GDPR (general processing: right to object to processing);

(c)   on a request under Article 15(1) of the GDPR (general processing: right of access by the data subject) for confirmation of whether personal data is being processed, the information would be withheld in reliance on a provision listed in subsection (4A)(a);

(d) on a request under section 45(1)(a) of the Data Protection Act 2018 (law enforcement processing: right of access by the data subject), the information would be withheld in reliance on subsection (4) of that section.

(7) In this section--

"the data protection principles" means the principles set out in--

(a) Article 5(1) of the GDPR, and

(b) section 34(1) of the Data Protection Act 2018;

"data subject" has the same meaning as in the Data Protection Act 2018 (see section 3 of that Act);

"the GDPR", "personal data", "processing" and references to a provision of Chapter 2 of Part 2 of the Data Protection Act 2018 have the same meaning as in Parts 5 to 7 of that Act (see section 3(2), (4), (10), (11) and (14) of that Act).

(8) In determining for the purposes of this section whether the lawfulness principle in Article 5(1)(a) of the GDPR would be contravened by the disclosure of information, Article 6(1) of the GDPR (lawfulness) is to be read as if the second sub-paragraph (disapplying the legitimate interests gateway in relation to public authorities) were omitted.

NOTES

Scottish public authority equivalent
FOI(S)A s 38

Exemption type
Absolute in relation to subsection (1); absolute in relation to subsection (2) so far as relating to cases where the first condition referred to in it is satisfied; not absolute otherwise: s 2(3)(fa)

Defined terms
"applicant": s 84

"data protection principles": subs.(7)
"data subject": subs (7), Data Protection Act 2018, s 3(5)
"duty to confirm or deny": s 1(6)
"exempt information": s 84
"GDPR" subs (7), Data Protection Act 2018 s 3(10)
"information": s 84
"personal data": subs (7), Data Protection Act 2018 s 3(2)
"processing": subs (7), Data Protection Act 2018 s 3(4)
"request for information": s 8

Information provided in confidence

41(1) Information is exempt information if—

(a) it was obtained by the public authority from any other person (including another public authority), and

(b) the disclosure of the information to the public (otherwise than under this Act) by the public authority holding it would constitute a breach of confidence actionable by that or any other person.

(2) The duty to confirm or deny does not arise if, or to the extent that, the confirmation or denial that would have to be given to comply with section 1(1)(a) would (apart from this Act) constitute an actionable breach of confidence.

NOTES

Scottish public authority equivalent
FOI(S)A s 36

Exemption type
Absolute: s 2(3)(g)

Defined terms
"duty to confirm or deny": s 1(6)
"exempt information": s 84
"information": s 84
"public authority": s 3(1)

Legal professional privilege

42(1) Information in respect of which a claim to legal professional privilege or, in Scotland, to confidentiality of communications could be maintained in legal proceedings is exempt information.

(2) The duty to confirm or deny does not arise if, or to the extent that, compliance with section 1(1)(a) would involve the disclosure of any information (whether or not already recorded) in respect of which such a claim could be maintained in legal proceedings.

NOTES

Scottish public authority equivalent	**Defined terms**
FOI(S)A s 36	"duty to confirm or deny": s 1(6)
Exemption type	"exempt information": s 84
Not absolute: s 2(3)	"information": s 84

Commercial interests

43(1) Information is exempt information if it constitutes a trade secret.

(2) Information is exempt information if its disclosure under this Act would, or would be likely to, prejudice the commercial interests of any person (including the public authority holding it).

(3) The duty to confirm or deny does not arise if, or to the extent that, compliance with section 1(1)(a) would, or would be likely to, prejudice the interests mentioned in subsection (2).

NOTES

Scottish public authority equivalent	**Defined terms**
FOI(S)A s 33	"duty to confirm or deny": s 1(6)
	"exempt information": s 84
Exemption type	"information": s 84
Not absolute: s 2(3)	"public authority": s 3(1)

Prohibitions on disclosure

44(1) Information is exempt information if its disclosure (otherwise than under this Act) by the public authority holding it—

    (a) is prohibited by or under any enactment,

    (b) is incompatible with any EU obligation, or

    (c) would constitute or be punishable as a contempt of court.

(2) The duty to confirm or deny does not arise if the confirmation or denial that would have to be given to comply with section 1(1)(a) would (apart from this Act) fall within any of paragraphs (a) to (c) of subsection (1).

NOTES

Scottish public authority equivalent	**Defined terms**
FOI(S)A s 26	"duty to confirm or deny": s 1(6)
	"enactment": s 84
Exemption type	"exempt information": s 84
Absolute: s 2(3)(h)	"information": s 84
	"public authority": s 3(1)

PART III

GENERAL FUNCTIONS OF MINISTER FOR THE CABINET OFFICE, SECRETARY OF STATE AND INFORMATION COMMISSIONER

Issue of code of practice by the Minister for the Cabinet Office

45(1) The Minister for the Cabinet Office shall issue, and may from time to time revise, a code of practice providing guidance to public authorities as to the practice which it would, in his opinion, be desirable for them to follow in connection with the discharge of the authorities' functions under Part I.

(2) The code of practice must, in particular, include provision relating to—

    (a)   the provision of advice and assistance by public authorities to persons who propose to make, or have made, requests for information to them,

    (b)   the transfer of requests by one public authority to another public authority by which the information requested is or may be held,

    (c)   consultation with persons to whom the information requested relates or persons whose interests are likely to be affected by the disclosure of information,

    (d)   the inclusion in contracts entered into by public authorities of terms relating to the disclosure of information,

    (da)   the disclosure by public authorities of datasets held by them, and

    (e)   the provision by public authorities of procedures for dealing with complaints about the handling by them of requests for information.

(2A) Provision of the kind mentioned in subsection (2)(da) may, in particular, include provision relating to-

    (a)   the giving of permission for datasets to be re-used,

    (b)   the disclosure of datasets in an electronic form which is capable of re-use,

    (c)   the making of datasets available for re-use in accordance with the terms of a licence,

    (d)   other matters relating to the making of datasets available for re-use,

    (e)   standards applicable to public authorities in connection with the disclosure of datasets.

(3) Any code under this section may make different provision for different public authorities.

(4) Before issuing or revising any code under this section, the Minister for the Cabinet Office shall consult the Commissioner.

(5) The Minister for the Cabinet Office shall lay before each House of Parliament any code or revised code made under this section.

Issue of code of practice by Secretary of State

46(1) The Secretary of State shall issue, and may from time to time revise, a code of practice providing guidance to relevant authorities as to the practice which it would, in his opinion, be desirable for them to follow in connection with the keeping, management and destruction of their records.

(2) For the purpose of facilitating the performance by the Public Record Office, the Public Record Office of Northern Ireland and other public authorities of their functions under this Act in relation to records which are public records for the purposes of the Public Records Act 1958 or the Public Records Act (Northern Ireland) 1923, the code may also include guidance as to—

    (a)   the practice to be adopted in relation to the transfer of records under section 3(4) of the Public Records Act 1958 or section 3 of the Public Records Act

(Northern Ireland) 1923, and

(b) the practice of reviewing records before they are transferred under those provisions.

(3) In exercising his functions under this section, the Secretary of State shall have regard to the public interest in allowing public access to information held by relevant authorities.

(4) The code may make different provision for different relevant authorities.

(5) Before issuing or revising any code under this section the Secretary of State shall consult—

(a) the Minister for the Cabinet Office,

(b) the Commissioner, and

(c) in relation to Northern Ireland, the appropriate Northern Ireland Minister.

(6) The Secretary of State shall lay before each House of Parliament any code or revised code made under this section.

(7) In this section "relevant authority" means—

(a) any public authority, and

(b) any office or body which is not a public authority but whose administrative and departmental records are public records for the purposes of the Public Records Act 1958 or the Public Records Act (Northern Ireland) 1923.

General functions of Commissioner

47(1) It shall be the duty of the Commissioner to promote the following of good practice by public authorities and, in particular, so to perform his functions under this Act as to promote the observance by public authorities of—

(a) the requirements of this Act, and

(b) the provisions of the codes of practice under sections 45 and 46.

(2) The Commissioner shall arrange for the dissemination in such form and manner as he considers appropriate of such information as it may appear to him expedient to give to the public—

(a) about the operation of this Act,

(b) about good practice, and

(c) about other matters within the scope of his functions under this Act,

and may give advice to any person as to any of those matters.

(3) The Commissioner may, with the consent of any public authority, assess whether that authority is following good practice.

(4) The Commissioner may charge such sums as he may determine for any relevant services provided by the Commissioner under this section.

(4A) In subsection (4) "relevant services" means-

(a) the provision to the same person of more than one copy of any published material where each of the copies of the material is either provided on paper, a portable disk which stores the material electronically or a similar medium,

   (b)   the provision of training, or

   (c)   the provision of conferences.

(4B)   The Minister for the Cabinet Office may by order amend subsection (4A).

(4C)   An order under subsection (4B) may include such transitional or saving provision as the Minister for the Cabinet Office considers appropriate.

(4D)   The Minister for the Cabinet Office must consult the Commissioner before making an order under subsection (4B).

(5)   The Commissioner shall from time to time as he considers appropriate—

   (a)   consult the Keeper of Public Records about the promotion by the Commissioner of the observance by public authorities of the provisions of the code of practice under section 46 in relation to records which are public records for the purposes of the Public Records Act 1958, and

   (b)   consult the Deputy Keeper of the Records of Northern Ireland about the promotion by the Commissioner of the observance by public authorities of those provisions in relation to records which are public records for the purposes of the Public Records Act (Northern Ireland) 1923.

(6)   In this section "good practice", in relation to a public authority, means such practice in the discharge of its functions under this Act as appears to the Commissioner to be desirable, and includes (but is not limited to) compliance with the requirements of this Act and the provisions of the codes of practice under sections 45 and 46.

NOTES

Scottish public authority equivalent	Defined terms
FOI(S)A s 43	"Commissioner": s 18(3)
	"good practice": subs (6)
	"public authority": s 3(1)

Recommendations as to good practice

48(1)   If it appears to the Commissioner that the practice of a public authority in relation to the exercise of its functions under this Act does not conform with that proposed in the codes of practice under sections 45 and 46, he may give to the authority a recommendation (in this section referred to as a "practice recommendation") specifying the steps which ought in his opinion to be taken for promoting such conformity.

(2)   A practice recommendation must be given in writing and must refer to the particular provisions of the code of practice with which, in the Commissioner's opinion, the public authority's practice does not conform.

(3)   Before giving to a public authority other than the Public Record Office a practice recommendation which relates to conformity with the code of practice under section 46 in respect of records which are public records for the purposes of the Public Records Act 1958, the Commissioner shall consult the Keeper of Public Records.

(4)   Before giving to a public authority other than the Public Record Office of Northern Ireland a practice recommendation which relates to conformity with the code of practice under section 46 in respect of records which are public records for the purposes of the Public Records Act (Northern Ireland) 1923, the Commissioner shall consult the Deputy Keeper of the Records of Northern Ireland.

NOTES

Commencement

Subsections (1), (2), 30 November 2002: SI
2002/2812

Subsections (3), (4), 1 January 2005: SI 2004/1909

Scottish public authority equivalent

FOI(S)A s 44

Defined terms

"Commissioner": s 18(3)

"code of practice": subs.(1), ss 45,46

"public authority": s 3(1)

"practice recommendation": subs (1)

49 .....

NOTES

Amendment

Repealed by the Data Protection Act 2018 s 211

Scottish public authority equivalent

FOI(S)A s 46

PART IV
ENFORCEMENT

Application for decision by Commissioner

50(1) Any person (in this section referred to as "the complainant") may apply to the Commissioner for a decision whether, in any specified respect, a request for information made by the complainant to a public authority has been dealt with in accordance with the requirements of Part I.

(2) On receiving an application under this section, the Commissioner shall make a decision unless it appears to him—

    (a) that the complainant has not exhausted any complaints procedure which is provided by the public authority in conformity with the code of practice under section 45,

    (b) that there has been undue delay in making the application,

    (c) that the application is frivolous or vexatious, or

    (d) that the application has been withdrawn or abandoned.

(3) Where the Commissioner has received an application under this section, he shall either—

    (a) notify the complainant that he has not made any decision under this section as a result of the application and of his grounds for not doing so, or

    (b) serve notice of his decision (in this Act referred to as a "decision notice") on the complainant and the public authority.

(4) Where the Commissioner decides that a public authority—

    (a) has failed to communicate information, or to provide confirmation or denial, in a case where it is required to do so by section 1(1), or

    (b) has failed to comply with any of the requirements of sections 11 and 17,

the decision notice must specify the steps which must be taken by the authority for complying with that requirement and the period within which they must be taken.

(5) A decision notice must contain particulars of the right of appeal conferred by section 57.

(6) Where a decision notice requires steps to be taken by the public authority within a specified period, the time specified in the notice must not expire before the end of the period within which an appeal can be brought against the notice and, if such an appeal is brought, no step which is affected by the appeal need be taken pending the

determination or withdrawal of the appeal.

(7) This section has effect subject to section 53.

NOTES

Scottish public authority equivalent
    FOI(S)A s 47

Defined terms
    "Commissioner": s 18(3)

"complainant": subs (1)
"decision notice": subs (3)
"information": s 84
"public authority": s 3(1)
"request for information": s 8

Information notices

51(1) If the Commissioner—

    (a)   has received an application under section 50, or

    (b)   reasonably requires any information—

        (i)   for the purpose of determining whether a public authority has complied or is complying with any of the requirements of Part I, or

        (ii)   for the purpose of determining whether the practice of a public authority in relation to the exercise of its functions under this Act conforms with that proposed in the codes of practice under sections 45 and 46,

he may serve the authority with a notice (in this Act referred to as "an information notice") requiring it, within such time as is specified in the notice, to furnish the Commissioner, in such form as may be so specified, with such information relating to the application, to compliance with Part I or to conformity with the code of practice as is so specified.

(2) An information notice must contain—

    (a)   in a case falling within subsection (1)(a), a statement that the Commissioner has received an application under section 50, or

    (b)   in a case falling within subsection (1)(b), a statement—

        (i)   that the Commissioner regards the specified information as relevant for either of the purposes referred to in subsection (1)(b), and

        (ii)   of his reasons for regarding that information as relevant for that purpose.

(3) An information notice must also contain particulars of the right of appeal conferred by section 57.

(4) The time specified in an information notice must not expire before the end of the period within which an appeal can be brought against the notice and, if such an appeal is brought, the information need not be furnished pending the determination or withdrawal of the appeal.

(5) An authority shall not be required by virtue of this section to furnish the Commissioner with any information in respect of—

    (a)   any communication between a professional legal adviser and his client in connection with the giving of legal advice to the client with respect to his obligations, liabilities or rights under this Act, or

    (b)   any communication between a professional legal adviser and his client, or between such an adviser or his client and any other person, made in connection with or in contemplation of proceedings under or arising out of this Act (including proceedings before the Tribunal) and for the purposes of such proceedings.

(6) In subsection (5) references to the client of a professional legal adviser include references to any person representing such a client.

(7) The Commissioner may cancel an information notice by written notice to the authority on which it was served.

(8) In this section "information" includes unrecorded information.

Enforcement notices

52(1) If the Commissioner is satisfied that a public authority has failed to comply with any of the requirements of Part I, the Commissioner may serve the authority with a notice (in this Act referred to as "an enforcement notice") requiring the authority to take, within such time as may be specified in the notice, such steps as may be so specified for complying with those requirements.

(2) An enforcement notice must contain—

(a) a statement of the requirement or requirements of Part I with which the Commissioner is satisfied that the public authority has failed to comply and his reasons for reaching that conclusion, and

(b) particulars of the right of appeal conferred by section 57.

(3) An enforcement notice must not require any of the provisions of the notice to be complied with before the end of the period within which an appeal can be brought against the notice and, if such an appeal is brought, the notice need not be complied with pending the determination or withdrawal of the appeal.

(4) The Commissioner may cancel an enforcement notice by written notice to the authority on which it was served.

(5) This section has effect subject to section 53.

Exception from duty to comply with decision notice or enforcement notice

53(1) This section applies to a decision notice or enforcement notice which—

(a) is served on—

(i) a government department,

(ii) the Welsh Assembly Government, or

(iii) any public authority designated for the purposes of this section by an order made by the Minister for the Cabinet Office, and

(b) relates to a failure, in respect of one or more requests for information—

       (i)   to comply with section 1(1)(a) in respect of information which falls within any provision of Part II stating that the duty to confirm or deny does not arise, or

      (ii)   to comply with section 1(1)(b) in respect of exempt information.

(2)   A decision notice or enforcement notice to which this section applies shall cease to have effect if, not later than the twentieth working day following the effective date, the accountable person in relation to that authority gives the Commissioner a certificate signed by him stating that he has on reasonable grounds formed the opinion that, in respect of the request or requests concerned, there was no failure falling within subsection (1)(b).

(3)   Where the accountable person gives a certificate to the Commissioner under subsection (2) he shall as soon as practicable thereafter lay a copy of the certificate before—

     (a)   each House of Parliament,

     (b)   the Northern Ireland Assembly, in any case where the certificate relates to a decision notice or enforcement notice which has been served on a Northern Ireland department or any Northern Ireland public authority, or

     (c)   the National Assembly for Wales, in any case where the certificate relates to a decision notice or enforcement notice which has been served on—

        (i)   the Welsh Assembly Government,

       (ii)   the National Assembly for Wales, or

      (iii)   any Welsh public authority.

(4)   In subsection (2) "the effective date", in relation to a decision notice or enforcement notice, means—

     (a)   the day on which the notice was given to the public authority, or

     (b)   where an appeal under section 57 is brought, the day on which that appeal (or any further appeal arising out of it) is determined or withdrawn.

(5)   Before making an order under subsection (1)(a)(iii), the Minister for the Cabinet Office shall—

     (a)   if the order relates to a Welsh public authority, consult the Welsh Ministers,

   (aa)   if the order relates to the National Assembly for Wales, consult the Presiding Officer of that Assembly,

     (b)   if the order relates to the Northern Ireland Assembly, consult the Presiding Officer of that Assembly, and

     (c)   if the order relates to a Northern Ireland public authority, consult the First Minister and deputy First Minister in Northern Ireland.

(6)   Where the accountable person gives a certificate to the Commissioner under subsection (2) in relation to a decision notice, the accountable person shall, on doing so or as soon as reasonably practicable after doing so, inform the person who is the complainant for the purposes of section 50 of the reasons for his opinion.

(7)   The accountable person is not obliged to provide information under subsection (6) if, or to the extent that, compliance with that subsection would involve the disclosure of exempt information.

(8)   In this section "the accountable person"—

     (a)   in relation to a Northern Ireland department or any Northern Ireland public authority, means the First Minister and deputy First Minister in Northern Ireland acting jointly,

  (b) in relation the Welsh Assembly Government, the National Assembly for Wales or any Welsh public authority, means the First Minister for Wales, and

  (c) in relation to any other public authority, means—

    (i) a Minister of the Crown who is a member of the Cabinet, or

    (ii) the Attorney General, the Advocate General for Scotland or the Attorney General for Northern Ireland.

(9) In this section "working day" has the same meaning as in section 10.

NOTES

Scottish public authority equivalent
 FOI(S)A s 52

Defined terms
 "accountable person": subs (8)
 "Commissioner": s 18(3)
 "complainant": s 50(1)
 "decision notice": s 50(3)
 "duty to confirm or deny": s 1(6)

"enforcement notice": s 52(1)
"exempt information": s 84, Part II
"government department": s 84
"information": s 84
"Minister of the Crown": s 84, Ministers of the
 Crown Act 1975
"Northern Ireland public authority": s 84
"public authority": s 3(1)
"request for information": s 8
"working day": s 10(6)

Failure to comply with notice

54(1) If a public authority has failed to comply with—

  (a) so much of a decision notice as requires steps to be taken,

  (b) an information notice, or

  (c) an enforcement notice,

the Commissioner may certify in writing to the court that the public authority has failed to comply with that notice.

(2) For the purposes of this section, a public authority which, in purported compliance with an information notice—

  (a) makes a statement which it knows to be false in a material respect, or

  (b) recklessly makes a statement which is false in a material respect,

is to be taken to have failed to comply with the notice.

(3) Where a failure to comply is certified under subsection (1), the court may inquire into the matter and, after hearing any witness who may be produced against or on behalf of the public authority, and after hearing any statement that may be offered in defence, deal with the authority as if it had committed a contempt of court.

(4) In this section "the court" means the High Court or, in Scotland, the Court of Session.

NOTES

Scottish public authority equivalent
 FOI(S)A s 53

Defined terms
 "Commissioner": s 18(3)

"decision notice": s 50(3)
"enforcement notice": s 52(1)
"information notice": s 51(1)
"public authority": s 3(1)

Powers of entry and inspection

55 Schedule 3 (powers of entry and inspection) has effect.

NOTES

Scottish public authority equivalent
 FOI(S)A s 54

No action against public authority

56(1) This Act does not confer any right of action in civil proceedings in respect of any failure to comply with any duty imposed by or under this Act.

(2) Subsection (1) does not affect the powers of the Commissioner under section 54.

NOTES

Scottish public authority equivalent	**Defined terms**
FOI(S)A s 55	"Commissioner": s 18(3)

PART V

APPEALS

Appeal against notices served under Part IV

57(1) Where a decision notice has been served, the complainant or the public authority may appeal to the Tribunal against the notice.

(2) A public authority on which an information notice or an enforcement notice has been served by the Commissioner may appeal to the Tribunal against the notice.

(3) In relation to a decision notice or enforcement notice which relates—
    (a) to information to which section 66 applies, and
    (b) to a matter which by virtue of subsection (3) or (4) of that section falls to be determined by the responsible authority instead of the appropriate records authority,
subsections (1) and (2) shall have effect as if the reference to the public authority were a reference to the public authority or the responsible authority.

NOTES

Scottish public authority equivalent	"decision notice": s 50(3)
FOI(S)A s 56	"enforcement notice": s 52(1)
	"information notice": s 51(1)
Defined terms	"public authority": s 3(1)
"appropriate records authority": s 15(5)	"responsible authority": s 15(5)
"Commissioner": s 18(3)	"Tribunal": s 18(3)
"complainant": s 50(1)	

Determination of appeals

58(1) If on an appeal under section 57 the Tribunal considers—
    (a) that the notice against which the appeal is brought is not in accordance with the law, or
    (b) to the extent that the notice involved an exercise of discretion by the Commissioner, that he ought to have exercised his discretion differently,
the Tribunal shall allow the appeal or substitute such other notice as could have been served by the Commissioner; and in any other case the Tribunal shall dismiss the appeal.

(2) On such an appeal, the Tribunal may review any finding of fact on which the notice in question was based.

NOTES

Scottish public authority equivalent	**Defined terms**
FOI(S)A s 57	"Commissioner": s 18(3)
	"Tribunal": s 18(3)

59 ....

Appeals against national security certificate

60(1)   Where a certificate under section 23(2) or 24(3) has been issued—

    (a)   the Commissioner, or

    (b)   any applicant whose request for information is affected by the issue of the certificate,

may appeal to the Tribunal against the certificate.

(2)   If on an appeal under subsection (1) relating to a certificate under section 23(2), the Tribunal finds that the information referred to in the certificate was not exempt information by virtue of section 23(1), the Tribunal may allow the appeal and quash the certificate.

(3)   If on an appeal under subsection (1) relating to a certificate under section 24(3), the Tribunal finds that, applying the principles applied by the court on an application for judicial review, the Minister did not have reasonable grounds for issuing the certificate, the Tribunal may allow the appeal and quash the certificate.

(4)   Where in any proceedings under this Act it is claimed by a public authority that a certificate under section 24(3) which identifies the information to which it applies by means of a general description applies to particular information, any other party to the proceedings may appeal to the Tribunal on the ground that the certificate does not apply to the information in question and, subject to any determination under subsection (5), the certificate shall be conclusively presumed so to apply.

(5)   On any appeal under subsection (4), the Tribunal may determine that the certificate does not so apply.

NOTES

Defined terms
  "applicant": s 84
  "Commissioner": s 18(3)
  "exempt information": s 84 and Pt.II

  "information": s 84
  "Tribunal": s 18(3)

Appeal proceedings

61(1)   Tribunal Procedure Rules may make provision for regulating the exercise of rights of appeal conferred by sections 57(1) and (2) and 60(1) and (4).

(2)   In relation to appeals under those provisions, Tribunal Procedure Rules may make provision about–

    (a)   securing the production of material used for the processing of personal data, and

    (b)   the inspection, examination, operation and testing of equipment or material used in connection with the processing of personal data.

(3)   Subsection (4) applies where--

    (a)   a person does something, or fails to do something, in relation to proceedings before the First-tier Tribunal on an appeal under those provisions, and

    (b)   if those proceedings were proceedings before a court having power to commit for contempt, the act or omission would constitute contempt of court.

(4)   The First-tier Tribunal may certify the offence to the Upper Tribunal.

(5)   Where an offence is certified under subsection (4), the Upper Tribunal may--

    (a)   inquire into the matter, and

    (b)   deal with the person charged with the offence in any manner in which it could deal with the person if the offence had been committed in relation to the Upper Tribunal.

(6)   Before exercising the power under subsection (5)(b), the Upper Tribunal must--

    (a)   hear any witness who may be produced against or on behalf of the person charged with the offence, and

    (b)   hear any statement that may be offered in defence.

(7)   In this section, "personal data" and "processing" have the same meaning as in Parts 5 to 7 of the Data Protection Act 2018 (see section 3(2), (4) and (14) of that Act).

PART VI
HISTORICAL RECORDS AND RECORDS IN PUBLIC RECORD OFFICE OR PUBLIC RECORD OFFICE OF NORTHERN IRELAND

Interpretation of Part VI

62(1)   For the purposes of this Part, a record becomes a "historical record" at the end of the period of twenty years beginning with the year following that in which it was created.

(2)   Where records created at different dates are for administrative purposes kept together in one file or other assembly, all the records in that file or other assembly are to be treated for the purposes of this Part as having been created when the latest of those records was created.

(2A)   Until the end of the period of 10 years beginning with the commencement of paragraph 4 of Schedule 7 to the Constitutional Reform and Governance Act 2010, subsection (1) has effect subject to any order made under section 46(2) of that Act.

(3)   In this Part "year" means a calendar year.

NOTES

Scottish public authority equivalent
   FOI(S)A s 57

Defined terms
   "historical record": subs (1)

Removal of exemptions: historical records generally

63(1)   Information contained in a historical record cannot be exempt information by virtue of section 30(1), 32, 33, 35 or 42.

(2)   Compliance with section 1(1)(a) in relation to a historical record is not to be taken to be capable of having any of the effects referred to in section 33(3) or 42(2).

(2A)   Information contained in a historical record cannot be exempt information by virtue of section 36 except-

    (a)   in a case falling within subsection (2)(a)(ii) of that section, or

    (b)   in a case falling within subsection (2)(c) of that section where the prejudice or likely prejudice relates to the effective conduct of public affairs in Northern Ireland.

(2B)   Compliance with section 1(1)(a) in relation to a historical record is not to be taken to have any of the effects referred to in subsection (3) of section 36, except where the effect-

    (a)   falls within subsection (2)(a)(ii) of that section, or

(b)   falls within subsection (2)(c) of that section and relates to the effective conduct of public affairs in Northern Ireland.

(2C)   Information cannot be exempt information-

    (a)   by virtue of section 28 or 43, or

    (b)   by virtue of section 36 in the excepted cases mentioned in subsection (2A),

after the end of the period of thirty years beginning with the year following that in which the record containing the information was created.

(2D)   Compliance with section 1(1)(a) in relation to any record is not to be taken, at any time after the end of the period of thirty years beginning with the year following that in which the record was created, to be capable-

    (a)   of prejudicing any of the matters referred to in section 28(1) or 43(2), or

    (b)   of having any of the effects referred to in section 36(3) in the excepted cases mentioned in subsection (2B).

(2E)   Information cannot be exempt information by virtue of any of paragraphs (a) to (ad) of section 37(1) after whichever is the later of-

    (a)   the end of the period of five years beginning with the date of the relevant death, and

    (b)   the end of the period of twenty years beginning with the date on which the record containing the information was created.

(2F)   In subsection (2E)(a) "the relevant death" means-

    (a)   for the purposes of any of paragraphs (a) to (ac) of section 37(1), the death of the person referred to in the paragraph concerned, or

    (b)   for the purposes of section 37(1)(ad), the death of the Sovereign reigning when the record containing the information was created

(3)   Information cannot be exempt information by virtue of section 37(1)(b) after the end of the period of sixty years beginning with the year following that in which the record containing the information was created.

(4)   Information cannot be exempt information by virtue of section 31 after the end of the period of one hundred years beginning with the year following that in which the record containing the information was created.

(5)   Compliance with section 1(1)(a) in relation to any record is not to be taken, at any time after the end of the period of one hundred years beginning with the year following that in which the record was created, to be capable of prejudicing any of the matters referred to in section 31(1).

NOTES

Scottish public authority equivalent	Defined terms
FOI(S)A s 58	"exempt information": s 84 and Pt II
	"historical information": s 62(1)
	"information": s 84

Removal of exemptions: historical records in public record offices

64(1)   Information contained in a historical record in the Public Record Office or the Public Record Office of Northern Ireland cannot be exempt information by virtue of section 21 or 22.

(2)   In relation to any information falling within section 23(1) which is contained in a historical record in the Public Record Office or the Public Record Office of Northern Ireland,

section 2(3) shall have effect with the omission of the reference to section 23.

NOTES

Defined terms
  "exempt information": s 84

"historical record": s 62(1)
"information": s 84

Decisions as to refusal of discretionary disclosure of historical records

65(1)   Before refusing a request for information relating to information which is contained in a historical record and is exempt information only by virtue of a provision not specified in section 2(3), a public authority shall—

  (a)   if the historical record is a public record within the meaning of the Public Records Act 1958, consult the Secretary of State, or

  (b)   if the historical record is a public record to which the Public Records Act (Northern Ireland) 1923 applies, consult the appropriate Northern Ireland Minister.

(2)   This section does not apply to information to which section 66 applies.

NOTES

Defined terms
  "appropriate Northern Ireland Minister": s 84
  "exempt information": s 84 and Part II
  "historical record": s 62(1)
  "information": s 84
  "public authority": s 3(1)
  "request for information": s 8

Decisions relating to certain transferred public records

66(1)   This section applies to any information which is (or, if it existed, would be) contained in a transferred public record, other than information which the responsible authority has designated as open information for the purposes of this section.

(2)   Before determining whether—

  (a)   information to which this section applies falls within any provision of Part II relating to the duty to confirm or deny, or

  (b)   information to which this section applies is exempt information,
  the appropriate records authority shall consult the responsible authority.

(3)   Where information to which this section applies falls within a provision of Part II relating to the duty to confirm or deny but does not fall within any of the provisions of that Part relating to that duty which are specified in subsection (3) of section 2, any question as to the application of subsection (1)(b) of that section is to be determined by the responsible authority instead of the appropriate records authority.

(4)   Where any information to which this section applies is exempt information only by virtue of any provision of Part II not specified in subsection (3) of section 2, any question as to the application of subsection (2)(b) of that section is to be determined by the responsible authority instead of the appropriate records authority.

(5)   Before making by virtue of subsection (3) or (4) any determination that subsection (1)(b) or (2)(b) of section 2 applies, the responsible authority shall consult—

  (a)   where the transferred public record is a public record within the meaning of the Public Records Act 1958, the Secretary of State, and

  (b)   where the transferred public record is a public record to which the Public Records Act (Northern Ireland) 1923 applies, the appropriate Northern Ireland

Minister.

(6) Where the responsible authority in relation to information to which this section applies is not (apart from this subsection) a public authority, it shall be treated as being a public authority for the purposes of Parts III, IV and V of this Act so far as relating to—

(a) the duty imposed by section 15(3), and

(b) the imposition of any requirement to furnish information relating to compliance with Part I in connection with the information to which this section applies.

NOTES

Defined terms
  "appropriate Northern Ireland Minister": s 84
  "appropriate records authority": s 15(5)
  "duty to confirm or deny": s 1(6)
  "exempt information": s 84

"information": s 84
"public authority": s 3(1)
"responsible authority": s 15(5)
"transferred public record": s 15(4)

Amendments of public records legislation

67 Schedule 5 (which amends the Public Records Act 1958 and the Public Records Act (Northern Ireland) 1923) has effect.

NOTES

Scottish public authority equivalent
  FOI(S)A s 70

PART VII

AMENDMENTS OF DATA PROTECTION ACT 1998

Amendments relating to personal information held by public authorities

Extension of meaning of "data"

68(1) Section 1 of the Data Protection Act 1998 (basic interpretative provisions) is amended in accordance with subsections (2) and (3).

(2) In subsection (1)—

(a) in the definition of "data", the word "or" at the end of paragraph (c) is omitted and after paragraph (d) there is inserted

"or

(e) is recorded information held by a public authority and does not fall within any of paragraphs (a) to (d);", and

(b) after the definition of "processing" there is inserted—

"'public authority' has the same meaning as in the Freedom of Information Act 2000;".

(3) After subsection (4) there is inserted—

"(5) In paragraph (e) of the definition of "data" in subsection (1), the reference to information "held" by a public authority shall be construed in accordance with section 3(2) of the Freedom of Information Act 2000.

(6) Where section 7 of the Freedom of Information Act 2000 prevents Parts I to V of that Act from applying to certain information held by a public authority, that information is not to be treated for the purposes of paragraph (e) of the definition of "data" in subsection (1) as held by a public authority."

(4) In section 56 of that Act (prohibition of requirement as to production of certain records),

after subsection (6) there is inserted—

"(6A)   A record is not a relevant record to the extent that it relates, or is to relate, only to personal data falling within paragraph (e) of the definition of "data" in section 1(1)."

(5)   In the Table in section 71 of that Act (index of defined expressions) after the entry relating to processing there is inserted—

"public authority   section 1(1)".

Right of access to unstructured personal data held by public authorities

69(1)   In section 7(1) of the Data Protection Act 1998 (right of access to personal data), for "sections 8 and 9" there is substituted "sections 8, 9 and 9A".

(2)   After section 9 of that Act there is inserted—

"9A Unstructured personal data held by public authorities

(1)   In this section "unstructured personal data" means any personal data falling within paragraph (e) of the definition of "data" in section 1(1), other than information which is recorded as part of, or with the intention that it should form part of, any set of information relating to individuals to the extent that the set is structured by reference to individuals or by reference to criteria relating to individuals.

(2)   A public authority is not obliged to comply with subsection (1) of section 7 in relation to any unstructured personal data unless the request under that section contains a description of the data.

(3)   Even if the data are described by the data subject in his request, a public authority is not obliged to comply with subsection (1) of section 7 in relation to unstructured personal data if the authority estimates that the cost of complying with the request so far as relating to those data would exceed the appropriate limit.

(4)   Subsection (3) does not exempt the public authority from its obligation to comply with paragraph (a) of section 7(1) in relation to the unstructured personal data unless the estimated cost of complying with that paragraph alone in relation to those data would exceed the appropriate limit.

(5)   In subsections (3) and (4) "the appropriate limit" means such amount as may be prescribed by the Secretary of State by regulations, and different amounts may be prescribed in relation to different cases.

(6)   Any estimate for the purposes of this section must be made in accordance with regulations under section 12(5) of the Freedom of Information Act 2000.".

(3)   In section 67(5) of that Act (statutory instruments subject to negative resolution procedure), in paragraph (c), for "or 9(3)" there is substituted ", 9(3) or 9A(5)".

Exemptions applicable to certain manual data held by public authorities

70(1)   After section 33 of the Data Protection Act 1998 there is inserted—

"33A Manual data held by public authorities

(1)   Personal data falling within paragraph (e) of the definition of "data" in section 1(1) are exempt from—

(a)   the first, second, third, fifth, seventh and eighth data protection principles,

(b)   the sixth data protection principle except so far as it relates to the rights conferred on data subjects by sections 7 and 14,

      (c) sections 10 to 12,

      (d) section 13, except so far as it relates to damage caused by a contravention of section 7 or of the fourth data protection principle and to any distress which is also suffered by reason of that contravention,

      (e) Part III, and

      (f) section 55.

  (2) Personal data which fall within paragraph (e) of the definition of "data" in section 1(1) and relate to appointments or removals, pay, discipline, superannuation or other personnel matters, in relation to—

      (a) service in any of the armed forces of the Crown,

      (b) service in any office or employment under the Crown or under any public authority, or

      (c) service in any office or employment, or under any contract for services, in respect of which power to take action, or to determine or approve the action taken, in such matters is vested in Her Majesty, any Minister of the Crown, the National Assembly for Wales, any Northern Ireland Minister (within the meaning of the Freedom of Information Act 2000) or any public authority, are also exempt from the remaining data protection principles and the remaining provisions of Part II."

(2) In section 55 of that Act (unlawful obtaining etc of personal data) in subsection (8) after "section 28" there is inserted "or 33A".

(3) In Part III of Schedule 8 to that Act (exemptions available after 23rd October 2001 but before 24th October 2007) after paragraph 14 there is inserted—

"14A

    (1) This paragraph applies to personal data which fall within paragraph (e) of the definition of "data" in section 1(1) and do not fall within paragraph 14(1)(a), but does not apply to eligible manual data to which the exemption in paragraph 16 applies.

    (2) During the second transitional period, data to which this paragraph applies are exempt from—

      (a) the fourth data protection principle, and

      (b) section 14(1) to (3)."

(4) In Schedule 13 to that Act (modifications of Act having effect before 24th October 2007) in subsection (4)(b) of section 12A to that Act as set out in paragraph 1, after "paragraph 14" there is inserted "or 14A".

71 .....

Availability under Act disregarded for purpose of exemption

72 In section 34 of the Data Protection Act 1998 (information available to the public by or under enactment), after the word "enactment" there is inserted "other than an enactment contained in the Freedom of Information Act 2000".

Other amendments

Further amendments of Data Protection Act 1998

73 Schedule 6 (which contains further amendments of the Data Protection Act 1998) has effect.

PART VIII
MISCELLANEOUS AND SUPPLEMENTAL

Power to make provision relating to environmental information

74(1) In this section "the Aarhus Convention" means the Convention on Access to Information, Public Participation in Decision-making and Access to Justice in Environmental Matters signed at Aarhus on 25th June 1998.

(2) For the purposes of this section "the information provisions" of the Aarhus Convention are Article 4, together with Articles 3 and 9 so far as relating to that Article.

(3) The Secretary of State may by regulations make such provision as he considers appropriate—

    (a) for the purpose of implementing the information provisions of the Aarhus Convention or any amendment of those provisions made in accordance with Article 14 of the Convention, and

    (b) for the purpose of dealing with matters arising out of or related to the implementation of those provisions or of any such amendment.

(4) Regulations under subsection (3) may in particular—

    (a) enable charges to be made for making information available in accordance with the regulations,

    (b) provide that any obligation imposed by the regulations in relation to the disclosure of information is to have effect notwithstanding any enactment or rule of law,

    (c) make provision for the issue by the Secretary of State of a code of practice,

    (d) provide for sections 47 and 48 to apply in relation to such a code with such modifications as may be specified,

    (e) provide for any of the provisions of Parts IV and V to apply, with such modifications as may be specified in the regulations, in relation to compliance with any requirement of the regulations, and

    (f) contain such transitional or consequential provision (including provision modifying any enactment) as the Secretary of State considers appropriate.

(5) This section has effect subject to section 80.

NOTES

Scottish public authority equivalent	Defined terms
FOI(S)A s 62	"Aarhus Convention": subs (1)
	"information provisions": subs (2)

Power to amend or repeal enactments prohibiting disclosure of information

75(1) If, with respect to any enactment which prohibits the disclosure of information held by a public authority, it appears to the Secretary of State or the Minister for the Cabinet Office that by virtue of section 44(1)(a) the enactment is capable of preventing the disclosure of information under section 1, he may by order repeal or amend the enactment for the purpose of removing or relaxing the prohibition.

(2) In subsection (1)—

"enactment" means—

    (a) any enactment contained in an Act passed before or in the same Session as this Act, or

    (b) any enactment contained in Northern Ireland legislation or subordinate

legislation passed or made before the passing of this Act;
"information" includes unrecorded information

(3) An order under this section may do all or any of the following—

  (a) make such modifications of enactments as, in the opinion of the Secretary of State or the Minister for the Cabinet Office, are consequential upon, or incidental to, the amendment or repeal of the enactment containing the prohibition;

  (b) contain such transitional provisions and savings as appear to the Secretary of State or the Minister for the Cabinet Office to be appropriate;

  (c) make different provision for different cases.

NOTES

Scottish public authority equivalent
  FOI(S)A s 64

Defined terms
  "enactment": s 84 and subs (2)
  "information": s 84 and subs (2)
  "public authority": s 3(1)

Subordinate legislation
  Freedom of Information (Removal and Relaxation of Statutory Prohibitions on Disclosure of Information) Order 2004, SI 2004/3363

Disclosure of information between Commissioner and ombudsmen

76(1) The Commissioner may disclose to a person specified in the first column of the Table below any information obtained by, or furnished to, the Commissioner under or for the purposes of this Act or the data protection legislation if it appears to the Commissioner that the information relates to a matter which could be the subject of an investigation by that person under the enactment specified in relation to that person in the second column of that Table.

TABLE

Ombudsman	*Enactment*
The Parliamentary Commissioner for Administration.	The Parliamentary Commissioner Act 1967 (c 13).
The Health Service Commissioner for England.	The Health Service Commissioners Act 1993 (c 46).
A Local Commissioner as defined by section 23(3) of the Local Government Act 1974.	Part III or Part 3A of the Local Government Act 1974 (c 7).
The Scottish Public Services Ombudsman	The Scottish Public Services Ombudsman Act 2002 (asp 11)
The Public Services Ombudsman for Wales	Part 2 of the Public Services Ombudsman (Wales) Act 2005
	Part 3 of the Public Services Ombudsman (Wales) Act 2019
The Northern Ireland Commissioner for Complaints.	The Commissioner for Complaints (Northern Ireland) Order 1996 (SI 1996/1297 (NI 7)).
The Assembly Ombudsman for Northern Ireland.	The Ombudsman (Northern Ireland) Order 1996 (SI 1996/1298 (NI 8)).
The Commissioner for Older People in Wales.	The Commissioner for Older People (Wales) Act 2006.

(2) Schedule 7 (which contains amendments relating to information disclosed to ombudsmen under subsection (1) and to the disclosure of information by ombudsmen to the Commissioner) has effect.

NOTES

Defined terms
"Commissioner": s 18(3)
"data protection legislation": s 84
"information": s 84

Disclosure between Commissioner and Scottish Information Commissioner

76A The Commissioner may disclose to the Scottish Information Commissioner any information obtained or furnished as mentioned in section 76(1) of this Act if it appears to the Commissioner that the information is of the same type that could be obtained by, or furnished to, the Scottish Information Commissioner under or for the purposes of the Freedom of Information (Scotland) Act.

NOTES

Defined terms
"Commissioner": s 18(3)
"information": s 84

Disclosure of information to Tribunal

76B(1) No enactment or rule of law prohibiting or restricting the disclosure of information precludes a person from providing the First-tier Tribunal or the Upper Tribunal with information necessary for the discharge of their functions in connection with appeals under section 60 of this Act.

(2) But this section does not authorise the making of a disclosure which is prohibited by any of Parts 1 to 7 or Chapter 1 of Part 9 of the Investigatory Powers Act 2016.

(3) Until the repeal of Part 1 of the Regulation of Investigatory Powers Act 2000 by paragraphs 45 and 54 of Schedule 10 to the Investigatory Powers Act 2016 is fully in force, subsection (2) has effect as if it included a reference to that Part

NOTES

Defined terms
"enactment": Interpretation Act 1978, Sch 1
"information": s 84

Offence of altering etc records with intent to prevent disclosure

77(1) Where—

    (a) a request for information has been made to a public authority, and

    (b) under section 1 of this Act, the applicant would have been entitled (subject to payment of any fee) to communication of any information in accordance with that section,

any person to whom this subsection applies is guilty of an offence if he alters, defaces, blocks, erases, destroys or conceals any record held by the public authority, with the intention of preventing the disclosure by that authority of all, or any part, of the information to the communication of which the applicant would have been entitled.

(2) Subsection (1) applies to the public authority and to any person who is employed by, is an officer of, or is subject to the direction of, the public authority.

(3) A person guilty of an offence under this section is liable on summary conviction to a fine not exceeding level 5 on the standard scale.

(4) No proceedings for an offence under this section shall be instituted—

(a) in England or Wales, except by the Commissioner or by or with the consent of the Director of Public Prosecutions;

(b) in Northern Ireland, except by the Commissioner or by or with the consent of the Director of Public Prosecutions for Northern Ireland.

Saving for existing powers

78 Nothing in this Act is to be taken to limit the powers of a public authority to disclose information held by it.

Defamation

79 Where any information communicated by a public authority to a person ("the applicant") under section 1 was supplied to the public authority by a third person, the publication to the applicant of any defamatory matter contained in the information shall be privileged unless the publication is shown to have been made with malice.

Scotland

80(1) No order may be made under section 4(1) or 5 in relation to any of the bodies specified in subsection (2); and the power conferred by section 74(3) does not include power to make provision in relation to information held by any of those bodies.

(2) The bodies referred to in subsection (1) are—

(a) the Scottish Parliament,
(b) any part of the Scottish Administration,
(c) the Scottish Parliamentary Corporate Body, or
(d) any Scottish public authority with mixed functions or no reserved functions (within the meaning of the Scotland Act 1998).

(3) Section 50 of the Copyright, Designs and Patents Act 1988 and paragraph 6 of Schedule 1 to the Copyright and Rights in Databases Regulations 1997 apply in relation to the Freedom of Information (Scotland) Act 2002 as they apply in relation to this Act.

Information held by Northern Ireland bodies

80A(1) *Repealed*

Application to government departments, etc

81(1) For the purposes of this Act each government department is to be treated as a person separate from any other government department.

(2) Subsection (1) does not enable—

    (a) a government department which is not a Northern Ireland department to claim for the purposes of section 41(1)(b) that the disclosure of any information by it would constitute a breach of confidence actionable by any other government department (not being a Northern Ireland department), or

    (b) a Northern Ireland department to claim for those purposes that the disclosure of information by it would constitute a breach of confidence actionable by any other Northern Ireland department.

(3) A government department or the Welsh Assembly Government is not liable to prosecution under this Act, but section 77 and paragraph 12 of Schedule 3 apply to a person in the public service of the Crown as they apply to any other person.

(4) The provisions specified in subsection (3) also apply to a person acting on behalf of either House of Parliament or on behalf of the Northern Ireland Assembly or the National Assembly for Wales as they apply to any other person.

NOTES

Defined terms

"government department": s 84
"information": s 84

Orders and regulations

82(1) Any power of the Secretary of State or the Minister for the Cabinet Office to make an order or regulations under this Act shall be exercisable by statutory instrument.

(2) A statutory instrument containing (whether alone or with other provisions)—

    (a) an order under section 5, 7(3) or (8), 53(1)(a)(iii) or 75, or

    (b) regulations under section 10(4) or 74(3),

shall not be made unless a draft of the instrument has been laid before, and approved by a resolution of, each House of Parliament.

(3) A statutory instrument which contains (whether alone or with other provisions)—

    (a) an order under section 4(1) or 47(4B), or

    (b) regulations under any provision of this Act not specified in subsection (2)(b),

and which is not subject to the requirement in subsection (2) that a draft of the instrument be laid before and approved by a resolution of each House of Parliament, shall be subject to annulment in pursuance of a resolution of either House of Parliament.

(4) An order under section 4(5) shall be laid before Parliament after being made.

(5) If a draft of an order under section 5 or 7(8) would, apart from this subsection, be treated for the purposes of the Standing Orders of either House of Parliament as a hybrid instrument, it shall proceed in that House as if it were not such an instrument.

Meaning of "Welsh public authority"

83(1) In this Act "Welsh public authority" means—

   (a) any public authority which is listed in Part II, III, IV or VI of Schedule 1 and whose functions are exercisable only or mainly in or as regards Wales, other than an excluded authority, or

   (b) any public authority which is—

       (i) a subsidiary of the Welsh Ministers (as defined by section 134(4) of the Government of Wales Act 2006), or

       (ii) a subsidiary of the Assembly Commission (as defined by section 139(4) of that Act).

(2) In paragraph (a) of subsection (1) "excluded authority" means a public authority which is designated by the Secretary of State or the Minister for the Cabinet Office by order as an excluded authority for the purposes of that paragraph.

(3) Before making an order under subsection (2), the Secretary of State or the Minister for the Cabinet Office shall consult the First Minister for Wales.

Interpretation

84 In this Act, unless the context otherwise requires—

"applicant", in relation to a request for information, means the person who made the request;

"appropriate Northern Ireland Minister" means the Northern Ireland Minister in charge of the Department of Culture, Arts and Leisure in Northern Ireland;

"appropriate records authority", in relation to a transferred public record, has the meaning given by section 15(5);

"body" includes an unincorporated association;

"the Commissioner" means the Information Commissioner;

"the data protection legislation" has the same meaning as in the Data Protection Act 2018 (see section 3 of that Act);

"dataset" has the meaning given by section 11(5);

"decision notice" has the meaning given by section 50;

"the duty to confirm or deny" has the meaning given by section 1(6);

"enactment" includes an enactment contained in Northern Ireland legislation;

"enforcement notice" has the meaning given by section 52;

"exempt information" means information which is exempt information by virtue of any provision of Part II;

"fees notice" has the meaning given by section 9(1);

"government department" includes a Northern Ireland department, the Northern Ireland Court Service and any other body or authority exercising statutory functions on behalf of the Crown, but does not include—

     (a) any of the bodies specified in section 80(2),

     (b) the Security Service, the Secret Intelligence Service or the Government Communications Headquarters,

     (ba) the National Crime Agency, or

     (c) the Welsh Assembly Government;

"information" (subject to sections 51(8) and 75(2)) means information recorded in any form;

"information notice" has the meaning given by section 51;

"Minister of the Crown" has the same meaning as in the Ministers of the Crown Act 1975;

"Northern Ireland Minister" includes the First Minister and deputy First Minister in Northern Ireland;

"Northern Ireland public authority" means any public authority, other than the Northern Ireland Assembly or a Northern Ireland department, whose functions are exercisable only or mainly in or as regards Northern Ireland and relate only or mainly to transferred matters;

"prescribed" means prescribed by regulations made by the Minister for the Cabinet Office;

"public authority" has the meaning given by section 3(1);

"public record" means a public record within the meaning of the Public Records Act 1958 or a public record to which the Public Records Act (Northern Ireland) 1923 applies;

"publication scheme" has the meaning given by section 19;

"request for information" has the meaning given by section 8;

"responsible authority", in relation to a transferred public record, has the meaning given by section 15(5);

"the special forces" means those units of the armed forces of the Crown the maintenance of whose capabilities is the responsibility of the Director of Special Forces or which are for the time being subject to the operational command of that Director;

"subordinate legislation" has the meaning given by subsection (1) of section 21 of the Interpretation Act 1978, except that the definition of that term in that subsection shall have effect as if "Act" included Northern Ireland legislation;

"transferred matter", in relation to Northern Ireland, has the meaning given by section 4(1) of the Northern Ireland Act 1998;

"transferred public record" has the meaning given by section 15(4);

"the Tribunal", in relation to any appeal under this Act, means—

    (a) the Upper Tribunal, in any case where it is determined by or under Tribunal Procedure Rules that the Upper Tribunal is to hear the appeal; or

    (b) the First-tier Tribunal, in any other case;

"Welsh public authority" has the meaning given by section 83.

NOTES

Scottish public authority equivalent
  FOI(S)A s 73

Expenses

85 There shall be paid out of money provided by Parliament—

    (a) any increase attributable to this Act in the expenses of the Secretary of State in respect of the Commissioner, the Tribunal or the members of the Tribunal,

    (b) any administrative expenses of the Secretary of State or the Minister for the Cabinet Office attributable to this Act,

    (c) any other expenses incurred in consequence of this Act by a Minister of the Crown or government department or by either House of Parliament, and

    (d) any increase attributable to this Act in the sums which under any other Act are payable out of money so provided.

NOTES

Defined terms   "government department": s 84
  "Commissioner": s 18(3)

"Minister of the Crown": s 84 of the Ministers of
the Crown Act 1975
"Tribunal": s 18(3)

Repeals

86   Schedule 8 (repeals) has effect.

Commencement

87(1)   The following provisions of this Act shall come into force on the day on which this Act is passed—

    (a)   sections 3 to 8 and Schedule 1,

    (b)   section 19 so far as relating to the approval of publication schemes,

    (c)   section 20 so far as relating to the approval and preparation by the Commissioner of model publication schemes,

    (d)   section 47(2) to (6),

    (e)   section 49,

    (f)   section 74,

    (g)   section 75,

    (h)   sections 78 to 85 and this section,

    (i)   paragraphs 2 and 17 to 22 of Schedule 2 (and section 18(4) so far as relating to those paragraphs),

    (j)   paragraph 4 of Schedule 5 (and section 67 so far as relating to that paragraph),

    (k)   paragraph 8 of Schedule 6 (and section 73 so far as relating to that paragraph),

    (l)   Part I of Schedule 8 (and section 86 so far as relating to that Part), and

    (m)   so much of any other provision of this Act as confers power to make any order, regulations or code of practice.

(2)   The following provisions of this Act shall come into force at the end of the period of two months beginning with the day on which this Act is passed—

    (a)   section 18(1),

    (b)   section 76 and Schedule 7,

    (c)   paragraphs 1(1), 3(1), 4, 6, 7, 8(2), 9(2), 10(a), 13(1) and (2), 14(a) and 15(1) and (2) of Schedule 2 (and section 18(4) so far as relating to those provisions), and

    (d)   Part II of Schedule 8 (and section 86 so far as relating to that Part).

(3)   Except as provided by subsections (1) and (2), this Act shall come into force at the end of the period of five years beginning with the day on which this Act is passed or on such day before the end of that period as the Secretary of State may by order appoint; and different days may be appointed for different purposes.

(4)   An order under subsection (3) may contain such transitional provisions and savings (including provisions capable of having effect after the end of the period referred to in that subsection) as the Secretary of State considers appropriate.

(5)   During the twelve months beginning with the day on which this Act is passed, and during each subsequent complete period of twelve months in the period beginning with that day and ending with the first day on which all the provisions of this Act are fully in force, the Secretary of State shall—

    (a)   prepare a report on his proposals for bringing fully into force those provisions of this Act which are not yet fully in force, and

    (b)   lay a copy of the report before each House of Parliament.

NOTES

Subordinate legislation

Freedom of Information Act 2000 (Commencement No 1) Order 2001, SI 2001/1637

Freedom of Information Act 2000 (Commencement No 2) Order 2002, SI 2002/2812

Freedom of Information Act 2000 (Commencement No 3) Order 2003, SI 2003/2603

Freedom of Information Act 2000 (Commencement No 4) Order 2004, SI 2004/1909

Freedom of Information Act 2000 (Commencement No 5) Order 2004, SI 2004/3122

Short title and extent

88(1) This Act may be cited as the Freedom of Information Act 2000.

(2) Subject to subsection (3), this Act extends to Northern Ireland.

(3) The amendment or repeal of any enactment by this Act has the same extent as that enactment.

NOTES

Scottish public authority equivalent

FOI(S)A s 76

SCHEDULE 1
PUBLIC AUTHORITIES

Section 3(1)(a)(i)

PART I
GENERAL

1 Any government department other than—

(a) the Competition and Markets Authority,

(b) the Office for Standards in Education, Children's Services and Skills.

1ZA The Competition and Markets Authority, in respect of information held otherwise than as a tribunal.

1A The Office for Standards in Education, Children's Services and Skills, in respect of information held for purposes other than those of the functions exercisable by Her Majesty's Chief Inspector of Education, Children's Services and Skills by virtue of section 5(1)(a)(iii) of the Care Standards Act 2000.

2 The House of Commons, in respect of information other than—

(a) information relating to any residential address of a member of either House of Parliament,

(b) information relating to travel arrangements of a member of either House of Parliament, where the arrangements relate to travel that has not yet been undertaken or is regular in nature,

(c) information relating to the identity of any person who delivers or has delivered goods, or provides or has provided services, to a member of either House of Parliament at any residence of the member,

(d) information relating to expenditure by a member of either House of Parliament on security arrangements,

(e) information held by the Intelligence and Security Committee of Parliament.

Paragraph (b) does not except information relating to the total amount of expenditure incurred on regular travel during any month.

3 The House of Lords, in respect of information other than—
    (a) information relating to any residential address of a member of either House of Parliament,
    (b) information relating to travel arrangements of a member of either House of Parliament, where the arrangements relate to travel that has not yet been undertaken or is regular in nature,
    (c) information relating to the identity of any person who delivers or has delivered goods, or provides or has provided services, to a member of either House of Parliament at any residence of the member,
    (d) information relating to expenditure by a member of either House of Parliament on security arrangements,
    (e) information held by the Intelligence and Security Committee of Parliament.
    Paragraph (b) does not except information relating to the total amount of expenditure incurred on regular travel during any month.

4 The Northern Ireland Assembly.

5 The National Assembly for Wales, in respect of information other than—
    (a) information relating to any residential address of a member of the Assembly,
    (b) information relating to travel arrangements of a member of the Assembly, where the arrangements relate to travel that has not yet been undertaken or is regular in nature,
    (c) information relating to the identity of any person who delivers or has delivered goods, or provides or has provided services, to a member of the Assembly at any residence of the member,
    (d) information relating to expenditure by a member of the Assembly on security arrangements.
    Paragraph (b) does not except information relating to the total amount of expenditure incurred on regular travel during any month.

5A The Welsh Assembly Government.

6 The armed forces of the Crown, except—
    (a) the special forces, and
    (b) any unit or part of a unit which is for the time being required by the Secretary of State to assist the Government Communications Headquarters in the exercise of its functions.

PART II
LOCAL GOVERNMENT

England and Wales

7 A local authority within the meaning of the Local Government Act 1972, namely—
    (a) in England, a county council, a London borough council, a district council or a parish council,
    (b) in Wales, a county council, a county borough council or a community council.

8 The Greater London Authority.

9 The Common Council of the City of London, in respect of information held in its capacity as a local authority, police authority or port health authority.

10 The Sub-Treasurer of the Inner Temple or the Under-Treasurer of the Middle Temple, in respect of information held in his capacity as a local authority.

11 The Council of the Isles of Scilly.

12 A parish meeting constituted under section 13 of the Local Government Act 1972.

13 Any charter trustees constituted under section 246 of the Local Government Act 1972.

14 A fire and rescue authority constituted by a scheme under section 2 of the Fire and Rescue Services Act 2004 or a scheme to which section 4 of that Act applies.

14A A fire and rescue authority created by order under section 4A of that Act.

15 A waste disposal authority established by virtue of an order under section 10(1) of the Local Government Act 1985.

15A *Repealed*

16 A port health authority constituted by an order under section 2 of the Public Health (Control of Disease) Act 1984.

17 *Repealed*

18 An internal drainage board which is continued in being by virtue of section 1 of the Land Drainage Act 1991.

19 A joint authority established under Part IV of the Local Government Act 1985 (fire and rescue services and transport).

19A An economic prosperity board established under section 88 of the Local Democracy, Economic Development and Construction Act 2009.

19B A combined authority established under section 103 of that Act.

20 The London Fire Commissioner.

21 A joint fire authority established by virtue of an order under section 42(2) of the Local Government Act 1985 (reorganisation of functions).

22 A body corporate established pursuant to an order under section 67 of the Local Government Act 1985 (transfer of functions to successors of residuary bodies, etc).

23 A body corporate established pursuant to an order under section 17 of the Local Government and Public Involvement in Health Act 2007 (residuary bodies).

24 The Broads Authority established by section 1 of the Norfolk and Suffolk Broads Act 1988.

25 A joint committee constituted in accordance with section 102(1)(b) of the Local Government Act 1972.

26 A joint board which is continued in being by virtue of section 263(1) of the Local Government Act 1972.

27 A joint authority established under section 21 of the Local Government Act 1992.

28 A Passenger Transport Executive for an integrated transport area for the purposes of Part 2 of the Transport Act 1968.

28A A sub-national transport body established under section 102E of the Local Transport Act 2008.

29 Transport for London.

30 The London Transport Users Committee.

31 A joint board the constituent members of which consist of any of the public authorities described in paragraphs 8, 9, 10, 12, 15, 16, 20 to 31, 57 and 58.

32 A National Park authority established by an order under section 63 of the Environment Act 1995.

33 A joint planning board constituted for an area in Wales outside a National Park by an order under section 2(1B) of the Town and Country Planning Act 1990.

33A A strategic planning panel established under section 60D of the Planning and Compulsory Purchase Act 2004

34 *Repealed.*

35 *Repealed.*

35A *Repealed.*

35B An inshore fisheries and conservation authority for a district established under section 149 of the Marine and Coastal Access Act 2009.

35C An urban development corporation established under section 135 of the Local Government, Planning and Land Act 1980.

35D A Mayoral development corporation established under section 198 of the Localism Act 2011.

35E A Local Healthwatch organisation, in respect of information held in connection with–

    (a) arrangements made under section 221(1) of the Local Government and Public Involvement with Health Act 2007, or

    (b) arrangements made in pursuance of arrangements made under section 221(1) of that Act.

Northern Ireland

36 A district council within the meaning of the Local Government Act (Northern Ireland) 1972.

PART III
THE NATIONAL HEALTH SERVICE

England and Wales

36A *Repealed.*

37 *Repealed.*

37A The National Health Service Commissioning Board.

37B A clinical commissioning group established under section 14D of the National Health Service Act 2006.

38 A special health authority established under section 28 of the National Health Service Act 2006 or section 22 of the National Health Service (Wales) Act 2006.

39 *Repealed.*

39A A Local Health Board established under section 11 of the National Health Service (Wales) Act 2006.

40 A National Health Service trust established under section 25 of the National Health Service Act 2006 or section 18 of the National Health Service (Wales) Act 2006.

40A An NHS foundation trust.

41 A Community Health Council established under section 182 of the National Health Service (Wales) Act 2006.

41A *Repealed.*

42 *Repealed.*

43 *Repealed.*

43A Any person providing primary medical services, primary dental services or primary ophthalmic services—

    (a) in accordance with arrangements made under section 92 or 107 of the National Health Service Act 2006, or section 50 or 64 of the National Health Service (Wales) Act 2006; or

    (b) under a contract under section 84, 100 or 117 of the National Health Service Act 2006 or

section 42 or 57 of the National Health Service (Wales) Act 2006;
  in respect of information relating to the provision of those services.

44 Any person providing general medical services, general dental services, general ophthalmic services or pharmaceutical services under the National Health Service Act 2006 or the National Health Service (Wales) Act 2006, in respect of information relating to the provision of those services.

45 *Repealed.*

45A Any person providing local pharmaceutical services under—
  (a) a pilot scheme established under section 134 of the National Health Service Act 2006 or section 92 of the National Health Service (Wales) Act 2006; or
  (b) an LPS scheme established under Schedule 12 to the National Health Service Act 2006 or Schedule 7 to the National Health Service (Wales) Act 2006,
  in respect of information relating to the provision of those services.

45B *Repealed*

45C Health Education England

Northern Ireland

46 *Repealed*

47 *Repealed.*

48 A Health and Social Services Trust established under Article 10 of the Health and Personal Social Services (Northern Ireland) Order 1991.

49 A special agency established under Article 3 of the Health and Personal Social Services (Special Agencies) (Northern Ireland) Order 1990.

50 *Repealed.*

51 Any person providing primary medical services, general dental services, general ophthalmic services or pharmaceutical services under Part VI of the Health and Personal Social Services (Northern Ireland) Order 1972, in respect of information relating to the provision of those services.

51A The Regional Business Services Organisation established under section 14 of the Health and Social Services (Reform) Act (Northern Ireland) 2009.

51B The Patient and Client Council established under section 16 of the Health and Social Care (Reform) Act (Northern Ireland) 2009.

51C The Regional Health and Social Care Board established under section 7 of the Health and Social Care (Reform) Act (Northern Ireland) 2009.

51D The Regional Agency for Public Health and Social Well-being established under section 12 of the Health and Social Care (Reform) Act (Northern Ireland) 2009.

PART IV
MAINTAINED SCHOOLS AND OTHER EDUCATIONAL INSTITUTIONS

England and Wales

52 The governing body of—
  (a) a maintained school, as defined by section 20(7) of the School Standards and Framework Act 1998, or
  (b) a maintained nursery school, as defined by section 22(9) of that Act.

52A(1)   The proprietor of an Academy, in respect of information held for the purposes of the proprietor's functions under Academy arrangements.

(2)   In sub-paragraph (1)—

"Academy arrangements" has the meaning given by section 1 of the Academies Act 2010;

"proprietor" has the meaning given by section 579(1) of the Education Act 1996.

53(1) The governing body of—
(a) an institution within the further education sector,
(aa) a registered higher education provider of a description prescribed by regulations made by the Secretary of State for the purposes of section 39(1) of the Higher Education and Research Act 2017.
(b) a university receiving financial support under section 65 of the Further and Higher Education Act 1992,
(c) an institution in Wales conducted by a higher education corporation,
(d) a designated institution for the purposes of Part II of the Further and Higher Education Act 1992 as defined by section 72(3) of that Act, or
(e) any college, school, hall or other institution of a registered higher education provider which falls within paragraph (aa) or a university which falls within paragraph (b).

53(2) In sub-paragraph (1)—
(a) "governing body" is to be interpreted in accordance with subsection (1) of section 90 of the Further and Higher Education Act 1992 but without regard to subsection (2) of that section,
(aa) "registered higher education provider" has the meaning given by section 3(10) of the Higher Education and Research Act 2017,
(b) in paragraph (a), the reference to an institution within the further education sector is to be construed in accordance with section 91(3) of the Further and Higher Education Act 1992,
(c) in paragraph (c), the reference to an institution in Wales is to be construed in accordance with section 62(7) of that Act, and "higher education corporation" has the meaning given by section 90(1) of that Act, and
(d) in paragraph (e) "college" includes any institution in the nature of a college.

Northern Ireland

54(1) The managers of—
(a) a controlled school, voluntary school or grant-maintained integrated school within the meaning of Article 2(2) of the Education and Libraries (Northern Ireland) Order 1986, or
(b) a pupil referral unit as defined by Article 87(1) of the Education (Northern Ireland) Order 1998.

54(2) In sub-paragraph (1) "managers" has the meaning given by Article 2(2) of the Education and Libraries (Northern Ireland) Order 1986.

55(1) The governing body of—
(a) a university receiving financial support under Article 30 of the Education and Libraries (Northern Ireland) Order 1993,
(b) a college of education in respect of which grants are paid under Article 66(2) or (3) of the Education and Libraries (Northern Ireland) Order 1986, or
(c) an institution of further education within the meaning of the Further Education (Northern Ireland) Order 1997.

55(2) In sub-paragraph (1) "governing body" has the meaning given by Article 30(3) of the Education and Libraries (Northern Ireland) Order 1993.

56 Any person providing further education to whom grants, loans or other payments are made under

Article 5(1)(b) of the Further Education (Northern Ireland) Order 1997.

PART V
POLICE

England and Wales

57 A police and crime commissioner.

58 The Mayor's Office for Policing and Crime.

59 A chief officer of police of a police force in England or Wales.

Northern Ireland.

60 The Northern Ireland Policing Board.

61 The Chief Constable of the Police Service of Northern Ireland.

Miscellaneous

62 The British Transport Police.

63 The Ministry of Defence Police established by section 1 of the Ministry of Defence Police Act 1987.

63A The Civil Nuclear Police Authority.

63B The chief constable of the Civil Nuclear Constabulary.

64 Any person who—
   (a) by virtue of any enactment has the function of nominating individuals who may be appointed as special constables by justices of the peace, and
   (b) is not a public authority by virtue of any other provision of this Act,
in respect of information relating to the exercise by any person appointed on his nomination of the functions of a special constable.

PART VI
OTHER PUBLIC BODIES AND OFFICES: GENERAL

The Adjudication Panel for Wales.

The adjudicators appointed under section 25 of the School Standards and Framework Act 1998.

The Administration of Radioactive Substances Advisory Committee.

The Advisory Board on Restricted Patients.

The Advisory Board on the Registration of Homoeopathic Products.

The Advisory Committee on Clinical Excellence Awards.

The Advisory Committee for Disabled People in Employment and Training.

The Advisory Committee for the Public Lending Right.

The Advisory Committee on Animal Feedingstuffs.

The Advisory Committee on Borderline Substances.

The Advisory Committee on Business and the Environment.

The Advisory Committee on Business Appointments.

The Advisory Committee on Conscientious Objectors.

The Advisory Committee on Dangerous Pathogens.

The Advisory Committee on the Government Art Collection.

The Advisory Committee on Historic Wreck Sites.

An Advisory Committee on Justices of the Peace in England and Wales.

The Advisory Committee on the Microbiological Safety of Food.

The Advisory Committee on Novel Foods and Processes.

The Advisory Committee on Organic Standards.

The Advisory Committee on Overseas Economic and Social Research.

The Advisory Committee on Packaging.

The Advisory Committee on Releases to the Environment.

The Advisory Committee on Statute Law.

The Advisory Committee on Telecommunications for the Disabled and Elderly.

The Advisory Council on Historical Manuscripts.

The Advisory Council on the Misuse of Drugs.

The Advisory Council on National Records and Archives.

The Advisory Council on Public Records.

The Advisory Group on Hepatitis.

The Advisory Group on Medical Countermeasures.

The Advisory Panel on Beacon Councils.

The Advisory Panel on Public Sector Information.

The Advisory Panel on Standards for the Planning Inspectorate.

The Aerospace Committee.

An Agricultural Dwelling House Advisory Committee.

An Agricultural Wages Committee.

The Agriculture and Environment Biotechnology Commission.

The Agriculture and Horticulture Development Board.

The Air Quality Expert Group.

The Airborne Particles Expert Group.

The All-Wales Medicines Strategy Group.

The Animal Procedures Committee.

The Animal Welfare Advisory Committee.

The Architects Registration Board.

The Armed Forces Pay Review Body.

The Arts and Humanities Research Council

The Arts Council of England.

The Arts Council of Wales.

An assessor appointed for the purposes of section 133 of the Criminal Justice Act 1988 in its application to England and Wales.

The Auditor General for Wales.

The Bank of England (including the Bank in its capacity as the Prudential Regulation Authority), in respect of information held for purposes other than those of its functions with respect to—

    (a)   monetary policy,

    (b)   financial operations intended to support financial institutions for the purposes of maintaining stability, and

    (c)   the provision of private banking services and related services.

The Better Regulation Task Force.

The Big Lottery Fund.

The Biotechnology and Biological Sciences Research Council.

The Board of the Pension Protection Fund.

The Britain-Russia Centre and East-West Centre.

The British Association for Central and Eastern Europe.

The British Broadcasting Corporation, in respect of information held for purposes other than those of journalism, art or literature.

The British Coal Corporation.

The British Council.

The British Educational Communications and Technology Agency.

The British Hallmarking Council.

The British Library.

The British Museum.

The British Pharmacopoeia Commission.

The British Railways Board.

The British Tourist Authority.

The British Transport Police Authority.

The British Wool Marketing Board.

The Broadcasting Standards Commission.

The Building Regulations Advisory Committee for England.

The Building Regulations Advisory Committee for Wales.

Canal & River Trust, in respect of information held by it relating to functions exercisable by it by virtue of the British Waterways Board (Transfer of Functions) Order 2012 (SI 2012/1659).

The Care Council for Wales.

The Care Quality Commission.

The Central Advisory Committee on War Pensions.

The Central Rail Users' Consultative Committee.

The Certification Officer.

The Channel Four Television Corporation, in respect of information held for purposes other than those of journalism, art or literature.

The chief inspector of constabulary appointed under section 54(1) of the Police Act 1996.

The Chief Inspector of the UK Border Agency.

The Children and Family Court Advisory and Support Service.

The Children's Commissioner.

The Children's Commissioner for Wales.

The Civil Aviation Authority.

The Civil Justice Council.

The Civil Procedure Rule Committee.

The Civil Service Appeal Board.

The Civil Service Commission.

The Coal Authority.

The College of Policing.

Comisiynydd y Gymraeg (The Welsh Language Commission).

The Commission for Architecture and the Built Environment.

The Commission for Equality and Human Rights.

The Commission on Human Medicines.

The Commission for Integrated Transport.

The Commission for Local Administration in England.

The Commissioner for Older People in Wales.

The Commissioner for Public Appointments.

The Commissioner for Victims and Witnesses.

The Commissioners of Northern Lighthouses.

The Committee on Agricultural Valuation.

The Committee on Carcinogenicity of Chemicals in Food, Consumer Products and the Environment.

The Committee on Climate Change.

The Committee on Medical Aspects of Radiation in the Environment.

The Committee on Mutagenicity of Chemicals in Food, Consumer Products and the Environment.

The Committee on Radioactive Waste Management.

The Committee on Safety of Devices.

The Committee on Standards in Public Life.

The Committee on Toxicity of Chemicals in Food, Consumer Products and the Environment.

The Committee on the Medical Effects of Air Pollutants.

The Commonwealth Scholarship Commission in the United Kingdom.

Communications for Business.

The company formed under section 3 of the Parliamentary Buildings (Restoration and Renewal) Act 2019

The Competition Commission, in relation to information held by it otherwise than as a tribunal.

The Competition Service.

Compliance Officer for the Independent Parliamentary Standards Authority.

The Comptroller and Auditor General.

A conservation board established under section 86 of the Countryside and Rights of Way Act 2000.

The Construction Industry Training Board.

Consumer Communications for England.

The Consumer Council for Water.

The Consumer Panel established under section 16 of the Communications Act 2003.

The Council for Science and Technology.

The Covent Garden Market Authority.

The Criminal Cases Review Commission.

The Criminal Injuries Compensation Authority.

The Criminal Justice Consultative Council.

The Criminal Procedure Rule Committee.

The Dartmoor Steering Group and Working Party.

The Darwin Advisory Committee.

The Defence Nuclear Safety Committee.

The Defence Scientific Advisory Council.

The Design Council.

The Diplomatic Service Appeal Board.

The Director of Fair Access to Higher Education.

The Director General of the Independent Office for Police Conduct

Director of Labour Market Enforcement

The Disability Employment Advisory Committee.

The Disabled Persons Transport Advisory Committee.

The Disclosure and Barring Service.

The Distributed Generation Co-Ordinating Group.

The East of England Industrial Development Board.

The Economic and Social Research Council.

The Electoral Commission.

The Engineering Construction Industry Training Board.

The Engineering and Physical Sciences Research Council.

The English Sports Council.

The English Tourist Board.

The Environment Agency.

Equality 2025.

The Ethnic Minority Business Forum.

The Expert Advisory Group on AIDS.

An Expert Panel on Air Quality Standards.

The Export Guarantees Advisory Council.

The Family Justice Council.

The Family Procedure Rule Committee.

The Family Proceedings Rules Committee.

The Farm Animal Welfare Council.

The Film Industry Training Board for England and Wales.

The Financial Conduct Authority.

The Financial Reporting Advisory Board.

The Fire Services Examination Board.

The Firearms Consultative Committee.

Flood and Coastal Erosion Committee of Pwyllgor Llifogydd ac Erydu Arfordirol.

The Fuel Cell Advisory Panel.

The Fuel Poverty Advisory Group.

The Gaelic Media Service, in respect of information held for purposes other than those of journalism, art or literature.

The Gambling Commission.

Gangmasters and Labour Abuse Authority.

The Gene Therapy Advisory Committee.

The General Chiropractic Council.

The General Dental Council.

The General Medical Council.

The General Optical Council.

The General Osteopathic Council.

The General Pharmaceutical Council.

The General Teaching Council for England.

The General Teaching Council for Wales.

The Government Hospitality Advisory Committee for the Purchase of Wine.

The Government-Industry Forum on Non-Food Use of Crops.

The Government Chemist.

The Great Britain-China Centre.

Groceries Code Adjudicator.

The Health and Care Professions Council.

The Health Research Authority.

The Health and Safety Commission.

The Health and Safety Executive.

The Health and Social Care Information Centre.

The Health Service Commissioner for England.

Her Majesty's Chief Inspector of Education and Training in Wales or Prif Arolygydd Ei Mawrhydi dros Addysg a Hyfforddiant yng Nghymru.

Her Majesty's Chief Inspector of Prisons.

Her Majesty's Commissioners for Judicial Appointments.

Her Majesty's Inspectorate of Probation for England and Wales.

The Herbal Medicines Advisory Committee.

The Higher Education Funding Council for England.

The Higher Education Funding Council for Wales.

The Historic Buildings and Monuments Commission for England.

The Historic Royal Palaces Trust.

The Homes and Communities Agency.

The Horserace Betting Levy Board.

Horticulture Research International.

The House of Lords Appointments Commission.

Any housing action trust established under Part III of the Housing Act 1988.

The Human Fertilisation and Embryology Authority.

The Human Genetics Commission.

The Human Tissue Authority.

The Immigration Services Commissioner.

The Imperial War Museum.

The Independent Anti-slavery Commissioner.

The Independent Advisory Committee on Development Impact.

The Independent Advisory Group on Teenage Pregnancy.

The Independent Board of Visitors for Military Corrective Training Centres.

The Independent Case Examiner for the Child Support Agency.

The Independent Groundwater Complaints Administrator.

The Independent Living Funds.

Any Independent Monitoring Board established under section 6(2) of the Prison Act 1952.

The Independent Monitoring Authority for Citizens' Rights Agreements.

The Independent Office for Police Conduct.

The Independent Parliamentary Standards Authority.

The Independent Remuneration Board of the Senedd.

The Independent Remuneration Panel for Wales.

The Independent Review Panel for Advertising.

The Independent Review Panel for Borderline Products.

The Independent Scientific Group on Cattle Tuberculosis.

The Independent Television Commission.

The Industrial Development Advisory Board.

The Industrial Injuries Advisory Council.

The Information Commissioner.

The Inland Waterways Advisory Council.

The Insolvency Rules Committee.

The Institute for Apprenticeships and Technical Education.

The Integrated Administration and Controls System Appeals Panel.

The Intellectual Property Advisory Committee.

Investors in People UK.

The Joint Committee on Vaccination and Immunisation.

The Joint Nature Conservation Committee.

The Joint Prison/Probation Accreditation Panel.

The Judicial Appointments Commission.

The Judicial Appointments and Conduct Ombudsman.

The Judicial Studies Board.

The Land Registration Rule Committee.

The Law Commission.

The Legal Deposit Advisory Panel.

The Legal Services Board.

The Legal Services Commission.

The Local Government Boundary Commission for England.

The Local Government Boundary Commission for Wales.

A local probation board established under section 4 of the Criminal Justice and Court Services Act 2000.

The London and South East Industrial Development Board.

The London Pensions Fund Authority.

The Low Pay Commission.

The Marine Management Organisation.

The Marshall Aid Commemoration Commission.

The Measurement Advisory Committee.

The Medical Research Council.

The Migration Advisory Committee.

The Money and Pension Service

Monitor.

The Museum of London.

The National Army Museum.

The National Association of Citizens Advice Bureaux–

    (a)   in respect of information relating to the function exercisable by virtue of article 2 of the Public Bodies (The Office of Fair Trading of Consumer Advice Scheme Function and Modification of Enforcement Functions) Order 2013 SI 2013/783,

    (b)   in respect of information relation to the functions transferred to it by Article 3(1)(a), (b) or (c) of the Public Bodies (Abolition of the National Consumer Council and Transfer of the Office of Fair Trading's Functions in relation to Estate Agents etc) Order 2014.

The National Audit Office.

The National Citizen Service Trust.

The National DNA Database Ethics Group.

The National Employers' Liaison Committee.

The National Employment Panel.

The National Employment Savings Trust Corporation.

The National Forest Company.

The National Gallery.

The National Guardian for Health and Social Care.

The National Heritage Memorial Fund.

The National Institute for Health and Care Excellence.

The National Library of Wales.

The National Maritime Museum.

The National Museum of Science and Industry.

The National Museums and Galleries of Wales.

The National Museums and Galleries on Merseyside.

The National Non-Food Crops Centre.

The National Portrait Gallery.

Natural England.

The Natural Environment Research Council.

The Natural History Museum.

The Natural Resources Body for Wales.

The New Deal Task Force.

The NHS Pay Review Body.

The North East Industrial Development Board.

The North West Industrial Development Board.

The Northern Ireland Judicial Appointments Ombudsman.

The Nuclear Decommissioning Authority.

The Nuclear Research Advisory Council.

The Nursing and Midwifery Council.

The Office of Budget Responsibility.

The Office of Communications.

The Office for Legal Complaints.

The Office of Manpower Economics.

The Office for Nuclear Regulation.

The Office of the Renewable Fuels Agency.

The Office for Students.

The Office of Tax Simplification.

The Oil and Pipelines Agency.

The Olympic Delivery Authority.

The Olympic Lottery Distributor.

The Olympic Park Legacy Company.

The Ombudsman for the Board of the Pension Protection Fund.

The OSO Board.

The Panel on Standards for the Planning Inspectorate.

The Parliamentary Boundary Commission for England.

The Parliamentary Boundary Commission for Scotland.

The Parliamentary Boundary Commission for Wales.

The Parliamentary Commissioner for Administration.

The Parliamentary Works Estimates Commission.

The Parliamentary Works Sponsor Body.

The Parole Board.

The Passengers' Council.

The Payments Systems Regulator established under section 40 of the Financial Services (Banking Reform) Act 2013.

The Pensions Ombudsman.

The Pensions Regulator.

The Pesticide Residues Committee.

The Pesticides Forum.

The Police Advisory Board for England and Wales.

The Police Negotiating Board.

The Police Remuneration Review Body.

The Police Senior Appointments Panel.

The Political Honours Scrutiny Committee.

The Prison Service Pay Review Body.

The Prisons and Probation Ombudsman for England and Wales.

A probation trust.

The Professional Standards Authority for Health and Social Care.

The Public Private Partnership Agreement Arbiter.

The Public Services Ombudsman for Wales.

Pubs Code Adjudicator.

Qualifications Wales.

The Race Education and Employment Forum.

The Race Relations Forum.

The Radio Authority.

The Radioactive Waste Management Advisory Committee.

A Regional Cultural Consortium.

Any regional flood defence committee.

The Registrar of Consultant Lobbyists.

The Registrar General for England and Wales.

The Regulator of Community Interest Companies.

The Regulator of Social Housing.

Remploy Ltd.

The Renewable Energy Advisory Committee.

Resource: The Council for Museums, Archives and Libraries.

The Review Body on Doctors and Dentists Remuneration.

The Reviewing Committee on the Export of Works of Art.

The Royal Air Force Museum.

The Royal Armouries.

The Royal Botanic Gardens, Kew.

The Royal College of Veterinary Surgeons, in respect of information held by it otherwise than as a tribunal.

The Royal Commission on Ancient and Historical Monuments of Wales.

The Royal Commission on Environmental Pollution.

The Royal Commission on Historical Manuscripts.

The Royal Hospital at Chelsea.

The Royal Mint Advisory Committee on the Design of Coins, Medals, Seals and Decorations.

The School Teachers' Review Body.

The Science Advisory Council.

The Science and Technology Facilities Council.

The Scientific Advisory Committee on Nutrition.

The Scientific Committee on Tobacco and Health.

The Sea Fish Industry Authority.

The Security Industry Authority.

The Senior Salaries Review Body.

The Sentencing Council for England and Wales.

Sianel Pedwar Cymru, in respect of information held for purposes other than those of journalism, art or literature.

The Single Source Regulations Authority.

Sir John Soane's Museum.

Small Business Commissioner.

The Small Business Council.

The Small Business Investment Task Force.

The Social Care Institute for Excellence.

The social fund Commissioner appointed under section 65 of the Social Security Administration Act 1992.

The Social Mobility and Child Poverty Commission.

The Social Security Advisory Committee.

Social Work England.

The South West Industrial Development Board.

The Spongiform Encephalopathy Advisory Committee.

The Sports Council for Wales.

The Sports Grounds Safety Authority.

The Standing Advisory Committee on Industrial Property.

The Standing Advisory Committee on Trunk Road Assessment.

The Standing Dental Advisory Committee.

The Steering Committee on Pharmacy Postgraduate Education.

The Strategic Investment Board.

The subsidence adviser appointed under section 46 of the Coal Industry Act 1994.

The Substance Misuse Advisory Panel.

The Sustainable Development Commission.

The Sustainable Energy Policy Advisory Board.

The Tate Gallery.

The TB Advisory Group.

The Technical Advisory Board.

The Technology Strategy Board.

The Theatres Trust.

The Traffic Commissioners, in respect of information held by them otherwise than as a tribunal.

The Training and Development Agency for Schools.

The Treasure Valuation Committee.

The Tribunal Procedure Committee.

The trustee corporation established by section 75 of the Pensions Act 2008.

The UK Advisory Panel for Health Care Workers Infected with Bloodborne Viruses.

The UK Chemicals Stakeholder Forum.

The UK Commission for Employment and Skills.

The UK Sports Council.

The United Kingdom Atomic Energy Authority.

United Kingdom Research and Innovation.

The University for Industry.

The Unlinked Anonymous Serosurveys Steering Group.

The Unrelated Live Transplant Regulatory Authority.

The Valuation Tribunal Service.

The verderers of the New Forest, in respect of information held by them otherwise than as a tribunal.

The Veterinary Products Committee.

The Veterinary Residues Committee.

The Victims' Payments Board, in relation to its administrative functions.

The Victoria and Albert Museum.

The Wales Audit Office.

The Wales Centre for Health.

The Wallace Collection.

The War Pensions Committees.

The Welsh Committee for Professional Development of Pharmacy.

The Welsh Dental Committee.

The Welsh Industrial Development Advisory Board.

The Welsh Medical Committee.

The Welsh Nursing and Midwifery Committee.

The Welsh Optometric Committee.

The Welsh Pharmaceutical Committee.

The Welsh Revenue Authority.

The Welsh Scientific Advisory Committee.

The Westminster Foundation for Democracy.

The West Midlands Industrial Development Board.

The Wilton Park Academic Council.

The Women's National Commission.

The Yorkshire and the Humber and the East Midlands Industrial Development Board.

The Youth Justice Board for England and Wales.

The Zoos Forum.

PART VII

OTHER PUBLIC BODIES AND OFFICES: NORTHERN IRELAND

An advisory committee established under paragraph 25 of the Health and Personal Social Services (Northern Ireland) Order 1972.

The Advisory Committee on Justices of the Peace in Northern Ireland.

The Agri-food and Biosciences Institute.

The Agricultural Wages Board for Northern Ireland.

The Arts Council of Northern Ireland.

The Assembly Ombudsman for Northern Ireland.

The Attorney General for Northern Ireland.

The Belfast Harbour Commissioners.

The Board of Trustees of National Museums and Galleries of Northern Ireland.

The Boundary Commission for Northern Ireland.

A central advisory committee established under paragraph 24 of the Health and Personal Social Services (Northern Ireland) Order 1972.

The Certification Officer for Northern Ireland.

The Charities Advisory Committee.

The Charity Commission for Northern Ireland

The Chief Electoral Officer for Northern Ireland.

The Chief Inspector of Criminal Justice in Northern Ireland.

The Civil Service Commissioners for Northern Ireland.

Comhairle na Gaelscolaíochta.

Commissioner for Children and Young People for Northern Ireland.

The Commissioner for Older People for Northern Ireland.

The Commissioner for Public Appointments for Northern Ireland.

The Commissioner for Survivors of Institutional Childhood Abuse.

The Commissioner for Victims and Survivors for Northern Ireland.

The Construction Industry Training Board.

The consultative Civic Forum referred to in section 56(4) of the Northern Ireland Act 1998.

The Council for Catholic Maintained Schools.

The Council for Nature Conservation and the Countryside.

The County Court Rules Committee (Northern Ireland).

The Criminal Injuries Compensation Appeals Panel for Northern Ireland, in relation to information held by it otherwise than as a tribunal.

A development corporation established under Part III of the Strategic Investment and Regeneration of Sites (Northern Ireland) Order 2003.

The Disability Living Allowance Advisory Board for Northern Ireland.

The discretionary support Commissioner appointed under Article 136 of the Welfare Reform (Northern Ireland) Order 2015.

The Distinction and Meritorious Service Awards Committee.

A district policing partnership.

The Drainage Council for Northern Ireland.

An Education and Library Board established under Article 3 of the Education and Libraries (Northern Ireland) Order 1986.

The Equality Commission for Northern Ireland.

The Family Proceedings Rules Committee (Northern Ireland).

The General Consumer Council for Northern Ireland.

The General Teaching Council for Northern Ireland.

The Governors of the Armargh Observatory and Planetarium.

The Harbour of Donaghadee Commissioners.

The Health and Safety Agency for Northern Ireland.

The Historic Buildings Council.

The Historic Monuments Council.

The Historical Institutional Abuse Redress Board.

The Independent Assessor of Military Complaints Procedures in Northern Ireland.

The Independent Financial Review Panel.

An independent monitoring board appointed under section 10 of the Prison Act (Northern Ireland) 1953.

The Independent Reviewer of the Northern Ireland (Emergency Provisions) Act.

The Independent Commissioner for Holding Centres.

Invest Northern Ireland.

The Labour Relations Agency.

The Laganside Corporation.

The Lay Observer for Northern Ireland.

The Livestock & Meat Commission for Northern Ireland.

The Local Government Staff Commission.

The Londonderry Port and Harbour Commissioners.

The Magistrates' Courts Rules Committee (Northern Ireland).

The Mental Health Commission for Northern Ireland.

The Northern Ireland Audit Office.

The Northern Ireland Authority for Utility Regulation.

The Northern Ireland Building Regulations Advisory Committee.

The Northern Ireland Civil Service Appeal Board.

The Northern Ireland Commissioner for Complaints.

The Northern Ireland Community Relations Council.

The Northern Ireland Council for the Curriculum, Examinations and Assessment.

The Northern Ireland Court of Judicature Rules Committee.

The Northern Ireland Crown Court Rules Committee.

The Northern Ireland Events Company.

The Northern Ireland Fire and Rescue Service Board.

The Northern Ireland Fishery Harbour Authority.

The Northern Ireland Health and Personal Social Services Regulation and Improvement Authority.

The Northern Ireland Higher Education Council.

The Northern Ireland Housing Executive.

The Northern Ireland Human Rights Commission.

The Northern Ireland Insolvency Rules Committee.

The Northern Ireland Judicial Appointments Commission.

The Northern Ireland Law Commission.

The Northern Ireland Legal Services Commission.

The Northern Ireland Local Government Officers' Superannuation Committee.

The Northern Ireland Museums Council.

The Northern Ireland Practice and Education Council for Nursing and Midwifery.

The Northern Ireland Social Care Council.

The Northern Ireland Tourist Board.

The Northern Ireland Transport Holding Company.

The Parades Commission.

Parole Commissioners for Northern Ireland.

The Pharmaceutical Society of Northern Ireland, in respect of information held by it otherwise than as a tribunal.

The Poisons Board (Northern Ireland).

The Police Ombudsman for Northern Ireland.

The Prisoner Ombudsman for Northern Ireland.

The Probation Board for Northern Ireland.

The Royal Ulster Constabulary George Cross Foundation.

The Rural Development Council for Northern Ireland.

The Safeguarding Board for Northern Ireland.

The Sentence Review Commissioners appointed under section 1 of the Northern Ireland (Sentences) Act 1998.

The social fund Commissioner appointed under Article 37 of the Social Security (Northern Ireland) Order 1998.

The Sports Council for Northern Ireland.

The Staff Commission for Education and Library Boards.

The Statistics Advisory Committee.

The Statute Law Committee for Northern Ireland.

A sub-group established under section 21 of the Police (Northern Ireland) Act 2000.

Ulster Supported Employment Ltd.

The Warrenpoint Harbour Authority.

The Waste Management Advisory Board.

The Youth Council for Northern Ireland.

SCHEDULE 2
THE COMMISSIONER AND THE TRIBUNAL

Section 18(4)

PART I
PROVISION CONSEQUENTIAL ON S 18(1) AND (2)

General

1(1)   Any reference in any enactment, instrument or document to the Data Protection Commissioner or the Data Protection Registrar shall be construed, in relation to any time after the commencement of section 18(1), as a reference to the Information Commissioner.

2(1)   Any reference in this Act or in any instrument under this Act to the Commissioner shall be construed, in relation to any time before the commencement of section 18(1), as a reference to the Data Protection Commissioner.

Remainder not reproduced

PART II
AMENDMENTS RELATING TO EXTENSION OF FUNCTIONS OF COMMISSIONER AND TRIBUNAL

Not reproduced

SCHEDULE 3
POWERS OF ENTRY AND INSPECTION

Section 55

Issue of warrants

1(1)   If a circuit judge or a District Judge (Magistrates' Courts) is satisfied by information on oath supplied by the Commissioner that there are reasonable grounds for suspecting—
    (a)   that a public authority has failed or is failing to comply with—
        (i)   any of the requirements of Part I of this Act,
        (ii)   so much of a decision notice as requires steps to be taken, or

(iii) an information notice or an enforcement notice, or

(b) that an offence under section 77 has been or is being committed,

and that evidence of such a failure to comply or of the commission of the offence is to be found on any premises specified in the information, he may, subject to paragraph 2, grant a warrant to the Commissioner.

(2) A warrant issued under sub-paragraph (1) shall authorise the Commissioner or any of his officers or staff at any time within seven days of the date of the warrant—

    (a) to enter and search the premises,

    (b) to inspect and seize any documents or other material found there which may be such evidence as is mentioned in that sub-paragraph, and

    (c) to inspect, examine, operate and test any equipment found there in which information held by the public authority may be recorded.

2(1) A judge shall not issue a warrant under this Schedule unless he is satisfied—

    (a) that the Commissioner has given seven days' notice in writing to the occupier of the premises in question demanding access to the premises, and

    (b) that either—

        (i) access was demanded at a reasonable hour and was unreasonably refused, or

        (ii) although entry to the premises was granted, the occupier unreasonably refused to comply with a request by the Commissioner or any of the Commissioner's officers or staff to permit the Commissioner or the officer or member of staff to do any of the things referred to in paragraph 1(2), and

    (c) that the occupier, has, after the refusal, been notified by the Commissioner of the application for the warrant and has had an opportunity of being heard by the judge on the question whether or not it should be issued.

(2) Sub-paragraph (1) shall not apply if the judge is satisfied that the case is one of urgency or that compliance with those provisions would defeat the object of the entry.

3 A judge who issues a warrant under this Schedule shall also issue two copies of it and certify them clearly as copies.

Execution of warrants

4 A person executing a warrant issued under this Schedule may use such reasonable force as may be necessary.

5 A warrant issued under this Schedule shall be executed at a reasonable hour unless it appears to the person executing it that there are grounds for suspecting that the evidence in question would not be found if it were so executed.

6(1) If the premises in respect of which a warrant is issued under this Schedule are occupied by a public authority and any officer or employee of the authority is present when the warrant is executed, he shall be shown the warrant and supplied with a copy of it; and if no such officer or employee is present a copy of the warrant shall be left in a prominent place on the premises.

(2) If the premises in respect of which a warrant is issued under this Schedule are occupied by a person other than a public authority and he is present when the warrant is executed, he shall be shown the warrant and supplied with a copy of it; and if that person is not present a copy of the warrant shall be left in a prominent place on the premises.

7(1) A person seizing anything in pursuance of a warrant under this Schedule shall give a receipt for it if asked to do so.

(2) Anything so seized may be retained for so long as is necessary in all the circumstances but the person in occupation of the premises in question shall be given a copy of anything that is seized if he so requests and the person executing the warrant considers that it can be done without undue delay.

Matters exempt from inspection and seizure

8   The powers of inspection and seizure conferred by a warrant issued under this Schedule shall not be exercisable in respect of information which is exempt information by virtue of section 23(1) or 24(1).

9(1)   Subject to the provisions of this paragraph, the powers of inspection and seizure conferred by a warrant issued under this Schedule shall not be exercisable in respect of—

(a)   any communication between a professional legal adviser and his client in connection with the giving of legal advice to the client with respect to his obligations, liabilities or rights under this Act, or

(b)   any communication between a professional legal adviser and his client, or between such an adviser or his client and any other person, made in connection with or in contemplation of proceedings under or arising out of this Act (including proceedings before the Tribunal) and for the purposes of such proceedings.

(2)   Sub-paragraph (1) applies also to—

(a)   any copy or other record of any such communication as is there mentioned, and

(b)   any document or article enclosed with or referred to in any such communication if made in connection with the giving of any advice or, as the case may be, in connection with or in contemplation of and for the purposes of such proceedings as are there mentioned.

(3)   This paragraph does not apply to anything in the possession of any person other than the professional legal adviser or his client or to anything held with the intention of furthering a criminal purpose.

(4)   In this paragraph references to the client of a professional legal adviser include references to any person representing such a client.

10   If the person in occupation of any premises in respect of which a warrant is issued under this Schedule objects to the inspection or seizure under the warrant of any material on the grounds that it consists partly of matters in respect of which those powers are not exercisable, he shall, if the person executing the warrant so requests, furnish that person with a copy of so much of the material in relation to which the powers are exercisable.

Return of warrants

11 A warrant issued under this Schedule shall be returned to the court from which it was issued—

(a)   after being executed, or

(b)   if not executed within the time authorised for its execution;

and the person by whom any such warrant is executed shall make an endorsement on it stating what powers have been exercised by him under the warrant.

Offences

12 Any person who—

(a)   intentionally obstructs a person in the execution of a warrant issued under this Schedule, or

(b)   fails without reasonable excuse to give any person executing such a warrant such assistance as he may reasonably require for the execution of the warrant,

is guilty of an offence.

Vessels, vehicles etc

13 In this Schedule "premises" includes any vessel, vehicle, aircraft or hovercraft, and references to the occupier of any premises include references to the person in charge of any vessel, vehicle, aircraft or hovercraft.

Scotland and Northern Ireland

14 In the application of this Schedule to Scotland—

(a)   for any reference to a circuit judge there is substituted a reference to the sheriff, and

(b)   for any reference to information on oath there is substituted a reference to evidence on oath.

15 In the application of this Schedule to Northern Ireland—
  (a) for any reference to a circuit judge there is substituted a reference to a county court judge, and
  (b) for any reference to information on oath there is substituted a reference to a complaint on oath.

SCHEDULE 4
APPEAL PROCEEDINGS: AMENDMENTS OF SCHEDULE 6
TO DATA PROTECTION ACT 1998

Repealed   Section 61(1)

SCHEDULE 5
AMENDMENTS OF PUBLIC RECORDS LEGISLATION

Not reproduced   Section 67

SCHEDULE 6
FURTHER AMENDMENTS OF DATA PROTECTION ACT 1998

Repealed   Section 73

SCHEDULE 7
DISCLOSURE OF INFORMATION BY OMBUDSMEN

Not reproduced   Section 76(2)

SCHEDULE 8
REPEALS

Not reproduced   Section 86

Freedom of Information (Scotland) Act 2002

(as amended to 1 February 2020)

2002 ASP 13

28 May 2002

An Act of the Scottish Parliament to make provision for the disclosure of information held by Scottish public authorities or by persons providing services for them; and for connected purposes.

PART 1
ACCESS TO INFORMATION HELD BY SCOTTISH PUBLIC AUTHORITIES

PART 2
EXEMPT INFORMATION

PART 3
THE SCOTTISH INFORMATION COMMISSIONER

PART 4
ENFORCEMENT

PART 5
HISTORICAL RECORDS

PART 6
CODES OF PRACTICE

PART 7
MISCELLANEOUS AND SUPPLEMENTAL

SCHEDULE 1
Scottish Public Authorities

SCHEDULE 2
The Scottish Information Commissioner

SCHEDULE 3
Powers of Entry and Inspection

SCHEDULE 4
Consequential Amendments to Scottish Public Services Ombudsman Act 2002

PART 1

ACCESS TO INFORMATION HELD BY SCOTTISH PUBLIC AUTHORITIES

Right to information

General entitlement

1 (1) A person who requests information from a Scottish public authority which holds it is entitled to be given it by the authority.

(2) The person who makes such a request is in this Part and in Parts 2 and 7 referred to as the "applicant".

(3) If the authority--
  (a) requires further information in order to identify and locate the requested information; and
  (b) has told the applicant so (specifying what the requirement for further information is),
then, provided that the requirement is reasonable, the authority is not obliged to give the requested information until it has the further information.

(4) The information to be given by the authority is that held by it at the time the request is received, except that, subject to subsection (5), any amendment or deletion which would have been made, regardless of the receipt of the request, between that time and the time it gives the information may be made before the information is given.

(5) The requested information is not, by virtue of subsection (4), to be destroyed before it can be given (unless the circumstances are such that it is not reasonably practicable to prevent such destruction from occurring).

(6) This section is subject to sections 2, 9, 12 and 14.

NOTES

FOIA 2000 equivalent
  s 1

Defined terms
  "information": s 73
  "Scottish public authority": ss 3(1), 73

Effect of exemptions

2(1) To information which is exempt information by virtue of any provision of Part 2, section 1 applies only to the extent that—
  (a) the provision does not confer absolute exemption; and
  (b) in all the circumstances of the case, the public interest in disclosing the information is not outweighed by that in maintaining the exemption.

(2) For the purposes of paragraph (a) of subsection (1), the following provisions of Part 2 (and no others) are to be regarded as conferring absolute exemption
  (a) section 25;
  (b) section 26;
  (c) section 36(2);
  (d) section 37; and
  (e) in subsection (1) of section 38
      (i)   paragraphs (a), (c) and (d); and
      (ii) paragraph (b) where the first condition referred to in that paragraph is

satisfied.

NOTES

FOIA 2000 equivalent
s 2

Defined terms
"exempt information": s 73
"information": s 73

Scottish public authorities

3(1) In this Act, "Scottish public authority" means
    (a) any body which, any other person who, or the holder of any office which
        (i) is listed in schedule 1; or
        (ii) is designated by order under section 5(1); or
    (b) a publicly-owned company, as defined by section 6.

(2) For the purposes of this Act but subject to subsection (4), information is held by an authority if it is held
    (a) by the authority otherwise than
        (i) on behalf of another person; or
        (ii) in confidence, having been supplied by a Minister of the Crown or by a department of the Government of the United Kingdom; or
    (b) by a person other than the authority, on behalf of the authority.

(3) Subsection (1)(a)(i) is subject to any qualification set out in schedule 1.

(4) Information is not held by the Keeper of the Records of Scotland if it is contained in a record transferred to the Keeper by a public authority within the meaning of the Freedom of Information Act 2000 (c 36) unless it is information
    (a) to which subsections (2) to (5) of section 22 apply by virtue of subsection (6) of that section; or
    (b) designated by that authority as open information for the purposes of this subsection.

(5) Where the public authority mentioned in subsection (4) is the Secretary of State for Scotland and the information is contained in a record transferred as is mentioned in subsection (6) of section 22 the reference in subsection (4)(b) to "that authority" is to be construed as a reference to the Scottish Ministers.

NOTES

FOIA 2000 equivalent
s 3

Defined terms
"body": s 73
"information": s 73
"Minister of the Crown": s 73
"publicly-owned company": s 6

Amendment of schedule 1

4(1) The Scottish Ministers may by order amend schedule 1 by
    (a) adding to that schedule a reference to
        (i) any body which; or
        (ii) the holder of any office which,
    is not for the time being listed there and is either a part of the Scottish Administration or a Scottish public authority with mixed functions or no reserved functions; or
    (b) removing from that schedule an entry for the time being listed there.

(2) The reference in paragraph (a) of subsection (1) to an authority with mixed functions or no reserved functions is to be construed in accordance with paragraphs 1(4) and 2 of Part III of Schedule 5 to the Scotland Act 1998 (c 46).

(3) An order under subsection (1) may relate to a specified person or office or to persons or offices falling within a specified description.

NOTES

FOIA 2000 equivalent
s 4

Defined terms
"body": s 73
"Scottish public authority": ss 3(1), 73

Further power to designate Scottish public authorities

5(1) The Scottish Ministers may by order designate as a Scottish public authority for the purposes of this Act any person mentioned in subsection (2) who
  (a) is neither for the time being listed in schedule 1 nor capable of being added to that schedule by order under section 4(1); and
  (b) is neither a public body nor the holder of any public office.

(2) The persons are those who either
  (a) appear to the Scottish Ministers to exercise functions of a public nature; or
  (b) are providing, under a contract made with a Scottish public authority, any service whose provision is a function of that authority.

(3) An order under subsection (1) may designate a specified person or persons falling within a specified description.

(4) An order under subsection (1) made by virtue of
  (a) subsection (2)(a) must specify the functions of a public nature which appear to be exercised;
  (b) subsection (2)(b) must specify the service being provided.

(5) Before making an order under subsection (1), the Scottish Ministers must
  (a) consult
    (i) every person to whom the order relates, or
    (ii) persons appearing to them to represent such persons, and
  (b) also consult such other persons as they consider appropriate.

NOTES

FOIA 2000 equivalent
s 5

Defined terms
"body": s 73
"Scottish public authority": ss 3(1), 73

Publicly-owned companies

6(1) A company is a "publicly-owned company" for the purposes of section 3(1)(b) if it is wholly owned
  (a) by the Scottish Ministers; or
  (b) by any other Scottish public authority listed in schedule 1, other than an authority so listed only in relation to information of a specified description.

(2) For the purposes of subsection (1), a company is wholly owned
  (a) by the Scottish Ministers if it has no members except
    (i) the Scottish Ministers or companies wholly owned by the Scottish Ministers;

or

 (ii) persons acting on behalf of the Scottish Ministers or of such companies; and

(b) by any other Scottish public authority if it has no members except

 (i) the authority or companies wholly owned by the authority; or

 (ii) persons acting on behalf of the authority or of such companies.

(3) In subsections (1) and (2), "company" includes any body corporate.

NOTES

FOIA 2000 equivalent
 s 6

Defined terms
 "information": s 73
 "Scottish public authority": ss 3(1), 73

Public authorities to which Act has limited application

7(1) An order under section 4(1)(a) may, in adding an entry to schedule 1, list the authority only in relation to information of a specified description; and where an authority is so listed nothing in this Act applies to any other information held by the authority.

(2) The Scottish Ministers may by order amend that schedule

(a) by limiting the entry relating to an authority to information of a specified description; or

(b) by removing or amending any such limitation for the time being contained in an entry so relating.

(3) Nothing in this Act applies to information held by a person designated as a Scottish public authority by order under subsection (1) of section 5 if the order is made by virtue of

(a) subsection (2)(a) of that section and the information does not relate to the functions; or

(b) subsection (2)(b) of that section and the information does not relate to the service, specified in the order.

(4) Nothing in this Act applies in relation to information

(a) held by a publicly-owned company; and

(b) of a description specified in relation to that company in an order made for the purposes of this subsection by the Scottish Ministers.

NOTES

FOIA 2000 equivalent
 s 7

Defined terms
 "information": s 73
 "publicly-owned company": s 6
 "Scottish public authority": ss 3(1), 73

Reports on section 5 power

7A(1) In accordance with this section, the Scottish Ministers must lay before the Parliament reports about the exercise of the section 5 power.

(2) The first report is to be laid on or before 31 October 2015.

(3) Each subsequent report is to be laid no later than 2 years after the date on which the previous report is laid.

(4) A report must

(a) state whether the section 5 power has been exercised during the reporting period,

and

(b) as the case may be

    (i) explain how the power has been exercised during the reporting period (and why), or

    (ii) give the reason for leaving the power unexercised during the reporting period.

(5) A report may

    (a) summarise any response to a consultation carried out during the reporting period as regards the exercise of the section 5 power,

    (b) indicate any intention to exercise the power in the future,

    (c) include such additional information as the Scottish Ministers consider appropriate.

(6) In this section

"reporting period" means

    (a) in the case of the first report, period of time from the date on which section 1 of the Freedom of Information (Amendment) (Scotland) Act 2013 comes into force until the date on which the first report is laid,

    (b) in the case of a subsequent report, period of time from the date on which the previous report is laid until the date on which the subsequent report is laid,

"section 5 power" means order-making power conferred by section 5(1).

NOTES

FOIA 2000 equivalent
n/a

Defined terms
"information": s 73

Requesting information

8(1) Any reference in this Act to "requesting" information is a reference to making a request which

    (a) is in writing or in another form which, by reason of its having some permanency, is capable of being used for subsequent reference (as, for example, a recording made on audio or video tape);

    (b) states the name of the applicant and an address for correspondence; and

    (c) describes the information requested.

(2) For the purposes of paragraph (a) of subsection (1) (and without prejudice to the generality of that paragraph), a request is to be treated as made in writing where the text of the request is

    (a) transmitted by electronic means;

    (b) received in legible form; and

    (c) capable of being used for subsequent reference.

NOTES

FOIA 2000 equivalent
s 8

Defined terms
"applicant": s 1(2)
"information": s 73

Fees

9(1) A Scottish public authority receiving a request which requires it to comply with section 1(1) may, within the time allowed by section 10 for so complying, give the applicant a notice in writing (in this Act referred to as a "fees notice") stating that a fee of an amount specified in the notice is to be charged by the authority for so complying.

(2) Subsection (1) is subject to section 19.

(3) If a fees notice is given to the applicant, the authority is not obliged to give the requested information unless the fee is duly paid; and for the purposes of this subsection and section 10(2) due payment is payment within the period of three months beginning with the day on which the notice is given.

(4) Subject to subsection (7), a fee charged under subsection (1) is to be determined by the authority in accordance with regulations made by the Scottish Ministers.

(5) Without prejudice to the generality of subsection (4), the regulations may in particular provide that
    (a) a fee is not to exceed such amount as may be specified in, or determined in accordance with, the regulations;
    (b) a fee is to be calculated in such manner as may be so specified; and
    (c) no fee is payable in a case so specified.

(6) Before making the regulations, the Scottish Ministers are to consult the Commissioner.

(7) Subsection (4) does not apply where provision is made, by or under any enactment, as to the fee that may be charged by the authority for the disclosure of the information.

NOTES

FOIA 2000 equivalent
s 9

Defined terms
  "applicant": s 1(2)
  "the Commissioner": s 73

"enactment": s 73
"information": s 73
"Scottish public authority": ss 3(1), 73

Subordinate legislation
  Freedom of Information (Fees for Required Disclosure) (Scotland) Regulations 2004, SSI 2004/467

Time for compliance

10(1) Subject to subsections (2) and (3), a Scottish public authority receiving a request which requires it to comply with section 1(1) must comply promptly; and in any event by not later than the twentieth working day after
    (a) in a case other than that mentioned in paragraph (b), the receipt by the authority of the request; or
    (b) in a case where section 1(3) applies, the receipt by it of the further information.

(2) If
    (a) the authority is the Keeper of the Records of Scotland; and
    (b) the information is information to which section 22(2) to (5) applies, subsection (1) applies with the substitution, for the reference to the twentieth working day, of a reference to the thirtieth working day.

(3) Where the authority gives a fees notice to the applicant and the fee is duly paid, the working days in the period
    (a) beginning with the day on which that notice is given; and
    (b) ending with the day on which the fee is received by the authority, are to be disregarded in calculating, for the purposes of subsection (1), the twentieth (or as the case may be the thirtieth) working day mentioned in that subsection.

(4) The Scottish Ministers may by regulations provide that subsections (1) and (3) are to have

effect as if references to the twentieth (or as the case may be the thirtieth) working day were references to such other working day, not later than the sixtieth, after receipt by the authority of the request as is specified in, or determined in accordance with, the regulations.

(5) Regulations under subsection (4) may

    (a) prescribe different days in relation to different cases; and

    (b) confer a discretion on the Scottish Information Commissioner, exercisable both at the request of the authority and where no such request has been made.

NOTES

FOIA 2000 equivalent
s 10

Defined terms
"applicant": s 1(2)
"the Commissioner": s 73

"fees notice": ss 9(1), 73
"information": s 73
"Scottish public authority": ss 3(1), 73
"working day": s 73

Subordinate legislation
Freedom of Information (Scotland) Act 2002 (Time for Compliance) Regulations 2016, SSI 2016/346

Means of providing information

11(1) Where, in requesting information from a Scottish public authority, the applicant expresses a preference for receiving it by any one or more of the means mentioned in subsection (2), the authority must, so far as is reasonably practicable, give effect to that preference.

(2) The means are

    (a) the provision to the applicant, in permanent form or in another form acceptable to the applicant, of a copy of the information;

    (b) such provision to the applicant of a digest or summary of the information; and

    (c) the provision to the applicant of a reasonable opportunity to inspect a record containing the information.

(3) In determining, for the purposes of subsection (1), what is reasonably practicable, the authority may have regard to all the circumstances, including cost; and where it determines that it is not reasonably practicable to give effect to the preference it must notify the applicant of the reasons for that determination.

(4) Subject to subsection (1), information given in compliance with section 1(1) may be given by any means which are reasonable in the circumstances.

(5) Such tests of reasonable practicability as are imposed by this section are not to be construed as detracting from any duty which a person has under or by virtue of section 29 of the Equality Act 2010 (provision of services etc) (duty to make adjustments to practices, policies, procedures or physical features so that use of services by disabled persons is facilitated or made possible).

NOTES

FOIA 2000 equivalent
s 11

Defined terms
"applicant": s 1(2)
"information": s 73
"requesting": s 8(1)
"Scottish public authority": ss 3(1), 73

Excessive cost of compliance

12(1)   Section 1(1) does not oblige a Scottish public authority to comply with a request for information if the authority estimates that the cost of complying with the request would exceed such amount as may be prescribed in regulations made by the Scottish Ministers; and different amounts may be so prescribed in relation to different cases.

(2)   The regulations may provide that, in such circumstances as they may specify, where two or more requests for information are made to the authority
(a)   by one person;
(b)   by different persons who appear to it to be acting in concert or whose requests appear to have been instigated wholly or mainly for a purpose other than the obtaining of the information itself; or
(c)   by different persons in circumstances where the authority considers it would be reasonable to make the information available to the public at large and elects to do so,
then if the authority estimates that the total cost of complying with both (or all) of the requests exceeds the amount prescribed, in relation to complying with either (or any) of those requests, under subsection (1), section 1(1) does not oblige the authority to comply with either (or any) of those requests.

(3)   The regulations may, in respect of an election made as mentioned in subsection (2)(c), make provision as to the means by which and the time within which the information is to be made available to the public at large.

(4)   The regulations may make provision as to
(a)   the costs to be estimated; and
(b)   the manner in which those costs are to be estimated.

(5)   Before making the regulations, the Scottish Ministers are to consult the Commissioner.

(6)   References in this section to the cost of complying with a request are not to be construed as including any reference to costs incurred in fulfilling any such duty under or by virtue of the Equality Act 2010 as is mentioned in section 11(5).

NOTES

FOIA 2000 equivalent
s 12
Defined terms
"the Commissioner": s 73

"information": s 73
"Scottish public authority": ss 3(1), 73

Subordinate legislation
Freedom of Information (Fees for Required Disclosure) (Scotland) Regulations 2004, SSI 2004/467

Fees for disclosure in certain circumstances

13(1)   A Scottish public authority may charge for the communication of any information
(a)   which by virtue of section 12(1) or (2) it is not obliged to communicate; and
(b)   which it is not otherwise required by law to communicate,
such fee as may be determined by it in accordance with regulations made by the Scottish Ministers.

(2)   Without prejudice to the generality of subsection (1), the regulations may in particular provide that a fee
(a)   is not to exceed such amount as may be specified in, or determined in accordance

with, the regulations; and

    (b) is to be calculated in such manner as may be so specified.

(3) Before making the regulations, the Scottish Ministers are to consult the Commissioner.

(4) Subsection (1) does not apply where provision is made, by or under any enactment, as to the fee that may be charged by the authority for the disclosure of the information.

NOTES

FOIA 2000 equivalent
  s 13

Defined terms
  "the Commissioner": s 73

"enactment": s 73
"information": s 73
"Scottish public authority": ss 3(1), 73

Subordinate legislation
  Freedom of Information (Fees for Required Disclosure) (Scotland) Regulations 2004, SSI 2004/467

Vexatious or repeated requests

14(1) Section 1(1) does not oblige a Scottish public authority to comply with a request for information if the request is vexatious.

(2) Where a Scottish public authority has complied with a request from a person for information, it is not obliged to comply with a subsequent request from that person which is identical or substantially similar unless there has been a reasonable period of time between the making of the request complied with and the making of the subsequent request.

NOTES

FOIA 2000 equivalent
  s 14

Defined terms
  "information": s 73
  "Scottish public authority": ss 3(1), 73

Duty to provide advice and assistance

15(1) A Scottish public authority must, so far as it is reasonable to expect it to do so, provide advice and assistance to a person who proposes to make, or has made, a request for information to it.

(2) A Scottish public authority which, in relation to the provision of advice or assistance in any case, conforms with the code of practice issued under section 60 is, as respects that case, to be taken to comply with the duty imposed by subsection (1).

NOTES

FOIA 2000 equivalent
  s 16

Defined terms
  "information": s 73
  "Scottish public authority": ss 3(1), 73

Refusal of request

16(1) Subject to section 18, a Scottish public authority which, in relation to a request for information which it holds, to any extent claims that, by virtue of any provision of Part 2, the information is exempt information must, within the time allowed by or by virtue of section 10 for complying with the request, give the applicant a notice in writing (in this Act referred to as a "refusal notice") which

    (a) discloses that it holds the information;

(b) states that it so claims;

(c) specifies the exemption in question; and

(d) states (if not otherwise apparent) why the exemption applies.

(2) Where the authority's claim is made only by virtue of a provision of Part 2 which does not confer absolute exemption, the notice must state the authority's reason for claiming that, in all the circumstances of the case, the public interest in maintaining the exemption outweighs that in disclosure of the information.

(3) The authority is not obliged to make a statement under subsection (1)(d) in so far as the statement would disclose information which would itself be exempt information.

(4) A Scottish public authority which, in relation to a request for information, claims that section 12(1) applies must, within the time allowed by or by virtue of section 10 for complying with the request, give the applicant a notice which states that it so claims.

(5) A Scottish public authority which, in relation to such a request, claims that section 14 applies must, within that time, give the applicant a notice which states that it so claims; except that the notice need not be given if

(a) the authority has, in relation to a previous identical or substantially similar such request, given the applicant a notice under this subsection; and

(b) it would in all the circumstances be unreasonable to expect it to serve a further such notice in relation to the current request.

(6) Subsections (1), (4) and (5) are subject to section 19.

NOTES

FOIA 2000 equivalent
  s 17

Defined terms
  "applicant": s 1(2)
  "exempt information": s 73
  "information": s 73
  "Scottish public authority": ss 3(1), 73

Notice that information is not held

17(1) Where

(a) a Scottish public authority receives a request which would require it either

(i)   to comply with section 1(1); or

(ii) to determine any question arising by virtue of paragraph (a) or (b) of section 2(1),

if it held the information to which the request relates; but

(b) the authority does not hold that information,

it must, within the time allowed by or by virtue of section 10 for complying with the request, give the applicant notice in writing that it does not hold it.

(2) Subsection (1) is subject to section 19.

(3) Subsection (1) does not apply if, by virtue of section 18, the authority instead gives the applicant a refusal notice.

NOTES

FOIA 2000 equivalent
  s 17

Defined terms
  "applicant": s 1(2)
  "information": s 73
  "refusal notice": ss 16(1), 73
  "Scottish public authority": ss 3(1), 73

Further provision as respects responses to request

18(1) Where, if information existed and was held by a Scottish public authority, the authority could give a refusal notice under section 16(1) on the basis that the information was exempt information by virtue of any of sections 28 to 35, 38, 39(1) or 41 but the authority considers that to reveal whether the information exists or is so held would be contrary to the public interest, it may (whether or not the information does exist and is held by it) give the applicant a refusal notice by virtue of this section.

(2) Neither paragraph (a) of subsection (1) of section 16 nor subsection (2) of that section applies as respects a refusal notice given by virtue of this section.

NOTES

FOIA 2000 equivalent
 s 17

Defined terms
 "applicant": s 1(2)

"exempt information": s 73
"information": s 73
"refusal notice": ss 16(1), 73
"Scottish public authority": ss 3(1), 73

Content of certain notices

19 A notice under section 9(1) or 16(1), (4) or (5) (including a refusal notice given by virtue of section 18(1)) or 17(1) must contain particulars
(a) of the procedure provided by the authority for dealing with complaints about the handling by it of requests for information; and
(b) about the rights of application to the authority and the Commissioner conferred by sections 20(1) and 47(1).

NOTES

FOIA 2000 equivalent
 s 17

Defined terms
 "the Commissioner": s 73
 "information": s 73
 "refusal notice": ss 16(1), 73

Requirement for review of refusal etc

20(1) An applicant who is dissatisfied with the way in which a Scottish public authority has dealt with a request for information made under this Part of this Act may require the authority to review its actions and decisions in relation to that request.

(2) A requirement under subsection (1) is referred to in this Act as a "requirement for review".

(3) A requirement for review must
(a) be in writing or in another form which, by reason of its having some permanency, is capable of being used for subsequent reference (as, for example, a recording made on audio or video tape);
(b) state the name of the applicant and an address for correspondence; and
(c) specify
(i) the request for information to which the requirement for review relates; and
(ii) the matter which gives rise to the applicant's dissatisfaction mentioned in subsection (1).

(4) For the purposes of paragraph (a) of subsection (3) (and without prejudice to the generality of that paragraph), a requirement for review is treated as made in writing where the text of the requirement is as mentioned in paragraphs (a) to (c) of section 8(2).

(5) Subject to subsection (6), a requirement for review must be made by not later than the fortieth working day after

    (a) the expiry of the time allowed by or by virtue of section 10 for complying with the request; or

    (b) in a case where the authority purports under this Act

        (i) to comply with a request for information; or

        (ii) to give the applicant a fees notice, a refusal notice or a notice under section 17(1) that information is not held,

    but does so outwith that time, the receipt by the applicant of the information provided or, as the case may be, the notice.

(6) A Scottish public authority may comply with a requirement for review made after the expiry of the time allowed by subsection (5) for making such a requirement if it considers it appropriate to do so.

(7) The Scottish Ministers may by regulations provide that subsections (5) and (6) are to have effect as if the reference in subsection (5) to the fortieth working day were a reference to such other working day as is specified in (or determined in accordance with) the regulations.

(8) Regulations under subsection (7) may

    (a) prescribe different days in relation to different cases; and

    (b) confer a discretion on the Scottish Information Commissioner.

(9) In subsection (1), the reference to "actions" and "decisions" includes inaction and failure to reach a decision.

NOTES

FOIA 2000 equivalent
  n/a

Defined terms
  "applicant": s 1(2)

"the Commissioner": s 73
"fees notice": ss 9(1), 73
"information": s 73
"refusal notice": ss 16(1), 73
"Scottish public authority": ss 3(1), 73
"working day": s 73

Review by Scottish public authority

21(1) Subject to subsection (2), a Scottish public authority receiving a requirement for review must (unless that requirement is withdrawn or is as mentioned in subsection (8)) comply promptly; and in any event by not later than the twentieth working day after receipt by it of the requirement.

(2) If

    (a) the authority is the Keeper of the Records of Scotland; and

    (b) a different authority is, by virtue of section 22(4), to review a decision to which the requirement relates,

subsection (1) applies with the substitution, for the reference to the twentieth working day, of a reference to the thirtieth working day.

(3) A requirement for review may be withdrawn by the applicant who made it, by notice in writing to the authority, at any time before the authority makes its decision on the requirement.

(4) The authority may, as respects the request for information to which the requirement

relates

   (a) confirm a decision complained of, with or without such modifications as it considers appropriate;

   (b) substitute for any such decision a different decision; or

   (c) reach a decision, where the complaint is that no decision had been reached.

(5) Within the time allowed by subsection (1) for complying with the requirement for review, the authority must give the applicant notice in writing of what it has done under subsection (4) and a statement of its reasons for so doing.

(6) The Scottish Ministers may by regulations provide that subsections (1) and (5) and section 47(4)(b) are to have effect as if the reference in subsection (1) to the twentieth (or as the case may be the thirtieth) working day were a reference to such other working day as is specified in (or determined in accordance with) the regulations.

(7) Regulations under subsection (6) may

   (a) prescribe different days in relation to different cases; and

   (b) confer a discretion on the Scottish Information Commissioner.

(8) Subsection (1) does not oblige a Scottish public authority to comply with a requirement for review if

   (a) the requirement is vexatious; or

   (b) the request for information to which the requirement for review relates was one with which, by virtue of section 14, the authority was not obliged to comply.

(9) Where the authority considers that paragraph (a) or (b) of subsection (8) applies, it must give the applicant who made the requirement for review notice in writing, within the time allowed by subsection (1) for complying with that requirement, that it so claims.

(10) A notice under subsection (5) or (9) must contain particulars about the rights of application to the Commissioner and of appeal conferred by sections 47(1) and 56.

NOTES

FOIA 2000 equivalent

   n/a

Defined terms

   "applicant": s 1(2)

   "the Commissioner": s 73

"information": s 73

"requirement for review": ss 20(2), 73

"Scottish public authority": ss 3(1), 73

"working day": s 73

Subordinate legislation

Freedom of Information (Scotland) Act 2002 (Time for Compliance) Regulations 2016, SSI 2016/346

Records transferred to the Keeper of the Records of Scotland

Special provisions relating to records transferred to Keeper

22(1) Subsections (2) to (5) apply to information which

   (a) is contained in a record transferred to the Keeper of the Records of Scotland by a Scottish public authority; and

   (b) has not been designated by the authority as open information for the purposes of this section.

(2) The Keeper must, as soon as practicable after receiving a request for information to which this subsection applies, send a copy of that request to the authority which transferred the information; and it is for the authority, instead of the Keeper, to come to a decision as to

whether the information is exempt information by virtue of any provision of Part 2 and to determine any question then arising by virtue of paragraph (a) or (b) of section 2(1) as respects the information.

(3) After receiving the copy, the authority must, within such time as will make it practicable for the Keeper to comply with section 10 as respects the request, inform the Keeper of the decision mentioned in subsection (2) and of any determination required by virtue of that decision.

(4) The Keeper must, as soon as practicable after receiving a requirement for review in which the specification under section 20(3)(c)(ii) relates to a decision made by the authority by virtue of subsection (2), send a copy of that requirement to the authority; and it is for the authority, instead of the Keeper, to review the decision and to do anything which is to be done under section 21(4).

(5) After receiving the requirement, the authority must, within such time as will make it practicable for the Keeper to comply with subsection (5) of section 21 as respects the requirement, inform the Keeper of what it has done under subsection (4) of that section and provide a statement of its reasons for so doing; and it is that information and statement which the Keeper shall, in the notice in writing, give in so complying.

(6) Subsections (2) to (5) also apply to information which is contained in a record transferred to the Keeper, before 1st July 1999, by the Secretary of State for Scotland and is not designated by the Scottish Ministers as open information for the purposes of section 3(4); but for the purposes of that application references in subsections (2) to (5) to "the authority" are to be construed as references to the Scottish Ministers.

FOIA 2000 equivalent
s 66

Defined terms
"exempt information": s 73
"information": s 73
"requirement for review": ss 20(2), 73
"Scottish public authority": ss 3(1), 73

Publication schemes

23(1) A Scottish public authority must
  (a) adopt and maintain a scheme (in this Act referred to as a "publication scheme") which relates to the publication of information by the authority and is approved by the Commissioner;
  (b) publish information in accordance with that scheme; and
  (c) from time to time review that scheme.

(2) A publication scheme must specify
  (a) classes of information which the authority publishes or intends to publish;
  (b) the manner in which information of each class is, or is intended to be, published; and
  (c) whether the published information is, or is intended to be, available to the public free of charge or on payment.

(3) In adopting or reviewing its publication scheme the authority must have regard to the public interest in
  (a) allowing public access to information held by it and in particular to information which

       (i)   relates to the provision of services by it, the cost to it of providing them or the standards attained by services so provided; or

       (ii)   consists of facts, or analyses, on the basis of which decisions of importance to the public have been made by it;

   (b) the publication of reasons for decisions made by it.

(4)   The authority must publish its publication scheme but may do so in such manner as it thinks fit.

(5)   The Commissioner may

   (a) when approving a publication scheme, provide that the approval expires at the end of a specified period; and

   (b) at any time give notice to an authority revoking, as from the end of the period of six months beginning at that time, approval of its publication scheme.

(6)   The Commissioner, when

   (a) refusing to approve a proposed publication scheme; or

   (b) revoking approval of a publication scheme,

must state the reason for doing so.

NOTES

FOIA 2000 equivalent
  s 19

Defined terms
  "the Commissioner": s 73
  "information": s 73
  "Scottish public authority": ss 3(1), 73

Model publication schemes

24(1)   The Commissioner may, in relation to Scottish public authorities falling within particular classes

   (a) prepare and approve model publication schemes; or

   (b) approve such schemes prepared by other persons.

(2)   If an authority which falls within the class to which an approved model publication scheme relates adopts that scheme without modification, no further approval of the Commissioner is required so long as that model scheme remains approved; but the approval of the Commissioner is required in relation to any modification of the scheme by an authority.

(3)   The Commissioner may

   (a) when approving a model publication scheme, provide that the approval expires at the end of a specified period; and

   (b) at any time publish, in such manner as the Commissioner thinks fit, a notice revoking, as from the end of the period of six months beginning at that time, approval of such a scheme.

(4)   The Commissioner, when

   (a) refusing to approve

       (i)   under subsection (1)(b), a proposed model scheme; or

       (ii)   any such modification as is mentioned in subsection (2),

      must state the reason for doing so; or

   (b) revoking approval of a model publication scheme, must include in the notice under subsection (3)(b) a statement of the reason for doing so.

NOTES

FOIA 2000 equivalent
  s 20

Defined terms
  "the Commissioner": s 73
  "publication scheme": ss 23(1), 73

PART 2

EXEMPT INFORMATION

Information otherwise accessible

25(1)   Information which the applicant can reasonably obtain other than by requesting it under section 1(1) is exempt information.

(2)   For the purposes of subsection (1), information

  (a) may be reasonably obtainable even if payment is required for access to it;

  (b) is to be taken to be reasonably obtainable if

   (i)   the Scottish public authority which holds it, or any other person, is obliged by or under any enactment to communicate it (otherwise than by making it available for inspection) to; or

   (ii)   the Keeper of the Records of Scotland holds it and makes it available for inspection and (in so far as practicable) copying by,

  members of the public on request, whether free of charge or on payment.

(3)   For the purposes of subsection (1), information is to be taken to be reasonably obtainable if

  (a) it is available

   (i)   on request from the Scottish public authority which holds it, and

   (ii)   in accordance with the authority's publication scheme, and

  (b) any associated payment required by the authority is specified in or determined under the scheme.

NOTES

FOIA 2000 equivalent
  s 21

Defined terms
  "applicant": s 1(2)

enactment": s 73
"information": s 73
"publication scheme": ss 23(1), 73
"requesting": s 8(1)
"Scottish public authority": ss 3(1), 73

Prohibitions on disclosure

26   Information is exempt information if its disclosure by a Scottish public authority (otherwise than under this Act)

  (a) is prohibited by or under an enactment;

  (b) is incompatible with an EU obligation; or

  (c) would constitute, or be punishable as, a contempt of court.

NOTES

FOIA 2000 equivalent
  s 44

Defined terms
  "enactment": s 73
  "information": s 73
  "Scottish public authority": ss 3(1), 73

Information intended for future publication

27(1) Information is exempt information if

(a) it is held with a view to its being published by

(i) a Scottish public authority; or

(ii) any other person,

at a date not later than twelve weeks after that on which the request for the information is made;

(b) when that request is made the information is already being held with that view; and

(c) it is reasonable in all the circumstances that the information be withheld from disclosure until such date as is mentioned in paragraph (a).

(2) Information obtained in the course of, or derived from, a programme of research is exempt information if

(a) the programme is continuing with a view to a report of the research(whether or not including a statement of that information) being published by

(i) a Scottish public authority; or

(ii) any other person; and

(b) disclosure of the information before the date of publication would, or would be likely to, prejudice substantially

(i) the programme;

(ii) the interests of any individual participating in the programme;

(iii) the interests of the authority which holds the information; or

(iv) the interests of the authority mentioned in sub-paragraph (i) of paragraph (a) (if it is a different authority from that which holds the information).

NOTES

FOIA 2000 equivalent
s 22

Defined terms
"information": s 73
"Scottish public authority": ss 3(1), 73

Relations within the United Kingdom

28(1) Information is exempt information if its disclosure under this Act would, or would be likely to, prejudice substantially relations between any administration in the United Kingdom and any other such administration.

(2) In subsection (1), "administration in the United Kingdom" means

(a) the Government of the United Kingdom;

(b) the Scottish Administration;

(c) the Executive Committee of the Northern Ireland Assembly; or

(d) the National Assembly for Wales.

NOTES

FOIA 2000 equivalent
s 28

Defined terms
"information": s 73

Formulation of Scottish Administration policy etc

29(1) Information held by the Scottish Administration is exempt information if it relates to

(a) the formulation or development of government policy;

(b) Ministerial communications;

(c) the provision of advice by any of the Law Officers or any request for the provision of such advice; or

(d) the operation of any Ministerial private office.

(2) Once a decision as to policy has been taken, any statistical information used to provide an informed background to the taking of the decision is not to be regarded, for the purposes of

(a) paragraph (a) of subsection (1), as relating to the formulation or development of the policy in question; or

(b) paragraph (b) of that subsection, as relating to Ministerial communications.

(3) In determining any question under section 2(1)(b) as respects information which is exempt information by virtue of subsection (1)(a), the Scottish Administration must have regard to the public interest in the disclosure of factual information which has been used, or is intended to be used, to provide an informed background to the taking of a decision.

(4) In this section

"government policy" means

(a) the policy of the Scottish Administration; and

(b) in relation to information created before 1st July 1999, the policy of the Government of the United Kingdom;

"the Law Officers" means the Lord Advocate, the Solicitor General for Scotland, the Advocate General for Scotland, the Attorney General, the Solicitor General and the Attorney General for Northern Ireland;"Ministerial communications" means any communications between Ministers and includes, in particular, communications relating to proceedings of the Scottish Cabinet (or of any committee of that Cabinet); and

"Ministerial private office" means any part of the Scottish Administration which provides personal administrative support to a Minister.

(5) In the definitions of "Ministerial communications" and "Ministerial private office" in subsection (4), "Minister" means a member of the Scottish Executive or a junior Scottish Minister.

NOTES

FOIA 2000 equivalent
s 35

Defined terms
"information": s 73

Prejudice to effective conduct of public affairs

30 Information is exempt information if its disclosure under this Act

(a) would, or would be likely to, prejudice substantially the maintenance of the convention of the collective responsibility of the Scottish Ministers;

(b) would, or would be likely to, inhibit substantially

(i) the free and frank provision of advice; or

(ii) the free and frank exchange of views for the purposes of deliberation; or

(c) would otherwise prejudice substantially, or be likely to prejudice substantially, the effective conduct of public affairs.

NOTES

FOIA 2000 equivalent
s 36

Defined terms
"information": s 73

National security and defence

31(1) Information is exempt information if exemption from section 1(1) is required for the purpose of safeguarding national security.

(2) A certificate signed by a member of the Scottish Executive certifying that such exemption is, or at any time was, required for the purpose of safeguarding national security is conclusive of that fact.

(3) Without prejudice to the generality of subsection (2), a certificate under that subsection may identify the information to which it applies by means of a general description and may be expressed to have prospective effect.

(4) Information is exempt information if its disclosure under this Act would, or would be likely to, prejudice substantially
    (a) the defence of the British Islands or of any colony; or
    (b) the capability, effectiveness or security of any relevant forces.

(5) In subsection (4)
    (a) in paragraph (a), "British Islands" and "colony" are to be construed in accordance with Schedule 1 to the Interpretation Act 1978 (c 30); and
    (b) in paragraph (b), "relevant forces" means
        (i)   the armed forces of the Crown; and
        (ii) any forces co-operating with those forces,
    or any part of the armed forces of the Crown or of any such co-operating forces.

NOTES

FOIA 2000 equivalent
ss 24, 26

Defined terms
"information": s 73

International relations

32(1) Information is exempt information if
    (a) its disclosure under this Act would, or would be likely to ,prejudice substantially
        (i)   relations between the United Kingdom and any other State;
        (ii)   relations between the United Kingdom and any international organisation or international court;
        (iii) the interests of the United Kingdom abroad; or
        (iv) the promotion or protection by the United Kingdom of its interests abroad; or
    (b) it is confidential information obtained from
        (i)   a State other than the United Kingdom; or
        (ii)   an international organisation or international court.

(2) For the purposes of subsection (1), information obtained from a State, organisation or court is confidential at any time while
    (a) the terms on which that information was obtained require it to beheld in confidence; or
    (b) the circumstances in which it was obtained make it reasonable for the State, organisation or court to expect that it will be so held.

(3) In subsection (1)
    "international court" means an international court which
        (a) is not an international organisation; and
        (b) is established
            (i)   by a resolution of an international organisation of which the United Kingdom is a member; or

(ii) by an international agreement to which the United Kingdom is a party;

"international organisation" means

(a) an international organisation whose members include any two or more States; or

(b) an organ of such an international organisation;

"State" includes

(a) the government of any State; and

(b) any organ of such a government,

and references to a State other than the United Kingdom include references to any territory outwith the United Kingdom.

NOTES

FOIA 2000 equivalent
s 27

Defined terms
"information": s 73

Commercial interests and the economy

33(1) Information is exempt information if

(a) it constitutes a trade secret; or

(b) its disclosure under this Act would, or would be likely to ,prejudice substantially the commercial interests of any person (including, without prejudice to that generality, a Scottish public authority).

(2) Information is exempt information if its disclosure under this Act would, or would be likely to, prejudice substantially

(a) the economic interests of the whole or part of the United Kingdom; or

(b) the financial interests of an administration in the United Kingdom.

(3) In subsection (2), "administration in the United Kingdom" has the same meaning as in section 28(2).

NOTES

FOIA 2000 equivalent
ss 29, 43

Defined terms
"information": s 73
"Scottish public authority": ss 3(1), 73

Investigations by Scottish public authorities and proceedings arising out of such investigations

34(1) Information is exempt information if it has at any time been held by a Scottish public authority for the purposes of

(a) an investigation which the authority has a duty to conduct to ascertain whether a person

(i) should be prosecuted for an offence; or

(ii) prosecuted for an offence is guilty of it;

(b) an investigation, conducted by the authority, which in the circumstances may lead to a decision by the authority to make a report to the procurator fiscal to enable it to be determined whether criminal proceedings should be instituted; or

(c) criminal proceedings instituted in consequence of a report made by the authority to the procurator fiscal.

(2) Information is exempt information if

(a) held by a Scottish public authority for the purposes of an inquiry instituted under the Inquiries into Fatal Accidents and Sudden Deaths etc(Scotland) Act 2016 but not for the time being concluded; or

    (b) held at any time by a Scottish public authority for the purposes of any other investigation being carried out

        (i)   by virtue of a duty to ascertain; or

        (ii)   for the purpose of making a report to the procurator fiscal as respects,

the cause of death of a person.

(3)   Information held by a Scottish public authority is exempt information if

    (a) it was obtained or recorded by the authority for the purposes of investigations (other than such investigations as are mentioned in subsection (1)) which are, by virtue either of Her Majesty's prerogative or of powers conferred by or under any enactment, conducted by the authority for any purpose specified in section 35(2); and

    (b) it relates to the obtaining of information from confidential sources.

(4)   Information is exempt information if obtained or recorded by a Scottish public authority for the purposes of civil proceedings, brought by or on behalf of the authority, which arise out of such investigations as are mentioned in subsection (1) or (3).

NOTES

FOIA 2000 equivalent
  s 30

Defined terms
  "enactment": s 73
  "information": s 73
  "Scottish public authority": ss 3(1), 73

Law enforcement

35(1)   Information is exempt information if its disclosure under this Act would, or would be likely to, prejudice substantially

    (a) the prevention or detection of crime;

    (b) the apprehension or prosecution of offenders;

    (c) the administration of justice;

    (d) the assessment or collection of any tax or duty (or of any imposition of a similar nature);

    (e) the operation of the immigration controls;

    (f) the maintenance of security and good order in prisons or in other institutions where persons are lawfully detained;

    (g) the exercise by any public authority (within the meaning of the Freedom of Information Act 2000 (c 36)) or Scottish public authority of its functions for any of the purposes mentioned in subsection (2);

    (h) any civil proceedings

        (i)   brought; and

        (ii)   arising out of an investigation conducted, for any such purpose,

by or on behalf of any such authority, by virtue either of Her Majesty's prerogative or of powers conferred by or under any enactment.

(2)   The purposes are

    (a) to ascertain whether a person has failed to comply with the law;

    (b) to ascertain whether a person is responsible for conduct which is improper;

    (c) to ascertain whether circumstances which would justify regulatory action in pursuance of any enactment exist or may arise;

    (d) to ascertain a person's fitness or competence in relation to (i)　the management of bodies corporate; or

(ii)　any profession or other activity which the person is, or seeks to become, authorised to carry on;

(e)　to ascertain the cause of an accident;

(f)　to protect a charity against misconduct or mismanagement (whether by trustees or other persons) in its administration;

(g)　to protect the property of a charity from loss or mismanagement;

(h)　to recover the property of a charity;

(i)　to secure the health, safety and welfare of persons at work; and

(j)　to protect persons, other than persons at work, against risk to health or safety where that risk arises out of, or in connection with, the actions of persons at work.

NOTES

FOIA 2000 equivalent
s 31

Defined terms
"enactment": s 73
"information": s 73
"Scottish public authority": ss 3(1), 73

Confidentiality

36(1)　Information in respect of which a claim to confidentiality of communications could be maintained in legal proceedings is exempt information.

(2)　Information is exempt information if

(a)　it was obtained by a Scottish public authority from another person(including another such authority); and

(b)　its disclosure by the authority so obtaining it to the public(otherwise than under this Act) would constitute a breach of confidence actionable by that person or any other person.

NOTES

FOIA 2000 equivalent
s 41

Defined terms
"information": s 73
"Scottish public authority": ss 3(1), 73

Court records, etc

37(1)　Information is exempt information if it is contained in

(a)　a document

(i)　lodged with, or otherwise placed in the custody of, a court for the purposes of proceedings in a cause or matter;

(ii)　served on, or by, a Scottish public authority for the purposes of such proceedings; or

(iii)　created by a court or a member of its administrative staff for the purposes of, or in the course of, such proceedings; or

(b)　a document

(i)　lodged with, or otherwise placed in the custody of, a person conducting an inquiry or arbitration, for the purposes of that inquiry or arbitration; or

(ii)　created by such a person for such purposes,

and a Scottish public authority holds the information solely because it is contained in such a document.

(2)　In this section

"court" includes a tribunal or body exercising the judicial power of the State; and "inquiry" means an inquiry or hearing held under a provision contained in, or made under, an enactment.

(3) This section does not apply to information held by a Scottish public authority for the purposes of an inquiry instituted under the Inquiries into Fatal Accidents and Sudden Deaths etc (Scotland) Act 2016.

NOTES

FOIA 2000 equivalent	Defined terms
s 32	"body": s 73
	"enactment": s 73
	"information": s 73
	"Scottish public authority": ss 3(1), 73

Personal information

38(1) Information is exempt information if it constitutes
    (a) personal data of which the applicant is the data subject;
    (b) personal data and the first, second or third condition is satisfied (see subsections (2A) to (3A));
    (c) personal census information; or
    (d) a deceased person's health record.

(2A) The first condition is that the disclosure of the information to a member of the public otherwise than under this Act—
    (a) would contravene any of the data protection principles, or
    (b) would do so if the exemptions in section 24(1) of the Data Protection Act 2018 (manual unstructured data held by public authorities) were disregarded.

(2B) The second condition is that the disclosure of the information to a member of the public otherwise than under this Act would contravene Article 21 of the GDPR (general processing: right to object to processing).

(3A) The third condition is that—
    (a) on a request under Article 15(1) of the GDPR (general processing: right of access by the data subject) for access to personal data, the information would be withheld in reliance on provision made by or under section 15, 16 or 26, or Schedule 2, 3, or 4 to, the Data Protection Act 2018, or
    (b) on a request under section 45(1)(b) of that Act (law enforcement processing: right of access by the data subject), the information would be withheld in relance n subsection (4) of that section.

(5) In this section
    "the data protection principles" means the principles set out in—
        (a) Article 5(1) of the GDPR, and;
        (b) section 34(1) of the Data Protection Act 2018;
    "data subject" has the same meaning as in the Data Protection Act 2018 (see section 3 of that Act;
    "the GDPR", "personal data", "processing" and references to a provision of Chapter 2 of Part 2 of the Data Protection Act 2018 have the same meaning as in Parts 5 to 7 of that Act (see section 3(2), (4), (10), (11) and (14) of that Act);
    "health record" has the meaning assigned to that term by section 1(1) of the Access to Health Records Act 1990 (c 23); and
    "personal census information" means any census information

(a) as defined in section 8(7) of the Census Act 1920 (c 41); or

(b) acquired or derived by virtue of sections 1 to 9 of the Census (Great Britain) Act 1910 (c 27),

which relates to an identifiable person or household.

(5A) In determining for the purposes of this section whether the lawfulness principle in Article 5(1)(a) of the GDPR would be contravened by the disclosure of information, Article 6(1) of the GDPR (lawfulness) is to be read as if the second sub-paragraph (disapplying the legitimate interests gateway in relation to public authorities) were omitted.

(6) In section 8(7) of the Census Act 1920 (penalties), in the definition of "personal census information", at the end there is added "but does not include information which, by virtue of section 58(2)(b) of the Freedom of Information (Scotland) Act 2002 (asp 13) (falling away of exemptions with time), is not exempt information within the meaning of that Act".

NOTES

FOIA 2000 equivalent
s 40

Defined terms
"applicant": s 1(2)
"information": s 73

Health, safety and the environment

39(1) Information is exempt information if its disclosure under this Act would, or would be likely to, endanger the physical or mental health or the safety of an individual.

(2) Information is exempt information if a Scottish public authority

(a) is obliged by regulations under section 62 to make it available to the public in accordance with the regulations; or

(b) would be so obliged but for any exemption contained in the regulations.

(3) Subsection (2)(a) is without prejudice to the generality of section 25(1).

NOTES

FOIA 2000 equivalent
s 38

Defined terms
"information": s 73
"Scottish public authority": ss 3(1), 73

Audit functions

40 Information is exempt information if its disclosure under this Act would, or would be likely to, prejudice substantially the exercise of a Scottish public authority's functions in relation to

(a) the audit of the accounts of other Scottish public authorities; or

(b) the examination of the economy, efficiency and effectiveness with which such authorities use their resources in discharging their functions.

NOTES

FOIA 2000 equivalent
s 40

Defined terms
"information": s 73
"Scottish public authority": ss 3(1), 73

Communications with Her Majesty etc and honours

41 Information is exempt information if it relates to

(a) communications with Her Majesty, with other members of the Royal Family or with the Royal Household; or

(b) the exercise by Her Majesty of Her prerogative of honour.

NOTES

FOIA 2000 equivalent
s 37

Defined terms
"information": s 73

PART 3
THE SCOTTISH INFORMATION COMMISSIONER

The Scottish Information Commissioner

42(1) For the purposes of this Act there is to be an officer known as the Scottish Information Commissioner (in this Act referred to as the "Commissioner") who is to be an individual appointed by Her Majesty on the nomination of the Parliament.

(1A) A person is disqualified from appointment as the Commissioner if the person is, or holds office in, or is an employee or appointee of, another Scottish public authority.

(1B) The Commissioner may not, without the approval of the Parliamentary corporation, also be, or hold office in, or be an employee or appointee of, another Scottish public authority.

(2) The Commissioner is entitled to
(a) a salary of such amount; and
(b) such allowances,
as the Parliamentary corporation may determine.

(3) Subject to subsection (4), the Commissioner is to hold office for such period not exceeding eight years as the Parliamentary corporation, at the time of appointment, may determine.

(3A) The Commissioner is to hold office otherwise on such terms and conditions as the Parliamentary corporation may determine.

(3B) Those terms and conditions may, without prejudice to subsection (1A)
(a) prohibit the Commissioner from holding any other specified office, employment or appointment or engaging in any other specified occupation,
(b) provide that the Commissioner's holding of any such office, employment or appointment or engagement in any such occupation is subject to the approval of the Parliamentary corporation.

(3C) In subsection (3B), "specified" means specified in the terms and conditions of office or within a description so specified.

(4) The Commissioner
(a) may be relieved of office by Her Majesty at that officer's request;
(b) . . .
(c) may be removed from office by Her Majesty if subsection (4A) applies . . .
(d) . . ..

(4A) This subsection applies if
(a) the Parliamentary corporation is satisfied that the Commissioner has breached the terms and conditions of office and the Parliament resolves that the Commissioner should be removed from office for that breach, or
(b) the Parliament resolves that it has lost confidence in the Commissioner's willingness, suitability or ability to perform the functions of the Commissioner,
and, in either case, the resolution is voted for by a number of members not fewer than two thirds of the total number of seats for members of the Parliament.

(5) A person who has held office as Commissioner is ineligible for reappointment at any time.

(6) The validity of any actings of the Commissioner is not affected by a defect in the nomination by the Parliament for that officer's appointment.

(7) The Commissioner, in the exercise of that officer's functions (except the function of preparing accounts), is not subject to the direction or control of the Parliamentary corporation, of any member of the Scottish Executive or of the Parliament; but this subsection is without prejudice to sections 42(9C) and 46(2A) and paragraphs 3(4), 4A, 6(2), 7 and 8 of schedule 2.

(8) Where the office of Commissioner is vacant, the Parliamentary corporation may appoint a person (who may or may not be a member of the Commissioner's staff) to discharge the functions of that office until a new Commissioner is appointed.

(9) A person appointed under subsection (8)
  (a) may be relieved of that appointment at that person's request;
  (b) may be removed from office by the Parliamentary corporation by notice in writing given by it;
  (c) in other respects, holds office on such terms and conditions as the Parliamentary corporation may determine; and
  (d) while holding that appointment, is to be treated for all purposes, except those of subsections (1) to (6) and those of paragraph 2 of schedule2, as the Commissioner.

(9A) The Commissioner may obtain advice, assistance or any other service from any person who, in the opinion of the Commissioner, is qualified to give it.

(9B) The Commissioner may pay to that person such fees and allowances as the Commissioner determines.

(9C) Any payment under subsection (9B) is subject to the approval of the Parliamentary corporation.

(10) Any function of the Commissioner may be exercised on behalf of that officer by any person (whether or not a member of that officer's staff) authorised by the Commissioner to do so (and to the extent so authorised).

(11) The Parliamentary corporation is to pay
  (a) the salary and allowances of the Commissioner;
  (b) any expenses properly incurred by that officer in the exercise of functions under this Act so far as those expenses are not met out of sums received and applied by that officer under section 43(6); and
  (c) any sums payable by virtue of subsection (9)(a) to (c) to, or in respect of, a person who
    (i) is appointed under subsection (8); or
    (ii) has ceased to hold office by virtue of having been so appointed.

(11A) Subsection (11)(b) does not require the Parliamentary corporation to pay any expenses incurred by the Commissioner which exceed or are otherwise not covered by a budget or, as the case may be, revised budget approved under paragraph 4A of schedule 2.

(11B) However, the Parliamentary corporation may pay those expenses.

(11C) The Parliamentary corporation is to indemnify the Commissioner in respect of any liabilities incurred by the Commissioner in the exercise of the Commissioner's functions under this Act. (12) Schedule 2 to this Act has effect with respect to the Commissioner.

NOTES

FOIA 2000 equivalent
s 18

Defined terms
"the Parliamentary corporation": s 73
"Scottish public authority": ss 3(1), 73

General functions of Commissioner

43(1)   The Commissioner, with a view in particular to promoting the observance by Scottish public authorities of the provisions of
    (a) this Act; and
    (b) the codes of practice issued under sections 60 and 61,
is to promote the following of good practice by those authorities.

(2)   The Commissioner
    (a) must determine what information it is expedient to give the public concerning the following matters
        (i)   the operation of this Act;
        (ii) good practice;
        (iii) other matters within the scope of that officer's functions,
    and must secure the dissemination of that information in an appropriate form and manner; and
    (b) may give advice to any person as to any of those matters.

(3)   The Commissioner may assess whether a Scottish public authority is following good practice.

(4)   The Commissioner may from time to time make proposals to the Scottish Ministers for the exercise by them of their functions under sections 4 and 5 of this Act.

(5)   The Commissioner may determine and charge reasonable sums for anything done or provided by the Commissioner in the performance of, or in connection with, the Commissioner's functions.

(6)   Any sum received by the Commissioner by virtue of subsection (5) is to be retained by that officer and applied to meet expenditure incurred in doing or providing whatever is charged for.

(7)   The Commissioner must from time to time consult the Keeper of the Records of Scotland about the promotion under subsection (1) of the observance by Scottish public authorities of the provisions of the code of practice issued under section 61.

(8)   In this section "good practice", in relation to a Scottish public authority, means such practice in the discharge of its functions under this Act as appears to the Commissioner to be desirable, and includes (but is not limited to) compliance with the requirements of this Act and the provisions of the codes of practice issued under sections 60 and 61.

NOTES

FOIA 2000 equivalent
s 47

Defined terms
"the Commissioner": s 73
"information": s 73
"Scottish public authority": ss 3(1), 73

Recommendations as to good practice

44(1) If it appears to the Commissioner that the practice of a Scottish public authority in relation to the exercise of its functions under this Act does not conform with the code of practice issued under section 60 or 61, the Commissioner may give the authority a recommendation (in this Act referred to as a "practice recommendation").

(2) A practice recommendation must
   (a) be in writing and specify the code and the provisions of that code with which, in the Commissioner's opinion, the authority's practice does not conform; and
   (b) specify the steps which that officer considers the authority ought to take in order to conform.

(3) The Commissioner must consult the Keeper of the Records of Scotland before giving a practice recommendation to a Scottish public authority (other than the Keeper) in relation to conformity with the code of practice issued under section 61.

NOTES

FOIA 2000 equivalent
s 48

Defined terms
"the Commissioner": s 73
"Scottish public authority": ss 3(1), 73

Confidentiality of information obtained by or furnished to Commissioner

45(1) A person who is or has been the Commissioner, a member of the Commissioner's staff or an agent of the Commissioner must not disclose any information which
   (a) has been obtained by, or furnished to, the Commissioner under or for the purposes of this Act; and
   (b) is not at the time of the disclosure, and has not previously been ,available to the public from another source,
unless the disclosure is made with lawful authority.

(2) For the purposes of subsection (1), disclosure is made with lawful authority only if, and to the extent that
   (a) the disclosure is made with the consent of the person from whom the information was so obtained or by whom it was so furnished;
   (b) the information was provided for the purpose of its being made available to the public (in whatever manner) under a provision of this Act;
   (c) the disclosure is made for the purpose of, and is necessary for, the discharge of
      (i) a function under this Act; or
      (ii) an EU obligation;
   (d) the disclosure is made for the purpose of proceedings, whether criminal or civil and whether arising under, or by virtue of, this Act or otherwise; or
   (e) either
      (i) in a case where the person mentioned in paragraph (a) is a Scottish public authority, had that person received on the day of disclosure a request for the information that person; or
      (ii) in any other case, had the Commissioner received on that day such a request the Commissioner,
   would, by virtue of section 1(1), have been under an obligation to give it.

(3) A person who knowingly or recklessly discloses information in contravention of subsection (1) is guilty of an offence.

(4) A person guilty of an offence under subsection (3) is liable

  (a) on summary conviction, to a fine not exceeding the statutory maximum; or

  (b) on conviction on indictment, to a fine.

NOTES

FOIA 2000 equivalent
  DPA s 59

Defined terms
  "the Commissioner": s 73
  "information": s 73
  "Scottish public authority": ss 3(1), 73

Laying and publication of reports

46(1) The Commissioner must lay annually before the Parliament a general report on the exercise during the reporting year of the functions conferred on that officer under this Act.

(1A) Each report must be so laid within 7 months after the end of the reporting year.

(1B) In this section, "reporting year" means the year beginning on 1 April.

(2) The report mentioned in subsection (1) (without prejudice to the generality of that subsection) must record the number of occasions, during the period covered by the report, on which the Commissioner failed to reach a decision on an application under section 47(1) (being an application on which a decision fell to be made) within the period of four months specified in section 49(3)(b).

(2A) In preparing a report under subsection (1), the Commissioner must comply with any direction given by the Parliamentary corporation as to the form and content of the report.

(3) The Commissioner may from time to time lay before the Parliament such other reports with respect to the functions conferred on that officer under this Act as that officer thinks fit.

(3A) The Commissioner must arrange for the publication of each report laid before the Parliament under this section.

NOTES

FOIA 2000 equivalent
  s 49

Defined terms
  "the Commissioner": s 73
  "the Parliamentary corporation": s 73

Strategic plans

46A(1) The Commissioner must, in respect of each 4 year period, lay before the Parliament a plan (referred to in this section as a "strategic plan") setting out how the Commissioner proposes to perform the Commissioner's functions during the 4 year period.

(2) A strategic plan must, in particular, set out

  (a) the Commissioner's objectives and priorities during the 4 year period,

  (b) how the Commissioner proposes to achieve them,

  (c) a timetable for doing so, and

  (d) estimates of the costs of doing so.

(3) Before laying a strategic plan before the Parliament, the Commissioner must provide a draft of it to and invite, and (if any are given) consider, comments on it from

  (a) the Parliamentary corporation,

  (b) the Keeper of the Records of Scotland, and

  (c) such other persons as the Commissioner thinks appropriate.

(4) The reference in subsection (3)(c) to other persons includes a committee of the Parliament.

(5) The Commissioner must lay each strategic plan before the Parliament not later than the beginning of the 4 year period to which the plan relates.

(6) The Commissioner must arrange for the publication of each strategic plan laid before the Parliament.

(7) The Commissioner may, at any time during a 4 year period, review the strategic plan for the period and lay a revised strategic plan before the Parliament.

(8) Subsections (2) to (7) apply to a revised strategic plan as they apply to a strategic plan.

(9) In that application, the reference in subsection (5) to the 4 year period is a reference to the period to which the revised strategic plan relates.

(10) In this section, "4 year period" means the period of 4 years beginning on 1 April next following the coming into force of this section and each subsequent period of 4 years.

NOTES

FOIA 2000 equivalent	**Defined terms**
n/a	"the Commissioner": s 73
	"the Parliamentary corporation": s 73

PART 4

ENFORCEMENT

Application for decision by Commissioner

47(1) A person who is dissatisfied with
    (a) a notice given under section 21(5) or (9); or
    (b) the failure of a Scottish public authority to which a requirement for review was made to give such a notice,
may make application to the Commissioner for a decision whether, in any respect specified in that application, the request for information to which the requirement relates has been dealt with in accordance with Part 1 of this Act.

(2) An application under subsection (1) must
    (a) be in writing or in another form which, by reason of its having some permanency, is capable of being used for subsequent reference (as, for example, a recording made on audio or video tape);
    (b) state the name of the applicant and an address for correspondence; and
    (c) specify
        (i) the request for information to which the requirement for review relates;
        (ii) the matter which was specified under sub-paragraph (ii) of section 20(3)(c); and
        (iii) the matter which gives rise to the dissatisfaction mentioned in subsection (1).

(3) For the purposes of paragraph (a) of subsection (2) (and without prejudice to the generality of that paragraph), an application under that subsection is treated as made in writing where the text of the application is as mentioned in paragraphs (a) to (c) of section 8(2).

(4) Subject to subsection (5), an application to the Commissioner under subsection (1) must be made
    (a) where the application concerns a matter mentioned in paragraph (a)of subsection

(1), before the expiry of six months after the date of receipt by the applicant of the notice complained of; or

(b) where the application concerns a matter mentioned in paragraph (b)of that subsection, before the expiry of six months after the period allowed in section 21(1) for complying with a requirement for review has elapsed.

(5) The Commissioner may consider an application under subsection (1) made after the expiry of the time allowed by subsection (4) for the making of that application if, in the opinion of the Commissioner, it is appropriate to do so.

(6) The Scottish Ministers may by regulations provide

(a) that a paragraph of subsection (4) is to have effect as if the reference in that paragraph to six months were a reference to such other period of months (being a period of not less than six months) as is specified in (or determined in accordance with) the regulations; and

(b) that subsection (5) is to have effect accordingly.

(7) Regulations under subsection (6) may

(a) prescribe different periods of months in relation to different cases; and

(b) confer a discretion on the Commissioner.

(8) This section is subject to section 48.

NOTES

FOIA 2000 equivalent
    s 50

Defined terms
    "applicant": s 1(2)
    "the Commissioner": s 73
    "information": s 73
    "requirement for review": ss 20(2), 73
    "Scottish public authority": ss 3(1), 73

When application excluded

48 No application may be made to the Commissioner for a decision under section 47(1) as respects a request for review made to

(a) the Commissioner;

(b) a procurator fiscal; or

(c) the Lord Advocate, to the extent that the information requested is held by the Lord Advocate as head of the systems of criminal prosecution and investigation of deaths in Scotland.

NOTES

FOIA 2000 equivalent
    n/a

Defined terms
    "the Commissioner": s 73
    "information": s 73

Commissioner's decision

49(1) The Commissioner must make a decision in relation to an application made in accordance with section 47(1) which is not excluded by section 48 unless

(a) in the opinion of the Commissioner, the application is frivolous or vexatious; or

(b) in the opinion of the Commissioner, the application appears to have been withdrawn or abandoned.

(2) In a case where the Commissioner determines that subsection (1) does not require a decision to be made, that officer must give the applicant and the Scottish public authority

in question notice in writing within one month of receipt of the application, or within such other period as is reasonable in the circumstances, specifying

(a) that no decision falls to be made in relation to the application; and

(b) the reasons why that is the case.

(3) In any other case, the Commissioner must

(a) give that authority notice in writing of the application and invite its comments; and

(b) if no settlement has in the meantime been effected, reach a decision on the application before the expiry of four months after receiving it, or before the expiry of such other period as is reasonable in the circumstances.

(4) The Commissioner may endeavour to effect a settlement between the applicant and that authority before the expiry of the period allowed by subsection (3) for reaching a decision on the application.

(5) The Commissioner must give the applicant and that authority, within the time allowed by subsection (3), notice in writing (referred to in this Act as a "decision notice") of any decision under paragraph (b) of that subsection.

(6) Where the Commissioner decides that that authority has not dealt with a request for information in accordance with Part 1 of this Act, the notice under subsection (5) must specify

(a) the provision of that Part with which the authority has failed to comply and the respect in which it has so failed;

(b) the steps which, in the opinion of the Commissioner, the authority must take to comply with the provision; and

(c) the time within which those steps must be taken.

(7) The time specified under subsection (6)(c) must not expire before the end of the period within which an appeal may be brought under section 56 against the decision of the Commissioner and, if such an appeal is brought, no step which is affected by the appeal need be taken before the cause is finally determined.

(8) A notice under subsection (2) or (5) must contain particulars of the right of appeal conferred by section 56.

(9) This section is subject to section 52.

NOTES

FOIA 2000 equivalent
s 50

Defined terms
"applicant": s 1(2)
"the Commissioner": s 73
"information": s 73
"Scottish public authority": ss 3(1), 73

Information notices

50(1) Where the Commissioner

(a) has received an application under section 47(1); or

(b) reasonably requires information

(i) for the purpose of determining whether a Scottish public authority has complied or is complying with the provisions of this Act; or

(ii) for the purpose of determining whether the practice of a Scottish public authority conforms with the code of practice issued under section 60 or 61,

that officer may give the authority notice in writing (referred to in this Act as "an information notice") requiring it, within such time as is specified in the notice, to give the officer, in such form as may be so specified, such information relating to the application, to compliance with this Act or to conformity with the code of practice as is so specified.

(2) An information notice must contain

(a) in a case mentioned in paragraph (a) of subsection (1) a statement that the Commissioner has received an application under section 47(1); or

(b) in a case mentioned in paragraph (b) of that subsection, a statement of

   (i) the purpose mentioned in that paragraph for which that officer regards the specified information as relevant;

   (ii) the officer's reasons for so regarding the information; and

   (iii) the time within which the information is to be given.

(3) An information notice must contain also particulars of the right of appeal conferred by section 56.

(4) The time specified under subsection (2)(b)(iii) in an information notice must not expire before the end of the period within which an appeal may be brought under section 56 against the notice; and, if such an appeal is brought, the information need not be given pending the determination or withdrawal of the appeal.

(5) A Scottish public authority is not obliged by virtue of this section to give the Commissioner information in respect of

(a) a communication between professional legal adviser and client in connection with the giving of legal advice to the client with respect to that client's obligations under this Act; or

(b) a communication between professional legal adviser and client, or between such adviser or client and another person, made in connection with or in contemplation of proceedings under or arising out of this Act and for the purpose of such proceedings.

(6) In subsection (5), references to the client of a professional legal adviser include references to a person representing such client.

(7) Subject to subsection (5), neither

(a) an obligation to maintain secrecy; nor

(b) any other restriction on disclosure,

however arising or imposed, affects the duty to comply with an information notice.

(8) The Commissioner may cancel an information notice by notice in writing given to the authority.

(9) In this section, "information" includes unrecorded information.

NOTES

FOIA 2000 equivalent
  s 51

Defined terms
  "the Commissioner": s 73
  "information": s 73
  "Scottish public authority": ss 3(1), 73

Enforcement notices

51(1) If the Commissioner is satisfied that a Scottish public authority has failed to comply with a provision of Part 1 of this Act, the Commissioner may give the authority a notice (referred to in this Act as "an enforcement notice") requiring the authority to take, within such time as is specified in the notice, such steps as are so specified for so complying.

(2) An enforcement notice must contain

(a) a statement of the provision with which the Commissioner is satisfied that the authority has failed to comply and the respect in which it has not done so; and

(b) particulars of the right of appeal conferred by section 56.

(3) The time specified under subsection (1) must not expire before the end of the period within which an appeal may be brought under section 56 against the notice and, if such an appeal is brought, the notice need not be complied with before the cause is finally determined.

(4) The Commissioner may cancel an enforcement notice by notice in writing given to the authority.

(5) This section is subject to section 52.

NOTES

FOIA 2000 equivalent
  s 52

Defined terms
"the Commissioner": s 73
"Scottish public authority": ss 3(1), 73

Exception from duty to comply with certain notices

52(1) This section applies to a decision notice or enforcement notice which

(a) is given to the Scottish Administration; and

(b) relates to a perceived failure, in respect of one or more requests for information, to comply with section 1(1) in respect of information which, by virtue of section 29, 31(1), 32(1)(b), 34, 36(1) or 41(b), is exempt information.

(2) A decision notice or enforcement notice to which this section applies ceases to have effect, in so far as it relates to the perceived failure, if, not later than the thirtieth working day following the effective date, the First Minister of the Scottish Executive, after consulting the other members of that Executive, signs and gives the Commissioner a certificate stating that the First Minister has on reasonable grounds formed, after such consultation, the opinion both that

(a) there was no such failure; and

(b) the information requested is of exceptional sensitivity.

(3) The First Minister is, by not later than the tenth working day after such a certificate

(a) is given, to lay a copy of it before the Parliament; and

(b) is given in relation to a decision notice, to inform the person to whose application the notice relates of the reasons for the opinion formed,

except that the First Minister is not obliged to provide information under paragraph (b) if, or to the extent that, compliance with that paragraph would necessitate the disclosure of exempt information.

(4) In subsection (2), "the effective date", in relation to a notice, means

(a) the day on which the notice was given to the Scottish Administration; or

(b) where an appeal under section 56 is brought, the day on which the cause is finally determined.

Failure to comply with notice

53(1) If a Scottish public authority has failed to comply with

 (a) so much of a notice given to it by the Commissioner under subsection(5) of section 49 as, by virtue of subsection (6)(b) of that section, requires steps to be taken by the authority;

 (b) an information notice; or

 (c) an enforcement notice,

the Commissioner may certify in writing to the court that the authority has failed to comply with the notice.

(2) For the purposes of this section, a Scottish public authority which, in purported compliance with an information notice

 (a) makes a statement which it knows to be false in a material respect; or

 (b) recklessly makes a statement which is false in a material respect,

is to be taken to have failed to comply with the notice.

(3) Where a failure to comply is certified under subsection (1), the court may inquire into the matter and, after hearing any witness who may be produced against or on behalf of the authority, and after hearing any statement that may be offered in defence, may deal with the authority as if it had committed a contempt of court.

(4) In this section, "the court" means the Court of Session.

Powers of entry and inspection

54 Schedule 3, which makes provision as to powers of entry and inspection, has effect.

No civil right of action against Scottish public authority

55(1) This Act does not confer a right of action in civil proceedings in respect of failure by a Scottish public authority to comply with a duty imposed by, under or by virtue of this Act.

(2) Subsection (1) does not affect the powers of the Commissioner under section 53(1).

NOTES

FOIA 2000 equivalent
s 56

Defined terms
"the Commissioner": s 73
"Scottish public authority": ss 3(1), 73

Appeal against notices under Part 4

56   An appeal, on a point of law, to the Court of Session may be made
  (a)   against a decision by the Commissioner under subsection (2) of section 49, by the person who applied for that decision;
  (b)   against a decision by the Commissioner under subsection (3)(b) of that section
      (i)   by that person; or
      (ii)   by the Scottish public authority in respect of which the decision was made; or
  (c)   against the decision which resulted in the giving of
      (i)   an information notice; or
      (ii)   an enforcement notice,
    to a Scottish public authority, by that authority.

NOTES

FOIA 2000 equivalent
s 57

Defined terms
"the Commissioner": s 73
"enforcement notice": ss 51(1), 73
"information": s 73
"information notice": ss 50(1), 73
"Scottish public authority": ss 3(1), 73

PART 5
HISTORICAL RECORDS

The expression "historical record"

57(1)   For the purposes of this Part, a record becomes a "historical record" in accordance with subsections (1A) to (1C).

(1A)   A record becomes one at the end of the period of 15 years beginning with 1st January in the calendar year following the date on which the record is created.

(1B)   A record containing information which would be exempt by virtue of section 36 becomes one at the end of the period of 30 years beginning with 1st January in the calendar year following the date on which the record is created.

(1C)   A record containing information which would be exempt by virtue of section 41(a) becomes one at the end of the later-ending of
  (a)   the period of 20 years beginning with the date on which the record is created,
  (b)   the period of 5 years beginning with
      (i)   in relation to communications with Her Majesty, the date of the death of Her Majesty,
      (ii)   in relation to communications with another member of the Royal Family, the date of the death of that member,
      (iii)   in relation to communications with the Royal Household, the date of the death of the Sovereign reigning when the record is created.

(1D)   In the application of subsections (1A) to (1C)
  (a)   the general rule in subsection (1A) is subject to the operation of subsections (1B)

and (1C) so far as relevant,

    (b) a record to which both subsections (1B) and (1C) relate becomes a historical record at the end of the later-ending of

        (i)   the period provided for in subsection (1B),

        (ii)   the period provided for in subsection (1C)(b).

(2)   Where records created at different dates are for administrative purposes kept together in one file or other assemblage, all the records in that file or assemblage are to be treated for the purposes of this Part as created when the latest of those records is created.

NOTES

FOIA 2000 equivalent
  s 62

Defined terms
  "information": s 73

Falling away of exemptions with time

58(1)   Information contained in a historical record cannot be exempt information by virtue of any of sections 28 to 30, 33(1), 36, 37, 40 and 41(a).

(2)   Information cannot be exempt information by virtue of

    (a) section 41(b) after the end of that period of sixty years; or

    (b) section 34(2)(b), 35 or 38(1)(c) or (d) after the end of that period of one hundred years,

which commences at the beginning of the calendar year following that in which the record containing the information is created.

NOTES

FOIA 2000 equivalent
  s 63

Defined terms
  "exempt information": s 73
  "historical record": s 57(1)
  "information": s 73

Power to vary periods mentioned in sections 57 and 58

59(1)   The Scottish Ministers may by order amend . . . paragraph (a) or (b) of subsection (2) of section 58 so as to substitute for the number of years for the time being mentioned in the provision in question such other number of years (not being a number which exceeds that mentioned in the provision as originally enacted) as may be specified in the order.

(1A)   The Scottish Ministers may by order

    (a) make provision modifying any enactment in accordance with which a record becomes a "historical record" for the purposes of this Part, and

    (b) do so by amending this Part or otherwise.

(1B)   Provision by virtue of subsection (1A) may (in particular) state that a record becomes such a "historical record"

    (a) in relation to the exemption under section 41(a), at the end of

        (i)   a specified period (not exceeding 30 years) beginning with the date on which the record is created or a particular date in the calendar year following that date, or

        (ii)   a specified period (not exceeding 30 years) beginning with the occurrence of an event apart from the creation of the record,

    (b) in relation to any other exemption under Part 2, at the end of a specified period (not exceeding 30 years) beginning with the date on which the record is created or a particular date in the calendar year following that date.

(1C) An order under subsection (1) or (1A) may make different provision for
    (a) records of different descriptions,
    (b) exemptions of different kinds,
    (c) different purposes in other respects.

(2) An order under subsection (1) or (1A) may contain such supplemental, incidental, consequential, transitional, transitory or saving provision as the Scottish Ministers think fit.

NOTES

FOIA 2000 equivalent
  s 62(2A)

Defined terms
  "enactment": s 73
  "historical record": s 57(1)

PART 6
CODES OF PRACTICE

Code of practice as to functions under this Act

60(1) The Scottish Ministers are to issue, and may from time to time revise, a code of practice providing guidance to Scottish public authorities as to the practice which it would, in the opinion of the Ministers, be desirable for the authorities to follow in connection with the discharge of the authorities' functions under this Act.

(2) The code must, in particular, include provision relating to
    (a) the provision of advice and assistance by the authorities to persons who propose to make, or have made, requests for information;
    (b) the transfer of requests by one of the authorities to another by which the information requested is or may be held;
    (c) consultation with persons to whom information requested relates or with persons whose interests are likely to be affected by the disclosure of such information;
    (d) the inclusion in contracts entered into by the authorities of terms relating to the disclosure of information;
    (e) the provision by the authorities of procedures for dealing with complaints about the handling by the authorities of requests for information; and
    (f) the collection and recording by the authorities of statistics as respects the discharge by them of their functions under this Act.

(3) The code may make different provision for different Scottish public authorities.

(4) Before issuing or revising the code, the Scottish Ministers are to consult the Commissioner.

(5) The Scottish Ministers must lay the code, and any revised code made under this section, before the Parliament.

NOTES

FOIA 2000 equivalent
  s 45

Defined terms
  "the Commissioner": s 73
  "information": s 73

Code of practice as to the keeping, management and destruction of records

61(1) The Scottish Ministers are to issue, and may from time to time revise, a code of practice providing guidance to Scottish public authorities as to the practice which it would, in the opinion of the Ministers, be desirable for the authorities to follow in connection with the keeping, management and destruction of the authorities' records.

(2) The code may also include guidance as to the practice

(a) to be adopted in relation to the transfer of records to the Keeper of the Records of Scotland;

(b) of reviewing records before they are so transferred; and

(c) to be adopted where one Scottish public authority holds records on behalf of another such authority.

(3) In exercising their functions under this section, the Scottish Ministers are to have regard to the public interest in allowing public access to information held by Scottish public authorities.

(4) The code may make different provision for different Scottish public authorities.

(5) Before issuing or revising the code the Scottish Ministers are to consult

(a) the Commissioner; and

(b) the Keeper of the Records of Scotland.

(6) The Scottish Ministers must lay the code, and any revised code made under this section, before the Parliament.

NOTES

FOIA 2000 equivalent
   s 46

Defined terms
   "the Commissioner": s 73
   "information": s 73
   "Scottish public authority": ss 3(1), 73

PART 7
MISCELLANEOUS AND SUPPLEMENTAL

Power to make provision relating to environmental information

62(1) In this section "the Aarhus Convention" means the Convention on Access to Information, Public Participation in Decision making and Access to Justice in Environmental Matters signed at Aarhus on 25th June 1998.

(2) For the purposes of this section, "the information provisions" of the Aarhus Convention are Article 4, together with Articles 3 and 9 so far as relating to that Article.

(3) The Scottish Ministers may, in relation to information held by or requested from any Scottish public authority, by regulations make such provision as they consider appropriate

(a) for the purpose of implementing the information provisions of the Aarhus Convention or any amendment of those provisions made in accordance with Article 14 of the Convention; and

(b) for the purpose of dealing with matters arising out of, or related to, the implementation of those provisions or of any such amendment.

(4) Regulations under subsection (3) may in particular

(a) enable charges to be made for making information available in accordance with the regulations;

(b) provide that any obligation imposed by the regulations in relation to the disclosure of information is to have effect notwithstanding any enactment or rule of law;

(c) make provision for the issue by the Scottish Ministers of a code of practice;

(d) provide for sections 43 and 44 to apply in relation to such a code with such modifications as may be specified in the regulations;

(e) provide for all or any of the provisions of Part 4 to apply, with such modifications as may be so specified, in relation to compliance with any requirement of the regulations; and

(f) contain such transitional or consequential provision (including provision modifying any enactment) as the Scottish Ministers consider appropriate.

NOTES

FOIA 2000 equivalent
s 39

Defined terms
"enactment": s 73
"information": s 73
"Scottish public authority": ss 3(1), 73

Disclosure of information to Scottish Public Services Ombudsman or to Information Commissioner

63   The Commissioner may disclose to

(a) the Scottish Public Services Ombudsman any information obtained by, or furnished to, the Commissioner under or for the purposes of this Act if it appears to the Commissioner that the information relates to a matter which is, or could be, the subject of an investigation by the Ombudsman under the Scottish Public Services Ombudsman Act 2002 (asp 11); or

(b) the Information Commissioner any information so obtained or furnished if it appears to the Commissioner that the information so relates as is mentioned in paragraph (a) or (b) of section 11AA(1) of the Parliamentary Commissioner Act 1967 (c 13) (disclosure of information by Parliamentary Commissioner to Information Commissioner).

NOTES

FOIA 2000 equivalent
ss 76, 76A

Defined terms
"the Commissioner": s 73
"information": s 73

Power to amend or repeal enactments prohibiting disclosure of information

64(1)   If it appears to the Scottish Ministers that by virtue of section 26(a) a relevant enactment is capable of preventing the disclosure of information under section 1, they may by order repeal or amend that enactment, in so far as it relates to any Scottish public authority, so as to remove or relax the prohibition.

(2)   In subsection (1)

"relevant enactment" means an Act of Parliament, or Act of the Scottish Parliament, which receives Royal Assent before the end of the calendar year in which this Act receives Royal Assent or any subordinate legislation made before the date on which this Act receives Royal Assent; and

"information" includes unrecorded information.

(3)   An order under subsection (1) may do all or any of the following

(a) make such modifications of enactments as, in the opinion of the Scottish Ministers, are consequential upon, or incidental to, the repeal or amendment of the relevant enactment;

(b) contain such transitional provisions and savings as appear to them to be appropriate;

(c) make different provision in relation to different cases.

NOTES

FOIA 2000 equivalent
s 75

Defined terms
"enactment": s 73

"information": s 73
"Scottish public authority": ss 3(1), 73
"subordinate legislation": s 73

Subordinate legislation
Freedom of Information (Relaxation of Statutory Prohibitions on Disclosure of Information) (Scotland) Order 2008, SSI 2008/339

Offence of altering etc records with intent to prevent disclosure

65(1) Where

(a) a request for information is made to a Scottish public authority; and

(b) the applicant is, under section 1, entitled to be given the information or any part of it,

a person to whom this subsection applies who, with the intention of preventing the disclosure by the authority of the information, or part, to which the entitlement relates, alters, defaces, blocks, erases, destroys or conceals a record held by the authority, is guilty of an offence.

(2) Subsection (1) applies to the authority and to any person who is employed by, is an officer of, or is subject to the direction of, the authority.

(3) A person guilty of an offence under subsection (1) is liable, on summary conviction, to a fine not exceeding level 5 on the standard scale.

NOTES

FOIA 2000 equivalent
s 77

Defined terms
"applicant": s 1(2)
"information": s 73
"Scottish public authority": ss 3(1), 73

Time limit for proceedings

65A(1) Proceedings for an offence under section 65(1) may be commenced within the period of 6 months beginning with the date on which evidence that the prosecutor believes is sufficient to justify the proceedings came to the prosecutor's knowledge.

(2) No such proceedings may be commenced more than 3 years

(a) after the commission of the offence, or

(b) in the case of a continuous contravention, after the last date on which the offence was committed.

(3) In the case of a continuous contravention, the complaint may specify the entire period during which the offence was committed.

(4) A certificate signed by or on behalf of the prosecutor stating the date on which the evidence referred to in subsection (1) came to the prosecutor's knowledge is conclusive as to that fact (and such a certificate purporting to be so signed is to be regarded as being so signed unless the contrary is proved).

(5) Section 136(3) of the Criminal Procedure (Scotland) Act 1995 applies for the purposes of this section as it does for those of that section.

FOIA 2000 equivalent
   n/a

Saving for existing powers of disclosure

66   Nothing in this Act is to be taken to limit the powers of a Scottish public authority to disclose information held by it.

FOIA 2000 equivalent   **Defined terms**
   s 78   "information": s 73
                                    "Scottish public authority": ss 3(1), 73

Protection from actions for defamation

67   Where, in compliance with a request for information, information supplied to a Scottish public authority by a third party is communicated by the authority, under section 1, to the applicant, the publication to the applicant of any defamatory matter contained in the information so supplied is privileged unless that publication is shown to have been made with malice.

FOIA 2000 equivalent   **Defined terms**
   s 79   "applicant": s 1(2)
                                    "information": s 73
                                    "Scottish public authority": ss 3(1), 73

Scottish Parliament and Scottish Administration

68   Section 65 and paragraph 10 of schedule 3 apply to
   (a) a member of the staff of, or a person acting on behalf of, the Parliament or the Parliamentary corporation; or
   (b) a member of the staff of the Scottish Administration,
as they apply to any other person; but none of those bodies is liable to prosecution under this Act.

FOIA 2000 equivalent   **Defined terms**
   n/a   "the Parliamentary corporation": s 73

Exercise of rights by children

69(1)   Where a question falls to be determined as to the legal capacity of a person who has not attained the age of sixteen years to exercise any right conferred by any provision of this Act, any such person is to be taken to have that capacity who has a general understanding of what it means to exercise the right.

(2)   Without prejudice to the generality of subsection (1), a person who has attained the age of twelve years is to be presumed to be of sufficient age and maturity to have such understanding as is mentioned in that subsection.

FOIA 2000 equivalent
   n/a

Amendment of Public Records (Scotland) Act 1937

70(1)   The Public Records (Scotland) Act 1937 (c 43) is amended as follows.

(2)   ...

(3)   After section 12 there is inserted
"12A Duty to afford facilities for inspection etc of certain records
It shall be the duty of the Keeper to arrange that reasonable facilities are available to the public for
(a) inspecting; and
(b) obtaining copies of,
such records held by the Keeper as either fall to be disclosed in accordance with the Freedom of Information (Scotland) Act 2002 (asp 13) or comprise information which is exempt information (within the meaning of that Act) by virtue of section 25(2)(b)(ii) of that Act.".

NOTES

FOIA 2000 equivalent
n/a

Defined terms
"exempt information": s 73
"information": s 73

Amendment of Scottish Public Services Ombudsman Act 2002

71(1)   In Part 2 of schedule 2 to the Scottish Public Services Ombudsman Act 2002 (asp 11) (persons listed as liable to investigation under that Act), after paragraph 45 there is inserted
"45A
The Scottish Information Commissioner.".

(2)   Schedule 4 to this Act, which contains amendments to that Act consequential on the provisions of this Act, has effect.

NOTES

FOIA 2000 equivalent
n/a

Orders and regulations

72(1)   Any power of the Scottish Ministers to make an order or regulations under this Act is exercisable by statutory instrument.

(2)   A statutory instrument
(a) made in exercise of any of the powers conferred by sections 4(1)(except in the case mentioned in subsection (3)), 13(1) or 62(3) is subject to annulment in pursuance of a resolution of the Parliament;
(b) containing an order under section 4(1) (but only in the case so mentioned), 5(1), 7(2) or (4)(b), 59(1) or (1A) or 64(1) or regulation sunder section 9(4), 10(4), 12, 20(7), 21(6) or 47(6) is not made unless a draft of the instrument has been
(i)   laid before; and
(ii)   approved by resolution of,
the Parliament.

(3) The case is that the instrument contains an order under paragraph (a) of section 4(1) and lists an authority in the way mentioned in section 7(1).

NOTES

FOIA 2000 equivalent
n/a

Interpretation

73   In this Act, unless the context requires a different interpretation

"the Commissioner" means the Scottish Information Commissioner;

"body" includes an unincorporated association;

"decision notice" has the meaning given by section 49(5);

"enactment" includes an enactment comprised in, or in an instrument made under, an Act of the Scottish Parliament;

"enforcement notice" has the meaning given by section 51(1);

"exempt information" means information which is so described in any provision of Part 2;

"fees notice" has the meaning given by section 9(1);

"information" (subject to sections 50(9) and 64(2)) means information recorded in any form;

"information notice" has the meaning given by section 50(1);

"Minister of the Crown" has the same meaning as in the Ministers of the Crown Act 1975 (c 26);

"the Parliamentary corporation" means the Scottish Parliamentary Corporate Body;

"publication scheme" has the meaning given by section 23(1)(a);

"refusal notice" has the meaning given by section 16(1) (including that section as read with section 18(2));

"requirement for review" has the meaning given by section 20(2);

"Scottish public authority" has the meaning given by section 3(1);

"subordinate legislation" has the same meaning as in the Interpretation Act1978 (c 30) but includes an instrument made under an Act of the Scottish Parliament; and

"working day" means any day other than a Saturday, a Sunday, Christmas Day or a day which, under the Banking and Financial Dealings Act 1971 (c 80), is a bank holiday in Scotland.

NOTES

FOIA 2000 equivalent
s 84

Giving of notice etc

74(1)   In this Act, any reference to

(a) a notice being given is to be construed as a reference to its being

(i)   delivered; or

(ii)   posted; and

(b) a request for information, a requirement for review or an application being made, or a certificate being given, is to be construed asa reference to its being

(i)   delivered;

(ii)   posted; or

(iii)   transmitted by electronic means.

(2)   For the purposes of any provision of this Act, a thing

(a) posted is presumed not to be received until the third day after the day of posting;

and

(b) transmitted by electronic means is presumed to be received on the day of transmission.

NOTES

FOIA 2000 equivalent
n/a

Defined terms
"information": s 73

Commencement

75(1) This section and sections 72 and 76 come into force on Royal Assent; and the other provisions of this Act come into force

(a) on such day as the Scottish Ministers may by order appoint, that day being, subject to paragraph (b), a day no later than 31st December 2005; or

(b) if the Commissioner recommends to the Scottish Ministers that a day after 31st December 2005 and specified in the recommendation be so appointed and they accept that recommendation, then on the specified day as so appointed,

and different days may be so appointed (or as the case may be recommended and appointed) for different provisions, for different persons or categories of person and for different purposes.

(2) An order under paragraph (b) of subsection (1) may contain such transitional provisions and savings (including provisions capable of having effect after the coming into force of provisions of this Act other than this section and sections 72 and 76) as the Scottish Ministers consider appropriate.

(3) During

(a) that period of twelve months which begins with the date of Royal Assent; and

(b) each subsequent period of twelve months until all the provisions of this Act are fully in force,

the Scottish Ministers are to prepare, and lay before the Parliament, a report of their proposals (including their response to any recommendations made under subsection (1)(b)) for bringing fully into force the provisions of this Act.

NOTES

FOIA 2000 equivalent
s 87

Defined terms
"the Commissioner": s 73

Short title

76 This Act may be cited as the Freedom of Information (Scotland) Act 2002.

SCHEDULE 1
SCOTTISH PUBLIC AUTHORITIES

Part 1
Ministers, the Parliament

1 The Scottish Ministers.

2 The Scottish Parliament.

3 The Scottish Parliamentary Corporate Body.

Part 2

Non Ministerial Office Holders in the Scottish Administration

4   The Chief Dental Officer of the Scottish Administration.

5   The Chief Medical Officer of the Scottish Administration.

6   Her Majesty's Inspectors of Constabulary.

7   Her Majesty's Chief Inspector of Prisons for Scotland.

7A   The Drinking Water Quality Regulator for Scotland.

7B   Food Standards Scotland.

8   Her Majesty's Inspector of Anatomy for Scotland.

9   Her Majesty's Chief Inspector of the Scottish Fire and Rescue Service.

10   Her Majesty's inspectors of schools (that is to say, the inspectors of schools appointed by Her Majesty on the recommendation of the Scottish Ministers under the Education (Scotland) Act 1980 (c 44)).

11   The Keeper of the Records of Scotland.

12   The Keeper of the Registers of Scotland.

12A   The Office of the Scottish Charity Regulator.

13   A procurator fiscal.

14   The Queen's and Lord Treasurer's Remembrancer.

15   The Queen's Printer for Scotland.

16   The Registrar General of Births, Deaths and Marriages for Scotland.

17   The Registrar of Independent Schools in Scotland.

18   A rent officer appointed under section 43(3) of the Rent (Scotland) Act 1984 (c 58).

18ZA Revenue Scotland

18A   The Scottish Court Service.

18AA The Scottish Fiscal Commission.

18B   The Scottish Housing Regulator.

19   . . .

Part 3

Local Government

20   An assessor appointed under section 27(2) of the Local Government etc (Scotland) Act 1994 (c 39).

21   A council constituted by section 2 of that Act.

22   A joint board, within the meaning of section 235(1) of the Local Government (Scotland) Act 1973 (c 65).

23   A licensing board continued in existence by or established under section 5 of the Licensing (Scotland) Act 2005 (asp 16).

24   The Strathclyde Passenger Transport Authority.

24A   A Transport Partnership created under the Transport (Scotland) Act 2005 (asp 12).

Part 4

The National Health Service

25   . . .

26   The Common Services Agency for the Scottish Health Service.

27   A Health Board, constituted under section 2 of the National Health Service (Scotland) Act 1978.

27A   Healthcare Improvement Scotland.

28   . . .

29   ...

29A   The National Waiting Times Centre Board.

30   A local health council, established under section 7 of the National Health Service (Scotland) Act 1978.

31   A National Health Service trust.

32   NHS 24.

32A   NHS Education for Scotland.

32B   NHS Health Scotland.

32C   ...

33   A person providing primary medical services under a general medical services contract (within the meaning of the National Health Service (Scotland) Act 1978) or general dental services, general ophthalmic services or pharmaceutical services under Part II of that Act, but only in respect of information relating to the provision of those services.

34   A person providing primary medical services or personal dental services under arrangements made under section 17C of that Act, but only in respect of information relating to the provision of those services.

35   A person providing, in Scotland, piloted services within the meaning of the National Health Service (Primary Care) Act 1997 (c 46), but only in respect of information relating to the provision of those services.

36   ...

37   The Scottish Advisory Committee on Distinction Awards.

38   ...

39   The Scottish Ambulance Service Board.

40   ...

41   The Scottish Dental Practice Board.

42   ...

43   ...

44   ...

45   The State Hospitals Board for Scotland.

46   ...

Part 5
Educational Institutions

47   The board of management of a college of further education (expressions used in this paragraph having the same meaning as in section 36(1) of the Further and Higher Education (Scotland) Act 1992 (c 37)).

48   A central institution within the meaning of the Education (Scotland) Act 1980.

49   An institution in receipt of funding from the Scottish Further and Higher Education Funding Council or a regional strategic body (within the meaning of the Further and Higher Education (Scotland) Act 2005) other than any institution whose activities are principally carried on outwith Scotland.

Part 6
Police

50   A chief constable of the Police Service of Scotland.

50A   The Scottish Police Authority.

50B   The Police Negotiating Board for Scotland.

51   ...

52   . . .

52A   . . .

Part 7
Others

53   The Accounts Commission for Scotland.

54   . . .

55   . . .

56   . . .

57   Audit Scotland.

58   The Auditor General for Scotland.

59   The Board of Trustees for the National Galleries of Scotland.

60   The Board of Trustees of the National Museums of Scotland.

61   The Board of Trustees of the Royal Botanic Garden, Edinburgh.

61A   Bòrd na Gàidhlig.

61B   The British Waterways Board.

62   . . .

62ZZZA Children's Hearings Scotland.

62ZZA   The Commissioner for Ethical Standards in Public Life in Scotland.

62ZA   The Commissioner for Children and Young People in Scotland.

62A   . . .

62B   . . .

62ZZC   Community Justice Scotland.

62ZC   The Convener of the School Closure Review Panels.

62C   Creative Scotland.

62D   The Criminal Courts Rules Council.

63   The Crofters Commission.

63A   Crown Estate Scotland.

64   . . .

65   . . .

66   The General Teaching Council for Scotland.

66A   Her Majesty's Chief Inspector of Prosecution in Scotland.

67   Highlands and Islands Enterprise.

67ZA   Historic Environment Scotland.

67ZB   ILF Scotland.

67A   . . .

67B   An integration joint board established by order under section 9(2) of the Public Bodies Joint Working) (Scotland) Act 2014.

68   . . .

68ZA   The James Hutton Institute.

68A   The Judicial Appointments Board for Scotland.

69   A Justice of the Peace Advisory Committee established under the Justices of the Peace Scotland) Order 2007.

70   Learning and Teaching Scotland.

71   The Local Government Boundary Commission for Scotland.

71A   The Moredun Research Institute.

72   The Mental Welfare Commission for Scotland.

72A   Mobility and Access Committee for Scotland.

73   A National Park authority, established by virtue of schedule 1 to the National Parks Scotland) Act 2000 (asp 10).

74   The Parole Board for Scotland.

75   A person appointed for Scotland under section 3(1) of the Local Government and Housing Act 1989 (c 42).

75ZA . . .

75A   . . .

75AB The Police Investigations and Review Commissioner.

75AC The Poverty and Inequality Commission.

75B   Quality Meat Scotland.

75C   The Risk Management Authority.

76   . . .

76A   A School Closure Review Panel constituted under section 17A(3) of the Schools Consultation) (Scotland) Act 2010.

77   The Scottish Agricultural Wages Board.

78   . . .

79   . . .

79A   The Scottish Association of Citizens Advice Bureaux, but only in respect of information relating to the functions exercisable by virtue of article 2 of the Public Bodies (The Office of Fair Trading Transfer of Consumer Advice Scheme Function and Modification of Enforcement Functions) Order 2013 SI 2013/783 and articles 3(1)(a), (b) and (d) of the Public Bodies (Abolition of the National Consumer Council and the Transfer of the Office of Fair Trading's Functions in relation to Estate Agents etc) Order 2014 (SI 2014/631).

80   The Scottish Children's Reporter Administration.

80A   . . .

80AA The Scottish Civil Justice Council.

80B   The Scottish Commission for Human Rights.

80C   The Scottish Commission on Social Security.

81   . . .

81A   The Scottish Committee on Climate Change.

82   . . .

83   The Scottish Criminal Cases Review Commission.

84   Scottish Enterprise.

85   The Scottish Environment Protection Agency.

85ZA The Scottish Fire and Rescue Service.

85A   The Scottish Further and Higher Education Funding Council.

85B   . . .

86   . . .

87   . . .

88   . . .

89   . . .

90   The Scottish Information Commissioner.

90A   The Scottish Land Commission.

91   The Scottish Law Commission.

92   The Scottish Legal Aid Board.

92A   The Scottish Legal Complaints Commission.

92B   The Scottish Local Authorities Remuneration Committee.

93   Scottish Natural Heritage.

94   . . .

95   The Scottish Public Services Ombudsman.

96   The Scottish Qualifications Authority.

97   . . .

97A   The Scottish Road Works Commissioner.

98   . . .

98A   The Scottish Sentencing Council.

99   The Scottish Social Services Council.

100   The Scottish Sports Council.

101   . . .

102   Scottish Water.

102A   Social Care and Social Work Improvement Scotland.

102B   South of Scotland Enterprise.

103   . . .

104   The Standards Commission for Scotland.

105   The National Library of Scotland

105A   Visit Scotland.

106   The Water Industry Commission for Scotland.

SCHEDULE 2
THE SCOTTISH INFORMATION COMMISSIONER

Status

1(1)   The Commissioner and that officer's staff are not to be regarded as servants or agents of the Crown or as having any status, immunity or privilege of the Crown; and the Commissioner's property is not to be regarded as property of, or property held on behalf of, the Crown.

(2)   The Commissioner is, as such, to be regarded as a juristic person distinct from the natural person holding the office.

Pensions, allowances, etc

2(1)   The Parliamentary corporation may make arrangements for the payment of pensions, allowances or gratuities to, or in respect of, any person who has ceased to hold the office of Commissioner and (without prejudice to that generality) may

    (a) make contributions or payments towards provision for such pensions, allowances or gratuities; and

    (b) for the purposes of this sub-paragraph, establish and administer one or more pension schemes.

(2)   The references in sub-paragraph (1) to pensions, allowances and gratuities include references to, as the case may be, pensions, allowances or gratuities by way of compensation for loss of office.

Staff

3(1) The Commissioner may appoint such staff, on such terms and conditions, as that officer may determine.

(2) The Commissioner may make arrangements for the payment of pensions, allowances or gratuities to, or in respect of, any person who has ceased to be a member of such staff and (without prejudice to that generality) may

(a) make contributions or payments towards provision for such pensions, allowances or gratuities; and

(b) for the purposes of this sub-paragraph, establish and administer one or more pension schemes.

(3) The references in sub-paragraph (2) to pensions, allowances and gratuities include references to, as the case may be, pensions, allowances or gratuities by way of compensation for loss of employment.

(4) The exercise of a power in sub-paragraph (1) or (2) is subject to the approval of the Parliamentary corporation.

Accountable officer

4(1) The Parliamentary corporation is to designate the Commissioner or a member of that officer's staff as the accountable officer for the purposes of this paragraph.

(2) The functions of the accountable officer are

(a) those specified in sub-paragraph (3); and

(b) where the accountable officer is not the Commissioner, the duty set out in sub-paragraph (4),

and the accountable officer is answerable to the Parliament for the exercise of those functions.

(3) The functions referred to in sub-paragraph (2)(a) are

(a) signing the accounts of the expenditure and receipts of the Commissioner;

(b) ensuring the propriety and regularity of the finances of the Commissioner; and

(c) ensuring that the resources of the Commissioner are used economically, efficiently and effectively.

(4) The duty referred to in sub-paragraph (2)(b) is a duty, where the accountable officer is required to act in some way but considers that to do so would be inconsistent with the proper performance of the functions specified in sub-paragraph (3), to

(a) obtain written authority from the Commissioner before taking the action; and

(b) send a copy of that authority as soon as possible to the Auditor General.

Budget

4A(1) The Commissioner must, before the start of each financial year, prepare proposals for the Commissioner's use of resources and expenditure during the year (a "budget") and, by such date as the Parliamentary corporation determines, send the budget to the Parliamentary corporation for approval.

(2) The Commissioner may, in the course of a financial year, prepare a revised budget for the remainder of the year and send it to the Parliamentary corporation for approval.

(3) In preparing a budget or revised budget, the Commissioner must ensure that the resources

of the Commissioner will be used economically, efficiently and effectively.

(4)　A budget or revised budget must contain a statement that the Commissioner has complied with the duty under sub-paragraph (3).

Accounts

5(1)　The Commissioner must
　　　　(a) keep accounts; and
　　　　(b) prepare annual accounts in respect of each financial year,
in accordance with such directions as the Scottish Ministers may give that officer.

(2)　The Commissioner must send a copy of the annual accounts to the Auditor General for Scotland for auditing.

(3)　The financial year of the Commissioner is
　　　　(a) the period beginning with the date on which the Commissioner is appointed and ending with 31st March next following that date; and
　　　　(b) each successive period of twelve months ending with 31st March.

(4)　If requested by any person, the Commissioner must make available at any reasonable time, without charge, in printed or in electronic form, the audited accounts, so that they may be inspected by that person.

General powers

6(1)　The Commissioner may do anything which appears necessary or expedient for the purpose of, or in connection with, or which appears conducive to, the exercise of that officer's functions; and without prejudice to that generality, may in particular
　　　　(a) acquire and dispose of land and other property; and
　　　　(b) enter into contracts.

(2)　The exercise of the power to acquire or dispose of land is subject to the approval of the Parliamentary corporation.

Location of office

7　The Commissioner must comply with any direction given by the Parliamentary corporation as to the location of the Commissioner's office.

Sharing of premises, staff, services and other resources

8　The Commissioner must comply with any direction given by the Parliamentary corporation as to the sharing of premises, staff, services or other resources with any other officeholder or any public body.

Restrictions on subsequent appointments etc

9(1)　A person who has ceased being the Commissioner may not, without the approval of the Parliamentary corporation
　　　　(a) be employed or appointed in any other capacity by the Commissioner,
　　　　(b) be a Scottish public authority or hold office in, or be an employee or appointee of, a Scottish public authority, or
　　　　(c) hold any other office, employment or appointment or engage in any other

occupation, being an office, employment, appointment or occupation which, by virtue of section 42(3B)(a), that person could not have held or, as the case may be, engaged in when Commissioner.

(2) The restriction in sub-paragraph (1)

    (a) starts when the person ceases to be the Commissioner, and

    (b) ends on the expiry of the financial year next following the one in which it started.

SCHEDULE 3
POWERS OF ENTRY AND INSPECTION

Grant of warrants

1(1) If a sheriff is satisfied by evidence on oath supplied by the Commissioner that there are reasonable grounds for suspecting

    (a) that a Scottish public authority has failed or is failing to comply with

        (i) any of the requirements of Part 1 of this Act;

        (ii) so much of a notice given to it by the Commissioner under subsection (5) of section 49 as, by virtue of subsection (6)(b) of that section, requires steps to be taken; or

        (iii) an information notice or an enforcement notice; or

    (b) that an offence under section 65(1) has been or is being committed, and that evidence of such a failure to comply or of the commission of the offence is to be found on any premises specified as part of that evidence, the sheriff, subject to paragraph 2, may grant to the Commissioner such warrant as is mentioned in sub-paragraph (2).

(2) The warrant is one which authorises the Commissioner, or any member of the Commissioner's staff, at any time within seven days after the date of the warrant

    (a) to enter and search the premises;

    (b) to inspect and seize any documents or other material found there which may constitute the evidence in question; and

    (c) to inspect, examine, operate and test any equipment found there in which information held by the authority may be recorded.

2(1) A sheriff must not grant the warrant unless satisfied

    (a) that the Commissioner has given seven days' notice in writing to the occupier of the premises demanding access to them; and

    (b) that either

        (i) access was demanded at a reasonable hour and was unreasonably refused; or

        (ii) although entry to the premises was granted, the occupier unreasonably refused to comply with a request by the Commissioner, or any member of the Commissioner's staff, to permit the Commissioner or any such member of staff to do any of the things referred to in paragraph 1(2); and

    (c) that the occupier has, after the refusal, been notified by the Commissioner of the application for the warrant and has had an opportunity of being heard by the sheriff on the question of whether or not it should be granted.

(2) Sub-paragraph (1) does not apply if the sheriff is satisfied that the case is one of urgency

or that compliance with the provisions of that sub-paragraph would defeat the object of the entry.

Execution of warrants

3 A person executing the warrant may use such reasonable force as may be necessary.

4 The warrant must be executed at a reasonable hour, unless it appears to the person executing it that there are grounds for suspecting that the evidence in question would not be found if it were so executed.

5(1) If the premises in respect of which the warrant is granted are occupied by a Scottish public authority and any officer or employee of the authority is present when the warrant is executed, that officer or employee must be shown the warrant and supplied with a copy of it; and if no such officer or employee is present a copy of the warrant must be left in a prominent place on the premises.

(2) If the premises in respect of which the warrant is granted are occupied by a person other than a Scottish public authority and that person is present when the warrant is executed, the person must be shown the warrant and supplied with a copy of it; and if the person is not present a copy of the warrant must be left in a prominent place on the premises.

6(1) A person seizing anything in pursuance of the warrant must give a receipt for it if asked to do so.

(2) Anything so seized may be retained for so long as is necessary in all the circumstances; but the person in occupation of the premises must be given a copy of anything that is seized if that person so requests and the person executing the warrant considers that it can be done without undue delay.

Matters exempt from inspection and seizure

7 The powers of inspection and seizure conferred by the warrant are not exercisable in respect of information which is exempt information by virtue of section 31(1).

8(1) Subject to the provisions of this paragraph, the powers of inspection and seizure conferred by the warrant are not exercisable in respect of
   (a) a communication between professional legal adviser and client in connection with the giving of legal advice to the client with respect to the client's obligations, liabilities or rights under this Act; or
   (b) a communication between professional legal adviser and client, or between such adviser or client and another person, made in connection with or in contemplation of proceedings under or arising out of this Act and for the purpose of such proceedings.

(2) Sub-paragraph (1) applies also to
   (a) a copy or other record of such communication as is there mentioned; and
   (b) a document or article enclosed with or referred to in such communication if made in connection with the giving of any advice or, as the case may be, in connection with or in contemplation of and for the purpose of such proceedings as are there

mentioned.

(3) This paragraph does not apply to anything in the possession of a person other than the professional legal adviser or client or to anything held with the intention of furthering a criminal purpose.

(4) In this paragraph references to the client of a professional legal adviser include references to a person representing such a client.

9 If the person in occupation of premises in respect of which the warrant is granted objects to the inspection or seizure under it of any material on the grounds that the material consists partly of matters in respect of which those powers are not exercisable, that person must, if requested, provide in response to the warrant a copy of so much of the material as is material in relation to which the powers are exercisable.

Offences

10(1) A person who
    (a) intentionally obstructs a person who is executing the warrant; or
    (b) fails, without reasonable excuse, to give the person who is executing the warrant such assistance as that person may reasonably require for executing it,
is guilty of an offence.

(2) A person guilty of an offence under sub-paragraph (1) is liable, on summary conviction, to a fine not exceeding level 5 on the standard scale.

Vessels, vehicles etc

11 In this schedule, "premises" includes vessel, vehicle, aircraft or hovercraft, and references to the occupier of premises include references to the person in charge of a vessel, vehicle, aircraft or hovercraft.

SCHEDULE 4
CONSEQUENTIAL AMENDMENTS TO
SCOTTISH PUBLIC SERVICES OMBUDSMAN ACT 2002

Not reproduced

Freedom of Information and Data Protection (Appropriate Limit and Fees) Regulations 2004 (SI 2004/3244)

Made 7th December 2004
Laid before Parliament 9th December 2004
Coming into force 1st January 2005

The Secretary of State, in exercise of the powers conferred upon him by sections 9(3) and (4), 12(3), (4) and (5), and 13(1) and (2) of the Freedom of Information Act 2000, and by sections 9A(5) and 67(2) of the Data Protection Act 1998, and having consulted the Information Commissioner in accordance with section 67(3) of the Data Protection Act 1998, hereby makes the following Regulations:

Citation and commencement

1   These Regulations may be cited as the Freedom of Information and Data Protection (Appropriate Limit and Fees) Regulations 2004 and come into force on 1st January 2005.

Interpretation

2   In these Regulations–
"the 2000 Act" means the Freedom of Information Act 2000;
"the 1998 Act" means the Data Protection Act 1998; and
"the appropriate limit" is to be construed in accordance with the provision made in regulation 3.

The appropriate limit

3(1)   This regulation has effect to prescribe the appropriate limit referred to in section 12(1) and (2) of the 2000 Act.

(2)   In the case of a public authority which is listed in Part I of Schedule 1 to the 2000 Act, the appropriate limit is £600.

(3)   In the case of any other public authority, the appropriate limit is £450.

Estimating the cost of complying with a request – general

4(1)   This regulation has effect in any case in which a public authority proposes to estimate whether the cost of complying with a relevant request would exceed the appropriate limit.

(2)   A relevant request is any request to the extent that it is a request–
  (a)   for unstructured personal data within the meaning of section 9A(1) of the 1998 Act, and to which section 7(1) of that Act would, apart from the appropriate limit, to any extent apply, or
  (b)   information to which section 1(1) of the 2000 Act would, apart from the appropriate limit, to any extent apply.

(3)   In a case in which this regulation has effect, a public authority may, for the purpose of its estimate, take account only of the costs it reasonably expects to incur in relation to the request in–
  (a)   determining whether it holds the information,
  (b)   locating the information, or a document which may contain the information,
  (c)   retrieving the information, or a document which may contain the information,

and

(d)   extracting the information from a document containing it.

(4)   To the extent to which any of the costs which a public authority takes into account are attributable to the time which persons undertaking any of the activities mentioned in paragraph (3) on behalf of the authority are expected to spend on those activities, those costs are to be estimated at a rate of £25 per person per hour.

Estimating the cost of complying with a request – aggregation of related requests

5(1)   In circumstances in which this regulation applies, where two or more requests for information to which section 1(1) of the 2000 Act would, apart from the appropriate limit, to any extent apply, are made to a public authority–

(a)   by one person, or

(b)   by different persons who appear to the public authority to be acting in concert or in pursuance of a campaign,

the estimated cost of complying with any of the requests is to be taken to be the total costs which may be taken into account by the authority, under regulation 4, of complying with all of them.

(2)   This regulation applies in circumstances in which–

(a)   the two or more requests referred to in paragraph (1) relate, to any extent, to the same or similar information, and

(b)   those requests are received by the public authority within any period of sixty consecutive working days.

(3)   In this regulation, "working day" means any day other than a Saturday, a Sunday, Christmas Day, Good Friday or a day which is a bank holiday under the Banking and Financial Dealings Act 1971 in any part of the United Kingdom.

Maximum fee for complying with section 1(1) of the 2000 Act

6(1)   Any fee to be charged under section 9 of the 2000 Act by a public authority to whom a request for information is made is not to exceed the maximum determined by the public authority in accordance with this regulation.

(2)   Subject to paragraph (4), the maximum fee is a sum equivalent to the total costs the public authority reasonably expects to incur in relation to the request in–

(a)   informing the person making the request whether it holds the information, and

(b)   communicating the information to the person making the request.

(3)   Costs which may be taken into account by a public authority for the purposes of this regulation include, but are not limited to, the costs of–

(a)   complying with any obligation under section 11(1) of the 2000 Act as to the means or form of communicating the information,

(b)   reproducing any document containing the information, and

(c)   postage and other forms of transmitting the information.

(4)   But a public authority may not take into account for the purposes of this regulation any costs which are attributable to the time which persons undertaking activities mentioned in paragraph (2) on behalf of the authority are expected to spend on those activities.

Maximum fee for communication of information under section 13 of the 2000 Act

7(1) Any fee to be charged under section 13 of the 2000 Act by a public authority to whom a request for information is made is not to exceed the maximum determined by a public authority in accordance with this regulation.

(2) The maximum fee is a sum equivalent to the total of—

    (a) the costs which the public authority may take into account under regulation 4 in relation to that request, and

    (b) the costs it reasonably expects to incur in relation to the request in—

        (i) informing the person making the request whether it holds the information, and

        (ii) communicating the information to the person making the request.

(3) But a public authority is to disregard, for the purposes of paragraph(2)(a), any costs which it may take into account under regulation 4 solely by virtue of the provision made by regulation 5.

(4) Costs which may be taken into account by a public authority for the purposes of paragraph (2)(b) include, but are not limited to, the costs of—

    (a) giving effect to any preference expressed by the person making the request as to the means or form of communicating the information,

    (b) reproducing any document containing the information, and

    (c) postage and other forms of transmitting the information.

(5) For the purposes of this regulation, the provision for the estimation of costs made by regulation 4(4) is to be taken to apply to the costs mentioned in paragraph (2)(b) as it does to the costs mentioned in regulation 4(3).

Freedom of Information
(Definition of Historical Records)
(Transitional and Saving Provisions) Order 2012
(SI 2012/3029)

Made: 5th December 2012

The Secretary of State makes the following Order in exercise of the powers conferred by section 46(2) and (3) of the Constitutional Reform and Governance Act 2010(1):

Citation, commencement and interpretation

1(1) This Order may be cited as the Freedom of Information (Definition of Historical Records) (Transitional and Saving Provisions) Order 2012 and shall come into force on 1st January 2013.

(2) In this Order—

"the 2000 Act" means the Freedom of Information Act 2000(2);

"relevant record" means a record which, by virtue of the coming into force on 1st January 2013 of paragraph 4 of Schedule 7 (amendments of Freedom of Information Act 2000: meaning of historical record) to the Constitutional Reform and Governance Act 2010(3) and but for this Order, becomes a historical record for the purposes of Part 6 (historical records and records in Public Record Office or Public Record Office of Northern Ireland) of the 2000 Act at the end of the period of twenty years beginning with the year following that in which it was created.

Transitional provision

2(1) Notwithstanding the coming into force on 1st January 2013 of paragraph 4 of Schedule 7 to the Constitutional Reform and Governance Act 2010, for the period of 10 years beginning on that day the time when a relevant record becomes a historical record for the purposes of Part 6 of the 2000 Act is that provided for by paragraph (2).

(2) A relevant record created in a year specified in column 1 of the table in the Schedule to this Order shall become a historical record from the end of the year specified in the corresponding entry in column 2 of that table.

Saving provision

3 Section 62(1) (meaning of historical record for purposes of Part 6 of Freedom of Information Act 2000) of the 2000 Act continues to apply as it did immediately before 1st January 2013 in relation to a relevant record created in 1983.

McNally
Minister of State
Ministry of Justice
5th December 2012

SCHEDULE

Article 2(2)

Transitional arrangements for relevant records becoming historical records in accordance with the Freedom of Information Act 2000

Column 1	Column 2
1984	2013
1985	2014
1986	2014
1987	2015
1988	2015
1989	2016
1990	2016
1991	2017
1992	2017
1993	2018
1994	2018
1995	2019
1996	2019
1997	2020
1998	2020
1999	2021
2000	2021
2001	2022

Freedom of Information (Designation as Public Authorities) Order 2011 (SI 2011/2598)

Made: 31st October 2011

The Secretary of State makes the following Order in exercise of the powers conferred by sections 5(1)(a) and (2) and 7(5) of the Freedom of Information Act 2000.

Citation and commencement

1(1) This Order may be cited as the Freedom of Information (Designation as Public Authorities) Order 2011.

(2) This Order comes into force on the day after the day on which it is made.

Persons designated as Public Authorities

2. The persons listed in column 1 of the Schedule are designated as public authorities under section 5(1)(a) of the Freedom of Information Act 2000 with respect to the function or functions specified in column 2.

Signed by the authority of the Secretary of State
McNally
Minister of State
Ministry of Justice
31st October 2011

SCHEDULE
Persons designated as Public Authorites

Column 1	Column 2
The Financial Ombudsman Service Limited	The administration of an ombudsman scheme in accordance with Part 16 of, and Schedule 17 to, the Financial Services and Markets Act 2000
The Universities and Colleges Admissions Service	The provision and maintenance of a central applications and admissions service in relation to: a an institution listed in paragraphs 53(1)(a) to (e) and 55(1)(a) and (b) of Part 4 of Schedule 1 to the Freedom of Information Act 2000; b an institution listed in Part 5 of Schedule 1 to the Freedom of Information (Scotland) Act 2002; c the College of Agriculture, Food and Rural Enterprise.

Freedom of Information (Designation as Public Authorities) Order 2015 (SI 2015/851)

Made   23rd March 2015

The Secretary of State makes the following Order in exercise of the powers conferred by sections 5(1)(a) and (2) and 7(5) of the Freedom of Information Act 2000.

Citation, commencement and interpretation

(1) This Order may be cited as the Freedom of Information (Designation as Public Authorities) Order 2015.

(2) This Order comes into force on the day after the day on which it is made.

(3) In this Order–
    (a) "the 1993 Act" means the Railways Act 1993;
    (b) "light maintenance depots" has the meaning given by section 83 of the 1993 Act;
    (c) "light maintenance services", "network services" and "station services" have the meaning given by section 82 of the 1993 Act; and
    (d) "operator" and "railway asset" have the meaning given by section 6(2) of the 1993 Act.

Persons designated as public authorities

2(1) Subject to article 2(2), each person listed in column 1 of the table in the Schedule is designated as a public authority under section 5(1)(a) of the Freedom of Information Act 2000 with respect to the functions specified in the corresponding entry in column 2.

(2) The functions in column 2 exclude any function in connection with which a person listed in column 1 makes a charge or obtains consideration of any kind, unless the purpose of exercising the function is to enable an operator to use or operate a railway asset.

Simon Hughes
Minister of State
Ministry of Justice
23rd March 2015

SCHEDULE
Persons Designated as Public Authorities

Column 1	Column 2
Network Rail Limited	(a) The acquisition, ownership, management, provision, operation and development of network services. (b) The acquisition, ownership, management, provision, operation and development of station services.

Network Rail Infrastructure Limited	(a) The acquisition, ownership, management, provision, operation and development of network services. (b) The acquisition, ownership, management, provision, operation and development of station services. (c) The provision and operation of light maintenance depots for the use of light maintenance services.
Network Rail Holdco Limited	(a) The acquisition and ownership of network services. (b) The acquisition and ownership of station services.

Freedom of Information (Designation as Public Authority and Amendment) Order 2018 (SI 2018/1212)

Made: 21st November 2018

The Secretary of State makes the following Order in exercise of the powers conferred by sections 5(1)(a) and (2) and 7(5) of the Freedom of Information Act 2000(1).

In accordance with section 5(3) of that Act(2), the Secretary of State has consulted persons appearing to the Secretary of State to represent the persons to whom the Order relates.

In accordance with section 82(2)(a) of that Act, a draft of this Order was laid before, and approved by a resolution of, each House of Parliament.

Citation and commencement

1(1) This Order may be cited as the Freedom of Information (Designation as Public Authority and Amendment) Order 2018.

(2) This Order comes into force on the day after the day on which it is made.

Person designated as a public authority

2(1) The National Police Chiefs' Council is designated as a public authority under section 5(1)(a) of the Freedom of Information Act 2000 with respect to the following of its functions—

    (a) the co-ordination of national operations;

    (b) the command of counter-terrorism operations and delivery of counter-terrorist policing through any collaboration agreement relating to counter-terrorism activities entered into under section 22A of the Police Act 1996(3);

    (c) the co-ordination of the national police response to national emergencies and the co-ordination of the mobilisation of resources across force borders and internationally;

    (d) the national operational implementation of standards and policy as set by the College of Policing(4) or by any government department;

    (e) the development, in collaboration with the College of Policing, of joint national approaches on criminal justice, value for money, service transformation, information management, performance management and technology; and

    (f) the development, in collaboration with the College of Policing, of joint national approaches to staff and human resource issues, including misconduct and discipline.

(2) In this article, "National Police Chiefs' Council" has the meaning given by section 101 of the Police Act 1996.

Freedom of Information
(Excluded Welsh Authorities) Order 2002
(SI 2002/2832)

Made 11th November 2002
Coming into force 30th November 2002

The Lord Chancellor, in exercise of the powers conferred upon him by section 83(2) of the Freedom of Information Act 2000, and after consultation with the National Assembly for Wales in accordance with section 83(3) of that Act, hereby makes the following Order:

1 This Order may be cited as the Freedom of Information (Excluded Welsh Authorities) Order 2002 and shall come into force on 30th November 2002.

2 The public authorities listed in the Schedule to this Order are designated as excluded authorities for the purposes of section 83(1)(a) of the Freedom of Information Act 2000.

SCHEDULE
EXCLUDED AUTHORITIES

Article 2

PART I
LOCAL GOVERNMENT

The magistrates' court committee established under section 27 of the Justices of the Peace Act 1997 for each of the following areas:
    Dyfed Powys;
    Gwent;
    North Wales; and
    South Wales.

PART II

OTHER BODIES AND OFFICES: GENERAL

The Advisory Committee on Justices of the Peace for each of the following areas:
    Clwyd;
    Dyfed-Carmarthen;
    Dyfed-Ceredigion;
    Dyfed-Pembroke;
    Gwent;
    Gwynedd;
    Mid Glamorgan;
    Powys;
    South Glamorgan; and
    West Glamorgan.

The Parliamentary Boundary Commission for Wales.

Sianel Pedwar Cymru, in respect of information held for purposes other than those of journalism, art or literature.

The Traffic Commissioner for the Welsh Traffic Area, in respect of information held otherwise than as a tribunal.

Freedom of Information
(Release of Datasets for Re-use) (Fees) Regulations 2013 (SI 2013/1977)

Made: 7th August 2013

The Secretary of State makes the following Regulations in exercise of the powers conferred upon him by section 11B(1), (2) and (3) of the Freedom of Information Act 2000(1) and with the consent of the Treasury:

Citation, commencement and interpretation

1 These Regulations may be cited as the Freedom of Information (Release of Datasets for Re-use) (Fees) Regulations 2013 and come into force on 1st September 2013.

Fees for release of datasets for re-use

2(1) A public authority may charge a fee for making a relevant copyright work available for re-use—

    (a) under section 11A(2) (release of datasets for re-use)(2) of the Act, or

    (b) in accordance with a requirement imposed by virtue of section 19(2A)(c) (publication schemes: datasets)(3) of the Act.

(2) The total fee shall not exceed the sum of—

    (a) the cost of collection, production, reproduction and dissemination of the relevant copyright work, and

    (b) a reasonable return on investment.

(3) A fee shall be determined, so far as is reasonably practicable,—

    (a) in accordance with the accounting principles applicable to the public authority from time to time, and

    (b) on the basis of a reasonable estimate of the demand for a relevant copyright work over the appropriate accounting period.

(4) A fee charged by a public authority for a relevant copyright work shall not include the cost of an activity mentioned in paragraph (2)(a) if that cost has been included in any other fee charged under the Act to the same applicant by that authority in respect of that work.

(5) Where a public authority charges fees it shall, so far as is reasonably practicable, establish standard fees.

(6) The public authority shall specify in writing the basis on which a standard fee has been determined, if requested at any time to do so by the applicant.

(7) Where a standard fee has not been established, the public authority shall specify in writing the factors that will be taken into account in determining a fee, if requested at any time to do so by the applicant.

(8) The public authority may not charge a fee by virtue of this regulation in relation to a relevant copyright work where it has a power under an enactment other than the Act to charge a fee in connection with making that work available for re-use.

(9) In this regulation "the Act" means the Freedom of Information Act 2000.

Freedom of Information (Time for Compliance with Request) Regulations 2004 (SI 2004/3364)

Made 16th December 2004
Coming into force 1st January 2005

Whereas a draft of these Regulations has been approved by resolution of both Houses of Parliament in pursuance of section 82(2) of the Freedom of Information Act 2000;

Now, therefore, the Secretary of State, in exercise of the powers conferred by section 10(4) and (5) of the Freedom of Information Act 2000, hereby makes the following Regulations:

Citation and commencement

1   These Regulations may be cited as the Freedom of Information (Time for Compliance with Request) Regulations 2004 and come into force on 1st January 2005.

Interpretation

2   In these Regulations, "the Act" means the Freedom of Information Act 2000.

Governing body of a maintained school or maintained nursery school and schools maintained by the Secretary of State for Defence

3(1)   This regulation applies—

    (a)   to a request for information that is received by the governing body of a maintained school or a maintained nursery school; and

    (b)   to a request for information which is held by the public authority only by virtue of the information being situated in a school which is maintained by the Secretary of State for Defence and which provides primary or secondary education, (or both primary and secondary education).

(2)   Where this regulation applies, subsections (1) and (2) of section 10 of the Act have effect as if any reference to the twentieth working day following the date of receipt were a reference to either—

    (a)   the twentieth working day following the date of receipt, disregarding any working day which, in relation to the school referred to in paragraph (1), is not a school day, or

    (b)   the sixtieth working day following the date of receipt,

whichever occurs first.

(3)   "School day", for the purposes of this regulation, means any day on which, at the school referred to in paragraph (1) above, there is a session.

Archives

4(1)   This regulation applies where—

    (a)   a request for information is received by an appropriate records authority or by a person at a place of deposit appointed under section 4(1) of the Public Records Act 1958; and

    (b)   the request relates wholly or partly to information:

        (i)   that may be contained in a transferred public record, and

        (ii)   that has not been designated as open information for the purposes of section

66 of the Act.

(2)   Where this regulation applies, subsections (1) and (2) of section 10 of the Act have effect as if any reference to the twentieth working day following the date of receipt were a reference to the thirtieth working day following the date of receipt.

Operations of armed forces of the Crown

5(1)   This regulation applies, in relation to a request for information, where–

    (a)   a public authority cannot comply with section 1(1) of the Act without obtaining information (whether or not recorded) from any individual (whether or not a member of the armed forces of the Crown) who is actively involved in an operation of the armed forces of the Crown, or in the preparations for such an operation, and

    (b)   for that reason, the public authority would not be able to obtain the information within such time as to enable it to comply with the request within the time referred to in subsections (1) and (2) of section 10 of the Act.

(2)   Where this regulation applies, subsections (1) and (2) of section 10 of the Act have effect as if any reference to the twentieth working day following the date of receipt were a reference to such other day, not being later than the sixtieth working day following the date of receipt, as the Information Commissioner may specify in accordance with paragraph (3).

(3)   Where–

    (a)   the public authority applies to the Information Commissioner for specification of a day in accordance with this regulation, and

    (b)   that application is made within twenty working days following the date of receipt of the request,

the Information Commissioner shall specify such day as he considers reasonable in all the circumstances.

Information held outside the United Kingdom

6(1)   This regulation applies to a request for information which–

    (a)   may

        (i)   relate to information not held in the United Kingdom, or

        (ii)   require information (including information held by a person who is not a public authority) that is not held in the United Kingdom to be obtained in order to comply with it, and

    (b)   for that reason, the public authority would not be able to obtain the information within such time as to enable it to comply with the request within the time referred to in subsections (1) and (2) of section 10 of the Act.

(2)   Where this regulation applies, subsections (1) and (2) of section 10 of the Act have effect as is any reference to the twentieth working day following the date of receipt were a reference to such other day, not being later than the sixtieth working day following the date of receipt, as the Information Commissioner may specify in accordance with paragraph (3).

(3)   Where–

    (a)   the public authority applies to the Information Commissioner for specification of a day in accordance with this regulation, and

    (b)   that application is made within twenty working days following the date of receipt of the request, the Information Commissioner shall specify such day as he considers reasonable in all the circumstances.

Freedom of Information
(Time for Compliance with Request) Regulations 2009
(SI 2009/1369)

Made: 3rd June 2009

The Secretary of State makes the following Regulations in exercise of the power conferred by section 10(4) of the Freedom of Information Act 2000(1).

A draft of these Regulations was laid before Parliament and approved by a resolution of each House of Parliament in accordance with section 82(2)(b) of that Act.

Citation and commencement

1(1) These Regulations may be cited as the Freedom of Information (Time for Compliance with Request) Regulations 2009.

(2) These Regulations come into force on 26th June 2009.

Managers of a controlled school, voluntary school, grant-maintained integrated school or pupil referral unit

2(1) This regulation applies to a request for information that is received by the managers of—

    (a) a controlled school, voluntary school or grant-maintained integrated school within the meaning of Article 2(2) of the Education and Libraries (Northern Ireland) Order 1986(2), or

    (b) a pupil referral unit as defined by Article 87(1) of the Education (Northern Ireland) Order 1998(3).

(2) Where this regulation applies, subsections (1) and (2) of section 10 of the Freedom of Information Act 2000 have effect as if any reference to the twentieth working day following the date of receipt were a reference to either—

    (a) the twentieth working day following the date of receipt, disregarding any working day which, in relation to the school or unit referred to in paragraph (1), is not a school day, or

    (b) the sixtieth working day following the date of receipt,

whichever occurs first.

(3) "School day", for the purposes of this regulation, means any day on which, at the school or unit referred to in paragraph (1) above, there is a session.

Freedom of Information
(Time for Compliance with Request) Regulations 2010
(SI 2010/2768)

Made: 17th November 2010

The Secretary of State, in exercise of the powers conferred by section 10(4) of the Freedom of Information Act 2000(1), makes the following Regulations.

In accordance with section 82(2)(b) of that Act, a draft of this instrument was laid before Parliament and approved by a resolution of each House of Parliament.

Citation and Commencement

1(1) These Regulations may be cited as the Freedom of Information (Time for Compliance with Request) Regulations 2010.

(2) These Regulations come into force on the day after the day on which they are made.

Proprietors of Academies

2(1) This regulation applies to a request for information that is received by the proprietor of an Academy.

(2) Where this regulation applies, subsections (1) and (2) of section 10 of the Freedom of Information Act 2000 have effect as if any reference to the twentieth working day following the date of receipt were a reference to either—

(a) the twentieth working day following the date of receipt, disregarding any working day which, in relation to the Academy referred to in paragraph (1), is not a school day, or

(b) the sixtieth working day following the date of receipt,

whichever occurs first.

(3) "School day", for the purposes of this regulation, has the same meaning as in section 579(1) of the Education Act 1996(2).

Signed by authority of the Secretary of State for Justice

Minister for the Cabinet Office's Code of Practice on the discharge of public authorities' functions under Part I of the Freedom of Information Act 2000

Issued under section 45 of the Freedom of Information Act 2000.

4 July 2018

Foreword

Freedom of Information is one of the pillars upon which open government operates. The Government is committed to supporting the effective operation of the Freedom of Information Act. For any Freedom of Information regime to be truly effective it is important that both its users and those subject to it have faith in it.

This Code of Practice provides guidance for public authorities on best practice in meeting their responsibilities under Part I of the Act. It sets the standard for all public authorities when considering how to respond to Freedom of Information requests.

The Information Commissioner also has a statutory duty to promote good practice by public authorities, including following this Code of Practice. In addition to this Code of Practice, public authorities should also consult the Commissioner's own guidance regarding best practice which can be found at .

The Commissioner can issue practice recommendations where he or she considers that public authorities have not conformed with the guidance set out in this Code. The Commissioner can also refer to non-compliance with the Code in decision and enforcement notices.

This foreword does not form part of the Code itself.

Introduction

This Code of Practice provides guidance to public authorities on the discharge of their functions and responsibilities under Part I (Access to information held by public authorities) of the Freedom of Information Act 2000 ("the Act'). It is issued under section 45 of the Act. Right of Access

1. Right of Access

Information

1.1 The Freedom of Information (FOI) Act 2000 ('the Act') gives a right of access to information. Any person who makes a request to a public authority for information is entitled:

- To be informed in writing by a public authority whether it holds information meeting the description set out in the request; and

- To have information the public authority holds relating to the request communicated to them.

These rights apply unless an exemption in Part II of the Act applies, or the request can be refused under sections 12 or 14, as set out in the legislation.

1.2 Section 84 of the Act defines the 'information' a public authority can be asked to provide under the Act. It makes clear that it means recorded information held in any form, electronic or paper.

1.3 Public authorities are not required to create new information in order to comply with a request for information under the Act. They only need to consider information already in existence at the time a request is received.

1.4 A request to a public authority for recorded information will be treated as a request under the Act, other than:

- information given out as part of routine business, for example, standard responses to general enquiries;
- a request for environmental information; or
- the requester's own personal data.

1.5 A request for environmental information only should be dealt with under the Environmental Information Regulations 2004 ,[2] and a request for a person's own personal data should be dealt with under the subject access provisions of the Data Protection Act 2018. Sometimes it may be necessary to consider a request under more than one access regime.

1.6 The Act provides a right to information. Disclosing existing documents will often be the most straightforward way of providing information. However, in other cases it may be appropriate to extract the relevant information for disclosure and put in a single document rather than redact the existing document that contains it.

1.7 There will be occasions where a request is made under the Act but does not in fact meet the above description of being a request for recorded information. This may include requests for explanations, clarification of policy, comments on the public authority's business, and any other correspondence that does not follow the definition of a valid request in section 8. It is best practice to provide an applicant with an explanation of why their request will not be treated under the Act if this is the case and to respond to their correspondence through other channels as appropriate. It is open to the applicant to appeal the handling of their correspondence to the Information Commissioner's Office.

Information held

1.8 In order to respond to a request for information public authorities need to consider whether the requested information is 'held' for the purposes of the Act. This is because

---

[2]   Public authorities may wish to refer to the Information Commissioner's *Regulation 16 Code of Practice: Discharge of Obligations of Public Authorities under the EIR.*

there may be instances when a public authority possesses information, either electronically or in physical copy, that does not meet the criteria for information 'held' set out in the Act and to which the obligations set out in the Act therefore do not apply.

1.9 Section 3(2) sets out the criteria for when information is held by a public authority for the purposes of the Act. This includes:

- information held by a public authority at the time of the request;
- information stored in off-site servers or cloud storage; and
- information held by other organisations and authorities on behalf of the public authority including, for example, off-site storage or information provided to lawyers for the purposes of litigation.

1.10 Information is 'held' by the public authority if it is retained for the purposes of the public authority's business. Purely personal, political, constituency, or trade union information, for example, will not be 'held' for the purposes of the Act and so will not be relevant for the purposes of the request. Where a public authority holds or stores information solely on behalf of another person or body that material will also not be 'held' by that authority for the purposes of the Act.

1.11 Information created after a request is received is not within the scope of the application and is therefore not "held" for the purposes of the Act. A search for information which has been deleted from a public authority's records before a request is received, and is only held in electronic back up files, should generally be regarded as not being held.[3]

1.12 Public authorities need to search for requested information in order to communicate to the applicant whether the information they are seeking is held or not held by that public authority. These searches should be conducted in a reasonable and intelligent way based on an understanding of how the public authority manages its records. Public authorities should concentrate their efforts on areas most likely to hold the requested information. If a reasonable search in the areas most likely to hold the requested information does not reveal the information sought, the public authority may consider that on the balance of probabilities the information is not held.

Section 77 (Offence of altering records etc. with intent to prevent disclosure)

1.13 Public authorities should make sure that their staff are aware that under section 77 of the Act it is a criminal offence to alter, deface, block, erase, destroy or conceal any information held by the public authority with the intention of preventing disclosure following a request under the Act for the information.

Valid requests

1.14 Section 8 sets out the criteria for what constitutes a valid request under the Act:

- Section 8(1)(a) requires that a request for information must be made in writing. This can either be in hard copy or electronically;
- Section 8(1)(b) requires that a request for information must state the name of the applicant and an address for correspondence. Applicants must provide their real name and not use a pseudonym. Both email and postal addresses are acceptable;
- Section 8(1)(c) requires that a request for information must also adequately describe the information sought.

---

[3] Public authorities should make sure they are also aware of the guidance provided in the Lord Chancellor's Code of Practice on the management of records issued under section 46 of the Freedom of Information Act 2000.

1.15 Public authorities do not have to comply with requests that do not meet the requirements set out in section 8. It is good practice to write to the applicant and explain this if this is the case.

1.16 A request submitted through social media will be valid where it meets the requirements of section 8 by providing an applicant's name and address for correspondence and a clear request for information. Addresses for correspondence can take the form of an email address or a unique name or identifier on a social media platform (for example a Twitter handle), as well as postal addresses. Requests must be addressed directly to the public authority the applicant is seeking information from, which includes elected officials and appointed representatives, when acting in their formal capacity. In order to be addressed directly, a public authority must have a formal, monitorable presence on the particular platform being used by an applicant.

1.17 Requests submitted in a foreign language are not generally considered valid requests. Public authorities are not expected to obtain translations of suspected requests for information. It is good practice when receiving a request in a foreign language to ask the applicant to provide their request in English or Welsh in order for the request to be processed.

Fees

1.18 It is open to public authorities, as a result of Regulations made under sections 9 and 13 of the Act, to charge for the cost of providing information requested under the Act. However, the majority of public authorities do not currently do so. It is also only possible to charge where information will be released. It is not possible for public authorities to charge for requests where, for example, information is being withheld under exemptions.

1.19 Where the public authority intends to charge for the cost of providing information, they should send a fees notice stating the amount to be paid, including how this has been calculated, as soon as possible within the 20 working day response period. The notice should inform applicants:
- that the 20 working day period for responding to the request will be paused until payment is received (it is reasonable to set a deadline of three months in which the fee should be paid);
- how to pay the fee; and
- their rights of complaint via internal review and to the Information Commissioner about the fee levied.

1.20 Public authorities may charge for:
- actual production expenses (e.g. redacting exempt information, printing or photocopying);
- transmission costs (e.g. postage); and
- complying with the applicant's preferences about the format in which they would like to receive the information (section 11) (e.g. scanning to a CD).

1.21 It is not possible to charge for any staff time where the cost of compliance falls below the cost limit (see Chapter 6). There is no obligation to comply with any request exceeding the cost limit. However, should a public authority decide to respond to a request that exceeds the cost limit on a voluntary basis it can charge for the staff time needed to do so. In such circumstances staff time is chargeable at a standard rate, including the cost of making redactions (but only the physical cost of making redactions and not staff time for considering whether exemptions apply), to be included in the initial fees notice.

1.22 Public authorities may already charge for supplying specific categories of information on a different statutory basis to the fees they are allowed to charge under the Act. They can continue to do this even when these charges are higher than the fees that can be charged under the Act. However, public authorities may not charge where a statutory obligation to provide information free of charge already exists.

1.23 Once the fee is received, the public authority should process it promptly and inform the applicant of the revised 20 working day response deadline. It is permissible to wait until a cheque clears before recommencing work. Should a public authority underestimate the costs to be charged, it should not issue a second fees notice and should bear the additional cost itself.

Means of communication

1.24 Section 11 of the Act says that if an applicant states a preference for receiving information in a specific format a public authority shall, if they are required to disclose information, aim to meet this preference as far as is reasonably practicable. Applicants may, for instance, request to receive the information in an electronic or hard copy format.

1.25 When considering whether it is reasonable to meet an applicant's wishes under section 11, public authorities may, for instance, consider the cost and complexity of providing information in the format requested and the resources they have available.

1.26 If an applicant doesn't state a preference, public authorities can communicate information by "any means which are reasonable in the circumstances" as set out in section 11(4). For example, where the platform used by an applicant to make their request imposes restrictions on the format of a response (for example, Twitter restricts the length of a response and does not allow the direct attachment of documents) it would be reasonable to respond in another format.

1.27 Guidance on additional requirements in relation to datasets is provided in Chapter 11 and for model communications in Chapter 10.

2. Advice and assistance

2.1 Section 16 of the Act sets out a duty for public authorities to provide reasonable advice and assistance to applicants requesting information. This duty to advise and assist is enforceable by the Information Commissioner. If a public authority does not meet this duty, the Commissioner may issue a decision notice under section 50, or an enforcement notice under section 52.

2.2. Public authorities should bear in mind that other Acts of Parliament may also be relevant to the way in which they provide advice and assistance to applicants or potential applicants, for example, compliance with duties under the Equality Act 2010.

Advice and assistance to prospective requesters

2.3   Public authorities should, as a matter of best practice, publish a postal address and email address (or appropriate online alternative) to which applicants can send requests for information or for assistance.

2.4   There is no requirement for a request for recorded information specifically to mention the Act in order to be a valid FOI request. Where an applicant asks a public authority to disclose recorded information but does not specifically mention the Act, and the request complies with section 8 (see paragraph 1.14 above), the public authority should consider the request under the Act in any case and let the applicant know that this is how the request is being handled. Where a person seeks to make a request orally they should be advised to put their application in writing in accordance with section 8(1)(a) of the Act.

2.5   There may be circumstances where a person is unable to frame their request in writing, for example owing to a disability. In these instances the public authority should make sure that assistance is given to enable them to make a request for information. For example, advising the person that another person or agency (such as a Citizens Advice Bureau) may be able to assist them with the application, or make the application on their behalf. Public authorities may also consider, in exceptional circumstances, offering to take a note of the application over the telephone and sending the note to the applicant for confirmation. Once verified by the applicant this would constitute a written request for information and the statutory time limit for reply would begin when the written confirmation was received.

Clarifying the request

2.6   There may be instances when a public authority needs to contact an applicant to seek clarification either regarding their name or the information they are seeking in order for the request they have made to meet the requirements set out in section 8 of the Act.

2.7   If a public authority considers the applicant has not provided their real name the public authority can make the applicant aware it does not intend to respond to the request until further information is received from the applicant. For example, this may be the case when an applicant appears to have used a pseudonym rather than their own name.

2.8   There may also be occasions when a request is not clear enough to adequately describe the information sought by the applicant in such a way that the public authority can conduct a search for it. In these cases, public authorities may ask for more detail to enable them to identify the information sought.

2.9   Where a public authority asks for further information or clarification to enable the requester to meet the requirements of section 8, the 20 working day response period will not start until a satisfactory reply constituting a valid request is received. Letters should make clear that if no response is received the request will be considered closed by the public authority. Two months would be an appropriate length of time to wait to receive clarification before closing a request.

Reducing the cost of a request

2.10   Where it is estimated the cost of answering a request would exceed the "cost limit" beyond which the public authority is not required to answer a request (and the authority is not prepared to answer it), public authorities should provide applicants with advice and assistance to help them reframe or refocus their request with a view to bringing it within the costs limit. Further guidance on the appropriate "cost limit" can be found in Chapter 6.

Transferring requests for information

2.11   There will be occasions when a public authority is not able to comply with a request (or to comply with it in full) because it does not hold the information requested.

2.12   In most cases where a public authority does not hold the information, but thinks that another public authority does, they should respond to the applicant to inform them that the requested information is not held by them, and that it may be held by another public authority. The public authority should, as best practice where they can, provide the contact details for the public authority they believe holds the requested information.

2.13   Where the public authority who originally received the request wishes to ask a different public authority directly to deal with the request by transferring it to them, this should only be done with the applicant's agreement in case the requester objects to their details being passed on. This is because public authorities have a duty to respond to a requester and confirm whether or not they hold information in scope of the request as set out in paragraph 2.12 above.

3.   Consultation with Third Parties

3.1   There will be circumstances when a public authority should consult third parties about information held in scope of a request in order to consider whether information is suitable for disclosure. These may include:
- when requests for information relate to persons or bodies who are not the applicant and/or the public authority; or
- when disclosure of information is likely to affect the interests of persons or bodies who are not the applicant or the authority.

3.2   Public authorities may want to directly consult third parties in these circumstances particularly if, for example, there are contractual obligations which require consultation before information is released. In other circumstances it may be good practice to consult third parties, for example, where a public authority proposes to disclose information relating to third parties, or information which is likely to affect their business or private interests.

3.3   Consultation will often be necessary because third parties who have created or provided the information may have a better understanding of its sensitivity than the public authority. On this basis it is important the public authority understands the views provided by the third party and gives them appropriate weight. The expert view of a third party may, as long as it is reasonable, be helpful if the applicant appeals against any refusal. The views of third parties will be especially relevant in cases where it is necessary to consider the prejudice and public interest tests.

3.4   Public authorities are not required to accept views provided to them from third parties about whether or not information should be released. It is ultimately for the public authority handling the request to take the final decision on release following any consultation it undertakes.

3.5   If a decision is made to release information following consultation with a third party it will generally be best practice to give the third party advance notice or to draw it to their attention as soon as possible.

3.6   There may be occasions where information being considered by a public authority relates to a large number of third parties. If a public authority intends to release information that relates to a large number of third parties it may be helpful to contact a representative organisation who can express views on these parties' behalf rather than contacting each third party individually. Alternatively, if no representative organisation exists, public authorities can also consider only notifying or consulting a representative sample of third parties regarding the disclosure of information, but these will be case by case judgements for the relevant public authority.

4.   Time limits for responding to requests

Statutory deadlines

4.1   The statutory deadlines for public authorities to respond to requests for information are set out in section 10(1) of the Act. These make clear that public authorities must respond to requests for information promptly and within 20 working days following the date of receipt of the request.

4.2   The date on which a request is received is the day on which it arrives or, if this is not a working day, the first working day following its arrival. Non-working days include weekends and public holidays anywhere in the UK.

4.3   Some public authorities are subject to different deadlines as a result of regulations made under section 10(4) of the Act. For example, maintained schools, academies, archives, the armed forces (frontline units) and information held outside the United Kingdom at for example, embassies, have had the initial 20 working day deadline extended in certain circumstances as they may sometimes find it difficult to deal with requests under the standard deadlines. These initial deadlines cannot go beyond 60 working days following receipt of a request, except where payment of a fee is awaited (paragraph 1.19).

Public interest test extensions

4.4   Public authorities may exceed the 20 working day deadline (or, where permitted by section 10(4) regulations, longer) if information falls within the scope of a qualified exemption and additional time is required to consider the public interest test. This is set out in Section 10(3) of the Act. This is normally described as a public interest test extension.

4.5   An extension is permitted "until such time as is reasonable in the circumstances", taking account, for example, of where the information is especially complex or voluminous, or where a public authority needs to consult third parties.

4.6   In general, it is best practice for an extension to be for no more than a further 20 working days although this will depend on the circumstances of the case, including again the complexity and volume of the material, and in some circumstances a longer extension may be appropriate.

4.7 Where public authorities decide a public interest test extension is required they should write to the applicant to inform them that this is the case, stating which exemption(s) it is rely on, and why, and ideally provide the applicant with a new deadline for when they should receive their response. If the deadline has to be further extended they should write again to the applicant.

5. Internal reviews

5.1 It is best practice for each public authority to have a procedure in place for dealing with disputes about its handling of requests for information. These disputes will usually be dealt with as a request for an "internal review" of the original decision. Public authorities should distinguish between a request for an internal review, which seeks to challenge either the outcome or the process of the handling of the initial response, and a general complaint, which should be handled as general correspondence.

5.2 Public authorities are obliged, under section 17(7) of the Act, when responding to a request for information, to notify applicants of whether they have an internal review process and, if they do, to set out the details of their review procedures, including details of how applicants request an internal review. They should also inform the applicant of their right to complain to the Information Commissioner under section 50 if they are still dissatisfied following the outcome of the public authority's internal review.

5.3 It is usual practice to accept a request for an internal review made within 40 working days from the date a public authority has issued an initial response to a request and this should be made clear in that response to the applicant. Public authorities are not obliged to accept internal reviews after this date. Internal review requests should be made in writing to a public authority.

5.4 Requests for internal review should be acknowledged and the applicant informed of the target date for responding. This should normally be within 20 working days of receipt.

5.5 If an internal review is complex, requires consultation with third parties or the relevant information is of a high volume, public authorities may need longer than 20 working days to consider the issues and respond. In these instances, the public authority should inform the applicant and provide a reasonable target date by which they will be able to respond to the internal review. It is best practice for this to be no more than an additional 20 working days, although there will sometimes be legitimate reasons why a longer extension is needed.

5.6 In the event that clarification of an internal review request is required from the applicant, the normal 20 working day time period will not begin until it is received.

5.7 Public authorities who are allowed to exceed the normal 20 working day deadline as a result of regulations made under section 10(4), for example maintained schools and the armed forces, should apply the same time scales to internal reviews.

5.8   The internal review procedure should provide a fair and thorough review of procedures and decisions taken in relation to the Act. This includes decisions taken about where the public interest lies if a qualified exemption has been used. It might also include applying a different or additional exemption(s).

5.9   It is best practice, wherever possible, for the internal review to be undertaken by someone other than the person who took the original decision. The public authority should in all cases re-evaluate their handling of the request, and pay particular attention to concerns raised by the applicant.

5.10   The applicant should be informed of the outcome of their internal review and a record should be kept of all such reviews and the final decision made.

5.11   If the outcome of an internal review is a decision that information previously withheld should now be disclosed, the information should normally be provided at the same time as the applicant is informed of the outcome of the review. If this is not possible, the applicant should be informed how soon the information will be provided.

5.12   In responding to a request for an internal review, the applicant should again be informed of their right to apply to the Information Commissioner for a review of whether the public authority has met the requirements of the Act.

6.   Cost limit

6.1   Section 12 of the Act allows public authorities to refuse to deal with any requests where they estimate that responding to the request would exceed the "appropriate limit", or 'cost limit' as it is more commonly known.

6.2   If a public authority calculates that responding to a request will take it over the cost limit it is not obliged to provide a substantive response. The cost limit is calculated at a flat rate of £25 per hour. For central government departments the cost limit is £600 (24 hours) and for all other public authorities is £450 (18 hours).

6.3   Public authorities can only include certain activities when estimating whether responding to a request would breach the cost limit. These are:
- establishing whether information is held;
- locating and retrieving information; and
- extracting relevant information from the document containing it.

6.4   Other factors including redaction time or any other expenses likely to occur in cost limit calculations cannot be included when estimating whether the response would exceed the cost limit.

6.5   When calculating the cost limit public authorities can aggregate requests which ask for the same or similar information and are received within a 60 working day period. These requests can either be from the same person or a group of people acting together.

6.6   Public authorities do not have to search for information in scope of a request until the cost limit is reached, even if the applicant requests that they do so. If responding to one part of a request would exceed the cost limit, public authorities do not have to provide a response to any other parts of the request.

6.7 The cost limit can be applied on the basis of a reasonable estimate at the time the request is received. Public authorities are not under any obligation to make a precise calculation although estimates should be sensible and realistic.

6.8 Public authorities should generally focus their attention on the locations most likely to hold the relevant information. Searches may take longer, for example, where information is only held in paper records or they are organised in a way that does not lend itself to the request in question. In some cases it may be helpful to conduct a sampling exercise to help establish likely cost but this is not essential.

6.9 Where a request is refused under section 12, public authorities should consider what advice and assistance can be provided to help the applicant reframe or refocus their request with a view to bringing it within the cost limit. This may include suggesting that the subject or timespan of the request is narrowed. Any refined request should be treated as a new request for the purposes of the Act.

6.10 The cost limit should be applied before any exemption in Part II of the Act. This is because it will generally be necessary to establish whether information is held and to collate it before applying an exemption.

Vexatious requests

7.1 Under section 14(1) of the Act a public authority is not obliged to provide a substantive response to a request if the request is vexatious. Like section 12, section 14 should be considered before consideration of any exemption in Part II of the Act.

7.2 The Act does not define what makes a vexatious request, though there are a number of Tribunal cases which have offered clarity and guidance on this issue. The Information Commissioner's Office's guidance for dealing with vexatious requests gives details of these. Public authorities should consider each case on its own facts, taking into consideration the best practice factors below. Section 14(1) may be used in a number of circumstances where a request, or the impact of a request, is not justifiable or reasonable.

7.3 Public authorities should always think carefully about applying section 14. However, Section 14(1) should not be considered as something to be applied as a last resort or in exceptional circumstances.

7.4 There will be times when a request is so unreasonable or objectionable that it is clear it is a vexatious request. For example, an abusive or offensive request that causes an unjustifiable level of distress or where threats are, or have been, made against staff.

7.5 In other circumstances it may be less immediately obvious that a request should be considered as vexatious. A public authority should consider a request vexatious where the request is likely to cause a disproportionate or unjustified level of disruption, irritation or distress. Factors public authorities might therefore want to consider include:

- the burden it places on a public authority and its staff;
- the likely motives for the request;
- the potential value or purpose of the request;
- any harassment or distress to staff.

7.6   It may be helpful for a public authority to ask itself the following questions when considering whether a request is vexatious:
- What is the burden imposed on the public authority by the request?
- Is there a personal grudge behind the request?
- Is the requester unreasonably persisting in seeking information in relation to issues already addressed by the public authority?
- Does the request have any serious purpose or value?

7.7   Public authorities can also take into account the wider context of a request to help them identify whether a request should be considered vexatious. For example:
- what other requests have been made by the same requester to the public authority;
- the number and subject matter of the requests if there are multiple requests; and
- previous dealings with the requester.

Having looked at the wider context, it is then important to assess whether the evidence supports or weakens the vexatious argument.

7.8   There may also be times when a public authority considers that responding to a new request following a series of previous requests would engage section 14(1) because doing so would be disruptive or burdensome to the public authority given the volume of previous correspondence.

7.9   The following are examples public authorities may want to use when considering whether a request is vexatious:
- When an applicant has engaged in a large volume of sustained correspondence over a number of years in abusive or confrontational language.
- Contact with a public authority that can be classified as long, detailed and overlapping. For example, a scenario when a requester has written to a series of officers on the same matters, repeating requests before a public authority has had the opportunity to answer an initial request and where responding to this correspondence would be a significant distraction from the public authority's main functions.
- Where a public authority considers that there is a deliberate 'campaign' by a number of requesters to purposefully disrupt the public authority's activities and functions via a high volume of requests on the same or similar topics.

These examples should not limit public authorities from using section 14 in other circumstances, as the reasons why a request might be considered vexatious will depend on the specific factors in each case. The website of the Information Commissioner's Office publishes examples of case law on this issue which may also be helpful to public authorities when considering whether a request is vexatious.

7.10   Public authorities should also keep in mind the requirements of section 8, in particular, the requirement for applicants to provide their real name and not use a pseudonym. As set out in paragraphs 1.14 and 1.15 pseudonymous requests are not valid requests under the Act. However, the use of pseudonyms may also form part of broader considerations when considering whether or not a request, or a series of requests, should be considered vexatious.

7.11   Finally, public authorities should note that the public interest in obtaining the material does not act as a 'trump card', overriding the vexatious elements of the request and requiring the public authority to respond to the request.

Interaction between section 12 (cost limit) and 14(1) (vexatious requests)

7.12   In some cases, responding to the request is so burdensome for the public authority in terms of resources and time that the request can be refused under section 14(1). This is likely to apply in cases where it would create a very significant burden for the public authority to:

- prepare the information for publication;
- redact the information for disclosure;
- consult third parties;
- apply exemptions.

7.13   It is not possible to use section 12 (cost limit) to refuse a request based on the above factors. In these cases, public authorities may want to instead consider using section 14 to refuse to respond to the request based on the burden that responding to the request would create.

7.14   Public authorities should avoid using section 14 for burdensome requests unnecessarily. On this basis they should always consider whether section 12 applies in the first instance. For example, if a public authority considers that locating and extracting the information in scope would exceed the cost limit, section 12 is likely to be most appropriate. However, if, for the reasons set out in paragraphs 7.12 to 7.13 above, section 12 cannot apply they should consider refusing the request using section 14(1).

7.15   An example of when this may happen may include the burden of redacting multiple entries on a large database as, although it may be possible to locate the database easily, redacting relevant entries (if there are thousands of entries) may create an unsustainable burden for the authority.

Repeated requests

7.16   Under section 14(2) of the Act, if a public authority has previously complied with a request for information (i.e. provided the information sought), it does not need to comply with a further request for the same information made by the same person, unless a reasonable interval has elapsed between compliance with the first request and receipt of the second. A repeated request should be interpreted as an identical or substantially similar request. This will depend on the circumstances and each case should be considered on its own merits.

Section 14 responses

7.17   If a public authority considers section 14 applies in any circumstances other than that referred in paragraph 7.14 they should provide a refusal notice to the applicant. This should be issued within 20 working days and explain that the public authority considers section 14 to be engaged. Public authorities should also include details of their internal review procedures and the right to appeal to the Information Commissioner. There is no obligation to explain why the request is vexatious, though public authorities may wish to do so as part of their section 16 duty to provide advice and assistance.

7.18 There will be some circumstances when a public authority does not need to provide a refusal notice. Section 17(6) sets out that a public authority is not obliged to issue a refusal notice where it considers that it is unreasonable in all the circumstances to do so. For example, if a refusal notice has previously been issued for an earlier vexatious or repeated request, and the public authority does not consider it reasonable to issue a further notice. It is worth noting that although section 17(6) excludes a public authority from the duty to provide a refusal notice, the public authority is still required to establish that each request is vexatious.

7.19 Public authorities should consider keeping an ongoing evidence log to record relevant correspondence or behaviour that has been taken into account when using section 14. This will be helpful in the event the applicant complains about the handling of the request.

8.   Publication Schemes

8.1 Section 19 of the FOI Act requires all public authorities to adopt and maintain a publication scheme. This element of the Act is designed to increase transparency and allow members of the public to routinely access information relating to the functions of a public authority.

8.2 The Information Commissioner's Office has approved a model publication scheme which public authorities should use in the first instance.
Public authorities should also produce a guide to the scheme setting out:
- what information is published and by what means;
- a schedule of fees, which should set out clearly any charges for obtaining any of the information.

8.3 Publication schemes must be updated and maintained, so public authorities must have a process for reviewing published information in order to ensure it is updated at appropriate intervals. Public authorities should also follow the timescales for publication of particular types of information as set out in the Information Commissioner's Office guidance.

8.4 This Code of Practice provides more specific guidance on two areas to supplement the existing guidance by the Information Commissioner's Office.

Compliance Statistics

8.5 Public authorities with over 100 Full Time Equivalent (FTE) employees should, as a matter of best practice, publish details of their performance on handling requests for information under the Act. The information should include:
- The number of requests received during the period;
- The number of the received requests that have not yet been processed (you may also wish to show how many of these outstanding requests have extended deadlines or a stopped clock, e.g. because a fee notice has been issued);
- The number of the received requests that were processed in full (including numbers

for those that were met within the statutory deadline, those where the deadline was extended and those where the processing took longer than the statutory deadline);

- The number of requests where the information was granted in full;
- The number of requests where the information was refused in full (you may wish to separately identify those where this was because the information was not held);
- The number of requests where the information was granted in part and refused in part;
- The number of requests received that have been referred for internal review (this needs only reporting annually).

8.6   It is for individual public authorities to decide whether they wish to publish more detailed information than that set out above (they may, for example, wish to show a breakdown of the exemptions they have used for refusing requests or to show a breakdown of the outcomes for their internal reviews). When public authorities publish their statistics, they should do so on a quarterly basis, in line with central government. Publication schemes are likely to form the best vehicle for publishing this information. A guide on producing a suitable publication scheme can be found on the Information Commissioner's website.

Senior Executive Pay & Benefits

8.7   Public authorities should also ensure publication schemes contain data to deliver sufficient transparency regarding the pay and benefits of senior executives and their equivalents.

8.8   In recent years, central government departments have increased the range of data published in respect of senior officials and primarily those at Director level (SCS2) and above. There will not always be a direct read-across for other public authorities but when considering what type of information should be published, authorities should consider those at management board level as a minimum equivalent.

8.9   Public authorities should publish information that covers the following four areas:

- Pay. Senior staff who form a public authority's senior management team; for central government departments this would be staff at Director level and above. Many other public sectors have published guidance, which set out sector-relevant salary levels suitable for publication (for example, the Local Government Association's *"Local Transparency Guidance - Publishing Organisation Information"*). The Information Commissioner's Office also publishes sector-relevant advice on this issue. Names and/or job titles should also be included (see 8.10 below).
- Expenses. As above, staff on the senior management team, including elected officials and appointed representatives, if these are not already covered elsewhere. This should cover details of international and domestic travel and business expenses.
- Benefits in kind. As above. Benefits in kind refer to benefits employees receive from their employment but which are not included in their salary. Examples include, company cars, private medical insurance paid for by an employer or cheap loans. Data should be published to the nearest £100.
- Hospitality. As above. This should include any gifts, hospitality and benefits that are received from third parties (though this does not need to include small and insignificant items of hospitality, such as refreshments). This should include the name of the person or organisation that offered the gift or hospitality and the type of gift or hospitality received. This may also include additional information, such

as whether the staff member was accompanied by a spouse, family member or friend.

8.10 When publishing the names and other details of individual staff, public authorities need to bear in mind the general principle that it is acceptable to name senior managers who expect to be held publicly accountable, but that this does not extend to junior staff who do not have that same expectation. The Information Commissioner's Office generally upholds this distinction.

8.11 Public authorities should publish this type of information at regular intervals. It is recommended that information about pay should be published annually, expenses quarterly and benefits in kind annually. Public authorities can refer to the Information Commissioner's Office guidance as direction to the expected minimum level of detail. Local authorities should follow the publication requirements in the statutory Local Government Transparency Code on senior salary.

9. Transparency and confidentiality obligations in contracts and outsourced services

Transparency

9.1 As more public services are contracted out to the private sector it is important that they are delivered in a transparent way, to ensure accountability to the user and taxpayer. There will be some circumstances when contractors hold information about contractual arrangements on behalf of a public authority which will then be subject to the Act.

9.2 It is important that contractors and public authorities are clear what this information is, and that it is made readily available to the contracting public authority when it receives requests under the Act.

Information held on behalf of a contracting public authority

9.3 When entering into a contract with a third party it is likely that both the public authority and the contractor will hold information about these contractual arrangements. If a contractor holds information relating to the contract "on behalf" of a public authority, this information should be considered in the same way as information held by a public authority and so will be subject to the Act (as explained in Chapter 1). Such information would, for example, include that which a public authority has placed in the custody of a contractor (e.g. record storage) or where a contract stipulates that certain information about service delivery is held on behalf of an authority for FOI purposes.

9.4 When entering into a contract the public authority and the contractor should agree what types of information they consider will be held by the contractor on behalf of the public authority and indicate this in the contract or in an annex or schedule. They should also think about putting in place appropriate arrangements for the public authority to gain access to the information if a request is made under the Act.

9.5 These appropriate arrangements may include:
- how and when the contractor should be approached for information, and who the

contact points in each organisation are;

- how quickly the information should be provided to the public authority bearing in mind the statutory deadline for responding to the request;

- how any disagreement about disclosure between the public authority and contractor will be addressed;

- how any request for internal review or subsequent appeal to the Information Commissioner will be handled;

- the contractor's responsibility for maintaining adequate systems for record keeping in relation to information held on behalf of the public authority; and

- where the public authority itself holds the requested information, the circumstances under which the public authority must consult the contractor about disclosure and the process to be adopted in such cases.

9.6   These arrangements should, as good practice, be set out in the contract or in a related Memorandum of Understanding.

9.7   Given the statutory obligations of public authorities to respond to requests under the Act, and the fact that information held on their behalf by contractors is information subject to the Act, contractors must comply with requests by a public authority for access to such information, and must do so in a timely manner.

9.8   Requests for information held by contractors on behalf of a public authority should be answered by the public authority. Contractors receiving requests should pass them to the public authority for consideration or respond to the applicant to let them know they should direct their request to the relevant public authority.

Contract clauses

9.9   Where contractors deliver services on behalf of a public authority the contract with the public authority will need to make clear that contractors will need to fully assist the public authority with their obligations under the Act in line with the guidance set out in this chapter. The contract should include details of how non-compliance with these obligations will be dealt with. This should apply to both new and amended contracts.

9.10   If existing contracts do not set out these provisions, public authorities and contractors should consider alternatives to ensuring that the contractor provides the public authority access to information held on the public authority's behalf. Options to consider include a supplementary Memorandum of Understanding.

9.11   Public authorities may be asked to accept confidentiality clauses when entering into a contract with a third party. Public authorities should carefully consider whether these agreements are compatible with their obligations under the Act and the public interest in accountability. It is important that both the public authority and the contractor are aware of the legal limits placed on the enforceability of such confidentiality clauses [4] and the importance of making sure that the public can gain access to a wide range of information about contracts and their delivery. Public authorities should be mindful of any broader transparency obligations to publish regular details of spending, tenders and contracts on external suppliers; contracts should not hinder such transparency reporting.

---

[4]   Under common law a breach of a duty of confidentiality is not enforceable in the courts where an overriding public interest justifies the breach.

9.12 Where there is good reason to include non-disclosure provisions in a contract, however, it may be helpful for public authorities and contractors to agree the types of information which should not be disclosed within a contract and the reasons for this confidentiality.

9.13 There may also be circumstances when public authorities offer or accept confidentiality arrangements that are not set out within a contract. Public authorities should also follow the guidance set out in this chapter in these circumstances. There will be circumstances when these agreements will be appropriate in order for the public authority to receive information from a third party; hence, this information may be protected by the exemptions in the Act. It will be important that both the public authority and the third party are aware of the legal limits placed on the enforceability of expectations of confidentiality and the public interest in transparency, as well as for authorities to ensure that such expectations are created only where it is appropriate to do so.

10. Communicating with a requester

10.1 Public authorities may find the following guidance helpful for ensuring responses to requests for information and internal reviews meet the requirements set out in the Act.

10.2 Any initial response to a request for information under the Act should contain:
- A statement that the request has been dealt with under the Act;
- Confirmation that the requested information is held or not held by the public authority or a statement neither confirming or denying whether the information is held;
- The process, contact details and timescales for the public authority's internal review appeals process;
- Information about the applicant's further right of appeal to the Information Commissioner and contact details for the Information Commissioner's Office.
- If some or all of the information cannot be disclosed, details setting out why this is the case, including the sections (with subsections) the public authority is relying on if relevant. When explaining the application of named exemptions, however, public authorities are not expected to provide any information which is itself exempt.

10.3 The response to a request for an Internal Review should contain:
- Whether the Internal Reviewer agrees with the original response or not;
- Whether the reviewer considers that new exemptions are applicable and, if so, details of these exemptions and why they are engaged (to the extent they can without providing exempt information);
- Information about the applicant's further right of appeal to the Information Commissioner and contact details for the Information Commissioner's Office.

11. Datasets

11.1 Sections 11, 11A, 11B and 19 of Part I of the Act provide additional rights in relation to the disclosure and, in some cases, re-use of datasets.

11.2   The provisions governing the release of a dataset apply to all datasets held by any public authority subject to the Act.

11.3   Provisions relating to <u>re-use</u> only apply to the relatively small proportion of datasets not subject to the Re-use of Public Sector Information (PSI) Regulations 2015 . Guidance about the re-use of datasets under the FOI Act is provided in Annex B to this Code of Practice.

11.4   The Act does not require the creation of datasets for publication, nor does it require datasets to be updated if they would not otherwise have been updated as part of the public authority's function. In deciding whether to release a dataset, a public authority should consider any exemptions which may apply and in particular, the exemption in section 40 of the Act relating to personal data and the Information Commissioner's Code of Practice on Anonymisation.

11.5   These considerations should also be taken into account when considering the release of an incomplete or draft dataset. When releasing an incomplete dataset it is good practice to explain the dataset is not complete and the likely implications of this.

i.   Scope

11.6   The definition of dataset is limited to the criteria specified at section 11(5) of the Act.

11.7   The first part of the definition (subsection (5)(a)) means that the datasets caught by the Act are those datasets which a public authority has originally obtained or recorded for the purposes of providing services or carrying out its functions, including decision-making.

11.8   The second part of the definition limits datasets to factual information subject to the two criteria in subsection (5)(b). The intention behind the first criterion is to catch 'raw' or 'source' data. Calculation of information within the dataset does not count as 'analysis' or 'interpretation'. Therefore aggregated data forming a high-level dataset (such as the creation of annual figures from data that were collected weekly), form a dataset within the definition of the Act.

11.9   The second criterion excludes official statistics which are subject to their own regime of disclosure and publication, including under the Statistics and Registration Service Act 2007.

11.10 Subsection 5(c) is also intended to ensure only 'raw' or 'source' data is captured within the meaning of a dataset. The key consideration here is whether the reorganisation or adaptation represents a 'material alteration' to the original presentation of the dataset. Minor or insignificant changes to a dataset will not take it outside the definition.

11.11 The other key consideration in the definition is how much, if any, of the data in the dataset has been changed or altered. If 'all or most' of the data in the dataset meet the criteria set out in subsection 5, then the dataset will fall within the definition. Examples of where datasets will continue to fall under the definition within the Act include:
   - The original dataset used to form a new dataset;
   - Amended datasets where work has been undertaken to improve the quality of a dataset;

- Datasets that have been anonymised, or otherwise had exempt information removed.

11.12 Where information requested meets the definition of a dataset, the authority will be under a duty to provide the dataset in a re-usable format where reasonably practicable.

ii.   Disclosing datasets in an electronic form which is capable of re-use

11.13 When releasing any dataset under the Act public authorities must, as far as reasonably practicable, provide it in a re-usable format. A re-usable format is one that is machine readable, such as Comma-separated Value (CSV) format.

11.14 Where datasets are only held in non-re-usable formats, the public authority is not obliged to convert the dataset before releasing it where it is not reasonably practicable to do so.

11.15 In deciding whether it would be practicable to provide the dataset in a re-usable format, the public authority can take account of all the relevant circumstances. These circumstances may include the time and the cost involved in converting the dataset from a proprietary to a re-usable format, and the resources available to the public authority.

11.16 If the public authority concludes that it would not be reasonably practicable to provide the dataset in a re-usable format, then the public authority must still provide the dataset in another format.

iii. Standards applicable to public authorities in connection with the disclosure of a dataset

11.17 When releasing datasets public authorities should adhere to the Public Data Principles where possible. These principles are expected good practice for central government departments and recommended for the wider public sector.

11.18 It is recommended good practice that datasets will be accompanied by sufficient metadata and contextual information about how and why the dataset was compiled or created.

11.19 When procuring new data processing systems, public authorities should reference the Government Principles for Open Standards in new government information technology specifications for software interoperability, data and document formats. The Principles are compulsory for central government departments, their agencies, non-departmental public bodies and any other bodies for which they are responsible.

iv.   Cost of providing the dataset in a reusable format

11.20 If the cost of complying with the request would not exceed the appropriate limit and the information is not otherwise exempt, the public authority must provide the dataset (subject to any right to charge a fee). If the requester expresses a preference for the dataset in electronic form, the public authority must provide it in a reusable format, so far as reasonably practicable. A public authority may not charge for the cost of providing the dataset in a reusable format, but, in deciding whether it would be reasonably practicable to provide it in that format, it can take account of the cost, time and resources that would be involved.

v.   Publication of datasets as part of a publication scheme

11.21 Public authorities should consider publishing existing and newly created datasets as part of their publication scheme. If the dataset would be released on request, the public authority should consider publishing it through the public authority's publication scheme.

11.22 Public authorities should consider their long term plans and processes for the collection and storage of datasets, keeping in mind that they should be made easily accessible and in a re-usable format for requests or publication as part of their publication scheme as well as for normal business purposes.

11.23 When publishing a dataset on their website, public authorities, should, where possible, publish it in a machine readable format, so that the data can be directly downloaded from a given URL.

11.24 If a dataset has been requested from a public authority under the Act, then the authority must publish that dataset in accordance with its publication scheme unless the public authority is satisfied that it would not be appropriate to publish it. If the public authority holds an updated version of the dataset it must also publish the updated version, unless it is satisfied that it is not appropriate to do so.

11.25 When the public authority publishes the dataset under its publication scheme, it must (as for responding to a request) provide it in an electronic form that is capable of re-use, where it is reasonably practicable to do so.

Annex A – Table of FOI Act Exemption Clauses

Not reproduced

Annex B – Re-use of datasets

As well as providing additional rights in relation to the disclosure of datasets, the Act also provides for the re-use of datasets not subject to the Re-use of Public Sector Information (PSI) Regulations 2015. The National Archives has provided separate guidance about the re-use of information in accordance with those Regulations.

Only where the PSI Regulations do not apply, should re-use be considered under the Act. They do not apply to datasets held by educational and research establishments, public service broadcasters, cultural or performing arts bodies (other than public sector museums, libraries and archives), or when held by other public authorities for purposes unrelated to their public task. The easiest way for a public authority to comply with the licensing requirements of both FOI and PSI is to make datasets available for re-use under the Open Government Licence, where appropriate.

Giving permission for datasets to be re-used

Public authorities should release datasets with accompanying details of licence conditions that apply to the re-use of the dataset or any limitation on re-use by virtue of third party intellectual property rights.

Consideration should also be given to the extent to which such information is exempt from disclosure under sections 41 and 43(2) of the Act.

The public authority should ascertain whether copyright and/or database rights ('intellectual property') in the dataset are owned solely by the authority or whether there is a third party interest. Nothing in the Act's re-use provisions overrides the rights of any third parties who may own intellectual property contained in the datasets. If a public authority grants a licence to re-use a dataset or part of a dataset containing third party intellectual property without the owner's permission it may constitute an infringement of the third party's rights.

Where there is a third party interest any re-use licence must permit re-use only of those parts of the dataset that the public authority owns. If possible, and subject to any confidentiality requirements, the public authority should identify the requester who owns the remainder of the rights.

In some cases the public authority may be able to obtain the third party's permission to grant the re-use of the third party intellectual property outside the Act.

UK government policy is that, wherever possible, Crown Copyright material should be made available for re-use. If in doubt it is advisable to seek legal advice.

Licensing

If the dataset that is being provided, or any part of it, is a relevant copyright work owned solely by the public authority, the public authority must make that work available for re-use in accordance with the terms of one of the licences specified in the following paragraphs. The UK Government Licensing Framework (UKGLF) provides an overview of the arrangements for licensing the use and re-use of public sector information. The starting point is that public authorities are encouraged to use the Open Government Licence for datasets which can be re-used without charge.

The Open Government Licence is the default licensing model for most Crown copyright information produced by the UK Government and supplied without charge. It is a non-transactional open licence which enables use and re-use with virtually no restrictions. It is applicable when use and re-use, including for commercial purposes, is at no cost to the user/re-user. Established as part of a wider UK Government Licensing Framework, it is hosted on The National Archives website .

It is recognised that the Open Government Licence will not be appropriate in all cases, for example, in circumstances where information may only be used for non-commercial purposes. The Non-Commercial Government Licence was developed to incorporate that situation. As with the Open Government Licence, public authorities can link to the Non-Commercial Government Licence on The National Archives website. Where a public authority charges a fee for the re-use of a dataset, it must do so in accordance with the Charged Licence. The licence consists of standard licensing terms and, like the above licences, forms part of the UK Government Licensing Framework. It can also be accessed on The National Archives website .

Costs and fees

It is important to distinguish between the cost to the public authority of disclosing a dataset (including in a re-usable format), and the fees that can be charged to the applicant for making a dataset available for re-use under section 11A (or, where relevant, the equivalent charging provisions in the PSI).

The Freedom of Information (Fees for Re-use of Datasets) Regulations 2013 provide that public authorities may charge a fee for making relevant copyright works available for re-use, unless it already has another applicable statutory power to charge. If a public authority wishes to charge a fee, and is already entitled to do so under any other applicable legislation for the re-use of the relevant copyright work, then it must do so on that other statutory basis instead of these regulations.

Lord Chancellor's Code of Practice
on the management of records

Issued under section 46 of the Freedom of Information Act 2000

Presented to Parliament by the Lord Chancellor pursuant to
section 46(6) of the Freedom of Information Act 2000

Code of Practice

Foreword

Introduction

(i)   The Code of Practice ("the Code") which follows fulfils the duty of the Lord Chancellor set out in section 46 of the Freedom of Information Act 20001 (the Act). This foreword provides background but does not form part of the Code itself.

(ii)   The Code is in two parts. In Part 1, the Code provides guidance to all relevant authorities as to the practice which it would, in the opinion of the Lord Chancellor, be desirable for them to follow in connection with the keeping, management and destruction of their records. This applies not only to public authorities but also to other bodies that are subject to the Public Records Act 1958 or the Public Records Act (Northern Ireland) 1923. Collectively they are called relevant authorities.

(iii)   The Code also describes, in Part 2, the procedure to be followed for timely and effective review and transfer of public records to The National Archives or to a place of deposit (as defined in section 4 of the Public Records Act 1958) or to the Public Record Office of Northern Ireland under the Public Records Act 1958 or the Public Records Act (Northern Ireland) 1923.

Importance of records management

(iv)   Freedom of information legislation is only as good as the quality of the records and other information to which it provides access. Access rights are of limited value if information cannot be found when requested or, when found, cannot be relied upon as authoritative. Good records and information management benefits those requesting information because it provides some assurance that the information provided will be complete and reliable. It benefits those holding the requested information because it enables them to locate and retrieve it easily within the statutory timescales or to explain why it is not held. It also supports control and delivery of information promised in an authority's Publication Scheme or required to be published by the Environmental Information Regulations 2004 (the EIR).

(v)   Records management is important for many other reasons. Records and information are the lifeblood of any organisation. They are the basis on which decisions are made, services provided and policies developed and communicated. Effective management of records and other information brings the following additional benefits:

- It supports an authority's business and discharge of its functions, promotes business efficiency and underpins service delivery by ensuring that authoritative information about past activities can be retrieved, used and relied upon in current business;

- It supports compliance with other legislation which requires records and information to be kept, controlled and accessible, such as the Data Protection Act 1998, employment legislation and health and safety legislation;

- It improves accountability, enabling compliance with legislation and other rules and requirements to be demonstrated to those with a right to audit or otherwise investigate the organisation and its actions;

- It enables protection of the rights and interests of an authority, its staff and its stakeholders;

- It increases efficiency and cost-effectiveness by ensuring that records are disposed of when no longer needed. This enables more effective use of resources, for example space within buildings and information systems, and saves staff time searching for information that may not be there;

- It provides institutional memory.

(vi) Poor records and information management create risks for the authority, such as:

- Poor decisions based on inaccurate or incomplete information; . Inconsistent or poor levels of service;

- Financial or legal loss if information required as evidence is not available or cannot be relied upon;

- Non-compliance with statutory or other regulatory requirements, or with standards that apply to the sector to which it belongs;

- Failure to handle confidential information with an appropriate level of security and the possibility of unauthorised access or disposal taking place;

- Failure to protect information that is vital to the continued functioning of the organisation, leading to inadequate business continuity planning;

- Unnecessary costs caused by storing records and other information for longer than they are needed;

- Staff time wasted searching for records;

- Staff time wasted considering issues that have previously been addressed and resolved;

- Loss of reputation as a result of all of the above, with damaging effects on public trust.

(vii) The Code is a supplement to the provisions in the Act and its adoption will help authorities comply with their duties under the Act. Consequently, all relevant authorities are strongly encouraged to pay heed to the guidance in the Code. The Code is complemented by the Code of Practice under section 45 of the Act and the Code of Practice under Regulation 16 of the EIR.

(viii) Authorities should note that if they fail to comply with the Code, they may also fail to comply with legislation relating to the creation, management, disposal, use and re-use of records and information, for example the Public Records Act 1958, the Data Protection Act 1998, and the of their statutory obligations.

Role of the Information Commissioner

(ix) The Information Commissioner has a duty under section 47 of the Act to promote the following of good practice by public authorities and in particular to promote observance of the requirements of the Act and the provisions of this Code of Practice. In order to carry out that duty specifically in relation to the Code, the Act confers a number of powers on the Commissioner.

Practice recommendations

(x) If it appears to the Information Commissioner that the practice of an authority in relation to the exercise of its functions under the Act does not conform to that set out in the Code, the Commissioner may issue a practice recommendation under section 48 of the Act. A practice recommendation will be in writing and will specify the provisions of the Code that have not been met and the steps that should, in the Commissioner's opinion, be taken to promote conformity with the Code. A practice recommendation cannot be directly enforced by the Information Commissioner. However, a failure to comply with a practice recommendation may lead to a failure to comply with the Act or could lead to an adverse comment in a report to Parliament by the Information Commissioner.

Information Notices

(xi)   If the Information Commissioner reasonably requires any information in order to determine whether the practice of an authority conforms with that recommended in the Code, he may serve on the authority a notice (known as an 'information notice') under section 51 of the Act. An information notice will be in writing and will require the authority to provide the Information Commissioner with specified information relating to conformity with the Code. It will also contain particulars of the rights of appeal conferred by section 57 of the Act.

Enforcement of information notices

(xii)   Under section 54 of the Act, if an authority fails to comply with an information notice, the Information Commissioner may certify in writing to the court that the authority has failed to comply. The court may then inquire into the matter and, after hearing any witnesses who may be produced against or on behalf of the authority, and after hearing any statement that may be offered in defence, deal with the authority as if it had committed a contempt of court.

Authorities subject to the Public Records Acts

(xiii) The Code should be read in the context of existing legislation affecting the management of records. In particular, the Public Records Act 1958 (as amended) gives duties to bodies subject to that Act in respect of the records they create or hold. It also requires the Chief Executive of The National Archives to supervise the discharge of those duties.

(xiv)   The Public Records Act (Northern Ireland) 1923 sets out the duties of public record bodies in Northern Ireland in respect of the records they create and requires that records should be transferred to, and preserved by, the Public Record Office of Northern Ireland. The title 'Keeper of Public Records' is used in the Public Records Act 1958 and the Freedom of Information Act 2000. This is one of the titles of the Chief Executive of The National Archives. The title 'Chief Executive of The National Archives' is used in this Code in recognition of the fact that it is the title used for operational purposes.

(xv)   The Information Commissioner will promote the observance of the Code in consultation with the Chief Executive of The National Archives when dealing with bodies which are subject to the Public Records Act 1958 and with the Deputy Keeper of the Records of Northern Ireland for bodies subject to the Public Records Act (Northern Ireland) 1923. Before issuing a practice recommendation under section 48 of the Act to a body subject to either of the Public Records Acts, the Information Commissioner will consult the Chief Executive of The National Archives or the Deputy Keeper of the Records of Northern Ireland as appropriate.

Role of the Lord Chancellor's Advisory Council on National Records and Archives and the

Sensitivity Review Group in Northern Ireland

(xvi) The Advisory Council on National Records and Archives (hereafter 'the Advisory Council') has a statutory role to advise the Lord Chancellor on matters concerning public records in general and on the application of the Act to information in public records that are historical records. The Lord Chancellor, having received the advice of his Advisory Council, may prepare and issue guidance. The guidance may include advice on the review of public records and on the periods of time for which the Advisory Council considers it appropriate to withhold categories of sensitive records after they have become historical records.

(xvii) The National Archives provides support as appropriate to the Advisory Council in its consideration of applications from authorities relating to retention or access to public records and in its preparation of guidance for the Lord Chancellor to issue to authorities.

(xviii) In Northern Ireland the Sensitivity Review Group, consisting of representatives of Northern Ireland departments, provides advice on the release of public records. The Public Record Office of Northern Ireland provides support to the Group. Guidance may be issued by the Deputy Keeper of the Records of Northern Ireland following consultation with the Departments responsible for the records affected by the guidance. The legal entity to which this provision applies is the Advisory Council on Public Records. Since April 2003 the Council has functioned as The Advisory Council on National Records and Archives and so that name is used in this Code. 7In this context, the term 'public records' applies only to the records of bodies that are subject to the Public Records Act 1958. The term 'historical record' is defined at section 62 of the Act.

Code of Practice

The Lord Chancellor, having consulted the Information Commissioner and the appropriate Northern Ireland Minister, issues the following Code of Practice pursuant to section 46 of the Freedom of Information Act 2000.

Laid before Parliament on 16 July 2009 pursuant to section 46(6) of the Freedom of Information Act 2000.

INTRODUCTION

Aims of the Code

1.1 The aims of the Code are:

- To set out the practices which relevant authorities should follow in relation to the creation, keeping, management and destruction of their records (Part 1 of the Code); and

- To describe the arrangements which bodies responsible for public records should follow in reviewing public records and transferring them to The National Archives or to a place of deposit for public records, or to the Public Record Office of Northern Ireland (Part 2 of the Code).

1.2. Part 1 of the Code provides a framework for relevant authorities to manage their records. It sets out recommended good practice for the organisational arrangements, decisions and processes required for effective records and information management.

1.3   Part 2 provides a framework for the review and transfer of public records that have been selected for permanent preservation at The National Archives, a place of deposit for public records or the Public Record Office of Northern Ireland. It sets out the process by which records due for transfer are assessed to determine whether the information they contain can be designated as open information or, if this is not possible, to identify the exemptions that apply and indicate for how long they should apply. Relevant authorities is the collective term used in the Act for bodies that are public authorities under the Freedom of Information Act and bodies that are not subject to that Act but are subject to the Public Records Act 1958 or the Public Records Act (Northern Ireland) 1923. Public records are the records of bodies that are subject to the Public Records 1958 or the Public Records Act (Northern Ireland) 1923. For the avoidance of doubt, the term 'public records' includes Welsh public records as defined by section 148 of the Government of Wales Act 2006. The legal entity to which this provision applies is the Public Record Office. Since April 2003 the Public Record Office has functioned as part of The National Archives and is known by that name. For that reason the name 'The National Archives' is used in this Code. In the Environmental Information Regulations 2004 (the EIR), exemptions are called exceptions. For simplicity the term exemption is used throughout the Code and should be taken to apply also to exceptions in the EIR.

Scope of the Code

2.   The Code applies to all records irrespective of the technology used to create and store them or the type of information they contain. It includes, therefore, not only paper files series and digital records management systems but also business and information systems (for example case management, finance and geographical information systems) and the contents of websites. The Code's focus is on records and the systems that contain them but the principles and recommended practice can be applied also to other information held by an authority.

Interpretation

3.   For the purposes of this Code, 'records' are defined as in the relevant British Standard13, namely 'information created, received, and maintained as evidence and information by an organization or person, in pursuance of legal obligations or in the transaction of business'. Some specific terms which are not defined in the Act have been included in the Glossary at Annex A. Other words and expressions used in this Code have the same meaning as the same words and expressions used in the Act.

Supplementary guidance

4.   More detailed guidance on both parts of the Code has been published separately. Standards and guidance which support the objectives of this Code most directly are listed at Annex B.

PART 1: RECORDS MANAGEMENT

Summary of recommended good practice in records management

5.1   Good practice in records management is made up of a number of key elements. The following list summarises the good practice recommended in Part 1 of the Code. Guidance on each element is given in sections 6-14 of this Part.

a) Authorities should have in place organisational arrangements that support records management (see section 6);

b) Authorities should have in place a records management policy, either as a separate policy or as part of a wider information or knowledge management policy (see section 7);

c) Authorities should ensure they keep the records they will need for business, regulatory, legal and accountability purposes (see section 8);

d) Authorities should keep their records in systems that enable records to be stored and retrieved as necessary (see section 9);

e) Authorities should know what records they hold and where they are, and should ensure that they remain usable for as long as they are required (see section 10);

f) Authorities should ensure that records are stored securely and that access to them is controlled (see section 11);

g) Authorities should define how long they need to keep particular records, should dispose of them when they are no longer needed and should be able to explain why records are no longer held (see section 12);

h) Authorities should ensure that records shared with other bodies or held on their behalf by other bodies are managed in accordance with the Code (see section 13);

i) Authorities should monitor compliance with the Code and assess the overall effectiveness of the programme (see section 14).

Organisational arrangements to support records management

6. Authorities should have in place organisational arrangements that support records management.

6.1 These arrangements should include:

a) Recognition of records management as a core corporate function, either separately or as part of a wider information or knowledge management function. The function should cover records in all formats throughout their lifecycle, from planning and creation through to disposal and should include records managed on behalf of the authority by an external body such as a contractor;

b) Inclusion of records and information management in the corporate risk management framework. Information and records are a corporate asset and loss of the asset could cause disruption to business. The level of risk will vary according to the strategic and operational value of the asset to the authority and risk management should reflect the probable extent of disruption and resulting damage;

c) A governance framework that includes defined roles and lines of responsibility. This should include allocation of lead responsibility for the records and information management function to a designated member of staff at sufficiently senior level to act as a records management champion, for example a board member, and allocation of operational responsibility to a member of staff with the necessary knowledge and skills. In small authorities it may be more practicable to combine these roles. Ideally the same people will be responsible also for compliance with other information legislation, for example the Data Protection Act 1998 and the

Re-use of Public Sector Information Regulations 2005, or will work closely with those people;

d) Clearly defined instructions, applying to staff at all levels of the authority, to create, keep and manage records. In larger organisations the responsibilities of managers, and in particular heads of business units, could be differentiated from the responsibilities of other staff by making it clear that managers are responsible for ensuring that adequate records are kept of the activities for which they are accountable;

e) Identification of information and business systems that hold records and provision of the resources needed to maintain and protect the integrity of those systems and the information they contain;

f) Consideration of records management issues when planning or implementing ICT systems, when extending staff access to new technologies and during re-structuring or major changes to the authority;

g) Induction and other training to ensure that all staff are aware of the authority's records management policies, standards, procedures and guidelines and understand their personal responsibilities. This should be extended to temporary staff, contractors and consultants who are undertaking work that it has been decided should be documented in the authority's records. If the organisation is large enough to employ staff whose work is primarily about records and information management, they should be given opportunities for professional development;

h) An agreed programme for managing records in accordance with this part of the Code;

i) Provision of the financial and other resources required to achieve agreed objectives in the records management programme.

Records management policy

7. Authorities should have in place a records management policy, either as a separate policy or as part of a wider information or knowledge management policy.

7.1 The policy should be endorsed by senior management, for example at board level, and should be readily available to staff at all levels.

7.2 The policy provides a mandate for the records and information management function and a framework for supporting standards, procedures and guidelines. The precise contents will depend on the particular needs and culture of the authority but it should as a minimum:

a) Set out the authority's commitment to create, keep and manage records which document its principal activities;

b) Outline the role of records management and its relationship to the authority's overall business strategy;

c) Identify and make appropriate connections to related policies, such as those dealing with email, information security and data protection;

d) Define roles and responsibilities, including the responsibility of individuals to document their work in the authority's records to the extent that, and in the way that, the authority has decided their work should be documented, and to use those records appropriately;

e) Indicate how compliance with the policy and the supporting standards, procedures and guidelines will be monitored.

7.3 The policy should be kept up-to-date so that it reflects the current needs of the authority. One way of ensuring this is to review it at agreed intervals, for example every three or five years, and after major organisational or technological changes, in order to assess whether it needs amendment.

7.4 The authority should consider publishing the policy so that members of the public can see the basis on which it manages its records.

Keeping records to meet corporate requirements
8. Authorities should ensure they keep the records they will need for business, regulatory, legal and accountability purposes.

Deciding what records should be kept
8.1 Authorities should consider what records they are likely to need about their activities, and the risks of not having those records, taking into account the following factors:

a) The legislative and regulatory environment within which they operate. This will be a mixture of generally applicable legislation, such as health and safety legislation and the Data Protection Act 1998, and specific legislation applying to the sector or authority. For example, the Charity Commission is required by its legislation to keep an accurate and up-to-date register of charities. This factor also includes standards applying to the sector or authority or to particular functions such as finance;

b) The need to refer to authoritative information about past actions and decisions for current business purposes. For example, problems such as outbreaks of foot and mouth disease may recur and in order to deal with each new outbreak a local authority needs reliable information about what it did during previous outbreaks and who was responsible for specific measures, such as closing public footpaths;

c) The need to protect legal and other rights of the authority, its staff and its stakeholders. For example, a local authority needs to know what land and buildings it owns in order to ensure proper control of its assets and to protect itself if challenged;

d) The need to explain, and if necessary justify, past actions in the event of an audit, public inquiry or other investigation. For example, the Audit Commission will expect to find accurate records of expenditure of public funds. Or, if an applicant complains to the Information Commissioner's Office (ICO) about the handling or outcome of an FOI request, the ICO will expect the authority to provide details of how the request was handled and, if applicable, why it refused to provide the information.

8.2 Having considered these factors, authorities should set business rules identifying:

a) What records should be kept, for example which decisions or actions should be recorded;

b) By whom this should be done, for example, by the sender or recipient of an email or voicemail;

c) At what point in the process or transaction this should be done, for example when drafts of a document should be frozen and kept as a record;

d) What those records should contain;

e) Where and how they should be stored, for example in a case file.

8.3   As part of this process authorities should consider whether any of these records should be subject to particular controls so as to ensure their evidential value can demonstrated if required by showing them to:

a) Be authentic, that is, they are what they say they are;

b) Be reliable, that is, they can be trusted as a full and accurate record;

c) Have integrity, that is, they have not been altered since they were created or filed;

d) Be usable, that is, they can be retrieved, read and used.

Ensuring those records are kept

8.4   All staff should be aware of which records the authority has decided to keep and of their personal responsibility to follow the authority's business rules and keep accurate and complete records as part of their daily work. Managers of business units, programmes and projects should take responsibility for ensuring that the agreed records of the unit, programme or project's work are kept and are available for corporate use.

8.5   Authorities should ensure that staff creating or filing records are aware of the need to give those records titles that reflect their specific nature and contents so as to facilitate retrieval.

8.6   Staff should also be aware of the need to dispose of ephemeral material on a routine basis. For example, print-outs of electronic documents should not be kept after the meeting for which they were printed, trivial emails should be deleted after being read, and keeping multiple or personal copies of documents should be discouraged.

Records systems

9.   Authorities should keep their records in systems that enable records to be stored and retrieved as necessary.

Choosing, implementing and using records systems

9.1   Authorities should decide the format in which their records are to be stored. There is no requirement in this Code for records and information to be created and held electronically, but if the authority is operating electronically, for example using email for internal and external communications or creating documents through word processing software, it is good practice to hold the resulting records electronically. In addition, authorities should note that the EIR require them progressively to make environmental information available to the public by electronic means (Regulation 4).

9.2   Authorities are likely to hold records and other information in a number of different systems. These systems could include a dedicated electronic document and records management system, business systems such as a case management, finance or geographical information system, a website, shared workspaces, audio-visual material and sets of paper files with related registers. In some cases related records of the same business activities may be held in different formats, for example digital files and supporting paper material.

9.3   Records systems should be designed to meet the authority's operational needs and using them should be an integral part of business operations and processes. Records systems should have the following characteristics:

a) They should be easy to understand and use so as to reduce the effort required of those who create and use the records within them. Ease of use is an important consideration when developing or selecting a system;

b) They should enable quick and easy retrieval of information. With digital systems this should include the capacity to search for information requested under the Act;

c) They should be set up in a way that enables routine records management processes to take place. For example, digital systems should be able to delete specified information in accordance with agreed disposal dates and leave the rest intact;

d) They should enable the context of each record and its relationship to other records to be understood. In a records management system this can be achieved by classifying and indexing records within a file plan or business classification scheme to bring together related records and enable the sequence of actions and context of each document to be understood. This approach has the added benefit of enabling handling decisions, for example relating to access or disposal, to be applied to groups of records instead of to individual records;

e) They should contain both information and metadata. Metadata enables the system to be understood and operated efficiently, the records within the system to be managed and the information within the records to be interpreted;

f) They should protect records in digital systems from accidental or unauthorised alteration, copying, movement or deletion;

g) They should provide secure storage to the level of protection required by the nature, contents and value of the information in them. For digital systems this includes a capacity to control access to particular information if necessary, for example by limiting access to named individuals or by requiring passwords. With paper files this includes a capacity to lock storage cupboards or areas and to log access to them and any withdrawal of records from them;

h) They should enable an audit trail to be produced of occasions on which selected records have been seen, used, amended and deleted.

9.4   Records systems should be documented to facilitate staff training, maintenance of the system and its reconstruction in the event of an emergency.

Limiting the active life of records within record systems

9.5   Folders, files and similar record assemblies should not remain live indefinitely with a capacity for new records to be added to them. They should be closed, that is, have their contents frozen, at an appropriate time.

9.6   The trigger for closure will vary according to the nature and function of the records, the extent to which they reflect ongoing business and the technology used to store them. For example, completion of the annual accounting process could be a trigger for closing financial records, completion of a project could be a trigger for closing project records, and completion of formalities following the death of a patient could be a trigger for closing that person's health record. Size is a factor and a folder should not be too big to be handled or scrutinised easily. For digital records a trigger could be migration to a new system. Authorities should decide the appropriate trigger for each records system and put arrangements in place to apply the trigger.

9.7 New continuation or part files should be opened if necessary. It should be clear to anyone looking at a record where the story continues, if applicable.

Storage and maintenance of records

10. Authorities should know what records they hold and where they are, and should ensure that they remain usable for as long as they are required.

Knowing what records are held

10.1 The effectiveness of records systems depends on knowledge of what records are held, what information they contain, in what form they are made accessible, what value they have to the organisation and how they relate to organisational functions. Without this knowledge an authority will find it difficult to:

    a) Locate and retrieve information required for business purposes or to respond to an information request;

    b) Produce a Publication Scheme or a reliable list of information assets available for re-use;

    c) Apply the controls required to manage risks associated with the records; d) Ensure records are disposed of when no longer needed.

10.2 Authorities should gather and maintain data on records and information assets. This can be done in various ways, for example through surveys or audits of the records and information held by the authority. It should be held in an accessible format and should be kept up to date.

10.3 Authorities should consider publishing details of the types of records they hold to help members of the public planning to make a request for information under the Act.

Storing records

10.4 Storage should provide protection to the level required by the nature, contents and value of the information in them. Records and information will vary in their strategic and operational value to the authority, and in their residual value for historical research, and storage and preservation arrangements reflecting their value should be put in place.

10.5 Authorities should be aware of any specific requirements for records storage that apply to them. For example, the Adoption National Minimum Standards issued by the Department of Health and the Welsh Assembly Government in 2003 require indexes and case files for children to be securely stored to minimise the risk of damage from fire or water.

10.6 Storage should follow accepted standards in respect of the storage environment, fire precautions, health and safety and, if applicable, physical organisation. It should allow easy and efficient retrieval of information but also minimise the risk of damage, loss or unauthorised access.

10.7   Records that are no longer required for frequent reference can be removed from current systems to off-line or near off-line (for digital media) or to off-site (for paper) storage where this is a more economical and efficient way to store them. They should continue to be subject to normal records management controls and procedures.

10.8   The whereabouts of records should be known at all times and movement of files and other physical records between storage areas and office areas should be logged.

Ensuring records remain usable

10.9   Records should remain usable for as long as they are required. This means that it should continue to be possible to retrieve, use and rely on them.

10.10 Records in digital systems will not remain usable unless precautions are taken. Authorities should put in place a strategy for their continued maintenance designed to ensure that information remains intact, reliable and usable for as long as it is required. The strategy should provide for updating of the storage media and migration of the software format within which the information and metadata are held, and for regular monitoring of integrity and usability.

10.11 Records in digital systems are particularly vulnerable to accidental or unauthorised alteration, copying, movement or deletion which can happen without trace. This puts at risk the reliability of the records which could damage the authority's interests. Authorities should assess these risks and put appropriate safeguards in place.

10.12 Back-up copies of records in digital systems should be kept and stored securely in a separate location. They should be checked regularly to ensure that the storage medium has not degraded and the information remains intact and capable of being restored to operational use. Back-ups should be managed in a way that enables disposal decisions to be applied securely without compromising the authority's capacity to recover from system failures and major disasters.

10.13 Physical records such as paper files may also require regular monitoring. For example, formats such as early photocopies may be at risk of fading, and regular checks should be made of any information in such formats that is of continuing value to the authority.

10.14 Metadata for records in any format should be kept in such a way that it remains reliable and accessible for as long as it is required, which will be at least for the life of the records.

Business continuity plans

10.15 Business continuity plans should identify and safeguard records considered vital to the organisation, that is:

    a) Records that would be essential to the continued functioning or reconstitution of the organisation in the event of a disaster;

    b) Records that are essential to ongoing protection of the organisation's legal and financial rights.

The plans should include actions to protect and recover these records in particular.

Security and access

11.   Authorities should ensure that records are stored securely and that access to them is controlled.

11.1   Authorities should ensure that their storage arrangements, handling procedures and arrangements for transmission of records reflect accepted standards and good practice in information security. It is good practice to have an information security policy addressing these points.

11.2   Ease of internal access will depend on the nature and sensitivity of the records. Access restrictions should be applied when necessary to protect the information concerned and should be kept up to date. Particular care should be taken with personal information about living individuals in order to comply with the 7th data protection principle, which requires precautions against unauthorised or unlawful processing, damage, loss or destruction. Within central Government, particular care should be taken with information bearing a protective marking. Other information, such as information obtained on a confidential basis, may also require particular protection.

11.3   Transmission of records, especially outside the authority's premises, should require authorisation. The method of transmission should be subject to risk assessment before a decision is made.

11.4   External access should be provided in accordance with relevant legislation.

11.5   An audit trail should be kept of provision of access, especially to people outside the immediate work area.

Disposal of records

12.   Authorities should define how long they need to keep particular records, should dispose of them when they are no longer needed and should be able to explain why records are no longer held.

12.1   For the purpose of this Code, disposal means the decision as to whether the record should be destroyed, transferred to an archives service for permanent preservation or presented, and the putting into effect of that decision.

General principle

12.2   As a general principle, records should be kept for as long as they are needed by the authority: for reference or accountability purposes, to comply with regulatory requirements or to protect legal and other rights and interests. Destruction at the end of this period ensures that office and server space are not used and costs are not incurred in maintaining records that are no longer required. For records containing personal information it also ensures compliance with the 5th data protection principle which requires that personal data is kept only for as long as it is needed.

12.3   Records should not be kept after they have ceased to be of use to the authority unless:

a)   They are known to be the subject of litigation or a request for information. If so, destruction should be delayed until the litigation is complete or, in the case of a request for information, all relevant complaint and appeal provisions have been exhausted;

b)   They have long-term value for historical or other research and have been or should be selected for permanent preservation. (Note that records containing personal information can be kept indefinitely for historical research purposes because they thereby become exempt from the 5th data protection principle.)

c)   They contain or relate to information recently released in response to a request under the Act. This may indicate historical value and destruction should be delayed while this is re-assessed.

Making disposal decisions

12.4 Disposal of records should be undertaken only in accordance with clearly established policies that:

a) Reflect the authority's continuing need for access to the information or the potential value of the records for historical or other research;

b) Are based on consultation between records management staff, staff of the relevant business unit and, where appropriate, others such as legal advisers, archivists or external experts;

c) Have been formally adopted by the authority;

d) Are applied by properly authorised staff;

e) Take account of security and confidentiality needs.

12.5 The policies should take the form of:

a) An overall policy, stating in broad terms the types of records likely to be selected for permanent preservation. The policy could be a separate policy, part of the records management policy or a preamble to a disposal schedule;

b) Disposal schedules which identify and describe records to which a pre-defined disposal action can be applied, for example destroy x years after [trigger event]; review after y years, transfer to archives for permanent preservation after z years.

12.6 Disposal schedules should contain sufficient details about the records to enable the records to be easily identified and the disposal action applied to them on a routine and timely basis. The amount of detail in disposal schedules will depend on the authority's needs but they should at least:

a) Describe the records, including any relevant reference numbers;

b) Identify the function to which the records relate and the business unit for that function (if that is not clear);

c) Specify the retention period, i.e. how long they are to be kept;

d) Specify what is to happen to them at the end of that period, i.e. the disposal action;

e) Note the legal, regulatory or other reason for the disposal period and action, for example a statutory provision.

Disposal schedules should be arranged in the way that best meets the authority's needs.

12.7 Disposal schedules should be kept up to date and should be amended if a relevant statutory provision changes. However, authorities should consider keeping information about previous provisions so that the basis on which records were previously destroyed can be explained.

12.8 If any records are not included in disposal schedules, special arrangements should be made to review them and decide whether they can be destroyed or should be selected for permanent preservation. Decisions of this nature should be documented and kept to provide evidence of which records have been identified for destruction, when the decision was made, and the reasons for the decision, where this is not apparent from the overall policy.

Implementing disposal decisions

12.9   Disposal schedules and disposal decisions should be implemented by properly authorised staff. Implementation arrangements should take account of variations caused by, for example, outstanding requests for information or litigation.

12.10   Records scheduled for destruction should be destroyed in as secure a manner as required by the level of confidentiality or security markings they bear. For example, records containing personal information about living individuals should be destroyed in a way that prevents unauthorised access (this is required to comply with the 7th data protection principle). With digital records it may be necessary to do more than overwrite the data to ensure the information is destroyed. Some authorities use the term 'retention schedules'. Because 'retention' has a specific meaning in Part 2 of the Code, the term disposal schedules is used throughout the Code.

12.11   When destruction is carried out by an external contractor, the contract should stipulate that the security and access arrangements established for the records will continue to be applied until destruction has taken place.

12.12   In some cases there will be more than one copy of a record. For example, there are likely to be back-up copies of digital records, or there may be digital copies of paper records. A record cannot be considered to have been completely destroyed until all copies, including back-up copies, have been destroyed, if there is a possibility that the data could be recovered.

Documenting the destruction of records

12.13   Details of destruction of records should be kept, either as part of the audit trail metadata or separately. Ideally, some evidence of destruction should be kept indefinitely because the previous existence of records may be relevant information. However, the level of detail and for how long it should be kept will depend on an assessment of the costs and the risks to the authority if detailed information cannot be produced on request.

12.14   At the very least it should be possible to provide evidence that as part of routine records management processes destruction of a specified type of record of a specified age range took place in accordance with a specified provision of the disposal schedule. Evidence of this nature will enable an authority and its staff to explain why records specified in a court order cannot be provided or to defend themselves against a charge under section 77 of the Act that records were destroyed in order to prevent their disclosure in response to a request for information.

Records for permanent preservation

12.15   Records selected for permanent preservation and no longer required by the authority should be transferred to an archives service that has adequate storage and public access facilities. Transfer should take place in an orderly manner and with a level of security appropriate to the confidentiality of the records.

12.16   Part 2 of the Code sets out the arrangements that apply to the review and transfer of public records. The approach set out in Part 2 may be relevant to the review and transfer of other types of records also.

Records created in the course of collaborative working or through out-sourcing

13. Authorities should ensure that records shared with other bodies or held on their behalf by other bodies are managed in accordance with the Code.

13.1 When authorities are working in partnership with other organisations, sharing information and contributing to a joint records system, they should ensure that all parties agree protocols that specify:

   a) What information should be contributed and kept, and by whom;

   b) What level of information security should be applied;

   c) Who should have access to the records;

   d) What disposal arrangements should be in place;

   e) Which body holds the information for the purposes of the Act.

13.2 Instructions and training should be provided to staff involved in such collaborative working.

13.3 Records management controls should be applied to information being shared with or passed to other bodies. Particular protection should be given to confidential or personal information. Protocols should specify when, and under what conditions, information will be shared or passed, and details should be kept of when this information has been shared or passed. Details should be kept also of how undertakings given to the original source of the information have been respected.

13.4 Some of an authority's records may be held on its behalf by another body, for example a body carrying out work for the authority under contract. The authority on whose behalf the records are held is responsible for ensuring that the provisions of the Code are applied to those records.

Monitoring and reporting on records and information management

14. Authorities should monitor compliance with the Code and assess the overall effectiveness of the programme.

14.1 Authorities should identify performance measures that reflect their information management needs and arrangements and the risks that non-compliance with the Code would present to the authority, including the impact on risks identified in the overall risk management framework.

14.2 The performance measures could be general in nature, for example that a policy has been issued, or could refer to processes, such as the application of disposal schedules to relevant records with due authorisation of destruction, or could use metrics such as retrieval times for paper records held off-site that have been requested under the Act.

14.3 Authorities should put in place the means by which performance can be measured. For example, if metrics are to be used, the data from which statistics will be generated must be kept. Qualitative indicators, for example whether guidance is being followed, can be measured by spot checks or by interviews.

14.4 Monitoring should be undertaken on a regular basis and the results reported to the person with lead responsibility for records management so that risks can be assessed and appropriate action taken.

14.5   Assessing whether the records management programme meets the needs of the organisation is a more complex task and requires consideration of what the programme is intended to achieve and how successful it is being. This requires consideration of business benefits in relation to corporate objectives as well as risks and should include consultation throughout the authority.

PART 2: REVIEW AND TRANSFER OF PUBLIC RECORDS

Purpose of Part 2

15.1   This part of the Code applies only to authorities which are subject to the Public Records Act 1958 or the Public Records Act (Northern Ireland) 1923. Under those Acts, authorities are required to identify records worthy of permanent preservation and transfer them to The National Archives, a place of deposit for public records or the Public Record Office of Northern Ireland as appropriate. This part of the Code sets out the arrangements which those authorities should follow to ensure the timely and effective review and transfer of public records. Arrangements should be established and operated under the supervision of The National Archives or, in Northern Ireland, in conjunction with the Public Record Office of Northern Ireland.

15.2   The general purpose of this part of the Code is to facilitate the performance by the authorities, The National Archives, the Public Record Office of Northern Ireland and places of deposit of their functions under the Act. In reviewing records for public access, authorities should ensure that public records become available at the earliest possible time in accordance with the Act and the EIR.

Selection of public records for permanent preservation

16.1   Section 12 of the Code describes the arrangements that authorities should follow for the disposal of records. In this context, disposal means the decision as to whether the record should be destroyed, transferred to an archives service for permanent preservation or presented and the putting into effect of that decision.

16.2   Authorities that have created or are otherwise responsible for public records should ensure that they operate effective arrangements to determine which records should be selected for permanent preservation in accordance with the guidance in section 12.

Retention or transfer of public records

Records subject to the Public Records Act 1958

17.1   Under the Public Records Act 1958, records selected for preservation must be transferred by the time they are 30 years old unless the Lord Chancellor gives authorisation for them to be retained in the department for a further period under section 3(4) of the Public Records Act 1958. Records may be transferred earlier by agreement between the parties involved.

17.2   Public records may be transferred either to The National Archives or to a place of deposit for public records appointed by the Lord Chancellor under section 4 of that Act. For guidance on which records may be transferred to which archives service, and on the transfer of UK public records relating to Northern Ireland, see Annex B. For the avoidance of doubt, Part 2 of the Code applies to all such transfers.

17.3 Authorities should submit applications to retain records for a further period to The National Archives for review and advice. The Lord Chancellor's Advisory Council will then consider the case in favour of retention for a further period. The Advisory Council will consider the case for retaining individual records, or coherent batches of records, on the basis of the guidance in chapter 9 of the White Paper Open Government (Cm 2290, 1993) or subsequent revisions of Government policy. Some categories of records are covered by a standard authorisation by the Lord Chancellor (known as 'blanket retentions') which are reviewed every 10 years.

Records subject to the Public Records Act (Northern Ireland) 1923

17.4 In Northern Ireland, transfer under the Public Records Act (Northern Ireland) 1923 to the Public Record Office of Northern Ireland takes place normally at 20 years. Under section 3 of that Act, records may be retained for a further period if the principal officer of the department, or a judge if court records are involved, certifies to the Minister responsible for Northern Ireland public records that they should be retained.

Determining the access status of public records before transfer

The access review

18.1 Authorities preparing public records for transfer to The National Archives, a place of deposit for public records or the Public Record Office of Northern Ireland should review the access status of those records. The purpose of this review is to:

    a) Consider which information must be available to the public on transfer because no exemptions under the Act or the EIR apply;

    b) Consider whether the information must be released in the public interest, notwithstanding the application of an exemption under the Act or the EIR;

    c) Consider which information must be available to the public at 30 years because relevant exemptions in the Act have ceased to apply;

    d) Consider which information should be withheld from public access through the application of an exemption under the Act or the EIR.

18.2 Those undertaking the review should ensure that adequate consultation takes place, both within the authority and with other authorities that might be affected by the decision, for example authorities that originally supplied the information. This is particularly advisable for records being transferred earlier than required.

Public records to be transferred as open

18.3 If the outcome of the review is that records are to be transferred as open, the transferring department should designate the records as open. There will be no formal review of this designation by The National Archives, places of deposit or the Public Record Office of Northern Ireland.

Public records to be transferred as subject to an exemption – general

18.4 If the outcome of the review is identification of specified information which the authority considers ought not to be released under the terms of the Act or the EIR, the authority should prepare a schedule that:

    a) Identifies the information precisely;

    b) Cites the relevant exemption(s);

c) Explains why the information may not be released;

d) Identifies a date at which either release would be appropriate or the case for release should be reconsidered.

18.5 Authorities should consider whether parts of records might be released if the sensitive information were redacted, i.e. rendered invisible or blanked out. Information that has been redacted should be stored securely and should be returned to the parent record when the exemption has ceased to apply.

Public records to be transferred as subject to an exemption – The National Archives

18.6 The schedule described above should be submitted to The National Archives for review and advice prior to transfer. If the outcome of the review is that some or all of the information in the records should be closed after it is 30 years old, the schedule will be considered by the Advisory Council. The Advisory Council may respond as follows

a) By accepting that the information may be withheld for longer than 30 years and earmarking the records for release or re-review at the date identified by the authority;

b) By accepting that the information may be withheld for longer than 30 years but asking the authority to reconsider the later date designated for release or re-review;

c) By questioning the basis on which it is considered that the information may be withheld for longer than 30 years and asking the authority to reconsider the case;

18.7 If the Advisory Council accepts that the information should be withheld, the records will be transferred as closed (in whole or in part as appropriate) and the relevant closure period applied.

Public records to be transferred as subject to an exemption – the Public Record Office of Northern Ireland

18.8 The schedule described at paragraph 18.4 should be submitted to the Public Record Office of Northern Ireland for review and advice.

18.9 If the outcome of the review is that the records should be closed after transfer, the schedule will be considered by the Sensitivity Review Group. The Sensitivity Review Group may respond as follows:

a) By accepting that the information should be withheld for longer than 30 years and earmarking the records for release or re-review at the date identified on the schedule;

b) By questioning the basis on which it is considered that the information may be withheld for longer than 30 years and asking the responsible authority to reconsider the case.

18.10 If the Sensitivity Review Group accepts that the information should be withheld, the records will be transferred as closed (in whole or in part as appropriate) and the relevant closure period applied.

Public records to be transferred as subject to an exemption – places of deposit for public records

18.11 Places of deposit should be informed which records cannot be made publicly available on transfer, which exemptions apply to the information they contain and for what reason, and for how long those exemptions should be applied.

Transmission of public records

19.1   It is the responsibility of authorities transferring records to ensure that those records are adequately prepared and are transferred with the level of security appropriate to the confidentiality of the information they contain.

Access after transfer of public records

Freedom of Information requests after transfer

20.1   For the avoidance of doubt, none of the actions described in this Code affects the statutory rights of access established under the Act or the EIR. Requests for exempt information in public records transferred to The National Archives, a place of deposit for public records or the Public Record Office of Northern Ireland will be dealt with on a case by case basis in accordance with the provisions of the Act or the EIR.

Expiry of closure periods

20.2   When an exemption has ceased to apply under section 63 of the Act the records will become automatically available to members of the public at the date specified in the finalised schedule (i.e. the schedule after it has been reviewed by the Advisory Council or the Sensitivity Review Group as appropriate).

20.3   In other cases, if the authority concerned wishes to extend the period during which the information is to be withheld, it should submit a further schedule explaining the sensitivity of the information. This is to be done before the expiry of the period stated in the earlier schedule. The process outlined at paragraphs 18.6–18.10 will then be applied. In Northern Ireland, Ministerial agreement is required for any further extension of the closure period and referral to the Minister will be an additional stage in the process.

Annex A Glossary

Disposal –   the decision as to whether the record should be destroyed, transferred to an archives service for permanent preservation or presented and the putting into effect of that decision.

Disposal schedules –   schedules that identify types of records and specify for how long they will be kept before they are destroyed, designated for permanent preservation or subjected to a further review.

Keeping records –   in the context of this Code, keeping records includes recording the authority's activities by creating documents and other types of records as well as handling material received.

Metadata –   information about the context within which records were created, their structure and how they have been managed over time. Metadata can refer to records within digital systems, for example event log data. It can also refer to systems such as paper files that are controlled either from a digital system or by a register or card index, for example the title and location.

Place of deposit –   an archives office appointed to receive, preserve and provide access to public records that have been selected for preservation but are not to be transferred to The National Archives. The power of appointment has been delegated by the Lord Chancellor to the Chief Executive of The National

Archives or an officer of appropriate seniority.

Presentation – an arrangement under the Public Records Act 1958 whereby records that have not been selected for permanent preservation are presented to an appropriate body by The National Archives.

Public records – records that are subject to the Public Records Act 1958 or the Public Records Act (Northern Ireland) 1923. The records of government departments and their executive agencies, some non-departmental public bodies, the courts, the NHS and the armed forces are public records. Local government records are not public records in England and Wales but those in Northern Ireland are.

Records – information created, received, and maintained as evidence and information by an organization or person, in pursuance of legal obligations or in the transaction of business. 21

Retention – an arrangement under the Public Records Act 1958 whereby authorities are permitted to delay the transfer of specified public records for an agreed period and to retain them until the end of that period.

Records system – the term used for an information or process system that contains records and other information. It can be either a paper-based system or a digital system. Examples are correspondence file series, digital records management systems, case management systems, function-specific systems such as finance systems, etc.

Annex B Standards and guidance supporting the Code
Not reproduced

Part III

Environmental Information

Environmental Information Regulations 2004
(SI 2004/3391)

Made 21st December 2004

Coming into force 1st January 2005

(as amended to 1 February 2020)

Whereas a draft of these Regulations has been approved by resolution of each House of Parliament in pursuance of paragraph 2(2) of Schedule 2 to the European Communities Act 1972;

Now, therefore, the Secretary of State, being a Minister designated for the purposes of section 2(2) of the European Communities Act 1972 in relation to freedom of access to, and dissemination of, information on the environment held by or for public authorities or other bodies, in exercise of the powers conferred on her by that section, makes the following Regulations:

PART 1
INTRODUCTORY

1 Citation and commencement

These Regulations may be cited as the Environmental Information Regulations 2004 and shall come into force on 1st January 2005.

NOTES

Scottish public authority equivalent

EI(S)R reg 1

2 Interpretation

(1) In these Regulations--

"the Act" means the Freedom of Information Act 2000;

"applicant", in relation to a request for environmental information, means the person who made the request;

"appropriate records authority", in relation to a transferred public record, has the same meaning as in section 15(5) of the Act;

"the Commissioner" means the Information Commissioner;

"the Directive" means Council Directive 2003/4/EC on public access to environmental information and repealing Council Directive 90/313/EEC;

"the data protection principles means the principles set out in—

    (a) Article 5(1) of the GDPR,

    (b) section 34(1) of the Data Protection Act 2018, and

    (c) section 85(1) of that Act;

"data subject" has the same meaning as in the Data Protection Act 2018 (see section 3 of that Act);

"environmental information" has the same meaning as in Article 2(1) of the Directive, namely any information in written, visual, aural, electronic or any other material form on--

    (a)   the state of the elements of the environment, such as air and atmosphere, water, soil, land, landscape and natural sites including wetlands, coastal and marine areas, biological diversity and its components, including genetically modified organisms, and the interaction among these elements;

(b)   factors, such as substances, energy, noise, radiation or waste, including radioactive waste, emissions, discharges and other releases into the environment, affecting or likely to affect the elements of the environment referred to in (a);

(c)   measures (including administrative measures), such as policies, legislation, plans, programmes, environmental agreements, and activities affecting or likely to affect the elements and factors referred to in (a) and (b) as well as measures or activities designed to protect those elements;

(d)   reports on the implementation of environmental legislation;

(e)   cost-benefit and other economic analyses and assumptions used within the framework of the measures and activities referred to in (c); and

(f)   the state of human health and safety, including the contamination of the food chain, where relevant, conditions of human life, cultural sites and built structures inasmuch as they are or may be affected by the state of the elements of the environment referred to in (a) or, through those elements, by any of the matters referred to in (b) and (c);

"the GDPR" and references to a provision of Chapter 2 of Part 2 of the Data Protection Act 2018 have the same meaning as in Parts 5 to 7 of that Act (see section 3(10), (11) and (14) of that Act);

"historical record" has the same meaning as in section 62(1) of the Act;

"personal data" has the same meaning as in Parts 5 to 7 of the Data Protection Act 2018 (see section 3(2) and (14) of that Act);

"public authority" has the meaning given by paragraph (2);

"public record" has the same meaning as in section 84 of the Act;

"responsible authority", in relation to a transferred public record, has the same meaning as in section 15(5) of the Act;

"Scottish public authority" means--

(a)   a body referred to in section 80(2) of the Act; and

(b)   insofar as not such a body, a Scottish public authority as defined in section 3 of the Freedom of Information (Scotland) Act 2002;

"transferred public record" has the same meaning as in section 15(4) of the Act; and

"working day" has the same meaning as in section 10(6) of the Act.

(2)   Subject to paragraph (3), "public authority" means--

    (a)   government departments;

    (b)   any other public authority as defined in section 3(1) of the Act, disregarding for this purpose the exceptions in paragraph 6 of Schedule 1 to the Act, but excluding--

        (i)   any body or office-holder listed in Schedule 1 to the Act only in relation to information of a specified description; or

        (ii)   any person designated by Order under section 5 of the Act;

    (c)   any other body or other person, that carries out functions of public administration; or

    (d)   any other body or other person, that is under the control of a person falling within sub-paragraphs (a), (b) or (c) and--

        (i)   has public responsibilities relating to the environment;

        (ii)   exercises functions of a public nature relating to the environment; or

        (iii)   provides public services relating to the environment.

(3)   Except as provided by regulation 12(10) a Scottish public authority is not a "public

authority" for the purpose of these Regulations.

(4A) In these Regulations, references to the Data Protection Act 2018 have effect as if in Chapter 3 of Part 2 of that Act (other general processing)—

    (a)   the references to an FOI public authority were references to a public authority as defined in these Regulations, and

    (b)   the references to personal data held by such an authority were to be interpreted in accordance with regulation 3(2).

(5) Except as provided by this regulation, expressions in these Regulations which appear in the Directive have the same meaning in these Regulations as they have in the Directive.

NOTES

Scottish public authority equivalent
  EI(S)R reg 2(1) but excluding definitions of "appropriate records authority" , "historical

record" , "public record" , "responsible authority" and "transferred public record."

Application

3(1) Subject to paragraphs (3) and (4), these Regulations apply to public authorities.

(2) For the purposes of these Regulations, environmental information is held by a public authority if the information--

    (a)   is in the authority's possession and has been produced or received by the authority; or

    (b)   is held by another person on behalf of the authority.

(3) These Regulations shall not apply to any public authority to the extent that it is acting in a judicial or legislative capacity.

(4) These Regulations shall not apply to either House of Parliament to the extent required for the purpose of avoiding an infringement of the privileges of either House.

(5) Each government department is to be treated as a person separate from any other government department for the purposes of Parts 2, 4 and 5 of these Regulations.

NOTES

Scottish public authority equivalent
  EI(S)R regs 2(2), 3

Defined terms
  "environmental information": reg 2(1)
  "public authority": regs 2(1)-(3) and 12(10); Freedom of Information Act 2000, s 3(1) and Sch 1

PART 2
ACCESS TO ENVIRONMENTAL INFORMATION HELD BY PUBLIC AUTHORITIES

Dissemination of environmental information

4(1) Subject to paragraph (3), a public authority shall in respect of environmental information that it holds–

    (a)   progressively make the information available to the public by electronic means which are easily accessible; and

    (b)   take reasonable steps to organize the information relevant to its functions with a view to the active and systematic dissemination to the public of the information.

(2) For the purposes of paragraph (1) the use of electronic means to make information available or to organize information shall not be required in relation to information

collected before 1st January 2005 in non-electronic form.

(3)   Paragraph (1) shall not extend to making available or disseminating information which a public authority would be entitled to refuse to disclose under regulation 12.

(4)   The information under paragraph (1) shall include at least–
      (a)   the information referred to in Article 7(2) of the Directive; and
      (b)   facts and analyses of facts which the public authority considers relevant and important in framing major environmental policy proposals.

NOTES

Scottish public authority equivalent
  EI(S)R reg 4

Defined terms
  "the Act": reg 2(1)
  "the Directive": reg 2(1)
  "environmental information": reg 2(1)

"information held by a public authority": reg 2(5); Council Directive 2003/4/EC, art 2(3)
"public": reg 2(5); Council Directive 2003/4/EC, art 2(6)
"public authority": reg 2(1)-(3) and 12(10); Freedom of Information Act 2000, s.3(1) and Sch 1

Duty to make available environmental information on request

5(1)   Subject to paragraph (3) and in accordance with paragraphs (2), (4), (5) and (6) and the remaining provisions of this Part and Part 3 of these Regulations, a public authority that holds environmental information shall make it available on request.

(2)   Information shall be made available under paragraph (1) as soon as possible and no later than 20 working days after the date of receipt of the request.

(3)   To the extent that the information requested includes personal data of which the applicant is the data subject, paragraph (1) shall not apply to those personal data.

(4)   For the purposes of paragraph (1), where the information made available is compiled by or on behalf of the public authority it shall be up to date, accurate and comparable, so far as the public authority reasonably believes.

(5)   Where a public authority makes available information in paragraph (b) of the definition of environmental information, and the applicant so requests, the public authority shall, insofar as it is able to do so, either inform the applicant of the place where information, if available, can be found on the measurement procedures, including methods of analysis, sampling and pre-treatment of samples, used in compiling the information, or refer the applicant to a standardised procedure used.

(6)   Any enactment or rule of law that would prevent the disclosure of information in accordance with these Regulations shall not apply.

NOTES

Scottish public authority equivalent
  EI(S)R regs 5, 11(1)

Defined terms
  "applicant": reg 2(1)
  "data": reg 2(4); Data Protection Act 1998, s 1(1)
  "data subject": reg 2(4); Data Protection Act 1998, s 1(1)
  "environmental information": reg 2(1)

"personal data": reg 2(4); Data Protection Act 1998, s 1(1)
"public authority": regs 2(1)-(3) and 12(10); Freedom of Information Act 2000, s 3(1) and Sch 1
"working day": reg 2(1); Freedom of Information Act 2000, s 10(6)

Form and format of information

6(1)   Where an applicant requests that the information be made available in a particular form or format, a public authority shall make it so available, unless–

    (a)   it is reasonable for it to make the information available in another form or format; or

    (b)   the information is already publicly available and easily accessible to the applicant in another form or format.

(2)   If the information is not made available in the form or format requested, the public authority shall–

    (a)   explain the reason for its decision as soon as possible and no later than 20 working days after the date of receipt of the request for the information;

    (b)   provide the explanation in writing if the applicant so requests; and

    (c)   inform the applicant of the provisions of regulation 11 and of the enforcement and appeal provisions of the Act applied by regulation 18.

NOTES

Scottish public authority equivalent
EI(S)R reg 6

Defined terms
"the Act": reg 2(1)
"applicant": reg 2(1)
"information held by a public authority": reg 2(5); Council Directive 2003/4/EC, art 2(3)

"public": reg 2(5); Council Directive 2003/4/EC, art 2(6)
"public authority": regs 2(1)-(3) and 12(10); Freedom of Information Act 2000, s 3(1) and Sch 1
"working day": reg 2(1); Freedom of Information Act 2000, s 10(6)

Extension of time

7(1)   Where a request is made under regulation 5, the public authority may extend the period of 20 working days referred to in the provisions in paragraph (2) to 40 working days if it reasonably believes that the complexity and volume of the information requested means that it is impracticable either to comply with the request within the earlier period or to make a decision to refuse to do so.

(2)   The provisions referred to in paragraph (1) are–

    (a)   regulation 5(2);

    (b)   regulation 6(2)(a); and

    (c)   regulation 14(2).

(3)   Where paragraph (1) applies the public authority shall notify the applicant accordingly as soon as possible and no later than 20 working days after the date of receipt of the request.

NOTES

Scottish public authority equivalent
EI(S)R reg 7

Defined terms
"applicant": reg 2(1)

"public authority": regs 2(1)-(3) and 12(10); Freedom of Information Act 2000, s 3(1) and Sch 1
"working day": reg 2(1); Freedom of Information Act 2000, s 10(6)

Charging

8(1)   Subject to paragraphs (2) to (8), where a public authority makes environmental information available in accordance with regulation 5(1) the authority may charge the applicant for making the information available.

(2) A public authority shall not make any charge for allowing an applicant–

    (a) to access any public registers or lists of environmental information held by the public authority; or

    (b) to examine the information requested at the place which the public authority makes available for that examination.

(3) A charge under paragraph (1) shall not exceed an amount which the public authority is satisfied is a reasonable amount.

(4) A public authority may require advance payment of a charge for making environmental information available and if it does it shall, no later than 20 working days after the date of receipt of the request for the information, notify the applicant of this requirement and of the amount of the advance payment.

(5) Where a public authority has notified an applicant under paragraph (4) that advance payment is required, the public authority is not required–

    (a) to make available the information requested; or

    (b) to comply with regulations 6 or 14,unless the charge is paid no later than 60 working days after the date on which it gave the notification.

(6) The period beginning with the day on which the notification of a requirement for an advance payment is made and ending on the day on which that payment is received by the public authority is to be disregarded for the purposes of determining the period of 20 working days referred to in the provisions in paragraph (7), including any extension to those periods under regulation 7(1).

(7) The provisions referred to in paragraph (6) are–

    (a) regulation 5(2);

    (b) regulation 6(2)(a); and

    (c) regulation 14(2).

(8) A public authority shall publish and make available to applicants–

    (a) a schedule of its charges; and

    (b) information on the circumstances in which a charge may be made or waived.

NOTES

Scottish public authority equivalent
EI(S)R reg 8

Defined terms
"applicant": reg 2(1)
"environmental information": reg 2(1)
"information held by a public authority": reg 2(5);

Council Directive 2003/4/EC, art 2(3)
"public": reg 2(5); Council Directive 2003/4/EC, art 2(6)
"public authority": reg 2(1)-(3) and 12(10); Freedom of Information Act 2000, s 3(1) and Sch 1
"working day": reg 2(1); Freedom of Information Act 2000, s 10(6)

Advice and assistance

9(1) A public authority shall provide advice and assistance, so far as it would be reasonable to expect the authority to do so, to applicants and prospective applicants.

(2) Where a public authority decides that an applicant has formulated a request in too general a manner, it shall–

    (a) ask the applicant as soon as possible and in any event no later than 20 working days after the date of receipt of the request, to provide more particulars in relation to the request; and

(b)   assist the applicant in providing those particulars.

(3)   Where a code of practice has been made under regulation 16, and to the extent that a public authority conforms to that code in relation to the provision of advice and assistance in a particular case, it shall be taken to have complied with paragraph (1) in relation to that case.

(4)   Where paragraph (2) applies, in respect of the provisions in paragraph (5), the date on which the further particulars are received by the public authority shall be treated as the date after which the period of 20 working days referred to in those provisions shall be calculated.

(5)   The provisions referred to in paragraph (4) are–
    (a)   regulation 5(2);
    (b)   regulation 6(2)(a); and
    (c)   regulation 14(2).

NOTES

Scottish public authority equivalent
EI(S)R reg 9

Defined terms
"applicant": reg 2(1)

"public authority": regs 2(1)-(3) and 12(10); Freedom of Information Act 2000, s 3(1) and Sch 1
"working day": reg 2(1); Freedom of Information Act 2000, s 10(6)

Transfer of a request

10(1)   Where a public authority that receives a request for environmental information does not hold the information requested but believes that another public authority or a Scottish public authority holds the information, the public authority shall either–
    (a)   transfer the request to the other public authority or Scottish public authority; or
    (b)   supply the applicant with the name and address of that authority, and inform the applicant accordingly with the refusal sent under regulation 14(1).

(2)   Where a request is transferred to a public authority, for the purposes of the provisions referred to in paragraph (3) the request is received by that public authority on the date on which it receives the transferred request.

(3)   The provisions referred to in paragraph (2) are–
    (a)   regulation 5(2);
    (b)   regulation 6(2)(a); and
    (c)   regulation 14(2).

NOTES

Scottish public authority equivalent
EI(S)R reg 14

Defined terms
"applicant": reg 2(1)
"environmental information": reg 2(1)

"information held by a public authority": reg 2(5); Council Directive 2003/4/EC, art 2(3)
"public authority": regs 2(1)-(3) and 12(10); Freedom of Information Act 2000, s 3(1) and Sch 1
"Scottish public authority": reg 2(1); Freedom of Information Act 2000, s 80(2)

Representations and reconsideration

11(1)   Subject to paragraph (2), an applicant may make representations to a public authority in relation to the applicant's request for environmental information if it appears to the applicant that the authority has failed to comply with a requirement of these Regulations in relation to the request.

(2) Representations under paragraph (1) shall be made in writing to the public authority no later than 40 working days after the date on which the applicant believes that the public authority has failed to comply with the requirement.

(3) The public authority shall on receipt of the representations and free of charge–

    (a) consider them and any supporting evidence produced by the applicant; and

    (b) decide if it has complied with the requirement.

(4) A public authority shall notify the applicant of its decision under paragraph (3) as soon as possible and no later than 40 working days after the date of receipt of the representations.

(5) Where the public authority decides that it has failed to comply with these Regulations in relation to the request, the notification under paragraph (4) shall include a statement of–

    (a) the failure to comply;

    (b) the action the authority has decided to take to comply with the requirement; and

    (c) the period within which that action is to be taken.

NOTES

Scottish public authority equivalent
  EI(S)R reg 16

Defined terms
  "the Act": reg 2(1)
  "applicant": reg 2(1)

"environmental information": reg 2(1)
"public authority": regs 2(1)-(3) and 12(10); Freedom of Information Act 2000, s 3(1) and Sch 1
"working day": reg 2(1); Freedom of Information Act 2000, s 10(6)

PART 3
EXCEPTIONS TO THE DUTY TO DISCLOSE ENVIRONMENTAL INFORMATION

Exceptions to the duty to disclose environmental information

12(1) Subject to paragraphs (2), (3) and (9), a public authority may refuse to disclose environmental information requested if–

    (a) an exception to disclosure applies under paragraphs (4) or (5); and

    (b) in all the circumstances of the case, the public interest in maintaining the exception outweighs the public interest in disclosing the information.

(2) A public authority shall apply a presumption in favour of disclosure.

(3) To the extent that the information requested includes personal data of which the applicant is not the data subject, the personal data shall not be disclosed otherwise than in accordance with regulation 13.

(4) For the purposes of paragraph (1)(a), a public authority may refuse to disclose information to the extent that–

    (a) it does not hold that information when an applicant's request is received;

    (b) the request for information is manifestly unreasonable;

    (c) the request for information is formulated in too general a manner and the public authority has complied with regulation 9;

    (d) the request relates to material which is still in the course of completion, to unfinished documents or to incomplete data; or

    (e) the request involves the disclosure of internal communications.

(5)   For the purposes of paragraph (1)(a), a public authority may refuse to disclose information to the extent that its disclosure would adversely affect–

    (a)   international relations, defence, national security or public safety;

    (b)   the course of justice, the ability of a person to receive a fair trial or the ability of a public authority to conduct an inquiry of a criminal or disciplinary nature;

    (c)   intellectual property rights;

    (d)   the confidentiality of the proceedings of that or any other public authority where such confidentiality is provided by law;

    (e)   the confidentiality of commercial or industrial information where such confidentiality is provided by law to protect a legitimate economic interest;

    (f)   the interests of the person who provided the information where that person–

        (i)   was not under, and could not have been put under, any legal obligation to supply it to that or any other public authority;

        (ii)   did not supply it in circumstances such that that or any other public authority is entitled apart from these Regulations to disclose it; and

        (iii)   has not consented to its disclosure; or

    (g)   the protection of the environment to which the information relates.

(6)   For the purposes of paragraph (1), a public authority may respond to a request by neither confirming nor denying whether such information exists and is held by the public authority, whether or not it holds such information, if that confirmation or denial would involve the disclosure of information which would adversely affect any of the interests referred to in paragraph (5)(a) and would not be in the public interest under paragraph (1)(b).

(7)   For the purposes of a response under paragraph (6), whether information exists and is held by the public authority is itself the disclosure of information.

(8)   For the purposes of paragraph (4)(e), internal communications includes communications between government departments.

(9)   To the extent that the environmental information to be disclosed relates to information on emissions, a public authority shall not be entitled to refuse to disclose that information under an exception referred to in paragraphs (5)(d) to (g).

(10) For the purposes of paragraphs (5)(b), (d) and (f), references to a public authority shall include references to a Scottish public authority.

(11) Nothing in these Regulations shall authorise a refusal to make available any environmental information contained in or otherwise held with other information which is withheld by virtue of these Regulations unless it is not reasonably capable of being separated from the other information for the purpose of making available that information.

NOTES

Scottish public authority equivalent
  EI(S)R reg 10

Defined terms
  "applicant": reg 2(1)
  "data": reg 2(4);
  "data subject": reg 2(4)

"environmental information": reg 2(1)
"public": reg 2(5); Council Directive 2003/4/EC, art 2(6)
"public authority": rr2(1)-(3) and 12(10); Freedom of Information Act 2000, s 3(1) and Sch 1
"Scottish public authority": reg 2(1); Freedom of Information Act 2000, s 80(2)

Personal data

13(1) To the extent that the information requested includes personal data of which the applicant is not the data subject, a public authority must not disclose the personal data if--

(a) the first condition is satisfied, or

(b) the second or third condition is satisfied and, in all the circumstances of the case, the public interest in not disclosing the information outweighs the public interest in disclosing it.

(2A) The first condition is that the disclosure of the information to a member of the public otherwise than under these Regulations—

(a) would contravene any of the data protection principles, or

(b) would do so if the exemptions in section 24(1) of the Data Protection Act 2018 (manual unstructured data held by public authorities) were disregarded.

(2B) The second condition is that the disclosure of the information to a member of the public otherwise than under these Regulations would contravene--

(a) Article 21 of the GDPR (general processing: right to object to processing), or

(b) section 99 of the Data Protection Act 2018 (intelligence services processing: right to object to processing).

(3A) The third condition is that—

(a) on a request under Article 15(1) of the GDPR (general processing: right of access by the data subject) for access to personal data, the information would be withheld in reliance on provision made by or under section 15, 16 or 26 of, or Schedule 2, 3 or 4 to, the Data Protection Act 2018,

(b) on a request under section 45(1)(b) of that Act (law enforcement processing: right of access by the data subject), the information would be withheld in reliance on subsection (4) of that section, or

(c) on a request under section 94(1)(b) of that Act (intelligence services processing: rights of access by the data subject), the information would be withheld in reliance on a provision of Chapter 6 of Part 4 of that Act..

(5A) For the purposes of this regulation a public authority may respond to a request by neither con-firming nor denying whether such information exists and is held by the public authority, whether or not it holds such information, to the extent that--

(a) the condition in paragraph (5B)(a) is satisfied, or

(b) a condition in paragraph (5B)(b) to (e) is satisfied and in all the circumstances of the case, the public interest in not confirming or denying whether the information exists outweighs the public interest in doing so.

(5B) The conditions mentioned in paragraph (5A) are--

(a) giving a member of the public the confirmation or denial--

(i) would (apart from these Regulations) contravene any of the data protection principles, or

(ii) would do so if the exemptions in section 24(1) of the Data Protection Act 2018 (manual un-structured data held by public authorities) were disregarded;

(b) giving a member of the public the confirmation or denial would (apart from these Regulations) contravene Article 21 of the GDPR or section 99 of the Data Protection Act 2018 (right to object to processing);

(c) on a request under Article 15(1) of the GDPR (general processing: right of access by the data subject) for confirmation of whether personal data is being processed, the information would be withheld in reliance on a provision listed in paragraph (3A)(a);

(d) on a request under section 45(1)(a) of the Data Protection Act 2018 (law enforcement pro-cessing: right of access by the data subject), the information would be withheld in reliance on subsection (4) of that section;

(e) on a request under section 94(1)(a) of that Act (intelligence services processing: rights of access by the data subject), the information would be withheld in reliance on a provision of Chapter 6 of Part 4 of that Act.

(6) In determining for the purposes of this regulation whether the lawfulness principle in Article 5(1)(a) of the GDPR would be contravened by the disclosure of information, Article 6(1) of the GDPR (lawfulness) is to be read as if the second sub-paragraph (disapplying the legitimate interests gateway in relation to public authorities) were omitted.

NOTES

Scottish public authority equivalent
  EI(S)R reg 11

Defined terms
  "applicant": reg 2(1)
  "data": reg 2(4);
  "data protection principles": reg 2(4);

"information held by a public authority": reg 2(5); Council Directive 2003/4/EC, art 2(3)
"personal data": reg 2(4);
"public": reg 2(5); Council Directive 2003/4/EC, art 2(6)
"public authority": regs 2(1)-(3) and 12(10); Freedom of Information Act 2000, s 3(1) and Sch 1

Refusal to disclose information

14(1) If a request for environmental information is refused by a public authority under regulations 12(1) or 13(1), the refusal shall be made in writing and comply with the following provisions of this regulation.

(2) The refusal shall be made as soon as possible and no later than 20 working days after the date of receipt of the request.

(3) The refusal shall specify the reasons not to disclose the information requested, including–

  (a) any exception relied on under regulations 12(4), 12(5) or 13; and

  (b) the matters the public authority considered in reaching its decision with respect to the public interest under regulation 12(1)(b) or, where these apply, regulations 13(1)(b) or (5A)).

(4) If the exception in regulation 12(4)(d) is specified in the refusal, the authority shall also specify, if known to the public authority, the name of any other public authority preparing the information and the estimated time in which the information will be finished or completed.

(5) The refusal shall inform the applicant–

  (a) that he may make representations to the public authority under regulation 11; and

  (b) of the enforcement and appeal provisions of the Act applied by regulation 18.

NOTES

Scottish public authority equivalent
  EI(S)R reg 13

Defined terms
  "the Act": reg 2(1)

"applicant": reg 2(1)
"environmental information": reg 2(1)
"public authority": regs 2(1)-(3) and 12(10); Freedom of Information Act 2000, s 3(1) and Sch 1
"working day": reg 2(1); Freedom of Information Act 2000, s 10(6)

Ministerial certificates

15(1) A Minister of the Crown may certify that a refusal to disclose information under regulation 12(1) is because the disclosure–

    (a)   would adversely affect national security; and

    (b)   would not be in the public interest under regulation 12(1)(b).

(2) For the purposes of paragraph (1)--

    (a)   a Minister of the Crown may designate a person to certify the matters in that paragraph on his behalf; and

    (b)   a refusal to disclose information under regulation 12(1) includes a response under regulation 12(6).

(3) A certificate issued in accordance with paragraph (1)--

    (a)   shall be conclusive evidence of the matters in that paragraph; and

    (b)   may identify the information to which it relates in general terms.

(4) A document purporting to be a certificate under paragraph (1) shall be received in evidence and deemed to be such a certificate unless the contrary is proved.

(5) A document which purports to be certified by or on behalf of a Minister of the Crown as a true copy of a certificate issued by that Minister under paragraph (1) shall in any legal proceedings be evidence (or, in Scotland, sufficient evidence) of that certificate.

(6) In paragraphs (1), (2) and (5), a "Minister of the Crown" has the same meaning as in section 25(3) of the Act.

NOTES

Scottish public authority equivalent
  EI(S)R reg 12

"the Act": reg 2(1)
"public": reg 2(5); Council Directive 2003/4/EC, art 2(6)

Defined terms

Issue of a code of practice and functions of the Commissioner

16(1) The Secretary of State may issue, and may from time to time revise, a code of practice providing guidance to public authorities as to the practice which it would, in the Secretary of State's opinion, be desirable for them to follow in connection with the discharge of their functions under these Regulations.

(2) The code may make different provision for different public authorities.

(3) Before issuing or revising any code under this regulation, the Secretary of State shall consult the Commissioner.

(4) The Secretary of State shall lay before each House of Parliament any code issued or revised under this regulation.

(5) The general functions of the Commissioner under section 47 of the Act and the power of the Commissioner to give a practice recommendation under section 48 of the Act shall apply for the purposes of these Regulations as they apply for the purposes of the Act but with the modifications specified in paragraph (6).

(6) For the purposes of the application of sections 47 and 48 of the Act to these Regulations, any reference to–

    (a)   a public authority is a reference to a public authority within the meaning of these Regulations;

(b)   the requirements or operation of the Act, or functions under the Act, includes a reference to the requirements or operation of these Regulations, or functions under these Regulations; and

(c)   a code of practice made under section 45 of the Act includes a reference to a code of practice made under this regulation.

NOTES

Scottish public authority equivalent
  EI(S)R reg 18

Defined terms
  "the Act": reg 2(1)

"the Commissioner": reg 2(1)
"public authority": regs 2(1)-(3) and 12(10); Freedom
    of Information Act 2000, s 3(1) and Sch 1

Historical and transferred public records

17(1) Where a request relates to information contained in a historical record other than one to which paragraph (2) applies and the public authority considers that it may be in the public interest to refuse to disclose that information under regulation 12(1)(b), the public authority shall consult–

(a)   the Secretary of State, if it is a public record within the meaning of the Public Records Act 1958; or

(b)   the appropriate Northern Ireland Minister, if it is a public record to which the Public Records Act (Northern Ireland) 1923 applies, before it decides whether the information may or may not be disclosed.

(2) Where a request relates to information contained in a transferred public record, other than information which the responsible authority has designated as open information for the purposes of this regulation, the appropriate records authority shall consult the responsible authority on whether there may be an exception to disclosure of that information under regulation 12(5).

(3) If the appropriate records authority decides that such an exception applies–

(a)   subject to paragraph (4), a determination on whether it may be in the public interest to refuse to disclose that information under regulation 12(1)(b) shall be made by the responsible authority;

(b)   the responsible authority shall communicate its determination to the appropriate records authority within such time as is reasonable in all the circumstances; and

(c)   the appropriate records authority shall comply with regulation 5 in accordance with that determination.

(4) Where a responsible authority is required to make a determination under paragraph (3), it shall consult–

(a)   the Secretary of State, if the transferred public record is a public record within the meaning of the Public Records Act 1958; or

(b)   the appropriate Northern Ireland Minister, if the transferred public record is a public record to which the Public Records Act (Northern Ireland) 1923 applies, before it determines whether the information may or may not be disclosed.

(5) A responsible authority which is not a public authority under these Regulations shall be treated as a public authority for the purposes of–

(a)   the obligations of a responsible authority under paragraphs (3)(a) and (b) and (4); and

(b)   the imposition of any requirement to furnish information relating to compliance with regulation 5.

Enforcement and appeal provisions

18(1)   The enforcement and appeals provisions of the Act shall apply for the purposes of these Regulations as they apply for the purposes of the Act but with the modifications specified in this regulation.

(2)   In this regulation, "the enforcement and appeals provisions of the Act" means–

(a)   Part IV of the Act (enforcement), including Schedule 3 (powers of entry and inspection) which has effect by virtue of section 55 of the Act; and

(b)   Part V of the Act (appeals).

(3)   Part IV of the Act shall not apply in any case where a certificate has been issued in accordance with regulation 15(1).

(4)   For the purposes of the application of the enforcement and appeals provisions of the Act–

(a)   for any reference to–

(i)   "this Act" there shall be substituted a reference to "these Regulations"; and

(ii)   "Part I" there shall be substituted a reference to "Parts 2 and 3 of these Regulations";

(b)   any reference to a public authority is a reference to a public authority within the meaning of these Regulations;

(c)   for any reference to the code of practice under section 45 of the Act (issue of a code of practice by the Secretary of State) there shall be substituted a reference to any code of practice issued under regulation 16(1);

(d)   in section 50(4) of the Act (contents of decision notice)--

(i)   in paragraph (a) for the reference to "section 1(1)" there shall be substituted a reference to "regulation 5(1)"; and

(ii)   in paragraph (b) for the references to "sections 11 and 17" there shall be substituted references to "regulations 6, 11 or 14";

(e)   in section 56(1) of the Act (no action against public authority) for the words "This Act does not confer" there shall be substituted the words "These Regulations do not confer";

(f)   in section 57(3)(a) of the Act (appeal against notices served under Part IV) for the reference to "section 66" of the Act (decisions relating to certain transferred public records) there shall be substituted a reference to "regulations 17(2) to (5)";

(g)   in paragraph 1 of Schedule 3 to the Act (issue of warrants) for the reference to "section 77" (offence of altering etc records with intent to prevent disclosure) there shall be substituted a reference to "regulation 19"; and

(h)   in paragraph 8 of Schedule 3 to the Act (matters exempt from inspection and seizure) for the reference to "information which is exempt information by virtue of section 23(1) or 24(1)" (bodies and information relating to national security) there shall be substituted a reference to "information whose disclosure would adversely affect national security".

(5)   In section 50(4)(a) of the Act (contents of decision notice) the reference to confirmation or denial applies to a response given by a public authority under regulation 12(6) or regulation 13(5A).

(6)   Section 53 of the Act (exception from duty to comply with decision notice or enforcement notice) applies to a decision notice or enforcement notice served under Part IV of the Act as applied to these Regulations on any of the public authorities referred to in section 53(1)(a); and in section 53(7) for the reference to "exempt information" there shall be substituted a reference to "information which may be refused under these Regulations".

(7)   Section 60 of the Act (appeals against national security certificate) shall apply with the following modifications–

(a)   for the reference to a certificate under section 24(3) of the Act (national security) there shall be substituted a reference to a certificate issued in accordance with regulation 15(1);

(b)   subsection (2) shall be omitted; and

(c)   in subsection (3), for the words, "the Minister did not have reasonable grounds for issuing the certificate" there shall be substituted the words "the Minister or person designated by him did not have reasonable grounds for issuing the certificate under regulation 15(1)".

(8)   A person found guilty of an offence under paragraph 12 of Schedule 3 to the Act (offences relating to obstruction of the execution of a warrant) is liable on summary conviction to a fine not exceeding level 5 on the standard scale.

(9)   A government department is not liable to prosecution in relation to an offence under paragraph 12 of Schedule 3 to the Act but that offence shall apply to a person in the public service of the Crown and to a person acting on behalf of either House of Parliament or on behalf of the Northern Ireland Assembly as it applies to any other person.

(10) Section 76(1) of the Act (disclosure of information between Commissioner and ombudsmen) shall apply to any information obtained by, or furnished to, the Commissioner under or for the purposes of these Regulations.

NOTES

Scottish public authority equivalent
EI(S)R reg 17

Defined terms
"the Act": reg 2(1)
"the Commissioner": reg 2(1)
"public authority": regs 2(1)-(3) and 12(10); Freedom of Information Act 2000, s 3(1) and Sch 1

Offence of altering records with intent to prevent disclosure

19(1) Where–

(a)   a request for environmental information has been made to a public authority under regulation 5; and

    (b)   the applicant would have been entitled (subject to payment of any charge) to that information in accordance with that regulation,

any person to whom this paragraph applies is guilty of an offence if he alters, defaces, blocks, erases, destroys or conceals any record held by the public authority, with the intention of preventing the disclosure by that authority of all, or any part, of the information to which the applicant would have been entitled.

(2)   Subject to paragraph (5), paragraph (1) applies to the public authority and to any person who is employed by, is an officer of, or is subject to the direction of, the public authority.

(3)   A person guilty of an offence under this regulation is liable on summary conviction to a fine not exceeding level 5 on the standard scale.

(4)   No proceedings for an offence under this regulation shall be instituted–
    (a)   in England and Wales, except by the Commissioner or by or with the consent of the Director of Public Prosecutions; or
    (b)   in Northern Ireland, except by the Commissioner or by or with the consent of the Director of Public Prosecutions for Northern Ireland.

(5)   A government department is not liable to prosecution in relation to an offence under paragraph (1) but that offence shall apply to a person in the public service of the Crown and to a person acting on behalf of either House of Parliament or on behalf of the Northern Ireland Assembly as it applies to any other person.

NOTES

Scottish public authority equivalent
  EI(S)R reg 19

Defined terms
  "applicant": reg 2(1)

"the Commissioner": reg 2(1)
"environmental information": reg 2(1)
"public authority": regs 2(1)-(3) and 12(10); Freedom of Information Act 2000, s 3(1) and Sch 1

Amendment

20(1)   Section 39 of the Act is amended as follows.

(2)   In subsection (1)(a), for "regulations under section 74" there is substituted "environmental information regulations".

(3)   After subsection (1) there is inserted–
    "(1A) In subsection (1) "environmental information regulations" means–
      (a) regulations made under section 74, or
      (b) regulations made under section 2(2) of the European Communities Act 1972 for the purpose of implementing any Community obligation relating to public access to, and the dissemination of, information on the environment.".

NOTES

Defined terms
  "the Act": reg 2(1)

Revocation

21   The following are revoked–
    (a)   The Environmental Information Regulations 1992 and the Environmental Information (Amendment) Regulations 1998 except insofar as these apply to Scottish public authorities; and

(b)   The Environmental Information Regulations (Northern Ireland) 1993 and the Environmental Information (Amendment) Regulations (Northern Ireland) 1998.

NOTES

Scottish public authority equivalent
  EI(S)R reg 21

Environmental Information (Scotland) Regulations 2004
SSI 2004/520

Made 30th November 2004
Laid before the Scottish Parliament 2nd December 2004
Coming into force 1st January 2005

(as amended to 1 February 2020)

The Scottish Ministers, in exercise of the powers conferred by section 2(2) of the European Communities Act 1972, and of all other powers enabling them in that behalf, hereby make the following Regulations:

Citation, commencement and extent

1(1) These Regulations may be cited as the Environmental Information (Scotland) Regulations 2004 and shall come into force on 1st January 2005.

(2) These Regulations extend to Scotland only.

Interpretation

2(1) In these Regulations—

"the Act" means the Freedom of Information (Scotland) Act 2002;

"applicant" means any person who requests that environmental information be made available;

"the Commissioner" means the Scottish Information Commissioner constituted by section 42 of the Act;

"the data protection principles" means the principles set out in—

(a) Article 5(1) of the GDPR, and

(b) section 34(1) of the Data Protection Act 2018;

"data subject" has the same meaning as in the Data Protection Act 2018 (see section 3 of that Act);

"the Directive" means Directive 2003/4/EC of the European Parliament and of the Council on public access to environmental information and repealing Council Directive 90/313/EEC;

"environmental information" has the same meaning as in Article 2(1) of the Directive, namely any information in written, visual, aural, electronic or any other material form on—

(a) the state of the elements of the environment, such as air and atmosphere, water, soil, land, landscape and natural sites including wetlands, coastal and marine areas, biological diversity and its components, including genetically modified organisms, and the interaction among these elements;

(b) factors, such as substances, energy, noise, radiation or waste, including radioactive waste, emissions, discharges and other releases into the environment, affecting or likely to affect the elements of the environment referred to in paragraph (a);

(c) measures (including administrative measures), such as policies, legislation, plans, programmes, environmental agreements, and activities affecting or likely to affect the elements and factors referred to in paragraphs (a) and (b) as well as measures or activities designed to protect those elements;

(d) reports on the implementation of environmental legislation;

(e) costs benefit and other economic analyses and assumptions used within the framework of the measures and activities referred to in paragraph (c); and

(f) the state of human health and safety, including the contamination of the food chain, where relevant, conditions of human life, cultural sites and built structures inasmuch as they are or may be affected by the state of the elements of the environment referred to in paragraph (a) or, through those elements, by any of the matters referred to in paragraphs (b) and (c);

"the GDPR" and references to a provision of Chapter 2 of Part 2 of the Data Protection Act 2018 have the same meaning as in Parts 5 to 7 of that Act (see section 3(10), (11) and (14) of that Act);

"personal data" has the same meaning as in Parts 5 to 7 of the Data Protection Act 2018 (see section 3(2) and (14) of that Act);

"Scottish public authority" means—

(a) any body which, any other person who, or the holder of any office which is—

(i) listed in schedule 1 to the Act (but subject to any qualification in that schedule), or

(ii) designated by order under section 5(1) of the Act;

(b) a publicly-owned company as defined by section 6 of the Act;

(c) any other Scottish public authority with mixed functions or no reserved functions (within the meaning of the Scotland Act 1998); and

(d) any other person who is neither a public body nor the holder of a public office and who is under the control of a person or body falling within paragraphs (a), (b) or (c) of this definition and—

(i) has public responsibilities relating to the environment;

(ii) exercises functions of a public nature relating to the environment; or

(iii) provides public services relating to the environment; and

"working day" has the same meaning as in section 73 of the Act.

(2) For the purpose of these Regulations, environmental information is held by a Scottish public authority if it is—

(a) in its possession and it has been produced or received by that authority; or

(b) held by another person on that authority's behalf,

and, in either case, it has not been supplied by a Minister of the Crown or department of the Government of the United Kingdom and held in confidence.

(3) The following expressions have the same meaning in these Regulations as they have in the Data Protection Act 1998, namely—

(a) "data", except that for the purposes of regulation 10(3) and 11, a public authority referred to in paragraph (e) of the definition of data in section 1(1) of that Act means a Scottish public authority within the meaning of these Regulations;

(b) "the data protection principles";

(c) "data subject"; and

(d) "personal data".

(3A) In these Regulations, references to the Data Protection Act 2018 have effect as if in Chapter 3 of Part 2 of that Act (other general processing)—

(a) the references to an FOI public authority were references to a Scottish public authority as defined in these Regulations, and

(b) the references to personal data held by such an authority were to be interpreted in accordance with paragraph (2) of this regulation.

(4)   Subject to paragraphs (1), (2) and (3), expressions in these Regulations which appear in the Directive have the same meaning in these Regulations as they have in the Directive.

Application

3(1)   Subject to paragraph (2), these Regulations apply to Scottish public authorities.

(2)   These Regulations shall not apply to any Scottish public authority to the extent that it is acting in a judicial or legislative capacity.

(3)   Nothing in these Regulations is to be taken to limit the powers of a Scottish public authority to disclose environmental information held by it.

Active dissemination of environmental information

4(1)   A Scottish public authority shall take reasonable steps to organise and keep up to date the environmental information, relevant to its functions, which it holds and at least the types of information listed in paragraph (2), with a view to the active and systematic dissemination of that information to the public and shall make that information progressively available to the public by electronic means unless it was collected before 14th February 2003 and is not available in electronic form.

(2)   The types of information referred to in paragraph (1) are—
    (a) texts of international treaties, conventions or agreements, and of Community, national, regional or local legislation, on the environment or relating to it;
    (b) policies, plans and programmes relating to the environment;
    (c) progress reports on the implementation of the items referred to in sub paragraphs (a) and (b) when prepared or held by a Scottish public authority in electronic form;
    (d) reports on the state of the environment;
    (e) data or summaries of data derived from the monitoring of activities that affect or are likely to affect the environment;
    (f) authorisations with a significant impact on the environment and environmental agreements or a reference to the place where such information can be requested or found;
    (g) environmental impact studies and risk assessments concerning those elements of the environment referred to in paragraph (a) of the definition of "environmental information" in regulation 2(1); and
    (h) facts and analyses of facts which the authority considers relevant and important in framing major environmental policy proposals.

Duty to make available environmental information on request

5(1)   Subject to paragraph (2), a Scottish public authority that holds environmental information shall make it available when requested to do so by any applicant.

(2)   The duty under paragraph (1)—
    (a) shall be complied with as soon as possible and in any event no later than 20 working days after the date of receipt of the request; and
    (b) is subject to regulations 6 to 12.

(3)   Any enactment or rule of law which would prevent the making available of information in accordance with these Regulations shall not apply.

(4)   A Scottish public authority shall, in making environmental information compiled by it available in accordance with paragraph (1), ensure so far as practicable that that information is up to date, accurate and comparable.

(5)   Where information of the kind referred to in paragraph (b) of the definition of "environmental information" in regulation 2(1) is made available, the authority shall, if the applicant so requests, provide such information as is available to it of the place where information can be found on the measurement procedures, including methods of analysis, sampling and pre treatment of samples, used in compiling the information, or refer the applicant to the standardised procedure used.

Form and format of information

6(1)   Where an applicant requests that environmental information be made available in a particular form or format, a Scottish public authority shall comply with that request unless—

(a) it is reasonable for it to make the information available in another form or format; or

(b) the information is already publicly available and easily accessible to the applicant in another form or format.

(2)   Where a Scottish public authority relies on a provision of paragraph (1) not to make the information available in the form or format requested it shall—

(a) give its reasons for that decision as soon as possible and in any event no later than 20 working days after the date of receipt of the request for the information;

(b) give its reasons in writing if the applicant so requests;

(c) inform the applicant of the review provisions under regulation 16 and of the enforcement and appeal provisions available in accordance with regulation 17.

Extension of time

7(1)   The period of 20 working days referred to in—

(a) regulation 5(2)(a);

(b) regulation 6(2)(a); and

(c) regulation 13(a),

may be extended by a Scottish public authority by a further period of up to 20 working days if the volume and complexity of the information requested makes it impracticable for the authority either to comply with the request within the earlier period or to make a decision to refuse to do so.

(2)   Where paragraph (1) applies the Scottish public authority shall notify the applicant accordingly as soon as possible and in any event no later than 20 working days after the date of receipt of the request for the information.

(3)   Notification under paragraph (2) shall—

(a) be in writing;

(b) give the authority's reasons for considering the information to be voluminous and complex; and

(c) inform the applicant of the review provisions under regulation 16 and of the enforcement and appeal provisions available in accordance with regulation 17.

Charging

8(1) Subject to paragraphs (2) to (8), where a Scottish public authority is under a duty to make environmental information available under regulation 5(1), it may charge a fee for so doing.

(2) A Scottish public authority shall not charge a fee for allowing an applicant to—
    (a) access any public registers or lists of environmental information held by it; or
    (b) examine the information requested at a place which the authority makes available for that purpose.

(3) Fees charged under paragraph (1) shall not exceed a reasonable amount and in any event shall not exceed the costs to the authority of producing the information requested.

(4) A Scottish public authority may require that payment of the whole or part of a fee under paragraph (1) be made in advance of making information available.

(5) Where a Scottish public authority imposes a requirement under paragraph (4) it shall notify the applicant in writing.

(6) Where a Scottish public authority has notified an applicant that advance payment is required under paragraph (5) then that authority is not obliged to—
    (a) make the information requested available under regulation 5(1); or
    (b) comply with regulations 6, 7 or 13,
unless the fee is paid; and any such fee must be paid within a period of 60 working days beginning with the day on which the authority gave such notification.

(7) No working day from and including the day on which notice under paragraph (5) is given up to and including the day on which a fee is paid shall count for the purposes of determining any period of working days in accordance with regulations 5(2)(a), 6(2)(a) and 13(a).

(8) A Scottish public authority shall publish and make available to applicants—
    (a) a schedule of its fees; and
    (b) information on the circumstances in which a fee may be charged, waived or required to be paid in advance.

Duty to provide advice and assistance

9(1) A Scottish public authority shall provide advice and assistance, so far as it would be reasonable to expect the authority to do so, to applicants and prospective applicants.

(2) Where a request has been formulated in too general a manner, the authority shall—
    (a) ask the applicant as soon as possible, and in any event no later than 20 working days after the date of receipt of request, to provide more particulars in relation to the request; and
    (b) assist the applicant in providing those particulars.

(3) To the extent that a Scottish public authority conforms to a code of practice under regulation 18 in relation to the provision of advice and assistance in a particular case, it shall be taken to have complied with the duty imposed by paragraph (1) in relation to that case.

(4) In any case to which paragraph (2) applies, the date on which the further particulars are received by the authority shall be treated as the date of the request for the purposes of

regulations 5(2)(a), 6(2)(a) and 13(a) and any period within which the authority is required to respond to that request by these Regulations shall begin on the day following that date.

Exceptions from duty to make environmental information available

10(1) A Scottish public authority may refuse a request to make environmental information available if—
    (a) there is an exception to disclosure under paragraphs (4) or (5); and
    (b) in all the circumstances, the public interest in making the information available is outweighed by that in maintaining the exception.

(2) In considering the application of the exceptions referred to in paragraphs (4) and (5), a Scottish public authority shall—
    (a) interpret those paragraphs in a restrictive way; and
    (b) apply a presumption in favour of disclosure.

(3) Where the environmental information requested includes personal data, the authority shall not make those personal data available otherwise than in accordance with regulation 11.

(4) A Scottish public authority may refuse to make environmental information available to the extent that—
    (a) it does not hold that information when an applicant's request is received;
    (b) the request for information is manifestly unreasonable;
    (c) the request for information is formulated in too general a manner and the authority has complied with its duty under regulation 9;
    (d) the request relates to material which is still in the course of completion, to unfinished documents or to incomplete data; or
    (e) the request involves making available internal communications.

(5) A Scottish public authority may refuse to make environmental information available to the extent that its disclosure would, or would be likely to, prejudice substantially—
    (a) international relations, defence, national security or public safety;
    (b) the course of justice, the ability of a person to receive a fair trial or the ability of any public authority to conduct an inquiry of a criminal or disciplinary nature;
    (c) intellectual property rights;
    (d) the confidentiality of the proceedings of any public authority where such confidentiality is provided for by law;
    (e) the confidentiality of commercial or industrial information where such confidentiality is provided for by law to protect a legitimate economic interest;
    (f) the interests of the person who provided the information where that person—
        (i) was not under, and could not have been put under, any legal obligation to supply the information;
        (ii) did not supply it in circumstances such that it could, apart from these Regulations, be made available; and
        (iii) has not consented to its disclosure; or
    (g) the protection of the environment to which the information relates.

(6) To the extent that the environmental information to be made available relates to information on emissions, a Scottish public authority shall not be entitled to refuse to make it available under an exception referred to in paragraph (5)(d) to (g).

(7) Nothing in these Regulations shall authorise a refusal to make available any environmental information contained in or otherwise held with other information which

is not made available by virtue of these Regulations unless it is not reasonably capable of being separated from that other information.

(8) For the purposes of this regulation, a Scottish public authority may respond to a request by not revealing whether such information exists or is held by it, whether or not it holds such information, if to do so would involve making information available which would, or would be likely to, prejudice substantially any of the interests referred to in paragraph (5)(a) and would not be in the public interest under paragraph (1)(b).

(9) For the purposes of a response under paragraph (8), whether information exists and is held by the public authority is itself making information available.

Personal data

11(1) To the extent that environmental information requested includes personal data of which the applicant is the data subject then the duty under regulation 5(1) to make it available shall not apply to those personal data.

(2) To the extent that environmental information requested includes personal data of which the applicant is not the data subject, a Scottish public authority must not make the personal data available if—

    (a) the first condition set out in paragraph (3A) is satisfied, or

    (b) the second or third condition set out in paragraph (3B) or (4A) is satisfied and, in all the circumstances of the case, the public interest in making the information available is outweighed by that in not doing so.

(3A) The first condition is that the disclosure of the information to a member of the public otherwise than under these Regulations—

    (a) would contravene any of the data protection principles, or

    (b) would do so if the exemptions in section 24(1) of the Data Protection Act 2018 (manual unstructured data held by public authorities) were disregarded.

(3B) The second condition is that the disclosure of the information to a member of the public otherwise than under these Regulations would contravene Article 21 of the GDPR (general processing: right to object to processing).

(4A) The third condition is that any of the following applies to the information—

    (a) it is exempt from the obligation under Article 15(1) of the GDPR (general processing: right of access by the data subject) to provide access to, and information about, personal data by virtue of provision made by or under section 15, 16 or 26 of, or Schedule 2, 3 or 4 to, the Data Protection Act 2018, or

    (b) on a request under section 45(1)(b) of that Act (law enforcement processing: right of access by the data subject), the information would be withheld in reliance on subsection (4) of that section.

(6) For the purposes of this regulation, a Scottish public authority may respond to a request by not revealing whether information exists or is held by it, whether or not it holds such information, if to do so would involve making information available in contravention of this regulation.

(7) In determining, for the purposes of this regulation, whether the lawfulness principle in Article 5(1)(a) of the GDPR would be contravened by the disclosure of information, Article 6(1) of the GDPR (lawfulness) is to be read as if the second sub-paragraph (disapplying the legitimate interests gateway in relation to public authorities) were

omitted.

Ministerial certificates

12(1) The Scottish Ministers may, for the purposes of regulation 10, certify that making environmental information available would, or would be likely to, prejudice substantially national security; and such a certificate is conclusive of that fact.

(2) A certificate under this regulation may identify the information to which it applies by means of a general description and may be expressed to have prospective effect.

Refusal to make information available

13 Subject to regulations 10(8) and 11(6), if a request to make environmental information available is refused by a Scottish public authority in accordance with regulation 10, the refusal shall—

(a) be given in writing as soon as possible and in any event no later than 20 working days after the date of receipt of the request for the information;

(b) specify the reasons for the refusal including, as appropriate, any exception under regulation 10(4) or (5) or provision of regulation 11 and how the Scottish public authority has reached its decision with respect to the public interest under regulation 10(1)(b);

(c) state the basis on which any exception relied on under regulation 10(4) or (5) or provision of regulation 11 applies if it would not otherwise be apparent;

(d) if the exception in regulation 10(4)(d) is relied on, state the time by which the authority considers that the information will be finished or completed; and

(e) inform the applicant of the review provisions under regulation 16 and of the enforcement and appeal provisions available in accordance with regulation 17.

Transfer of a request

14(1) Where a Scottish public authority has received a request to make environmental information available and does not hold that information but believes that another public authority holds the information requested then it shall either—

(a) transfer the request to the other authority; or

(b) supply the applicant with the name and address of that other authority,

and inform the applicant accordingly with the refusal sent in accordance with regulation 13.

(2) Where a request is transferred, in accordance with this regulation, to a Scottish public authority, the request shall be treated as received by the receiving authority for the purposes of regulations 5(2), 6(2)(a) and 13(a) on the date that it is so received and any period within which the authority is required to respond to that request by these Regulations shall begin on the day following that date.

Records transferred to the Keeper

15(1) This regulation applies to environmental information, other than open information, which is contained in a record transferred to the Keeper of the Records of Scotland ("the Keeper") by a Scottish public authority.

(2) Where environmental information is contained in a record—

(a) to which this regulation applies; and;

(b) a request has been made for that information to be made available by the Keeper under regulation 5(1),

the Keeper shall, as soon as practicable after receiving the request, send a copy of it to the authority which transferred the information.

(3) That authority, instead of the Keeper, shall come to a decision as to whether the information is subject to an exception under regulation 10(1)(a) and determine any question then arising under regulation 10(1)(b).

(4) After receiving the copy, that authority shall, within such time as will make it practicable for the Keeper to comply with these Regulations as respects the request, inform the Keeper of the decision and of any determination required by virtue of that decision as mentioned in paragraph(3).

(5) The Keeper shall, as soon as practicable after receiving representations in accordance with regulation 16, send a copy of those representations to the authority and the authority, instead of the Keeper, shall review the decision and do anything which is to be done under that regulation.

(6) After receiving the copy representations, the authority must, within such time as will make it practicable for the Keeper to comply with these Regulations, inform the Keeper of its decision and provide a statement of its reasons for so doing and it is that decision and statement which the Keeper shall notify to the applicant.

(7) Paragraphs (2) to (6) also apply to information which is contained in a record transferred to the Keeper, before 1st July 1999, by the Secretary of State for Scotland; but for that purpose references in those paragraphs to "the Scottish public authority" and "the authority" are to be construed as references to the Scottish Ministers.

(8) In this regulation, "open information" means environmental information which is transferred to the Keeper and which the transferor has authorised the Keeper to make available in the event of a request being made in accordance with regulation 5(1).

Review by Scottish public authority

16(1) Subject to paragraph (2), an applicant may make representations to a Scottish public authority if it appears to the applicant that the authority has not complied with any requirement of these Regulations in relation to the applicant's request.

(2) Representations under paragraph (1) shall be made in writing to the Scottish public authority no later than 40 working days after either the date that the applicant receives any decision or notification which the applicant believes does not comply with these Regulations or the date by which such a decision or notification should have been made, or any other action should have been taken, by the authority but was not made or taken.

(3) The Scottish public authority shall on receipt of such representations—
　　(a) consider them and any supporting evidence produced by the applicant; and
　　(b) review the matter and decide whether it has complied with these Regulations.

(4) The Scottish public authority shall as soon as possible and no later than 20 working days after the date of receipt of the representations notify the applicant of its decision.

(5) Where the Scottish public authority decides that it has not complied with its duty under these Regulations, it shall immediately take steps to remedy the breach of duty.

Enforcement and appeal provisions

17(1) The provisions of Part 4 of the Act (Enforcement) including schedule 3 (powers of entry and inspection), shall apply for the purposes of these Regulations as they apply for the purposes of the Act but with the modifications specified in paragraph (2).

(2) In the application of any provision of the Act by paragraph (1) any reference to—
  (a) the Act is deemed to be a reference to these Regulations;
  (b) the requirements of Part 1 of the Act is deemed to be a reference to the requirements of these Regulations;
  (c) a Scottish public authority is deemed to be a reference to a Scottish public authority within the meaning of these Regulations;
  (d) the code of practice under section 60 or 61 of the Act (issue of a code of practice by the Scottish Ministers) is deemed to be a reference to any code of practice issued under regulation 18(1);
  (e) sections 29 (formulation of Scottish Administration policy), 31(1) (national security and defence), 32(1)(b) (international relations), 34 (investigations by Scottish public authorities and proceedings arising out of such investigations), 36(1) (confidentiality) and 41(b) (communications with Her Majesty etc and honours), in section 52(1)(b) (exception from duty to comply with certain notices) of the Act is deemed to be reference to regulations 10(4)(e) and 10(5)(a), (b), (d) and (e);
  (f) a notice under section 21(5) or (9) (review by a Scottish public authority) of the Act is deemed to be a reference to a notice under regulation 16(4); and
  (g) the period allowed in section 21(1) of the Act is deemed to be a reference to the period specified in regulation 16(4).

Code of practice and functions of the Commissioner

18(1) The Scottish Ministers may issue, and may from time to time revise, a code of practice providing guidance to Scottish public authorities as to the practice which it would, in the opinion of the Ministers, be desirable for those authorities to follow in connection with the discharge of their functions under these Regulations and with the keeping, management and destruction of their records.

(2) The code may make different provision for different Scottish public authorities.

(3) Before issuing or revising any code under this regulation, the Scottish Ministers shall consult the Commissioner.

(4) The Scottish Ministers shall lay before the Scottish Parliament any code or revised code issued under this regulation.

(5) Sections 43(1) to (3) and (5) to (8) (general functions of Commissioner), 44 (recommendations as to good practice), 45 (confidentiality of information obtained by or furnished to Commissioner), 46 (laying of reports) and 63 (disclosure of information to Scottish Public Services Ombudsman or to Information Commissioner) of the Act shall have effect for the purposes of these Regulations as they have effect for the purposes of the Act but with the modifications specified in paragraph (6).

(6) In the application of any provision of the Act by paragraph (5) any reference to—
  (a) the Act is deemed to be a reference to these Regulations;
  (b) a Scottish public authority is deemed to be a reference to a Scottish public authority within the meaning of these Regulations;
  (c) the code of practice under section 60 of the Act (issue of a code of practice by the

Scottish Ministers) is deemed to be reference to any code of practice issued under paragraph (1);

(d) the code of practice under section 61 of the Act (code of practice as to the keeping, management and destruction of records) is deemed to be a reference to a code of practice under paragraph (1); and

(e) section 1(1) of the Act is deemed to be a reference to regulation 5(1).

Offences

19(1) Where—

(a) a request for environmental information has been made to a Scottish public authority under regulation 5; and

(b) the applicant would have been entitled to that information in accordance with that regulation,

any person to whom this paragraph applies who alters, defaces, blocks, erases, destroys or conceals any record held by the Scottish public authority, with the intention of preventing the disclosure by that authority of all, or any part, of the information to which the applicant would have been entitled, is guilty of an offence.

(2) Subject to paragraph (4), paragraph (1) applies to the Scottish public authority and to any person who is employed by, is an officer of or is subject to the direction of, that authority.

(3) A person guilty of an offence under paragraph (1) is liable on summary conviction to a fine not exceeding level 5 on the standard scale.

(4) Paragraph (2) applies to—

(a) a member of the staff, or a person acting on behalf of, the Scottish Parliament or the Scottish Parliamentary Corporate Body;

(b) a member of the staff of the Scottish Administration,

as it applies to any other person, but none of those bodies is liable to prosecution under these Regulations.

Time limit for proceedings

19A(1) Proceedings for an offence under regulation 19(1) committed on or after 31st May 2013 may be commenced within the period of 6 months beginning with the date on which evidence that the prosecutor believes is sufficient to justify the proceedings came to the prosecutor's knowledge.

(2) No proceedings for an offence referred to in paragraph (1) may be commenced more than 3 years—

(a) after the commission of the offence; or

(b) in the case of a continuous contravention, after the last date on which the offence was committed.

(3) In the case of a continuous contravention, the complaint may specify the entire period during which the offence was committed.

(4) A certificate signed by or on behalf of the prosecutor stating the date on which the evidence referred to in paragraph (1) came to the prosecutor's knowledge is conclusive as to that fact (and such a certificate purporting to be so signed is to be regarded as being signed unless the contrary is proved).

(5) Section 136(3) Criminal Procedure (Scotland) Act 1995 applies for the purposes of this

regulation as it does for those of that section.

Application of the Act

20 Section 39(2) and (3) of the Act shall apply to these Regulations as they apply to regulations made under section 62 of the Act.

Revocation of Regulations

21 The Environmental Information Regulations 1992 and the Environmental Information (Amendment) Regulations 1998 are hereby revoked so far as they have effect in relation to Scottish public authorities.

Convention on Access to Information, Public Participation in Decision-making and Access to Justice in Environmental Matters
done at Aarhus, Denmark, on 25 June 1998

The Parties to this Convention,

Recalling principle 1 of the Stockholm Declaration on the Human Environment,

Recalling also principle 10 of the Rio Declaration on Environment and Development,

Recalling further General Assembly resolutions 37/7 of 28 October 1982 on the World Charter for Nature and 45/94 of 14 December 1990 on the need to ensure a healthy environment for the well-being of individuals,

Recalling the European Charter on Environment and Health adopted at the First European Conference on Environment and Health of the World Health Organization in Frankfurt-am-Main, Germany, on 8 December 1989,

Affirming the need to protect, preserve and improve the state of the environment and to ensure sustainable and environmentally sound development,

Recognizing that adequate protection of the environment is essential to human well-being and the enjoyment of basic human rights, including the right to life itself,

Recognizing also that every person has the right to live in an environment adequate to his or her health and well-being, and the duty, both individually and in association with others, to protect and improve the environment for the benefit of present and future generations,

Considering that, to be able to assert this right and observe this duty, citizens must have access to information, be entitled to participate in decision-making and have access to justice in environmental matters, and acknowledging in this regard that citizens may need assistance in order to exercise their rights,

Recognizing that, in the field of the environment, improved access to information and public participation in decision-making enhance the quality and the implementation of decisions, contribute to public awareness of environmental issues, give the public the opportunity to express its concerns and enable public authorities to take due account of such concerns,

Aiming thereby to further the accountability of and transparency in decision-making and to strengthen public support for decisions on the environment,

Recognizing the desirability of transparency in all branches of government and inviting legislative bodies to implement the principles of this Convention in their proceedings,

Recognizing also that the public needs to be aware of the procedures for participation in environmental decision-making, have free access to them and know how to use them,

Recognizing further the importance of the respective roles that individual citizens, non-governmental organizations and the private sector can play in environmental protection,

Desiring to promote environmental education to further the understanding of the environment and sustainable development and to encourage widespread public awareness of, and participation in, decisions affecting the environment and sustainable development,

Noting, in this context, the importance of making use of the media and of electronic or other, future forms of communication,

Recognizing the importance of fully integrating environmental considerations in governmental decision-making and the consequent need for public authorities to be in possession of accurate, comprehensive and up-to- date environmental information,

Acknowledging that public authorities hold environmental information in the public interest,

Concerned that effective judicial mechanisms should be accessible to the public, including organizations, so that its legitimate interests are protected and the law is enforced,

Noting the importance of adequate product information being provided to consumers to enable them to make informed environmental choices,

Recognizing the concern of the public about the deliberate release of genetically modified organisms into the environment and the need for increased transparency and greater public participation in decision-making in this field,

Convinced that the implementation of this Convention will contribute to strengthening democracy in the region of the United Nations Economic
Commission for Europe (ECE),

Conscious of the role played in this respect by ECE and recalling, inter alia, the ECE Guidelines on Access to Environmental Information and Public Participation in Environmental Decision-making endorsed in the Ministerial Declaration adopted at the Third Ministerial Conference "Environment for Europe" in Sofia, Bulgaria, on 25 October 1995,

Bearing in mind the relevant provisions in the Convention on Environmental Impact Assessment in a Transboundary Context, done at Espoo, Finland, on 25 February 1991, and the Convention on the Transboundary Effects of Industrial Accidents and the Convention on the Protection and Use of Transboundary Watercourses and International Lakes, both done at Helsinki on 17 March 1992, and other regional conventions,

Conscious that the adoption of this Convention will have contributed to the further strengthening of the "Environment for Europe" process and to the results of the Fourth Ministerial Conference in Aarhus, Denmark, in June 1998,

Have agreed as follows:

Article 1 — Objective
In order to contribute to the protection of the right of every person of present and future generations to live in an environment adequate to his or her health and well-being, each Party shall guarantee the rights of access to information, public participation in decision-making, and access to justice in environmental matters in accordance with the provisions of this Convention.

Article 2 — Definitions
For the purposes of this Convention,

1. "Party" means, unless the text otherwise indicates, a Contracting Party to this Convention;

2. "Public authority" means:

   (a) Government at national, regional and other level;

   (b) Natural or legal persons performing public administrative functions under national law, including specific duties, activities or services in relation to the environment;

(c) Any other natural or legal persons having public responsibilities or functions, or providing public services, in relation to the environment, under the control of a body or person falling within subparagraphs (a) or (b) above;

(d) The institutions of any regional economic integration organization referred to in article 17 which is a Party to this Convention.

This definition does not include bodies or institutions acting in a judicial or legislative capacity;

3. "Environmental information" means any information in written, visual, aural, electronic or any other material form on:

(a) The state of elements of the environment, such as air and atmosphere, water, soil, land, landscape and natural sites, biological diversity and its components, including genetically modified organisms, and the interaction among these elements;

(b) Factors, such as substances, energy, noise and radiation, and activities or measures, including administrative measures, environmental agreements, policies, legislation, plans and programmes, affecting or likely to affect the elements of the environment within the scope of subparagraph (a) above, and cost-benefit and other economic analyses and assumptions used in environmental decision-making;

(c) The state of human health and safety, conditions of human life, cultural sites and built structures, inasmuch as they are or may be affected by the state of the elements of the environment or, through these elements, by the factors, activities or measures referred to in subparagraph (b) above;

4. "The public" means one or more natural or legal persons, and, in accordance with national legislation or practice, their associations, organizations or groups;

5. "The public concerned" means the public affected or likely to be affected by, or having an interest in, the environmental decision-making; for the purposes of this definition, non-governmental organizations promoting environmental protection and meeting any requirements under national law shall be deemed to have an interest.

Article 3 — General Provisions

1. Each Party shall take the necessary legislative, regulatory and other measures, including measures to achieve compatibility between the provisions implementing the information, public participation and access-to-justice provisions in this Convention, as well as proper enforcement measures, to establish and maintain a clear, transparent and consistent framework to implement the provisions of this Convention.

2. Each Party shall endeavour to ensure that officials and authorities assist and provide guidance to the public in seeking access to information, in facilitating participation in decision-making and in seeking access to justice in environmental matters.

3. Each Party shall promote environmental education and environmental awareness among the public, especially on how to obtain access to information, to participate in decision-making and to obtain access to justice in environmental matters.

4. Each Party shall provide for appropriate recognition of and support to associations, organizations or groups promoting environmental protection and ensure that its national legal system is consistent with this obligation.

5. The provisions of this Convention shall not affect the right of a Party to maintain or introduce measures providing for broader access to information, more extensive public participation in decision-making and wider access to justice in environmental matters than required by this Convention.

6. This Convention shall not require any derogation from existing rights of access to information, public participation in decision-making and access to justice in environmental matters.

7. Each Party shall promote the application of the principles of this Convention in international environmental decision-making processes and within the framework of international organizations in matters relating to the environment.

8. Each Party shall ensure that persons exercising their rights in conformity with the provisions of this Convention shall not be penalized, persecuted or harassed in any way for their involvement. This provision shall not affect the powers of national courts to award reasonable costs in judicial proceedings.

9. Within the scope of the relevant provisions of this Convention, the public shall have access to information, have the possibility to participate in decision-making and have access to justice in environmental matters without discrimination as to citizenship, nationality or domicile and, in the case of a legal person, without discrimination as to where it has its registered seat or an effective centre of its activities.

Article 4 — Access to Environmental Information

1. Each Party shall ensure that, subject to the following paragraphs of this article, public authorities, in response to a request for environmental information, make such information available to the public, within the framework of national legislation, including, where requested and subject to subparagraph (b) below, copies of the actual documentation containing or comprising such information:

   (a) Without an interest having to be stated;

   (b) In the form requested unless:

      (i) It is reasonable for the public authority to make it available in another form, in which case reasons shall be given for making it available in that form; or

      (ii) The information is already publicly available in another form.

2. The environmental information referred to in paragraph 1 above shall be made available as soon as possible and at the latest within one month after the request has been submitted, unless the volume and the complexity of the information justify an extension of this period up to two months after the request. The applicant shall be informed of any extension and of the reasons justifying it.

3. A request for environmental information may be refused if:

   (a) The public authority to which the request is addressed does not hold the environmental information requested;

   (b) The request is manifestly unreasonable or formulated in too general a manner; or

   (c) The request concerns material in the course of completion or concerns internal communications of public authorities where such an exemption is provided for in national law or customary practice, taking into account the public interest served by disclosure.

4. A request for environmental information may be refused if the disclosure would adversely affect:

   (a) The confidentiality of the proceedings of public authorities, where such confidentiality is provided for under national law;

   (b) International relations, national defence or public security;

   (c) The course of justice, the ability of a person to receive a fair trial or the ability of a public authority to conduct an enquiry of a criminal or disciplinary nature;

   (d) The confidentiality of commercial and industrial information, where such confidentiality is protected by law in order to protect a legitimate economic interest. Within this framework, information on emissions which is relevant for the protection of the environment shall be disclosed;

   (e) Intellectual property rights;

   (f) The confidentiality of personal data and/or files relating to a natural person where that person has not consented to the disclosure of the information to the public, where such confidentiality is provided for in national law;

   (g) The interests of a third party which has supplied the information requested without that party being under or capable of being put under a legal obligation to do so, and where that party does not consent to the release of the material; or

   (h) The environment to which the information relates, such as the breeding sites of rare species.

   The aforementioned grounds for refusal shall be interpreted in a restrictive way, taking into account the public interest served by disclosure and taking into account whether the information requested relates to emissions into the environment.

5. Where a public authority does not hold the environmental information requested, this public authority shall, as promptly as possible, inform the applicant of the public authority to which it believes it is possible to apply for the information requested or transfer the request to that authority and inform the applicant accordingly.

6. Each Party shall ensure that, if information exempted from disclosure under paragraphs 3 (c) and 4 above can be separated out without prejudice to the confidentiality of the information exempted, public authorities make available the remainder of the environmental information that has been requested.

7. A refusal of a request shall be in writing if the request was in writing or the applicant so requests. A refusal shall state the reasons for the refusal and give information on access to the review procedure provided for in accordance with article 9. The refusal shall be made as soon as possible and at the latest within one month, unless the complexity of the information justifies an extension of this period up to two months after the request. The applicant shall be informed of any extension and of the reasons justifying it.

8. Each Party may allow its public authorities to make a charge for supplying information, but such charge shall not exceed a reasonable amount. Public authorities intending to make such a charge for supplying information shall make available to applicants a schedule of charges which may be levied, indicating the circumstances in which they may be levied or waived and when the supply of information is conditional on the advance payment of such a charge.

Article 5 — Collection and Dissemination of Environmental Information

1. Each Party shall ensure that:

   (a) Public authorities possess and update environmental information which is relevant to their functions;

   (b) Mandatory systems are established so that there is an adequate flow of information to public authorities about proposed and existing activities which may significantly affect the environment;

   (c) In the event of any imminent threat to human health or the environment, whether caused by human activities or due to natural causes, all information which could enable the public to take measures to prevent or mitigate harm arising from the threat and is held by a public authority is disseminated immediately and without delay to members of the public who may be affected.

2. Each Party shall ensure that, within the framework of national legislation, the way in which public authorities make environmental information available to the public is transparent and that environmental information is effectively accessible, inter alia, by:

   (a) Providing sufficient information to the public about the type and scope of environmental information held by the relevant public authorities, the basic terms and conditions under which such information is made available and accessible, and the process by which it can be obtained;

   (b) Establishing and maintaining practical arrangements, such as:

      (i) Publicly accessible lists, registers or files;

      (ii) Requiring officials to support the public in seeking access to information under this Convention; and

      (iii) The identification of points of contact; and

   (c) Providing access to the environmental information contained in lists, registers or files as referred to in subparagraph (b) (i) above free of charge.

3. Each Party shall ensure that environmental information progressively becomes available in electronic databases which are easily accessible to the public through public telecommunications networks. Information accessible in this form should include:

   (a) Reports on the state of the environment, as referred to in paragraph 4 below;

   (b) Texts of legislation on or relating to the environment;

   (c) As appropriate, policies, plans and programmes on or relating to the environment, and environmental agreements; and

   (d) Other information, to the extent that the availability of such information in this form would facilitate the application of national law implementing this Convention,

   provided that such information is already available in electronic form.

4. Each Party shall, at regular intervals not exceeding three or four years, publish and disseminate a national report on the state of the environment, including information on the quality of the environment and information on pressures on the environment.

5. Each Party shall take measures within the framework of its legislation for the purpose of disseminating, inter alia:

   (a) Legislation and policy documents such as documents on strategies, policies, programmes and action plans relating to the environment, and progress reports on their implementation, prepared at various levels of government;

   (b) International treaties, conventions and agreements on environmental issues; and

   (c) Other significant international documents on environmental issues, as appropriate.

6. Each Party shall encourage operators whose activities have a significant impact on the environment to inform the public regularly of the environmental impact of their activities and products, where appropriate within the framework of voluntary eco-labelling or eco-auditing schemes or by other means.

7. Each Party shall:

   (a) Publish the facts and analyses of facts which it considers relevant and important in framing major environmental policy proposals;

   (b) Publish, or otherwise make accessible, available explanatory material on its dealings with the public in matters falling within the scope of this Convention; and

   (c) Provide in an appropriate form information on the performance of public functions or the provision of public services relating to the environment by government at all levels.

8. Each Party shall develop mechanisms with a view to ensuring that sufficient product information is made available to the public in a manner which enables consumers to make informed environmental choices.

9. Each Party shall take steps to establish progressively, taking into account international processes where appropriate, a coherent, nationwide system of pollution inventories or registers on a structured, computerized and publicly accessible database compiled through standardized reporting. Such a system may include inputs, releases and transfers of a specified range of substances and products, including water, energy and resource use, from a specified range of activities to environmental media and to on-site and off-site treatment and disposal sites.

10. Nothing in this article may prejudice the right of Parties to refuse to disclose certain environmental information in accordance with article 4, paragraphs 3 and 4.

Article 6 — Public Participation in Decisions on Specific Activities

1. Each Party:

   (a) Shall apply the provisions of this article with respect to decisions on whether to permit proposed activities listed in annex I;

   (b) Shall, in accordance with its national law, also apply the provisions of this article to decisions on proposed activities not listed in annex I which may have a significant effect on the environment. To this end, Parties shall determine whether such a proposed activity is subject to these provisions; and

   (c) May decide, on a case-by-case basis if so provided under national law, not to apply the provisions of this article to proposed activities serving national defence purposes, if that Party deems that such application would have an adverse effect on these purposes.

2. The public concerned shall be informed, either by public notice or individually as appropriate, early in an environmental decision-making procedure, and in an adequate, timely and effective manner, inter alia, of:

   (a) The proposed activity and the application on which a decision will be taken;

   (b) The nature of possible decisions or the draft decision;

   (c) The public authority responsible for making the decision;

   (d) The envisaged procedure, including, as and when this information can be provided:

      (i) The commencement of the procedure;

      (ii) The opportunities for the public to participate;

      (iii) The time and venue of any envisaged public hearing;

      (iv) An indication of the public authority from which relevant information can be obtained and where the relevant information has been deposited for examination by the public;

      (v) An indication of the relevant public authority or any other official body to which comments or questions can be submitted and of the time schedule for transmittal of comments or questions; and

      (vi) An indication of what environmental information relevant to the proposed activity is available; and

   (e) The fact that the activity is subject to a national or transboundary environmental impact assessment procedure.

3. The public participation procedures shall include reasonable time-frames for the different phases, allowing sufficient time for informing the public in accordance with paragraph 2 above and for the public to prepare and participate effectively during the environmental decision-making.

4. Each Party shall provide for early public participation, when all options are open and effective public participation can take place.

5. Each Party should, where appropriate, encourage prospective applicants to identify the public concerned, to enter into discussions, and to provide information regarding the objectives of their application before applying for a permit.

6. Each Party shall require the competent public authorities to give the public concerned access for examination, upon request where so required under national law, free of charge and as soon as it becomes available, to all information relevant to the decision-making referred to in this article that is available at the time of the public participation procedure, without prejudice to the right of Parties to refuse to disclose certain information in accordance with article 4, paragraphs 3 and 4. The relevant information shall include at least, and without prejudice to the provisions of article 4:

   (a) A description of the site and the physical and technical characteristics of the proposed activity, including an estimate of the expected residues and emissions;

   (b) A description of the significant effects of the proposed activity on the environment;

   (c) A description of the measures envisaged to prevent and/or reduce the effects, including emissions;

(d) A non-technical summary of the above;

(e) An outline of the main alternatives studied by the applicant; and

(f) In accordance with national legislation, the main reports and advice issued to the public authority at the time when the public concerned shall be informed in accordance with paragraph 2 above.

7. Procedures for public participation shall allow the public to submit, in writing or, as appropriate, at a public hearing or inquiry with the applicant, any comments, information, analyses or opinions that it considers relevant to the proposed activity.

8. Each Party shall ensure that in the decision due account is taken of the outcome of the public participation.

9. Each Party shall ensure that, when the decision has been taken by the public authority, the public is promptly informed of the decision in accordance with the appropriate procedures. Each Party shall make accessible to the public the text of the decision along with the reasons and considerations on which the decision is based.

10. Each Party shall ensure that, when a public authority reconsiders or updates the operating conditions for an activity referred to in paragraph 1, the provisions of paragraphs 2 to 9 of this article are applied mutatis mutandis, and where appropriate.

11. Each Party shall, within the framework of its national law, apply, to the extent feasible and appropriate, provisions of this article to decisions on whether to permit the deliberate release of genetically modified organisms into the environment.

Article 7 — Public Participation Concerning Plans, Programmes and Policies Relating to the Environment

Each Party shall make appropriate practical and/or other provisions for the public to participate during the preparation of plans and programmes relating to the environment, within a transparent and fair framework, having provided the necessary information to the public. Within this framework, article 6, paragraphs 3, 4 and 8, shall be applied. The public which may participate shall be identified by the relevant public authority, taking into account the objectives of this Convention. To the extent appropriate, each Party shall endeavour to provide opportunities for public participation in the preparation of policies relating to the environment.

Article 8 — Public Participation During the Preparation of Executive Regulations And/or Generally Applicable Legally Binding Normative Instruments

Each Party shall strive to promote effective public participation at an appropriate stage, and while options are still open, during the preparation by public authorities of executive regulations and other generally applicable legally binding rules that may have a significant effect on the environment. To this end, the following steps should be taken:

(a) Time-frames sufficient for effective participation should be fixed;

(b) Draft rules should be published or otherwise made publicly available; and

(c) The public should be given the opportunity to comment, directly or through representative consultative bodies.

The result of the public participation shall be taken into account as far as possible.

Article 9 — Access to Justice

1. Each Party shall, within the framework of its national legislation, ensure that any person who considers that his or her request for information under article 4 has been ignored, wrongfully refused, whether in part or in full, inadequately answered, or otherwise not dealt with in accordance with the provisions of that article, has access to a review procedure before a court of law or another independent and impartial body established by law.

   In the circumstances where a Party provides for such a review by a court of law, it shall ensure that such a person also has access to an expeditious procedure established by law that is free of charge or inexpensive for reconsideration by a public authority or review by an independent and impartial body other than a court of law.

   Final decisions under this paragraph 1 shall be binding on the public authority holding the information. Reasons shall be stated in writing, at least where access to information is refused under this paragraph.

2. Each Party shall, within the framework of its national legislation, ensure that members of the public concerned

   (a) Having a sufficient interest

   or, alternatively,

   (b) Maintaining impairment of a right, where the administrative procedural law of a Party requires this as a precondition,

   have access to a review procedure before a court of law and/or another independent and impartial body established by law, to challenge the substantive and procedural legality of any decision, act or omission subject to the provisions of article 6 and, where so provided for under national law and without prejudice to paragraph 3 below, of other relevant provisions of this Convention.

   What constitutes a sufficient interest and impairment of a right shall be determined in accordance with the requirements of national law and consistently with the objective of giving the public concerned wide access to justice within the scope of this Convention. To this end, the interest of any non-governmental organization meeting the requirements referred to in article 2, paragraph 5, shall be deemed sufficient for the purpose of subparagraph (a) above. Such organizations shall also be deemed to have rights capable of being impaired for the purpose of subparagraph (b) above.

   The provisions of this paragraph 2 shall not exclude the possibility of a preliminary review procedure before an administrative authority and shall not affect the requirement of exhaustion of administrative review procedures prior to recourse to judicial review procedures, where such a requirement exists under national law.

3. In addition and without prejudice to the review procedures referred to in paragraphs 1 and 2 above, each Party shall ensure that, where they meet the criteria, if any, laid down in its national law, members of the public have access to administrative or judicial procedures to challenge acts and omissions by private persons and public authorities which contravene provisions of its national law relating to the environment.

4. In addition and without prejudice to paragraph 1 above, the procedures referred to in paragraphs 1, 2 and 3 above shall provide adequate and effective remedies, including injunctive relief as appropriate, and be fair, equitable, timely and not prohibitively expensive. Decisions under this article shall be given or recorded in writing. Decisions of courts, and whenever possible of other bodies, shall be publicly accessible.

5. In order to further the effectiveness of the provisions of this article, each Party shall ensure that information is provided to the public on access to administrative and judicial review procedures and shall consider the establishment of appropriate assistance mechanisms to remove or reduce financial and other barriers to access to justice.

Article 10 — Meeting of the Parties

1. The first meeting of the Parties shall be convened no later than one year after the date of the entry into force of this Convention. Thereafter, an ordinary meeting of the Parties shall be held at least once every two years, unless otherwise decided by the Parties, or at the written request of any Party, provided that, within six months of the request being communicated to all Parties by the Executive Secretary of the Economic Commission for Europe, the said request is supported by at least one third of the Parties.

2. At their meetings, the Parties shall keep under continuous review the implementation of this Convention on the basis of regular reporting by the Parties, and, with this purpose in mind, shall:

   (a) Review the policies for and legal and methodological approaches to access to information, public participation in decision-making and access to justice in environmental matters, with a view to further improving them;

   (b) Exchange information regarding experience gained in concluding and implementing bilateral and multilateral agreements or other arrangements having relevance to the purposes of this Convention and to which one or more of the Parties are a party;

   (c) Seek, where appropriate, the services of relevant ECE bodies and other competent international bodies and specific committees in all aspects pertinent to the achievement of the purposes of this Convention;

   (d) Establish any subsidiary bodies as they deem necessary;

   (e) Prepare, where appropriate, protocols to this Convention;

   (f) Consider and adopt proposals for amendments to this Convention in accordance with the provisions of article 14;

   (g) Consider and undertake any additional action that may be required for the achievement of the purposes of this Convention;

   (h) At their first meeting, consider and by consensus adopt rules of procedure for their meetings and the meetings of subsidiary bodies;

   (i) At their first meeting, review their experience in implementing the provisions of article 5, paragraph 9, and consider what steps are necessary to develop further the system referred to in that paragraph, taking into account international processes and developments, including the elaboration of an appropriate instrument concerning pollution release and transfer registers or inventories which could be annexed to this Convention.

3. The Meeting of the Parties may, as necessary, consider establishing financial arrangements on a consensus basis.

4. The United Nations, its specialized agencies and the International Atomic Energy Agency, as well as any State or regional economic integration organization entitled under article 17 to sign this Convention but which is not a Party to this Convention, and any

intergovernmental organization qualified in the fields to which this Convention relates, shall be entitled to participate as observers in the meetings of the Parties.

5. Any non-governmental organization, qualified in the fields to which this Convention relates, which has informed the Executive Secretary of the Economic Commission for Europe of its wish to be represented at a meeting of the Parties shall be entitled to participate as an observer unless at least one third of the Parties present in the meeting raise objections.

6. For the purposes of paragraphs 4 and 5 above, the rules of procedure referred to in paragraph 2 (h) above shall provide for practical arrangements for the admittance procedure and other relevant terms.

Article 11 — Right to Vote

1. Except as provided for in paragraph 2 below, each Party to this Convention shall have one vote.

2. Regional economic integration organizations, in matters within their competence, shall exercise their right to vote with a number of votes equal to the number of their member States which are Parties to this Convention. Such organizations shall not exercise their right to vote if their member States exercise theirs, and vice versa.

Article 12 — Secretariat

The Executive Secretary of the Economic Commission for Europe shall carry out the following secretariat functions:

(a) The convening and preparing of meetings of the Parties;

(b) The transmission to the Parties of reports and other information received in accordance with the provisions of this Convention; and

(c) Such other functions as may be determined by the Parties.

Article 13 — Annexes

The annexes to this Convention shall constitute an integral part thereof.

Article 14 — Amendments to the Convention

1. Any Party may propose amendments to this Convention.

2. The text of any proposed amendment to this Convention shall be submitted in writing to the Executive Secretary of the Economic Commission for Europe, who shall communicate it to all Parties at least ninety days before the meeting of the Parties at which it is proposed for adoption.

3. The Parties shall make every effort to reach agreement on any proposed amendment to this Convention by consensus. If all efforts at consensus have been exhausted, and no agreement reached, the amendment shall as a last resort be adopted by a three-fourths majority vote of the Parties present and voting at the meeting.

4. Amendments to this Convention adopted in accordance with paragraph 3 above shall be communicated by the Depositary to all Parties for ratification, approval or acceptance. Amendments to this Convention other than those to an annex shall enter into force for Parties having ratified, approved or accepted them on the ninetieth day after the receipt by the Depositary of notification of their ratification, approval or acceptance by at least three fourths of these Parties. Thereafter they shall enter into force for any other Party on the ninetieth day after that Party deposits its instrument of ratification, approval or acceptance of the amendments.

5. Any Party that is unable to approve an amendment to an annex to this Convention shall so notify the Depositary in writing within twelve months from the date of the communication of the adoption. The Depositary shall without delay notify all Parties of any such notification received. A Party may at any time substitute an acceptance for its previous notification and, upon deposit of an instrument of acceptance with the Depositary, the amendments to such an annex shall become effective for that Party.

6. On the expiry of twelve months from the date of its communication by the Depositary as provided for in paragraph 4 above an amendment to an annex shall become effective for those Parties which have not submitted a notification to the Depositary in accordance with the provisions of paragraph 5 above, provided that not more than one third of the Parties have submitted such a notification.

7. For the purposes of this article, "Parties present and voting" means Parties present and casting an affirmative or negative vote.

Article 15 — Review of Compliance

The Meeting of the Parties shall establish, on a consensus basis, optional arrangements of a non-confrontational, non-judicial and consultative nature for reviewing compliance with the provisions of this Convention. These arrangements shall allow for appropriate public involvement and may include the option of considering communications from members of the public on matters related to this Convention.

Article 16 — Settlement of Disputes

1. If a dispute arises between two or more Parties about the interpretation or application of this Convention, they shall seek a solution by negotiation or by any other means of dispute settlement acceptable to the parties to the dispute.

2. When signing, ratifying, accepting, approving or acceding to this Convention, or at any time thereafter, a Party may declare in writing to the Depositary that, for a dispute not resolved in accordance with paragraph 1 above, it accepts one or both of the following means of dispute settlement as compulsory in relation to any Party accepting the same obligation:

    (a) Submission of the dispute to the International Court of Justice;

    (b) Arbitration in accordance with the procedure set out in annex II.

3. If the parties to the dispute have accepted both means of dispute settlement referred to in paragraph 2 above, the dispute may be submitted only to the International Court of Justice, unless the parties agree otherwise.

Article 17 — Signature

This Convention shall be open for signature at Aarhus (Denmark) on 25 June 1998, and thereafter at United Nations Headquarters in New York until 21 December 1998, by States members of the Economic Commission for Europe as well as States having consultative status with the Economic Commission for Europe pursuant to paragraphs 8 and 11 of Economic and Social Council resolution 36 (IV) of 28 March 1947, and by regional economic integration organizations constituted by sovereign States members of the Economic Commission for Europe to which their member States have transferred competence over matters governed by this Convention, including the competence to enter into treaties in respect of these matters.

Article 18 — Depositary

The Secretary-General of the United Nations shall act as the Depositary of this Convention.

Article 19 — Ratification, Acceptance, Approval and Accession

1. This Convention shall be subject to ratification, acceptance or approval by signatory States and regional economic integration organizations.

2. This Convention shall be open for accession as from 22 December 1998 by the States and regional economic integration organizations referred to in article 17.

3. Any other State, not referred to in paragraph 2 above, that is a Member of the United Nations may accede to the Convention upon approval by the Meeting of the Parties.

4. Any organization referred to in article 17 which becomes a Party to this Convention without any of its member States being a Party shall be bound by all the obligations under this Convention. If one or more of such an organization's member States is a Party to this Convention, the organization and its member States shall decide on their respective responsibilities for the performance of their obligations under this Convention. In such cases, the organization and the member States shall not be entitled to exercise rights under this Convention concurrently.

5. In their instruments of ratification, acceptance, approval or accession, the regional economic integration organizations referred to in article 17 shall declare the extent of their competence with respect to the matters governed by this Convention. These organizations shall also inform the Depositary of any substantial modification to the extent of their competence.

Article 20 — Entry Into Force

1. This Convention shall enter into force on the ninetieth day after the date of deposit of the sixteenth instrument of ratification, acceptance, approval or accession.

2. For the purposes of paragraph 1 above, any instrument deposited by a regional economic integration organization shall not be counted as additional to those deposited by States members of such an organization.

3. For each State or organization referred to in article 17 which ratifies, accepts or approves this Convention or accedes thereto after the deposit of the sixteenth instrument of ratification, acceptance, approval or accession, the Convention shall enter into force on the ninetieth day after the date of deposit by such State or organization of its instrument of ratification, acceptance, approval or accession.

Article 21 — Withdrawal

At any time after three years from the date on which this Convention has come into force with respect to a Party, that Party may withdraw from the Convention by giving written notification to the Depositary. Any such withdrawal shall take effect on the ninetieth day after the date of its receipt by the Depositary.

Article 22 — Authentic Texts

The original of this Convention, of which the English, French and Russian texts are equally authentic, shall be deposited with the Secretary-General of the United Nations.

IN WITNESS WHEREOF the undersigned, being duly authorized thereto, have signed this Convention.

DONE at Aarhus (Denmark), this twenty-fifth day of June, one thousand nine hundred and ninety-eight.

Annex I

LIST OF ACTIVITIES REFERRED TO IN ARTICLE 6, PARAGRAPH 1 (a)

1. Energy sector:

   – Mineral oil and gas refineries;

   – Installations for gasification and liquefaction;

   – Thermal power stations and other combustion installations with a heat input of 50 megawatts (MW) or more;

   – Coke ovens;

   – Nuclear power stations and other nuclear reactors including the dismantling or decommissioning of such power stations or reactors 1/ (except research installations for the production and conversion of fissionable and fertile materials whose maximum power does not exceed 1 kW continuous thermal load);

   – Installations for the reprocessing of irradiated nuclear fuel;

   – Installations designed:

     – For the production or enrichment of nuclear fuel;

     – For the processing of irradiated nuclear fuel or high–level radioactive waste;

     – For the final disposal of irradiated nuclear fuel;

     – Solely for the final disposal of radioactive waste;

     – Solely for the storage (planned for more than 10 years) of irradiated nuclear fuels or radioactive waste in a different site than the production site.

2. Production and processing of metals:

   – Metal ore (including sulphide ore) roasting or sintering installations;

   – Installations for the production of pig–iron or steel (primary or secondary fusion) including continuous casting, with a capacity exceeding 2.5 tons per hour;

   – Installations for the processing of ferrous metals:

     (i) Hot–rolling mills with a capacity exceeding 20 tons of crude steel per hour;

     (ii) Smitheries with hammers the energy of which exceeds 50 kilojoules per hammer, where the calorific power used exceeds 20 MW;

     (iii) Application of protective fused metal coats with an input exceeding 2 tons of crude steel per hour;

   – Ferrous metal foundries with a production capacity exceeding 20 tons per day;

   – Installations:

     (i) For the production of non–ferrous crude metals from ore, concentrates or secondary raw materials by metallurgical, chemical or electrolytic processes;

     (ii) For the smelting, including the alloying, of non–ferrous metals, including recovered products (refining, foundry casting, etc.), with a melting capacity exceeding 4 tons per day for lead and cadmium or 20 tons per day for all other metals;

– Installations for surface treatment of metals and plastic materials using an electrolytic or chemical process where the volume of the treatment vats exceeds 30 m^3.

3. Mineral industry:

– Installations for the production of cement clinker in rotary kilns with a production capacity exceeding 500 tons per day or lime in rotary kilns with a production capacity exceeding 50 tons per day or in other furnaces with a production capacity exceeding 50 tons per day;

– Installations for the production of asbestos and the manufacture of asbestos–based products;

– Installations for the manufacture of glass including glass fibre with a melting capacity exceeding 20 tons per day;

– Installations for melting mineral substances including the production of mineral fibres with a melting capacity exceeding 20 tons per day;

– Installations for the manufacture of ceramic products by firing, in particular roofing tiles, bricks, refractory bricks, tiles, stoneware or porcelain, with a production capacity exceeding 75 tons per day, and/or with a kiln capacity exceeding 4 m^3 and with a setting density per kiln exceeding 300 kg/m^3.

4. Chemical industry: Production within the meaning of the categories of activities contained in this paragraph means the production on an industrial scale by chemical processing of substances or groups of substances listed in subparagraphs (a) to (g):

(a) Chemical installations for the production of basic organic chemicals, such as:

(i) Simple hydrocarbons (linear or cyclic, saturated or unsaturated, aliphatic or aromatic);

(ii) Oxygen–containing hydrocarbons such as alcohols, aldehydes, ketones, carboxylic acids, esters, acetates, ethers, peroxides, epoxy resins;

(iii) Sulphurous hydrocarbons;

(iv) Nitrogenous hydrocarbons such as amines, amides, nitrous compounds, nitro compounds or nitrate compounds, nitriles, cyanates, isocyanates;

(v) Phosphorus–containing hydrocarbons;

(vi) Halogenic hydrocarbons;

(vii) Organometallic compounds;

(viii) Basic plastic materials (polymers, synthetic fibres and cellulose–based fibres);

(ix) Synthetic rubbers;

(x) Dyes and pigments;

(xi) Surface–active agents and surfactants;

(b) Chemical installations for the production of basic inorganic chemicals, such as:

(i) Gases, such as ammonia, chlorine or hydrogen chloride, fluorine or hydrogen fluoride, carbon oxides, sulphur compounds, nitrogen oxides, hydrogen, sulphur dioxide, carbonyl chloride;

(ii) Acids, such as chromic acid, hydrofluoric acid, phosphoric acid, nitric acid, hydrochloric acid, sulphuric acid, oleum, sulphurous acids;

(iii) Bases, such as ammonium hydroxide, potassium hydroxide, sodium hydroxide;

(iv) Salts, such as ammonium chloride, potassium chlorate, potassium carbonate, sodium carbonate, perborate, silver nitrate;

(v) Non-metals, metal oxides or other inorganic compounds such as calcium carbide, silicon, silicon carbide;

(c) Chemical installations for the production of phosphorous–, nitrogen–or potassium–based fertilizers (simple or compound fertilizers);

(d) Chemical installations for the production of basic plant health products and of biocides;

(e) Installations using a chemical or biological process for the production of basic pharmaceutical products;

(f) Chemical installations for the production of explosives;

(g) Chemical installations in which chemical or biological processing is used for the production of protein feed additives, ferments and other protein substances.

5. Waste management:

    – Installations for the incineration, recovery, chemical treatment or landfill of hazardous waste;

    – Installations for the incineration of municipal waste with a capacity exceeding 3 tons per hour;

    – Installations for the disposal of non–hazardous waste with a capacity exceeding 50 tons per day;

    – Landfills receiving more than 10 tons per day or with a total capacity exceeding 25 000 tons, excluding landfills of inert waste.

6. Waste–water treatment plants with a capacity exceeding 150 000 population equivalent.

7. Industrial plants for the:

(a) Production of pulp from timber or similar fibrous materials;

(b) Production of paper and board with a production capacity exceeding 20 tons per day.

8. (a) Construction of lines for long–distance railway traffic and of airports 2/ with a basic runway length of 2 100 m or more;

(b) Construction of motorways and express roads; 3/

(c) Construction of a new road of four or more lanes, or realignment and/or widening of an existing road of two lanes or less so as to provide four or more lanes, where such new road, or realigned and/or widened section of road, would be 10 km or more in a continuous length.

9. (a) Inland waterways and ports for inland–waterway traffic which permit the passage of vessels of over 1 350 tons;

(b) Trading ports, piers for loading and unloading connected to land and outside ports (excluding ferry piers) which can take vessels of over 1 350 tons.

10. Groundwater abstraction or artificial groundwater recharge schemes where the annual volume of water abstracted or recharged is equivalent to or exceeds 10 million cubic metres.

11. (a) Works for the transfer of water resources between river basins where this transfer aims at preventing possible shortages of water and where the amount of water transferred exceeds 100 million cubic metres/year;

(b) In all other cases, works for the transfer of water resources between river basins where the multiannual average flow of the basin of abstraction exceeds 2 000 million cubic metres/year and where the amount of water transferred exceeds 5% of this flow.

In both cases transfers of piped drinking water are excluded.

12. Extraction of petroleum and natural gas for commercial purposes where the amount extracted exceeds 500 tons/day in the case of petroleum and 500 000 cubic metres/day in the case of gas.

13. Dams and other installations designed for the holding back or permanent storage of water, where a new or additional amount of water held back or stored exceeds 10 million cubic metres.

14. Pipelines for the transport of gas, oil or chemicals with a diameter of more than 800 mm and a length of more than 40 km.

15. Installations for the intensive rearing of poultry or pigs with more than:

(a) 40 000 places for poultry;

(b) 2 000 places for production pigs (over 30 kg); or

(c) 750 places for sows.

16. Quarries and opencast mining where the surface of the site exceeds 25 hectares, or peat extraction, where the surface of the site exceeds 150 hectares.

17. Construction of overhead electrical power lines with a voltage of 220 kV or more and a length of more than 15 km.

18. Installations for the storage of petroleum, petrochemical, or chemical products with a capacity of 200 000 tons or more.

19. Other activities:

– Plants for the pretreatment (operations such as washing, bleaching, mercerization) or dyeing of fibres or textiles where the treatment capacity exceeds 10 tons per day;

– Plants for the tanning of hides and skins where the treatment capacity exceeds 12 tons of finished products per day;

(a) Slaughterhouses with a carcass production capacity greater than 50 tons per day;

(b) Treatment and processing intended for the production of food products from:

(i) Animal raw materials (other than milk) with a finished product production capacity greater than 75 tons per day;

(ii) Vegetable raw materials with a finished product production capacity greater than 300 tons per day (average value on a quarterly basis);

(c) Treatment and processing of milk, the quantity of milk received being greater than 200 tons per day (average value on an annual basis);

– Installations for the disposal or recycling of animal carcasses and animal waste with a treatment capacity exceeding 10 tons per day;

– Installations for the surface treatment of substances, objects or products using organic solvents, in particular for dressing, printing, coating, degreasing, waterproofing, sizing, painting, cleaning or impregnating, with a consumption capacity of more than 150 kg per hour or more than 200 tons per year;

– Installations for the production of carbon (hard–burnt coal) or electrographite by means of incineration or graphitization.

20. Any activity not covered by paragraphs 1–19 above where public participation is provided for under an environmental impact assessment procedure in accordance with national legislation.

21. The provision of article 6, paragraph 1 (a) of this Convention, does not apply to any of the above projects undertaken exclusively or mainly for research, development and testing of new methods or products for less than two years unless they would be likely to cause a significant adverse effect on environment or health.

22. Any change to or extension of activities, where such a change or extension in itself meets the criteria/thresholds set out in this annex, shall be subject to article 6, paragraph 1 (a) of this Convention. Any other change or extension of activities shall be subject to article 6, paragraph 1 (b) of this Convention.

Notes

1. Nuclear power stations and other nuclear reactors cease to be such an installation when all nuclear fuel and other radioactively contaminated elements have been removed permanently from the installation site.

2. For the purposes of this Convention, "airport" means an airport which complies with the definition in the 1944 Chicago Convention setting up the International Civil Aviation Organization (Annex 14).

3. For the purposes of this Convention, "express road" means a road which complies with the definition in the European Agreement on Main International Traffic Arteries of 15 November 1975.

Annex II
ARBITRATION

1. In the event of a dispute being submitted for arbitration pursuant to article 16, paragraph 2, of this Convention, a party or parties shall notify the secretariat of the subject matter of arbitration and indicate, in particular, the articles of this Convention whose interpretation or application is at issue. The secretariat shall forward the information received to all Parties to this Convention.

2. The arbitral tribunal shall consist of three members. Both the claimant party or parties and the other party or parties to the dispute shall appoint an arbitrator, and the two arbitrators

so appointed shall designate by common agreement the third arbitrator, who shall be the president of the arbitral tribunal. The latter shall not be a national of one of the parties to the dispute, nor have his or her usual place of residence in the territory of one of these parties, nor be employed by any of them, nor have dealt with the case in any other capacity.

3. If the president of the arbitral tribunal has not been designated within two months of the appointment of the second arbitrator, the Executive Secretary of the Economic Commission for Europe shall, at the request of either party to the dispute, designate the president within a further two–month period.

4. If one of the parties to the dispute does not appoint an arbitrator within two months of the receipt of the request, the other party may so inform the Executive Secretary of the Economic Commission for Europe, who shall designate the president of the arbitral tribunal within a further two–month period. Upon designation, the president of the arbitral tribunal shall request the party which has not appointed an arbitrator to do so within two months. If it fails to do so within that period, the president shall so inform the Executive Secretary of the Economic Commission for Europe, who shall make this appointment within a further two–month period.

5. The arbitral tribunal shall render its decision in accordance with international law and the provisions of this Convention.

6. Any arbitral tribunal constituted under the provisions set out in this annex shall draw up its own rules of procedure.

7. The decisions of the arbitral tribunal, both on procedure and on substance, shall be taken by majority vote of its members.

8. The tribunal may take all appropriate measures to establish the facts.

9. The parties to the dispute shall facilitate the work of the arbitral tribunal and, in particular, using all means at their disposal, shall:

   (a) Provide it with all relevant documents, facilities and information;

   (b) Enable it, where necessary, to call witnesses or experts and receive their evidence.

10. The parties and the arbitrators shall protect the confidentiality of any information that they receive in confidence during the proceedings of the arbitral tribunal.

11. The arbitral tribunal may, at the request of one of the parties, recommend interim measures of protection.

12. If one of the parties to the dispute does not appear before the arbitral tribunal or fails to defend its case, the other party may request the tribunal to continue the proceedings and to render its final decision. Absence of a party or failure of a party to defend its case shall not constitute a bar to the proceedings.

13. The arbitral tribunal may hear and determine counter–claims arising directly out of the subject matter of the dispute.

14. Unless the arbitral tribunal determines otherwise because of the particular circumstances of the case, the expenses of the tribunal, including the remuneration of its members, shall be borne by the parties to the dispute in equal shares. The tribunal shall keep a record of all its expenses, and shall furnish a final statement thereof to the parties.

15. Any Party to this Convention which has an interest of a legal nature in the subject matter of the dispute, and which may be affected by a decision in the case, may intervene in the

proceedings with the consent of the tribunal.

16. The arbitral tribunal shall render its award within five months of the date on which it is established, unless it finds it necessary to extend the time limit for a period which should not exceed five months.

17. The award of the arbitral tribunal shall be accompanied by a statement of reasons. It shall be final and binding upon all parties to the dispute. The award will be transmitted by the arbitral tribunal to the parties to the dispute and to the secretariat. The secretariat will forward the information received to all Parties to this Convention.

18. Any dispute which may arise between the parties concerning the interpretation or execution of the award may be submitted by either party to the arbitral tribunal which made the award or, if the latter cannot be seized thereof, to another tribunal constituted for this purpose in the same manner as the first.

Directive 2003/4/EC of the
European Parliament and of the Council
of 28 January 2003
on public access to environmental information
and repealing Council Directive 90/313/EEC

THE EUROPEAN PARLIAMENT AND THE COUNCIL OF THE EUROPEAN UNION,

Having regard to the Treaty establishing the European Community, and in particular Article 175(1) thereof,

Having regard to the proposal from the Commission,

Having regard to the opinion of the European Economic and Social Committee,

Having regard to the opinion of the Committee of the Regions,

Acting in accordance with the procedure laid down in Article 251 of the Treaty in the light of the joint text approved by the Conciliation Committee on 8 November 2002,

Whereas:

(1) Increased public access to environmental information and the dissemination of such information contribute to a greater awareness of environmental matters, a free exchange of views, more effective participation by the public in environmental decision-making and, eventually, to a better environment.

(2) Council Directive 90/313/EEC of 7 June 1990 on the freedom of access to information on the environment initiated a process of change in the manner in which public authorities approach the issue of openness and transparency, establishing measures for the exercise of the right of public access to environmental information which should be developed and continued. This Directive expands the existing access granted under Directive 90/313/EEC.

(3) Article 8 of that Directive requires Member States to report to the Commission on the experience gained, in the light of which the Commission is required to make a report to the European Parliament and to the Council together with any proposal for revision of the Directive which it may consider appropriate.

(4) The report produced under Article 8 of that Directive identifies concrete problems encountered in the practical application of the Directive.

(5) On 25 June 1998 the European Community signed the UN/ECE Convention on Access to Information, Public Participation in Decision-Making and Access to Justice in Environmental Matters ('the Aarhus Convention'). Provisions of Community law must be consistent with that Convention with a view to its conclusion by the European Community.

(6) It is appropriate in the interest of increased transparency to replace Directive 90/313/EEC rather than to amend it, so as to provide interested parties with a single, clear and coherent legislative text.

(7) Disparities between the laws in force in the Member States concerning access to environmental information held by public authorities can create inequality within the Community as regards access to such information or as regards conditions of competition.

(8) It is necessary to ensure that any natural and legal person has a right of access to

environmental information held by or for public authorities without his having to state an interest.

(9) It is also necessary that public authorities make available and disseminate environmental information to the general public to the widest extent possible, in particular by using information and communication technologies. The future development of these technologies should be taken into account in the reporting on, and reviewing of, this Directive.

(10) The definition of environmental information should be clarified so as to encompass information in any form on the state of the environment, on factors, measures or activities affecting or likely to affect the environment or designed to protect it, on cost-benefit and economic analyses used within the framework of such measures or activities and also information on the state of human health and safety, including the contamination of the food chain, conditions of human life, cultural sites and built structures in as much as they are, or may be, affected by any of those matters.

(11) To take account of the principle in Article 6 of the Treaty, that environmental protection requirements should be integrated into the definition and implementation of Community policies and activities, the definition of public authorities should be expanded so as to encompass government or other public administration at national, regional or local level whether or not they have specific responsibilities for the environment. The definition should likewise be expanded to include other persons or bodies performing public administrative functions in relation to the environment under national law, as well as other persons or bodies acting under their control and having public responsibilities or functions in relation to the environment.

(12) Environmental information which is physically held by other bodies on behalf of public authorities should also fall within the scope of this Directive.

(13) Environmental information should be made available to applicants as soon as possible and within a reasonable time and having regard to any timescale specified by the applicant.

(14) Public authorities should make environmental information available in the form or format requested by an applicant unless it is already publicly available in another form or format or it is reasonable to make it available in another form or format. In addition, public authorities should be required to make all reasonable efforts to maintain the environmental information held by or for them in forms or formats that are readily reproducible and accessible by electronic means.

(15) Member States should determine the practical arrangements under which such information is effectively made available. These arrangements shall guarantee that the information is effectively and easily accessible and progressively becomes available to the public through public telecommunications networks, including publicly accessible lists of public authorities and registers or lists of environmental information held by or for public authorities.

(16) The right to information means that the disclosure of information should be the general rule and that public authorities should be permitted to refuse a request for environmental information in specific and clearly defined cases. Grounds for refusal should be interpreted in a restrictive way, whereby the public interest served by disclosure should be weighed against the interest served by the refusal. The reasons for a refusal should be provided to the applicant within the time limit laid down in this Directive.

(17) Public authorities should make environmental information available in part where it is

possible to separate out any information falling within the scope of the exceptions from the rest of the information requested.

(18) Public authorities should be able to make a charge for supplying environmental information but such a charge should be reasonable. This implies that, as a general rule, charges may not exceed actual costs of producing the material in question. Instances where advance payment will be required should be limited. In particular cases, where public authorities make available environmental information on a commercial basis, and where this is necessary in order to guarantee the continuation of collecting and publishing such information, a market-based charge is considered to be reasonable; an advance payment may be required. A schedule of charges should be published and made available to applicants together with information on the circumstances in which a charge may be levied or waived.

(19) Applicants should be able to seek an administrative or judicial review of the acts or omissions of a public authority in relation to a request.

(20) Public authorities should seek to guarantee that when environmental information is compiled by them or on their behalf, the information is comprehensible, accurate and comparable. As this is an important factor in assessing the quality of the information supplied the method used in compiling the information should also be disclosed upon request.

(21) In order to increase public awareness in environmental matters and to improve environmental protection, public authorities should, as appropriate, make available and disseminate information on the environment which is relevant to their functions, in particular by means of computer telecommunication and/or electronic technology, where available.

(22) This Directive should be evaluated every four years, after its entry into force, in the light of experience and after submission of the relevant reports by the Member States, and be subject to revision on that basis. The Commission should submit an evaluation report to the European Parliament and the Council.

(23) Since the objectives of the proposed Directive cannot be sufficiently achieved by the Member States and can therefore be better achieved at Community level, the Community may adopt measures, in accordance with the principle of subsidiarity as set out in Article 5 of the Treaty. In accordance with the principle of proportionality, as set out in that Article, this Directive does not go beyond what is necessary in order to achieve those objectives.

(24) The provisions of this Directive shall not affect the right of a Member State to maintain or introduce measures providing for broader access to information than required by this Directive,

HAVE ADOPTED THIS DIRECTIVE:

Article 1 — Objectives

The objectives of this Directive are:

(a) to guarantee the right of access to environmental information held by or for public authorities and to set out the basic terms and conditions of, and practical arrangements for, its exercise; and

(b) to ensure that, as a matter of course, environmental information is progressively made available and disseminated to the public in order to achieve the widest possible systematic availability and dissemination to the public of environmental information. To this end the use, in particular, of computer telecommunication and/or electronic technology, where available, shall be promoted.

Article 2 — Definitions

For the purposes of this Directive:

1. 'Environmental information' shall mean any information in written, visual, aural, electronic or any other material form on:

    (a) the state of the elements of the environment, such as air and atmosphere, water, soil, land, landscape and natural sites including wetlands, coastal and marine areas, biological diversity and its components, including genetically modified organisms, and the interaction among these elements;

    (b) factors, such as substances, energy, noise, radiation or waste, including radioactive waste, emissions, discharges and other releases into the environment, affecting or likely to affect the elements of the environment referred to in (a);

    (c) measures (including administrative measures), such as policies, legislation, plans, programmes, environmental agreements, and activities affecting or likely to affect the elements and factors referred to in (a) and (b) as well as measures or activities designed to protect those elements;

    (d) reports on the implementation of environmental legislation;

    (e) cost-benefit and other economic analyses and assumptions used within the framework of the measures and activities referred to in (c); and

    (f) the state of human health and safety, including the contamination of the food chain, where relevant, conditions of human life, cultural sites and built structures inasmuch as they are or may be affected by the state of the elements of the environment referred to in (a) or, through those elements, by any of the matters referred to in (b) and (c).

2. 'Public authority' shall mean:

    (a) government or other public administration, including public advisory bodies, at national, regional or local level;

    (b) any natural or legal person performing public administrative functions under national law, including specific duties, activities or services in relation to the environment; and

    (c) any natural or legal person having public responsibilities or functions, or providing public services, relating to the environment under the control of a body or person falling within (a) or (b).

Member States may provide that this definition shall not include bodies or institutions when acting in a judicial or legislative capacity. If their constitutional provisions at the date of adoption of this Directive make no provision for a review procedure within the meaning of Article 6, Member States may exclude those bodies or institutions from that definition.

3. 'Information held by a public authority' shall mean environmental information in its

possession which has been produced or received by that authority.

4   'Information held for a public authority' shall mean environmental information which is physically held by a natural or legal person on behalf of a public authority.

5. 'Applicant' shall mean any natural or legal person requesting environmental information.

6. 'Public' shall mean one or more natural or legal persons, and, in accordance with national legislation or practice, their associations, organisations or groups.

Article 3 — Access to environmental information upon request

1. Member States shall ensure that public authorities are required, in accordance with the provisions of this Directive, to make available environmental information held by or for them to any applicant at his request and without his having to state an interest.

2. Subject to Article 4 and having regard to any timescale specified by the applicant, environmental information shall be made available to an applicant:

    (a) as soon as possible or, at the latest, within one month after the receipt by the public authority referred to in paragraph 1 of the applicant's request; or

    (b) within two months after the receipt of the request by the public authority if the volume and the complexity of the information is such that the one-month period referred to in (a) cannot be complied with. In such cases, the applicant shall be informed as soon as possible, and in any case before the end of that one-month period, of any such extension and of the reasons for it.

3. If a request is formulated in too general a manner, the public authority shall as soon as possible, and at the latest within the timeframe laid down in paragraph 2(a), ask the applicant to specify the request and shall assist the applicant in doing so, e.g. by providing information on the use of the public registers referred to in paragraph 5(c). The public authorities may, where they deem it appropriate, refuse the request under Article 4(1)(c).

4. Where an applicant requests a public authority to make environmental information available in a specific form or format (including in the form of copies), the public authority shall make it so available unless:

    (a) it is already publicly available in another form or format, in particular under Article 7, which is easily accessible by applicants; or

    (b) it is reasonable for the public authority to make it available in another form or format, in which case reasons shall be given for making it available in that form or format.

    For the purposes of this paragraph, public authorities shall make all reasonable efforts to maintain environmental information held by or for them in forms or formats that are readily reproducible and accessible by computer telecommunications or by other electronic means.

    The reasons for a refusal to make information available, in full or in part, in the form or format requested shall be provided to the applicant within the time limit referred to in paragraph 2(a).

5. For the purposes of this Article, Member States shall ensure that:

    (a) officials are required to support the public in seeking access to information;

    (b) lists of public authorities are publicly accessible; and

    (c) the practical arrangements are defined for ensuring that the right of access to environmental information can be effectively exercised, such as:

— the designation of information officers;

— the establishment and maintenance of facilities for the examination of the information required,

— registers or lists of the environmental information held by public authorities or information points, with clear indications of where such information can be found.

Member States shall ensure that public authorities inform the public adequately of the rights they enjoy as a result of this Directive and to an appropriate extent provide information, guidance and advice to this end.

Article 4 — Exceptions

1. Member States may provide for a request for environmental information to be refused if:

(a) the information requested is not held by or for the public authority to which the request is addressed. In such a case, where that public authority is aware that the information is held by or for another public authority, it shall, as soon as possible, transfer the request to that other authority and inform the applicant accordingly or inform the applicant of the public authority to which it believes it is possible to apply for the information requested;

(b) the request is manifestly unreasonable;

(c) the request is formulated in too general a manner, taking into account Article 3(3);

(d) the request concerns material in the course of completion or unfinished documents or data;

(e) the request concerns internal communications, taking into account the public interest served by disclosure.

Where a request is refused on the basis that it concerns material in the course of completion, the public authority shall state the name of the authority preparing the material and the estimated time needed for completion.

2. Member States may provide for a request for environmental information to be refused if disclosure of the information would adversely affect:

(a) the confidentiality of the proceedings of public authorities, where such confidentiality is provided for by law;

(b) international relations, public security or national defence;

(c) the course of justice, the ability of any person to receive a fair trial or the ability of a public authority to conduct an enquiry of a criminal or disciplinary nature;

(d) the confidentiality of commercial or industrial information where such confidentiality is provided for by national or Community law to protect a legitimate economic interest, including the public interest in maintaining statistical confidentiality and tax secrecy;

(e) intellectual property rights;

(f) the confidentiality of personal data and/or files relating to a natural person where that person has not consented to the disclosure of the information to the public, where such confidentiality is provided for by national or Community law;

(g) the interests or protection of any person who supplied the information requested on a voluntary basis without being under, or capable of being put under, a legal obligation to do so, unless that person has consented to the release of the information concerned;

(h) the protection of the environment to which such information relates, such as the location of rare species.

The grounds for refusal mentioned in paragraphs 1 and 2 shall be interpreted in a restrictive way, taking into account for the particular case the public interest served by disclosure. In every particular case, the public interest served by disclosure shall be weighed against the interest served by the refusal. Member States may not, by virtue of paragraph 2(a), (d), (f), (g) and (h), provide for a request to be refused where the request relates to information on emissions into the environment.

Within this framework, and for the purposes of the application of subparagraph (f), Member States shall ensure that the requirements of Directive 95/46/EC of the European Parliament and of the Council of 24 October 1995 on the protection of individuals with regard to the processing of personal data and on the free movement of such data are complied with.

3. Where a Member State provides for exceptions, it may draw up a publicly accessible list of criteria on the basis of which the authority concerned may decide how to handle requests.

4. Environmental information held by or for public authorities which has been requested by an applicant shall be made available in part where it is possible to separate out any information falling within the scope of paragraphs 1(d) and (e) or 2 from the rest of the information requested.

5. A refusal to make available all or part of the information requested shall be notified to the applicant in writing or electronically, if the request was in writing or if the applicant so requests, within the time limits referred to in Article 3(2)(a) or, as the case may be, (b). The notification shall state the reasons for the refusal and include information on the review procedure provided for in accordance with Article 6.

Article 5 — Charges

1. Access to any public registers or lists established and maintained as mentioned in Article 3(5) and examination in situ of the information requested shall be free of charge.

2. Public authorities may make a charge for supplying any environmental information but such charge shall not exceed a reasonable amount.

3. Where charges are made, public authorities shall publish and make available to applicants a schedule of such charges as well as information on the circumstances in which a charge may be levied or waived.

Article 6 — Access to justice

1. Member States shall ensure that any applicant who considers that his request for information has been ignored, wrongfully refused (whether in full or in part), inadequately answered or otherwise not dealt with in accordance with the provisions of Articles 3, 4 or 5, has access to a procedure in which the acts or omissions of the public authority concerned can be reconsidered by that or another public authority or reviewed administratively by an independent and impartial body established by law. Any such procedure shall be expeditious and either free of charge or inexpensive.

2. In addition to the review procedure referred to in paragraph 1, Member States shall ensure that an applicant has access to a review procedure before a court of law or another independent and impartial body established by law, in which the acts or omissions of the public authority concerned can be reviewed and whose decisions may become final. Member States may furthermore provide that third parties incriminated by the disclosure of information may also have access to legal recourse.

3. Final decisions under paragraph 2 shall be binding on the public authority holding the information. Reasons shall be stated in writing, at least where access to information is refused under this Article.

Article 7 — Dissemination of environmental information

1. Member States shall take the necessary measures to ensure that public authorities organise the environmental information which is relevant to their functions and which is held by or for them, with a view to its active and systematic dissemination to the public, in particular by means of computer telecommunication and/or electronic technology, where available.

The information made available by means of computer telecommunication and/or electronic technology need not include information collected before the entry into force of this Directive unless it is already available in electronic form.

Member States shall ensure that environmental information progressively becomes available in electronic databases which are easily accessible to the public through public telecommunication networks.

2. The information to be made available and disseminated shall be updated as appropriate and shall include at least:

   (a) texts of international treaties, conventions or agreements, and of Community, national, regional or local legislation, on the environment or relating to it;

   (b) policies, plans and programmes relating to the environment;

   (c) progress reports on the implementation of the items referred to in (a) and (b) when prepared or held in electronic form by public authorities;

   (d) the reports on the state of the environment referred to in paragraph 3;

   (e) data or summaries of data derived from the monitoring of activities affecting, or likely to affect, the environment;

   (f) authorisations with a significant impact on the environment and environmental agreements or a reference to the place where such information can be requested or found in the framework of Article 3;

   (g) environmental impact studies and risk assessments concerning the environmental elements referred to in Article 2(1)(a) or a reference to the place where the information can be requested or found in the framework of Article 3.

3. Without prejudice to any specific reporting obligations laid down by Community legislation, Member States shall take the necessary measures to ensure that national, and, where appropriate, regional or local reports on the state of the environment are published at regular intervals not exceeding four years; such reports shall include information on the quality of, and pressures on, the environment.

4. Without prejudice to any specific obligation laid down by Community legislation, Member

States shall take the necessary measures to ensure that, in the event of an imminent threat to human health or the environment, whether caused by human activities or due to natural causes, all information held by or for public authorities which could enable the public likely to be affected to take measures to prevent or mitigate harm arising from the threat is disseminated, immediately and without delay.

5. The exceptions in Article 4(1) and (2) may apply in relation to the duties imposed by this Article.

6. Member States may satisfy the requirements of this Article by creating links to Internet sites where the information can be found.

Article 8 — Quality of environmental information
1. Member States shall, so far as is within their power, ensure that any information that is compiled by them or on their behalf is up to date, accurate and comparable.

2. Upon request, public authorities shall reply to requests for information pursuant to Article 2(1)b, reporting to the applicant on the place where information, if available, can be found on the measurement procedures, including methods of analysis, sampling, and pre-treatment of samples, used in compiling the information, or referring to a standardised procedure used.

Article 9 — Review procedure
1. Not later than 14 February 2009, Member States shall report on the experience gained in the application of this Directive.

They shall communicate the report to the Commission not later than 14 August 2009.

No later than 14 February 2004, the Commission shall forward to the Member States a guidance document setting out clearly the manner in which it wishes the Member States to report.

2. In the light of experience and taking into account developments in computer telecommunication and/or electronic technology, the Commission shall make a report to the European Parliament and to the Council together with any proposal for revision, which it may consider appropriate.

Article 10 — Implementation
Member States shall bring into force the laws, regulations and administrative provisions necessary to comply with this Directive by 14 February 2005. They shall forthwith inform the Commission thereof.

When Member States adopt these measures, they shall contain a reference to this Directive or shall be accompanied by such reference on the occasion of their official publication. The methods of making such reference shall be laid down by Member States.

Article 11 — Repeal
Directive 90/313/EEC is hereby repealed with effect from 14 February 2005.

References to the repealed Directive shall be construed as referring to this Directive and shall be read in accordance with the correlation table in the Annex.

Article 12 — Entry into force
This Directive shall enter into force on the day of its publication in the Official Journal of the European Union.

Article 13 — Addressees
This Directive is addressed to the Member States.

Done at Brussels, 28 January 2003.

Code of Practice on the discharge of the obligations of public authorities under the Environmental Information Regulations 2004
SI 2004 No. 3391

laid before Parliament on 16 February 2005

Issued under Regulation 16 of the Regulations, February 2005

FOREWORD TO THE CODE OF PRACTICE

Introduction

1. The Code of Practice, to which this is a foreword, is prepared in accordance with Regulation 16 of the Environmental Information Regulations 2004 (EIR) and provides guidance to public authorities as to the practice that would be desirable for them to follow in connection with discharging their functions under the EIR. However, if public authorities do not follow the Code's recommendations it will be difficult for them to meet their obligations under the Regulations.

2. The definition of 'public authority' for the purposes of the EIR is wider than that under section 3(1) of the Freedom of Information Act 2000 (FOIA). Those bodies subject to both the FOIA and the EIR will need to consider the Code provisions relevant to the appropriate regime (this Code or the FOIA section 45 Code). Public authorities covered only by the EIR need only consider this Code of Practice on access to information.

Recommendations for EIR public authorities on record keeping, management and destruction are set out in the FOIA section 46 Code of Practice.

3. This Code applies where a request for environmental information is received, as defined in the EIR. Any request for other information should be handled in accordance with the FOIA and other access regimes such as the Data Protection Act as appropriate. Where a request relates to information, part of which is environmental and part of which is not, then each part of the request should be handled in accordance with the relevant legislation.

4. This foreword does not form part of the Code itself.

5. An access to environmental information regime has been in place since 1992, in the form of the Environmental Information Regulations 1992, as amended by the Environmental Information (Amendment) Regulations 1998, and also the Environmental Information Regulations (Northern Ireland) 1993 and 1998. The introduction of replacement Regulations in England, Wales and Northern Ireland (and of similar regulations in Scotland) enables compliance with the UK's commitments under the UNECE Convention on Access to Information, Public Participation in Decision-making, and Access to Justice in Environmental Matters (the "Aarhus" Convention), and with EU Directive 2003/4/EC. Increased public access to environmental information and the dissemination of such information contribute to a greater awareness of environmental matters, a free exchange of views, more effective participation by the public in environmental decision- making and, eventually, to a better environment (Recital 1, Directive 2003/4/EC).

6. The Government is committed to greater openness in the public sector. FOIA and EIR will further this aim by helping to transform the culture of the public sector to one of greater openness, enabling members of the public to scrutinise the decisions of public authorities

759

more closely and ensure that services provided by the public sector are more efficiently and properly delivered. Conformity with the Code will assist this.

7. The Code is a supplement to the provisions in the EIR. It is not a substitute for legislation. Public authorities should seek legal advice as considered necessary on general issues relating to the implementation of the EIR or its application to individual cases. They should also refer to the Government's Guidance on the EIR and to any guidance issued by the Information Commissioner.

8. The provisions of the EIR granting a general right of access came into force on 1st January 2005 and the Commissioner's powers to handle appeals and issue guidance will also took effect on 1st January 2005.

9. This code of practice outlines to public authorities the practice that it would, in the opinion of the Secretary of State, be desirable for them to follow in connection with the discharge of their duties under the Environmental Information Regulations 2004 (EIR).

10. The aims of the Code are to:

– facilitate the disclosure of information under the EIR by setting out good administrative practice that it is desirable for public authorities to follow when handling requests for information including, where appropriate, the transfer of a request to a different authority;

– to set out good practice in proactive dissemination of environmental information;

– to protect the interests of applicants by setting out standards of advice and assistance that should be followed as a matter of good practice;

– to ensure that third party rights are considered and that authorities consider the implications for access to environmental information before agreeing to confidentiality provisions in contracts and accepting information in confidence from a third party;

– to encourage, as matter of good practice, the development of effective review and appeal procedures of decisions taken under the EIR.

11. Although there is a power under EIR for the Secretary of State to issue the Code, the provisions of the Code are not legislation. However, authorities are expected to abide by the Code unless there are good reasons, capable of being justified to the Information Commissioner, why it would be inappropriate to do so.

12. The requirements for dealing with requests for environmental information are contained in the EIR and public authorities must comply with these provisions at all times. However, Regulation 16 applies section 47 of the FOIA, which places a duty on the Information Commissioner to promote good practice by public authorities ("good practice" includes compliance with the provisions of the Code), and section 48 of the FOIA which enables the Information Commissioner to issue a "practice recommendation" to a public authority if it appears to him that the practice of the authority does not conform with that proposed in the Code.

13. Public authorities and others are encouraged to contact the Information Commissioner's Office for advice and assistance about their duties under the Regulations. The Information Commissioner can provide valuable, detailed assistance to help organisations achieve compliance through the development of good practice. Further, Regulation 9 of the EIR

places a duty on public authorities to provide advice and assistance to applicants and potential applicants. Authorities will have complied with this duty in any particular case if they have conformed with the Code in relation to the provision of advice or assistance in that case.

Main differences between requirements under the FOIA and EIR that must be reflected in this code

14. The main differences are:

    i. the range of bodies covered by the EIR is wider to allow for consistency with the EC Directive, and includes public utilities and certain public private partnerships and private companies, such as those in the water, waste, transport and energy sectors;

    ii. requests for environmental information need not be in writing;

    iii. the information held by a public authority includes holding information held on behalf of any other person;

    iv. the duty to provide advice and assistance requires a public authority to respond within 20 working days when requesting more particulars from the applicant;

    v. the time limits for responding to a request apply to ALL requests including those involving consideration of the public interest. Regulation 7 allows for an extension from 20 to 40 working days for complex and high volume requests;

    vi no exception is made for requests that will involve costs in excess of the 'appropriate limit' within the meaning of the Fees Regulations made under sections 9, 12 and 13 of the FOIA. Except in specified limited circumstances, ALL requests must be dealt with and any charges imposed must be reasonable;

    vii there are differences in the exceptions available under EIR and the exemptions available under FOIA; viii the requirement for public authorities to have in place a complaints and reconsideration procedure to deal with representations alleging non-compliance with the EIR is mandatory. Each of these differences is explained in greater detail in the EIR Guidance that can be found at http://www.defra.gov.uk/environment/pubaccess/ . The Guidance also explains the scope of environmental information and provides further information on terminology, including "emissions" and "held by or for".

Duty to provide advice and assistance

15. Regulation 9 of the EIR places a duty on public authorities to provide advice and assistance to applicants. A public authority is deemed to have complied with this duty in any particular case if it has conformed with this Code in relation to the provision of advice and assistance in that case. The duty to assist and advise is enforceable by the Information Commissioner. If a public authority fails in its statutory duty, the Commissioner may issue a decision notice under section 50, or an enforcement notice under section 52 of the FOIA.

16. Public Authorities should not forget that other Acts of Parliament may be relevant to the way in which authorities provide advice and assistance to applicants or potential applicants, e.g. the Disability Discrimination Act 1995 and the Race Relations Act 1976 (as amended by the Race Relations (Amendment) Act 2000).

Copyright

17. Public authorities should be aware that information that is disclosed under the EIR might be subject to copyright protection. If an applicant wishes to use any such information in a way that would infringe copyright, for example by making multiple copies, or issuing copies to the public, he or she would require a licence from the copyright holder. HMSO have issued guidance, which is available at:
http://www.hmso.gov.uk/copyright/managing_copyright.htm
or by telephone on 01603 621000.

18 http://www.hmso.gov.uk/copyright/guidance/gn_19.htm explains more fully the distinction between the supply of information held by public authorities under Freedom of Information legislation and the re- use of that information and those circumstances where formal licensing is required.

19. Reports on the environment may be commissioned by public authorities from outside organisations. In general, public authorities should seek to ensure that the copyright of any such reports rests with them. If not, it should be made clear to the outside organisation that under the terms of the EIR, the public authority will likely be making copies of their reports, or parts thereof, available to the public in response to EIR applications, and it may not be solely environmental information contained in reports that will be disclosed.

Practice recommendations

20. The Information Commissioner has a duty to enforce compliance and promote good practice. The following (described in paragraphs 21-24) are the principal tools at his disposal. The Information Commissioner (the Commissioner) is issuing guidance for public authorities on dealing with requests for environmental information, which may be helpful in setting out in more detail the Commissioner's enforcement powers.

21. In accordance with the powers provided in section 74 of the FOIA, Regulation 16(5) of EIR provides that the general functions of the Commissioner under sections 47-49 of the FOIA shall apply under EIR. Under section 47 of the FOIA, the Information Commissioner has a duty to promote the observance of this Code by public authorities. If it appears to the Commissioner that the practice of a public authority in the exercise of its functions under the EIR does not conform with that proposed in the Code of Practice, he may give to the authority a recommendation, under section 48 (known as a "practice recommendation"), specifying the steps which should, in his opinion, be taken to promote such conformity. Unless the public authority appeals against the decision of the Commissioner the public authority must comply with the recommendation of the Commissioner. There is no statutory time limit for this; it will depend on the circumstances of the case but the Commissioner can specify a particular time limit for compliance in the recommendation in question, and will take into consideration the measurements of Articles 9(1) and 9(4) of the Aarhus Convention in setting any time limit.

22. A practice recommendation must be given in writing and must refer to the particular provisions of the Code of Practice with which, in the Commissioner's opinion, the public authority's practice does not conform. A practice recommendation is simply a recommendation and cannot be directly enforced by the Commissioner. However, a failure to comply with a practice recommendation may lead to a failure to comply with the EIR. Further, a failure to take account of a practice recommendation may lead to an adverse comment in a report to Parliament by the Commissioner.

Information notices

23. Regulation 18 of the EIR applies the enforcement and appeal provisions of FOIA to environmental information. The Information Commissioner determines whether the practice of a public authority conforms to this Code. Where an application has been received under section 50 of the FOIA, under section 51 of the FOIA, he may serve an information notice on the authority requiring it to provide information relating to its conformity with the Code.

24. Under the provisions of section 54 of the FOIA, if a public authority fails to comply with an information notice the Commissioner may certify in writing to the court that the public authority has failed to comply with that notice. The court may then inquire into the matter and, after hearing any witnesses who may be produced against or on behalf of the public authority, and after hearing any statement that may be offered in defence, deal with the authority as if it had committed a contempt of court.

Code of Practice on the Discharge of the Obligations of Public Authorities Under the Environmental Information Regulations 2004 (SI 2004 No 3391)

The Secretary of State, after consulting the Information Commissioner, issues the following Code of Practice pursuant to Regulation 16 of the Environmental Information Regulations 2004. Laid before Parliament on 16 February 2005 pursuant to Regulation 16 of the Environmental Information Regulations.

I TRAINING

1. All communications to a public authority, including those not in writing and those transmitted by electronic means, potentially amount to a request for information within the meaning of the EIR, and if they do they must be dealt with in accordance with the provisions of the EIR. It is therefore essential that everyone working in a public authority who deals with correspondence, or who otherwise may be required to provide information, is familiar with the requirements of the EIR and this Code in addition to the FOIA and the other Codes of Practice issued under its provisions, and takes account of any relevant guidance on good practice issued by the Commissioner. Authorities should also ensure that proper training is provided.

2. Requests for environmental information may come in the form of verbal requests which has specific implications for training provision.

3. In planning and delivering training, authorities should be aware of other provisions affecting the disclosure of information such as the FOIA, the Data Protection Act 1998, and anti-discrimination legislation (such as the Disability Discrimination Act).

II PROACTIVE DISSEMINATION OF INFORMATION

4. Under Regulation 4, a public authority has a duty to progressively make the information available to the public by electronic means which are easily accessible, and to take reasonable steps to organize information relevant to its functions with a view to active and systematic dissemination.

5. Consideration should be given to making web sites accessible to all and simple to use, so that information can be readily found, for example by enabling search functions and having an

alphabetical directory as well as tree structures. Information should not be 'buried' on a site.

6. Public authorities should consider how to publicise applicants' rights to information, for example as part of general information on services provided by the authority.

7. When public authorities are considering what information to disseminate proactively, they should not restrict themselves to the minimum requirements as listed in the Directive. For example, consideration should be given to disseminating frequently requested information, which will reduce individual requests for such information in the future.

III THE PROVISION OF ADVICE AND ASSISTANCE TO PERSONS MAKING REQUESTS FOR INFORMATION

8. The provision of advice and assistance to persons making requests for environmental information differs from that provided to those making general requests for information under FOIA:

   – requests for environmental information need not be in writing;

   – EIR contains no equivalent to the 'appropriate limit' exemption under section 12 of the FOIA; and

   – the duty to provide advice and assistance under EIR requires the public authority to request that the applicant provide more particulars within 20 working days of the request where a request is formulated in too general a manner.

9. Every public authority should be ready to provide advice and assistance, including but not necessarily limited to the steps set out below. This advice and assistance should be available to those who propose to make, or have made requests and help them to make good use of the Regulations. The duty on the public authority is to provide advice and assistance "so far as it would be reasonable to expect the authority to do so".

10. Appropriate assistance might include:

    – providing an outline of the different kinds of information that might meet the terms of the request;

    – providing access to detailed catalogues and indexes, where these are available, to help the applicant ascertain the nature and extent of the information held by the authority; and

    – providing a general response to the request setting out options for further information that could be provided on request.

    – advising the person that another person or agency (such as a Citizens Advice Bureau) may be able to assist them with the application or make the application on their behalf.

11. This list is not exhaustive and public authorities should be flexible in offering advice and assistance most appropriate to the circumstances of the applicant.

12. Public authorities should publish their procedures for dealing with requests for information. These procedures may include what the public authority's usual procedure will be where it does not hold the information requested. (See also VI - "Transferring requests for information"). It may also alert potential applicants to the fact that the public authority may want to consult other public authorities and/or third parties in order to

reach a decision on whether the requested information can be released. Potential applicants may wish to be notified before any transfer of request or consultation is made. If this is the case, the published procedure should therefore alert them to say so in their applications. (See also VII - "Consultation with third parties".) The procedures should include an address or addresses (including an e-mail address where possible) to which applicants may direct requests for information or for assistance. A telephone number should also be provided and where possible the name of an individual who can provide assistance. These procedures should be referred to in the authority's publication scheme where it has one.

13. Public authorities may wish to consider publishing their procedures for reviewing refusals for requests. In addition, public authorities will also wish to consider providing information about other access regimes (where appropriate), provide guidance about frequently requested information, and provide information relating to previous disclosures.

14. Staff in public authorities in contact with the public should bear in mind that not everyone will be aware of the EIR or the FOIA and they should draw the legislation to the attention of potential applicants who appear unaware of them. Any question which cannot be dealt with on the spot should be treated as a request for information.

15. A request for information under the EIR can be in any form and need not be in writing. However, for a response to be made by the public authority it will need contact details to either provide the information or refuse the request. A request in writing includes a request transmitted by electronic means. Where a person finds it difficult to specify very clearly the nature of their request, the public authority should ensure that appropriate assistance is given to enable that person to make a request for information. For example, if a request is formulated in too general a manner the public authority shall, as soon as possible and not later than 20 working days after receipt of the request, ask the applicant to provide more particulars and shall assist them in doing so. However, Public Authorities should be aware of the dangers of over- bureaucratising procedures when responding to requests for routine information.

Clarifying the Request

16. Where the applicant does not describe the information sought in a way which would enable the public authority to identify or locate it, or the request is ambiguous, the authority should, as far as practicable, provide assistance to the applicant to enable him or her to describe more clearly the information requested. Authorities should be aware that the aim of providing assistance is to clarify the nature of the information sought, not to determine the aims or motivation of the applicant. Care should be taken not to give the applicant the impression that he or she is obliged to disclose the nature of his or her interest or that he or she will be treated differently if he or she does. It is important that the applicant is contacted as soon as possible, preferably by telephone, fax or e-mail, where more information is needed to clarify what is sought. Public authorities should also be prepared to explain why they are asking for additional information. The 20 day time limit stops running when a request for clarification is issued.

17. In seeking to clarify what is sought, public authorities should bear in mind that applicants cannot reasonably be expected to possess identifiers such as a file reference number, or a description of a particular record, unless this information is made available by the authority for the use of applicants.

18. If, following the provision of such assistance, the applicant is still unable to describe the

information requested in a way that would enable the authority to identify and locate it, the authority is not expected to seek further clarification. The authority should disclose any information relating to the application that has been successfully identified and found that it can disclose. It should also explain to the applicant why it cannot take the request any further and provide details of the authority's complaints procedure and where applicable the applicant's rights under section 50 of the FOIA (see "Complaints Procedure" in section XII below).

19. Where the applicant indicates that he or she is not prepared to pay any charge requested, the authority should consider whether there is any information that may be of interest to the applicant that is available free of charge.

20. There is no EIR equivalent to the 'appropriate limit' under section 12 of the FOIA. A public authority is expected to deal with all requests for environmental information. However, cost may be relevant when considering whether to apply the exceptions relating to 'manifestly unreasonable' or 'too general'. . Where the applicant makes a request that is clear but which involves the provision of a very large volume of information, and specifies a cost ceiling, the authority should consider providing an indication of what information could be provided within the cost ceiling.

21. There are no special provisions for dealing with requests that appear to be part of an organised campaign. Such requests are to be expected and dealt with in the usual way. Repeatedly requested information may be best made available by means of a publication scheme. Being part of a campaign does not necessarily make a request 'manifestly unreasonable'.

Form and Format

22. Regulation 6 allows for the applicant to be given the information available in a particular form or format unless there is another reasonable approach to supplying the information. A public authority should be flexible, as far as is reasonable, with respect to form and format, taking into account the fact, for example, that some IT users may not be able to read attachments in certain formats, and that some members of the public may prefer paper to electronic copies.

23. Although there is no specific reference in the Regulations to the provision of information in the form of a summary or digest, a request for environmental information may include a request for information to be provided in the form of a digest or summary. This should generally be provided so long as it is reasonably practical to do so, taking into account the cost. Many applicants will find a summary more useful than masses of data, and this should be taken into account when considering proactive dissemination.

IV TIMELINESS IN DEALING WITH REQUESTS FOR INFORMATION

24. Requests for information must be responded to within 20 working days. The 20 day time limit can be extended to 40 working days if the complexity and volume of the information requested means that the 20 working days deadline cannot be complied with. Unlike FOIA, there is no provision to further extend the time limit for cases where the public interest has to be balanced.

25. Public authorities are required to comply with all requests for information as soon as possible and they must not delay responding until the end of the 20 working day period

under Regulation 5(2)(b) if the information could reasonably have been provided earlier.

26. Public authorities must aim to make all decisions as soon as possible and in any case within 20 working days, including in cases where a public authority needs to consider where the public interest lies. However, it is recognised there will be some instances where, because of the complexity and volume of the information requested it will not be possible to deal with an application within 20 working days. In such cases a public authority is expected to inform the applicant of this as soon as possible and within 20 working days, and should, be as specific as possible in their response to the applicant indicating when they will receive the information and the reasons for the delay. The 20 days will halt at the point that the authority issues a request for payment of an advance charge, and commences again at the point payment is received, Authorities must in any case comply with or refuse the request within 40 working days. Authorities may find it helpful to formulate a policy about how to apply the provision on making a time extension.

27. It is of critical importance for the body receiving a request to identify the request for environmental information in the first instance, and then to meet the timetable. Monitoring the timeliness of responses is easiest where requests for information are in writing. Where requests for environmental information are made otherwise than in writing (e.g. by telephone or in person) public authorities will need a system for recording the request. This may, for example, involve making a written note of the request and asking the applicant to confirm its accuracy.

V CHARGES

28. The EIR does not require charges to be made but public authorities have discretion to make a reasonable charge for environmental information. However, if they are providing access to a public register, or if the applicant examines the information at the offices of the public authority or in a drop in library or other place which the public authority makes available for that examination, access to the information shall be free of charge. When making a charge, whether for information that is proactively disseminated or provided on request, the charge must not exceed the cost of producing the information unless that public authority is one entitled to levy a market-based charge for the information, such as a trading fund.

29. Where a public authority proposes to make a charge, a schedule of charges should be made available (including, e.g. a price list for publications, or the charge per unit of work which will be incurred to meet a request). When an advance payment is required, the applicant should be notified and the public authority should invite the applicant to say whether they wish to proceed with the request, or their request, or part of it, or whether the request may be met in some other way (for example, by visiting the offices of the public authority to inspect the information or by making use of more easily identifiable data). Where a requirement for advance payment has been notified, the period between the notification and the receipt of payment will be disregarded in determining the response times for meeting requests (Regulation 8(5)). The request will remain active for up to 60 working days from the date of notification. If no payment is received during this time the request lapses but the applicant may make a new application at any time. When a fee payment is received the public authority should release the information promptly and within the appropriate time limit.

30. Public authorities should ensure that any charges they make are reasonable, and in

accordance with the EIR and the guidance.

VI TRANSFERRING REQUESTS FOR INFORMATION

31. A request whether in writing or received in any other form can only be transferred where a public authority receives a request for environmental information that it does not itself hold and which is not held by any other person on its behalf. If a public authority in receipt of a request holds some of the information requested, a transfer can only be made in respect of the information it does not hold but is held by another public authority.

32. Public authorities should bear in mind that "holding" environmental information under the EIR includes holding a copy of a record produced or supplied by another person or body and, unlike FOIA, it extends to holding a record on behalf of another person or body. Where information is held on behalf of another person or body it will be appropriate to consult on whether the environmental information requested should be supplied unless the outcome can be predicted with reasonable confidence. (See also VII – Consultation with Third Parties). (Special provisions apply to the National Archives and other public record holding bodies under Regulation 17 including the Public Records Office Northern Ireland).

33. The authority receiving the initial request must always deal with that request in accordance with the EIR. When the authority receiving the original request does not hold all the information requested it must still deal with the request for information it does hold. The authority must also advise the applicant that it does not hold part of the requested information, or all of it, whichever applies. However, before doing this, the authority must be certain as to the extent of information requested that it holds itself. If information is freely available via a third party's public register, an authority may point to that register as part of providing advice and assistance, but this does not alter the authority's responsibility to respond to the request, for example if the applicant requests the information in the format in which it is held by the authority.

34. If the authority to whom the initial request was made believes that some or all of the information requested is held by another public authority, the authority should consider what would be the most helpful and expeditious way of assisting the applicant with his or her request. In most cases this is likely to involve:

    – contacting the applicant and informing him or her that the information requested may be held by another public authority;

    – suggesting that the applicant re-applies to the authority that is believed to hold the information;

    – providing him or her with contact details for that authority;

    – if the public authority receiving the request and the authority holding the information are publicly perceived as indelibly linked, explaining to the applicant the difference between the two authorities.

35. However, in some cases the authority to whom the original request is made may consider it to be more appropriate to transfer the request for information that it does not itself hold to another authority. In such cases, the authority should always consult with the other authority with a view to ascertaining whether it does hold the information and, if so, whether it should transfer the request to it. A request (or part of a request) should not be

transferred if there is any reason to doubt that the second authority holds the information. When consulting a second authority the identity of the person requesting the information should not be disclosed unless that person has consented.

36. Before transferring a request for information to another authority, the authority should firstly consider whether a transfer is appropriate. If a transfer is appropriate the authority should first obtain the consent of the applicant who may have valid reasons for not wishing their request to be transferred to a third party. If consent is given the applicant should always be provided with sufficient details concerning the date and destination of transfer.

37. Where a request or part of a request is transferred from one public authority to another, the receiving authority must comply with its obligations under the EIR in the same way as it would for a request that is received direct from an applicant. The time for complying with such a request will be measured from the day that the receiving authority receives the request.

38. All transfers of requests should take place as soon as is practicable, and the applicant should be notified as soon as possible once this has been done by issuing a refusal letter under Regulation 14.

39. Where a public authority is unable either to advise the applicant which public authority holds, or may hold, the requested information or to facilitate the transfer of the request to another authority (or considers it inappropriate to do so) it should consider what advice, if any, it can provide to the applicant to enable him or her to pursue his or her request. In this event the public authority should also issue a refusal letter in accordance with Regulation 14. The refusal letter should explain that the public authority does not hold the information.

VII CONSULTATION WITH THIRD PARTIES

40. Public authorities must always remember that unless an exception is provided for in the EIR in relation to any particular information, they will be obliged to disclose that information in response to a request. Authorities are not obliged by the EIR to consult in respect of information which may be wholly or jointly owned by third parties, but may make a commitment to do so.

41. All EIR exceptions are subject to the public interest test; unlike FOIA, the EIR contains no 'absolute' exceptions. Moreover, lack of consent of a third party does not necessarily preclude disclosure, as in each case the public interest must be balanced. If the public interest in disclosing the information outweighs the public interest in withholding it, the information must be disclosed. (Information on emissions must be disclosed in accordance with Regulation 12 and personal data must be considered in accordance with DPA requirements).

42. A public authority may consider that consultation is not appropriate where the cost of consulting with third parties would be disproportionate because, for example, many third parties are involved or there has been earlier consultation on the status and sensitivity of the information. It should be noted that in this context 'third party' is specifically a person or body affected by the information that is the subject of the consultation. In such cases the authority should consider what is the most reasonable course of action for it to take in light of the requirements of the EIR, the potential effects of disclosure, and the public interest.

43. Where the consent of a number of third parties may be relevant and those parties have a representative organisation that can express views on behalf of those parties the authority may, if it considers consultation appropriate, consider that it would be sufficient to consult that representative organisation. If there is no representative organisation, the authority may consider that it would be sufficient to consult a representative sample of the third parties in question.

44. The fact that the third party has not responded to consultation does not relieve the authority of its duty to disclose information under the EIR, or its duty to reply within the time specified in the EIR.

45. In all cases, it is for the public authority that received the request, not the third party (or representative of the third party) to weigh the public interest and to determine whether or not information should be disclosed under the EIR. A refusal to consent to disclosure by a third party does not in itself mean information should be withheld, although it may indicate interests involved. Note that in the case of public records transferred to a public record office there is a requirement to consult (see Regulation 17).

VIII ENVIRONMENTAL INFORMATION REGULATIONS AND PUBLIC SECTOR CONTRACTS

46. When entering into contracts public authorities should refuse to include contractual terms that purport to restrict the disclosure of environmental information held by the authority and relating to the contract beyond the restrictions permitted by the EIR. Public authorities cannot "contract out" of their obligations under the Regulations. This means that they cannot sign a contract that gives an undertaking to a private firm (or anyone else) that they will not comply with their obligations under the Regulations. Unless an exception provided for under the EIR is applicable in relation to any particular information and the balancing of public interest favours refusal, a public authority will be obliged to disclose that information in response to a request, regardless of the terms of any contract. Where personal data is concerned this will be done in accordance with the requirements of Regulation 13 and the Data Protection Act 1998.

47. When entering into contracts with non-public authority contractors, public authorities may be under pressure to accept confidentiality clauses so that information relating to the terms of the contract, its value and performance will be exempt from disclosure. Public authorities should reject such clauses wherever possible and explain the relevance of the public interest test. Where, exceptionally, it is necessary to include non-disclosure provisions in a contract, an option could be to agree with the contractor a schedule of the contract that clearly identifies information that should not be disclosed. But authorities will need to take care when drawing up any such schedule, and be aware that any restrictions on disclosure provided for could potentially be overridden by their obligations under the EIR, as described above.

48. In any event, public authorities should not agree to hold information 'in confidence' which is not in fact confidential in nature. Authorities should be aware that certain exceptions including those for commercial confidentiality, and voluntarily supplied data, are not available when the information requested is about emissions into the environment.

49. Any acceptance of confidentiality provisions must be for good reasons and capable of being justified to the Commissioner.

50. It is for the public authority to disclose information pursuant to the EIR, and not the non-public authority contractor, unless that contractor received the request and is, itself, a body subject to the EIR. However, a public authority may have concerns regarding contractual matters and not wish the contractor to release information without consulting them. In these cases, contracts or other working arrangements should be made to ensure appropriate consultation about the handling of requests for information exchanged between the parties. Any such constraints should be drawn as narrowly as possible and according to the individual circumstances of the case. Apart from such cases, public authorities should not impose terms of secrecy on contractors.

51. With contracts in existence prior to EIR 2004 being enacted, if an authority receives a request for information whose release would mean an actionable breach of confidence, the authority should refer to the guidance issued by the Information Commissioner.Public authorities in this position should seek their own legal advice as appropriate.

52. Under the EIR, some contractors, including public utilities that have been privatised, are subject to the requirements of the EIR.

IX ACCEPTING INFORMATION IN CONFIDENCE FROM THIRD PARTIES

53. A public authority should only accept information from third parties in confidence if it is essential to obtain that information in connection with the exercise of any of the authority's functions and it would not otherwise be provided. Even in these circumstances it will be necessary to explain the relevance of the public interest test and the fact that there could be circumstances in which the public interest in disclosure equals or outweighs the adverse effects of disclosure on a third party. In addition, public authorities should not agree to hold information received from third parties "in confidence" which is not confidential in nature (paragraph 47). Again, acceptance of any confidentiality provisions must be for good reasons, capable of being justified to the Commissioner. (Special provisions apply to archives (paragraph 32).

X CONSULTATION WITH DEVOLVED ADMINISTRATIONS

54. Public authorities should consult with the relevant devolved administration before disclosing information provided by or directly concerning that administration, except where:

- the views of the devolved administration can have no effect on the decision of the authority (for example where there is no applicable exception so the information must be disclosed under EIR); or

- where the outcome may be predicted with reasonable confidence and in the circumstances, consultation would be too costly or time consuming.

55. Similarly, the devolved administrations should consult with the relevant non-devolved public authority before disclosing information provided by or directly concerning that authority, except where the views of the public authority can have no effect on the decision whether to disclose, or where consultation would be disproportionate in the circumstances.

XI REFUSAL OF REQUEST

Advice on withholding of information is covered in Chapter 7 of the Guidance.

56. Where a request for information is refused or partially refused in accordance with an exception, the EIR requires that the authority notify the applicant which exception has been claimed and why that exception applies. Public authorities should not unless the statement would involve the disclosure of information which would itself be withheld in accordance with the EIR merely paraphrase the wording of the exception. They should state clearly in the decision letter the reason why they have decided to apply that exception in the case in question. The EIR also requires authorities, when withholding information, to state the reasons for claiming that the public interest in maintaining the exception outweighs the public interest in disclosure. Public authorities should specify the public interest factors (for and against disclosure) that they have taken into account before reaching the decision (again, unless the statement would involve the disclosure of information which would itself be withheld in accordance with the EIR). They should also include details of the complaints procedure.

57. For monitoring purposes public authorities should keep a record of all applications where either all or part of the requested information is withheld, the basis on which it was withheld (including the exception or exceptions which were applied), and, where relevant, a full explanation of how the public interest test was applied and the factors which were considered. Public authorities should also keep copies of redacted information, together with a copy of the information that the applicant actually received in case of a subsequent complaint. Senior managers in each public authority will need this information to determine whether cases are being properly considered and whether the reasons for refusals are sound. The information will also be required if the applicant appeals against the refusal, or refers the case to the Information Commissioner. This could be done by requiring all staff that refuse a request for information to forward the details to a central point in the organisation for collation. Details of information on complaints about applications which have been refused (see XII – "Complaints procedure") could be collected at the same central point.

XII REVIEW AND COMPLAINTS PROCEDURES

58. Each public authority must have a review procedure in place. This procedure may be used by any person who considers that their request has not been properly handled or who are otherwise dissatisfied with the outcome of the consideration of their request and where the issue is such that it cannot be resolved informally in discussion with the official dealing with the request. Information relating to the complaints procedure should be included in an authority's publication scheme if it has one, or made readily available elsewhere. Under Regulation 18, the enforcement and appeal provisions of the FOIA will apply in respect of a complaint made after 1st January 2005.

59. Any decision made in relation to a request under the EIR that contains a refusal must be in writing and public authorities are obliged under Regulations 14 (5) to notify the applicant of his or her right of complaint. They should provide details of their own complaints procedure, including how to make a complaint and inform the applicant of the right to complain to the Commissioner under section 50 of the FOIA if he or she is still dissatisfied following the authority's review. However, as a matter of good practice authorities should provide details of their complaints procedure when responding to all requests. It is for the applicant to decide whether they are content with the response they

receive; they may have concerns that they wish to pursue in circumstances where the public authority claims to have fully complied with their request.

60. Any written reply from the applicant (including one transmitted electronically) expressing dissatisfaction with an authority's response to a valid request for information should be treated as a complaint, as should any written communication from a person who perceives the authority is not complying with its publication scheme where it has one. These communications should be handled in accordance with the authority's review procedure pursuant to Regulation 11, even if the applicant does not state his or her desire for the authority to review their decision or the handling of their application.

61. The complaints procedure should be a fair and impartial means of dealing with handling problems and reviewing decisions taken pursuant to the EIR, including decisions taken about where the public interest lies. It should be possible to reverse or otherwise amend decisions previously taken. Complaints procedures should be clear and not unnecessarily bureaucratic. They should be capable of producing a prompt determination of the complaint.

62. In all cases, complaints should be acknowledged and the complainant should be informed of the authority's target date for determining the complaint. Where it is apparent that determination of the complaint will take longer than the target time (for example because of the complexity of the particular case), the authority should inform the applicant and explain the reason for the delay. The complainant should always be informed of the outcome of his or her complaint.

63. Authorities must consider each complaint, decide whether they have complied with their requirements under EIR and respond to the complainant within 40 working days from the time when the complaint was received.

64. Records should be kept of all complaints and of their outcome. Authorities should have procedures in place for monitoring complaints and for reviewing, and if necessary amending procedures for dealing with requests for information where such action is indicated by more than occasional reversals of initial decisions.

65. Where the outcome of a complaint is that information should be disclosed which was previously withheld, the information in question should be disclosed with immediate effect.

66. Where the outcome of a complaint is that the procedures within an authority have not been properly followed by the authority's staff, the authority should apologise to the applicant. The authority should also take appropriate steps to prevent similar errors occurring in future.

67. Where the outcome of a complaint is that an initial decision to withhold information is upheld or is otherwise in the authority's favour, the applicant should be informed of his or her right to apply to the Commissioner and be given details of how to make an application for a decision on whether the request for information has been dealt with in accordance with the requirements of the EIR. As failure to deal with a complaint promptly may be grounds for complaint to the Information Commissioner, authorities should set out details of the timescale for dealing with complaints in their complaints procedure, which should be made readily available.

Part IV

Other Rights to Information

Public Records Act 1958

CHAPTER 51

(as amended to 1 February 2020)

An Act to make new provision with respect to public records and the Public Record Office, and for connected purposes

23rd July 1958

BE IT ENACTED by the Queen's most Excellent Majesty, by and with the advice and consent of the Lords Spiritual and Temporal, and Commons, in this present Parliament assembled, and by the authority of the same, as follows:–

TABLE OF PROVISIONS

General responsibility of the Secretary of State for public records

1(1)   The Secretary of State shall be generally responsible for the execution of this Act and shall supervise the care and preservation of public records..

(2)   There shall be an Advisory Council on Public Records to advise the Secretary of State on matters concerning public records in general and, in particular, on those aspects of the work of the Public Record Office which affect members of the public who make use of the facilities provided by the Public Record Office.
The Master of the Rolls shall be chairman of the said Council and the remaining members of the Council shall be appointed by the Secretary of State on such terms as he may specify.

(2A)   The matters on which the Advisory Council on Public Records may advise the Secretary of State include matters relating to the application of the Freedom of Information Act 2000 to information contained in public records which are historical records within the meaning of Part VI of that Act.

(3)   The Secretary of State shall in every year lay before both Houses of Parliament a report on the work of the Public Record Office, which shall include any report made to him by the Advisory Council on Public Records.

NOTES

Defined terms
"public records" s 10(1) and Sch 1;

"records" s 10(1)

The Public Record Office

2(1)   The Secretary of State may appoint a Keeper of Public Records to take charge under his direction of the Public Record Office and of the records therein and may, with the concurrence of the Treasury as to numbers and conditions of service, appoint such other persons to serve in the Public Record Office as he may think fit.

(2)   The Keeper of Public Records and other persons appointed under this Act shall receive such salaries and remuneration as the Treasury may from time to time direct.

(3)   It shall be the duty of the Keeper of Public Records to take all practicable steps for the preservation of records under his charge.

(4)   The Keeper of Public Records shall have power to do all such things as appear to him necessary or expedient for maintaining the utility of the Public Record Office and may in particular--

   (a)   compile and make available indexes and guides to, and calendars and texts of, the records in the Public Record Office;

   (b)   prepare publications concerning the activities of and facilities provided by the Public Record Office;

   (c)   regulate the conditions under which members of the public may inspect public and other records or use the other facilities of the Public Record Office;

   (d)   provide for the making and authentication of copies of and extracts from records required as evidence in legal proceedings or for other purposes;

   (e)   accept responsibility for the safe keeping of records other than public records;

   (f)   make arrangements for the separate housing of films and other records which have to be kept under special conditions;

   (g)   lend records, in a case where the Secretary of State gives his approval, for display at commemorative exhibitions or for other special purposes;

   (h)   acquire records and accept gifts and loans.

(5)   The Secretary of State may by regulations made with the concurrence of the Treasury and contained in a statutory instrument prescribe the fees which may be charged for the inspection of records under the charge of the Keeper of Public Records, for authenticated copies or extracts from such records and for other services afforded by officers of the Public Record Office and authorise the remission of the fees in prescribed cases.

(6)   Fees received under the last foregoing subsection shall be paid into the Exchequer.

NOTES

Defined terms	Subordinate legislation
"public records" s 10(1) and Sch 1; "records" s 10(1)	Public Record Office (Fees) Regulations 2015, SI 2015/2042

Selection and preservation of public records

3(1)   It shall be the duty of every person responsible for public records of any description which are not in the Public Record Office or a place of deposit appointed by the Secretary of State under this Act to make arrangements for the selection of those records which ought to be permanently preserved and for their safe-keeping.

(2)   Every person shall perform his duties under this section under the guidance of the Keeper of Public Records and the said Keeper shall be responsible for co-ordinating and supervising all action taken under this section.

(3)   All public records created before the year sixteen hundred and sixty shall be included

among those selected for permanent preservation.

(4) Public records selected for permanent preservation under this section shall be transferred not later than 20 years after their creation either to the Public Record Office or to such other place of deposit appointed by the Secretary of State under this Act as the Secretary of State may direct:

Provided that any records may be retained after the said period if, in the opinion of the person who is responsible for them, they are required for administrative purposes or ought to be retained for any other special reason and, where that person is not the Secretary of State, the Secretary of State has been informed of the facts and given his approval.

(4A) Until the end of the period of 10 years beginning with the commencement of section 45 of the Constitutional Reform and Governance Act 2010, subsection (4) has effect subject to any order made under subsection (2) of that section.

(5) The Secretary of State may, if it appears to him in the interests of the proper administration of the Public Record Office, direct that the transfer of any class of records under this section shall be suspended until arrangements for their reception have been completed.

(6) Public records which, following the arrangements made in pursuance of this section, have been rejected as not required for permanent preservation shall be destroyed or, subject, in the case of records for which some person other than the Secretary of State is responsible, to the approval of the Secretary of State, disposed of in any other way.

(7) Any question as to the person whose duty it is to make arrangements under this section with respect to any class of public records shall be referred to the Secretary of State for his decision.

(8) The provisions of this section shall not make it unlawful for the person responsible for any public record to transmit it to the Keeper of the Records of Scotland or to the Public Record Office of Northern Ireland.

NOTES

Defined terms
"public records" s 10(1) and Sch 1;
"records" s 10(1)

Place of deposit of public records

4(1) If it appears to the Secretary of State that a place outside the Public Record Office affords suitable facilities for the safe-keeping and preservation of records and their inspection by the public he may, with the agreement of the authority who will be responsible for records deposited in that place, appoint it as a place of deposit as respects any class of public records selected for permanent preservation under this Act.

(2) In choosing a place of deposit under this section for public records of—
  (a)   courts of quarter sessions or magistrates' courts, or
  (b)   courts of coroners of counties or boroughs,
the Secretary of State shall have regard to any arrangements made by the person for the time being responsible for the records with respect to the place where those records are to be kept and, where he does not follow any such arrangements, shall, so far as practicable, proceed on the principle that the records of any such court ought to be kept in the area of the administrative county or county borough comprising the area for which the court acts or where it sits, except in a case where the authorities or persons appearing

to the Secretary of State to be mainly concerned consent to the choice of a place of deposit elsewhere.

(3) The Secretary of State may at any time direct that public records shall be transferred from the Public Record Office to a place of deposit appointed under this section or from such a place of deposit to the Public Record Office or another place of deposit.

(4) Before appointing a place of deposit under this section as respects public records of a class for which the Secretary of State is not himself responsible, he shall consult with the Minister or other person if any who appears to him to be primarily concerned and, where the records are records of a court of quarter sessions the records of which are, apart from the provisions of this Act, subject to the directions of a custos rotulorum, the Secretary of State shall consult him.

(5) Public records in the Public Record Office shall be in the custody of the Keeper of Public Records and public records in a place of deposit appointed under this Act shall be in the custody of such officer as the Secretary of State may appoint.

(6) Public records in the Public Record Office or other place of deposit appointed by the Secretary of State under this Act shall be temporarily returned at the request of the person by whom or department or office from which they were transferred.

NOTES

Defined terms   "records" s 10(1)
"public records" s 10(1) and Sch 1;

Access to public records

5(3) It shall be the duty of the Keeper of Public Records to arrange that reasonable facilities are available to the public for inspecting and obtaining copies of those public records in the Public Record Office which fall to be disclosed in accordance with the Freedom of Information Act 2000.

(5) The Secretary of State shall as respects all public records in places of deposit appointed by him under this Act outside the Public Record Office require arrangements to be made for their inspection by the public comparable to those made for public records in the Public Record Office.

NOTES

Defined terms   "records" s 10(1)
"public records" s 10(1) and Sch 1;

Office or other place of deposit

6 If as respects any public records in the Public Record Office or any place of deposit appointed under this Act it appears to the Keeper of Public Records that they are duplicated by other public records which have been selected for permanent preservation or that there is some other special reason why they should not be permanently preserved, he may, with the approval of the Secretary of State and of the Minister or other person, if any, who appears to the Secretary of State to be primarily concerned with public records of the class in question, authorise the destruction of those records or, with that approval, their disposal in any other way.

NOTES

Defined terms   "records" s 10(1)
"public records" s 10(1) and Sch 1;

Records for which Master of the Rolls remains responsible

7(1) Subject to the provisions of this section, the Master of the Rolls shall continue to be responsible for, and to have custody of, the records of the Chancery of England, including those created after the commencement of this Act, and shall have power to determine where the said records or any of them are for the time being to be deposited.

(2) Section three and subsection (6) of section four of this Act shall not apply to any of the said records but if and so long as any of them are deposited in the Public Record Office those records shall be in the custody of the Keeper of Public Records and subject to the directions of the Secretary of State as in the case of any other records in the Public Record Office.

(3) Subject to the foregoing provisions of this section, the Master of the Rolls shall not have charge and superintendence over, or custody of, any public records and any public records which at the commencement of this Act were in the custody of the Master of the Rolls (other than records of the Chancery of England) shall thereafter be in the custody of the Keeper of Public Records or such other officer as the Secretary of State may from time to time appoint.

NOTES

Defined terms "records" s 10(1)
   "public records" s 10(1) and Sch 1;

Court records

8(1) The Lord Chanellor shall be responsible for the public records of every court of record or magistrates' court which are not in the Public Record Office or a place of deposit appointed by him under this Act and shall have power to determine in the case of any such records other than records of the Supreme Court, the officer in whose custody they are for the time being to be:

(1A) Records of the Supreme Court for which the Lord Chancellor is responsible under subsection (1) shall be in the custody of the chief executive of that court.

(4) Where any private documents have remained in the custody of a court in England or Wales for more than fifty years without being claimed, the Keeper of Public Records may, with the approval of the Master of the Rolls, require the documents to be transferred to the Public Record Office and thereupon the documents shall become public records for the purposes of this Act.

(5) Section three of this Act shall not apply to such of the records of ecclesiastical courts described in paragraph (n) of sub-paragraph (1) of paragraph 4 of the First Schedule to this Act as are not held in any office of the Senior Courts or in the Public Record Office, but, if the Lord Chancellor after consulting the President of the Family Division so directs as respects any of those records, those records shall be transferred to such place of deposit as may be appointed by the Secretary of State and shall thereafter be in the custody of such officer as may be so appointed.

(6) The public records which at the commencement of this Act are in the custody of the University of Oxford and which are included in the index a copy of which was transmitted to the principal probate registrar under section two of the Oxford University Act 1860 shall not be required to be transferred under the last foregoing subsection but the Lord Chancellor shall make arrangements with the University of Oxford as to the conditions under which those records may be inspected by the public.

NOTES

Legal validity of public records and authenticated copies

9(1)   The legal validity of any record shall not be affected by its removal under the provisions of this Act, or of the Public Record Office Acts 1838 to 1898, or by any provisions in those Acts with respect to its legal custody.

(2)   A copy of or extract from a public record in the Public Record Office purporting to be examined and certified as true and authentic by the proper officer and to be sealed or stamped with the seal of the Public Record Office shall be admissible as evidence in any proceedings without any further or other proof thereof if the original record would have been admissible as evidence in those proceedings.

(3)   An electronic copy of or extract from a public record in the Public Record Office which--
   (a)   purports to have been examined and certified as true and authentic by the proper officer; and
   (b)   appears on a website purporting to be one maintained by or on behalf of the Public Record Office, shall, when viewed on that website, be admissible as evidence in any proceedings without further or other proof if the original record would have been admissible as evidence in those proceedings.

(4)   In this section any reference to the proper officer is a reference to the Keeper of Public Records or any other officer of the Public Record Office authorised in that behalf by the Keeper of Public Records, and, in the case of copies and extracts made before the commencement of this Act, the deputy keeper of the records or any assistant record keeper appointed under the Public Record Office Act 1838.

Interpretation

10(1)   In this Act "public records" has the meaning assigned to it by the First Schedule to this Act and "records" includes not only written records but records conveying information by any other means whatsoever.

(2)   Where records created at different dates are for administrative purposes kept together in one file or other assembly all the records in that file or other assembly shall be treated for the purposes of this Act as having been created when the latest of those records was created.

Northern Ireland

12(1)   It shall be lawful for any government department or other body or person having the custody of any public records relating exclusively or mainly to Northern Ireland to transmit those records to the Public Record Office of Northern Ireland.

Short title, repeals and commencement

13(1)   This Act may be cited as the Public Records Act 1958.

(3)   This Act shall come into force on the first day of January, nineteen hundred and fifty-nine.

SCHEDULE 1
Definition of Public Records

Section 10

1.   The provisions of this Schedule shall have effect for determining what are public records for the purposes of this Act.

Departmental records

2(1)   Subject to the provisions of this paragraph, administrative and departmental records belonging to Her Majesty, whether in the United Kingdom or elsewhere, in right of Her Majesty's Government in the United Kingdom and, in particular,--

    (a)   records of, or held in, any department of Her Majesty's Government in the United Kingdom, or

    (b)   records of any office, commission or other body or establishment whatsoever under Her Majesty's Government in the United Kingdom,

shall be public records.

(2)   Sub-paragraph (1) of this paragraph shall not apply--

    (a)   to records of any government department or body which is wholly or mainly concerned with Scottish affairs, or which carries on its activities wholly or mainly in Scotland, or

    (b)   to registers, or certified copies of entries in registers, being registers or certified copies kept or deposited in the General Register Office under or in pursuance of any enactment, whether past or future, which provides for the registration of births, deaths, marriages, civil partnerships or adoptions, or

    (c)   except so far as provided by paragraph 4 of this Schedule, to records of the Duchy of Lancaster, or

    (d)   to records of the office of the Public Trustee relating to individual trusts or

    (e)   to Welsh public records (as defined in the Government of Wales Act 2006).

3(1)   Without prejudice to the generality of sub-paragraph (1) of the last foregoing paragraph, the administrative and departmental records of bodies and establishments set out in the Table at the end of this paragraph shall be public records, whether or not they are records belonging to Her Majesty.

(2)   The provisions of this paragraph shall not be taken as applying to records in any museum or gallery mentioned in the said Table which form part of its permanent collections (that is to say records which the museum or gallery has acquired otherwise than by transfer from or arrangements with a government department).

Table not reproduced

PART II
OTHER ESTABLISHMENTS AND ORGANISATIONS

Anglo-Egyptian Resettlement Board.
Armouries.
The Authorised Conveyancing Practitioners Board.
The Big Lottery Fund.

The Board of the Pension Protection Fund.

The Board of Trustees of the National Museums and Galleries on Merseyside.

British Coal Corporation.

British Council.

British Museum (including the Natural History Museum).

British Telecommunications.

Care Council for Wales.

the Care Quality Commission and the Healthwatch England Committee.

Catering Wages Commission.

Central Police Training and Development Authority.

Child Maintenance and Enforcement Commission.

Civil Nuclear Police Authority.

Coal Authority.

Coal Industry Social Welfare Organisation.

Commission for Architecture and the Built Environment.

The Commission for Equality and Human Rights.

Commission for Health Improvement.

Commission for Patient and Public Involvement in Health.

Commission for Rural Communities.

Commission on Industrial Relations.

Commissioner for Parliamentary Investigations.

The Committee on Climate Change.

Competition and Markets Authority

Competition Service.

Consumer Council for Water.

The Conveyancing Ombudsman.

Criminal Cases Review Commission.

Crown Agents for Oversea Governments and Administrations (before and after their reconstitution as a body corporate) except when acting for governments or authorities outside Her Majesty's Dominions.

Crown Agents Holding and Realisation Board.

Council for Healthcare Regulatory Excellence.

A development agency established under section 1 of the Regional Development Agencies Act 1998.

Development Commission.

Electoral Commission.

The Environment Agency.

Funding Agency for Schools.

Further Education Funding Council for England.

Gambling Commission.

Gangmasters Licensing Authority.

General Social Care Council.

General Teaching Council for England.

General Teaching Council for Wales.

Health Education England.

Health Research Authority.

Historic Buildings and Monuments Commission for England.

The Homes and Communities Agency.

Human Tissue Authority.

Imperial War Museum.
Independent Monitoring Authority for Citizens' Rights.
Independent Office for Police Conduct.
The Independent Parliamentary Standards Authority.
Information Commissioner.
Infrastructure Planning Commission.
Irish Sailors' and Soldiers' Land Trust.
Learning and Skills Council for England.
The Legal Services Board.
The Legal Services Consultative Panel.
The Legal Services Ombudsman.
Local Better Regulation Office.
Local Government Boundary Commission for England.
London Museum.
The Lord Chancellor's Advisory Committee on Legal Education and Conduct.
The Marine Management Organisation.
Money and Pension Service.
National Audit Office.
National Citizen Service Trust.
The National Data Guardian for Health and Social Care.
National Gallery.
National Maritime Museum.
National Portrait Gallery.
National Savings Committee.
Natural England.
Nuclear Decommissioning Authority.
Occupational Pensions Regulatory Authority.
Office of Communications.
The Office of the Health Professions Adjudicator.
The Office for Legal Complaints.
Office for Nuclear Regulation.
Office for Students.
Office for Tenants and Social Landlords.
The Ombudsman for the Board of the Pension Protection Fund.
Pensions Compensation Board.
Pensions Ombudsman.
The Pensions Regulator.
Police Information Technology Organisation.
Post Office.
Post Office company (within the meaning of Part IV of the Postal Services Act 2000).
Qualifications and Curriculum Authority.
Qualifications and Curriculum Development Agency.
Rail Passengers' Committees.
Rail Passengers' Council.
The Registrar of Consultant Lobbyists.
The Regulator of Social Housing.
Remploy Limited.
Royal Botanic Gardens, Kew.
Royal Greenwich Observatory.
School Curriculum and Assessment Authority.

Science Museum.
Scottish Criminal Cases Review Commission.
Security Industry Authority.
Serious Organised Crime Agency.
The Simpler Trade Procedures Board.
A strategic highways company for the time being appointed under Part 1 of the Infrastructure Act 2015.
Tate Gallery
Training and Development Agency for Schools.
Teacher Training Agency.
Traffic Director for London.
The trustee corporation established by section 75 of the Pensions Act 2008.
Trustee Savings Banks Inspection Committee.
United Kingdom Atomic Energy Authority.
United Kingdom Research and Innovation.
University Grants Committee.
Valuation Tribunal Service.
Victoria and Albert Museum.
Wallace Collection.
War Works Commission.
Any body established for the purpose of determining the boundaries of constituencies of the Parliament of the United Kingdom, or of local authorities in England.

3A(1) Her Majesty may by Order in Council amend the Table at the end of paragraph 3 of this Schedule by adding to either Part of the Table an entry relating to any body or establishment--

    (a)   which, at the time when the Order is made, is specified in Schedule 2 to the Parliamentary Commissioner Act 1967 (departments, etc subject to investigation), or

    (b)   in respect of which an entry could, at that time, be added to Schedule 2 to that Act by an Order in Council under section 4 of that Act (which confers power to amend that Schedule).

  (2) An Order in Council under this paragraph may relate to a specified body or establishment or to bodies or establishments falling within a specified description.

  (3) An Order in Council under this paragraph shall be subject to annulment in pursuance of a resolution of either House of Parliament.

Records of courts and tribunals.

4(1) Subject to the provisions of this paragraph, records of the following descriptions shall be public records for the purposes of this Act:–

    (za)   records of the Supreme Court;

    (a)   records of, or held in any department of, the Senior Courts (including any court held under a commission of assize);

    (aa)   records of the family court;

    (b)   records of county courts and of any other superior or inferior court of record established since the passing of the County Courts Act 1846;

    (d)   records of courts of quarter sessions;

(e)   records of magistrates' courts;

(f)   records of coroners' courts;

(fa)   records of the Court Martial, the Summary Appeal Court or the Service Civilian Court;

(g)   records of courts-martial held whether within or outside the United Kingdom by any of Her Majesty's forces raised in the United Kingdom;

(h)   records of naval courts held whether within or outside the United Kingdom under the enactments relating to merchant shipping;

(i)   records of any court exercising jurisdiction held by Her Majesty within a country outside Her dominions;

(j)   records of any tribunal (by whatever name called)--

      (i)   which has jurisdiction connected with any functions of a department of Her Majesty's Government in the United Kingdom; or

      (ii)   which has jurisdiction in proceedings to which such a Government department is a party or to hear appeals from decisions of such a Government department;

(k)   records of any Rent Tribunal or Local Valuation Court;

(kk)   records of any Conveyancing Appeal Tribunal;

(l)   records of the Industrial Court, of the Industrial Disputes Tribunal, and of the National Arbitration Tribunal (which was replaced by the Industrial Disputes Tribunal);

(m)   records of umpires and deputy-umpires appointed under the National Service Act 1948 or the Reinstatement in Civil Employment Act 1944;

(n)   records of ecclesiastical courts when exercising the testamentary and matrimonial jurisdiction removed from them by the Court of Probate Act 1857 and the Matrimonial Causes Act 1857 respectively;

(o)   records of such other courts or tribunals (by whatever name called) as the Lord Chancellor may by order contained in a statutory instrument specify.

(1A)   Records of, or held in any department of, the Senior Courts within sub-paragraph (1)(a) of this paragraph include the records of the Chancery Court of the county palatine of Lancaster and the Chancery Court of the county palatine of Durham (which were abolished by the Courts Act 1971).

(1B)   Records of county courts within sub-paragraph (1)(b) of this paragraph include the records of the following courts (which were abolished by the Courts Act 1971)--

      (a)   the Tolzey and Pie Poudre Courts of the City and County of Bristol;

      (b)   the Liverpool Court of Passage;

      (c)   the Norwich Guildhall Court; and

      (d)   the Court of Record for the Hundred of Salford.

(2)   This paragraph shall not apply to any court or tribunal whose jurisdiction extends only to Scotland or Northern Ireland.

(3)   In this paragraph "records" includes records of any proceedings in the court or tribunal in question and includes rolls, writs, books, decrees, bills, warrants and accounts of, or in the custody of, the court or tribunal in question.

Records of the Chancery of England

5   The records of the Chancery of England, other than any which are Welsh public records (as defined in the Government of Wales Act 2006), shall be public records for the purposes of this Act.

Records in Public Record Office

6 Without prejudice to the foregoing provisions of this Schedule, public records for the purposes of this Act shall include--

    (a)   all records within the meaning of the Public Record Office Act 1838, or to which that Act was applied, which at the commencement of this Act are in the custody of the Master of the Rolls in pursuance of that Act, and

    (b)   all records (within the meaning of the said Act or to which that Act was applied) which at the commencement of this Act are in the Public Record Office and, in pursuance of the said Act, under the charge and superintendence of the Master of the Rolls, and

    (c)   all records forming part of the same series as any series of documents falling under sub-paragraph (a) or sub-paragraph (b) of this paragraph

other than any which are Welsh public records (as defined in the Government of Wales Act 2006).

Power to add further categories of records and to determine cases of doubt

7(1) Without prejudice to the Lord Chancellor's power of making orders under paragraph 4 of this Schedule, Her Majesty may by Order in Council direct that any description of records not falling within the foregoing provisions of this Schedule and not being Welsh public records (as defined in the Government of Wales Act 2006) shall be treated as public records for the purposes of this Act but no recommendation shall be made to Her Majesty in Council to make an Order under this sub-paragraph unless a draft of the Order has been laid before Parliament and approved by resolution of each House of Parliament.

(2) A question whether any records or description of records are public records for the purposes of this Act shall be referred to and determined by the Secretary of State and the Secretary of State shall include his decisions on such questions in his annual report to Parliament and shall from time to time compile and publish lists of the departments, bodies, establishments, courts and tribunals comprised in paragraphs 2, 3 and 4 of this Schedule and lists describing more particularly the categories of records which are, or are not, public records as defined in this Schedule.

Interpretation

8 It is hereby declared that any description of government department, court, tribunal or other body or establishment in this Schedule by reference to which a class of public records is framed extends to a government department, court, tribunal or other body or establishment, as the case may be, which has ceased to exist, whether before or after the passing of this Act.

Local Government Act 1972

(as amended to 1 February 2020)

PART VA
ACCESS TO MEETINGS AND DOCUMENTS OF CERTAIN AUTHORITIES, COMMITTEES AND SUB-COMMITTEES

Admission to meetings of principal councils.

100A(1) A meeting of a principal council shall be open to the public except to the extent that they are excluded (whether during the whole or part of the proceedings) under subsection (2) below or by resolution under subsection (4) below.

(2) The public shall be excluded from a meeting of a principal council during an item of business whenever it is likely, in view of the nature of the business to be transacted or the nature of the proceedings, that, if members of the public were present during that item, confidential information would be disclosed to them in breach of the obligation of confidence; and nothing in this Part shall be taken to authorise or require the disclosure of confidential information in breach of the obligation of confidence.

(3) For the purposes of subsection (2) above, "confidential information" means–

   (a) information furnished to the council by a Government department upon terms (however expressed) which forbid the disclosure of the information to the public; and

   (b) information the disclosure of which to the public is prohibited by or under any enactment or by the order of a court;

and, in either case, the reference to the obligation of confidence is to be construed accordingly.

(4) A principal council may by resolution exclude the public from a meeting during an item of business whenever it is likely, in view of the nature of the business to be transacted or the nature of the proceedings, that if members of the public were present during that item there would be disclosure to them of exempt information, as defined in section 100I below.

(5) A resolution under subsection (4) above shall–

   (a) identify the proceedings, or the part of the proceedings, to which it applies, and

   (b) state the description, in terms of Schedule 12A to this Act, of the exempt information giving rise to the exclusion of the public,

and where such a resolution is passed this section does not require the meeting to be open to the public during proceedings to which the resolution applies.

(5A) Where the public are excluded from a meeting of a principal council in England under subsection (2) or (4), the council may also prevent any person from reporting on the meeting using methods

   (a) which can be used without that person's presence at the meeting, and

   (b) which enable persons not present at the meeting to see or hear the proceedings at the meeting as it takes place or later.

(6) The following provisions shall apply in relation to a meeting of a principal council, that is to say–

   (a) public notice of the time and place of the meeting shall be given by posting it

789

at the offices of the council five clear days at least before the meeting or, if the meeting is convened at shorter notice, then at the time it is convened;

(b) while the meeting is open to the public, the council shall not have power to exclude members of the public from the meeting; and

(c) subject to subsection (7D), while the meeting is open to the public, duly accredited representatives of newspapers attending the meeting for the purpose of reporting the proceedings for those newspapers shall, so far as practicable, be afforded reasonable facilities for taking their report and, unless the meeting is held in premises not belonging to the council or not on the telephone, for telephoning the report at their own expense.

(7) Subject to subsection (7A), nothing in this section shall require a principal council to permit the taking of photographs of any proceedings, or the use of any means to enable persons not present to see or hear any proceedings (whether at the time or later), or the making of any oral report on any proceedings as they take place.

(7A) While a meeting of a principal council in England is open to the public, any person attending is to be permitted to report on the meeting.

(7B) Subsection (7A) does not require a principal council in England to permit oral reporting or oral commentary on a meeting as it takes place if the person reporting or providing the commentary is present at the meeting.

(7C) A person attending a meeting of a principal council in England for the purpose of reporting on the meeting must, so far as practicable, be afforded reasonable facilities for doing so.

(7D) Subsection (7C) applies in place of subsection (6)(c) in the case of a principal council in England.

(7E) Any person who attends a meeting of a principal council in England for the purpose of reporting on the meeting may use any communication method, including the internet, to publish, post or otherwise share the results of the person's reporting activities.

(7F) Publication and dissemination may take place at the time of the meeting or occur after the meeting.

(8) This section is without prejudice to any power of exclusion to suppress or prevent disorderly conduct or other misbehaviour at a meeting.

(9) In this section "reporting" means—

(a) filming, photographing or making an audio recording of proceedings at a meeting,

(b) using any other means for enabling persons not present to see or hear proceedings at a meeting as it takes place or later, or

(c) reporting or providing commentary on proceedings at a meeting, orally or in writing, so that the report or commentary is available as the meeting takes place or later to persons not present.

NOTES

Defined terms
"England": s 269
"exempt information":ss 100I, 100K(1)
"information": s 100K(1)

"meeting": s 100K(2)
"newspaper": s 100K(1)
"principal council": ss 100J, 100K(1), 270(1)

Access to agenda and connected reports.

100B(1) Copies of the agenda for a meeting of a principal council and, subject to subsection (2) below, copies of any report for the meeting shall be open to inspection by members of the public at the offices of the council in accordance with subsection (3) below.

(2) If the proper officer thinks fit, there may be excluded from the copies of reports provided in pursuance of subsection (1) above the whole of any report which, or any part which, relates only to items during which, in his opinion, the meeting is likely not to be open to the public.

(3) Any document which is required by subsection (1) above to be open to inspection shall be so open at least five clear days before the meeting, except that–

    (a)   where the meeting is convened at shorter notice, the copies of the agenda and reports shall be open to inspection from the time the meeting is convened, and

    (b)   where an item is added to an agenda copies of which are open to inspection by the public, copies of the item (or of the revised agenda), and the copies of any report for the meeting relating to the item, shall be open to inspection from the time the item is added to the agenda;

but nothing in this subsection requires copies of any agenda, item or report to be open to inspection by the public until copies are available to members of the council.

(4) An item of business may not be considered at a meeting of a principal council unless either–

    (a)   a copy of the agenda including the item (or a copy of the item) is open to inspection by members of the public in pursuance of subsection (1) above for at least five clear days before the meeting or, where the meeting is convened at shorter notice, from the time the meeting is convened; or

    (b)   by reason of special circumstances, which shall be specified in the minutes, the chairman of the meeting is of the opinion that the item should be considered at the meeting as a matter of urgency.

(5) Where by virtue of subsection (2) above the whole or any part of a report for a meeting is not open to inspection by the public under subsection (1) above–

    (a)   every copy of the report or of the part shall be marked "Not for publication"; and

    (b)   there shall be stated on every copy of the whole or any part of the report the description, in terms of Schedule 12A to this Act, of the exempt information by virtue of which the council are likely to exclude the public during the item to which the report relates.

(6) Where a meeting of a principal council is required by section 100A above to be open to the public during the proceedings or any part of them, there shall be made available for the use of members of the public present at the meeting a reasonable number of copies of the agenda and, subject to subsection (8) below, of the reports for the meeting.

(7) There shall, on request and on payment of postage or other necessary charge for transmission, be supplied for the benefit of any newspaper–

    (a)   a copy of the agenda for a meeting of a principal council and, subject to subsection (8) below, a copy of each of the reports for the meeting;

    (b)   such further statements or particulars, if any, as are necessary to indicate the nature of the items included in the agenda; and

    (c)   if the proper officer thinks fit in the case of any item, copies of any other documents supplied to members of the council in connection with the item.

(8) Subsection (2) above applies in relation to copies of reports provided in pursuance of subsection (6) or (7) above as it applies in relation to copies of reports provided in pursuance of subsection (1) above.

NOTES

Defined terms
"copy": s 100K(1)
"exempt information": ss 100I, 100K(1)
"meeting": s 100K(2)

"newspaper": s 100K(1)
"principal council": ss 100J, 100K(1), 270(1)
"proper officer": s 270(3), (4)(c)

Inspection of minutes and other documents after meetings.

100C(1) After a meeting of a principal council the following documents shall be open to inspection by members of the public at the offices of the council until the expiration of the period of six years beginning with the date of the meeting, namely–

  (a)   the minutes, or a copy of the minutes, of the meeting, excluding so much of the minutes of proceedings during which the meeting was not open to the public as discloses exempt information;

  (b)   where applicable, a summary under subsection (2) below;

  (c)   a copy of the agenda for the meeting; and

  (d)   a copy of so much of any report for the meeting as relates to any item during which the meeting was open to the public.

(2) Where, in consequence of the exclusion of parts of the minutes which disclose exempt information, the document open to inspection under subsection (1)(a) above does not provide members of the public with a reasonably fair and coherent record of the whole or part of the proceedings, the proper officer shall make a written summary of the proceedings or the part, as the case may be, which provides such a record without disclosing the exempt information.

NOTES

Defined terms
"copy": s 100K(1)
"exempt information": ss 100I, 100K(1)

"meeting": s 100K(2)
"principal council": ss 100J, 100K(1), 270(1)
"proper officer": s 270(3), (4)(c)

Inspection of background papers.

100D(1) Subject, in the case of section 100C(1), to subsection (2) below, if and so long as copies of the whole or part of a report for a meeting of a principal council are required by section 100B(1) or 100C(1) above to be open to inspection by members of the public–

  (a)   those copies shall each include a copy of a list, compiled by the proper officer, of the background papers for the report or the part of the report, and

  (b)   at least one copy of each of the documents included in that list shall also be open to inspection at the offices of the council.

(2) Subsection (1) above does not require a copy of any document included in the list, to be open to inspection after the expiration of the period of four years beginning with the date of the meeting.

(3) Where a copy of any of the background papers for a report is required by subsection (1) above to be open to inspection by members of the public, the copy shall be taken for the

purposes of this Part to be so open if arrangements exist for its production to members of the public as soon as is reasonably practicable after the making of a request to inspect the copy.

(4) Nothing in this section–

    (a) requires any document which discloses exempt information to be included in the list referred to in subsection (1) above; or

    (b) without prejudice to the generality of subsection (2) of section 100A above, requires or authorises the inclusion in the list of any document which, if open to inspection by the public, would disclose confidential information in breach of the obligation of confidence, within the meaning of that subsection.

(5) For the purposes of this section the background papers for a report are those documents relating to the subject matter of the report which–

    (a) disclose any facts or matters on which, in the opinion of the proper officer, the report or an important part of the report is based, and

    (b) have, in his opinion, been relied on to a material extent in preparing the report,

but do not include any published works.

NOTES

Defined terms
"copy": s 100K(1)
"exempt information": ss 100I, 100K(1)

"meeting": s 100K(2)
"principal council": ss 100J, 100K(1), 270(1)
"proper officer": s 270(3), (4)(c)

Application to committees and sub-committees.

100E(1) Sections 100A to 100D above shall apply in relation to a committee or sub-committee of a principal council as they apply in relation to a principal council.

(1A) But in section 100A, subsections (5A), (7A) to (7F) and (9) do not apply to a committee which is appointed or established jointly by one or more principal councils in England and one or more principal councils in Wales, or a sub-committee of such a committee.

(2) In the application by virtue of this section of sections 100A to 100D above in relation to a committee or sub-committee–

    (a) section 100A(6)(a) shall be taken to have been complied with if the notice is given by posting it at the time there mentioned at the offices of every constituent principal council and, if the meeting of the committee or sub-committee to which that section so applies is to be held at premises other than the offices of such a council, at those premises;

    (b) for the purposes of section 100A(6)(c), premises belonging to a constituent principal council shall be treated as belonging to the committee or sub-committee; and

    (c) for the purposes of sections 100B(1), 100C(1) and 100D(1), offices of any constituent principal council shall be treated as offices of the committee or sub-committee.

(3) Any reference in this Part to a committee or sub-committee of a principal council is a reference to–

    (a) a committee which is constituted under an enactment specified in section 101(9) below or which is appointed by one or more principal councils under section 102 below; or

(b)   a joint committee not falling within paragraph (a) above which is appointed or established under any enactment by two or more principal councils and is not a body corporate; or

(bb)   the Navigation Committee of the Broads Authority;

(bba)   a committee in place by virtue of section 107D(3)(c)(ii) of the Local Democracy, Economic Development and Construction Act 2009;

(bbb)   a joint committee in place by virtue of section 107E of that Act; or

(c)   a sub-committee appointed or established under any enactment by one or more committees falling within paragraphs(a) to (bb) 3 above.

(4) Any reference in this Part to a constituent principal council, in relation to a committee or sub-committee, is a reference–

(a)   in the case of a committee, to the principal council, or any of the principal councils, of which it is a committee; and

(b)   in the case of a sub-committee, to any principal council which, by virtue of paragraph (a) above, is a constituent principal council in relation to the committee, or any of the committees, which established or appointed the sub-committee.

NOTES

Defined terms
"England": s 269
"meeting": s 100K(2)

"principal council": ss 100J, 100K(1), 270(1)
"Wales": s 269

Inspection of records relating to functions exercisable by members

100EA(1) The appropriate authority may by regulations make provision for written records of decisions made or action taken by a member of a local authority, in exercise of a function of the authority by virtue of arrangements made under section 236 of the Local Government and Public Involvement in Health Act 2007 or under section 56 of the Local Government (Wales) Measure 2011, to be made and provided to the authority by the member.

(2) Any written record provided to the authority under regulations under subsection (1) shall be open to inspection by members of the public at the offices of the authority for the period of six years beginning with the date on which the decision was made or action was taken.

(2A) In this section "appropriate authority" means–

(a)   in relation to local authorities in England, the Secretary of State;

(b)   in relation to local authorities in Wales, the Welsh Ministers.

(3) A statutory instrument containing regulations under subsection (1) shall be subject to annulment in pursuance of a resolution of either House of Parliament (in the case of regulations made by the Secretary of State) or a resolution of the National Assembly for Wales (in the case of regulations made by the Welsh Ministers).

NOTES

Defined terms
"England": s 269

"local authority": s 270(1)
"Wales": s 269

Additional rights of access to documents for members of principal councils.

100F(1) Any document which is in the possession or under the control of a principal council and contains material relating to any business to be transacted at a meeting of the council or a committee or sub-committee of the council shall, subject to subsections (2) to (2E) below, be open to inspection by any member of the council.

(2) In relation to a principal council in England, subsection (1) above does not require the document to be open to inspection if it appears to the proper officer that it discloses exempt information.

(2A) But subsection (1) above does require (despite subsection (2) above) the document to be open to inspection if the information is information of a description for the time being falling within–

    (a) paragraph 3 of Schedule 12A to this Act (except to the extent that the information relates to any terms proposed or to be proposed by or to the authority in the course of negotiations for a contract), or

    (b) paragraph 6 of Schedule 12A to this Act.

(2B) In subsection (2A) above, "the authority"has the meaning given in paragraph 11(2) of Schedule 12A to this Act.

(2C) In relation to a principal council in Wales, subsection (1) above does not require the document to be open to inspection if it appears to the proper officer that it discloses exempt information.

(2D) But subsection (1) above does require (despite subsection (2C) above) the document to be open to inspection if the information is information of a description for the time being falling within–

    (a) paragraph 14 of Schedule 12A to this Act (except to the extent that the information relates to any terms proposed or to be proposed by or to the authority in the course of negotiations for a contract), or

    (b) paragraph 17 of Schedule 12A to this Act.

(2E) In subsection (2D) above, "the authority"has the meaning given in paragraph 22(2) of Schedule 12A to this Act.

(3) The appropriate person may by order amend subsections (2) to (2E) above–

    (a) by adding to the descriptions of exempt information to which those subsections refer for the time being; or

    (b) by removing any description of exempt information to which those subsections refer for the time being.

(3A) In subsection (3) above "the appropriate person" means–

    (a) in relation to England, the Secretary of State;

    (b) in relation to Wales, the National Assembly for Wales.

(4) Any statutory instrument containing an order under subsection (3) above made by the Secretary of State shall be subject to annulment in pursuance of a resolution of either House of Parliament.

(5) The rights conferred by this section on a member of a principal council are in addition to any other rights he may have apart from this section.

NOTES

Defined terms

"committee or sub-committee of a principal council": ss 100E(3), 100J(3YA), (3ZA)(b), (3ZAA), 100K(1)

"England": s 269

"exempt information": ss 100I, 100K(1)

"meeting": s 100K(2)

"principal council": ss 100J, 100K(1), 270(1)

"proper officer": s 270(3), (4)(c)

"Wales": s 269

Principal councils to publish additional information.

100G(1) A principal council shall maintain a register stating–

    (a) the name and address of every member of the council for the time being together with, in the case of a councillor, the ward or division which he represents; and

    (b) in respect of every committee or sub-committee of the council–

        (i) the members of the council who are members of the committee or sub-committee or who are entitled, in accordance with any standing orders relating to the committee or sub-committee, to speak at its meetings or any of them;

        (ii) the name and address of every other person who is a member of the committee or sub-committee or who is entitled, in accordance with any standing orders relating to the committee or sub-committee, to speak at its meetings or any of them otherwise than in the capacity of an officer of the council; and

        (iii) the functions in relation to the committee or sub-committee of every person falling within sub-paragraph (i) above who is not a member of the committee or sub-committee and of every person falling within subparagraph (ii) above.

(2) A principal council shall maintain a list–

    (a) specifying those powers of the council which, for the time being,are exercisable from time to time by officers of the council in pursuance of arrangements made under this Act or any other enactment for their discharge by those officers; and

    (b) stating the title of the officer by whom each of the powers so specified is for the time being so exercisable;

but this subsection does not require a power to be specified in the list if the arrangements for its discharge by the officer are made for a specified period not exceeding six months.

(3) There shall be kept at the offices of every principal council a written summary of the rights–

    (a) to attend meetings of a principal council and of committees and sub-committees of a principal council, and

    (b) to inspect and copy documents and to be furnished with documents,

which are for the time being conferred by this Part, Part XI below and such other enactments as the Secretary of State by order specifies.

(4) The register maintained under subsection (1) above, the list maintained under subsection (2) above and the summary kept under subsection (3) above shall be open to inspection by the public at the offices of the council.

NOTES

Defined terms

"meeting": s 100K(2)

"committee or sub-committee of a principal council": ss 100E(3), 100J(3YA), (3ZA)(b), (3ZAA), 100K(1)

"principal council": ss 100J, 100K(1), 270(1)

Supplemental provisions and offences.

100H(1) A document directed by any provision of this Part to be open to inspection shall be so open at all reasonable hours and–

    (a)   in the case of a document open to inspection by virtue of section 100D(1) above, upon payment of such reasonable fee as may be required for the facility; and

    (b)   in any other case, without payment.

(2) Where a document is open to inspection by a person under any provisions of this Part, the person may, subject to subsection (3) below–

    (a)   make copies of or extracts from the document, or

    (b)   require the person having custody of the document to supply to him a photographic copy of or of extracts from the document,

upon payment of such reasonable fee as may be required for the facility.

(3) Subsection (2) above does not require or authorise the doing of any act which infringes the copyright in any work except that, where the owner of the copyright is a principal council, nothing done in pursuance of that subsection shall constitute an infringement of the copyright.

(4) If, without reasonable excuse, a person having the custody of a document which is required by section 100B(1), 100C(1) or 100EA(2) above to be open to inspection by the public–

    (a)   intentionally obstructs any person exercising a right conferred by this Part to inspect, or to make a copy of or extracts from, the document, or

    (b)   refuses to furnish copies to any person entitled to obtain them under any provision of this Part,

he shall be liable on summary conviction to a fine not exceeding level 1 on the standard scale.

(5) Where any accessible document for a meeting to which this subsection applies–

    (a)   is supplied to, or open to inspection by, a member of the public,or

    (b)   is supplied for the benefit of any newspaper, in pursuance of section 100B(7) above,

the publication thereby of any defamatory matter contained in the document shall be privileged unless the publication is proved to be made with malice.

(6) Subsection (5) above applies to any meeting of a principal council and any meeting of a committee or sub-committee of a principal council; and, for the purposes of that subsection, the "accessible documents" for a meeting are the following–

    (a)   any copy of the agenda or of any item included in the agenda for the meeting;

    (b)   any such further statements or particulars for the purpose of indicating the nature of any item included in the agenda as are mentioned in section 100B(7)(b) above;

    (c)   any copy of a document relating to such an item which is supplied for the benefit of a newspaper in pursuance of section 100B(7)(c) above;

    (d)   any copy of the whole or part of a report for the meeting;

(e) any copy of the whole or part of any background papers for a report for the meeting, within the meaning of section 100D above.

(7) The rights conferred by this Part to inspect, copy and be furnished with documents are in addition, and without prejudice, to any such rights conferred by or under any other enactment.

Exempt information and power to vary Schedule 12A.

100I(1) In relation to principal councils in England, the descriptions of information which are, for the purposes of this Part, exempt information are those for the time being specified in Part I of Schedule 12A to this Act, but subject to any qualifications contained in Part II of that Schedule; and Part III has effect for the interpretation of Parts 1 to 3 of that Schedule.

(1A) In relation to principal councils in Wales, the descriptions of information which are, for the purposes of this Part, exempt information are those for the time being specified in Part 4 of Schedule 12A to this Act, but subject to any qualifications contained in Part 5 of that Schedule; and Part 6 has effect for the interpretation of Parts 4 to 6 of that Schedule.

(2) The appropriate person may by order vary Schedule 12A to this Act by adding to it any description or other provision or by deleting from it or varying any description or other provision for the time being specified or contained in it.

(3) The appropriate person may exercise the power conferred by subsection (2) above by amending any Part of Schedule 12A to this Act, with or without amendment of any other Part.

(3A) In this section "the appropriate person" means–
    (a) in relation to England, the Secretary of State;
    (b) in relation to Wales, the National Assembly for Wales.

(4) Any statutory instrument containing an order under this section made by the Secretary of State shall be subject to annulment in pursuance of a resolution of either House of Parliament.

Application to new authorities, Common Council, etc.

100J(1) Except in this section, and subject as follows, any reference in this Part to a principal council includes a reference to–
    (a) ...
    (b) a joint authority;
    (ba) ....;
    (bb) the London Fire and Emergency Planning Authority;
    (bc) an economic prosperity board;

(bd) a combined authority;

(be) Transport for London;

(bf) a sub-national transport body;

(c) the Common Council;

(cc) the Broads Authority;

(cd) a National Park authority;

(d) a joint board or joint committee falling within subsection (2) below;

(f) a fire and rescue authority constituted by a scheme under section 2 of the Fire and Rescue Services Act 2004 or a scheme to which section 4 of that Act applies ;

(g) the Homes and Communities Agency so far as it is exercising functions conferred on it in relation to a designated area by virtue of a designation order;

(h) a Mayoral development corporation.

(2) A joint board or joint committee falls within this subsection if–

  (a) it is constituted under any enactment as a body corporate; and

  (b) it discharges functions of two or more principal councils;

and for the purposes of this subsection any body falling within paragraph (a), (bc), (bd) or (c) of subsection (1) above shall be treated as a principal council.

(2A) In its application by virtue of subsection (1)(g) above in relation to the Homes and Communities Agency, a reference in this Part to the offices of the council (however expressed)–

  (a) is to be treated as a reference to such premises located within the designated area as the Homes and Communities Agency considers appropriate, and

  (b) in the application of section 100A(6)(a) above to a case where the meeting is to be held at premises other than those mentioned in paragraph (a) above, includes a reference to those other premises.

(2B) In section 100A, subsections (5A), (7A) to (7F) and (9) do not apply to—

  (a) ....

  (b) the Common Council other than in its capacity as a local authority or police authority;

  (c) a joint board or a joint committee falling within subsection (2) above;

  (d) the Homes and Communities Agency; or

  (e) a Mayoral development corporation.

(3) In its application by virtue of subsection (1) above in relation to a body falling within paragraph (b), (ba), (bb), (bc), (bd), (be), (bf), (cc), (cd), (d), (f) or (h) of that subsection, section 100A (6)(a) above shall have effect with the insertion after the word "council" of the words "(and, if the meeting is to be held at premises other than those offices, at those premises)".

(3YA) In its application by virtue of subsection (1)(be) above in relation to Transport for London, section 100E(3) has effect as if for paragraph (bb) there were substituted–

  "(bb) a committee of Transport for London (with "committee", in relation to Transport for London, here having the same meaning as in Schedule 10 to the Greater London Authority Act 1999); or".

(3ZA) In its application by virtue of subsection (1)(g) above in relation to the Homes and Communities Agency, section 100E above shall have effect as if–

(a)   in subsection (2), paragraph (c) was omitted, and

(b)   in subsection (3), for paragraphs (a) to (c) there were substituted–

"(a) a committee established under paragraph 6(1) of Schedule 1 to the Housing and Regeneration Act 2008 for the purpose of exercising functions conferred on the Homes and Communities Agency in relation to a designated area by virtue of a designation order; or

(b)   a sub-committee of such a committee established under paragraph 6(2) of that Schedule to that Act for that purpose."

(3ZAA) In its application by virtue of subsection (1)(h) above in relation to a Mayoral development corporation, section 100E(3) has effect as if for paragraphs (a) to (c) there were substituted–

"(a)   a committee which is established under Schedule 21 to the Localism Act 2011 by a principal council, or

(b)   a sub-committee established under that Schedule by a committee within paragraph (a)."

(3ZB) In its application by virtue of subsection (1)(g) above in relation to the Homes and Communities Agency, section 100G(1) above shall have effect as if paragraph (a) was omitted.

(4)   In its application by virtue of subsection (1) above, section 100G(1)(a) above shall have effect–

(a)   in relation to a joint authority, a joint waste authority, an economic prosperity board, or a combined authority with the substitution for the words after "together with" of the words the name or description of the body or other person that appointed him; and

(aa)   in relation to the Broads Authority or its Navigation Committee or any National Park authority, with the substitution for the words after "together with" of the words"the name of the person who appointed him"; and

(b)   in relation to a Mayoral development corporation, or joint board or joint committee falling within subsection (2) above, with the omission of the words after "for the time being"; and

(c)   in relation to a fire and rescue authority falling within subsection (1)(f) above 12 , with the substitution for the words" , in the case of a councillor, the ward or division" of the words " the constituent area".

(4A)   ....

(4AA) In its application by virtue of subsection (1)(be) above in relation to Transport for London, section 100G shall have effect–

(a)   with the substitution for subsection (1)(a) and (b) of–

"(a)   the name of every member of the council for the time being; and

(b)   the name of every member of each committee or subcommittee of the council for the time being.", and

(b)   with the insertion in subsection (2)(b) after ""exercisable"" of "", but not an officer by whom such a power is exercisable at least partly as a result of sub-delegation by any officer"".

(4B)   In this section "designated area" and "designation order"have the same meanings as in Part 1 of the Housing and Regeneration Act 2008.

NOTES

Defined terms   "economic prosperity board": s 270(1)

"combined authority": s 270(1) "joint authority": s 270(1)
"Common Council": s 270(1) "sub-national transport body": s 270(1)

Interpretation and application of Part VA.

100K(1) In this Part—

"committee or sub-committee of a principal council" shall be construed in accordance with section 100E(3) above (and see section 100J(3YA), (3ZA)(b) and (3ZAA) above);

"constituent principal council" shall be construed in accordance with section 100E(4) above;

"copy", in relation to any document, includes a copy made from a copy;

"exempt information"has the meaning given by section 100I above;

"information" includes an expression of opinion, any recommendations and any decision taken;

"newspaper" includes—

(a) a news agency which systematically carries on the business of selling and supplying reports or information to newspapers; and

(b) any organisation which is systematically engaged in collecting news—
(i) for sound or television broadcasts; or
(ii) for inclusion in programmes to be included in any programme service (within the meaning of the Broadcasting Act 1990) other than a sound or television broadcasting service;

"principal council"shall be construed in accordance with section 100J above.

(2) Any reference in this Part to a meeting is a reference to a meeting held after 1st April 1986.

(3) The Secretary of State may by order amend sections 100A(6)(a) and 100B(3) and (4)(a) above so as to substitute for each reference to three clear days such greater number of days as may be specified in the order.

(4) Any statutory instrument containing an order under subsection (3) above shall be subject to annulment in pursuance of a resolution of either House of Parliament.

SCHEDULE 12A
ACCESS TO INFORMATION: EXEMPT INFORMATION

PART I DESCRIPTIONS OF EXEMPT INFORMATION: ENGLAND

1. Information relating to any individual.

2. Information which is likely to reveal the identity of an individual.

3. Information relating to the financial or business affairs of any particular person (including the authority holding that information).

4. Information relating to any consultations or negotiations, or contemplated consultations or negotiations, in connection with any labour relations matter arising between the authority or a Minister of the Crown and employees of, or office holders under, the authority.

5. Information in respect of which a claim to legal professional privilege could be maintained in legal proceedings.

6. Information which reveals that the authority proposes–
    (a) to give under any enactment a notice under or by virtue of which requirements are imposed on a person; or
    (b) to make an order or direction under any enactment.

7. Information relating to any action taken or to be taken in connection with the prevention, investigation or prosecution of crime.

PART II QUALIFICATIONS: ENGLAND

8. Information falling within paragraph 3 above is not exempt information by virtue of that paragraph if it is required to be registered under–
    (a) the Companies Acts (as defined in section 2 of the Companies Act 2006);
    (b) the Friendly Societies Act 1974;
    (c) the Friendly Societies Act 1992;
    (d) the Co-operative and Community Benefit Societies Act 2014;
    (e) the Building Societies Act 1986; or
    (f) the Charities Act 2011.

9. Information is not exempt information if it relates to proposed development for which the local planning authority may grant itself planning permission or permission in principle pursuant to regulation 3 of the Town and Country Planning General Regulations 1992.

10. Information which–
    (a) falls within any of paragraphs 1 to 7 above; and
    (b) is not prevented from being exempt by virtue of paragraph 8 or 9 above,
is exempt information if and so long, as in all the circumstances of the case, the public interest in maintaining the exemption outweighs the public interest in disclosing the information.

PART III INTERPRETATION: ENGLAND

11(1)   In Parts 1 and 2 and this Part of this Schedule–
    "employee" means a person employed under a contract of service;
    "financial or business affairs"includes contemplated, as well as past or current, activities;
    "labour relations matter" means–
    (a) any of the matters specified in paragraphs (a) to (g) of section 218(1) of the Trade Union and Labour Relations (Consolidation) Act 1992 (matters which may be the subject of a trade dispute, within the meaning of that Act); or
    (b) any dispute about a matter falling within paragraph (a) above;
    and for the purposes of this definition the enactments mentioned in paragraph (a) above, with the necessary modifications, shall apply in relation to office-holders under the authority as they apply in relation to employees of the authority;
    "office-holder", in relation to the authority, means the holder of any paid office appointments to which are or may be made or confirmed by the authority or by any joint board on which the authority is represented or by any person who holds any such

office or is an employee of the authority;

"registered" in relation to information required to be registered under the Building Societies Act 1986, means recorded in the public file of any building society (within the meaning of that Act).

(2) Any reference in Parts 1 and 2 and this Part of this Schedule to "the authority" is a reference to the principal council or, as the case may be, the committee or sub-committee in relation to whose proceedings or documents the question whether information is exempt or not falls to be determined and includes a reference–

   (a)   in the case of a principal council, to any committee or sub-committee of the council; and

   (b)   in the case of a committee, to–

      (i)   any constituent principal council;

      (ii)   any other principal council by which appointments are made to the committee or whose functions the committee discharges; and

      (iii)   any other committee or sub-committee of a principal council falling within sub-paragraph (i) or (ii) above; and

   (c)   in the case of a sub-committee, to–

      (i)   the committee, or any of the committees, of which it is a sub-committee; and

      (ii)   any principal council which falls within paragraph (b) above in relation to that committee.

PART IV DESCRIPTIONS OF EXEMPT INFORMATION: WALES

14. Information relating to the financial or business affairs of any particular person (including the authority holding that information).

15. Information relating to any consultations or negotiations, or contemplated consultations or negotiations, in connection with any labour relations matter arising between the authority or a Minister of the Crown and employees of, or office holders under, the authority.

16. Information in respect of which a claim to legal professional privilege could be maintained in legal proceedings.

17. Information which reveals that the authority proposes–

   (a)   to give under any enactment a notice under or by virtue of which requirements are imposed on a person; or

   (b)   to make an order or direction under any enactment.

18. Information relating to any action taken or to be taken in connection with the prevention, investigation or prosecution of crime.

PART V QUALIFICATIONS: WALES

19. Information falling within paragraph 14 above is not exempt information by virtue of that paragraph if it is required to be registered under–

   (a)   the Companies Acts (as defined in section 2 of the Companies Act 2006);

   (b)   the Friendly Societies Act 1974;

(c) the Friendly Societies Act 1992;

(d) the Co-operative and Community Benefit Societies Act 2014;

(e) the Building Societies Act 1986; or

(f) the Charities Act 2011.

20. Information is not exempt information if it relates to proposed development for which the local planning authority may grant itself planning permission pursuant to regulation 3 of the Town and Country Planning General Regulations 1992.

21. Information which–

(a) falls within any of paragraphs 12 to 15, 17 and 18 above; and

(b) is not prevented from being exempt by virtue of paragraph 19 or 20 above,

is exempt information if and so long, as in all the circumstances of the case, the public interest in maintaining the exemption outweighs the public interest in disclosing the information.

PART VI INTERPRETATION: WALES

22(1) In Parts 4 and 5 and this Part of this Schedule–

"employee" means a person employed under a contract of service;

"financial or business affairs"includes contemplated, as well as past or current, activities;

"labour relations matter" means–

(a) any of the matters specified in paragraphs (a) to (g) of section 218(1) of the Trade Union and Labour Relations (Consolidation) Act 1992 (matters which may be the subject of a trade dispute, within the meaning of that Act); or

(b) any dispute about a matter falling within paragraph (a) above;

and for the purposes of this definition the enactments mentioned in paragraph (a) above, with the necessary modifications, shall apply in relation to office-holders under the authority as they apply in relation to employees of the authority;

"office-holder", in relation to the authority, means the holder of any paid office appointments to which are or may be made or confirmed by the authority or by any joint board on which the authority is represented or by any person who holds any such office or is an employee of the authority;

"registered" in relation to information required to be registered under the Building Societies Act 1986, means recorded in the public file of any building society (within the meaning of that Act).

(2) Any reference in Parts 4 and 5 and this Part of this Schedule to "the authority" is a reference to the principal council or, as the case may be, the committee or sub-committee in relation to whose proceedings or documents the question whether information is exempt or not falls to be determined and includes a reference

(a) in the case of a principal council, to any committee or sub-committee of the council; and

(b) in the case of a committee, to–

(i) any constituent principal council;

(ii) any other principal council by which appointments are made to the committee or whose functions the committee discharges; and

      (iii) any other committee or sub-committee of a principal council falling within sub-paragraph (i) or (ii) above; and

  (c) in the case of a sub-committee, to–

      (i) the committee, or any of the committees, of which it is a sub-committee; and

      (ii) any principal council which falls within paragraph (b) above in relation to that committee.

Access to Health Records Act 1990

(as amended to 1 February 2020)
This version is applicable to England only.
There are different versions for Scotland and Wales.

An Act to establish a right of access to health records by the individuals to whom they relate and other persons; to provide for the correction of inaccurate health records and for the avoidance of certain contractual obligations; and for connected purposes.

13th July 1990

BE IT ENACTED by the Queen's most Excellent Majesty, by and with the advice and consent of the Lords Spiritual and Temporal, and Commons, in this present Parliament assembled, and by the authority of the same, as follows:—

Preliminary

"Health record" and related expressions

1(1). In this Act "health record" means a record which—

    (a)   consists of information relating to the physical or mental health of an individual who can be identified from that information, or from that and other information in the possession of the holder of the record; and

    (b)   has been made by or on behalf of a health professional in connection with the care of that individual.

(2) In this Act "holder", in relation to a health record, means—

    (a)   in the case of a record made by a health professional performing primary medical services under a general medical services contract made with the National Health Service Commissioning Board or a Local Health Board, the person or body who entered into the contract with the Board (or, in a case where more than one person so entered into the contract, any such person);

(aa)   in the case of a record made by a health professional performing such services in accordance with arrangements under section 92 or 107 of the National Health Service Act 2006, or section 50 or 64 of the National Health Service (Wales) Act 2006, with the National Health Service Commissioning Board or a Local Health Board, the person or body which made the arrangements with the Board (or, in a case where more than one person so made the arrangements, any such person);

(b)   in the case of a record made by a health professional for purposes connected with the provision of health services by a health service body (and not falling within paragraph (aa) above), the health service body by which or on whose behalf the record is held;

(c)   in any other case, the health professional by whom or on whose behalf the record is held.

(3)   In this Act "patient", in relation to a health record, means the individual in connection with whose care the record has been made.

Health Professionals

2.   In this Act, "health professional" has the same meaning as in the Data Protection Act 2018 (see section 204 of that Act).

Main provisions

Right of access to health records

3 (1)   An application for access to a health record, or to any part of a health record, may be made to the holder of the record by any of the following, namely--

(a)   ...

(b)   ...

(cc)   ...

(e)   ...

(ee)   where the record is held in Scotland and the patient is incapable, within the meaning of the Adults with Incapacity (Scotland) Act 2000 (asp 4) in relation to making or authorising the application, any person entitled to act on behalf of the patient under that Act;

(f)   where the patient has died, the patient's personal representative and any person who may have a claim arising out of the patient's death;

(g)   where the patient has died, a medical examiner exercising functions by virtue of section 20 of the Coroners and Justice Act 2009 in relation to the death.

(2)   Subject to section 4 below, where an application is made under subsection (1) above the holder shall, within the requisite period, give access to the record, or the part of a record, to which the application relates–

(a)   in the case of a record, by allowing the applicant to inspect the record or, where section 5 below applies, an extract setting out so much of the record as is not excluded by that section;

(b)   in the case of a part of a record, by allowing the applicant to inspect an extract setting out that part or, where that section applies, so much of that part as is not so excluded; or

(c)   in either case, if the applicant so requires, by supplying him with a copy of the record or extract.

(3)   Where any information contained in a record or extract which is so allowed to be inspected, or a copy of which is so supplied, is expressed in terms which are not intelligible

without explanation, an explanation of those terms shall be provided with the record or extract, or supplied with the copy.

(4) No fee shall be required for giving access under subsection (2) above other than the following, namely–

    (a)   where access is given to a record, or part of a record, none of which was made after the beginning of the period of 40 days immediately preceding the date of the application, a fee not exceeding such maximum as may be prescribed for the purposes of this section by regulations under section 7 of the Data Protection Act 1998; and

    (b)   where a copy of a record or extract is supplied to the applicant, a fee not exceeding the cost of making the copy and (where applicable) the cost of posting it to him.

Paragraphs (a) and (b) above do not apply in the case of access for which an application is made under subsection (1)(g) above.

(5) For the purposes of subsection (2) above the requisite period is–

    (a)   where the application relates to a record, or part of a record, none of which was made before the beginning of the period of 40 days immediately preceding the date of the application, the period of 21 days beginning with that date;

    (b)   in any other case, the period of 40 days beginning with that date.

(6) Where–

    (a)   an application under subsection (1) above does not contain sufficient information to enable the holder of the record to identify the patient or, to satisfy himself that the applicant is entitled to make the application; and

    (b)   within the period of 14 days beginning with the date of the application, the holder of the record requests the applicant to furnish him with such further information as he may reasonably require for that purpose,

subsection (5) above shall have effect as if for any reference to that date there were substituted a reference to the date on which that further information is so furnished.

Cases where right of access may be wholly excluded

4(1) ...

(2) ...

(3) Where an application is made under subsection (1)(f) of section 3 above, access shall not be given under subsection (2) of that section if the record includes a note, made at the patient's request, that he did not wish access to be given on such an application.

Cases where right of access may be partially excluded

5(1) Access shall not be given under section 3(2) above to any part of a health record–

    (a)   which, in the opinion of the holder of the record, would disclose–

        (i)   information likely to cause serious harm to the physical or mental health of any individual; or

        (ii)   information relating to or provided by an individual, other than the patient, who could be identified from that information; or

    (b)   which was made before the commencement of this Act.

(2) Subsection (1)(a)(ii) above shall not apply–

    (a)   where the individual concerned has consented to the application; or

    (b)   where that individual is a health professional who has been involved in the care of the patient;

and subsection (1)(b) above shall not apply where and to the extent that, in the opinion of the holder of the record, the giving of access is necessary in order to make intelligible any part of the record to which access is required to be given under section 3(2) above.

(3)   Access shall not be given under section 3(2) to any part of a health record which, in the opinion of the holder of the record, would disclose–

    (a)   information provided by the patient in the expectation that it would not be disclosed to the applicant; or

    (b)   information obtained as a result of any examination or investigation to which the patient consented in the expectation that the information would not be so disclosed.

(4)   Where an application is made under subsection (1)(f) of section 3 above, access shall not be given under subsection (2) of that section to any part of the record which, in the opinion of the holder of the record, would disclose information which is not relevant to any claim which may arise out of the patient's death.

(5)   The Secretary of State may by regulations provide that, in such circumstances as may be prescribed by the regulations, access shall not be given under section 3(2) above to any part of a health record which satisfies such conditions as may be so prescribed.

Correction of inaccurate health records

6(1)   Where a person considers that any information contained in a health record, or any part of a health record, to which he has been given access under section 3(2) above is inaccurate, he may apply to the holder of the record for the necessary correction to be made.

(2)   On an application under subsection (1) above, the holder of the record shall–

    (a)   if he is satisfied that the information is inaccurate, make the necessary correction;

    (b)   if he is not so satisfied, make in the part of the record in which the information is contained a note of the matters in respect of which the information is considered by the applicant to be inaccurate; and

    (c)   in either case, without requiring any fee, supply the applicant with a copy of the correction or note.

(3)   In this section "inaccurate" means incorrect, misleading or incomplete.

Duty of health service bodies etc to take advice

7(1)   A health service body shall take advice from the appropriate health professional before they decide whether they are satisfied as to any matter for the purposes of this Act, or form an opinion as to any matter for those purposes.

(2)   In this section "the appropriate health professional", in relation to a health service body, means–

    (a)   where, for purposes connected with the provision of health services by the body, one or more medical or dental practitioners are currently responsible for the clinical care of the patient, that practitioner or, as the case may be, such one of those practitioners as is the most suitable to advise the body on the matter in question;

    (b)   where paragraph (a) above does not apply but one or more medical or dental practitioners are available who, for purposes connected with the provision of such services by the body, have been responsible for the clinical care of the patient, that practitioner or, as the case may be, such one of those practitioners as was most recently so responsible, and

    (c)   where neither paragraph (a) nor paragraph (b) above applies, a health professional who has the necessary experience and qualifications to advise the body on the matter in question.

(3) ...

Supplemental

Applications to the court

8(1) Subject to subsection (2) below, where the court is satisfied, on an application made by the person concerned within such period as may be prescribed by rules of court, that the holder of a health record has failed to comply with any requirement of this Act, the court may order the holder to comply with that requirement.

(2) The court shall not entertain an application under subsection (1) above unless it is satisfied that the applicant has taken all such steps to secure compliance with the requirement as may be prescribed by regulations made by the Secretary of State.

(3) For the purposes of subsection (2) above, the Secretary of State may by regulations require the holders of health records to make such arrangements for dealing with complaints that they have failed to comply with any requirements of this Act as may be prescribed by the regulations.

(4) For the purposes of determining any question whether an applicant is entitled to be given access under section 3(2) above to any health record, or any part of a health record, the court—

    (a) may require the record or part to be made available for its own inspection; but

    (b) shall not, pending determination of that question in the applicant's favour, require the record or part to be disclosed to him or his representatives whether by discovery (or, in Scotland, recovery) or otherwise.

(5) The jurisdiction conferred by this section shall be exercisable by the High Court or the county court or, in Scotland, by the Court of Session or the sheriff.

Avoidance of certain contractual terms

9. Any term or condition of a contract shall be void in so far as it purports to require an individual to supply any other person with a copy of a health record, or of an extract from a health record, to which he has been given access under section 3(2) above.

Regulations and orders

10(1) Regulations under this Act may make different provision for different cases or classes of cases including, in particular, different provision for different health records or classes of health records.

(2) Any power to make regulations under this Act shall be exercisable by statutory instrument.

(3) Any statutory instrument containing regulations under this Act shall be subject to annulment in pursuance of a resolution of either House of Parliament.

Interpretation

11. In this Act—

    "application" means an application in writing and "apply" shall be construed accordingly;

    "care" includes examination, investigation, diagnosis and treatment;

    "general medical services contract" means a contract under section 84 of the National Health Service Act 2006 or section 42 of the National Health Service (Wales) Act 2006;

    "Health Board" has the same meaning as in the National Health Service (Scotland) Act 1978;

"health service body" means–

(a)   a Health Authority or Special Health Authority , Special Health Authority or Local Health Board;

(b)   a Health Board;

(c)   ......

(d)   a National Health Service trust first established under section 5 of the National Health Service and Community Care Act 1990, section 25 of the National Health Service Act 2006 or section 18 of the National Health Service (Wales) Act 2006 or section 12A of the National Health Service (Scotland) Act 1978;

(e)   an NHS foundation trust;

(f)   the Health and Social Care Information Centre;

"information", in relation to a health record, includes any expression of opinion about the patient;

"Local Health Board" means a Local Health Board established under section 11 of the National Health Service (Wales) Act 2006;

"make", in relation to such a record, includes compile;

"Special Health Authority" means a Special Health Authority established under section 28 of the National Health Service Act 2006 or section 22 of the National Health Service (Wales) Act 2006.

Short title, commencement and extent

12(1)   This Act may be cited as the Access to Health Records Act 1990.

(2)   This Act shall come into force on 1st November 1991.

(3)   This Act does not extend to Northern Ireland.

Regulation (EC) No 1049/2001 of the European Parliament and of the Council of 30 May 2001 regarding public access to European Parliament, Council and Commission documents

THE EUROPEAN PARLIAMENT AND THE COUNCIL OF THE EUROPEAN UNION,

Having regard to the Treaty establishing the European Community, and in particular Article 255(2) thereof,

Having regard to the proposal from the Commission

Acting in accordance with the procedure referred to in Article 251 of the Treaty

Whereas:

(1) The second subparagraph of Article 1 of the Treaty on European Union enshrines the concept of openness, stating that the Treaty marks a new stage in the process of creating an ever closer union among the peoples of Europe, in which decisions are taken as openly as possible and as closely as possible to the citizen.

(2) Openness enables citizens to participate more closely in the decision-making process and guarantees that the administration enjoys greater legitimacy and is more effective and more accountable to the citizen in a democratic system. Openness contributes to strengthening the principles of democracy and respect for fundamental rights as laid down in Article 6 of the EU Treaty and in the Charter of Fundamental Rights of the European Union.

(3) The conclusions of the European Council meetings held at Birmingham, Edinburgh and Copenhagen stressed the need to introduce greater transparency into the work of the Union institutions. This Regulation consolidates the initiatives that the institutions have already taken with a view to improving the transparency of the decision-making process.

(4) The purpose of this Regulation is to give the fullest possible effect to the right of public access to documents and to lay down the general principles and limits on such access in accordance with Article 255(2) of the EC Treaty.

(5) Since the question of access to documents is not covered by provisions of the Treaty establishing the European Coal and Steel Community and the Treaty establishing the European Atomic Energy Community, the European Parliament, the Council and the Commission should, in accordance with Declaration No 41 attached to the Final Act of the Treaty of Amsterdam, draw guidance from this Regulation as regards documents concerning the activities covered by those two Treaties.

(6) Wider access should be granted to documents in cases where the institutions are acting in their legislative capacity, including under delegated powers, while at the same time preserving the effectiveness of the institutions' decision-making process. Such documents should be made directly accessible to the greatest possible extent.

(7) In accordance with Articles 28(1) and 41(1) of the EU Treaty, the right of access also applies to documents relating to the common foreign and security policy and to police and judicial cooperation in criminal matters. Each institution should respect its security rules.

(8) In order to ensure the full application of this Regulation to all activities of the Union, all agencies established by the institutions should apply the principles laid down in this

Regulation.

(9) On account of their highly sensitive content, certain documents should be given special treatment. Arrangements for informing the European Parliament of the content of such documents should be made through interinstitutional agreement.

(10) In order to bring about greater openness in the work of the institutions, access to documents should be granted by the European Parliament, the Council and the Commission not only to documents drawn up by the institutions, but also to documents received by them. In this context, it is recalled that Declaration No 35 attached to the Final Act of the Treaty of Amsterdam provides that a Member State may request the Commission or the Council not to communicate to third parties a document originating from that State without its prior agreement.

(11) In principle, all documents of the institutions should be accessible to the public. However, certain public and private interests should be protected by way of exceptions. The institutions should be entitled to protect their internal consultations and deliberations where necessary to safeguard their ability to carry out their tasks. In assessing the exceptions, the institutions should take account of the principles in Community legislation concerning the protection of personal data, in all areas of Union activities.

(12) All rules concerning access to documents of the institutions should be in conformity with this Regulation.

(13) In order to ensure that the right of access is fully respected, a two-stage administrative procedure should apply, with the additional possibility of court proceedings or complaints to the Ombudsman.

(14) Each institution should take the measures necessary to inform the public of the new provisions in force and to train its staff to assist citizens exercising their rights under this Regulation. In order to make it easier for citizens to exercise their rights, each institution should provide access to a register of documents.

(15) Even though it is neither the object nor the effect of this Regulation to amend national legislation on access to documents, it is nevertheless clear that, by virtue of the principle of loyal cooperation which governs relations between the institutions and the Member States, Member States should take care not to hamper the proper application of this Regulation and should respect the security rules of the institutions.

(16) This Regulation is without prejudice to existing rights of access to documents for Member States, judicial authorities or investigative bodies.

(17) In accordance with Article 255(3) of the EC Treaty, each institution lays down specific provisions regarding access to its documents in its rules of procedure. Council Decision 93/731/EC of 20 December 1993 on public access to Council documents, Commission Decision 94/90/ECSC, EC, Euratom of 8 February 1994 on public access to Commission documents, European Parliament Decision 97/632/EC, ECSC, Euratom of 10 July 1997 on public access to European Parliament documents, and the rules on confidentiality of Schengen documents should therefore, if necessary, be modified or be repealed,

HAVE ADOPTED THIS REGULATION:

Article 1 — Purpose

The purpose of this Regulation is:

    (a) to define the principles, conditions and limits on grounds of public or private interest governing the right of access to European Parliament, Council and Commission (hereinafter referred to as 'the institutions') documents provided for in Article 255 of the EC Treaty in such a way as to ensure the widest possible access to documents,

(b) to establish rules ensuring the easiest possible exercise of this right, and

(c) to promote good administrative practice on access to documents.

Article 2 — Beneficiaries and scope

1. Any citizen of the Union, and any natural or legal person residing or having its registered office in a Member State, has a right of access to documents of the institutions, subject to the principles, conditions and limits defined in this Regulation.

2. The institutions may, subject to the same principles, conditions and limits, grant access to documents to any natural or legal person not residing or not having its registered office in a Member State.

3. This Regulation shall apply to all documents held by an institution, that is to say, documents drawn up or received by it and in its possession, in all areas of activity of the European Union.

4. Without prejudice to Articles 4 and 9, documents shall be made accessible to the public either following a written application or directly in electronic form or through a register. In particular, documents drawn up or received in the course of a legislative procedure shall be made directly accessible in accordance with Article 12.

5. Sensitive documents as defined in Article 9(1) shall be subject to special treatment in accordance with that Article.

6. This Regulation shall be without prejudice to rights of public access to documents held by the institutions which might follow from instruments of international law or acts of the institutions implementing them.

Article 3 — Definitions

For the purpose of this Regulation:

(a) 'document' shall mean any content whatever its medium (written on paper or stored in electronic form or as a sound, visual or audiovisual recording) concerning a matter relating to the policies, activities and decisions falling within the institution's sphere of responsibility;

(b) 'third party' shall mean any natural or legal person, or any entity outside the institution concerned, including the Member States, other Community or non-Community institutions and bodies and third countries.

Article 4 — Exceptions

1. The institutions shall refuse access to a document where disclosure would undermine the protection of:

(a) the public interest as regards:

— public security,

— defence and military matters,

— international relations,

— the financial, monetary or economic policy of the Community or a Member State;

(b) privacy and the integrity of the individual, in particular in accordance with Community legislation regarding the protection of personal data.

2. The institutions shall refuse access to a document where disclosure would undermine the protection of:

— commercial interests of a natural or legal person, including intellectual property,

— court proceedings and legal advice,

— the purpose of inspections, investigations and audits,

unless there is an overriding public interest in disclosure.

3. Access to a document, drawn up by an institution for internal use or received by an institution, which relates to a matter where the decision has not been taken by the institution, shall be refused if disclosure of the document would seriously undermine the institution's decision-making process, unless there is an overriding public interest in disclosure.

Access to a document containing opinions for internal use as part of deliberations and preliminary consultations within the institution concerned shall be refused even after the decision has been taken if disclosure of the document would seriously undermine the institution's decision-making process, unless there is an overriding public interest in disclosure.

4. As regards third-party documents, the institution shall consult the third party with a view to assessing whether an exception in paragraph 1 or 2 is applicable, unless it is clear that the document shall or shall not be disclosed.

5. A Member State may request the institution not to disclose a document originating from that Member State without its prior agreement.

6. If only parts of the requested document are covered by any of the exceptions, the remaining parts of the document shall be released.

7. The exceptions as laid down in paragraphs 1 to 3 shall only apply for the period during which protection is justified on the basis of the content of the document. The exceptions may apply for a maximum period of 30 years. In the case of documents covered by the exceptions relating to privacy or commercial interests and in the case of sensitive documents, the exceptions may, if necessary, continue to apply after this period.

Article 5 — Documents in the Member States

Where a Member State receives a request for a document in its possession, originating from an institution, unless it is clear that the document shall or shall not be disclosed, the Member State shall consult with the institution concerned in order to take a decision that does not jeopardise the attainment of the objectives of this Regulation.

The Member State may instead refer the request to the institution.

Article 6 — Applications

1. Applications for access to a document shall be made in any written form, including electronic form, in one of the languages referred to in Article 314 of the EC Treaty and in

a sufficiently precise manner to enable the institution to identify the document. The applicant is not obliged to state reasons for the application.

2. If an application is not sufficiently precise, the institution shall ask the applicant to clarify the application and shall assist the applicant in doing so, for example, by providing information on the use of the public registers of documents.

3. In the event of an application relating to a very long document or to a very large number of documents, the institution concerned may confer with the applicant informally, with a view to finding a fair solution.

4. The institutions shall provide information and assistance to citizens on how and where applications for access to documents can be made.

Article 7 — Processing of initial applications

1. An application for access to a document shall be handled promptly. An acknowledgement of receipt shall be sent to the applicant. Within 15 working days from registration of the application, the institution shall either grant access to the document requested and provide access in accordance with Article 10 within that period or, in a written reply, state the reasons for the total or partial refusal and inform the applicant of his or her right to make a confirmatory application in accordance with paragraph 2 of this Article.

2. In the event of a total or partial refusal, the applicant may, within 15 working days of receiving the institution's reply, make a confirmatory application asking the institution to reconsider its position.

3. In exceptional cases, for example in the event of an application relating to a very long document or to a very large number of documents, the time-limit provided for in paragraph 1 may be extended by 15 working days, provided that the applicant is notified in advance and that detailed reasons are given.

4. Failure by the institution to reply within the prescribed time-limit shall entitle the applicant to make a confirmatory application.

Article 8 — Processing of confirmatory applications

1. A confirmatory application shall be handled promptly. Within 15 working days from registration of such an application, the institution shall either grant access to the document requested and provide access in accordance with Article 10 within that period or, in a written reply, state the reasons for the total or partial refusal. In the event of a total or partial refusal, the institution shall inform the applicant of the remedies open to him or her, namely instituting court proceedings against the institution and/or making a complaint to the Ombudsman, under the conditions laid down in Articles 230 and 195 of the EC Treaty, respectively.

2. In exceptional cases, for example in the event of an application relating to a very long document or to a very large number of documents, the time limit provided for in paragraph 1 may be extended by 15 working days, provided that the applicant is notified in advance and that detailed reasons are given.

3. Failure by the institution to reply within the prescribed time limit shall be considered as a negative reply and entitle the applicant to institute court proceedings against the institution and/or make a complaint to the Ombudsman, under the relevant provisions of the EC

Treaty.

Article 9 — Treatment of sensitive documents

1. Sensitive documents are documents originating from the institutions or the agencies established by them, from Member States, third countries or International Organisations, classified as 'TRÈS SECRET/TOP SECRET', 'SECRET' or 'CONFIDENTIEL' in accordance with the rules of the institution concerned, which protect essential interests of the European Union or of one or more of its Member States in the areas covered by Article 4(1)(a), notably public security, defence and military matters.

2. Applications for access to sensitive documents under the procedures laid down in Articles 7 and 8 shall be handled only by those persons who have a right to acquaint themselves with those documents. These persons shall also, without prejudice to Article 11(2), assess which references to sensitive documents could be made in the public register.

3. Sensitive documents shall be recorded in the register or released only with the consent of the originator.

4. An institution which decides to refuse access to a sensitive document shall give the reasons for its decision in a manner which does not harm the interests protected in Article 4.

5. Member States shall take appropriate measures to ensure that when handling applications for sensitive documents the principles in this Article and Article 4 are respected.

6. The rules of the institutions concerning sensitive documents shall be made public.

7. The Commission and the Council shall inform the European Parliament regarding sensitive documents in accordance with arrangements agreed between the institutions.

Article 10 — Access following an application

1. The applicant shall have access to documents either by consulting them on the spot or by receiving a copy, including, where available, an electronic copy, according to the applicant's preference. The cost of producing and sending copies may be charged to the applicant. This charge shall not exceed the real cost of producing and sending the copies. Consultation on the spot, copies of less than 20 A4 pages and direct access in electronic form or through the register shall be free of charge.

2. If a document has already been released by the institution concerned and is easily accessible to the applicant, the institution may fulfil its obligation of granting access to documents by informing the applicant how to obtain the requested document.

3. Documents shall be supplied in an existing version and format (including electronically or in an alternative format such as Braille, large print or tape) with full regard to the applicant's preference.

Article 11 — Registers

1. To make citizens' rights under this Regulation effective, each institution shall provide public access to a register of documents. Access to the register should be provided in electronic form. References to documents shall be recorded in the register without delay.

2. For each document the register shall contain a reference number (including, where applicable, the interinstitutional reference), the subject matter and/or a short description of the content of the document and the date on which it was received or drawn up and

recorded in the register. References shall be made in a manner which does not undermine protection of the interests in Article 4.

3. The institutions shall immediately take the measures necessary to establish a register which shall be operational by 3 June 2002.

Article 12 — Direct access in electronic form or through a register

1. The institutions shall as far as possible make documents directly accessible to the public in electronic form or through a register in accordance with the rules of the institution concerned.

2. In particular, legislative documents, that is to say, documents drawn up or received in the course of procedures for the adoption of acts which are legally binding in or for the Member States, should, subject to Articles 4 and 9, be made directly accessible.

3. Where possible, other documents, notably documents relating to the development of policy or strategy, should be made directly accessible.

4. Where direct access is not given through the register, the register shall as far as possible indicate where the document is located.

Article 13 — Publication in the Official Journal

1. In addition to the acts referred to in Article 254(1) and (2) of the EC Treaty and the first paragraph of Article 163 of the Euratom Treaty, the following documents shall, subject to Articles 4 and 9 of this Regulation, be published in the Official Journal:

    (a) Commission proposals;

    (b) common positions adopted by the Council in accordance with the procedures referred to in Articles 251 and 252 of the EC Treaty and the reasons underlying those common positions, as well as the European Parliament's positions in these procedures;

    (c) framework decisions and decisions referred to in Article 34(2) of the EU Treaty;

    (d) conventions established by the Council in accordance with Article 34(2) of the EU Treaty;

    (e) conventions signed between Member States on the basis of Article 293 of the EC Treaty;

    (f) international agreements concluded by the Community or in accordance with Article 24 of the EU Treaty.

2. As far as possible, the following documents shall be published in the Official Journal:

    (a) initiatives presented to the Council by a Member State pursuant to Article 67(1) of the EC Treaty or pursuant to Article 34(2) of the EU Treaty;

    (b) common positions referred to in Article 34(2) of the EU Treaty;

    (c) directives other than those referred to in Article 254(1) and (2) of the EC Treaty, decisions other than those referred to in Article 254(1) of the EC Treaty, recommendations and opinions.

3. Each institution may in its rules of procedure establish which further documents shall be published in the Official Journal.

Article 14 — Information

1. Each institution shall take the requisite measures to inform the public of the rights they enjoy under this Regulation.

2. The Member States shall cooperate with the institutions in providing information to the citizens.

Article 15 — Administrative practice in the institutions

1. The institutions shall develop good administrative practices in order to facilitate the exercise of the right of access guaranteed by this Regulation.

2. The institutions shall establish an interinstitutional committee to examine best practice, address possible conflicts and discuss future developments on public access to documents.

Article 16 — Reproduction of documents

This Regulation shall be without prejudice to any existing rules on copyright which may limit a third party's right to reproduce or exploit released documents.

Article 17 — Reports

1. Each institution shall publish annually a report for the preceding year including the number of cases in which the institution refused to grant access to documents, the reasons for such refusals and the number of sensitive documents not recorded in the register.

2. At the latest by 31 January 2004, the Commission shall publish a report on the implementation of the principles of this Regulation and shall make recommendations, including, if appropriate, proposals for the revision of this Regulation and an action programme of measures to be taken by the institutions.

Article 18 — Application measures

1. Each institution shall adapt its rules of procedure to the provisions of this Regulation. The adaptations shall take effect from 3 December 2001.

2. Within six months of the entry into force of this Regulation, the Commission shall examine the conformity of Council Regulation (EEC, Euratom) No 354/83 of 1 February 1983 concerning the opening to the public of the historical archives of the European Economic Community and the European Atomic Energy Community with this Regulation in order to ensure the preservation and archiving of documents to the fullest extent possible.

3. Within six months of the entry into force of this Regulation, the Commission shall examine the conformity of the existing rules on access to documents with this Regulation.

Article 19 — Entry into force

This Regulation shall enter into force on the third day following that of its publication in the *Official Journal of the European Communities*.

It shall be applicable from 3 December 2001.

This Regulation shall be binding in its entirety and directly applicable in all Member States.

Done at Brussels, 30 May 2001.

Part V

Data Protection
(post-EU Exit Day)

Data Protection, Privacy and Electronic Communications (Amendments etc) (EU Exit) Regulations 2019/419

(not in force as at 1 February 2020)

Made: 28 February 2019

The Secretary of State makes these Regulations in exercise of the powers conferred by sections 8(1) and 23(1) of, paragraph 1(1) of Schedule 4 to and paragraph 21 of Schedule 7 to the European Union (Withdrawal) Act 2018, section 211(2) of the Data Protection Act 2018 and section 2(2) of the European Communities Act 1972¹.

In accordance with paragraph 3(1) of Schedule 4 to the European Union (Withdrawal) Act 2018, these Regulations are made with the consent of the Treasury.

The Secretary of State is a Minister designated for purposes of section 2(2) of the European Communities Act 1972 in respect of matters relating to electronic communications.

In accordance with paragraphs 1(1) and 12(1) of Schedule 7 to the European Union (Withdrawal) Act 2018, section 211(5) of the Data Protection Act 2018 and paragraph 2(2) of Schedule 2 to the European Communities Act 1972 a draft of this instrument has been laid before, and approved by a resolution of, each House of Parliament.

Citation, commencement and extent

1(1) These Regulations may be cited as the Data Protection, Privacy and Electronic Communications (Amendments etc) (EU Exit) Regulations 2019.

(2) Subject to paragraph (3), they come into force on exit day.

(3) Regulations 7 and 8 and Schedule 4 come into force on 29th March 2019.

(4) An amendment, repeal or revocation made by these Regulations has the same extent in the United Kingdom as the provision to which it relates.

Interpretation

2 In these Regulations—

"the 2018 Act" means the Data Protection Act 2018;

"the UK GDPR" means Regulation (EU) 2016/679 of the European Parliament and of the Council of 27th April 2016 on the protection of natural persons with regard to the processing of personal data and on the free movement of such data (General Data Protection Regulation) as it forms part of the law of England and Wales, Scotland and Northern Ireland by virtue of section 3 of the European Union (Withdrawal) Act 2018.

Amendment of the UK GDPR

3 Schedule 1 amends the UK GDPR.

Amendment of the Data Protection Act 2018

4 Schedule 2 amends the 2018 Act.

GDPR merger modifications

5(1) Schedules 1 and 2 include modifications ("the GDPR merger modifications") that merge the provisions relating to the processing of personal data that, immediately before exit day, are found in the EU GDPR and the applied GDPR, read with the 2018 Act.

(2) Retained case law and retained general principles of EU law falling within paragraph (3) are not, by virtue of the GDPR merger modifications, to be treated as relevant to the UK GDPR or the 2018 Act as they apply to applied GDPR processing on and after exit day.

(3) Retained case law and retained general principles of EU law fall within this paragraph so far as they are, or are derived from, principles or decisions that are not relevant to any of the following immediately before exit day—

(a) the applied GDPR,

(b) the applied Chapter 2, or

(c) Parts 5 to 7 of the 2018 Act so far as they apply to applied GDPR processing,

having regard (among other things) to the limits of EU competence immediately before exit day.

(4) In this regulation—

"the applied Chapter 2" means Chapter 2 of Part 2 of the 2018 Act as applied by Chapter 3 of that Part immediately before exit day (see section 22 of that Act);

"the applied GDPR" means the EU GDPR as applied by Chapter 3 of Part 2 of the 2018 Act as it has effect immediately before exit day (see section 22 of that Act);

"applied GDPR processing" means the processing of personal data to which the applied GDPR applied immediately before exit day (see section 21 of the 2018 Act);

"the EU GDPR" means Regulation (EU) 2016/679 of the European Parliament and of the Council of 27th April 2016 on the protection of natural persons with regard to the processing of personal data and on the free movement of such data (General Data Protection Regulation) as it has effect in EU law immediately before exit day;

"retained case law" and "retained general principles of EU law" have the same meaning as in the European Union (Withdrawal) Act 2018 (see section 6(7) of that Act).

Consequential amendments of other legislation

6 In Schedule 3—

(a) Part 1 revokes certain retained EU law;

(b) Part 2 contains amendments of primary legislation (as defined in section 211(7) of the 2018 Act) that are consequential on Schedules 1 and 2;

(c) Part 3 contains amendments of other legislation that are consequential on those Schedules;

(d) Part 4 contains modifications of legislation that are consequential on those Schedules;

(e) Part 5 contains supplementary provision.

Amendments consequential on provisions of the 2018 Act

7 Schedule 4 contains amendments consequential on provisions of the 2018 Act.

Amendment of the Privacy and Electronic Communications Regulations 2003

8(1) Regulation 2 of the Privacy and Electronic Communications (EC Directive) Regulations 2003 is amended as follows.

(2) In paragraph (1), at the appropriate place, insert—

"consent" by a user or subscriber corresponds to the data subject's consent in the GDPR (as defined in section 3(10) of the Data Protection Act 2018);1."

(3) Omit paragraph (3).

We consent to the making of these Regulations

Paul Maynard
Jeremy Quin
27 February 2019   Two of the Lords Commissioners of Her Majesty's Treasury

Margot James
Minister of State
28 February 2019   Department for Digital, Culture, Media and Sport

SCHEDULE 1
AMENDMENTS OF THE UK GDPR

Regulation 3

Introduction

1. The UK GDPR is amended as follows.

2. In the title of the Regulation, for ", and repealing Directive 95/46/EC (General Data Protection Regulation)" substitute "(United Kingdom General Data Protection Regulation)".

Chapter 1 (general provisions)

3. In Article 1, omit paragraph 3.

4(1) Article 2 is amended as follows.

(2) For paragraph 1 substitute—

"1 This Regulation applies to the automated or structured processing of personal data, including—

(a) processing in the course of an activity which, immediately before exit day, fell outside the scope of EU law, and

(b) processing in the course of an activity which, immediately before exit day, fell within the scope of Chapter 2 of Title 5 of the Treaty on European Union (common foreign and security policy activities).

1A This Regulation also applies to the manual unstructured processing of personal data held by an FOI public authority.".

(3) For paragraph 2 substitute—

"2 This Regulation does not apply to—

(a)   the processing of personal data by an individual in the course of a purely personal or household activity;

(b)   the processing of personal data by a competent authority for any of the law enforcement purposes (see Part 3 of the 2018 Act);

(c)   the processing of personal data to which Part 4 of the 2018 Act (intelligence services processing) applies.".

(4)   Omit paragraph 3.

(5)   In paragraph 4, for "Directive 2000/31/EC"1 to the end substitute "the Electronic Commerce (EC Directive) Regulations 2002, in particular the provisions about mere conduits, caching and hosting (see regulations 17 to 19 of those Regulations).".

(6)   After paragraph 4 insert—
    "5   In this Article—
        (a)   'the automated or structured processing of personal data' means—
            (i)   the processing of personal data wholly or partly by automated means, and
            (ii)   the processing otherwise than by automated means of personal data which forms part of a filing system or is intended to form part of a filing system;
        (b)   'the manual unstructured processing of personal data' means the processing of personal data which is not the automated or structured processing of personal data;
        (c)   'FOI public authority' has the same meaning as in Chapter 3 of Part 2 of the 2018 Act (see section 21(5) of that Act);
        (d)   references to personal data 'held' by an FOI public authority are to be interpreted in accordance with section 21(6) and (7) of the 2018 Act;
        (e)   'competent authority' and 'law enforcement purposes' have the same meaning as in Part 3 of the 2018 Act (see sections 30 and 31 of that Act).".

5(1)   Article 3 is amended as follows.

(2)   In paragraph 1, for "the Union" (in both places) substitute "the United Kingdom".

(3)   In paragraph 2—
    (a) before "processing" (in the first place) insert "relevant";
    (b) for "the Union" (in each place) substitute "the United Kingdom".

(4)   After paragraph 2 insert—
    "2A   In paragraph 2, "relevant processing of personal data" means processing to which this Regulation applies, other than processing described in Article 2(1)(a) or (b) or (1A).".

(5)   In paragraph 3—
    (a) for "the Union" substitute "the United Kingdom";
    (b) for "Member State law" substitute "domestic law".

6(1)   Article 4 is amended as follows.

(2)   Before paragraph (1) insert—
    "(A1)   'the 2018 Act' means the Data Protection Act 2018;

826

(A2) 'domestic law' means the law of the United Kingdom or of a part of the United Kingdom;

(A3) 'the Commissioner' means the Information Commissioner (see section 114 of the 2018 Act);".

(3) In paragraph (7), for "; where the purposes and means of such processing are determined by Union or Member State law, the controller or the specific criteria for its nomination may be provided for by Union or Member State law" substitute "(but see section 6 of the 2018 Act)".

(4) In paragraph (9), for "Union or Member State law" substitute "domestic law".

(5) After paragraph (10) insert—

"(10A) 'public authority' and 'public body' are to be interpreted in accordance with section 7 of the 2018 Act and provision made under that section;".

(6) Omit paragraph (16).

(7) In paragraph (17), for "the Union" substitute "the United Kingdom".

(8) In paragraph (20), for "on the territory of a Member State" substitute "in the United Kingdom".

(9) Omit paragraph (21).

(10) After paragraph (21) insert—

"(21A) 'foreign designated authority' means an authority designated for the purposes of Article 13 of the Data Protection Convention (as defined in section 3 of the 2018 Act) by a party, other than the United Kingdom, which is bound by that Convention;".

(11) Omit paragraphs (22), (23) and (24).

(12) In paragraph (25), at the end insert "as it has effect immediately before exit day".

(13) After paragraph (26) insert—

"(27) 'third country' means a country or territory outside the United Kingdom;

(28) references to a fundamental right or fundamental freedom (however expressed) are to a fundamental right or fundamental freedom which continues to form part of domestic law on and after exit day by virtue of section 4 of the European Union (Withdrawal) Act 2018, as the right or freedom is amended or otherwise modified by domestic law from time to time on or after exit day.".

7(1) Article 6 is amended as follows.

(2) Omit paragraph 2.

(3) In paragraph 3—

(a) in the first subparagraph, for points (a) and (b) (and the colon before them) substitute "domestic law";

(b) in the second subparagraph, for "The Union or Member State law" substitute "The domestic law".

(4) In paragraph 4—

(a) for "a Union or Member State law" substitute "domestic law";

(b) after "safeguard" insert "national security, defence or any of".

8(1)   Article 8 is amended as follows.

  (2)   In paragraph 1—
          (a) for "16 years old" substitute "13 years old";
          (b) for "of 16 years" substitute "of 13 years";
          (c) omit the second subparagraph.

  (3)   In paragraph 3, for "of Member States" substitute "as it operates in domestic law".

  (4)   After paragraph 3 insert—
          "4. In paragraph 1, the reference to information society services does not include
          preventive or counselling services.".

9(1)   Article 9 is amended as follows.

  (2)   In paragraph 2(a), for "Union or Member State law provide" substitute "domestic law
          provides".

  (3)   In paragraph 2(b)—
          (a) for "Union or Member State law" substitute "domestic law";
          (b) for "to Member State law" substitute "to domestic law".

  (4)   In paragraph 2(g), for "Union or Member State law" substitute "domestic law".

  (5)   In paragraph 2(h), for "Union or Member State law" substitute "domestic law".

  (6)   In paragraph 2(i), for "Union or Member State law" substitute "domestic law".

  (7)   paragraph 2(j)—
          (a) after "Article 89(1)" insert "(as supplemented by section 19 of the 2018 Act)";
          (b) for "Union or Member State law" substitute "domestic law".

  (8)   In paragraph 3, for "Union or Member State law" (in both places) substitute "domestic
          law".

  (9)   After that paragraph insert—
          "3A   In paragraph 3, 'national competent bodies' means competent bodies of the
          United Kingdom or a part of the United Kingdom.".

  (10)   Omit paragraph 4.

  (11)   After that paragraph insert—
          "5 In the 2018 Act—
          (a)   section 10 makes provision about when the requirement in paragraph 2(b),
                 (g), (h), (i) or (j) of this Article for authorisation by, or a basis in, domestic
                 law is met;
          (b)   section 11(1) makes provision about when the processing of personal data
                 is carried out in circumstances described in paragraph 3 of this Article.".

10(1)   Article 10 is amended as follows.

  (2)   The existing text becomes paragraph 1.

  (3)   In that paragraph, for "Union or Member State law" substitute "domestic law".

(4)   After that paragraph insert—
    "2 In the 2018 Act—
       (a)   section 10 makes provision about when the requirement in paragraph 1 of this Article for authorisation by domestic law is met;
       (b)   section 11(2) makes provision about the meaning of "personal data relating to criminal convictions and offences or related security measures".".

11(1)   Article 12 is amended as follows.

(2)   In paragraph 4, for "a supervisory authority" substitute "the Commissioner".

(3)   After paragraph 6 insert—
    "6A   The Commissioner may publish (and amend or withdraw)—
       (a)   standardised icons for use in combination with information provided to data subjects under Articles 13 and 14;
       (b)   a notice stating that other persons may publish (and amend or withdraw) such icons, provided that the icons satisfy requirements specified in the notice as to the information to be presented by the icons and the procedures for providing the icons.
    6B The Commissioner must not publish icons or a notice under paragraph 6A unless satisfied (as appropriate) that the icons give a meaningful overview of the intended processing in an easily visible, intelligible and clearly legible manner or that the notice will result in icons that do so.".

(4)   In paragraph 7
    (a) for "The information" substitute "If standardised icons are published as described in paragraph 6A (and not withdrawn), the information";
    (b) for "standardised" to "processing" substitute "the icons".

(5)   Omit paragraph 8.

12(1)   Article 13 is amended as follows.

(2)   In paragraph 1(f), for "an adequacy decision by the Commission" substitute "relevant adequacy regulations under section 17A of the 2018 Act1".

(3)   In paragraph 2(d), for "a supervisory authority" substitute "the Commissioner".

13(1)   Article 14 is amended as follows.

(2)   In paragraph 1(f), for "an adequacy decision by the Commission" substitute "relevant adequacy regulations under section 17A of the 2018 Act".

(3)   In paragraph 2(e), for "a supervisory authority" substitute "the Commissioner".

(4)   In paragraph 5(c), for "Union or Member State law to which the controller is subject and" substitute "a provision of domestic law".

(5)   In paragraph 5(d), for "Union or Member State law" substitute "domestic law".

14   In Article 15(1)(f), for "a supervisory authority" substitute "the Commissioner".

15(1)   Article 17 is amended as follows.

(2)   In paragraph 1(e), for "in Union or Member State law to which the controller is subject" substitute "under domestic law".

(3)   In paragraph 3(b), for "by Union or Member State law to which the controller is subject" substitute "under domestic law".

16   In Article 18(2), omit "of the Union or of a Member State".

17   In Article 21(5)—
(a)   omit "and notwithstanding Directive 2002/58/EC1,";
(b)   at the end insert ", notwithstanding domestic law made before exit day implementing Directive 2002/58/EC of the European Parliament and of the Council of 12th July 2002 concerning the processing of personal data and the protection of privacy in the electronic communications sector"

18(1)   Article 22 is amended as follows.

(2)   In paragraph 2(b), for "authorised by Union or Member State law to which the controller is subject and" substitute "required or authorised by domestic law".

(3)   After paragraph 3 insert—
"3A   Section 14 of the 2018 Act, and regulations under that section, make provision to safeguard data subjects' rights, freedoms and legitimate interests in cases that fall within point (b) of paragraph 2 (but not within point (a) or (c) of that paragraph).".

19(1)   Article 23 is amended as follows.

(2)   In paragraph 1—
(a)   for "Union or Member State law to which the data controller or processor is subject may restrict by way of legislative measure" substitute "The Secretary of State may restrict";
(b)   omit points (a) and (b);
(c)   in point (e)—
(i)   omit "of the Union or of a Member State" in the first place it occurs;
(ii)   for "of the Union or of a Member State", in the second place it occurs, substitute "of the United Kingdom".

(3)   In paragraph 2, for "any legislative measure referred to in" substitute "provision made in exercise of the power under".

(4)   After that paragraph insert—
"3   The Secretary of State may exercise the power under paragraph 1 only by making regulations under section 16 of the 2018 Act.".

20   In Article 26(1), for "Union or Member State law to which the controllers are subject" substitute "domestic law".

21(1) Article 27 is amended as follows.

(2) In the heading, for "the Union" substitute "the United Kingdom.

(3) In paragraph 1, for "the Union" substitute "the United Kingdom.

(4) Omit paragraph 3.

(5) In paragraph 4, for "supervisory authorities" substitute "the Commissioner".

22(1) Article 28 is amended as follows.

(2) In paragraph 3—
    (a) in the opening words, for "Union or Member State law" substitute "domestic law";
    (b) in point (a), for "Union or Member State law to which the processor is subject" substitute "domestic law";
    (c) in point (g), for "Union or Member State law" substitute "domestic law";
    (d) in the second subparagraph, for "other Union or Member State data protection provisions" substitute "other domestic law relating to data protection".

(3) In paragraph 4, "for Union or Member State law" substitute "domestic law".

(4) In paragraph 6, for "paragraphs 7 and 8" substitute "paragraph 8".

(5) Omit paragraph 7.

(6) In paragraph 8—
    (a) for "A supervisory authority" substitute "The Commissioner";
    (b) omit "and in accordance with the consistency mechanism referred to in Article 63".

23 In Article 29, for "Union or Member State law" substitute "domestic law".

24(1) Article 30 is amended as follows.

(2) In paragraph 1(g), after "Article 32(1)" insert "or, as appropriate, the security measures referred to in section 28(3) of the 2018 Act".

(3) In paragraph 2(d), after "Article 32(1)" insert "or, as appropriate, the security measures referred to in section 28(3) of the 2018 Act".

(4) In paragraph 4, for "the supervisory authority" substitute "the Commissioner".

25(1) Article 31 is amended as follows.

(2) In the heading, for "the supervisory authority" substitute "the Commissioner".

(3) For "the supervisory authority in the performance of its tasks" substitute "the Commissioner in the performance of the Commissioner's tasks".

26 In Article 32(4), for "Union or Member State law" substitute "domestic law".

27(1) Article 33 is amended as follows.

(2) In the heading, for "the supervisory authority" substitute "the Commissioner".

(3) In paragraph 1—
    (a) for "the supervisory authority competent in accordance with Article 55" substitute "the Commissioner";
    (b) for "the notification to the supervisory authority" substitute "the notification under this paragraph".

(4) In paragraph 5, for "the supervisory authority" substitute "the Commissioner".

28 In Article 34(4), for "the supervisory authority" substitute "the Commissioner".

29 Article 35 is amended as follows.
    (2) In paragraph 4—
        (a)   in the first sentence, for "The supervisory authority" substitute "The Commissioner";
        (b)   omit the second sentence.
    (3) In paragraph 5—
        (a)   in the first sentence, for "The supervisory authority" substitute "The Commissioner";
        (b)   omit the second sentence.
    (4) Omit paragraph 6.
    (5) For paragraph 10 substitute—
        "10   In the case of processing pursuant to point (c) or (e) of Article 6(1), paragraphs 1 to 7 of this Article do not apply if a data protection impact assessment has already been carried out for the processing as part of a general impact assessment required by domestic law, unless domestic law provides otherwise.".

30(1) Article 36 is amended as follows.

(2) In paragraph 1, for "the supervisory authority" substitute "the Commissioner".

(3) In paragraph 2—
    (a) in the first sentence, for "the supervisory authority" (in both places) substitute "the Commissioner";
    (b) in the third sentence, for "The supervisory authority" substitute "The Commissioner";
    (c) in the last sentence, for "the supervisory authority has obtained information it" substitute "the Commissioner has obtained information the Commissioner".

(4) In paragraph 3—
    (a) in the opening words, for "the supervisory authority" (in both places) substitute "the Commissioner";
    (b) in point (f), for "the supervisory authority" substitute "the Commissioner".

(5) In paragraph 4—
    (a) for "Members States shall consult the supervisory authority" substitute "The relevant authority must consult the Commissioner";
    (b) for "a national parliament" substitute "Parliament, the National Assembly for

Wales, the Scottish Parliament or the Northern Ireland Assembly".

(6) After that paragraph insert—
"4A In paragraph 4, "the relevant authority" means —
(a) in relation to a legislative measure adopted by Parliament, or a regulatory measure based on such a legislative measure, the Secretary of State;
(b) in relation to a legislative measure adopted by the National Assembly for Wales, or a regulatory measure based on such a legislative measure, the Welsh Ministers;
(c) in relation to a legislative measure adopted by the Scottish Parliament, or a regulatory measure based on such a legislative measure, the Scottish Ministers;
(d) in relation to a legislative measure adopted by the Northern Ireland Assembly, or a regulatory measure based on such a legislative measure, the relevant Northern Ireland department.".

(7) Omit paragraph 5.

31(1) Article 37 is amended as follows.

(2) In paragraph 4, omit "or, where required by Union or Member State law shall,".

(3) In paragraph 7, for "the supervisory authority" substitute "the Commissioner".

32 In Article 38(5), for "Union or Member State law" substitute "domestic law".

33(1) Article 39 is amended as follows.

(2) In paragraph 1(a) and (b), for "other Union or Member State data protection provisions" substitute "other domestic law relating to data protection".

(3) In paragraph 1(d) and (e), for "the supervisory authority" substitute "the Commissioner".

34(1) Article 40 is amended as follows.

(2) In paragraph 1, for "The Member States, the supervisory authorities, the Board and the Commission" substitute "The Commissioner".

(3) In paragraph 2(i), for "supervisory authorities" substitute "the Commissioner".

(4) In paragraph 3, omit "and having general validity pursuant to paragraph 9 of this Article".

(5) In paragraph 4, for "supervisory authorities competent pursuant to Article 55 or 56" substitute "the Commissioner".

(6) In paragraph 5—
(a) for "the supervisory authority which is competent pursuant to Article 55. The supervisory authority" substitute "the Commissioner, who";
(b) for "it finds" substitute "the Commissioner finds".

(7) In paragraph 6, for "and where the code of conduct concerned does not relate to processing activities in several Member States, the supervisory authority" substitute "the Commissioner".

(8) Omit paragraphs 7, 8, 9, 10 and 11.

35(1) Article 41 is amended as follows.

(2) In paragraph 1, for "the competent supervisory authority" (in both places) substitute "the Commissioner".

(3) In paragraph 2(a) and (d), for "the competent supervisory authority" substitute "the Commissioner".

(4) Omit paragraph 3.

(5) In paragraph 4, for "the competent supervisory authority" (in both places) substitute "the Commissioner".

(6) In paragraph 5, for "The competent supervisory authority" substitute "The Commissioner".

36(1) Article 42 is amended as follows.

(2) In paragraph 1—
    (a) for "The Member States, the supervisory authorities, the Board and the Commission" substitute "The Commissioner";
    (b) omit ", in particular at Union level,".

(3) In paragraph 4, for "the supervisory authorities which are competent pursuant to Article 55 or 56" substitute "the Commissioner".

(4) In paragraph 5—
    (a) for "the competent supervisory authority" substitute "the Commissioner";
    (b) for "that competent supervisory authority" substitute "the Commissioner";
    (c) omit "or by the Board pursuant to Article 63" and the second sentence.

(5) In paragraph 6, for "the competent supervisory authority" substitute "the Commissioner".

(6) In paragraph 7, for "the competent supervisory authority" substitute "the Commissioner".

(7) In paragraph 8, for "The Board" substitute "The Commissioner".

37(1) Article 43 is amended as follows.

(2) In paragraph 1—
    (a) in the opening words—
        (i) for "the competent supervisory authority" substitute "the Commissioner";
        (ii) for "the supervisory authority" substitute "the Commissioner";
        (iii) for "Members States shall ensure that those certification bodies are" substitute "In accordance with section 17 of the 2018 Act, those certification bodies may only be";
    (b) for point (a) substitute—
      "(a)   the Commissioner;";
    (c) in point (b)—
        (i) for "the national accreditation body" substitute "the UK national accreditation body";
        (ii) for "the supervisory authority which is competent pursuant to Article 55 or

56" substitute "the Commissioner".

(3) In paragraph 2—

  (a) in point (a), for "the competent supervisory authority" substitute "the Commissioner";

  (b) in point (b), for "the supervisory authority" to the end substitute "the Commissioner";

  (c) in point (e), for "the competent supervisory authority" substitute "the Commissioner".

(4) In paragraph 3, for "the supervisory authority which is competent pursuant to Article 55 or 56 or by the Board pursuant to Article 63" substitute "the Commissioner".

(5) In paragraph 5, for "the competent supervisory authorities" substitute "the Commissioner".

(6) In paragraph 6—

  (a) for "the supervisory authority" substitute "the Commissioner";

  (b) omit from "The supervisory authorities" to the end.

(7) In paragraph 7, for "the competent supervisory authority or the national accreditation body" substitute "the Commissioner or the UK national accreditation body".

(8) Omit paragraphs 8 and 9.

38(1) Article 45 is amended as follows.

(2) In paragraph 1, for "where the Commission" to the end of the first sentence substitute "where it is based on adequacy regulations (see section 17A of the 2018 Act)".

(3) In paragraph 2—

  (a) for ", the Commission" substitute "for the purposes of sections 17A and 17B1 of the 2018 Act, the Secretary of State";

  (b) in point (b), for "the supervisory authorities of the Member States" substitute "the Commissioner".

(4) Omit paragraphs 3, 4, 5 and 6.

(5) In paragraph 7, for "A decision pursuant to paragraph 5 of this Article" substitute "The amendment or revocation of regulations under section 17A of the 2018 Act".

(6) Omit paragraphs 8 and 9.

39(1) Article 46 is amended as follows.

(2) In paragraph 1, for "a decision pursuant to Article 45(3)" substitute "adequacy regulations under section 17A of the 2018 Act".

(3) In paragraph 2—

  (a) for "a supervisory authority" substitute "the Commissioner";

  (b) for paragraph (c) substitute—

    "(c)   standard data protection clauses specified in regulations made by the Secretary of State under section 17C1 of the 2018 Act and for the time being in force;";

  (c) for paragraph (d) substitute—

"(d) standard data protection clauses specified in a document issued (and not withdrawn) by the Commissioner under section 119A2 of the 2018 Act and for the time being in force;".

(4) In paragraph 3, for "Subject to the authorisation from the competent supervisory authority" substitute "With authorisation from the Commissioner".

(5) Omit paragraphs 4 and 5.

40(1) Article 47 is amended as follows.

(2) In paragraph 1—
    (a) for "The competent supervisory authority" substitute "The Commissioner";
    (b) omit "in accordance with the consistency mechanism set out in Article 63".

(3) In paragraph 2(e), for "the competent supervisory authority and before the competent courts of the Member States in accordance with Article 79" substitute "the Commissioner and before a court in accordance with Article 79 (see section 180 of the 2018 Act)".

(4) In paragraph 2(f)—
    (a) for "established on the territory of a Member State" substitute "established in the United Kingdom";
    (b) for "not established in the Union" substitute "not established in the United Kingdom".

(5) In paragraph 2(j), for "the competent supervisory authority" substitute "the Commissioner".

(6) In paragraph 2(k), for "the supervisory authority" substitute "the Commissioner".

(7) In paragraph 2(l), for "the supervisory authority" (in both places) substitute "the Commissioner".

(8) In paragraph 2(m), for "the competent supervisory authority" substitute "the Commissioner".

(9) Omit paragraph 3.

41 Omit Article 48.

42(1) Article 49 is amended as follows.

(2) In paragraph 1—
    (a) in the opening words, for "an adequacy decision pursuant to Article 45(3)" substitute "adequacy regulations under section 17A of the 2018 Act";
    (b) in point (g), for "Union or Member State law" (in both places) substitute "domestic law";
    (c) in the second subparagraph, for "the supervisory authority" substitute "the Commissioner".

(3) In paragraph 4, for "shall be recognised in Union law or in the law of the Member State to which the controller is subject" substitute "must be public interest that is recognised in domestic law (whether in regulations under section 18(1) of the 2018 Act or otherwise)".

(4) Omit paragraph 5.

(5) After that paragraph insert—

> "5A This Article and Article 46 are subject to restrictions in regulations under section 18(2) of the 2018 Act.".

43 In Article 50, for "the Commission and supervisory authorities" substitute "the Commissioner".

44 For the heading of Chapter 6 substitute "The Commissioner".

45(1) Article 51 is amended as follows.

(2) For the heading, substitute "Monitoring the application of this Regulation".

(3) In paragraph 1—

    (a) for "Each Member State shall provide for one or more independent public authorities to be" substitute "The Commissioner is";

    (b) omit "within the Union ("supervisory authority")".

(4) Omit paragraphs 2, 3 and 4.

46(1) Article 52 is amended as follows.

(2) In paragraph 1—

    (a) for "Each supervisory authority" substitute "The Commissioner";

    (b) omit "its" (in both places).

(3) In paragraph 2—

    (a) for "The member or members of each supervisory authority" substitute "The Commissioner";

    (b) omit "their" (in both places).

(4) In paragraph 3—

    (a) for "Member or members of each supervisory authority" substitute "The Commissioner";

    (b) for "their duties" substitute "the Commissioner's duties";

    (c) for "during their term of office" substitute "while holding office".

(5) Omit paragraphs 4, 5 and 6.

47 Omit Article 53.

48 Omit Article 54.

49 In the heading of section 2 of Chapter 6, for "Competence, tasks" substitute "Tasks".

50 Omit Article 55.

51 Omit Article 56.

52(1)   Article 57 is amended as follows.

(2)   In paragraph 1—

    (a)   for "each supervisory authority shall on its territory" substitute "the Commissioner must";

    (b)   in point (c), for ", in accordance with Member State law, the national parliament" substitute "Parliament";

    (c)   in point (e), for "the supervisory authorities in other Member States" substitute "foreign designated authorities";

    (d)   in point (f), for "another supervisory authority" substitute "a foreign designated authority";

    (e)   omit point (g);

    (f)   in point (h), for "another supervisory authority" substitute "a foreign designated authority";

    (g)   in point (j), after "and" insert "issue standard data protection clauses referred to";

    (h)   after point (o) insert—

      "(oa)   maintain a public register of certification mechanisms and data protection seals and marks pursuant to Article 42(8) and of controllers or processors established in third countries and certified pursuant to Article 42(7);";

    (i)   omit point (t).

(3)   In paragraph 2, for "Each supervisory authority" substitute "The Commissioner".

(4)   In paragraph 3, for "the tasks of each supervisory authority shall be" substitute "the Commissioner's tasks is to be".

(5)   In paragraph 4, for "supervisory authority" (in both places) substitute "Commissioner".

53(1)   Article 58 is amended as follows.

(2)   In paragraph 1—

    (a)   for "Each supervisory authority shall have" substitute "The Commissioner has";

    (b)   in point (e), for "its" substitute "the Commissioner's";

    (c)   in point (f), for "Union or Member State procedural law" substitute "domestic law".

(3)   In paragraph 2, for "Each supervisory authority shall have" substitute "The Commissioner has".

(4)   In paragraph 3—

    (a)   for "Each supervisory authority shall have" substitute "The Commissioner has";

    (b)   in point (b)—

      (i)   for "its" substitute "the Commissioner's";

      (ii)   for "the national parliament, the Member State government or, in accordance with Member State law, to" substitute "Parliament, the government or";

    (c)   omit point (c).

(5)   After paragraph 3 insert—

    "3A   In the 2018 Act, section 115(4) to (9) provide that the Commissioner's functions under this Article are subject to certain safeguards.".

(6)   Omit paragraphs 4, 5 and 6.

54   In Article 59—

    (a) for "Each supervisory authority" substitute "The Commissioner";

    (b) for "its" substitute "the Commissioner's";

    (c) for the second sentence substitute "The Commissioner must arrange for those reports to be laid before Parliament and send a copy to the Secretary of State.";

    (d) omit ", to the Commission and to the Board".

55   Omit Articles 60 to 76 and the headings for, and for the sections of, Chapter 7.

56(1) Article 77 is amended as follows.

  (2) In the heading, for "a supervisory authority" substitute "the Commissioner".

  (3) In paragraph 1, for "a supervisory authority, in particular in the Member State of his or her habitual residence, place of work or place of the alleged infringement" substitute "the Commissioner".

  (4) In paragraph 2, for "The supervisory authority with which the complaint has been lodged" substitute "The Commissioner".

57(1) Article 78 is amended as follows.

  (2) In the heading, for "a supervisory authority" substitute "the Commissioner".

  (3) In paragraph 1, for "a supervisory authority" substitute "the Commissioner".

  (4) In paragraph 2, for "the supervisory authority which is competent pursuant to Articles 55 and 56" substitute "the Commissioner".

  (5) Omit paragraph 3.

  (6) Omit paragraph 4.

58(1) Article 79 is amended as follows.

  (2) In paragraph 1, for "a supervisory authority" substitute "the Commissioner".

  (3) Omit paragraph 2.

59(1) Article 80 is amended as follows.

  (2) In paragraph 1—

    (a) for the words from "a not-for profit" to "their personal data" substitute "a body or other organisation which meets the conditions in section 187(3) and (4) of the 2018 Act";

    (b) omit "where provided for by Member State law".

  (3) In paragraph 2—

    (a) for "Member States" substitute "The Secretary of State";

    (b) omit ", in that Member State,";

    (c) for "the supervisory authority which is competent pursuant to Article 77" substitute "the Commissioner".

(4) After that paragraph insert—

"3.

The Secretary of State may exercise the power under paragraph 2 of this Article only by making regulations under section 190 of the 2018 Act.".

60 Omit Article 81.

61 In Article 82, omit paragraph 6.

62(1) Article 83 is amended as follows.

(2) In paragraph 1, for "Each supervisory authority" substitute "The Commissioner".

(3) In paragraph 2—

(a) in point (f), for "the supervisory authority" substitute "the Commissioner";

(b) in point (h), for "the supervisory authority" substitute "the Commissioner".

(4) In paragraph 4, for "10 000 000 EUR" substitute "£8,700,000".

(5) In paragraph 5—

(a) for "20 000 000 EUR" substitute "£17,500,000";

(b) for point (d) substitute—

"(d) any obligations under Part 5 or 6 of Schedule 2 to the 2018 Act or regulations made under section 16(1)(c) of the 2018 Act;";

(c) in point (e), for "the supervisory authority" substitute "the Commissioner".

(6) In paragraph 6—

(a) for "the supervisory authority" substitute "the Commissioner";

(b) for "20 000 000 EUR" substitute "£17,500,000".

(7) Omit paragraphs 7, 8 and 9.

(8) After paragraph 9 insert—

"10 In the 2018 Act, section 115(9) makes provision about the exercise of the Commissioner's functions under this Article.".

63 In Article 84, for paragraphs 1 and 2 substitute—

"Part 6 of the 2018 Act makes further provision about penalties applicable to infringements of this Regulation."

64(1) Article 85 is amended as follows.

(2) Omit paragraph 1.

(3) In paragraph 2—

(a) for "Members States shall" substitute "the Secretary of State may";

(b) for "independent supervisory authorities" substitute "the Commissioner";

(c) omit ", Chapter VII (cooperation and consistency)".

(4) After that paragraph insert—

"2A The Secretary of State may exercise the power under paragraph 2 of this Article only by making regulations under section 16 of the 2018 Act.".

(5) Omit paragraph 3.

65(1) Article 86 is amended as follows.

(2) The existing text becomes paragraph 1.

(3) In that paragraph, for "Union or Member State law" substitute "domestic law".

(4) After that paragraph insert—
"2.
Chapter 3 of Part 2 of the 2018 Act makes provision about the application of this Regulation to the manual unstructured processing of personal data held by an FOI public authority (as defined in Article 2).".

66 After Article 86 insert—
"Article 86A Processing and national security and defence
Chapter 3 of Part 2 of the 2018 Act makes provision about the application of this Regulation where processing is carried out, or exemption from a provision of this Regulation is required, for the purposes of safeguarding national security or for defence purposes.".

67 Omit Article 87.

68 Omit Article 88.

69(1) Article 89 is amended as follows.

(2) After paragraph 1 insert—
"1A   In the 2018 Act, section 19 makes provision about when the requirements in paragraph 1 are satisfied.".

(3) Omit paragraphs 2, 3 and 4.

70 Omit Article 90.

71 Omit Article 91.

72 Omit Articles 92 and 93 and the heading for Chapter 10.

73(1) Article 94 is amended as follows.

(2) Omit paragraph 1.

(3) In paragraph 2—
(a) in the first sentence, for "the repealed Directive" substitute "Directive 95/46/EC of the European Parliament and of the Council of 24th October 1995 on the protection of individuals with regard to the processing of personal data and on the free movement of such data (which ceased to have effect on 25th May 2018)";
(b) in the second sentence, for "by this Regulation" substitute "by the EU GDPR (as

defined in section 3 of the 2018 Act)"1.

74(1)   Article 95 is amended as follows.

(2)   For "the Union" substitute "the United Kingdom".

(3)   For "Directive 2002/58/EC" substitute "domestic law made before exit day implementing Directive 2002/58/EC of the European Parliament and of the Council of 12th July 2002 concerning the processing of personal data and the protection of privacy in the electronic communications sector".

75(1)   Article 96 is amended as follows.

(2)   For "Member States" substitute "the United Kingdom or the Commissioner".

(3)   For "Union law" substitute "domestic law".

76   Omit Article 97.

77   Omit Article 98.

78   Omit Article 99.

79   Omit the sentence following Article 99.

80   It is not to be presumed, by virtue of the revocation of a provision by this Schedule, that the provision was applicable to the United Kingdom immediately before exit day (and so would, but for this Schedule, be part of the UK GDPR).

SCHEDULE 2
AMENDMENTS OF THE DATA PROTECTION ACT 2018

Regulation 4

1   The Data Protection Act 2018 is amended as follows.

2(1)   Section 1 is amended as follows.

(2)   In subsection (2), for "GDPR" substitute "UK GDPR".

(3)   In subsection (3), for "GDPR" to the end substitute "UK GDPR".

(4)   In subsection (4), omit "and implements the Law Enforcement Directive".

3   In section 2(1) and (2), for "GDPR, the applied GDPR" substitute "UK GDPR".

4(1)   Section 3 is amended as follows.

(2)   In subsection (6), omit "Chapter 2 or 3 of" and "Chapter or".

(3) In subsection (9)—
  (a) for paragraph (a) substitute—
      "(a)   the UK GDPR,";
  (b) Omit paragraph (b);
  (c) in paragraph (e), for "the GDPR" substitute "the EU GDPR".

(4) In subsection (10)—
  (a) for "The GDPR" substitute "The UK GDPR";
  (b) for "(General Data Protection Regulation)" substitute "(United Kingdom General Data Protection Regulation), as it forms part of the law of England and Wales, Scotland and Northern Ireland by virtue of section 3 of the European Union (Withdrawal) Act 2018 (and see section 205(4)1)".

(5) After subsection (10) insert—
      "(10A) "The EU GDPR" means Regulation (EU) 2016/679 of the European Parliament and of the Council of 27th April 2016 on the protection of natural persons with regard to the processing of personal data and on the free movement of such data (General Data Protection Regulation) as it has effect in EU law.".

(6) Omit subsection (11).

(7) In subsection (14)—
  (a) for paragraph (a) substitute—
      "(a)   references to the UK GDPR are to the UK GDPR read with Part 2;";
  (b) Omit paragraph (b);
  (c) in paragraphs (c) and (d), omit "Chapter 2 or 3 of".

5(1) Section 4 is amended as follows.

(2) In subsection (2)—
  (a) for "Chapter 2 of this Part" substitute "This Part";
  (b) for "GDPR" (in each place) substitute "UK GDPR".

(3) Omit subsection (3).

6(1) Section 5 is amended as follows.

(2) In subsection (1)—
  (a) omit "Chapter 2 of";
  (b) for "GDPR" (in both places) substitute "UK GDPR";
  (c) for "Chapter 2 as" substitute "this Part as".

(3) In subsection (2)—
  (a) for "GDPR" (in each place) substitute "UK GDPR";
  (b) for "Chapter 2" substitute "this Part".

(4) In subsection (3), for "Chapter 2" substitute "this Part".

(5) Omit subsections (4), (5) and (6).

(6) In subsection (7)—
  (a) omit "Chapter 2 or Chapter 3 of";

(b) for "the Chapter" substitute "this Part".

7   For the heading of Chapter 2 substitute "The UK GDPR".

8   In the italic heading before section 6, for "GDPR" substitute "UK GDPR".

9   In section 6(1) and (2), for "GDPR" substitute "UK GDPR".

10(1)   Section 7 is amended as follows.

(2)   In subsection (1)—
      (a) for "GDPR" substitute "UK GDPR";
      (b) omit "under the law of the United Kingdom".

(3)   In subsections (2) and (4), for "GDPR" substitute "UK GDPR".

11   In section 8, for "GDPR" substitute "UK GDPR".

12   Omit section 9.

13(1)   Section 10 is amended as follows.

(2)   In subsections (1), (2) and (3), for "GDPR" substitute "UK GDPR".

(3)   In subsection (5), for "10 of the GDPR" substitute "10(1) of the UK GDPR".

14   In section 11, in subsection (1) (in both places) and in subsection (2), for "GDPR" substitute "UK GDPR".

15   In section 12(1)(a) and (b), for "GDPR" substitute "UK GDPR".

16   In section 13(2) and (3), for "GDPR" substitute "UK GDPR".

17(1)   Section 14 is amended as follows.

(2)   In subsection (1)—
      (a) for "GDPR" (in both places) substitute "UK GDPR";
      (b) for "authorised by law" substitute "required or authorised under the law of the United Kingdom or a part of the United Kingdom".

(3)   In subsections (3)(c), (5) and (6) (in both places), for "GDPR" substitute "UK GDPR".

18   For the italic heading before section 15 substitute "Exemptions etc".

19(1)   Section 15 is amended as follows.

(2)   In subsection (1), for "GDPR" substitute "UK GDPR".

(3) In subsection (2)(a)—
    (a) for "GDPR" (in the first place) substitute "UK GDPR";
    (b) for ", as allowed for by" substitute "(of a kind described in";
    (c) for "GDPR" (in the second place) substitute "UK GDPR)".

(4) In subsection (2)(b)—
    (a) for "GDPR" (in the first place) substitute "UK GDPR";
    (b) for ", as allowed for by" substitute "(of a kind described in";
    (c) for "GDPR" (in the second place) substitute "UK GDPR)".

(5) In subsection (2)(c)—
    (a) for "GDPR" (in the first place) substitute "UK GDPR";
    (b) for ", as allowed for by" substitute "(of a kind described in";
    (c) for "GDPR" (in the second place) substitute "UK GDPR)".

(6) In subsection (2)(d)—
    (a) for "GDPR" (in the first place) substitute "UK GDPR";
    (b) for ", as allowed for by" substitute "(of a kind described in";
    (c) for "GDPR" (in the second place) substitute "UK GDPR)".

(7) In subsection (2)(e)—
    (a) for ", V and VII of the GDPR" substitute "and V of the UK GDPR";
    (b) for ", as allowed for by Article 85(2) of the GDPR" substitute "(of a kind described in Article 85(2) of the UK GDPR)".

(8) In subsection (2)(f)—
    (a) for "GDPR" (in the first place) substitute "UK GDPR";
    (b) omit ", as allowed for by Article 89(2) and (3) of the GDPR".

(9) In subsection (3)—
    (a) for "GDPR" (in the first place) substitute "UK GDPR";
    (b) for ", as allowed for by" substitute "(of a kind described in";
    (c) for "GDPR" (in the second place) substitute "UK GDPR)".

(10) In subsection (4) —
    (a) for "GDPR" (in the first place) substitute "UK GDPR";
    (b) for ", as allowed for by" substitute "(of a kind described in";
    (c) for "GDPR" (in the second place) substitute "UK GDPR)".

(11) After subsection (4) insert—
    "(4A) In connection with the manual unstructured processing of personal data held by an FOI public authority, see Chapter 3 of this Part (sections 21, 24 and 25).".

(12) In subsection (5), for "and the exemption in section 26" substitute "(sections 26 to 28)".

20(1) Section 16 is amended as follows.

(2) In subsection (1)—
    (a) in the opening words, for "GDPR" substitute "UK GDPR";
    (b) in paragraph (a)—
        (i) omit "for Member State law";
        (ii) for "GDPR" substitute "UK GDPR";
    (c) in paragraph (b), for "a legislative measure" substitute "provision";

(d) in paragraph (c), for "GDPR" substitute "UK GDPR".

(3) In subsection (2)—

    (a) omit "and" at the end of paragraph (a)(ii);

    (b) after paragraph (b) insert—

        ", and

    (c) consequentially amend the UK GDPR by adding, varying or omitting a reference to section 15, Schedule 2, 3 or 4, this section or regulations under this section.".

21   For the italic heading before section 17 substitute "Certification".

22(1)   Section 17 is amended as follows.

(2)   In subsection (1)(b), for "national accreditation body" substitute "UK national accreditation body".

(3)   In subsection (3), for "national accreditation body" substitute "UK national accreditation body".

(4)   In subsection (6)—

    (a) for "national accreditation body" substitute "UK national accreditation body";

    (b) for "GDPR" substitute "UK GDPR".

(5)   In subsection (7)—

    (a) for "national accreditation body" substitute "UK national accreditation body";

    (b) for "GDPR" substitute "UK GDPR".

(6)   In subsection (8)—

    (a) for "GDPR" substitute "UK GDPR";

    (b) for "national accreditation body" (in both places) substitute "UK national accreditation body".

23   Before section 18 (but after the italic heading before it) insert—

    "Transfers based on adequacy regulations

    17A(1)   The Secretary of State may by regulations specify any of the following which the Secretary of State considers ensures an adequate level of protection of personal data—

        (a)   a third country,

        (b)   a territory or one or more sectors within a third country,

        (c)   an international organisation, or

        (d)   a description of such a country, territory, sector or organisation.

        (2)   For the purposes of the UK GDPR and this Part of this Act, a transfer of personal data to a third country or an international organisation is based on adequacy regulations if, at the time of the transfer, regulations made under this section are in force which specify, or specify a description which includes—

        (a)   in the case of a third country, the country or a relevant territory or sector within the country, or

        (b)   in the case of an international organisation, the organisation.

        (3)   Regulations under this section may specify that the Secretary of State considers that an adequate level of protection of personal data is ensured

only for a transfer specified or described in the regulations and, if they do so, only such a transfer may rely on those regulations for the purposes of subsection (2).

(4) Article 45(2) of the UK GDPR makes provision about the assessment of the adequacy of the level of protection for the purposes of this section and section 17B.

(5) Regulations under this section—

    (a) where they relate to a third country, must specify their territorial and sectoral application;

    (b) where applicable, must specify the independent supervisory authority or authorities referred to in Article 45(2)(b) of the UK GDPR.

(6) Regulations under this section may, among other things—

    (a) provide that in relation to a country, territory, sector, organisation or transfer specified, or falling within a description specified, in the regulations, section 17B(1) has effect as if it required the reviews described there to be carried out at such shorter intervals as are specified in the regulations;

    (b) identify a transfer of personal data by any means, including by reference to the controller or processor, the recipient, the personal data transferred or the means by which the transfer is made or by reference to relevant legislation, lists or other documents, as they have effect from time to time;

    (c) confer a discretion on a person.

(7) Regulations under this section are subject to the negative resolution procedure.

Transfers based on adequacy regulations: review etc

17B(1) For so long as regulations under section 17A are in force which specify, or specify a description which includes, a third country, a territory or sector within a third country or an international organisation, the Secretary of State must carry out a review of whether the country, territory, sector or organisation ensures an adequate level of protection of personal data at intervals of not more than 4 years.

(2) Each review under subsection (1) must take into account all relevant developments in the third country or international organisation.

(3) The Secretary of State must, on an ongoing basis, monitor developments in third countries and international organisations that could affect decisions to make regulations under section 17A or to amend or revoke such regulations.

(4) Where the Secretary of State becomes aware that a country, territory, sector or organisation specified, or falling within a description specified, in regulations under section 17A no longer ensures an adequate level of protection of personal data, whether as a result of a review under this section or otherwise, the Secretary of State must, to the extent necessary, amend or revoke the regulations.

(5) Where regulations under section 17A are amended or revoked in accordance with subsection (4), the Secretary of State must enter into consultations with the third country or international organisation concerned with a view to remedying the lack of an adequate level of protection.

(6) The Secretary of State must publish—

      (a)   a list of the third countries, territories and specified sectors within a third country and international organisations, and the descriptions of such countries, territories, sectors and organisations, which are for the time being specified in regulations under section 17A, and

      (b)   a list of the third countries, territories and specified sectors within a third country and international organisations, and the descriptions of such countries, territories, sectors and organisations, which have been but are no longer specified in such regulations.

(7)   In the case of regulations under section 17A which specify that an adequate level of protection of personal data is ensured only for a transfer specified or described in the regulations—

      (a)   the duty under subsection (1) is only to carry out a review of the level of protection ensured for such a transfer, and

      (b)   the lists published under subsection (6) must specify or describe the relevant transfers.

Standard data protection clauses

17C(1)   The Secretary of State may by regulations specify standard data protection clauses which the Secretary of State considers provide appropriate safeguards for the purposes of transfers of personal data to a third country or an international organisation in reliance on Article 46 of the UK GDPR (and see also section 119A).

(2)   The Secretary of State must keep under review the standard data protection clauses specified in regulations under this section that are for the time being in force.

(3)   Regulations under this section are subject to the negative resolution procedure.".

24(1)   Section 18 is amended as follows.

(2)   In the heading, at the end insert ": public interest".

(3)   In subsection (1), for "GDPR" substitute "UK GDPR".

(4)   In subsection (2), for paragraph (a) (but not the final "and") substitute—
"(a)the transfer cannot take place based on adequacy regulations (see section 17A),".

25   In section 19(2), for "GDPR" substitute "UK GDPR".

26   In section 20—
    (a) for "this Chapter" (in both places) substitute "this Part";
    (b) for "GDPR" substitute "UK GDPR".

27   For the heading of Chapter 3 substitute "Exemptions for manual unstructured processing and for national security and defence purposes".

28   For the italic heading before section 21 substitute "Definitions".

29(1)   Section 21 is amended as follows.

(2) For the heading substitute "Definitions".

(3) Omit subsections (1), (2), (3) and (4).

30 Omit section 22 and the italic heading before it.

31 Omit section 23.

32(1) Section 24 is amended as follows.

(2) In subsection (1)—
    (a) for "the applied GDPR" substitute "the UK GDPR";
    (b) for "this Chapter" substitute "the UK GDPR";
    (c) for "section 21(2)" substitute "Article 2(1A)".

(3) In subsection (2)—
    (a) in paragraphs (a), (b) and (c), for "the applied GDPR" substitute "the UK GDPR";
    (b) after paragraph (c) insert—
      "(ca)   in Part 2 of this Act, sections 17A, 17B and 17C (transfers to third countries);
      (cb)   in Part 5 of this Act, section 119A (standard clauses for transfers to third countries);";
    (c) for paragraph (d) substitute—
      "(d)   in Part 7 of this Act, sections 170 and 171 (offences relating to personal data).".

(4) In subsection (3)—
    (a) for "the applied GDPR" substitute "the UK GDPR";
    (b) for "this Chapter" substitute "the UK GDPR";
    (c) for "section 21(2)" substitute "Article 2(1A)".

(5) In subsection (5)—
    (a) for "the applied GDPR" substitute "the UK GDPR";
    (b) for "this Chapter" substitute "the UK GDPR";
    (c) for "section 21(2)" substitute "Article 2(1A)";
    (d) in paragraph (a), for "that Article" substitute "Article 15".

33(1) Section 25 is amended as follows.

(2) In subsection (1)—
    (a) for "the applied GDPR" substitute "the UK GDPR";
    (b) for "this Chapter" substitute "the UK GDPR";
    (c) for "section 21(2)" substitute "Article 2(1A)".

(3) In subsection (2)(a) and (b), omit "of the applied GDPR".

34(1) Section 26 is amended as follows.

(2) In subsection (1)—
    (a) for "the applied GDPR" substitute "the UK GDPR";
    (b) for "this Chapter" substitute "the UK GDPR".

(3) In subsection (2)—

    (a) in paragraphs (a), (b), (c) and (d), for "the applied GDPR" substitute "the UK GDPR";

    (b) in paragraph (e), for "the applied GDPR" (in both places) substitute "the UK GDPR";

    (c) in paragraph (f), for "the applied GDPR" substitute "the UK GDPR";

    (d) after paragraph (f) insert—

        "(fa)   in Part 2 of this Act, sections 17A, 17B and 17C (transfers to third countries);";

    (e) in paragraph (g)—

        (i)   in sub-paragraph (ii), for "the applied GDPR" substitute "the UK GDPR";

        (ii)   after sub-paragraph (iii) insert—

            "(iv)   section 119A (standard clauses for transfers to third countries);".

35   In section 27(5), for "the applied GDPR" substitute "the UK GDPR".

36(1)   Section 28 is amended as follows.

(2)   In the heading, for "applied GDPR" substitute "UK GDPR".

(3)   In subsections (1) and (2)—

    (a) for "the applied GDPR" substitute "the UK GDPR";

    (b) for "this Chapter" substitute "the UK GDPR".

(4)   In subsection (3), for "the applied GDPR" substitute "the UK GDPR".

(5)   After subsection (4) insert—

    "(5)   The functions conferred on the Commissioner in relation to the UK GDPR by Articles 57(1)(a), (d), (e), (h) and (u) and 58(1)(d) and (2)(a) to (d) of the UK GDPR (which are subject to safeguards set out in section 115) include functions in relation to subsection (3).".

37   In section 33(7), for "other than a member State" substitute "outside the United Kingdom".

38   In section 48, omit subsection (8).

39   In section 67, omit subsection (8).

40(1)   Section 73 is amended as follows.

(2)   In subsection (1)(b), omit "other than the United Kingdom".

(3)   In subsection (3)—

    (a) in paragraph (a) for "an adequacy decision (see section 74)" substitute "adequacy regulations (see section 74A)";

    (b) in paragraphs (b) and (c), for "an adequacy decision" substitute "adequacy regulations".

(4)   In subsection (5)(a), omit "a member State or".

41   Omit section 74.

42   After section 74 insert—

"Transfers based on adequacy regulations

74A(1)   The Secretary of State may by regulations specify any of the following which the Secretary of State considers ensures an adequate level of protection of personal data—

    (a)   a third country,

    (b)   a territory or one or more sectors within a third country,

    (c)   an international organisation, or

    (d)   a description of such a country, territory, sector or organisation.

(2)   For the purposes of this Part of this Act, a transfer of personal data to a third country or an international organisation is based on adequacy regulations if, at the time of the transfer, regulations made under this section are in force which specify, or specify a description which includes—

    (a)   in the case of a third country, the country or a relevant territory or sector within the country, and

    (b)   in the case of an international organisation, the organisation,

and such a transfer does not require specific authorisation.

(3)   Regulations under this section may specify that the Secretary of State considers that an adequate level of protection of personal data is ensured only for a transfer specified or described in the regulations and, if they do so, only such a transfer may rely on those regulations for the purposes of subsection (2).

(4)   When assessing the adequacy of the level of protection for the purposes of this section or section 74B, the Secretary of State must, in particular, take account of—

    (a)   the rule of law, respect for human rights and fundamental freedoms, relevant legislation, both general and sectoral, including concerning public security, defence, national security and criminal law and the access of public authorities to personal data, as well as the implementation of such legislation, data protection rules, professional rules and security measures, including rules for the onward transfer of personal data to another third country or international organisation, which are complied with in that country or international organisation, case-law, as well as effective and enforceable data subject rights and effective administrative and judicial redress for the data subjects whose personal data is transferred,

    (b)   the existence and effective functioning of one or more independent supervisory authorities in the third country or to which an international organisation is subject, with responsibility for ensuring and enforcing compliance with data protection rules, including adequate enforcement powers, for assisting and advising data subjects in exercising their rights and for cooperation with the Commissioner, and

    (c)   the international commitments the third country or international organisation concerned has entered into, or other obligations arising from legally binding conventions or instruments as well as from its participation in multilateral or regional systems, in particular in relation to the protection of personal data.

(5)   Regulations under this section—

(a)   where they relate to a third country, must specify their territorial and sectoral application;

(b)   where applicable, must specify the independent supervisory authority or authorities referred to in subsection (4)(b).

(6)   Regulations under this section may, among other things—

(a)   provide that, in relation to a country, territory, sector, organisation or territory specified, or falling within a description specified, in the regulations, section 74B(1) has effect as if it required the reviews described there to be carried out at such shorter intervals as are specified in the regulations;

(b)   identify a transfer of personal data by any means, including by reference to the controller or processor, the recipient, the personal data transferred or the means by which the transfer is made or by reference to relevant legislation, lists or other documents, as they have effect from time to time;

(c)   confer a discretion on a person.

(7)   Regulations under this section are subject to the negative resolution procedure.

Transfers based on adequacy regulations: review etc

74B(1)   For so long as regulations under section 74A are in force which specify, or specify a description which includes, a third country, a territory or sector within a third country or an international organisation, the Secretary of State must carry out a review of whether the country, territory, sector or organisation ensures an adequate level of protection of personal data at intervals of not more than 4 years.

(2)   Each review under subsection (1) must take into account all relevant developments in the third country or international organisation.

(3)   The Secretary of State must, on an ongoing basis, monitor developments in third countries and international organisations that could affect decisions to make regulations under section 74A or to amend or revoke such regulations.

(4)   Where the Secretary of State becomes aware that a country, territory, sector or organisation specified, or falling within a description specified, in regulations under section 74A no longer ensures an adequate level of protection of personal data, whether as a result of a review under this section or otherwise, the Secretary of State must, to the extent necessary, amend or revoke the regulations.

(5)   Where regulations under section 74A are amended or revoked in accordance with subsection (4), the Secretary of State must enter into consultations with the third country or international organisation concerned with a view to remedying the lack of an adequate level of protection.

(6)   The Secretary of State must publish—

(a)   a list of the third countries, territories and specified sectors within a third country and international organisations, and the descriptions of such countries, territories, sectors and organisations, which are for the time being specified in regulations under section 74A, and

(b) a list of the third countries, territories and specified sectors within a third country and international organisations, and the descriptions of such countries, territories, sectors and organisations, which have been but are no longer specified in such regulations.

(7) In the case of regulations under section 74A which specify that an adequate level of protection of personal data is ensured only for a transfer specified or described in the regulations—

(a) the duty under subsection (1) is only to carry out a review of the level of protection ensured for such a transfer, and

(b) the lists published under subsection (6) must specify or describe the relevant transfers.".

43 In section 76(1)(c), omit "a member State or".

44 Section 77(8), for "member States" substitute "the United Kingdom".

45(1) Section 78 is amended as follows.

(2) In subsection (4), omit "other than the United Kingdom".

(3) In subsection (5)(a), omit "a member State or".

46(1) Section 80 is amended as follows.

(2) In subsection (1), for "an EU recipient or a non-EU recipient" substitute "a non-UK recipient".

(3) In subsection (2)—

(a) omit the definition of "EU recipient";

(b) for "non-EU recipient" substitute "non-UK recipient".

(4) In subsection (4), for "the EU recipient or non-EU recipient" substitute "the non-UK recipient".

(5) Omit subsections (5), (6) and (7).

47(1) Section 115 is amended as follows.

(2) In the heading, for "GDPR" substitute "UK GDPR".

(3) Omit subsection (1).

(4) In subsection (2)—

(a) in paragraphs (a) and (b), for "GDPR" substitute "UK GDPR";

(b) after "section 2" insert "and section 28(5)".

(5) In subsections (3) and (4), for "GDPR" substitute "UK GDPR".

(6) In subsection (5), for "GDPR" (in both places) substitute "UK GDPR".

(7) In subsection (6), for "GDPR" substitute "UK GDPR".

(8) In subsection (7), for "GDPR" (in both places) substitute "UK GDPR".

(9) In subsection (8)(a) and (b), for "GDPR" substitute "UK GDPR".

(10) In subsections (9) and (10), for "GDPR" substitute "UK GDPR".

48(1) Section 116 is amended as follows.

(2) Before subsection (1) insert—

"(A1) The Commissioner is responsible for monitoring the application of Part 3 of this Act, in order to protect the fundamental rights and freedoms of individuals in relation to processing by a competent authority for any of the law enforcement purposes (as defined in Part 3) and to facilitate the free flow of personal data.".

(3) In subsection (1), omit paragraph (a) (including the final "and").

(4) In subsection (2), for "GDPR" substitute "UK GDPR".

49(1) Section 117 is amended as follows.

(2) After "this Act" insert "or the UK GDPR".

(3) Omit "(and see also Article 55(3) of the GDPR)" (and the comma before those words).

50(1) Section 118 is amended as follows.

(2) For the heading substitute "Co-operation between parties to the Data Protection Convention".

(3) Omit subsections (1), (2), (3) and (4).

51 After section 119 insert—

"Standard clauses for transfers to third countries etc

119A(1) The Commissioner may issue a document specifying standard data protection clauses which the Commissioner considers provide appropriate safeguards for the purposes of transfers of personal data to a third country or an international organisation in reliance on Article 46 of the UK GDPR (and see also section 17C).

(2) The Commissioner may issue a document that amends or withdraws a document issued under subsection (1).

(3) A document issued under this section—

    (a) must specify when it comes into force,

    (b) may make different provision for different purposes, and

    (c) may include transitional provision or savings.

(4) Before issuing a document under this section, the Commissioner must consult the Secretary of State and such of the following as the Commissioner considers appropriate—

    (a) trade associations;

    (b) data subjects;

    (c) persons who appear to the Commissioner to represent the interests of data subjects.

(5)   After a document is issued under this section—

    (a)   the Commissioner must send a copy to the Secretary of State, and

    (b)   the Secretary of State must lay it before Parliament.

(6)   If, within the 40-day period, either House of Parliament resolves not to approve the document then, with effect from the end of the day on which the resolution is passed, the document is to be treated as not having been issued under this section (so that the document, and any amendment or withdrawal made by the document, is to be disregarded for the purposes of Article 46(2)(d) of the UK GDPR).

(7)   Nothing in subsection (6)—

    (a)   affects any transfer of personal data previously made in reliance on the document, or

    (b)   prevents a further document being laid before Parliament.

(8)   The Commissioner must publish—

    (a)   a document issued under this section, and

    (b)   a notice identifying any document which, under subsection (6), is treated as not having been issued under this section.

(9)   The Commissioner must keep under review the clauses specified in a document issued under this section for the time being in force.

(10)   In this section, "the 40-day period" means—>

    (a)   if the document is laid before both Houses of Parliament on the same day, the period of 40 days beginning with that day, or

    (b)   if the document is laid before the Houses of Parliament on different days, the period of 40 days beginning with the later of those days.

(11)   In calculating the 40-day period, no account is to be taken of any period during which Parliament is dissolved or prorogued or during which both Houses of Parliament are adjourned for more than 4 days.

(12)   In this section, "trade association" includes a body representing controllers or processors.".

52(1)   Section 120 is amended as follows.

(2)   In subsection (2), for "GDPR" (in each place) substitute "UK GDPR".

(3)   After subsection (2) insert—

    "(2A) The Commissioner may contribute to the activities of international organisations with data protection functions.".

(4)   In subsection (6), in the definition of "third country", for "that is not a member State" substitute "outside the United Kingdom".

53   In section 123(7), for "GDPR" (in both places) substitute "UK GDPR".

54   In section 129(1), for "GDPR" substitute "UK GDPR".

55   In section 132(2), omit paragraph (d).

56   In section 135(4), for "GDPR" substitute "UK GDPR".

57   In section 136(1)(b), for "GDPR" substitute "UK GDPR".

58   In section 139(2), for "GDPR" substitute "UK GDPR".

59   In section 142(9)—
      (a) for "GDPR" (in both places) substitute "UK GDPR";
      (b) for "the European Union" substitute "the United Kingdom".

60   In section 143(9), for "GDPR" substitute "UK GDPR".

61   In section 149(2)(a), (b), (c) and (e), (3) and (4)(b) and (c), for "GDPR" substitute "UK
     GDPR".

62   In section 151(1)(b) and (8)(a), for "GDPR" substitute "UK GDPR".

63   In section 155(2)(a), for "GDPR" (in both places) substitute "UK GDPR".

64(1) Section 157 is amended as follows.

  (2) In subsection (1), for "GDPR" (in both places) substitute "UK GDPR";

  (3) In subsection (2)(a), omit "74,".

  (4) In subsection (5), for "20 million Euros" (in both places) substitute "£17,500,000".

  (5) In subsection (6), for "10 million Euros" (in both places) substitute "£8,700,000".

  (6) Omit subsection (7).

65   In section 159(1) and (2), for "GDPR" substitute "UK GDPR".

66(1) Section 165 is amended as follows.

  (2) In subsection (1), for "GDPR" (in both places) substitute "UK GDPR".

  (3) In subsection (5)(b), for "another supervisory authority or" substitute "a".

  (4) Omit subsection (6).

  (5) In subsection (7), omit the definition of "supervisory authority".

67   In section 166(1), for "GDPR" substitute "UK GDPR".

68   In section 167(4), for "GDPR" substitute "UK GDPR".

69(1) Section 168 is amended as follows.

(2) In the heading, for "GDPR" substitute "UK GDPR".

(3) In subsections (1) and (2), for "GDPR" substitute "UK GDPR".

70 In section 169(1), for "GDPR" substitute "UK GDPR".

71 In section 170(7), for "GDPR" substitute "UK GDPR".

72 In section 171(8)(a), for "GDPR" substitute "UK GDPR".

73 In section 173(2)(a) and (b), for "GDPR" substitute "UK GDPR".

74 In section 174(2)(a) and (b), for "GDPR" substitute "UK GDPR".

75 In section 180(2)(d) and (e), for "GDPR" substitute "UK GDPR".

76 In section 181, in the definition of "representative", for "GDPR" (in both places) substitute "UK GDPR".

77 In section 182(3), omit paragraph (a).

78(1) Section 183 is amended as follows.

(2) In subsection (2)(d), for "processing of personal data to which Chapter 3 of Part 2 or Part 4 of this Act applies" substitute "relevant processing of personal data".

(3) After subsection (2) insert—
"(2A) In subsection (2)(d), "relevant processing of personal data" means —
  (a) processing of personal data described in Article 2(1)(a) or (b) or (1A) of the UK GDPR, and
  (b) processing of personal data to which Part 4 of this Act applies.".

79 In section 185(4)(a) and (b), for "GDPR" substitute "UK GDPR".

80(1) Section 186 is amended as follows.

(2) In subsection (2)(a), for "GDPR" substitute "UK GDPR".

(3) In subsection (3)(b), omit "23,".

81(1) Section 187 is amended as follows.

(2) In subsection (1), in the opening words, for "GDPR applies" insert "UK GDPR applies, Article 80(1) of the UK GDPR (representation of data subjects)".

(3) In subsection (1)(a)—
  (a) omit "Article 80(1) of the GDPR (representation of data subjects)";

(b) for "that Article" substitute "subsections (3) and (4)";

(c) for "GDPR" (in the second place) substitute "UK GDPR".

(4) In subsection (1)(b)—

(a) for "a data subject may also authorise" substitute "also authorises";

(b) for "GDPR" substitute "UK GDPR".

(5) In subsection (2)—

(a) for "GDPR" substitute "UK GDPR";

(b) in paragraph (a), for ", (4)(d) and (6)(c)" substitute "and (4)(d)".

(6) In subsection (5), for "GDPR" substitute "UK GDPR".

82 In section 188(2), for "GDPR" substitute "UK GDPR".

83(1) Section 189 is amended as follows.

(2) In subsection (2), for "GDPR" (in each place) substitute "UK GDPR".

(3) In subsection (4)(c) and (d), for "GDPR" substitute "UK GDPR".

84 In section 190(1), for "GDPR" (in each place) substitute "UK GDPR".

85(1) Section 205 is amended as follows.

(2) In subsection (1), in the definition of "enactment"—

(a) omit "and" at the end of paragraph (d);

(b) after paragraph (e) insert—

"and

(f) any retained direct EU legislation;".

(3) In subsection (1), in the definition of "international obligation of the United Kingdom",
Omit paragraph (a).

(4) After subsection (1) insert—

"(1A) In this Act, references to a fundamental right or fundamental freedom (however
expressed) are to a fundamental right or fundamental freedom which continues
to form part of domestic law on and after exit day by virtue of section 4 of the
European Union (Withdrawal) Act 2018, as the right or freedom is amended or
otherwise modified by the law of the United Kingdom, or of a part of the
United Kingdom, from time to time on or after exit day.".

(5) In subsection (2)—

(a) before paragraph (a) insert—

"(za) Section 119A(10) and (11);";

(b) omit "Chapter 2 or 3 of".

(6) Omit subsection (3).

(7) After subsection (3) insert—

"(4) In the definition of "the UK GDPR" in section 3(10)—

(a) the reference to Regulation (EU) 2016/679 as it forms part of the law of
England and Wales, Scotland and Northern Ireland by virtue of section 3

of the European Union (Withdrawal) Act 2018 is to be treated as a reference to that Regulation as modified by Schedule 1 to the Data Protection, Privacy and Electronic Communications (Amendments etc) (EU Exit) Regulations 2019 ("the 2019 Regulations"), but

(b)   nothing in the definition or in paragraph (a) determines whether, where Regulation (EU) 2016/679 is modified on or after exit day by the law of England and Wales, Scotland or Northern Ireland (other than by Schedule 1 to the 2019 Regulations), the reference to Regulation (EU) 2016/679 is then to be read as a reference to that Regulation as modified.

(5) Subsection (4) is not to be read as implying anything about how other references to Regulation (EU) 2016/679 or references to other retained EU law are to be interpreted.".

86(1)   The Table in section 206 is amended as follows.

(2)   Omit the entries for "the applied Chapter 2" and "the applied GDPR".

(3)   After the entry for "enforcement notice" insert—
"the EU GDPR
Section 3".

(4)   Omit the entry for "the GDPR".

(5)   In the entries for "public authority" and "public body", for "GDPR" substitute "UK GDPR".

(6)   At the end insert—
"the UK GDPR
Section 3".

87(1)   Section 207 is amended as follows.

(2)   In subsection (1), for "(2) and (3)" substitute "(1A) and (2)".

(3)   After subsection (1) insert—
"(1A) In the case of the processing of personal data to which Part 2 (the UK GDPR) applies, it applies to the types of such processing to which the UK GDPR applies by virtue of Article 3 of the UK GDPR.".

(4)   In subsection (2), for "It applies to the processing of personal data" substitute "In the case of the processing of personal data to which Part 2 does not apply, it applies where such processing is carried out".

(5)   Omit subsection (3).

(6)   In subsection (4), for "Subsections (1) to (3)" substitute "Subsections (1), (1A) and (2)".

(7)   Omit subsection (6).

(8)   In subsection (7), omit the words after paragraph (d).

88   In section 209(2), (3) and (4), for "GDPR" substitute "UK GDPR".

89   In section 210(2) and (3), for "GDPR" substitute "UK GDPR".

90(1)   Section 213 is amended as follows.

(2)   In subsection (2), for "GDPR" substitute "EU GDPR".

(3)   At the end insert—
    "(4)   Schedule 21 contains further transitional, transitory and saving provision made in connection with the amendment of this Act and the UK GDPR by regulations under section 8 of the European Union (Withdrawal) Act 2018.".

91(1)   Schedule 1 is amended as follows.

(2)   In paragraph 2(3), for "GDPR" substitute "UK GDPR".

(3)   In paragraph 4(b), for "GDPR" substitute "UK GDPR".

(4)   In paragraph 39(a), for "GDPR" substitute "UK GDPR".

(5)   In paragraph 41, for "GDPR" (in both places) substitute "UK GDPR".

92(1)   Schedule 2 is amended as follows.

(2)   In the heading, for "GDPR" substitute "UK GDPR".

(3)   In the heading of Part 1, for "based on" substitute "as described in".

(4)   In the italic heading before paragraph 1, for "GDPR" (in the first place) substitute "UK GDPR".

(5)   In paragraph 1—
    (a) in sub-paragraph (a), for "GDPR" (in both places) substitute "UK GDPR";
    (b) in sub-paragraph (b), for "GDPR" (in both places) substitute "UK GDPR".

(6)   In paragraph 2—
    (a) in sub-paragraph (1), for "GDPR" (in the second place) substitute "UK GDPR";
    (b) in sub-paragraph (3), for "GDPR" substitute "UK GDPR".

(7)   In paragraph 3—
    (a) in sub-paragraph (1), for "GDPR" substitute "UK GDPR";
    (b) in sub-paragraph (3), for "GDPR" (in each place) substitute "UK GDPR".

(8)   In paragraph 4—
    (a) in sub-paragraph (1), for "GDPR" substitute "UK GDPR";
    (b) in sub-paragraph (2), in the opening words (but not the words following paragraph (g)), for "GDPR" (in each place) substitute "UK GDPR";
    (c) in sub-paragraph (4), for "GDPR" substitute "UK GDPR".

(9)   In the heading of Part 2, for "based on" substitute "as described in".

(10)   In the italic heading before paragraph 6, for "GDPR" (in the first place) substitute "UK GDPR".

(11)   In paragraph 6, for "GDPR" (in the second and third places) substitute "UK GDPR".

(12)   In paragraph 13, for "GDPR" (in the second place) substitute "UK GDPR".

(13)   In the heading of Part 3, for "based on Article 23(1):" substitute "for the".

(14)   In paragraph 16(1), for "GDPR" (in both places) substitute "UK GDPR".

(15)   In the heading of Part 4, for "based on" substitute "as described in".

(16)   In the italic heading before paragraph 18, for "GDPR" (in the first place) substitute "UK GDPR".

(17)   In paragraph 18, for "GDPR" (in the second and third places) substitute "UK GDPR".

(18)   In paragraph 20(3), for "GDPR" substitute "UK GDPR".

(19)   In paragraph 25—
    (a) in sub-paragraph (2), for "GDPR" (in both places) substitute "UK GDPR";
    (b) in sub-paragraph (3), for "GDPR" substitute "UK GDPR".

(20)   In the heading of Part 5, omit "based on Article 85(2)".

(21)   In paragraph 26(9)—
    (a) in the opening words, for "GDPR" (in the second and third places) substitute "UK GDPR";
    (b) in paragraphs (a), (b), (c) and (d), for "GDPR" substitute "UK GDPR";
    (c) Omit paragraph (e).

(22)   In the heading of Part 6, omit "based on Article 89".

(23)   In paragraph 27—
    (a) in sub-paragraph (1), for "sub-paragraph (3)" substitute "sub-paragraphs (3) and (4)";
    (b) in sub-paragraph (2), for "GDPR (the rights in which may be derogated from by virtue of Article 89(2) of the GDPR)" substitute "UK GDPR";
    (c) in sub-paragraph (3)(a), for "GDPR" substitute "UK GDPR";
    (d) after sub-paragraph (3) insert—
        "(4)   Where processing for a purpose described in sub-paragraph (1) serves at the same time another purpose, the exemption in sub-paragraph (1) is available only where the personal data is processed for a purpose referred to in that sub-paragraph.".

(24)   In paragraph 28—
    (a) in sub-paragraph (1), for "sub-paragraph (3)" substitute "sub-paragraphs (3) and (4)";
    (b) in sub-paragraph (2), for "GDPR (the rights in which may be derogated from by virtue of Article 89(3) of the GDPR)" substitute "UK GDPR";
    (c) in sub-paragraph (3), for "GDPR" substitute "UK GDPR";
    (d) after sub-paragraph (3) insert—
        "(4)   Where processing for a purpose described in sub-paragraph (1) serves at the same time another purpose, the exemption in sub-paragraph (1) is available only where the personal data is processed for a purpose referred to in that sub-paragraph.".

93(1)   Schedule 3 is amended as follows.

(2)   In the heading, for "GDPR" substitute "UK GDPR".

(3)   In the heading of Part 1, for "GDPR" substitute "UK GDPR".

(4) In paragraph 1, for "GDPR" (in the second and third places) substitute "UK GDPR".

(5) In paragraph 2(2), for "GDPR" substitute "UK GDPR".

(6) In the italic heading before paragraph 5, for "GDPR" substitute "UK GDPR".

(7) In paragraph 5(1), for "GDPR" substitute "UK GDPR".

(8) In the italic heading before paragraph 6, for "GDPR" substitute "UK GDPR".

(9) In paragraph 6(1), for "GDPR" substitute "UK GDPR".

(10) In paragraph 7(2), for "GDPR" substitute "UK GDPR".

(11) In the italic heading before paragraph 11, for "GDPR" substitute "UK GDPR".

(12) In paragraph 11, for "GDPR" substitute "UK GDPR".

(13) In the italic heading before paragraph 12, for "GDPR" substitute "UK GDPR".

(14) In paragraph 12(1)(a) and (3), for "GDPR" substitute "UK GDPR".

(15) In paragraph 17(2), for "GDPR" substitute "UK GDPR".

(16) In the italic heading before paragraph 19, for "GDPR" substitute "UK GDPR".

(17) In paragraph 19, for "GDPR" substitute "UK GDPR".

(18) In the italic heading before paragraph 20, for "GDPR" substitute "UK GDPR".

(19) In paragraph 20(1)(a) and (3), for "GDPR" substitute "UK GDPR".

(20) In the italic heading before paragraph 21, for "GDPR" substitute "UK GDPR".

(21) In paragraph 21(2), for "GDPR" substitute "UK GDPR".

94(1) Schedule 4 is amended as follows.

(2) In the heading, for "GDPR" substitute "UK GDPR".

(3) In the italic heading before paragraph 1, for "GDPR" (in the first place) substitute "UK GDPR".

(4) In paragraph 1, for "GDPR" (in the second and third places) substitute "UK GDPR".

95 In Schedule 5, in the following provisions, for "national accreditation body" substitute "UK national accreditation body"—
    (a) paragraph 1(2) (in both places);
    (b) paragraph 4(4) (in both places);
    (c) paragraph 6(4).

96 Omit Schedule 6.

97(1) Schedule 13 is amended as follows.

(2) In paragraph 1(1)—
    (a) in paragraph (e), omit "LED supervisory authorities and";
    (b) in paragraph (f), omit "LED supervisory authorities and" and "the Law

Enforcement Directive and";

    (c) in paragraph (g), omit "an LED supervisory authority,";

    (d) Omit paragraph (i).

(3) In paragraph 3, omit the definition of "LED supervisory authority".

98 In Schedule 14, omit Part 1.

99(1) Schedule 18 is amended as follows.

(2) In paragraph 1(2), for "section 21(2)" substitute "Article 2(1A) of the UK GDPR".

(3) In paragraph 5(a) and (b), for "GDPR" substitute "UK GDPR".

100(1) Schedule 19 is amended as follows.

(2) In paragraph 431(3), for "the GDPR or the applied GDPR" substitute "the UK GDPR".

(3) In paragraph 432(5)(a), for "the GDPR or the applied GDPR" substitute "the UK GDPR".

101(1) Schedule 20 is amended as follows.

(2) In the heading of Part 3, for "GDPR" substitute "UK GDPR".

(3) In the italic heading before paragraph 12, for "GDPR" (in both places) substitute "UK GDPR".

(4) In paragraph 18—

    (a) in sub-paragraphs (2)(b) and (6)(b), for "applied GDPR" substitute "UK GDPR";

    (b) after sub-paragraph (7) insert—

        "(8) In this paragraph, references to the UK GDPR do not include the EU GDPR as it was directly applicable to the United Kingdom before exit day (see paragraph 2 of Schedule 21).".

(5) In paragraph 50, for "GDPR" substitute "UK GDPR".

102 After Schedule 20 insert—

"SCHEDULE 21

Further transitional provision etc   (Section 213)

PART 1

Interpretation

1 The applied GPDR

In this Schedule, "the applied GDPR" means the EU GDPR as applied by Chapter 3 of Part 2 before exit day.

PART 2

CONTINUATION OF EXISTING ACTS ETC

Merger of the directly applicable GDPR and the applied GDPR

2(1) On and after exit day, references in an enactment to the UK GDPR (including the reference in the definition of "the data protection legislation" in section 3(9)) include—

    (a)   the EU GDPR as it was directly applicable to the United Kingdom before exit day, read with Chapter 2 of Part 2 of this Act as it had effect before exit day, and

    (b)   the applied GDPR, read with Chapter 3 of Part 2 of this Act as it had effect before exit day.

(2)   On and after exit day, references in an enactment to, or to a provision of, Chapter 2 of Part 2 of this Act (including general references to this Act or to Part 2 of this Act) include that Chapter or that provision as applied by Chapter 3 of Part 2 of this Act as it had effect before exit day.

(3)   Sub-paragraphs (1) and (2) have effect—

    (a)   in relation to references in this Act, except as otherwise provided;

    (b)   in relation to references in other enactments, unless the context otherwise requires.

3(1)   Anything done in connection with the EU GDPR as it was directly applicable to the United Kingdom before exit day, the applied GDPR or this Act—

    (a)   if in force or effective immediately before exit day, continues to be in force or effective on and after exit day, and

    (b)   if in the process of being done immediately before exit day, continues to be done on and after exit day.

(2)   References in this paragraph to anything done include references to anything omitted to be done.

PART 3

TRANSFERS TO THIRD COUNTRIES AND INTERNATIONAL ORGANISATIONS

UK GDPR: adequacy decisions and adequacy regulations

4(1)   On and after exit day, for the purposes of the UK GDPR and Part 2 of this Act, a transfer of personal data to a third country or an international organisation is based on adequacy regulations if, at the time of the transfer, paragraph 5 specifies, or specifies a description which includes—

    (a)   in the case of a third country, the country or a relevant territory or sector within the country, or

    (b)   in the case of an international organisation, the organisation.

(2)   Sub-paragraph (1) has effect subject to provision in paragraph 5 providing that only particular transfers to the country, territory, sector or organisation may rely on a particular provision of paragraph 5 for the purposes of sub-paragraph (1).

(3)   The Secretary of State may by regulations—

    (a)   repeal sub-paragraphs (1) and (2) and paragraph 5;

    (b)   amend paragraph 5 so as to omit a third country, territory, sector or international organisation specified, or of a description specified, in that paragraph;

    (c)   amend paragraph 5 so as to replace a reference to, or description of, a third country, territory, sector or organisation with a narrower reference or description, including by specifying or describing particular transfers of personal data and making provision described in sub-paragraph (2).

(4)   Regulations under this paragraph may, among other things——

(a)   identify a transfer of personal data by any means, including by reference to the controller or processor, the recipient, the personal data transferred or the means by which the transfer is made or by reference to relevant legislation, lists or other documents, as they have effect from time to time;

(b)   confer a discretion on a person.

(5)   Regulations under this paragraph are subject to the negative resolution procedure.

(6)   Sub-paragraphs (1) and (2) have effect in addition to section 17A(2) and (3).

5(1)   The following are specified for the purposes of paragraph 4(1)—

(a)   an EEA state;

(b)   Gibraltar;

(c)   a Union institution, body, office or agency set up by, or on the basis of, the Treaty on the European Union, the Treaty on the Functioning of the European Union or the Euratom Treaty;

(d)   an equivalent institution, body, office or agency set up by, or on the basis of, the Treaties establishing the European Economic Area;

(e)   a third country which is the subject of a decision listed in sub-paragraph (2), other than a decision that, immediately before exit day, had been repealed or was suspended;

(f)   a third country, territory or sector within a third country or international organisation which is the subject of an adequacy decision made by the European Commission before exit day on the basis of Article 45(3) of the EU GDPR, other than a decision that, immediately before exit day, had been repealed or was suspended.

(2)   The decisions mentioned in sub-paragraph (1)(e) are the following—

(a)   Commission Decision 2000/518/EC1 of 26th July 2000 pursuant to Directive 95/46/EC of the European Parliament and of the Council on the adequate protection of personal data provided in Switzerland;

(b)   Commission Decision 2002/2/EC2 of 20th December 2001 pursuant to Directive 95/46/EC of the European Parliament and of the Council on the adequate protection of personal data provided by the Canadian Personal Information Protection and Electronic Documents Act;

(c)   Commission Decision 2003/490/EC3 of 30th June 2003 pursuant to Directive 95/46/EC of the European Parliament and of the Council on the adequate protection of personal data in Argentina;

(d)   Commission Decision 2003/821/EC4 of 21st November 2003 on the adequate protection of personal data in Guernsey;

(e)   Commission Decision 2004/411/EC5 of 28th April 2004 on the adequate protection of personal data in the Isle of Man;

(f)   Commission Decision 2008/393/EC6 of 8th May 2008 pursuant to Directive 95/46/EC of the European Parliament and of the Council on the adequate protection of personal data in Jersey;

(g)   Commission Decision 2010/146/EU7 of 5th March 2010 pursuant to Directive 95/46/EC of the European Parliament and of the

Council on the adequate protection provided by the Faeroese Act on processing of personal data;

(h) Commission Decision 2010/625/EU8 of 19th October 2010 pursuant to Directive 95/46/EC of the European Parliament and of the Council on the adequate protection of personal data in Andorra;

(i) Commission Decision 2011/61/EU9 of 31st January 2011 pursuant to Directive 95/46/EC of the European Parliament and of the Council on the adequate protection of personal data by the State of Israel with regard to automated processing of personal data;

(j) Commission Implementing Decision 2012/484/EU10 of 21st August 2012 pursuant to Directive 95/46/EC of the European Parliament and of the Council on the adequate protection of personal data by the Eastern Republic of Uruguay with regard to automated processing of personal data;

(k) Commission Implementing Decision 2013/65/EU11 of 19th December 2012 pursuant to Directive 95/46/EC of the European Parliament and of the Council on the adequate protection of personal data by New Zealand;

(l) Commission Implementing Decision (EU) 2016/125012 of 12th July 2016 pursuant to Directive 95/46/EC of the European Parliament and of the Council on the adequacy of the protection provided by the EU-U.S. Privacy Shield.

(3) Where a decision described in sub-paragraph (1)(e) or (f) states that an adequate level of protection of personal data is ensured only for a transfer specified or described in the decision, only such a transfer may rely on that provision and that decision for the purposes of paragraph 4(1).

(4) The references to a decision in sub-paragraphs (1)(e) and (f) and (2) are to the decision as it had effect in EU law immediately before exit day, subject to sub-paragraphs (5) and (6).

(5) For the purposes of this paragraph, where a reference to legislation, a list or another document in a decision described in sub-paragraph (1)(e) or (f) is a reference to the legislation, list or document as it has effect from time to time, it is to be treated as a reference to the legislation, list or other document as it has effect at the time of the transfer.

(6) For the purposes of this paragraph, where a decision described in sub-paragraph (1)(e) or (f) relates to—

(a) transfers from the European Union (or the European Community) or the European Economic Area, or

(b) transfers to which the EU GDPR applies,

it is to be treated as relating to equivalent transfers to or from the United Kingdom or transfers to which the UK GDPR applies (as appropriate).

6(1) In the provisions listed in sub-paragraph (2)—

(a) references to regulations made under section 17A (other than references to making such regulations) include the provision made in paragraph 5;

(b) references to the revocation of such regulations include the repeal of all or part of paragraph 5.

(2) Those provisions are—

(a)   Articles 13(1)(f), 14(1)(f), 45(1) and (7), 46(1) and 49(1) of the UK GDPR;

(b)   sections 17B(1), (3), (6) and (7) and 18(2) of this Act.

UK GDPR: transfers subject to appropriate safeguards
provided by standard data protection clauses

7(1)   Subject to paragraph 8, the appropriate safeguards referred to in Article 46(1) of the UK GDPR may be provided for on and after exit day as described in this paragraph.

(2)   The safeguards may be provided for by any standard data protection clauses included in an arrangement which, if the arrangement had been entered into immediately before exit day, would have provided for the appropriate safeguards referred to in Article 46(1) of the EU GDPR by virtue of Article 46(2)(c) or (d) or (5) of the EU GDPR.

(3)   The safeguards may be provided for by a version of standard data protection clauses described in sub-paragraph (2) incorporating changes where—

    (a)   all of the changes are made in consequence of the withdrawal of the United Kingdom from the EU or provision made by regulations under section 8 or 23 of the European Union (Withdrawal) Act 2018 (or both), and

    (b)   none of the changes alters the effect of the clauses.

(4)   The following changes are to be treated as falling within sub-paragraph (3)(a) and (b)—

    (a)   changing references to adequacy decisions made by the European Commission into references to equivalent provision made by regulations under section 17A or by or under paragraphs 4 to 6 of this Schedule;

    (b)   changing references to transferring personal data outside the European Union or the European Economic Area into references to transferring personal data outside the United Kingdom.

(5)   In the case of a transfer of personal data made under arrangements entered into before exit day, the safeguards may be provided for on and after exit day by standard data protection clauses not falling within sub-paragraph (2) which—

    (a)   formed part of the arrangements immediately before exit day, and

    (b)   at that time, provided for the appropriate safeguards referred to in Article 46(1) of the EU GDPR by virtue of Article 46(2)(c) or (d) or (5) of the EU GDPR.

(6)   The Secretary of State and the Commissioner must keep the operation of this paragraph under review.

(7)   In this paragraph, "adequacy decision" means a decision made on the basis of—

    (a)   Article 45(3) of the EU GDPR, or

    (b)   Article 25(6) of Directive 95/46/EC of the European Parliament and of the Council of 24th October 1995 on the protection of individuals with regard to the processing of personal data and on the free movement of such data.

(8)   This paragraph has effect in addition to Article 46(2) and (3) of the UK GDPR.

8(1) Paragraph 7 does not apply to the extent that it has been disapplied by—

    (a) regulations made by the Secretary of State, or

    (b) a document issued by the Commissioner.

(2) Regulations under this paragraph are subject to the negative resolution procedure.

(3) Subsections (3) to (8) and (10) to (12) of section 119A apply in relation to a document issued by the Commissioner under this paragraph as they apply to a document issued by the Commissioner under section 119A(2).

UK GDPR: transfers subject to appropriate
safeguards provided by binding corporate rules

9(1) The appropriate safeguards referred to in Article 46(1) of the UK GDPR may be provided for on and after exit day as described sub-paragraphs (2) to (4), subject to sub-paragraph (5).

(2) The safeguards may be provided for by any binding corporate rules authorised by the Commissioner which, immediately before exit day, provided for the appropriate safeguards referred to in Article 46(1) of the EU GDPR by virtue of Article 46(5) of the EU GDPR.

(3) The safeguards may be provided for by a version of binding corporate rules described in sub-paragraph (2) incorporating changes where—

    (a) all of the changes are made in consequence of the withdrawal of the United Kingdom from the EU or provision made by regulations under section 8 or 23 of the European Union (Withdrawal) Act 2018 (or both), and

    (b) none of the changes alters the effect of the rules.

(4) The following changes are to be treated as falling within sub-paragraph (3)(a) and (b)—

    (a) changing references to adequacy decisions made by the European Commission into references to equivalent provision made by regulations under section 17A or by or under paragraphs 4 to 6 of this Schedule;

    (b) changing references to transferring personal data outside the European Union or the European Economic Area into references to transferring personal data outside the United Kingdom.

(5) Sub-paragraphs (2) to (4) cease to apply in relation to binding corporate rules if, on or after exit day, the Commissioner withdraws the authorisation of the rules (or, where sub-paragraph (3) is relied on, the authorisation of the rules mentioned in sub-paragraph (2)).

(6) The Commissioner must keep the operation of this paragraph under review.

(7) In this paragraph—

    "adequacy decision" means a decision made on the basis of—

        (a) Article 45(3) of the EU GDPR, or

        (b) Article 25(6) of Directive 95/46/EC of the European Parliament and of the Council of 24th October 1995 on the protection of individuals with regard to the processing of personal data and on the free movement of such data;

    "binding corporate rules" has the meaning given in Article 4(20) of the UK GDPR.

(8)   This paragraph has effect in addition to Article 46(2) and (3) of the UK GDPR.

Part 3 (law enforcement processing):
adequacy decisions and adequacy regulations

10(1)   On and after exit day, for the purposes of Part 3 of this Act, a transfer of personal data to a third country or an international organisation is based on adequacy regulations if, at the time of the transfer, paragraph 11 specifies, or specifies a description which includes—

    (a)   in the case of a third country, the country or a relevant territory or sector within the country, or

    (b)   in the case of an international organisation, the organisation.

(2)   Sub-paragraph (1) has effect subject to provision in paragraph 11 providing that only particular transfers to the country, territory, sector or organisation may rely on a particular provision of paragraph 11 for the purposes of sub-paragraph (1).

(3)   The Secretary of State may by regulations—

    (a)   repeal sub-paragraphs (1) and (2) and paragraph 11;

    (b)   amend paragraph 11 so as to omit a third country, territory, sector or international organisation specified, or of a description specified, in that paragraph;

    (c)   amend paragraph 11 so as to replace a reference to, or description of, a third country, territory, sector or organisation with a narrower reference or description, including by specifying or describing particular transfers of personal data and by making provision described in sub-paragraph (2).

(4)   Regulations under this paragraph may, among other things—

    (a)   identify a transfer of personal data by any means, including by reference to the controller or processor, the recipient, the personal data transferred or the means by which the transfer is made or by reference to relevant legislation, lists or other documents, as they have effect from time to time;

    (b)   confer a discretion on a person.

(5)   Regulations under this paragraph are subject to the negative resolution procedure.

(6)   Sub-paragraphs (1) and (2) have effect in addition to section 74A(2) and (3).

11(1)   The following are specified for the purposes of paragraph 10(1)—

    (a)   a member State;

    (b)   Gibraltar;

    (c)   a third country, a territory or sector within a third country or an international organisation which is the subject of an adequacy decision made by the European Commission before exit day on the basis of Article 36(3) of the Law Enforcement Directive, other than a decision that, immediately before exit day, had been repealed or was suspended.

(2)   Where a decision described in sub-paragraph (1)(c) states that an adequate level of protection of personal data is ensured only for a transfer specified or described in the decision, only such a transfer may rely on that provision and

that decision for the purposes of paragraph 10(1).

(3)   The reference to a decision in sub-paragraph (1)(c) is to the decision as it had effect in EU law immediately before exit day, subject to sub-paragraphs (4) and (5).

(4)   For the purposes of this paragraph, where a reference to legislation, a list or another document in a decision described in sub-paragraph (1)(c) is a reference to the legislation, list or document as it has effect from time to time, it is to be treated as a reference to the legislation, list or other document as it has effect at the time of the transfer.

(5)   For the purposes of this paragraph, where a decision described in sub-paragraph (1)(c) relates to—

(a)   transfers from the European Union (or the European Community) or the European Economic Area, or

(b)   transfers to which the Law Enforcement Directive applies,

it is to be treated as relating to equivalent transfers from the United Kingdom or transfers to which Part 3 of this Act applies (as appropriate).

12   In section 74B(1), (3), (6) and (7)—

(a)   references to regulations made under section 74A (other than references to making such regulations) include the provision made in paragraph 11;

(b)   references to the revocation of such regulations include the repeal of all or part of paragraph 11.

PART 4
REPEAL OF PROVISIONS IN CHAPTER 3 OF PART 2

Applied GDPR: power to make provision in consequence of GDPR regulations

13(1)   Regulations made under section 23 before exit day continue in force until they are revoked, despite the repeal of that section by the Data Protection, Privacy and Electronic Communications (Amendments etc) (EU Exit) Regulations 2019.

(2)   The provisions listed in section 186(3) include regulations made under section 23 before exit day (and not revoked).

(3)   Sub-paragraphs (1) and (2) do not have effect so far as otherwise provided by the law of England and Wales, Scotland or Northern Ireland.

Applied GDPR: national security certificates

14(1)   This paragraph applies to a certificate issued under section 27 of this Act which has effect immediately before exit day.

(2)   A reference in the certificate to a provision of the applied GDPR has effect, on and after exit day, as it if were a reference to the corresponding provision of the UK GDPR or this Act.

PART 5
THE INFORMATION COMMISSIONER

Confidentiality of information

15   The repeal of section 132(2)(d) by the Data Protection, Privacy and

Electronic Communications (Amendments etc) (EU Exit) Regulations 2019 has effect only in relation to a disclosure of information made on or after exit day.

PART 6

ENFORCEMENT

GDPR: maximum amount of penalties

16   In relation to an infringement, before exit day, of a provision of the EU GDPR (as it was directly applicable to the United Kingdom) or the applied GDPR—

    (a)   Article 83(5) and (6) of the UK GDPR and section 157(5)(a) and (b) of this Act have effect as if for "£17,500,000" there were substituted "20 million Euros";

    (b)   Article 83(4) of the UK GDPR and section 157(6)(a) and (b) of this Act have effect as if for "£8,700,000" there were substituted "10 million Euros";

    (c)   the maximum amount of a penalty in sterling must be determined by applying the spot rate of exchange set by the Bank of England on the day on which the penalty notice is given under section 155 of this Act.

GDPR: right to an effective remedy against the Commissioner

17(1)   This paragraph applies where—

    (a)   proceedings are brought against a decision made by the Commissioner before exit day, and

    (b)   the Commissioner's decision was preceded by an opinion or decision of the European Data Protection Board in accordance with the consistency mechanism referred to in Article 63 of the EU GDPR.

    (2)   The Commissioner must forward the Board's opinion or decision to the court or tribunal dealing with the proceedings.".

SCHEDULE 3

CONSEQUENTIAL AMENDMENTS OF OTHER LEGISLATION

Regulation 6

PART 1

REVOCATION OF RETAINED EU LAW

Revocation of Regulations and Decisions

1   The following Regulations and Decisions are revoked in so far as they are retained EU law—

    (a) Commission Decision 2000/518/EC of 26th July 2000 pursuant to Directive 95/46/EC of the European Parliament and of the Council on the adequate protection of personal data provided in Switzerland;

    (b) Commission Decision 2001/497/EC1 of 15th June 2001 on standard contractual clauses for the transfer of personal data to third countries, under Directive 95/46/EC;

    (c) Commission Decision 2002/2/EC of 20th December 2001 pursuant to Directive

95/46/EC of the European Parliament and of the Council on the adequate protection of personal data provided by the Canadian Personal Information Protection and Electronic Documents Act;

(d) Commission Decision 2003/490/EC of 30th June 2003 pursuant to Directive 95/46/EC of the European Parliament and of the Council on the adequate protection of personal data in Argentina;

(e) Commission Decision 2003/821/EC of 21st November 2003 on the adequate protection of personal data in Guernsey;

(f) Commission Decision 2004/411/EC of 28th April 2004 on the adequate protection of personal data in the Isle of Man;

(g) Commission Decision 2004/915/EC2 of 27th December 2004 amending Decision 2001/497/EC as regards the introduction of an alternative set of standard contractual clauses for the transfer of personal data to third countries;

(h) Commission Decision 2008/393/EC of 8th May 2008 pursuant to Directive 95/46/EC of the European Parliament and of the Council on the adequate protection of personal data in Jersey;

(i) Commission Decision 2010/87/EU3 of 5th February 2010 on standard contractual clauses for the transfer of personal data to processors established in third countries under Directive 95/46/EC of the European Parliament and of the Council;

(j) Commission Decision 2010/146/EU of 5th March 2010 pursuant to Directive 95/46/EC of the European Parliament and of the Council on the adequate protection provided by the Faeroese Act on processing of personal data;

(k) Commission Decision 2010/625/EU of 19th October 2010 pursuant to Directive 95/46/EC of the European Parliament and of the Council on the adequate protection of personal data in Andorra;

(l) Commission Decision 2011/61/EU of 31st January 2011 pursuant to Directive 95/46/EC of the European Parliament and of the Council on the adequate protection of personal data by the State of Israel with regard to automated processing of personal data;

(m) Commission Implementing Decision 2012/484/EU of 21st August 2012 pursuant to Directive 95/46/EC of the European Parliament and of the Council on the adequate protection of personal data by the Eastern Republic of Uruguay with regard to automated processing of personal data;

(n) Commission Implementing Decision 2013/65/EU of 19th December 2012 pursuant to Directive 95/46/EC of the European Parliament and of the Council on the adequate protection of personal data by New Zealand;

(o) Commission Implementing Decision (EU) 2016/1250 of 12th July 2016 pursuant to Directive 95/46/EC of the European Parliament and of the Council on the adequacy of the protection provided by the EU-U.S. Privacy Shield;

(p) Commission Implementing Decision (EU) 2016/22954 of 16th December 2016 amending Decisions 2000/518/EC, 2002/2/EC, 2003/490/EC, 2003/821/EC, 2004/411/EC, 2008/393/EC, 2010/146/EU, 2010/625/EU, 2011/61/EU and Implementing Decisions 2012/484/EU, 2013/65/EU on the adequate protection of personal data by certain countries, pursuant to Article 25(6) of Directive 95/46/EC of the European Parliament and of the Council;

(q) Commission Implementing Decision (EU) 2016/22975 of 16th December 2016 amending Decisions 2001/497/EC and 2010/87/EU on standard contractual clauses for the transfer of personal data to third countries and to processors established in such countries, under Directive 95/46/EC of the European Parliament and of the

Council;

(r) Regulation (EU) 2018/1725 of the European Parliament and of the Council of 23rd October 2018 on the protection of natural persons with regard to the processing of personal data by the Union institutions, bodies, offices and agencies and on the free movement of such data, and repealing Regulation (EC) No 45/2001 and Decision No 1247/2002/EC.

Revocation of provisions of EEA agreement

2 Paragraphs 5e, 5ea, 5ed, 5ee, 5ef, 5eg, 5eh, 5ei, 5ek, 5el, 5em, 5en, 5eo, 5ep and 5eq of Annex 11 to the EEA agreement, as it forms part of the law of England and Wales, Scotland or Northern Ireland on and after exit day by virtue of section 3(1) of the European Union (Withdrawal) Act 2018, are revoked in so far as they are retained EU law.

PART 2

AMENDMENTS OF PRIMARY LEGISLATION

3-19 *Not reproduced*

20(1) Section 40 of the Freedom of Information Act 2000 (personal information) is amended as follows.

(2) In subsections (3B), (4A)(a) and (5B)(b) and (c), for "GDPR" substitute "UK GDPR".

(3) In subsection (7)—

    (a) in the definition of "the data protection principles", for "GDPR" substitute "UK GDPR";

    (b) omit the words from "the GDPR", "personal data", "processing"" to the "(14) of that Act);";

    (c) at the appropriate places insert—

"personal data" and "processing" have the same meaning as in Parts 5 to 7 of the Data Protection Act 2018 (see section 3(2), (4) and (14) of that Act);"

"the UK GDPR" has the same meaning as in Parts 5 to 7 of the Data Protection Act 2018 (see section 3(10) and (14) of that Act)."

(4) In subsection (8), for "GDPR" (in both places) substitute "UK GDPR".

21 *Not reproduced*

22(1) Section 38 of the Freedom of Information (Scotland) Act 2002 (personal information)1 is amended as follows.

(2) In subsections (2B) and (3A)(a), for "GDPR" substitute "UK GDPR".

(3) In subsection (5)—

    (a) in the definition of "the data protection principles", for "GDPR" substitute "UK GDPR";

    (b) omit the words from "the GDPR", "personal data", "processing"" to "(14) of that Act);";

    (c) at the appropriate places insert—

"personal data" and "processing" have the same meaning as in Parts 5 to 7 of the Data

Protection Act 2018 (see section 3(2), (4) and (14) of that Act);"

"the UK GDPR" has the same meaning as in Parts 5 to 7 of the Data Protection Act 2018 (see section 3(10) and (14) of that Act)."

(4) In subsection (5A), for "GDPR" (in both places) substitute "UK GDPR".

23-110 *Not reproduced*

PART 4
MODIFICATION

111(1) Legislation described in sub-paragraph (2) has effect on and after exit day as if it were modified in accordance with sub-paragraphs (3) and (4) (but see sub-paragraph (5)).

(2) That legislation is—
    (a) subordinate legislation made on or before exit day;
    (b) primary legislation passed or made on or before exit day.

(3) The following have effect as references to the UK GDPR—
    (a) references to the GDPR as defined in section 3(10) of the 2018 Act or as defined for the purposes of Parts 5 to 7 of the 2018 Act;
    (b) other references to Regulation (EU) 2016/679 of the European Parliament and of the Council of 27th April 2016 on the protection of natural persons with regard to the processing of personal data and on the free movement of such data (General Data Protection Regulation).

(4) References described in sub-paragraph (3) which are references to the GDPR or the Regulation read with Chapter 2 of Part 2 of the 2018 Act have effect as references to the UK GDPR read with Part 2 of that Act.

(5) Sub-paragraphs (1) to (4) have effect unless the context otherwise requires and, in particular, do not affect references to the Regulation mentioned in sub-paragraph (3)(b) as it has effect in EU law.

(6) paragraph 2 of Schedule 21 to the 2018 Act (inserted by these Regulations) has effect in relation to references to the UK GDPR arising as a result of this paragraph as it has effect in relation of other references to the UK GDPR.

(7) In this paragraph—
    "primary legislation" has the meaning given in section 211 of the 2018 Act;
    "references" includes any references, however expressed;
    "subordinate legislation" has the meaning given in the Interpretation Act 1978.

PART 5
SUPPLEMENTARY

Interpretation of references to enactments

112 Nothing in Parts 2 to 4 of this Schedule is to be read as implying anything about whether references to an enactment or statutory provision (whether in Acts or instruments amended by those Parts of this Schedule or elsewhere) include the UK GDPR or other retained direct EU legislation.

SCHEDULE 4

AMENDMENTS CONSEQUENTIAL ON PROVISIONS OF THE 2018 ACT

Regulation 7

1-2   *Not reproduced*

Data Protection Act 2018

3   In Schedule 19 to the Data Protection Act 2018 (minor and consequential amendments), omit paragraphs 76 and 201.

Part VI

Data Protection
(pre-25 May 2018)

Data Protection Act 1998

(as amended to 24 May 2018)

CHAPTER 29

An Act to make new provision for the regulation of the processing of information relating to individuals, including the obtaining, holding, use or disclosure of such information.

16 July 1998

BE IT ENACTED by the Queen's most Excellent Majesty, by and with the advice and consent of the Lords Spiritual and Temporal, and Commons, in this present Parliament assembled, and by the authority of the same, as follows:–

PART I
PRELIMINARY

PART II
RIGHTS OF DATA SUBJECTS AND OTHERS

PART III
NOTIFICATION BY DATA CONTROLLERS

PART I
PRELIMINARY

Basic interpretative provisions

1(1) In this Act, unless the context otherwise requires–
    "data" means information which–
    (a)   is being processed by means of equipment operating automatically in response
          to instructions given for that purpose,
    (b)   is recorded with the intention that it should be processed by means of such
          equipment,
    (c)   is recorded as part of a relevant filing system or with the intention that it
          should form part of a relevant filing system,
    (d)   does not fall within paragraph (a), (b) or (c) but forms part of an accessible
          record as defined by section 68; or
    (e)   is recorded information held by a public authority and does not fall within any
          of paragraphs (a) to (d);

"data controller" means, subject to subsection (4), a person who (either alone or jointly or in common with other persons) determines the purposes for which and the manner in which any personal data are, or are to be, processed;

"data processor", in relation to personal data, means any person (other than an employee of the data controller) who processes the data on behalf of the data controller;

"data subject" means an individual who is the subject of personal data;

"personal data" means data which relate to a living individual who can be identified–

    (a)   from those data, or

    (b)   from those data and other information which is in the possession of, or is likely to come into the possession of, the data controller,

and includes any expression of opinion about the individual and any indication of the intentions of the data controller or any other person in respect of the individual;

"processing", in relation to information or data, means obtaining, recording or holding the information or data or carrying out any operation or set of operations on the information or data, including–

    (a)   organisation, adaptation or alteration of the information or data,

    (b)   retrieval, consultation or use of the information or data,

    (c)   disclosure of the information or data by transmission, dissemination or otherwise making available, or

    (d)   alignment, combination, blocking, erasure or destruction of the information or data;

"public authority" means a public authority as defined by the Freedom of Information Act 2000 or a Scottish public authority as defined by the Freedom of Information (Scotland) Act 2002;

"relevant filing system" means any set of information relating to individuals to the extent that, although the information is not processed by means of equipment operating automatically in response to instructions given for that purpose, the set is structured, either by reference to individuals or by reference to criteria relating to individuals, in such a way that specific information relating to a particular individual is readily accessible.

(2)   In this Act, unless the context otherwise requires–

    (a)   "obtaining" or "recording", in relation to personal data, includes obtaining or recording the information to be contained in the data, and

    (b)   "using" or "disclosing", in relation to personal data, includes using or disclosing the information contained in the data.

(3)   In determining for the purposes of this Act whether any information is recorded with the intention–

    (a)   that it should be processed by means of equipment operating automatically in response to instructions given for that purpose, or

    (b)   that it should form part of a relevant filing system,

it is immaterial that it is intended to be so processed or to form part of such a system only after being transferred to a country or territory outside the European Economic Area.

(4)   Where personal data are processed only for purposes for which they are required by or under any enactment to be processed, the person on whom the obligation to process the data is imposed by or under that enactment is for the purposes of this Act the data controller.

(5)   In paragraph (e) of the definition of "data" in subsection (1), the reference to information

"held" by a public authority shall be construed in accordance with section 3(2) of the Freedom of Information Act 2000 or section 3(2), (4) and (5) of the Freedom of Information (Scotland) Act 2002.

(6) Where

    (a)   section 7 of the Freedom of Information Act 2000 prevents Parts I to V of that Act or

    (b)   section 7(1) of the Freedom of Information (Scotland) Act 2002 prevents that Act,

from applying to certain information held by a public authority, that information is not to be treated for the purposes of paragraph (e) of the definition of "data" in subsection (1) as held by a public authority.

NOTES

Defined terms

"accessible record": s 68 and Schs 11 and 12
"the Commissioner": s 70(1)
"data": s 1(1)
"data controller": ss1(1) and (4) and 63(3)
"data processor": s 1(1)
"data protection principles": s 4 and Sch1
"data subject": s 1(1)
"disclosing": s 1(2)(b)
"EEA State": s 70(1)
"enactment": s 70(1)
"held": s 1(6) and Freedom of Information Act

"obtaining": s 1(2)(a)
"personal data": s 1(1)
"processing": s 1(1)
"public authority": s 1(1) and Freedom of Information Act 2000, s 3(1)
"recording": s 1(2)(a)
"relevant filing system": s 1(1)
"sensitive personal data": s 2
"the special purposes": s 3
"the Tribunal": s 70(1)
"using": s 1(2)(b)

2000, s 3(2),

Sensitive personal data

2   In this Act "sensitive personal data" means personal data consisting of information as to–

    (a)   the racial or ethnic origin of the data subject,

    (b)   his political opinions,

    (c)   his religious beliefs or other beliefs of a similar nature,

    (d)   whether he is a member of a trade union (within the meaning of the Trade Union and Labour Relations (Consolidation) Act 1992,

    (e)   his physical or mental health or condition,

    (f)   his sexual life,

    (g)   the commission or alleged commission by him of any offence, or

    (h)   any proceedings for any offence committed or alleged to have been committed by him, the disposal of such proceedings or the sentence of any court in such proceedings.

NOTES

Defined terms
"data subject": s 1(1)

"sensitive personal data": s 2

The special purposes

3   In this Act "the special purposes" means any one or more of the following–

    (a)   the purposes of journalism,

    (b)   artistic purposes, and

    (c)   literary purposes.

The data protection principles

4(1)   References in this Act to the data protection principles are to the principles set out in Part I of Schedule 1.

(2)   Those principles are to be interpreted in accordance with Part II of Schedule 1.

(3) Schedule 2 (which applies to all personal data) and Schedule 3 (which applies only to sensitive personal data) set out conditions applying for the purposes of the first principle; and Schedule 4 sets out cases in which the eighth principle does not apply.

(4) Subject to section 27(1), it shall be the duty of a data controller to comply with the data protection principles in relation to all personal data with respect to which he is the data controller.

NOTES

Defined terms
  "data controller": s 1(1)
  "data protection principles": s 4 and Sch1

"personal data": s 1(1)
"sensitive personal data": s 2

Application of Act

5(1) Except as otherwise provided by or under section 54, this Act applies to a data controller in respect of any data only if–

(a) the data controller is established in the United Kingdom and the data are processed in the context of that establishment, or

(b) the data controller is established neither in the United Kingdom nor in any other EEA State but uses equipment in the United Kingdom for processing the data otherwise than for the purposes of transit through the United Kingdom.

(2) A data controller falling within subsection (1)(b) must nominate for the purposes of this Act a representative established in the United Kingdom.

(3) For the purposes of subsections (1) and (2), each of the following is to be treated as established in the United Kingdom–

(a) an individual who is ordinarily resident in the United Kingdom,

(b) a body incorporated under the law of, or of any part of, the United Kingdom,

(c) a partnership or other unincorporated association formed under the law of any part of the United Kingdom, and

(d) any person who does not fall within paragraph (a), (b) or (c) but maintains in the United Kingdom–

(i) an office, branch or agency through which he carries on any activity, or

(ii) a regular practice;

and the reference to establishment in any other EEA State has a corresponding meaning.

NOTES

Defined terms
  "data": s 1(1)
  "data controller": s 1(1)
  "EEA State": s 70(1)

"established": s 5(3)
"processing": s 1(1)

The Commissioner and the Tribunal

6(1) For the purposes of this Act and of the Freedom of Information Act 2000 there shall be an officer known as the Information Commissioner (in this Act referred to as "the Commissioner").

(2) The Commissioner shall be appointed by Her Majesty by Letters Patent.

(7) Schedule 5 has effect in relation to the Commissioner .

Defined terms
"processing": s 1(1)
"Commissioner": s 6(1)

"data controller": s 1(1)
"data subject": s 1(1)
"Tribunal": s 6(3)

PART II
RIGHTS OF DATA SUBJECTS AND OTHERS

Right of access to personal data

7(1) Subject to the following provisions of this section and to sections 8, 9 and 9A, an individual is entitled–

    (a) to be informed by any data controller whether personal data of which that individual is the data subject are being processed by or on behalf of that data controller,

    (b) if that is the case, to be given by the data controller a description of–

        (i) the personal data of which that individual is the data subject,

        (ii) the purposes for which they are being or are to be processed, and

        (iii) the recipients or classes of recipients to whom they are or may be disclosed,

    (c) to have communicated to him in an intelligible form–

        (i) the information constituting any personal data of which that individual is the data subject, and

        (ii) any information available to the data controller as to the source of those data, and

    (d) where the processing by automatic means of personal data of which that individual is the data subject for the purpose of evaluating matters relating to him such as, for example, his performance at work, his creditworthiness, his reliability or his conduct, has constituted or is likely to constitute the sole basis for any decision significantly affecting him, to be informed by the data controller of the logic involved in that decision-taking.

(2) A data controller is not obliged to supply any information under subsection (1) unless he has received–

    (a) a request in writing, and

    (b) except in prescribed cases, such fee (not exceeding the prescribed maximum) as he may require.

(3) Where a data controller–

    (a) reasonably requires further information in order to satisfy himself as to the identity of the person making a request under this section and to locate the information which that person seeks, and

    (b) has informed him of that requirement,

the data controller is not obliged to comply with the request unless he is supplied with that further information.

(4) Where a data controller cannot comply with the request without disclosing information relating to another individual who can be identified from that information, he is not obliged to comply with the request unless–

    (a) the other individual has consented to the disclosure of the information to the person making the request, or

    (b) it is reasonable in all the circumstances to comply with the request without the consent of the other individual.

(5) In subsection (4) the reference to information relating to another individual includes a reference to information identifying that individual as the source of the information sought by the request; and that subsection is not to be construed as excusing a data controller from communicating so much of the information sought by the request as can be communicated without disclosing the identity of the other individual concerned, whether by the omission of names or other identifying particulars or otherwise.

(6) In determining for the purposes of subsection (4)(b) whether it is reasonable in all the circumstances to comply with the request without the consent of the other individual concerned, regard shall be had, in particular, to–

    (a) any duty of confidentiality owed to the other individual,

    (b) any steps taken by the data controller with a view to seeking the consent of the other individual,

    (c) whether the other individual is capable of giving consent, and

    (d) any express refusal of consent by the other individual.

(7) An individual making a request under this section may, in such cases as may be prescribed, specify that his request is limited to personal data of any prescribed description.

(8) Subject to subsection (4), a data controller shall comply with a request under this section promptly and in any event before the end of the prescribed period beginning with the relevant day.

(9) If a court is satisfied on the application of any person who has made a request under the foregoing provisions of this section that the data controller in question has failed to comply with the request in contravention of those provisions, the court may order him to comply with the request.

(10) In this section–

"prescribed" means prescribed by the Secretary of State by regulations;

"the prescribed maximum" means such amount as may be prescribed;

"the prescribed period" means forty days or such other period as may be prescribed;

"the relevant day", in relation to a request under this section, means the day on which the data controller receives the request or, if later, the first day on which the data controller has both the required fee and the information referred to in subsection (3).

(11) Different amounts or periods may be prescribed under this section in relation to different cases.

NOTES

Defined terms

"court" s 15(1)

"data controller": s 1(1)

"data subject": s 1(1)

"personal data": s 1(1)

"prescribed": s 7(10)

"prescribed maximum": s 7(10)

"prescribed period": s 7(10)

"processing": s 1(1)

"recipients": s 70(1)

"relevant day": s 7(10)

Subordinate legislation

Data Protection (Subject Access) (Fees and Miscellaneous Provisions) Regulations 2000, SI 2000/191.

Provisions supplementary to section 7

8(1) The Secretary of State may by regulations provide that, in such cases as may be prescribed, a request for information under any provision of subsection (1) of section 7 is to be treated as extending also to information under other provisions of that subsection.

(2) The obligation imposed by section 7(1)(c)(i) must be complied with by supplying the data subject with a copy of the information in permanent form unless–

    (a)   the supply of such a copy is not possible or would involve disproportionate effort, or

    (b)   the data subject agrees otherwise;

and where any of the information referred to in section 7(1)(c)(i) is expressed in terms which are not intelligible without explanation the copy must be accompanied by an explanation of those terms.

(3) Where a data controller has previously complied with a request made under section 7 by an individual, the data controller is not obliged to comply with a subsequent identical or similar request under that section by that individual unless a reasonable interval has elapsed between compliance with the previous request and the making of the current request.

(4) In determining for the purposes of subsection (3) whether requests under section 7 are made at reasonable intervals, regard shall be had to the nature of the data, the purpose for which the data are processed and the frequency with which the data are altered.

(5) Section 7(1)(d) is not to be regarded as requiring the provision of information as to the logic involved in any decision-taking if, and to the extent that, the information constitutes a trade secret.

(6) The information to be supplied pursuant to a request under section 7 must be supplied by reference to the data in question at the time when the request is received, except that it may take account of any amendment or deletion made between that time and the time when the information is supplied, being an amendment or deletion that would have been made regardless of the receipt of the request.

(7) For the purposes of section 7(4) and (5) another individual can be identified from the information being disclosed if he can be identified from that information, or from that and any other information which, in the reasonable belief of the data controller, is likely to be in, or to come into, the possession of the data subject making the request.

NOTES

Defined terms
"data": s 1(1)
"data controller": s 1(1)
"data subject": s 1(1)
"processing": s 1(1)

Subordinate legislation
Data Protection (Subject Access) (Fees and Miscellaneous Provisions) Regulations 2000, SI 2000/191.

Application of section 7 where data controller is credit reference agency

9(1) Where the data controller is a credit reference agency, section 7 has effect subject to the provisions of this section.

(2) An individual making a request under section 7 may limit his request to personal data relevant to his financial standing, and shall be taken to have so limited his request unless the request shows a contrary intention.

(3) Where the data controller receives a request under section 7 in a case where personal data of which the individual making the request is the data subject are being processed by or on behalf of the data controller, the obligation to supply information under that section includes an obligation to give the individual making the request a statement, in such form as may be prescribed by the Secretary of State by regulations, of the individual's rights–

    (a)   under section 159 of the Consumer Credit Act 1974 , and

    (b)   to the extent required by the prescribed form, under this Act.

NOTES

Defined terms

"credit reference agency": s 70(1)
"data controller": s 1(1)
"data subject": s 1(1)
"personal data": s 1(1)
"prescribed": s 7(10)

Subordinate legislation

Data Protection (Subject Access) (Fees and Miscellaneous Provisions) Regulations 2000, SI 2000/191.

Unstructured personal data held by public authorities

9A(1) In this section "unstructured personal data" means any personal data falling within paragraph (e) of the definition of "data" in section 1(1), other than information which is recorded as part of, or with the intention that it should form part of, any set of information relating to individuals to the extent that the set is structured by reference to individuals or by reference to criteria relating to individuals.

(2) A public authority is not obliged to comply with subsection (1) of section 7 in relation to any unstructured personal data unless the request under that section contains a description of the data.

(3) Even if the data are described by the data subject in his request, a public authority is not obliged to comply with subsection (1) of section 7 in relation to unstructured personal data if the authority estimates that the cost of complying with the request so far as relating to those data would exceed the appropriate limit.

(4) Subsection (3) does not exempt the public authority from its obligation to comply with paragraph (a) of section 7(1) in relation to the unstructured personal data unless the estimated cost of complying with that paragraph alone in relation to those data would exceed the appropriate limit.

(5) In subsections (3) and (4) "the appropriate limit" means such amount as may be prescribed by the Secretary of State by regulations, and different amounts may be prescribed in relation to different cases.

(6) Any estimate for the purposes of this section must be made in accordance with regulations under section 12(5) of the Freedom of Information Act 2000.

NOTES

Defined terms

"data": s 1(1)
"data subject": s 1(1)

"personal data": s 1(1)
"public authority": FOIA s 3(1)

Right to prevent processing likely to cause damage or distress

10(1) Subject to subsection (2), an individual is entitled at any time by notice in writing to a data controller to require the data controller at the end of such period as is reasonable in the circumstances to cease, or not to begin, processing, or processing for a specified purpose or in a specified manner, any personal data in respect of which he is the data subject, on the ground that, for specified reasons–

    (a) the processing of those data or their processing for that purpose or in that manner is causing or is likely to cause substantial damage or substantial distress to him or to another, and

    (b) that damage or distress is or would be unwarranted.

(2) Subsection (1) does not apply–

    (a) in a case where any of the conditions in paragraphs 1 to 4 of Schedule 2 is met, or

(b)   in such other cases as may be prescribed by the Secretary of State by order.

(3)   The data controller must within twenty-one days of receiving a notice under subsection (1) ("the data subject notice") give the individual who gave it a written notice–

(a)   stating that he has complied or intends to comply with the data subject notice, or

(b)   stating his reasons for regarding the data subject notice as to any extent unjustified and the extent (if any) to which he has complied or intends to comply with it.

(4)   If a court is satisfied, on the application of any person who has given a notice under subsection (1) which appears to the court to be justified (or to be justified to any extent), that the data controller in question has failed to comply with the notice, the court may order him to take such steps for complying with the notice (or for complying with it to that extent) as the court thinks fit.

(5)   The failure by a data subject to exercise the right conferred by subsection (1) or section 11(1) does not affect any other right conferred on him by this Part.

NOTES

Defined terms
"court": s 15(1)
"data": s 1(1)
"data controller": s 1(1)
"data subject": s 1(1)
"data subject notice": s 10(3)

"personal data": s 1(1)
"prescribed": s 7(10)
"processing": s 1(1)

Right to prevent processing for purposes of direct marketing

11(1)   An individual is entitled at any time by notice in writing to a data controller to require the data controller at the end of such period as is reasonable in the circumstances to cease, or not to begin, processing for the purposes of direct marketing personal data in respect of which he is the data subject.

(2)   If the court is satisfied, on the application of any person who has given a notice under subsection (1), that the data controller has failed to comply with the notice, the court may order him to take such steps for complying with the notice as the court thinks fit.

(2A)   This section shall not apply in relation to the processing of such data as are mentioned in paragraph (1) of regulation 8 of the Telecommunications (Data Protection and Privacy) Regulations 1999 (processing of telecommunications billing data for certain marketing purposes) for the purposes mentioned in paragraph (2) of that regulation.

(3)   In this section "direct marketing" means the communication (by whatever means) of any advertising or marketing material which is directed to particular individuals.

NOTES

Defined terms
"court": s 15(1)
"data controller": s 1(1)
"direct marketing": s 11(3)

"data subject": s 1(1)
"personal data": s 1(1)
"processing": s 1(1)

Rights in relation to automated decision-taking

12(1)   An individual is entitled at any time, by notice in writing to any data controller, to require the data controller to ensure that no decision taken by or on behalf of the data controller which significantly affects that individual is based solely on the processing by automatic means of personal data in respect of which that individual is the data subject for the purpose of evaluating matters relating to him such as, for example, his performance at work, his creditworthiness, his reliability or his conduct.

(2) Where, in a case where no notice under subsection (1) has effect, a decision which significantly affects an individual is based solely on such processing as is mentioned in subsection (1)–

    (a)   the data controller must as soon as reasonably practicable notify the individual that the decision was taken on that basis, and

    (b)   the individual is entitled, within twenty-one days of receiving that notification from the data controller, by notice in writing to require the data controller to reconsider the decision or to take a new decision otherwise than on that basis.

(3) The data controller must, within twenty-one days of receiving a notice under subsection (2)(b) ("the data subject notice") give the individual a written notice specifying the steps that he intends to take to comply with the data subject notice.

(4) A notice under subsection (1) does not have effect in relation to an exempt decision; and nothing in subsection (2) applies to an exempt decision.

(5) In subsection (4) "exempt decision" means any decision–

    (a)   in respect of which the condition in subsection (6) and the condition in subsection (7) are met, or

    (b)   which is made in such other circumstances as may be prescribed by the Secretary of State by order.

(6) The condition in this subsection is that the decision–

    (a)   is taken in the course of steps taken–

        (i)   for the purpose of considering whether to enter into a contract with the data subject,

        (ii)   with a view to entering into such a contract, or

        (iii)   in the course of performing such a contract, or

    (b)   is authorised or required by or under any enactment.

(7) The condition in this subsection is that either–

    (a)   the effect of the decision is to grant a request of the data subject, or

    (b)   steps have been taken to safeguard the legitimate interests of the data subject (for example, by allowing him to make representations).

(8) If a court is satisfied on the application of a data subject that a person taking a decision in respect of him ("the responsible person") has failed to comply with subsection (1) or (2)(b), the court may order the responsible person to reconsider the decision, or to take a new decision which is not based solely on such processing as is mentioned in subsection (1).

(9) An order under subsection (8) shall not affect the rights of any person other than the data subject and the responsible person.

NOTES

Defined terms

  "court": s 15(1)
  "data controller": s 1(1)
  "data subject": s 1(1)
  "data subject notice": s 12(3)
  "enactment": s 70(1)

  "exempt decision": s 12(5)
  "personal data": s 1(1)
  "prescribed": s 7(10)
  "processing": s 1(1)
  "responsible person": s 12(8)

Compensation for failure to comply with certain requirements

13(1) An individual who suffers damage by reason of any contravention by a data controller of any of the requirements of this Act is entitled to compensation from the data controller for that damage.

(2) An individual who suffers distress by reason of any contravention by a data controller of any of the requirements of this Act is entitled to compensation from the data controller for that distress if—

    (a)   the individual also suffers damage by reason of the contravention, or

    (b)   the contravention relates to the processing of personal data for the special purposes.

(3) In proceedings brought against a person by virtue of this section it is a defence to prove that he had taken such care as in all the circumstances was reasonably required to comply with the requirement concerned.

NOTES

Defined terms
"data controller": s 1(1)
"personal data": s 1(1)

"processing": s 1(1)
"special purposes": s 3

Rectification, blocking, erasure and destruction

14(1) If a court is satisfied on the application of a data subject that personal data of which the applicant is the subject are inaccurate, the court may order the data controller to rectify, block, erase or destroy those data and any other personal data in respect of which he is the data controller and which contain an expression of opinion which appears to the court to be based on the inaccurate data.

(2) Subsection (1) applies whether or not the data accurately record information received or obtained by the data controller from the data subject or a third party but where the data accurately record such information, then—

    (a)   if the requirements mentioned in paragraph 7 of Part II of Schedule 1 have been complied with, the court may, instead of making an order under subsection (1), make an order requiring the data to be supplemented by such statement of the true facts relating to the matters dealt with by the data as the court may approve, and

    (b)   if all or any of those requirements have not been complied with, the court may, instead of making an order under that subsection, make such order as it thinks fit for securing compliance with those requirements with or without a further order requiring the data to be supplemented by such a statement as is mentioned in paragraph (a).

(3) Where the court

    (a)   makes an order under subsection (1), or

    (b)   is satisfied on the application of a data subject that personal data of which he was the data subject and which have been rectified, blocked, erased or destroyed were inaccurate,

it may, where it considers it reasonably practicable, order the data controller to notify third parties to whom the data have been disclosed of the rectification, blocking, erasure or destruction.

(4) If a court is satisfied on the application of a data subject—

    (a)   that he has suffered damage by reason of any contravention by a data controller of any of the requirements of this Act in respect of any personal data, in circumstances entitling him to compensation under section 13, and

    (b)   that there is a substantial risk of further contravention in respect of those data in such circumstances,

the court may order the rectification, blocking, erasure or destruction of any of those data.

(5) Where the court makes an order under subsection (4) it may, where it considers it reasonably practicable, order the data controller to notify third parties to whom the data have been disclosed of the rectification, blocking, erasure or destruction.

(6) In determining whether it is reasonably practicable to require such notification as is mentioned in subsection (3) or (5) the court shall have regard, in particular, to the number of persons who would have to be notified.

NOTES

Defined terms
 "court": s 15(1)
 "data" s 1(1)
 "data controller": s 1(1)

"data subject": s 1(1)
"inaccurate (in relation to data)": s 70(2)
"personal data": s 1(1)
"third party": s 70(1)

Jurisdiction and procedure

15(1) The jurisdiction conferred by sections 7 to 14 is exercisable by the High Court or a county court or, in Scotland, by the Court of Session or the sheriff.

(2) For the purpose of determining any question whether an applicant under subsection (9) of section 7 is entitled to the information which he seeks (including any question whether any relevant data are exempt from that section by virtue of Part IV) a court may require the information constituting any data processed by or on behalf of the data controller and any information as to the logic involved in any decision-taking as mentioned in section 7(1)(d) to be made available for its own inspection but shall not, pending the determination of that question in the applicant's favour, require the information sought by the applicant to be disclosed to him or his representatives whether by discovery (or, in Scotland, recovery) or otherwise.

NOTES

Defined terms
 "data": s 1(1)

"data controller": s 1(1)
"processing": s 1(1)

PART III
NOTIFICATION BY DATA CONTROLLERS

Preliminary

16(1) In this Part "the registrable particulars", in relation to a data controller, means–

    (a)   his name and address,

    (b)   if he has nominated a representative for the purposes of this Act, the name and address of the representative,

    (c)   a description of the personal data being or to be processed by or on behalf of the data controller and of the category or categories of data subject to which they relate,

    (d)   a description of the purpose or purposes for which the data are being or are to be processed,

    (e)   a description of any recipient or recipients to whom the data controller intends or may wish to disclose the data,

    (f)   the names, or a description of, any countries or territories outside the European Economic Area to which the data controller directly or indirectly transfers, or intends or may wish directly or indirectly to transfer, the data,

    (ff)   where the data controller is a public authority, a statement of that fact

    (g)   in any case where–

(i)   personal data are being, or are intended to be, processed in circumstances in which the prohibition in subsection (1) of section 17 is excluded by subsection (2) or (3) of that section, and

(ii)   the notification does not extend to those data,

a statement of that fact, and

(h)   such information about the data controller as may be prescribed under section 18(5A).

(2)   In this Part–

"fees regulations" means regulations made by the Secretary of State under section 18(5) or 19(4) or (7);

"notification regulations" means regulations made by the Secretary of State under the other provisions of this Part;

"prescribed", except where used in relation to fees regulations, means prescribed by notification regulations.

(3)   For the purposes of this Part, so far as it relates to the addresses of data controllers–

(a)   the address of a registered company is that of its registered office, and

(b)   the address of a person (other than a registered company) carrying on a business is that of his principal place of business in the United Kingdom.

NOTES

Defined terms
"address": s 16(3)
"business": s 70(1)
"data": s 1(1)
"data controller": s 1(1) and (4) and 63(3).
"data subject": s 1(1)
"disclosing": s 1(2)(b)
"EEA State": s 70(1)

"fees regulations": s 16(2)
"notification regulations": s 16(2)
"personal data": s 1(1)
"prescribed": s 16(2)
"processing": s 1(1)
"recipient": s 70(1)
"registered company": s 70(1)
"registrable particulars": s 16(1)

Prohibition on processing without registration

17(1)   Subject to the following provisions of this section, personal data must not be processed unless an entry in respect of the data controller is included in the register maintained by the Commissioner under section 19 (or is treated by notification regulations made by virtue of section 19(3) as being so included).

(2)   Except where the processing is assessable processing for the purposes of section 22, subsection (1) does not apply in relation to personal data consisting of information which falls neither within paragraph (a) of the definition of "data" in section 1(1) nor within paragraph (b) of that definition.

(3)   If it appears to the Secretary of State that processing of a particular description is unlikely to prejudice the rights and freedoms of data subjects, notification regulations may provide that, in such cases as may be prescribed, subsection (1) is not to apply in relation to processing of that description.

(4)   Subsection (1) does not apply in relation to any processing whose sole purpose is the maintenance of a public register.

NOTES

Defined terms
"accessible record": s 68
"assessable processing": s 22(1)
"the Commissioner": s 70(1)
"data": s 1(1)
"data controller": ss1(1) and (4) and 63(3)
"data subject": s 1(1)
"notification regulations": s 16(2)

"personal data": s 1(1)
"prescribed": s 16(2)
"processing": s 1(1)
"public register": s 70(1)

Subordinate legislation
Data Protection (Notification and Notification Fees) Regulations 2000, SI 2000/188.

Notification by data controllers

18(1) Any data controller who wishes to be included in the register maintained under section 19 shall give a notification to the Commissioner under this section.

(2) A notification under this section must specify in accordance with notification regulations–

(a) the registrable particulars, and

(b) a general description of measures to be taken for the purpose of complying with the seventh data protection principle.

(3) Notification regulations made by virtue of subsection (2) may provide for the determination by the Commissioner, in accordance with any requirements of the regulations, of the form in which the registrable particulars and the description mentioned in subsection (2)(b) are to be specified, including in particular the detail required for the purposes of section 16(1)(c), (d), (e) and (f) and subsection (2)(b).

(4) Notification regulations may make provision as to the giving of notification–

(a) by partnerships, or

(b) in other cases where two or more persons are the data controllers in respect of any personal data.

(5) The notification must be accompanied by such fee as may be prescribed by fees regulations.

(5A) Notification regulations may prescribe the information about the data controller which is required for the purpose of verifying the fee payable under subsection (5).

(6) Notification regulations may provide for any fee paid under subsection (5) or section 19(4) to be refunded in prescribed circumstances.

NOTES

Defined terms

"the Commissioner": s 70(1)

"data controller": ss 1(1) and (4) and 63(3)

"data protection principles": s 4 and Schedule 1

"fees regulations": s 16(2)

"notification regulations": s 16(2)

"personal data": s 1(1)

"prescribed": s 16(2)

"registrable particulars": s 16(1)

Subordinate legislation

Data Protection (Notification and Notification Fees) Regulations 2000, SI 2000/188.

Register of notifications

19(1) The Commissioner shall–

(a) maintain a register of persons who have given notification under section 18, and

(b) make an entry in the register in pursuance of each notification received by him under that section from a person in respect of whom no entry as data controller was for the time being included in the register.

(2) Each entry in the register shall consist of–

(a) the registrable particulars notified under section 18 or, as the case requires, those particulars as amended in pursuance of section 20(4), and

(b) such other information as the Commissioner may be authorised or required by notification regulations to include in the register.

(3) Notification regulations may make provision as to the time as from which any entry in respect of a data controller is to be treated for the purposes of section 17 as having been

made in the register.

(4) No entry shall be retained in the register for more than the relevant time except on payment of such fee as may be prescribed by fees regulations.

(5) In subsection (4) "the relevant time" means twelve months or such other period as may be prescribed by notification regulations; and different periods may be prescribed in relation to different cases.

(6) The Commissioner–

    (a) shall provide facilities for making the information contained in the entries in the register available for inspection (in visible and legible form) by members of the public at all reasonable hours and free of charge, and

    (b) may provide such other facilities for making the information contained in those entries available to the public free of charge as he considers appropriate.

(7) The Commissioner shall, on payment of such fee, if any, as may be prescribed by fees regulations, supply any member of the public with a duly certified copy in writing of the particulars contained in any entry made in the register.

(8) Nothing in subsection (6) or (7) applies to information which is included in an entry in the register only by reason of it falling within section 16(1)(h).

NOTES

Defined terms
"the Commissioner": s 70(1)
"data controller": ss1(1) and (4) and 63(3)
"fees regulations": s 16(2)
"notification regulations": s 16(2)
"prescribed": s 16(2)

Subordinate legislation
Data Protection (Fees under section 19(7)) Regulations 2000, SI 2000/187.
Data Protection (Notification and Notification Fees) Regulations 2000, SI 2000/188

Duty to notify changes

20(1) For the purpose specified in subsection (2), notification regulations shall include provision imposing on every person in respect of whom an entry as a data controller is for the time being included in the register maintained under section 19 a duty to notify to the Commissioner, in such circumstances and at such time or times and in such form as may be prescribed, such matters relating to the registrable particulars and measures taken as mentioned in section 18(2)(b) as may be prescribed.

(2) The purpose referred to in subsection (1) is that of ensuring, so far as practicable, that at any time–

    (a) that at any time the entries in the register maintained under section 19 contain current names and addresses and describe the current practice or intentions of the data controller with respect to the processing of personal data,

    (aa) that the correct fee is paid under section 19(4), and

    (b) that at any time the Commissioner is provided with a general description of measures currently being taken as mentioned in section 18(2)(b).

(3) Subsection (3) of section 18 has effect in relation to notification regulations made by virtue of subsection (1) as it has effect in relation to notification regulations made by virtue of subsection (2) of that section.

(4) On receiving any notification under notification regulations made by virtue of subsection (1), the Commissioner shall make such amendments of the relevant entry in the register maintained under section 19 as are necessary to take account of the notification.

NOTES

Defined terms
  "address": s 70(1)
  "Commissioner": s 70(1)
  "data controller": s 1(1)
  "notification regulations": s 16(2)

"personal data": s 1(1)
"prescribed": s 16(2)
"processing": s 1(1)
"registrable particulars": s 16(1)

Offences

21(1) If section 17(1) is contravened, the data controller is guilty of an offence.

(2) Any person who fails to comply with the duty imposed by notification regulations made by virtue of section 20(1) is guilty of an offence.

(3) It shall be a defence for a person charged with an offence under subsection (2) to show that he exercised all due diligence to comply with the duty.

NOTES

Defined terms
  "data controller": s 1(1)

"notification regulations": s 16(2)

Preliminary assessment by Commissioner

22(1) In this section "assessable processing" means processing which is of a description specified in an order made by the Secretary of State as appearing to him to be particularly likely–
    (a) to cause substantial damage or substantial distress to data subjects, or
    (b) otherwise significantly to prejudice the rights and freedoms of data subjects.

(2) On receiving notification from any data controller under section 18 or under notification regulations made by virtue of section 20 the Commissioner shall consider–
    (a) whether any of the processing to which the notification relates is assessable processing, and
    (b) if so, whether the assessable processing is likely to comply with the provisions of this Act.

(3) Subject to subsection (4), the Commissioner shall, within the period of twenty-eight days beginning with the day on which he receives a notification which relates to assessable processing, give a notice to the data controller stating the extent to which the Commissioner is of the opinion that the processing is likely or unlikely to comply with the provisions of this Act.

(4) Before the end of the period referred to in subsection (3) the Commissioner may, by reason of special circumstances, extend that period on one occasion only by notice to the data controller by such further period not exceeding fourteen days as the Commissioner may specify in the notice.

(5) No assessable processing in respect of which a notification has been given the Commissioner as mentioned in subsection (2) shall be carried on unless either–
    (a) the period of twenty-eight days beginning with the day on which the notification is received by the Commissioner (or, in a case falling within subsection (4), that period as extended under that subsection) has elapsed, or
    (b) before the end of that period (or that period as so extended) the data controller has received a notice from the Commissioner under subsection (3) in respect of the processing.

(6) Where subsection (5) is contravened, the data controller is guilty of an offence.

(7) The Secretary of State may by order amend subsections (3), (4) and (5) by substituting for the number of days for the time being specified there a different number specified in the

order.

Power to make provision for appointment of data protection supervisors

23(1) The Secretary of State may by order–

    (a)   make provision under which a data controller may appoint a person to act as a data protection supervisor responsible in particular for monitoring in an independent manner the data controller's compliance with the provisions of this Act, and

    (b)   provide that, in relation to any data controller who has appointed a data protection supervisor in accordance with the provisions of the order and who complies with such conditions as may be specified in the order, the provisions of this Part are to have effect subject to such exemptions or other modifications as may be specified in the order.

(2) An order under this section may–

    (a)   impose duties on data protection supervisors in relation to the Commissioner, and

    (b)   confer functions on the Commissioner in relation to data protection supervisors.

Duty of certain data controllers to make certain information available

24(1) Subject to subsection (3), where personal data are processed in a case where–

    (a)   by virtue of subsection (2) or (3) of section 17, subsection (1) of that section does not apply to the processing, and

    (b)   the data controller has not notified the relevant particulars in respect of that processing under section 18,

the data controller must, within twenty-one days of receiving a written request from any person, make the relevant particulars available to that person in writing free of charge.

(2) In this section "the relevant particulars" means the particulars referred to in paragraphs (a) to (f) of section 16(1).

(3) This section has effect subject to any exemption conferred for the purposes of this section by notification regulations.

(4) Any data controller who fails to comply with the duty imposed by subsection (1) is guilty of an offence.

(5) It shall be a defence for a person charged with an offence under subsection (4) to show that he exercised all due diligence to comply with the duty.

Functions of Commissioner in relation to making of notification regulations

25(1) As soon as practicable after the passing of this Act, the Commissioner shall submit to the Secretary of State proposals as to the provisions to be included in the first notification regulations.

(2)   The Commissioner shall keep under review the working of notification regulations and may from time to time submit to the Secretary of State proposals as to amendments to be made to the regulations.

(3)   The Secretary of State may from time to time require the Commissioner to consider any matter relating to notification regulations and to submit to him proposals as to amendments to be made to the regulations in connection with that matter.

(4)   Before making any notification regulations, the Secretary of State shall–

(a)   consider any proposals made to him by the Commissioner under subsection (2) or (3), and

(b)   consult the Commissioner.

NOTES

Defined terms	**Subordinate legislation**
"Commissioner": s 70(1)	Data Protection (Notification and Notification Fees)
"notification regulations": s 16(2)	Regulations 2000, SI 2000/188

Fees regulations

26(1)   Fees regulations prescribing fees for the purposes of any provision of this Part may provide for different fees to be payable in different cases.

(2)   In making any fees regulations, the Secretary of State shall have regard to the desirability of securing that the fees payable to the Commissioner are sufficient to offset–

(a)   the expenses incurred by the Commissioner in discharging his functions under this Act and any expenses of the Secretary of State in respect of the Commissioner so far as attributable to those functions; and

(b)   to the extent that the Secretary of State considers appropriate–

(i)   any deficit previously incurred (whether before or after the passing of this Act) in respect of the expenses mentioned in paragraph (a), and

(ii)   expenses incurred or to be incurred by the Secretary of State in respect of the inclusion of any officers or staff of the Commissioner in any scheme under section 1 of the Superannuation Act 1972.

NOTES

Defined terms	"Tribunal": s 70(1)
"Commissioner": s 70(1)	
"fees regulations": s 16(2)	

PART IV
EXEMPTIONS

Preliminary

27(1)   References in any of the data protection principles or any provision of Parts II and III to personal data or to the processing of personal data do not include references to data or processing which by virtue of this Part are exempt from that principle or other provision.

(2)   In this Part "the subject information provisions" means–

(a)   the first data protection principle to the extent to which it requires compliance with paragraph 2 of Part II of Schedule 1, and

(b)   section 7.

(3)   In this Part "the non-disclosure provisions" means the provisions specified in subsection (4)

to the extent to which they are inconsistent with the disclosure in question.

(4) The provisions referred to in subsection (3) are–

    (a)   the first data protection principle, except to the extent to which it requires compliance with the conditions in Schedules 2 and 3,

    (b)   the second, third, fourth and fifth data protection principles, and

    (c)   sections 10 and 14(1) to (3).

(5) Except as provided by this Part, the subject information provisions shall have effect notwithstanding any enactment or rule of law prohibiting or restricting the disclosure, or authorising the withholding, of information.

National security

28(1) Personal data are exempt from any of the provisions of–

    (a)   the data protection principles,

    (b)   Parts II, III and V, and

    (c)   sections 54A and 55,

if the exemption from that provision is required for the purpose of safeguarding national security.

(2) Subject to subsection (4), a certificate signed by a Minister of the Crown certifying that exemption from all or any of the provisions mentioned in subsection (1) is or at any time was required for the purpose there mentioned in respect of any personal data shall be conclusive evidence of that fact.

(3) A certificate under subsection (2) may identify the personal data to which it applies by means of a general description and may be expressed to have prospective effect.

(4) Any person directly affected by the issuing of a certificate under subsection (2) may appeal to the Tribunal against the certificate.

(5) If on an appeal under subsection (4), the Tribunal finds that, applying the principles applied by the court on an application for judicial review, the Minister did not have reasonable grounds for issuing the certificate, the Tribunal may allow the appeal and quash the certificate.

(6) Where in any proceedings under or by virtue of this Act it is claimed by a data controller that a certificate under subsection (2) which identifies the personal data to which it applies by means of a general description applies to any personal data, any other party to the proceedings may appeal to the Tribunal on the ground that the certificate does not apply to the personal data in question and, subject to any determination under subsection (7), the certificate shall be conclusively presumed so to apply.

(7) On any appeal under subsection (6), the Tribunal may determine that the certificate does not so apply.

(8) A document purporting to be a certificate under subsection (2) shall be received in evidence and deemed to be such a certificate unless the contrary is proved.

(9) A document which purports to be certified by or on behalf of a Minister of the Crown as a true copy of a certificate issued by that Minister under subsection (2) shall in any legal proceedings be evidence (or, in Scotland, sufficient evidence) of that certificate.

(10) The power conferred by subsection (2) on a Minister of the Crown shall not be exercisable except by a Minister who is a member of the Cabinet or by the Attorney General or the Advocate General for Scotland.

(11) No power conferred by any provision of Part V may be exercised in relation to personal data which by virtue of this section are exempt from that provision.

(12) Schedule 6 shall have effect in relation to appeals under subsection (4) or (6) and the proceedings of the Tribunal in respect of any such appeal.

NOTES

Defined terms
"data controller": s 1(1) and (4) and 63(3)
"data protection principles": s 4 and Schedule 1

"Minister of the Crown": s 70(1)
"personal data" : s 1(1)
"the Tribunal": s 70(1)

Crime and taxation

29(1) Personal data processed for any of the following purposes–
    (a)   the prevention or detection of crime,
    (b)   the apprehension or prosecution of offenders, or
    (c)   the assessment or collection of any tax or duty or of any imposition of a similar nature,
are exempt from the first data protection principle (except to the extent to which it requires compliance with the conditions in Schedules 2 and 3) and section 7 in any case to the extent to which the application of those provisions to the data would be likely to prejudice any of the matters mentioned in this subsection.

(2) Personal data which–
    (a)   are processed for the purpose of discharging statutory functions, and
    (b)   consist of information obtained for such a purpose from a person who had it in his possession for any of the purposes mentioned in subsection (1),
are exempt from the subject information provisions to the same extent as personal data processed for any of the purposes mentioned in that subsection.

(3) Personal data are exempt from the non-disclosure provisions in any case in which–
    (a)   the disclosure is for any of the purposes mentioned in subsection (1), and
    (b)   the application of those provisions in relation to the disclosure would be likely to prejudice any of the matters mentioned in that subsection.

(4) Personal data in respect of which the data controller is a relevant authority and which–
    (a)   consist of a classification applied to the data subject as part of a system of risk assessment which is operated by that authority for either of the following purposes–
        (i)   the assessment or collection of any tax or duty or any imposition of a similar nature, or
        (ii)   the prevention or detection of crime, or apprehension or prosecution of offenders, where the offence concerned involves any unlawful claim for any payment out of, or any unlawful application of, public funds, and
    (b)   are processed for either of those purposes,
are exempt from section 7 to the extent to which the exemption is required in the interests of the operation of the system.

(5) In subsection (4)–

"public funds" includes funds provided by any EU institution;

"relevant authority" means–

    (a)   a government department,

    (b)   a local authority, or

    (c)   any other authority administering housing benefit or council tax benefit.

NOTES

Defined terms

"data": s 1(1)

"data controller": ss1(1) and (4) and 63(3)

"data subject": s 1(1)

"data protection principles": s 4 and Sch1

"disclosing": s 1(2)(b)

"government department": s 70(1)

"the non-disclosure provisions": s 27(3)

"personal data": s 1(1)

"processing": s 1(1) and para5 of Sch8

"public funds": s 29(5)

"relevant authority": s 29(5)

"the subject information provisions": s 27(2)

Health, education and social work

30(1)   The Secretary of State may by order exempt from the subject information provisions, or modify those provisions in relation to, personal data consisting of information as to the physical or mental health or condition of the data subject.

(2)   The Secretary of State may by order exempt from the subject information provisions, or modify those provisions in relation to–

    (a)   personal data in respect of which the data controller is the proprietor of, or a teacher at, a school, and which consist of information relating to persons who are or have been pupils at the school, or

    (b)   personal data in respect of which the data controller is an education authority in Scotland, and which consist of information relating to persons who are receiving, or have received, further education provided by the authority.

(3)   The Secretary of State may by order exempt from the subject information provisions, or modify those provisions in relation to, personal data of such other descriptions as may be specified in the order, being information–

    (a)   processed by government departments or local authorities or by voluntary organisations or other bodies designated by or under the order, and

    (b)   appearing to him to be processed in the course of, or for the purposes of, carrying out social work in relation to the data subject or other individuals;

but the Secretary of State shall not under this subsection confer any exemption or make any modification except so far as he considers that the application to the data of those provisions (or of those provisions without modification) would be likely to prejudice the carrying out of social work.

(4)   An order under this section may make different provision in relation to data consisting of information of different descriptions.

(5)   In this section–

"education authority" and "further education" have the same meaning as in the Education (Scotland) Act 1980 ("the 1980 Act"), and

"proprietor"–

    (a)   in relation to a school in England or Wales, has the same meaning as in the Education Act 1996,

    (b)   in relation to a school in Scotland, means–

        (ii)   in the case of an independent school, the proprietor within the meaning of the 1980 Act,

        (iii)   in the case of a grant-aided school, the managers within the meaning of the 1980 Act, and

        (iv)   in the case of a public school, the education authority within the meaning of the 1980 Act, and

(c) in relation to a school in Northern Ireland, has the same meaning as in the Education and Libraries (Northern Ireland) Order 1986 and includes, in the case of a controlled school, the Board of Governors of the school.

NOTES

Defined terms
"data": s 1(1)
"data controller": ss 1(1) and (4) and 63(3)
"data subject": s 1(1)
"educational record": Schedule 11, paragraph 1
"government department": s 70(1)
"health professional": s 69(1)
"personal data": s 1(1)
"processing": s 1(1)
"proprietor": s 30(5)
"pupil": s 70(1)
"school": s 70(1)

"teacher": s 70(1)
"the subject information provisions": s 27(2)

Subordinate legislation
Data Protection (Subject Access Modification) (Health) Order 2000, SI 2000/413.
Data Protection (Subject Access Modification) (Education) Order 2000, SI 2000/414.
Data Protection (Subject Access Modification) (Social Work) Order 2000, SI 2000/415.

Regulatory activity

31(1) Personal data processed for the purposes of discharging functions to which this subsection applies are exempt from the subject information provisions in any case to the extent to which the application of those provisions to the data would be likely to prejudice the proper discharge of those functions.

(2) Subsection (1) applies to any relevant function which is designed–
    (a) for protecting members of the public against–
        (i) financial loss due to dishonesty, malpractice or other seriously improper conduct by, or the unfitness or incompetence of, persons concerned in the provision of banking, insurance, investment or other financial services or in the management of bodies corporate,
        (ii) financial loss due to the conduct of discharged or undischarged bankrupts, or
        (iii) dishonesty, malpractice or other seriously improper conduct by, or the unfitness or incompetence of, persons authorised to carry on any profession or other activity,
    (b) for protecting charities or community interest companies against misconduct or mismanagement (whether by trustees, directors or other persons) in their administration,
    (c) for protecting the property of charities or community interest companies from loss or misapplication,
    (d) for the recovery of the property of charities or community interest companies,
    (e) for securing the health, safety and welfare of persons at work, or
    (f) for protecting persons other than persons at work against risk to health or safety arising out of or in connection with the actions of persons at work.

(3) In subsection (2) "relevant function" means–
    (a) any function conferred on any person by or under any enactment,
    (b) any function of the Crown, a Minister of the Crown or a government department, or
    (c) any other function which is of a public nature and is exercised in the public interest.

(4) Personal data processed for the purpose of discharging any function which–

(a)   is conferred by or under any enactment on–
    (i)   the Parliamentary Commissioner for Administration,
    (ii)   the Commission for Local Administration in England,
    (iii)   the Health Service Commissioner for England,
    (iv)   the Public Services Ombudsman for Wales,
    (v)   the Assembly Ombudsman for Northern Ireland.
    (vi)   the Northern Ireland Commissioner for Complaints, or
    (vii)   the Scottish Public Services Ombudsman, and
(b)   is designed for protecting members of the public against–
    (i)   maladministration by public bodies,
    (ii)   failures in services provided by public bodies, or
    (iii)   a failure of a public body to provide a service which it was a function of the body to provide,

are exempt from the subject information provisions in any case to the extent to which the application of those provisions to the data would be likely to prejudice the proper discharge of that function.

(4A)   Personal data processed for the purpose of discharging any function which is conferred by or under Part XVI of the Financial Services and Markets Act 2000 on the body established by the Financial Services Authority for the purposes of that Part are exempt from the subject information provisions in any case to the extent to which the application of those provisions to the data would be likely to prejudice the proper discharge of the function.

(4B)   Personal data processed for the purposes of discharging any function of the Legal Services Board are exempt from the subject information provisions in any case to the extent to which the application of those provisions to the data would be likely to prejudice the proper discharge of the function.

(4C)   Personal data processed for the purposes of the function of considering a complaint under the scheme established under Part 6 of the Legal Services Act 2007 (legal complaints) are exempt from the subject information provisions in any case to the extent to which the application of those provisions to the data would be likely to prejudice the proper discharge of the function.

(5)   Personal data processed for the purpose of discharging any function which–
(a)   is conferred by or under any enactment on the Office of Fair Trading, and
(b)   is designed–
    (i)   for protecting members of the public against conduct which may adversely affect their interests by persons carrying on a business,
    (ii)   for regulating agreements or conduct which have as their object or effect the prevention, restriction or distortion of competition in connection with any commercial activity, or
    (iii)   for regulating conduct on the part of one or more undertakings which amounts to the abuse of a dominant position in a market,

are exempt from the subject information provisions in any case to the extent to which the application of those provisions to the data would be likely to prejudice the proper discharge of that function.

(5A)   Personal data processed by a CPC enforcer for the purpose of discharging any function conferred on such a body by or under the CPC Regulation are exempt from the subject information provisions in any case to the extent to which the application of those provisions to the data would be likely to prejudice the proper discharge of that function.

(5B)   In subsection (5A)–
(a)   "CPC enforcer" has the meaning given to it in section 213(5A) of the

Enterprise Act 2002 but does not include the Office of Fair Trading;
    (b)   "CPC Regulation" has the meaning given to it in section 235A of that Act.

(6)   Personal data processed for the purpose of the function of considering a complaint under section 14 of the NHS Redress Act 2006, section 113(1) or (2) or 114(1) or (3) of the Health and Social Care (Community Health and Standards) Act 2003, or section 24D, 26 or 26ZB of the Children Act 1989, are exempt from the subject information provisions in any case to the extent to which the application of those provisions to the data would be likely to prejudice the proper discharge of that function.

(7)   Personal data processed for the purpose of discharging any function which is conferred by or under Part 3 of the Local Government Act 2000 on–
    (a)   the monitoring officer of a relevant authority,
    (b)   ..., or
    (c)   the Public Services Ombudsman for Wales,
are exempt from the subject information provisions in any case to the extent to which the application of those provisions to the data would be likely to prejudice the proper discharge of that function.

(8)   In subsection (7)–
    (a)   "relevant authority" has the meaning given by section 49(6) of the Local Government Act 2000, and
    (b)   any reference to the monitoring officer of a relevant authority, or to an ethical standards officer, has the same meaning as in Part 3 of that Act.

NOTES

Defined terms
"business": s 70(1)
"data": s 1(1)
"enactment": s 70(1)
"government department": s 70(1)

"Minister of the Crown": s 70(1)
"personal data": s 1(1)
"processing": s 1(1)
"relevant function": s 31(3)
"the subject information provisions": s 27(2)

Journalism, literature and art

32(1)   Personal data which are processed only for the special purposes are exempt from any provision to which this subsection relates if–
    (a)   the processing is undertaken with a view to the publication by any person of any journalistic, literary or artistic material,
    (b)   the data controller reasonably believes that, having regard in particular to the special importance of the public interest in freedom of expression, publication would be in the public interest, and
    (c)   the data controller reasonably believes that, in all the circumstances, compliance with that provision is incompatible with the special purposes.

(2)   Subsection (1) relates to the provisions of–
    (a)   the data protection principles except the seventh data protection principle,
    (b)   section 7,
    (c)   section 10,
    (d)   section 12, and
    (e)   section 14(1) to (3).

(3)   In considering for the purposes of subsection (1)(b) whether the belief of a data controller that publication would be in the public interest was or is a reasonable one, regard may be had to his compliance with any code of practice which–

(a) is relevant to the publication in question, and

(b) is designated by the Secretary of State by order for the purposes of this subsection.

(4) Where at any time ("the relevant time") in any proceedings against a data controller under section 7(9), 10(4), 12(8) or 14 or by virtue of section 13 the data controller claims, or it appears to the court, that any personal data to which the proceedings relate are being processed–

(a) only for the special purposes, and

(b) with a view to the publication by any person of any journalistic, literary or artistic material which, at the time twenty-four hours immediately before the relevant time, had not previously been published by the data controller,

the court shall stay the proceedings until either of the conditions in subsection (5) is met.

(5) Those conditions are–

(a) that a determination of the Commissioner under section 45 with respect to the data in question takes effect, or

(b) in a case where the proceedings were stayed on the making of a claim, that the claim is withdrawn.

(6) For the purposes of this Act "publish", in relation to journalistic, literary or artistic material, means make available to the public or any section of the public.

NOTES

Defined terms
"the Commissioner": s 70(1)
"data": s 1(1)
"data controller": ss1(1) and (4) and 63(3)
"data protection principles": s 4 and Sch1
"exempt manual data": Sch13, para1(4)
"personal data": s 1(1)
"processing": s 1(1)
"publish": s 32(6)

"relevant time": s 32(4)
"the special purposes": s 3

Subordinate legislation
Data Protection (Designated Codes of Practice) (No 2) Order 2000

Research, history and statistics

33(1) In this section–

"research purposes" includes statistical or historical purposes;

"the relevant conditions", in relation to any processing of personal data, means the conditions–

(a) that the data are not processed to support measures or decisions with respect to particular individuals, and

(b) that the data are not processed in such a way that substantial damage or substantial distress is, or is likely to be, caused to any data subject.

(2) For the purposes of the second data protection principle, the further processing of personal data only for research purposes in compliance with the relevant conditions is not to be regarded as incompatible with the purposes for which they were obtained.

(3) Personal data which are processed only for research purposes in compliance with the relevant conditions may, notwithstanding the fifth data protection principle, be kept indefinitely.

(4) Personal data which are processed only for research purposes are exempt from section 7 if–

(a) they are processed in compliance with the relevant conditions, and

(b) the results of the research or any resulting statistics are not made available in a form which identifies data subjects or any of them.

(5) For the purposes of subsections (2) to (4) personal data are not to be treated as processed otherwise than for research purposes merely because the data are disclosed–

 (a) to any person, for research purposes only,

 (b) to the data subject or a person acting on his behalf,

 (c) at the request, or with the consent, of the data subject or a person acting on his behalf, or

 (d) in circumstances in which the person making the disclosure has reasonable grounds for believing that the disclosure falls within paragraph (a), (b) or (c).

NOTES

Defined terms
"data": s 1(1)
"data protection principles": s 4 and Sch 1
"data subject": s 1(1)
"disclosing" (of personal data): s 1(2)(b)

"personal data": s 1(1)
"processing": s 1(1)
"relevant conditions": s 33(1)
"research purposes": s 33(1)

Manual data held by public authorities

33A(1) Personal data falling within paragraph (e) of the definition of "data" in section 1(1) are exempt from–

 (a) the first, second, third, fifth, seventh and eighth data protection principles,

 (b) the sixth data protection principle except so far as it relates to the rights conferred on data subjects by sections 7 and 14,

 (c) sections 10 to 12,

 (d) section 13, except so far as it relates to damage caused by a contravention of section 7 or of the fourth data protection principle and to any distress which is also suffered by reason of that contravention,

 (e) Part III, and

 (f) section 55.

(2) Personal data which fall within paragraph (e) of the definition of "data" in section 1(1) and relate to appointments or removals, pay, discipline, superannuation or other personnel matters, in relation to–

 (a) service in any of the armed forces of the Crown,

 (b) service in any office or employment under the Crown or under any public authority, or

 (c) service in any office or employment, or under any contract for services, in respect of which power to take action, or to determine or approve the action taken, in such matters is vested in Her Majesty, any Minister of the Crown, the National Assembly for Wales, any Northern Ireland Minister (within the meaning of the Freedom of Information Act 2000) or any public authority,

are also exempt from the remaining data protection principles and the remaining provisions of Part II.

NOTES

Defined terms
"data": s 1(1)
"data protection principles": s 4 and Sch 1

"data subject": s 1(1)
"personal data": s 1(1)
"public authority": FOIA s 3(1)

Information available to the public by or under enactment

34 Personal data are exempt from–

 (a) the subject information provisions,

 (b) the fourth data protection principle and section 14(1) to (3), and

(c)   the non-disclosure provisions,

if the data consist of information which the data controller is obliged by or under any enactment other than an enactment contained in the Freedom of Information Act 2000 to make available to the public, whether by publishing it, by making it available for inspection, or otherwise and whether gratuitously or on payment of a fee.

NOTES

Defined terms
"data": s 1(1)
"data controller": ss1(1) and (4) and 63(3)
"data protection principles": s 4 and Sch1

"enactment": s 70(1)
"the non-disclosure provisions": s 27(3)
"personal data": s 1(1)
"the subject information provisions": s 27(2)

Disclosures required by law or made in connection with legal proceedings etc

35(1)   Personal data are exempt from the non-disclosure provisions where the disclosure is required by or under any enactment, by any rule of law or by the order of a court.

(2)   Personal data are exempt from the non-disclosure provisions where the disclosure is necessary–

(a)   for the purpose of, or in connection with, any legal proceedings (including prospective legal proceedings), or

(b)   for the purpose of obtaining legal advice,

or is otherwise necessary for the purposes of establishing, exercising or defending legal rights.

NOTES

Defined terms
"disclosing": s 1(2)(b)
"enactment": s 70(1)
"the non-disclosure provisions": s 27(3)

"personal data": s 1(1)

Parliamentary privilege

35A   Personal data are exempt from–

(a)   the first data protection principle, except to the extent to which it requires compliance with the conditions in Schedules 2 and 3,

(b)   the second, third, fourth and fifth data protection principles,

(c)   section 7, and

(d)   sections 10 and 14(1) to (3),

if the exemption is required for the purpose of avoiding an infringement of the privileges of either House of Parliament.

NOTES

Defined terms
"data protection principles": s 4 and Sch1

"personal data": s 1(1)

Domestic purposes

36   Personal data processed by an individual only for the purposes of that individual's personal, family or household affairs (including recreational purposes) are exempt from the data protection principles and the provisions of Parts II and III.

NOTES

Defined terms
"data protection principles": s 4 and Sch1

"personal data": s 1(1)
"processing": s 1(1) Sch8, para5

Miscellaneous exemptions

37   Schedule 7 (which confers further miscellaneous exemptions) has effect.

Powers to make further exemptions by order

38(1) The Secretary of State may by order exempt from the subject information provisions personal data consisting of information the disclosure of which is prohibited or restricted by or under any enactment if and to the extent that he considers it necessary for the safeguarding of the interests of the data subject or the rights and freedoms of any other individual that the prohibition or restriction ought to prevail over those provisions.

(2) The Secretary of State may by order exempt from the non-disclosure provisions any disclosures of personal data made in circumstances specified in the order, if he considers the exemption is necessary for the safeguarding of the interests of the data subject or the rights and freedoms of any other individual.

NOTES

Defined terms
"data subject": s 1(1)
"disclosing": s 1(2)(b)
"enactment": s 70(1)
"the non-disclosure provisions": s 27(3)
"personal data": s 1(1)

"the subject information provisions": s 27(2)

Subordinate legislation
Data Protection (Miscellaneous Subject Access Exemptions) Order 2000, SI 2000/419.

Transitional relief
39 Schedule 8 (which confers transitional exemptions) has effect.

PART V
ENFORCEMENT

Enforcement notices
40(1) If the Commissioner is satisfied that a data controller has contravened or is contravening any of the data protection principles, the Commissioner may serve him with a notice (in this Act referred to as "an enforcement notice") requiring him, for complying with the principle or principles in question, to do either or both of the following–

(a) to take within such time as may be specified in the notice, or to refrain from taking after such time as may be so specified, such steps as are so specified, or

(b) to refrain from processing any personal data, or any personal data of a description specified in the notice, or to refrain from processing them for a purpose so specified or in a manner so specified, after such time as may be so specified.

(2) In deciding whether to serve an enforcement notice, the Commissioner shall consider whether the contravention has caused or is likely to cause any person damage or distress.

(3) An enforcement notice in respect of a contravention of the fourth data protection principle which requires the data controller to rectify, block, erase or destroy any inaccurate data may also require the data controller to rectify, block, erase or destroy any other data held by him and containing an expression of opinion which appears to the Commissioner to be based on the inaccurate data.

(4) An enforcement notice in respect of a contravention of the fourth data protection principle, in the case of data which accurately record information received or obtained by the data controller from the data subject or a third party, may require the data controller either–

(a) to rectify, block, erase or destroy any inaccurate data and any other data held by him and containing an expression of opinion as mentioned in subsection (3), or

(b)   to take such steps as are specified in the notice for securing compliance with the requirements specified in paragraph 7 of Part II of Schedule 1 and, if the Commissioner thinks fit, for supplementing the data with such statement of the true facts relating to the matters dealt with by the data as the Commissioner may approve.

(5)   Where–

(a)   an enforcement notice requires the data controller to rectify, block, erase or destroy any personal data, or

(b)   the Commissioner is satisfied that personal data which have been rectified, blocked, erased or destroyed had been processed in contravention of any of the data protection principles,

an enforcement notice may, if reasonably practicable, require the data controller to notify third parties to whom the data have been disclosed of the rectification, blocking, erasure or destruction; and in determining whether it is reasonably practicable to require such notification regard shall be had, in particular, to the number of persons who would have to be notified.

(6)   An enforcement notice must contain–

(a)   a statement of the data protection principle or principles which the Commissioner is satisfied have been or are being contravened and his reasons for reaching that conclusion, and

(b)   particulars of the rights of appeal conferred by section 48.

(7)   Subject to subsection (8), an enforcement notice must not require any of the provisions of the notice to be complied with before the end of the period within which an appeal can be brought against the notice and, if such an appeal is brought, the notice need not be complied with pending the determination or withdrawal of the appeal.

(8)   If by reason of special circumstances the Commissioner considers that an enforcement notice should be complied with as a matter of urgency he may include in the notice a statement to that effect and a statement of his reasons for reaching that conclusion; and in that event subsection (7) shall not apply but the notice must not require the provisions of the notice to be complied with before the end of the period of seven days beginning with the day on which the notice is served.

(9)   Notification regulations (as defined by section 16(2)) may make provision as to the effect of the service of an enforcement notice on any entry in the register maintained under section 19 which relates to the person on whom the notice is served.

(10)   This section has effect subject to section 46(1).

Cancellation of an enforcement notice

41(1)   If the Commissioner considers that all or any of the provisions of an enforcement notice need not be complied with in order to ensure compliance with the data protection principle or principles to which it relates, he may cancel or vary the notice by written notice to the person on whom it was served.

(2)   A person on whom an enforcement notice has been served may, at any time after the

expiry of the period during which an appeal can be brought against that notice, apply in writing to the Commissioner for the cancellation or variation of that notice on the ground that, by reason of a change of circumstances, all or any of the provisions of that notice need not be complied with in order to ensure compliance with the data protection principle or principles to which that notice relates.

NOTES

Defined terms

"the Commissioner": s 70(1)

"data protection principles": s 4 and Sch 1

"enforcement notice": s 40(1)

Assessment notices

41A(1)   The Commissioner may serve a data controller within subsection (2) with a notice (in this Act referred to as an "assessment notice") for the purpose of enabling the Commissioner to determine whether the data controller has complied or is complying with the data protection principles.

(2)   A data controller is within this subsection if the data controller is–

    (a)   a government department,

    (b)   a public authority designated for the purposes of this section by an order made by the Secretary of State, or

    (c)   a person of a description designated for the purposes of this section by such an order.

(3)   An assessment notice is a notice which requires the data controller to do all or any of the following–

    (a)   permit the Commissioner to enter any specified premises;

    (b)   direct the Commissioner to any documents on the premises that are of a specified description;

    (c)   assist the Commissioner to view any information of a specified description that is capable of being viewed using equipment on the premises;

    (d)   comply with any request from the Commissioner for–

        (i)   a copy of any of the documents to which the Commissioner is directed;

        (ii)   a copy (in such form as may be requested) of any of the information which the Commissioner is assisted to view;

    (e)   direct the Commissioner to any equipment or other material on the premises which is of a specified description;

    (f)   permit the Commissioner to inspect or examine any of the documents, information, equipment or material to which the Commissioner is directed or which the Commissioner is assisted to view;

    (g)   permit the Commissioner to observe the processing of any personal data that takes place on the premises;

    (h)   make available for interview by the Commissioner a specified number of persons of a specified description who process personal data on behalf of the data controller (or such number as are willing to be interviewed).

(4)   In subsection (3) references to the Commissioner include references to the Commissioner's officers and staff.

(5)   An assessment notice must, in relation to each requirement imposed by the notice, specify–

    (a)   the time at which the requirement is to be complied with, or

    (b)   the period during which the requirement is to be complied with.

(6)   An assessment notice must also contain particulars of the rights of appeal conferred by

section 48.

(7) The Commissioner may cancel an assessment notice by written notice to the data controller on whom it was served.

(8) Where a public authority has been designated by an order under subsection (2)(b) the Secretary of State must reconsider, at intervals of no greater than 5 years, whether it continues to be appropriate for the authority to be designated.

(9) The Secretary of State may not make an order under subsection (2)(c) which designates a description of persons unless–

    (a)   the Commissioner has made a recommendation that the description be designated, and

    (b)   the Secretary of State has consulted–

        (i)   such persons as appear to the Secretary of State to represent the interests of those that meet the description;

        (ii)   such other persons as the Secretary of State considers appropriate.

(10) The Secretary of State may not make an order under subsection (2)(c), and the Commissioner may not make a recommendation under subsection (9)(a), unless the Secretary of State or (as the case may be) the Commissioner is satisfied that it is necessary for the description of persons in question to be designated having regard to–

    (a)   the nature and quantity of data under the control of such persons, and

    (b)   any damage or distress which may be caused by a contravention by such persons of the data protection principles.

(11) Where a description of persons has been designated by an order under subsection (2)(c) the Secretary of State must reconsider, at intervals of no greater than 5 years, whether it continues to be necessary for the description to be designated having regard to the matters mentioned in subsection (10).

(12) In this section–

"public authority" includes any body, office-holder or other person in respect of which–

    (a)   an order may be made under section 4 or 5 of the Freedom of Information Act 2000, or

    (b)   an order may be made under section 4 or 5 of the Freedom of Information (Scotland) Act 2002;

"specified" means specified in an assessment notice.

NOTES

Defined terms
  "business": s 70(1)
  "the Commissioner": s 70(1)
  "data": s 1(1)
  "data controller": s 1(1)

"data protection principles": s 4 and Sch 1
"government department": s 70(1)
"personal data": s 1(1)
"processing": s 1(1)

Assessment notices: limitations

41B(1) A time specified in an assessment notice under section 41A(5) in relation to a requirement must not fall, and a period so specified must not begin, before the end of the period within which an appeal can be brought against the notice, and if such an appeal is brought the requirement need not be complied with pending the determination or withdrawal of the appeal.

(2) If by reason of special circumstances the Commissioner considers that it is necessary for the data controller to comply with a requirement in an assessment notice as a matter of urgency, the Commissioner may include in the notice a statement to that effect and a statement of the reasons for that conclusion; and in that event subsection (1) applies in

912

relation to the requirement as if for the words from "within" to the end there were substituted "of 7 days beginning with the day on which the notice is served".

(3) A requirement imposed by an assessment notice does not have effect in so far as compliance with it would result in the disclosure of–

    (a) any communication between a professional legal adviser and the adviser's client in connection with the giving of legal advice with respect to the client's obligations, liabilities or rights under this Act, or

    (b) any communication between a professional legal adviser and the adviser's client, or between such an adviser or the adviser's client and any other person, made in connection with or in contemplation of proceedings under or arising out of this Act (including proceedings before the Tribunal) and for the purposes of such proceedings.

(4) In subsection (3) references to the client of a professional legal adviser include references to any person representing such a client.

(5) Nothing in section 41A authorises the Commissioner to serve an assessment notice on–

    (a) a judge,

    (b) a body specified in section 23(3) of the Freedom of Information Act 2000 (bodies dealing with security matters), or

    (c) the Office for Standards in Education, Children's Services and Skills in so far as it is a data controller in respect of information processed for the purposes of functions exercisable by Her Majesty's Chief Inspector of Education, Children's Services and Skills by virtue of section 5(1)(a) of the Care Standards Act 2000.

(6) In this section "judge" includes–

    (a) a justice of the peace (or, in Northern Ireland, a lay magistrate),

    (b) a member of a tribunal, and

    (c) a clerk or other officer entitled to exercise the jurisdiction of a court or tribunal;

and in this subsection "tribunal" means any tribunal in which legal proceedings may be brought.

NOTES

Defined terms

"assessment notice": s 41A(1)
"the Commissioner": s 70(1)
"data": s 1(1)

"data controller": s 1(1)
"government department": s 70(1)
"personal data": s 1(1)
"processing": s 1(1)

Code of practice about assessment notices

41C(1) The Commissioner must prepare and issue a code of practice as to the manner in which the Commissioner's functions under and in connection with section 41A are to be exercised.

(2) The code must in particular–

    (a) specify factors to be considered in determining whether to serve an assessment notice on a data controller;

    (b) specify descriptions of documents and information that–

        (i) are not to be examined or inspected in pursuance of an assessment notice, or

        (ii) are to be so examined or inspected only by persons of a description specified in the code;

      (c)   deal with the nature of inspections and examinations carried out in pursuance of an assessment notice;

      (d)   deal with the nature of interviews carried out in pursuance of an assessment notice;

      (e)   deal with the preparation, issuing and publication by the Commissioner of assessment reports in respect of data controllers that have been served with assessment notices.

(3)   The provisions of the code made by virtue of subsection (2)(b) must, in particular, include provisions that relate to–

      (a)   documents and information concerning an individual's physical or mental health;

      (b)   documents and information concerning the provision of social care for an individual.

(4)   An assessment report is a report which contains–

      (a)   a determination as to whether a data controller has complied or is complying with the data protection principles,

      (b)   recommendations as to any steps which the data controller ought to take, or refrain from taking, to ensure compliance with any of those principles, and

      (c)   such other matters as are specified in the code.

(5)   The Commissioner may alter or replace the code.

(6)   If the code is altered or replaced, the Commissioner must issue the altered or replacement code.

(7)   The Commissioner may not issue the code (or an altered or replacement code) without the approval of the Secretary of State.

(8)   The Commissioner must arrange for the publication of the code (and any altered or replacement code) issued under this section in such form and manner as the Commissioner considers appropriate.

(9)   In this section "social care" has the same meaning as in Part 1 of the Health and Social Care Act 2008 (see section 9(3) of that Act).

NOTES

Request for assessment

42(1)   A request may be made to the Commissioner by or on behalf of any person who is, or believes himself to be, directly affected by any processing of personal data for an assessment as to whether it is likely or unlikely that the processing has been or is being carried out in compliance with the provisions of this Act.

(2)   On receiving a request under this section, the Commissioner shall make an assessment in such manner as appears to him to be appropriate, unless he has not been supplied with such information as he may reasonably require in order to–

      (a)   satisfy himself as to the identity of the person making the request, and

      (b)   enable him to identify the processing in question.

(3)   The matters to which the Commissioner may have regard in determining in what manner it is appropriate to make an assessment include–

      (a)   the extent to which the request appears to him to raise a matter of substance,

      (b)   any undue delay in making the request, and

      (c)   whether or not the person making the request is entitled to make an application under section 7 in respect of the personal data in question.

(4) Where the Commissioner has received a request under this section he shall notify the person who made the request–

    (a) whether he has made an assessment as a result of the request, and

    (b) to the extent that he considers appropriate, having regard in particular to any exemption from section 7 applying in relation to the personal data concerned, of any view formed or action taken as a result of the request.

Information notices

43(1) If the Commissioner–

    (a) has received a request under section 42 in respect of any processing of personal data, or

    (b) reasonably requires any information for the purpose of determining whether the data controller has complied or is complying with the data protection principles,

he may serve the data controller with a notice (in this Act referred to as "an information notice") requiring the data controller, within such time as is specified in the notice, to furnish the Commissioner, in such form as may be so specified, with such information relating to the request or to compliance with the principles as is so specified to furnish the Commissioner with specified information relating to the request or to compliance with the principles.

(1A) In subsection (1) "specified information" means information–

    (a) specified, or described, in the information notice, or

    (b) falling within a category which is specified, or described, in the information notice.

(1B) The Commissioner may also specify in the information notice–

    (a) the form in which the information must be furnished;

    (b) the period within which, or the time and place at which, the information must be furnished.

(2) An information notice must contain–

    (a) in a case falling within subsection (1)(a), a statement that the Commissioner has received a request under section 42 in relation to the specified processing, or

    (b) in a case falling within subsection (1)(b), a statement that the Commissioner regards the specified information as relevant for the purpose of determining whether the data controller has complied, or is complying, with the data protection principles and his reasons for regarding it as relevant for that purpose.

(3) An information notice must also contain particulars of the rights of appeal conferred by section 48.

(4) Subject to subsection (5), the time specified in an information notice shall not expire a period specified in an information notice under subsection (1B)(b) must not end, and a time so specified must not fall, before the end of the period within which an appeal can be

brought against the notice and, if such an appeal is brought, the information need not be furnished pending the determination or withdrawal of the appeal.

(5) If by reason of special circumstances the Commissioner considers that the information is required as a matter of urgency, he may include in the notice a statement to that effect and a statement of his reasons for reaching that conclusion; and in that event subsection (4) shall not apply, but the notice shall not require the information to be furnished before the end of the period of seven days beginning with the day on which the notice is served.

(6) A person shall not be required by virtue of this section to furnish the Commissioner with any information in respect of–

    (a) any communication between a professional legal adviser and his client in connection with the giving of legal advice to the client with respect to his obligations, liabilities or rights under this Act, or

    (b) any communication between a professional legal adviser and his client, or between such an adviser or his client and any other person, made in connection with or in contemplation of proceedings under or arising out of this Act (including proceedings before the Tribunal) and for the purposes of such proceedings.

(7) In subsection (6) references to the client of a professional legal adviser include references to any person representing such a client.

(8) A person shall not be required by virtue of this section to furnish the Commissioner with any information if the furnishing of that information would, by revealing evidence of the commission of any offence other than an offence under this Act, , other than an offence under this Act or an offence within subsection (8A), expose him to proceedings for that offence.

(8A) The offences mentioned in subsection (8) are–

    (a) an offence under section 5 of the Perjury Act 1911 (false statements made otherwise than on oath),

    (b) an offence under section 44(2) of the Criminal Law (Consolidation) (Scotland) Act 1995 (false statements made otherwise than on oath), or

    (c) an offence under Article 10 of the Perjury (Northern Ireland) Order 1979 (false statutory declarations and other false unsworn statements).

(8B) Any relevant statement provided by a person in response to a requirement under this section may not be used in evidence against that person on a prosecution for any offence under this Act (other than an offence under section 47) unless in the proceedings–

    (a) in giving evidence the person provides information inconsistent with it, and

    (b) evidence relating to it is adduced, or a question relating to it is asked, by that person or on that person's behalf.

(8C) In subsection (8B) "relevant statement", in relation to a requirement under this section, means–

    (a) an oral statement, or

    (b) a written statement made for the purposes of the requirement.

(9) The Commissioner may cancel an information notice by written notice to the person on whom it was served.

(10) This section has effect subject to section 46(3).

NOTES

Defined terms
"the Commissioner": s 70(1)
"data controller": ss1(1) and (4) and 63(3)

"data protection principles": s 4 and Sch1
"information notice": s 43(1)
"personal data": s 1(1)

Special information notices

44   If the Commissioner–

> (a)   has received a request under section 42 in respect of any processing of personal data, or
>
> (b)   has reasonable grounds for suspecting that, in a case in which proceedings have been stayed under section 32, the personal data to which the proceedings relate–
>
>> (i)   are not being processed only for the special purposes, or
>>
>> (ii)   are not being processed with a view to the publication by any person of any journalistic, literary or artistic material which has not previously been published by the data controller,

he may serve the data controller with a notice (in this Act referred to as a "special information notice") requiring the data controller, within such time as is specified in the notice, to furnish the Commissioner, in such form as may be so specified, with such information as is so specified for the purpose specified in subsection (2) to furnish the Commissioner with specified information for the purpose specified in subsection (2).

(1A)   In subsection (1) "specified information" means information–

> (a)   specified, or described, in the special information notice, or
>
> (b)   falling within a category which is specified, or described, in the special information notice.

(1B)   The Commissioner may also specify in the special information notice–

> (a)   the form in which the information must be furnished;
>
> (b)   the period within which, or the time and place at which, the information must be furnished.

(2)   That purpose is the purpose of ascertaining–

> (a)   whether the personal data are being processed only for the special purposes, or
>
> (b)   whether they are being processed with a view to the publication by any person of any journalistic, literary or artistic material which has not previously been published by the data controller.

(3)   A special information notice must contain–

> (a)   in a case falling within paragraph (a) of subsection (1), a statement that the Commissioner has received a request under section 42 in relation to the specified processing, or
>
> (b)   in a case falling within paragraph (b) of that subsection, a statement of the Commissioner's grounds for suspecting that the personal data are not being processed as mentioned in that paragraph.

(4)   A special information notice must also contain particulars of the rights of appeal conferred by section 48.

(5)   Subject to subsection (6), the time specified in a special information notice shall not expire a period specified in a special information notice under subsection (1B)(b) must not end, and a time so specified must not fall, before the end of the period within which an appeal can be brought against the notice and, if such an appeal is brought, the information need not be furnished pending the determination or withdrawal of the appeal.

(6) If by reason of special circumstances the Commissioner considers that the information is required as a matter of urgency, he may include in the notice a statement to that effect and a statement of his reasons for reaching that conclusion; and in that event subsection (5) shall not apply, but the notice shall not require the information to be furnished before the end of the period of seven days beginning with the day on which the notice is served.

(7) A person shall not be required by virtue of this section to furnish the Commissioner with any information in respect of–

    (a)   any communication between a professional legal adviser and his client in connection with the giving of legal advice to the client with respect to his obligations, liabilities or rights under this Act, or

    (b)   any communication between a professional legal adviser and his client, or between such an adviser or his client and any other person, made in connection with or in contemplation of proceedings under or arising out of this Act (including proceedings before the Tribunal) and for the purposes of such proceedings.

(8) In subsection (7) references to the client of a professional legal adviser include references to any person representing such a client.

(9) A person shall not be required by virtue of this section to furnish the Commissioner with any information if the furnishing of that information would, by revealing evidence of the commission of any offence other than an offence under this Act, , other than an offence under this Act or an offence within subsection (9A), expose him to proceedings for that offence.

(9A) The offences mentioned in subsection (9) are–

    (a)   an offence under section 5 of the Perjury Act 1911 (false statements made otherwise than on oath),

    (b)   an offence under section 44(2) of the Criminal Law (Consolidation) (Scotland) Act 1995 (false statements made otherwise than on oath), or

    (c)   an offence under Article 10 of the Perjury (Northern Ireland) Order 1979 (false statutory declarations and other false unsworn statements).

(9B) Any relevant statement provided by a person in response to a requirement under this section may not be used in evidence against that person on a prosecution for any offence under this Act (other than an offence under section 47) unless in the proceedings–

    (a)   in giving evidence the person provides information inconsistent with it, and

    (b)   evidence relating to it is adduced, or a question relating to it is asked, by that person or on that person's behalf.

(9C) In subsection (9B) "relevant statement", in relation to a requirement under this section, means–

    (a)   an oral statement, or

    (b)   a written statement made for the purposes of the requirement.

(10) The Commissioner may cancel a special information notice by written notice to the person on whom it was served.

NOTES

Defined terms
"the Commissioner": s 70(1)
"data controller": ss1(1) and (4) and 63(3)
"personal data": s 1(1)
"processing": s 1(1)

"publish": s 32(6)
"special information notice": s 44(1)
"the special purposes": s 3
"the Tribunal": s 70(1)

Determination by Commissioner as to the special purposes

45(1)   Where at any time it appears to the Commissioner (whether as a result of the service of a special information notice or otherwise) that any personal data–

    (a)   are not being processed only for the special purposes, or

    (b)   are not being processed with a view to the publication by any person of any journalistic, literary or artistic material which has not previously been published by the data controller,

he may make a determination in writing to that effect.

(2)   Notice of the determination shall be given to the data controller; and the notice must contain particulars of the right of appeal conferred by section 48.

(3)   A determination under subsection (1) shall not take effect until the end of the period within which an appeal can be brought and, where an appeal is brought, shall not take effect pending the determination or withdrawal of the appeal.

NOTES

Defined terms
  "the Commissioner": s 70(1)
  "data controller": ss 1(1) and (4) and 63(3)
  "personal data": s 1(1)

  "processing": s 1(1)
  "publish": s 32(6)
  "special information notice": s 44(1)
  "the special purposes": s 3

Restriction on enforcement in case of processing for the special purposes

46(1)   The Commissioner may not at any time serve an enforcement notice on a data controller with respect to the processing of personal data for the special purposes unless–

    (a)   a determination under section 45(1) with respect to those data has taken effect, and

    (b)   the court has granted leave for the notice to be served.

(2)   The court shall not grant leave for the purposes of subsection (1)(b) unless it is satisfied–

    (a)   that the Commissioner has reason to suspect a contravention of the data protection principles which is of substantial public importance, and

    (b)   except where the case is one of urgency, that the data controller has been given notice, in accordance with rules of court, of the application for leave.

(3)   The Commissioner may not serve an information notice on a data controller with respect to the processing of personal data for the special purposes unless a determination under section 45(1) with respect to those data has taken effect.

NOTES

Defined terms
  "the Commissioner": s 70(1)
  "data controller": ss 1(1) and (4) and 63(3)
  "data protection principles": s 4 and Sch 1
  "enforcement notice": s 40(1)

  "information notice": s 43(1)
  "personal data": s 1(1)
  "processing": s 1(1)
  "the special purposes": s 3

Failure to comply with notice

47(1)   A person who fails to comply with an enforcement notice, an information notice or a special information notice is guilty of an offence.

(2)   A person who, in purported compliance with an information notice or a special information notice–

    (a)   makes a statement which he knows to be false in a material respect, or

    (b)   recklessly makes a statement which is false in a material respect,

is guilty of an offence.

(3) It is a defence for a person charged with an offence under subsection (1) to prove that he exercised all due diligence to comply with the notice in question.

NOTES

Defined terms
"enforcement notice": s 40(1)

"information notice": s 43(1)
"special information notice": s 44(1)

Rights of appeal

48(1) A person on whom an enforcement notice, an assessment notice, an information notice or a special information notice has been served may appeal to the Tribunal against the notice.

(2) A person on whom an enforcement notice has been served may appeal to the Tribunal against the refusal of an application under section 41(2) for cancellation or variation of the notice.

(3) Where an enforcement notice, an assessment notice, an information notice or a special information notice contains a statement by the Commissioner in accordance with section 40(8), 41B(2), 43(5) or 44(6) then, whether or not the person appeals against the notice, he may appeal against–
    (a) the Commissioner's decision to include the statement in the notice, or
    (b) the effect of the inclusion of the statement as respects any part of the notice.

(4) A data controller in respect of whom a determination has been made under section 45 may appeal to the Tribunal against the determination.

(5) Schedule 6 has effect in relation to appeals under this section and the proceedings of the Tribunal in respect of any such appeal.

NOTES

Defined terms
"assessment notice": s 41A(1)
"the Commissioner": s 70(1)
"enforcement notice": s 40(1)

"information notice": s 43(1)
"special information notice": s 44(1)
"the Tribunal": s 70(1)

Determination of appeals

49(1) If on an appeal under section 48(1) the Tribunal considers–
    (a) that the notice against which the appeal is brought is not in accordance with the law, or
    (b) to the extent that the notice involved an exercise of discretion by the Commissioner, that he ought to have exercised his discretion differently,
the Tribunal shall allow the appeal or substitute such other notice or decision as could have been served or made by the Commissioner; and in any other case the Tribunal shall dismiss the appeal.

(2) On such an appeal, the Tribunal may review any determination of fact on which the notice in question was based.

(3) If on an appeal under section 48(2) the Tribunal considers that the enforcement notice ought to be cancelled or varied by reason of a change in circumstances, the Tribunal shall cancel or vary the notice.

(4) On an appeal under subsection (3) of section 48 the Tribunal may direct–
    (a) that the notice in question shall have effect as if it did not contain any such statement as is mentioned in that subsection, or
    (b) that the inclusion of the statement shall not have effect in relation to any part of the notice,
and may make such modifications in the notice as may be required for giving effect to the direction.

(5) On an appeal under section 48(4), the Tribunal may cancel the determination of the Commissioner.

NOTES

Defined terms
"address": s 49(7)
"the Commissioner": s 70(1)

"enforcement notice": s 40(1)
"the Tribunal": s 70(1)

Powers of entry and inspection

50 Schedule 9 (powers of entry and inspection) has effect.

PART VI
MISCELLANEOUS AND GENERAL

Functions of Commissioner

General duties of Commissioner

51(1) It shall be the duty of the Commissioner to promote the following of good practice by data controllers and, in particular, so to perform his functions under this Act as to promote the observance of the requirements of this Act by data controllers.

(2) The Commissioner shall arrange for the dissemination in such form and manner as he considers appropriate of such information as it may appear to him expedient to give to the public about the operation of this Act, about good practice, and about other matters within the scope of his functions under this Act, and may give advice to any person as to any of those matters.

(3) Where–

    (a)   the Secretary of State so directs by order, or

    (b)   the Commissioner considers it appropriate to do so,

the Commissioner shall, after such consultation with trade associations, data subjects or persons representing data subjects as appears to him to be appropriate, prepare and disseminate to such persons as he considers appropriate codes of practice for guidance as to good practice.

(4) The Commissioner shall also–

    (a)   where he considers it appropriate to do so, encourage trade associations to prepare, and to disseminate to their members, such codes of practice, and

    (b)   where any trade association submits a code of practice to him for his consideration, consider the code and, after such consultation with data subjects or persons representing data subjects as appears to him to be appropriate, notify the trade association whether in his opinion the code promotes the following of good practice.

(5) An order under subsection (3) shall describe the personal data or processing to which the code of practice is to relate, and may also describe the persons or classes of persons to whom it is to relate.

(5A) In determining the action required to discharge the duties imposed by subsections (1) to (4), the Commissioner may take account of any action taken to discharge the duty imposed by section 52A (data-sharing code).

(6) The Commissioner shall arrange for the dissemination in such form and manner as he

considers appropriate of–

    (a)   any Community finding as defined by paragraph 15(2) of Part II of Schedule 1,

    (b)   any decision of the European Commission, under the procedure provided for in Article 31(2) of the Data Protection Directive, which is made for the purposes of Article 26(3) or (4) of the Directive, and

    (c)   such other information as it may appear to him to be expedient to give to data controllers in relation to any personal data about the protection of the rights and freedoms of data subjects in relation to the processing of personal data in countries and territories outside the European Economic Area.

(7) The Commissioner may, with the consent of the data controller, assess any processing of personal data for the following of good practice and shall inform the data controller of the results of the assessment.

(8) The Commissioner may charge such sums as he may with the consent of the Secretary of State determine for any services provided by the Commissioner by virtue of this Part.

(9) In this section–

"good practice" means such practice in the processing of personal data as appears to the Commissioner to be desirable having regard to the interests of data subjects and others, and includes (but is not limited to) compliance with the requirements of this Act;

"trade association" includes any body representing data controllers.

NOTES

Defined terms
  "Commissioner": s 70(1)
  "data controller": ss1(1) and (4) and 63(3)
  "Data Protection Directive": s 70(1)
  "data subject": s 1(1)

  "good practice": s 51(a)
  "personal data": s 1(1)
  "processing": s 1(1)
  "trade association": s 51(a)

Reports and codes of practice to be laid before Parliament

52(1) The Commissioner shall lay annually before each House of Parliament a general report on the exercise of his functions under this Act.

(2) The Commissioner may from time to time lay before each House of Parliament such other reports with respect to those functions as he thinks fit.

(3) The Commissioner shall lay before each House of Parliament any code of practice prepared under section 51(3) for complying with a direction of the Secretary of State, unless the code is included in any report laid under subsection (1) or (2).

NOTES

Defined terms
  "Commissioner": s 70(1)

Data-sharing code

52A(1) The Commissioner must prepare a code of practice which contains–

    (a)   practical guidance in relation to the sharing of personal data in accordance with the requirements of this Act, and

    (b)   such other guidance as the Commissioner considers appropriate to promote good practice in the sharing of personal data.

(2) For this purpose "good practice" means such practice in the sharing of personal data as appears to the Commissioner to be desirable having regard to the interests of data subjects and others, and includes (but is not limited to) compliance with the requirements of this Act.

(3) Before a code is prepared under this section, the Commissioner must consult such of the following as the Commissioner considers appropriate–

    (a)   trade associations (within the meaning of section 51);

    (b)   data subjects;

    (c)   persons who appear to the Commissioner to represent the interests of data subjects.

(4) In this section a reference to the sharing of personal data is to the disclosure of the data by transmission, dissemination or otherwise making it available.

NOTES

Defined terms

"Commissioner": s 70(1)

"data controller": ss1(1) and (4) and 63(3)

"Data Protection Directive": s 70(1)

"data subject": s 1(1)

"personal data": s 1(1)

"processing": s 1(1)

"trade association": s 51(a)

Data-sharing code: procedure

52B(1) When a code is prepared under section 52A, it must be submitted to the Secretary of State for approval.

(2) Approval may be withheld only if it appears to the Secretary of State that the terms of the code could result in the United Kingdom being in breach of any of its Community obligations or any other international obligation.

(3) The Secretary of State must–

    (a)   if approval is withheld, publish details of the reasons for withholding it;

    (b)   if approval is granted, lay the code before Parliament.

(4) If, within the 40-day period, either House of Parliament resolves not to approve the code, the code is not to be issued by the Commissioner.

(5) If no such resolution is made within that period, the Commissioner must issue the code.

(6) Where–

    (a)   the Secretary of State withholds approval, or

    (b)   such a resolution is passed,

the Commissioner must prepare another code of practice under section 52A.

(7) Subsection (4) does not prevent a new code being laid before Parliament.

(8) A code comes into force at the end of the period of 21 days beginning with the day on which it is issued.

(9) A code may include transitional provision or savings.

(10) In this section "the 40-day period" means the period of 40 days beginning with the day on which the code is laid before Parliament (or, if it is not laid before each House of Parliament on the same day, the later of the 2 days on which it is laid).

(11) In calculating the 40-day period, no account is to be taken of any period during which Parliament is dissolved or prorogued or during which both Houses are adjourned for more than 4 days.

NOTES

Defined terms

"Commissioner": s 70(1)

Alteration or replacement of data-sharing code

52C(1) The Commissioner–

    (a)   must keep the data-sharing code under review, and

    (b)   may prepare an alteration to that code or a replacement code.

(2) Where, by virtue of a review under subsection (1)(a) or otherwise, the Commissioner becomes aware that the terms of the code could result in the United Kingdom being in breach of any of its Community obligations or any other international obligation, the Commissioner must exercise the power under subsection (1)(b) with a view to remedying the situation.

(3) Before an alteration or replacement code is prepared under subsection (1), the Commissioner must consult such of the following as the Commissioner considers appropriate–

    (a)   trade associations (within the meaning of section 51);

    (b)   data subjects;

    (c)   persons who appear to the Commissioner to represent the interests of data subjects.

(4) Section 52B (other than subsection (6)) applies to an alteration or replacement code prepared under this section as it applies to the code as first prepared under section 52A.

(5) In this section "the data-sharing code" means the code issued under section 52B(5) (as altered or replaced from time to time).

NOTES

Defined terms

  "Commissioner": s 70(1)

  "data controller": ss1(1) and (4) and 63(3)

  "data subject": s 1(1)

"personal data": s 1(1)

"processing": s 1(1)

"trade association": s 51(a)

Publication of data-sharing code

52D(1) The Commissioner must publish the code (and any replacement code) issued under section 52B(5).

(2) Where an alteration is so issued, the Commissioner must publish either–

    (a)   the alteration, or

    (b)   the code or replacement code as altered by it.

NOTES

Defined terms

  "Commissioner": s 70(1)

Effect of data-sharing code

52E(1) A failure on the part of any person to act in accordance with any provision of the data-sharing code does not of itself render that person liable to any legal proceedings in any court or tribunal.

(2) The data-sharing code is admissible in evidence in any legal proceedings.

(3) If any provision of the data-sharing code appears to–

    (a)   the Tribunal or a court conducting any proceedings under this Act,

    (b)   a court or tribunal conducting any other legal proceedings, or

    (c)   the Commissioner carrying out any function under this Act,

to be relevant to any question arising in the proceedings, or in connection with the exercise of that jurisdiction or the carrying out of those functions, in relation to any time when it was in force, that provision of the code must be taken into account in determining that question.

(4)   In this section "the data-sharing code" means the code issued under section 52B(5) (as altered or replaced from time to time).

NOTES

Defined terms
"Commissioner": s 70(1)

"the Tribunal": s 70(1)

Assistance by Commissioner in cases involving processing for the special purposes

53(1)   An individual who is an actual or prospective party to any proceedings under section 7(9), 10(4), 12(8) or 14 or by virtue of section 13 which relate to personal data processed for the special purposes may apply to the Commissioner for assistance in relation to those proceedings.

(2)   The Commissioner shall, as soon as reasonably practicable after receiving an application under subsection (1), consider it and decide whether and to what extent to grant it, but he shall not grant the application unless, in his opinion, the case involves a matter of substantial public importance.

(3)   If the Commissioner decides to provide assistance, he shall, as soon as reasonably practicable after making the decision, notify the applicant, stating the extent of the assistance to be provided.

(4)   If the Commissioner decides not to provide assistance, he shall, as soon as reasonably practicable after making the decision, notify the applicant of his decision and, if he thinks fit, the reasons for it.

(5)   In this section–
  (a)   references to "proceedings" include references to prospective proceedings, and
  (b)   "applicant", in relation to assistance under this section, means an individual who applies for assistance.

(6)   Schedule 10 has effect for supplementing this section.

NOTES

Defined terms
"applicant": s 53(5)(b)
"Commissioner": s 70(1)
"personal data": s 1(1)

"proceedings": s 53(5)
"special purposes": s 3

International co-operation

54(1)   The Commissioner–
  (a)   shall continue to be the designated authority in the United Kingdom for the purposes of Article 13 of the Convention, and
  (b)   shall be the supervisory authority in the United Kingdom for the purposes of the Data Protection Directive.

(2)   The Secretary of State may by order make provision as to the functions to be discharged by the Commissioner as the designated authority in the United Kingdom for the purposes of Article 13 of the Convention.

(3)   The Secretary of State may by order make provision as to co-operation by the Commissioner with the European Commission and with supervisory authorities in other EEA States in connection with the performance of their respective duties and, in particular,

as to–

    (a)   the exchange of information with supervisory authorities in other EEA States or with the European Commission, and

    (b)   the exercise within the United Kingdom at the request of a supervisory authority in another EEA State, in cases excluded by section 5 from the application of the other provisions of this Act, of functions of the Commissioner specified in the order.

(4)   The Commissioner shall also carry out any data protection functions which the Secretary of State may by order direct him to carry out for the purpose of enabling Her Majesty's Government in the United Kingdom to give effect to any international obligations of the United Kingdom.

(5)   The Commissioner shall, if so directed by the Secretary of State, provide any authority exercising data protection functions under the law of a colony specified in the direction with such assistance in connection with the discharge of those functions as the Secretary of State may direct or approve, on such terms (including terms as to payment) as the Secretary of State may direct or approve.

(6)   Where the European Commission makes a decision for the purposes of Article 26(3) or (4) of the Data Protection Directive under the procedure provided for in Article 31(2) of the Directive, the Commissioner shall comply with that decision in exercising his functions under paragraph 9 of Schedule 4 or, as the case may be, paragraph 8 of that Schedule.

(7)   The Commissioner shall inform the European Commission and the supervisory authorities in other EEA States–

    (a)   of any approvals granted for the purposes of paragraph 8 of Schedule 4, and

    (b)   of any authorisations granted for the purposes of paragraph 9 of that Schedule.

(8)   In this section–

"the Convention" means the Convention for the Protection of Individuals with regard to Automatic Processing of Personal Data which was opened for signature on 28th January 1981;

"data protection functions" means functions relating to the protection of individuals with respect to the processing of personal information.

NOTES

Defined terms
"the Commissioner": s 70(1)
"the Convention": s 54(8)
"the Data Protection Directive": s 70(1)
"data protection functions": s 54(8)
"EEA State": s 70(1)

Subordinate legislation
Data Protection (Functions of Designated Authority) Order 2000.
Data Protection (International Co-operation) Order 2000

Inspection of overseas information systems

54A(1)   The Commissioner may inspect any personal data recorded in–

    (a)   the Schengen information system,

    (b)   the Europol information system,

    (c)   the Customs information system.

(2)   The power conferred by subsection (1) is exercisable only for the purpose of assessing whether or not any processing of the data has been or is being carried out in compliance with this Act.

(3)   The power includes power to inspect, operate and test equipment which is used for the processing of personal data.

(4)   Before exercising the power, the Commissioner must give notice in writing of his intention to do so to the data controller.

(5)   But subsection (4) does not apply if the Commissioner considers that the case is one of urgency.

(6)   Any person who–

    (a)   intentionally obstructs a person exercising the power conferred by subsection (1), or

    (b)   fails without reasonable excuse to give any person exercising the power any assistance he may reasonably require,

is guilty of an offence.

(7)   In this section–

"the Customs information system" means the information system established under Chapter II of the Convention on the Use of Information Technology for Customs Purposes,

"the Europol information system" means the information system established under Title II of the Convention on the Establishment of a European Police Office,

"the Schengen information system" means the information system established under Title IV of the Convention implementing the Schengen Agreement of 14th June 1985, or any system established in its place in pursuance of any Community obligation.

NOTES

Defined terms
  "Commissioner": s 70(1)
  "data controller": ss 1(1) and (4) and 63(3)

"data subject": s 1(1)
"processing": s 1(1)

Unlawful obtaining etc of personal data

55(1)   A person must not knowingly or recklessly, without the consent of the data controller–

    (a)   obtain or disclose personal data or the information contained in personal data, or

    (b)   procure the disclosure to another person of the information contained in personal data.

(2)   Subsection (1) does not apply to a person who shows–

    (a)   that the obtaining, disclosing or procuring–

        (i)   was necessary for the purpose of preventing or detecting crime, or

        (ii)   was required or authorised by or under any enactment, by any rule of law or by the order of a court,

    (b)   that he acted in the reasonable belief that he had in law the right to obtain or disclose the data or information or, as the case may be, to procure the disclosure of the information to the other person,

    (c)   that he acted in the reasonable belief that he would have had the consent of the data controller if the data controller had known of the obtaining, disclosing or procuring and the circumstances of it,

    (ca)   that he acted–

        (i)   for the special purposes,

        (ii)   with a view to the publication by any person of any journalistic, literary or artistic material, and

        (iii)   in the reasonable belief that in the particular circumstances the obtaining, disclosing or procuring was justified as being in the public interest, or

(d)   that in the particular circumstances the obtaining, disclosing or procuring was justified as being in the public interest.

(3)   A person who contravenes subsection (1) is guilty of an offence.

(4)   A person who sells personal data is guilty of an offence if he has obtained the data in contravention of subsection (1).

(5)   A person who offers to sell personal data is guilty of an offence if–

(a)   he has obtained the data in contravention of subsection (1), or

(b)   he subsequently obtains the data in contravention of that subsection.

(6)   For the purposes of subsection (5), an advertisement indicating that personal data are or may be for sale is an offer to sell the data.

(7)   Section 1(2) does not apply for the purposes of this section; and for the purposes of subsections (4) to (6), "personal data" includes information extracted from personal data.

(8)   References in this section to personal data do not include references to personal data which by virtue of section 28 or 33A are exempt from this section.

Power of Commissioner to impose monetary penalty

55A(1) The Commissioner may serve a data controller with a monetary penalty notice if the Commissioner is satisfied that–

(a)   there has been a serious contravention of section 4(4) by the data controller,

(b)   the contravention was of a kind likely to cause substantial damage or substantial distress, and

(c)   subsection (2) or (3) applies.

(2)   This subsection applies if the contravention was deliberate.

(3)   This subsection applies if the data controller–

(a)   knew or ought to have known–

(i)   that there was a risk that the contravention would occur, and

(ii)   that such a contravention would be of a kind likely to cause substantial damage or substantial distress, but

(b)   failed to take reasonable steps to prevent the contravention.

(3A) The Commissioner may not be satisfied as mentioned in subsection (1) by virtue of any matter which comes to the Commissioner's attention as a result of anything done in pursuance of–

(a)   an assessment notice;

(b)   an assessment under section 51(7).

(4)   A monetary penalty notice is a notice requiring the data controller to pay to the Commissioner a monetary penalty of an amount determined by the Commissioner and specified in the notice.

(5)   The amount determined by the Commissioner must not exceed the prescribed amount.

(6)   The monetary penalty must be paid to the Commissioner within the period specified in the notice.

(7) The notice must contain such information as may be prescribed.

(8) Any sum received by the Commissioner by virtue of this section must be paid into the Consolidated Fund.

(9) In this section–
"data controller" does not include the Crown Estate Commissioners or a person who is a data controller by virtue of section 63(3);
"prescribed" means prescribed by regulations made by the Secretary of State.

NOTES

Defined terms
"assessment notice": s 41A(1)

"the Commissioner": s 70(1)
"data controller": ss1(1) and (4) and 63(3)

Monetary penalty notices: procedural rights

55B(1) Before serving a monetary penalty notice, the Commissioner must serve the data controller with a notice of intent.

(2) A notice of intent is a notice that the Commissioner proposes to serve a monetary penalty notice.

(3) A notice of intent must–
   (a) inform the data controller that he may make written representations in relation to the Commissioner's proposal within a period specified in the notice, and
   (b) contain such other information as may be prescribed.

(4) The Commissioner may not serve a monetary penalty notice until the time within which the data controller may make representations has expired.

(5) A person on whom a monetary penalty notice is served may appeal to the Tribunal against–
   (a) the issue of the monetary penalty notice;
   (b) the amount of the penalty specified in the notice.

(6) In this section, "prescribed" means prescribed by regulations made by the Secretary of State.

NOTES

Defined terms
"the Commissioner": s 70(1)

"data controller": ss1(1) and (4) and 63(3)

Guidance about monetary penalty notices

55C(1) The Commissioner must prepare and issue guidance on how he proposes to exercise his functions under sections 55A and 55B.

(2) The guidance must, in particular, deal with–
   (a) the circumstances in which he would consider it appropriate to issue a monetary penalty notice, and
   (b) how he will determine the amount of the penalty.

(3) The Commissioner may alter or replace the guidance.

(4) If the guidance is altered or replaced, the Commissioner must issue the altered or replacement guidance.

(5) The Commissioner may not issue guidance under this section without the approval of the Secretary of State.

(6)   The Commissioner must lay any guidance issued under this section before each House of Parliament.

(7)   The Commissioner must arrange for the publication of any guidance issued under this section in such form and manner as he considers appropriate.

(8)   In subsections (5) to (7), "guidance" includes altered or replacement guidance.

NOTES
Defined terms
   "the Commissioner": s 70(1)

Monetary penalty notices: enforcement

55D(1)   This section applies in relation to any penalty payable to the Commissioner by virtue of section 55A.

(2)   In England and Wales, the penalty is recoverable–
   (a)   if a county court so orders, as if it were payable under an order of that court;
   (b)   if the High Court so orders, as if it were payable under an order of that court.

(3)   In Scotland, the penalty may be enforced in the same manner as an extract registered decree arbitral bearing a warrant for execution issued by the sheriff court of any sheriffdom in Scotland.

(4)   In Northern Ireland, the penalty is recoverable–
   (a)   if a county court so orders, as if it were payable under an order of that court;
   (b)   if the High Court so orders, as if it were payable under an order of that court.

NOTES
Defined terms
   "the Commissioner": s 70(1)

Notices under sections 55A and 55B: supplemental

55E(1)   The Secretary of State may by order make further provision in connection with monetary penalty notices and notices of intent.

(2)   An order under this section may in particular–
   (a)   provide that a monetary penalty notice may not be served on a data controller with respect to the processing of personal data for the special purposes except in circumstances specified in the order;
   (b)   make provision for the cancellation or variation of monetary penalty notices;
   (c)   confer rights of appeal to the Tribunal against decisions of the Commissioner in relation to the cancellation or variation of such notices;
   (e)   make provision for the determination of appeals made by virtue of paragraph (c);

(3)   An order under this section may apply any provision of this Act with such modifications as may be specified in the order.

(4)   An order under this section may amend this Act.

NOTES
Defined terms
   "the Commissioner": s 70(1)

"special purposes": s 3
"the Tribunal": s 70(1)

Records obtained under data subject's right of access

Prohibition of requirement as to production of certain records

56(1)   A person must not, in connection with–

(a)   the recruitment of another person as an employee,

(b)   the continued employment of another person, or

(c)   any contract for the provision of services to him by another person,

require that other person or a third party to supply him with a relevant record or to produce a relevant record to him.

(2)   A person concerned with the provision (for payment or not) of goods, facilities or services to the public or a section of the public must not, as a condition of providing or offering to provide any goods, facilities or services to another person, require that other person or a third party to supply him with a relevant record or to produce a relevant record to him.

(3)   Subsections (1) and (2) do not apply to a person who shows–

(a)   that the imposition of the requirement was required or authorised by or under any enactment, by any rule of law or by the order of a court, or

(b)   that in the particular circumstances the imposition of the requirement was justified as being in the public interest.

(4)   Having regard to the provisions of Part V of the Police Act 1997 (certificates of criminal records etc), the imposition of the requirement referred to in subsection (1) or (2) is not to be regarded as being justified as being in the public interest on the ground that it would assist in the prevention or detection of crime.

(5)   A person who contravenes subsection (1) or (2) is guilty of an offence.

(6)   In this section "a relevant record" means any record which–

(a)   has been or is to be obtained by a data subject from any data controller specified in the first column of the Table below in the exercise of the right conferred by section 7, and

(b)   contains information relating to any matter specified in relation to that data controller in the second column,

and includes a copy of such a record or a part of such a record.

TABLE

Data controller	Subject-matter
1 Any of the following persons–	(a) Convictions.
(a) a chief officer of police of a police force in England and Wales.	(b) Cautions
(b) a chief constable of a police force in Scotland.	
(c) the Chief Constable of the Police Service of Northern Ireland.	
(d) the Director General of the Serious Organised Crime Agency.	
2 The Secretary of State.	(a) Convictions.
	(b) Cautions.
	(c) His functions under section 92 of the Powers of Criminal Courts (Sentencing) Act 2000, section 205(2) or 208 of the Criminal Procedure (Scotland) Act 1995 or section 73 of the Children and Young Persons Act

(Northern Ireland) 1968 in relation to any person sentenced to detention.

(d) His functions under the Prison Act 1952, the Prisons (Scotland) Act 1989 or the Prison Act (Northern Ireland) 1953 in relation to any person imprisoned or detained.

(e) His functions under the Social Security Contributions and Benefits Act 1992, the Social Security Administration Act 1992 or the Jobseekers Act 1995.

(f) His functions under Part V of the Police Act 1997.

(g) His functions under the Safeguarding Vulnerable Groups Act 2006 or the Safeguarding Vulnerable Groups (Northern Ireland) Order 2007.

3 The Department of Health and Social Services for Northern Ireland.	Its functions under the Social Security Contributions and Benefits (Northern Ireland) Act 1992, the Social Security Administration (Northern Ireland) Act 1992 or the Jobseekers (Northern Ireland) Order 1995.
4 The Independent Barring Board.	Its functions under the Safeguarding Vulnerable Groups Act 2006 or the Safeguarding Vulnerable Groups (Northern Ireland) Order 2007.

(6A) A record is not a relevant record to the extent that it relates, or is to relate, only to personal data falling within paragraph (e) of the definition of "data" in section 1(1).

(7) In the Table in subsection (6)–
"caution" means a caution given to any person in England and Wales or Northern Ireland in respect of an offence which, at the time when the caution is given, is admitted;
"conviction" has the same meaning as in the Rehabilitation of Offenders Act 1974 or the Rehabilitation of Offenders (Northern Ireland) Order 1978.

(8) The Secretary of State may by order amend–
    (a)   the Table in subsection (6), and
    (b)   subsection (7).

(9) For the purposes of this section a record which states that a data controller is not processing any personal data relating to a particular matter shall be taken to be a record containing information relating to that matter.

(10) In this section "employee" means an individual who–
    (a)   works under a contract of employment, as defined by section 230(2) of the Employment Rights Act 1996, or
    (b)   holds any office,
whether or not he is entitled to remuneration; and "employment" shall be construed accordingly.

NOTES

Defined terms
"data controller": ss1(1) and (4) and 63(3)
"enactment": s 70(1)

"personal data": s 1(1)
"third party": s 70(1)

Avoidance of certain contractual terms relating to health records

57(1) Any term or condition of a contract is void in so far as it purports to require an individual–

(a) to supply any other person with a record to which this section applies, or with a copy of such a record or a part of such a record, or

(b) to produce to any other person such a record, copy or part.

(2) This section applies to any record which–

(a) has been or is to be obtained by a data subject in the exercise of the right conferred by section 7, and

(b) consists of the information contained in any health record as defined by section 68(2).

NOTES

Defined terms
"data subject": s 1(1)

"health record": s 68(2)

Information provided to Commissioner or Tribunal

Disclosure of information

58 No enactment or rule of law prohibiting or restricting the disclosure of information shall preclude a person from furnishing the Commissioner or the Tribunal with any information necessary for the discharge of their functions under this Act or the Freedom of Information Act 2000.

NOTES

Defined terms
"Commissioner": s 70(1)
"enactment": s 70(1)

"Tribunal": s 70(1)

Confidentiality of information

59(1) No person who is or has been the Commissioner, a member of the Commissioner's staff or an agent of the Commissioner shall disclose any information which–

(a) has been obtained by, or furnished to, the Commissioner under or for the purposes of the information Acts,

(b) relates to an identified or identifiable individual or business, and

(c) is not at the time of the disclosure, and has not previously been, available to the public from other sources,

unless the disclosure is made with lawful authority.

(2) For the purposes of subsection (1) a disclosure of information is made with lawful authority only if, and to the extent that–

(a) the disclosure is made with the consent of the individual or of the person for the time being carrying on the business,

(b) the information was provided for the purpose of its being made available to the public (in whatever manner) under any provision of the information Acts,

(c) the disclosure is made for the purposes of, and is necessary for, the discharge of–

(i) any functions under the information Acts, or

(ii) any Community obligation,

(d) the disclosure is made for the purposes of any proceedings, whether criminal or civil and whether arising under, or by virtue of, the information Acts or otherwise, or

    (e)   having regard to the rights and freedoms or legitimate interests of any person, the disclosure is necessary in the public interest.

(3) Any person who knowingly or recklessly discloses information in contravention of subsection (1) is guilty of an offence.

(4) In this section "the information Acts" means this Act and the Freedom of Information Act 2000.

NOTES

Defined terms
  "Commissioner": s 70(1)

General provisions relating to offences

Prosecutions and penalties

60(1) No proceedings for an offence under this Act shall be instituted--

    (a)   in England or Wales, except by the Commissioner or by or with the consent of the Director of Public Prosecutions;

    (b)   in Northern Ireland, except by the Commissioner or by or with the consent of the Director of Public Prosecutions for Northern Ireland.

(2) A person guilty of an offence under any provision of this Act other than section 54A and paragraph 12 of Schedule 9 is liable–

    (a)   on summary conviction, to a fine not exceeding the statutory maximum, or

    (b)   on conviction on indictment, to a fine.

(3) A person guilty of an offence under section 54A and paragraph 12 of Schedule 9 is liable on summary conviction to a fine not exceeding level 5 on the standard scale.

(4) Subject to subsection (5), the court by or before which a person is convicted of–

    (a)   an offence under section 21(1), 22(6), 55 or 56,

    (b)   an offence under section 21(2) relating to processing which is assessable processing for the purposes of section 22, or

    (c)   an offence under section 47(1) relating to an enforcement notice,

may order any document or other material used in connection with the processing of personal data and appearing to the court to be connected with the commission of the offence to be forfeited, destroyed or erased.

(5) The court shall not make an order under subsection (4) in relation to any material where a person (other than the offender) claiming to be the owner of or otherwise interested in the material applies to be heard by the court, unless an opportunity is given to him to show cause why the order should not be made.

NOTES

Defined terms
  "Commissioner": s 70(1)

"personal data": s 1(1)
"processing": s 1(1)

Liability of directors etc

61(1) Where an offence under this Act has been committed by a body corporate and is proved to have been committed with the consent or connivance of or to be attributable to any neglect on the part of any director, manager, secretary or similar officer of the body corporate or any person who was purporting to act in any such capacity, he as well as the body corporate shall be guilty of that offence and be liable to be proceeded against and punished accordingly.

(2) Where the affairs of a body corporate are managed by its members subsection (1) shall apply in relation to the acts and defaults of a member in connection with his functions of management as if he were a director of the body corporate.

(3) Where an offence under this Act has been committed by a Scottish partnership and the contravention in question is proved to have occurred with the consent or connivance of, or to be attributable to any neglect on the part of, a partner, he as well as the partnership shall be guilty of that offence and shall be liable to be proceeded against and punished accordingly.

Amendments of Consumer Credit Act 1974

Amendments of Consumer Credit Act 1974

62(1) *Not reproduced*

General

Application to Crown

63(1) This Act binds the Crown.

(2) For the purposes of this Act each government department shall be treated as a person separate from any other government department.

(3) Where the purposes for which and the manner in which any personal data are, or are to be, processed are determined by any person acting on behalf of the Royal Household, the Duchy of Lancaster or the Duchy of Cornwall, the data controller in respect of those data for the purposes of this Act shall be–

    (a)   in relation to the Royal Household, the Keeper of the Privy Purse,

    (b)   in relation to the Duchy of Lancaster, such person as the Chancellor of the Duchy appoints, and

    (c)   in relation to the Duchy of Cornwall, such person as the Duke of Cornwall, or the possessor for the time being of the Duchy of Cornwall, appoints.

(4) Different persons may be appointed under subsection (3)(b) or (c) for different purposes.

(5) Neither a government department nor a person who is a data controller by virtue of subsection (3) shall be liable to prosecution under this Act, but sections 54A and 55 and paragraph 12 of Schedule 9 shall apply to a person in the service of the Crown as they apply to any other person.

NOTES

Defined terms
"data controller": ss1(1) and (4) and 63(3)
"government department": s 70(1)

"personal data": s 1(1)
"processing": s 1(1)

Application to Parliament

63A(1) Subject to the following provisions of this section and to section 35A, this Act applies to the processing of personal data by or on behalf of either House of Parliament as it applies to the processing of personal data by other persons

(2) Where the purposes for which and the manner in which any personal data are, or are to be, processed are determined by or on behalf of the House of Commons, the data controller in respect of those data for the purposes of this Act shall be the Corporate Officer of that House.

(3) Where the purposes for which and the manner in which any personal data are, or are to be, processed are determined by or on behalf of the House of Lords, the data controller in respect of those data for the purposes of this Act shall be the Corporate Officer of that House.

(4) Nothing in subsection (2) or (3) is to be taken to render the Corporate Officer of the House of Commons or the Corporate Officer of the House of Lords liable to prosecution under this Act, but section 55 and paragraph 12 of Schedule 9 shall apply to a person acting on behalf of either House as they apply to any other person.

NOTES

Defined terms
  "data controller": ss1(1) and (4) and 63(3)
  "data protection principles": s 4 and Sch 1

"personal data": s 1(1)
"processing": s 1(1)

Transmission of notices etc by electronic or other means

64(1) This section applies to
  (a) a notice or request under any provision of Part II,
  (b) a notice under subsection (1) of section 24 or particulars made available under that subsection, or
  (c) an application under section 41(2),
but does not apply to anything which is required to be served in accordance with rules of court.

(2) The requirement that any notice, request, particulars or application to which this section applies should be in writing is satisfied where the text of the notice, request, particulars or application–
  (a) is transmitted by electronic means,
  (b) is received in legible form, and
  (c) is capable of being used for subsequent reference.

(3) The Secretary of State may by regulations provide that any requirement that any notice, request, particulars or application to which this section applies should be in writing is not to apply in such circumstances as may be prescribed by the regulations.

Service of notices by Commissioner

65(1) Any notice authorised or required by this Act to be served on or given to any person by the Commissioner may–
  (a) if that person is an individual, be served on him–
     (i) by delivering it to him, or
     (ii) by sending it to him by post addressed to him at his usual or last-known place of residence or business, or
     (iii) by leaving it for him at that place;
  (b) if that person is a body corporate or unincorporate, be served on that body–
     (i) by sending it by post to the proper officer of the body at its principal office, or
     (ii) by addressing it to the proper officer of the body and leaving it at that office;
  (c) if that person is a partnership in Scotland, be served on that partnership–
     (i) by sending it by post to the principal office of the partnership, or
     (ii) by addressing it to that partnership and leaving it at that office.

(2) In subsection (1)(b) "principal office", in relation to a registered company, means its registered office and "proper officer", in relation to any body, means the secretary or other executive officer charged with the conduct of its general affairs.

936

(3)   This section is without prejudice to any other lawful method of serving or giving a notice.

NOTES

Defined terms
"the Commissioner": s 70(1)

Exercise of rights in Scotland by children

66(1)   Where a question falls to be determined in Scotland as to the legal capacity of a person under the age of sixteen years to exercise any right conferred by any provision of this Act, that person shall be taken to have that capacity where he has a general understanding of what it means to exercise that right.

(2)   Without prejudice to the generality of subsection (1), a person of twelve years of age or more shall be presumed to be of sufficient age and maturity to have such understanding as is mentioned in that subsection.

Orders, regulations and rules

67(1)   Any power conferred by this Act on the Secretary of State to make an order, regulations or rules shall be exercisable by statutory instrument.

(2)   Any order, regulations or rules made by the Secretary of State under this Act may–
    (a)   make different provision for different cases, and
    (b)   make such supplemental, incidental, consequential or transitional provision or savings as the Secretary of State considers appropriate;
and nothing in section 7(11), 19(5), 26(1) or 30(4) limits the generality of paragraph (a).

(3)   Before making–
    (a)   an order under any provision of this Act other than section 75(3),
    (b)   any regulations under this Act other than notification regulations (as defined by section 16(2)),
the Secretary of State shall consult the Commissioner.

(4)   A statutory instrument containing (whether alone or with other provisions) an order under–
    section 10(2)(b),
    section 12(5)(b),
    section 22(1),
    section 30,
    section 32(3),
    section 38,
    section 41A(2)(c),
    section 55E(1),
    section 56(8),
    paragraph 10 of Schedule 3, or
    paragraph 4 of Schedule 7,
shall not be made unless a draft of the instrument has been laid before and approved by a resolution of each House of Parliament.

(5)   A statutory instrument which contains (whether alone or with other provisions)–
    (a)   an order under–
        section 22(7),
        section 23,
        section 41A(2)(b),

section 51(3),

section 54(2), (3) or (4),

paragraph 3, 4 or 14 of Part II of Schedule 1,

paragraph 6 of Schedule 2,

paragraph 2, 7 or 9 of Schedule 3,

paragraph 4 of Schedule 4,

paragraph 6 of Schedule 7,

  (b)   regulations under section 7 which–

      (i)   prescribe cases for the purposes of subsection (2)(b),

      (ii) are made by virtue of subsection (7), or

      (iii) relate to the definition of "the prescribed period",

  (c)   regulations under section 8(1) , 9(3) or 9A(5),

  (ca)   regulations under section 55A(5) or (7) or 55B(3)(b),

  (d)   regulations under section 64,

  (e)   notification regulations (as defined by section 16(2)), or

  (f)   rules under paragraph 7 of Schedule 6,

and which is not subject to the requirement in subsection (4) that a draft of the instrument be laid before and approved by a resolution of each House of Parliament, shall be subject to annulment in pursuance of a resolution of either House of Parliament.

(6)   A statutory instrument which contains only–

      (a)   regulations prescribing fees for the purposes of any provision of this Act, or

      (b)   regulations under section 7 prescribing fees for the purposes of any other enactment,

shall be laid before Parliament after being made.

NOTES

Defined terms

"the Commissioner": s.70(1)

Meaning of "accessible record"

68(1) In this Act "accessible record" means–

      (a)   a health record as defined by subsection (2),

      (b)   an educational record as defined by Schedule 11, or

      (c)   an accessible public record as defined by Schedule 12.

(2)   In subsection (1)(a) "health record" means any record which–

      (a)   consists of information relating to the physical or mental health or condition of an individual, and

      (b)   has been made by or on behalf of a health professional in connection with the care of that individual.

Meaning of "health professional"

69(1) In this Act "health professional" means any of the following–

      (a)   a registered medical practitioner,

      (b)   a registered dentist as defined by section 53(1) of the Dentists Act 1984,

      (c)   a registered dispensing optician or a registered optometrist within the meaning of the Opticians Act 1989,

      (d)   a registered pharmacist or registered pharmacy technician within the meaning of the Pharmacists and Pharmacy Technicians Order 2007 or a registered person as defined by Article 2(2) of the Pharmacy (Northern Ireland) Order 1976,

      (e)   a registered nurse or midwife,

(f)   a registered osteopath as defined by section 41 of the Osteopaths Act 1993,

(g)   a registered chiropractor as defined by section 43 of the Chiropractors Act 1994,

(h)   any person who is registered as a member of a profession to which the Health Professions Order 2001 for the time being extends,

(i)   a child psychotherapist, and

(j)   ...

(k)   a scientist employed by such a body as head of a department.

(2)   In subsection (1)(a) "registered medical practitioner" includes any person who is provisionally registered under section 15 or 21 of the Medical Act 1983 and is engaged in such employment as is mentioned in subsection (3) of that section.

(3)   In subsection (1) "health service body" means–

(a)   a Strategic Health Authority established under section 13 of the National Health Service Act 2006,

(b)   a Special Health Authority established under section 28 of that Act, or section 22 of the National Health Service (Wales) Act 2006,

(bb)   a Primary Care Trust established under section 18 of the National Health Service Act 2006,

(bbb)   a Local Health Board established under section 11 of the National Health Service (Wales) Act 2006,

(c)   a Health Board within the meaning of the National Health Service (Scotland) Act 1978,

(d)   a Special Health Board within the meaning of that Act,

(e)   the managers of a State Hospital provided under section 102 of that Act,

(f)   a National Health Service trust first established under section 5 of the National Health Service and Community Care Act 1990, section 25 of the National Health Service Act 2006, section 18 of the National Health Service (Wales) Act 2006 or section 12A of the National Health Service (Scotland) Act 1978,

(fa)   an NHS foundation trust;

(g)   a Health and Social Services Board established under Article 16 of the Health and Personal Social Services (Northern Ireland) Order 1972,

(h)   a special health and social services agency established under the Health and Personal Social Services (Special Agencies) (Northern Ireland) Order 1990, or

(i)   a Health and Social Services trust established under Article 10 of the Health and Personal Social Services (Northern Ireland) Order 1991.

Supplementary definitions

70(1)   In this Act, unless the context otherwise requires–

"business" includes any trade or profession;

"the Commissioner" means the Information Commissioner;

"credit reference agency" has the same meaning as in the Consumer Credit Act 1974;

"the Data Protection Directive" means Directive 95/46/EC on the protection of individuals with regard to the processing of personal data and on the free movement of such data;

"EEA State" means a State which is a contracting party to the Agreement on the European Economic Area signed at Oporto on 2nd May 1992 as adjusted by the Protocol signed at Brussels on 17th March 1993;

"enactment" includes an enactment passed after this Act and any enactment comprised in, or in any instrument made under, an Act of the Scottish Parliament;

"government department" includes a Northern Ireland department and any body or authority exercising statutory functions on behalf of the Crown;

"government department" includes–

    (a) any part of the Scottish Administration;

    (b) a Northern Ireland department;

    (c) the Welsh Assembly Government;

    (d) any body or authority exercising statutory functions on behalf of the Crown;

"Minister of the Crown" has the same meaning as in the Ministers of the Crown Act 1975;

"public register" means any register which pursuant to a requirement imposed–

    (a) by or under any enactment, or

    (b) in pursuance of any international agreement,

is open to public inspection or open to inspection by any person having a legitimate interest;

"pupil"–

    (a) in relation to a school in England and Wales, means a registered pupil within the meaning of the Education Act 1996,

    (b) in relation to a school in Scotland, means a pupil within the meaning of the Education (Scotland) Act 1980, and

    (c) in relation to a school in Northern Ireland, means a registered pupil within the meaning of the Education and Libraries (Northern Ireland) Order 1986;

"recipient", in relation to any personal data, means any person to whom the data are disclosed, including any person (such as an employee or agent of the data controller, a data processor or an employee or agent of a data processor) to whom they are disclosed in the course of processing the data for the data controller, but does not include any person to whom disclosure is or may be made as a result of, or with a view to, a particular inquiry by or on behalf of that person made in the exercise of any power conferred by law;

"registered company" means a company registered under the enactments relating to companies for the time being in force in the United Kingdom;

"school"–

    (a) in relation to England and Wales, has the same meaning as in the Education Act 1996,

    (b) in relation to Scotland, has the same meaning as in the Education (Scotland) Act 1980, and

    (c) in relation to Northern Ireland, has the same meaning as in the Education and Libraries (Northern Ireland) Order 1986;

"teacher" includes–

    (a) in Great Britain, head teacher, and

    (b) in Northern Ireland, the principal of a school;

"third party", in relation to personal data, means any person other than–

    (a) the data subject,

    (b) the data controller, or

    (c) any data processor or other person authorised to process data for the data controller or processor;

"the Tribunal" in relation to any appeal under this Act, means—

    (a) the Upper Tribunal, in any case where it is determined by or under Tribunal Procedure Rules that the Upper Tribunal is to hear the appeal; or

(b)   the First-tier Tribunal, in any other case.

(2)   For the purposes of this Act data are inaccurate if they are incorrect or misleading as to any matter of fact.

Index of defined expressions

71   The following Table shows provisions defining or otherwise explaining expressions used in this Act (other than provisions defining or explaining an expression only used in the same section or Schedule)–

accessible record   section 68

address (in Part III)   section 16(3)

business   section 70(1)

the Commissioner   section 70(1)

credit reference agency   section 70(1)

data   section 1(1)

data controller   sections 1(1) and (4) and 63(3)

data processor   section 1(1)

the Data Protection Directive   section 70(1)

data protection principles   section 4 and Schedule 1

data subject   section 1(1)

disclosing (of personal data)   section 1(2)(b)

EEA State   section 70(1)

enactment   section 70(1)

enforcement notice   section 40(1)

fees regulations (in Part III)   section 16(2)

government department   section 70(1)

health professional   section 69

inaccurate (in relation to data)   section 70(2)

information notice   section 43(1)

Minister of the Crown   section 70(1)

the non-disclosure provisions (in Part IV)   section 27(3)

notification regulations (in Part III)   section 16(2)

obtaining (of personal data)   section 1(2)(a)

personal data   section 1(1)

prescribed (in Part III)   section 16(2)

processing (of information or data)   section 1(1) and paragraph 5 of Schedule 8

public authority   section 1(1)

public register   section 70(1)

publish (in relation to journalistic, literary or artistic material)   section 32(6)

pupil (in relation to a school)   section 70(1)

recipient (in relation to personal data)   section 70(1)

recording (of personal data)   section 1(2)(a)

registered company   section 70(1)

registrable particulars (in Part III)   section 16(1)

relevant filing system   section 1(1)

school   section 70(1)

sensitive personal data   section 2

special information notice   section 44(1)

the special purposes   section 3

the subject information provisions (in Part IV)   section 27(2) teacher   section 70(1)

third party (in relation to processing of personal data)   section 70(1)

the Tribunal   section 70(1)

using (of personal data)   section 1(2)(b).

Modifications of Act

72   During the period beginning with the commencement of this section and ending with 23rd October 2007, the provisions of this Act shall have effect subject to the modifications set out in Schedule 13.

Transitional provisions and savings

73   Schedule 14 (which contains transitional provisions and savings) has effect.

Minor and consequential amendments and repeals and revocations

74(1)   Schedule 15 (which contains minor and consequential amendments) has effect.

(2)   The enactments and instruments specified in Schedule 16 are repealed or revoked to the extent specified.

Short title, commencement and extent

75(1)   This Act may be cited as the Data Protection Act 1998.

(2)   The following provisions of this Act–

    (a)   sections 1 to 3,

    (b)   section 25(1) and (4),

    (c)   section 26,

    (d)   sections 67 to 71,

    (e)   this section,

    (f)   paragraph 17 of Schedule 5,

    (g)   Schedule 11,

    (h)   Schedule 12, and

    (i)   so much of any other provision of this Act as confers any power to make subordinate legislation,

shall come into force on the day on which this Act is passed.

(3)   The remaining provisions of this Act shall come into force on such day as the Secretary of State may by order appoint; and different days may be appointed for different purposes.

(4)   The day appointed under subsection (3) for the coming into force of section 56 must not be earlier than the first day on which sections 112, 113 and 115 of the Police Act 1997 (which provide for the issue by the Secretary of State of criminal conviction certificates, criminal record certificates and enhanced criminal record certificates) are all in force.

(4A)   Subsection (4) does not apply to section 56 so far as that section relates to a record containing information relating to–

    (a)   the Secretary of State's functions under the Safeguarding Vulnerable Groups Act 2006 or the Safeguarding Vulnerable Groups (Northern Ireland) Order 2007, or

    (b)   the Independent Barring Board's functions under that Act or that Order.

(5)   Subject to subsection (6), this Act extends to Northern Ireland.

(6)   Any amendment, repeal or revocation made by Schedule 15 or 16 has the same extent as that of the enactment or instrument to which it relates.

SCHEDULE 1
THE DATA PROTECTION PRINCIPLES

Section 4(1) and (2)

PART I
THE PRINCIPLES

1. Personal data shall be processed fairly and lawfully and, in particular, shall not be processed unless–

    (a)   at least one of the conditions in Schedule 2 is met, and

    (b)   in the case of sensitive personal data, at least one of the conditions in Schedule 3 is also met.

2. Personal data shall be obtained only for one or more specified and lawful purposes, and shall not be further processed in any manner incompatible with that purpose or those purposes.

3. Personal data shall be adequate, relevant and not excessive in relation to the purpose or purposes for which they are processed.

4. Personal data shall be accurate and, where necessary, kept up to date.

5. Personal data processed for any purpose or purposes shall not be kept for longer than is necessary for that purpose or those purposes.

6. Personal data shall be processed in accordance with the rights of data subjects under this Act.

7. Appropriate technical and organisational measures shall be taken against unauthorised or unlawful processing of personal data and against accidental loss or destruction of, or damage to, personal data.

8. Personal data shall not be transferred to a country or territory outside the European Economic Area unless that country or territory ensures an adequate level of protection for the rights and freedoms of data subjects in relation to the processing of personal data.

PART II
INTERPRETATION OF THE PRINCIPLES IN PART I

The first principle

1(1) In determining for the purposes of the first principle whether personal data are processed fairly, regard is to be had to the method by which they are obtained, including in particular whether any person from whom they are obtained is deceived or misled as to the purpose or purposes for which they are to be processed.

(2) Subject to paragraph 2, for the purposes of the first principle data are to be treated as obtained fairly if they consist of information obtained from a person who–

    (a)   is authorised by or under any enactment to supply it, or

    (b)   is required to supply it by or under any enactment or by any convention or other instrument imposing an international obligation on the United Kingdom.

2(1)   Subject to paragraph 3, for the purposes of the first principle personal data are not to be treated as processed fairly unless–

    (a)   in the case of data obtained from the data subject, the data controller ensures so far as practicable that the data subject has, is provided with, or has made readily available to him, the information specified in sub-paragraph (3), and

    (b)   in any other case, the data controller ensures so far as practicable that, before the relevant time or as soon as practicable after that time, the data subject has, is provided with, or has made readily available to him, the information specified in sub-paragraph (3).

(2)   In sub-paragraph (1)(b) "the relevant time" means–

    (a)   the time when the data controller first processes the data, or

    (b)   in a case where at that time disclosure to a third party within a reasonable period is envisaged–

       (i)   if the data are in fact disclosed to such a person within that period, the time when the data are first disclosed,

       (ii)   if within that period the data controller becomes, or ought to become, aware that the data are unlikely to be disclosed to such a person within that period, the time when the data controller does become, or ought to become, so aware, or

      (iii)   in any other case, the end of that period.

(3)   The information referred to in sub-paragraph (1) is as follows, namely–

    (a)   the identity of the data controller,

    (b)   if he has nominated a representative for the purposes of this Act, the identity of that representative,

    (c)   the purpose or purposes for which the data are intended to be processed, and

    (d)   any further information which is necessary, having regard to the specific circumstances in which the data are or are to be processed, to enable processing in respect of the data subject to be fair.

3(1)   Paragraph 2(1)(b) does not apply where either of the primary conditions in sub-paragraph (2), together with such further conditions as may be prescribed by the Secretary of State by order, are met.

(2)   The primary conditions referred to in sub-paragraph (1) are–

    (a)   that the provision of that information would involve a disproportionate effort, or

    (b)   that the recording of the information to be contained in the data by, or the disclosure of the data by, the data controller is necessary for compliance with any legal obligation to which the data controller is subject, other than an obligation imposed by contract.

4(1)   Personal data which contain a general identifier falling within a description prescribed by the Secretary of State by order are not to be treated as processed fairly and lawfully unless they are processed in compliance with any conditions so prescribed in relation to general identifiers of that description.

(2)   In sub-paragraph (1) "a general identifier" means any identifier (such as, for example, a number or code used for identification purposes) which–

    (a)   relates to an individual, and

    (b)   forms part of a set of similar identifiers which is of general application.

The second principle

5.   The purpose or purposes for which personal data are obtained may in particular be

specified–

    (a)   in a notice given for the purposes of paragraph 2 by the data controller to the data subject, or

    (b)   in a notification given to the Commissioner under Part III of this Act.

6.   In determining whether any disclosure of personal data is compatible with the purpose or purposes for which the data were obtained, regard is to be had to the purpose or purposes for which the personal data are intended to be processed by any person to whom they are disclosed.

The fourth principle

7.   The fourth principle is not to be regarded as being contravened by reason of any inaccuracy in personal data which accurately record information obtained by the data controller from the data subject or a third party in a case where–

    (a)   having regard to the purpose or purposes for which the data were obtained and further processed, the data controller has taken reasonable steps to ensure the accuracy of the data, and

    (b)   if the data subject has notified the data controller of the data subject's view that the data are inaccurate, the data indicate that fact.

The sixth principle

8.   A person is to be regarded as contravening the sixth principle if, but only if–

    (a)   he contravenes section 7 by failing to supply information in accordance with that section,

    (b)   he contravenes section 10 by failing to comply with a notice given under subsection (1) of that section to the extent that the notice is justified or by failing to give a notice under subsection (3) of that section,

    (c)   he contravenes section 11 by failing to comply with a notice given under subsection (1) of that section, or

    (d)   he contravenes section 12 by failing to comply with a notice given under subsection (1) or (2)(b) of that section or by failing to give a notification under subsection (2)(a) of that section or a notice under subsection (3) of that section.

The seventh principle

9.   Having regard to the state of technological development and the cost of implementing any measures, the measures must ensure a level of security appropriate to–

    (a)   the harm that might result from such unauthorised or unlawful processing or accidental loss, destruction or damage as are mentioned in the seventh principle, and

    (b)   the nature of the data to be protected.

10.   The data controller must take reasonable steps to ensure the reliability of any employees of his who have access to the personal data.

11.   Where processing of personal data is carried out by a data processor on behalf of a data controller, the data controller must in order to comply with the seventh principle–

    (a)   choose a data processor providing sufficient guarantees in respect of the technical and organisational security measures governing the processing to be carried out, and

    (b)   take reasonable steps to ensure compliance with those measures.

12.   Where processing of personal data is carried out by a data processor on behalf of a data

controller, the data controller is not to be regarded as complying with the seventh principle unless–

    (a)   the processing is carried out under a contract–

        (i)   which is made or evidenced in writing, and

        (ii) under which the data processor is to act only on instructions from the data controller, and

    (b)   the contract requires the data processor to comply with obligations equivalent to those imposed on a data controller by the seventh principle.

The eighth principle

13.   An adequate level of protection is one which is adequate in all the circumstances of the case, having regard in particular to–

    (a)   the nature of the personal data,

    (b)   the country or territory of origin of the information contained in the data,

    (c)   the country or territory of final destination of that information,

    (d)   the purposes for which and period during which the data are intended to be processed,

    (e)   the law in force in the country or territory in question,

    (f)   the international obligations of that country or territory,

    (g)   any relevant codes of conduct or other rules which are enforceable in that country or territory (whether generally or by arrangement in particular cases), and

    (h)   any security measures taken in respect of the data in that country or territory.

14.   The eighth principle does not apply to a transfer falling within any paragraph of Schedule 4, except in such circumstances and to such extent as the Secretary of State may by order provide.

15(1)   Where–

    (a)   in any proceedings under this Act any question arises as to whether the requirement of the eighth principle as to an adequate level of protection is met in relation to the transfer of any personal data to a country or territory outside the European Economic Area, and

    (b)   a Community finding has been made in relation to transfers of the kind in question,

that question is to be determined in accordance with that finding.

(2)   In sub-paragraph (1) "Community finding" means a finding of the European Commission, under the procedure provided for in Article 31(2) of the Data Protection Directive, that a country or territory outside the European Economic Area does, or does not, ensure an adequate level of protection within the meaning of Article 25(2) of the Directive.

SCHEDULE 2

CONDITIONS RELEVANT FOR PURPOSES OF THE FIRST PRINCIPLE: PROCESSING OF ANY PERSONAL DATA

Section 4(3)

1.   The data subject has given his consent to the processing.

2.   The processing is necessary–

    (a)   for the performance of a contract to which the data subject is a party, or

    (b)   for the taking of steps at the request of the data subject with a view to entering into a contract.

3.   The processing is necessary for compliance with any legal obligation to which the data controller is subject, other than an obligation imposed by contract.

4.   The processing is necessary in order to protect the vital interests of the data subject.

5.   The processing is necessary–
   (a)   for the administration of justice,
   (aa) for the exercise of any functions of either House of Parliament,
   (b)   for the exercise of any functions conferred on any person by or under any enactment,
   (c)   for the exercise of any functions of the Crown, a Minister of the Crown or a government department, or
   (d)   for the exercise of any other functions of a public nature exercised in the public interest by any person.

6(1)   The processing is necessary for the purposes of legitimate interests pursued by the data controller or by the third party or parties to whom the data are disclosed, except where the processing is unwarranted in any particular case by reason of prejudice to the rights and freedoms or legitimate interests of the data subject.

(2)   The Secretary of State may by order specify particular circumstances in which this condition is, or is not, to be taken to be satisfied.

SCHEDULE 3
CONDITIONS RELEVANT FOR PURPOSES OF THE FIRST PRINCIPLE: PROCESSING OF SENSITIVE PERSONAL DATA

Section 4(3)

1.   The data subject has given his explicit consent to the processing of the personal data.

2(1)   The processing is necessary for the purposes of exercising or performing any right or obligation which is conferred or imposed by law on the data controller in connection with employment.

(2)   The Secretary of State may by order–
   (a)   exclude the application of sub-paragraph (1) in such cases as may be specified, or
   (b)   provide that, in such cases as may be specified, the condition in subparagraph (1) is not to be regarded as satisfied unless such further conditions as may be specified in the order are also satisfied.

3.   The processing is necessary–
   (a)   in order to protect the vital interests of the data subject or another person, in a case where–
      (i)   consent cannot be given by or on behalf of the data subject, or
      (ii) the data controller cannot reasonably be expected to obtain the consent of the data subject, or
   (b)   in order to protect the vital interests of another person, in a case where consent by or on behalf of the data subject has been unreasonably withheld.

4.   The processing–
   (a)   is carried out in the course of its legitimate activities by any body or association

which–
>>(i) is not established or conducted for profit, and
>>(ii) exists for political, philosophical religious or trade-union purposes,
>(b) is carried out with appropriate safeguards for the rights and freedoms of data subjects,
>(c) relates only to individuals who either are members of the body or association or have regular contact with it in connection with its purposes, and
>(d) does not involve disclosure of the personal data to a third party without the consent of the data subject.

5. The information contained in the personal data has been made public as a result of steps deliberately taken by the data subject.

6. The processing–
>(a) is necessary for the purpose of, or in connection with, any legal proceedings (including prospective legal proceedings),
>(b) is necessary for the purpose of obtaining legal advice, or
>(c) is otherwise necessary for the purposes of establishing, exercising or defending legal rights.

7(1) The processing is necessary–
>(a) for the administration of justice,
>(aa) for the exercise of any functions of either House of Parliament,
>(b) for the exercise of any functions conferred on any person by or under an enactment, or
>(c) for the exercise of any functions of the Crown, a Minister of the Crown or a government department.

(2) The Secretary of State may by order–
>(a) exclude the application of sub-paragraph (1) in such cases as may be specified, or
>(b) provide that, in such cases as may be specified, the condition in subparagraph (1) is not to be regarded as satisfied unless such further conditions as may be specified in the order are also satisfied.

7A(1) The processing–
>(a) is either–
>>(i) the disclosure of sensitive personal data by a person as a member of an anti-fraud organisation or otherwise in accordance with any arrangements made by such an organisation; or
>>(ii) any other processing by that person or another person of sensitive personal data so disclosed; and
>(b) is necessary for the purposes of preventing fraud or a particular kind of fraud.

(2) In this paragraph "an anti-fraud organisation" means any unincorporated association, body corporate or other person which enables or facilitates any sharing of information to prevent fraud or a particular kind of fraud or which has any of these functions as its purpose or one of its purposes.

8(1) The processing is necessary for medical purposes and is undertaken by–
>(a) a health professional, or
>(b) a person who in the circumstances owes a duty of confidentiality which is equivalent to that which would arise if that person were a health professional.

(2) In this paragraph "medical purposes" includes the purposes of preventative medicine, medical diagnosis, medical research, the provision of care and treatment and the

management of healthcare services.

9(1)   The processing–

    (a)   is of sensitive personal data consisting of information as to racial or ethnic origin,

    (b)   is necessary for the purpose of identifying or keeping under review the existence or absence of equality of opportunity or treatment between persons of different racial or ethnic origins, with a view to enabling such equality to be promoted or maintained, and

    (c)   is carried out with appropriate safeguards for the rights and freedoms of data subjects.

(2)   The Secretary of State may by order specify circumstances in which processing falling within sub-paragraph (1)(a) and (b) is, or is not, to be taken for the purposes of sub-paragraph (1)(c) to be carried out with appropriate safeguards for the rights and freedoms of data subjects.

10.   The personal data are processed in circumstances specified in an order made by the Secretary of State for the purposes of this paragraph.

SCHEDULE 4
CASES WHERE THE EIGHTH PRINCIPLE DOES NOT APPLY

Section 4(3)

1.   The data subject has given his consent to the transfer.

2.   The transfer is necessary–

    (a)   for the performance of a contract between the data subject and the data controller, or

    (b)   for the taking of steps at the request of the data subject with a view to his entering into a contract with the data controller.

3.   The transfer is necessary–

    (a)   for the conclusion of a contract between the data controller and a person other than the data subject which–

        (i)   is entered into at the request of the data subject, or

        (ii)   is in the interests of the data subject, or

    (b)   for the performance of such a contract.

4(1)   The transfer is necessary for reasons of substantial public interest.

(2)   The Secretary of State may by order specify–

    (a)   circumstances in which a transfer is to be taken for the purposes of subparagraph (1) to be necessary for reasons of substantial public interest, and

    (b)   circumstances in which a transfer which is not required by or under an enactment is not to be taken for the purpose of sub-paragraph (1) to be necessary for reasons of substantial public interest.

5.   The transfer–

    (a)   is necessary for the purpose of, or in connection with, any legal proceedings (including prospective legal proceedings),

    (b)   is necessary for the purpose of obtaining legal advice, or

(c) is otherwise necessary for the purposes of establishing, exercising or defending legal rights.

6. The transfer is necessary in order to protect the vital interests of the data subject.

7. The transfer is of part of the personal data on a public register and any conditions subject to which the register is open to inspection are complied with by any person to whom the data are or may be disclosed after the transfer.

8. The transfer is made on terms which are of a kind approved by the Commissioner as ensuring adequate safeguards for the rights and freedoms of data subjects.

9. The transfer has been authorised by the Commissioner as being made in such a manner as to ensure adequate safeguards for the rights and freedoms of data subjects.

SCHEDULE 5
THE INFORMATION COMMISSIONER AND THE INFORMATION TRIBUNAL

Section 6(7)

PART I
THE COMMISSIONER

Status and capacity

1(1) The corporation sole by the name of the Data Protection Registrar established by the Data Protection Act 1984 shall continue in existence by the name of the Information Commissioner.

(2) The Commissioner and his officers and staff are not to be regarded as servants or agents of the Crown.

Tenure of office

2(1) Subject to the provisions of this paragraph, the Commissioner shall hold office for such term not exceeding five years as may be determined at the time of his appointment.

(2) The Commissioner may be relieved of his office by Her Majesty at his own request.

(3) The Commissioner may be removed from office by Her Majesty in pursuance of an Address from both Houses of Parliament.

(4) The Commissioner shall in any case vacate his office–
    (a) on completing the year of service in which he attains the age of sixty-five years, or
    (b) if earlier, on completing his fifteenth year of service.

(5) Subject to sub-paragraph (4), a person who ceases to be Commissioner on the expiration of his term of office shall be eligible for re-appointment, but a person may not be re-appointed for a third or subsequent term as Commissioner unless, by reason of special circumstances, the person's re-appointment for such a term is desirable in the public interest.

Salary etc

3(1) There shall be paid–
    (a) to the Commissioner such salary, and
    (b) to or in respect of the Commissioner such pension,
as may be specified by a resolution of the House of Commons.

(2) A resolution for the purposes of this paragraph may–

    (a) specify the salary or pension,

    (b) provide that the salary or pension is to be the same as, or calculated on the same basis as, that payable to, or to or in respect of, a person employed in a specified office under, or in a specified capacity in the service of, the Crown, or

    (c) specify the salary or pension and provide for it to be increased by reference to such variables as may be specified in the resolution.

(3) A resolution for the purposes of this paragraph may take effect from the date on which it is passed or from any earlier or later date specified in the resolution.

(4) A resolution for the purposes of this paragraph may make different provision in relation to the pension payable to or in respect of different holders of the office of Commissioner.

(5) Any salary or pension payable under this paragraph shall be charged on and issued out of the Consolidated Fund.

(6) In this paragraph "pension" includes an allowance or gratuity and any reference to the payment of a pension includes a reference to the making of payments towards the provision of a pension.

Officers and staff

4(1) The Commissioner–

    (a) shall appoint a deputy commissioner or two deputy commissioners, and

    (b) may appoint such number of other officers and staff as he may determine.

(1A) The Commissioner shall, when appointing any second deputy commissioner, specify which of the Commissioner's functions are to be performed, in the circumstances referred to in paragraph 5(1), by each of the deputy commissioners.

(2) The remuneration and other conditions of service of the persons appointed under this paragraph shall be determined by the Commissioner.

(3) The Commissioner may pay such pensions, allowances or gratuities to or in respect of the persons appointed under this paragraph, or make such payments towards the provision of such pensions, allowances or gratuities, as he may determine.

(4) The references in sub-paragraph (3) to pensions, allowances or gratuities to or in respect of the persons appointed under this paragraph include references to pensions, allowances or gratuities by way of compensation to or in respect of any of those persons who suffer loss of office or employment.

(5) Any determination under sub-paragraph (1)(b), (2) or (3) shall require the approval of the Secretary of State.

(6) The Employers' Liability (Compulsory Insurance) Act 1969 shall not require insurance to be effected by the Commissioner.

5(1) The deputy commissioner or deputy commissioners shall perform the functions conferred by this Act or the Freedom of Information Act 2000 on the Commissioner during any vacancy in that office or at any time when the Commissioner is for any reason unable to act.

(2) Without prejudice to sub-paragraph (1), any functions of the Commissioner under this Act

or the Freedom of Information Act 2000 may, to the extent authorised by him, be performed by any of his officers or staff.

Authentication of seal of the Commissioner

6. The application of the seal of the Commissioner shall be authenticated by his signature or by the signature of some other person authorised for the purpose.

Presumption of authenticity of documents issued by the Commissioner

7. Any document purporting to be an instrument issued by the Commissioner and to be duly executed under the Commissioner's seal or to be signed by or on behalf of the Commissioner shall be received in evidence and shall be deemed to be such an instrument unless the contrary is shown.

Money

8. The Secretary of State may make payments to the Commissioner out of money provided by Parliament.

9(1) All fees and other sums received by the Commissioner in the exercise of his functions under this Act, under section 159 of the Consumer Credit Act 1974 or under the Freedom of Information Act 2000 shall be paid by him to the Secretary of State.

(2) Sub-paragraph (1) shall not apply where the Secretary of State, with the consent of the Treasury, otherwise directs.

(3) Any sums received by the Secretary of State under sub-paragraph (1) shall be paid into the Consolidated Fund.

Accounts

10(1) It shall be the duty of the Commissioner–
    (a)   to keep proper accounts and other records in relation to the accounts,
    (b)   to prepare in respect of each financial year a statement of account in such form as the Secretary of State may direct, and
    (c)   to send copies of that statement to the Comptroller and Auditor General on or before 31st August next following the end of the year to which the statement relates or on or before such earlier date after the end of that year as the Treasury may direct.

(2) The Comptroller and Auditor General shall examine and certify any statement sent to him under this paragraph and lay copies of it together with his report thereon before each House of Parliament.

(3) In this paragraph "financial year" means a period of twelve months beginning with 1st April.

Application of Part I in Scotland

11. Paragraphs 1(1), 6 and 7 do not extend to Scotland.

PART II
THE TRIBUNAL

Tenure of office

12(1) Subject to the following provisions of this paragraph, a member of the Tribunal shall hold and vacate his office in accordance with the terms of his appointment and shall, on ceasing to hold office, be eligible for re-appointment.

(2) Any member of the Tribunal may at any time resign his office by notice in writing to the Lord Chancellor (in the case of the chairman or a deputy chairman) or to the Secretary of State (in the case of any other member).

(3) A person who is the chairman or deputy chairman of the Tribunal shall vacate his office on the day on which he attains the age of seventy years; but this sub-paragraph is subject to section 26(4) to (6) of the Judicial Pensions and Retirement Act 1993 (power to authorise continuance in office up to the age of seventy-five years).

Salary etc

13. The Secretary of State shall pay to the members of the Tribunal out of money provided by Parliament such remuneration and allowances as he may determine.

Officers and staff

14. The Secretary of State may provide the Tribunal with such officers and staff as he thinks necessary for the proper discharge of its functions.

Expenses

15. Such expenses of the Tribunal as the Secretary of State may determine shall be defrayed by the Secretary of State out of money provided by Parliament.

SCHEDULE 6
APPEAL PROCEEDINGS

Sections 28(12), 48(5)

Tribunal Procedure Rules

7(1) Tribunal Procedure Rules may make provision for regulating the exercise of the rights of appeal conferred–

    (a)   by sections 28(4) and (6) and 48 of this Act, and

    (b)   by sections 47(1) and (2) and 60(1) and (4) of the Freedom of Information Act 2000.

(2) In the case of appeals under this Act and the Freedom of Information Act 2000, Tribunal Procedure Rules may make provision–

    (a)   for securing the production of material used for the processing of personal data;

    (b)   for the inspection, examination, operation and testing of any equipment or material used in connection with the processing of personal data;

    (c)   for hearing an appeal in the absence of the appellant or for determining an appeal without a hearing.

Obstruction etc

8(1) If any person is guilty of any act or omission in relation to proceedings before the Tribunal which, if those proceedings were proceedings before a court having power to commit for contempt, would constitute contempt of court, the Tribunal may certify the offence to the High Court or, in Scotland, the Court of Session.

(2) Where an offence is so certified, the court may inquire into the matter and, after hearing any witness who may be produced against or on behalf of the person charged with the offence, and after hearing any statement that may be offered in defence, deal with him in

any manner in which it could deal with him if he had committed the like offence in relation to the court.

SCHEDULE 7
MISCELLANEOUS EXEMPTIONS

Section 37

Confidential references given by the data controller

1. Personal data are exempt from section 7 if they consist of a reference given or to be given in confidence by the data controller for the purposes of–

    (a) the education, training or employment, or prospective education, training or employment, of the data subject,

    (b) the appointment, or prospective appointment, of the data subject to any office, or

    (c) the provision, or prospective provision, by the data subject of any service.

Armed forces

2. Personal data are exempt from the subject information provisions in any case to the extent to which the application of those provisions would be likely to prejudice the combat effectiveness of any of the armed forces of the Crown.

Judicial appointments and honours

3. Personal data processed for the purposes of–

    (a) assessing any person's suitability for judicial office or the office of Queen's Counsel, or

    (b) the conferring by the Crown of any honour or dignity,

are exempt from the subject information provisions.

Crown employment and Crown or Ministerial appointments

4(1) The Secretary of State may by order exempt from the subject information provisions personal data processed for the purposes of assessing any person's suitability for–

    (a) employment by or under the Crown, or

    (b) any office to which appointments are made by Her Majesty, by a Minister of the Crown or by a Northern Ireland authority.

(2) In this paragraph "Northern Ireland authority" means the First Minister, the deputy First Minister, a Northern Ireland Minister or a Northern Ireland department.

Management forecasts etc

5. Personal data processed for the purposes of management forecasting or management planning to assist the data controller in the conduct of any business or other activity are exempt from the subject information provisions in any case to the extent to which the application of those provisions would be likely to prejudice the conduct of that business or other activity.

Corporate finance

6(1) Where personal data are processed for the purposes of, or in connection with, a corporate finance service provided by a relevant person–

    (a) the data are exempt from the subject information provisions in any case to the extent to which either–

        (i) the application of those provisions to the data could affect the price of any instrument which is already in existence or is to be or may be created, or

(ii) the data controller reasonably believes that the application of those provisions to the data could affect the price of any such instrument, and

(b) to the extent that the data are not exempt from the subject information provisions by virtue of paragraph (a), they are exempt from those provisions if the exemption is required for the purpose of safeguarding an important economic or financial interest of the United Kingdom.

(2) For the purposes of sub-paragraph (1)(b) the Secretary of State may by order specify–

(a) matters to be taken into account in determining whether exemption from the subject information provisions is required for the purpose of safeguarding an important economic or financial interest of the United Kingdom, or

(b) circumstances in which exemption from those provisions is, or is not, to be taken to be required for that purpose.

(3) In this paragraph–

"corporate finance service" means a service consisting in–

(a) underwriting in respect of issues of, or the placing of issues of, any instrument,

(b) advice to undertakings on capital structure, industrial strategy and related matters and advice and service relating to mergers and the purchase of undertakings, or

(c) services relating to such underwriting as is mentioned in paragraph (a);

"instrument" means any instrument listed in section C of Annex I to Directive 2004/39/EC of the European Parliament and of the Council of 21 April 2004 on markets in financial instruments;

"price" includes value;

"relevant person" means–

(a) any person who, by reason of any permission he has under Part IV of the Financial Services and Markets Act 2000, is able to carry on a corporate finance service without contravening the general prohibition, within the meaning of section 19 of that Act,

(b) an EEA firm of the kind mentioned in paragraph 5(a) or (b) of Schedule 3 to that Act which has qualified for authorisation under paragraph 12 of that Schedule, and may lawfully carry on a corporate finance service,

(c) any person who is exempt from the general prohibition in respect of any corporate finance service–

(i) as a result of an exemption order made under section 38(1) of that Act, or

(ii) by reason of section 39(1) of that Act (appointed representatives),

(cc) any person, not falling within paragraph (a), (b) or (c) who may lawfully carry on a corporate finance service without contravening the general prohibition,

(d) any person who, in the course of his employment, provides to his employer a service falling within paragraph (b) or (c) of the definition of "corporate finance service", or

(e) any partner who provides to other partners in the partnership a service falling within either of those paragraphs.

Negotiations

7. Personal data which consist of records of the intentions of the data controller in relation to any negotiations with the data subject are exempt from the subject information provisions in any case to the extent to which the application of those provisions would be likely to prejudice those negotiations.

8(1)   Section 7 shall have effect subject to the provisions of sub-paragraphs (2) to (4) in the case of personal data consisting of marks or other information processed by a data controller–

     (a)   for the purpose of determining the results of an academic, professional or other examination or of enabling the results of any such examination to be determined, or

     (b)   in consequence of the determination of any such results.

(2)   Where the relevant day falls before the day on which the results of the examination are announced, the period mentioned in section 7(8) shall be extended until–

     (a)   the end of five months beginning with the relevant day, or

     (b)   the end of forty days beginning with the date of the announcement,

whichever is the earlier.

(3)   Where by virtue of sub-paragraph (2) a period longer than the prescribed period elapses after the relevant day before the request is complied with, the information to be supplied pursuant to the request shall be supplied both by reference to the data in question at the time when the request is received and (if different) by reference to the data as from time to time held in the period beginning when the request is received and ending when it is complied with.

(4)   For the purposes of this paragraph the results of an examination shall be treated as announced when they are first published or (if not published) when they are first made available or communicated to the candidate in question.

(5)   In this paragraph–

"examination" includes any process for determining the knowledge, intelligence, skill or ability of a candidate by reference to his performance in any test, work or other activity;

"the prescribed period" means forty days or such other period as is for the time being prescribed under section 7 in relation to the personal data in question;

"relevant day" has the same meaning as in section 7.

9(1)   Personal data consisting of information recorded by candidates during an academic, professional or other examination are exempt from section 7.

(2)   In this paragraph "examination" has the same meaning as in paragraph 8.

10   Personal data are exempt from the subject information provisions if the data consist of information in respect of which a claim to legal professional privilege or, in Scotland, to confidentiality of communications could be maintained in legal proceedings.

11(1)   A person need not comply with any request or order under section 7 to the extent that compliance would, by revealing evidence of the commission of any offence other than an offence under this Act, , other than an offence under this Act or an offence within sub-paragraph (1A), expose him to proceedings for that offence.

(1A)   The offences mentioned in sub-paragraph (1) are–

     (a)   an offence under section 5 of the Perjury Act 1911 (false statements made otherwise than on oath),

     (b)   an offence under section 44(2) of the Criminal Law (Consolidation) (Scotland) Act 1995 (false statements made otherwise than on oath), or

     (c)   an offence under Article 10 of the Perjury (Northern Ireland) Order 1979 (false statutory declarations and other false unsworn statements).

(2) Information disclosed by any person in compliance with any request or order under section 7 shall not be admissible against him in proceedings for an offence under this Act.

SCHEDULE 8
TRANSITIONAL RELIEF

Section 39

PART I
INTERPRETATION OF SCHEDULE

1(1) For the purposes of this Schedule, personal data are "eligible data" at any time if, and to the extent that, they are at that time subject to processing which was already under way immediately before 24th October 1998.

(2) In this Schedule–

"eligible automated data" means eligible data which fall within paragraph (a) or (b) of the definition of "data" in section 1(1);

"eligible manual data" means eligible data which are not eligible automated data;

"the first transitional period" means the period beginning with the commencement of this Schedule and ending with 23rd October 2001;

"the second transitional period" means the period beginning with 24th October 2001 and ending with 23rd October 2007.

PART II
EXEMPTIONS AVAILABLE BEFORE 24TH OCTOBER 2001

2-13 *Not reproduced*

PART III
EXEMPTIONS AVAILABLE AFTER 23RD OCTOBER 2001 BUT BEFORE 24TH OCTOBER 2007

14 *Not reproduced*

PART IV
EXEMPTIONS AFTER 23RD OCTOBER 2001 FOR HISTORICAL RESEARCH

15. In this Part of this Schedule "the relevant conditions" has the same meaning as in section 33.

16(1) Eligible manual data which are processed only for the purpose of historical research in compliance with the relevant conditions are exempt from the provisions specified in sub-paragraph (2) after 23rd October 2001.

(2) The provisions referred to in sub-paragraph (1) are–

(a) the first data protection principle except in so far as it requires compliance with paragraph 2 of Part II of Schedule 1,

(b)   the second, third, fourth and fifth data protection principles, and

(c)   section 14(1) to (3).

17(1)   After 23rd October 2001 eligible automated data which are processed only for the purpose of historical research in compliance with the relevant conditions are exempt from the first data protection principle to the extent to which it requires compliance with the conditions in Schedules 2 and 3.

(2)   Eligible automated data which are processed–

(a)   only for the purpose of historical research,

(b)   in compliance with the relevant conditions, and

(c)   otherwise than by reference to the data subject,

are also exempt from the provisions referred to in sub-paragraph (3) after 23rd October 2001.

(3)   The provisions referred to in sub-paragraph (2) are–

(a)   the first data protection principle except in so far as it requires compliance with paragraph 2 of Part II of Schedule 1,

(b)   the second, third, fourth and fifth data protection principles, and

(c)   section 14(1) to (3).

18   For the purposes of this Part of this Schedule personal data are not to be treated as processed otherwise than for the purpose of historical research merely because the data are disclosed–

(a)   to any person, for the purpose of historical research only,

(b)   to the data subject or a person acting on his behalf,

(c)   at the request, or with the consent, of the data subject or a person acting on his behalf, or

(d)   in circumstances in which the person making the disclosure has reasonable grounds for believing that the disclosure falls within paragraph (a), (b) or (c).

PART V
EXEMPTION FROM SECTION 22

19   Processing which was already under way immediately before 24th October 1998 is not assessable processing for the purposes of section 22.

SCHEDULE 9
POWERS OF ENTRY AND INSPECTION

Section 50

Issue of warrants

1(1)   If a circuit judge or a District Judge (Magistrates' Courts) is satisfied by information on oath supplied by the Commissioner that there are reasonable grounds for suspecting–

(a)   that a data controller has contravened or is contravening any of the data protection principles, or

(b)   that an offence under this Act has been or is being committed,

and that evidence of the contravention or of the commission of the offence is to be found on any premises specified in the information, he may, subject to subparagraph (2) and paragraph 2, grant a warrant to the Commissioner.

(1A)   Sub-paragraph (1B) applies if a circuit judge or a District Judge (Magistrates' Courts) is satisfied by information on oath supplied by the Commissioner that a data controller has failed to comply with a requirement imposed by an assessment notice.

(1B) The judge may, for the purpose of enabling the Commissioner to determine whether the data controller has complied or is complying with the data protection principles, grant a warrant to the Commissioner in relation to any premises that were specified in the assessment notice; but this is subject to sub-paragraph (2) and paragraph 2.

(2) A judge shall not issue a warrant under this Schedule in respect of any personal data processed for the special purposes unless a determination by the Commissioner under section 45 with respect to those data has taken effect.

(3) A warrant issued under sub-paragraph (1) this Schedule shall authorise the Commissioner or any of his officers or staff at any time within seven days of the date of the warrant to enter the premises, to search them, to inspect, examine, operate and test any equipment found there which is used or intended to be used for the processing of personal data and to inspect and seize any documents or other material found there which may be such evidence as is mentioned in that sub-paragraph –

    (a)   to enter the premises;

    (b)   to search the premises;

    (c)   to inspect, examine, operate and test any equipment found on the premises which is used or intended to be used for the processing of personal data;

    (d)   to inspect and seize any documents or other material found on the premises which–

        (i)   in the case of a warrant issued under sub-paragraph (1), may be such evidence as is mentioned in that paragraph;

        (ii)   in the case of a warrant issued under sub-paragraph (1B), may enable the Commissioner to determine whether the data controller has complied or is complying with the data protection principles;

    (e)   to require any person on the premises to provide an explanation of any document or other material found on the premises;

    (f)   to require any person on the premises to provide such other information as may reasonably be required for the purpose of determining whether the data controller has contravened, or is contravening, the data protection principles.

2(1) A judge shall not issue a warrant under this Schedule unless he is satisfied–

    (a)   that the Commissioner has given seven days' notice in writing to the occupier of the premises in question demanding access to the premises, and

    (b)   that either–

        (i)   access was demanded at a reasonable hour and was unreasonably refused, or

        (ii)   although entry to the premises was granted, the occupier unreasonably refused to comply with a request by the Commissioner or any of the Commissioner's officers or staff to permit the Commissioner or the officer or member of staff to do any of the things referred to in paragraph 1(3), and

    (c)   that the occupier, has, after the refusal, been notified by the Commissioner of the application for the warrant and has had an opportunity of being heard by the judge on the question whether or not it should be issued.

(1A) In determining whether the Commissioner has given an occupier the seven days' notice referred to in sub-paragraph (1)(a) any assessment notice served on the occupier is to be disregarded.

(2) Sub-paragraph (1) shall not apply if the judge is satisfied that the case is one of urgency or that compliance with those provisions would defeat the object of the entry.

3 A judge who issues a warrant under this Schedule shall also issue two copies of it and certify them clearly as copies.

Execution of warrants

4 A person executing a warrant issued under this Schedule may use such reasonable force as may be necessary.

5 A warrant issued under this Schedule shall be executed at a reasonable hour unless it appears to the person executing it that there are grounds for suspecting that the evidence in question would not be found object of the warrant would be defeated if it were so executed.

6 If the person who occupies the premises in respect of which a warrant is issued under this Schedule is present when the warrant is executed, he shall be shown the warrant and supplied with a copy of it; and if that person is not present a copy of the warrant shall be left in a prominent place on the premises.

7(1) A person seizing anything in pursuance of a warrant under this Schedule shall give a receipt for it if asked to do so.

(2) Anything so seized may be retained for so long as is necessary in all the circumstances but the person in occupation of the premises in question shall be given a copy of anything that is seized if he so requests and the person executing the warrant considers that it can be done without undue delay.

Matters exempt from inspection and seizure

8 The powers of inspection and seizure conferred by a warrant issued under this Schedule shall not be exercisable in respect of personal data which by virtue of section 28 are exempt from any of the provisions of this Act.

9(1) Subject to the provisions of this paragraph, the powers of inspection and seizure conferred by a warrant issued under this Schedule shall not be exercisable in respect of–

    (a) any communication between a professional legal adviser and his client in connection with the giving of legal advice to the client with respect to his obligations, liabilities or rights under this Act, or

    (b) any communication between a professional legal adviser and his client, or between such an adviser or his client and any other person, made in connection with or in contemplation of proceedings under or arising out of this Act (including proceedings before the Tribunal) and for the purposes of such proceedings.

(2) Sub-paragraph (1) applies also to–

    (a) any copy or other record of any such communication as is there mentioned, and

    (b) any document or article enclosed with or referred to in any such communication if made in connection with the giving of any advice or, as the case may be, in connection with or in contemplation of and for the purposes of such proceedings as are there mentioned.

(3) This paragraph does not apply to anything in the possession of any person other than the professional legal adviser or his client or to anything held with the intention of furthering

a criminal purpose.

(4) In this paragraph references to the client of a professional legal adviser include references to any person representing such a client.

10 If the person in occupation of any premises in respect of which a warrant is issued under this Schedule objects to the inspection or seizure under the warrant of any material on the grounds that it consists partly of matters in respect of which those powers are not exercisable, he shall, if the person executing the warrant so requests, furnish that person with a copy of so much of the material as is not exempt from those powers.

Return of warrants

11 A warrant issued under this Schedule shall be returned to the court from which it was issued–
    (a)   after being executed, or
    (b)   if not executed within the time authorised for its execution;
and the person by whom any such warrant is executed shall make an endorsement on it stating what powers have been exercised by him under the warrant.

Offences

12 Any person who–
    (a)   intentionally obstructs a person in the execution of a warrant issued under this Schedule, or
    (b)   fails without reasonable excuse to give any person executing such a warrant such assistance as he may reasonably require for the execution of the warrant,
    (c)   makes a statement in response to a requirement under paragraph (e) or (f) of paragraph 1(3) which that person knows to be false in a material respect, or
    (d)   recklessly makes a statement in response to such a requirement which is false in a material respect,
is guilty of an offence.

Vessels, vehicles etc

13 In this Schedule "premises" includes any vessel, vehicle, aircraft or hovercraft, and references to the occupier of any premises include references to the person in charge of any vessel, vehicle, aircraft or hovercraft.

Scotland and Northern Ireland

14 In the application of this Schedule to Scotland–
    (a)   for any reference to a circuit judge there is substituted a reference to the sheriff,
    (b)   for any reference to information on oath there is substituted a reference to evidence on oath, and
    (c)   for the reference to the court from which the warrant was issued there is substituted a reference to the sheriff clerk.

15 In the application of this Schedule to Northern Ireland–
    (a)   for any reference to a circuit judge there is substituted a reference to a county court judge, and
    (b)   for any reference to information on oath there is substituted a reference to a complaint on oath.

Self-incrimination

16 An explanation given, or information provided, by a person in response to a requirement

under paragraph (e) or (f) of paragraph 1(3) may only be used in evidence against that person—

    (a)   on a prosecution for an offence under—

        (i)   paragraph 12,

        (ii)   section 5 of the Perjury Act 1911 (false statements made otherwise than on oath),

        (iii)   section 44(2) of the Criminal Law (Consolidation) (Scotland) Act 1995 (false statements made otherwise than on oath), or

        (iv)   Article 10 of the Perjury (Northern Ireland) Order 1979 (false statutory declarations and other false unsworn statements), or

    (b)   on a prosecution for any other offence where—

        (i)   in giving evidence that person makes a statement inconsistent with that explanation or information, and

        (ii)   evidence relating to that explanation or information is adduced, or a question relating to it is asked, by that person or on that person's behalf.

SCHEDULE 10
FURTHER PROVISIONS RELATING TO ASSISTANCE UNDER SECTION 53

Section 53(6)

1   In this Schedule "applicant" and "proceedings" have the same meaning as in section 53.

2   The assistance provided under section 53 may include the making of arrangements for, or for the Commissioner to bear the costs of—

    (a)   the giving of advice or assistance by a solicitor or counsel, and

    (b)   the representation of the applicant, or the provision to him of such assistance as is usually given by a solicitor or counsel—

        (i)   in steps preliminary or incidental to the proceedings, or

        (ii)   in arriving at or giving effect to a compromise to avoid or bring an end to the proceedings.

3   Where assistance is provided with respect to the conduct of proceedings—

    (a)   it shall include an agreement by the Commissioner to indemnify the applicant (subject only to any exceptions specified in the notification) in respect of any liability to pay costs or expenses arising by virtue of any judgment or order of the court in the proceedings,

    (b)   it may include an agreement by the Commissioner to indemnify the applicant in respect of any liability to pay costs or expenses arising by virtue of any compromise or settlement arrived at in order to avoid the proceedings or bring the proceedings to an end, and

    (c)   it may include an agreement by the Commissioner to indemnify the applicant in respect of any liability to pay damages pursuant to an undertaking given on the grant of interlocutory relief (in Scotland, an interim order) to the applicant.

4   Where the Commissioner provides assistance in relation to any proceedings, he shall do so on such terms, or make such other arrangements, as will secure that a person against whom the proceedings have been or are commenced is informed that assistance has been or is being provided by the Commissioner in relation to them.

5   In England and Wales or Northern Ireland, the recovery of expenses incurred by the Commissioner in providing an applicant with assistance (as taxed or assessed in such manner as may be prescribed by rules of court) shall constitute a first charge for the benefit of the Commissioner—

(a)   on any costs which, by virtue of any judgment or order of the court, are payable to the applicant by any other person in respect of the matter in connection with which the assistance is provided, and

(b)   on any sum payable to the applicant under a compromise or settlement arrived at in connection with that matter to avoid or bring to an end any proceedings.

6   In Scotland, the recovery of such expenses (as taxed or assessed in such manner as may be prescribed by rules of court) shall be paid to the Commissioner, in priority to other debts–

(a)   out of any expenses which, by virtue of any judgment or order of the court, are payable to the applicant by any other person in respect of the matter in connection with which the assistance is provided, and

(b)   out of any sum payable to the applicant under a compromise or settlement arrived at in connection with that matter to avoid or bring to an end any proceedings.

SCHEDULE 11
EDUCATIONAL RECORDS

Section 68(1)(b)

Meaning of "educational record"

1   For the purposes of section 68 "educational record" means any record to which paragraph 2, 5 or 7 applies.

England and Wales

2   This paragraph applies to any record of information which–

(a)   is processed by or on behalf of the governing body of, or a teacher at, any school in England and Wales specified in paragraph 3,

(b)   relates to any person who is or has been a pupil at the school, and

(c)   originated from or was supplied by or on behalf of any of the persons specified in paragraph 4,

other than information which is processed by a teacher solely for the teacher's own use.

3   The schools referred to in paragraph 2(a) are–

(a)   a school maintained by a local education authority, and

(b)   a special school, as defined by section 6(2) of the Education Act 1996, which is not so maintained.

4   The persons referred to in paragraph 2(c) are–

(a)   an employee of the local education authority which maintains the school,

(b)   in the case of–

(i)   a voluntary aided, foundation or foundation special school (within the meaning of the School Standards and Framework Act 1998), or

(ii)   a special school which is not maintained by a local education authority,

a teacher or other employee at the school (including an educational psychologist engaged by the governing body under a contract for services),

(c)   the pupil to whom the record relates, and

(d)   a parent, as defined by section 576(1) of the Education Act 1996, of that pupil.

Scotland

5   This paragraph applies to any record of information which is processed-

(a)   by an education authority in Scotland, and

(b)   for the purpose of the relevant function of the authority,

other than information which is processed by a teacher solely for the teacher's own use.

6   For the purposes of paragraph 5–

(a)   "education authority" means an education authority within the meaning of the Education (Scotland) Act 1980 ("the 1980 Act"),

(b)   "the relevant function" means, in relation to each of those authorities, their function under section 1 of the 1980 Act and section 7(1) of the 1989 Act, and

(c)   information processed by an education authority is processed for the purpose of the relevant function of the authority if the processing relates to the discharge of that function in respect of a person–

(i)   who is or has been a pupil in a school provided by the authority, or

(ii)   who receives, or has received, further education (within the meaning of the 1980 Act) so provided.

Northern Ireland

7(1)   This paragraph applies to any record of information which–

(a)   is processed by or on behalf of the Board of Governors of, or a teacher at, any grant-aided school in Northern Ireland,

(b)   relates to any person who is or has been a pupil at the school, and

(c)   originated from or was supplied by or on behalf of any of the persons specified in paragraph 8,

other than information which is processed by a teacher solely for the teacher's own use.

(2)   In sub-paragraph (1) "grant-aided school" has the same meaning as in the Education and Libraries (Northern Ireland) Order 1986.

8   The persons referred to in paragraph 7(1) are–

(a)   a teacher at the school,

(b)   an employee of an education and library board, other than such a teacher,

(c)   the pupil to whom the record relates, and

(d)   a parent (as defined by Article 2(2) of the Education and Libraries (Northern Ireland) Order 1986) of that pupil.

England and Wales: transitory provisions

Not reproduced

SCHEDULE 12
ACCESSIBLE PUBLIC RECORDS

Section 68(1)(c)

Meaning of "accessible public record"

1   For the purposes of section 68 "accessible public record" means any record which is kept by an authority specified–

(a)   as respects England and Wales, in the Table in paragraph 2,

(b)   as respects Scotland, in the Table in paragraph 4, or

(c)   as respects Northern Ireland, in the Table in paragraph 6,

and is a record of information of a description specified in that Table in relation to that authority.

Housing and social services records: England and Wales

2   The following is the Table referred to in paragraph 1(a).

TABLE OF AUTHORITIES AND INFORMATION

The authorities	*The accessible information*
Housing Act local authority.	Information held for the purpose of any of the authority's tenancies.
Local social services authority.	Information held for any purpose of the authority's social services functions.

3(1)   The following provisions apply for the interpretation of the Table in paragraph 2.

(2)   Any authority which, by virtue of section 4(e) of the Housing Act 1985, is a local authority for the purpose of any provision of that Act is a "Housing Act local authority" for the purposes of this Schedule, and so is any housing action trust established under Part III of the Housing Act 1988.

(3)   Information contained in records kept by a Housing Act local authority is "held for the purpose of any of the authority's tenancies" if it is held for any purpose of the relationship of landlord and tenant of a dwelling which subsists, has subsisted or may subsist between the authority and any individual who is, has been or, as the case may be, has applied to be, a tenant of the authority.

(4)   Any authority which, by virtue of section 1 or 12 of the Local Authority Social Services Act 1970, is or is treated as a local authority for the purposes of that Act is a "local social services authority" for the purposes of this Schedule; and information contained in records kept by such an authority is "held for any purpose of the authority's social services functions" if it is held for the purpose of any past, current or proposed exercise of such a function in any case.

(5)   Any expression used in paragraph 2 or this paragraph and in Part II of the Housing Act 1985 or the Local Authority Social Services Act 1970 has the same meaning as in that Act.

Housing and social services records: Scotland

4   The following is the Table referred to in paragraph 1(b).

TABLE OF AUTHORITIES AND INFORMATION

The authorities	*The accessible information*
Local authority.	Information held for any purpose of any of the body's tenancies.
Scottish Homes.	
Social work authority.	Information held for any purpose of the authority's functions under the Social Work (Scotland) Act 1968 and the enactments referred to in section 5(1B) of that Act.

5(1)   The following provisions apply for the interpretation of the Table in paragraph 4.

(2) "Local authority" means–

    (a) a council constituted under section 2 of the Local Government etc (Scotland) Act 1994,

    (b) a joint board or joint committee of two or more of those councils, or

    (c) any trust under the control of such a council.

(3) Information contained in records kept by a local authority or Scottish Homes is held for the purpose of any of their tenancies if it is held for any purpose of the relationship of landlord and tenant of a dwelling-house which subsists, has subsisted or may subsist between the authority or, as the case may be, Scottish Homes and any individual who is, has been or, as the case may be, has applied to be a tenant of theirs.

(4) "Social work authority" means a local authority for the purposes of the Social Work (Scotland) Act 1968; and information contained in records kept by such an authority is held for any purpose of their functions if it is held for the purpose of any past, current or proposed exercise of such a function in any case.

Housing and social services records: Northern Ireland

6   The following is the Table referred to in paragraph 1(c).

TABLE OF AUTHORITIES AND INFORMATION

The authorities	The accessible information
The Northern Ireland Housing Executive.	Information held for the purpose of any of the Executive's tenancies.
A Health and Social Services Board.	Information held for the purpose of any past, current or proposed exercise by the Board of any function exercisable, by virtue of directions under Article 17(1) of the Health and Personal Social Services (Northern Ireland) Order 1972, by the Board on behalf of the Department of Health and Social Services with respect to the administration of personal social services under– (a) the Children and Young Persons Act (Northern Ireland) 1968; (b) the Health and Personal Social Services (Northern Ireland) Order 1972; (c) Article 47 of the Matrimonial Causes (Northern Ireland) Order 1978; (d) Article 11 of the Domestic Proceedings (Northern Ireland) Order 1980; (e) the Adoption (Northern Ireland) Order 1987; or (f) the Children (Northern Ireland) Order 1995.
An HSS trust.	Information held for the purpose of any past, current or proposed exercise by the trust of any function exercisable, by virtue of an authorisation under Article 3(1) of the Health and Personal Social Services (Northern Ireland) Order 1994, by the trust on behalf of a Health and Social Services Board with respect to the administration of personal social services under any statutory provision mentioned in the last preceding entry.

7(1) This paragraph applies for the interpretation of the Table in paragraph 6.

(2) Information contained in records kept by the Northern Ireland Housing Executive is "held for the purpose of any of the Executive's tenancies" if it is held for any purpose of the relationship of landlord and tenant of a dwelling which subsists, has subsisted or may subsist between the Executive and any individual who is, has been or, as the case may be, has applied to be, a tenant of the Executive.

SCHEDULE 13
MODIFICATIONS OF ACT HAVING EFFECT BEFORE 24TH OCTOBER 2007

Not reproduced   Section 72

SCHEDULE 14
TRANSITIONAL PROVISIONS AND SAVINGS

Not reproduced   Section 73

SCHEDULE 15
MINOR AND CONSEQUENTIAL AMENDMENTS

Not reproduced   Section 74(1)

SCHEDULE 16
REPEALS AND REVOCATIONS

Not reproduced   Section 74(2)

Directive 95/46/EC of the European Parliament and of the Council of 24 October 1995 on the protection of individuals with regard to the processing of personal data and on the free movement of such data

THE EUROPEAN PARLIAMENT AND THE COUNCIL OF THE EUROPEAN UNION,

Having regard to the Treaty establishing the European Community, and in particular Article 100a thereof,

Having regard to the proposal from the Commission,

Having regard to the opinion of the Economic and Social Committee,

Acting in accordance with the procedure referred to in Article 189b of the Treaty,

(1) Whereas the objectives of the Community, as laid down in the Treaty, as amended by the Treaty on European Union, include creating an ever closer union among the peoples of Europe, fostering closer relations between the States belonging to the Community, ensuring economic and social progress by common action to eliminate the barriers which divide Europe, encouraging the constant improvement of the living conditions of its peoples, preserving and strengthening peace and liberty and promoting democracy on the basis of the fundamental rights recognized in the constitution and laws of the Member States and in the European Convention for the Protection of Human Rights and Fundamental Freedoms;

(2) Whereas data-processing systems are designed to serve man; whereas they must, whatever the nationality or residence of natural persons, respect their fundamental rights and freedoms, notably the right to privacy, and contribute to economic and social progress, trade expansion and the well-being of individuals;

(3) Whereas the establishment and functioning of an internal market in which, in accordance with Article 7a of the Treaty, the free movement of goods, persons, services and capital is ensured require not only that personal data should be able to flow freely from one Member State to another, but also that the fundamental rights of individuals should be safeguarded;

(4) Whereas increasingly frequent recourse is being had in the Community to the processing of personal data in the various spheres of economic and social activity; whereas the progress made in information technology is making the processing and exchange of such data considerably easier;

(5) Whereas the economic and social integration resulting from the establishment and functioning of the internal market within the meaning of Article 7a of the Treaty will necessarily lead to a substantial increase in cross-border flows of personal data between all those involved in a private or public capacity in economic and social activity in the Member States; whereas the exchange of personal data between undertakings in different Member States is set to increase; whereas the national authorities in the various Member States are being called upon by virtue of Community law to collaborate and exchange personal data so as to be able to perform their duties or carry out tasks on behalf of an authority in another Member State within the context of the area without internal frontiers as constituted by the internal market;

(6) Whereas, furthermore, the increase in scientific and technical cooperation and the coordinated introduction of new telecommunications networks in the Community necessitate and facilitate cross-border flows of personal data;

(7) Whereas the difference in levels of protection of the rights and freedoms of individuals, notably the right to privacy, with regard to the processing of personal data afforded in the Member States may prevent the transmission of such data from the territory of one Member State to that of another Member State; whereas this difference may therefore constitute an obstacle to the pursuit of a number of economic activities at Community level, distort competition and impede authorities in the discharge of their responsibilities under Community law; whereas this difference in levels of protection is due to the existence of a wide variety of national laws, regulations and administrative provisions;

(8) Whereas, in order to remove the obstacles to flows of personal data, the level of protection of the rights and freedoms of individuals with regard to the processing of such data must be equivalent in all Member States; whereas this objective is vital to the internal market but cannot be achieved by the Member States alone, especially in view of the scale of the divergences which currently exist between the relevant laws in the Member States and the need to coordinate the laws of the Member States so as to ensure that the cross-border flow of personal data is regulated in a consistent manner that is in keeping with the objective of the internal market as provided for in Article 7a of the Treaty; whereas Community action to approximate those laws is therefore needed;

(9) Whereas, given the equivalent protection resulting from the approximation of national laws, the Member States will no longer be able to inhibit the free movement between them of personal data on grounds relating to protection of the rights and freedoms of individuals, and in particular the right to privacy; whereas Member States will be left a margin for manoeuvre, which may, in the context of implementation of the Directive, also be exercised by the business and social partners; whereas Member States will therefore be able to specify in their national law the general conditions governing the lawfulness of data processing; whereas in doing so the Member States shall strive to improve the protection currently provided by their legislation; whereas, within the limits of this margin for manoeuvre and in accordance with Community law, disparities could arise in the implementation of the Directive, and this could have an effect on the movement of data within a Member State as well as within the Community;

(10) Whereas the object of the national laws on the processing of personal data is to protect fundamental rights and freedoms, notably the right to privacy, which is recognized both in Article 8 of the European Convention for the Protection of Human Rights and Fundamental Freedoms and in the general principles of Community law; whereas, for that reason, the approximation of those laws must not result in any lessening of the protection they afford but must, on the contrary, seek to ensure a high level of protection in the Community;

(11) Whereas the principles of the protection of the rights and freedoms of individuals, notably the right to privacy, which are contained in this Directive, give substance to and amplify those contained in the Council of Europe Convention of 28 January 1981 for the Protection of Individuals with regard to Automatic Processing of Personal Data;

(12) Whereas the protection principles must apply to all processing of personal data by any person whose activities are governed by Community law; whereas there should be excluded the processing of data carried out by a natural person in the exercise of activities which are

exclusively personal or domestic, such as correspondence and the holding of records of addresses;

(13) Whereas the activities referred to in Titles V and VI of the Treaty on European Union regarding public safety, defence, State security or the activities of the State in the area of criminal laws fall outside the scope of Community law, without prejudice to the obligations incumbent upon Member States under Article 56 (2), Article 57 or Article 100a of the Treaty establishing the European Community; whereas the processing of personal data that is necessary to safeguard the economic well-being of the State does not fall within the scope of this Directive where such processing relates to State security matters;

(14) Whereas, given the importance of the developments under way, in the framework of the information society, of the techniques used to capture, transmit, manipulate, record, store or communicate sound and image data relating to natural persons, this Directive should be applicable to processing involving such data;

(15) Whereas the processing of such data is covered by this Directive only if it is automated or if the data processed are contained or are intended to be contained in a filing system structured according to specific criteria relating to individuals, so as to permit easy access to the personal data in question;

(16) Whereas the processing of sound and image data, such as in cases of video surveillance, does not come within the scope of this Directive if it is carried out for the purposes of public security, defence, national security or in the course of State activities relating to the area of criminal law or of other activities which do not come within the scope of Community law;

(17) Whereas, as far as the processing of sound and image data carried out for purposes of journalism or the purposes of literary or artistic expression is concerned, in particular in the audiovisual field, the principles of the Directive are to apply in a restricted manner according to the provisions laid down in Article 9;

(18) Whereas, in order to ensure that individuals are not deprived of the protection to which they are entitled under this Directive, any processing of personal data in the Community must be carried out in accordance with the law of one of the Member States; whereas, in this connection, processing carried out under the responsibility of a controller who is established in a Member State should be governed by the law of that State;

(19) Whereas establishment on the territory of a Member State implies the effective and real exercise of activity through stable arrangements; whereas the legal form of such an establishment, whether simply branch or a subsidiary with a legal personality, is not the determining factor in this respect; whereas, when a single controller is established on the territory of several Member States, particularly by means of subsidiaries, he must ensure, in order to avoid any circumvention of national rules, that each of the establishments fulfils the obligations imposed by the national law applicable to its activities;

(20) Whereas the fact that the processing of data is carried out by a person established in a third country must not stand in the way of the protection of individuals provided for in this Directive; whereas in these cases, the processing should be governed by the law of the Member State in which the means used are located, and there should be guarantees to ensure that the rights and obligations provided for in this Directive are respected in practice;

(21) Whereas this Directive is without prejudice to the rules of territoriality applicable in criminal matters;

(22) Whereas Member States shall more precisely define in the laws they enact or when

bringing into force the measures taken under this Directive the general circumstances in which processing is lawful; whereas in particular Article 5, in conjunction with Articles 7 and 8, allows Member States, independently of general rules, to provide for special processing conditions for specific sectors and for the various categories of data covered by Article 8;

(23) Whereas Member States are empowered to ensure the implementation of the protection of individuals both by means of a general law on the protection of individuals as regards the processing of personal data and by sectorial laws such as those relating, for example, to statistical institutes;

(24) Whereas the legislation concerning the protection of legal persons with regard to the processing data which concerns them is not affected by this Directive;

(25) Whereas the principles of protection must be reflected, on the one hand, in the obligations imposed on persons, public authorities, enterprises, agencies or other bodies responsible for processing, in particular regarding data quality, technical security, notification to the supervisory authority, and the circumstances under which processing can be carried out, and, on the other hand, in the right conferred on individuals, the data on whom are the subject of processing, to be informed that processing is taking place, to consult the data, to request corrections and even to object to processing in certain circumstances;

(26) Whereas the principles of protection must apply to any information concerning an identified or identifiable person; whereas, to determine whether a person is identifiable, account should be taken of all the means likely reasonably to be used either by the controller or by any other person to identify the said person; whereas the principles of protection shall not apply to data rendered anonymous in such a way that the data subject is no longer identifiable; whereas codes of conduct within the meaning of Article 27 may be a useful instrument for providing guidance as to the ways in which data may be rendered anonymous and retained in a form in which identification of the data subject is no longer possible;

(27) Whereas the protection of individuals must apply as much to automatic processing of data as to manual processing; whereas the scope of this protection must not in effect depend on the techniques used, otherwise this would create a serious risk of circumvention; whereas, nonetheless, as regards manual processing, this Directive covers only filing systems, not unstructured files; whereas, in particular, the content of a filing system must be structured according to specific criteria relating to individuals allowing easy access to the personal data; whereas, in line with the definition in Article 2 (c), the different criteria for determining the constituents of a structured set of personal data, and the different criteria governing access to such a set, may be laid down by each Member State; whereas files or sets of files as well as their cover pages, which are not structured according to specific criteria, shall under no circumstances fall within the scope of this Directive;

(28) Whereas any processing of personal data must be lawful and fair to the individuals concerned; whereas, in particular, the data must be adequate, relevant and not excessive in relation to the purposes for which they are processed; whereas such purposes must be explicit and legitimate and must be determined at the time of collection of the data; whereas the purposes of processing further to collection shall not be incompatible with the purposes as they were originally specified;

(29) Whereas the further processing of personal data for historical, statistical or scientific purposes is not generally to be considered incompatible with the purposes for which the

data have previously been collected provided that Member States furnish suitable safeguards; whereas these safeguards must in particular rule out the use of the data in support of measures or decisions regarding any particular individual;

(30) Whereas, in order to be lawful, the processing of personal data must in addition be carried out with the consent of the data subject or be necessary for the conclusion or performance of a contract binding on the data subject, or as a legal requirement, or for the performance of a task carried out in the public interest or in the exercise of official authority, or in the legitimate interests of a natural or legal person, provided that the interests or the rights and freedoms of the data subject are not overriding; whereas, in particular, in order to maintain a balance between the interests involved while guaranteeing effective competition, Member States may determine the circumstances in which personal data may be used or disclosed to a third party in the context of the legitimate ordinary business activities of companies and other bodies; whereas Member States may similarly specify the conditions under which personal data may be disclosed to a third party for the purposes of marketing whether carried out commercially or by a charitable organization or by any other association or foundation, of a political nature for example, subject to the provisions allowing a data subject to object to the processing of data regarding him, at no cost and without having to state his reasons;

(31) Whereas the processing of personal data must equally be regarded as lawful where it is carried out in order to protect an interest which is essential for the data subject's life;

(32) Whereas it is for national legislation to determine whether the controller performing a task carried out in the public interest or in the exercise of official authority should be a public administration or another natural or legal person governed by public law, or by private law such as a professional association;

(33) Whereas data which are capable by their nature of infringing fundamental freedoms or privacy should not be processed unless the data subject gives his explicit consent; whereas, however, derogations from this prohibition must be explicitly provided for in respect of specific needs, in particular where the processing of these data is carried out for certain health-related purposes by persons subject to a legal obligation of professional secrecy or in the course of legitimate activities by certain associations or foundations the purpose of which is to permit the exercise of fundamental freedoms;

(34) Whereas Member States must also be authorized, when justified by grounds of important public interest, to derogate from the prohibition on processing sensitive categories of data where important reasons of public interest so justify in areas such as public health and social protection - especially in order to ensure the quality and cost-effectiveness of the procedures used for settling claims for benefits and services in the health insurance system - scientific research and government statistics; whereas it is incumbent on them, however, to provide specific and suitable safeguards so as to protect the fundamental rights and the privacy of individuals;

(35) Whereas, moreover, the processing of personal data by official authorities for achieving aims, laid down in constitutional law or international public law, of officially recognized religious associations is carried out on important grounds of public interest;

(36) Whereas where, in the course of electoral activities, the operation of the democratic system requires in certain Member States that political parties compile data on people's political opinion, the processing of such data may be permitted for reasons of important public interest, provided that appropriate safeguards are established;

(37) Whereas the processing of personal data for purposes of journalism or for purposes of literary of artistic expression, in particular in the audiovisual field, should qualify for

exemption from the requirements of certain provisions of this Directive in so far as this is necessary to reconcile the fundamental rights of individuals with freedom of information and notably the right to receive and impart information, as guaranteed in particular in Article 10 of the European Convention for the Protection of Human Rights and Fundamental Freedoms; whereas Member States should therefore lay down exemptions and derogations necessary for the purpose of balance between fundamental rights as regards general measures on the legitimacy of data processing, measures on the transfer of data to third countries and the power of the supervisory authority; whereas this should not, however, lead Member States to lay down exemptions from the measures to ensure security of processing; whereas at least the supervisory authority responsible for this sector should also be provided with certain ex-post powers, e.g. to publish a regular report or to refer matters to the judicial authorities;

(38) Whereas, if the processing of data is to be fair, the data subject must be in a position to learn of the existence of a processing operation and, where data are collected from him, must be given accurate and full information, bearing in mind the circumstances of the collection;

(39) Whereas certain processing operations involve data which the controller has not collected directly from the data subject; whereas, furthermore, data can be legitimately disclosed to a third party, even if the disclosure was not anticipated at the time the data were collected from the data subject; whereas, in all these cases, the data subject should be informed when the data are recorded or at the latest when the data are first disclosed to a third party;

(40) Whereas, however, it is not necessary to impose this obligation of the data subject already has the information; whereas, moreover, there will be no such obligation if the recording or disclosure are expressly provided for by law or if the provision of information to the data subject proves impossible or would involve disproportionate efforts, which could be the case where processing is for historical, statistical or scientific purposes; whereas, in this regard, the number of data subjects, the age of the data, and any compensatory measures adopted may be taken into consideration;

(41) Whereas any person must be able to exercise the right of access to data relating to him which are being processed, in order to verify in particular the accuracy of the data and the lawfulness of the processing; whereas, for the same reasons, every data subject must also have the right to know the logic involved in the automatic processing of data concerning him, at least in the case of the automated decisions referred to in Article 15 (1); whereas this right must not adversely affect trade secrets or intellectual property and in particular the copyright protecting the software; whereas these considerations must not, however, result in the data subject being refused all information;

(42) Whereas Member States may, in the interest of the data subject or so as to protect the rights and freedoms of others, restrict rights of access and information; whereas they may, for example, specify that access to medical data may be obtained only through a health professional;

(43) Whereas restrictions on the rights of access and information and on certain obligations of the controller may similarly be imposed by Member States in so far as they are necessary to safeguard, for example, national security, defence, public safety, or important economic or financial interests of a Member State or the Union, as well as criminal investigations and prosecutions and action in respect of breaches of ethics in the regulated professions; whereas the list of exceptions and limitations should include the tasks of monitoring,

inspection or regulation necessary in the three last-mentioned areas concerning public security, economic or financial interests and crime prevention; whereas the listing of tasks in these three areas does not affect the legitimacy of exceptions or restrictions for reasons of State security or defence;

(44) Whereas Member States may also be led, by virtue of the provisions of Community law, to derogate from the provisions of this Directive concerning the right of access, the obligation to inform individuals, and the quality of data, in order to secure certain of the purposes referred to above;

(45) Whereas, in cases where data might lawfully be processed on grounds of public interest, official authority or the legitimate interests of a natural or legal person, any data subject should nevertheless be entitled, on legitimate and compelling grounds relating to his particular situation, to object to the processing of any data relating to himself; whereas Member States may nevertheless lay down national provisions to the contrary;

(46) Whereas the protection of the rights and freedoms of data subjects with regard to the processing of personal data requires that appropriate technical and organizational measures be taken, both at the time of the design of the processing system and at the time of the processing itself, particularly in order to maintain security and thereby to prevent any unauthorized processing; whereas it is incumbent on the Member States to ensure that controllers comply with these measures; whereas these measures must ensure an appropriate level of security, taking into account the state of the art and the costs of their implementation in relation to the risks inherent in the processing and the nature of the data to be protected;

(47) Whereas where a message containing personal data is transmitted by means of a telecommunications or electronic mail service, the sole purpose of which is the transmission of such messages, the controller in respect of the personal data contained in the message will normally be considered to be the person from whom the message originates, rather than the person offering the transmission services; whereas, nevertheless, those offering such services will normally be considered controllers in respect of the processing of the additional personal data necessary for the operation of the service;

(48) Whereas the procedures for notifying the supervisory authority are designed to ensure disclosure of the purposes and main features of any processing operation for the purpose of verification that the operation is in accordance with the national measures taken under this Directive;

(49) Whereas, in order to avoid unsuitable administrative formalities, exemptions from the obligation to notify and simplification of the notification required may be provided for by Member States in cases where processing is unlikely adversely to affect the rights and freedoms of data subjects, provided that it is in accordance with a measure taken by a Member State specifying its limits; whereas exemption or simplification may similarly be provided for by Member States where a person appointed by the controller ensures that the processing carried out is not likely adversely to affect the rights and freedoms of data subjects; whereas such a data protection official, whether or not an employee of the controller, must be in a position to exercise his functions in complete independence;

(50) Whereas exemption or simplification could be provided for in cases of processing operations whose sole purpose is the keeping of a register intended, according to national law, to provide information to the public and open to consultation by the public or by any person demonstrating a legitimate interest;

(51) Whereas, nevertheless, simplification or exemption from the obligation to notify shall not release the controller from any of the other obligations resulting from this Directive;

(52) Whereas, in this context, ex post facto verification by the competent authorities must in general be considered a sufficient measure;

(53) Whereas, however, certain processing operation are likely to pose specific risks to the rights and freedoms of data subjects by virtue of their nature, their scope or their purposes, such as that of excluding individuals from a right, benefit or a contract, or by virtue of the specific use of new technologies; whereas it is for Member States, if they so wish, to specify such risks in their legislation;

(54) Whereas with regard to all the processing undertaken in society, the amount posing such specific risks should be very limited; whereas Member States must provide that the supervisory authority, or the data protection official in cooperation with the authority, check such processing prior to it being carried out; whereas following this prior check, the supervisory authority may, according to its national law, give an opinion or an authorization regarding the processing; whereas such checking may equally take place in the course of the preparation either of a measure of the national parliament or of a measure based on such a legislative measure, which defines the nature of the processing and lays down appropriate safeguards;

(55) Whereas, if the controller fails to respect the rights of data subjects, national legislation must provide for a judicial remedy; whereas any damage which a person may suffer as a result of unlawful processing must be compensated for by the controller, who may be exempted from liability if he proves that he is not responsible for the damage, in particular in cases where he establishes fault on the part of the data subject or in case of force majeure; whereas sanctions must be imposed on any person, whether governed by private of public law, who fails to comply with the national measures taken under this Directive;

(56) Whereas cross-border flows of personal data are necessary to the expansion of international trade; whereas the protection of individuals guaranteed in the Community by this Directive does not stand in the way of transfers of personal data to third countries which ensure an adequate level of protection; whereas the adequacy of the level of protection afforded by a third country must be assessed in the light of all the circumstances surrounding the transfer operation or set of transfer operations;

(57) Whereas, on the other hand, the transfer of personal data to a third country which does not ensure an adequate level of protection must be prohibited;

(58) Whereas provisions should be made for exemptions from this prohibition in certain circumstances where the data subject has given his consent, where the transfer is necessary in relation to a contract or a legal claim, where protection of an important public interest so requires, for example in cases of international transfers of data between tax or customs administrations or between services competent for social security matters, or where the transfer is made from a register established by law and intended for consultation by the public or persons having a legitimate interest; whereas in this case such a transfer should not involve the entirety of the data or entire categories of the data contained in the register and, when the register is intended for consultation by persons having a legitimate interest, the transfer should be made only at the request of those persons or if they are to be the recipients;

(59) Whereas particular measures may be taken to compensate for the lack of protection in a third country in cases where the controller offers appropriate safeguards; whereas, moreover, provision must be made for procedures for negotiations between the Community and such third countries;

(60) Whereas, in any event, transfers to third countries may be effected only in full compliance with the provisions adopted by the Member States pursuant to this Directive, and in particular Article 8 thereof;

(61) Whereas Member States and the Commission, in their respective spheres of competence, must encourage the trade associations and other representative organizations concerned to draw up codes of conduct so as to facilitate the application of this Directive, taking account of the specific characteristics of the processing carried out in certain sectors, and respecting the national provisions adopted for its implementation;

(62) Whereas the establishment in Member States of supervisory authorities, exercising their functions with complete independence, is an essential component of the protection of individuals with regard to the processing of personal data;

(63) Whereas such authorities must have the necessary means to perform their duties, including powers of investigation and intervention, particularly in cases of complaints from individuals, and powers to engage in legal proceedings; whereas such authorities must help to ensure transparency of processing in the Member States within whose jurisdiction they fall;

(64) Whereas the authorities in the different Member States will need to assist one another in performing their duties so as to ensure that the rules of protection are properly respected throughout the European Union;

(65) Whereas, at Community level, a Working Party on the Protection of Individuals with regard to the Processing of Personal Data must be set up and be completely independent in the performance of its functions; whereas, having regard to its specific nature, it must advise the Commission and, in particular, contribute to the uniform application of the national rules adopted pursuant to this Directive;

(66) Whereas, with regard to the transfer of data to third countries, the application of this Directive calls for the conferment of powers of implementation on the Commission and the establishment of a procedure as laid down in Council Decision 87/373/EEC (1);

(67) Whereas an agreement on a modus vivendi between the European Parliament, the Council and the Commission concerning the implementing measures for acts adopted in accordance with the procedure laid down in Article 189b of the EC Treaty was reached on 20 December 1994;

(68) Whereas the principles set out in this Directive regarding the protection of the rights and freedoms of individuals, notably their right to privacy, with regard to the processing of personal data may be supplemented or clarified, in particular as far as certain sectors are concerned, by specific rules based on those principles;

(69) Whereas Member States should be allowed a period of not more than three years from the entry into force of the national measures transposing this Directive in which to apply such new national rules progressively to all processing operations already under way; whereas, in order to facilitate their cost-effective implementation, a further period expiring 12 years after the date on which this Directive is adopted will be allowed to Member States to ensure the conformity of existing manual filing systems with certain of the Directive's provisions; whereas, where data contained in such filing systems are manually processed during this extended transition period, those systems must be brought into conformity with these provisions at the time of such processing;

(70) Whereas it is not necessary for the data subject to give his consent again so as to allow the controller to continue to process, after the national provisions taken pursuant to this Directive enter into force, any sensitive data necessary for the performance of a contract

concluded on the basis of free and informed consent before the entry into force of these provisions;

(71) Whereas this Directive does not stand in the way of a Member State's regulating marketing activities aimed at consumers residing in territory in so far as such regulation does not concern the protection of individuals with regard to the processing of personal data;

(72) Whereas this Directive allows the principle of public access to official documents to be taken into account when implementing the principles set out in this Directive,

HAVE ADOPTED THIS DIRECTIVE:

CHAPTER I
GENERAL PROVISIONS

Article 1 — Object of the Directive

1. In accordance with this Directive, Member States shall protect the fundamental rights and freedoms of natural persons, and in particular their right to privacy with respect to the processing of personal data.

2. Member States shall neither restrict nor prohibit the free flow of personal data between Member States for reasons connected with the protection afforded under paragraph 1.

Article 2 — Definitions

For the purposes of this Directive:

(a) 'personal data' shall mean any information relating to an identified or identifiable natural person ('data subject'); an identifiable person is one who can be identified, directly or indirectly, in particular by reference to an identification number or to one or more factors specific to his physical, physiological, mental, economic, cultural or social identity;

(b) 'processing of personal data' ('processing') shall mean any operation or set of operations which is performed upon personal data, whether or not by automatic means, such as collection, recording, organization, storage, adaptation or alteration, retrieval, consultation, use, disclosure by transmission, dissemination or otherwise making available, alignment or combination, blocking, erasure or destruction;

(c) 'personal data filing system' ('filing system') shall mean any structured set of personal data which are accessible according to specific criteria, whether centralized, decentralized or dispersed on a functional or geographical basis;

(d) 'controller' shall mean the natural or legal person, public authority, agency or any other body which alone or jointly with others determines the purposes and means of the processing of personal data; where the purposes and means of processing are determined by national or Community laws or regulations, the controller or the specific criteria for his nomination may be designated by national or Community law;

(e) 'processor' shall mean a natural or legal person, public authority, agency or any other body which processes personal data on behalf of the controller;

(f) 'third party' shall mean any natural or legal person, public authority, agency or any other body other than the data subject, the controller, the processor and the persons who, under the direct authority of the controller or the processor, are authorized to process the data;

(g) 'recipient' shall mean a natural or legal person, public authority, agency or any other body to whom data are disclosed, whether a third party or not; however, authorities which may receive data in the framework of a particular inquiry shall not be regarded as recipients;

(h) 'the data subject's consent' shall mean any freely given specific and informed indication of his wishes by which the data subject signifies his agreement to personal data relating to him being processed.

Article 3 — Scope

1. This Directive shall apply to the processing of personal data wholly or partly by automatic means, and to the processing otherwise than by automatic means of personal data which form part of a filing system or are intended to form part of a filing system.

2. This Directive shall not apply to the processing of personal data:
   - in the course of an activity which falls outside the scope of Community law, such as those provided for by Titles V and VI of the Treaty on European Union and in any case to processing operations concerning public security, defence, State security (including the economic well-being of the State when the processing operation relates to State security matters) and the activities of the State in areas of criminal law,
   - by a natural person in the course of a purely personal or household activity.

Article 4 — National law applicable

1. Each Member State shall apply the national provisions it adopts pursuant to this Directive to the processing of personal data where:

   (a) the processing is carried out in the context of the activities of an establishment of the controller on the territory of the Member State; when the same controller is established on the territory of several Member States, he must take the necessary measures to ensure that each of these establishments complies with the obligations laid down by the national law applicable;

   (b) the controller is not established on the Member State's territory, but in a place where its national law applies by virtue of international public law;

   (c) the controller is not established on Community territory and, for purposes of processing personal data makes use of equipment, automated or otherwise, situated on the territory of the said Member State, unless such equipment is used only for purposes of transit through the territory of the Community.

2. In the circumstances referred to in paragraph 1 (c), the controller must designate a representative established in the territory of that Member State, without prejudice to legal actions which could be initiated against the controller himself.

CHAPTER II
GENERAL RULES ON THE LAWFULNESS OF THE PROCESSING OF PERSONAL DATA

Article 5

Member States shall, within the limits of the provisions of this Chapter, determine more precisely the conditions under which the processing of personal data is lawful.

SECTION I
PRINCIPLES RELATING TO DATA QUALITY

Article 6

1. Member States shall provide that personal data must be:

    (a) processed fairly and lawfully;

    (b) collected for specified, explicit and legitimate purposes and not further processed in a way incompatible with those purposes. Further processing of data for historical, statistical or scientific purposes shall not be considered as incompatible provided that Member States provide appropriate safeguards;

    (c) adequate, relevant and not excessive in relation to the purposes for which they are collected and/or further processed;

    (d) accurate and, where necessary, kept up to date; every reasonable step must be taken to ensure that data which are inaccurate or incomplete, having regard to the purposes for which they were collected or for which they are further processed, are erased or rectified;

    (e) kept in a form which permits identification of data subjects for no longer than is necessary for the purposes for which the data were collected or for which they are further processed. Member States shall lay down appropriate safeguards for personal data stored for longer periods for historical, statistical or scientific use.

2. It shall be for the controller to ensure that paragraph 1 is complied with.

SECTION II
CRITERIA FOR MAKING DATA PROCESSING LEGITIMATE

Article 7

Member States shall provide that personal data may be processed only if:

(a) the data subject has unambiguously given his consent; or

(b) processing is necessary for the performance of a contract to which the data subject is party or in order to take steps at the request of the data subject prior to entering into a contract; or

(c) processing is necessary for compliance with a legal obligation to which the controller is subject; or

(d) processing is necessary in order to protect the vital interests of the data subject; or

(e) processing is necessary for the performance of a task carried out in the public interest

979

or in the exercise of official authority vested in the controller or in a third party to whom the data are disclosed; or

(f) processing is necessary for the purposes of the legitimate interests pursued by the controller or by the third party or parties to whom the data are disclosed, except where such interests are overridden by the interests for fundamental rights and freedoms of the data subject which require protection under Article 1 (1).

SECTION III
SPECIAL CATEGORIES OF PROCESSING

Article 8 — The processing of special categories of data

1. Member States shall prohibit the processing of personal data revealing racial or ethnic origin, political opinions, religious or philosophical beliefs, trade-union membership, and the processing of data concerning health or sex life.

2. Paragraph 1 shall not apply where:

   (a) the data subject has given his explicit consent to the processing of those data, except where the laws of the Member State provide that the prohibition referred to in paragraph 1 may not be lifted by the data subject's giving his consent; or

   (b) processing is necessary for the purposes of carrying out the obligations and specific rights of the controller in the field of employment law in so far as it is authorized by national law providing for adequate safeguards; or

   (c) processing is necessary to protect the vital interests of the data subject or of another person where the data subject is physically or legally incapable of giving his consent; or

   (d) processing is carried out in the course of its legitimate activities with appropriate guarantees by a foundation, association or any other non-profit-seeking body with a political, philosophical, religious or trade-union aim and on condition that the processing relates solely to the members of the body or to persons who have regular contact with it in connection with its purposes and that the data are not disclosed to a third party without the consent of the data subjects; or

   (e) the processing relates to data which are manifestly made public by the data subject or is necessary for the establishment, exercise or defence of legal claims.

3. Paragraph 1 shall not apply where processing of the data is required for the purposes of preventive medicine, medical diagnosis, the provision of care or treatment or the management of health-care services, and where those data are processed by a health professional subject under national law or rules established by national competent bodies to the obligation of professional secrecy or by another person also subject to an equivalent obligation of secrecy.

4. Subject to the provision of suitable safeguards, Member States may, for reasons of substantial public interest, lay down exemptions in addition to those laid down in paragraph 2 either by national law or by decision of the supervisory authority.

5. Processing of data relating to offences, criminal convictions or security measures may be carried out only under the control of official authority, or if suitable specific safeguards are provided under national law, subject to derogations which may be granted by the Member State under national provisions providing suitable specific safeguards. However, a complete register of criminal convictions may be kept only under the control of official authority.

   Member States may provide that data relating to administrative sanctions or judgements in civil cases shall also be processed under the control of official authority.

6. Derogations from paragraph 1 provided for in paragraphs 4 and 5 shall be notified to the Commission.

7. Member States shall determine the conditions under which a national identification number or any other identifier of general application may be processed.

Article 9 — Processing of personal data and freedom of expression

Member States shall provide for exemptions or derogations from the provisions of this Chapter, Chapter IV and Chapter VI for the processing of personal data carried out solely for journalistic purposes or the purpose of artistic or literary expression only if they are necessary to reconcile the right to privacy with the rules governing freedom of expression.

SECTION IV
INFORMATION TO BE GIVEN TO THE DATA SUBJECT

Article 10 — Information in cases of collection of data from the data subject

Member States shall provide that the controller or his representative must provide a data subject from whom data relating to himself are collected with at least the following information, except where he already has it:

   (a) the identity of the controller and of his representative, if any;

   (b) the purposes of the processing for which the data are intended;

   (c) any further information such as

   − the recipients or categories of recipients of the data,

   − whether replies to the questions are obligatory or voluntary, as well as the possible consequences of failure to reply,

   − the existence of the right of access to and the right to rectify the data concerning him

   in so far as such further information is necessary, having regard to the specific circumstances in which the data are collected, to guarantee fair processing in respect of the data subject.

Article 11 — Information where the data have not been obtained from the data subject

1. Where the data have not been obtained from the data subject, Member States shall provide that the controller or his representative must at the time of undertaking the recording of personal data or if a disclosure to a third party is envisaged, no later than the time when the data are first disclosed provide the data subject with at least the following information, except where he already has it:

   (a) the identity of the controller and of his representative, if any;

   (b) the purposes of the processing;

   (c) any further information such as

- the categories of data concerned,

- the recipients or categories of recipients,

- the existence of the right of access to and the right to rectify the data concerning him

in so far as such further information is necessary, having regard to the specific circumstances in which the data are processed, to guarantee fair processing in respect of the data subject.

2. Paragraph 1 shall not apply where, in particular for processing for statistical purposes or for the purposes of historical or scientific research, the provision of such information proves impossible or would involve a disproportionate effort or if recording or disclosure is expressly laid down by law. In these cases Member States shall provide appropriate safeguards.

SECTION V
THE DATA SUBJECT'S RIGHT OF ACCESS TO DATA

Article 12 — Right of access
Member States shall guarantee every data subject the right to obtain from the controller:

(a) without constraint at reasonable intervals and without excessive delay or expense:

- confirmation as to whether or not data relating to him are being processed and information at least as to the purposes of the processing, the categories of data concerned, and the recipients or categories of recipients to whom the data are disclosed,

- communication to him in an intelligible form of the data undergoing processing and of any available information as to their source,

- knowledge of the logic involved in any automatic processing of data concerning him at least in the case of the automated decisions referred to in Article 15 (1);

(b) as appropriate the rectification, erasure or blocking of data the processing of which does not comply with the provisions of this Directive, in particular because of the incomplete or inaccurate nature of the data;

(c) notification to third parties to whom the data have been disclosed of any rectification, erasure or blocking carried out in compliance with (b), unless this proves impossible or involves a disproportionate effort.

SECTION VI
EXEMPTIONS AND RESTRICTIONS

Article 13 — Exemptions and restrictions
1. Member States may adopt legislative measures to restrict the scope of the obligations and rights provided for in Articles 6 (1), 10, 11 (1), 12 and 21 when such a restriction constitutes a necessary measures to safeguard:

(a) national security;

(b) defence;

(c) public security;

(d) the prevention, investigation, detection and prosecution of criminal offences, or of breaches of ethics for regulated professions;

(e) an important economic or financial interest of a Member State or of the European Union, including monetary, budgetary and taxation matters;

(f) a monitoring, inspection or regulatory function connected, even occasionally, with the exercise of official authority in cases referred to in (c), (d) and (e);

(g) the protection of the data subject or of the rights and freedoms of others.

2. Subject to adequate legal safeguards, in particular that the data are not used for taking measures or decisions regarding any particular individual, Member States may, where there is clearly no risk of breaching the privacy of the data subject, restrict by a legislative measure the rights provided for in Article 12 when data are processed solely for purposes of scientific research or are kept in personal form for a period which does not exceed the period necessary for the sole purpose of creating statistics.

SECTION VII
THE DATA SUBJECT'S RIGHT TO OBJECT

Article 14 — The data subject's right to object
Member States shall grant the data subject the right:

(a) at least in the cases referred to in Article 7 (e) and (f), to object at any time on compelling legitimate grounds relating to his particular situation to the processing of data relating to him, save where otherwise provided by national legislation. Where there is a justified objection, the processing instigated by the controller may no longer involve those data;

(b) to object, on request and free of charge, to the processing of personal data relating to him which the controller anticipates being processed for the purposes of direct marketing, or to be informed before personal data are disclosed for the first time to third parties or used on their behalf for the purposes of direct marketing, and to be expressly offered the right to object free of charge to such disclosures or uses.

Member States shall take the necessary measures to ensure that data subjects are aware of the existence of the right referred to in the first subparagraph of (b).

Article 15 — Automated individual decisions
1. Member States shall grant the right to every person not to be subject to a decision which produces legal effects concerning him or significantly affects him and which is based solely on automated processing of data intended to evaluate certain personal aspects relating to him, such as his performance at work, creditworthiness, reliability, conduct, etc.

2. Subject to the other Articles of this Directive, Member States shall provide that a person may be subjected to a decision of the kind referred to in paragraph 1 if that decision:

(a) is taken in the course of the entering into or performance of a contract, provided the request for the entering into or the performance of the contract, lodged by the data subject, has been satisfied or that there are suitable measures to safeguard his legitimate interests, such as arrangements allowing him to put his point of view; or

(b) is authorized by a law which also lays down measures to safeguard the data subject's legitimate interests.

SECTION VIII
CONFIDENTIALITY AND SECURITY OF PROCESSING

Article 16 — Confidentiality of processing

Any person acting under the authority of the controller or of the processor, including the processor himself, who has access to personal data must not process them except on instructions from the controller, unless he is required to do so by law.

Article 17 — Security of processing

1. Member States shall provide that the controller must implement appropriate technical and organizational measures to protect personal data against accidental or unlawful destruction or accidental loss, alteration, unauthorized disclosure or access, in particular where the processing involves the transmission of data over a network, and against all other unlawful forms of processing.

    Having regard to the state of the art and the cost of their implementation, such measures shall ensure a level of security appropriate to the risks represented by the processing and the nature of the data to be protected.

2. The Member States shall provide that the controller must, where processing is carried out on his behalf, choose a processor providing sufficient guarantees in respect of the technical security measures and organizational measures governing the processing to be carried out, and must ensure compliance with those measures.

3. The carrying out of processing by way of a processor must be governed by a contract or legal act binding the processor to the controller and stipulating in particular that:

    — the processor shall act only on instructions from the controller,

    — the obligations set out in paragraph 1, as defined by the law of the Member State in which the processor is established, shall also be incumbent on the processor.

4. For the purposes of keeping proof, the parts of the contract or the legal act relating to data protection and the requirements relating to the measures referred to in paragraph 1 shall be in writing or in another equivalent form.

SECTION IX
NOTIFICATION

Article 18 — Obligation to notify the supervisory authority

1. Member States shall provide that the controller or his representative, if any, must notify the supervisory authority referred to in Article 28 before carrying out any wholly or partly automatic processing operation or set of such operations intended to serve a single purpose or several related purposes.

2. Member States may provide for the simplification of or exemption from notification only in the following cases and under the following conditions:

    — where, for categories of processing operations which are unlikely, taking account of the data to be processed, to affect adversely the rights and freedoms of data subjects, they specify the purposes of the processing, the data or categories of data undergoing processing, the category or categories of data subject, the recipients or categories of recipient to whom the data are to be disclosed and the length of time the data are to be stored, and/or

    — where the controller, in compliance with the national law which governs him, appoints a personal data protection official, responsible in particular:

– for ensuring in an independent manner the internal application of the national provisions taken pursuant to this Directive

– for keeping the register of processing operations carried out by the controller, containing the items of information referred to in Article 21 (2),

thereby ensuring that the rights and freedoms of the data subjects are unlikely to be adversely affected by the processing operations.

3. Member States may provide that paragraph 1 does not apply to processing whose sole purpose is the keeping of a register which according to laws or regulations is intended to provide information to the public and which is open to consultation either by the public in general or by any person demonstrating a legitimate interest.

4. Member States may provide for an exemption from the obligation to notify or a simplification of the notification in the case of processing operations referred to in Article 8 (2) (d).

5. Member States may stipulate that certain or all non-automatic processing operations involving personal data shall be notified, or provide for these processing operations to be subject to simplified notification.

Article 19 — Contents of notification

1. Member States shall specify the information to be given in the notification. It shall include at least:

(a) the name and address of the controller and of his representative, if any;

(b) the purpose or purposes of the processing;

(c) a description of the category or categories of data subject and of the data or categories of data relating to them;

(d) the recipients or categories of recipient to whom the data might be disclosed;

(e) proposed transfers of data to third countries;

(f) a general description allowing a preliminary assessment to be made of the appropriateness of the measures taken pursuant to Article 17 to ensure security of processing.

2. Member States shall specify the procedures under which any change affecting the information referred to in paragraph 1 must be notified to the supervisory authority.

Article 20 — Prior checking

1. Member States shall determine the processing operations likely to present specific risks to the rights and freedoms of data subjects and shall check that these processing operations are examined prior to the start thereof.

2. Such prior checks shall be carried out by the supervisory authority following receipt of a notification from the controller or by the data protection official, who, in cases of doubt, must consult the supervisory authority.

3. Member States may also carry out such checks in the context of preparation either of a

measure of the national parliament or of a measure based on such a legislative measure, which define the nature of the processing and lay down appropriate safeguards.

Article 21 — Publicizing of processing operations

1. Member States shall take measures to ensure that processing operations are publicized.

2. Member States shall provide that a register of processing operations notified in accordance with Article 18 shall be kept by the supervisory authority.

   The register shall contain at least the information listed in Article 19 (1) (a) to (e).

   The register may be inspected by any person.

3. Member States shall provide, in relation to processing operations not subject to notification, that controllers or another body appointed by the Member States make available at least the information referred to in Article 19 (1) (a) to (e) in an appropriate form to any person on request.

   Member States may provide that this provision does not apply to processing whose sole purpose is the keeping of a register which according to laws or regulations is intended to provide information to the public and which is open to consultation either by the public in general or by any person who can provide proof of a legitimate interest.

CHAPTER III
JUDICIAL REMEDIES, LIABILITY AND SANCTIONS

Article 22 — Remedies

Without prejudice to any administrative remedy for which provision may be made, inter alia before the supervisory authority referred to in Article 28, prior to referral to the judicial authority, Member States shall provide for the right of every person to a judicial remedy for any breach of the rights guaranteed him by the national law applicable to the processing in question.

Article 23 — Liability

1. Member States shall provide that any person who has suffered damage as a result of an unlawful processing operation or of any act incompatible with the national provisions adopted pursuant to this Directive is entitled to receive compensation from the controller for the damage suffered.

2. The controller may be exempted from this liability, in whole or in part, if he proves that he is not responsible for the event giving rise to the damage.

Article 24 — Sanctions

The Member States shall adopt suitable measures to ensure the full implementation of the provisions of this Directive and shall in particular lay down the sanctions to be imposed in case of infringement of the provisions adopted pursuant to this Directive.

CHAPTER IV
TRANSFER OF PERSONAL DATA TO THIRD COUNTRIES

Article 25 — Principles

1. The Member States shall provide that the transfer to a third country of personal data which are undergoing processing or are intended for processing after transfer may take place only if, without prejudice to compliance with the national provisions adopted pursuant to the other

provisions of this Directive, the third country in question ensures an adequate level of protection.

2. The adequacy of the level of protection afforded by a third country shall be assessed in the light of all the circumstances surrounding a data transfer operation or set of data transfer operations; particular consideration shall be given to the nature of the data, the purpose and duration of the proposed processing operation or operations, the country of origin and country of final destination, the rules of law, both general and sectoral, in force in the third country in question and the professional rules and security measures which are complied with in that country.

3. The Member States and the Commission shall inform each other of cases where they consider that a third country does not ensure an adequate level of protection within the meaning of paragraph 2.

4. Where the Commission finds, under the procedure provided for in Article 31 (2), that a third country does not ensure an adequate level of protection within the meaning of paragraph 2 of this Article, Member States shall take the measures necessary to prevent any transfer of data of the same type to the third country in question.

5. At the appropriate time, the Commission shall enter into negotiations with a view to remedying the situation resulting from the finding made pursuant to paragraph 4.

6. The Commission may find, in accordance with the procedure referred to in Article 31 (2), that a third country ensures an adequate level of protection within the meaning of paragraph 2 of this Article, by reason of its domestic law or of the international commitments it has entered into, particularly upon conclusion of the negotiations referred to in paragraph 5, for the protection of the private lives and basic freedoms and rights of individuals.

   Member States shall take the measures necessary to comply with the Commission's decision.

Article 26 — Derogations

1. By way of derogation from Article 25 and save where otherwise provided by domestic law governing particular cases, Member States shall provide that a transfer or a set of transfers of personal data to a third country which does not ensure an adequate level of protection within the meaning of Article 25 (2) may take place on condition that:

   (a) the data subject has given his consent unambiguously to the proposed transfer; or

   (b) the transfer is necessary for the performance of a contract between the data subject and the controller or the implementation of precontractual measures taken in response to the data subject's request; or

   (c) the transfer is necessary for the conclusion or performance of a contract concluded in the interest of the data subject between the controller and a third party; or

   (d) the transfer is necessary or legally required on important public interest grounds, or for the establishment, exercise or defence of legal claims; or

   (e) the transfer is necessary in order to protect the vital interests of the data subject; or

   (f) the transfer is made from a register which according to laws or regulations is intended to provide information to the public and which is open to consultation either by the public in general or by any person who can demonstrate legitimate interest, to the extent that the conditions laid down in law for consultation are fulfilled in the particular case.

2. Without prejudice to paragraph 1, a Member State may authorize a transfer or a set of transfers of personal data to a third country which does not ensure an adequate level of protection within the meaning of Article 25 (2), where the controller adduces adequate safeguards with respect to the protection of the privacy and fundamental rights and freedoms of individuals and as regards the exercise of the corresponding rights; such safeguards may in particular result from appropriate contractual clauses.

3. The Member State shall inform the Commission and the other Member States of the authorizations it grants pursuant to paragraph 2.

   If a Member State or the Commission objects on justified grounds involving the protection of the privacy and fundamental rights and freedoms of individuals, the Commission shall take appropriate measures in accordance with the procedure laid down in Article 31 (2).

   Member States shall take the necessary measures to comply with the Commission's decision.

4. Where the Commission decides, in accordance with the procedure referred to in Article 31 (2), that certain standard contractual clauses offer sufficient safeguards as required by paragraph 2, Member States shall take the necessary measures to comply with the Commission's decision.

CHAPTER V
CODES OF CONDUCT

Article 27

1. The Member States and the Commission shall encourage the drawing up of codes of conduct intended to contribute to the proper implementation of the national provisions adopted by the Member States pursuant to this Directive, taking account of the specific features of the various sectors.

2. Member States shall make provision for trade associations and other bodies representing other categories of controllers which have drawn up draft national codes or which have the intention of amending or extending existing national codes to be able to submit them to the opinion of the national authority.

   Member States shall make provision for this authority to ascertain, among other things, whether the drafts submitted to it are in accordance with the national provisions adopted pursuant to this Directive. If it sees fit, the authority shall seek the views of data subjects or their representatives.

3. Draft Community codes, and amendments or extensions to existing Community codes, may be submitted to the Working Party referred to in Article 29. This Working Party shall determine, among other things, whether the drafts submitted to it are in accordance with the national provisions adopted pursuant to this Directive. If it sees fit, the authority shall seek the views of data subjects or their representatives. The Commission may ensure appropriate publicity for the codes which have been approved by the Working Party.

CHAPTER VI

SUPERVISORY AUTHORITY AND WORKING PARTY ON THE PROTECTION OF INDIVIDUALS WITH REGARD TO THE PROCESSING OF PERSONAL DATA

Article 28 — Supervisory authority

1. Each Member State shall provide that one or more public authorities are responsible for monitoring the application within its territory of the provisions adopted by the Member States pursuant to this Directive.

   These authorities shall act with complete independence in exercising the functions entrusted to them.

2. Each Member State shall provide that the supervisory authorities are consulted when drawing up administrative measures or regulations relating to the protection of individuals' rights and freedoms with regard to the processing of personal data.

3. Each authority shall in particular be endowed with:

   – investigative powers, such as powers of access to data forming the subject-matter of processing operations and powers to collect all the information necessary for the performance of its supervisory duties,

   – effective powers of intervention, such as, for example, that of delivering opinions before processing operations are carried out, in accordance with Article 20, and ensuring appropriate publication of such opinions, of ordering the blocking, erasure or destruction of data, of imposing a temporary or definitive ban on processing, of warning or admonishing the controller, or that of referring the matter to national parliaments or other political institutions,

   – the power to engage in legal proceedings where the national provisions adopted pursuant to this Directive have been violated or to bring these violations to the attention of the judicial authorities.

   Decisions by the supervisory authority which give rise to complaints may be appealed against through the courts.

4. Each supervisory authority shall hear claims lodged by any person, or by an association representing that person, concerning the protection of his rights and freedoms in regard to the processing of personal data. The person concerned shall be informed of the outcome of the claim.

   Each supervisory authority shall, in particular, hear claims for checks on the lawfulness of data processing lodged by any person when the national provisions adopted pursuant to Article 13 of this Directive apply. The person shall at any rate be informed that a check has taken place.

5. Each supervisory authority shall draw up a report on its activities at regular intervals. The report shall be made public.

6. Each supervisory authority is competent, whatever the national law applicable to the processing in question, to exercise, on the territory of its own Member State, the powers conferred on it in accordance with paragraph 3. Each authority may be requested to exercise its powers by an authority of another Member State.

   The supervisory authorities shall cooperate with one another to the extent necessary for the performance of their duties, in particular by exchanging all useful information.

7. Member States shall provide that the members and staff of the supervisory authority, even after their employment has ended, are to be subject to a duty of professional secrecy with regard to confidential information to which they have access.

Article 29 — Working Party on the Protection of Individuals with regard to the Processing of Personal Data

1. A Working Party on the Protection of Individuals with regard to the Processing of Personal Data, hereinafter referred to as 'the Working Party', is hereby set up.

   It shall have advisory status and act independently.

2. The Working Party shall be composed of a representative of the supervisory authority or authorities designated by each Member State and of a representative of the authority or authorities established for the Community institutions and bodies, and of a representative of the Commission.

   Each member of the Working Party shall be designated by the institution, authority or authorities which he represents. Where a Member State has designated more than one supervisory authority, they shall nominate a joint representative. The same shall apply to the authorities established for Community institutions and bodies.

3. The Working Party shall take decisions by a simple majority of the representatives of the supervisory authorities.

4. The Working Party shall elect its chairman. The chairman's term of office shall be two years. His appointment shall be renewable.

5. The Working Party's secretariat shall be provided by the Commission.

6. The Working Party shall adopt its own rules of procedure.

7. The Working Party shall consider items placed on its agenda by its chairman, either on his own initiative or at the request of a representative of the supervisory authorities or at the Commission's request.

Article 30

1. The Working Party shall:

   (a) examine any question covering the application of the national measures adopted under this Directive in order to contribute to the uniform application of such measures;

   (b) give the Commission an opinion on the level of protection in the Community and in third countries;

   (c) advise the Commission on any proposed amendment of this Directive, on any additional or specific measures to safeguard the rights and freedoms of natural persons with regard to the processing of personal data and on any other proposed Community measures affecting such rights and freedoms;

   (d) give an opinion on codes of conduct drawn up at Community level.

2. If the Working Party finds that divergences likely to affect the equivalence of protection for persons with regard to the processing of personal data in the Community are arising between the laws or practices of Member States, it shall inform the Commission accordingly.

3. The Working Party may, on its own initiative, make recommendations on all matters relating

to the protection of persons with regard to the processing of personal data in the Community.

4. The Working Party's opinions and recommendations shall be forwarded to the Commission and to the committee referred to in Article 31.

5. The Commission shall inform the Working Party of the action it has taken in response to its opinions and recommendations. It shall do so in a report which shall also be forwarded to the European Parliament and the Council. The report shall be made public.

6. The Working Party shall draw up an annual report on the situation regarding the protection of natural persons with regard to the processing of personal data in the Community and in third countries, which it shall transmit to the Commission, the European Parliament and the Council. The report shall be made public.

CHAPTER VII
COMMUNITY IMPLEMENTING MEASURES

Article 31 — The Committee

1. The Commission shall be assisted by a committee composed of the representatives of the Member States and chaired by the representative of the Commission.

2. The representative of the Commission shall submit to the committee a draft of the measures to be taken. The committee shall deliver its opinion on the draft within a time limit which the chairman may lay down according to the urgency of the matter.

   The opinion shall be delivered by the majority laid down in Article 148 (2) of the Treaty. The votes of the representatives of the Member States within the committee shall be weighted in the manner set out in that Article. The chairman shall not vote.

   The Commission shall adopt measures which shall apply immediately. However, if these measures are not in accordance with the opinion of the committee, they shall be communicated by the Commission to the Council forthwith. It that event:

   – the Commission shall defer application of the measures which it has decided for a period of three months from the date of communication,

   – the Council, acting by a qualified majority, may take a different decision within the time limit referred to in the first indent.

FINAL PROVISIONS

Article 32

1. Member States shall bring into force the laws, regulations and administrative provisions necessary to comply with this Directive at the latest at the end of a period of three years from the date of its adoption.

   When Member States adopt these measures, they shall contain a reference to this Directive or be accompanied by such reference on the occasion of their official publication. The methods of making such reference shall be laid down by the Member States.

2. Member States shall ensure that processing already under way on the date the national provisions adopted pursuant to this Directive enter into force, is brought into conformity with these provisions within three years of this date.

By way of derogation from the preceding subparagraph, Member States may provide that the processing of data already held in manual filing systems on the date of entry into force of the national provisions adopted in implementation of this Directive shall be brought into conformity with Articles 6, 7 and 8 of this Directive within 12 years of the date on which it is adopted. Member States shall, however, grant the data subject the right to obtain, at his request and in particular at the time of exercising his right of access, the rectification, erasure or blocking of data which are incomplete, inaccurate or stored in a way incompatible with the legitimate purposes pursued by the controller.

3. By way of derogation from paragraph 2, Member States may provide, subject to suitable safeguards, that data kept for the sole purpose of historical research need not be brought into conformity with Articles 6, 7 and 8 of this Directive.

4. Member States shall communicate to the Commission the text of the provisions of domestic law which they adopt in the field covered by this Directive.

Article 33

The Commission shall report to the Council and the European Parliament at regular intervals, starting not later than three years after the date referred to in Article 32 (1), on the implementation of this Directive, attaching to its report, if necessary, suitable proposals for amendments. The report shall be made public.

The Commission shall examine, in particular, the application of this Directive to the data processing of sound and image data relating to natural persons and shall submit any appropriate proposals which prove to be necessary, taking account of developments in information technology and in the light of the state of progress in the information society.

Article 34

This Directive is addressed to the Member States.

Done at Luxembourg, 24 October 1995.

For the European Parliament

Data Protection (Conditions under Paragraph 3 of Part II of Schedule 1) Order 2000
(SI 2000/185)

Made 31st January 2000
Laid before Parliament 7th February 2000
Coming into force 1st March 2000

The Secretary of State, in exercise of the powers conferred upon him by section 67(2) of, and paragraph 3(1) of Part II of Schedule 1 to, the Data Protection Act 1998, and after consultation with the Data Protection Commissioner in accordance with section 67(3) of that Act, hereby makes the following Order:

Citation and commencement

1 This Order may be cited as the Data Protection (Conditions under Paragraph 3 of Part II of Schedule 1) Order 2000 and shall come into force on 1st March 2000.

Interpretation

2 In this Order, "Part II" means Part II of Schedule 1 to the Data Protection Act 1998.

General provisions

3(1) In cases where the primary condition referred to in paragraph 3(2)(a) of Part II is met, the provisions of articles 4 and 5 apply.

(2) In cases where the primary condition referred to in paragraph 3(2)(b) of that Part is met by virtue of the fact that the recording of the information to be contained in the data by, or the disclosure of the data by, the data controller is not a function conferred on him by or under any enactment or an obligation imposed on him by order of a court, but is necessary for compliance with any legal obligation to which the data controller is subject, other than an obligation imposed by contract, the provisions of article 4 apply.

Notices in writing

4(1) One of the further conditions prescribed in paragraph (2) must be met if paragraph 2(1)(b) of Part II is to be disapplied in respect of any particular data subject.

(2) The conditions referred to in paragraph (1) are that—

    (a) no notice in writing has been received at any time by the data controller from an individual, requiring that data controller to provide the information set out in paragraph 2(3) of that Part before the relevant time (as defined in paragraph 2(2) of that Part) or as soon as practicable after that time; or

    (b) where such notice in writing has been received but the data controller does not have sufficient information about the individual in order readily to determine whether he is processing personal data about that individual, the data controller shall send to the individual a written notice stating that he cannot provide the information set out in paragraph 2(3) of that Part because of his inability to make that determination, and explaining the reasons for that inability.

(3) The requirement in paragraph (2) that notice should be in writing is satisfied where the text of the notice—

    (a) is transmitted by electronic means,

(b)   is received in legible form, and

(c)   is capable of being used for subsequent reference.

Further condition in cases of disproportionate effort

5(1)   The further condition prescribed in paragraph (2) must be met for paragraph 2(1)(b) of Part II to be disapplied in respect of any data.

(2)   The condition referred to in paragraph (1) is that the data controller shall record the reasons for his view that the primary condition referred to in article 3(1) is met in respect of the data.

Data Protection (Crown Appointments) Order 2000 (SI 2000/416)

Made 17th February 2000
Coming into force 1st March 2000

Whereas a draft of this Order has been laid before and approved by a resolution of each House of Parliament:

Now, therefore, the Secretary of State, in exercise of the powers conferred upon him by paragraph 4 of Schedule 7 to the Data Protection Act 1998, and after consultation with the Data Protection Commissioner in accordance with section 67(3) of that Act, hereby makes the following Order:

1   This Order may be cited as the Data Protection (Crown Appointments) Order 2000 and shall come into force on 1st March 2000.

2   There shall be exempted from the subject information provisions of the Data Protection Act 1998 (as defined by section 27(2) of that Act) personal data processed for the purposes of assessing any person's suitability for any of the offices listed in the Schedule to this Order.

SCHEDULE

EXEMPTIONS FROM SUBJECT INFORMATION PROVISIONS

Article 2

Offices to which appointments are made by Her Majesty:–

(a) Archbishops, diocesan and suffragan bishops in the Church of England
(b) Deans of cathedrals of the Church of England
(c) Deans and Canons of the two Royal Peculiars
(d) The First and Second Church Estates Commissioners
(e) Lord-Lieutenants
(f) Masters of Trinity College and Churchill College, Cambridge
(g) The Provost of Eton
(h) The Poet Laureate
(i) The Astronomer Royal

Data Protection (Fees under section 19(7)) Regulations 2000 (SI 2000/187)

Made 31st January 2000
Laid before Parliament 7th February 2000
Coming into force 1st March 2000

The Secretary of State, in exercise of the powers conferred upon him by section 19(7) of the Data Protection Act 1998, having regard to the definition of "fees regulations" in section 16(2) of that Act, and after consultation with the Data Protection Commissioner in accordance with section 67(3) of the Act, hereby makes the following Regulations:

1   These Regulations may be cited as the Data Protection (Fees under section 19(7)) Regulations 2000 and shall come into force on 1st March 2000.

2   The fee payable by a member of the public for the supply by the Information Commissioner under section 19(7) of the Data Protection Act 1998 of a duly certified written copy of the particulars contained in any entry made in the register maintained under section 19(1) of that Act shall be £2.

Data Protection
(Functions of Designated Authority) Order 2000
(SI 2000/186)

Made 31st January 2000
Laid before Parliament 7th February 2000
Coming into force 1st March 2000

The Secretary of State, in exercise of the powers conferred upon him by sections 54(2) and 67(2) of the Data Protection Act 1998 and after consultation with the Data Protection Commissioner in accordance with section 67(3) of that Act, hereby makes the following Order:

Citation and commencement

1   This Order may be cited as the Data Protection (Functions of Designated Authority) Order 2000 and shall come into force on 1st March 2000.

Interpretation

2(1)   In this Order:"the Act" means the Data Protection Act 1998;"foreign designated authority" means an authority designated for the purposes of Article 13 of the Convention by a party (other than the United Kingdom) which is bound by that Convention;"register" means the register maintained under section 19(1) of the Act;"request", except in article 3, means a request for assistance under Article 14 of the Convention which states–

(a)   the name and address of the person making the request;

(b)   particulars which identify the personal data to which the request relates;

(c)   the rights under Article 8 of the Convention to which the request relates;

(d)   the reasons why the request has been made;

and "requesting person" means a person making such a request.

(2)   In this Order, references to the Commissioner are to the Commissioner as the designated authority in the United Kingdom for the purposes of Article 13 of the Convention.

Co-operation between the Commissioner and foreign designated authorities

3(1)   The Commissioner shall, at the request of a foreign designated authority, furnish to that foreign designated authority such information referred to in Article 13(3)(a) of the Convention, and in particular the data protection legislation in force in the United Kingdom at the time the request is made, as is the subject of the request.

(2)   The Commissioner shall, at the request of a foreign designated authority, take appropriate measures in accordance with Article 13(3)(b) of the Convention, for furnishing to that foreign designated authority information relating to the processing of personal data in the United Kingdom.

(3)   The Commissioner may request a foreign designated authority to furnish to him or, as the case may be, to take appropriate measures for furnishing to him, the information referred to in Article 13(3) of the Convention.

Persons resident outside the United Kingdom

4(1)   This article applies where a person resident outside the United Kingdom makes a request to the Commissioner under Article 14 of the Convention, including a request forwarded to the Commissioner through the Secretary of State or a foreign designated authority, seeking assistance in exercising any of the rights under Article 8 of the Convention.

(2) If the request—

    (a)   seeks assistance in exercising the rights under section 7 of the Act; and

    (b)   does not indicate that the data controller has failed, contrary to section 7 of the Act, to comply with the same request on a previous occasion,

the Commissioner shall notify the requesting person of the data controller's address for the receipt of notices from data subjects exercising their rights under that section and of such other information as the Commissioner considers necessary to enable that person to exercise his rights under that section.

(3) If the request indicates that a data protection principle has been contravened by a data controller the Commissioner shall either—

    (a)   notify the requesting person of the rights of data subjects and the remedies available to them under Part II of the Act together with such particulars as are contained in the data controller's entry in the register as are necessary to enable the requesting person to avail himself of those remedies; or

    (b)   if the Commissioner considers that notification in accordance with sub-paragraph (a) would not assist the requesting person or would, for any other reason, be inappropriate, treat the request as if it were a request for an assessment which falls to be dealt with under section 42 of the Act.

(4) The Commissioner shall not be required, in response to any request referred to in paragraphs (2) and (3) above, to supply to the requesting person a duly certified copy in writing of the particulars contained in any entry made in the register other than on payment of such fee as is prescribed for the purposes of section 19(7) of the Act.

Persons resident in the United Kingdom

5(1) Where a request for assistance in exercising any of the rights referred to in Article 8 of the Convention in a country or territory (other than the United Kingdom) specified in the request is made by a person resident in the United Kingdom and submitted through the Commissioner under Article 14(2) of the Convention, the Commissioner shall, if he is satisfied that the request contains all necessary particulars referred to in Article 14(3) of the Convention, send it to the foreign designated authority in the specified country or territory.

(2) If the Commissioner decides that he is not required by paragraph (1) above to render assistance to the requesting person he shall, where practicable, notify that person of the reasons for his decision.

Restrictions on use of information

6 Where the Commissioner receives information from a foreign designated authority as a result of either—

    (a)   a request made by him under article 3(3) above; or

    (b)   a request received by him under articles 3(2) or 4 above,

the Commissioner shall use that information only for the purposes specified in the request.

Data Protection (Miscellaneous Subject Access Exemptions) Order 2000 (SI 2000/419)

Made 17th February 2000
Coming into force 1st March 2000

Whereas a draft of this Order has been laid before and approved by a resolution of each House of Parliament:

Whereas the Secretary of State considers it necessary for the safeguarding of the interests of data subjects or the rights and freedoms of other individuals that the prohibitions or restrictions on disclosure contained in the enactments and instruments listed in the Schedule to this Order ought to prevail over section 7 of the Data Protection Act 1998:

Now, therefore, the Secretary of State, in exercise of the powers conferred on him by sections 38(1) and 67(2) of the Data Protection Act 1998, and after consultation with the Data Protection Commissioner in accordance with section 67(3) of that Act, hereby makes the following Order:

1   This Order may be cited as the Data Protection (Miscellaneous Subject Access Exemptions) Order 2000 and shall come into force on 1st March 2000.

2   Personal data consisting of information the disclosure of which is prohibited or restricted by the enactments and instruments listed in the Schedule to this Order are exempt from section 7 of the Data Protection Act 1998.

SCHEDULE

EXEMPTIONS FROM SECTION 7

Article 2

PART 1

ENACTMENTS AND INSTRUMENTS EXTENDING TO THE UNITED KINGDOM

PART II

ENACTMENTS AND INSTRUMENTS EXTENDING TO ENGLAND AND WALES

(a) *Adoption records and reports*
Sections 57 to 62, 77 and 79 of, and Schedule 2 to, the Adoption and Children Act 2002.
Regulation 14 of the Adoption Agencies Regulations 1983.
Regulation 41 of the Adoption Agencies Regulations 2005.
Regulation 42 of the Adoption Agencies (Wales) Regulations 2005.
Rules 5, 6, 9, 17, 18, 21, 22 and 53 of the Adoption Rules 1984.
Rules 5, 6, 9, 17, 18, 21, 22 and 32 of the Magistrates' Courts (Adoption) Rules 1984.
Rules 24, 29, 30, 65, 72, 73, 77, 78 and 83 of the Family Procedure (Adoption) Rules 2005.

(b) *Statement of child's special educational needs*
Regulation 19 of the Education (Special Educational Needs) Regulations 1994.

(c) *Parental order records and reports*

Sections 50 and 51 of the Adoption Act 1976 as modified by paragraphs 4(a) and (b) of Schedule 1 to the Parental Orders (Human Fertilisation and Embryology) Regulations 1994 in relation to parental orders made under section 30 of the Human Fertilisation and Embryology Act 1990.

Rules 4A.5 and 4A.9 of the Family Proceedings Rules 1991.

Rules 21E and 21I of the Family Proceedings Courts (Children Act 1989) Rules 1991.

PART III

ENACTMENTS AND INSTRUMENTS EXTENDING TO SCOTLAND

(a) *Adoption records and reports*

Section 45 of the Adoption (Scotland) Act 1978.

Regulation 23 of the Adoption Agencies (Scotland) Regulations 1996.

Rule 67.3 of the Act of Sederunt (Rules of the Court of Session 1994) 1994.

Rules 2.12, 2.14, 2.30 and 2.33 of the Act of Sederunt (Child Care and Maintenance Rules) 1997.

Regulation 8 of the Adoption Allowance (Scotland) Regulations 1996.

(b) *Information provided by principal reporter for children's hearing*

Rules 5 and 21 of the Children's Hearings (Scotland) Rules 1996.

(c) *Record of child or young person's special educational needs*

Section 60(4) of the Education (Scotland) Act 1980.

Proviso (bb) to regulation 7(2) of the Education (Record of Needs) (Scotland) Regulations 1982.

(d) *Parental order records and reports*

Section 45 of the Adoption (Scotland) Act 1978 as modified by paragraph 10 of Schedule 1 to the Parental Orders (Human Fertilisation and Embryology) (Scotland) Regulations 1994 in relation to parental orders made under section 30 of the Human Fertilisation and Embryology Act 1990.

Rules 2.47 and 2.59 of the Act of Sederunt (Child Care and Maintenance Rules) 1997.

Rules 81.3 and 81.18 of the Act of Sederunt (Rules of the Court of Session 1994) 1994.

PART IV

ENACTMENTS AND INSTRUMENTS EXTENDING TO NORTHERN IRELAND

(a) *Adoption records and reports*

Articles 50 and 54 of the Adoption (Northern Ireland) Act 1987.

Rule 53 of Order 84 of the Rules of the Court of Judicature (Northern Ireland) 1980.

Rule 22 of the County Court (Adoption) Rules (Northern Ireland) 1980.

Rule 32 of Order 50 of the County Court Rules (Northern Ireland) 1981.

(b) *Statement of child's special educational needs*

Regulation 17 of the Education (Special Educational Needs) Regulations (Northern Ireland) 1997.

(c) *Parental order records and reports*

Articles 50 and 54 of the Adoption (Northern Ireland) Order 1987 as modified by paragraph 5(a) and (e) of Schedule 2 to the Parental Orders (Human Fertilisation and Embryology) Regulations 1994 in respect of parental orders made under section 30 of the Human Fertilisation and Embryology Act 1990.

Rules 4, 5 and 16 of Order 84A of the Rules of the Court of Judicature (Northern Ireland) 1980.

Rules 3, 4 and 15 of Order 50A of the County Court Rules (Northern Ireland) 1981.

Data Protection (Monetary Penalties) Order 2010
(SI 2010/910)

Made: 22nd March 2010

The Secretary of State has consulted the Information Commissioner in accordance with section 67(3) of the Data Protection Act 1998(1).

In accordance with section 67(4) of that Act, a draft of this instrument was laid before Parliament and approved by a resolution of each House of Parliament.

Accordingly the Secretary of State, in exercise of the powers conferred by section 55E(2) of that Act, makes the following Order:

Citation, commencement and interpretation

1(1)   This Order may be cited as the Data Protection (Monetary Penalties) Order 2010 and comes into force on 6th April 2010.

(2)   In this Order references to sections and Schedules are references to sections of and Schedules to the Data Protection Act 1998.

Monetary penalty notices: procedure: written representations

2   The Commissioner must consider any written representations made in relation to a notice of intent when deciding whether to serve a monetary penalty notice.

Monetary penalty notices: procedure: supplementary provisions

3(1)   The period specified by the Commissioner for making written representations in accordance with section 55B(3)(a) must not be less than 21 days beginning with the first day after the date of service of the notice of intent.

(2)   The Commissioner may not serve a monetary penalty notice relating to a notice of intent if a period of 6 months has elapsed beginning with the first day after the service of the notice of intent.

(3)   The period specified in accordance with section 55A(6) must be at least 28 days beginning with the first day after the date of service of the monetary penalty notice.

Monetary penalty notices: variation

4(1)   The Commissioner may vary a monetary penalty notice by written notice to the person on whom it was served.

(2)   A notice under paragraph (1) must specify—
(a)the notice concerned; and
(b)how the notice is varied.

(3)   The Commissioner may not vary a monetary penalty notice so as to reduce the period specified in accordance with section 55A(6).

(4)   The Commissioner may not vary a monetary penalty notice so as to increase the amount of the monetary penalty, or otherwise vary a monetary penalty notice to the detriment of the person on whom it was served.

(5)   A person on whom a notice under paragraph (1) is served may appeal to the Tribunal

against that notice.

(6) Where the Commissioner varies a monetary penalty notice so as to reduce the amount of the monetary penalty, the Commissioner must repay any amount that has already been paid that exceeds the amount of the reduced monetary penalty.

Monetary penalty notices: cancellation

5(1) The Commissioner may cancel a monetary penalty notice by written notice to the person on whom it was served.

(2) Where a monetary penalty notice has been cancelled, the Commissioner may not take any further action under section 55A, 55B or 55D in relation to the contravention to which that monetary penalty notice relates.

(3) Where a monetary penalty notice has been cancelled, the Commissioner must repay any amount that has been paid pursuant to that notice.

Monetary penalty notices: enforcement

6 The Commissioner must not take action to enforce a monetary penalty unless—

(a) the period specified in accordance with section 55A(6) has expired and all or any of the monetary penalty has not been paid;

(b) all relevant appeals against the monetary penalty notice and any variation of it have been either been decided or withdrawn; and

(c) the period for the data controller to appeal against the monetary penalty and any variation of it has expired.

Appeals

7 Section 49 and Schedule 6 have effect in relation to appeals under section 55B(5) and article 4(5) as they have effect in relation to appeals under section 48(1).

Michael Wills
Minister of State
Ministry of Justice
22nd March 2010

Data Protection (Monetary Penalties) (Maximum Penalty and Notices) Regulations 2010 (SI 2010/31)

Made: 6th January 2010

The Secretary of State has consulted the Information Commissioner in accordance with section 67(3)(b) of the Data Protection Act 1998(1).

Accordingly, the Secretary of State, in exercise of the powers conferred by sections 55A(5) and (7) and 55B(3)(b) of that Act(2), makes the following Regulations:

Citation, commencement and interpretation

1(1) These Regulations may be cited as the Data Protection (Monetary Penalties) (Maximum Penalty and Notices) Regulations 2010 and come into force on 6th April 2010.

(2) In these Regulations references to sections are references to sections of the Data Protection Act 1998.

(3) In these Regulations—
"address" is construed in accordance with section 16(3);
"contravention" is construed in accordance with section 55A.

Prescribed amount

2 The prescribed amount for the purposes of section 55A(5) is £500,000.

Notices of intent

3 For the purposes of section 55B(3)(b) the prescribed information is—
  (a) the name and address of the data controller;
  (b) the grounds on which the Commissioner proposes to serve a monetary penalty notice, including—
    (i) the nature of the personal data involved in the contravention,
    (ii) a description of the circumstances of the contravention,
    (iii) the reason the Commissioner considers that the contravention is serious,
    (iv) the reason the Commissioner considers that the contravention is of a kind likely to cause substantial damage or substantial distress, and
    (v) whether the Commissioner considers that section 55A(2) applies or that section 55A(3) applies, and the reason the Commissioner has taken this view;
  (c) an indication of the amount of the monetary penalty the Commissioner proposes to impose and any aggravating or mitigating features the Commissioner has taken into account; and
  (d) the date on which the Commissioner proposes to serve the monetary penalty notice.

Monetary penalty notices

4 For the purposes of section 55A(7) the prescribed information is—
  (a) the name and address of the data controller;
  (b) details of the notice of intent served on the data controller;
  (c) whether the Commissioner received written representations following the service of the notice of intent;

(d) the grounds on which the Commissioner imposes the monetary penalty, including—

    (i) the nature of the personal data involved in the contravention,

    (ii) a description of the circumstances of the contravention,

    (iii) the reason the Commissioner is satisfied that the contravention is serious,

    (iv) the reason the Commissioner is satisfied that the contravention is of a kind likely to cause substantial damage or substantial distress, and

    (v) whether the Commissioner is satisfied that section 55A(2) applies, or that section 55A(3) applies, and the reason the Commissioner is so satisfied;

(e) the reasons for the amount of the monetary penalty including any aggravating or mitigating features the Commissioner has taken into account when setting the amount;

(f) details of how the monetary penalty is to be paid;

(g) details of, including the time limit for, the data controller's right of appeal against—

    (i) the imposition of the monetary penalty, and

    (ii) the amount of the monetary penalty; and

(h) details of the Commissioner's enforcement powers under section 55D(3).

Michael Wills

Minister of State
Ministry of Justice
6th January 2010

Data Protection (Processing of
Sensitive Personal Data) Order 2000
(SI 2000/417)

Made 17th February 2000
Coming into force 1st March 2000

Whereas a draft of this Order has been laid before and approved by a resolution of each House of Parliament:

Now, therefore, the Secretary of State, in exercise of the powers conferred on him by section 67(2) of, and paragraph 10 of Schedule 3 to, the Data Protection Act 1998 and after consultation with the Data Protection Commissioner in accordance with section 67(3) of that Act, hereby makes the following Order:

1(1) This Order may be cited as the Data Protection (Processing of Sensitive Personal Data) Order 2000 and shall come into force on 1st March 2000.

(2) In this Order, "the Act" means the Data Protection Act 1998.

2 For the purposes of paragraph 10 of Schedule 3 to the Act, the circumstances specified in any of the paragraphs in the Schedule to this Order are circumstances in which sensitive personal data may be processed.

SCHEDULE

CIRCUMSTANCES IN WHICH SENSITIVE PERSONAL DATA MAY BE PROCESSED

Article 2

1(1) The processing–
- (a) is in the substantial public interest;
- (b) is necessary for the purposes of the prevention or detection of any unlawful act; and
- (c) must necessarily be carried out without the explicit consent of the data subject being sought so as not to prejudice those purposes.

(2) In this paragraph, "act" includes a failure to act.

2 The processing–
- (a) is in the substantial public interest;
- (b) is necessary for the discharge of any function which is designed for protecting members of the public against–
  - (i) dishonesty, malpractice, or other seriously improper conduct by, or the unfitness or incompetence of, any person, or
  - (ii) mismanagement in the administration of, or failures in services provided by, any body or association; and
- (c) must necessarily be carried out without the explicit consent of the data subject being sought so as not to prejudice the discharge of that function.

3(1) The disclosure of personal data–

(a) is in the substantial public interest;

(b) is in connection with–

    (i) the commission by any person of any unlawful act (whether alleged or established),

    (ii) dishonesty, malpractice, or other seriously improper conduct by, or the unfitness or incompetence of, any person (whether alleged or established), or

    (iii) mismanagement in the administration of, or failures in services provided by, any body or association (whether alleged or established);

(c) is for the special purposes as defined in section 3 of the Act; and

(d) is made with a view to the publication of those data by any person and the data controller reasonably believes that such publication would be in the public interest.

(2) In this paragraph, "act" includes a failure to act.

4 The processing–

(a) is in the substantial public interest;

(b) is necessary for the discharge of any function which is designed for the provision of confidential counselling, advice, support or any other service; and

(c) is carried out without the explicit consent of the data subject because the processing–

    (i) is necessary in a case where consent cannot be given by the data subject,

    (ii) is necessary in a case where the data controller cannot reasonably be expected to obtain the explicit consent of the data subject, or

    (iii) must necessarily be carried out without the explicit consent of the data subject being sought so as not to prejudice the provision of that counselling, advice, support or other service.

5(1) The processing–

(a) is necessary for the purpose of–

    (i) carrying on insurance business, or

    (ii) making determinations in connection with eligibility for, and benefits payable under, an occupational pension scheme as defined in section 1 of the Pension Schemes Act 1993;

(b) is of sensitive personal data consisting of information falling within section 2(e) of the Act relating to a data subject who is the parent, grandparent, great grandparent or sibling of–

    (i) in the case of paragraph (a)(i), the insured person, or

    (ii) in the case of paragraph (a)(ii), the member of the scheme;

(c) is necessary in a case where the data controller cannot reasonably be expected to obtain the explicit consent of that data subject and the data controller is not aware of the data subject withholding his consent; and

(d) does not support measures or decisions with respect to that data subject.

(2) In this paragraph–

(a) insurance business" means business which consists of effecting or carrying out contracts of insurance of the following kind–

    (i) life and annuity,

    (ii) linked long term,

    (iii) permanent health,

    (iv) accident, or

    (v) sickness; and
(b) "insured" and "member" includes an individual who is seeking to become an insured person or member of the scheme respectively.

(2A) The definition of "insurance business" in sub-paragraph (2) above must be read with–
 (a) section 22 of the Financial Services and Markets Act 2000;
 (b) any relevant order under that section; and
 (c) Schedule 2 to that Act.

6 The processing–
 (a) is of sensitive personal data in relation to any particular data subject that are subject to processing which was already under way immediately before the coming into force of this Order;
 (b) is necessary for the purpose of–
  (i) effecting or carrying out contracts of long-term insurance of the kind mentioned in sub-paragraph (2)(a)(i), (ii) or (iii) of paragraph 5 above;] or
  (ii) establishing or administering an occupational pension scheme as defined in section 1 of the Pension Schemes Act 1993; and
 (c) either–
  (i) is necessary in a case where the data controller cannot reasonably be expected to obtain the explicit consent of the data subject and that data subject has not informed the data controller that he does not so consent, or
  (ii) must necessarily be carried out even without the explicit consent of the data subject so as not to prejudice those purposes.

7(1) Subject to the provisions of sub-paragraph (2), the processing–
 (a) is of sensitive personal data consisting of information falling within section 2(c) or (e) of the Act;
 (b) is necessary for the purpose of identifying or keeping under review the existence or absence of equality of opportunity or treatment between persons–
  (i) holding different beliefs as described in section 2(c) of the Act, or
  (ii) of different states of physical or mental health or different physical or mental conditions as described in section 2(e) of the Act,
with a view to enabling such equality to be promoted or maintained;
 (c) does not support measures or decisions with respect to any particular data subject otherwise than with the explicit consent of that data subject; and
 (d) does not cause, nor is likely to cause, substantial damage or substantial distress to the data subject or any other person.

(2) Where any individual has given notice in writing to any data controller who is processing personal data under the provisions of sub-paragraph (1) requiring that data controller to cease processing personal data in respect of which that individual is the data subject at the end of such period as is reasonable in the circumstances, that data controller must have ceased processing those personal data at the end of that period.

8(1) Subject to the provisions of sub-paragraph (2), the processing–
 (a) is of sensitive personal data consisting of information falling within section 2(b) of the Act;
 (b) is carried out by any person or organisation included in the register maintained

pursuant to section 1 of the Registration of Political Parties Act 1998 in the course of his or its legitimate political activities; and

(c) does not cause, nor is likely to cause, substantial damage or substantial distress to the data subject or any other person.

(2) Where any individual has given notice in writing to any data controller who is processing personal data under the provisions of sub-paragraph (1) requiring that data controller to cease processing personal data in respect of which that individual is the data subject at the end of such period as is reasonable in the circumstances, that data controller must have ceased processing those personal data at the end of that period.

9 The processing–

(a) is in the substantial public interest;

(b) is necessary for research purposes (which expression shall have the same meaning as in section 33 of the Act);

(c) does not support measures or decisions with respect to any particular data subject otherwise than with the explicit consent of that data subject; and

(d) does not cause, nor is likely to cause, substantial damage or substantial distress to the data subject or any other person.

10 The processing is necessary for the exercise of any functions conferred on a constable by any rule of law.

Data Protection (Processing of Sensitive Personal Data) Order 2006 (SI 2006/2068)

Made 25th July 2006
Coming into force in accordance with article 1(1)

The Secretary of State makes the following Order in exercise of the powers conferred by section 67(2) of and paragraph 10 of Schedule 3 to the Data Protection Act 1998;

In accordance with section 67(3), he has consulted the Information Commissioner;

In accordance with section 67(4) of that Act, a draft of this instrument was laid before Parliament and approved by a resolution of each House of Parliament.

Citation, commencement and interpretation

1(1) This Order may be cited as the Data Protection (Processing of Sensitive Personal Data) Order 2006 and shall come into force on the day after the day on which it is made.

(2) In this Order–

"the Act" means the Data Protection Act 1998;

"caution" means a caution given to any person in England and Wales or Northern Ireland in respect of an offence which, at the time when the caution is given, is admitted and includes a reprimand or warning to which section 65 of the Crime and Disorder Act 1998 applies;

"conviction" has the same meaning as in section 56 of the Act;

"payment card" includes a credit card, a charge card and a debit card;

"pseudo-photograph" includes an image, whether made by computer-graphics or otherwise howsoever, which appears to be a photograph.

Condition relevant for purposes of the First Principle: processing of sensitive personal data

2(1) For the purposes of paragraph 10 of Schedule 3 to the Act, the circumstances specified in paragraph (2) are circumstances in which sensitive personal data may be processed.

(2) The processing of information about a criminal conviction or caution for an offence listed in paragraph (3) relating to an indecent photograph or pseudo-photograph of a child is necessary for the purpose of administering an account relating to the payment card used in the commission of the offence or for cancelling that payment card.

(3) The offences listed are those under–

    (a)   section 1 of the Protection of Children Act 1978,

    (b)   section 160 of the Criminal Justice Act 1988,

    (c)   article 15 of the Criminal Justice (Evidence etc) (Northern Ireland) Order 1988,

    (d)   article 3 of the Protection of Children (Northern Ireland) Order 1978,

    (e)   section 52 of the Civic Government (Scotland) Act 1982, or

    (f)   incitement to commit any of the offences in sub-paragraphs (a)–(e).

Data Protection (Processing of Sensitive Personal Data) Order 2009
(SI 2009/1811)

Made 7th July 2009

Coming into force in accordance with article 1(1)

The Secretary of State, in exercise of the powers conferred by section 67(2) of and paragraph 10 of Schedule 3 to the Data Protection Act 1998, makes the following Order;

In accordance with section 67(3) of the Data Protection Act 1998, the Secretary of State has consulted the Information Commissioner;

In accordance with section 67(4) of the Data Protection Act 1998, a draft of this instrument was laid before Parliament and approved by a resolution of each House of Parliament;

Citation, commencement and interpretation

1(1) This Order may be cited as the Data Protection (Processing of Sensitive Personal Data) Order 2009 and shall come into force on the day after the day on which it is made.

(2) In this Order "prison" includes young offender institutions, remand centres and secure training centres and "prisoner" includes a person detained in a young offender institution, remand centre or secure training centre.

Condition relevant for purpose of the First Principle: processing of sensitive personal data

2(1) For the purposes of paragraph 10 of Schedule 3 to the Data Protection Act 1998, the circumstance specified in paragraph (2) is a circumstance in which sensitive personal data may be processed.

(2) The processing of information about a prisoner, including information relating to the prisoner's release from prison, for the purpose of informing a Member of Parliament about the prisoner and arrangements for the prisoner's release.

Data Protection (Processing of Sensitive Personal Data) (Elected Representatives) Order 2002
(SI 2002/2905)

Made 19th November 2002
Coming into force 17th December 2002

Whereas a draft of this Order has been laid before and approved by a resolution of each House of Parliament:

Now, therefore, the Lord Chancellor, in exercise of the powers conferred upon him by section 67(2) of, and paragraph 10 of Schedule 3 to, the Data Protection Act 1998, and after consultation with the Information Commissioner in accordance with section 67(3) of that Act, hereby makes the following Order:

1   This Order may be cited as the Data Protection (Processing of Sensitive Personal Data) (Elected Representatives) Order 2002 and shall come into force on the twenty-eighth day after the day on which it is made.

2   For the purposes of paragraph 10 of Schedule 3 to the Data Protection Act 1998, the circumstances specified in any of paragraphs 3, 4, 5 or 6 in the Schedule to this Order are circumstances in which sensitive personal data may be processed.

SCHEDULE
CIRCUMSTANCES IN WHICH SENSITIVE PERSONAL DATA MAY BE PROCESSED

Interpretation

1   In this Schedule, "elected representative" means–

   (a)   a Member of the House of Commons, a Member of the National Assembly for Wales, a Member of the Scottish Parliament or a Member of the Northern Ireland Assembly;

   (b)   a Member of the European Parliament elected in the United Kingdom;

   (c)   an elected member of a local authority within the meaning of section 270(1) of the Local Government Act 1972, namely–

   (i)   in England, a county council, a district council, a London borough council or a parish council,

   (ii)   in Wales, a county council, a county borough council or a community council;

   (d)   an elected mayor of a local authority within the meaning of Part II of the Local Government Act 2000;

   (e)   the Mayor of London or an elected member of the London Assembly;

   (f)   an elected member of–

   (i)   the Common Council of the City of London, or

   (ii)   the Council of the Isles of Scilly;

   (g)   an elected member of a council constituted under section 2 of the Local Government etc (Scotland) Act 1994; or

   (h)   an elected member of a district council within the meaning of the Local Government Act (Northern Ireland) 1972.

2   For the purposes of paragraph 1 above–

(a) a person who is—
    (i) a Member of the House of Commons immediately before Parliament is dissolved,
    (ii) a Member of the Scottish Parliament immediately before that Parliament is dissolved, or
    (iii) a Member of the Northern Ireland Assembly immediately before that Assembly is dissolved,

shall be treated as if he were such a member until the end of the fourth day after the day on which the subsequent general election in relation to that Parliament or Assembly is held;

(b) a person who is a Member of the National Assembly for Wales and whose term of office comes to an end, in accordance with section 2(5)(b) of the Government of Wales Act 1998, at the end of the day preceding an ordinary election (within the meaning of section 2(4) of that Act), shall be treated as if he were such a member until the end of the fourth day after the day on which that ordinary election is held; and

(c) a person who is an elected member of the Common Council of the City of London and whose term of office comes to an end at the end of the day preceding the annual Wardmotes shall be treated as if he were such a member until the end of the fourth day after the day on which those Wardmotes are held.

Processing by elected representatives

3 The processing—
    (a) is carried out by an elected representative or a person acting with his authority;
    (b) is in connection with the discharge of his functions as such a representative;
    (c) is carried out pursuant to a request made by the data subject to the elected representative to take action on behalf of the data subject or any other individual; and
    (d) is necessary for the purposes of, or in connection with, the action reasonably taken by the elected representative pursuant to that request.

4 The processing—
    (a) is carried out by an elected representative or a person acting with his authority;
    (b) is in connection with the discharge of his functions as such a representative;
    (c) is carried out pursuant to a request made by an individual other than the data subject to the elected representative to take action on behalf of the data subject or any other individual;
    (d) is necessary for the purposes of, or in connection with, the action reasonably taken by the elected representative pursuant to that request; and
    (e) is carried out without the explicit consent of the data subject because the processing—
        (i) is necessary in a case where explicit consent cannot be given by the data subject,
        (ii) is necessary in a case where the elected representative cannot reasonably be expected to obtain the explicit consent of the data subject,
        (iii) must necessarily be carried out without the explicit consent of the data subject being sought so as not to prejudice the action taken by the elected representative, or
        (iv) is necessary in the interests of another individual in a case where the explicit consent of the data subject has been unreasonably withheld.

Processing limited to disclosures to elected representatives

5   The disclosure–

   (a)   is made to an elected representative or a person acting with his authority;

   (b)   is made in response to a communication to the data controller from the elected representative, or a person acting with his authority, acting pursuant to a request made by the data subject;

   (c)   is of sensitive personal data which are relevant to the subject matter of that communication; and

   (d)   is necessary for the purpose of responding to that communication.

6   The disclosure–

   (a)   is made to an elected representative or a person acting with his authority;

   (b)   is made in response to a communication to the data controller from the elected representative, or a person acting with his authority, acting pursuant to a request made by an individual other than the data subject;

   (c)   is of sensitive personal data which are relevant to the subject matter of that communication;

   (d)   is necessary for the purpose of responding to that communication; and

   (e)   is carried out without the explicit consent of the data subject because the disclosure–

      (i)   is necessary in a case where explicit consent cannot be given by the data subject,

      (ii)   is necessary in a case where the data controller cannot reasonably be expected to obtain the explicit consent of the data subject,

      (iii)   must necessarily be carried out without the explicit consent of the data subject being sought so as not to prejudice the action taken by the elected representative, or

      (iv)   is necessary in the interests of another individual in a case where the explicit consent of the data subject has been unreasonably withheld.

Data Protection (Subject Access)
(Fees and Miscellaneous Provisions) Regulations 2000
(SI 2000/191)

Made 31st January 2000
Laid before Parliament 7th February 2000
Coming into force 1st March 2000

The Secretary of State, in exercise of the powers conferred on him by sections 7(2), (7), (8) and (11) (having regard to the definitions of "prescribed", "the prescribed maximum" and "the prescribed period" in section 7(10)), 8(1) and 67(2) of the Data Protection Act 1998 and having consulted the Data Protection Commissioner in accordance with section 67(3) of that Act, hereby makes the following Regulations:

Citation, commencement and interpretation

1(1) These Regulations may be cited as the Data Protection (Subject Access) (Fees and Miscellaneous Provisions) Regulations 2000 and shall come into force on 1st March 2000.

(2) In these Regulations "the Act" means the Data Protection Act 1998.

Extent of subject access requests

2(1) A request for information under any provision of section 7(1)(a), (b) or (c) of the Act is to be treated as extending also to information under all other provisions of section 7(1)(a), (b) and (c).

(2) A request for information under any provision of section 7(1) of the Act is to be treated as extending to information under the provisions of section 7(1)(d) only where the request shows an express intention to that effect.

(3) A request for information under the provisions of section 7(1)(d) of the Act is to be treated as extending also to information under any other provision of section 7(1) only where the request shows an express intention to that effect.

Maximum subject access fee

3 Except as otherwise provided by regulations 4, 5 and 6 below, the maximum fee which may be required by a data controller under section 7(2)(b) of the Act is £10.4 Limited requests for subject access where data controller is credit reference agency

Limited requests for subject access where data controller is credit reference agency

4(1) In any case in which a request under section 7 of the Act has been made to a data controller who is a credit reference agency, and has been limited, or by virtue of section 9(2) of the Act is taken to have been limited, to personal data relevant to an individual's financial standing–

   (a)   the maximum fee which may be required by a data controller under section 7(2)(b) of the Act is £2, and

   (b)   the prescribed period for the purposes of section 7(8) of the Act is seven working days.

(2) In this regulation "working day" means any day other than–

   (a)   Saturday or Sunday,

   (b)   Christmas Day or Good Friday,

    (c)   a bank holiday, within the meaning of section 1 of the Banking and Financial Dealings Act 1971, in the part of the United Kingdom in which the data controller's address is situated.

(3) For the purposes of paragraph (2)(c) above–

    (a)   the address of a registered company is that of its registered office, and

    (b)   the address of a person (other than a registered company) carrying on a business is that of his principal place of business in the United Kingdom.

Subject access requests in respect of educational records

5(1) This regulation applies to any case in which a request made under section 7 of the Act relates wholly or partly to personal data forming part of an accessible record which is an educational record within the meaning of Schedule 11 to the Act.

(2) Except as provided by paragraph (3) below, a data controller may not require a fee under section 7(2)(b) of the Act in any case to which this regulation applies.

(3) Where, in a case to which this regulation applies, the obligation imposed by section 7(1)(c)(i) of the Act is to be complied with by supplying the data subject with a copy of information in permanent form, the maximum fee which may be required by a data controller under section 7(2)(b) of the Act is that applicable to the case under the Schedule to these Regulations.

(4) In any case to which this regulation applies, and in which the address of the data controller to whom the request is made is situated in England and Wales, the prescribed period for the purposes of section 7(8) of the Act is fifteen school days within the meaning of section 579(1) of the Education Act 1996.

Certain subject access requests in respect of health records

6(1) This regulation applies only to cases in which a request made under section 7 of the Act–

    (a)   relates wholly or partly to personal data forming part of an accessible record which is a health record within the meaning of section 68(2) of the Act, and

    (b)   does not relate exclusively to data within paragraphs (a) and (b) of the definition of "data" in section 1(1) of the Act.

(2) Where in a case to which this regulation applies, the obligation imposed by section 7(1)(c)(i) of the Act is to be complied with by supplying the data subject with a copy of information in permanent form, the maximum fee which may be required by a data controller under section 7(2)(b) of the Act is £50.

(3) Except in a case to which paragraph (2) above applies, a data controller may not require a fee under section 7(2)(b) of the Act where, in a case to which this regulation applies, the request relates solely to personal data which–

    (a)   form part of an accessible record–

        (i)   which is a health record within the meaning of section 68(2) of the Act, and

        (ii) at least some of which was made after the beginning of the period of 40 days immediately preceding the date of the request; and

    (b)   do not fall within paragraph (a) or (b) of the definition of "data" in section 1(1) of the Act.

(4) For the purposes of paragraph (3) above, an individual making a request in any case to which this regulation applies may specify that his request is limited to personal data of the

description set out in that paragraph.

SCHEDULE
MAXIMUM SUBJECT ACCESS FEES WHERE A COPY OF INFORMATION CONTAINED IN AN EDUCATIONAL RECORD IS SUPPLIED IN PERMANENT FORM

Regulation 5(3)

1 In any case in which the copy referred to in regulation 5(3) includes material in any form other than a record in writing on paper, the maximum fee applicable for the purposes of regulation 5(3) is £50.

2 In any case in which the copy referred to in regulation 5(3) consists solely of a record in writing on paper, the maximum fee applicable for the purposes of regulation 5(3) is set out in the table below.

TABLE

number of pages of information comprising the copy	maximum fee
fewer than 20	£1
20-29	£2
30-39	£3
40-49	£4
50-59	£5
60-69	£6
70-79	£7
80-89	£8
90-99	£9
100-149	£10
150-199	£15
200-249	£20
250-299	£25
300-349	£30
350-399	£35
400-449	£40
450-499	£45
500 or more	£50

Data Protection (Subject Access Modification) (Education) Order 2000 (SI 2000/414)

Made 17th February 2000
Coming into force 1st March 2000

Whereas a draft of this Order has been laid before and approved by a resolution of each House of Parliament:

Now, therefore, the Secretary of State, in exercise of powers conferred upon him by sections 30(2) and (4) and 67(2) of the Data Protection Act 1998, and after consultation with the Data Protection Commissioner in accordance with section 67(3) of the Act, hereby makes the following Order:

Citation and commencement

1 This Order may be cited as the Data Protection (Subject Access Modification) (Education) Order 2000 and shall come into force on 1st March 2000.

Interpretation

2 In this Order–

"the Act" means the Data Protection Act 1998;

"education authority" in article 6 has the same meaning as in paragraph 6 of Schedule 11 to the Act;

"Principal Reporter" means the Principal Reporter appointed under section 127 of the Local Government etc (Scotland) Act 1994 or any officer of the Scottish Children's Reporter Administration to whom there is delegated under section 131(1) of that Act any function of the Principal Reporter;

"request" means a request made under section 7; and

"section 7" means section 7 of the Act.

Personal data to which the Order applies

3(1) Subject to paragraph (2), this Order applies to personal data consisting of information constituting an educational record as defined in paragraph 1 of Schedule 11 to the Act.

(2) This Order does not apply–

    (a) to any data consisting of information as to the physical or mental health or condition of the data subject to which the Data Protection (Subject Access Modification) (Health) Order 2000 applies; or

    (b) to any data which are exempted from section 7 by an order made under section 38(1) of the Act.

Exemption from the subject information provisions

4(1) Personal data falling within paragraph (2) and to which this Order applies are exempt from the subject information provisions.

(2) This paragraph applies to personal data processed by a court and consisting of information supplied in a report or other evidence given to the court in the course of proceedings to which the Magistrates' Courts (Children and Young Persons) Rules 1992, the Magistrates' Courts (Criminal Justice (Children)) Rules (Northern Ireland) 1999, the Act of Sederunt (Child Care and Maintenance Rules) 1997 or the Children's Hearings (Scotland) Rules

1996 apply where, in accordance with a provision of any of those Rules, the information may be withheld by the court in whole or in part from the data subject.

Exemptions from section 7

5(1) Personal data to which this Order applies are exempt from section 7 in any case to the extent to which the application of that section would be likely to cause serious harm to the physical or mental health or condition of the data subject or any other person.

(2) In circumstances where the exemption in paragraph (1) does not apply, where any person falling within paragraph (3) is enabled by or under any enactment or rule of law to make a request on behalf of a data subject and has made such a request, personal data consisting of information as to whether the data subject is or has been the subject of or may be at risk of child abuse are exempt from section 7 in any case to the extent to which the application of that section would not be in the best interests of that data subject.

(3) A person falls within this paragraph if–

    (a)   the data subject is a child, and that person has parental responsibility for that data subject; or

    (b)   the data subject is incapable of managing his own affairs and that person has been appointed by a court to manage those affairs.

(4) For the purposes of paragraph (2), "child abuse" includes physical injury (other than accidental injury) to, and physical and emotional neglect, ill-treatment and sexual abuse of, a child.

(5) Paragraph (2) shall not apply in Scotland.

Modification of section 7 relating to Principal Reporter

6 Where in Scotland a data controller who is an education authority receives a request relating to information constituting data to which this Order applies and which the education authority believes to have originated from or to have been supplied by or on behalf of the Principal Reporter acting in pursuance of his statutory duties, other than information which the data subject is entitled to receive from the Principal Reporter, section 7 shall be modified so that–

(a) the data controller shall, within fourteen days of the relevant day (as defined by section 7(10) of the Act), inform the Principal Reporter that a request has been made; and

    (b)   the data controller shall not communicate information to the data subject pursuant to that section unless the Principal Reporter has informed that data controller that, in his opinion, the exemption specified in article 5(1) does not apply with respect to the information.

Further modifications of section 7

7(1) In relation to data to which this Order applies–

    (a)   section 7(4) of the Act shall have effect as if there were inserted after paragraph (b) of that subsection "or (c) the other individual is a relevant person";

    (b)   section 7(9) shall have effect as if–

        (i)   there was substituted–

"(9) If a court is satisfied on the application of–

(a) any person who has made a request under the foregoing provisions of this section, or

(b) any person to whom serious harm to his physical or mental health or condition would be likely to be caused by compliance with any such request in contravention of those provisions,

that the data controller in question is about to comply with or has failed to comply with the request in contravention of those provisions, the court may order him not to comply or, as the case may be, to comply with the request."; and

>> (ii) the reference to a contravention of the foregoing provisions of that section included a reference to a contravention of the provisions contained in this Order.

(2) After section 7(ii) of the Act insert–

"(12) A person is a relevant person for the purposes of subsection (4)(c) if he–

(a) is a person referred to in paragraph 4(a) or (b) or paragraph 8(a) or (b) of Schedule 11;

(b) is employed by an education authority (within the meaning of paragraph 6 of Schedule 11) in pursuance of its functions relating to education and the information relates to him, or he supplied the information in his capacity as such an employee; or

(c) is the person making the request."

Data Protection (Subject Access Modification) (Health) Order 2000 (SI 2000/413)

Made 17th February 2000
Coming into force 1st March 2000

Whereas a draft of this Order has been laid before and approved by a resolution of each House of Parliament:

Now, therefore, the Secretary of State, in exercise of the powers conferred on him by sections 30(1) and (4) and 67(2) of the Data Protection Act 1998 and after consultation with the Data Protection Commissioner in accordance with section 67(3) of that Act, hereby makes the following Order:

Citation and commencement

1   This Order may be cited as the Data Protection (Subject Access Modification) (Health) Order 2000 and shall come into force on 1st March 2000.

Interpretation

2   In this Order–

"the Act" means the Data Protection Act 1998;

"the appropriate health professional" means–

(a)   the health professional who is currently or was most recently responsible for the clinical care of the data subject in connection with the matters to which the information which is the subject of the request relates; or

(b)   where there is more than one such health professional, the health professional who is the most suitable to advise on the matters to which the information which is the subject of the request relates; or

(c)   where–

(i)   there is no health professional available falling within paragraph (a) or (b), or

(ii)   the data controller is the Secretary of State and data to which this Order applies are processed in connection with the exercise of the functions conferred on him by or under the Child Support Act 1991 and the Child Support Act 1995 or his functions in relation to social security or war pensions,

a health professional who has the necessary experience and qualifications to advise on the matters to which the information which is the subject of the request relates;

"care" includes examination, investigation, diagnosis and treatment;

"request" means a request made under section 7;

"section 7" means section 7 of the Act; and

"war pension" has the same meaning as in section 25 of the Social Security Act 1989 (establishment and functions of war pensions committees).

Personal data to which Order applies

3(1)   Subject to paragraph (2), this Order applies to personal data consisting of information as to the physical or mental health or condition of the data subject.

(2)   This Order does not apply to any data which are exempted from section 7 by an order made under section 38(1) of the Act.

Exemption from the subject information provisions

4(1) Personal data falling within paragraph (2) and to which this Order applies are exempt from the subject information provisions.

(2) This paragraph applies to personal data processed by a court and consisting of information supplied in a report or other evidence given to the court by a local authority, Health and Social Services Board, Health and Social Services Trust, probation officer or other person in the course of any proceedings to which the Family Proceedings Courts (Children Act 1989) Rules 1991, the Magistrates' Courts (Children and Young Persons) Rules 1992, the Magistrates' Courts (Criminal Justice (Children)) Rules (Northern Ireland) 1999, the Act of Sederunt (Child Care and Maintenance Rules) 1997 or the Children's Hearings (Scotland) Rules 1996 apply where, in accordance with a provision of any of those Rules, the information may be withheld by the court in whole or in part from the data subject.

Exemptions from section 7

5(1) Personal data to which this Order applies are exempt from section 7 in any case to the extent to which the application of that section would be likely to cause serious harm to the physical or mental health or condition of the data subject or any other person.

(2) Subject to article 7(1), a data controller who is not a health professional shall not withhold information constituting data to which this Order applies on the ground that the exemption in paragraph (1) applies with respect to the information unless the data controller has first consulted the person who appears to the data controller to be the appropriate health professional on the question whether or not the exemption in paragraph (1) applies with respect to the information.

(3) Where any person falling within paragraph (4) is enabled by or under any enactment or rule of law to make a request on behalf of a data subject and has made such a request, personal data to which this Order applies are exempt from section 7 in any case to the extent to which the application of that section would disclose information–

    (a) provided by the data subject in the expectation that it would not be disclosed to the person making the request;

    (b) obtained as a result of any examination or investigation to which the data subject consented in the expectation that the information would not be so disclosed; or

    (c) which the data subject has expressly indicated should not be so disclosed,

provided that sub-paragraphs (a) and (b) shall not prevent disclosure where the data subject has expressly indicated that he no longer has the expectation referred to therein.

(4) A person falls within this paragraph if–

    (a) except in relation to Scotland, the data subject is a child, and that person has parental responsibility for that data subject;

    (b) in relation to Scotland, the data subject is a person under the age of sixteen, and that person has parental responsibilities for that data subject; or

    (c) the data subject is incapable of managing his own affairs and that person has been appointed by a court to manage those affairs.

Modification of section 7 relating to data controllers who are not health professionals

6(1) Subject to paragraph (2) and article 7(3), section 7 of the Act is modified so that a data controller who is not a health professional shall not communicate information constituting data to which this Order applies in response to a request unless the data controller has first consulted the person who appears to the data controller to be the appropriate health professional on the question whether or not the exemption in article 5(1) applies with respect to the information.

(2) Paragraph (1) shall not apply to the extent that the request relates to information which the data controller is satisfied has previously been seen by the data subject or is already within the knowledge of the data subject.

Additional provision relating to data controllers who are not health professionals

7(1) Subject to paragraph (2), article 5(2) shall not apply in relation to any request where the data controller has consulted the appropriate health professional prior to receiving the request and obtained in writing from that appropriate health professional an opinion that the exemption in article 5(1) applies with respect to all of the information which is the subject of the request.

(2) Paragraph (1) does not apply where the opinion either–

    (a)   was obtained before the period beginning six months before the relevant day (as defined by section 7(10) of the Act) and ending on that relevant day, or

    (b)   was obtained within that period and it is reasonable in all the circumstances to re-consult the appropriate health professional.

(3) Article 6(1) shall not apply in relation to any request where the data controller has consulted the appropriate health professional prior to receiving the request and obtained in writing from that appropriate health professional an opinion that the exemption in article 5(1) does not apply with respect to all of the information which is the subject of the request.

Further modifications of section 7

7 In relation to data to which this Order applies–

    (a)   section 7(4) of the Act shall have effect as if there were inserted after paragraph (b) of that subsection "or, (c) the information is contained in a health record and the other individual is a health professional who has compiled or contributed to the health record or has been involved in the care of the data subject in his capacity as a health professional";

    (b)   section 7(9) shall have effect as if–

        (i)   there was substituted–

        "(9) If a court is satisfied on the application of–

            (a)   any person who has made a request under the foregoing provisions of this section, or

            (b)   any other person to whom serious harm to his physical or mental health or condition would be likely to be caused by compliance with any such request in contravention of those provisions,

        that the data controller in question is about to comply with or has failed to comply with the request in contravention of those provisions, the court may order him not to comply or, as the case may be, to comply with the request."; and

        (ii)   the reference therein to a contravention of the foregoing provisions of that section included a reference to a contravention of the provisions contained in this Order.

Data Protection (Subject Access Modification) (Social Work) Order 2000 (SI 2000/415)

Made 17th February 2000
Coming into force 1st March 2000

Whereas a draft of this Order has been laid before and approved by a resolution of each House of Parliament:

Whereas the Secretary of State considers that the application of the subject information provisions (or those provisions without modification) in the circumstances and to the extent specified in this Order would be likely to prejudice the carrying out of social work:

Now, therefore, the Secretary of State, in exercise of the powers conferred on him by sections 30(3) and (4) and 67(2) of the Data Protection Act 1998, and after consultation with the Data Protection Commissioner in accordance with section 67(3) of that Act, hereby makes the following Order:

Citation and commencement

1 This Order may be cited as the Data Protection (Subject Access Modification) (Social Work) Order 2000 and shall come into force on 1st March 2000.

Interpretation

(1) In this Order–

"the Act" means the Data Protection Act 1998;

"compulsory school age" in paragraph 1(f) of the Schedule has the same meaning as in section 8 of the Education Act 1996, and in paragraph 1(g) of the Schedule has the same meaning as in Article 46 of the Education and Libraries (Northern Ireland) Order 1986;

"Health and Social Services Board" means a Health and Social Services Board established under Article 16 of the Health and Personal Social Services (Northern Ireland) Order 1972;

"Health and Social Services Trust" means a Health and Social Services Trust established under the Health and Personal Social Services (Northern Ireland) Order 1991;

"Principal Reporter" means the Principal Reporter appointed under section 127 of the Local Government etc (Scotland) Act 1994 or any officer of the Scottish Children's Reporter Administration to whom there is delegated under section 131(1) of that Act any function of the Principal Reporter;

"request" means a request made under section 7;

"school age" in paragraph 1(h) of the Schedule has the same meaning as in section 31 of the Education (Scotland) Act 1980;

"section 7" means section 7 of the Act; and

"social work authority" in article 6 means a local authority for the purposes of the Social Work (Scotland) Act 1968.

(2) Any reference in this Order to a local authority in relation to data processed or formerly processed by it includes a reference to the Council of the Isles of Scilly in relation to data processed or formerly processed by the Council in connection with any functions mentioned in paragraph 1(a)(ii) of the Schedule which are or have been conferred upon the Council by or under any enactment.

Personal data to which Order applies

3(1) Subject to paragraph (2), this Order applies to personal data falling within any of the descriptions set out in paragraphs 1 and 2 of the Schedule.

(2) This Order does not apply–

    (a) to any data consisting of information as to the physical or mental health or condition of the data subject to which the Data Protection (Subject Access Modification) (Health) Order 2000 or the Data Protection (Subject Access Modification) (Education) Order 2000 applies; or

    (b) to any data which are exempted from section 7 by an order made under section 38(1) of the Act.

Exemption from subject information provisions

4 Personal data to which this Order applies by virtue of paragraph 2 of the Schedule are exempt from the subject information provisions.

Exemption from section 7

5(1) Personal data to which this Order applies by virtue of paragraph 1 of the Schedule are exempt from the obligations in section 7(1)(b) to (d) of the Act in any case to the extent to which the application of those provisions would be likely to prejudice the carrying out of social work by reason of the fact that serious harm to the physical or mental health or condition of the data subject or any other person would be likely to be caused.

(2) In paragraph (1) the "carrying out of social work" shall be construed as including–

    (a) the exercise of any functions mentioned in paragraph 1(a)(i), (d), (f) to (j), (m), (o), (r), (s) or (t) of the Schedule;

    (b) the provision of any service mentioned in paragraph 1(b), (c) or (k) of the Schedule; and

    (c) the exercise of the functions of any body mentioned in paragraph 1(e) of the Schedule or any person mentioned in paragraph 1(p) or (q) of the Schedule.

(3) Where any person falling within paragraph (4) is enabled by or under any enactment or rule of law to make a request on behalf of a data subject and has made such a request, personal data to which this Order applies are exempt from section 7 in any case to the extent to which the application of that section would disclose information–

    (a) provided by the data subject in the expectation that it would not be disclosed to the person making the request;

    (b) obtained as a result of any examination or investigation to which the data subject consented in the expectation that the information would not be so disclosed; or

    (c) which the data subject has expressly indicated should not be so disclosed,

provided that sub-paragraphs (a) and (b) shall not prevent disclosure where the data subject has expressly indicated that he no longer has the expectation referred to therein.

(4) A person falls within this paragraph if–

    (a) except in relation to Scotland, the data subject is a child, and that person has parental responsibility for that data subject;

    (b) in relation to Scotland, the data subject is a person under the age of sixteen, and that person has parental responsibilities for that data subject; or

    (c) the data subject is incapable of managing his own affairs and that person has been appointed by a court to manage those affairs.

Modification of section 7 relating to Principal Reporter

6   Where in Scotland a data controller who is a social work authority receives a request relating to information constituting data to which this Order applies and which originated from or was supplied by the Principal Reporter acting in pursuance of his statutory duties, other than information which the data subject is entitled to receive from the Principal Reporter, section 7 shall be modified so that–

    (a)   the data controller shall, within fourteen days of the relevant day (within the meaning of section 7(10) of the Act), inform the Principal Reporter that a request has been made; and

    (b)   the data controller shall not communicate information to the data subject pursuant to that section unless the Principal Reporter has informed that data controller that, in his opinion, the exemption specified in article 5(1) does not apply with respect to the information.

Further modifications of section 7

7(1)   In relation to data to which this Order applies by virtue of paragraph 1 of the Schedule–

    (a)   section 7(4) shall have effect as if there were inserted after paragraph (b) of that subsection "or, (c) the other individual is a relevant person";

    (b)   section 7(9) shall have effect as if–

       (i)   there was substituted–

"(9)   If a court is satisfied on the application of–

(a) any person who has made a request under the foregoing provisions of this section, or

(b) any person to whom serious harm to his physical or mental health or condition would be likely to be caused by compliance with any such request in contravention of those provisions,that the data controller in question is about to comply with or has failed to comply with the request in contravention of those provisions, the court may order him not to comply or, as the case may be, to comply with the request."; and

       (ii)   the reference to a contravention of the foregoing provisions of that section included a reference to a contravention of the provisions contained in this Order.

(2)   In relation to data to which this Order applies by virtue of paragraph 1 of the Schedule, section 7 shall have effect as if after subsection (11) there were inserted–

"(12)   A person is a relevant person for the purposes of subsection (4)(c) if he–

(a) is a person referred to in paragraph 1(p), (q), (r), (s) or (t) of the Schedule to the Data Protection (Subject Access Modification) (Social Work) Order 2000; or

(b) is or has been employed by any person or body referred to in paragraph 1 of that Schedule in connection with functions which are or have been exercised in relation to the data consisting of the information; or

(c) has provided for reward a service similar to a service provided in the exercise of any functions specified in paragraph 1(a)(i), (b), (c) or (d) of that Schedule,

and the information relates to him or he supplied the information in his official capacity or, as the case may be, in connection with the provision of that service.".

SCHEDULE
PERSONAL DATA TO WHICH THIS ORDER APPLIES

Article 31

1.   This paragraph applies to personal data falling within any of the following descriptions–

(a) data processed by a local authority–

    (i) in connection with its social services functions within the meaning of the Local Authority Social Services Act 1970 or any functions exercised by local authorities under the Social Work (Scotland) Act 1968 or referred to in section 5(1B) of that Act, or

    (ii) in the exercise of other functions but obtained or consisting of information obtained in connection with any of those functions;

(b) data processed by a Health and Social Services Board in connection with the provision of personal social services within the meaning of the Health and Personal Social Services (Northern Ireland) Order 1972 or processed by the Health and Social Services Board in the exercise of other functions but obtained or consisting of information obtained in connection with the provision of those services;

(c) data processed by a Health and Social Services Trust in connection with the provision of personal social services within the meaning of the Health and Personal Social Services (Northern Ireland) Order 1972 on behalf of a Health and Social Services Board by virtue of an authorisation made under Article 3(1) of the Health and Personal Social Services (Northern Ireland) Order 1994 or processed by the Health and Social Services Trust in the exercise of other functions but obtained or consisting of information obtained in connection with the provision of those services;

(d) data processed by a council in the exercise of its functions under Part II of Schedule 9 to the Health and Social Services and Social Security Adjudications Act 1983;

(e) data processed by a probation committee established by section 3 of the Probation Service Act 1993 or the Probation Board for Northern Ireland established by the Probation Board (Northern Ireland) Order 1982;

(f) data processed by a local education authority in the exercise of its functions under section 36 of the Children Act 1989 or Chapter II of Part VI of the Education Act 1996 so far as those functions relate to ensuring that children of compulsory school age receive suitable education whether by attendance at school or otherwise;

(g) data processed by an education and library board in the exercise of its functions under article 55 of the Children (Northern Ireland) Order 1995 or article 45 of, and Schedule 13 to, the Education and Libraries (Northern Ireland) Order 1986 so far as those functions relate to ensuring that children of compulsory school age receive efficient full-time education suitable to their age, ability and aptitude and to any special educational needs they may have, either by regular attendance at school or otherwise;

(h) data processed by an education authority in the exercise of its functions under sections 35 to 42 of the Education (Scotland) Act 1980 so far as those functions relate to ensuring that children of school age receive efficient education suitable to their age, ability and aptitude, whether by attendance at school or otherwise;

(i) data relating to persons detained in a special hospital provided under section 4 of the National Health Service Act 1977 and processed by a special health authority established under section 11 of that Act in the exercise of any functions similar to any social services functions of a local authority;

(j) data relating to persons detained in special accommodation provided under article 110 of the Mental Health (Northern Ireland) Order 1986 and processed by a Health and Social Services Trust in the exercise of any functions similar to any social services functions of a local authority;

(k) data processed by the National Society for the Prevention of Cruelty to Children or by any other voluntary organisation or other body designated under this sub-paragraph by the Secretary of State or the Department of Health, Social Services and Public Safety and appearing to the Secretary of State or the Department, as the case may be, to be processed for the purposes of the provision of any service similar to a service provided in the exercise of any functions specified in sub-paragraphs (a)(i), (b), (c) or (d) above;

(l) data processed by–

   (zi) a Strategic Health Authority established under section 8 of the National Health Service Act 1977;

   (i) a Health Authority established under section 8 of the National Health Service Act 1977;

   (ii) an NHS Trust established under section 5 of the National Health Service and Community Care Act 1990;

   (iiza) an NHS foundation trust within the meaning of section 1(1) of the Health and Social Care (Community Health and Standards) Act 2003;

   (iia) a Primary Care Trust established under section 16A of the National Health Service Act 1977; or

   (iii) a Health Board established under section 2 of the National Health Service (Scotland) Act 1978,which were obtained or consisted of information which was obtained from any authority or body mentioned above or government department and which, whilst processed by that authority or body or government department, fell within any sub-paragraph of this paragraph;

(m) data processed by an NHS Trust as referred to in sub-paragraph (l)(ii) above in the exercise of any functions similar to any social services functions of a local authority;

(mm) data processed by an NHS foundation trust as referred to in sub-paragraph (l)(iiza) above in the exercise of any functions similar to any social services functions of a local authority;

(n) data processed by a government department and obtained or consisting of information obtained from any authority or body mentioned above and which, whilst processed by that authority or body, fell within any of the preceding sub-paragraphs of this paragraph;

(o) data processed for the purposes of the functions of the Secretary of State pursuant to section 82(5) of the Children Act 1989;

(p) data processed by any children's guardian appointed under rule 4.10 of the Family Proceedings Rules 1991 or rule 10 of the Family Proceedings Courts (Children Act 1989) Rules 1991, by any guardian ad litem appointed under Article 60 of the Children (Northern Ireland) Order 1995 or Article 66 of the Adoption (Northern Ireland) Order 1987 or by a safeguarder appointed under section 41 of the Children (Scotland) Act 1995;

(q) data processed by the Principal Reporter;

(r) data processed by any officer of the Children and Family Court Advisory and Support Service for the purpose of his functions under section 7 of the Children Act 1989, rules 4.11 and 4.11B of the Family Proceedings Rules 1991, and rules 11 and 11B of the Family Proceedings Courts (Children Act 1989) Rules 1991;

(s) data processed by any officer of the service appointed as guardian ad litem under rule 9.5(1) of the Family Proceedings Rules 1991;

(t) data processed by the Children and Family Court Advisory and Support Service for the purpose of its functions under section 12(1) and (2) and section 13(1), (2) and (4) of the Criminal Justice and Court Services Act 2000;

(u) data processed for the purposes of the functions of the appropriate Minister pursuant to section 12 of the Adoption and Children Act 2002 (independent review of determinations).

2 This paragraph applies to personal data processed by a court and consisting of information supplied in a report or other evidence given to the court by a local authority, Health and Social Services Board, Health and Social Services Trust, probation officer, officer of the Children and Family Court Advisory and Support Service or other person in the course of any proceedings to which the Family Proceedings Courts (Children Act 1989) Rules 1991, the Magistrates' Courts (Children and Young Persons) Rules 1992, the Magistrates' Courts (Criminal Justice (Children)) Rules (Northern Ireland) 1999, the Act of Sederunt (Child Care and Maintenance Rules) 1997, the Children's Hearings (Scotland) Rules 1996 or the Family Proceedings Rules 1991 apply where, in accordance with a provision of any of those Rules, the information may be withheld by the court in whole or in part from the data subject.

Part VII

Procedural Material

Tribunals, Courts and Enforcement Act 2007

as amended to 1 February 2020

CONTENTS

PART 1
TRIBUNALS AND INQUIRIES

CHAPTER 1
TRIBUNAL JUDICIARY: INDEPENDENCE AND SENIOR PRESIDENT

CHAPTER 2
FIRST-TIER TRIBUNAL AND UPPER TRIBUNAL

Establishment

Members and composition of tribunals

Review of decisions and appeals

"Judicial review"

Tribunals, Courts and Enforcement Act 2007

2007 CHAPTER 15

An Act to make provision about tribunals and inquiries; to establish an Administrative Justice and Tribunals Council; to amend the law relating to judicial appointments and appointments to the Law Commission; to amend the law relating to the enforcement of judgments and debts; to make further provision about the management and relief of debt; to make provision protecting cultural objects from seizure or forfeiture in certain circumstances; to amend the law relating to the taking of possession of land affected by compulsory purchase; to alter the powers of the High Court in judicial review applications; and for connected purposes.

19th July 2007

BE IT ENACTED by the Queen's most Excellent Majesty, by and with the advice and consent of the Lords Spiritual and Temporal, and Commons, in this present Parliament assembled, and by the authority of the same, as follows:—

PART 1
TRIBUNALS AND INQUIRIES
CHAPTER 2
FIRST-TIER TRIBUNAL AND UPPER TRIBUNAL

Establishment

The First-tier Tribunal and the Upper Tribunal

3(1) There is to be a tribunal, known as the First-tier Tribunal, for the purpose of exercising the functions conferred on it under or by virtue of this Act or any other Act.

 (2) There is to be a tribunal, known as the Upper Tribunal, for the purpose of exercising the functions conferred on it under or by virtue of this Act or any other Act.

 (3) Each of the First-tier Tribunal, and the Upper Tribunal, is to consist of its judges and other members.

 (4) The Senior President of Tribunals is to preside over both of the First-tier Tribunal and the Upper Tribunal.

 (5) The Upper Tribunal is to be a superior court of record.

Members and composition of tribunals

Judges and other members of the First-tier Tribunal

4(1) A person is a judge of the First-tier Tribunal if the person—

    (a) is a judge of the First-tier Tribunal by virtue of appointment under paragraph 1(1) of Schedule 2,

    (b) is a transferred-in judge of the First-tier Tribunal (see section 31(2)),

    (c) is a judge of the Upper Tribunal,

    (ca) is within section 6A,

    (d) .....; or

    (e) is a member of a panel of Employment Judges.

 (2) A person is also a judge of the First-tier Tribunal, but only as regards functions of the

tribunal in relation to appeals such as are mentioned in subsection (1) of section 5 of the Criminal Injuries Compensation Act 1995, if the person is an adjudicator appointed under that section by the Scottish Ministers.

(3) A person is one of the other members of the First-tier Tribunal if the person—

    (a) is a member of the First-tier Tribunal by virtue of appointment under paragraph 2(1) of Schedule 2,

    (b) is a transferred-in other member of the First-tier Tribunal (see section 31(2)),

    (c) is one of the other members of the Upper Tribunal, or

    (d) is a member of a panel of members of employment tribunals that is not a panel of Employment Judges.

(4) Schedule 2—

    contains provision for the appointment of persons to be judges or other members of the First-tier Tribunal, and makes further provision in connection with judges and other members of the First-tier Tribunal.

Judges and other members of the Upper Tribunal

5(1) A person is a judge of the Upper Tribunal if the person—

    (a) is the Senior President of Tribunals,

    (b) is a judge of the Upper Tribunal by virtue of appointment under paragraph 1(1) of Schedule 3,

    (c) is a transferred-in judge of the Upper Tribunal (see section 31(2)),

    (d) .....

    (e) is the Chief Social Security Commissioner, or any other Social Security Commissioner, appointed under section 50(1) of the Social Security Administration (Northern Ireland) Act 1992,

    (f) is a Social Security Commissioner appointed under section 50(2) of that Act (deputy Commissioners),

    (g) is within section 6(1),

    (h) is a deputy judge of the Upper Tribunal (whether under paragraph 7 of Schedule 3 or under section 31(2)), or

    (i) is a Chamber President or a Deputy Chamber President, whether of a chamber of the Upper Tribunal or of a chamber of the First-tier Tribunal, and does not fall within any of paragraphs (a) to (h).

(2) A person is one of the other members of the Upper Tribunal if the person—

    (a) is a member of the Upper Tribunal by virtue of appointment under paragraph 2(1) of Schedule 3,

    (b) is a transferred-in other member of the Upper Tribunal (see section 31(2)), or

    (c) is a member of the Employment Appeal Tribunal appointed under section 22(1)(c) of the Employment Tribunals Act 1996. . .

    (d) ....

(3) Schedule 3—

    contains provision for the appointment of persons to be judges (including deputy judges), or other members, of the Upper Tribunal, and makes further provision in connection with judges and other members of the Upper Tribunal.

Certain judges who are also judges of First-tier Tribunal and Upper Tribunal

6(1) A person is within this subsection (and so, by virtue of sections 4(1)(c) and 5(1)(g), is a judge of the First-tier Tribunal and of the Upper Tribunal) if the person—

(za) is the Lord Chief Justice of England and Wales,

(zb) is the Master of the Rolls,

(zc) is the President of the Queen's Bench Division of the High Court in England and Wales,

(zd) is the President of the Family Division of the High Court in England and Wales,

(ze) is the Chancellor of the High Court in England and Wales,

(a) is an ordinary judge of the Court of Appeal in England and Wales (including the vice-president, if any, of either division of that Court),

(b) is a Lord Justice of Appeal in Northern Ireland,

(c) is a judge of the Court of Session,

(d) is a puisne judge of the High Court in England and Wales or Northern Ireland,

(da) is a deputy judge of the High Court in England and Wales,

(db) is the Judge Advocate General,

(e) is a circuit judge,

(ea) is a Recorder,

(f) is a sheriff in Scotland,

(g) is a county court judge in Northern Ireland,

(h) is a district judge in England and Wales or Northern Ireland, . . .

(i) is a District Judge (Magistrates' Courts),

(j) is the President of Employment Tribunals (England and Wales),

(k) is the President of Employment Tribunals (Scotland),

(l) is the Vice President of Employment Tribunals (Scotland), or

(m) is a Regional Employment Judge.

(2) References in subsection (1)(c) to (i) to office-holders do not include deputies or temporary office-holders.

Certain judges who are also judges of the First-tier Tribunal

6A A person is within this section (and so, by virtue of section 4(1)(ca), is a judge of the First-tier Tribunal) if the person—

(a) is a deputy Circuit judge,

(b) ...

(c) is a person who holds an office listed—

(i) in the first column of the table in section 89(3C) of the Senior Courts Act 1981 (senior High Court Masters etc), or

(ii) in column 1 of Part 2 of Schedule 2 to that Act (High Court Masters etc),

(d) is a deputy district judge appointed under section 102 of that Act or section 8 of the County Courts Act 1984,

(e) is a Deputy District Judge (Magistrates' Courts), or

(f) is a person appointed under section 30(1)(a) or (b) of the Courts-Martial (Appeals) Act 1951 (assistants to the Judge Advocate General).

Chambers: jurisdiction and Presidents

7(1) The Lord Chancellor may, with the concurrence of the Senior President of Tribunals, by order make provision for the organisation of each of the First-tier Tribunal and the Upper Tribunal into a number of chambers.

(2) There is—
    (a) for each chamber of the First-tier Tribunal, and
    (b) for each chamber of the Upper Tribunal,
to be a person, or two persons, to preside over that chamber.

(3) A person may at a particular time—
    (a) preside over more than one chamber of the First-tier Tribunal;
    (b) preside over more than one chamber of the Upper Tribunal;
    (c) preside over—
        (i) one or more chambers of the First-tier Tribunal, and
        (ii) one or more chambers of the Upper Tribunal.

(4) A person appointed under this section to preside over a chamber is to be known as a Chamber President.

(5) Where two persons are appointed under this section to preside over the same chamber, any reference in an enactment to the Chamber President of the chamber is a reference to a person appointed under this section to preside over the chamber.

(6) The Senior President of Tribunals may (consistently with subsection (2)) appoint a person who is the Chamber President of a chamber to preside instead, or to preside also, over another chamber.

(7) The Senior President of Tribunals may (consistently with subsection (2)) appoint a person who is not a Chamber President to preside over a chamber.

(8) Schedule 4 (eligibility for appointment under subsection (7), appointment of Deputy Chamber Presidents and Acting Chamber Presidents, assignment of judges and other members of the First-tier Tribunal and Upper Tribunal, and further provision about Chamber Presidents and chambers) has effect.

(9) Each of the Lord Chancellor and the Senior President of Tribunals may, with the concurrence of the other, by order—
    (a) make provision for the allocation of the First-tier Tribunal's functions between its chambers;
    (b) make provision for the allocation of the Upper Tribunal's functions between its chambers;
    (c) amend or revoke any order made under this subsection.

Senior President of Tribunals: power to delegate

8(1) The Senior President of Tribunals may delegate any function he has in his capacity as Senior President of Tribunals—
    (a) to any judge, or other member, of the Upper Tribunal or First-tier Tribunal;
    (b) to staff appointed under section 40(1).

(1A) A function under paragraph 1(1) or 2(1) of Schedule 2 may be delegated under subsection (1) only to a Chamber President of a chamber of the Upper Tribunal.

(2) Subsection (1) does not apply to functions of the Senior President of Tribunals under any of the following—
    section 7(7);
    section 7(9);

section 29B;

section 29D;

paragraph 2(1) of Schedule 3;

paragraph 3 of Schedule 5;

paragraph 7(1) of Schedule 3;

paragraph 2 of Schedule 4;

paragraph 5(1) and (3) of Schedule 4;

paragraph 5(5) to (8) of Schedule 4;

paragraph 5A(2)(a) of Schedule 4;

paragraph 5A(3)(a) of Schedule 4.

(3) A delegation under subsection (1) is not revoked by the delegator's becoming incapacitated.

(4) Any delegation under subsection (1) that is in force immediately before a person ceases to be Senior President of Tribunals continues in force until varied or revoked by a subsequent holder of the office of Senior President of Tribunals.

(5) The delegation under this section of a function shall not prevent the exercise of the function by the Senior President of Tribunals.

Review of decisions and appeals

Review of decision of First-tier Tribunal

9(1) The First-tier Tribunal may review a decision made by it on a matter in a case, other than a decision that is an excluded decision for the purposes of section 11(1) (but see subsection (9)).

(2) The First-tier Tribunal's power under subsection (1) in relation to a decision is exercisable—

    (a) of its own initiative, or

    (b) on application by a person who for the purposes of section 11(2) has a right of appeal in respect of the decision.

(3) Tribunal Procedure Rules may—

    (a) provide that the First-tier Tribunal may not under subsection (1) review (whether of its own initiative or on application under subsection (2)(b)) a decision of a description specified for the purposes of this paragraph in Tribunal Procedure Rules;

    (b) provide that the First-tier Tribunal's power under subsection (1) to review a decision of a description specified for the purposes of this paragraph in Tribunal Procedure Rules is exercisable only of the tribunal's own initiative;

    (c) provide that an application under subsection (2)(b) that is of a description specified for the purposes of this paragraph in Tribunal Procedure Rules may be made only on grounds specified for the purposes of this paragraph in Tribunal Procedure Rules;

    (d) provide, in relation to a decision of a description specified for the purposes of this paragraph in Tribunal Procedure Rules, that the First-tier Tribunal's power under subsection (1) to review the decision of its own initiative is exercisable only on grounds specified for the purposes of this paragraph in Tribunal Procedure Rules.

(4) Where the First-tier Tribunal has under subsection (1) reviewed a decision, the First-tier Tribunal may in the light of the review do any of the following—

    (a) correct accidental errors in the decision or in a record of the decision;

    (b) amend reasons given for the decision;

    (c) set the decision aside.

(5) Where under subsection (4)(c) the First-tier Tribunal sets a decision aside, the First-tier Tribunal must either—

    (a) re-decide the matter concerned, or

    (b) refer that matter to the Upper Tribunal.

(6) Where a matter is referred to the Upper Tribunal under subsection (5)(b), the Upper Tribunal must re-decide the matter.

(7) Where the Upper Tribunal is under subsection (6) re-deciding a matter, it may make any decision which the First-tier Tribunal could make if the First-tier Tribunal were re-deciding the matter.

(8) Where a tribunal is acting under subsection (5)(a) or (6), it may make such findings of fact as it considers appropriate.

(9) This section has effect as if a decision under subsection (4)(c) to set aside an earlier decision were not an excluded decision for the purposes of section 11(1), but the First-tier Tribunal's only power in the light of a review under subsection (1) of a decision under subsection (4)(c) is the power under subsection (4)(a).

(10) A decision of the First-tier Tribunal may not be reviewed under subsection (1) more than once, and once the First-tier Tribunal has decided that an earlier decision should not be reviewed under subsection (1) it may not then decide to review that earlier decision under that subsection.

(11) Where under this section a decision is set aside and the matter concerned is then re-decided, the decision set aside and the decision made in re-deciding the matter are for the purposes of subsection (10) to be taken to be different decisions.

Review of decision of Upper Tribunal

10(1) The Upper Tribunal may review a decision made by it on a matter in a case, other than a decision that is an excluded decision for the purposes of section 13(1) (but see subsection (7)).

(2) The Upper Tribunal's power under subsection (1) in relation to a decision is exercisable—

    (a) of its own initiative, or

    (b) on application by a person who for the purposes of section 13(2) has a right of appeal in respect of the decision.

(3) Tribunal Procedure Rules may—

    (a) provide that the Upper Tribunal may not under subsection (1) review (whether of its own initiative or on application under subsection (2)(b)) a decision of a description specified for the purposes of this paragraph in Tribunal Procedure Rules;

    (b) provide that the Upper Tribunal's power under subsection (1) to review a decision of a description specified for the purposes of this paragraph in Tribunal Procedure Rules is exercisable only of the tribunal's own initiative;

    (c) provide that an application under subsection (2)(b) that is of a description specified for the purposes of this paragraph in Tribunal Procedure Rules may be made only on grounds specified for the purposes of this paragraph in Tribunal Procedure Rules;

    (d)   provide, in relation to a decision of a description specified for the purposes of this paragraph in Tribunal Procedure Rules, that the Upper Tribunal's power under subsection (1) to review the decision of its own initiative is exercisable only on grounds specified for the purposes of this paragraph in Tribunal Procedure Rules.

(4)   Where the Upper Tribunal has under subsection (1) reviewed a decision, the Upper Tribunal may in the light of the review do any of the following—

    (a)   correct accidental errors in the decision or in a record of the decision;

    (b)   amend reasons given for the decision;

    (c)   set the decision aside.

(5)   Where under subsection (4)(c) the Upper Tribunal sets a decision aside, the Upper Tribunal must re-decide the matter concerned.

(6)   Where the Upper Tribunal is acting under subsection (5), it may make such findings of fact as it considers appropriate.

(7)   This section has effect as if a decision under subsection (4)(c) to set aside an earlier decision were not an excluded decision for the purposes of section 13(1), but the Upper Tribunal's only power in the light of a review under subsection (1) of a decision under subsection (4)(c) is the power under subsection (4)(a).

(8)   A decision of the Upper Tribunal may not be reviewed under subsection (1) more than once, and once the Upper Tribunal has decided that an earlier decision should not be reviewed under subsection (1) it may not then decide to review that earlier decision under that subsection.

(9)   Where under this section a decision is set aside and the matter concerned is then re-decided, the decision set aside and the decision made in re-deciding the matter are for the purposes of subsection (8) to be taken to be different decisions.

Right to appeal to Upper Tribunal

11(1)   For the purposes of subsection (2), the reference to a right of appeal is to a right to appeal to the Upper Tribunal on any point of law arising from a decision made by the First-tier Tribunal other than an excluded decision.

(2)   Any party to a case has a right of appeal, subject to subsection (8).

(3)   That right may be exercised only with permission (or, in Northern Ireland, leave).

(4)   Permission (or leave) may be given by—

    (a)   the First-tier Tribunal, or

    (b)   the Upper Tribunal,

on an application by the party.

(5)   For the purposes of subsection (1), an "excluded decision" is—

    (a)   any decision of the First-tier Tribunal on an appeal made in exercise of a right conferred by the Criminal Injuries Compensation Scheme in compliance with section 5(1)(a) of the Criminal Injuries Compensation Act 1995 (appeals against decisions on reviews),

    (aa) any decision of the First-tier Tribunal on an appeal made in exercise of a right conferred by the Victims of Overseas Terrorism Compensation Scheme in compliance with section 52(3) of the Crime and Security Act 2010,

  (b) any decision of the First-tier Tribunal on an appeal under section 27(3) or (5), 79(5) or (7) or 111(3) or (5) of the Data Protection Act 2018 (appeals against national security certificate),

  (c) any decision of the First-tier Tribunal on an appeal under section 60(1) or (4) of the Freedom of Information Act 2000 (appeals against national security certificate),

  (ca) any decision of the First-tier Tribunal under section 88, 89(3) or 92(3) of the Tax Collection and Management (Wales) Act 2016 (anaw 6) (approval for Welsh Revenue Authority to issue certain information notices),

  (cb) any decision of the First-tier Tribunal under section 108 of that Act (approval for Welsh Revenue Authority to inspect premises),

  (cc) any decision of the First-tier Tribunal under section 181E or 181F of that Act (appeals relating to postponement requests),

  (d) a decision of the First-tier Tribunal under section 9—

    (i) to review, or not to review, an earlier decision of the tribunal,

    (ii) to take no action, or not to take any particular action, in the light of a review of an earlier decision of the tribunal,

    (iii) to set aside an earlier decision of the tribunal, or

    (iv) to refer, or not to refer, a matter to the Upper Tribunal,

  (e) a decision of the First-tier Tribunal that is set aside under section 9 (including a decision set aside after proceedings on an appeal under this section have been begun), or

  (f) any decision of the First-tier Tribunal that is of a description specified in an order made by the Lord Chancellor.

(6) A description may be specified under subsection (5)(f) only if—

  (a) in the case of a decision of that description, there is a right to appeal to a court, the Upper Tribunal or any other tribunal from the decision and that right is, or includes, something other than a right (however expressed) to appeal on any point of law arising from the decision, or

  (b) decisions of that description are made in carrying out a function transferred under section 30 and prior to the transfer of the function under section 30(1) there was no right to appeal from decisions of that description.

(7) Where—

  (a) an order under subsection (5)(f) specifies a description of decisions, and

  (b) decisions of that description are made in carrying out a function transferred under section 30,

the order must be framed so as to come into force no later than the time when the transfer under section 30 of the function takes effect (but power to revoke the order continues to be exercisable after that time, and power to amend the order continues to be exercisable after that time for the purpose of narrowing the description for the time being specified).

(8) The Lord Chancellor may by order make provision for a person to be treated as being, or to be treated as not being, a party to a case for the purposes of subsection (2).

Proceedings on appeal to Upper Tribunal

12(1) Subsection (2) applies if the Upper Tribunal, in deciding an appeal under section 11, finds that the making of the decision concerned involved the making of an error on a point of law.

(2) The Upper Tribunal—

    (a) may (but need not) set aside the decision of the First-tier Tribunal, and

    (b) if it does, must either—

        (i) remit the case to the First-tier Tribunal with directions for its reconsideration, or

        (ii) re-make the decision.

(3) In acting under subsection (2)(b)(i), the Upper Tribunal may also—

    (a) direct that the members of the First-tier Tribunal who are chosen to reconsider the case are not to be the same as those who made the decision that has been set aside;

    (b) give procedural directions in connection with the reconsideration of the case by the First-tier Tribunal.

(4) In acting under subsection (2)(b)(ii), the Upper Tribunal—

    (a) may make any decision which the First-tier Tribunal could make if the First-tier Tribunal were re-making the decision, and

    (b) may make such findings of fact as it considers appropriate.

Right to appeal to Court of Appeal etc

13(1) For the purposes of subsection (2), the reference to a right of appeal is to a right to appeal to the relevant appellate court on any point of law arising from a decision made by the Upper Tribunal other than an excluded decision.

(2) Any party to a case has a right of appeal, subject to subsection (14).

(3) That right may be exercised only with permission (or, in Northern Ireland, leave).

(4) Permission (or leave) may be given by—

    (a) the Upper Tribunal, or

    (b) the relevant appellate court,

on an application by the party.

(5) An application may be made under subsection (4) to the relevant appellate court only if permission (or leave) has been refused by the Upper Tribunal.

(6) The Lord Chancellor may, as respects an application under subsection (4) that falls within subsection (7) and for which the relevant appellate court is the Court of Appeal in England and Wales or the Court of Appeal in Northern Ireland, by order make provision for permission (or leave) not to be granted on the application unless the Upper Tribunal or (as the case may be) the relevant appellate court considers—

    (a) that the proposed appeal would raise some important point of principle or practice, or

    (b) that there is some other compelling reason for the relevant appellate court to hear the appeal.

(6A) Rules of court may make provision for permission not to be granted on an application under subsection (4) to the Court of Session that falls within subsection (7) unless the court considers—

    (a) that the proposed appeal would raise some important point of principle or practice, or

    (b) that there is some other compelling reason for the court to hear the appeal.

(7) An application falls within this subsection if the application is for permission (or leave) to appeal from any decision of the Upper Tribunal on an appeal under section 11.

(8) For the purposes of subsection (1), an "excluded decision" is—

    (a) any decision of the Upper Tribunal on an appeal under section 27(3) or (5), 79(5) or (7) or 111(3) or (5) of the Data Protection Act 2018 (appeals against national security certificate),

    (b) any decision of the Upper Tribunal on an appeal under section 60(1) or (4) of the Freedom of Information Act 2000 (appeals against national security certificate),

    (ba) any decision of the Upper Tribunal under section 88, 89(3) or 92(3) of the Tax Collection and Management (Wales) Act 2016 (anaw 6) (approval for Welsh Revenue Authority to issue certain information notices),

    (bb) any decision of the Upper Tribunal under section 108 of that Act (approval for Welsh Revenue Authority to inspect premises),

    (bc) any decision of the Upper Tribunal under section 181E or 181F of that Act (appeals relating to postponement requests),

    (c) any decision of the Upper Tribunal on an application under section 11(4)(b) (application for permission or leave to appeal),

    (d) a decision of the Upper Tribunal under section 10—

        (i) to review, or not to review, an earlier decision of the tribunal,

        (ii) to take no action, or not to take any particular action, in the light of a review of an earlier decision of the tribunal, or

        (iii) to set aside an earlier decision of the tribunal,

    (e) a decision of the Upper Tribunal that is set aside under section 10 (including a decision set aside after proceedings on an appeal under this section have been begun), or

    (f) any decision of the Upper Tribunal that is of a description specified in an order made by the Lord Chancellor.

(9) A description may be specified under subsection (8)(f) only if—

    (a) in the case of a decision of that description, there is a right to appeal to a court from the decision and that right is, or includes, something other than a right (however expressed) to appeal on any point of law arising from the decision, or

    (b) decisions of that description are made in carrying out a function transferred under section 30 and prior to the transfer of the function under section 30(1) there was no right to appeal from decisions of that description.

(10) Where—

    (a) an order under subsection (8)(f) specifies a description of decisions, and

    (b) decisions of that description are made in carrying out a function transferred under section 30,

    the order must be framed so as to come into force no later than the time when the transfer under section 30 of the function takes effect (but power to revoke the order continues to be exercisable after that time, and power to amend the order continues to be exercisable after that time for the purpose of narrowing the description for the time being specified).

(11) Before the Upper Tribunal decides an application made to it under subsection (4), the Upper Tribunal must specify the court that is to be the relevant appellate court as respects the proposed appeal.

(12) The court to be specified under subsection (11) in relation to a proposed appeal is whichever of the following courts appears to the Upper Tribunal to be the most appropriate—

(a) the Court of Appeal in England and Wales;

(b) the Court of Session;

(c) the Court of Appeal in Northern Ireland.

(13) In this section except subsection (11), "the relevant appellate court", as respects an appeal, means the court specified as respects that appeal by the Upper Tribunal under subsection (11).

(14) The Lord Chancellor may by order make provision for a person to be treated as being, or to be treated as not being, a party to a case for the purposes of subsection (2).

(15) Rules of court may make provision as to the time within which an application under subsection (4) to the relevant appellate court must be made.

Proceedings on appeal to Court of Appeal etc

14(1) Subsection (2) applies if the relevant appellate court, in deciding an appeal under section 13, finds that the making of the decision concerned involved the making of an error on a point of law.

(2) The relevant appellate court—

(a) may (but need not) set aside the decision of the Upper Tribunal, and

(b) if it does, must either—

(i) remit the case to the Upper Tribunal or, where the decision of the Upper Tribunal was on an appeal or reference from another tribunal or some other person, to the Upper Tribunal or that other tribunal or person, with directions for its reconsideration, or

(ii) re-make the decision.

(3) In acting under subsection (2)(b)(i), the relevant appellate court may also—

(a) direct that the persons who are chosen to reconsider the case are not to be the same as those who—

(i) where the case is remitted to the Upper Tribunal, made the decision of the Upper Tribunal that has been set aside, or

(ii) where the case is remitted to another tribunal or person, made the decision in respect of which the appeal or reference to the Upper Tribunal was made;

(b) give procedural directions in connection with the reconsideration of the case by the Upper Tribunal or other tribunal or person.

(4) In acting under subsection (2)(b)(ii), the relevant appellate court—

(a) may make any decision which the Upper Tribunal could make if the Upper Tribunal were re-making the decision or (as the case may be) which the other tribunal or person could make if that other tribunal or person were re-making the decision, and

(b) may make such findings of fact as it considers appropriate.

(5) Where—

(a) under subsection (2)(b)(i) the relevant appellate court remits a case to the Upper Tribunal, and

(b) the decision set aside under subsection (2)(a) was made by the Upper Tribunal on an appeal or reference from another tribunal or some other person,

the Upper Tribunal may (instead of reconsidering the case itself) remit the case to that other tribunal or person, with the directions given by the relevant appellate court for its reconsideration.

(6) In acting under subsection (5), the Upper Tribunal may also—

    (a) direct that the persons who are chosen to reconsider the case are not to be the same as those who made the decision in respect of which the appeal or reference to the Upper Tribunal was made;

    (b) give procedural directions in connection with the reconsideration of the case by the other tribunal or person.

(7) In this section "the relevant appellate court", as respects an appeal under section 13, means the court specified as respects that appeal by the Upper Tribunal under section 13(11).

Appeal to Supreme Court: grant of certificate by Upper Tribunal

14A(1) If the Upper Tribunal is satisfied that—

    (a) the conditions in subsection (4) or (5) are fulfilled in relation to the Upper Tribunal's decision in any proceedings, and

    (b) as regards that decision, a sufficient case for an appeal to the Supreme Court has been made out to justify an application under section 14B,

the Upper Tribunal may grant a certificate to that effect.

(2) The Upper Tribunal may grant a certificate under this section only on an application made by a party to the proceedings.

(3) The Upper Tribunal may grant a certificate under this section only if the relevant appellate court as regards the proceedings is—

    (a) the Court of Appeal in England and Wales, or

    (b) the Court of Appeal in Northern Ireland.

(4) The conditions in this subsection are that a point of law of general public importance is involved in the decision of the Upper Tribunal and that point of law is—

    (a) a point of law that—

        (i) relates wholly or mainly to the construction of an enactment or statutory instrument, and

        (ii) has been fully argued in the proceedings and fully considered in the judgment of the Upper Tribunal in the proceedings, or

    (b) a point of law—

        (i) in respect of which the Upper Tribunal is bound by a decision of the relevant appellate court or the Supreme Court in previous proceedings, and

        (ii) that was fully considered in the judgments given by the relevant appellate court or, as the case may be, the Supreme Court in those previous proceedings.

(5) The conditions in this subsection are that a point of law of general public importance is involved in the decision of the Upper Tribunal and that—

    (a) the proceedings entail a decision relating to a matter of national importance or consideration of such a matter,

    (b) the result of the proceedings is so significant (whether considered on its own or together with other proceedings or likely proceedings) that, in the opinion of the

Upper Tribunal, a hearing by the Supreme Court is justified, or

   (c)   the Upper Tribunal is satisfied that the benefits of earlier consideration by the Supreme Court outweigh the benefits of consideration by the Court of Appeal.

(6)   Before the Upper Tribunal decides an application made to it under this section, the Upper Tribunal must specify the court that would be the relevant appellate court if the application were an application for permission (or leave) under section 13.

(7)   In this section except subsection (6) and in sections 14B and 14C, "the relevant appellate court", as respects an application, means the court specified as respects that application by the Upper Tribunal under subsection (6).

(8)   No appeal lies against the grant or refusal of a certificate under subsection (1).

Appeal to Supreme Court: permission to appeal

14B(1)   If the Upper Tribunal grants a certificate under section 14A in relation to any proceedings, a party to those proceedings may apply to the Supreme Court for permission to appeal directly to the Supreme Court.

(2)   An application under subsection (1) must be made—

   (a)   within one month from the date on which that certificate is granted, or

   (b)   within such time as the Supreme Court may allow in a particular case.

(3)   If on such an application it appears to the Supreme Court to be expedient to do so, the Supreme Court may grant permission for such an appeal.

(4)   If permission is granted under this section—

   (a)   no appeal from the decision to which the certificate relates lies to the relevant appellate court, but

   (b)   an appeal lies from that decision to the Supreme Court.

(5)   An application under subsection (1) is to be determined without a hearing.

(6)   Subject to subsection (4), no appeal lies to the relevant appellate court from a decision of the Upper Tribunal in respect of which a certificate is granted under section 14A until—

   (a)   the time within which an application can be made under subsection (1) has expired, and

   (b)   where such an application is made, that application has been determined in accordance with this section.

Appeal to Supreme Court: exclusions

14C(1)   No certificate may be granted under section 14A in respect of a decision of the Upper Tribunal in any proceedings where, by virtue of any enactment (other than sections 14A and 14B), no appeal would lie from that decision of the Upper Tribunal to the relevant appellate court, with or without the permission (or leave) of the Upper Tribunal or the relevant appellate court.

(2)   No certificate may be granted under section 14A in respect of a decision of the Upper Tribunal in any proceedings where, by virtue of any enactment, no appeal would lie from a decision of the relevant appellate court on that decision of the Upper Tribunal to the Supreme Court, with or without the permission (or leave) of the relevant appellate court or the Supreme Court.

(3)   Where no appeal would lie to the relevant appellate court from the decision of the Upper

Tribunal except with the permission (or leave) of the Upper Tribunal or the relevant appellate court, no certificate may be granted under section 14A in respect of a decision of the Upper Tribunal unless it appears to the Upper Tribunal that it would be a proper case for giving permission (or leave) to appeal to the relevant appellate court.

(4)　No certificate may be granted under section 14A in respect of a decision or order of the Upper Tribunal made by it in the exercise of its jurisdiction to punish for contempt.

"Judicial review"

Upper Tribunal's "judicial review" jurisdiction

15(1)　The Upper Tribunal has power, in cases arising under the law of England and Wales or under the law of Northern Ireland, to grant the following kinds of relief—

(a)　a mandatory order;

(b)　a prohibiting order;

(c)　a quashing order;

(d)　a declaration;

(e)　an injunction.

(2)　The power under subsection (1) may be exercised by the Upper Tribunal if—

(a)　certain conditions are met (see section 18), or

(b)　the tribunal is authorised to proceed even though not all of those conditions are met (see section 19(3) and (4)).

(3)　Relief under subsection (1) granted by the Upper Tribunal—

(a)　has the same effect as the corresponding relief granted by the High Court on an application for judicial review, and

(b)　is enforceable as if it were relief granted by the High Court on an application for judicial review.

(4)　In deciding whether to grant relief under subsection (1)(a), (b) or (c), the Upper Tribunal must apply the principles that the High Court would apply in deciding whether to grant that relief on an application for judicial review.

(5)　In deciding whether to grant relief under subsection (1)(d) or (e), the Upper Tribunal must—

(a)　in cases arising under the law of England and Wales apply the principles that the High Court would apply in deciding whether to grant that relief under section 31(2) of the Senior Courts Act 1981 on an application for judicial review, and

(b)　in cases arising under the law of Northern Ireland apply the principles that the High Court would apply in deciding whether to grant that relief on an application for judicial review.

(5A)　In cases arising under the law of England and Wales, subsections (2A) and (2B) of section 31 of the Senior Courts Act 1981 apply to the Upper Tribunal when deciding whether to grant relief under subsection (1) as they apply to the High Court when deciding whether to grant relief on an application for judicial review.

(5B)　If the tribunal grants relief in reliance on section 31(2B) of the Senior Courts Act 1981 as applied by subsection (5A), the tribunal must certify that the condition in section 31(2B) as so applied is satisfied.

(6)　For the purposes of the application of subsection (3)(a) in relation to cases arising under the law of Northern Ireland—

 (a) a mandatory order under subsection (1)(a) shall be taken to correspond to an order of mandamus,

 (b) a prohibiting order under subsection (1)(b) shall be taken to correspond to an order of prohibition, and

 (c) a quashing order under subsection (1)(c) shall be taken to correspond to an order of certiorari.

Application for relief under section 15(1)

16(1) This section applies in relation to an application to the Upper Tribunal for relief under section 15(1).

 (2) The application may be made only if permission (or, in a case arising under the law of Northern Ireland, leave) to make it has been obtained from the tribunal.

 (3) The tribunal may not grant permission (or leave) to make the application unless—

  (a) it considers that the applicant has a sufficient interest in the matter to which the application relates, and

  (b) in cases arising under the law of England and Wales, the applicant has provided the tribunal with any information about the financing of the application that is specified in Tribunal Procedure Rules for the purposes of this paragraph.

(3A) The information that may be specified for the purposes of subsection (3)(b) includes—

  (a) information about the source, nature and extent of financial resources available, or likely to be available, to the applicant to meet liabilities arising in connection with the application, and

  (b) if the applicant is a body corporate that is unable to demonstrate that it is likely to have financial resources available to meet such liabilities, information about its members and about their ability to provide financial support for the purposes of the application.

(3B) Tribunal Procedure Rules under subsection (3)(b) that specify information identifying those who are, or are likely to be, sources of financial support must provide that only a person whose financial support (whether direct or indirect) exceeds, or is likely to exceed, a level set out in the rules has to be identified.

This subsection does not apply to rules that specify information described in subsection (3A)(b).

(3C) In cases arising under the law of England and Wales, when considering whether to grant permission to make the application, the tribunal—

  (a) may of its own initiative consider whether the outcome for the applicant would have been substantially different if the conduct complained of had not occurred, and

  (b) must consider that question if the respondent asks it to do so.

(3D) In subsection (3C) "the conduct complained of" means the conduct (or alleged conduct) of the respondent that the applicant claims justifies the tribunal in granting relief.

(3E) If, on considering the question mentioned in subsection (3C)(a) and (b), it appears to the tribunal to be highly likely that the outcome for the applicant would not have been substantially different, the tribunal must refuse to grant permission.

(3F) The tribunal may disregard the requirement in subsection (3E) if it considers that it is appropriate to do so for reasons of exceptional public interest.

(3G) If the tribunal grants permission in reliance on subsection (3F), the tribunal must certify that the condition in subsection (3F) is satisfied.

(4) Subsection (5) applies where the tribunal considers—

(a) that there has been undue delay in making the application, and

(b) that granting the relief sought on the application would be likely to cause substantial hardship to, or substantially prejudice the rights of, any person or would be detrimental to good administration.

(5) The tribunal may—

(a) refuse to grant permission (or leave) for the making of the application;

(b) refuse to grant any relief sought on the application.

(6) The tribunal may award to the applicant damages, restitution or the recovery of a sum due if—

(a) the application includes a claim for such an award arising from any matter to which the application relates, and

(b) the tribunal is satisfied that such an award would have been made by the High Court if the claim had been made in an action begun in the High Court by the applicant at the time of making the application.

(6A) In cases arising under the law of England and Wales, subsections (2A) and (2B) of section 31 of the Senior Courts Act 1981 apply to the Upper Tribunal as regards the making of an award under subsection (6) as they apply to the High Court as regards the making of an award under section 31(4) of the Senior Courts Act 1981.

(6B) If the tribunal makes an award in reliance on section 31(2B) of the Senior Courts Act 1981 as applied by subsection (6A), the tribunal must certify that the condition in section 31(2B) as so applied is satisfied.

(7) An award under subsection (6) may be enforced as if it were an award of the High Court.

(8) Where—

(a) the tribunal refuses to grant permission (or leave) to apply for relief under section 15(1),

(b) the applicant appeals against that refusal, and

(c) the Court of Appeal grants the permission (or leave),

the Court of Appeal may go on to decide the application for relief under section 15(1).

(9) Subsections (4) and (5) do not prevent Tribunal Procedure Rules from limiting the time within which applications may be made.

Quashing orders under section 15(1): supplementary provision

17(1) If the Upper Tribunal makes a quashing order under section 15(1)(c) in respect of a decision, it may in addition—

(a) remit the matter concerned to the court, tribunal or authority that made the decision, with a direction to reconsider the matter and reach a decision in accordance with the findings of the Upper Tribunal, or

(b) substitute its own decision for the decision in question.

(2) The power conferred by subsection (1)(b) is exercisable only if—

(a) the decision in question was made by a court or tribunal,

(b) the decision is quashed on the ground that there has been an error of law, and

(c) without the error, there would have been only one decision that the court or tribunal could have reached.

(3) Unless the Upper Tribunal otherwise directs, a decision substituted by it under subsection (1)(b) has effect as if it were a decision of the relevant court or tribunal.

Limits of jurisdiction under section 15(1)

18(1) This section applies where an application made to the Upper Tribunal seeks (whether or not alone)—

(a) relief under section 15(1), or

(b) permission (or, in a case arising under the law of Northern Ireland, leave) to apply for relief under section 15(1).

(2) If Conditions 1 to 4 are met, the tribunal has the function of deciding the application.

(3) If the tribunal does not have the function of deciding the application, it must by order transfer the application to the High Court.

(4) Condition 1 is that the application does not seek anything other than—

(a) relief under section 15(1);

(b) permission (or, in a case arising under the law of Northern Ireland, leave) to apply for relief under section 15(1);

(c) an award under section 16(6);

(d) interest;

(e) costs.

(5) Condition 2 is that the application does not call into question anything done by the Crown Court.

(6) Condition 3 is that the application falls within a class specified for the purposes of this subsection in a direction given in accordance with Part 1 of Schedule 2 to the Constitutional Reform Act 2005.

(7) The power to give directions under subsection (6) includes—

(a) power to vary or revoke directions made in exercise of the power, and

(b) power to make different provision for different purposes.

(8) Condition 4 is that the judge presiding at the hearing of the application is either—

(a) a judge of the High Court or the Court of Appeal in England and Wales or Northern Ireland, or a judge of the Court of Session, or

(b) such other persons as may be agreed from time to time between the Lord Chief Justice, the Lord President, or the Lord Chief Justice of Northern Ireland, as the case may be, and the Senior President of Tribunals.

(9) Where the application is transferred to the High Court under subsection (3)—

(a) the application is to be treated for all purposes as if it—

(i) had been made to the High Court, and

(ii) sought things corresponding to those sought from the tribunal, and

(b) any steps taken, permission (or leave) given or orders made by the tribunal in relation to the application are to be treated as taken, given or made by the High Court.

(10) Rules of court may make provision for the purpose of supplementing subsection (9).

(11) The provision that may be made by Tribunal Procedure Rules about amendment of an application for relief under section 15(1) includes, in particular, provision about amendments that would cause the application to become transferrable under subsection (3).

(12) For the purposes of subsection (9)(a)(ii), in relation to an application transferred to the High Court in Northern Ireland—

    (a) an order of mandamus shall be taken to correspond to a mandatory order under section 15(1)(a),

    (b) an order of prohibition shall be taken to correspond to a prohibiting order under section 15(1)(b), and

    (c) an order of certiorari shall be taken to correspond to a quashing order under section 15(1)(c).

Transfer of judicial review applications from High Court

19 *not reproduced*

Transfer of judicial review applications from the Court of Session

20(1) Where an application is made to the supervisory jurisdiction of the Court of Session, the Court—

    (a) must, if Conditions 1 and 2 are met, and, ...

    (aa) ...

    (b) may, if Conditions 1 and 3 are met, but Condition 2 is not,

by order transfer the application to the Upper Tribunal.

(2) Condition 1 is that the application does not seek anything other than an exercise of the supervisory jurisdiction of the Court of Session.

(3) Condition 2 is that the application falls within a class specified for the purposes of this subsection by act of sederunt made with the consent of the Lord Chancellor.

(4) Condition 3 is that the subject matter of the application is not a devolved Scottish matter.

(5) ....

(5A) ....

(6) There may not be specified under subsection (3) any class of application which includes an application the subject matter of which is a devolved Scottish matter.

(7) For the purposes of this section, the subject matter of an application is a devolved Scottish matter if it—

    (a) concerns the exercise of functions in or as regards Scotland, and

    (b) does not relate to a reserved matter within the meaning of the Scotland Act 1998.

(8) In subsection (2), the reference to the exercise of the supervisory jurisdiction of the Court of Session includes a reference to the making of any order in connection with or in consequence of the exercise of that jurisdiction.

Procedural steps where application transferred

20A(1) This section applies where the Court of Session transfers an application under section

20(1).

(2) It is for the Upper Tribunal to determine—
   (a) whether the application has been made timeously, and
   (b) whether to grant permission for the application to proceed under section 27B of the Court of Session Act 1988 ("the 1988 Act") (requirement for permission).

(3) Accordingly—
   (a) the Upper Tribunal has the same powers in relation to the application as the Court of Session would have had in relation to it under sections 27A to 27C of the 1988 Act,
   (b) sections 27C and 27D of that Act apply in relation to a decision of the Upper Tribunal under section 27B(1) of that Act as they apply in relation to such a decision of the Court of Session.

(4) The references in section 27C(3) and (4) of the 1988 Act (oral hearings where permission refused) to a different Lord Ordinary from the one who granted or refused permission are to be read as references to different members of the Tribunal from those of whom it was composed when it refused or granted permission.

Upper Tribunal's "judicial review" jurisdiction: Scotland

21(1) The Upper Tribunal has the function of deciding applications transferred to it from the Court of Session under section 20(1).

(2) The powers of review of the Upper Tribunal in relation to such applications are the same as the powers of review of the Court of Session in an application to the supervisory jurisdiction of that Court.

(3) In deciding an application by virtue of subsection (1), the Upper Tribunal must apply principles that the Court of Session would apply in deciding an application to the supervisory jurisdiction of that Court.

(4) An order of the Upper Tribunal by virtue of subsection (1)—
   (a) has the same effect as the corresponding order granted by the Court of Session on an application to the supervisory jurisdiction of that Court, and
   (b) is enforceable as if it were an order so granted by that Court.

(5) Where an application is transferred to the Upper Tribunal by virtue of section 20(1), any steps taken or orders made by the Court of Session in relation to the application (other than the order to transfer the application under section 20(1)) are to be treated as taken or made by the tribunal.

(6) Tribunal Procedure Rules may make further provision for the purposes of supplementing subsection (5).

Miscellaneous

Tribunal Procedure Rules

22(1) There are to be rules, to be called "Tribunal Procedure Rules", governing—
   (a) the practice and procedure to be followed in the First-tier Tribunal, and
   (b) the practice and procedure to be followed in the Upper Tribunal.

(2) Tribunal Procedure Rules are to be made by the Tribunal Procedure Committee.

(3) In Schedule 5—

Part 1 makes further provision about the content of Tribunal Procedure Rules,

Part 2 makes provision about the membership of the Tribunal Procedure Committee,

Part 3 makes provision about the making of Tribunal Procedure Rules by the Committee, and

Part 4 confers power to amend legislation in connection with Tribunal Procedure Rules.

(4) Power to make Tribunal Procedure Rules is to be exercised with a view to securing—

    (a) that, in proceedings before the First-tier Tribunal and Upper Tribunal, justice is done,

    (b) that the tribunal system is accessible and fair,

    (c) that proceedings before the First-tier Tribunal or Upper Tribunal are handled quickly and efficiently,

    (d) that the rules are both simple and simply expressed, and

    (e) that the rules where appropriate confer on members of the First-tier Tribunal, or Upper Tribunal, responsibility for ensuring that proceedings before the tribunal are handled quickly and efficiently.

(5) In subsection (4)(b) "the tribunal system" means the system for deciding matters within the jurisdiction of the First-tier Tribunal or the Upper Tribunal.

Practice directions

23(1) The Senior President of Tribunals may give directions—

    (a) as to the practice and procedure of the First-tier Tribunal;

    (b) as to the practice and procedure of the Upper Tribunal.

(2) A Chamber President may give directions as to the practice and procedure of the chamber over which he presides.

(3) A power under this section to give directions includes—

    (a) power to vary or revoke directions made in exercise of the power, and

    (b) power to make different provision for different purposes (including different provision for different areas).

(4) Directions under subsection (1) may not be given without the approval of the Lord Chancellor.

(5) Directions under subsection (2) may not be given without the approval of—

    (a) the Senior President of Tribunals, and

    (b) the Lord Chancellor.

(6) Subsections (4) and (5)(b) do not apply to directions to the extent that they consist of guidance about any of the following—

    (a) the application or interpretation of the law;

    (b) the making of decisions by members of the First-tier Tribunal or Upper Tribunal.

(7) Subsections (4) and (5)(b) do not apply to directions to the extent that they consist of criteria for determining which members of the First-tier Tribunal or Upper Tribunal may be chosen to decide particular categories of matter; but the directions may, to that extent, be given only after consulting the Lord Chancellor.

Mediation

24(1) A person exercising power to make Tribunal Procedure Rules or give practice directions must, when making provision in relation to mediation, have regard to the following principles—

(a) mediation of matters in dispute between parties to proceedings is to take place only by agreement between those parties;

(b) where parties to proceedings fail to mediate, or where mediation between parties to proceedings fails to resolve disputed matters, the failure is not to affect the outcome of the proceedings.

(2) Practice directions may provide for members to act as mediators in relation to disputed matters in a case that is the subject of proceedings.

(3) The provision that may be made by virtue of subsection (2) includes provision for a member to act as a mediator in relation to disputed matters in a case even though the member has been chosen to decide matters in the case.

(4) Once a member has begun to act as a mediator in relation to a disputed matter in a case that is the subject of proceedings, the member may decide matters in the case only with the consent of the parties.

(5) Staff appointed under section 40(1) may, subject to their terms of appointment, act as mediators in relation to disputed matters in a case that is the subject of proceedings.

(6) In this section—

"member" means a judge or other member of the First-tier Tribunal or a judge or other member of the Upper Tribunal;

"practice direction" means a direction under section 23(1) or (2);

"proceedings" means proceedings before the First-tier Tribunal or proceedings before the Upper Tribunal.

Supplementary powers of Upper Tribunal

25(1) In relation to the matters mentioned in subsection (2), the Upper Tribunal—

(a) has, in England and Wales or in Northern Ireland, the same powers, rights, privileges and authority as the High Court, and

(b) has, in Scotland, the same powers, rights, privileges and authority as the Court of Session.

(2) The matters are—

(a) the attendance and examination of witnesses,

(b) the production and inspection of documents, and

(c) all other matters incidental to the Upper Tribunal's functions.

(3) Subsection (1) shall not be taken—

(a) to limit any power to make Tribunal Procedure Rules;

(b) to be limited by anything in Tribunal Procedure Rules other than an express limitation.

(4) A power, right, privilege or authority conferred in a territory by subsection (1) is available for purposes of proceedings in the Upper Tribunal that take place outside that territory (as well as for purposes of proceedings in the tribunal that take place within that territory).

First-tier Tribunal and Upper Tribunal: sitting places

26 Each of the First-tier Tribunal and the Upper Tribunal may decide a case—

    (a) in England and Wales,

    (b) in Scotland, or

    (c) in Northern Ireland,

even though the case arises under the law of a territory other than the one in which the case is decided.

Enforcement

27(1) A sum payable in pursuance of a decision of the First-tier Tribunal or Upper Tribunal made in England and Wales—

    (a) shall be recoverable as if it were payable under an order of the county court in England and Wales;

    (b) shall be recoverable as if it were payable under an order of the High Court in England and Wales.

(2) An order for the payment of a sum payable in pursuance of a decision of the First-tier Tribunal or Upper Tribunal made in Scotland (or a copy of such an order certified in accordance with Tribunal Procedure Rules) may be enforced as if it were an extract registered decree arbitral bearing a warrant for execution issued by the sheriff court of any sheriffdom in Scotland.

(3) A sum payable in pursuance of a decision of the First-tier Tribunal or Upper Tribunal made in Northern Ireland—

    (a) shall be recoverable as if it were payable under an order of a county court in Northern Ireland;

    (b) shall be recoverable as if it were payable under an order of the High Court in Northern Ireland.

(4) This section does not apply to a sum payable in pursuance of—

    (a) an award under section 16(6), or

    (b) an order by virtue of section 21(1).

(5) The Lord Chancellor may by order make provision for subsection (1) or (3) to apply in relation to a sum of a description specified in the order with the omission of one (but not both) of paragraphs (a) and (b).

(6) Tribunal Procedure Rules—

    (a) may make provision as to where, for purposes of this section, a decision is to be taken to be made;

    (b) may provide for all or any of subsections (1) to (3) to apply only, or not to apply except, in relation to sums of a description specified in Tribunal Procedure Rules.

Assessors

28(1) If it appears to the First-tier Tribunal or the Upper Tribunal that a matter before it requires special expertise not otherwise available to it, it may direct that in dealing with that matter it shall have the assistance of a person or persons appearing to it to have relevant knowledge or experience.

(2) The remuneration of a person who gives assistance to either tribunal as mentioned in subsection (1) shall be determined and paid by the Lord Chancellor.

(3) The Lord Chancellor may—

    (a) establish panels of persons from which either tribunal may (but need not) select persons to give it assistance as mentioned in subsection (1);

    (b) under paragraph (a) establish different panels for different purposes;

    (c) after carrying out such consultation as he considers appropriate, appoint persons to a panel established under paragraph (a);

    (d) remove a person from such a panel.

Costs or expenses

29(1) The costs of and incidental to—

    (a) all proceedings in the First-tier Tribunal, and

    (b) all proceedings in the Upper Tribunal,

shall be in the discretion of the Tribunal in which the proceedings take place.

(2) The relevant Tribunal shall have full power to determine by whom and to what extent the costs are to be paid.

(3) Subsections (1) and (2) have effect subject to Tribunal Procedure Rules.

(4) In any proceedings mentioned in subsection (1), the relevant Tribunal may—

    (a) disallow, or

    (b) (as the case may be) order the legal or other representative concerned to meet,

the whole of any wasted costs or such part of them as may be determined in accordance with Tribunal Procedure Rules.

(5) In subsection (4) "wasted costs" means any costs incurred by a party—

    (a) as a result of any improper, unreasonable or negligent act or omission on the part of any legal or other representative or any employee of such a representative, or

    (b) which, in the light of any such act or omission occurring after they were incurred, the relevant Tribunal considers it is unreasonable to expect that party to pay.

(6) In this section "legal or other representative", in relation to a party to proceedings, means any person exercising a right of audience or right to conduct the proceedings on his behalf.

(7) In the application of this section in relation to Scotland, any reference in this section to costs is to be read as a reference to expenses.

CHAPTER 2A

EXERCISE OF TRIBUNAL FUNCTIONS BY AUTHORISED PERSONS

Meaning of "authorised person" and "judicial office holder"

29A In this Chapter—

    "authorised person" means a person authorised under paragraph 3 of Schedule 5 to exercise functions of the First-tier Tribunal or Upper Tribunal;

    "judicial office holder" has the meaning given by section 109(4) of the Constitutional Reform Act 2005.

Directions and independence: authorised persons

29B(1) The Senior President of Tribunals may give directions to an authorised person.

(2) Apart from such directions, an authorised person exercising a function by virtue of paragraph 3 of Schedule 5 is not subject to the direction of the Lord Chancellor or any

other person when exercising the function.

(3) The Senior President of Tribunals may delegate to one or more of the following the Senior President of Tribunals' functions under subsection (1)—

  (a) a judicial office holder;

  (b) a person appointed under section 2(1) of the Courts Act 2003 or section 40(1) of this Act.

(4) A person to whom functions of the Senior President of Tribunals are delegated under subsection (3)(b) is not subject to the direction of any person other than—

  (a) the Senior President of Tribunals, or

  (b) a judicial office holder nominated by the Senior President of Tribunals,

when exercising the functions.

(5) Subsections (3) to (5) of section 8 apply to—

  (a) a delegation under subsection (3) of this section, and

  (b) a nomination under subsection (4) of this section,

as they apply to a delegation under subsection (1) of that section.

Protection of authorised persons

29C(1) No action lies against an authorised person in respect of what the person does or omits to do—

  (a) in the execution of the person's duty as an authorised person exercising, by virtue of paragraph 3 of Schedule 5, functions of a tribunal, and

  (b) in relation to a matter within the person's jurisdiction.

(2) An action lies against an authorised person in respect of what the person does or omits to do—

  (a) in the purported execution of the person's duty as an authorised person exercising, by virtue of paragraph 3 of Schedule 5, functions of a tribunal, but

  (b) in relation to a matter not within the person's jurisdiction,

if, but only if, it is proved that the person acted in bad faith.

(3) If an action is brought in a court in Scotland in circumstances in which subsection (1) or (2) provides that no action lies, the court in which the action is brought—

  (a) may, on the application of the defender, dismiss the action, and

  (b) if it does so, may find the person bringing the action liable in expenses.

(4) If an action is brought in any other court in circumstances in which subsection (1) or (2) provides that no action lies, the court in which the action is brought—

  (a) may, on the application of the defendant, strike out the proceedings in the action, and

  (b) if it does so, may if it thinks fit order the person bringing the action to pay costs.

Costs or expenses in legal proceedings: authorised persons

29D(1) A court may not order an authorised person to pay costs in any proceedings in respect of what the person does or omits to do in the execution (or purported execution) of the person's duty as an authorised person exercising, by virtue of paragraph 3 of Schedule 5, a function of a tribunal.

(2) But subsection (1) does not apply in relation to any proceedings in which an authorised person—

(a) is being tried for an offence or is appealing against a conviction, or

(b) is proved to have acted in bad faith in respect of the matters giving rise to the proceedings.

(3) A court which is prevented by subsection (1) from ordering an authorised person to pay costs in any proceedings may instead order the Lord Chancellor to make a payment in respect of the costs of a person in the proceedings.

(4) The Lord Chancellor may, after consulting the Senior President of Tribunals, make regulations specifying—

(a) circumstances in which a court must or must not exercise the power conferred on it by subsection (3), and

(b) how the amount of any payment ordered under subsection (3) is to be determined.

(5) The power to make regulations under subsection (4) includes power to make—

(a) any supplementary, incidental or consequential provision, and

(b) any transitory, transitional or saving provision,

which the Lord Chancellor considers necessary or expedient.

(6) The Senior President of Tribunals may delegate the Senior President of Tribunals' functions under subsection (4) to a person who is a judicial office holder.

(7) Subsections (3) to (5) of section 8 apply to a delegation under subsection (6) of this section as they apply to a delegation under subsection (1) of that section.

(8) In the application of this section to Scotland—

(a) references to a court ordering an authorised person to pay costs are to be read as references to a court finding an authorised person liable in expenses, and

(b) the second reference to costs in subsection (3) is to be read as a reference to expenses.

Indemnification of authorised persons

29E(1) "Indemnifiable amounts", in relation to an authorised person, means—

(a) costs which the person reasonably incurs in or in connection with proceedings in respect of anything done or omitted to be done in the exercise (or purported exercise) of the person's duty as an authorised person,

(b) costs which the person reasonably incurs in taking steps to dispute a claim which might be made in such proceedings,

(c) damages awarded against the person or costs ordered to be paid by the person in such proceedings, or

(d) sums payable by the person in connection with a reasonable settlement of such proceedings or such a claim.

(2) The Lord Chancellor must indemnify an authorised person in respect of indemnifiable amounts if, in respect of the matters giving rise to the proceedings or claim, the person acted reasonably and in good faith.

(3) The Lord Chancellor may indemnify an authorised person in respect of other indemnifiable amounts unless it is proved, in respect of the matters giving rise to the proceedings or claim, that the person acted in bad faith.

(4) Any question whether, or to what extent, an authorised person is to be indemnified under this section is to be determined by the Lord Chancellor.

(5) The Lord Chancellor may, if an authorised person claiming to be indemnified so requests, make a determination for the purposes of this section with respect to—

    (a) costs such as are mentioned in subsection (1)(a) or (b), or

    (b) sums such as are mentioned in subsection (1)(d),

before the costs are incurred or the settlement in connection with which the sums are payable is made.

(6) But a determination under subsection (5) before costs are incurred—

    (a) is subject to such limitations (if any) as the Lord Chancellor thinks proper and to the subsequent determination of the costs reasonably incurred, and

    (b) does not affect any other determination which may fall to be made in connection with the proceedings or claim in question.

(7) In the application of this section to Scotland, references to costs are to be read as references to expenses.

CHAPTER 3
TRANSFER OF TRIBUNAL FUNCTIONS

Transfer of functions of certain tribunals

30(1) The Lord Chancellor may by order provide for a function of a scheduled tribunal to be transferred—

    (a) to the First-tier Tribunal,

    (b) to the Upper Tribunal,

    (c) to the First-tier Tribunal and the Upper Tribunal with the question as to which of them is to exercise the function in a particular case being determined by a person under provisions of the order,

    (d) to the First-tier Tribunal to the extent specified in the order and to the Upper Tribunal to the extent so specified,

    (e) to the First-tier Tribunal and the Upper Tribunal with the question as to which of them is to exercise the function in a particular case being determined by, or under, Tribunal Procedure Rules,

    (f) to an employment tribunal,

    (g) to the Employment Appeal Tribunal,

    (h) to an employment tribunal and the Employment Appeal Tribunal with the question as to which of them is to exercise the function in a particular case being determined by a person under provisions of the order, or

    (i) to an employment tribunal to the extent specified in the order and to the Employment Appeal Tribunal to the extent so specified.

(2) In subsection (1) "scheduled tribunal" means a tribunal in a list in Schedule 6 that has effect for the purposes of this section.

(3) The Lord Chancellor may, as respects a function transferred under subsection (1) or this subsection, by order provide for the function to be further transferred as mentioned in any of paragraphs (a) to (i) of subsection (1).

(4) An order under subsection (1) or (3) may include provision for the purposes of or in consequence of, or for giving full effect to, a transfer under that subsection.

(5) A function of a tribunal may not be transferred under subsection (1) or (3) if, or to the

extent that, the provision conferring the function—

    (a) would be within the legislative competence of the Scottish Parliament if it were included in an Act of that Parliament, or

    (b) would be within the legislative competence of the Northern Ireland Assembly if it were included in an Act of that Assembly.

(6) Subsection (5) does not apply to—

    (a) the Secretary of State's function of deciding appeals under section 41 of the Consumer Credit Act 1974,

    (b) functions of the Consumer Credit Appeals Tribunal,

    (c) the Secretary of State's function of deciding appeals under section 7(1) of the Estate Agents Act 1979, or

    (d) functions of an adjudicator under section 5 of the Criminal Injuries Compensation Act 1995 (but see subsection.

(7) Functions of an adjudicator under section 5 of the Criminal Injuries Compensation Act 1995, so far as they relate to Scotland, may be transferred under subsection (1) or (3) only with the # (8) "relevant function", in relation to a tribunal, means a function which relates—

    (a) to the operation of the tribunal (including, in particular, its membership, administration, staff, accommodation and funding, and payments to its members or staff), or

    (b) to the provision of expenses and allowances to persons attending the tribunal or attending elsewhere in connection with proceedings before the tribunal.

Transfers under section 30: supplementary powers

31(1) The Lord Chancellor may by order make provision for abolishing the tribunal by whom a function transferred under section 30(1) is exercisable immediately before its transfer.

(2) The Lord Chancellor may by order make provision, where functions of a tribunal are transferred under section 30(1), for a person—

    (a) who is the tribunal (but is not the Secretary of State), or

    (b) who is a member of the tribunal, or

    (c) who is an authorised decision-maker for the tribunal,

to (instead or in addition) be the holder of an office specified in subsection (3).

(3) Those offices are—

    (a) transferred-in judge of the First-tier Tribunal,

    (b) transferred-in other member of the First-tier Tribunal,

    (c) transferred-in judge of the Upper Tribunal,

    (d) transferred-in other member of the Upper Tribunal, and

    (e) deputy judge of the Upper Tribunal.

(4) Where functions of a tribunal are transferred under section 30(1), the Lord Chancellor must exercise the power under subsection (2) so as to secure that each person who immediately before the end of the tribunal's life—

    (a) is the tribunal,

    (b) is a member of the tribunal, or

    (c) is an authorised decision-maker for the tribunal,

becomes the holder of an office specified in subsection (3) with effect from the end of the tribunal's life (if the person is not then already the holder of such an office).

(5) Subsection (4) does not apply in relation to a person—
  (a) by virtue of the person's being the Secretary of State, or
  (b) by virtue of the person's being a Commissioner for the general purposes of the income tax;
  and a reference in subsection (4) to the end of a tribunal's life is to when the tribunal is abolished or (without being abolished) comes to have no functions.

(6) For the purposes of this section, a person is an "authorised decision-maker" for a tribunal if—
  (a) the tribunal is listed in column 1 of an entry in the following Table, and
  (b) the person is of the description specified in column 2 of that entry.

1 Tribunal	2 Authorised decision-maker
Adjudicator to Her Majesty's Land Registry	Member of the Adjudicator's staff who is authorised by the Adjudicator to carry out functions of the Adjudicator which are not of an administrative character
The Secretary of State as respects his function of deciding appeals under section 41 of the Consumer Credit Act 1974	Person who is a member of a panel under regulation 24 of the Consumer Credit Licensing (Appeals) Regulations 1998 (SI 1998/1203)
The Secretary of State as respects his function of deciding appeals under section 7(1) of the Estate Agents Act 1979	Person appointed, at any time after 2005, under regulation 19(1) of the Estate Agents (Appeals) Regulations 1981 (SI 1981/1518) to hear an appeal on behalf of the Secretary of State

(7) Where a function of a tribunal is transferred under section 30(1), the Lord Chancellor may by order provide for procedural rules in force immediately before the transfer to have effect, or to have effect with appropriate modifications, after the transfer (and, accordingly, to be capable of being varied or revoked) as if they were—
  (a) Tribunal Procedure Rules, or
  (b) employment tribunal procedure regulations, or Appeal Tribunal procedure rules, within the meaning given by section 42(1) of the Employment Tribunals Act 1996.

(8) In subsection (7)—
  "procedural rules" means provision (whether called rules or not)—
    (a) regulating practice or procedure before the tribunal, and
    (b) applying for purposes connected with the exercise of the function;
  "appropriate modifications" means modifications (including additions and omissions) that appear to the Lord Chancellor to be necessary to secure, or expedient in connection with securing, that the procedural rules apply in relation to the exercise of the function after the transfer.

(9) The Lord Chancellor may, in connection with provision made by order under section 30 or the preceding provisions of this section, make by order such incidental, supplemental, transitional or consequential provision, or provision for savings, as the Lord Chancellor thinks fit, including provision applying only in relation to cases selected by a member—
  (a) of the First-tier Tribunal,

    (b) of the Upper Tribunal,

    (c) of the Employment Appeal Tribunal, or

    (d) of a panel of members of employment tribunals.

(10)   Subsections (1), (2) and (7) are not to be taken as prejudicing the generality of subsection (9).

Power to provide for appeal to Upper Tribunal from tribunals in Wales

32(1)   Subsection (2) applies if—

    (a) a function is transferred under section 30(1)(a), (c), (d) or (e) in relation to England but is not transferred under section 30(1) in relation to Wales, or

    (b) a function that is not exercisable in relation to Wales is transferred under section 30(1)(a), (c), (d) or (e) in relation to England and, although there is a corresponding function that is exercisable in relation to Wales, that corresponding function is not transferred under section 30(1) in relation to Wales.

(2)   The Lord Chancellor may by order—

    (a) provide for an appeal against a decision to be made to the Upper Tribunal instead of to the court to which an appeal would otherwise fall to be made where the decision is made in exercising, in relation to Wales, the function mentioned in subsection (1)(a) or (as the case may be) the corresponding function mentioned in subsection (1)(b);

    (b) provide for a reference of any matter to be made to the Upper Tribunal instead of to the court to which a reference would otherwise fall to be made where the matter arises in exercising, in relation to Wales, the function mentioned in subsection (1)(a) or (as the case may be) the corresponding function mentioned in subsection (1)(b).

(3)   The Lord Chancellor may by order provide for an appeal against a decision of a scheduled tribunal to be made to the Upper Tribunal, instead of to the court to which an appeal would otherwise fall to be made, where the decision is made by the tribunal in exercising a function in relation to Wales.

(4)   In subsection (3) "scheduled tribunal" means a tribunal in a list in Schedule 6 that has effect for the purposes of that subsection.

(5)   An order under subsection (2) or (3)—

    (a) may include provision for the purposes of or in consequence of, or for giving full effect to, provision made by the order;

    (b) may include such incidental, supplemental, transitional or consequential provision or savings as the Lord Chancellor thinks fit.

Power to provide for appeal to Upper Tribunal from tribunals in Scotland

33(1)   Subsection (2) applies if—

    (a) a function is transferred under section 30(1)(a), (c), (d) or (e) in relation to England (whether or not also in relation to Wales) but is not transferred under section 30(1) in relation to Scotland,

    (b) an appeal may be made to the Upper Tribunal against any decision, or any decision of a particular description, made in exercising the transferred function in relation to England, and

    (c) no appeal may be made against a corresponding decision made in exercising the function in relation to Scotland.

(2)   The Lord Chancellor may by order provide for an appeal against any such corresponding decision to be made to the Upper Tribunal.

(3)   An order under subsection (2)—

    (a)   may include provision for the purposes of or in consequence of, or for giving full effect to, provision made by the order;

    (b)   may include such incidental, supplemental, transitional or consequential provision or savings as the Lord Chancellor thinks fit.

(4)   An order under subsection (2) does not cease to have effect, and power to vary or revoke the order does not cease to be exercisable, just because either or each of the conditions in subsection (1)(b) and (c) ceases to be satisfied in relation to the function and decisions concerned.

Power to provide for appeal to Upper Tribunal from tribunals in Northern Ireland

34(1)   Subsection (2) applies if—

    (a)   a function is transferred under section 30(1)(a), (c), (d) or (e) in relation to England (whether or not also in relation to Wales) but is not transferred under section 30(1) in relation to Northern Ireland,

    (b)   an appeal may be made to the Upper Tribunal against any decision, or any decision of a particular description, made in exercising the transferred function in relation to England, and

    (c)   no appeal may be made against a corresponding decision made in exercising the function in relation to Northern Ireland.

(2)   The Lord Chancellor may by order provide for an appeal against any such corresponding decision to be made to the Upper Tribunal.

(3)   An order under subsection (2)—

    (a)   may include provision for the purposes of or in consequence of, or for giving full effect to, provision made by the order;

    (b)   may include such incidental, supplemental, transitional or consequential provision or savings as the Lord Chancellor thinks fit.

(4)   An order under subsection (2) does not cease to have effect, and power to vary or revoke the order does not cease to be exercisable, just because either or each of the conditions in subsection (1)(b) and (c) ceases to be satisfied in relation to the function and decisions concerned.

Transfer of Ministerial responsibilities for certain tribunals

35(1)   The Lord Chancellor may by order—

    (a)   transfer any relevant function, so far as that function is exercisable by a Minister of the Crown—

        (i)   to the Lord Chancellor, or

        (ii)   to two (or more) Ministers of the Crown of whom one is the Lord Chancellor;

    (b)   provide for any relevant function that is exercisable by a Minister of the Crown other than the Lord Chancellor to be exercisable by the other Minister of the Crown concurrently with the Lord Chancellor;

    (c)   provide for any relevant function that is exercisable by the Lord Chancellor concurrently with another Minister of the Crown to cease to be exercisable by the other Minister of the Crown.

(2) In this section "relevant function" means a function, in relation to a scheduled tribunal, which relates—

    (a) to the operation of the tribunal (including, in particular, its membership, administration, staff, accommodation and funding, and payments to its members or staff), or

    (b) to the provision of expenses and allowances to persons attending the tribunal or attending elsewhere in connection with proceedings before the tribunal.

(3) In subsection (2) "scheduled tribunal" means a tribunal in a list in Schedule 6 that has effect for the purposes of this section.

(4) A relevant function may not be transferred under subsection (1) if, or to the extent that, the provision conferring the function—

    (a) would be within the legislative competence of the Scottish Parliament if it were included in an Act of that Parliament, or

    (b) would be within the legislative competence of the Northern Ireland Assembly if it were included in an Act of that Assembly.

(5) Subsection (4) does not apply to any relevant function of the Secretary of State—

    (a) under section 41 of the Consumer Credit Act 1974 (appeals), or

    (b) under section 7 of the Estate Agents Act 1979 (appeals).

(6) Any reference in subsection (1) to a Minister of the Crown includes a reference to a Minister of the Crown acting jointly.

(7) An order under subsection (1)—

    (a) may relate to a function either wholly or in cases (including cases framed by reference to areas) specified in the order;

    (b) may include provision for the purposes of, or in consequence of, or for giving full effect to, the transfer or (as the case may be) other change as regards exercise;

    (c) may include such incidental, supplementary, transitional or consequential provision or savings as the Lord Chancellor thinks fit;

    (d) may include provision for the transfer of any property, rights or liabilities of the person who loses functions or whose functions become shared with the Lord Chancellor.

(8) An order under subsection (1), so far as it—

    (a) provides under paragraph (a) for the transfer of a function, or

    (b) provides under paragraph (b) for a function to become exercisable by the Lord Chancellor, or

    (c) provides under paragraph (c) for a function to cease to be exercisable by a Minister of the Crown other than the Lord Chancellor,

may not, after that transfer or other change has taken place, be revoked by another order under that subsection.

(9) Section 1 of the 1975 Act (power to transfer Ministerial functions) does not apply to a function of the Lord Chancellor—

    (a) so far as it is a function transferred to the Lord Chancellor under subsection (1)(a),

    (b) so far as it is a function exercisable by the Lord Chancellor as a result of provision under subsection (1)(b), or

(c)   so far as it is a function that has become exercisable by the Lord Chancellor alone as a result of provision under subsection (1)(c).

(10) In this section—

"Minister of the Crown" has the meaning given by section 8(1) of the 1975 Act but includes the Commissioners for Her Majesty's Revenue and Customs;

"the 1975 Act" means the Ministers of the Crown Act 1975.

Transfer of powers to make procedural rules for certain tribunals

36(1) The Lord Chancellor may by order transfer any power to make procedural rules for a scheduled tribunal to—

(a) himself, or

(b) the Tribunal Procedure Committee.

(2) A power may not be transferred under subsection (1) if, or to the extent that, the provision conferring the power—

(a) would be within the legislative competence of the Scottish Parliament if it were included in an Act of that Parliament, or

(b) would be within the legislative competence of the Northern Ireland Assembly if it were included in an Act of that Assembly.

(3) Subsection (2) does not apply to—

(a) power conferred by section 40A(3) . . . of the Consumer Credit Act 1974 (power to make provision with respect to appeals), or

(b) power conferred by section 7(3) of the Estate Agents Act 1979 (duty of Secretary of State to make regulations with respect to appeals under section 7(1) of that Act).

(4) An order under subsection (1)(b)—

(a) may not alter any parliamentary procedure relating to the making of the procedural rules concerned, but

(b) may otherwise include provision for the purpose of assimilating the procedure for making them to the procedure for making Tribunal Procedure Rules.

(5) An order under subsection (1)(b) may include provision requiring the Tribunal Procedure Committee to make procedural rules for purposes notified to it by the Lord Chancellor.

(6) An order under this section—

(a) may relate to a power either wholly or in cases (including cases framed by reference to areas) specified in the order;

(b) may include provision for the purposes of or in consequence of, or for giving full effect to, the transfer;

(c) may include such incidental, supplementary, transitional or consequential provision or savings as the Lord Chancellor thinks fit.

(7) A power to make procedural rules for a tribunal that is exercisable by the Tribunal Procedure Committee by virtue of an order under this section must be exercised by the committee with a view to securing—

(a) that the system for deciding matters within the jurisdiction of that tribunal is accessible and fair,

(b) that proceedings before that tribunal are handled quickly and efficiently,

(c) that the rules are both simple and simply expressed, and

(d) that the rules where appropriate confer on persons who are, or who are members of, that tribunal responsibility for ensuring that proceedings before that tribunal are handled quickly and efficiently.

(8) In this section—

"procedural rules", in relation to a tribunal, means provision (whether called rules or not) regulating practice or procedure before the tribunal;

"scheduled tribunal" means a tribunal in a list in Schedule 6 that has effect for the purposes of this section.

Power to amend lists of tribunals in Schedule 6

37(1) The Lord Chancellor may by order amend Schedule 6—

    (a) for the purpose of adding a tribunal to a list in the Schedule;

    (b) for the purpose of removing a tribunal from a list in the Schedule;

    (c) for the purpose of removing a list from the Schedule;

    (d) for the purpose of adding to the Schedule a list of tribunals that has effect for the purposes of any one or more of sections 30, 32(3), 35 and 36.

(2) The following rules apply to the exercise of power under subsection (1)—

    (a) a tribunal may not be added to a list, or be in an added list, if the tribunal is established otherwise than by or under an enactment;

    (b) a tribunal established by an enactment passed or made after the last day of the Session in which this Act is passed must not be added to a list, or be in an added list, that has effect for the purposes of section 30;

    (c) if any relevant function is exercisable in relation to a tribunal by the Welsh Ministers (whether by the Welsh Ministers alone, or by the Welsh Ministers jointly or concurrently with any other person), the tribunal may be added to a list, or be in an added list, only with the consent of the Welsh Ministers;

    (d) a tribunal may be in more than one list.

(3) In subsection (2)(c) "relevant function", in relation to a tribunal, means a function which relates—

    (a) to the operation of the tribunal (including, in particular, its membership, administration, staff, accommodation and funding, and payments to its members or staff), or

    (b) to the provision of expenses and allowances to persons attending the tribunal or attending elsewhere in connection with proceedings before the tribunal.

(4) In subsection (1) "tribunal" does not include an ordinary court of law.

(5) In this section "enactment" means any enactment whenever passed or made, including an enactment comprised in subordinate legislation (within the meaning of the Interpretation Act 1978).

Orders under sections 30 to 36: supplementary

38(1) Provision in an order under any of sections 30 to 36 may take the form of amendments, repeals or revocations of enactments.

(2) In this section "enactment" means any enactment whenever passed or made, including an enactment comprised in subordinate legislation (within the meaning of the Interpretation Act 1978).

(3) Any power to extend enactments to a territory outside the United Kingdom shall have effect as if it included—

    (a) power to extend those enactments as they have effect with any amendments and repeals made in them by orders under any of sections 30 to 36, and

    (b) power to extend those enactments as if any amendments and repeals made in them under those sections had not been made.

CHAPTER 4

ADMINISTRATIVE MATTERS IN RESPECT OF CERTAIN TRIBUNALS

The general duty

39(1) The Lord Chancellor is under a duty to ensure that there is an efficient and effective system to support the carrying on of the business of—

    (a) the First-tier Tribunal,

    (b) the Upper Tribunal,

    (c) employment tribunals, and

    (d) the Employment Appeal Tribunal. . .

    (e) ...

and that appropriate services are provided for those tribunals (referred to in this section and in sections 40 and 41 as "the tribunals").

(2) Any reference in this section, or in section 40 or 41, to the Lord Chancellor's general duty in relation to the tribunals is to his duty under subsection (1).

(3) The Lord Chancellor must annually prepare and lay before each House of Parliament a report as to the way in which he has discharged his general duty in relation to the tribunals.

Tribunal staff and services

40(1) The Lord Chancellor may appoint such staff as appear to him appropriate for the purpose of discharging his general duty in relation to the tribunals.

(2) Subject to subsections (3) and (4), the Lord Chancellor may enter into such contracts with other persons for the provision, by them or their sub-contractors, of staff or services as appear to him appropriate for the purpose of discharging his general duty in relation to the tribunals.

(3) The Lord Chancellor may not enter into contracts for the provision of staff to discharge functions which involve making judicial decisions or exercising any judicial discretion.

(4) The Lord Chancellor may not enter into contracts for the provision of staff to carry out the administrative work of the tribunals unless an order made by the Lord Chancellor authorises him to do so.

(5) Before making an order under subsection (4) the Lord Chancellor must consult the Senior President of Tribunals as to what effect (if any) the order might have on the proper and efficient administration of justice.

(6) An order under subsection (4) may authorise the Lord Chancellor to enter into contracts for the provision of staff to discharge functions—

    (a) wholly or to the extent specified in the order,

    (b) generally or in cases or areas specified in the order, and

    (c) unconditionally or subject to the fulfilment of conditions specified in the order.

Provision of accommodation

41(1) The Lord Chancellor may provide, equip, maintain and manage such tribunal buildings, offices and other accommodation as appear to him appropriate for the purpose of discharging his general duty in relation to the tribunals.

(2) The Lord Chancellor may enter into such arrangements for the provision, equipment, maintenance or management of tribunal buildings, offices or other accommodation as appear to him appropriate for the purpose of discharging his general duty in relation to the tribunals.

(3) The powers under—
  (a) section 2 of the Commissioners of Works Act 1852 (acquisition by agreement), and
  (b) section 228(1) of the Town and Country Planning Act 1990 (compulsory acquisition),
  to acquire land necessary for the public service are to be treated as including power to acquire land for the purpose of its provision under arrangements entered into under subsection (2).

(4) In this section "tribunal building" means any place where any of the tribunals sits, including the precincts of any building in which it sits.

Fees

42(1) The Lord Chancellor may by order prescribe fees payable in respect of—
  (a) anything dealt with by the First-tier Tribunal,
  (b) anything dealt with by the Upper Tribunal,
  (c) ....
  (d) anything dealt with by an added tribunal, and
  (e) mediation conducted by staff appointed under section 40(1).

(2) An order under subsection (1) may, in particular, contain provision as to—
  (a) scales or rates of fees;
  (b) exemptions from or reductions in fees;
  (c) remission of fees in whole or in part.

(3) In subsection (1)(d) "added tribunal" means a tribunal specified in an order made by the Lord Chancellor.

(4) A tribunal may be specified in an order under subsection (3) only if—
  (a) it is established by or under an enactment, whenever passed or made, and
  (b) is not an ordinary court of law.

(5) Before making an order under this section, the Lord Chancellor must consult—
  (a) the Senior President of Tribunals, . . .
  (b) .. ..

(6) The making of an order under subsection (1) requires the consent of the Treasury except where the order contains provision only for the purpose of altering amounts payable by way of fees already prescribed under that subsection.

(7) The Lord Chancellor must take such steps as are reasonably practicable to bring information about fees under subsection (1) to the attention of persons likely to have to pay them.

(8) Fees payable under subsection (1) are recoverable summarily as a civil debt.

(9) Subsection (8) does not apply to the recovery in Scotland of fees payable under this section.

(10) ...

Report by Senior President of Tribunals

43(1) Each year the Senior President of Tribunals must give the Lord Chancellor a report covering, in relation to relevant tribunal cases—

    (a) matters that the Senior President of Tribunals wishes to bring to the attention of the Lord Chancellor, and

    (b) matters that the Lord Chancellor has asked the Senior President of Tribunals to cover in the report.

(2) The Lord Chancellor must publish each report given to him under subsection (1).

(3) In this section "relevant tribunal cases" means—

    (a) cases coming before the First-tier Tribunal,

    (b) cases coming before the Upper Tribunal,

    (c) cases coming before the Employment Appeal Tribunal, . . . and

    (d) cases coming before employment tribunals. . .

    (e) ...

CHAPTER 5

44 *repealed*

45 *repealed*

CHAPTER 6
SUPPLEMENTARY

Delegation of functions by Lord Chief Justice etc

46(1) The Lord Chief Justice of England and Wales may nominate a judicial office holder (as defined in section 109(4) of the Constitutional Reform Act 2005) to exercise any of his functions under the provisions listed in subsection (2).

(2) The provisions are—

    paragraphs 3(4) and 6(3)(a) of Schedule 2;

    paragraphs 3(4) and 6(3)(a) of Schedule 3;

    paragraphs 2(2) and 5(5) of Schedule 4;

    paragraphs 21(2), 22, 24 and 25(2)(a) of Schedule 5.

(3) The Lord President of the Court of Session may nominate any of the following to exercise any of his functions under the provisions listed in subsection (4)—

    (a) a judge who is a member of the First or Second Division of the Inner House of the Court of Session;

    (b) the Senior President of Tribunals.

(4) The provisions are—

    paragraphs 3(2) and 6(3)(b) of Schedule 2;

    paragraphs 3(2) and 6(3)(b) of Schedule 3;

    paragraphs 2(3) and 5(6) of Schedule 4;

paragraphs 23, 24, 25(2)(b) and (c) and 28(1)(b) of Schedule 5.

(5) The Lord Chief Justice of Northern Ireland may nominate any of the following to exercise any of his functions under the provisions listed in subsection (6)—

    (a) the holder of one of the offices listed in Schedule 1 to the Justice (Northern Ireland) Act 2002;

    (b) a Lord Justice of Appeal (as defined in section 88 of that Act);

    (c) the Senior President of Tribunals.

(6) The provisions are—

paragraphs 3(3) and 6(3)(c) of Schedule 2;

paragraphs 3(3) and 6(3)(c) of Schedule 3;

paragraphs 2(4) and 5(7) of Schedule 4;

paragraphs 24 and 25(2)(c) of Schedule 5.

(7) In Schedules 2 to 4 "senior judge" means—

    (a) the Lord Chief Justice of England and Wales,

    (b) the Lord President of the Court of Session,

    (c) the Lord Chief Justice of Northern Ireland, or

    (d) the Senior President of Tribunals.

Co-operation in relation to judicial training, guidance and welfare

47(1) Persons with responsibilities in connection with a courts-related activity, and persons with responsibilities in connection with the corresponding tribunals activity, must co-operate with each other in relation to the carrying-on of those activities.

(2) In this section "courts-related activity" and "corresponding tribunals activity" are to be read as follows—

    (a) making arrangements for training of judiciary of a territory is a courts-related activity, and the corresponding tribunals activity is making arrangements for training of tribunal members;

    (b) making arrangements for guidance of judiciary of a territory is a courts-related activity, and the corresponding tribunals activity is making arrangements for guidance of tribunal members;

    (c) making arrangements for the welfare of judiciary of a territory is a courts-related activity, and the corresponding tribunals activity is making arrangements for the welfare of tribunal members.

(3) Subsection (1) applies to a person who has responsibilities in connection with a courts-related activity only if—

    (a) the person is the chief justice of the territory concerned, or

    (b) what the person does in discharging those responsibilities is done (directly or indirectly) on behalf of the chief justice of that territory.

(4) Subsection (1) applies to a person who has responsibilities in connection with a corresponding tribunals activity only if—

    (a) the person is the Senior President of Tribunals or the President of Welsh Tribunals, or

    (b) what the person does in discharging those responsibilities is done (directly or indirectly) on behalf of the Senior President of Tribunals or the President of Welsh Tribunals.

(5) For the purposes of this section—

(a) "territory" means—
    (i) England and Wales,
    (ii) Scotland, or
    (iii) Northern Ireland;
(b) the "chief justice"—
    (i) of England and Wales is the Lord Chief Justice of England and Wales,
    (ii) of Scotland is the Lord President of the Court of Session, and
    (iii) of Northern Ireland is the Lord Chief Justice of Northern Ireland;
(c) a person is a "tribunal member" if the person is—
    (i) a judge, or other member, of the First-tier Tribunal or Upper Tribunal,
    (ii) a judge, or other member, of the Employment Appeal Tribunal, or
    (iii) a member of a panel of members of employment tribunals (whether or not a panel of Employment Judges). . .
    (iv) . . . , or
    (v) a judge, or other member, of a tribunal listed in section 59 of the Wales Act 2017 (the Welsh tribunals).

Orders and regulations under Part 1: supplemental and procedural provisions

49(1) Power—
    (a) of the Lord Chancellor to make an order, or regulations, under this Part,
    (b) of the Senior President of Tribunals to make an order under section 7(9), or
    (c) of the Scottish Ministers, or the Welsh Ministers, to make an order under paragraph 25(2) of Schedule 7,
is exercisable by statutory instrument.

(2) The Statutory Instruments Act 1946 shall apply in relation to the power to make orders conferred on the Senior President of Tribunals by section 7(9) as if the Senior President of Tribunals were a Minister of the Crown.

(3) Any power mentioned in subsection (1) includes power to make different provision for different purposes.

(4) Without prejudice to the generality of subsection (3), power to make an order under section 30 or 31 includes power to make different provision in relation to England, Scotland, Wales and Northern Ireland respectively.

(5) None of the orders or regulations mentioned in subsection (6) may be made unless a draft of the statutory instrument containing the order or regulations (whether alone or with other provision) has been laid before, and approved by a resolution of, each House of Parliament.

(6) The orders and regulations are—
    (a) an order under section 11(8), 13(6) or (14), 30, 31(1), 32, 33, 34, 35, 36, 37 or 42(3);
    (aa) regulations under section 29D(4);
    (b) an order under paragraph 15 of Schedule 4;
    (c) an order under section 42(1)(a) to (d) that provides for fees to be payable in respect of things for which fees have never been payable;
    (d) an order under section 31(2), (7) or (9), or paragraph 30(1) of Schedule 5, that contains provision taking the form of an amendment or repeal of an enactment comprised in an Act.

(7) A statutory instrument that—
  (a) contains—
    (i) an order mentioned in subsection (8), or
    (ii) regulations under Part 3 of Schedule 9, and
  (b) is not subject to any requirement that a draft of the instrument be laid before, and approved by a resolution of, each House of Parliament,
  is subject to annulment in pursuance of a resolution of either House of Parliament.

(8) Those orders are—
  (a) an order made by the Lord Chancellor under this Part;
  (b) an order made by the Senior President of Tribunals under section 7(9).

(9) A statutory instrument that contains an order made by the Scottish Ministers under paragraph 25(2) of Schedule 7 is subject to annulment in pursuance of a resolution of the Scottish Parliament.

(10) A statutory instrument that contains an order made by the Welsh Ministers under paragraph 25(2) of Schedule 7 is subject to annulment in pursuance of a resolution of the National Assembly for Wales.

PARTS 2 - 6

Not reproduced

SCHEDULE 1
SENIOR PRESIDENT OF TRIBUNALS

not reproduced

SCHEDULE 2
JUDGES AND OTHER MEMBERS OF THE FIRST-TIER TRIBUNAL

Section 4

Power to appoint judges of First-tier Tribunal

1(1) The Senior President of Tribunals may appoint a person to be one of the judges of the First-tier Tribunal.

(2) A person is eligible for appointment under sub-paragraph (1) only if the person—
  (a) satisfies the judicial-appointment eligibility condition on a 5-year basis,
  (b) is an advocate or solicitor in Scotland of at least five years' standing,
  (c) is a barrister or solicitor in Northern Ireland of at least five years' standing, or
  (d) in the opinion of the Senior President of Tribunals, has gained experience in law which makes the person as suitable for appointment as if the person satisfied any of paragraphs (a) to (c).
    (3) Section 52(2) to (5) (meaning of "gain experience in law") apply for the purposes of sub-paragraph (2)(d), but as if section 52(4)(i) referred to the Senior President of Tribunals instead of to the relevant decision-maker.

Power to appoint other members of First-tier Tribunal

2(1) The Senior President of Tribunals may appoint a person to be one of the members of the First-tier Tribunal who are not judges of the tribunal.

(2) A person is eligible for appointment under sub-paragraph (1) only if the person has qualifications prescribed in an order made by the Lord Chancellor with the concurrence

of the Senior President of Tribunals.

Appointed and transferred-in judges and other members: removal from office

3(1) This paragraph applies to any power by which—

    (a) a person appointed under paragraph 1(1) or 2(1),

    (b) a transferred-in judge of the First-tier Tribunal, or

    (c) a transferred-in other member of the First-tier Tribunal,

may be removed from office.

(2) If the person exercises functions wholly or mainly in Scotland, the power may be exercised only with the concurrence of the Lord President of the Court of Session.

(3) If the person exercises functions wholly or mainly in Northern Ireland, the power may be exercised only with the concurrence of the Lord Chief Justice of Northern Ireland.

(4) If neither of sub-paragraphs (2) and (3) applies, the power may be exercised only with the concurrence of the Lord Chief Justice of England and Wales.

Terms of appointment

4(1) This paragraph applies—

    (a) to a person appointed under paragraph 1(1) or 2(1),

    (b) to a transferred-in judge of the First-tier Tribunal, and

    (c) to a transferred-in other member of the First-tier Tribunal.

(2) If the terms of the person's appointment provide that he is appointed on a salaried (as opposed to fee-paid) basis, the person may be removed from office—

    (a) only by the Lord Chancellor (and in accordance with paragraph 3), and

    (b) only on the ground of inability or misbehaviour.

(2A) If the terms of the person's appointment provide that the person is appointed on a fee-paid basis, the person may be removed from office—

    (a) only by the Lord Chancellor (and in accordance with paragraph 3), and

    (b) only on—

        (i) the ground of inability or misbehaviour, or

        (ii) a ground specified in the person's terms of appointment.

(2B) If the period (or extended period) for which the person is appointed ends before—

    (a) the day on which the person attains the age of 70, or

    (b) if different, the day that for the purposes of section 26 of the Judicial Pensions and Retirement Act 1993 is the compulsory retirement date for the office concerned in the person's case,

then, subject to sub-paragraph (2C), the Lord Chancellor must extend the period of the person's appointment (including a period already extended under this sub-paragraph) before it ends.

(2C) Extension under sub-paragraph (2B)—

    (a) requires the person's agreement,

    (b) is to be for such period as the Lord Chancellor considers appropriate, and

    (c) may be refused on—

        (i) the ground of inability or misbehaviour, or

        (ii) a ground specified in the person's terms of appointment,

but only with any agreement of a senior judge (see section 46(7)), or a nominee of a senior judge, that may be required by those terms.

(3) Subject to the preceding provisions of this paragraph (but subject in the first place to the Judicial Pensions and Retirement Act 1993, the person is to hold and vacate office in accordance with the terms of his appointment, which are to be such as the Lord Chancellor may determine.

Remuneration, allowances and expenses

5(1) Sub-paragraph (2) applies—

   (a) to a person appointed under paragraph 1(1) or 2(1),

   (b) to a transferred-in judge of the First-tier Tribunal, and

   (c) to a transferred-in other member of the First-tier Tribunal.

(2) The Lord Chancellor may pay to a person to whom this sub-paragraph applies such amounts (if any) as the Lord Chancellor may determine by way of—

   (a) remuneration;

   (b) allowances;

   (c) expenses.

Certain judges neither appointed under paragraph 1(1) nor transferred in

6(1) In this paragraph "judge by request of the First-tier Tribunal" means a person who is a judge of the First-tier Tribunal but who—

   (a) is not the Senior President of Tribunals,

   (b) is not a judge of the First-tier Tribunal appointed under paragraph 1(1),

   (c) is not a transferred-in judge of the First-tier Tribunal,

   (d) is not a Chamber President, or Acting Chamber President or Deputy Chamber President, of a chamber of the First-tier Tribunal,

   (e) is not a judge of the First-tier Tribunal by virtue of section 4(1)(e) (Employment Judge),

   (f) ... and

   (g) is not a judge of the First-tier tribunal by virtue of section 4(2) (criminal injuries compensation adjudicator appointed by the Scottish Ministers).

(2) A judge by request of the First-tier Tribunal may act as a judge of the First-tier Tribunal only if requested to do so by the Senior President of Tribunals.

(3) Such a request made to a person who is a judge of the First-tier Tribunal by virtue of the combination of sections 4(1)(c) and 5(1)(g) may be made only with—

   (a) the concurrence of the Lord Chief Justice of England and Wales where the person is—

     (i) an ordinary judge of the Court of Appeal in England and Wales,

     (ii) a puisne judge of the High Court in England and Wales,

     (iii) a circuit judge,

     (iv) a district judge in England and Wales, ...

     (v) a District Judge (Magistrates' Courts),

     (vi) the Master of the Rolls,

     (vii) the President of the Queen's Bench Division of the High Court of England and Wales,

     (viii) the President of the Family Division of that court,

     (ix) the Chancellor of that court,

     (x) a deputy judge of that court, or

     (xi) the Judge Advocate General;

(b) the concurrence of the Lord President of the Court of Session where the person is—

    (i) a judge of the Court of Session, or

    (ii) a sheriff;

(c) the concurrence of the Lord Chief Justice of Northern Ireland where the person is—

    (i) a Lord Justice of Appeal in Northern Ireland,

    (ii) a puisne judge of the High Court in Northern Ireland,

    (iii) a county court judge in Northern Ireland, or

    (iv) a district judge in Northern Ireland.

(3A) A request made under sub-paragraph (2) to a person who is a judge of the First-tier Tribunal by virtue of section 4(1)(ca) may be made only with the concurrence of the Lord Chief Justice of England and Wales.

(4) Sub-paragraph (5) applies—

(a) to a judge by request of the First-tier Tribunal, and

(b) to a person who is a judge of the First-tier Tribunal by virtue of section 4(1)(e) (Employment Judge). . .

(c) . . ..

(5) The Lord Chancellor may pay to a person to whom this sub-paragraph applies such amounts (if any) as the Lord Chancellor may determine by way of—

(a) remuneration;

(b) allowances;

(c) expenses.

Other members neither appointed under paragraph 2(1) nor transferred in

7(1) In this paragraph "ex officio member of the First-tier Tribunal" means a person who is a member of the First-tier Tribunal by virtue of—

(a) section 4(3)(d) (members of employment tribunals who are not Employment Judges), or

(b) the combination of sections 4(3)(c) and 5(2)(c) (members of Employment Appeal Tribunal appointed under section 22(1)(c) of the Employment Tribunals Act 1996). . .

(c) . . ..

(2) The Lord Chancellor may pay to an ex officio member of the First-tier Tribunal such amounts (if any) as the Lord Chancellor may determine by way of—

(a) remuneration;

(b) allowances;

(c) expenses.

Training etc

8 The Senior President of Tribunals is responsible, within the resources made available by the Lord Chancellor, for the maintenance of appropriate arrangements for the training, guidance and welfare of judges and other members of the First-tier Tribunal (in their capacities as such judges and other members).

Oaths

9(1) Sub-paragraph (2) applies to a person ("J")—

     (a) who is appointed under paragraph 1(1) or 2(1), or

     (b) who becomes a transferred-in judge, or a transferred-in other member, of the First-tier Tribunal and has not previously taken the required oaths after accepting another office.

(2) J must take the required oaths before—

     (a) the Senior President of Tribunals, or

     (b) an eligible person who is nominated by the Senior President of Tribunals for the purpose of taking the oaths from J.

(3) A person is eligible for the purposes of sub-paragraph (2)(b) if any one or more of the following paragraphs applies to him—

     (a) he holds high judicial office (as defined in section 60(2) of the Constitutional Reform Act 2005);

     (b) he holds judicial office (as defined in section 109(4) of that Act);

     (c) he holds (in Scotland) the office of sheriff.

(4) In this paragraph "the required oaths" means (subject to sub-paragraph (5))—

     (a) the oath of allegiance, and

     (b) the judicial oath,

as set out in the Promissory Oaths Act 1868.

(5) Where it appears to the Lord Chancellor that J will carry out functions as a judge or other member of the First-tier Tribunal wholly or mainly in Northern Ireland, the Lord Chancellor may direct that in relation to J "the required oaths" means—

     (a) the oath as set out in section 19(2) of the Justice (Northern Ireland) Act 2002, or

     (b) the affirmation and declaration as set out in section 19(3) of that Act.

SCHEDULE 3
JUDGES AND OTHER MEMBERS OF THE UPPER TRIBUNAL

Section 5

Power to appoint judges of Upper Tribunal

1(1) Her Majesty, on the recommendation of the Lord Chancellor, may appoint a person to be one of the judges of the Upper Tribunal.

(2) A person is eligible for appointment under sub-paragraph (1) only if the person—

     (a) satisfies the judicial-appointment eligibility condition on a 7-year basis,

     (b) is an advocate or solicitor in Scotland of at least seven years' standing,

     (c) is a barrister or solicitor in Northern Ireland of at least seven years' standing, or

     (d) in the opinion of the Senior President of Tribunals, has gained experience in law which makes the person as suitable for appointment as if the person satisfied any of paragraphs (a) to (c).

(3) Section 52(2) to (5) (meaning of "gain experience in law") apply for the purposes of sub-paragraph (2)(d), but as if section 52(4)(i) referred to the Lord Chancellor instead of to the relevant decision-maker.

Power to appoint other members of Upper Tribunal

2(1) The Senior President of Tribunals may appoint a person to be one of the members of the Upper Tribunal who are not judges of the tribunal.

(2) A person is eligible for appointment under sub-paragraph (1) only if the person has

qualifications prescribed in an order made by the Lord Chancellor with the concurrence of the Senior President of Tribunals.

Appointed and transferred-in judges and other members: removal from office

3(1) This paragraph applies to any power by which—

    (a) a person appointed under paragraph 1(1) or 2(1),

    (b) a transferred-in judge of the Upper Tribunal,

    (ba) a person who is a deputy judge of the Upper Tribunal (whether by appointment under paragraph 7(1) or as a result of provision under section 31(2)), or

    (c) a transferred-in other member of the Upper Tribunal,

may be removed from office.

(2) If the person exercises functions wholly or mainly in Scotland, the power may be exercised only with the concurrence of the Lord President of the Court of Session.

(3) If the person exercises functions wholly or mainly in Northern Ireland, the power may be exercised only with the concurrence of the Lord Chief Justice of Northern Ireland.

(4) If neither of sub-paragraphs (2) and (3) applies, the power may be exercised only with the concurrence of the Lord Chief Justice of England and Wales.

Terms of appointment

4(1) This paragraph applies—

    (a) to a person appointed under paragraph 1(1) or 2(1),

    (b) to a transferred-in judge of the Upper Tribunal, and

    (c) to a transferred-in other member of the Upper Tribunal.

(2) If the terms of the person's appointment provide that he is appointed on a salaried (as opposed to fee-paid) basis, the person may be removed from office—

    (a) only by the Lord Chancellor (and in accordance with paragraph 3), and

    (b) only on the ground of inability or misbehaviour.

(2A) If the terms of the person's appointment provide that the person is appointed on a fee-paid basis, the person may be removed from office—

    (a) only by the Lord Chancellor (and in accordance with paragraph 3), and

    (b) only on—

        (i) the ground of inability or misbehaviour, or

        (ii) a ground specified in the person's terms of appointment.

(2B) If the period (or extended period) for which the person is appointed ends before—

    (a) the day on which the person attains the age of 70, or

    (b) if different, the day that for the purposes of section 26 of the Judicial Pensions and Retirement Act 1993 is the compulsory retirement date for the office concerned in the person's case,

then, subject to sub-paragraph (2C), the Lord Chancellor must extend the period of the person's appointment (including a period already extended under this sub-paragraph) before it ends.

(2C) Extension under sub-paragraph (2B)—

    (a) requires the person's agreement,

    (b) is to be for such period as the Lord Chancellor considers appropriate, and

    (c) may be refused on—

        (i) the ground of inability or misbehaviour, or

(ii) a ground specified in the person's terms of appointment,

but only with any agreement of a senior judge (see section 46(7)), or a nominee of a senior judge, that may be required by those terms.

(3) Subject to the preceding provisions of this paragraph (but subject in the first place to the Judicial Pensions and Retirement Act 1993, the person is to hold and vacate office as a judge, or other member, of the Upper Tribunal in accordance with the terms of his appointment, which are to be such as the Lord Chancellor may determine.

Remuneration, allowances and expenses

5(1) Sub-paragraph (2) applies—

    (a) to a person appointed under paragraph 1(1) or 2(1),

    (b) to a transferred-in judge of the Upper Tribunal, and

    (c) to a transferred-in other member of the Upper Tribunal.

(2) The Lord Chancellor may pay to a person to whom this sub-paragraph applies such amounts (if any) as the Lord Chancellor may determine by way of—

    (a) remuneration;

    (b) allowances;

    (c) expenses.

Certain judges neither appointed under paragraph 1(1) nor transferred in

6(1) In this paragraph "judge by request of the Upper Tribunal" means a person who is a judge of the Upper Tribunal but—

    (a) is not the Senior President of Tribunals,

    (b) is not a judge of the Upper Tribunal appointed under paragraph 1(1),

    (c) is not a transferred-in judge of the Upper Tribunal,

    (d) ....

    (e) is not a deputy judge of the Upper Tribunal, and

    (f) is not a Chamber President, or Acting Chamber President or Deputy Chamber President, of a chamber of the Upper Tribunal.

(2) A judge by request of the Upper Tribunal may act as a judge of the Upper Tribunal only if requested to do so by the Senior President of Tribunals.

(3) Such a request made to a person who is a judge of the Upper Tribunal by virtue of section 5(1)(g) may be made only with—

    (a) the concurrence of the Lord Chief Justice of England and Wales where the person is—

        (i) an ordinary judge of the Court of Appeal in England and Wales,

        (ii) a puisne judge of the High Court in England and Wales,

        (iii) a circuit judge,

        (iv) a district judge in England and Wales, . . .

        (v) a District Judge (Magistrates' Courts),

        (vi) the Master of the Rolls,

        (vii) the President of the Queen's Bench Division of the High Court of England and Wales,

        (viii) the President of the Family Division of that court,

        (ix) the Chancellor of that court,

        (x) a deputy judge of that court, or

        (xi) the Judge Advocate General;

    (b) the concurrence of the Lord President of the Court of Session where the person is—

        (i) a judge of the Court of Session, or

        (ii) a sheriff;

    (c) the concurrence of the Lord Chief Justice of Northern Ireland where the person is—

        (i) a Lord Justice of Appeal in Northern Ireland,

        (ii) a puisne judge of the High Court in Northern Ireland,

        (iii) a county court judge in Northern Ireland, or

        (iv) a district judge in Northern Ireland.

(4) The Lord Chancellor may pay to a judge by request of the Upper Tribunal, or a person who is a judge of the Upper Tribunal by virtue of section 5(1)(d), such amounts (if any) as the Lord Chancellor may determine by way of—

    (a) remuneration;

    (b) allowances;

    (c) expenses.

Deputy judges of the Upper Tribunal

7(1) The Senior President of Tribunals may appoint a person to be a deputy judge of the Upper Tribunal for such period as the Lord Chancellor considers appropriate.

(2) A person is eligible for appointment under sub-paragraph (1) only if he is eligible to be appointed under paragraph 1(1) (see paragraph 1(2)).

(3) The following provisions of this paragraph apply—

    (a) to a person appointed under sub-paragraph (1), and

    (b) to a person who becomes a deputy judge of the Upper Tribunal as a result of provision under section 31(2).

(3A) The person may be removed from office—

    (a) only by the Lord Chancellor (and in accordance with paragraph 3), and

    (b) only on—

        (i) the ground of inability or misbehaviour, or

        (ii) a ground specified in the person's terms of appointment.

(3B) If the period (or extended period) for which the person is appointed ends before—

    (a) the day on which the person attains the age of 70, or

    (b) if different, the day that for the purposes of section 26 of the Judicial Pensions and Retirement Act 1993 is the compulsory retirement date for the office concerned in the person's case,

then, subject to sub-paragraph (3C), the Lord Chancellor must extend the period of the person's appointment (including a period already extended under this sub-paragraph) before it ends.

(3C) Extension under sub-paragraph (3B)—

    (a) requires the person's agreement,

    (b) is to be for such period as the Lord Chancellor considers appropriate, and

    (c) may be refused on—

        (i) the ground of inability or misbehaviour, or

        (ii) a ground specified in the person's terms of appointment,

but only with any agreement of a senior judge (see section 46(7)), or a nominee of a senior judge, that may be required by those terms.

(4) Subject to the previous provisions of this paragraph (but subject in the first place to the Judicial Pensions and Retirement Act 1993), a person is to hold and vacate office as a deputy judge of the Upper Tribunal in accordance with the person's terms of appointment, which are to be such as the Lord Chancellor may determine.

(5) The Lord Chancellor may pay to a person to whom this sub-paragraph applies such amounts (if any) as the Lord Chancellor may determine by way of—

    (a) remuneration;

    (b) allowances;

    (c) expenses.

Other members neither appointed under paragraph 2(1) nor transferred in

8(1) In this paragraph "ex officio member of the Upper Tribunal" means—

    (a) a person who is a member of the Upper Tribunal by virtue of section 5(2)(c) (member of Employment Appeal Tribunal appointed under section 22(1)(c) of the Employment Tribunals Act 1996. . .

    (b) .....

(2) The Lord Chancellor may pay to an ex officio member of the Upper Tribunal such amounts (if any) as the Lord Chancellor may determine by way of—

    (a) remuneration;

    (b) allowances;

    (c) expenses.

Training etc

9 The Senior President of Tribunals is responsible, within the resources made available by the Lord Chancellor, for the maintenance of appropriate arrangements for the training, guidance and welfare of judges and other members of the Upper Tribunal (in their capacities as such judges and other members).

Oaths

10(1) Sub-paragraph (2) applies to a person ("J")—

    (a) who is appointed under paragraph 1(1), 2(1) or 7(1), or

    (b) who—

        (i) becomes a transferred-in judge, or a transferred-in other member, of the Upper Tribunal, or

        (ii) becomes a deputy judge of the Upper Tribunal as a result of provision under section 31(2),

and has not previously taken the required oaths after accepting another office.

(2) J must take the required oaths before—

    (a) the Senior President of Tribunals, or

    (b) an eligible person who is nominated by the Senior President of Tribunals for the purpose of taking the oaths from J.

(3) A person is eligible for the purposes of sub-paragraph (2)(b) if any one or more of the following paragraphs applies to him—

    (a) he holds high judicial office (as defined in section 60(2) of the Constitutional Reform Act 2005;

    (b) he holds judicial office (as defined in section 109(4) of that Act);

  (c) he holds (in Scotland) the office of sheriff.

(4) In this paragraph "the required oaths" means (subject to sub-paragraph (5))—

  (a) the oath of allegiance, and

  (b) the judicial oath,

as set out in the Promissory Oaths Act 1868.

(5) Where it appears to the Lord Chancellor that J will carry out functions as a judge or other member of the Upper Tribunal wholly or mainly in Northern Ireland, the Lord Chancellor may direct that in relation to J "the required oaths" means—

  (a) the oath as set out in section 19(2) of the Justice (Northern Ireland) Act 2002, or

  (b) the affirmation and declaration as set out in section 19(3) of that Act.

SCHEDULE 4
CHAMBERS AND CHAMBER PRESIDENTS: FURTHER PROVISION

Section 7

PART 1
CHAMBER PRESIDENTS: APPOINTMENT, DELEGATION, DEPUTIES AND FURTHER PROVISION

Eligibility for appointment as Chamber President under section 7(7)

1 A person is eligible for appointment under section 7(7) only if—

  (a) he is a judge of the Upper Tribunal, or

  (b) he does not fall within paragraph (a) but is eligible to be appointed under paragraph 1(1) of Schedule 3 as a judge of the Upper Tribunal (see paragraph 1(2) of that Schedule).

Appointment as Chamber President under section 7(7): consultation and nomination

2(1) The Senior President of Tribunals must consult the Lord Chancellor before the Senior President of Tribunals appoints under section 7(7) a person within—

  section 6(1)(a) (ordinary judge of Court of Appeal in England and Wales),

  section 6(1)(b) (Lord Justice of Appeal in Northern Ireland),

  section 6(1)(c) (judge of the Court of Session), or

  section 6(1)(d) (puisne judge of the High Court in England and Wales or Northern Ireland).

(2) If the Senior President of Tribunals, in exercise of his power under section 7(7) in a particular case, wishes that the person appointed should be drawn from among the ordinary judges of the Court of Appeal in England and Wales or the puisne judges of the High Court in England and Wales, the Lord Chancellor must first ask the Lord Chief Justice of England and Wales to nominate one of those judges for the purpose.

(3) If the Senior President of Tribunals, in exercise of his power under section 7(7) in a particular case, wishes that the person appointed should be drawn from among the judges of the Court of Session, the Lord Chancellor must first ask the Lord President of the Court of Session to nominate one of those judges for the purpose.

(4) If the Senior President of Tribunals, in exercise of his power under section 7(7) in a particular case, wishes that the person appointed should be drawn from among the Lords Justices of Appeal in Northern Ireland or the puisne judges of the High Court in Northern

Ireland, the Lord Chancellor must first ask the Lord Chief Justice of Northern Ireland to nominate one of those judges for the purpose.

(4A)   The Senior President of Tribunals may make a request under sub-paragraph (2), (3) or (4) only with the Lord Chancellor's concurrence.

(5)   If a judge is nominated under sub-paragraph (2), (3) or (4) in response to a request under that sub-paragraph, the Senior President of Tribunals must appoint the nominated judge as Chamber President of the chamber concerned.

Chamber Presidents: duration of appointment, remuneration etc

3(1)   A Chamber President is to hold and vacate office as a Chamber President in accordance with the terms of his appointment as a Chamber President but subject to paragraph 5A (and subject in the first place to the Judicial Pensions and Retirement Act 1993, and those terms are to be such as the Lord Chancellor may determine.

(2)   The Lord Chancellor may pay to a Chamber President such amounts (if any) as the Lord Chancellor may determine by way of—
    (a)   remuneration;
    (b)   allowances;
    (c)   expenses.

Delegation of functions by Chamber Presidents

4(1)   The Chamber President of a chamber of the First-tier Tribunal or Upper Tribunal may delegate any function he has in his capacity as the Chamber President of the chamber—
    (a)   to any judge, or other member, of either of those tribunals;
    (b)   to staff appointed under section 40(1).

(2)   A delegation under sub-paragraph (1) is not revoked by the delegator's becoming incapacitated.

(3)   Any delegation made by a person under sub-paragraph (1) that is in force immediately before the person ceases to be the Chamber President of a chamber continues in force until subsequently varied or revoked by another holder of the office of Chamber President of that chamber.

(4)   The delegation under sub-paragraph (1) of a function shall not prevent the exercise of the function by the Chamber President of the chamber concerned.

(5)   In this paragraph "delegate" includes further delegate.

Deputy Chamber Presidents

5(1)   The Senior President of Tribunals may appoint a person who is not a Deputy Chamber President of a chamber to be a Deputy Chamber President of a chamber.

(2)   The Senior President of Tribunals may appoint a person who is a Deputy Chamber President of a chamber to be instead, or to be also, a Deputy Chamber President of another chamber.

(3)   The power under sub-paragraph (1) is exercisable in any particular case only if the Senior President of Tribunals—
    (a)   has consulted the Lord Chancellor about whether a Deputy Chamber President should be appointed for the chamber concerned, and
    (b)   considers, in the light of the consultation, that a Deputy Chamber President of the

chamber should be appointed.

(4) A person is eligible for appointment under sub-paragraph (1) only if—

    (a) he is a judge of the Upper Tribunal by virtue of appointment under paragraph 1(1) of Schedule 3,

    (b) he is a transferred-in judge of the Upper Tribunal (see section 31(2)),

    (c) he is a judge of the Upper Tribunal by virtue of—

        . . .

        section 5(1)(e) (Social Security Commissioner for Northern Ireland),

        section 5(1)(g) (certain judges of courts in the United Kingdom), or

        section 5(1)(h) (deputy judge of the Upper Tribunal), or

    (d) he falls within none of paragraphs (a) to (c) but is eligible to be appointed under paragraph 1(1) of Schedule 3 as a judge of the Upper Tribunal (see paragraph 1(2) of that Schedule).

(5) If the Senior President of Tribunals, in exercise of his power under sub-paragraph (1) in a particular case, wishes that the person appointed should be drawn from among the ordinary judges of the Court of Appeal in England and Wales or the puisne judges of the High Court in England and Wales, the Senior President of Tribunals must first ask the Lord Chief Justice of England and Wales to nominate one of those judges for the purpose.

(6) If the Senior President of Tribunals, in exercise of his power under sub-paragraph (1) in a particular case, wishes that the person appointed should be drawn from among the judges of the Court of Session, the Senior President of Tribunals must first ask the Lord President of the Court of Session to nominate one of those judges for the purpose.

(7) If the Senior President of Tribunals, in exercise of his power under sub-paragraph (1) in a particular case, wishes that the person appointed should be drawn from among the Lords Justices of Appeal in Northern Ireland or the puisne judges of the High Court in Northern Ireland, the Lord Senior President of Tribunals must first ask the Lord Chief Justice of Northern Ireland to nominate one of those judges for the purpose.

(7A) The Senior President of Tribunals may make a request under sub-paragraph (5), (6) or (7) only with the Lord Chancellor's concurrence.

(8) If a judge is nominated under sub-paragraph (5), (6) or (7) in response to a request under that sub-paragraph, the Senior President of Tribunals must appoint the nominated judge as a Deputy Chamber President of the chamber concerned.

(9) A Deputy Chamber President is to hold and vacate office as a Deputy Chamber President in accordance with the terms of his appointment but subject to paragraph 5A (and subject in the first place to the Judicial Pensions and Retirement Act 1993, and those terms are to be such as the Lord Chancellor may determine.

(10) The Lord Chancellor may pay to a Deputy Chamber President such amounts (if any) as the Lord Chancellor may determine by way of—

    (a) remuneration;

    (b) allowances;

    (c) expenses.

(11) In sub-paragraphs (1) and (2) "chamber" means chamber of the First-tier Tribunal or chamber of the Upper Tribunal.

Chamber Presidents and Deputies: removal from office and extension of appointment

5A(1)   This paragraph applies to a person—

    (a)   appointed under section 7(6) or (7) as a Chamber President, or

    (b)   appointed under paragraph 5(1) or (2) as a Deputy Chamber President of a chamber.

(2)   If the terms of the person's appointment provide that the person is appointed otherwise than on a fee-paid basis, the person may be removed from office—

    (a)   only by the Lord Chancellor with the concurrence of the Senior President of Tribunals, and

    (b)   only on the ground of inability or misbehaviour.

(3)   If the terms of the person's appointment provide that the person is appointed on a fee-paid basis, the person may be removed from office—

    (a)   only by the Lord Chancellor with the concurrence of the Senior President of Tribunals, and

    (b)   only on—

       (i)   the ground of inability or misbehaviour, or

       (ii)   a ground specified in the person's terms of appointment.

(4)   If the period (or extended period) for which the person is appointed ends before—

    (a)   the day on which the person attains the age of 70, or

    (b)   if different, the day that for the purposes of section 26 of the Judicial Pensions and Retirement Act 1993 is the compulsory retirement date for the office concerned in the person's case,

then, subject to sub-paragraph (5), the Lord Chancellor must extend the period of the person's appointment (including a period already extended under this sub-paragraph) before it ends.

(5)   Extension under sub-paragraph (4)—

    (a)   requires the person's agreement,

    (b)   is to be for such period as the Lord Chancellor considers appropriate, and

    (c)   may be refused on—

       (i)   the ground of inability or misbehaviour, or

       (ii)   a ground specified in the person's terms of appointment,

but only with any agreement of a senior judge (see section 46(7)), or a nominee of a senior judge, that may be required by those terms.

Acting Chamber Presidents

6(1)   If in the case of a particular chamber of the First-tier Tribunal or Upper Tribunal there is no-one appointed under section 7 to preside over the chamber, the Senior President of Tribunals may appoint a person to preside over the chamber during the vacancy.

(2)   A person appointed under sub-paragraph (1) is to be known as an Acting Chamber President.

(3)   A person who is the Acting Chamber President of a chamber is to be treated as the Chamber President of the chamber for all purposes other than—

    (a)   the purposes of this paragraph of this Schedule, and

    (b)   the purposes of the Judicial Pensions and Retirement Act 1993.

(4)   A person is eligible for appointment under sub-paragraph (1) only if he is eligible for appointment as a Chamber President.

(5) An Acting Chamber President is to hold and vacate office as an Acting Chamber President in accordance with the terms of his appointment.

(6) The Lord Chancellor may pay to an Acting Chamber President such amounts (if any) as the Lord Chancellor may determine by way of—

    (a) remuneration;

    (b) allowances;

    (c) expenses.

Guidance

7 The Chamber President of a chamber of the First-tier Tribunal or the Upper Tribunal is to make arrangements for the issuing of guidance on changes in the law and practice as they relate to the functions allocated to the chamber.

Oaths

8(1) Sub-paragraph (2) applies to a person ("the appointee")—

    (a) appointed under section 7(7) as a Chamber President,

    (b) appointed under paragraph 5(1) as a Deputy Chamber President of a chamber, or

    (c) appointed as an Acting Chamber President.

(2) The appointee must take the required oaths before—

    (a) the Senior President of Tribunals, or

    (b) an eligible person who is nominated by the Senior President of Tribunals for the purpose of taking the oaths from the appointee.

(3) A person is eligible for the purposes of sub-paragraph (2)(b) if any one or more of the following paragraphs applies to him—

    (a) he holds high judicial office (as defined in section 60(2) of the Constitutional Reform Act 2005;

    (b) he holds judicial office (as defined in section 109(4) of that Act);

    (c) he holds (in Scotland) the office of sheriff.

(4) Sub-paragraph (2) does not apply to the appointee if he has previously taken the required oaths in compliance with a requirement imposed on him under paragraph 9 of Schedule 2 or paragraph 10 of Schedule 3.

(5) In this paragraph "the required oaths" means (subject to sub-paragraph (6))—

    (a) the oath of allegiance, and

    (b) the judicial oath,

as set out in the Promissory Oaths Act 1868.

(6) Where it appears to the Lord Chancellor that the appointee will carry out functions under his appointment wholly or mainly in Northern Ireland, the Lord Chancellor may direct that in relation to the appointee "the required oaths" means—

    (a) the oath as set out in section 19(2) of the Justice (Northern Ireland) Act 2002, or

    (b) the affirmation and declaration as set out in section 19(3) of that Act.

PART 2
JUDGES AND OTHER MEMBERS OF CHAMBERS: ASSIGNMENT AND JURISDICTION

Assignment is function of Senior President of Tribunals

9(1) The Senior President of Tribunals has—

> (a) the function of assigning judges and other members of the First-tier Tribunal (including himself) to chambers of the First-tier Tribunal, and
>
> (b) the function of assigning judges and other members of the Upper Tribunal (including himself) to chambers of the Upper Tribunal.

(2) The functions under sub-paragraph (1) are to be exercised in accordance with the following provisions of this Part of this Schedule.

Deemed assignment of Chamber Presidents and Deputy Chamber Presidents

10(1) The Chamber President, or a Deputy Chamber President, of a chamber—

> (a) is to be taken to be assigned to that chamber;
>
> (b) may be assigned additionally to one or more of the other chambers;
>
> (c) may be assigned under paragraph (b) to different chambers at different times.

(2) Paragraphs 11(1) and (2) and 12(2) and (3) do not apply to assignment of a person who is a Chamber President or a Deputy Chamber President.

(3) In sub-paragraph (1) "chamber" means chamber of the First-tier Tribunal or the Upper Tribunal.

Assigning members of First-tier Tribunal to its chambers

11(1) Each person who is a judge or other member of the First-tier Tribunal by virtue of appointment under paragraph 1(1) or 2(1) of Schedule 2 or who is a transferred-in judge, or transferred-in other member, of the First-tier Tribunal—

> (a) is to be assigned to at least one of the chambers of the First-tier Tribunal, and
>
> (b) may be assigned to different chambers of the First-tier Tribunal at different times.

(2) A judge or other member of the First-tier Tribunal to whom sub-paragraph (1) does not apply—

> (a) may be assigned to one or more of the chambers of the First-tier Tribunal, and
>
> (b) may be assigned to different chambers of the First-tier Tribunal at different times.

(3) The Senior President of Tribunals may assign a judge or other member of the First-tier Tribunal to a particular chamber of the First-tier Tribunal only with the concurrence—

> (a) of the Chamber President of the chamber, and
>
> (b) of the judge or other member.

(4) The Senior President of Tribunals may end the assignment of a judge or other member of the First-tier Tribunal to a particular chamber of the First-tier Tribunal only with the concurrence of the Chamber President of the chamber.

(5) Sub-paragraph (3)(a) does not apply where the judge, or other member, concerned is not assigned to any of the chambers of the First-tier Tribunal.

(6) Sub-paragraphs (3)(a) and (4) do not apply where the judge concerned is within section 6(1)(a) to (d) (judges of Courts of Appeal, Court of Session and High Courts).

(7) Sub-paragraphs (3) and (4) do not apply where the judge concerned is the Senior President of Tribunals himself.

Assigning members of Upper Tribunal to its chambers

12(1) Sub-paragraph (2) applies to a person if—

> (a) he is a judge of the Upper Tribunal by virtue of appointment under paragraph 1(1) of Schedule 3, or

    (b) he is a transferred-in judge of the Upper Tribunal, or

    (c) he is a deputy judge of the Upper Tribunal, or

    (d) he is a member of the Upper Tribunal by virtue of appointment under paragraph 2(1) of Schedule 3, or

    (e) he is a transferred-in other member of the Upper Tribunal.

(2) Each person to whom this sub-paragraph applies—

    (a) is to be assigned to at least one of the chambers of the Upper Tribunal, and

    (b) may be assigned to different chambers of the Upper Tribunal at different times.

(3) A judge or other member of the Upper Tribunal to whom sub-paragraph (2) does not apply—

    (a) may be assigned to one or more of the chambers of the Upper Tribunal, and

    (b) may be assigned to different chambers of the Upper Tribunal at different times.

(4) The Senior President of Tribunals may assign a judge or other member of the Upper Tribunal to a particular chamber of the Upper Tribunal only with the concurrence—

    (a) of the Chamber President of the chamber, and

    (b) of the judge or other member.

(5) The Senior President of Tribunals may end the assignment of a judge or other member of the Upper Tribunal to a particular chamber of the Upper Tribunal only with the concurrence of the Chamber President of the chamber.

(6) Sub-paragraph (4)(a) does not apply where the judge, or other member, concerned is not assigned to any of the chambers of the Upper Tribunal.

(7) Sub-paragraphs (4)(a) and (5) do not apply where the judge concerned is within section 6(1)(a) to (d) (judges of Courts of Appeal, Court of Session and High Courts).

(8) Sub-paragraphs (4) and (5) do not apply where the judge concerned is the Senior President of Tribunals himself.

Policy of Senior President of Tribunals as respects assigning members to chambers etc

13(1) The Senior President of Tribunals must publish a document recording the policy adopted by him in relation to—

    (a) the assigning of persons to chambers in exercise of his functions under paragraph 9,

    (b) . . . and

    (c) the nominating of persons to act as members of panels of members of employment tribunals in exercise of his functions under any such provision as is mentioned in section 5D(1) of the Employment Tribunals Act 1996.

(2) That policy must be such as to secure—

    (a) that appropriate use is made of the knowledge and experience of the judges and other members of the First-tier Tribunal and Upper Tribunal, and

    (b) that, in the case of a chamber (of the First-tier Tribunal or Upper Tribunal) whose business consists of, or includes, cases likely to involve the application of the law of Scotland or Northern Ireland, sufficient knowledge and experience of that law is to be found among persons assigned to the chamber.

(3) No policy may be adopted by the Senior President of Tribunals for the purposes of sub-paragraph (1) unless the Lord Chancellor concurs in the policy.

(4)   The Senior President of Tribunals must keep any policy adopted for the purposes of sub-paragraph (1) under review.

Choosing members to decide cases

14(1)   The First-tier Tribunal's function, or the Upper Tribunal's function, of deciding any matter in a case before the tribunal is to be exercised by a member or members of the chamber of the tribunal to which the case is allocated.

(2)   The member or members must be chosen by the Senior President of Tribunals.

(3)   A person choosing under sub-paragraph (2)—
   (a)   must act in accordance with any provision under paragraph 15;
   (b)   may choose himself.

(4)   In this paragraph "member", in relation to a chamber of a tribunal, means a judge or other member of the tribunal who is assigned to the chamber.

Composition of tribunals

15(1)   The Lord Chancellor must by order make provision, in relation to every matter that may fall to be decided by the First-tier Tribunal or the Upper Tribunal, for determining the number of members of the tribunal who are to decide the matter.

(2)   Where an order under sub-paragraph (1) provides for a matter to be decided by a single member of a tribunal, the order—
   (a)   must make provision for determining whether the matter is to be decided by one of the judges, or by one of the other members, of the tribunal, and
   (b)   may make provision for determining, if the matter is to be decided by one of the other members of the tribunal, what qualifications (if any) that other member must have.

(3)   Where an order under sub-paragraph (1) provides for a matter to be decided by two or more members of a tribunal, the order—
   (a)   must make provision for determining how many (if any) of those members are to be judges of the tribunal and how many (if any) are to be other members of the tribunal, and
   (b)   may make provision for determining—
      (i)   if the matter is to be decided by persons who include one or more of the other members of the tribunal, or
      (ii)   if the matter is to be decided by two or more of the other members of the tribunal,
   what qualifications (if any) that other member or any of those other members must have.

(4)   A duty under sub-paragraph (1), (2) or (3) to provide for the determination of anything may be discharged by providing for the thing to be determined by the Senior President of Tribunals, or a Chamber President, in accordance with any provision made under that sub-paragraph.

(5)   Power under paragraph (b) of sub-paragraph (2) or (3) to provide for the determination of anything may be exercised by giving, to the Senior President of Tribunals or a Chamber President, power to determine that thing in accordance with any provision made under that paragraph.

(6)   Where under sub-paragraphs (1) to (4) a matter is to be decided by two or more members

Tribunals, Courts and Enforcement Act 2007
Schedule 5 – Procedure in First-tier Tribunal & Upper Tribunal
Part 1 – Tribunal procedure rules

of a tribunal, the matter may, if the parties to the case agree, be decided in the absence of one or more (but not all) of the members chosen to decide the matter.

(7)   Where the member, or any of the members, of a tribunal chosen to decide a matter does not have any qualification that he is required to have under sub-paragraphs (2)(b), or (3)(b), and (5), the matter may despite that, if the parties to the case agree, be decided by the chosen member or members.

(8)   Before making an order under this paragraph, the Lord Chancellor must consult the Senior President of Tribunals.

(9)   In this paragraph "qualification" includes experience.

SCHEDULE 5

PROCEDURE IN FIRST-TIER TRIBUNAL AND UPPER TRIBUNAL

Section 22

PART 1

TRIBUNAL PROCEDURE RULES

Introductory

1(1)   This Part of this Schedule makes further provision about the content of Tribunal Procedure Rules.

(2)   The generality of section 22(1) is not to be taken to be prejudiced by—
   (a)   the following paragraphs of this Part of this Schedule, or
   (b)   any other provision (including future provision) authorising or requiring the making of provision by Tribunal Procedure Rules.

(3)   In the following paragraphs of this Part of this Schedule "Rules" means Tribunal Procedure Rules.

Concurrent functions

2   Rules may make provision as to who is to decide, or as to how to decide, which of the First-tier Tribunal and Upper Tribunal is to exercise, in relation to any particular matter, a function that is exercisable by the two tribunals on the basis that the question as to which of them is to exercise the function is to be determined by, or under, Rules.

Delegation of functions to staff

3(1)   Rules may provide for functions—
   (a)   of the First-tier Tribunal, or
   (b)   of the Upper Tribunal,
to be exercised by staff appointed under section *40(1)* 2(1) of the Courts Act 2003 or section 40(1) of this Act.

(2)   In making provision of the kind mentioned in sub-paragraph (1) in relation to a function, Rules may (in particular)—
   (a)   provide for the function to be exercisable by a member of staff only if the member of staff is, or is of a description, specified in exercise of a discretion conferred by Rules;
   (b)   provide for the function to be exercisable by a member of staff only if the member

of staff is approved, or is of a description approved, for the purpose by a person specified in Rules.

(3) A person may exercise functions by virtue of this paragraph only if authorised to do so by the Senior President of Tribunals.

(4) An authorisation under this paragraph—
    (a) may be subject to conditions, and
    (b) may be varied or revoked by the Senior President of Tribunals at any time.

(5) The Senior President of Tribunals may delegate to one or more of the following the Senior President of Tribunals' functions under the preceding provisions of this paragraph—
    (a) a judicial office holder;
    (b) a person appointed under section 2(1) of the Courts Act 2003 or section 40(1) of this Act.

(6) A person to whom functions of the Senior President of Tribunals are delegated under sub-paragraph (5)(b) is not subject to the direction of any person other than—
    (a) the Senior President of Tribunals, or
    (b) a judicial office holder nominated by the Senior President of Tribunals,
when exercising the functions.

(7) Subsections (3) to (5) of section 8 apply to—
    (a) a delegation under sub-paragraph (5), and
    (b) a nomination under sub-paragraph (6),
as they apply to a delegation under subsection (1) of that section.

(8) In this paragraph—
    "function" does not include—
        (a) any function so far as its exercise involves authorising a person's committal to prison or arrest;
        (b) any function of granting an injunction;
    "judicial office holder" has the meaning given by section 109(4) of the Constitutional Reform Act 2005.

Time limits

4 Rules may make provision for time limits as respects initiating, or taking any step in, proceedings before the First-tier Tribunal or the Upper Tribunal.

Repeat applications

5 Rules may make provision restricting the making of fresh applications where a previous application in relation to the same matter has been made.

Tribunal acting of its own initiative

6 Rules may make provision about the circumstances in which the First-tier Tribunal, or the Upper Tribunal, may exercise its powers of its own initiative.

Hearings

7 Rules may—
    (a) make provision for dealing with matters without a hearing;
    (b) make provision as respects allowing or requiring a hearing to be in private or as respects allowing or requiring a hearing to be in public.

Tribunals, Courts and Enforcement Act 2007
Schedule 5 – Procedure in First-tier Tribunal & Upper Tribunal
Part 1 – Tribunal procedure rules

Proceedings without notice

8   Rules may make provision for proceedings to take place, in circumstances described in Rules, at the request of one party even though the other, or another, party has had no notice.

Representation

9   Rules may make provision conferring additional rights of audience before the First-tier Tribunal or the Upper Tribunal.

Evidence, witnesses and attendance

10(1)   Rules may make provision about evidence (including evidence on oath and administration of oaths).

 (2)   Rules may modify any rules of evidence provided for elsewhere, so far as they would apply to proceedings before the First-tier Tribunal or Upper Tribunal.

 (3)   Rules may make provision, where the First-tier Tribunal has required a person—
    (a)   to attend at any place for the purpose of giving evidence,
    (b)   otherwise to make himself available to give evidence,
    (c)   to swear an oath in connection with the giving of evidence,
    (d)   to give evidence as a witness,
    (e)   to produce a document, or
    (f)   to facilitate the inspection of a document or any other thing (including any premises),
   for the Upper Tribunal to deal with non-compliance with the requirement as though the requirement had been imposed by the Upper Tribunal.

 (4)   Rules may make provision for the payment of expenses and allowances to persons giving evidence, producing documents, attending proceedings or required to attend proceedings.

Use of information

11(1)   Rules may make provision for the disclosure or non-disclosure of information received during the course of proceedings before the First-tier Tribunal or Upper Tribunal.

 (2)   Rules may make provision for imposing reporting restrictions in circumstances described in Rules.

Costs and expenses

12(1)   Rules may make provision for regulating matters relating to costs, or (in Scotland) expenses, of proceedings before the First-tier Tribunal or Upper Tribunal.

 (2)   The provision mentioned in sub-paragraph (1) includes (in particular)—
    (a)   provision prescribing scales of costs or expenses;
    (b)   provision for enabling costs to undergo detailed assessment in England and Wales by the county court or the High Court;
    (c)   provision for taxation in Scotland of accounts of expenses by an Auditor of Court;
    (d)   provision for enabling costs to be taxed in Northern Ireland in a county court or the High Court;
    (e)   provision for costs or expenses—
       (i)   not to be allowed in respect of items of a description specified in Rules;

(ii) not to be allowed in proceedings of a description so specified;

(f) provision for other exceptions to either or both of subsections (1) and (2) of section 29.

Set-off and interest

13(1) Rules may make provision for a party to proceedings to deduct, from amounts payable by him, amounts payable to him.

(2) Rules may make provision for interest on sums awarded (including provision conferring a discretion or provision in accordance with which interest is to be calculated).

Arbitration

14 Rules may provide for any of the provisions of sections 1 to 15 of and schedule 1 to the Arbitration (Scotland) Act 2010 (which extends to Scotland) or Part 1 of the Arbitration Act 1996 (which extends to England and Wales, and Northern Ireland, but not Scotland) not to apply, or not to apply except so far as is specified in Rules, where the First-tier Tribunal, or Upper Tribunal, acts as arbitrator.

Correction of errors and setting-aside of decisions on procedural grounds

15(1) Rules may make provision for the correction of accidental errors in a decision or record of a decision.

(2) Rules may make provision for the setting aside of a decision in proceedings before the First-tier Tribunal or Upper Tribunal—

(a) where a document relating to the proceedings was not sent to, or was not received at an appropriate time by, a party to the proceedings or a party's representative,

(b) where a document relating to the proceedings was not sent to the First-tier Tribunal or Upper Tribunal at an appropriate time,

(c) where a party to the proceedings, or a party's representative, was not present at a hearing related to the proceedings, or

(d) where there has been any other procedural irregularity in the proceedings.

(3) Sub-paragraphs (1) and (2) shall not be taken to prejudice, or to be prejudiced by, any power to correct errors or set aside decisions that is exercisable apart from rules made by virtue of those sub-paragraphs.

Ancillary powers

16 Rules may confer on the First-tier Tribunal, or the Upper Tribunal, such ancillary powers as are necessary for the proper discharge of its functions.

Rules may refer to practice directions

17 Rules may, instead of providing for any matter, refer to provision made or to be made about that matter by directions under section 23.

Presumptions

18 Rules may make provision in the form of presumptions (including, in particular, presumptions as to service or notification).

Differential provision

19 Rules may make different provision for different purposes or different areas.

Tribunals, Courts and Enforcement Act 2007
Schedule 5 – Procedure in First-tier Tribunal & Upper Tribunal
Part 2 – Tribunal procedure committee

PART 2
TRIBUNAL PROCEDURE COMMITTEE

Membership

20   The Tribunal Procedure Committee is to consist of—

   (a)   the Senior President of Tribunals or a person nominated by him,

   (b)   the persons currently appointed by the Lord Chancellor under paragraph 21,

   (c)   the persons currently appointed by the Lord Chief Justice of England and Wales under paragraph 22,

   (d)   the person currently appointed by the Lord President of the Court of Session under paragraph 23, and

   (e)   any person currently appointed under paragraph 24 at the request of the Senior President of Tribunals.

Lord Chancellor's appointees

21(1)   The Lord Chancellor must appoint—

   (a)   three persons each of whom must be a person with experience of—

      (i)   practice in tribunals, or

      (ii)   advising persons involved in tribunal proceedings, . . .

   (b)   . . ..

   (2)   Before making an appointment under sub-paragraph (1), the Lord Chancellor must consult the Lord Chief Justice of England and Wales.

   (3)   . . .

Lord Chief Justice's appointees

22(1)   The Lord Chief Justice of England and Wales must appoint—

   (a)   one of the judges of the First-tier Tribunal,

   (b)   one of the judges of the Upper Tribunal, and

   (c)   one person who is a member of the First-tier Tribunal, or is a member of the Upper Tribunal, but is not a judge of the First-tier Tribunal and is not a judge of the Upper Tribunal.

   (2)   Before making an appointment under sub-paragraph (1), the Lord Chief Justice of England and Wales must consult the Lord Chancellor.

Lord President's appointee

23(1)   The Lord President of the Court of Session must appoint one person with experience in and knowledge of the Scottish legal system.

   (2)   Before making an appointment under sub-paragraph (1), the Lord President of the Court of Session must consult the Lord Chancellor.

Persons appointed at request of Senior President of Tribunals

24(1)   At the request of the Senior President of Tribunals, an appropriate senior judge may appoint a person or persons with experience in and knowledge of—

   (a)   a particular issue, or

   (b)   a particular subject area in relation to which the First-tier Tribunal or the Upper Tribunal has, or is likely to have, jurisdiction, for the purpose of assisting the Committee with regard to that issue or subject area.

(2)   In sub-paragraph (1) "an appropriate senior judge" means any of—
    (a)   the Lord Chief Justice of England and Wales,
    (b)   the Lord President of the Court of Session, and
    (c)   the Lord Chief Justice of Northern Ireland.

(3)   The total number of persons appointed at any time under sub-paragraph (1) must not exceed four.

(4)   Before making an appointment under sub-paragraph (1), the person making the appointment must consult the Lord Chancellor.

(5)   The terms of appointment of a person appointed under sub-paragraph (1) may (in particular) authorise him to act as a member of the Committee only in relation to matters specified by those terms.

Power to amend paragraphs 20 to 24

25(1)   The Lord Chancellor may by order—
    (a)   amend any of paragraphs 20, 21(1), 22(1), 23(1) and 24(1), and
    (b)   make consequential amendments in any other provision of paragraphs 21 to 24 or in paragraph 28(7).

(2)   The making of an order under this paragraph—
    (a)   requires the concurrence of the Lord Chief Justice of England and Wales,
    (b)   if the order amends paragraph 23(1), requires also the concurrence of the Lord President of the Court of Session, and
    (c)   if the order amends paragraph 24(1), requires also the concurrence of the Lord President of the Court of Session and the Lord Chief Justice of Northern Ireland.

Committee members' expenses

26   The Lord Chancellor may reimburse members of the Tribunal Procedure Committee their travelling and out-of-pocket expenses.

PART 3
MAKING OF TRIBUNAL PROCEDURE RULES BY TRIBUNAL PROCEDURE COMMITTEE

Meaning of "Rules" and "the Committee"

27   In the following provisions of this Part of this Schedule—
    "the Committee" means the Tribunal Procedure Committee;
    "Rules" means Tribunal Procedure Rules.

Process for making Rules

28(1)   Before the Committee makes Rules, the Committee must—
    (a)   consult such persons (including such of the Chamber Presidents) as it considers appropriate,
    (b)   consult the Lord President of the Court of Session if the Rules contain provision relating to proceedings in Scotland, and
    (c)   meet (unless it is inexpedient to do so).

(2)   Rules made by the Committee must be—
    (a)   signed by a majority of the members of the Committee, and

Tribunals, Courts and Enforcement Act 2007
Schedule 5 – Procedure in First-tier Tribunal & Upper Tribunal
Part 3 – Making of tribunal procedure rules by committee

(b) submitted to the Lord Chancellor.

(3) The Lord Chancellor may allow or disallow Rules so made.

(4) If the Lord Chancellor disallows Rules so made, he must give the Committee written reasons for doing so.

(5) Rules so made and allowed—

    (a) come into force on such day as the Lord Chancellor directs, and

    (b) are to be contained in a statutory instrument to which the Statutory Instruments Act 1946 applies as if the instrument contained rules made by a Minister of the Crown.

(6) A statutory instrument containing Rules made by the Committee is subject to annulment in pursuance of a resolution of either House of Parliament.

(7) In the case of a member of the Committee appointed under paragraph 24, the terms of his appointment may (in particular) provide that, for the purposes of sub-paragraph (2)(a), he is to count as a member of the Committee only in relation to matters specified in those terms.

Delegation of functions to staff: reconsideration of decisions

28A(1) Before making Rules that provide for the exercise of functions of the First-tier Tribunal or Upper Tribunal by authorised persons by virtue of paragraph 3, the Committee must take the following steps in relation to each of the functions in question.

(2) The Committee must consider whether the Rules should include a right for the parties to proceedings in which a decision is made by an authorised person exercising the function to have the decision reconsidered by a judicial office holder.

(3) If the Committee considers that the rules should include such a right, it must include provision to that effect when it makes the Rules.

(4) If the Committee does not consider that the rules should include such a right, it must inform the Lord Chancellor of—

    (a) its decision, and

    (b) its reasons for reaching that decision.

(5) In this paragraph "authorised person" and "judicial office holder" have the same meanings as in Chapter 2A of Part 1 of this Act (see section 29A).

Power of Lord Chancellor to require Rules to be made

29(1) This paragraph applies if the Lord Chancellor gives the Committee written notice that he thinks it is expedient for Rules to include provision that would achieve a purpose specified in the notice.

(2) The Committee must make such Rules, in accordance with paragraph 28, as it considers necessary to achieve the specified purpose.

(3) Those Rules must be made—

    (a) within such period as may be specified by the Lord Chancellor in the notice, or

    (b) if no period is so specified, within a reasonable period after the Lord Chancellor gives the notice to the Committee.

PART 4

POWER TO AMEND LEGISLATION IN CONNECTION WITH TRIBUNAL PROCEDURE RULES

Lord Chancellor's power

30 (1) The Lord Chancellor may by order amend, repeal or revoke any enactment to the extent he considers necessary or desirable—

    (a) in order to facilitate the making of Tribunal Procedure Rules, or

    (b) in consequence of—

        (i) section 22,

        (ii) Part 1 or 3 of this Schedule, or

        (iii) Tribunal Procedure Rules.

(2) In this paragraph "enactment" means any enactment whenever passed or made, including an enactment comprised in subordinate legislation (within the meaning of the Interpretation Act 1978).

SCHEDULE 6

TRIBUNALS FOR THE PURPOSES OF SECTIONS 30 TO 36

Sections 30 to 37

PART 1

TRIBUNALS FOR THE PURPOSES OF SECTIONS 30, 35 AND 36

Tribunal	Enactment
Information Tribunal	Section 6 of the Data Protection Act 1998 (c 29)

PART 2

TRIBUNALS FOR THE PURPOSES OF SECTIONS 30 AND 35

not reproduced

PART 3

TRIBUNALS FOR THE PURPOSES OF SECTIONS 30 AND 36

not reproduced

PART 4

TRIBUNALS FOR THE PURPOSES OF SECTION 30

not reproduced

PART 5

TRIBUNALS FOR THE PURPOSES OF SECTIONS 35 AND 36

not reproduced

PART 6

TRIBUNALS FOR THE PURPOSES OF SECTION 35

not reproduced

PART 7

TRIBUNALS FOR THE PURPOSES OF SECTION 32(3)

not reproduced

Tribunal Procedure (First-tier Tribunal) (General Regulatory Chamber) Rules 2009 (SI 2009/1976)

TABLE OF PROVISIONS

PART 1 – INTRODUCTION

PART 2 – GENERAL POWERS AND PROVISIONS

PART 3 – PROCEEDINGS BEFORE THE TRIBUNAL

CHAPTER 1: BEFORE THE HEARING
CASES OTHER THAN CHARITIES CASES OR CERTIFICATION CASES

CHAPTER 2: BEFORE THE HEARING – CHARITIES CASES

Tribunal Procedure (First-tier Tribunal) (General Regulatory Chamber) Rules 2009 (SI 2009/1976)

as amended to 1 February 2020

Made 16th July 2009
Laid before Parliament 21st July 2009
Coming into force 1st September 2009

After consulting in accordance with paragraph 28(1) of Schedule 5 to the Tribunals, Courts and Enforcement Act 2007, the Tribunal Procedure Committee has made the following Rules in exercise of the power conferred by sections 9(3), 22 and 29(3) and (4) of, and Schedule 5 to, that Act.

The Lord Chancellor has allowed the Rules in accordance with paragraph 28(3) of Schedule 5 to the Tribunals, Courts and Enforcement Act 2007.

Part 1 – Introduction

Citation, commencement, application and interpretation

1(1) These Rules may be cited as the Tribunal Procedure (First-tier Tribunal) (General Regulatory Chamber) Rules 2009 and come into force on 1st September 2009.

(2) These Rules apply to proceedings before the General Regulatory Chamber of the First-tier Tribunal, including where the Tribunal exercises its jurisdiction under section 61(4) of the Freedom of Information Act 2000 and section 202(2) of the Data Protection Act 2018.

(3) In these Rules—

"the 2007 Act" means the Tribunals, Courts and Enforcement Act 2007;

"agricultural product or foodstuff decision" means a decision of the Secretary of State specified in the first column of the table in Annex 3 to Regulation (EU) No 1151/2012 of the European Parliament and of the Council on quality schemes for agricultural products and foodstuffs;

"appellant" means a person who—

    (a) commences Tribunal proceedings, whether by making an appeal, an application, a claim, a complaint, a reference or otherwise; or

    (b) is added or substituted as an appellant under rule 9 (addition, substitution and removal of parties);

"aromatised wine decision" means a decision of the Secretary of State specified in column 1 of the table in Annex 4 to Regulation (EU) No 251/2014 of the European Parliament and of the Council on the definition, description, presentation, labelling and the protection of geographical indications of aromatised wine products;

"certification case" means a case in which the Tribunal may certify an offence to the Upper Tribunal under section 61(4) of the Freedom of Information Act 2000 or section 202(2) of the Data Protection Act 2018;

"charities case" means an appeal or application in respect of a decision, order or direction of the Charity Commission, or a reference under Schedule 1D of the Charities Act 1993;

"document" means anything in which information is recorded in any form, and an obligation under these Rules or any practice direction or direction to provide or allow access to a document or a copy of a document for any purpose means, unless the Tribunal directs otherwise, an obligation to provide or allow access to such document or copy in a legible form or in a form which can be readily made into a legible form;

"hearing" means an oral hearing and includes a hearing conducted in whole or in part by video link, telephone or other means of instantaneous two-way electronic communication;

"notice of appeal" means a document which starts proceedings;

"party" means—
    (a) a person who is an appellant or a respondent;
    (b) if the proceedings have been concluded, a person who was an appellant or a respondent when the Tribunal finally disposed of all issues in the proceedings;

"practice direction" means a direction given under section 23 of the 2007 Act;

"respondent" means—
    (a) in proceedings appealing against or challenging a decision, direction or order, the person who made the decision, direction or order appealed against or challenged;
    (b) a person against whom an appellant otherwise brings proceedings; or
    (c) a person added or substituted as a respondent under rule 9 (addition, substitution and removal of parties);

"transport case" means proceedings under the Road Traffic Act 1988, the Road Traffic Offenders Act 1988, the Greater London Authority Act 1999, the Postal Services Act 2000, the Vehicle Drivers (Certificates of Professional Competence) Regulations 2007, the European Communities (Recognition of Professional Qualifications) Regulations 2007 and the European Union (Recognition of Professional Qualifications) Regulations 2015;

"Tribunal" means the First-tier Tribunal.

Overriding objective and parties' obligation to co-operate with the tribunal

2(1)   The overriding objective of these Rules is to enable the Tribunal to deal with cases fairly and justly.

(2)   Dealing with a case fairly and justly includes—
    (a) dealing with the case in ways which are proportionate to the importance of the case, the complexity of the issues, the anticipated costs and the resources of the parties;
    (b) avoiding unnecessary formality and seeking flexibility in the proceedings;
    (c) ensuring, so far as practicable, that the parties are able to participate fully in the proceedings;
    (d) using any special expertise of the Tribunal effectively; and
    (e) avoiding delay, so far as compatible with proper consideration of the issues.

(3)   The Tribunal must seek to give effect to the overriding objective when it—
    (a) exercises any power under these Rules; or
    (b) interprets any rule or practice direction.

(4)   Parties must—
    (a) help the Tribunal to further the overriding objective; and
    (b) co-operate with the Tribunal generally.

Alternative dispute resolution and arbitration

3(1) The Tribunal should seek, where appropriate—

    (a) to bring to the attention of the parties the availability of any appropriate alternative procedure for the resolution of the dispute; and

    (b) if the parties wish, and provided that it is compatible with the overriding objective, to facilitate the use of the procedure.

(2) Part 1 of the Arbitration Act 1996 does not apply to proceedings before the Tribunal.

PART 2 – GENERAL POWERS AND PROVISIONS

Delegation to staff

4(1) Staff appointed under section 40(1) of the 2007 Act (tribunal staff and services) may, with the approval of the Senior President of Tribunals, carry out functions of a judicial nature permitted or required to be done by the Tribunal.

(2) The approval referred to at paragraph (1) may apply generally to the carrying out of specified functions by members of staff of a specified description in specified circumstances.

(3) Within 14 days after the date that the Tribunal sends notice of a decision made by a member of staff pursuant to an approval under paragraph (1) to a party, that party may apply in writing to the Tribunal for that decision to be considered afresh by a judge.

Case management powers

5(1) Subject to the provisions of the 2007 Act and any other enactment, the Tribunal may regulate its own procedure.

(2) The Tribunal may give a direction in relation to the conduct or disposal of proceedings at any time, including a direction amending, suspending or setting aside an earlier direction.

(3) In particular, and without restricting the general powers in paragraphs (1) and (2), the Tribunal may—

    (a) extend or shorten the time for complying with any rule, practice direction or direction, unless such extension or shortening would conflict with a provision of another enactment containing a time limit;

    (b) consolidate or hear together two or more sets of proceedings or parts of proceedings raising common issues, or treat a case as a lead case (whether under rule 18 or otherwise);

    (c) permit or require a party to amend a document;

    (d) permit or require a party or another person to provide documents, information or submissions to the Tribunal or a party;

    (e) deal with an issue in the proceedings as a preliminary issue;

    (f) hold a hearing to consider any matter, including a case management issue;

    (g) decide the form of any hearing;

    (h) adjourn or postpone a hearing;

    (i) require a party to produce a bundle for a hearing;

    (j) stay (or, in Scotland, sist) proceedings;

    (k) transfer proceedings to another court or tribunal if that other court or tribunal has jurisdiction in relation to the proceedings and—

        (i) because of a change of circumstances since the proceedings were started, the

Tribunal no longer has jurisdiction in relation to the proceedings; or

(ii) the Tribunal considers that the other court or tribunal is a more appropriate forum for the determination of the case;

(l) suspend the effect of its own decision pending the determination by the Tribunal or the Upper Tribunal of an application for permission to appeal against, and any appeal or review of, that decision.

Procedure for applying for and giving directions

6(1) The Tribunal may give a direction on the application of one or more of the parties or on its own initiative.

(2) An application for a direction may be made—

(a) by sending or delivering a written application to the Tribunal; or

(b) orally during the course of a hearing.

(3) An application for a direction must include the reason for making that application.

(4) Unless the Tribunal considers that there is good reason not to do so, the Tribunal must send written notice of any direction to every party and to any other person affected by the direction.

(5) If a party or any other person sent notice of the direction under paragraph (4) wishes to challenge a direction which the Tribunal has given, they may do so by applying for another direction which amends, suspends or sets aside the first direction.

Failure to comply with rules, practice directions or tribunal directions

7(1) An irregularity resulting from a failure to comply with any provision of these Rules, a practice direction or a direction does not of itself render void the proceedings or any step taken in the proceedings.

(2) If a party has failed to comply with a requirement in these Rules, a practice direction or a direction, the Tribunal may take such action as the Tribunal considers just, which may include—

(a) waiving the requirement;

(b) requiring the failure to be remedied;

(c) exercising its power under rule 8 (striking out a party's case);

(d) exercising its power under paragraph (3); or

(e) barring or restricting a party's participation in the proceedings.

(3) The Tribunal may refer to the Upper Tribunal, and ask the Upper Tribunal to exercise its power under section 25 of the 2007 Act in relation to, any failure by a person to comply with a requirement imposed by the Tribunal—

(a) to attend at any place for the purpose of giving evidence;

(b) otherwise to make themselves available to give evidence;

(c) to swear an oath in connection with the giving of evidence;

(d) to give evidence as a witness;

(e) to produce a document; or

(f) to facilitate the inspection of a document or any other thing (including any premises).

Certification

7A(1) This rule applies to certification cases.

(2) An application for the Tribunal to certify an offence to the Upper Tribunal must be made in writing and must be sent or delivered to the Tribunal so that it is received no later than 28 days after the relevant act or omission (as the case may be) first occurs.

(3) The application must include—

    (a) details of the proceedings giving rise to the application;

    (b) details of the act or omission (as the case may be) relied on;

    (c) if the act or omission (as the case may be) arises following, and in relation to, a decision of the Tribunal, a copy of any written record of that decision;

    (d) if the act or omission (as the case may be) arises following, and in relation to, an order of the Tribunal under section 166(2) of the Data Protection Act 2018 (orders to progress complaints), a copy of the order;

    (e) the grounds relied on in contending that if the proceedings in question were proceedings before a court having power to commit for contempt, the act or omission (as the case may be) would constitute contempt of court;

    (f) a statement as to whether the applicant would be content for the case to be dealt with without a hearing if the Tribunal considers it appropriate, and

    (g) any further information or documents required by a practice direction.

(4) If an application is provided to the Tribunal later than the time required by paragraph (2) or by any extension of time under rule 5(3)(a) (power to extend time)—

    (a) the application must include a request for an extension of time and the reason why the application was not provided in time, and

    (b) unless the Tribunal extends time for the application, the Tribunal must not admit the application.

(5) When the Tribunal admits the application, it must send a copy of the application and any accompanying documents to the respondent and must give directions as to the procedure to be followed in the consideration and disposal of the application.

(6) A decision disposing of the application will be treated by the Tribunal as a decision which finally disposes of all issues in the proceedings comprising the certification case and rule 38 (decisions) will apply.

Striking out a party's case

8(1) The proceedings, or the appropriate part of them, will automatically be struck out if the appellant has failed to comply with a direction that stated that failure by the appellant to comply with the direction would lead to the striking out of the proceedings or that part of them.

(2) The Tribunal must strike out the whole or a part of the proceedings if the Tribunal—

    (a) does not have jurisdiction in relation to the proceedings or that part of them; and

    (b) does not exercise its power under rule 5(3)(k)(i) (transfer to another court or tribunal) in relation to the proceedings or that part of them.

(3) The Tribunal may strike out the whole or a part of the proceedings if—

    (a) the appellant has failed to comply with a direction which stated that failure by the appellant to comply with the direction could lead to the striking out of the proceedings or part of them;

    (b) the appellant has failed to co-operate with the Tribunal to such an extent that the Tribunal cannot deal with the proceedings fairly and justly; or

    (c) the Tribunal considers there is no reasonable prospect of the appellant's case, or part of it, succeeding.

(4) The Tribunal may not strike out the whole or a part of the proceedings under paragraph (2) or (3)(b) or (c) without first giving the appellant an opportunity to make representations in relation to the proposed striking out.

(5) If the proceedings, or part of them, have been struck out under paragraph (1) or (3)(a), the appellant may apply for the proceedings, or part of them, to be reinstated.

(6) An application under paragraph (5) must be made in writing and received by the Tribunal within 28 days after the date on which the Tribunal sent notification of the striking out to that party.

(7) This rule applies to a respondent as it applies to an appellant except that—
   (a) a reference to the striking out of the proceedings is to be read as a reference to the barring of the respondent from taking further part in the proceedings; and
   (b) a reference to an application for the reinstatement of proceedings which have been struck out is to be read as a reference to an application for the lifting of the bar on the respondent from taking further part in the proceedings.

(8) If a respondent has been barred from taking further part in proceedings under this rule and that bar has not been lifted, the Tribunal need not consider any response or other submission made by that respondent, and may summarily determine any or all issues against that respondent.

Addition, substitution and removal of parties

9(1) The Tribunal may give a direction adding, substituting or removing a party as an appellant or a respondent.

(2) If the Tribunal gives a direction under paragraph (1) it may give such consequential directions as it considers appropriate.

(3) Any person who is not a party may apply to the Tribunal to be added or substituted as a party.

(4) If a person who is entitled to be a party to proceedings by virtue of another enactment applies to be added as a party, and any conditions applicable to that entitlement have been satisfied, the Tribunal must give a direction adding that person as a respondent or, if appropriate, as an appellant.

(5) An application by a person to be added as a party to a reference under Schedule 1D of the Charities Act 1993 must be made within 42 days of the date on which the Tribunal publishes details of the reference in accordance with rule 26(4).

Orders for costs

10(1) Subject to paragraph (1A) the Tribunal may make an order in respect of costs (or, in Scotland, expenses) only—

(a) under section 29(4) of the 2007 Act (wasted costs) and costs incurred in applying for such costs;

(b) if the Tribunal considers that a party has acted unreasonably in bringing, defending or conducting the proceedings; or

(c) where the Charity Commission,,the Gambling Commission or the Information Commissioner is the respondent and a decision, direction or order of the Commission or the Commissioner is the subject of the proceedings, if the Tribunal considers that the decision, direction or order was unreasonable.

(1A) If the Tribunal allows an appeal against a decision of the Gambling Commission, the Tribunal must, unless it considers that there is a good reason not to do so, order the Commission to pay to the appellant an amount equal to any fee paid by the appellant under the First-tier Tribunal (Gambling) Fees Order 2010 that has neither been included in an order made under paragraph (1) nor refunded.

(2) The Tribunal may make an order under paragraph (1) on an application or on its own initiative.

(3) A person making an application for an order under this rule must—
  (a) send or deliver a written application to the Tribunal and to the person against whom it is proposed that the order be made; and
  (b) send or deliver a schedule of the costs or expenses claimed with the application.

(4) An application for an order under paragraph (1) may be made at any time during the proceedings but may not be made later than 14 days after the date on which the Tribunal sends—
  (a) a decision notice recording the decision which finally disposes of all issues in the proceedings; or
  (b) notice under rule 17(5) that a withdrawal which ends the proceedings has taken effect.

(5) The Tribunal may not make an order under paragraph (1) or (1A) against a person("the paying person") without first—
  (a) giving that person an opportunity to make representations; and
  (b) if the paying person is an individual, considering that person's financial means.

(6) The amount of costs or expenses to be paid under an order under paragraph (1) may be ascertained by—
  (a) summary assessment by the Tribunal;
  (b) agreement of a specified sum by the paying person and the person entitled to receive the costs or expenses ("the receiving person"); or
  (c) assessment of the whole or a specified part of the costs or expenses, including the costs or expenses of the assessment, incurred by the receiving person, if not agreed.

(7) Following an order under paragraph (6)(c) a party may apply—
  (a) in England and Wales, to the county court for a detailed assessment of costs in accordance with the Civil Procedure Rules 1998 on the standard basis or, if specified in the order, on the indemnity basis;
  (b) in Scotland, to the Auditor of the Court of Session for the taxation of the expenses according to the fees payable in the Court of Session; or
  (c) in Northern Ireland, to the county court for the costs to be taxed.

(8) Upon making an order for the assessment of costs, the Tribunal may order an amount to be paid on account before the costs or expenses are assessed.

Representatives

11(1) A party may appoint a representative (whether legally qualified or not) to represent that party in the proceedings.

(2) If a party appoints a representative, that party must send or deliver to the Tribunal and to each other party written notice of the representative's name and address.

(3) Anything permitted or required to be done by or provided to a party under these Rules, a practice direction or a direction may be done by or provided to the representative of that party except—

    (a) signing a witness statement; or

    (b) sending or delivering a notice under paragraph (2), if the representative is not a person who, for the purposes of the Legal Services Act 2007, is an authorised person in relation to an activity which constitutes the exercise of a right of audience or the conduct of litigation within the meaning of that Act, an advocate or solicitor in Scotland or a barrister or solicitor in Northern Ireland.

(4) A person who receives due notice of the appointment of a representative—

    (a) must provide to the representative any document which is required to be sent to the represented party, and need not provide that document to the represented party; and

    (b) may assume that the representative is and remains authorised until receiving written notification to the contrary from the representative or the represented party.

(5) At a hearing a party may be accompanied by another person whose name and address has not been notified under paragraph (2) but who, with the permission of the Tribunal, may act as a representative or otherwise assist in presenting the party's case at the hearing.

(6) Paragraphs (2) to (4) do not apply to a person who accompanies a party under paragraph (5).

Calculating time

12(1) An act required by these Rules, a practice direction or a direction to be done on or by a particular day must be done before 5pm on that day.

(2) If the time specified by these Rules, a practice direction or a direction for doing any act ends on a day other than a working day, the act is done in time if it is done on the next working day.

(3) In this rule "working day" means any day except a Saturday or Sunday, Christmas Day, Good Friday or a bank holiday under section 1 of the Banking and Financial Dealings Act 1971.

Sending and delivery of documents

13(1) Any document to be provided to the Tribunal under these Rules, a practice direction or a direction must be—

    (a) sent by prepaid post or by document exchange, or delivered by hand to the address specified for the proceedings;

    (b) sent by fax to the number specified for the proceedings; or

    (c) sent or delivered by such other method as the Tribunal may permit or direct.

(2) Subject to paragraph (3), if a party provides a fax number, email address or other details for the electronic transmission of documents to them, that party must accept delivery of documents by that method.

(3) If a party informs the Tribunal and all other parties that a particular form of communication, other than pre-paid post or delivery by hand, should not be used to provide documents to that party, that form of communication must not be so used.

(4) If the Tribunal or a party sends a document to a party or the Tribunal by email or any other electronic means of communication, the recipient may request that the sender provide a hard copy of the document to the recipient. The recipient must make such a request as soon as reasonably practicable after receiving the document electronically.

(5) The Tribunal and each party may assume that the address provided by a party or its representative is and remains the address to which documents should be sent or delivered until receiving written notification to the contrary.

Prevention of disclosure or publication of documents and information

14(1) The Tribunal may make an order prohibiting the disclosure or publication of—

    (a) specified documents or information relating to the proceedings; or

    (b) any matter likely to lead members of the public to identify any person whom the Tribunal considers should not be identified.

(2) The Tribunal may give a direction prohibiting the disclosure of a document or information to a person if—

    (a) the Tribunal is satisfied that such disclosure would be likely to cause that person or some other person serious harm; and

    (b) the Tribunal is satisfied, having regard to the interests of justice, that it is proportionate to give such a direction.

(3) If a party ("the first party") considers that the Tribunal should give a direction under paragraph (2) prohibiting the disclosure of a document or information to another party ("the second party"), the first party must—

    (a) exclude the relevant document or information from any documents that will be provided to the second party; and

    (b) provide to the Tribunal the excluded document or information, and the reason for its exclusion, so that the Tribunal may decide whether the document or information should be disclosed to the second party or should be the subject of a direction under paragraph (2).

(4) If the Tribunal gives a direction under paragraph (2) which prevents disclosure to a party who has appointed a representative, the Tribunal may give a direction that the documents or information be disclosed to that representative if the Tribunal is satisfied that—

    (a) disclosure to the representative would be in the interests of the party; and

    (b) the representative will act in accordance with paragraph (5).

(5) Documents or information disclosed to a representative in accordance with a direction under paragraph (4) must not be disclosed either directly or indirectly to any other person without the Tribunal's consent.

(6) The Tribunal may give a direction that certain documents or information must or may be disclosed to the Tribunal on the basis that the Tribunal will not disclose such documents or information to other persons, or specified other persons.

(7) A party making an application for a direction under paragraph (6) may withhold the relevant documents or information from other parties until the Tribunal has granted or refused the application.

(8) Unless the Tribunal considers that there is good reason not to do so, the Tribunal must send notice that a party has made an application for a direction under paragraph (6) to each other party.

(9)   In a case involving matters relating to national security, the Tribunal must ensure that information is not disclosed contrary to the interests of national security.

(10)   The Tribunal must conduct proceedings and record its decision and reasons appropriately so as not to undermine the effect of an order made under paragraph (1), a direction given under paragraph (2) or (6) or the duty imposed by paragraph (9).

Disclosure, evidence and submissions

15(1)   Without restriction on the general powers in rule 5(1) and (2) (case management powers), the Tribunal may give directions as to—

    (a)   the exchange between parties of lists of documents which are relevant to the appeal, or relevant to particular issues, and the inspection of such documents;

    (b)   the provision by parties of statements of agreed matters;

    (c)   issues on which it requires evidence or submissions;

    (d)   the nature of the evidence or submissions it requires;

    (e)   whether the parties are permitted or required to provide expert evidence, and if so whether the parties must jointly appoint a single expert to provide such evidence;

    (f)   any limit on the number of witnesses whose evidence a party may put forward, whether in relation to a particular issue or generally;

    (g)   the manner in which any evidence or submissions are to be provided, which may include a direction for them to be given—

        (i)   orally at a hearing; or

        (ii)   by written submissions or witness statement; and

    (h)   the time at which any evidence or submissions are to be provided.

(2)   The Tribunal may—

    (a)   admit evidence whether or not—

        (i)   the evidence would be admissible in a civil trial in the United Kingdom; or

        (ii)   the evidence was available to a previous decision maker; or

    (b)   exclude evidence that would otherwise be admissible where—

        (i)   the evidence was not provided within the time allowed by a direction or a practice direction;

        (ii)   the evidence was otherwise provided in a manner that did not comply with a direction or a practice direction; or

        (iii)   it would otherwise be unfair to admit the evidence.

(3)   The Tribunal may consent to a witness giving, or require any witness to give, evidence on oath, and may administer an oath for that purpose.

Summoning or citation of witnesses and orders to answer questions or produce documents

16(1)   On the application of a party or on its own initiative, the Tribunal may—

    (a)   by summons (or, in Scotland, citation) require any person to attend as a witness at a hearing at the time and place specified in the summons or citation; or

    (b)   order any person to answer any questions or produce any documents in that person's possession or control which relate to any issue in the proceedings.

(2)   A summons or citation under paragraph (1)(a) must—

    (a)   give the person required to attend 14 days' notice of the hearing or such shorter period as the Tribunal may direct; and

    (b)   where the person is not a party, make provision for the person's necessary expenses of attendance to be paid, and state who is to pay them.

(3) No person may be compelled to give any evidence or produce any document that the person could not be compelled to give or produce on a trial of an action in a court of law in the part of the United Kingdom where the proceedings are due to be determined.

(4) A summons, citation or order under this rule must—

    (a) state that the person on whom the requirement is imposed may apply to the Tribunal to vary or set aside the summons, citation or order, if they have not had an opportunity to object to it; and

    (b) state the consequences of failure to comply with the summons, citation or order.

Withdrawal

17(1) Subject to paragraph (2), and, in the case of a withdrawal of a reference from an ethical standards officer, to the provisions of regulation 5 of the Case Tribunals (England) Regulations 2008, a party may give notice of the withdrawal of its case, or any part of it—

    (a) by sending or delivering to the Tribunal a written notice of withdrawal; or

    (b) orally at a hearing.

(2) Notice of withdrawal will not take effect unless the Tribunal consents to the withdrawal.

(3) A party who has withdrawn their case may apply to the Tribunal for the case to be reinstated.

(4) An application under paragraph (3) must be made in writing and be received by the Tribunal within 28 days after—

    (a) the date on which the Tribunal received the notice under paragraph (1)(a); or

    (b) the date of the hearing at which the case was withdrawn orally under paragraph (1)(b).

(5) The Tribunal must notify each party in writing that a withdrawal has taken effect under this rule.

Lead cases

18(1) This rule applies if—

    (a) two or more cases have been started before the Tribunal;

    (b) in each such case the Tribunal has not made a decision disposing of the proceedings; and

    (c) the cases give rise to common or related issues of fact or law.

(2) The Tribunal may give a direction—

    (a) specifying one or more cases falling under paragraph (1) as a lead case or lead cases; and

    (b) staying (or, in Scotland, sisting) the other cases falling under paragraph (1) ("the related cases").

(3) When the Tribunal makes a decision in respect of the common or related issues—

    (a) the Tribunal must send a copy of that decision to each party in each of the related cases; and

    (b) subject to paragraph (4), that decision shall be binding on each of those parties.

(4) Within 28 days after the date on which the Tribunal sent a copy of the decision to a party under paragraph (3)(a), that party may apply in writing for a direction that the decision does not apply to, and is not binding on the parties to, a particular related case.

(5) The Tribunal must give directions in respect of cases which are stayed (or, in Scotland, sisted) under paragraph (2)(b), providing for the disposal of or further directions in those cases.

(6) If the lead case or cases lapse or are withdrawn before the Tribunal makes a decision in respect of the common or related issues, the Tribunal must give directions as to—

    (a) whether another case or other cases are to be specified as a lead case or lead cases; and

    (b) whether any direction affecting the related cases should be set aside or amended.

Entry directions

18A(1) This rule applies to an appeal against a decision of, or notice issued by, the Information Commissioner.

(2) The Tribunal may give a direction ("an entry direction") requiring the occupier of any premises ("the occupier"), including a party, to permit entry to specified persons in order to allow such persons to—

    (a) inspect, examine, operate or test relevant equipment;

    (b) inspect, examine or test relevant materials.

(3) In paragraph (2)—

    "relevant equipment" means equipment on the premises used or intended to be used in connection with the processing of personal data, or the storage, recording or deletion of other information; and

    "relevant materials" means any documents and other materials on the premises connected with the processing of personal data, or the storage, recording or deletion of other information.

(4) A direction under paragraph (2) may not require a person to permit the inspection, examination or testing of any document or other materials which a person could not be compelled to produce in the trial of an action in a court of law in the part of the United Kingdom where the proceedings are due to be determined.

(5) A direction under paragraph (2) must specify the date and time at which the entry is to take place.

(6) The Tribunal must send a copy of the direction to the occupier so that it is received at least 7 days before the date specified for the entry.

Transfer of cases to the Upper Tribunal

19(1) This rule applies to charities cases and proceedings under the Data Protection Act 1998, the Data Protection Act 2018 and the Freedom of Information Act 2000 (including those Acts as applied and modified by the Privacy and Electronic Communications (EC Directive) Regulations 2003 and the Environmental Information Regulations 2004).

(1A) On receiving a notice of appeal in an appeal under section 28 of the Data Protection Act 1998, sections 27, 79 or 111 of the Data Protection Act 2018 or section 60 of the Freedom of Information Act 2000 (including that section as applied and modified by regulation 18 of the Environmental Information Regulations 2004) (appeals in relation to national security certificates) the Tribunal must transfer the case to the Upper Tribunal without taking further action in relation to the appeal.

(2) In any other case, the Tribunal may refer a case or a preliminary issue to the President of

the General Regulatory Chamber of the First-tier Tribunal with a request that the case or issue be considered for transfer to the Upper Tribunal.

(3) If a case or issue has been referred by the Tribunal under paragraph (2), the President of the General Regulatory Chamber may, with the concurrence of the President of the appropriate Chamber of the Upper Tribunal, direct that the case or issue be transferred to and determined by the Upper Tribunal.

Power to stay or sist decision pending an appeal to, or decision by, the Tribunal

19A(1) The Tribunal may suspend the effect of a decision of the Gambling Commission (whether or not the decision has already taken effect) while an appeal against that decision—

(a) could be brought within the time required by these Rules; or

(b) has been brought and has not yet been finally determined or withdrawn.

(2) In an appeal against a decision of the Immigration Services Commissioner, the Tribunal may direct that while the appeal is being dealt with the decision appealed against shall have—

(a) no effect; or

(b) only such limited effect as is specified in the direction.

(3) If the Tribunal makes a direction under paragraph (2), the Tribunal must consider any application by the Immigration Services Commissioner for the cancellation or variation of the direction.

(4) The Tribunal may vary or cancel a direction made under paragraph 9(3) of Schedule 5 to the Immigration and Asylum Act 1999 (interim directions pending the decision of the Tribunal).

Procedure for applying for a stay of a decision pending an appeal

20(1) This rule applies where rule 19A or another enactment provides in any terms for the Tribunal to stay (or, in Scotland, sist) or suspend, or to lift a stay (or, in Scotland, sist) or suspension of, a decision which is or may be the subject of an appeal to the Tribunal ("the substantive decision") pending such appeal, including an enactment which provides for—

(a) an appeal to the Tribunal against a decision not to stay (or, in Scotland, sist) the effect of the substantive decision pending an appeal; or

(b) an application to the Tribunal for an order that the substantive decision shall take effect immediately.

(2) A person who wishes the Tribunal to decide whether the substantive decision should be stayed (or, in Scotland, sisted) or suspended must make a written application to the Tribunal which must include—

(a) the name and address of the person making the application;

(b) the name and address of any representative of that person;

(c) the address to which documents for that person should be sent or delivered;

(d) the name and address of any person who will be a respondent to the appeal;

(e) details of the substantive decision and any decision as to when that decision is to take effect, and copies of any written record of, or reasons for, those decisions; and

(f) the grounds on which the person making the application relies.

(3) In the case of an appeal against a refusal by the registrar to stay (or, in Scotland, sist) a decision to refuse an application for registration as a driving instructor, an application under paragraph (2) must be sent or delivered to the Tribunal so that it is received within

10 days after the date on which the registrar sent notice of the refusal to the person making the application.

(4) If the Tribunal grants a stay (or, in Scotland, sist) or suspension following an application under this rule—

    (a) the Tribunal may give directions as to the conduct of the appeal of the substantive decision; and

    (b) the Tribunal may, where appropriate, grant the stay (or, in Scotland, sist) or suspension subject to conditions.

(5) Unless the Tribunal considers that there is good reason not to do so, the Tribunal must send written notice of any decision made under this rule to each party.

PART 3 – PROCEEDINGS BEFORE THE TRIBUNAL

CHAPTER 1: BEFORE THE HEARING
CASES OTHER THAN CHARITIES CASES OR CERTIFICATION CASES

Application of this Chapter

21 This Chapter applies to cases other than charities cases or certification cases (to which rule 7A applies).

The notice of appeal

22(1) An appellant must start proceedings before the Tribunal by sending or delivering to the Tribunal a notice of appeal so that it is received—

    (a) if a time for providing the notice of appeal is set out in paragraph (6), within that time;

    (b) otherwise, within 28 days of the date on which notice of the act or decision to which the proceedings relate was sent to the appellant.

(1A) The time limit in paragraph (1)(b) does not apply to—

    (a) the laying before the Tribunal by the Immigration Services Commissioner of a disciplinary charge under paragraph 9(1)(e) of Schedule 5 to the Immigration and Asylum Act 1999; or

    (b) an application by the Immigration Services Commissioner for suspension of a person's registration under paragraph 4B(1) of Schedule 6 to that Act.

(2) The notice of appeal must include—

    (a) the name and address of the appellant;

    (b) the name and address of the appellant's representative (if any);

    (c) an address where documents for the appellant may be sent or delivered;

    (d) the name and address of any respondent;

    (e) details of the decision or act, or failure to decide or act, to which the proceedings relate;

    (f) the result the appellant is seeking;

    (g) the grounds on which the appellant relies; and

    (h) any further information or documents required by a practice direction.

(2A) If the proceedings are an application under section 166(2) of the Data Protection Act 2018 (orders to progress complaints), the appellant must provide with the notice of appeal copies of—

     (a)   the complaint made to the Information Commissioner, and

     (b)   any information provided by the Information Commissioner to the appellant about progress on the complaint or of the outcome of the complaint.

(3)   If the proceedings challenge a decision, the appellant must provide with the notice of appeal a copy of any written record of that decision, and any statement of reasons for that decision that the appellant has or can reasonably obtain.

(3A)   If the appeal is brought under section 141 or 337(1) of the Gambling Act 2005, the appellant must provide with the notice of appeal any fee payable to the Tribunal.

(4)   If the appellant provides the notice of appeal to the Tribunal later than the time required by paragraph (1) or by any extension of time under rule 5(3)(a) (power to extend time)—

     (a)   the notice of appeal must include a request for an extension of time and the reason why the notice of appeal was not provided in time; and

     (b)   unless the Tribunal extends time for the notice of appeal under rule 5(3)(a) (power to extend time) the Tribunal must not admit the notice of appeal.

(5)   When the Tribunal receives the notice of appeal, subject to rule 19(1A) (national security appeals), it must send a copy of the notice of appeal and any accompanying documents to each respondent.

(6)   The time for providing the notice of appeal referred to in paragraph (1)(a) is as follows—

     (a)   in an appeal against a refusal or revocation of a licence to give driving instruction, within 14 days of the date on which notice of the decision was sent to the appellant;

     (b)   in an appeal under section 28(4) of the Data Protection Act 1998, sections 27(3), 79(5) or 111(3) of the Data Protection Act 2018 or section 60(1) of the Freedom of Information Act 2000 (including that subsection as applied and modified by regulation 18 of the Environmental Information Regulations 2004), at any time during the currency of the disputed certificate to which it relates;

     (c)   in an appeal under section 28(6) of the Data Protection Act 1998, sections 27(5), 79(7) or 111(5) of the Data Protection Act 2018 or section 60(4) of the Freedom of Information Act 2000 (including that subsection as applied and modified by regulation 18 of the Environmental Information Regulations 2004), within 28 days of the date on which the claim was made that the certificate applies to the information or data in question;

     (cc)   in an appeal under section 57(4) of the Freedom of Information Act 2000 as it applies by reason of regulation 19 of the Re-use of Public Sector Information Regulations 2015, within 28 days of the latest date by which the public sector body is required to comply with section 50(4) of that Act;

     (d)   in the case of a reference from an ethical standards officer made in accordance with sections 63(3)(b) or section 65(4) of the Local Government Act 2000, within 28 days of the completion of the report made in accordance with sections 63(3)(a) and 65(1) of that Act; . . .

     (e)   in the case of a reference from a Standards Committee under the Local Government Act 2000 within 28 days of the meeting which decided to make such a reference; or

     (f)   in the case of an application under section 166(2) of the Data Protection Act 2018 (orders to progress complaints), within 28 days of the expiry of six months from the date on which the Commissioner received the complaint

     (g)   in an appeal against a decision of the REACH Agency, within 90 days of the date on which the appellant was first notified, or otherwise became aware, of the decision;

(h) in an appeal against an agricultural product or foodstuff decision, within 28 days of the date on which the decision was published;

(i) in an appeal against an aromatised wine decision, within 28 days of the date on which the decision was published

(j) in an appeal against a PDO or PGI wine decision, within 28 days of the date on which the decision was published.

The response

23(1) Each respondent must send or deliver to the Tribunal a response to the notice of appeal so that it is received—

(a) in a transport case, within 14 days after the date on which the respondent received the notice of appeal;

(b) otherwise, within 28 days after the date on which the respondent received the notice of appeal.

(2) The response must include—

(a) the name and address of the respondent;

(b) the name and address of the respondent's representative (if any);

(c) an address where documents for the respondent may be sent or delivered;

(d) any further information or documents required by a practice direction or direction; and

(e) whether the respondent would be content for the case to be dealt with without a hearing if the Tribunal considers it appropriate.

(3) The response must include a statement as to whether the respondent opposes the appellant's case and, if so, any grounds for such opposition which are not contained in another document provided with the response.

(4) If the proceedings challenge a decision, the respondent must provide with the response a copy of any written record of that decision, and any statement of reasons for that decision, that the appellant did not provide with the notice of appeal and the respondent has or can reasonably obtain.

(5) If the respondent provides the response to the Tribunal later than the time required by paragraph (1) or by any extension of time under rule 5(3)(a) (power to extend time), the response must include a request for an extension of time and the reason why the response was not provided in time.

(6) In a transport case, the Tribunal must send a copy of the response and any accompanying documents to each other party.

(7) In any other case, the respondent must send or deliver a copy of the response and any accompanying documents to each other party at the same time as it provides the response to the Tribunal.

Appellant's reply

24(1) The appellant may make a written submission and provide further documents in reply to a response.

(2) Any reply and accompanying documents provided under paragraph (1) must be sent or delivered to the Tribunal within 14 days after the date on which the respondent or the Tribunal sent the response to the appellant.

(3) If the appellant provides the reply to the Tribunal later than the time required by paragraph (2) or by any extension of time under rule 5(3)(a) (power to extend time) the reply must include a request for an extension of time and the reason why the reply was not provided in time.

(4) In a transport case, the Tribunal must send a copy of any reply and any accompanying documents to each other party.

(5) In any other case, the appellant must send or deliver a copy of any reply and any accompanying documents to each other party at the same time as it provides the reply to the Tribunal.

CHAPTER 2: BEFORE THE HEARING—CHARITIES CASES

Application of this Chapter
25 This Chapter applies to charities cases.

The notice of appeal
26(1) An appellant must start proceedings before the Tribunal by sending or delivering to the Tribunal a notice of appeal so that it is received—
  (a) if the appellant was the subject of the decision to which the proceedings relate, within 42 days of the date on which notice of the decision was sent to the appellant; or
  (b) if the appellant was not the subject of the decision to which the proceedings relate, within 42 days of the date on which the decision was published.

(2) The notice of appeal must include—
  (a) the name and address of the appellant;
  (b) the name and address of the appellant's representative (if any);
  (c) an address where documents for the appellant may be sent or delivered;
  (d) the basis on which the appellant has standing to start proceedings before the Tribunal;
  (e) the name and address of any respondent;
  (f) details of the decision or act, or failure to decide or act, to which the proceedings relate;
  (g) the result the appellant is seeking;
  (h) the grounds on which the appellant relies; and
  (i) any further information or documents required by a practice direction.

(3) If the proceedings challenge a decision, the appellant must provide with the notice of appeal a copy of any written record of that decision, and any statement of reasons for that decision that the appellant has or can reasonably obtain.

(4) If the notice of appeal relates to a reference under Schedule 1D of the Charities Act 1993—
  (a) if the appellant is the Charity Commission, it must send evidence of the Attorney General's consent to the reference with the notice of appeal; and
  (b) on receiving the notice of appeal the Tribunal must publish details of the reference and information as to how a person likely to be affected by the reference can apply to be added as a party to the proceedings.

(5) If the appellant provides the notice of appeal to the Tribunal later than the time required

by paragraph (1) or by any extension of time under rule 5(3)(a) (power to extend time)—

    (a) the notice of appeal must include a request for an extension of time and the reason why the notice of appeal was not provided in time; and

    (b) unless the Tribunal extends time for the notice of appeal under rule 5(3)(a) (power to extend time) the Tribunal must not admit the notice of appeal.

(6) The appellant must send or deliver a copy of the notice of appeal and any accompanying documents to the respondent at the same time as it provides the notice of appeal to the Tribunal.

The response

27(1) The respondent must send or deliver to the Tribunal a response to the notice of appeal so that it is received within 28 days after the date on which the respondent received the notice of appeal.

(2) The response must include—

    (a) the name and address of the respondent;

    (b) the name and address of the respondent's representative (if any);

    (c) an address where documents for the respondent may be sent or delivered;

    (d) any further information or documents required by a practice direction or direction; and

    (e) whether the respondent would be content for the case to be dealt with without a hearing if the Tribunal considers it appropriate.

(3) The response must include a statement as to whether the respondent opposes the appellant's case and, if so, any grounds for such opposition which are not contained in another document provided with the response.

(4) If the proceedings challenge a decision, the respondent must provide with the response a copy of any written record of that decision, and any statement of reasons for that decision, that the appellant did not provide with the notice of appeal and the respondent has or can reasonably obtain.

(5) If the proceedings challenge a decision, the respondent must provide with the response a list of—

    (a) the documents relied upon by the respondent when reaching the decision; and

    (b) any other documents which the respondent considers could adversely affect its case or support the appellant's case.

(6) If the respondent provides the response to the Tribunal later than the time required by paragraph (1) or by any extension of time under rule 5(3)(a) (power to extend time), the response must include a request for an extension of time and the reason why the response was not provided in time.

(7) The respondent must send or deliver a copy of the response and any accompanying documents to each other party at the same time as it provides the response to the Tribunal.

Appellant's reply

28(1) The appellant may send or deliver to the Tribunal a reply to the respondent's response and any additional documents relied upon by the appellant.

(2) Any reply must be sent or delivered to the Tribunal so that it is received within 28 days

after the date on which the respondent sent the response to the appellant.

(3)   If the appellant provides a reply to the Tribunal later than the time required by paragraph (2) or by any extension of time under rule 5(3)(a) (power to extend time) the reply must include a request for an extension of time and the reason why the reply was not provided in time.

(4)   The appellant may provide with the reply a list of documents on which the appellant relies in support of the appeal or application, and which—

   (a)   the appellant did not provide with the notice of appeal; and

   (b)   the respondent did not include in any list of documents provided under rule 27(5).

(5)   The appellant must send or deliver a copy of any reply and any accompanying documents to each respondent at the same time as it provides the reply to the Tribunal.

Secondary disclosure by the respondent

29(1)   If the appellant provides a reply under rule 28, the respondent must send or deliver to the Tribunal, so that it is received within 14 days after the date on which the respondent received the appellant's reply, a list of any further material which—

   (a)   might reasonably be expected to assist that appellant's case as disclosed by that appellant's reply; and.

   (b)   was not included in a list of documents provided by the respondent with the response.

(2)   If the respondent provides the list to the Tribunal later than the time required by paragraph (1) or by any extension of time under rule 5(3)(a) (power to extend time), the response must include a request for an extension of time and the reason why the response was not provided in time.

(3)   The respondent must send or deliver a copy of the list to each other party at the same time as it provides the response to the Tribunal.

Provision of copy documents

30(1)   If a party has provided a list of documents under rule 27, 28 or 29, that party must within 7 days of receiving a request from another party—

   (a)   provide that other party with a copy of any document specified in the list; or

   (b)   make such document available to that party to read or copy.

Involvement of the Attorney General under section 2D of the Charities Act 1993

31(1)   If the Tribunal directs that all the necessary papers in proceedings be sent to the Attorney General under section 2D(2) and (3) of the Charities Act 1993, the Attorney General must notify the Tribunal whether the Attorney General intends to intervene in the proceedings within 28 days of receiving the papers.

(2)   The Attorney General may at any time notify the Tribunal that the Attorney General intends to intervene in the proceedings on the Attorney General's own initiative.

(3)   If the Tribunal requests that the Attorney General argue a question in relation to the proceedings under section 2D(4)(b) of the Charities Act 1993, the Tribunal must provide to the Attorney General—

   (a)   a statement of the question;

   (b)   an account of the proceedings to date;

   (c)   the reasons the Tribunal considers it necessary to have the question fully argued;

and

(d) copies of the documents the Tribunal considers necessary to enable the Attorney General to decide whether it is appropriate to argue the question.

(4) If the Attorney General notifies the Tribunal that the Attorney General intends to intervene in, or to argue a question in relation to, proceedings under section 2D(4) of the Charities Act 1993, the Tribunal must hold a case management hearing.

CHAPTER 3: HEARINGS

Decision with or without a hearing

32(1) Subject to paragraphs (2) and (3), the Tribunal must hold a hearing before making a decision which disposes of proceedings unless—

(a) each party has consented to the matter being determined without a hearing; and

(b) the Tribunal is satisfied that it can properly determine the issues without a hearing.

(2) This rule does not apply to a decision under Part 4 (correcting, setting aside, reviewing and appealing Tribunal decisions).

(3) The Tribunal may in any event dispose of proceedings without a hearing under rule 8 (striking out a party's case).

(4) Notwithstanding any other provision in these Rules, if the Tribunal holds a hearing to consider a preliminary issue, and following the disposal of that preliminary issue no further issue remains to be determined, the Tribunal may dispose of the proceedings without holding any further hearing.

Entitlement to attend and take part in a hearing

33(1) Subject to rule 35(4) (exclusion of a person from a hearing) each party is entitled to—

(a) attend any hearing that is held; and

(b) send written representations to the Tribunal and each other party prior to the hearing.

(2) The Tribunal may give a direction permitting or requesting any person to—

(a) attend and take part in a hearing to such extent as the Tribunal considers proper; or

(b) make written submissions in relation to a particular issue.

Notice of hearings

34(1) The Tribunal must give each person entitled, permitted or requested to attend a hearing (including any adjourned or postponed hearing) reasonable notice of the time and place of the hearing and any changes to the time and place of the hearing.

(2) The period of notice under paragraph (1) in relation to a hearing to consider disposal of the proceedings must be at least 14 days, except that the Tribunal may give shorter notice—

(a) with the parties' consent; or

(b) in urgent or exceptional circumstances.

Public and private hearings

35(1) Subject to the following paragraphs, all hearings must be held in public.

(2) The Tribunal may give a direction that a hearing, or part of it, is to be held in private.

(3) Where a hearing, or part of it, is to be held in private, the Tribunal may determine who is permitted to attend the hearing or part of it.

(4) The Tribunal may give a direction excluding from any hearing, or part of it—

    (a) any person whose conduct the Tribunal considers is disrupting or is likely to disrupt the hearing;

    (b) any person whose presence the Tribunal considers is likely to prevent another person from giving evidence or making submissions freely;

    (c) any person who the Tribunal considers should be excluded in order to give effect to the requirement at rule 14(10) (prevention of disclosure or publication of documents and information); or

    (d) any person where the purpose of the hearing would be defeated by the attendance of that person.

(5) The Tribunal may give a direction excluding a witness from a hearing until that witness gives evidence.

Hearings in a party's absence

36 If a party fails to attend a hearing the Tribunal may proceed with the hearing if the Tribunal—

    (a) is satisfied that the party has been notified of the hearing or that reasonable steps have been taken to notify the party of the hearing; and

    (b) considers that it is in the interests of justice to proceed with the hearing.

CHAPTER 4: DECISIONS

Consent orders

37(1) The Tribunal may, at the request of the parties but only if it considers it appropriate, make a consent order disposing of the proceedings and making such other appropriate provision as the parties have agreed.

(2) Notwithstanding any other provision of these Rules, the Tribunal need not hold a hearing before making an order under paragraph (1), or provide reasons for the order.

Decisions

38(1) The Tribunal may give a decision orally at a hearing.

(2) Subject to rule 14(10) (prevention of disclosure or publication of documents and information), the Tribunal must provide to each party as soon as reasonably practicable after making a decision which finally disposes of all issues in the proceedings (except a decision under Part 4)—

    (a) a decision notice stating the Tribunal's decision;

    (b) written reasons for the decision; and

    (c) notification of any right of appeal against the decision and the time within which, and manner in which, such right of appeal may be exercised.

(3) The Tribunal may provide written reasons for any decision to which paragraph (2) does not apply.

PART 4 – CORRECTING, SETTING ASIDE, REVIEWING AND APPEALING TRIBUNAL DECISIONS

Interpretation

39 In this Part—

"appeal" means the exercise of a right of appeal on a point of law under section 11 of the 2007 Act; and

"review" means the review of a decision by the Tribunal under section 9 of the 2007 Act.

Clerical mistakes and accidental slips or omissions

40 The Tribunal may at any time correct any clerical mistake or other accidental slip or omission in a decision, direction or any document produced by it, by—

(a) sending notification of the amended decision or direction, or a copy of the amended document, to each party; and

(b) making any necessary amendment to any information published in relation to the decision, direction or document.

Setting aside a decision which disposes of proceedings

41(1) The Tribunal may set aside a decision which disposes of proceedings, or part of such a decision, and re-make the decision or the relevant part of it, if—

(a) the Tribunal considers that it is in the interests of justice to do so; and

(b) one or more of the conditions in paragraph (2) are satisfied.

(2) The conditions are—

(a) a document relating to the proceedings was not sent to, or was not received at an appropriate time by, a party or a party's representative;

(b) a document relating to the proceedings was not sent to the Tribunal at an appropriate time;

(c) a party, or a party's representative, was not present at a hearing related to the proceedings; or

(d) there has been some other procedural irregularity in the proceedings.

(3) A party applying for a decision, or part of a decision, to be set aside under paragraph (1) must make a written application to the Tribunal so that it is received no later than 28 days after the date on which the Tribunal sent notice of the decision to the party.

Application for permission to appeal

42(1) A person seeking permission to appeal must make a written application to the Tribunal for permission to appeal.

(2) An application under paragraph (1) must be sent or delivered to the Tribunal so that it is received no later than 28 days after the latest of the dates that the Tribunal sends to the person making the application—

(a) written reasons for the decision;

(b) notification of amended reasons for, or correction of, the decision following a review; or

(c) notification that an application for the decision to be set aside has been unsuccessful.

(3) The date in paragraph (2)(c) applies only if the application for the decision to be set aside

was made within the time stipulated in rule 41 (setting aside a decision which disposes of proceedings) or any extension of that time granted by the Tribunal.

(4) If the person seeking permission to appeal sends or delivers the application to the Tribunal later than the time required by paragraph (2) or by any extension of time under rule 5(3)(a) (power to extend time)—

    (a) the application must include a request for an extension of time and the reason why the application was not provided in time; and

    (b) unless the Tribunal extends time for the application under rule 5(3)(a) (power to extend time) the Tribunal must not admit the application.

(5) An application under paragraph (1) must—

    (a) identify the decision of the Tribunal to which it relates;

    (b) identify the alleged error or errors of law in the decision; and

    (c) state the result the party making the application is seeking.

Tribunal's consideration of application for permission to appeal

43(1) On receiving an application for permission to appeal the Tribunal must first consider, taking into account the overriding objective in rule 2, whether to review the decision in accordance with rule 44 (review of a decision).

(2) If the Tribunal decides not to review the decision, or reviews the decision and decides to take no action in relation to the decision, or part of it, the Tribunal must consider whether to give permission to appeal in relation to the decision or that part of it.

(3) The Tribunal must send a record of its decision to the parties as soon as practicable.

(4) If the Tribunal refuses permission to appeal it must send with the record of its decision—

    (a) a statement of its reasons for such refusal; and

    (b) notification of the right to make an application to the Upper Tribunal for permission to appeal and the time within which, and the method by which, such application must be made.

(5) The Tribunal may give permission to appeal on limited grounds, but must comply with paragraph (4) in relation to any grounds on which it has refused permission.

Review of a decision

44(1) The Tribunal may only undertake a review of a decision—

    (a) pursuant to rule 43(1) (review on an application for permission to appeal); and

    (b) if it is satisfied that there was an error of law in the decision.

(2) The Tribunal must notify the parties in writing of the outcome of any review, and of any right of appeal in relation to the outcome.

(3) If the Tribunal takes any action in relation to a decision following a review without first giving every party an opportunity to make representations, the notice under paragraph (2) must state that any party that did not have an opportunity to make representations may apply for such action to be set aside and for the decision to be reviewed again.

Power to treat an application as a different type of application

45 The Tribunal may treat an application for a decision to be corrected, set aside or reviewed, or for permission to appeal against a decision, as an application for any other one of those things.

Tribunal Procedure (Upper Tribunal) Rules 2008
(SI 2008/2698)

PART 4 – JUDICIAL REVIEW PROCEEDINGS IN THE UPPER TRIBUNAL

PART 5 – HEARINGS

PART 6 – DECISIONS

PART 7 – CORRECTING, SETTING ASIDE, REVIEWING AND APPEALING DECISIONS OF THE UPPER TRIBUNAL

SCHEDULES

Tribunal Procedure (Upper Tribunal) Rules 2008 (SI 2008/2698)

as amended to 1 February 2020

Made 9th October 2008
Laid before Parliament 15th October 2008
Coming into force 3rd November 2008

After consulting in accordance with paragraph 28(1) of Schedule 5 to, the Tribunals, Courts and Enforcement Act 2007 the Tribunal Procedure Committee has made the following Rules in exercise of the power conferred by sections 10(3), 16(9), 22 and 29(3) and (4) of, and Schedule 5 to, that Act.

The Lord Chancellor has allowed the Rules in accordance with paragraph 28(3) of Schedule 5 to the Tribunals, Courts and Enforcement Act 2007.

PART 1
INTRODUCTION

Citation, commencement, application and interpretation

1(1) These Rules may be cited as the Tribunal Procedure (Upper Tribunal) Rules 2008 and come into force on 3rd November 2008.

(2) These Rules apply to proceedings before the Upper Tribunal except proceedings in the Lands Chamber.

(3) In these Rules—

"the 2007 Act" means the Tribunals, Courts and Enforcement Act 2007;
"appellant" means—

(a) a person who makes an appeal, or applies for permission to appeal, to the Upper Tribunal;

(b) in proceedings transferred or referred to the Upper Tribunal from the First-tier Tribunal, a person who started the proceedings in the First-tier Tribunal; or

(c) a person substituted as an appellant under rule 9(1) (substitution and addition of parties);

"applicant" means—

(a) a person who applies for permission to bring, or does bring, judicial review proceedings before the Upper Tribunal and, in judicial review proceedings transferred to the Upper Tribunal from a court, includes a person who was a claimant or petitioner in the proceedings immediately before they were transferred; or

(b) a person who refers a financial services case or a wholesale energy case to the Upper Tribunal;

"appropriate national authority" means, in relation to an appeal, the Secretary of State, the Scottish Ministers, the Department of the Environment in Northern Ireland or the Welsh Ministers, as the case may be;

"asylum case" means proceedings before the Upper Tribunal on appeal against a decision in proceedings under section 82, 83 or 83A of the Nationality,

Immigration and Asylum Act 2002 in which a person claims that removal from, or a requirement to leave, the United Kingdom would breach the United Kingdom's obligations under the Convention relating to the Status of Refugees done at Geneva on 28 July 1951 and the Protocol to the Convention;

"authorised person" means—

(a) an examiner appointed by the Secretary of State under section 66A of the Road Traffic Act 1988;

(b) an examiner appointed by the Department of the Environment in Northern Ireland under Article 74 of the Road Traffic (Northern Ireland) Order 1995; or

(c) any person authorised in writing by the Department of the Environment in Northern Ireland for the purposes of the Goods Vehicles (Licensing of Operators) Act (Northern Ireland) 2010;

and includes a person acting under the direction of such an examiner or other authorised person, who has detained the vehicle to which an appeal relates;

"disability discrimination in schools case" means proceedings concerning discrimination in the education of a child or young person or related matters;

"dispose of proceedings" includes, unless indicated otherwise, disposing of a part of the proceedings;

"document" means anything in which information is recorded in any form, and an obligation under these Rules or any practice direction or direction to provide or allow access to a document or a copy of a document for any purpose means, unless the Upper Tribunal directs otherwise, an obligation to provide or allow access to such document or copy in a legible form or in a form which can be readily made into a legible form;

"fast-track case" means an asylum case or an immigration case where the person who appealed to the First-tier Tribunal—

(a) was detained under the Immigration Acts at a place specified in rule 2(3) of the Schedule to the Tribunal Procedure (First-tier Tribunal) (Immigration and Asylum Chamber) Rules 2014 when the notice of decision that was the subject of the appeal to the First-tier Tribunal was served on the appellant;

(b) remains so detained; and

(c) the First-tier Tribunal or the Upper Tribunal has not directed that the case cease to be treated as a fast-track case;

"financial sanctions case" means an appeal to the Upper Tribunal under section 147(6) of the Policing and Crime Act 2017;

"financial services case" means a reference to the Upper Tribunal in respect of—

(a) a decision of the Financial Conduct Authority;

(aa) a decision of the Prudential Regulation Authority;

(b) a decision of the Bank of England;

(c) a decision of the Pensions Regulator;

(d) a decision of a person relating to the assessment of any compensation or consideration under the Banking (Special Provisions) Act 2008 or the Banking Act 2009; or

(e) any determination, calculation or dispute which may be referred to the Upper Tribunal under the Financial Services and Markets Act 2000 (Contribution to Costs of Special Resolution Regime) Regulations 2010 (and in these Rules a decision in respect of which a reference has been made to the Upper Tribunal in a financial services case includes any such determination, calculation or, except for the purposes of rule 5(5), dispute relating to the making of payments under the Regulations)

"hearing" means an oral hearing and includes a hearing conducted in whole or in part by video link, telephone or other means of instantaneous twoway electronic communication;

"immigration case" means proceedings before the Upper Tribunal on appeal against a decision in proceedings under section 40A of the British Nationality Act 1981, section 82 of the Nationality, Immigration and Asylum Act 2002, regulation 26 of the Immigration (European Economic Area) Regulations 2006 that are not an asylum case, or the Immigration (Citizens' Rights Appeals) (EU Exit) Regulations 2020;

"immigration judicial review proceedings" means judicial review proceedings which are designated as an immigration matter—

(a) in a direction made in accordance with Part 1 of Schedule 2 to the Constitutional Reform Act 2005 specifying a class of case for the purposes of section 18(6) of the 2007 Act; or

(b) in an order of the High Court in England and Wales made under section 31A(3) of the Senior Courts Act 1981, transferring to the Upper Tribunal an application of a kind described in section 31A(1) of that Act;

"interested party" means—

(a) a person who is directly affected by the outcome sought in judicial review proceedings, and has been named as an interested party under rule 28 or 29 (judicial review), or has been substituted or added as an interested party under rule 9 (addition, substitution and removal of parties);

(b) in judicial review proceedings transferred to the Upper Tribunal under section 25A(2) or (3) of the Judicature (Northern Ireland) Act 1978 or section 31A(2) or (3) of the Senior Courts Act 1981, a person who was an interested party in the proceedings immediately before they were transferred to the Upper Tribunal;

(c) in a financial services case or a wholesale energy case, any person other than the applicant who could have referred the case to the Upper Tribunal and who has been added or substituted as an interested party under rule 9 (addition, substitution and removal of parties);

(d) in a financial sanctions case, any person other than the appellant upon whom the Treasury has imposed a monetary penalty under Part 8 of the Policing and Crime Act 2017 in connection with the same matters as led to the decision that is the subject of the appeal and who has been added or substituted as an interested party under rule 9 (addition, substitution and removal of parties); and

(e) in a trade remedies case, any person other than the appellant who could have appealed to the Upper Tribunal and who has been added or substituted as an interested party under rule 9 (addition, substitution and removal of parties);

"judicial review proceedings" means proceedings within the jurisdiction of the Upper Tribunal pursuant to section 15 or 21 of the 2007 Act, whether such proceedings are started in the Upper Tribunal or transferred to the Upper Tribunal;

"mental health case" means proceedings before the Upper Tribunal on appeal against a decision in proceedings under the Mental Health Act 1983 or paragraph 5(2) of the Schedule to the Repatriation of Prisoners Act 1984;

"national security certificate appeal" means an appeal under section 28 of the Data

Protection Act 1998, sections 27, 79 or 111 of the Data Protection Act 2018 or section 60 of the Freedom of Information Act 2000 (including that section as applied and modified by regulation 18 of the Environmental Information Regulations 2004);

"party" means a person who is an appellant, an applicant, a respondent or an interested party in proceedings before the Upper Tribunal, a person who has referred a question or matter to the Upper Tribunal or, if the proceedings have been concluded, a person who was an appellant, an applicant, a respondent or an interested party when the Upper Tribunal finally disposed of all issues in the proceedings;

"permission" includes leave in cases arising under the law of Northern Ireland;

"practice direction" means a direction given under section 23 of the 2007 Act;

"QCS Board" means a Board constituted under Part 2 of the Transport Act 2000;

"quality contracts scheme" has the meaning provided for in section 124(3) (quality contracts scheme) of the Transport Act 2000;

"quality contracts scheme case" means proceedings in the Upper Tribunal under Part 2 of the Transport Act 2000;

"reference", in a financial services case, includes an appeal;

"relevant minister" means the Minister or designated person responsible for the signing of the certificate to which a national security certificate appeal relates;

"respondent" means—

(a) in an appeal, or application for permission to appeal, against a decision of another tribunal, any person other than the appellant who—

    (i) was a party before that other tribunal;

    (ii) ....

    (iii) otherwise has a right of appeal against the decision of the other tribunal and has given notice to the Upper Tribunal that they wish to be a party to the appeal;

(b) in any other any other application for permission to appeal, or any other appeal except a road transport case, the person who made the decision that has been challenged;

(c) in judicial review proceedings—

    (i) in proceedings started in the Upper Tribunal, the person named by the applicant as the respondent;

    (ii) in proceedings transferred to the Upper Tribunal under section 25A(2) or (3) of the Judicature (Northern Ireland) Act 1978 or section 31A(2) or (3) of the Senior Courts Act 1981, a person who was a defendant in the proceedings immediately before they were transferred;

    (iii) in proceedings transferred to the Upper Tribunal under section 20(1) of the 2007 Act, a person to whom intimation of the petition was made before the proceedings were transferred, or to whom the Upper Tribunal has required intimation to be made;

(ca) in proceedings transferred or referred to the Upper Tribunal from the First-tier Tribunal, a person who was a respondent in the proceedings in the First-tier Tribunal;

(d) in a reference under the Forfeiture Act 1982, the person whose eligibility for a benefit or advantage is in issue;

(da) in a financial services case—

    (i) where the case is a multiple regulator case, both the primary and secondary regulator as defined in Schedule 3 to these rules (but subject to the operation of paragraph 4A(3) of that Schedule);

    (ii) where the case is a single regulator case, the maker of the decision in respect of which a reference has been made; or

  (db) in a wholesale energy case, in relation to Great Britain, the Gas and Electricity Markets Authority or, in relation to Northern Ireland, the Northern Ireland Authority for Utility Regulation; or

  (e) a person substituted or added as a respondent under rule 9 (substitution and addition of parties);

"road transport case" means an appeal against a decision of—

  (a) a traffic commissioner, other than an appeal pursuant to—

    (i) section 6F of the Transport Act 1985, or

    (ii) section 123T of the Transport Act 2000, or

  (b) the Department of the Environment in Northern Ireland;

"special educational needs case" means proceedings concerning the education of a child or young person who has or may have special educational needs, including proceedings relating to—

  (a) an EHC needs assessment within the meaning of section 36(2) of the Children and Families Act 2014;

  (aa) a detained person's EHC needs assessment within the meaning of section 70(5) of the Children and Families Act 2014; or

  (b) an EHC plan within the meaning of section 37(2) of that Act,

of such a child or young person;

"TRA" means the Trade Remedies Authority;

"trade remedies case" means an appeal pursuant to the Trade Remedies (Reconsideration and Appeals) (EU Exit) Regulations 2019 against a decision made by the TRA or a determination of the Secretary of State;

"tribunal" does not include a traffic commissioner;

"wholesale energy case" means a reference to the Upper Tribunal in respect of a decision of—

  (a) in relation to Great Britain, the Gas and Electricity Markets Authority under the Electricity and Gas (Market Integrity and Transparency) (Enforcement etc) Regulations 2013; or

  (b) in relation to Northern Ireland, the Northern Ireland Authority for Utility Regulation under the Electricity and Gas (Market Integrity and Transparency) (Enforcement etc) Regulations (Northern Ireland) 2013;

"working day" means any day except a Saturday or Sunday, Christmas Day, Good Friday or a bank holiday under section 1 of the Banking and Financial Dealings Act 1971;

"young person" means, in relation to a special educational needs case or a disability discrimination in schools case, a person over compulsory school age but under 25.

Overriding objective and parties' obligation to co-operate with the Upper Tribunal

2(1) The overriding objective of these Rules is to enable the Upper Tribunal to deal with cases fairly and justly.

(2) Dealing with a case fairly and justly includes–

  (a) dealing with the case in ways which are proportionate to the importance of the case, the complexity of the issues, the anticipated costs and the resources of the parties;

    (b)   avoiding unnecessary formality and seeking flexibility in the proceedings;

    (c)   ensuring, so far as practicable, that the parties are able to participate fully in the proceedings;

    (d)   using any special expertise of the Upper Tribunal effectively; and

    (e)   avoiding delay, so far as compatible with proper consideration of the issues.

(3)   The Upper Tribunal must seek to give effect to the overriding objective when it–

    (a)   exercises any power under these Rules; or

    (b)   interprets any rule or practice direction.

(4)   Parties must–

    (a)   help the Upper Tribunal to further the overriding objective; and

    (b)   co-operate with the Upper Tribunal generally.

Alternative dispute resolution and arbitration

3(1)   The Upper Tribunal should seek, where appropriate–

    (a)   to bring to the attention of the parties the availability of any appropriate alternative procedure for the resolution of the dispute; and

    (b)   if the parties wish and provided that it is compatible with the overriding objective, to facilitate the use of the procedure.

(2)   Part 1 of the Arbitration Act 1996 does not apply to proceedings before the Upper Tribunal.

PART 2
GENERAL POWERS AND PROVISIONS

Delegation to staff

4(1)   Staff appointed under section 40(1) of the 2007 Act (tribunal staff and services) may, with the approval of the Senior President of Tribunals, carry out functions of a judicial nature permitted or required to be done by the Upper Tribunal.

(2)   The approval referred to at paragraph (1) may apply generally to the carrying out of specified functions by members of staff of a specified description in specified circumstances.

(3)   Within 14 days after the date on which the Upper Tribunal sends notice of a decision made by a member of staff under paragraph (1) to a party, that party may apply in writing to the Upper Tribunal for that decision to be considered afresh by a judge.

Case management powers

5(1)   Subject to the provisions of the 2007 Act and any other enactment, the Upper Tribunal may regulate its own procedure.

(2)   The Upper Tribunal may give a direction in relation to the conduct or disposal of proceedings at any time, including a direction amending, suspending or setting aside an earlier direction.

(3)   In particular, and without restricting the general powers in paragraphs (1) and (2), the Upper Tribunal may—

    (a)   extend or shorten the time for complying with any rule, practice direction or direction;

(b) consolidate or hear together two or more sets of proceedings or parts of proceedings raising common issues, or treat a case as a lead case;

(c) permit or require a party to amend a document;

(d) permit or require a party or another person to provide documents, information, evidence or submissions to the Upper Tribunal or a party;

(e) deal with an issue in the proceedings as a preliminary issue;

(f) hold a hearing to consider any matter, including a case management issue;

(g) decide the form of any hearing;

(h) adjourn or postpone a hearing;

(i) require a party to produce a bundle for a hearing;

(j) stay (or, in Scotland, sist) proceedings;

(k) transfer proceedings to another court or tribunal if that other court or tribunal has jurisdiction in relation to the proceedings and—

   (i) because of a change of circumstances since the proceedings were started, the Upper Tribunal no longer has jurisdiction in relation to the proceedings; or

   (ii) the Upper Tribunal considers that the other court or tribunal is a more appropriate forum for the determination of the case;

(l) suspend the effect of its own decision pending an appeal or review of that decision;

(m) in an appeal, or an application for permission to appeal, against the decision of another tribunal, suspend the effect of that decision pending the determination of the application for permission to appeal, and any appeal;

(n) require any person, body or other tribunal whose decision is the subject of proceedings before the Upper Tribunal to provide reasons for the decision, or other information or documents in relation to the decision or any proceedings before that person, body or tribunal.

(4) The Upper Tribunal may direct that a fast-track case cease to be treated as a fast-track case if—

(a) all the parties consent; or

(b) the Upper Tribunal is satisfied that the appeal or application could not be justly determined if it were treated as a fast-track case

(c) .....

(5) In a financial services case, the Upper Tribunal may direct that the effect of the decision in respect of which the reference has been made is to be suspended pending the determination of the reference, if it is satisfied that to do so would not prejudice—

(a) the interests of any persons (whether consumers, investors or otherwise) intended to be protected by that notice;

(b) the smooth operation or integrity of any market intended to be protected by that notice; or

(c) the stability of the financial system of the United Kingdom.

(5A) In a financial sanctions case, the Upper Tribunal may direct that the payment of a monetary penalty that is the subject of an appeal be suspended pending the determination of the appeal or its withdrawal.

(6) Paragraph (5) does not apply in the case of a reference in respect of a decision of the Pensions Regulator.

(7) In a wholesale energy case, the Upper Tribunal may direct that the effect of the decision in respect of which the reference has been made is to be suspended pending the determination of the reference.

Procedure for applying for and giving directions

6(1) The Upper Tribunal may give a direction on the application of one or more of the parties or on its own initiative.

(2) An application for a direction may be made–
  (a) by sending or delivering a written application to the Upper Tribunal; or
  (b) orally during the course of a hearing.

(3) An application for a direction must include the reason for making that application.

(4) Unless the Upper Tribunal considers that there is good reason not to do so, the Upper Tribunal must send written notice of any direction to every party and to any other person affected by the direction.

(5) If a party or any other person sent notice of the direction under paragraph (4) wishes to challenge a direction which the Upper Tribunal has given, they may do so by applying for another direction which amends, suspends or sets aside the first direction.

Failure to comply with rules etc

7(1) An irregularity resulting from a failure to comply with any requirement in these Rules, a practice direction or a direction, does not of itself render void the proceedings or any step taken in the proceedings.

(2) If a party has failed to comply with a requirement in these Rules, a practice direction or a direction, the Upper Tribunal may take such action as it considers just, which may include–
  (a) waiving the requirement;
  (b) requiring the failure to be remedied;
  (c) exercising its power under rule 8 (striking out a party's case); or
  (d) except in a mental health case, an asylum case or an immigration case, restricting a party's participation in the proceedings.

(3) Paragraph (4) applies where the First-tier Tribunal has referred to the Upper Tribunal a failure by a person to comply with a requirement imposed by the First-tier Tribunal–
  (a) to attend at any place for the purpose of giving evidence;
  (b) otherwise to make themselves available to give evidence;
  (c) to swear an oath in connection with the giving of evidence;
  (d) to give evidence as a witness;
  (e) to produce a document; or
  (f) to facilitate the inspection of a document or any other thing (including any premises).

(4) The Upper Tribunal may exercise its power under section 25 of the 2007 Act (supplementary powers of the Upper Tribunal) in relation to such non-compliance as if the requirement had been imposed by the Upper Tribunal.

Striking out a party's case

8(1A) Except for paragraph (2), this rule does not apply to an asylum case or an immigration case.

(1) The proceedings, or the appropriate part of them, will automatically be struck out—

(a) if the appellant or applicant has failed to comply with a direction that stated that failure by the appellant or applicant to comply with the direction would lead to the striking out of the proceedings or part of them; or

(b) in immigration judicial review proceedings, when a fee has not been paid, as required, in respect of an application under rule 30(4) or upon the grant of permission.

(2) The Upper Tribunal must strike out the whole or a part of the proceedings if the Upper Tribunal—

(a) does not have jurisdiction in relation to the proceedings or that part of them; and

(b) does not exercise its power under rule 5(3)(k)(i) (transfer to another court or tribunal) in relation to the proceedings or that part of them.

(3) The Upper Tribunal may strike out the whole or a part of the proceedings if—

(a) the appellant or applicant has failed to comply with a direction which stated that failure by the appellant or applicant to comply with the direction could lead to the striking out of the proceedings or part of them;

(b) the appellant or applicant has failed to cooperate with the Upper Tribunal to such an extent that the Upper Tribunal cannot deal with the proceedings fairly and justly; or

(c) in proceedings which are not an appeal from the decision of another tribunal or judicial review proceedings, the Upper Tribunal considers there is no reasonable prospect of the appellant's or the applicant's case, or part of it, succeeding.

(4) The Upper Tribunal may not strike out the whole or a part of the proceedings under paragraph (2) or (3)(b) or (c) without first giving the appellant or applicant an opportunity to make representations in relation to the proposed striking out.

(5) If the proceedings have been struck out under paragraph (1) or (3)(a), the appellant or applicant may apply for the proceedings, or part of them, to be reinstated.

(6) An application under paragraph (5) must be made in writing and received by the Upper Tribunal within 1 month after the date on which the Upper Tribunal sent notification of the striking out to the appellant or applicant.

(7) This rule applies to a respondent or an interested party as it applies to an appellant or applicant except that—

(a) a reference to the striking out of the proceedings is to be read as a reference to the barring of the respondent or interested party from taking further part in the proceedings; and

(b) a reference to an application for the reinstatement of proceedings which have been struck out is to be read as a reference to an application for the lifting of the bar on the respondent or interested party taking further part in the proceedings.

(8) If a respondent or an interested party has been barred from taking further part in proceedings under this rule and that bar has not been lifted, the Upper Tribunal need not consider any response or other submission made by that respondent or interested party, and may summarily determine any or all issues against that respondent or interested party.

Addition, substitution and removal of parties

9(1) The Upper Tribunal may give a direction adding, substituting or removing a party as an appellant, a respondent or an interested party.

(2)   If the Upper Tribunal gives a direction under paragraph (1) it may give such consequential directions as it considers appropriate.

(3)   A person who is not a party may apply to the Upper Tribunal to be added or substituted as a party.

(4)   If a person who is entitled to be a party to proceedings by virtue of another enactment applies to be added as a party, and any conditions applicable to that entitlement have been satisfied, the Upper Tribunal must give a direction adding that person as a respondent or, if appropriate, as an appellant.

(5)   In an asylum case, the United Kingdom Representative of the United Nations High Commissioner for Refugees ("the United Kingdom Representative") may give notice to the Upper Tribunal that the United Kingdom Representative wishes to participate in the proceedings.

(6)   If the United Kingdom Representative gives notice under paragraph (5)—
      (i)   the United Kingdom Representative is entitled to participate in any hearing; and
      (ii)   all documents which are required to be sent or delivered to parties must be sent or delivered to the United Kingdom Representative.

Orders for costs

10(1)   The Upper Tribunal may not make an order in respect of costs (or, in Scotland, expenses) in proceedings transferred or referred by, or on appeal from, another tribunal except—
      (aa)   in a national security certificate appeal, to the extent permitted by paragraph (1A);
      (a)   in proceedings transferred by, or on appeal from, the Tax Chamber of the First-tier Tribunal; or
      (b)   to the extent and in the circumstances that the other tribunal had the power to make an order in respect of costs (or, in Scotland, expenses).

(1A)   In a national security certificate appeal—
      (a)   the Upper Tribunal may make an order in respect of costs or expenses in the circumstances described at paragraph (3)(c) and (d);
      (b)   if the appeal is against a certificate, the Upper Tribunal may make an order in respect of costs or expenses against the relevant Minister and in favour of the appellant if the Upper Tribunal allows the appeal and quashes the certificate to any extent or the Minister withdraws the certificate;
      (c)   if the appeal is against the application of a certificate, the Upper Tribunal may make an order in respect of costs or expenses—
             (i)   against the appellant and in favour of any other party if the Upper Tribunal dismisses the appeal to any extent; or
             (ii)   in favour of the appellant and against any other party if the Upper Tribunal allows the appeal to any extent.

(2)   The Upper Tribunal may not make an order in respect of costs or expenses under section 4 of the Forfeiture Act 1982.

(3)   In other proceedings, the Upper Tribunal may not make an order in respect of costs or expenses except—
      (a)   in judicial review proceedings;
      (b)   ....
      (c)   under section 29(4) of the 2007 Act (wasted costs) and costs incurred in applying

for such costs;

   (d) if the Upper Tribunal considers that a party or its representative has acted unreasonably in bringing, defending or conducting the proceedings;

   (e) if, in a financial services case or a wholesale energy case, the Upper Tribunal considers that the decision in respect of which the reference was made was unreasonable; or

   (f) if, in a financial sanctions case, the Upper Tribunal considers that the decision to impose or uphold a monetary penalty in respect of which the appeal was made was unreasonable.

(4) The Upper Tribunal may make an order for costs (or, in Scotland, expenses) on an application or on its own initiative.

(5) A person making an application for an order for costs or expenses must—

   (a) send or deliver a written application to the Upper Tribunal and to the person against whom it is proposed that the order be made; and

   (b) send or deliver with the application a schedule of the costs or expenses claimed sufficient to allow summary assessment of such costs or expenses by the Upper Tribunal.

(6) An application for an order for costs or expenses may be made at any time during the proceedings but may not be made later than 1 month after the date on which the Upper Tribunal sends—

   (a) a decision notice recording the decision which finally disposes of all issues in the proceedings; or

   (b) notice under rule 17(5) that a withdrawal which ends the proceedings has taken effect.

(7) The Upper Tribunal may not make an order for costs or expenses against a person (the "paying person") without first—

   (a) giving that person an opportunity to make representations; and

   (b) if the paying person is an individual and the order is to be made under paragraph (3)(a), (b) or (d), considering that person's financial means.

(8) The amount of costs or expenses to be paid under an order under this rule may be ascertained by—

(a) summary assessment by the Upper Tribunal;

   (b) agreement of a specified sum by the paying person and the person entitled to receive the costs or expenses ("the receiving person"); or

   (c) assessment of the whole or a specified part of the costs or expenses, including the costs or expenses of the assessment, incurred by the receiving person, if not agreed.

(9) Following an order for assessment under paragraph (8)(c), the paying person or the receiving person may apply—

   (a) in England and Wales, to the High Court or the Costs Office of the Supreme Court (as specified in the order) for a detailed assessment of the costs on the standard basis or, if specified in the order, on the indemnity basis; and the Civil Procedure Rules 1998 shall apply, with necessary modifications, to that application and assessment as if the proceedings in the tribunal had been proceedings in a court to which the Civil Procedure Rules 1998 apply;

   (b) in Scotland, to the Auditor of the Court of Session for the taxation of the expenses according to the fees payable in that court; or

> (c)   in Northern Ireland, to the Taxing Office of the High Court of Northern Ireland for taxation on the standard basis or, if specified in the order, on the indemnity basis.

(10)   Upon making an order for the assessment of costs, the Upper Tribunal may order an amount to be paid on account before the costs or expenses are assessed.

Representatives

11(1)   Subject to paragraph (5A), a party may appoint a representative (whether a legal representative or not) to represent that party in the proceedings save that a party in an asylum or immigration case may not be represented by any person prohibited from representing by section 84 of the Immigration and Asylum Act 1999.

(2)   If a party appoints a representative, that party (or the representative if the representative is a legal representative) must send or deliver to the Upper Tribunal written notice of the representative's name and address.

(2A)   If the Upper Tribunal receives notice that a party has appointed a representative under paragraph (2), it must send a copy of that notice to each other party.

(3)   Anything permitted or required to be done by a party under these Rules, a practice direction or a direction may be done by the representative of that party, except signing a witness statement.

(4)   A person who receives due notice of the appointment of a representative—
> (a)   must provide to the representative any document which is required to be provided to the represented party, and need not provide that document to the represented party; and
> (b)   may assume that the representative is and remains authorised as such until they receive written notification that this is not so from the representative or the represented party.

(5)   Subject to paragraph (5B), at a hearing a party may be accompanied by another person whose name and address has not been notified under paragraph (2) but who, subject to paragraph (8) and with the permission of the Upper Tribunal, may act as a representative or otherwise assist in presenting the party's case at the hearing.

(5A)   In immigration judicial review proceedings, a party may appoint as a representative only a person authorised under the Legal Services Act 2007 to undertake the conduct of litigation in the High Court.

(5B)   At a hearing of immigration judicial review proceedings, rights of audience before the Upper Tribunal are restricted to persons authorised to exercise those rights in the High Court under the Legal Services Act 2007.

(6)   Paragraphs (2) to (4) do not apply to a person who accompanies a party under paragraph (5).

(7)   In a mental health case if the patient has not appointed a representative the Upper Tribunal may appoint a legal representative for the patient where—
> (a)   the patient has stated that they do not wish to conduct their own case or that they wish to be represented; or
> (b)   the patient lacks the capacity to appoint a representative but the Upper Tribunal believes that it is in the patient's best interests for the patient to be represented.

(8) In a mental health case a party may not appoint as a representative, or be represented or assisted at a hearing by—

    (a) a person liable to be detained or subject to guardianship or aftercare under supervision, or who is a community patient, under the Mental Health Act 1983; or

    (b) a person receiving treatment for mental disorder at the same hospital home as the patient.

(9) In this rule "legal representative" means a person who, for the purposes of the Legal Services Act 2007, is an authorised person in relation to an activity which constitutes the exercise of a right of audience or the conduct of litigation within the meaning of that Act, a qualified person as defined in section 84(2) of the Immigration and Asylum Act 1999, an advocate or solicitor in Scotland or a barrister or solicitor in Northern Ireland.

(10) In an asylum case or an immigration case, an appellant's representative before the First-tier Tribunal will be treated as that party's representative before the Upper Tribunal, unless the Upper Tribunal receives notice—

    (a) of a new representative under paragraph (2) of this rule; or

    (b) from the appellant stating that they are no longer represented.

Calculating time

12(1) An act required by these Rules, a practice direction or a direction to be done on or by a particular day must be done by 5pm on that day.

(2) If the time specified by these Rules, a practice direction or a direction for doing any act ends on a day other than a working day, the act is done in time if it is done on the next working day.

(3) In a special educational needs case or a disability discrimination in schools case, the following days must not be counted when calculating the time by which an act must be done—

    (a) 25th December to 1st January inclusive; and

    (b) any day in August.

(3A) In an asylum case or an immigration case, when calculating the time by which an act must be done, in addition to the days specified in the definition of "working days" in rule 1 (interpretation), the following days must also not be counted as working days—

    (a) 27th to 31st December inclusive

    (b) .....

(4) Paragraph (3) or (3A) does not apply where the Upper Tribunal directs that an act must be done by or on a specified date.

(5) ....

Sending and delivery of documents

13(1) Any document to be provided to the Upper Tribunal under these Rules, a practice direction or a direction must be—

    (a) sent by prepaid post or by document exchange, or delivered by hand, to the address specified for the proceedings;

    (b) sent by fax to the number specified for the proceedings; or

    (c) sent or delivered by such other method as the Upper Tribunal may permit or direct.

(2) Subject to paragraph (3), if a party provides a fax number, email address or other details for the electronic transmission of documents to them, that party must accept delivery of documents by that method.

(3) If a party informs the Upper Tribunal and all other parties that a particular form of communication, other than prepaid post or delivery by hand, should not be used to provide documents to that party, that form of communication must not be so used.

(4) If the Upper Tribunal or a party sends a document to a party or the Upper Tribunal by email or any other electronic means of communication, the recipient may request that the sender provide a hard copy of the document to the recipient. The recipient must make such a request as soon as reasonably practicable after receiving the document electronically.

(5) The Upper Tribunal and each party may assume that the address provided by a party or its representative is and remains the address to which documents should be sent or delivered until receiving written notification to the contrary.

(6) Subject to paragraph (7), if a document submitted to the Upper Tribunal is not written in English, it must be accompanied by an English translation.

(7) In proceedings that are in Wales or have a connection with Wales, a document or translation may be submitted to the Upper Tribunal in Welsh.

Use of documents and information

14(1) The Upper Tribunal may make an order prohibiting the disclosure or publication of—
    (a) specified documents or information relating to the proceedings; or
    (b) any matter likely to lead members of the public to identify any person whom the Upper Tribunal considers should not be identified.

(2) The Upper Tribunal may give a direction prohibiting the disclosure of a document or information to a person if—
    (a) the Upper Tribunal is satisfied that such disclosure would be likely to cause that person or some other person serious harm; and
    (b) the Upper Tribunal is satisfied, having regard to the interests of justice, that it is proportionate to give such a direction.

(3) If a party ("the first party") considers that the Upper Tribunal should give a direction under paragraph (2) prohibiting the disclosure of a document or information to another party ("the second party"), the first party must—
    (a) exclude the relevant document or information from any documents that will be provided to the second party; and
    (b) provide to the Upper Tribunal the excluded document or information, and the reason for its exclusion, so that the Upper Tribunal may decide whether the document or information should be disclosed to the second party or should be the subject of a direction under paragraph (2).

(4) ....

(5) If the Upper Tribunal gives a direction under paragraph (2) which prevents disclosure to a party who has appointed a representative, the Upper Tribunal may give a direction that the documents or information be disclosed to that representative if the Upper Tribunal

is satisfied that—
  (a) disclosure to the representative would be in the interests of the party; and
  (b) the representative will act in accordance with paragraph (6).

(6) Documents or information disclosed to a representative in accordance with a direction under paragraph (5) must not be disclosed either directly or indirectly to any other person without the Upper Tribunal's consent.

(7) Unless the Upper Tribunal gives a direction to the contrary, information about mental health cases and the names of any persons concerned in such cases must not be made public.

(8) The Upper Tribunal may, on its own initiative or on the application of a party, give a direction that certain documents or information must or may be disclosed to the Upper Tribunal on the basis that the Upper Tribunal will not disclose such documents or information to other persons, or specified other persons.

(8A) In a trade remedies case, the Upper Tribunal may give a direction under paragraph (8) if the Upper Tribunal is satisfied that—
  (a) where such documents or information have been supplied to the TRA, the TRA is treating such documents or information as confidential in accordance with—
     (i) regulation 45 of the Trade Remedies (Dumping and Subsidisation) (EU Exit) Regulations 2019;
     (ii) regulation 16 of the Trade Remedies (Increase in Imports Causing Serious Injury to UK Producers) (EU Exit) Regulations 2019; or
     (iii) regulation 5 of the Trade Remedies (Reconsideration and Appeals) (EU Exit) Regulations 2019; or
  (b) where such documents or information have not been supplied to the TRA, if such documents or information were to be supplied to the TRA in accordance with regulation 5 of the Trade Remedies (Reconsideration and Appeals) (EU Exit) Regulations 2019, the TRA would be entitled to treat such documents or information as confidential in accordance with that regulation,
  and the Upper Tribunal is not precluded from considering such documents or information in making its decision in the case.

(9) A party making an application for a direction under paragraph (8) may withhold the relevant documents or information from other parties until the Upper Tribunal has granted or refused the application.

(10) In a case involving matters relating to national security, the Upper Tribunal must ensure that information is not disclosed contrary to the interests of national security.

(11) The Upper Tribunal must conduct proceedings and record its decision and reasons appropriately so as not to undermine the effect of an order made under paragraph (1), a direction given under paragraph (2) or (8) or the duty imposed by paragraph (10).

Evidence and submissions

15(1) Without restriction on the general powers in rule 5(1) and (2) (case management powers), the Upper Tribunal may give directions as to—
  (a) issues on which it requires evidence or submissions;
  (b) the nature of the evidence or submissions it requires;
  (c) whether the parties are permitted or required to provide expert evidence, and if so whether the parties must jointly appoint a single expert to provide such evidence;

    (d) any limit on the number of witnesses whose evidence a party may put forward, whether in relation to a particular issue or generally;

    (e) the manner in which any evidence or submissions are to be provided, which may include a direction for them to be given—

        (i) orally at a hearing; or

       (ii) by written submissions or witness statement; and

    (f) the time at which any evidence or submissions are to be provided.

(2)   The Upper Tribunal may—

    (a) admit evidence whether or not—

        (i) the evidence would be admissible in a civil trial in the United Kingdom; or

       (ii) the evidence was available to a previous decision maker; or

    (b) exclude evidence that would otherwise be admissible where—

        (i) the evidence was not provided within the time allowed by a direction or a practice direction;

       (ii) the evidence was otherwise provided in a manner that did not comply with a direction or a practice direction; or

      (iii) it would otherwise be unfair to admit the evidence.

(2A) In an asylum case or an immigration case—

    (a) if a party wishes the Upper Tribunal to consider evidence that was not before the First-tier Tribunal, that party must send or deliver a notice to the Upper Tribunal and any other party—

        (i) indicating the nature of the evidence; and

       (ii) explaining why it was not submitted to the First-tier Tribunal; and

    (b) when considering whether to admit evidence that was not before the First-tier Tribunal, the Upper Tribunal must have regard to whether there has been unreasonable delay in producing that evidence.

(3)   The Upper Tribunal may consent to a witness giving, or require any witness to give, evidence on oath, and may administer an oath for that purpose.

Summoning or citation of witnesses and orders to answer questions or produce documents

16(1) On the application of a party or on its own initiative, the Upper Tribunal may—

    (a) by summons (or, in Scotland, citation) require any person to attend as a witness at a hearing at the time and place specified in the summons or citation; or

    (b) order any person to answer any questions or produce any documents in that person's possession or control which relate to any issue in the proceedings.

(2)   A summons or citation under paragraph (1)(a) must—

    (a) give the person required to attend 14 days' notice of the hearing or such shorter period as the Upper Tribunal may direct; and

    (b) where the person is not a party, make provision for the person's necessary expenses of attendance to be paid, and state who is to pay them.

(3)   No person may be compelled to give any evidence or produce any document that the person could not be compelled to give or produce on a trial of an action in a court of law in the part of the United Kingdom where the proceedings are due to be determined.

(4)   A person who receives a summons, citation or order may apply to the Upper Tribunal for it to be varied or set aside if they did not have an opportunity to object to it before it was

made or issued.

(5) A person making an application under paragraph (4) must do so as soon as reasonably practicable after receiving notice of the summons, citation or order.

(6) A summons, citation or order under this rule must—
  (a) state that the person on whom the requirement is imposed may apply to the Upper Tribunal to vary or set aside the summons, citation or order, if they did not have an opportunity to object to it before it was made or issued; and
  (b) state the consequences of failure to comply with the summons, citation or order.

Withdrawal

17(1) Subject to paragraph (2), a party may give notice of the withdrawal of its case, or any part of it—
  (a) by sending or delivering to the Upper Tribunal a written notice of withdrawal; or
  (b) orally at a hearing.

(2) Notice of withdrawal will not take effect unless the Upper Tribunal consents to the withdrawal except in relation to an application for permission to appeal.

(3) A party which has withdrawn its case may apply to the Upper Tribunal for the case to be reinstated.

(4) An application under paragraph (3) must be made in writing and be received by the Upper Tribunal within 1 month after—
  (a) the date on which the Upper Tribunal received the notice under paragraph (1)(a); or
  (b) the date of the hearing at which the case was withdrawn orally under paragraph (1)(b).

(5) The Upper Tribunal must notify each party in writing that a withdrawal has taken effect under this rule.

(6) Paragraph (3) does not apply to a financial services case other than a reference against a penalty.

Appeal treated as abandoned or finally determined in an asylum case or an immigration case

17A(1) A party to an asylum case or an immigration case before the Upper Tribunal must notify the Upper Tribunal if they are aware that—
  (a) the appellant has left the United Kingdom;
  (b) the appellant has been granted leave to enter or remain in the United Kingdom;
  (c) a deportation order has been made against the appellant; or
  (d) a document listed in paragraph 4(2) of Schedule 2 to the Immigration (European Economic Area) Regulations 2006 has been issued to the appellant.

(1A) A party to an appeal under the Immigration (Citizens' Rights Appeals) (EU Exit) Regulations 2020 ("the 2020 Regulations") before the Upper Tribunal must also notify the Upper Tribunal if they are aware that the appeal is to be treated as abandoned under regulation 13(3) of those Regulations.

(2) Where an appeal is treated as abandoned pursuant to section 104(4) or (4A) of the Nationality, Immigration and Asylum Act 2002 or paragraph 4(2) of Schedule 2 to the Immigration (European Economic Area) Regulations 2006 or regulation 13(3) of the 2020

Regulations, or as finally determined pursuant to section 104(5) of the Nationality, Immigration and Asylum Act 2002, the Upper Tribunal must send the parties a notice informing them that the appeal is being treated as abandoned or finally determined.

(3) Where an appeal would otherwise fall to be treated as abandoned pursuant to section 104(4A) of the Nationality, Immigration and Asylum Act 2002 or regulation 13(3) of the 2020 Regulations, but the appellant wishes to pursue their appeal, the appellant must send or deliver a notice, which must comply with any relevant practice directions, to the Upper Tribunal and the respondent so that it is received within thirty days of the date on which the notice of the grant of leave to enter or remain in the United Kingdom was sent to the appellant.

(4) Where a notice of grant of leave to enter or remain is sent electronically or delivered personally, the time limit in paragraph (3) is twenty eight days.

(5) Notwithstanding rule 5(3)(a) (case management powers) and rule 7(2) (failure to comply with rules etc), the Upper Tribunal must not extend the time limits in paragraph (3) and (4).

Notice of funding of legal services

18 If a party is granted funding of legal services at any time, that party must as soon as practicable—

    (a)
        (i) if civil legal services (within the meaning of section 8 of the Legal Aid, Sentencing and Punishment of Offenders Act 2012) are provided under arrangements made for the purposes of Part 1 of that Act or by the Northern Ireland Legal Services Commission, send a copy of the certificate or funding notice to the Upper Tribunal; or
        (ii) if funding is granted by the Scottish Legal Aid Board, send a copy of the legal aid certificate to the Upper Tribunal; and

    (b) notify every other party in writing that funding has been granted.

Confidentiality in social security and child support cases

19(1) Paragraph (4) applies to an appeal against a decision of the First-tier Tribunal—

    (a) in proceedings under the Child Support Act 1991 in the circumstances described in paragraph (2), other than an appeal against a reduced benefit decision (as defined in section 46(10)(b) of the Child Support Act 1991, as that section had effect prior to the commencement of section 15(b) of the Child Maintenance and Other Payments Act 2008); or

    (b) in proceedings where the parties to the appeal include former joint claimants who are no longer living together in the circumstances described in paragraph (3).

(2) The circumstances referred to in paragraph (1)(a) are that—

    (a) in the proceedings in the First-tier Tribunal in respect of which the appeal has been brought, there was an obligation to keep a person's address confidential; or

    (b) an absent parent, nonresident parent or person with care would like their address or the address of the child to be kept confidential and has given notice to that effect to the Upper Tribunal—
        (i) in an application for permission to appeal or notice of appeal;
        (ii) within 1 month after an enquiry by the Upper Tribunal; or
        (iii) when notifying any subsequent change of address after proceedings have been

started.

(3) The circumstances referred to in paragraph (1)(b) are that—

    (a) in the proceedings in the First-tier Tribunal in respect of which the appeal has been brought, there was an obligation to keep a person's address confidential; or

    (b) one of the former joint claimants would like their address to be kept confidential and has given notice to that effect to the Upper Tribunal—

        (i) in an application for permission to appeal or notice of appeal;

        (ii) within 1 month after an enquiry by the Upper Tribunal; or

        (iii) when notifying any subsequent change of address after proceedings have been started.

(4) Where this paragraph applies, the Secretary of State or other decision maker and the Upper Tribunal must take appropriate steps to secure the confidentiality of the address and of any information which could reasonably be expected to enable a person to identify the address, to the extent that the address or that information is not already known to each other party.

(5) In this rule—

    "absent parent", "nonresident parent" and "person with care" have the meanings set out in section 3 of the Child Support Act 1991;

    "joint claimants" means the persons who made a joint claim for a jobseeker's allowance under the Jobseekers Act 1995, a tax credit under the Tax Credits Act 2002 or in relation to whom an award of universal credit is made under Part 1 of the Welfare Reform Act 2012.

Power to pay expenses and allowances

20(1) In proceedings brought under section 4 of the Safeguarding Vulnerable Groups Act 2006, the Secretary of State may pay such allowances for the purpose of or in connection with the attendance of persons at hearings as the Secretary of State may, with the consent of the Treasury, determine.

(2) Paragraph (3) applies to proceedings on appeal from a decision of—

    (a) the First-tier Tribunal in proceedings under the Child Support Act 1991, section 12 of the Social Security Act 1998 or paragraph 6 of Schedule 7 to the Child Support, Pensions and Social Security Act 2000;

    (b) the First-tier Tribunal in a war pensions and armed forces case (as defined in the Tribunal Procedure (First-tier Tribunal) (War Pensions and Armed Forces Compensation Chamber) Rules 2008); or

    (c) a Pensions Appeal Tribunal for Scotland or Northern Ireland.

(3) The Lord Chancellor (or, in Scotland, the Secretary of State) may pay to any person who attends any hearing such travelling and other allowances, including compensation for loss of remunerative time, as the Lord Chancellor (or, in Scotland, the Secretary of State) may determine.

Procedure for applying for a stay of a decision pending an appeal

20A(1) This rule applies where another enactment provides in any terms for the Upper Tribunal to stay or suspend, or to lift a stay or suspension of, a decision which is or may be the subject of an appeal to the Upper Tribunal ("the substantive decision") pending such appeal.

(2) A person who wishes the Upper Tribunal to decide whether the substantive decision

should be stayed or suspended must make a written application to the Upper Tribunal which must include—

  (a) the name and address of the person making the application;
  (b) the name and address of any representative of that person;
  (c) the address to which documents for that person should be sent or delivered;
  (d) the name and address of any person who will be a respondent to the appeal;
  (e) details of the substantive decision and any decision as to when that decision is to take effect, and copies of any written record of, or reasons for, those decisions; and
  (f) the grounds on which the person making the application relies.

(3) In the case of an application under paragraph (2) in a road transport case—

  (a) the person making the application must notify the decision maker when making the application;
  (b) within 7 days of receiving notification of the application the decision maker must send or deliver written reasons for refusing or withdrawing the stay—
      (i) to the Upper Tribunal; and
      (ii) to the person making the application, if the decision maker has not already done so.

(4) If the Upper Tribunal grants a stay or suspension following an application under this rule—

  (a) the Upper Tribunal may give directions as to the conduct of the appeal of the substantive decision; and
  (b) the Upper Tribunal may, where appropriate, grant the stay or suspension subject to conditions.

(5) Unless the Upper Tribunal considers that there is good reason not to do so, the Upper Tribunal must send written notice of any decision made under this rule to each party.

PART 3
PROCEDURE FOR CASES IN THE UPPER TRIBUNAL

Application to the Upper Tribunal for permission to appeal

21(1) ....

(2) A person may apply to the Upper Tribunal for permission to appeal to the Upper Tribunal against a decision of another tribunal only if—

  (a) they have made an application for permission to appeal to the tribunal which made the decision challenged; and
  (b) that application has been refused or has not been admitted or has been granted only on limited grounds.

(3) An application for permission to appeal must be made in writing and received by the Upper Tribunal no later than—

  (a) in the case of an application under section 4 of the Safeguarding Vulnerable Groups Act 2006, 3 months after the date on which written notice of the decision being challenged was sent to the appellant;
  (aa) in an asylum case or an immigration case where the appellant is in the United Kingdom at the time that the application is made—
      (i) 14 days after the date on which notice of the First-tier Tribunal's refusal of permission was sent to the appellant; or

(ii) if the case is a fast-track case, four working days after the date on which notice of the First-tier Tribunal's refusal of permission was sent to the appellant;

(ab) ....

(b) otherwise, a month after the date on which the tribunal that made the decision under challenge sent notice of its refusal of permission to appeal, or refusal to admit the application for permission to appeal, to the appellant.

(3A) ....

(4) The application must state—

(a) the name and address of the appellant;

(b) the name and address of the representative (if any) of the appellant;

(c) an address where documents for the appellant may be sent or delivered;

(d) details (including the full reference) of the decision challenged;

(e) the grounds on which the appellant relies; and

(f) whether the appellant wants the application to be dealt with at a hearing.

(5) The appellant must provide with the application a copy of—

(a) any written record of the decision being challenged;

(b) any separate written statement of reasons for that decision; and

(c) if the application is for permission to appeal against a decision of another tribunal, the notice of refusal of permission to appeal, or notice of refusal to admit the application for permission to appeal, from that other tribunal.

(6) If the appellant provides the application to the Upper Tribunal later than the time required by paragraph (3) or by an extension of time allowed under rule 5(3)(a) (power to extend time)—

(a) the application must include a request for an extension of time and the reason why the application was not provided in time; and

(b) unless the Upper Tribunal extends time for the application under rule 5(3)(a) (power to extend time) the Upper Tribunal must not admit the application.

(7) If the appellant makes an application to the Upper Tribunal for permission to appeal against the decision of another tribunal, and that other tribunal refused to admit the appellant's application for permission to appeal because the application for permission or for a written statement of reasons was not made in time—

(a) the application to the Upper Tribunal for permission to appeal must include the reason why the application to the other tribunal for permission to appeal or for a written statement of reasons, as the case may be, was not made in time; and

(b) the Upper Tribunal must only admit the application if the Upper Tribunal considers that it is in the interests of justice for it to do so.

(8) In this rule, a reference to notice of a refusal of permission to appeal is to be taken to include a reference to notice of a grant of permission to appeal on limited grounds.

Decision in relation to permission to appeal

22(1) Except where rule 22A (special procedure for providing notice of a refusal of permission to appeal in an asylum case) applies, if the Upper Tribunal refuses permission to appeal or refuses to admit a late application for permission, it must send written notice of the refusal and of the reasons for the refusal to the appellant.

(2) If the Upper Tribunal gives permission to appeal—

(a) the Upper Tribunal must send written notice of the permission, and of the reasons for any limitations or conditions on such permission, to each party;

(b) subject to any direction by the Upper Tribunal, the application for permission to appeal stands as the notice of appeal and the Upper Tribunal must send to each respondent a copy of the application for permission to appeal and any documents provided with it by the appellant; and

(c) the Upper Tribunal may, with the consent of the appellant and each respondent, determine the appeal without obtaining any further response.

(3) Paragraph (4) applies where the Upper Tribunal, without a hearing, determines an application for permission to appeal—

(a) against a decision of—

(i) the Tax Chamber of the First-tier Tribunal;

(ii) the Health, Education and Social Care Chamber of the First-tier Tribunal;

(iia) the General Regulatory Chamber of the First-tier Tribunal;

(iib) ....

(iii) the Mental Health Review Tribunal for Wales; or

(iv) the Special Educational Needs Tribunal for Wales; or

(b) under section 4 of the Safeguarding Vulnerable Groups Act 2006.

(4) In the circumstances set out at paragraph (3) the appellant may apply for the decision to be reconsidered at a hearing if the Upper Tribunal—

(a) refuses permission to appeal or refuses to admit a late application for permission; or

(b) gives permission to appeal on limited grounds or subject to conditions.

(5) An application under paragraph (4) must be made in writing and received by the Upper Tribunal within 14 days after the date on which the Upper Tribunal sent written notice of its decision regarding the application to the appellant.

Special procedure for providing notice of a refusal of permission to appeal in an asylum case

22A(1) This rule applies to a decision in an asylum case to refuse permission to appeal or to refuse to admit a late application for permission to appeal, where—

(a) the appellant is not the Secretary of State;

(b) at the time the application is made the appellant is in the United Kingdom; and

(c) the decision is not made in a fast-track case.

(2) The Upper Tribunal must provide written notice of the refusal and of the reasons for the refusal ("the notice") to the Secretary of State as soon as reasonably practicable.

(3) The Secretary of State must—

(a) send the notice to the appellant not later than 30 days after the Upper Tribunal provided it to the Secretary of State; and

(b) as soon as practicable after doing so, inform the Upper Tribunal of the date on which, and the means by which, it was sent.

(4) If the Secretary of State does not give the Upper Tribunal the information required by paragraph (3)(b) within 31 days after the notice was provided to the Secretary of State, the Upper Tribunal must send the notice to the appellant as soon as reasonably practicable.

Notice of appeal

23(1) This rule applies—

    (a) to proceedings on appeal to the Upper Tribunal for which permission to appeal is not required, except proceedings to which rule 26A, 26B or 26C applies;

    (b) if another tribunal has given permission for a party to appeal to the Upper Tribunal; or

    (c) subject to any other direction by the Upper Tribunal, if the Upper Tribunal has given permission to appeal and has given a direction that the application for permission to appeal does not stand as the notice of appeal.

(1A) In an asylum case or an immigration case in which the First-tier Tribunal has given permission to appeal, subject to any direction of the First-tier Tribunal or the Upper Tribunal, the application for permission to appeal sent or delivered to the First-tier Tribunal stands as the notice of appeal and accordingly paragraphs (2) to (6) of this rule do not apply.

(2) The appellant must provide a notice of appeal to the Upper Tribunal so that it is received within 1 month after—

    (a) the date that the tribunal that gave permission to appeal sent notice of such permission to the appellant; or

    (b) if permission to appeal is not required, the date on which notice of decision to which the appeal relates—

        (i) was sent to the appellant;

        (ii) in a quality contracts scheme case, if the notice was not sent to the appellant, the date on which the notice was published in a newspaper in accordance with the requirement of section 125 (notice and consultation requirements) of the Transport Act 2000, or

        (iii) in a trade remedies case—

            (aa)   where the appeal is against a decision made by the TRA and notice is required to be published in accordance with the Trade Remedies (Reconsideration and Appeals) (EU Exit) Regulations 2019, the date of such publication or (if later) when the notice comes into effect;

            (bb)   where the appeal is against a decision made by the TRA and no notice is required to be published in accordance with the Trade Remedies (Reconsideration and Appeals) (EU Exit) Regulations 2019, the date on which the appellant is notified of the decision, or

            (cc)   where the appeal is against a determination of the Secretary of State under the Taxation (Crossborder Trade) Act 2018, the Trade Remedies (Dumping and Subsidisation) (EU Exit) Regulations 2019, the Trade Remedies (Increase in Imports Causing Serious Injury to UK Producers) (EU Exit) Regulations 2019 or the Trade Remedies (Reconsideration and Appeals) (EU Exit) Regulations 2019 (as the case may be), the date on which the notice is published in accordance with the relevant provision or (if later) when the notice comes into effect.

(3) The notice of appeal must include the information listed in rule 21(4)(a) to (e) (content of the application for permission to appeal) and, where the Upper Tribunal has given permission to appeal, the Upper Tribunal's case reference.

(4) If another tribunal has granted permission to appeal, the appellant must provide with the

notice of appeal a copy of—

    (a) any written record of the decision being challenged;

    (b) any separate written statement of reasons for that decision; and

    (c) the notice of permission to appeal.

(5) If the appellant provides the notice of appeal to the Upper Tribunal later than the time required by paragraph (2) or by an extension of time allowed under rule 5(3)(a) (power to extend time)—

    (a) the notice of appeal must include a request for an extension of time and the reason why the notice was not provided in time; and

    (b) unless the Upper Tribunal extends time for the notice of appeal under rule 5(3)(a) (power to extend time) the Upper Tribunal must not admit the notice of appeal.

(6) When the Upper Tribunal receives the notice of appeal it must send a copy of the notice and any accompanying documents—

    (a) to each respondent;

    (b) in a road transport case, to—

        (i) the decision maker;

        (ii) the appropriate national authority; and

        (iii) in a case relating to the detention of a vehicle, the authorised person; or

    (c) in an appeal against a decision of a traffic commissioner pursuant to section 6F of the Transport Act 1985 or section 123T of the Transport Act 2000, to—

        (i) the respondent, and

        (ii) the traffic commissioner who was the decision maker.

(6A) In a case to which paragraph (6)(c) applies, the Upper Tribunal must at the same time require such commissioner to—

    (a) send or deliver to the Upper Tribunal (within such time as the Upper Tribunal may specify)—

        (i) a copy of any written record of the decision under challenge, and any statement of reasons for that decision, and

        (ii) copies of all documents relevant to the case in such commissioner's possession, and

    (b) provide copies of such documents to each other party at the same time as they are provided to the Upper Tribunal.

(7) Paragraph (6)(a) does not apply in a quality contracts scheme case, in respect of which Schedule A1 makes alternative and further provision.

Response to the notice of appeal

24(1) This rule and rule 25 do not apply to—

    (a) a road transport case, in respect of which Schedule 1 makes alternative provision; or

    (b) a financial sanctions case in respect of which Schedule 4 makes alternative provision.

(1A) Subject to any direction given by the Upper Tribunal, a respondent may provide a response to a notice of appeal.

(2) Any response provided under paragraph (1A) must be in writing and must be sent or delivered to the Upper Tribunal so that it is received—

    (a) if an application for permission to appeal stands as the notice of appeal, no later than one month after the date on which the respondent was sent notice that permission to appeal had been granted;

(aa) in a fast-track case, two days before the hearing of the appeal;

(ab) in a quality contracts scheme case, no later than 1 month after the date on which a copy of the notice of appeal is sent to the respondent; or

(b) in any other case, no later than 1 month after the date on which the Upper Tribunal sent a copy of the notice of appeal to the respondent.

(3) The response must state—

  (a) the name and address of the respondent;

  (b) the name and address of the representative (if any) of the respondent;

  (c) an address where documents for the respondent may be sent or delivered;

  (d) whether the respondent opposes the appeal;

  (e) the grounds on which the respondent relies, including (in the case of an appeal against the decision of another tribunal) any grounds on which the respondent was unsuccessful in the proceedings which are the subject of the appeal, but intends to rely in the appeal; and

  (f) whether the respondent wants the case to be dealt with at a hearing.

(4) If the respondent provides the response to the Upper Tribunal later than the time required by paragraph (2) or by an extension of time allowed under rule 5(3)(a) (power to extend time), the response must include a request for an extension of time and the reason why the response was not provided in time.

(5) When the Upper Tribunal receives the response it must send a copy of the response and any accompanying documents to the appellant and each other party.

(6) Paragraph (5) does not apply in a quality contracts scheme case, in respect of which Schedule A1 makes alternative and further provision.

Appellant's reply

25(1) Subject to any direction given by the Upper Tribunal, the appellant may provide a reply to any response provided under rule 24 (response to the notice of appeal).

(2) Subject to paragraph (2A), any reply provided under paragraph (1) must be in writing and must be sent or delivered to the Upper Tribunal so that it is received within one month after the date on which the Upper Tribunal sent a copy of the response to the appellant.

(2A) In an asylum case or an immigration case, the time limit in paragraph (2) is—

  (a) one month after the date on which the Upper Tribunal sent a copy of the response to the appellant, or five days before the hearing of the appeal, whichever is the earlier; and

  (b) in a fast-track case, the day of the hearing.

(2B) In a quality contracts scheme case, the time limit in paragraph (2) is 1 month from the date on which the respondent sent a copy of the response to the appellant.

(3) When the Upper Tribunal receives the reply it must send a copy of the reply and any accompanying documents to each respondent.

(4) Paragraph (3) does not apply in a quality contracts scheme case, in respect of which Schedule A1 makes alternative and further provision.

References under the Forfeiture Act 1982

26(1) If a question arises which is required to be determined by the Upper Tribunal under section 4 of the Forfeiture Act 1982, the person to whom the application for the relevant benefit or advantage has been made must refer the question to the Upper Tribunal.

(2) The reference must be in writing and must include—
    (a) a statement of the question for determination;
    (b) a statement of the relevant facts;
    (c) the grounds upon which the reference is made; and
    (d) an address for sending documents to the person making the reference and each respondent.

(3) When the Upper Tribunal receives the reference it must send a copy of the reference and any accompanying documents to each respondent.

(4) Rules 24 (response to the notice of appeal) and 25 (appellant's reply) apply to a reference made under this rule as if it were a notice of appeal.

Cases transferred or referred to the Upper Tribunal, applications made directly to the Upper Tribunal, cases where an offence has been certified

26A(1) Paragraphs (2) and (3) apply to—
    (a) a case transferred or referred to the Upper Tribunal from the First-tier Tribunal;
    (b) a case, other than an appeal or a case to which rule 26 (references under the Forfeiture Act 1982) applies, which is started by an application made directly to the Upper Tribunal; or
    (c) a case where an offence has been certified to the Upper Tribunal.

(2) In a case to which this paragraph applies—
    (a) the Upper Tribunal must give directions as to the procedure to be followed in the consideration and disposal of the proceedings;
    (aa) in a reference under Schedule 1D of the Charities Act 1993, the Upper Tribunal may give directions providing for an application to join the proceedings as a party and the time within which it may be made; and
    (b) the preceding rules in this Part will only apply to the proceedings to the extent provided for by such directions.

(3) If a case or matter to which this paragraph applies is to be determined without notice to or the involvement of a respondent—
    (a) any provision in these Rules requiring a document to be provided by or to a respondent; and
    (b) any other provision in these Rules permitting a respondent to participate in the proceedings
does not apply to that case or matter.

(4) Schedule 2 makes further provision for national security certificate appeals transferred to the Upper Tribunal.

Financial services cases

26B Schedule 3 makes provision for financial services cases and wholesale energy cases.

Financial sanctions cases

26C Schedule 4 makes provision for financial sanctions cases.

PART 4
JUDICIAL REVIEW PROCEEDINGS IN THE UPPER TRIBUNAL

Application of this Part to judicial review proceedings transferred to the Upper Tribunal

27(1) When a court transfers judicial review proceedings to the Upper Tribunal, the Upper Tribunal—

    (a) must notify each party in writing that the proceedings have been transferred to the Upper Tribunal; and

    (b) must give directions as to the future conduct of the proceedings.

(2) The directions given under paragraph (1)(b) may modify or disapply for the purposes of the proceedings any of the provisions of the following rules in this Part.

(3) In proceedings transferred from the Court of Session under section 20(1) of the 2007 Act, the directions given under paragraph (1)(b) must—

    (a) if the Court of Session did not make a first order specifying the required intimation, service and advertisement of the petition, state the Upper Tribunal's requirements in relation to those matters;

    (b) state whether the Upper Tribunal will consider summary dismissal of the proceedings; and

    (c) where necessary, modify or disapply provisions relating to permission in the following rules in this Part.

Applications for permission to bring judicial review proceedings

28(1) A person seeking permission to bring judicial review proceedings before the Upper Tribunal under section 16 of the 2007 Act must make a written application to the Upper Tribunal for such permission.

(2) Subject to paragraph (3), an application under paragraph (1) must be made promptly and, unless any other enactment specifies a shorter time limit, must be sent or delivered to the Upper Tribunal so that it is received no later than 3 months after the date of the decision, action or omission to which the application relates.

(3) An application for permission to bring judicial review proceedings challenging a decision of the First-tier Tribunal may be made later than the time required by paragraph (2) if it is made within 1 month after the date on which the First-tier Tribunal sent—

    (a) written reasons for the decision; or

    (b) notification that an application for the decision to be set aside has been unsuccessful, provided that that application was made in time.

(4) The application must state—

    (a) the name and address of the applicant, the respondent and any other person whom the applicant considers to be an interested party;

    (b) the name and address of the applicant's representative (if any);

    (c) an address where documents for the applicant may be sent or delivered;

    (d) details of the decision challenged (including the date, the full reference and the identity of the decision maker);

    (e) that the application is for permission to bring judicial review proceedings;

    (f) the outcome that the applicant is seeking; and

    (g) the facts and grounds on which the applicant relies.

(5) If the application relates to proceedings in a court or tribunal, the application must name as an interested party each party to those proceedings who is not the applicant or a respondent.

(6) The applicant must send with the application—
    (a) a copy of any written record of the decision in the applicant's possession or control; and
    (b) copies of any other documents in the applicant's possession or control on which the applicant intends to rely.

(7) If the applicant provides the application to the Upper Tribunal later than the time required by paragraph (2) or (3) or by an extension of time allowed under rule 5(3)(a) (power to extend time)—
    (a) the application must include a request for an extension of time and the reason why the application was not provided in time; and
    (b) unless the Upper Tribunal extends time for the application under rule 5(3)(a) (power to extend time) the Upper Tribunal must not admit the application.

(8) Except where rule 28A(2)(a) (special provisions for immigration judicial review proceedings) applies, when the Upper Tribunal receives the application it must send a copy of the application and any accompanying documents to each person named in the application as a respondent or interested party.

Special provisions for immigration judicial review

28A(1) The Upper Tribunal must not accept an application for permission to bring immigration judicial review proceedings unless it is either accompanied by any required fee or the Upper Tribunal accepts an undertaking that the fee will be paid.

(2) Within 9 days of making an application referred to in paragraph (1), an applicant must provide—
    (a) a copy of the application and any accompanying documents to each person named in the application as a respondent or an interested party; and
    (b) the Upper Tribunal with a written statement of when and how this was done.

Acknowledgment of service

29(1) A person who is sent or provided with a copy of an application for permission under rule 28(8) (application for permission to bring judicial review proceedings) or rule 28A(2)(a) (special provisions for immigration judicial review proceedings) and wishes to take part in the proceedings must provide to the Upper Tribunal an acknowledgment of service so that it is received no later than 21 days after the date on which the Upper Tribunal sent, or in immigration judicial review proceedings the applicant provided, a copy of the application to that person.

(2) An acknowledgment of service under paragraph (1) must be in writing and state—
    (a) whether the person intends to support or oppose the application for permission;
    (b) their grounds for any support or opposition under subparagraph (a), or any other submission or information which they consider may assist the Upper Tribunal; and
    (c) the name and address of any other person not named in the application as a respondent or interested party whom the person providing the acknowledgment considers to be an interested party.

(2A) In immigration judicial review proceedings, a person who provides an acknowledgement of service under paragraph (1) must also provide a copy to—

    (a) the applicant; and

    (b) any other person named in the application under rule 28(4)(a) or acknowledgement of service under paragraph (2)(c)

no later than the time specified in paragraph (1).

(3) A person who is provided with a copy of an application for permission under rule 28(8) or 28A(2)(a) but does not provide an acknowledgment of service to the Upper Tribunal may not take part in the application for permission unless allowed to do so by the Upper Tribunal, but may take part in the subsequent proceedings if the application is successful.

Decision on permission or summary dismissal, and reconsideration of permission or summary dismissal at a hearing

30(1) The Upper Tribunal must send to the applicant, each respondent and any other person who provided an acknowledgment of service to the Upper Tribunal, and may send to any other person who may have an interest in the proceedings, written notice of—

    (a) its decision in relation to the application for permission; and

    (b) the reasons for any—

        (i) refusal of the application or refusal to admit the late application, or

        (ii) limitations or conditions on permission.

(2) In proceedings transferred from the Court of Session under section 20(1) of the 2007 Act, where the Upper Tribunal has considered whether summarily to dismiss of the proceedings, the Upper Tribunal must send to the applicant and each respondent, and may send to any other person who may have an interest in the proceedings, written notice of—

    (a) its decision in relation to the summary dismissal of proceedings; and

    (b) the reasons for any decision summarily to dismiss part or all of the proceedings, or any limitations or conditions on the continuation of such proceedings.

(3) Paragraph (4) applies where the Upper Tribunal, without a hearing—

    (a) determines an application for permission to bring judicial review proceedings by—

        (i) refusing permission or refusing to admit the late application, or

        (ii) giving permission on limited grounds or subject to conditions; or

    (b) in proceedings transferred from the Court of Session, summarily dismisses part or all of the proceedings, or imposes any limitations or conditions on the continuation of such proceedings.

(4) Subject to paragraph (4A), in the circumstances specified in paragraph (3) the applicant may apply for the decision to be reconsidered at a hearing.

(4A) Where the Upper Tribunal refuses permission to bring immigration judicial review proceedings or refuses to admit a late application for permission to bring such proceedings and considers the application to be totally without merit, it shall record that fact in its decision notice and, in those circumstances, the applicant may not request the decision to be reconsidered at a hearing.

(5) An application under paragraph (4) must be made in writing and must be sent or delivered to the Upper Tribunal so that it is received within 14 days, or in immigration judicial review proceedings 9 days, after the date on which the Upper Tribunal sent written notice of its decision regarding the application to the applicant.

Responses

31(1) Any person to whom the Upper Tribunal has sent notice of the grant of permission under rule 30(1) (notification of decision on permission), and who wishes to contest the application or support it on additional grounds, must provide detailed grounds for contesting or supporting the application to the Upper Tribunal.

(2) Any detailed grounds must be provided in writing and must be sent or delivered to the Upper Tribunal so that they are received not more than 35 days after the Upper Tribunal sent notice of the grant of permission under rule 30(1).

Applicant seeking to rely on additional grounds

32 The applicant may not rely on any grounds, other than those grounds on which the applicant obtained permission for the judicial review proceedings, without the consent of the Upper Tribunal.

Right to make representations

33 Each party and, with the permission of the Upper Tribunal, any other person, may—
  (a) submit evidence, except at the hearing of an application for permission;
  (b) make representations at any hearing which they are entitled to attend; and
  (c) make written representations in relation to a decision to be made without a hearing.

Amendments and additional grounds resulting in transfer of proceedings to the High Court in England and Wales

33A(1) This rule applies only to judicial review proceedings arising under the law of England and Wales.

(2) In relation to such proceedings—
  (a) the powers of the Upper Tribunal to permit or require amendments under rule 5(3)(c) extend to amendments which would, once in place, give rise to an obligation or power to transfer the proceedings to the High Court in England and Wales under section 18(3) of the 2007 Act or paragraph (3);
  (b) except with the permission of the Upper Tribunal, additional grounds may not be advanced, whether by an applicant or otherwise, if they would give rise to an obligation or power to transfer the proceedings to the High Court in England and Wales under section 18(3) of the 2007 Act or paragraph (3).

(3) Where the High Court in England and Wales has transferred judicial review proceedings to the Upper Tribunal under any power or duty and subsequently the proceedings are amended or any party advances additional grounds—
  (a) if the proceedings in their present form could not have been transferred to the Upper Tribunal under the relevant power or duty had they been in that form at the time of the transfer, the Upper Tribunal must transfer the proceedings back to the High Court in England and Wales;
  (b) subject to subparagraph (a), where the proceedings were transferred to the Upper Tribunal under section 31A(3) of the Senior Courts Act 1981(power to transfer judicial review proceedings to the Upper Tribunal), the Upper Tribunal may transfer proceedings back to the High Court in England and Wales if it appears just and convenient to do so.

PART 5
HEARINGS

Decision with or without a hearing

34(1) Subject to paragraphs (2) and (3), the Upper Tribunal may make any decision without a hearing.

(2) The Upper Tribunal must have regard to any view expressed by a party when deciding whether to hold a hearing to consider any matter, and the form of any such hearing.

(3) In immigration judicial review proceedings, the Upper Tribunal must hold a hearing before making a decision which disposes of proceedings.

(4) Paragraph (3) does not affect the power of the Upper Tribunal to—
   (a) strike out a party's case, pursuant to rule 8(1)(b) or 8(2);
   (b) consent to withdrawal, pursuant to rule 17;
   (c) determine an application for permission to bring judicial review proceedings, pursuant to rule 30; or
   (d) make a consent order disposing of proceedings, pursuant to rule 39,
   without a hearing.

Entitlement to attend a hearing

35(1) Subject to rule 37(4) (exclusion of a person from a hearing), each party is entitled to attend a hearing.

(2) In a national security certificate appeal the relevant Minister is entitled to attend any hearing.

Notice of hearings

36(1) The Upper Tribunal must give each party entitled to attend a hearing reasonable notice of the time and place of the hearing (including any adjourned or postponed hearing) and any change to the time and place of the hearing.

(2) The period of notice under paragraph (1) must be at least 14 days except that—
   (a) in applications for permission to bring judicial review proceedings, the period of notice must be at least 2 working days;
   (aa) in a fast-track case the period of notice must be at least one working day; and
   (b) in any case other than a fast-track case the Upper Tribunal may give shorter notice—
      (i) with the parties' consent; or
      (ii) in urgent or exceptional cases.

Special time limits for hearing an appeal in a fast-track case

36A(1) Subject to rule 36(2)(aa) (notice of hearings) and paragraph (2) of this rule, where permission to appeal to the Upper Tribunal has been given in a fast-track case, the Upper Tribunal must start the hearing of the appeal not later than—

(a) five working days after the date on which the First-tier Tribunal or the Upper Tribunal sent notice of its grant of permission to appeal to the appellant; or

(b) where the notice of its grant of permission to appeal is sent electronically or delivered personally, two working days after the date on which the First-tier Tribunal or the Upper

Tribunal sent notice of its grant of permission to appeal to the appellant.

(2) If the Upper Tribunal is unable to arrange for the hearing to start within the time specified in paragraph (1), it must set a date for the hearing as soon as is reasonably practicable.

Public and private hearings

37(1) Subject to the following paragraphs, all hearings must be held in public.

(2) The Upper Tribunal may give a direction that a hearing, or part of it, is to be held in private.

(2A) In a national security certificate appeal, the Upper Tribunal must have regard to its duty under rule 14(10) (no disclosure of information contrary to the interests of national security) when considering whether to give a direction that a hearing, or part of it, is to be held in private.

(3) Where a hearing, or part of it, is to be held in private, the Upper Tribunal may determine who is entitled to attend the hearing or part of it.

(4) The Upper Tribunal may give a direction excluding from any hearing, or part of it—
   (a) any person whose conduct the Upper Tribunal considers is disrupting or is likely to disrupt the hearing;
   (b) any person whose presence the Upper Tribunal considers is likely to prevent another person from giving evidence or making submissions freely;
   (c) any person who the Upper Tribunal considers should be excluded in order to give effect to the requirement at rule 14(11) (prevention of disclosure or publication of documents and information);
   (d) any person where the purpose of the hearing would be defeated by the attendance of that person; or
   (e) a person under 18, other than a young person who is a party in a special educational needs case or a disability discrimination in schools case.

(5) The Upper Tribunal may give a direction excluding a witness from a hearing until that witness gives evidence.

Hearings in a party's absence

38 If a party fails to attend a hearing, the Upper Tribunal may proceed with the hearing if the Upper Tribunal—
   (a) is satisfied that the party has been notified of the hearing or that reasonable steps have been taken to notify the party of the hearing; and
   (b) considers that it is in the interests of justice to proceed with the hearing.

PART 6
DECISIONS

Consent orders

39(1) The Upper Tribunal may, at the request of the parties but only if it considers it appropriate, make a consent order disposing of the proceedings and making such other appropriate provision as the parties have agreed.

(2) Notwithstanding any other provision of these Rules, the Upper Tribunal need not hold a hearing before making an order under paragraph (1).

Decisions

40(1) The Upper Tribunal may give a decision orally at a hearing.

(1A) Subject to paragraph (1B), in immigration judicial review proceedings, a decision which disposes of proceedings shall be given at a hearing.

(1B) Paragraph (1A) does not affect the power of the Upper Tribunal to—
  (a) strike out a party's case, pursuant to rule 8(1)(b) or 8(2);
  (b) consent to withdrawal, pursuant to rule 17;
  (c) determine an application for permission to bring judicial review proceedings, pursuant to rule 30; or
  (d) make a consent order disposing of proceedings, pursuant to rule 39,
  without a hearing.

(2) Except where rule 22 (decision in relation to permission to appeal) or rule 22A (special procedure for providing notice of a refusal of permission to appeal in an asylum case) applies, the Upper Tribunal must provide to each party as soon as reasonably practicable after making a decision (other than a decision under Part 7) which finally disposes of all issues in the proceedings or of a preliminary issue dealt with following a direction under rule 5(3)(e)—
  (a) a decision notice stating the Upper Tribunal's decision; and
  (b) notification of any rights of review or appeal against the decision and the time and manner in which such rights of review or appeal may be exercised.

(3) Subject to rule 14(11) (prevention of disclosure or publication of documents and information), the Upper Tribunal must provide written reasons for its decision with a decision notice provided under paragraph (2)(a) unless—
  (a) the decision was made with the consent of the parties; or
  (b) the parties have consented to the Upper Tribunal not giving written reasons.

(4) The Upper Tribunal may provide written reasons for any decision to which paragraph (2) does not apply.

(5) In a national security certificate appeal, when the Upper Tribunal provides a notice or reasons to the parties under this rule, it must also provide the notice or reasons to the relevant Minister and the Information Commissioner, if they are not parties.

40A ....

PART 7
CORRECTING, SETTING ASIDE, REVIEWING AND APPEALING DECISIONS OF THE UPPER TRIBUNAL

Interpretation

41 In this Part—
  "appeal", except in rule 44(2) (application for permission to appeal), means the exercise of a right of appeal under section 13 of the 2007 Act; and
  "review" means the review of a decision by the Upper Tribunal under section 10 of the 2007 Act.

Clerical mistakes and accidental slips or omissions

42 The Upper Tribunal may at any time correct any clerical mistake or other accidental slip or omission in a decision or record of a decision by—

  (a) sending notification of the amended decision, or a copy of the amended record, to all parties; and

  (b) making any necessary amendment to any information published in relation to the decision or record.

Setting aside a decision which disposes of proceedings

43(1) The Upper Tribunal may set aside a decision which disposes of proceedings, or part of such a decision, and remake the decision or the relevant part of it, if—

  (a) the Upper Tribunal considers that it is in the interests of justice to do so; and

  (b) one or more of the conditions in paragraph (2) are satisfied.

  (2) The conditions are—

  (a) a document relating to the proceedings was not sent to, or was not received at an appropriate time by, a party or a party's representative;

  (b) a document relating to the proceedings was not sent to the Upper Tribunal at an appropriate time;

  (c) a party, or a party's representative, was not present at a hearing related to the proceedings; or

  (d) there has been some other procedural irregularity in the proceedings.

  (3) Except where paragraph (4) applies, a party applying for a decision, or part of a decision, to be set aside under paragraph (1) must make a written application to the Upper Tribunal so that it is received no later than 1 month after the date on which the Upper Tribunal sent notice of the decision to the party.

  (4) In an asylum case or an immigration case, the written application referred to in paragraph (3) must be sent or delivered so that it is received by the Upper Tribunal—

  (a) where the person who appealed to the First-tier Tribunal is in the United Kingdom at the time that the application is made, no later than twelve days after the date on which the Upper Tribunal or, as the case may be in an asylum case, the Secretary of State for the Home Department, sent notice of the decision to the party making the application; or

  (b) where the person who appealed to the First-tier Tribunal is outside the United Kingdom at the time that the application is made, no later than thirty eight days after the date on which the Upper Tribunal sent notice of the decision to the party making the application.

  (5) Where a notice of decision is sent electronically or delivered personally, the time limits in paragraph (4) are ten working days.

Application for permission to appeal

44(1) Subject to paragraphs (4A) and (4B), a person seeking permission to appeal must make a written application to the Upper Tribunal for permission to appeal.

  (2) Paragraph (3) applies to an application under paragraph (1) in respect of a decision—

  (a) on an appeal against a decision in a social security and child support case (as defined in the Tribunal Procedure (First-tier Tribunal) (Social Entitlement Chamber) Rules 2008);

  (b) on an appeal against a decision in proceedings in the War Pensions and Armed

Forces Compensation Chamber of the First-tier Tribunal;

 (ba) on an appeal against a decision of a Pensions Appeal Tribunal for Scotland or Northern Ireland; or

 (c) in proceedings under the Forfeiture Act 1982.

(3) Where this paragraph applies, the application must be sent or delivered to the Upper Tribunal so that it is received within 3 months after the date on which the Upper Tribunal sent to the person making the application—

 (a) written notice of the decision;

 (b) notification of amended reasons for, or correction of, the decision following a review; or

 (c) notification that an application for the decision to be set aside has been unsuccessful.

(3A) An application under paragraph (1) in respect of a decision in an asylum case or an immigration case must be sent or delivered to the Upper Tribunal so that it is received within the appropriate period after the Upper Tribunal or, as the case may be in an asylum case, the Secretary of State for the Home Department, sent any of the documents in paragraph (3) to the party making the application.

(3B) The appropriate period referred to in paragraph (3A) is as follows—

 (a) where the person who appealed to the First-tier Tribunal is in the United Kingdom at the time that the application is made—

  (i) twelve working days; or

  (ii) if the party making the application is in detention under the Immigration Acts, seven working days; and

 (b) where the person who appealed to the First-tier Tribunal is outside the United Kingdom at the time that the application is made, thirty eight days.

(3C) Where a notice of decision is sent electronically or delivered personally, the time limits in paragraph (3B) are—

 (a) in subparagraph (a)(i), ten working days;

 (b) in subparagraph (a)(ii), five working days; and

 (c) in subparagraph (b), ten working days.

(3D) An application under paragraph (1) in respect of a decision in a financial services case must be sent or delivered to the Upper Tribunal so that it is received within 14 days after the date on which the Upper Tribunal sent to the person making the application—

 (a) written notice of the decision;

 (b) notification of amended reasons for, or correction of, the decision following a review; or

 (c) notification that an application for the decision to be set aside has been unsuccessful.

(4) Where paragraph (3), (3A), (3D) or (4C) does not apply, an application under paragraph (1) must be sent or delivered to the Upper Tribunal so that it is received within 1 month after the latest of the dates on which the Upper Tribunal sent to the person making the application—

 (a) written reasons for the decision;

 (b) notification of amended reasons for, or correction of, the decision following a review; or

 (c) notification that an application for the decision to be set aside has been unsuccessful.

(4A) Where a decision that disposes of immigration judicial review proceedings is given at a hearing, a party may apply at that hearing for permission to appeal, and the Upper Tribunal must consider at the hearing whether to give or refuse permission to appeal.

(4B) Where a decision that disposes of immigration judicial review proceedings is given at a hearing and no application for permission to appeal is made at that hearing—

(a) the Upper Tribunal must nonetheless consider at the hearing whether to give or refuse permission to appeal; and

(b) if permission to appeal is given to a party, it shall be deemed for the purposes of section 13(4) of the 2007 Act to be given on application by that party.

(4C) Where a decision that disposes of immigration judicial review proceedings is given pursuant to rule 30 and the Upper Tribunal records under rule 30(4A) that the application is totally without merit, an application under paragraph (1) must be sent or delivered to the Upper Tribunal so that it is received within 7 days after the later of the dates on which the Upper Tribunal sent to the applicant—

(a) written reasons for the decision; or

(b) notification of amended reasons for, or correction of, the decision following a review.

(5) The date in paragraph (3)(c) or (4)(c) applies only if the application for the decision to be set aside was made within the time stipulated in rule 43 (setting aside a decision which disposes of proceedings) or any extension of that time granted by the Upper Tribunal.

(6) If the person seeking permission to appeal provides the application to the Upper Tribunal later than the time required by paragraph (3), (3A), (3D) or (4), or by any extension of time under rule 5(3)(a) (power to extend time)—

(a) the application must include a request for an extension of time and the reason why the application notice was not provided in time; and

(b) unless the Upper Tribunal extends time for the application under rule 5(3)(a) (power to extend time) the Upper Tribunal must refuse the application.

(7) An application under paragraph (1) or (4A)(a) must—

(a) identify the decision of the Upper Tribunal to which it relates;

(b) identify the alleged error or errors of law in the decision; and

(c) state the result the party making the application is seeking.

Upper Tribunal's consideration of application for permission to appeal

45(1) On receiving an application for permission to appeal the Upper Tribunal may review the decision in accordance with rule 46 (review of a decision), but may only do so if—

(a) when making the decision the Upper Tribunal overlooked a legislative provision or binding authority which could have had a material effect on the decision; or

(b) since the Upper Tribunal's decision, a court has made a decision which is binding on the Upper Tribunal and which, had it been made before the Upper Tribunal's decision, could have had a material effect on the decision.

(2) If the Upper Tribunal decides not to review the decision, or reviews the decision and decides to take no action in relation to the decision or part of it, the Upper Tribunal must consider whether to give permission to appeal in relation to the decision or that part of it.

(3) The Upper Tribunal must provide a record of its decision to the parties as soon as

practicable.

(4) If the Upper Tribunal refuses permission to appeal it must provide with the record of its decision—

    (a) a statement of its reasons for such refusal; and

    (b) notification of the right to make an application to the relevant appellate court for permission to appeal and the time within which, and the method by which, such application must be made.

(5) The Upper Tribunal may give permission to appeal on limited grounds, but must comply with paragraph (4) in relation to any grounds on which it has refused permission.

Review of a decision

46(1) The Upper Tribunal may only undertake a review of a decision pursuant to rule 45(1) (review on an application for permission to appeal).

(2) The Upper Tribunal must notify the parties in writing of the outcome of any review and of any rights of review or appeal in relation to the outcome.

(3) If the Upper Tribunal decides to take any action in relation to a decision following a review without first giving every party an opportunity to make representations, the notice under paragraph (2) must state that any party that did not have an opportunity to make representations may apply for such action to be set aside and for the decision to be reviewed again.

Setting aside a decision in proceedings under the Forfeiture Act 1982

47(1) A person who referred a question to the Upper Tribunal under rule 26 (references under the Forfeiture Act 1982) must refer the Upper Tribunal's previous decision in relation to the question to the Upper Tribunal if they—

    (a) consider that the decision should be set aside and remade under this rule; or

    (b) have received a written application for the decision to be set aside and remade under this rule from the person to whom the decision related.

(2) The Upper Tribunal may set aside the decision, either in whole or in part, and remake it if—

    (a) ....

    (b) the decision was made in ignorance of, or was based on a mistake as to, some material fact; or

    (c) there has been a relevant change in circumstances since the decision was made.

(3) Rule 26(2) to (4), Parts 5 and 6 and this Part apply to a reference under this rule as they apply to a reference under rule 26(1).

Power to treat an application as a different type of application

48 The Upper Tribunal may treat an application for a decision to be corrected, set aside or reviewed, or for permission to appeal against a decision, as an application for any other one of those things.

SCHEDULE 1
PROCEDURE AFTER THE NOTICE OF APPEAL IN APPEALS AGAINST DECISIONS OF TRAFFIC COMMISSIONERS

Not reproduced

SCHEDULE 2
ADDITIONAL PROCEDURE IN NATIONAL SECURITY CERTIFICATE CASES

Rule 26A(4)

1   This Schedule applies only to national security certificate appeals.

2   Following the transfer of the appeal from the First-tier Tribunal, the Upper Tribunal must provide a copy of the notice of appeal to the respondent, the relevant Minister and the Information Commissioner.

3   The relevant Minister must send or deliver to the Upper Tribunal a copy of the certificate to which the appeal relates, and a response to the notice of appeal, not later than 42 days after the date on which the relevant Minister received a copy of the notice of appeal.

4   In an appeal under section 28(4) of the Data Protection Act 1998, sections 27(3), 79(5) or 111(3) of the Data Protection Act 2018 or section 60(1) of the Freedom of Information Act 2000 (including that subsection as applied and modified by regulation 18 of the Environmental Information Regulations 2004), the relevant Minister's response must state whether the relevant Minister intends to oppose the appeal and, if so set out—
    (a)   a summary of the circumstances relating to the issue of the certificate;
    (b)   the reason for the issue of the certificate;
    (c)   the grounds on which the relevant Minister relies in opposing the appeal; and
    (d)   a statement of the evidence on which the relevant Minister relies in support of those grounds.

5   In an appeal under section 28(6) of the Data Protection Act 1998, sections 27(5), 79(7) or 111(5) of the Data Protection Act 2018 or section 60(4) of the Freedom of Information Act 2000 (including that subsection as applied and modified by regulation 18 of the Environmental Information Regulations 2004), the relevant Minister's response must state whether the relevant Minister intends to make representations in relation to the appeal and, if so set out—
    (a)   the extent to which the relevant Minister intends to support or oppose the appeal;
    (b)   the grounds on which the relevant Minister relies in supporting or opposing the appeal; and
    (c)   a statement of the evidence on which the relevant Minister relies in support of those grounds.

6   The Upper Tribunal must—
    (a)   subject to paragraph 11, provide the relevant Minister's response and any other response to the appellant, the Information Commissioner and any respondent; and
    (b)   send a copy of any other response to the relevant Minister.

7   On grounds of the need to ensure that information is not disclosed contrary to the interests of national security, the relevant Minster may—
    (a)   object to the disclosure of the relevant Minister's response to the appellant, the

Information Commissioner or any respondent, by sending a notice to the Upper Tribunal with the response; or

(b) object to the disclosure of any other response to the Information Commissioner or any respondent, by sending a notice to the Upper Tribunal within 42 days of the date on which the relevant Minister received a copy of the response.

8 A notice under paragraph 7 must—

(a) state the reason for the objection; and

(b) in the case of a notice under paragraph 7(a) and to the extent that it is possible to do so, be accompanied by a version of the relevant Minister's response in a form that can be shown to the appellant, the Commissioner or, as the case may be, a respondent.

9 Before the Upper Tribunal gives a direction, issues a summons or citation, or produces or publishes a written record of, or reasons for, a decision—

(a) the Upper Tribunal must notify the relevant Minister of the proposed action; and

(b) if the relevant Minister considers that the proposal would cause information that is or would be exempt by virtue of a provision in Part 2 of the Freedom of Information Act 2000 to be disclosed, the relevant Minister may object to the proposal by sending a notice to the Upper Tribunal so that the Upper Tribunal receives the notice within 14 days of the date that the Minister received notice of the proposal.

10 When deciding whether to uphold an objection made by the relevant Minister—

(a) any hearing must take place in the absence of the parties;

(b) if the Upper Tribunal is minded to overrule the relevant Minister's objection, or to require the relevant Minister to provide a version of the relevant Minister's response in a form other than one provided under paragraph 8(b) above, the Upper Tribunal must invite the relevant Minister to make representations; and

(c) if the Upper Tribunal overrules an objection in relation to the disclosure of a response, the Upper Tribunal must not disclose, or require the relevant Minister to disclose, any material the subject of the objection unless the relevant Minister relies upon that material in opposing the appeal.

11 Where the relevant Minister may object to the disclosure of a response or proposed action by the Upper Tribunal, the Upper Tribunal may not proceed with that disclosure or that proposed action unless—

(a) the time for the relevant Minister to object has expired; and

(b) the relevant Minister has not objected, or the Upper Tribunal has overruled the relevant Minister's objection and, in the case of the disclosure of a response, may proceed with the disclosure under paragraph 10(c).

First-tier Tribunal and Upper Tribunal (Composition of Tribunal) Order 2008 (SI 2008/2835)

Made 29th October 2008

Coming into force 3rd November 2008

The Lord Chancellor makes the following Order in exercise of the powers conferred by section 145(1) of, and paragraph 15 of Schedule 4 to, the Tribunals, Courts and Enforcement Act 2007.

In accordance with paragraph 15(8) of that Act the Lord Chancellor has consulted the Senior President of Tribunals.

In accordance with section 49(5) of that Act a draft of this instrument was laid before Parliament and approved by a resolution of each House of Parliament.

Citation and commencement

1   This Order may be cited as the First-tier Tribunal and Upper Tribunal (Composition of Tribunal) Order 2008 and comes into force on 3rd November 2008.

Number of members of the First-tier Tribunal

2(1)   The number of members of the tribunal who are to decide any matter that falls to be decided by the First-tier Tribunal must be determined by the Senior President of Tribunals in accordance with paragraph (2).

(2)   The Senior President of Tribunals must have regard to—

    (a)   where the matter which falls to be decided by the tribunal fell to a tribunal in a list in Schedule 6 to the Tribunals, Courts and Enforcement Act 2007 before its functions were transferred by order under section 30(1) of that Act, any provision made by or under any enactment for determining the number of members of that tribunal; and

    (b)   the need for members of tribunals to have particular expertise, skills or knowledge.

Number of members of the Upper Tribunal

3(1)   The number of members of the tribunal who are to decide any matter that falls to be decided by the Upper Tribunal is one unless determined otherwise under paragraph (2).

(2)   The tribunal may consist of two or three members if the Senior President of Tribunals so determines.

Tribunal consisting of single member

4(1)   Where a matter is to be decided by a single member of a tribunal, it must be decided by a judge of the tribunal unless paragraph (2) applies.

(2)   The matter may be decided by one of the other members of the tribunal if the Senior President of Tribunals so determines.

Tribunal consisting of two or more members

5   The following articles apply where a matter is to be decided by two or more members of a tribunal.

6 The number of members who are to be judges of the tribunal and the number of members who are to be other members of the tribunal must be determined by the Senior President of Tribunals.

7 The Senior President of Tribunals must select one of the members (the "presiding member") to chair the tribunal.

8 If the decision of the tribunal is not unanimous, the decision of the majority is the decision of the tribunal; and the presiding member has a casting vote if the votes are equally divided.

First-tier Tribunal and Upper Tribunal (Chambers) Order 2010 (SI 2010/2655)

as amended to 1 February 2020

Made 28th October 2010
Coming into force 29th November 2010

The Lord Chancellor, with the concurrence of the Senior President of Tribunals, makes the following Order in exercise of the power conferred by section 7(1) and (9) of the Tribunals, Courts and Enforcement Act 2007.

CONTENTS

Citation, commencement and revocations

1(1)   This Order may be cited as the First-tier Tribunal and Upper Tribunal (Chambers) Order 2010 and comes into force on 29th November 2010.

(2)   The Orders listed in the first column of the Schedule to this Order are revoked to the extent specified in the second column.

First-tier Tribunal Chambers

2   The First-tier Tribunal shall be organised into the following chambers—
   (a) the General Regulatory Chamber;
   (b) the Health, Education and Social Care Chamber;
   (c) the Immigration and Asylum Chamber;
   (cc) the Property Chamber;
   (d)   the Social Entitlement Chamber;
   (e) the Tax Chamber;

(f) the War Pensions and Armed Forces Compensation Chamber.

Functions of the General Regulatory Chamber

3 To the General Regulatory Chamber are allocated all functions related to—
   (a) proceedings in respect of the decisions and actions of regulatory bodies which are not allocated to the Health, Education and Social Care Chamber by article 4 or to the Tax Chamber by article 7;
   (b) matters referred to the First-tier Tribunal under Schedule 1D to the Charities Act 1993 (references to Tribunal);
   (c) the determination of remuneration for carrying mail-bags in a ship or aircraft.

Functions of the Health, Education and Social Care Chamber

4 To the Health, Education and Social Care Chamber are allocated all functions related to—
   (a) an appeal against a decision related to children with special educational needs;
   (b) a claim of disability discrimination in the education of a child;
   (c) an application or an appeal against a decision or determination related to work with children or vulnerable adults;
   (d) an appeal against a decision related to registration in respect of the provision of health or social care;
   (e) an application in respect of, or an appeal against a decision related to, the provision of health care or health services;
   (f) an appeal against a decision related to registration in respect of social workers and social care workers;
   (g) an appeal against a decision related to the provision of childcare;
   (h) an appeal against a decision related to an independent school or other independent educational institution;
   (i) applications and references by and in respect of patients under the provisions of the Mental Health Act 1983 or paragraph 5(2) of the Schedule to the Repatriation of Prisoners Act 1984.

Functions of the Immigration and Asylum Chamber of the First-tier Tribunal

5 To the Immigration and Asylum Chamber of the First-tier Tribunal are allocated all functions related to immigration and asylum matters, with the exception of matters allocated to—
   (a) the Social Entitlement Chamber by article 6(a);
   (b) the General Regulatory Chamber by article 3(a).

Functions of the Property Chamber

5A To the Property Chamber are allocated all functions conferred on the First-tier Tribunal relating to—
   (a) a reference by the Chief Land Registrar and any other application, matter or appeal under the Land Registration Act 2002;
   (b) proceedings under any of the enactments referred to in section 6A(2) of the Agriculture (Miscellaneous Provisions) Act 1954 or the Hill Farming Act 1946;
   (c) housing etc, under the Housing Act 2004;
   (d) leasehold property;
   (e) residential property;
   (f) rents;

   (g) the right to buy;

   (h) proceedings relating to mobile homes and caravan sites;

   (i) proceedings for approval by the First-tier Tribunal of the exercise of a power of entry, made under paragraph 6B of Schedule 9 to the Local Government Finance Act 1988 or under section 25A of the Local Government Finance Act 1992.

Functions of the Social Entitlement Chamber

6   To the Social Entitlement Chamber are allocated all functions related to appeals—

   (a) in cases regarding support for asylum seekers, failed asylum seekers, persons designated under section 130 of the Criminal Justice and Immigration Act 2008, or the dependants of any such persons;

   (b) in criminal injuries compensation cases;

   (c) regarding entitlement to, payments of, or recovery or recoupment of payments of, social security benefits, child support, vaccine damage payments, health in pregnancy grant and tax credits, with the exception of—

      (i) appeals under section 11 of the Social Security Contributions (Transfer of Functions, etc) Act 1999 (appeals against decisions of Her Majesty's Revenue and Customs);

      (ii) appeals in respect of employer penalties or employer information penalties (as defined in section 63(11) and (12) of the Tax Credits Act 2002);

      (iii) appeals under regulation 28(3) of the Child Trust Funds Regulations 2004;

   (d) regarding saving gateway accounts with the exception of appeals against requirements to account for an amount under regulations made under section 14 of the Saving Gateway Accounts Act 2009;

   (e) regarding child trust funds with the exception of appeals against requirements to account for an amount under regulations made under section 22(4) of the Child Trust Funds Act 2004 in relation to section 13 of that Act;

   (ea) appealable decisions within the meaning of section 56(3) of the Childcare Payments Act 2014;

   (f) regarding payments in consequence of diffuse mesothelioma;

   (g) regarding a certificate or waiver decision in relation to NHS charges;

   (h) regarding entitlement to be credited with earnings or contributions;

   (i) against a decision as to whether an accident was an industrial accident.

Functions of the Tax Chamber

7   To the Tax Chamber are allocated all functions, except those functions allocated to the Social Entitlement Chamber by article 6 or to the Tax and Chancery Chamber of the Upper Tribunal by article 13, related to an appeal, application, reference or other proceeding in respect of—

   (a) a function of the Commissioners for Her Majesty's Revenue and Customs or an officer of Revenue and Customs;

   (b) the exercise by the National Crime Agency of general Revenue functions or Revenue inheritance tax functions (as defined in section 323 of the Proceeds of Crime Act 2002);

   (c) the exercise by the Director of Border Revenue of functions under section 7 of the Borders, Citizenship and Revenue Act 2009;

   (d) a function of the Compliance Officer for the Independent Parliamentary Standards Authority;

   (e) a function of the Welsh Revenue Authority.

Functions of the War Pensions and Armed Forces Compensation Chamber

8   To the War Pensions and Armed Forces Compensation Chamber are allocated all functions related to appeals under the War Pensions (Administrative Provisions) Act 1919 and the Pensions Appeal Tribunals Act 1943.

Upper Tribunal Chambers

9   The Upper Tribunal shall be organised into the following chambers—

    (a)   the Administrative Appeals Chamber;

    (b)   the Immigration and Asylum Chamber of the Upper Tribunal;

    (c)   the Lands Chamber;

    (d)   the Tax and Chancery Chamber.

Functions of the Administrative Appeals Chamber

10   To the Administrative Appeals Chamber are allocated all functions related to—

    (a)   an appeal—

        (i)   against a decision made by the First-tier Tribunal, except an appeal allocated to the Tax and Chancery Chamber by article 13(a) or the Immigration and Asylum Chamber of the Upper Tribunal by article 11(a);

        (ii)   under section 5 of the Pensions Appeal Tribunals Act 1943 (appeals against assessment of extent of disablement) against a decision of the Pensions Appeal Tribunal in Northern Ireland established under paragraph 1(3) of the Schedule to the Pensions Appeal Tribunals Act 1943 (constitution, jurisdiction and procedure of Pensions Appeal Tribunals);

        (iii)   against a decision of the Pensions Appeal Tribunal in Scotland established under paragraph 1(2) of the Schedule to the Pensions Appeal Tribunals Act 1943;

        (iv)   against a decision of the Mental Health Review Tribunal for Wales established under section 65 of the Mental Health Act 1983 (Mental Health Review Tribunals);

        (v)   against a decision of the Special Educational Needs Tribunal for Wales;

        (vi)   under section 4 of the Safeguarding Vulnerable Groups Act 2006 (appeals);

        (vii)   transferred to the Upper Tribunal from the First-tier Tribunal under Tribunal Procedure Rules, except an appeal allocated to the Tax and Chancery Chamber by article 13(1)(e);

        (viii)   against a decision in a road transport case;

    (b)   an application, except an application allocated to another chamber by article 11(c), (d) or (e), 12(c) or 13(g), for the Upper Tribunal—

        (i)   to grant the relief mentioned in section 15(1) of the Tribunals, Courts and Enforcement Act 2007 (Upper Tribunal's "judicial review" jurisdiction);

        (ii)   to exercise the powers of review under section 21(2) of that Act (Upper Tribunal's "judicial review" jurisdiction: Scotland);

    (c)   a matter referred to the Upper Tribunal by the First-tier Tribunal—

        (i)   under section 9(5)(b) of the Tribunals, Courts and Enforcement Act 2007 (review of decision of First-tier Tribunal), or

        (ii)   under Tribunal Procedure Rules relating to non-compliance with a requirement of the First-tier Tribunal,

        except where the reference is allocated to another chamber by article 11(b) or 13(f);

    (d)   a determination or decision under section 4 of the Forfeiture Act 1982;

(e) proceedings, or a preliminary issue, transferred under Tribunal Procedure Rules to the Upper Tribunal from the First-tier Tribunal, except those allocated to the Lands Chamber by article 12(cc) or to the Tax and Chancery Chamber by article 13(1)(e).

Functions of the Immigration and Asylum Chamber of the Upper Tribunal

11   To the Immigration and Asylum Chamber of the Upper Tribunal are allocated all functions related to—

(a) an appeal against a decision of the First-tier Tribunal made in the Immigration and Asylum Chamber of the First-tier Tribunal;

(b) a matter referred to the Upper Tribunal under section 9(5)(b) of the Tribunals, Courts and Enforcement Act 2007 or under Tribunal Procedure Rules by the Immigration and Asylum Chamber of the First-tier Tribunal;

(c) an application for the Upper Tribunal to grant relief mentioned in section 15(1) of the Tribunals, Courts and Enforcement Act 2007 (Upper Tribunal's "judicial review" jurisdiction), or to exercise the power of review under section 21(2) of that Act (Upper Tribunal's "judicial review" jurisdiction: Scotland), which is made by a person who claims to be a minor from outside the United Kingdom challenging a defendant's assessment of that person's age;

(d) an application for the Upper Tribunal to exercise the powers of review under section 21(2) of the Tribunals, Court and Enforcement Act (Upper Tribunal's "judicial review" jurisdiction: Scotland), which relates to a decision of the First-tier Tribunal mentioned in paragraph (a);

(e) an application for the Upper Tribunal to grant relief mentioned in section 15(1) of the Tribunals, Courts and Enforcement Act 2007 (Upper Tribunal's "judicial review" jurisdiction), which is designated as an immigration matter—

   (i) in a direction made in accordance with Part 1 of Schedule 2 to the Constitutional Reform Act 2005 specifying a class of case for the purposes of section 18(6) of the Tribunals, Courts and Enforcement Act 2007; or

   (ii) in an order of the High Court in England and Wales made under section 31A(3) of the Senior Courts Act 1981, transferring to the Upper Tribunal an application of a kind described in section 31A(1) of that Act.

Functions of the Lands Chamber

12   To the Lands Chamber are allocated—

(a) all functions related to—

   (i) compensation and other remedies for measures taken which affect the ownership, value, enjoyment or use of land or water, or of rights over or property in land or water;

   (ii) appeals from decisions of—

      (aa)   the First-tier Tribunal made in the Property Chamber . . .;

      (ab)   leasehold valuation tribunals in Wales, residential property tribunals in Wales, rent assessment committees in Wales, the Agricultural Land Tribunal in Wales or the Valuation Tribunal for Wales;

      (ac)   the Valuation Tribunal for England;

   (iii) the determination of questions of the value of land or an interest in land arising in tax proceedings;

   (iv) proceedings in respect of restrictive covenants, blight notices or the obstruction of light;

(v) proceedings under Schedule 3A to the Communications Act 2003;

(vi) proceedings under the Riot Compensation Act 2016;

(b) the Upper Tribunal's function as arbitrator under section 1(5) of the Lands Tribunal Act 1949;

(c) an application for the Upper Tribunal to grant the relief mentioned in section 15(1) of the Tribunals, Courts and Enforcement Act 2007 (Upper Tribunal's "judicial review" jurisdiction) which relates to a decision of a tribunal mentioned in sub-paragraph (a)(ii);

(cc) any case which may be transferred under Tribunal Procedure Rules to the Upper Tribunal from the Property Chamber of the First-tier Tribunal in relation to functions listed in article 5A(c) to (h);

(d) any other functions transferred to the Upper Tribunal by the Transfer of Tribunal Functions (Lands Tribunal and Miscellaneous Amendments) Order 2009.

Functions of the Tax and Chancery Chamber

13(1) To the Tax and Chancery Chamber are allocated all functions related to—

(a) an appeal against a decision of the First-tier Tribunal made—

(i) in the Tax Chamber;

(ii) in the General Regulatory Chamber in a charities case;

(b) a reference or appeal in respect of—

(i) a decision of the Financial Conduct Authority or the Prudential Regulation Authority;

(ii) a decision of the Bank of England;

(iii) a decision of a person related to the assessment of any compensation or consideration under the Banking (Special Provisions) Act 2008;

(iv) a determination or dispute within the meaning of regulation 14(5) or 15 of the Financial Services and Management Act 2000 (Contribution to Costs of Special Resolution Regime) Regulations 2010;

(ba) an appeal in respect of a decision of a Minister under section 147(4)(a) or (b) of the Policing and Crime Act 2017;

(c) a reference in respect of a decision of the Pensions Regulator;

(d) an application under paragraph 50(1)(d) of Schedule 36 to the Finance Act 2008;

(e) proceedings, or a preliminary issue, transferred to the Upper Tribunal under Tribunal Procedure Rules—

(i) from the Tax Chamber of the First-tier Tribunal;

(ii) from the General Regulatory Chamber of the First-tier Tribunal in a charities case;

(f) a matter referred to the Upper Tribunal under section 9(5)(b) of the Tribunals, Courts and Enforcement Act 2007 or under Tribunal Procedure Rules relating to non-compliance with a requirement of the First-tier Tribunal—

(i) by the Tax Chamber of the First-tier Tribunal;

(ii) by the General Regulatory Chamber of the First-tier Tribunal in a charities case;

(g) an application for the Upper Tribunal to grant the relief mentioned in section 15(1) of the Tribunals, Courts and Enforcement Act 2007 (Upper Tribunal's "judicial review" jurisdiction), or to exercise the powers of review under section 21(2) of that Act (Upper Tribunal's "judicial review" jurisdiction: Scotland), which relates to—

(i) a decision of the First-tier Tribunal mentioned in paragraph (1)(a)(i) or (ii);

(ii) a function of the Commissioners for Her Majesty's Revenue and Customs or an officer of Revenue and Customs, with the exception of any function in respect of which an appeal would be allocated to the Social Entitlement Chamber by article 6;

(iii) the exercise by the National Crime Agency of general Revenue functions or Revenue inheritance tax functions (as defined in section 323 of the Proceeds of Crime Act 2002), with the exception of any function in relation to which an appeal would be allocated to the Social Entitlement Chamber by article 6;

(iv) a function of the Charity Commission, or one of the bodies mentioned in sub-paragraph (b) or (c);

(h) ...

(i) an application under section 151, 181E or 181F of the Tax Collection and Management (Wales) Act 2016.

(2) In this article "a charities case" means an appeal or application in respect of a decision, order or direction of the Charity Commission, or a reference under Schedule 1D to the Charities Act 1993.

Resolution of doubt or dispute as to chamber

14 If there is any doubt or dispute as to the chamber in which a particular matter is to be dealt with, the Senior President of Tribunals may allocate that matter to the chamber which appears to the Senior President of Tribunals to be most appropriate.

Re-allocation of a case to another chamber

15 At any point in the proceedings, the Chamber President of the chamber to which a case or any issue in that case has been allocated by or under this Order may, with the consent of the corresponding Chamber President, allocate that case or that issue to another chamber within the same tribunal, by giving a direction to that effect.

SCHEDULE
REVOCATIONS

not reproduced

Qualifications for Appointment of Members to the First-tier Tribunal and Upper Tribunal Order 2008 (SI 2008/2692)

Made 15th October 2008
Laid before Parliament 15th October 2008
Coming into force 3rd November 2008

The Lord Chancellor, with the concurrence of the Senior President of Tribunals, makes the following Order in exercise of the powers conferred by paragraph 2(2) of Schedule 2 and paragraph 2(2) of Schedule 3 to the Tribunals, Courts and Enforcement Act 2007.

1(1) This Order may be cited as the Qualifications for Appointment of Members to the First-tier Tribunal and Upper Tribunal Order 2008 and shall come into force on 3rd November 2008.

(2) In this Order "registered medical practitioner" means a fully registered person within the meaning of the Medical Act 1983 whether or not they hold a licence to practise under that Act.

2(1) A person is eligible for appointment as a member of the First-tier Tribunal or the Upper Tribunal who is not a judge of those tribunals if paragraph (2), (3) or (4) applies.

(2) This paragraph applies to a person who is–
    (a)   a registered medical practitioner;
    (b)   a registered nurse;
    (c)   a registered dentist;
    (ca) a registered optometrist;
    (d)   a clinical psychologist;
    (e)   an educational psychologist;
    (f)   a pharmacologist;
    (g)   a veterinary surgeon or a veterinary practitioner registered under the Veterinary Surgeons Act 1966;
    (h)   a Member or Fellow of the Royal Institution of Chartered Surveyors; or
    (i)   an accountant who is a member of–
        (i)   the Institute of Chartered Accountants in England and Wales;
        (ii) the Institute of Chartered Accountants in Scotland;
        (iii) the Institute of Chartered Accountants in Ireland;
        (iv) the Institute of Certified Public Accountants in Ireland;
        (v) the Association of Chartered Certified Accountants;
        (vi) the Chartered Institute of Management Accountants; or
        (vii) the Chartered Institute of Public Finance and Accountancy.

(3) This paragraph applies to a person who is experienced in dealing with the physical or mental needs of disabled persons because they–
    (a)   work with disabled persons in a professional or voluntary capacity; or
    (b)   are themselves disabled.

(3A) A person is not eligible for appointment under paragraph (3) if they are a registered medical practitioner.

(4) This paragraph applies to a person who has substantial experience–
    (a)   of service in Her Majesty's naval, military, or air forces;

(b) of educational, child care, health, or social care matters;

(c) of dealing with victims of violent crime;

(d) in transport operations and its law and practice;

(e) in the regulatory field;

(f) in consumer affairs;

(g) in an industry, trade or business sector and the matters that are likely to arise as issues in the course of disputes with regulators of such industries, trades or businesses;

(h) in tax matters and related tax procedures;

(i) in a business, trade, charity or not-for-profit organisation;

(j) in immigration services or the law and procedure relating to immigration;

(k) of data protection;

(l) of freedom of information (including environmental information) rights;

(m) of service as a Member or Senior Officer of a local authority in England;

(n) in environmental matters;

(o) in the drainage of land;

(p) in farming and the ownership or management of agricultural property;

(q) in relation to housing or housing conditions;

(r) in matters relating to landlord and tenant relationships;

(s) in valuation.

Transfer of Tribunal Functions Order 2010
(SI 2010/22)

Made 6th January 2010

Coming into force in accordance with article 1

The Lord Chancellor makes the following Order in exercise of the powers conferred by sections 30(1) and (4), 31(1), (2) and (9) and 38 of, and paragraph 30 of Schedule 5 to, the Tribunals, Courts and Enforcement Act 2007.

The Welsh Ministers have consented to the making of this Order in so far as their consent is required by section 30(8) of that Act.

A draft of this Order was laid before Parliament and approved by a resolution of each House of Parliament in accordance with section 49(5) of that Act.

Citation, commencement and extent

1(1) This Order may be cited as the Transfer of Tribunal Functions Order 2010 and, subject to paragraph (2), comes into force on 18th January 2010.

(2) The following provisions of this Order come into force on 6th April 2010–

    (a) paragraph (5);

    (b) article 2(2), (3)(b) and (4);

    (c) article 3 in respect of the Financial Services and Markets Tribunal;

    (d) Schedule 1 in respect of the Financial Services and Markets Tribunal and the Pensions Regulator Tribunal;

    (e) in Schedule 2, paragraphs 3(c)(i), 4(c), 5 to 9, 12 to 14, 15(c), 17(b), 18(b), 20 to 23, 43 to 49, 74 to 89, 92(h) to (k) and 141 to 151;

    (f) in Schedule 3, paragraphs 16 to 38, 90 to 94, 140 to 142, 143(d), 144 to 146, 148 to 158, 176 to 189 and 191 to 200; and

    (g) Part 2 of Schedule 4.

(3) Subject as follows, this Order extends to England and Wales, Scotland and Northern Ireland.

(4) Except as provided by paragraph (5), an amendment, repeal or revocation of any enactment by any provision of Schedule 2, 3 or 4 extends to the part or parts of the United Kingdom to which the enactment extends.

(5) The amendments, repeals and revocations made by the following provisions do not extend to Northern Ireland–

    (a) in Schedule 2, paragraphs 5(b), 9(b), 77 to 79, 83 to 85, 88, 142(b) and 143(b);

    (b) in Schedule 3, paragraphs 90 to 94;

    (c) in Part 2 of Schedule 4, the entries relating to–

        (i) the Tribunals, Courts and Enforcement Act 2007 in so far as it relates to paragraph 40 of Schedule 10;

        (ii) the Pensions Act 2008;

        (iii) the Pensions Regulator Tribunal Rules 2005; and

        (iv) the Lord Chancellor (Transfer of Functions and Supplementary Provisions) (No 2) Order 2006.

Transfer of functions of certain tribunals

2(1) The functions of the following tribunals are transferred to the First-tier Tribunal–

    (a) tribunals drawn from the Adjudication Panel for England;

    (b)   the Claims Management Services Tribunal;

    (c)   the Gambling Appeals Tribunal;

    (d)   the Immigration Services Tribunal; and

    (e)   the Family Health Services Appeal Authority.

(2)   The functions of the Financial Services and Markets Tribunal are transferred to the Upper Tribunal.

(3)   The functions of the following tribunals are transferred to the First-tier Tribunal and the Upper Tribunal with the question as to which one of them is to exercise the functions in a particular case being determined by, or under, Tribunal Procedure Rules–

    (a)   the Information Tribunal; and

    (b)   subject to paragraph (4), the Pensions Regulator Tribunal.

(4)   The functions of the Pensions Regulator Tribunal exercisable in relation to Northern Ireland are not transferred.

Abolition of tribunals

3   The tribunals mentioned in article 2(1), (2) and (3)(a) are abolished.

Persons becoming judges and other members of the First-tier Tribunal and the Upper Tribunal

4   A person who, immediately before this Order comes into force, holds an office listed in a part of Schedule 1, is to hold the office or offices set out in the corresponding entry in the table below.

Table not reproduced

Consequential, transitional and saving provisions

5(1)   Schedule 2 contains amendments to primary legislation as a consequence of the transfers effected by this Order.

(2)   Schedule 3 contains amendments to secondary legislation as a consequence of the transfers effected by this Order.

(3)   Schedule 4 contains repeals and revocations as a consequence of the amendments in Schedules 2 and 3.

(4)   Schedule 5 contains transitional and saving provisions.

SCHEDULE 1

Persons Becoming Judges and Members of the First-tier Tribunal and Upper Tribunal

Not reproduced

SCHEDULE 2

Consequential Amendments to Primary Legislation

Not reproduced

SCHEDULE 3

CONSEQUENTIAL AMENDMENTS TO SECONDARY LEGISLATION

Not reproduced

SCHEDULE 4

REPEALS AND REVOCATIONS

Not reproduced

SCHEDULE 5

TRANSITIONAL AND SAVING PROVISIONS

Article 5(4)

Interpretation of Schedule 5

1   In this Schedule–

"old tribunal" means a tribunal, the functions of which are transferred by article 2, but does not include the Pensions Regulator Tribunal in respect of its functions exercisable in Northern Ireland;

"new tribunal" means–

    (a)   the Upper Tribunal, in respect of–

        (i)   the functions of the Financial Services and Markets Tribunal and the Pensions Regulator Tribunal;

        (ii)   the functions of the Information Tribunal of deciding appeals under section 28 of the Data Protection Act 1998 or section 60 of the Freedom of Information Act 2000 (including that section as applied and modified by regulation 18 of the Environmental Information Regulations 2004) (appeals in relation to national security certificates);

    (b)   the First-tier Tribunal, in respect of–

        (i)   the tribunal functions mentioned in article 2(1);

        (ii)   the functions of the Information Tribunal other than those mentioned in paragraph (a)(ii);

"transfer date" means the date on which the functions of an old tribunal are transferred to a new tribunal by article 2.

Transitional and saving provisions

2   Any proceedings before an old tribunal which are pending immediately before the transfer date shall continue on and after the transfer date as proceedings before the new tribunal.

3(1)   The following sub-paragraphs apply where proceedings are continued in a new tribunal by virtue of paragraph 2.

(2)   Where a hearing began before the transfer date but was not completed by that date, the new tribunal must be comprised for the continuation of that hearing of the person or persons who began it.

(3)   The new tribunal may give any direction to ensure that proceedings are dealt with fairly and, in particular, may–

    (a)   apply any provision in procedural rules which applied to the proceedings before the transfer date; or

(b)   disapply provisions of Tribunal Procedure Rules.

(4)   In sub-paragraph (3) "procedural rules" means provision (whether called rules or not) regulating practice or procedure before a tribunal.

(5)   Any direction or order given or made in proceedings which is in force immediately before the transfer date remains in force on and after that date as if it were a direction or order of the new tribunal.

(6)   A time period which has started to run before the transfer date and which has not expired shall continue to apply.

(7)   An order for costs may only be made if, and to the extent that, an order for costs could have been made by the old tribunal before the transfer date.4Paragraph 5 applies where–

(a)   an appeal lies to a court from any decision made by an old tribunal before the transfer date;

(b)   that right of appeal has not been exercised; and

(c)   the time to exercise that right of appeal has not expired prior to the transfer date.

5   In the circumstances set out at paragraph 4, such of the following provisions as is appropriate shall apply as if the decision were a decision made on or after the transfer date by the new tribunal–

(a)   section 11 of the Tribunals, Courts and Enforcement Act 2007 (right to appeal to Upper Tribunal);

(b)   section 13 of the Tribunals, Courts and Enforcement Act 2007 (right to appeal to Court of Appeal);

(c)   section 78(9A) to (9D) or section 78B(4) to (7) of the Local Government Act 2000 (as inserted or amended by Schedule 2 to this Order).

6   Any case to be remitted by a court on or after the transfer date and which, if it had been remitted before the transfer date, would have been remitted to an old tribunal, shall be remitted to the new tribunal.

7   Staff appointed to an old tribunal before the transfer date are to be treated on and after that date, for the purpose of any enactment, as if they had been appointed by the Lord Chancellor under section 40(1) of the Tribunals, Courts and Enforcement Act 2007 (tribunal staff and services).

8A   A decision made by an old tribunal before the transfer date is to be treated on or after the transfer date as a decision of the new tribunal.

Appeals from the Upper Tribunal to the Court of Appeal Order 2008
(SI 2008/2834)

Made 29th October 2008
Coming into force in accordance with article 1

The Lord Chancellor makes the following Order in exercise of the power conferred by section 13(6) of the Tribunals, Courts and Enforcement Act 2007.

A draft of this Order was laid before Parliament and approved by a resolution of each House of Parliament in accordance with section 49(5) of that Act.

1 This Order may be cited as the Appeals from the Upper Tribunal to the Court of Appeal Order 2008 and shall come into force on 3rd November 2008.

2 Permission to appeal to the Court of Appeal in England and Wales or leave to appeal to the Court of Appeal in Northern Ireland shall not be granted unless the Upper Tribunal or, where the Upper Tribunal refuses permission, the relevant appellate court, considers that–

    (a) the proposed appeal would raise some important point of principle or practice; or

    (b) there is some other compelling reason for the relevant appellate court to hear the appeal.

Civil Procedure Rules 1998
Part 53: Media and Communications Claims

53.1 Scope of this Part

(1) This Part contains rules about media and communications claims.

(2) A "media and communications claim" means a claim which—
   (a) satisfies the requirements of paragraph (3) or (4); and
   (b) has been issued in or transferred into the Media and Communications List.

(3) A High Court claim must be issued in the Media and Communications List if it is or includes a claim for defamation, or is or includes—
   (a) a claim for misuse of private information;
   (b) a claim in data protection law; or
   (c) a claim for harassment by publication.

(4) Subject to Part 63 and any other applicable provisions, a claim not falling within paragraph (3) may be issued in the Media and Communications List if the claim arises from—
   (a) the publication or threatened publication of information via the media, online or in speech; or
   (b) other activities of the media,
   and the claimant considers it is suitable for resolution in that list.

53.2 Specialist list

(1) The Media and Communications List is a specialist list of the High Court.

(2) One of the Judges of the Queen's Bench Division shall be the Judge in Charge of the Media and Communications List.

(3) A Media and Communications List Judge is a judge authorised by the President of the Queen's Bench Division, in consultation with the Chancellor of the High Court, to hear claims in the Media and Communications List.

(4) All proceedings in the Media and Communications List will be heard by a Media and Communications Judge, or by a Master of the Queen's Bench Division, except that—
   (a) another judge of the Queen's Bench Division or Chancery Division may hear urgent applications if no Media and Communications Judge is available; and
   (b) unless the court otherwise orders, any application relating to enforcement of a Media and Communications List order or judgment for the payment of money will be dealt with by a Master of the Queen's Bench Division or District Judge.

Practice Direction 53A
Transferring Proceedings to and from the Media and Communications List

This practice direction supplements Part 53

1   If a Media and Communications Judge orders proceedings to be transferred to the Media and Communications List—

    (1)   the judge will order them to be transferred to the Royal Courts of Justice; and

    (2)   the judge may give case management directions.

2   An application by a defendant, including a Part 30 defendant, for an order transferring proceedings to or from the Media and Communications List should be made promptly and normally not later than the first case management conference.

3   A party applying for an order transferring a claim to the Media and Communications List must give notice of the application to the court or list in which the claim is proceeding, and the Media and Communications Judge will not make an order for transfer unless and until satisfied that such notice and any applicable consent has been given.

4   A Media and Communications Judge may decide that the court should consider of its own motion whether a claim should be transferred from the Media and Communications List. If the judge does so, CPR rules 3.3 and 23.8(c) apply.

5   A Media and Communications List Judge deciding whether to transfer a claim to or from the Media and Communications List will consider whether the claim or any part of it—

    (1)   falls outside the scope of that list (whether or not it also falls within the scope of Part 63); or

    (2)   falls within the scope of the list but would more conveniently be dealt with in another court or list, and make such order as the court considers appropriate in the light of its conclusions.

6   This practice direction is subject to CPR rule 30.5.

Practice Direction 53B
Media and Communications Claims

This practice direction supplements Part 53

1 This practice direction applies to media and communications claims.
(Rule 53.1 defines "media and communications claim".)

Statements of case

2.1 Statements of case should be confined to the information necessary to inform the other party of the nature of the case they have to meet. Such information should be set out concisely and in a manner proportionate to the subject matter of the claim.
(Part 16 and the accompanying practice direction contain requirements for the contents of statements of case.)

2.2 A claimant must in the particulars of claim give full details of the facts and matters on which they rely in support of any claim for damages.
(Rule 16.4(1)(c) requires a claimant seeking aggravated or exemplary damages to include in the particulars of claim a statement to that effect and the grounds for claiming such damages.)

2.3 A claimant who wishes to advance any positive case in response to any facts or matters raised in a defence must file and serve a reply.
(Rule 15.8 contains the requirements for filing and serving a reply.)
(Further requirements as to the statements of case in particular types of claim are set out at paragraphs 4, 8, 9 and 10 below.)

Statements in open court

3.1 This paragraph only applies where a party wishes to accept a Part 36 offer or other offer of settlement in relation to a claim for—
    (1) libel;
    (2) slander;
    (3) malicious falsehood; or
    (4) misuse of private or confidential information.

3.2 A party may apply for permission to make a statement in open court before or after the Part 36 offer or other offer to settle the claim is accepted.

3.3 The statement that the applicant wishes to make must be submitted for the approval of the court and must accompany the notice of application.

3.4 The court may postpone the time for making the statement if other claims relating to the subject matter of the statement are still proceeding.

Statements of case

4.1(1) In a claim for libel the publication the subject of the claim must be identified in the claim form.

(2) In a claim for slander the claim form must so far as practicable identify the person or persons to whom the words were spoken and when.

4.2 The claimant must set out in the particulars of claim—

    (1) the precise words of the statement complained of, save where the length of the statement makes it impracticable to do so, in which case the words may be set out in a schedule annexed to the particulars of claim, or otherwise identified;

    (2) when, how and to whom the statement was published. If the claimant does not know to whom the statement was published or it is impracticable to set out all such persons, then the particulars of claim must include all facts and matters relied upon to show (a) that such publication took place, and (b) the extent of such publication;

    (3) the facts and matters relied upon in order to satisfy the requirement of section 1 of the Defamation Act 2013 that the publication of the statement complained of has caused or is likely to cause serious harm to the reputation of the claimant, or, in the case of a body that trades for profit, that it has caused or is likely to cause the body serious financial loss;

    (4) the imputation(s) which the claimant alleges that the statement complained of conveyed, both—

        (a) as to its natural and ordinary meaning; and

        (b) by way of any innuendo meaning (that is, a meaning alleged to be conveyed to some person by reason of knowing facts extraneous to the statement complained of). In the case of an innuendo meaning, the claimant must also identify the relevant extraneous facts;

    (5) full details of the facts and matters on which the claimant relies in support of the claim for damages. A claimant who seeks aggravated or exemplary damages must provide the information specified in rule 16.4(1)(c).

4.3 Where a defendant relies on the defence under section 2 of the Defamation Act 2013 that the imputation conveyed by the statement complained of is substantially true, they must—

    (1) specify the imputation they contend is substantially true; and

    (2) give details of the matters on which they rely in support of that contention.

4.4 Where a defendant relies on the defence under section 3 of the Defamation Act 2013 that the statement complained of was a statement of honest opinion, they must—

    (1) specify the imputation they seek to defend as honest opinion; and

    (2) set out the facts and matters relied on in support of their case that—

        (a) the statement complained of indicated, in general or specific terms, the basis of the opinion; and

        (b) an honest person could have held that opinion on the basis of any fact which existed at the time it was published or anything asserted to be a fact in a privileged statement published before the statement complained of.

4.5 Where a defendant alleges that the statement complained of was, or formed part of, a statement on a matter of public interest under section 4 of the Defamation Act 2013, they must—

    (1) specify the matter of public interest relied upon; and

    (2) give details of all matters relied on in support of any case that they reasonably believed that publishing the statement was in the public interest.

4.6 Where a defendant alleges that the statement complained of was published on a privileged occasion, they must specify the circumstances they rely on in support of that contention.

4.7 Where a defendant relies on a defence under section 2(truth), section 3 (honest opinion), or section 4 (publication on a matter of public interest) of the Defamation Act 2013, the claimant must serve a reply specifically admitting, not admitting, or denying that defence and setting out the claimant's case in response to each fact alleged by the defendant in respect of it.

4.8(1) If the defendant contends that any of the statement complained of, or any part thereof, was honest opinion, or was published on a privileged occasion, and the claimant intends to allege that the defendant did not hold the opinion or acted with malice (as applicable), the claimant must serve a reply giving details of the facts or matters relied on.

(2) If the defendant relies on any other defence, and the claimant intends to allege that the defence is not available because of the defendant's state of mind, the claimant must serve a reply giving details of the facts or matters relied on. This includes—
   (a) where a defendant relies on the defence under section 4 of the Defamation Act 2013 and the claimant intends to allege that the defendant did not reasonably believe that the publication was in the public interest;
   (b) where a defendant relies on the defence under section 4(2) of the Defamation Act 1996 (offer to make amends) and the claimant intends to allege that the defendant had the state of mind referred to in section 4(3) of the defamation Act 1996.

4.9 A defendant who relies on an offer to make amends under section 2 of the Defamation Act 1996 as their defence must—
   (1) state in their defence—
      (a) that they are relying on the offer in accordance with section 4(2) of the Defamation Act 1996; and
      (b) that it has not been withdrawn by them or been accepted; and
   (2) attach a copy of the offer made with their defence.

Court's powers in connection with an offer of amends
5.1 Sections 2 to 4 of the Defamation Act 1996 make provision for a person who has made a statement which is alleged to be defamatory to make an offer to make amends. Section 3 provides for the court to assist in the process of making amends.

5.2 A claim under section 3 of the Defamation Act 1996 made other than in existing proceedings may be made under CPR Part 8—
   (1) where the parties agree on the steps to make amends, and the sole purpose of the claim is for the court to make an order under section 3(3) for an order that the offer be fulfilled; or
   (2) where the parties do not agree—
      (a) on the steps to be taken by way of correction, apology and publication (see section 3(4));
      (b) on the amount to be paid by way of compensation (see section 3(5)); or
      (c) on the amount to be paid by way of costs (see section 3(6)).
(Applications in existing proceedings made under section 3 of the Defamation Act 1996 must be made in accordance with CPR Part 23.)

5.3(1) A claim or application under section 3 of the Defamation Act 1996 must be supported by written evidence.

(2) The evidence referred to in paragraph (1) must include—
     (a) a copy of the offer of amends;
     (b) details of the steps taken to fulfil the offer of amends;
     (c) a copy of the text of any correction and apology;
     (d) details of the publication of the correction and apology;
     (e) a statement of the amount of any sum paid as compensation;
     (f) a statement of the amount of any sum paid for costs;
     (g) why the offer is unsatisfactory.

(3) Where any step specified in section 2(4) of the Defamation Act 1996 has not been taken, then the evidence referred to in paragraph (2)(c) to (f) must state what steps are proposed by the party to fulfil the offer of amends and the date or dates on which each step will be fulfilled and, if none, that no proposal has been made to take that step.

Determination of meaning
6.1 At any time in a defamation claim the court may determine—
     (1) the meaning of the statement complained of;
     (2) whether the statement is defamatory of the claimant at common law;
     (3) whether the statement is a statement of fact or opinion.

6.2 An application for a determination of meaning may be made at any time after the service of particulars of claim. Such an application should be made promptly.

6.3 Where an application is made for a determination of meaning, the application notice must state that it is an application for a determination of meaning made in accordance with this practice direction.

6.4 An application made under this paragraph must be made to a Judge.
     (Rule 3.3 applies where the court exercises its powers on its own initiative.)
     (Following a determination of meaning the court may exercise its power under rule 3.4.)

Summary disposal
7.1 Where an application is made for summary disposal, the application notice must state—
     (1) that it is an application for summary disposal made in accordance with section 8 of the Defamation Act 1996; and
     (2) the matters set out in paragraph 2(3) of Practice Direction 24.

7.2 An application for summary disposal may be made at any time after the service of particulars of claim.
     (This provision disapplies for these applications the usual time restriction on making applications in rule 24.4.)

7.3(1) This paragraph applies where—
     (a) the court has ordered the defendant in defamation proceedings to agree and publish a correction and apology as summary relief under section 8(2) of the Defamation Act 1996; and
     (b) the parties are unable to agree its content within the time specified in the order.

(2) Where the court grants this type of summary relief under the Act, the order will specify the date by which the parties should reach agreement about the content, time, manner, form and place of publication of the correction and apology.

(3) Where the parties cannot agree the content of the correction and apology by the date specified in the order, then the claimant must prepare a summary of the judgment given by the court and serve it on all the other parties within 3 days following the date specified in the order.

(4) Where the parties cannot agree the summary of the judgment prepared by the claimant they must within 3 days of receiving the summary –
    (a) file with the court and serve on all the other parties a copy of the summary showing the revisions they wish to make to it; and
    (b) apply to the court for the court to settle the summary.

(5) The court will then itself settle the summary and the judge who delivered the judgment being summarised will normally do this.

MISUSE OF PRIVATE OR CONFIDENTIAL INFORMATION

8.1 In a claim for misuse of private information, the claimant must specify in the particulars of claim (in a confidential schedule if necessary to preserve privacy)—
    (1) the information as to which the claimant claims to have (or to have had) a reasonable expectation of privacy;
    (2) the facts and matters upon which the claimant relies in support of the contention that they had (or have) such a reasonable expectation;
    (3) the use (or threatened use) of the information by the defendant which the claimant claims was (or would be) a misuse; and
    (4) any facts and matters upon which the claimant relies in support of their contention that their rights not to have the specified information used by the defendant in the way alleged outweighed (or outweigh) any rights of the defendant to use the information in that manner.

8.2 In a claim for misuse of confidential information or breach of confidence, the claimant must specify in the particulars of claim (in a confidential schedule if necessary to preserve confidentiality)—
    (1) the information said to be confidential;
    (2) the facts and matters upon which the claimant relies in support of the contention that it was (or is) confidential information that the defendant held (or holds) under a duty or obligation of confidence;
    (3) the use (or threatened use) of the information by the defendant which the claimant claims was (or would be) a misuse of the information or breach of that obligation.

DATA PROTECTION

9. In any claim for breach of any data protection legislation the claimant must specify in the particulars of claim—
    (1) the legislation and the provision that the claimant alleges the defendant has breached;
    (2) any specific data or acts of processing to which the claim relates;

(3)   the specific acts or omissions said to amount to such a breach, and the claimant's grounds for that allegation; and

(4)   the remedies which the claimant seeks.

HARASSMENT

10.1   This paragraph applies to claims for harassment arising from publication or threatened publication via the media, online, or in speech.

10.2   Rule 65.28(1)(a) shall not apply, and the claim should be commenced under the Part 7 procedure.

10.3   The claimant must specify in the particulars of claim (in a schedule if necessary) the acts of the defendant alleged to constitute a course of conduct which amount to (and which were known or ought to have been known by the defendant to amount to) harassment, including specific details of any actual or threatened communications.

10.4   A defendant must in any defence specifically admit or deny each act alleged in the particulars of claim to constitute part of a course of conduct amounting to harassment.

(Rule 16.5 contains requirements as to the contents of defences.)

Practice Note

Protection of Confidential Information in Information Rights
Appeals Before the First-tier Tribunal in the General
Regulatory Tribunal on Or After 18 January 2010

1. This Practice Note sets out the arrangements for protecting confidential information in First-tier Tribunal (Information Rights) appeals and related matters. In this Practice Note references to Rules are references to the Tribunal Procedure (First-tier Tribunal) (General Regulatory Chamber) Rules 2009 as amended by the Tribunal Procedure (Amendment No 3) Rules 2010 (the Rules). Introduction

2. As with all courts and tribunals, it is of course essential that information which is relevant to proceedings is, as far as is possible, available to all parties to a case.

3. However, the nature of appeals to the First-tier Tribunal (Information Rights) under the Freedom of Information Act 2000 (FOIA) is such that the Tribunal will often require to see information which must be kept confidential from one or more of the other parties to the appeal. Amongst other things, this can mean that during the hearing the party requesting the information is asked to leave the room

4. For instance, there will be cases where a person who made a request for information under section 1(1) FOIA is a party to an appeal which examines the application of exemptions to the obligation to supply information. In many cases the Tribunal will need to see the information which has been withheld in order to reach its decision. However, in cases where disclosure has been refused, it would in most cases undermine the very object of the exemption if the information in question were to be disclosed, during the Tribunal proceedings, to the person who made the request. The Tribunal will need to ensure that that information is kept confidential. This is in accordance with the overriding objective under Rule 2 of dealing with cases fairly and justly.

5. Considerations of confidentiality can often also apply to other information which the Tribunal requires to see, such as written and oral evidence and submissions. For example, in considering whether exemptions have been applied correctly, the Tribunal may require evidence on why disclosure would result in prejudice. Such evidence will often also reveal something of the nature of the requested information in a way which would undermine the objectives of the exemption. Equally, it may reveal other information which the Tribunal requires in order to determine the case, but which would be exempt under FOIA, for example, commercially sensitive information that is revealed in documents recording a public authority s consultation with third parties under the Section 45 Code of Practice.

6. The legal basis for the Tribunal dealing with confidential information in proceedings was considered in the Ruling in Sugar v Information Commissioner and the BBC dated 12th May 2006. Although this Ruling was applied under the Information Tribunal (Enforcement Appeals) Rules 2005 as amended it is considered that the legal position is the same under the Rules.

7. This Practice Note covers:

   A. Confidentiality and Redaction
   B. Joinder
   C. Witnesses
   D. Documents
   E. Decisions

A. Confidentiality and Redaction

8. Where a party to proceedings claims that an exemption under Part II of FOIA has been applied, or would apply to information (such as documentary or oral evidence and submissions) and the Tribunal requires to see the information in order to determine the appeal, the Judge should ensure action is taken to maintain appropriate confidentiality. This applies in particular when the Tribunal is making directions under Rule 5 as to the disclosure of documents, statements of facts and evidence and skeleton arguments.

9. For example, on exchange between the parties of lists of relevant documents, the Judge should consider ensuring that directions provide, as necessary, for some entries to be kept confidential from one or more parties to the proceedings. This may require parties to prepare two versions of such documents one full version for the Tribunal, and one version to be exchanged with the other parties, which does not include information which needs to be kept confidential. See section D below.

10. Similar considerations apply to evidence and submissions which are prepared and put before the Tribunal. In order for the Tribunal to ensure that it has all the information that it requires, and that the parties provide it with as full oral evidence and submissions as possible, it may be necessary for some information to be kept confidential from one or more of the parties, or redacted if appropriate. See section C below.

11. For example, as the Notice of Appeal and replies to the Notice are required to be sent to all parties to the case, the Judge should consider whether the Tribunal requires further preliminary details of a party s case to be provided on a confidential basis.

12. Factors that should be considered when making directions, to ensure appropriate confidentiality include: The primary objective is to ensure that the Tribunal has all the information that it requires in order to make a just and fair decision in a case. The Judge will want to take necessary steps to ensure that the parties provide it with relevant documents and evidence, and that the parties are able to make full and frank submissions. Where a party claims that documents or evidence need to be kept confidential from one or more of the other parties to the case because they claim the documents or evidence are exempt under FOIA, or would be if a request were received, the Tribunal should consider ensuring appropriate confidentiality. Whether the hearing or part of the hearing should be held in private or a party excluded from part of the hearing as provided for under Rule 35. In relation to the latter the Tribunal must always consider the potential detrimental effect that an order to exclude may have on a party who may be denied the opportunities he would otherwise have in accordance with the overriding objective in particular as identified under Rule 2(2)(c) (ensuring, so far as practicable, that the parties are able to participate fully in the proceedings).

13. Parties should understand that at times the Judge may have to make directions during the hearing to hold part of it in private. This means that those who cannot see what is claimed to be confidential information, or hear evidence presented that needs to refer directly to its contents will be asked to leave the room for the minimum length of time necessary to examine such evidence. For the avoidance of doubt those excluded will be those from whom the information needs to be kept confidential, which normally will mean everyone other than those parties from whom the documents are requested and any related parties and those representing the Information Commissioner.

B. Joinder

14. It is essential that the Tribunal has before it all the information that it requires in order to take a decision on a case. In some cases, the Tribunal will require information from persons who are not automatically parties to an appeal.

15. For example, when the Information Commissioner issues a Decision Notice under section 50 FOIA he is seeking to resolve a complaint concerning a request for information that was made to a public authority. When a Decision Notice is appealed to the Tribunal, one of the parties to the original complaint (that is, the complainant or the public authority) will not automatically be a party to the appeal the parties will be the person bringing the appeal, and the Information Commissioner.

16. In particular where the public authority is not a party to the appeal, the Tribunal will very often require information from the public authority in order to determine a case. For example, if there is a dispute of fact over whether or not the public authority held information for the purposes of section 1(1) FOIA, the Tribunal may require evidence from the public authority on this point. In some cases, the Tribunal may need evidence from a public authority who is not the subject of the Information Commissioner s decision. For example, cases involving the National Archives and papers over 30 years old usually require input from the public authority that transferred files to the National Archives. Such considerations often apply if an appeal will potentially determine a person s liability under FOIA but that person is not an existing or original party. Third parties who have provided information to a public authority may also have an interest in an appeal.

17. While the requestor has an interest in the appeal, he or she may not be well placed to assist the Tribunal in its determination of the case.

18. The most straightforward options in this situation are for the Tribunal to invite that party to apply to be joined or for the Tribunal to order that the other person be joined as a party to the appeal. This will enable the Tribunal to give that person an opportunity to be heard or to ensure that the person provides it with all the information, evidence and submissions that it requires to determine the case. The Tribunal also has the power to receive evidence from people who are not parties. It is sometimes appropriate to receive letters from the requestor but not to join him/her as a party. Where the requestor is not a party, the arrangements to ensure confidentiality of documents are less complex and the hearing can be run more efficiently.

19. When making preliminary directions in a case, the Judge should consider whether it is advisable to invite a person to apply to be joined or to order that any person who has an interest in the proceedings, or can provide the Tribunal with information to enable it to determine the case, should be joined to the proceedings under Rule 9. This should be kept under review as the case proceeds.

20. Factors that a Judge might consider when deciding whether to invite to apply or make an order under Rule 9: The need to ensure that the Tribunal has before it all the information that it requires in order to determine the case and whether it can get that information without joining a party; Where it appears that an appeal may determine the rights or liabilities of a person who is not a party to an appeal, the desirability of that person having the opportunity to make representations; Any evidence or expertise which a person may be able to provide to the Tribunal, which would assist in the determination of the appeal; Whether the issues at stake in the appeal may be of significance beyond the facts of the particular case; Any representations made by a person who applies to be joined under Rule 9(3).

C. Witnesses

21.   The parties can call witnesses to give evidence before the Tribunal, but these witnesses need to be relevant to the case see ruling in Keston Ramblers Association v The Information Commissioner (1) and London Borough of Bromley (2) dated 7th June 2006. The Tribunal usually requires such evidence to be set out in written witness statements which are served on the other parties and filed with the Tribunal before the hearing in accordance with any directions. Where the statement deals with confidential information, two versions of the statement may need to be prepared.

22.   In the event that witness statements are to be filed, unless there is good reason, they should comply with the following requirements. Witness statements will not be rejected on the ground that they are not in a satisfactory form, but it is helpful for the Tribunal if the following requirements are adhered to:

   a. The witness statement should be headed with the title of the proceedings for example: Case Number EA 200X/XXXX A.B. Appellant Information Commissioner Respondent [name of additional parties of joined party, if any] [Joined Party/Additional Party]

   b. At the top right hand corner of the first page there should be clearly written:
       (i) the party on whose behalf the statement has been made, for example appellant or the name of the party, for example Mrs Smith ,
       (ii) if more than one statement has been filed, the number of the statement in relation to that witness, for example 2nd statement .

   c. The witness statement must, if possible, be in the intended witness's own words, the statement should be written in the first person and should also state:
       (i) the full name of the witness,
       (ii) their place of residence or, if they are making the statement in a professional, business or other occupational capacity, the address at which they work, the position they hold and the name of their firm or employer,
       (iii) their occupation or, they have none, their description, and
       (iv) the fact that they are a party to the proceedings or are employed by a party to the proceedings, if that is the case.

   d. Where a witness refers to an exhibit or exhibits, he/she should state "I refer to the (description of exhibit) marked "..." or where there is a reference to another document that should include the page number in any bundle.

   e. A witness statement should:
       (i) be produced in A4 format,
       (ii) be fully legible,
       (iii) have the pages numbered consecutively at the bottom of the page in the middle,
       (iv) be divided into numbered paragraphs.

   f. A witness statement is the equivalent of the oral evidence which that witness would, if called, give in evidence. The Tribunal may or may not require the witness at any hearing to give evidence on oath but any witness statement must contain a statement from the witness confirming that he or she believes the contents of the statement to be true. Something like: "I believe that the facts stated in this witness statement are true" or Insofar as the matters to which I refer are within my own knowledge they are true; insofar as they are not within my own knowledge they are true to the best of my knowledge, information and belief.

g. Where the witness refers to confidential information then either two versions of the statement should be prepared, one with the confidential information and one without it, or there should be a separate closed statement containing only the confidential material. The open statement or version should be served on all parties and the closed statement or version only on those parties who are entitled to see the confidential information at this stage in the proceedings. Parties must be careful to ensure that a separate closed statement does not contain additional non-confidential evidence which the other party is entitled to see. h. Any alteration to a witness statement must be initialled by the person making the statement. The completed statement must be signed by the witness. i. Witness statements should be filed electronically with the Tribunal in MS Word format if possible as well as being provided as part of the hard copy bundle of documents dealt with in section D. below.

23. Depending on the directions, witnesses may be called to appear before the Tribunal at an oral hearing. Usually the witness will not be required to repeat the evidence in their witness statement but will be subject to questioning by the other parties and the Tribunal. The witness may be required to swear an oath to tell the truth on a holy book of the witness choosing or affirm before giving evidence.

24. After a hearing, or where the case is being decided on the papers, it may in rare cases be necessary for the Tribunal to seek further evidence from the parties. The Tribunal may then seek more information through an additional written witness statement.

D. Documents

25. Where the Tribunal has ordered that a bundle is filed for any hearing or determination on the papers under Rule 13, unless there is good reason, the bundle should include a copy of:
   (a)   the Notice of Appeal,
   (b)   the Reply or Replies, including those put in by Additional Parties,
   (c)   the disputed [Decision] Notice,
   (d)   the document requesting the information, the public authority s response (i.e. s. 17 letter) and any document from the applicant requesting an internal review of the decision and the public authority s response to that request,
   (e)   copies of all orders and directions made by the Tribunal
   (f) any other necessary and relevant documents,
   (g)   all witness statements to be relied on,
   (h)   an agreed statement of facts, if applicable, and a chronology of events.

26. Parties should always aim to keep the bundle as relevant and compact as possible in order to minimise the size of bundles where possible.

27. The documents should be in the bundle in the sequence set out in paragraph 25 above and within (6) above any correspondence should be filed chronologically. It is not necessary or desirable for there to be more than one copy of any document in the bundle. For example, there is no need to include a copy of the Decision Notice separately if it has been annexed to the Notice of Appeal. However, any document which refers to another document (which if included in the bundle would otherwise be a duplicate) must be marked with a reference to where the copy of the document may be found within the bundle (for example see page XX of the bundle). The bundle should be paginated (continuously) throughout at the bottom right hand corner of the page, or else tabbed dividers should be used, with each section paginated. There should be an index with a description of each document

and the page number. Dividers should be used for the different sections, particularly if there is more than one lever arch file of documents.

28. The bundle should normally be contained in a ring binder or lever arch file. Where more than one bundle is supplied, they should be clearly distinguishable, for example, by different colours, letters or numbers. If there are numerous bundles, a core bundle should be prepared containing the core documents essential to the proceedings, with references to the supplementary documents in the other bundles.

29. If a document to be included in the bundle is illegible, a typed copy should be included in the bundle next to it, suitably cross-referenced.

30. Any documents (such as the requested information that is the subject of the appeal) that have been ordered to be disclosed to the Tribunal but not to one or more of the parties (see section A Confidentiality and Redaction) must be included in a separate bundle. This bundle should also contain any closed witness statement(s) or skeleton arguments which concern any confidential information (see section C. Witnesses). The document(s), witness statement(s), skeletons and bundle must be clearly marked as not to be disclosed to [name of relevant party] or to the public . This information should not be disclosed to any person except with the consent of the party who provided the information.

31. The Tribunal may wish to direct that the parties agree the final index to the bundle of documents after any witness statements have been submitted. Once written evidence has been submitted, the parties and the Tribunal are better placed to assess whether further documents are necessary to determine the issues on appeal.

E. Decisions

32. At the end of the hearing the Tribunal will give its decision or retire to consider its decision which will be given later, usually within 3 weeks of the hearing. The Tribunal will also provide any material findings of fact and reasons for the decision. The decision with reasons will be signed by the Judge and then sent to the parties and very soon afterwards will be published on the Tribunal s web site. Under Rule 38(2) the Tribunal must have regard to the desirability of safeguarding the privacy of data subjects, commercially sensitive information and any exempt information. As a result the decision may be part open and part closed. The closed part of a decision is usually contained in a confidential annex. The Tribunal should refer to the existence of a closed decision in its open decision, so that all parties are aware of the existence of a closed decision.

33. To help ensure that no confidential information is released through the Tribunal s decision, it is good practice to send a draft of the decision to the originator of the confidential information, which will usually be the public authority and the Information Commissioner if he has already had sight of the information. It will usually be sent to solicitors, lay clients and their advisors under an embargo1 so that that they have the opportunity to indicate if any confidential information is contained in the decision and at the same time ask them to check for any clerical mistakes or accidental slips or omissions. Usually only a short period of 3 to 5 days is given for the exercise. After having given those parties the opportunity to indicate whether any confidential information is contained in the open part of the decision, the Tribunal will often show the open part of the decision to the other parties for them to check for any clerical mistakes or accidental slips or omissions. Recipients must ensure that neither the draft decision nor its substance is disclosed more widely or used in the public domain before it is finalised and them

promulgated (signed by the Judge and published).

34. An example of the wording of an embargoed decision is as follows: We enclose the draft decision in the above named appeal, embargoed in order to give counsel, solicitors, lay clients and their advisors only, the opportunity to indicate if any parts of the decision need to be part of a confidential annex and to point out to the Tribunal any clerical mistakes or other accidental slips or omissions by 12 noon on 27th April 2010. The draft decision must under no circumstances be shown or the contents disclosed to others not covered by the embargo until promulgated. No extensions of time will be permitted.

35. In relation to the closed part of a decision if the public authority, which has provided the confidential information, desires to provide the closed part of 1 The CPR (see PD 40(e)) permits the draft decision to be shown to lay clients as well as solicitors. Lay clients are often best placed to check that the decision does not contain confidential information the person who gave oral evidence can often tell better than the solicitor whether a particular fact was given in open or closed session. the decision to a 3rd party, such as another public authority who was the source of the information, then the Tribunal is unlikely to object to such disclosure.

1 February 2010

Practice Note
Closed Material in Information Rights Cases

1. It is a general principle of tribunal practice that hearings are in public with all parties entitled to be present throughout; and that the documents provided to the tribunal by any party are seen also by all the other parties.

2. In the information rights jurisdiction, there are some cases in which this principle must be modified.

3. In some appeals, the tribunal is able to make its decision without looking at the information whose disclosure is disputed. These can and do proceed normally. Sometimes however, the public authority cannot properly explain its case without showing the disputed information to the tribunal. Put another way, sometimes the tribunal cannot check, on behalf of the citizen, that the public authority is entitled to an exemption under the Freedom of Information Act 2000 or the Environmental Information Regulations 2004, without seeing the disputed information for itself. Obviously, though, disclosure of the information to everyone in the proceedings would defeat the object of the exercise. There is no point in deciding whether information should or should not be disclosed, if it already has been. Similar difficulties can occur with supporting evidence and arguments.

4. In these circumstances the law permits the tribunal to deviate from the normal rule but only so far as is necessary to ensure that the purpose of the proceedings is not defeated. Any such deviation must be authorised by a judge.

5. Rule 14(6) GRC Rules empowers the tribunal to give a direction that certain documents or information be disclosed to the tribunal but not to the other parties to the appeal. The Information Commissioner and the public authority are normally under a duty to disclose to the tribunal all the material they hold which is relevant to the appeal. Should they wish any of that material to be withheld from the requester then one of them must apply to the judge for a direction to that effect.

6. The application must be in writing. It should include a draft of the requested direction and enclose a copy of material which the applicant seeks to withhold. The reasons for withholding the information must be given. In respect of the disputed information it will be sufficient to say that the tribunal needs to see it in order to evaluate the evidence properly. In the case of other material, greater explanation may be required. On receipt of the application, tribunal staff will, unless there is good reason not to do so, tell all the other parties that it has been made; but they will send a copy of the application only to the judge.

7. When considering the application, the judge will first ask whether it is possible for a hearing to take place within the normal rules of disclosure. If yes, (s)he will give directions accordingly. If not, the judge will make a direction under Rule 14(6) stating the information which is to be withheld. It is common to refer to the withheld information as "closed material".

8. Care must be taken, when drafting the direction, not to give away the nature or content of the withheld information. That said, it may be possible, by providing an index to the documents, for example, to give an idea of what material has been withheld. The public authority and the Information Commissioner will be expected to assist the Tribunal in this

respect.

9. The judge will limit non-disclosure to what is necessary. For example, it may be possible to edit a document so that at least some of it is disclosed even though some has to be withheld. If the judge's provisional view is that some but not all of the material should be withheld, tribunal staff will write to the requesting party with a new proposed draft. This is to give the applicant for the direction a chance to add further comments and to ensure that the later draft is clear and correct.

10. Once the judge makes a direction under Rule 14(6) the Tribunal must conduct the proceedings so as not to undermine its effect. All parties must co-operate in this. The judge will also be vigilant as to whether, as events unfold, the direction might require amendment.

11. There are likely to be consequences for any hearing which takes place. It may be that all the parties being present for all of the hearing would undermine the effects of a Rule 14(6) direction. If so, Rule 35(4)(c) permits the tribunal to exclude one of the parties for some of the time.

12. If this happens, the judge will explain to the excluded party, usually the citizen, what is likely to happen during the closed part of the hearing. The judge may ask if there are any particular questions or points which (s)he would like put to the other parties while (s)he is absent.

13. Before the closed part of the hearing ends, the tribunal should discuss with the remaining parties:- (a) What summary of the closed hearing can be given to the excluded party without undermining the Rule 14(6) direction. (b) Whether, in the course of the closed session, any new material has emerged which it is not necessary to withhold and which therefore should be disclosed.

14. The tribunal's final decision and reasons must also be recorded so as not to undermine the effect of any Rule 14(6) direction.

15. We are still perhaps working out the practical effects of Rules 38(2) and 14(10). They do not mean that a closed part of the decision is always needed whenever closed material has been seen. Where the Tribunal orders disclosure it may be necessary for part of the decision to remain closed until after the period for an appeal has expired.

16. It may be prudent in complex cases for a draft of the decision to be shared with the public authority/IC in advance to reduce the risk of inadvertent disclosure.

17. Tribunal practice may require further modification in cases involving matters relating to national security. See Rule 14(9).

May 2012

General Regulatory Chamber First-tier Tribunal GRC
Guidance Note 2
Permission to Appeal on or after 18 January 2010

1. The Tribunal Procedure (First-tier Tribunal) (General Regulatory Chamber) Rules 2009 as amended by the Tribunal Procedure (Amendment No 3) Rules 2010 (the Rules) provide for the correcting, setting aside, reviewing and appealing of First-tier Tribunal (FTT) decisions. When considering what should happen after a decision has been handed down the judge should bear in mind all of these various powers.

2. GRC jurisdictions will use a similar format for applications for permission to appeal to the Upper Tribunal (UT) with accompanying notes or their documentation must be approved by the President of the GRC. An example of the format and notes are contained in the annex to this Guidance Note.

3. Under paragraph 13 of the Senior President of Tribunals Practice Statement on the Composition of Tribunals dated 21st August 2009 (PS) where the Tribunal has given a decision that disposes of proceedings (the substantive decision), any matter decided under, or in accordance with, rule 5(3)(l) or Part 4 of the Tribunal Procedure (First-tier Tribunal) (General Regulatory Chamber) 2009 Rules as amended or section 9 of the Tribunals, Courts and Enforcement Act 2007 must be decided by one judge, unless the Chamber President considers it appropriate that it is decided either by:-

   a. the same members of the Tribunal as gave the substantive decision; or

   b. a Tribunal, constituted in accordance with paragraphs 4 to 12 [of the PS] comprised of different members of the Tribunal to that which gave the substantive decision.

4. In order for the Chamber President to consider whether it is appropriate for one judge to consider such an application under paragraph 13 of the PS all applications after the disposal of a case must be sent to the Principal Judge (PJ) of the jurisdiction in question. The PJ should then consider whether the matter should be referred to the Chamber President to exercise any of his powers under paragraph 13 a. and b. If there is no reason to think that it should be referred to the Chamber President then the PJ should decide whether an application should be dealt with by the judge who presided or the panel who heard the case, or some other judge including the PJ or new panel.

5. In order for the Chamber President to be aware of applications for permission which are granted or refused PJs are requested to notify the Chamber President of decisions to give or refuse permission to appeal to the UT by emailing him a copy of the decision together with a copy of the application for permission to appeal within 7 days of the decision at john.angel@judiciary.gsi.gov.uk.

John Angel Acting President General Regulatory Chamber

9 February 2010

Joint Office Note No. 2
General Regulatory Chamber of the First-tier Tribunal
Administrative Appeals Chamber of the Upper Tribunal
Discretionary Transfers of Information Rights Appeals on or after 18 January 2010

1. Rules 19(1), (2) and (3) of the Tribunal Procedure (First-tier Tribunal) (General Regulatory Chamber) 2009 apply to an appeal under the Data Protection Act 1998 (DPA) or the Freedom of Information Act 2000 (FOIA), including DPA and FOIA as applied and modified by the Privacy and Electronic Communications Regulations 2003 and the Environmental Information Regulations 2004. They enable some or all of the questions arising in such appeals (IR Appeals) to be dealt with in the Upper Tribunal (UT) rather than the First-tier Tribunal (FTT).

2. Rule 19(2) provides that the FTT may refer a case or preliminary issue to the President of the General Regulatory Chamber (GRC) with a request that the case or preliminary issue be considered for transfer to the UT. Under Rule 19(3) where such a request has been made the President of the GRC may, with the concurrence of the President of the appropriate chamber of the UT, direct that the case or issue be transferred to and determined by the UT. In IR Appeals the appropriate chamber of the UT will be the Administrative Appeals Chamber (AAC).

3. Ordinarily IR Appeals will be dealt with in the GRC, and the AAC will not become involved at the first-level appeal stage. Cases or issues will only be suitable for transfer where some special feature merits this course. Examples may be where a case is of considerable public importance or involves complex, sensitive or unusual issues.

4. Cases where no request for transfer is made by any party: If a GRC judge dealing with an IR appeal considers that that there is some special feature which may merit transfer, then that judge should advise the Principal Judge of the IR jurisdiction of the GRC and the President of the GRC. If the President of the GRC considers that transfer of the case or a preliminary issue may be appropriate, the next steps will involve the AAC as well as the GRC. First, the President of the GRC will advise the lead judge of the AAC s Information Rights judicial group (UT Judge Wikeley) (or, if he is unavailable, another judge of that Group) and the President of the AAC. Second, if the President of the AAC agrees that such transfer merits consideration then the GRC President will unless there is good reason to the contrary - invite observations from all actual or potential parties on the proposed transfer. Third, either the GRC president will, if thought appropriate and the AAC President concurs, make a direction that the case or issue be transferred to and determined by the AAC, or the parties will be advised that the proposed direction will not be made.

5. Cases where transfer is requested by one or more of the parties: Upon receipt of such a request the GRC judge dealing with the case should notify the Principal Judge of the IR jurisdiction of the GRC and the President of the GRC. Unless there is good reason to the contrary the President of the GRC should at this stage invite observations from all actual or potential parties. If in the light of those observations the President of the GRC considers that transfer of the case or a preliminary issue may be appropriate, the next steps will be as set out in the preceding paragraph, modified as appropriate.